P9-ARL-076

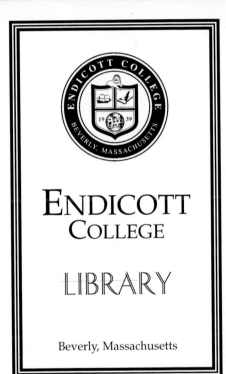

ENDICOTT COLLEGE

LIBRARY

Beverly, Massachusetts

Encyclopedia of the
AMERICAN
RELIGIOUS
EXPERIENCE

Encyclopedia of the
AMERICAN RELIGIOUS EXPERIENCE

Studies of Traditions and Movements

Charles H. Lippy and Peter W. Williams, *EDITORS*

Volume I

CHARLES SCRIBNER'S SONS · NEW YORK

Copyright © 1988 Charles Scribner's Sons

Library of Congress Cataloging-in-Publication Data

Encyclopedia of the American religious experience.

Bibliography: p.
Includes index.
1. United States—Religion.   2. North America—
Religion. I. Lippy, Charles H. II. Williams, Peter W.
BL2525.E53   1987   291′.0973   87-4781
ISBN 0-684-18062-6 Set
ISBN 0-684-18861-9 Volume I
ISBN 0-684-18862-7 Volume II
ISBN 0-684-18863-5 Volume III

Published simultaneously in Canada
by Collier Macmillan Canada, Inc.

3 5 7 9 11 13 15 17 19 Q/C 20 18 16 14 12 10 8 6 4 2

Printed in the United States of America.

The paper in this book meets the guidelines for permanence and
durability of the Committee on Production Guidelines for Book Longevity
of the Council on Library Resources

Editorial Staff

PREFACE

One of the most frequently quoted characterizations of America is G. K. Chesterton's remark that we are "the nation with the soul of a church." In a sense this is paradoxical, since the New Republic was the first in history in which government and organized religion were separated formally by law. Yet in this very separation lies a major clue to the prominent role that religion has played in the development of American society and culture. In no other nation, past or present, has such a diversity of religions existed among one people. In few other nations have religious groups competed so avidly with one another not only for adherents but for a chance to shape the broader society according to their own visions. In no other nation have religious events, issues, and personalities consistently claimed such a major share of public attention. One's appreciation of American society and culture is dramatically enriched by a grasp of the role religion has played throughout our history, from the time when Native American tribal cultures flourished to the age of the electronic church.

Scholars of earlier generations were often likely either to denigrate the role that religion played in American society, as in the caricatures of Puritanism offered by H. L. Mencken and Vernon Parrington, or else to employ a sort of tunnel vision in its study through which the development of one particular tradition was isolated from all other contexts. In this latter case, historians of a denomination saw themselves primarily as chronicling and celebrating the achievements of their own forebears, with little attention to how those achievements correlated with events in other traditions. More recently, however, those concerned with interpreting the broader contexts of the American story have come to emphasize the centrality of religion in the development of American society and culture as a whole. In the founding of most of the colonies that would eventually coalesce into the United States, religion was a major and often primary goal of these first settlements. "Nature's God," whom Jefferson invokes in the Declaration of Independence, was an essential idea of the Enlightenment that helped inspire a democratic and pluralistic new nation unlike any other in history. The fiction of Hawthorne and Melville is nearly unfathomable without an appreciation of the Calvinism lurking in those writers' backgrounds. Although the causes of the Civil War are complex, the prophetic zeal of abolitionists from John Brown to James Russell Lowell was doubtless a major component of its genesis. The towering figure of Martin Luther King, Jr., a Baptist preacher, stands at the center of the most dramatic social movements of the twentieth century. Contemporary issues of public policy—such as abortion, capital punishment, nuclear warfare, and the teaching of evolution in public schools—are unintelligible without a grasp of the religious issues at stake in these debates. At a time when critics of American education are lamenting the omission from texts and curricula of the religious dimension in our history, we hope that this collection of essays on virtually every aspect of that experience will help to rectify this neglect.

This encyclopedia offers a new approach to understanding the American religious experience. Most comprehensive works to date have tended to define

vii

PREFACE

"American" as referring only to the United States. The present three volumes seek to expand the range of vision to include all of the North American continent, although primary emphasis is put on developments within the United States. Many other reference works have told the story of the American religious experience from a perspective that reflects the dominance of Anglo-Saxon Protestantism in American religious life. These essays address more broadly the total scope of religious activity and the impact of that activity on American life. For example, we have included detailed treatment of several religions of Asian or Middle Eastern origin such as Islam, which may soon be exceeded only by Christianity in its number of American adherents. Similarly, we have devoted several essays to the various dimensions of worship, a topic generally slighted in historical surveys. We have also tried to recognize that religion is not confined to churches and synagogues and that it has had impact on aspects of American life ranging from the novel to the television evangelist.

The *Encyclopedia of the American Religious Experience* is organized by topical and thematic essays, rather than through a multitude of brief dictionary-like entries, to allow for more thorough discussion and analysis. All the essays have been composed with an eye not simply to thorough coverage of a particular topic but also to the significance of that subject in the development of American society and culture and the religious traditions and organizations within it. The cross-references and the detailed index are especially valuable to those who wish to survey the full scope of any given topic. Each essay also contains an extensive bibliography of pertinent works that point the reader to yet other perspectives.

The essays collected in these volumes make the best of current scholarship on religion in America available to a broad audience, including students, clergy, fellow scholars, and general readers. The authors come from Mexico, Canada, and all parts of the United States; their academic disciplines include American history, sociology, the history of religions, theology, philosophy, American studies, and others; and they themselves come from a great variety of religious backgrounds. The guiding principles of selection were the authors' achievements as scholars and their appropriateness in training and interest for the subjects. We have attempted to ensure that each essay satisfies some general requirements in covering the subject matter, while we have also encouraged all authors to contribute to original scholarship in their own unique voices, even when the viewpoint or interpretation presented may be controversial.

Essays from Part I of the *Encyclopedia,* which is entitled "Approaches to Religion in America," illustrate the cross-disciplinary nature of the study of religion in America. It is our belief that no single method of data gathering or interpretation can satisfactorily illuminate the nature of American religion, and we have therefore sought out this variety of interpretative stances. Similarly, as the titles in Part II ("North America: Contexts and Backgrounds") indicate, we believe that the religious experience of Americans cannot be understood in a cultural or historical vacuum, and we have therefore included essays that treat the various temporal, geographical, and ethnic contexts in which America's religious development has unfolded. In Part III and Part IV—"Jewish and Christian Traditions" and "Religions Outside the Jewish and Christian Traditions"—we have included discussions of a wide variety of organized religious denominations. However, in Part V and Part VI ("Movements in American Religion" and "American Religious Thought and Literature"), we have also tried to be mindful of the intellectual and social movements that have cut

PREFACE

across denominational lines and given rise to transformations and new configurations within older traditions, at times resulting in the birth of new denominations. Religious forces are not necessarily confined to explicitly religious structures, nor are such structures immune to the social and cultural currents of the broader society. In recognition of these influences, the third volume deals with these interactions from a wide variety of perspectives, as the organization indicates: "Liturgy, Worship and the Arts" (Part VII); "Religion and the Political and Social Orders" (Part VIII); and "The Dissemination of American Religion" (Part IX). Finally, the contemporary study of American religion has been characterized by the transcendence of narrowly denominational viewpoints, and these essays are offered as contributions to a common body of scholarship in which students of any or no individual religious commitment may participate.

In addition to the contributors themselves, we are indebted to a considerable number of people in the conceptualization, organization, and ultimate publication of these volumes. Special acknowledgment must be given to Martin E. Marty of the University of Chicago not only for his direct contributions but also for his helping to arrange a happy coming-together of editors and publishers. Next, the Reference Books Division of Charles Scribner's Sons has been consistently supportive of our work. Most recently this staff has included Jonathan Aretakis and Michael McGinley. Thanks are also due to their predecessors, who worked with us in earlier phases—Marshall DeBruhl, Christiane Deschamps, Laura Gross, Elizabeth Elston, and Kirk Reynolds. Each of us has received important logistical support from colleagues and staff at our respective universities: Sharon Barnes, Joseph Carter, Alan Schaffer, Flora Walker, and John Wunder at Clemson; and Stephen Day, Harold Forshey, Alan Miller, Kathi Fields, and Kathleen Grondin at Miami. Charles Lippy would also like especially to acknowledge Clemson's support in providing a sabbatical leave during the spring of 1984 and a Provost's Research Award. Among the contributors, Christa Klein, Albert Raboteau, and Baird Tipson have been involved with the project through its various metamorphoses and have been most supportive and helpful throughout. In addition, a number of scholars, though not able to contribute essays, provided valuable advice at various stages. They include Jeremy duQ. Adams of Southern Methodist University; John H. Erickson of St. Vladimir's Orthodox Theological Seminary; Philip Gleason of the University of Notre Dame; William Green of the University of Rochester; Robert T. Handy of Union Theological Seminary; Winthrop Hudson, of Chapel Hill, North Carolina; William R. Hutchison of Harvard University; Ronald L. Numbers of the University of Wisconsin; and John F. Wilson of Princeton University.

Finally, word came to us during this project's unfolding of the death of Yale's Sydney E. Ahlstrom, another longtime source of aid and encouragement. It is sobering for us to realize that, where we have assembled some hundred scholars for the task of synthesizing the story of religion in America, this one individual had created the previous generation's synthesis by himself.

Charles H. Lippy
Peter W. Williams

CONTENTS

CONTENTS

CONTENTS

CONTENTS

CONTENTS

CONTENTS

Encyclopedia of the
AMERICAN
RELIGIOUS
EXPERIENCE

Part I
APPROACHES TO RELIGION
IN AMERICA

THE HISTORIOGRAPHY OF
AMERICAN RELIGION

Henry Warner Bowden

UNTIL recently, all major historians of American religion have been advocates and participants in the events unfolding around them. For three centuries authors usually linked historical accounts with religious truth that they embraced as members of various ecclesiastical traditions. Although a separation has occurred in contemporary scholarship between historical and religious interests, earlier publications in this genre allowed for no difference between the two spheres. Historians identified themselves with churches and used history to defend the legitimacy of their respective causes. Perspectives in this earlier phase yielded religious histories, whereas more recent historiographical developments have produced histories of religion in America. In this latter stage questions of the ultimate truth in subjects under consideration have been left aside.

One of the earliest historians wrote a treatise based on first-hand observations, but his work was lost for many generations. William Bradford compiled *Of Plimoth Plantation* as a record of Pilgrim experiences from their voyage on the *Mayflower* in 1620 to the year 1647. This manuscript on the Plymouth colony became misplaced and, though mentioned by a few later chroniclers, did not appear in published form until 1841 (U.S. edition, 1856). Since then it has been issued in several printings as a valuable source on American religious beginnings. Another observer of Puritan settlement in the New World was Nathaniel Morton, whose *New England's Memorial* appeared in 1669. Probably the most influential authority on such affairs was Cotton Mather, whose *Magnalia Christi Americana* (1702) announced itself in subtitle as a cultural history, with religion paramount, covering events down to the year 1698. Mather's volume epitomized the pious historian's approach by describing personal virtue and ecclesiastical happenings in the service of a high purpose. He wrote to instruct readers about worthy antecedents, urging them to emulate sanctified habits and thus to perpetuate the commonwealth that had been established by earlier saints. A final example of this sort of history that featured seventeenth-century prototypes was *A Chronological History of New-England* (1736), written by Thomas Prince.

Developments in eighteenth-century America did not receive the same amount of historical attention from those who participated in them. Some think that the effect of Enlightenment categories gave priority to rationalism, considered timeless and uninterested in historical development. Others suggest that more immediate concerns such as revival experiences and political arguments over independence from England detracted from inquiry into the past. For these and more circumstantial reasons, few notable histories appeared during this period. The most important one, written by Samuel Miller, was entitled *A Brief Retrospect of the Eighteenth Century* (1803). Consisting of two volumes, this encyclopedic overview discusses the importance of religion in recent American developments, including advances in science, the arts, and literature. It also extols the priority of Presbyterian attitudes and principles, which Miller influenced as a clergyman of that denomination.

When romanticism succeeded the Enlightenment as a dominant cultural trend, intellectuals began to place more importance on historical background. In explaining a current state of affairs, they stressed origins as a determinant of subsequent characteristics. Historical development in the minds of most nineteenth-century writers constituted a gradual unfolding of the seed or germ that defined a subject's essential nature. One of the first authors to write a coordinated survey of American religion from this point of view was Robert Baird. His classic study, *Religion in America* (1843; unabridged reprint, 1856 and 1969; abridged reprint, 1970), attempted to explain the dynamics of church life in the United States to European observers. Baird clearly approved of such characteristics as separation of church and state, voluntary support for ecclesiastical programs, and revivals as the means to conversions and increased church membership. His stress on evangelical freedom allowed him to endorse mainstream Protestant churches as those embodying the true genius of American religion. The same perspective led him to reject Roman Catholics, Jews, Mormons, and Unitarians as marginal groups whose discordant traits could not hope to flourish in the republican atmosphere of American life. A similar bias in favor of "the voluntary principle," evangelical freedom, and gradual influence of religion on society can be seen in his *Progress and Prospects of Christianity in the United States of America* (1851) and *State and Prospects of Religion in America* (1855).

Another scholar who furthered the new interest in historical origins and progress was the Swiss-born, German-educated Philip Schaff. From a more ecumenical, broad-minded perspective, Schaff discussed religious developments in America against the backdrop of their relation to ancient, medieval, and Reformation occurrences. In *Principle of Protestantism* (1845; reprint, 1964) and *What Is Church History?* (1846) he laid the theoretical basis for a workable method in historical scholarship, justly acquiring the reputation as one of America's foremost church historians. Concentrating directly on the ecclesiastical scene of his adopted country, Schaff wrote *America: A Sketch of the Political, Social, and Religious Character of the United States of North America* (1855; reprint, 1961). In addition to articles and speeches on American themes made throughout his long career, he also published *Church and State in the United States,* a treatise first appearing in papers of the American Historical Association (1888) and reprinted as a separate volume in 1972. Like Baird, Schaff endorsed the Protestant principles of religious freedom, evangelical competition, and biblical authority that he saw operating in this country. But unlike

Baird, he discerned a pattern of growth where all churches contributed to progress. Schaff firmly believed that providential action guided developments in Catholic as well as Protestant groups. He foresaw a time when their variant versions of religious truth would eventually coalesce into a reunion of Christendom. This ecumenical achievement would, he thought, occur in America, the place where positive aspects of Old World heritages could combine without those specific elements of different traditions that heretofore had separated various communions. Schaff's irenic vision, historical accuracy, and emphasis on the providential direction of events had a lasting influence on his generation and the one to follow.

One of his contemporaries was made of sterner, more polemical stuff. John Gilmary Shea identified himself with the Roman Catholic church, and that church with exclusive religious truth. Perceiving himself primarily as an archivist who let documents speak for themselves, Shea compiled a wide range of materials for his *History of Catholic Missions Among the Indian Tribes of the United States, 1529–1854* (1855) and his four-volume magnum opus, *A History of the Catholic Church Within the Limits of the United States, from the First Attempted Colonization to the Present Time* (1886). In these works, as well as in many articles published in the *American Catholic Quarterly Review,* Shea wrote indefatigably to defend his church from the calumnies of Protestant critics. Assuming the rectitude of Catholic creeds and liturgy as unarguable truths, he labored to demonstrate his church's seniority in American experience. Compared with Spanish, French, and even English priestly efforts in the New World, Protestant activities were tardy attempts to transfer religious witness across the Atlantic. Shea was also concerned about the legitimacy of Catholic citizenship. After Protestants became preponderant in American affairs, they challenged Catholic loyalty to republican cultural values. Shea marshaled historical documents to argue that Catholics were genuinely American, qualified for full participation in communal life by their adherence to stable church life and by repeated support of governmental policy—especially through enlisting to defend American interests during wartime.

While Shea used history for apologetic purposes on behalf of Catholicism, Daniel Dorchester emerged as a spokesman for the dominant Protestant viewpoint. This Massachusetts Methodist minister shared a respect for historical data with his peers, but in his case it took two distinctive forms. Dorchester utilized statistical evidence for his surveys as no investigator had before, and his emphasis on progress inaugurated a new interpretive dimension. Instead of stressing early religious traits that continued through changing circumstances, legitimizing present practices through ties with an orthodox past, Dorchester emphasized progressive movement away from venerable origins. In *Problems of Religious Progress* (1881; rev. eds., 1895, 1900) he compiled tables, charts, and diagrams to authenticate the popular view that American Protestants had improved on earlier attempts to affect secular life with religious values. His *Christianity in the United States from the First Settlement down to the Present Time* (1888; rev. ed., 1895) also furnished massive documentation to prove that mainstream Protestant churches were improving moral and social conditions as never before. His optimistic conception of religious growth epitomized the high point of pan-Protestant dominance in American culture. Embracing a broad selection of Reformation traditions but eschewing minority voices such as Catholicism, Dorchester's imperialistic view championed progress of an exclusive sort. It also failed to note cultural developments such as immigration that would soon make his triumphalist conceptions obsolete.

Philip Schaff's broad historical vision and encouragement of scholarly endeavor bore fruit alongside Dorchester's parochial tabulations. Shortly after founding the American Society of Church History in 1888, Schaff began recruiting experts in denominational history to write for a contemplated *American Church History Series.* Thirteen volumes were published between 1893 and 1897 on various aspects of the nation's religious makeup. The series was at that time the most ambitious venture in historical studies of American religion, and its scope has not been equaled since. The shelf of books included separate studies of twenty denominations. Schaff urged authors to emphasize compatible elements among their several churches, the better to further common sympathies and shared goals for future growth. Most volumes featured careful use of denominational source materials, discussed

events against the background of larger intellectual and social movements, and softened interchurch polemics. Conspicuous among the others, *The Religious Forces of the United States* (1893; rev. eds., 1896, 1912; reprint, 1971) by Henry K. Carroll drew heavily on the government census of 1890 and used those statistics to discuss the condition and character of American Christianity for contemporaries. The final volume, *A History of American Christianity* (1897; reprint, 1971) by Leonard W. Bacon, provided a masterful summation of the various denominational episodes. Bacon took a major step in blending denominational chronicles with standard geographical and chronological categories, thus moving toward the production of a single religious history for Americans.

By the turn of the twentieth century, religious historiographical patterns had reached their most important transitional period. Some historians continued to produce narrowly focused, denominational apologetics. Others had begun to tackle interdenominational surveys of increased scope, but this focus still highlighted core Protestant groups such as Baptists, Methodists, Presbyterians, Congregationalists, and Episcopalians, with a nod toward Lutherans and Disciples of Christ for good measure. Attempts to align religious history with secular historical chronology and interpretive themes had more far-reaching consequences. As religious historians sought to incorporate contemporary scholarly standards in their providential narratives, they slowly learned that new rigors concerning documentary evidence required a shift in their customary approach. It became increasingly difficult to invoke divine guidance as a factor in history, and as more students of American religion were trained at American universities and abroad, new generations of investigators gradually abandoned references to providential causation. In its place they conformed to secular interpretive themes current among historians of social and political topics.

One important perspective that shaped historical interpretation at the beginning of this century has been termed "progressivism." This more recent type of progressivism differs from the earlier version by stressing conflict and embattled victory over obstacles rather than a gradual evolution of tendencies attributable to organic growth. Modern progressivism emphasized struggles that overcame vested interests, not an effortless exfoliation of characteristics whose inherent power made triumph inevitable. The exemplar of such a view applied to religion was *History of Religion in the United States* (1924) by Henry K. Rowe. Though it lacked scholarly references and a bibliography to aid further inquiry, Rowe's work stood within the tradition of secular progressivist historians. He chose episodes from American annals to chart the growth of liberty. For him the main themes of church development in this country had been the victory of free church ideals over ecclesiastical establishment, the triumph of evangelical enthusiasm over formalized preaching and worship, and the emergence of activist theological views over Calvinist dogmatism. Rowe's account of religious changes on the American continent celebrated both an upward movement of acquired freedoms and the emerging core of what could be called distinctive American religion, separable from other versions.

A scholar whose career shared the same timespan with Rowe was Peter K. Guilday, but his parochial interests place his contributions within a more specific, topical framework. Guilday succeeded Shea as the foremost historian of American Catholicism, and his concern to place ecclesiastical events in the larger context of this country's cultural progress added a dimension that made his publications interesting to a wider reading public. His concern to embody critical historical procedures also recommended his work within a scholarly constituency that was becoming increasingly professionalized.

Guilday produced a number of essays, lectures, and bibliographical guides on new studies of Catholic experience in the United States. In 1919 his spearheading efforts culminated in founding the American Catholic Historical Association. Concerning his own researches, a biographical focus yielded valuable studies of two early American prelates. His two-volume *Life and Times of John Carroll* (1922; reprint, 1954) portrayed the church's first bishop and archbishop amid all the difficulties of administering to the faithful while creating an adequate hierarchy. Similarly, his *Life and Times of John England* (1927), also in two volumes, depicted the travail of encouraging growth of a minority religion during the early national period. Guilday also wrote *A History of the Councils of Baltimore, 1791–*

1884 (1932), which discussed in a progressivist vein the gradual vindication of Catholic resilience in a country where nativist antagonisms had impaired its contribution to liberty.

Emerging alongside progressivists, other historians of American religion turned their attention to a different set of interpretive themes fostered by secular investigators. Though compatible with judgments about recent successes won at the expense of outmoded opposition, this historiographical focus chose to emphasize environmental factors as an explanation of how the process occurred. These historians preferred to describe the process and to underscore the role played by environmental context in various epochs. The American frontier was one of the most fruitful sets of conditioning factors that historians used for explanation and interpretation. At first the frontier was thought of in geographical and physical terms, but eventually this concept expanded to include all boundary experiences in social, cultural, and intellectual spheres. By concentrating on American culture as it moved west, frontier historians were free to select aspects of experience that were useful in furthering contemporary social reforms. Instead of dwelling on colonial origins, ageless principles, or organic unfolding, the frontier school looked at conflicts met when people moved west. That focus and changes born from struggles to survive contributed to improving the quality of American life.

Peter G. Mode was one of the earliest students of American religion to utilize the frontier theme as an organizing and interpretive principle. At the turn of this century Mode was convinced that environmental conditioning did not receive enough recognition as a factor in history. So he adopted the "frontier thesis," recently made popular by his fellow midwesterner Frederick Jackson Turner. Mode's inventive capacity showed itself by adapting much of the already familiar story of American denominational Protestantism to this powerful thesis. His book *The Frontier Spirit in American Christianity* (1923) stands at the head of a veritable flood of others that utilized frontier conditions to explain religious developments in this country. Mode did not influence these authors directly, nor did they consciously imitate his work. Frontier themes appeared so appropriate, so "right" as the distinctive explanatory factor for America, that many historians absorbed and reflected it unquestioningly. Mode was the first of this literary throng, and he charted the way for those who came after by issuing the *Source Book and Bibliographical Guide for American Church History* (1921). As researcher and author of pioneering books, he set a historiographical precedent that remained vigorous for the next half century.

Following the line of thought that Mode inaugurated, William W. Sweet expanded frontier elements to make that perspective a dominant theme in American religious scholarship. Sweet occupied the first chair of American church history in the country, at the University of Chicago, from 1927 until 1946. He strove to establish the integrity of what he considered a neglected field in religious studies. As an advocate of training in secular historical methods, Sweet also began a program of graduate studies that singled out American topics for research. He set about collecting documentary sources, making Chicago the richest depository of primary source materials in the country. Selected publications from this archive made representative sources available to the larger public. Sweet compiled four volumes for the *Religion on the American Frontier* series. *The Baptists, 1783–1830* (1931; reprint, 1964), *The Presbyterians, 1783–1840* (1936; reprint, 1964), *The Congregationalists, 1783–1850* (1939; reprint, 1964), and *The Methodists, 1783–1840* (1946; reprint, 1964) comprised a wealth of data regarding the largest and most active Protestant churches at work in America's westering experience.

Sweet provided many narratives and analyses in addition to these collected documents. As one fascinated with the New World, he argued that life on the American continent had elicited fresh beginnings. America in his view was new ground where innovative forms of institutional and intellectual life flourished. This viewpoint shaped his classic narrative, *The Story of Religions in America* (1930; rev. eds., 1939, 1950), which quickly captured the market as a textbook in this area. There he held that in the frontier context men from all stations of life worked out pragmatic approaches to the problems and opportunities confronting them. They eventually created new attitudes in which innovation and experimentation became a distinctive way of life. General characteristics accruing to this frontier environment were individualism, hard work, recklessness, an up-

wardly mobile and democratic social system, violence, and an ability to form lines of common defense in times of crisis. Many studies replicated these observations. *Religion in Colonial America* (1942), *Revivalism in America* (1944), *The American Churches: An Interpretation* (1947), *American Culture and Religion* (1951), and *Religion in the Development of American Culture, 1765–1840* (1952) all attest to Sweet's attachment to frontier experience as the key to a proper understanding of religious activity in the nation's collective past. These studies allowed him to put forth interpretations that stressed American religion as a force for applying moral discipline on lawless circumstances, a missionary activism that discounted theological precision, an evangelical context that valued revival techniques, and an atmosphere of freedom that encouraged tolerance and ecumenical cooperation.

While Sweet was producing his studies of the emergent characteristics of American religion, derived from pioneer experience, a few scholars began looking at the country's early beginnings again. Before the 1930s, studies of Puritan activities had ebbed to a very low point. Publications that mentioned religious influence in early American life, such as *Main Currents in American Thought* (1927, 1930) by Vernon L. Parrington, disparaged it to the point of insignificance or obscurantism. Most students of American religion at this time either accepted the prevailing viewpoint or ignored the topic to pursue more promising areas of research. But a resurgence of Puritan studies occurred largely because of one man, an individual not professionally connected with religion as an academic discipline and one utterly indifferent to possible truths found in any of its theological statements. Perry G. E. Miller was professor of American literature at Harvard University, and in that position he pursued a lifetime of inquiry into the intellectual roots of American culture. Noting that colonial influences were heavily shaped by religious considerations, Miller launched penetrating studies into that substratum. His most valuable contribution lay in trying to understand the full range of Puritan life for its own sake, not for purposes of edifying readers or of measuring later progress against initially principled rigidity.

Miller portrayed the full sweep of Puritan life with both erudition and wit. He contributed two biographies of major figures: *Jonathan Edwards*

(1949) and *Roger Williams* (1953). Those studies contained some controversial interpretations, but even more provocative ideas appeared in *Orthodoxy in Massachusetts* (1933) and in *Errand into the Wilderness* (1952), where Miller put forth a new appreciation of Puritan practice and purpose. All such occasional pieces formed a setting for two massive syntheses of colonial life. *The New England Mind: The Seventeenth Century* (1939) and *The New England Mind: From Colony to Province* (1953) allowed Miller enough room to detail every major aspect of religious thought and clerical duty. His careful tracing of intellectual roots in Britain and on the Continent helped clarify the framework of Puritan thinking. His empathetic recapitulation of vigorous theological articulation laid bare the tensions and power of religious influences amid burgeoning social development.

In addition to rehabilitating Puritan studies almost single-handedly with these seminal efforts, Miller also furnished new collections of sources for others to read. Sometimes alone, sometimes collaborating with other editors, he put together anthologies, such as *The Puritans* (1938; rev. ed., 1963), *The Transcendentalists* (1950), and *The Great Awakening* (1967), through which subsequent historians could appreciate the vital world of American religious thought.

Miller's success was due largely to the high quality of his analysis and the care with which he investigated historical details. But his independent explorations into a neglected field coincided with a larger historiographical trend, and this shift to broader priorities gave momentum to the perspective that Miller embodied. The new focus was intellectual history, or a return to the study of ideas. Historians have been interested in ideas one way or another for some time, of course, and earlier historical schools included some notice of human thought in their interpretive schemes.

Since the 1950s, however, intellectual historians have exhibited attitudes that distinguish them from earlier students of ideas. These perspectives harbored a basically new appreciation for complexity in American history, an awareness of multiple forces that earlier interpretations simplified for ulterior motives. With this awareness, intellectual historians defended ideas as factors that had to be recognized as part of causal explanations. They held that ideas were powerful determinants of action, as important in a given period as social, political, or economic considerations. Other historians took an even bolder stand and chose to study ideas or systems of thought with little concern for their utility or practical application. Miller fit more plausibly in this category because he usually looked at ideas for what they were rather than for what they did. So his initiative demonstrated to other historians of American religion that inquiries could savor the intrinsic worth of beliefs and not necessarily justify them by pragmatic assessment. Intellectual historians since his time have stressed either the inherent cogency of religious ideas or their practical consequences, and each approach has enlarged the horizons of professional scholarship and has enriched its content.

While Sweet led the way with writings on religion in frontier conditions and Miller patiently unfolded the Puritan intellectual world, some contemporaries attempted other synthetic overviews. H. Richard Niebuhr wrote *Social Sources of Denominationalism* (1929), where he applied sociological analysis to explain the constantly proliferating number of ecclesiastical groups in this country. He then supplemented that view with *The Kingdom of God in America* (1937), in which he used an avowedly theological perspective to conflate most differences found in American religion into three variations on that basic ideal. Taking a different interpretive tack, Winfred E. Garrison in *The March of Faith* (1933) focused on religious developments after the Civil War. Students of American life could grasp the really important conditions of modern existence, he said, by looking at recent developments such as urban growth and increased industrialization. Colonial beginnings were relatively insignificant for him. Another author of this period who made admirable efforts to comprehend general developmental patterns was Willard L. Sperry. His *Religion in America* (1946) represented the limited capacity of his generation of scholars to break with dated conceptions of Protestant hegemony and denominational interpretation.

Another major element affecting historiographical tendencies emerged in full force at midcentury. Instead of emphasizing progress through conflict, historians in this more recent era tried to locate a consensus of American values that could be salvaged from a turbulent past. In a more somber mood after World War II, historians reflected new concerns about finding some measure of reassuring continuity in American life. They became more conservative because awareness of death camps, aggressive Marxism, and the atomic bomb nurtured unsettling anxieties. Many turned to history as a means of singling out a better life in American experience, superior to the uncertainties of global competition. Instead of endorsing change as progress, many historians were apprehensive about the future, and that mind-set correspondingly affected their view of the past. Consensus historians no longer emphasized conflict or unsettling change in our collective experience but rather sought to locate a homogeneous culture where shared ideals had undergirded variation over time as a normative reality in American experience.

The perspective that highlighted a search for consensus found many supporters among American religious historians. Great numbers of works published in the middle decades of this century echoed with themes of continuity, together with those stressing doctrine or intellectual content and distinctive traits of American character. In religious studies these works featured another more practical quality too, namely, generalized synopses based on a solid foundation of monographic investigations. Broad synthetic histories subsumed the best of deeper inquiries into specific topics and presented those findings within an overall narrative of American religious life. Clifton E. Olmstead, for example, produced an overview in his *History of Religion in the United States* (1960) and followed it with a condensed version in *Religion in America: Past and Present* (1961). In amalgamating a large number of narrower scholarly investigations Olmstead succeeded in portraying American religion as an entity, greater than the sum of its disparate parts. Another author whose publications fit within this broad classification is Winthrop S. Hudson. In *The Great Tradition in American Churches* (1953) he emphasized a consensus of values since colonial times, and his *American Protestantism* (1961) as well as *Religion in America: An Historical Account of the Development of American Religious Life* (1965; rev. eds., 1973, 1981) made splendid use of more specialized studies for general survey purposes.

In considering this genre of synoptic, generic, catholic histories of religion in the American past, the figure of Sidney E. Mead must be reckoned with. Mead primarily utilized articles, reviews, and lectures to disseminate his ideas, and at least two generations of historians have carefully noted his suggestive contributions. Nine essays found their way into a small but weighty book, *The Lively Experiment: The Shaping of Christianity in America* (1963). There Mead displayed encyclopedic familiarity with both sources and interpretive opinions while wrestling with the implications of religious freedom as the spiritual force that interacted with other aspects of American culture. Democratic beliefs rooted in Christian faith, true religion embodied in democratic forms and ideals for the good society—these were the factors that fascinated Mead as central elements of a past that presented complex ambiguities for the present. If historians could untangle threads of pietism and rationalism in the American heritage, he hoped they might furnish future generations with the means of appropriating those traditions with contemporary effectiveness.

The latter half of this century has witnessed a veritable renaissance of historical writing about American Christianity. The study of religion definitively abandoned its attempt to edify readers with references to supernatural truth and providential causation. Most historians in recent times have preferred instead to define their subject as one of the many subheadings of humanistic inquiry. An outstanding and durable accomplishment embodying this modern viewpoint was a two-volume masterpiece by H. Shelton Smith, Robert T. Handy, and Lefferts A. Loetscher, *American Christianity: An Historical Interpretation with Representative Documents* (1960, 1963). The authors provided an extensive discussion of diverse religious developments in this country. They developed an independent chronology and reprinted 187 primary sources to show how the Christian religion helped fashion the larger context of American culture and was in turn shaped by this nurturing environment. The aptness of selected documents, accuracy of dates and spelling, wisdom of bibliographical choices, and balance of interpretive judgments sustain this work as one of the most important publications of the century.

Another collective effort worth mentioning was *Religion in American Life* (1961), a modest series edited by James W. Smith and A. Leland

Jamison. Their synthetic overview incorporated essays by specialists who discussed ways in which institutional and intellectual aspects of American religion have interacted with other facets of national life. Recurrent themes such as pluralism, scientific empiricism, and cultural accommodation received particular attention in separate volumes called *The Shaping of American Religion* and *Religious Perspectives in American Culture*. Also part of the series was the indispensable two-volume study *A Critical Bibliography of Religion in America* by Nelson R. Burr, who organized huge quantities of disparate material topically and according to historical periods. More a discussion of previous works than a mere listing of titles, this achievement was truly impressive for both its range of knowledge and its intriguing use of organizing techniques. It remains a trustworthy introduction to the field as well as a familiar guide for specialists.

Two of the coauthors of *American Christianity . . . Representative Documents* deserve mention for their independent work. H. Shelton Smith combined interests in religious thought and cultural conditions to aid historical interpretation at crucial junctures. His *Changing Conceptions of Original Sin: A Study in American Theology Since 1750* (1955) remains the best survey of intellectual convictions that began with Calvinist strictures and shifted gradually to Arminian affirmations. In line with these general tendencies Smith also brought out *Horace Bushnell* (1965), a sophisticated interpretation of and selection of writings by a subsequent theologian of note. His last great contribution focused on race relations within Protestant churches, a vexing problem that he described with sympathy and gentle impatience in *In His Image, But . . . : Racism in Southern Religion, 1780–1910* (1972). Robert T. Handy has also distinguished himself for decades as a scholar of the highest rank. In addition to essays, reviews, and popular lectures, Handy produced a study of Protestant dominance in nineteenth-century America that approached definitive status. In *A Christian America: Protestant Hopes and Historical Realities* (1971) he delineated early attempts by Protestants to control American values, and then he indicated which altered features of modern culture doomed those attempts increasingly to failure. His ambitious project *A History of the Churches in the United States and Canada* (1977) incorporated for the first time an account

of North American religious activities beyond this country's borders. Its successful introduction of a new integrative concept has challenged others to pursue further investigations along that line.

The search for new organizing principles or integrative techniques elicited two more significant contributions. Martin E. Marty has published extensively in American religious history, producing books and articles in such profusion that readers hardly know how to assimilate all of them. Standing out from the rest of Marty's work, however, was his *Righteous Empire: The Protestant Experience in America* (1970) wherein he crystallized an interpretive theme adumbrated in some of his earlier writings. There Marty boldly asserted that denominational classifications in modern America were less important than differences between members of the same church. He saw liberal and conservative clusters of adherents who resembled each other across denominational lines. This "two-party system" was, he suggested, more helpful than the old organizational labels for understanding religious patterns in contemporary times.

Another author who brought a different investigative principle to bear was Arthur C. Piepkorn, whose *Profiles of Belief: The Religious Bodies of the United States and Canada* (1977, 1979) consummated decades of dogged, painstaking research. In four volumes Piepkorn collated data on more than a thousand different religious bodies. He provided a short historical sketch of their institutional origins and then expounded central doctrines with rich ecumenical understanding. This encyclopedic work bids fair to supersede the earlier taxonomic success by Frank S. Mead, *Handbook of Denominations in the United States* (1951; 7th ed., 1980).

One of the foremost scholars in American religion during recent times has been Edwin S. Gaustad, whose contributions have set standards in both methodological dexterity and conceptual comprehensiveness. He provided a survey of pluralistic patterns in *A Religious History of America* (1966), which stood alongside several others in competition for a limited textbook market. A more original work was *Historical Atlas of Religion in America* (1962; rev. ed., 1976), which set Gaustad on an unparalleled plateau. With abundant charts and maps it constituted a narrative geographical history of American religion that portrayed the expansion and contractions of this country's denominations. In addition to noting specific groups, Gaustad also discussed American Christianity in a synoptic way that placed religious devotion within the larger social, political, economic, and military affairs of its time. More than a tracing of discrete church groupings, it ranks as one of the best generic histories of American religion. In reproducing primary sources for contemporary students, Gaustad has since issued two volumes that represent the very finest judgment about rich and variegated expressions over the past four hundred years. *A Documentary History of Religion in America* (1982–1983) reprinted materials from mainline traditions and sectarian innovations in two volumes. They included staid bureaucratic memoranda and passionate speeches from souls burning for a cause, comprising in their pages the finest collection of diverse material on the subject yet to be printed.

One final author culminated the long list of scholars who strove to correlate previous monographic studies into a single survey. Sydney E. Ahlstrom applied his interests in religious thought and in general American studies to create the fullest, most complete overview of spiritual experiences and expressions in the American context. *A Religious History of the American People* (1972) resulted from several decades of study in different aspects of the nation's religious past. It actually constituted three discernible but not separable emphases within the covers of a single, massive volume. On one level Ahlstrom produced an integrated discussion of religious activities associated with tangible structures. He depicted the life and thoughts of persons who for centuries worked within organized religious groups, and he analyzed their historical existence by reference to sociologically defined religious actions. On a second level Ahlstrom went beyond standard institutional history to recognize that many religious activities flourished outside of traditionally organized channels. This more comprehensive discussion touched on manifestations of religious sensibilities that have appeared in this country over the years. The third emphasis in his survey focused on religion and its reciprocal connections with American social and political life. Reminding his readers that religion has stimuli and outlets in a milieu larger than the confines of churches or

circles of believers, Ahlstrom dealt creatively with the complex relationships between faith and cultural behavior. He continued a historiographical tradition stemming from Robert Baird, which interpreted America as a nation with the soul of a church where evangelical Protestantism informed popular national ideals during much of its history.

Contemporary scholarship on Roman Catholicism has been enhanced tremendously by the efforts of one gifted historian, John T. Ellis. Trained originally in European church history, Ellis turned rather late to American affairs and achieved immediate recognition for his painstakingly thorough two-volume study *The Life of James Cardinal Gibbons, Archbishop of Baltimore, 1834–1921* (1952). His ability to match a talent for general interpretive discussion to narrow investigation became clear with the issuance of *American Catholicism* (1956; rev. ed., 1969), a brief and lucid overview that still circulates widely among new generations of readers. Ellis also put together a useful collection of primary sources related to his communion, entitled *Documents of American Catholic History* (1956; rev. ed., 1967). There he displayed a mastery of judicious choice among available materials as well as a capacity for explaining their significance in succinct introductory comments. A further comprehensive survey from his pen was *Catholics in Colonial America* (1965), in which he discussed comparatively the various Spanish, French, and English beginnings on this continent.

Since the heyday of Ellis' writing, Philip Gleason has released an edited collection of essays, *Catholicism in America* (1970), and David J. O'Brien has published *The Renewal of American Catholicism* (1972). A more recent volume attempts to build on these previous works and place Catholic studies on a more comprehensive level. James J. Hennesey in *American Catholics: A History of the Roman Catholic Community in the United States* (1981) strove to depict the heartbeat of common religious life that has always undergirded more academic topics such as diocesan, hierarchical, and institutional growth.

Judaism in American life did not elicit much study during the country's early centuries because Jewish communities were small. As this faith grew significantly with twentieth-century demographic expansion, historical studies have emerged to achieve both scope and sophistication of appreciable merit. Morris U. Schappes compiled *A Documentary History of the Jews in the United States, 1654–1875* (1950; rev. ed., 1971), which inaugurated a list of many other important studies. Jacob R. Marcus edited an impressive three volumes, *Memoirs of American Jews, 1775–1865* (1955–1956), and then issued a further compilation entitled *American Jewry: Documents* (1959). The collaborative work of Joseph L. Blau and Salo W. Baron yielded additional primary sources in their meticulous *Jews of the United States, 1790–1840* (1963). Industrious spadework of that sort provided the background for others who accepted the challenge of discussing Judaism in the larger context of American culture. Nathan Glazer produced a gem of a little book, *American Judaism* (1957; rev. ed., 1972), for the *History of American Civilization* series supervised by Daniel Boorstin. Winthrop S. Hudson and John T. Ellis also contributed volumes to that series, on Protestantism and Catholicism, respectively. Joseph L. Blau wrote a survey, *Judaism in America: From Curiosity to Third Faith* (1976), that stands as the latest general treatment of this ancient heritage in modern circumstances.

Sydney E. Ahlstrom's comprehensive discussion of American religious experience was the capstone of works going back thematically to Robert Baird and methodologically to William W. Sweet. From 1930 to 1972 many authors surveyed the whole field of religious developments in this country, but that historiographical era has now come to a close. The concern for consensus history has given way to new interests in topical diversity, methodological experimentation, and uncertainty regarding any integrative interpretive pattern. New energies motivate younger students of American religion in this last quarter of the twentieth century, and innovative questions together with fresh data enlarge the scope of learning. Minority voices such as those of blacks, Hispanics, and American Indians are causing historians to recover unknown historical elements from oblivion. Other minorities, long present but ignored, such as women in every ethnic group, are demanding fuller and more balanced understanding of their partially known activities. New hypotheses drawn from psychology, anthropology, and increased interdisciplinary amalgams call for additional interpretations of familiar documents. These and many more fac-

tors give contemporary historians greater opportunities to combine methodological techniques and avenues of approach to enrich their findings.

Of many creative studies in this contemporary genre three are striking examples of fresh discussion of religion. Peter W. Williams' *Popular Religion in America* (1980) posed a deliberate rejoinder to Ahlstrom, urging students to see that a great deal of important religious experience was excluded from even the most magisterial of inclusive surveys. Catherine L. Albanese echoed the point Williams made, and her *American Religions and Religion* (1981) provided additional proof that the pluralistic nature of the topic, viewed through a cumulative number of perspectives, could never be exhausted or given definitive treatment. Another publication of this sort that celebrates complexity and diversification is *American Religion: A Cultural Perspective* (1984) by Mary F. Bednarowski.

Among all the different perspectives developed during this century, that of social history has probably yielded the most fruitful consequences for religion studies. The new focal point was deliberately urged by scholars such as James H. Robinson and John F. Jameson in the early 1900s to counteract undue emphasis on military and political events. Social experience, dubbed "New History," allowed students to investigate the various aspects of everyday existence that constituted people's lives. Most historians who followed this broad avenue of inquiry had been raised in urban areas and had absorbed values after America reached mature levels of industrial and technological accomplishment. The pioneering study of urbanization was *The Rise of the City, 1878–1898* (1930), by Arthur M. Schlesinger, Sr. He suggested numerous ways in which social forces affected education, politics, the arts, and religion. Schlesinger helped shape successive generations through seminal essays and by advising graduate students. Another historian who opened many eyes to the importance of social development and the possible roles of religious influence was Richard Hofstadter, whose *Social Darwinism in American Thought, 1860–1915* (1944) explored the intellectual dynamics of the new age. After that, Hofstadter published studies of more contemporary times, taking a decidedly positive attitude toward social progress and humanitarian legislation in both *The Age of Reform:*

From Bryan to F.D.R. (1955) and *The Progressive Movement, 1900–1915* (1963).

Many students trained according to the canons of social history chose to focus specifically on religious groups and to investigate their contribution to social movements. Some of the more mature and sober assessments along this line include Aaron I. Abell's *The Urban Impact of American Protestantism, 1865–1900* (1943), Henry F. May's *Protestant Churches and Industrial America* (1949), and Arthur Mann's *Yankee Reformers in the Urban Age* (1954). Developing somewhat later in the sequence of scholarly publication, similar studies of Roman Catholic influence have now produced impressive achievements as well. Aaron Abell again led the way with his *American Catholicism and Social Action: A Search for Social Justice, 1865–1950* (1960); another landmark study was David J. O'Brien's *American Catholics and Social Reform: The New Deal Years* (1968).

Most aspects of social history produced in this century have had a "liberal" or "progressivist" flavor that accentuates the benefits of reform and social change. One facet of social history that did not applaud American experience or depict the dominant tendencies in policy and practice approvingly was immigration. While many historians have acknowledged immigration as a factor in American life, the modern scholar probably most responsible for pressing the point home has been Oscar Handlin. Beginning with *Boston's Immigrants, 1790–1880: A Study in Acculturation* (1941), Handlin spotlighted a field where religion played a significant role. His classic *The Uprooted: The Epic Story of the Great Migrations that Made the American People* (1951) and a later synthesis, *Race and Nationality in American Life* (1957), pointed out many levels where religious loyalty to imported traditions provided stability in the lives of people set in a context of bewildering new demands. Successive waves of immigration created a more complex society in this country and augmented its burgeoning religious pluralism. Many residents took a jaundiced view of the newcomers and their faiths brought from the Old World. Important studies by Ray A. Billington (*The Protestant Crusade 1800–1860: A Study of the Origins of American Nativism*, 1938) and John Higham (*Strangers in the Land: Patterns of American Nativism, 1850–1925*, 1955) pointed up the less attractive side of conservative Americans who

used religious prejudice to combat recently arrived citizens of the republic.

Another area where historians mined seams of social history to find ore that could be coined into greater understanding of religious experience was that of family life and collective biography. Edmund S. Morgan produced a landmark study in 1944, *The Puritan Family: Religion and Domestic Relations in Seventeenth-Century New England,* and that example has prompted many subsequent efforts in more circumscribed areas of inquiry. Morgan's works also included *The Puritan Dilemma: The Story of John Winthrop* (1958) and *Visible Saints: The History of a Puritan Idea* (1963), which also sparked a host of other investigations into the relationships between religion and colonial society. Two worth mentioning are Richard L. Bushman's *From Puritan to Yankee: Character and the Social Order in Connecticut, 1690–1765* (1967) and Robert Middlekauf's *The Mathers: Three Generations of Puritan Intellectuals, 1596–1728* (1971). These are just samples of the profound impact on religion studies made by the perspective that focuses on social experience and the role played by people's faith in their community setting.

In recent decades there has been a prodigious growth in monographs that concentrate on special questions of religious activity. They are far too numerous to list in any comprehensive way, but some of the most significant can be mentioned as representative of the rest. Since the days of Perry Miller, Puritan studies have once again risen to a critical intensity and thoroughness that define them as a field in itself. David D. Hall's *The Faithful Shepherd: A History of the New England Minister in the Seventeenth Century* (1972) provided a careful analysis of changes in clerical function and status in America's most influential class of religious leaders. E. Brooks Holifield's *The Covenant Sealed: The Development of Puritan Sacramental Theology in Old and New England, 1570–1720* (1974) traced the emergence of institutional patterns for a magisterial church over against challenges of sectarian dissenters. Sacvan Bercovitch combined a sensitivity to belles lettres and to religious expressions in his works *The Puritan Origins of the American Self* (1975) and *The American Jeremiad* (1978). There he probed for the early American consciousness of purpose and identity with the land that marked Puritans as archetypes of the people that eventually emerged. Emory Elliott's *Power and the Pulpit in Puritan New England* (1975) depicts changes in collective consciousness as generations of colonial Americans grew accustomed to their new surroundings. David E. Stannard (*The Puritan Way of Death: A Study in Religion, Culture, and Social Change,* 1977) and Mason I. Lowance, Jr. (*The Language of Canaan,* 1980) are more recent authors who show that investigations into Puritan life have not exhausted innovative ways of shedding light on the past.

Each denomination and colonial region has its special topics, together with authors who advance learning in those particular areas. Perhaps none of them, however, has benefited as much from a consistently high-quality scholarship as have the Quakers of the middle Atlantic region. In 1948 Frederick Tolles set the standard for modern historical students of the Society of Friends with his *Meetinghouse and Countinghouse: The Quaker Merchants of Colonial Philadelphia, 1682–1763.* Since then Mary M. Dunn has produced *William Penn: Politics and Conscience* (1967) and Melvin B. Endy, Jr., has written *William Penn and Early Quakerism* (1973), two complementary analyses of the complex founding father. New historical perspectives have further benefited studies of this group, as evidenced by J. William Frost's *The Quaker Family in Colonial America: A Portrait of the Society of Friends* (1973) and Jack D. Marietta's *The Reform of American Quakerism, 1748–1783* (1984).

Monographs in many other topical and chronological areas show that almost all contemporary scholarship is interdisciplinary. Historians combine a number of different perspectives to produce studies of great sophistication and subtle nuance. Recent studies of eighteenth-century experience include Alan Heimert's *Religion and the American Mind from the Great Awakening to the Revolution* (1966), which produced widespread reaction, both positive and negative. Catherine L. Albanese's work *Sons of the Fathers: The Civil Religion of the American Revolution* (1976) showed once again that this author is in the forefront of those who combine different insights to enhance our understanding of religion in both individual and collective action. Nathan O. Hatch published *The Sacred Cause of Liberty: Republican Thought and the Millennium in Revolutionary New England* (1977), while Mark A. Noll wrote *Christians in the American Revolution* (1977) to elu-

cidate further ramifications of religious motivation at work during the birth of this nation.

Religious experience in the early national period has also received close attention. The classic by William G. McLoughlin, *Modern Revivalism: Charles Grandison Finney to Billy Graham* (1959), set the stage for many solid studies of a widespread phenomenon in American life. Timothy L. Smith's *Revivalism and Social Reform: American Protestantism on the Eve of the Civil War* (1957) combined traditional attention to theological influences with new questions about social effectiveness. Interdisciplinary investigations reached a new peak with a brace of books that appeared the same year. Clifford S. Griffin wrote *Their Brothers' Keepers: Moral Stewardship in the United States, 1800–1865* (1960) and Charles I. Foster published *An Errand of Mercy: The Evangelical United Front, 1790–1837* (1960), separate investigations of social reform, expressing both republican optimism and conservative control. The debate has not ended yet, but the most sophisticated advance on the topic thus far has been by Fred J. Hood, in his *Reformed America: The Middle and Southern States, 1783–1837* (1980).

Developments later in the nineteenth century have also received the attention that befits their varied nature in both institutional forms and intellectual content. Some of the most impressive of these studies have concentrated on ideas that emerged into distinctive forms. Kenneth Cauthen opened new vistas on theological innovation with his *The Impact of American Religious Liberalism* (1962), and this work led to William R. Hutchison's *The Modernist Impulse in American Protestantism* (1976), which currently stands as the definitive study. In 1970 Ernest R. Sandeen pioneered studies of the theological counterpart to liberalism in *The Roots of Fundamentalism: British and American Millenarianism, 1800–1930.* Refinements in this area led to George R. Marsden's *Fundamentalism and American Culture: The Shaping of Twentieth Century Evangelicalism, 1870–1925* (1980), which still commands this field as the latest word on a difficult and complex subject.

Recent works on Roman Catholicism also reflect an interdisciplinary approach. Jay P. Dolan combined interests in traditional forms and social forces in *The Immigrant Church: New York's Irish and German Catholics, 1815–1865* (1975). He also blended that rather sacramentally rigid institution into American emotionalism with his ground-breaking study, *Catholic Revivalism: The American Experience, 1830–1900* (1977). Somewhat earlier Robert D. Cross conducted inquiries into the social side of this confession, producing *The Emergence of Liberal Catholicism in America* (1958). And recently Gary Wills, in *Bare Ruined Choirs: Doubt, Prophecy, and Radical Religion* (1972), provided both analysis and first-hand evidence of the growing intellectual ferment in Catholic circles.

Interdisciplinary studies with a particular focus on religion among black Americans have flourished impressively over recent decades. The dean of such historians was E. Franklin Frazier, whose *The Negro Church in America* (1963) encouraged a host of subsequent investigations. A decade later C. Eric Lincoln continued work along those lines with *The Black Church Since Frazier* (1974), complementing his own wider studies of optional faiths among these peoples, *The Black Muslims in America* (1961). Following the lead of such explorations, Joseph R. Washington, Jr., published *Black Sects and Cults* (1972), while in 1978 Albert J. Raboteau produced one of the most scholarly accomplishments in this genre, *Slave Religion: The "Invisible Institution" in the Antebellum South.* Rounding out the ideational side of a movement that had predominantly social overtones, James H. Cone offered a study entitled *Black Theology: A Documentary History* (1979).

The American religious scene after the Civil War witnessed resurgent interest in non-Christian and Eastern religions. A similar revival in the 1960s stimulated historians to recapture that part of religious diversity in this country's past. Jacob Needleman inaugurated a small set of valuable books on this diverse topic with his *The New Religions* (1970). Shortly thereafter a collection of twenty-seven scholarly essays on "marginal" religious movements appeared. This extraordinary anthology covering the very best of interdisciplinary treatments was edited by Irving I. Zaretsky and Mark P. Leone, appearing under the unpretentious title *Religious Movements in Contemporary America* (1974). More recently Robert S. Ellwood, Jr., produced a sensitive, eclectic study, *Alternative Altars: Unconventional and Eastern Spirituality in America* (1978), and Bruce F. Campbell issued an appreciative summation of the oldest Western organization that fostered many parallel expressions in his *Ancient Wisdom Revived: A History of the Theosophical Movement* (1980).

Schools of interpretation since Peter G. Mode have made vital contributions to historical scholarship in the twentieth century. Their successive changes and different, often overlapping emphases have helped contemporary students to reach a more complex appreciation of American religious history. At the present time we are able to employ a wide spectrum of viewpoints, applying them to new topics that call for investigation and utilizing innovative methods in interdisciplinary ways. An awareness of how we reached such a wealth of insights can help orient present-day students in the rudiments of optional approaches. Historiographical grounding also encourages us to blend resources from previous approaches, the better to produce new findings with accuracy and relevance for our age.

BIBLIOGRAPHY

Sydney E. Ahlstrom, "The Problem of the History of Religion in America," in *Church History,* 39 (1970); Herman Ausubel, *Historians and Their Craft: A Study of the Presidential Addresses of the American Historical Association, 1884–1945* (1950); Henry Warner Bowden, *Church History in the Age of Science: Historiographical Essays, 1876–1918* (1971); Henry J. Browne, "American Catholic History: A Progress Report on Research and Study," in *Church History,* 26 (1957); Paul A. Carter, "Recent Historiography of the Protestant Churches in America," in *Church History,* 37 (1968); Shirley Jackson Case, *The Christian Philosophy of History* (1943); Eric Cochrane, "What Is Catholic Historiography?" in *Catholic Historical Review,* 61 (1975); Merle Curti, ed., *American Scholarship in the Twentieth Century* (1953).

John Tracy Ellis, "The Ecclesiastical Historian in the Service of Clio," in *Church History,* 38 (1969); Adrian T. English, "The Historiography of American Catholic History, 1785–1884," in *Catholic Historical Review,* 5 (1926); Edwin S. Gaustad, *Religion in America: History and Historiography* (1973); John Higham, Leonard Krieger, and Felix Gilbert, *History* (1965); Richard Hofstadter, *The Progressive Historians: Turner, Beard, Parrington* (1968); Winthrop S. Hudson, "Shifting Trends in Church History," in *Journal of Bible and Religion,* 28 (1960); Michael Kammen, ed., *The Past Before Us: Contemporary Historical Writing in the United States* (1980); George Marsden and Frank Roberts, eds., *A Christian View of History?* (1975); Henry F. May, "The Recovery of American Religious History," in *American Historical Review,* 70 (1964), and "Intellectual History and Religious History," in *New Directions in American Intellectual History,* John Higham and Paul K. Conkin, eds. (1979); John T. McNeill, Matthew Spinka, and Harold R. Willoughby, eds., *Environmental Factors in Christian History* (1939); Sidney E. Mead, "Church History Explained," in *Church History,* 32 (1963).

David J. O'Brien, "American Catholic Historiography: A

Post-Conciliar Evaluation," in *Church History,* 37 (1968); Thomas F. O'Connor, "Trends and Portends in American Catholic Historiography," in *Catholic Historical Review,* 33 (1947); Robert Allen Skotheim, *American Intellectual Histories and Historians* (1966); Wendell H. Stephenson, "A Quarter Century of American Historiography," in *Mississippi Valley Historical Review,* 45 (1958); Joseph R. Strayer, ed., *The Interpretation of History* (1950); George H. Williams, "Church History," in *Protestant Thought in the Twentieth Century: Whence and Whither?* Arnold S. Nash, ed. (1951).

THE SOCIOLOGICAL STUDY
OF AMERICAN RELIGION

John Wilson

THE study of religion is one of the oldest sociological concerns. The nineteenth-century founders of the discipline saw religion as the mainspring of human societies, and they believed it explained major differences within and between them. They understood that, in traditional societies at least, religion had been the fundamental basis for social cohesion. Their own lifetimes witnessed rapid industrial and urban growth. New institutions emerged, and others changed their roles in society. Institutional differentiation posed a question that could not have been asked in traditional societies: What is the relationship of religion to society? Concomitantly, increasing class conflict and social mobility aroused concern about the future basis of social solidarity.

Sociologists today treat religion much as they do any other social institution; that is, as a stable cluster of values, norms, statuses, roles, and groups developed around a basic social need. Sociologists pay particular attention to how patterns of religious belief and practice vary and under what social structural conditions these variations occur. Their goal is to explain religious behavior by reference to broad theoretical propositions about social systems in general.

THEORY

The founder of sociology, Auguste Comte (1798–1857), believed that the society of human beings must be studied in the same scientific manner as the world of nature. Sociology was to follow natural science both in its empirical methods and in the function it would serve for society. Knowledge of the laws of society could be used to ameliorate the human condition. Comte's mentor, Claude Henri de Rouvroy, comte de Saint-Simon, referred to the emerging science of society as "the new Christianity." Whereas in traditional societies religion furnished the unifying principle, in the new positivist order that Comte attempted to inaugurate, science was to provide this unity. The two other giants of sociology's early years, Herbert Spencer (1820–1903) and Karl Marx (1818–1883), took a similar view of religion, both recognizing that religion performs the role of cementing social relations and legitimating social institutions and both anticipating a time when a science of society would replace religion in this role.

During this early period of great optimism about the promise of a new science of society, sociologists could be accused of treating religion in a reductionist manner, seeking to explain religion as an illusion born either of false ideas (Comte) or of material conditions (Spencer and Marx). However, their optimism about the role of science as a foundation for morals and their dismissive attitude toward religion did not survive the turn of the century. The sociologists of the discipline's classic age, Émile Durkheim (1858–1917) and Max Weber (1864–1920), rejected the argument that the nonrational was destined to disappear from social life as the age of positivism matured. Each sought, in different ways and with different results, to formulate a theory of society in which religious ideas and practices could be explained rather than explained away. Although their influence was rather late in reaching American shores, it is to them that the foundations of the sociological study of American religion must be traced.

Émile Durkheim. Durkheim dismissed theories of religion that locate the origins of religious sentiments in intrapsychic phenomena (such as trances or dreams) or in natural wonders (such as storms). He believed instead that "religious force is only the sentiment inspired by the group in its members, but projected outside of the consciousness that experienced them, and objectified." Thus, when the faithful believe in a moral power upon which they depend and from which they draw their ideas about appropriate behavior, they are not deceived, for such a power exists —it is society. Even the idea of a soul, of a divine spark within each individual that lives on after death, stems from our social being because it is from society that we obtain our sense of individuality.

Durkheim assumed a correspondence between the structure of the sacred world and the structure of the social world. Religious beliefs and values are templates for people's lives, while the structure of religious belief systems tends to correspond to the social structure. Types of religious personnel, of sacred entities, and of rituals and beliefs in themselves form a pattern and vary in correspondence with variations in economic, political, and kinship structures.

Religion, for Durkheim, plays a quasi-ethnic role, providing its adherents with a sense of identity and of belonging. This theme was articulated in Will Herberg's *Protestant–Catholic–Jew,* a popular sociological work of the 1960s. Herberg advanced the hypothesis that the religious differences that remain in the American population fall into three broad categories, Protestant, Catholic, and Jewish, and that the differences within these broad groups, especially to the extent that they arise from ethnic differences, are relatively residual and are slowly disappearing. Moreover, Herberg argues, the significance of these broad religious preferences lies in their social structural implications; that is, it lies in determining who associates with whom rather than in any fundamental differences of religious outlook. Studies confirm that although people are less inclined than before to expect their friends to be ethnically akin to themselves, they do appear to require their friends to be drawn from their own broad religious community.

Durkheim's influence is also evident in many community studies conducted by sociologists since the 1920s. They indicate that churchgoing has been the most important and visible community activity for small-town America. In the words of Arthur J. Vidich and Joseph Bensman

in *Small Town in Mass Society* (1958), church life "thickens" public life, adding a quality and depth to the more open and social side of community living. Involvement in community affairs is associated with involvement in the church; church members tend to belong to other voluntary associations; those who attend church most frequently are the most active in voluntary associations and also spend more time visiting their neighbors; and those with a clear sense of and attachment to the local community go to church most often.

The presence of competing religious denominations in a community does little to weaken the integrative function of the church. The denominations play down their differences during community celebrations, speak with a common voice on most social issues, and cooperate in many welfare and recreation programs. Indeed, communities define religion as that which is integrative. There is a feeling that something has to keep the community together, that the church is the best agency to do this, and that, accordingly, religious activities should not be divisive. To the degree that a community is integrated at all, the expression of that integration will occur in ways we have come to call religion.

Max Weber. Influenced by German idealism, Weber postulated a basic drive for meaning among human beings. Without a given, solely instinctual relationship to the world, human beings must first forge and then maintain their relationship to it. Human beings have an acute need to make sense of occurrences such as death, innocent suffering, and the elements of randomness in the distribution of life chances that appear unfathomable.

Like Durkheim, Weber saw religion as world-maintaining and legitimating, capable of making social events and processes more plausible. He observed that religious values underpin social organization and shape a variety of nominally secular activities, such as business, politics, and science. But Weber also saw religion as world-destroying, capable of making the social world seem illusory, a mere artifice to be rejected in favor of the real world of the spirit. He thus looked for religious ideas to create charismatic breakthroughs in social development and to play a major role in determining the direction of that development.

Weber's insights into the dual nature of reli-

18

gion have been extremely influential in the study of American religion. The work he inspired includes studies of religious change and political development (e.g., John Hammond's *The Politics of Benevolence,* 1979), religious authority systems and organization (e.g., Benjamin Zablocki's *Alienation and Charisma,* 1980), the shaping of social practices by religious ideas (e.g., Reinhard Bendix's *Work and Authority in Industry,* 1956), and the creation of divergent social structures by different religious ethics and their attendant claims of duty (e.g., Gary Schwartz's *Sect Ideologies and Social Status,* 1970).

SOCIOLOGY OF RELIGION IN THE UNITED STATES

Weber and Durkheim had little influence on the study of American religion until the 1940s. Nevertheless, most of the sociologists prominent in the development of the discipline in the United States turned their attention to religion. Some (e.g., William Graham Sumner, Lester Ward) were rather hostile to religion and either believed in its imminent demise or saw it as a mechanism of social control and oppression to be exposed and overturned. Many other early sociologists, however, were either clergymen or committed laymen filled with a sense of mission to use sociology to reshape social structure along lines indicated by Christian ethics. Charles A. Ellwood, Emory S. Bogardus, Howard W. Odum, and Albion W. Small were enthusiastic advocates of the Social Gospel, an American Protestant movement, attracted by its promise to reorder society rationally by using sociological ideas without having to sacrifice religious ideals.

The Social Gospel encouraged churches in America to use sociological techniques to examine their own organizations and their relationship to the social community at large. One enthusiastic advocate of the Social Gospel, John D. Rockefeller, Jr., provided the money to set up the Committee on Social and Religious Surveys in 1921. (The name was changed to the Institute of Social and Religious Research in 1923.) Directed by H. Paul Douglass, the institute conducted studies of Protestant congregations and church agencies in various cities throughout the United States until Rockefeller withdrew his support in 1934. Exemplars of scientific research,

Douglass' studies were, nevertheless, oriented exclusively to the practical problems of churches having to deal with the shift of population to the cities. Little effort was made to link this research with any developments in general sociological thinking.

During the 1920s sociology became increasingly secular in orientation and tone. Its links with the Social Gospel and with ethical reform movements in general attenuated. With sociology's retreat from a social reform orientation and greater stress on the scientific and professional basis of the discipline, the foundation on which religionists had formed a working alliance with academics began to collapse. The religionists, with their practical concerns and minimal knowledge of sociological theory and methods, either withdrew or were excluded from active participation in general sociology journals. As a result, the sociology of religion in the United States experienced a marked decline. When it was revived in the late 1940s, it had changed its character. As a result of the rise to prominence of Talcott Parsons and his functionalist paradigm, sociological interest in religion became much more abstract. There was no loss of commitment to the Weberian notion that human beings would always have ultimate concerns about which they would formulate beliefs, but Parsons was intent on integrating this insight into a more general and systematic theory of social systems.

The secularization of the sociology of religion in the United States is reflected in the history of professional associations of scholars working in this field. The first, the American Catholic Sociological Society (now the Association for the Sociology of Religion), was formed in 1938 specifically to combat this growing secularity. The Society for the Scientific Study of Religion, on the other hand, was formed in 1949 to encourage more positivist approaches in the sociology of religion, along the lines of a conventional specialty within the discipline. A third body, the Religious Research Association, was formed in 1959 to bridge the gap between ecclesiastics and academics. These professional associations form an uneasy alliance within the discipline, although a recent trend toward more theoretically informed and empirically based research programs seems to be bringing them closer together.

Readers of the journals of these professional associations will be struck as much by the sophistication of the methods of research employed in the papers published as by their theoretical richness. The period after World War II saw the rapid development of survey methods in sociology, aided in no small part by improvements in computer technology and, later, by new techniques for statistical analysis of the masses of data thus gathered. Several denominations and associations of denominations sponsored self-studies, using these new techniques, or otherwise sponsored the gathering of data on the linkage of religious involvement and social practice. Perhaps the most notable was the five-year study organized by Charles Y. Glock at the University of California in the 1960s that eventually produced seven volumes of published findings, the most influential of which were *Christian Beliefs and Anti-Semitism* by Glock and Rodney Stark (1966) and *American Piety: The Nature of Religious Commitment* (Stark and Glock, 1968).

During the 1960s and 1970s, sociologists of religion also began to take advantage of the masses of data being produced by general-purpose surveys such as those conducted by the University of Michigan (Detroit-area study) and by the National Opinion Research Center (general social survey). These data proved especially valuable in light of the absence of items on religion in the official census. The data have been used to determine the relationship of religious preference to occupation, income, and education; to race, sex, and age; and to individual attitudes and activities, such as political orientation, racial prejudice, work attitudes, child-rearing practices, and leisure pursuits.

INTERWEAVING OF RELIGIOUS AND NONRELIGIOUS ROLES

The differentiation of religious from nonreligious institutions in modern societies poses the question of how religious and nonreligious roles are interwoven. To what degree are differences in our religious roles reflected in differences in our secular roles?

The Religious Role. The religious role in the United States has a number of facets: membership in a religious organization; attendance at worship services; participation in activities of a religious nature outside worship services; listening to or watching religious broadcasts; con-

tributing money or other resources; holding religious beliefs; adhering to religious ethics; experiencing feelings defined as religious; performing private devotions; and celebrating crucial life transitions, such as marriage, with religious ceremonies. The meaning and significance of each of these facets vary by religion and even by specific denomination.

Trends in the number of people performing religious roles can be plotted at the societal level, at the denominational level, or at the level of the individual congregation. At the societal level, the data show period effects on overall religious activity. Church attendance was high in the 1920s, low in the 1930s, high in the late 1940s and early 1950s, low in the 1960s, and high again in the 1970s. International tensions and conservative political swings seem to have the closest association with greater religious activity. Higher church attendance is also affected by demographic changes, although the magnitudes are small. Most notably, there is a positive association between family size and religious activity; that is, the higher the average size of families in the population, the higher the rates of church attendance. High birthrates are an indication of commitment by young adults to traditional family life and other privatistic values, a commitment also expressed in church attendance.

At the denominational level, patterns of shifting allegiance are detectable as some denominations lose members and others gain. During the 1970s, for example, the more liberal denominations lost members while the more conservative ones gained. The reasons for shifts in allegiance are in part external to the denomination and in part internal. Among external reasons are swings in political and social attitudes, population migration, and changes in the characteristics of the population (e.g., higher education levels). Among internal reasons are organizational restructuring, alliances with other denominations, the adoption of policy positions on social issues, liturgical reform, and theological reinterpretations. A notable example of the impact of internal change (or lack of it) on denominational strength was the drop of almost twenty percentage points in Catholic church attendance as the laity reacted to the 1968 birth control encyclical *Humanae Vitae*.

Growth and decline in local congregations depend to some extent on such internal factors as the quality of the minister's role performance, the popularity of the worship services, the range and variety of church programs, the average age of the congregation, and the degree of harmony among its members. More important, however, are contextual factors. Growing congregations are more likely to have a local monopoly in neighborhoods experiencing a new influx of affluent residents who own their homes.

Using a variety of measures of religious role performance (but most often simply religious preference), sociologists have addressed themselves to the question of how religious and nonreligious roles interweave. Do religious people and nonreligious people differ in any other social respects? Do people of one religion exhibit secular role behavior different from that exhibited by people of another? The most attention has been paid to the interweaving of religious roles with family, workplace, and political roles.

Family Roles. Intensity of religious involvement is closely related to the family life cycle. In the years of late adolescence and early adulthood, people are usually less involved religiously. As they form families of their own and become parents, they tend to become more involved, largely for the sake of their children. Involvement declines once the children have grown and left the home.

In the primary stage of religious socialization, the principal instrument is the family. Parents initiate children into their particular view of what being religious means. The stages of human maturation are all marked by religious rituals. At these times the family reaffirms its religious beliefs and values. At the secondary stage, socialization occurs through participation in formal organizations and in peer groups. The primary influences do not wane, however; the effect of religious education through secondary associations is predicated on what has already been taught and continues to be affirmed by the family. Most Americans report the same religion as their parents. For example, in Muncie, Indiana, the Christian denomination with the highest retention rate is the Catholic Church. The most retentive of the Protestant denominations is the Methodist, with most others falling in the 50 to 57 percent range. Jews occur in Muncie in numbers too small for meaningful comparison, but nationwide Jewish retention rates are similar to those of Catholics.

Family roles are, in turn, shaped by religious commitment. Being religious increases the likelihood of marrying; religious preference defines the pool from which a marriage partner will be selected; religious involvement lowers the odds of a marriage ending in divorce and increases the level of marital satisfaction. There are, of course, differences between religions in their impact on family roles. Catholics are less likely to get divorced than Protestants. Among Protestants, the Episcopalians, Baptists, and Fundamentalists have higher divorce rates, even when socioeconomic differences are controlled for. Jews experience the lowest levels of marital dissolution. The Catholic fertility rate in the early decades of the twentieth century was significantly higher than the non-Catholic fertility rate. Between the 1920s and the 1940s, some convergence seems to have occurred, perhaps connected with the increased proportion of native-born Catholic Americans. This trend was reversed during the baby boom of the 1950s but resumed during the 1960s, to the extent that now there are negligible fertility rate differences between the two major faiths. Jews have the lowest birthrate of all, verging on zero population growth.

Religion also shapes the structure of the family. Jewish families tend to be democratic and very affectionate and supportive. The Catholic family is somewhat more patriarchal and less supportive. The Protestant family is democratic but the least supportive of any. Catholics tend to spend more time with their families and to visit family members outside the household more often than do either Protestants or Jews. Discipline, control, and obedience are more likely to be stressed in child training in Protestant and Jewish homes than in Catholic families.

By and large, religious institutions reinforce traditional sex roles. The traditional subservient role of women in society is reflected in the teachings of most Christian and Jewish groups, and their religious practices also mirror male dominance. Except in the most liberal denominations, there has been little impetus among religious bodies in the United States to alter the status of women, either in their own organizations or in society at large. Although the churches were among the first voluntary associations to allow women significant leadership roles and although women attend church more frequently than men, they are still underrepresented in positions of power and status. Women laity working in the church tend to be segmented into nurturant tasks (e.g., teaching Sunday school) and excluded from organizational responsibility and decision making. Few women enter the ministry, even in denominations where this is allowed. When women do become ministers, they tend to be paid less and assigned to less desirable posts.

Women are more likely than men to volunteer for church-sponsored activities, probably because such activities provide a sense of community and an opportunity to share with others. In this sense, church and family roles replicate each other and are, in fact, regarded by women as alike. The most important festivals—Easter and Christmas—are both religious rituals and celebrations of the family. It is also noteworthy that women are more likely than men to be affiliated with conservative religious denominations, in which the verities of home, family, and traditional sex roles are exalted.

Some family practices are dysfunctional for religious institutions, just as some religious practices are dysfunctional for kinship systems. Voluntarism and individualism posit a religious loyalty that transcends the claims of family. Many religious bodies offer the kind of interaction and personal satisfaction that compete with gratifications obtained at home. And many demand the kind of conversion experience that entails the burning of bridges, the most salient of which might be ties to other family members. Conversely, families are autonomous structures capable of resisting religious pressures. What distinguishes Catholic from Protestant families in the 1980s is not so much their behavior as the consonance between their behavior and their teaching. Mainline Protestants have changed their teaching to bring it into harmony with new forms of family living; the Catholic family is also changing, but with little or no sign that church leaders will modify their teaching to any significant degree.

Work Roles. On a visit to North Carolina in 1904, Weber observed an association between church membership and credit worthiness. Church membership, regular attendance at worship services, and officeholding were regarded as sure signs of a person's economic standing in the community. Subsequent sociological research revealed that church attendance was typically more common among the middle class than among the working class. As the most public religious observance, church attendance could be expected to correlate with other ways of affirming status in the community, such as dress, habitation, and transportation. The unusually high rate of officeholding could be attributed to the superior organizational skills, more extensive contact networks, and more abundant discretionary time enjoyed by white-collar workers.

Today there is little association between occupation and involvement in the religious role. There are no significant differences in occupation between those who attend church frequently and those who do not. Nor does church attendance vary with level of income. Substituting church membership for church attendance produces the same result.

Weber argued in *The Protestant Ethic and the Spirit of Capitalism* (1905) that some Protestant denominations, particularly those close to Calvinism, embodied in their doctrine a work ethic highly conducive to success in professional and managerial occupations, while Catholics placed little value on this kind of behavior. In Gerhard Lenski's *The Religious Factor* (1961), a study of male respondents to a survey conducted in Detroit during the spring of 1958, Weber's thesis is put to the test. Dividing the sample into four social classes—upper middle, lower middle, upper working, lower working—on the basis of collapsed census occupational categories, then matching respondents for class origins, Lenski discovered that more white Protestant men than Catholic men rose to the ranks of the upper middle class or retained that status. Catholic men were more likely to move into or to remain in the lower half of the working class. White Protestants also reported more positive attitudes toward work. There was little mobility out of the working class for black Protestants. Jews were excluded from the analysis because of the small size of the group.

Subsequent researchers, noting that the differences Lenski found were very small, have challenged his findings, using their own data. First, when the religion in which the individual was raised (rather than the currently reported religion) is used as the independent variable, the advantages enjoyed by Protestants disappear. Clearly, religious affiliation is just as likely to be a consequence as a cause of socioeconomic achievement. Second, when Catholics are divided into those who are third-generation and those who are first-generation Americans, the former enjoy much more success than the latter —more, indeed, than many Protestants. Inferior performance by Catholics is due to the fact that most of them came to the United States more recently than did most Protestants. Third, when Protestants are divided into different denominations, some perform much better than Catholics while others perform much worse. This reaffirms Weber's initial premise that there is no uniform Protestant ethic to which all Protestants subscribe.

Jews record the highest levels of socioeconomic achievement for the three major faiths, in large part because of the value Jews attach to formal education. However, while above average in education and income, Jews have experienced particular difficulty in securing adequate representation at the very highest echelons of the occupational structure. The suggestion is that Jews, together with Catholics, encounter discriminatory barriers to entry into jobs, despite their qualifications.

Political Roles. In a modern society, an individual's religious role (as church member or believer) and his political role (as citizen) are separate but interwoven. Sociologists in general take it for granted that religious institutions and political institutions affect each other in many complex ways. Religious practices that threaten the state will not be tolerated; a government without the sanction of religious institutions will lack legitimacy.

American history teaches that Protestants vote Republican and that Catholics and Jews vote Democratic. These differences persist although their magnitudes are small. Jews have been the most consistently Democratic group, followed by Catholics. The most Democratic of all Protestant bodies are the Baptists and the Neo-Fundamentalists, probably because of their strength in the South. Episcopalians are the most strongly Republican group, followed by Presbyterians. Lutherans and Methodists are middle of the road politically; if they leave the middle of the road, they are likely to veer to the right. Identification with a political party is stronger among the more devout: Protestants who attend church more frequently are more likely than Protestants who attend church infrequently to identify with the Republican party. These relationships hold even when socioeconomic status is controlled for. Indeed, the differences between religious groups with respect to political party preference are greater than the differences between classes. In other words, religion is a more powerful influence on party preference than social class; the correlation of religion with party preference is about half that of party identification with all other social characteristics (except race) combined.

Since World War II some significant changes have taken place in the relationship between religious affiliation and party preference. There have been sizable Republican gains among white Protestants in the South, while the loyalty of northern white Protestants to the Republican party has weakened. Both Catholics and Jews have shown an increasing disposition to identify themselves as independents. Black Protestants, however, remain firmly within the Democratic camp.

RELIGIOUS ORGANIZATION

Religion in the United States has largely been refracted through the ubiquitous organizational forms that structure so much of daily life. Sociologists wishing to apply their knowledge of organizations to religious bodies encounter a serious problem in that much popular thinking about religious collectivities is framed by concepts, like church and sect, taken from Christian ecclesiology. These concepts contain assumptions about the structure and function of religion in society (e.g., that there will be a dominant church) that sociologists should avoid making. The history of sociology's preoccupation with religious organizations is largely the story of efforts to shake free of these value-laden concepts.

Church–Sect Models. Weber first suggested to sociologists that the internal organization of groups founded with the primary and deliberate purpose of cultivating religious interests constitutes an object worthy of study. It was Weber who first distinguished between sects, "associations that accept only religious qualified persons in their midst," and the church, "a community organized by officials into an institution which bestows gifts of grace."

Weber's pupil Ernst Troeltsch spelled out the

internal logic of the interrelations between doctrinal, moral, and social characteristics in three types of Christian groupings—the church, the sect, and the mystical group (or cult)—and, described briefly the organizational forms congruent with them. In *The Social Sources of Denominationalism* (1929), Helmut Richard Niebuhr advanced Troeltsch's scheme in two ways. He decided that a new type, the denomination, was necessary to describe the most common form of religious organization in a pluralist society like the United States. The denomination does not claim universal allegiance coterminous with the state, as does the church. Like the sect, it emphasizes voluntary allegiance but, unlike the sect, it makes no claim on monopoly of the truth; nor does it make such stringent demands on its members by way of doctrine and morals. Niebuhr detected a tendency for many sects, especially those preoccupied with converting individuals, to become denominations. He believed that sects cater predominantly to the dispossessed, while denominations are typically religions of the middle class.

In his *Millhands and Preachers* (1942), Liston Pope accepted and employed Niebuhr's argument that organizational differences reflect lines of socioeconomic division in the United States. Pope discovered that religious behavior and ideology differed quite markedly between the uptown people and the millworkers in his study of Gaston County, North Carolina; the forms of religious worship were also different. He thus perpetuated the notion that church, denomination, and sect are defined, in part, by their socioeconomic base.

Models of Bureaucracy. Thinking about religious organizations as ranging along a continuum from sect to church continues to dominate the sociological perspective on American religion. Efforts have recently been made to incorporate theoretical models of secular organizations into the sociology of religion. A landmark is Paul Harrison's *Authority and Power in the Free Church Tradition* (1959). In this study of the American Baptist Convention, Harrison used a model of formal bureaucracy to understand the convention's authority structure, demonstrating the power of rational-legal authority in a church ostensibly subscribing to congregational or democratic values.

Harrison contended that a social system cannot operate over an extended period of time on the basis of power alone. Leaders must establish a legitimate right to exercise their power. Weber had claimed that such legitimacy may be rooted in devotion to tradition, law, or the charismatic qualities of the leader. He believed that modern organization could be characterized as possessing legal authority within a bureaucratic organization; it involves the exercise of control by the occupants of legally sanctioned offices on the basis of factual knowledge.

Harrison discovered that bureaucrats had supplanted charismatics in the American Baptist Convention, a denomination with a strong tradition of voluntarism and a rejection of external authority. The executives had assumed considerable responsibilities and no little power in the organization, making decisions with regard to its educational enterprises, fund-raising activities, and missionary work. Harrison surmised that the accumulation of power by bureaucrats in a religious organization is cumulative. The bureaucrat, once appointed, is in an excellent position to assume effective policy-making responsibilities, even though the denomination officially has a democratic or congregational polity. The bureaucrat tends to have a much more detailed knowledge of the kinds of issues that come before the decision-making bodies and usually influences the choice of issues to be discussed. The power of the bureaucracy may even extend to determining the composition of the decision-making boards.

Open-Systems Models. Harrison assumed that religious organizations, like their secular counterparts, would exhibit a tendency toward increasing rationalization. On the vertical dimension, this would mean an increase in the degree of integration between upper and lower levels of the organization, with local congregations suffering reduced autonomy. On the horizontal dimension, this would mean an increase in the degree of integration at the same level of operation, as agencies, committees, and offices are subsumed under one policy-making and administrative unit.

More recently, sociologists have questioned the assumption that religious bodies must inevitably bureaucratize in this way. They have looked, instead, to an open-systems model to explain religious organizations. This model assumes that changes in an organization's environment will produce changes in its internal structure. The model also assumes, however, that certain structures, not all of them bureaucratic, can exploit their environment in order to survive better than others. Thus certain kinds of exchanges between the organization and its environment encourage bureaucratization: where the organization is in competition with others for funds or resources; where formal teaching and instruction of a "clientele" are the aim; where there is a high turnover of "seekers" to be processed; and where the organization is situated within a stable environment in which a balance of demands can be met through specialized agencies whose work needs to be coordinated. On the other hand, bureaucracy will be discouraged where the organization is competing with kinship systems for allegiance, where the state is cooptive or oppressive, or where resources (including the intangible resources of skills and aptitudes) are lacking.

Their goals being less tangible than those of secular organizations, religious bodies confront a number of organizational dilemmas as they try to cope with routine management problems. Religious organizations provide the stability and reliability necessary for the expression, communication, and regeneration of religious ideas and sentiments, but they tend to become ossified and rigid and, instead of providing an orderly context to life, constrain religion's creative energies.

Organization means rules, offices, and record-keeping, which tend to impair an organization's ability to adapt to change. More formal organization means a stable set of statuses and roles and a stratified set of rewards, such as prestige and material compensation. These rewards often result in the subtle transformation of the goals and values of the organization toward the maintenance of the organization itself.

The goal of membership increase to which many religious organizations give priority may become an end in itself, the urge to expand subordinating a more long-range concern: the quality of fellowship for existing members. Religious organizations, like secular organizations, face problems of undercommitment, but they also confront the problem of overcommitment. "True believers" make demands on the organization for action that it does not have the resources to meet. Finally, many faiths—Judaism would be one—fail to separate organization for

"churchly" purposes from organization for other communal needs because they do not distinguish them. Organic ties (family, neighborhood) must somehow be made compatible with more bureaucratic imperatives.

The Congregation. Most sociological studies of religious organizations take the denomination as the unit of observation. However, a long tradition of research treats the congregation in organizational terms. Congregation research has been dominated by an ecological model portraying the congregation as a territorially based organization with roots in the social life of the community, possibly in competition with, or symbiotically related to, other forms of organization in that territory. Thus, in the 1920's H. Paul Douglass studied congregations in both rural and urban settings, arguing that the proliferation of competing voluntary organizations in cities would impel greater specialization within a congregation, increasing the number and diversity of its programs and activities.

Douglass' research signaled a departure from ad hoc description and a beginning of systematic theorizing about the relationship between a religious congregation (treated as another example of an urban voluntary organization) and the surrounding community. In their formative years, congregations reflect the social and economic homogeneity of the surrounding community. A denomination may have several congregations within the same city, each with a different style and ethos reflecting the particular characteristics of its ecological niche. As time passes, communities change. The original residents leave or die and new residents move in, often with socioeconomic characteristics and cultural backgrounds different from those of the previous residents.

Some congregations are able to incorporate the newcomers, especially if they are compatible socially. Other congregations become commuter churches, with most of those attending services traveling from some distance. The residents who leave the inner city usually relocate in the suburbs. Here churches are less oriented to the immediate community, which has vague territorial boundaries. Lacking the strong "tribal" ties of ethnic churches, the localism of small-town churches, or the moral community of sects, suburban congregations are notable for their openness, tolerance of individual freedom of action, and low level of commitment.

25

Congregational studies in the 1950s and 1960s relied less on simple ecological models, looking not only at demographics but also at changing attitudes and needs in various communities, treating the congregation as an active, purposive body. Whether a congregation adapts to the environment or actively seeks to mold that environment to meet its own purposes depends in large part on the characteristics of its membership, the resources it commands, and its organizational strength. The latest congregational studies pay more attention not only to the internal dynamics of the congregation but also to its linkages with the parent denomination and with other voluntary associations in the local community.

The patterns observed at the denominational level also appear at the congregational level. The same kind of goal-substitution tendency is found. Where congregational goals are vaguely defined, it is easy for the congregation to be subverted to an emphasis on survival goals. The same kind of organizational dilemmas appear. For example, internal conflicts can be avoided and solidarity increased by focusing on a goal related to group survival (e.g., building a new church). However, too much attention to external goals can undermine the expressive functions that, to many, are the primary purpose of the local congregation. Persistent money-raising can impoverish affective, familylike relationships.

The Minister. Sociologists treat the occupation of minister as the archetype of the professional role, with its idea of having been "called" to serve, its self-regulation, its autonomy, and its use of a professional association as the major reference for ethical standards. And yet sociologists are aware that ministers increasingly find themselves working in bureaucracies. How is it possible for the minister to fulfill a professional role while respecting the rules and operating procedures of the bureaucracy for which he or she works?

The tensions begin prior to entry into the ministry. Studies reveal that for many entrants the ministry is a channel of upward mobility. However, the professional ethic denigrates the pursuit of personal advancement. What are the correct motivations for the aspiring minister, and what actions are appropriate to them? Other tensions arise when much of the formal training inculcates a more idealized concept of the ministry than that which exists in real life. Young people choose the ministry with one set of ideals and occupational images; they are introduced to a radically different set in training; when they emerge as neophyte ministers in the local parish, they discover additional roles and obligations for which they were never trained. Administrative tasks are the most salient of these. Ministers of the larger churches typically resemble corporate executives. Backed by church equivalents of junior executives, administrative assistants, and secretaries, they oversee and orchestrate a multitude of religious, educational, recreational, welfare, and fund-raising activities.

Further tensions arise once the minister accepts a post. Then he or she typically discovers a gap between personal goals and values and those of the congregation. The congregation stresses the expressive functions of congregational life, while the minister emphasizes outreach and the fulfillment of social responsibilities. The congregation will usually want to be comforted; the minister will want to challenge it. Additional tensions will arise for the religious professional if the denomination has developed an elaborate administrative structure, staffed not by ministers but by full-time administrators. Two hierarchies will be created, one based on charisma, the other on rational–legal criteria. As the power of the latter increases, ministerial autonomy diminishes.

For the ambitious minister, there are further dilemmas. In the world of professions, superior role performance according to universalistic criteria recognized by the professional's peers determines intraoccupational mobility. But pastoral role performance is less visible to professional colleagues than is, say, the work of a scientist. The minister and the congregation are tempted to attach significance to less spiritual achievements, such as membership increase and budget expansion.

Finally, ministers experience the strains of working in an occupation that cannot completely control entry into its own ranks. The profusion of religious bodies, the commitment of many of those religious bodies to the principle of priesthood of all believers, the diffuseness of the role, and the presence of part-time ministers make control over expertise and the practice of that expertise (the hallmark of any profession) almost impossible.

SOCIAL TRENDS

Pluralism. In the United States religious bodies stand in fair competition with one another, each trying to mobilize more vigorous support, maintain more attractive premises, provide more stimulating services, furnish ampler support facilities, and present a more favorable public image than its competitors. And, in a society where pragmatism is a virtue, religious bodies must compete with secular organizations by offering themselves as more supportive, more helpful, and better at solving a person's problems. The formal equality of religious groups replicates the formal equality of individuals. The mobility people enjoy is there for organizations to enjoy, too.

Religion in the United States has probably become more pluralistic since the turn of the century. The series of studies of "Middletown" (Muncie, Indiana) carried out in 1924, 1934, and 1976 indicate that the growth in the number of different religious bodies has outstripped the increase in population. Today there are 59 different religious bodies in Muncie and 165 different churches serving a population of 120,000. Most of Muncie's religious bodies agree on strictly doctrinal issues. Theirs is largely an experiential religion, not founded on formal proofs and requiring none to be sustained. There is little connection with the theological positions that originally set the religions apart.

The major line of difference between America's religious bodies is between liberal and conservative theologies; a gulf separates the more public, socially conscious religions from the more personal, privatistic religions. However, in a community like Muncie, even these differences are of little significance. Its citizens do not hesitate to attend worship services at a denomination other than their own.

The two lines rarely crossed in this denominational switching are the lines that separate blacks from whites and Jews from Gentiles. Most Americans attend churches in which there are no members of a race other than their own. The black church has been a largely separate institution since the early nineteenth century, the product of white discrimination and exclusion, and perpetuated in some part by blacks anxious to find a haven in a hostile world.

The fact that most practicing Jews have been born Jewish forces them together for self-protection. The Jewish way of life is a matter of familial solidarity first, but it must also be understood in the light of the active will of many Jews to function as a community. It is not simply association with a synagogue that enables an individual to become part of the Jewish community. Affiliation with a whole range of organizations—philanthropic, educational, charitable, cultural—is also customary. This is perhaps particularly true in the Jewish community in the United States, for there is reluctance on the part of all Americans to think themselves bound to anything by birth.

Jews record extremely high rates of endogamy. In 1979, 25 percent of Jews married outside the faith, up from 5 percent in 1950 but still a low figure considering that Jews constitute only 3 percent of the population. Marriages between Protestants and Catholics, on the other hand, are by no means uncommon, and the trend is toward even higher rates of intermarriage. The same degree of Jewish exclusiveness is found with regard to friendships. More so than either Protestants or Catholics, Jews are likely to draw their friends from their own faith.

Privatization. Comte, Spencer, and Marx were alike in thinking that the social conditions that made religion necessary would soon disappear and that science in the future would provide the world view by which social development and individual actions would be guided. Beginning with Weber and Durkheim, sociologists have questioned the accuracy of this projection, contending that religion is a functional requisite for the existence of social life and should not be thought of as a practice that will one day disappear. They do not claim, however, that religion and its relation to society will be unchanged. Rather, most sociologists have assumed that religious ideas and actions will become less directly connected to the public world of politics and business and will form part of the private sphere in which people make decisions about their personal affairs.

This privatization thesis finds two kinds of

sociological advocates. Some, like Talcott Parsons, believe that the separation of public and private spheres is a natural part of the evolutionary differentiation of social structures. Society's institutions become increasingly specialized in the functions they perform and, therefore, more adaptive or efficient. Political and economic institutions operate mainly in the public sphere, while kinship and religious institutions operate mainly in the private sphere. The intense concern with individual problems that this more privatistic religion encourages does not weaken but strengthens the hold of religious thinking on social life.

Other sociologists see in privatization a weakening of the connection between religion and society. They cite the results of polls showing little relation between religious preference and political attitudes except when an issue of personal morality (e.g., abortion) becomes important in an election. They also draw comfort from studies such as those conducted in Muncie showing that sermons are typically homilies or exhortations to faith that touch on public issues only obliquely. Muncie's religion is intensely privatistic—diffuse, hopeful, absorbed in personal experiences and in moral improvement. People no longer expect the churches to prepare them for public involvement. Churches no longer have clear channels through which they may advance persons from their midst into the public arena. Religion is practiced not out of obedience to tradition or principle but for pleasure. People choose a church because they like it and want to go; otherwise they stay away altogether, simply because they dislike something about the services or prefer some other activity on Sunday morning.

In tune with these sentiments, the most popular religious denominations tend to be those that maximize self-realization and personal growth and reward primary relationships. Divine commandments are transformed into instrumental strategies for achieving personal satisfaction. This type of self-examination goes beyond the traditional Christian pietistic exercise of searching heart and soul; it is more preoccupied with the emotional and psychological dimensions of human experience and with individual problems such as anxiety, stress, depression, and tension. Denominations, which people join voluntarily

and which are composed entirely of self-selected, impersonally related, and segmentally associated individuals, encourage this privatism.

Privatization has not gone unresisted. Many of the new religious movements of the 1960s sought to re-create small-scale, intimate, collegial, relatively self-supporting communes that would break down the barriers between public and private spheres. Collective goals and strong interpersonal relations were stressed over individual achievement. The resurgence of evangelicalism in the 1970s also marked a protest against privatization. In this case, the rightness of a religious tradition in which private and public spheres had never been separated was reaffirmed in a series of militant initiatives in the political arena, including foreign policy.

NEW RELIGIOUS MOVEMENTS

The great efflorescence of new religious movements during the 1960s, unmatched since the 1920s, saw two broad groups emerge. Dualistic movements (e.g., evangelicals) reaffirmed traditional moral absolutism and preached a political and social conservatism. Monistic movements (many drawing inspiration from the East) affirmed relativism and a subjectivist moral meaning system. Preaching a vision of the universe in which there is an ultimate metaphysical unity or oneness, monistic movements emphasized self-discovery, enlightenment, and therapy. They were somewhat more liberal.

A number of theories have been put forward to explain new religious movements. Some see in such movements a quest for community in a society characterized by large cities, bureaucratized work, and nucleated families. Structures that traditionally mediated relations between the individual and large-scale formal structures have been eroded. Religious movements that offer new communities arise to take their place. They combine the diffuse affectivity of familial roles with universalistic values. Some see in new religious movements a search for moral certitude in a time of great moral indeterminacy during which public institutions are losing their legitimacy. Others see in new religious movements a reaction to the increasingly secular nature of conventional religion. In a society becoming more and more rationalized and bureaucratized, sects appear in the institutional interstices of modern life.

Common to all theories of new religious movements is the idea that such movements can be traced to some form of deprivation, a condition in which legitimate expectations exceed actuality. The assumption is that new religious movements are a form of protest against present conditions, likely to attract the support of those who feel deprived in economic, social, or organismic terms, or in a combination of these.

Relative deprivation theories were criticized during the 1970s by scholars who believed that new religious movements could only partly be explained by reference to deprivations. Just as important, they said, is the group's ability to command and use resources, such as money, facilities, and means of communication, as well as less tangible assets, such as the organizational and legal skills of members.

This new emphasis on resource mobilization also altered the sociological treatment of the process by which individuals join new religious movements. The conventional model saw conversion to new religions as consisting of several stages. The earliest stage occurs during the person's original religious socialization when, for example, he or she is taught to be more credulous of individualist than of collectivist understandings of problems. A second phase is the experiencing of personal difficulties or problems, often of a chronic nature. These difficulties are naturally explained in terms instilled during prior socialization. The third phase involves the perception that a certain religious movement might furnish a way to resolve the perceived difficulties, possibly through initial contact with a movement participant who focuses the prospective convert's needs. The fourth phase is a loss of positive or rewarding ties with the larger society. The fifth phase is the development of affective ties with the new group. Conversion, in the end, is a matter of coming to accept the opinion of one's friends.

Although there is some truth to this conventional model of conversion, it has proved very difficult to use in sociological research. One difficulty is that past events are routinely reinterpreted during the course of conversion; personal biographies are reconstructed in the light of new

experiences, often at the prompting of the group itself. It is difficult to decide whether deprivations actually existed or whether conditions previously considered normal are now defined as problematic. The same can be said of events that, in retrospect, are considered turning points. The sociological researcher must treat interviews with converts as having dubious validity and not providing a truthful record of past experiences.

Besides these methodological difficulties, the step-sequence model of conversion exaggerates the importance of life crises or deprivation as a trigger for conversion. Converts, even by their own telling, do not report markedly higher rates of personal troubles than the general population. And many seem as much concerned with social problems (e.g., rising divorce rates) that have no more effect on them than they do on the general population. Although it is likely that deprivation will be salient in cases of conversion to highly nonconformist groups (in which a high level of commitment is usually expected), in most instances deprivation is probably of minor importance.

In view of these problems, the social psychological emphasis in the study of conversion has given way to an approach that emphasizes the function of bridging structures in connecting prospective with existing members. Kinship and friendship networks, for example, link converts to new groups and facilitate conversion. Ties such as these seem to be more important in determining rates of conversion than any change in world view that might have accompanied a personal crisis. The new model also attaches less importance to a group's teachings. The appeal contained in a group's teaching is not self-evident. Nor is it brought to the fore by the force of some personal crisis. Rather, the appeal is contingent on intellectual and emotional exposure, as in social networks. Rather than being drawn to a group because of its teachings, people are drawn to teachings because of their ties to the group.

CONCLUSION

The continued vitality of religion in modern societies has obliged even those sociologists inclined to dismiss it as a lingering superstition to renew the efforts begun by Weber and Durkheim to comprehend the nature and function of charismatic or sacred phenomena. The efflorescence of new religions continually renews this challenge to understanding. Sociologists have responded to this challenge in ways as varied as the discipline itself. Perhaps the most vigorous and sustained of these responses has been to apply increasingly sophisticated statistical procedures to assess the several antecedents and particular consequences of individual religiosity. This, in turn, has intensified efforts to improve the measurement of religiosity by multidimensional scaling.

In a discipline so closely identified with the study of social groups and collectivities, it is to be expected that religious movements and organizations should also be subjected to sociological scrutiny. After a long period of time shackled by concepts drawn almost unmodified from ecclesiology, sociologists have begun to turn to more general and formal theories of organizational development and interorganizational relations to understand sectarian and denominational behavior. There is great promise for the future in a line of research in which structures, rather than individuals, are the unit of analysis. The recent replication of the Lynds' "Middletown" studies also indicates that the tradition of studying religion in its ecological context remains alive.

Finally, given the macrosociological work of their founding fathers, it is unlikely that sociologists of religion would abandon the efforts to obtain a clearer picture of the part played by religion in societal development. The role of religious ideas in the emergence and disappearance of economic and political systems, the changing relation of church and state, and the impact of religious values on movements for social reform occupy center stage and will continue to do so as long as institution-building remains a preoccupation of the sociological profession.

The nineteenth-century opinion that religion and the new science of society must conflict is now rarely expressed. Sociologists, having abandoned the strident positivism of their founder, have found ways of thinking about and discussing religion in its social context that do not deny its existence and force. Most religions, on the other hand, have come to appreciate the insights sociologists provide into the individual and structural limitations placed on the social expression of religious beliefs and experiences. Much remains to be learned about the social patterns religious behavior forms, but that these patterns exist and can be revealed is a lesson unlikely to be forgotten.

BIBLIOGRAPHY

Reinhard Bendix, *Work and Authority in Industry: Ideologies of Management in the Course of Industrialization* (1956); Peter L. Berger, *The Sacred Canopy: Elements of a Sociological Theory of Religion* (1967); Theodore Caplow, Howard M. Bahr, Bruce H. Chadwick et al., *All Faithful People: Change and Continuity in Middletown's Religion* (1983); William V. D'Antonio and Joan Aldous, eds., *Families and Religions: Conflict and Change in Modern Society* (1983); Émile Durkheim, *The Elementary Forms of the Religious Life,* Joseph Ward Swain, trans. (1915; 2nd ed., 1976); John R. Earle, Dean D. Knudsen, and Donald W. Shriver, Jr., *Spindles and Spires: A Re-Study of Religion and Social Change in Gastonia* (1976).

Andrew M. Greeley, *The American Catholic: A Social Portrait* (1977); John L. Hammond, *The Politics of Benevolence: Revival Religion and American Voting Behavior* (1979); Paul M. Harrison, *Authority and Power in the Free Church Tradition: A Social Case Study of the American Baptist Convention* (1959); Will Herberg, *Protestant–Catholic–Jew: An Essay in American Religious Sociology* (1955; rev. ed., 1960); Dean R. Hoge and David A. Roozen, eds., *Understanding Church Growth and Decline, 1950–1978* (1979); Gerhard E. Lenski, *The Religious Factor: A Sociological Study of Religion's Impact on Politics, Economics, and Family Life* (1961; rev. ed., 1963); Frank Newport, "The Religious Switcher of the United States," in *American Sociological Review,* 44 (1979).

Talcott Parsons, "Christianity and Modern Industrial Society," in Edward A. Tiryakian, ed., *Sociological Theory, Values, and Sociocultural Change: Essays in Honor of Pitirim A. Sorokin* (1963); Liston Pope, *Millhands and Preachers: A Study of Gastonia* (1942); Harold E. Quinley, *The Prophetic Clergy: Social Activism Among Protestant Ministers* (1974); Ross P. Scherer, ed., *American Denominational Organization: A Sociological View* (1980); Gary Schwartz, *Sect Ideologies and Social Status* (1970); Rodney Stark and Charles Y. Glock, *American Piety: The Nature of Religious Commitment* (1968); Bryan R. Wilson, ed., *The Social Impact of New Religious Movements* (1983); John Wilson, *Religion in American Society: The Effective Presence* (1978); Robert Wuthnow, ed., *The Religious Dimension: New Directions in Quantitative Research* (1979); Benjamin Zablocki, *Alienation and Charisma: A Study of Contemporary American Communes* (1980).

[See also INSTITUTIONAL FORMS OF RELIGION.]

INSTITUTIONAL FORMS

OF RELIGION

Russell E. Richey

THE study of American religious institutions appears to be a battlefield rather than an academic field. For unlike fields of study in which scholars from different disciplines work collaboratively on common ground, share the tools and the yield, and improve the theory and method in the process, this one is a contested terrain across which five scholarly units move, sometimes occupying, sometimes skirmishing, seldom working at peacemaking, and virtually never respecting one another's claims.

The five scholarly claimants are denominational or confessional history; interdisciplinary discussions of voluntary association; organizational studies; the ideal typology of church, denomination, sect, and cult; and studies of religious institutions as ethnic groups. Although these approaches do, at places, draw upon one another, they tend to do so mainly on the empirical level. For theory, and hence in the conceptualization and study of religious institutions, the approaches show little attention to one another. For example, those from both the denominational and organizational perspectives reject the church/denomination/sect/cult typology; yet the typological approach is the one that beginning students of religion first meet. Melton (1977) complains of its normative (rather than objective or descriptive) character and pejorative overtones and of the lack of consensus among its users. Beckford (1973) concurs, insisting further that the revisions and reformulations indicate basic design problems and divert attention to conceptual issues so as to create a methodological quagmire. Viewing the typology as distorted by theological and ethical concerns and as anachronistic, he calls for a moratorium on its use.

These criticisms make the point that the study of institutional forms of religion has been fragmented into tunnel-like perspectives. The invitation to the topic beckons the student into one of the several approaches. This essay seeks to promote scholarly conversation on the topic by highlighting the distinctive contributions and weaknesses of each approach and then suggesting possible lines of convergence.

The five scholarly trends show little sign of convergence and only modest interaction because each claims self-sufficiency. Each trend offers an interpretive model, an internally consistent method (or methods), and a language for analysis. Each boasts a sizable literature, continuing intradisciplinary discussion, and recent sophisticated restatement. The approaches vary in their capacity to analyze and assess what might be termed American organizational culture, with interactions among national bodies, with the distinct levels of organization and the relations among them, with the networks of paradenominational or quasi-denominational associations, with commonalities among national bodies, and with institutional and cultural changes over time. Even in the face of these complexities, however, each model proves sufficient to continue to claim followers.

In this essay we shall review each of the theories of religious institutions in the sequence in which it came to prominence in American religious scholarship; trace its emergence for the insight this provides into both the nature and changes in institutional configurations; exhibit major features of religious institutions as they are brought into relief by the theory; note primary strengths and weaknesses of each and points of convergence or dissonance among the theories; and conclude by pointing toward an evolutionary model of religious institutions that draws on all five theories.

DENOMINATIONAL HISTORY

Although scorned by many academic students of religion, denominational history prospers both as a mode of sustaining and renewing the self-consciousness of individual bodies and as a framework for examining religious institutions in general. Pursued by amateur as well as professional historians, sustained by the impulse of each judicatorial or organizational level of every body to legitimize itself, aired in every conceivable form from mimeograph handout and Sunday school literature to TV docudrama and university press monograph, churned out in profusion by denominational press and journal, denominational history functions like other popular forms of historical investigation, like genealogy and local history, to gather and order the memories and records that belong to the past of institution, individual, or place. Its investigatory procedures do not always please the social scientist, who not infrequently finds himself dependent upon these often normatively governed efforts for data. Such displeasure doubtless hampers academic pursuit of denominational history. Yet it also stimulates alternative and more sophisticated analyses of religious institutions, many of which belong to the four other approaches surveyed here but a few of which might be classified with this one. At any rate, denominational data lies in denominational hands, and on that fact rest both the past and the prospects of denominational history. It will thrive as a means of recovering and ordering the stuff of institutional life.

Before reflecting on denominational history as a framework for analysis of religious institutions, we should note several characteristics of the approach that are seen most clearly in the histories, especially the early histories, of single denominations. The very first histories are especially revealing as they typically indicate the presence of denominational consciousness. That is, they indicate that the religious movement which produced this history recognizes itself as conditioned by time and space (that is, as a historical not a transcendent reality) and as surrounded by other religious bodies with equivalent claims to legitimacy. So, for instance, the publication of Jesse Lee's *A Short History of the Methodists* (1810) should be read as a sign that Methodism should be classified as a denomination. The peculiarities

of denominational history derive from its role in shaping and being shaped by denominational self-consciousness.

Denominational history assumes as appropriate, true, and defensible the distinctive aspects of ethos, belief, ethic, ritual, and structure defining the movement. It may, in fact often initially did, take an apologetic or defensive stance. It functions less to persuade outsiders of its truth claims than to address outside criticism in such a way that insiders remain persuaded. In so doing it may account for denominational distinctions by tracing them back into earlier history, perhaps to the period in which sacred texts were delivered. Yet such a longer historical perspective and also the comparative or critical comment on other traditions reinforces rather than abandons the internal analytical stance. Most of the other marks of denominational history follow from its both shaping and being shaped by denominational consciousness.

Denominational history is idiosyncratic, internal, continuous, self-contained, and developmental. It is idiosyncratic in that its language of analysis is the denomination's own, often heavily laden with terminology by which the movement established itself on American shores, terminology only marginally adjusted to subsequent dramatic growth, greater complexity, transformed authority systems, and changed relations to society. While this language functions to reconnect the present-day movement with its origins, it may mark later developments. Its very familiarity as well as its normative character may inhibit this language's value for analytical purposes. For instance, when Baptist language explains Baptist history, insiders sometimes fail to recognize their own patterns as conditioned by and shared with outside religious and nonreligious bodies; and outsiders sometimes fail to appreciate the functionality, variety, and nuance in denominational language. To illustrate, both internal critics and social scientists compare the "religious" quality of original goals with the supposedly secular present-day bureaucracy and thereby dramatically oversimplify the ways in which the body has come to terms with change.

The fact that denominational history has traditionally been written by and for insiders (until recently mainly clergy at that), sometimes by commission, and has been made available under denominational auspices further reinforced its internal quality. Contemporary practitioners try to eliminate or control the triumphal tone that colored earlier efforts. Although denominational history currently respects standards of historical objectivity, aims at impartiality, and often bends over backward to be self-critical, still the parochial perspective remains.

While the normative, internal quality of denominational history often reinforces the status quo, it has played and continues to play prophetic as well as legitimating roles. Indeed, reformist parties often discover imprisoned in the denominational past just the vision to which they would move. And schisms typically foster competition between mother and daughter churches to claim the record. See, for instance, historical accounts produced by Old and New School Presbyterians and by Northern and Southern Methodists.

Like Whiggish history, denominational history is presentistic in that the boundaries and constituencies of the denomination as they exist at the point of writing shape the conceptualization of history itself. The past is ordered so as to establish a continuity of denominational self-consciousness between the present denominational configurations and the accepted points of origin. The denominational histories of Methodism written before and after the merger of the Methodist church with the Evangelical and United Brethren illustrate this reshaping of the past. Historians revised the Methodist past so as to write the Brethren in. Although it is not uncommon for the largest or dominant body in a family of denominations to provide in its denominational history some attention to smaller bodies, the dominant body is still treated as self-contained. While the denominational historian carefully charts change, he assumes a continuity of denominational identity. The approach, then, is continuous and developmental. Even major schisms or divisions do not part the fabric of the movement but only tear away the fringe.

As our discussion of other approaches will suggest, this tunnel view of history rather severely distorts the record. It minimizes discontinuities within religious traditions. It also minimizes continuities with other religious traditions and with American culture. On the other hand, for certain phases in the life of many movements —sectarian, ethnic, or confessional periods—

when interaction with the outside world is minimized, the introspection of denominational history has a definite but unintended utility. Then in one of its most distinctive contributions to the study of religious institutions, it exemplifies important aspects of denominational consciousness at those crucial periods in the life of the body. Denominational history then serves, perhaps best serves, as primary rather than secondary resource. It becomes data for other assessments of the movement.

Often the initial assessment of a religious movement, denominational history provided one of the earliest, nontheological modes for analyzing American religious institutions in general. From Branagan (1811) through Rupp (1844) and Gorrie (1850), through the thirteen-volume *American Church History Series* edited by Schaff (1893–1897), down to Piepkorn's four volumes (1977–1979) and Melton's two (1978), Americans have surveyed religious institutions by proceeding from one national body to another. Early ventures such as Rupp's and Schaff's simply commissioned and incorporated accounts by eminent denominational spokespersons. Recent interpreters such as Milton Backman (*Christian Churches of America,* 1976, 1983) content themselves with advisers from the several traditions. The important point is that like individual denominational histories, such aggregate efforts rely upon the conceptual systems generated by the bodies studied. This means that religious institutions are not so much brought within a single framework as they are juxtaposed. To be sure, certain important issues surface and certain findings result from that procedure. Many of these are cogently stated by Melton (1977).

How are religious institutions to be analyzed? Are they to be brought within some one controlling paradigm? dissected for comparison of internal characteristics? arranged in several types or classifications? Melton insists that an analytic scheme must be "empirically based," attentive to the variety of religious forms, productive of "meaningful data," and constructed in terms of "the group in itself." He posits that the shaping characteristics, "life style," "thought world," and "heritage," permit such a meaningful classification. Rejecting the church/denomination/sect/cult typology, he instead proposes the phrase "primary religious group" to cover all "associations which seek the primary religious allegiance of . . . members." "Secondary" refers to service, supplementary, or subsidiary agencies and "tertiary" to "groups of groups." On the basis of these considerations he classifies primary groups into those persistent, largely endogamous but evolving aggregations termed "families." In some, like the Lutheran-liturgical family, heritage distinguishes; life-style and/or religious experience mark Communal, Holiness-Pentecostal, and Psychic families; thought world identifies Protestants, Adventists, and Fundamentalists. Other families include Liberal, Mormon, Independent Fundamentalist, European Free Church, New Thought, Magical, and Non-Christian. Such classifications are quite common. For analogous schemes, based respectively on historical and historical-theological considerations, see below and Piepkorn (1977–1979).

Among the chief virtues of this scheme, as Melton notes, is its elasticity. First, the classification is indeed open and developmental. Additional families can be readily added as they emerge on the American religious scene. In the event of major ecumenical ventures or inter-family "marriages" the scheme alters readily to fit the new pattern. It is really a classification not a typology. Second, the notion of family permits the identification of the dominant member(s) whose size, influence, and priority establish familial image and self-image. That dominant role may shift, as has occurred within the Baptist fold with the growth to national prominence of the Southern Baptist Convention. Third, Melton recognizes an American religious establishment in which he places ten of the families.

These considerations point to the value of the denominational history approach, its continuing popularity, and its attractiveness to historians. It surveys the religious landscape, performing what Marty (1976) calls "mapping." It is geographic rather than geologic, showing interest in underlying features of the religious terrain only as they affect life on the surface. Here, it evidences history's sense of obligation to the topography of human experience.

Sociologists might well be appalled that Melton would gather the major world religions under a single, nonestablishment category of Classical Non-Christian Family. Yet his point is that whatever schemes may be appropriate to analysis of these religions in other contexts, their institutional life in the United States should be portrayed in appositional terms. Some bodies enjoy preeminence and some marginal status. Institutions reflect the religious power realities. However, denominational history is only one way of analyzing this dimension of religious institutionalization. Like diary or autobiography for the biographer, denominational history functions for the student of religious organization as a vital entrée to the interior world of religious groups. Whether it is a sufficient resource, we can better say after examination of other approaches.

THE STUDY OF VOLUNTARISM

The treatment of religious institutions—from congregations and societies through denominational and interdenominational associations—as instances of the voluntary principle is, in one sense, coeval with American political consciousness. John Locke's definition of the church as a voluntary society, the reinforcement of this definition through the liberal or British Commonwealth tradition, which in recent years has been conceded as of decisive importance in shaping American political thought (Edmund Burke recognized this "dissidence of dissent" in the Revolutionary cause), its prominence in the political discourse surrounding the Constitution, and its employment as analytical tool by Alexis de Tocqueville have made voluntarism a central precept in American reflection on religious institutions and their relation to public order. As such, this conception has been of a piece with other aspects of American pluralism and decentralism—laissez-faire, localism, provincialism, states' rights, agrarianism, individualism.

In the nineteenth century, European visitors and spokespersons for Protestantism acclaimed the voluntary principle as the grand point of distinction for the American church. It was, in fact, in explaining this distinguishing mark of American institutions that American apologists gave the concept formal analytical significance. Notably Baird (1844) and Schaff (1855), who wrote for Europeans, made the voluntary principle the very essence of American religion and the organizing principle of its history. Embraced by both interpreters and practitioners (particularly Baptists, who proclaimed it their own), voluntarism has been featured as the American institutional principle. Recent publications exemplifying this approach include Gustafson (1961, 1970), Powell (1967), Pennock and Chapman (1969), and Smith and Freedman (1972). The monumental contributions of Adams and Hudson to the study of voluntary associations are celebrated and itemized in festschrifts dedicated to them by Robertson (1966) and Ban and Dekar (1982). The centrality of voluntarism to the Reagan presidency should suggest both its salience in American ideology and something of its fate in more recent years.

It is, in part, the longevity and vigor of this tradition that argue for the distinction of voluntarism as an approach in its own right. Some, however, would relegate the concept of voluntary association to a subcategory, subsuming voluntarism (and the study of American religion) under organizational studies. For two reasons we prefer to make voluntarism a separate theoretical option. First, the concept and topic are by no means the property of sociologists who study organization. Political scientists, social ethicists, and historians have used, and continue to use, this rubric. Their contributions to our understanding of religious institutions are not well comprehended under organizational studies. In fact, they tend to be simply ignored. Second, many who favor this rubric function at one level or another with a pluralist understanding—of truth, of politics, of society, of religion. To recognize this as a distinct approach gives that vision its day in court.

The fruit of this pluralist perspective is, ironically, a kind of monism. Its advocates see Judaism and Catholicism as well as Protestantism, episcopal and presbyterian patterns as well as congregational, and bodies of European and Asian as well as British origin adopting a common voluntaristic form. That is, the religious environment fosters institutional convergence. The realities of the American scene—religious freedom, separation of church and state, pluralism—condition the nature of membership, resource mechanisms, authority systems, structure, internal dynamics, purpose, ethos, and leadership patterns. Some who discern the increasing uniformity of religious institutions worry that traditions, orthodoxies, pieties, and polities have been compromised. The fact that this uniformity extends beyond religion and typifies voluntary association in general in-

creases that worry. In the individual act of joining and supporting, in the configurations of local gatherings, in the regional structures and national offices, religious patterns resemble those of the March of Dimes, the Odd Fellows, or the PTA. And societal function is assessed, as well, in similar terms. See, for instance, the extensive catalog by Schindler-Rainman and Lippitt (1971) of requisites of democratic societies dependent upon voluntary associations. Frequently cited socio-political functions include: providing smaller belonging units that mediate between citizen and centralized state or mass society; training in self-government, citizenship, and democratic values; initiating improvements in and conserving the overall quality of life; serving as basis of or reinforcement for law, order, social cohesion; shaping personal identity; and fostering communication, innovation, and planning.

Several significant aspects of religious institutions and of this approach surface in this itemization. First, as opposed to denominational history, which makes the national organization primary, this approach regards the individual act of consent and the local body that elicits that consent as the foundation of religious institutions and indeed religious life. Consent establishes religious institutions. Hence voluntarism means the freedom to join or not but also the explicit *willing* that creates institutions in the first place.

Second, institutions are stamped in subtle but important ways by consent. Consensual exigencies "distort" authority, politics, and structure. The degree to which this has occurred is a matter of some dispute. Winter (1968) argues convincingly that the actual differences are of degree rather than kind and locates religious systems on a spectrum with Roman Catholicism on the right, Protestantism in the middle, and Judaism on the left. Institutional convergence, then, is partially moderated, partially obscured by polities that formally locate authority in clerical, centralized, or hierarchical fashion. Nevertheless, the prevalence of the voluntary principle and its relation to the democratic ethos of American society put great pressure on institutions, their authority structures, and their sources of legitimacy. Typically, though, religious bodies have found ways of accommodating the right of consent; even those with clerical, centralized, or hierarchical authority have succeeded. The forms of that accommodation, though, have varied.

The Southern Baptist Convention has a well-earned reputation for congregationalism and individualism, is zealous for lay prerogatives as exercised by deacons, and in the past kept the barriers into ministry low, yet can lodge quite formidable power in pastors (Winthrop Still Hudson, *Baptists in Transition*, 1979). Presbyterians, on the other hand, whose successive levels of church courts, high barriers to ordination, and framework of laws suggest more aristocratic patterns, balance structural hierarchy by including laity at every level and by carefully circumscribing clerical authority. Strains of black and white Methodism, at least in the past, vested considerable power and prerogative in episcopacy and clerical conferences but fostered lay activism and preached a very contagious Gospel. The Episcopal church, in a sense, resolved the issue in the seventeenth century by learning to live with powerful lay vestries. Roman Catholicism has certainly formalized consensual practices since Vatican II (1962–1965), but, Protestant impressions to the contrary, earlier found quite subtle ways of establishing consent without altering church law, particularly by legitimating various languages and cultures. Judaism, at least in the estimation of Blau (1976), has come to embody American institutional culture in quite striking ways. Blau proposes four terms, all consensual marks, to characterize both American religion in general and American Judaism—voluntarism, pluralism, protestantism, and moralism.

Many immigrant religious communities have felt the consensual pressures of voluntarism. That dynamic in turn thrust itself into self-perception and historical reflection. Many histories of immigrant religious bodies make Americanization the central dynamic. The inner meaning of institutional life became progressive democratization. To Americanize meant to yield increasingly to consensualism. But does this historical commonplace exhaust the nature of consent and the meaning of America?

To illustrate, in the Delaware Valley, where toleration and pluralism prevailed, the initial phase of eighteenth-century denominational development increased authority, reversing more democratic tendencies of the European sending churches (Butler, 1978). Comparable patterns occurred in the same period in Puritanism. Furthermore, as we shall see, the organizational revolution in the late nineteenth and early twentieth centuries created powerful centralized bureaucracies in many communions. Was democratization confined to the intervening period? Was it illusory? Did it represent a nineteenth-century aberration? Not really. The force of these several apparent countertrends derives from an expectation, a highly normative, progressive conception of Americanization that is itself problematic.

The historical assumption that European hierarchy (little effort has been made to fit African or Asian traditions into the pattern) gave way to American democracy fails to recognize that both forms of authority and the types of consent appropriate to them are quite diverse. Max Weber distinguished three bases of authority—tradition, legal or bureaucratic framework, and charisma of the leader. Any of these (traditional, legal, charismatic) might be related to factors having to do with its exercise—whether authority is lay or clerical, centralized or decentralized, hierarchical or not. Quite complicated combinations have existed, as some of the illustrations cited above should suggest.

First, both the historical arguments positing a one-directional flow from hierarchy to freedom and revisionist discoveries of the contrary fail to discriminate expressions of authority. Second, both the traditional and revisionist readings assume authority and consent to be mutually exclusive. However, the Anglo-American fear that authority always seeks to encroach on liberty, which underlies the historiography of Americanization, does injustice to the relation of consent and authority. They prove to have been interdependent. Religious groups seemed to have served a vital society-building role in providing through their authority a basis for order, community, justice, and culture. Consent to that authority effectively established the new society. Once established, that authority was indeed pressed to retain consent and forced over time to accommodate new consensual patterns. Yet at all times the two required one another. Finally, the conception of Americanization in this formula is as simplistic as the notion of authority and as problematic as the purported movement from order to freedom. Quite simply it makes Anglo-Saxon Protestant evangelicalism the telos of American history and presumes that assimilation to that religio-cultural pattern is normative.

While that perception was sufficiently vivid in both Anglo-Saxon and immigrant culture for it to be given some historical credence, we still need to be careful not to impose that reading where nonexistent. In short, we should be wary of simplistic statements about the nature of consent and about the direction of the historical process.

Third, because persons join freely and because they consent by their joining to that for which the institution stands, the voluntary associations of American religion have been defined by their purposes. That is especially striking in the nineteenth-century voluntary societies and evangelical denominations that tended to be single-minded in their endeavor to stamp locality, nation, and world with a revivalist imprint. They were, as Handy (1984) and others have shown, intent upon building Christian culture. Handy makes patent that changes in purpose—mainstream Protestants in the early nineteenth century sought a Christian culture as a "means"; the late nineteenth century accepted it as an "end"; in the twentieth century the ideal collapsed altogether—had dramatic impact upon religious institutions. In a sense, mainstream Protestant bodies lost their primary reason for being. For good or ill, these denominations had over the years gathered unto themselves other purposes and hence have survived the loss of that overarching goal. Ironically, the recent growth of evangelical bodies demonstrates that purposiveness is highly functional and even that the purpose disavowed by mainstream Protestantism—Christianizing nation and world—remains highly efficacious as a recruitment device whatever its plausibility for world history.

The salience of purpose has made religious institutions highly brittle, unyielding, and schism prone. Congregation, missions society, denomination, and cooperative agency could, like the railroads, build incredible steam for motion along a single track. They were groups of individuals consenting to an overriding purpose. To reorient or divert them to another purpose threatened their consensual basis, particularly when the new issue was as divisive as antislavery.

Fourth, because consent has to be continually reestablished around the purpose or purposes of the voluntary association, religious institutions demand considerable political skill in their leaders and politics in their common life. This point is particularly important because many in the churches cultivate the conceit that in policy formation, decision making, and leadership selection, religious institutions should not be political. They sometimes combine this conceit with the distinguishable notion that religious institutions should not be political and should refrain from lobbying, organizing, or persuading in civil politics. Occasionally denominational leaders active in one or both political senses nevertheless advance this conceit, thereby cloaking their exercises of power. This deception (and self-deception) derives plausibility because religious political activity often combines several political cultures.

Each of the five kinds of institutional understandings under review in this essay actually prescribes a code of political behavior. Each represents a distinct type of political culture, with its own leadership styles, codes of acceptable interaction, and sanctions. Denominational political behavior can be that appropriate for a charismatic entity, a particular denominational tradition, an ethnic heritage, a voluntary association, a complex organization, or some combination thereof. The person proscribing politics in religious institutions may feel that only one of these political cultures is legitimate or may seek to return the movement to an earlier self-understanding. If successful, he doesn't rid the denomination of politics but only legislates or imposes one political culture.

As voluntary associations, then, American religious institutions must of necessity be political entities, at least internally. Without politics, institutions can neither maintain their organization nor sustain their direction. Voluntarism does not necessitate, however, that the politics exercised must be identical to that elsewhere prevailing in the contemporary voluntary culture—that to be found in other voluntary associations of the day. This was the point at issue in the trusteeism controversy in nineteenth-century Roman Catholicism. Would the church structure its political interactions according to emergent (largely Protestant) American patterns of association? Would it vest property in local boards of trustees like its Congregational or Baptist neighbors? To protect its ecclesial self-understanding and episcopal authority the church refused. So also the Old Order Amish and the Unification Church function with distinctive political cultures deemed essential to their continued existence and quite at odds with surrounding cultural patterns.

Finally, those groups that *did* accept the voluntary culture itself *and were welcomed* into it claimed the right to structure American society. Mathews (in Mulder and Wilson, 1978), McLoughlin (1978), Singleton (1979), and others have studied the process by which seemingly competitive, voluntary associations defined the boundaries, codes, rituals, symbols, and networks that created a nineteenth-century Protestant establishment. In recognizing the churchlike role of "voluntaristic churches," Singleton proclaims it incorrect to term them denominations. "They assumed they were—and to a large extent they in fact were—coextensive with their society" (p. xix). While his denial does not seem fully persuasive, it serves to underscore his positive point, which students of voluntary associations have long made, beginning at least with Alexis de Tocqueville, that the threads that bound Americans in these small units also held the society together.

The social functions and effects outlined above may or may not have been fully intended —the degree to which the Protestant denominations through revivals and through the complex of voluntary societies sought dominion over American society was and remains in dispute— but the fact is that voluntary religious institutions served to orient their membership to American society as a whole. In the early nineteenth century that orientation assumed the transparency of nation, culture, and society. These latter were but means to the kingdom. By the end of the nineteenth century the kingdom glowed within culture, and religious institutions reoriented themselves to cultural goals. In the middle third of the twentieth century those institutions that had sought the kingdom through voluntary means abandoned the goal of a Christian America. But the vision of a voluntary establishment lives on in conservative Protentantism, in Republican party rhetoric, and in national programs of voluntary action. This passing of the mantle of voluntarism, change in goals, and secularization, epitomized by the YMCA, should not obscure the importance of voluntary religious institutions in nineteenth-century America and, for our purposes the more important point, the impor-tance of voluntarism as a culture in American religion.

RELIGIOUS ORGANIZATION

While pluralism and voluntarism certainly have had defenders, they have also had critics. In the nineteenth century Roman Catholics, theologically sensitive representatives of Lutheran and Reformed traditions, anti-mission Baptists, Christians, and individuals like the Presbyterian (later Episcopalian) Calvin Colton and the Unitarian William Ellery Channing—strange bedfellows obviously—concurred in opposing the seductive and coercive features of voluntary culture. In this century their sentiments have been developed by religion scholars into a full-fledged social control theory of American history.

Sociologists Robert Michels, C. Wright Mills, and Floyd Hunter and political scientists Grant McConnell, Henry Kariel, Theodore Lowi, and Herbert Marcuse, among others, attack voluntary associations for elitism and oligarchy and indict religious institutions on two counts. First, as part of the voluntary culture, they have created and must take responsibility for a society in which power is exercised by privately organized, "irresponsible" organizations and elites. Recent interpreters of this private government do not depict religious hands at the controls, as did Colton in the nineteenth century when he termed the array of voluntary societies, with their interlocking boards, "Protestant Jesuitism." They decry instead the arbitrary and oppressive power of corporations, unions, and professional organizations. Such private power is deemed dangerous because it is politically unaccountable, beyond the controls of the democratic process, and not subservient to the protections granted individuals under the Constitution. Second, religious institutions prove to be susceptible to similar charges of elitism, bureaucracy, and popular disenfranchisement. Here, too, professionalism, managerial procedures, and corporate structures permit elites to establish dominion.

One strand of organization studies virtually attacks religious bureaucracy; draws contrasts between formal, traditional conceptions of religious authority on the one hand, and operative informal power on the other; and pits lay or local expectations of consensus against the reality of national expertise and elitism. This scholarship, sometimes with the allure of an exposé (Fry, 1975; Mickey and Wilson, 1977), reflects profound discomfort with the growth in denominational bureaucracy that has occurred in this century, as well as preferences for other models of religious organization. Another strand of organization studies proves a better resource for understanding these changes. These organization studies rest on two important developments, one societal, the other academic.

The societal development stems from what Alfred D. Chandler, Jr., terms "the managerial revolution," the reconstruction of American business from single units whose enterprise was "coordinated" by the invisible hand of the market to multiunit enterprises, administered by hierarchies of professional managers whose visible hand and rational-technical expertise coordinate those "market" functions. This entrepreneurial capitalism Chandler distinguishes from the earlier financial and family forms of capitalism. The triumph of the manager had occurred by World War I but was anticipated by such nineteenth-century developments as railroad organization and the professionalization of important sectors of American society. In underscoring the enormity of the changes, Chandler remarks that "the American businessman of 1840 would find the environment of fifteenth-century Italy more familiar than that of his own nation seventy years later" (1977, p. 455). The import of business changes for American society as a whole has been captured in phrases like "the organizational society" and "the organizational revolution" (Presthus, 1962; Boulding, 1953). Wiebe (1967) has effectively charted the reshaping of American society as managerial patterns, the identity and linkage of persons through professions and corporation, large-scale hierarchical organization, and various forms of regulation spread from business into government and private sectors.

The academic development reflects these societal changes. Indeed, it would be an interesting exercise in the sociology of knowledge to depict the various stages in organization studies as an evolving societal consciousness of the phases of the organizational revolution. From Max Weber's studies of bureaucracy and rationality, to Robert Michels' iron law of oligarchy, to Frederick W. Taylor's scientific management, to Fritz J. Roethlisberger and William J. Dickson's emphasis on human relations and Chester I. Barnard's on cooperation, to Talcott Parsons' theory of social systems, and to more recent theory—functional (Peter M. Blau), decision-making (James G. March and Herbert A. Simon), compliance (Amitai Etzioni), exchange (Peter M. Blau), and open systems (Daniel Katz and Robert L. Kahn)—the study of organizations has had both analytic and exemplificative value. The phases of organization studies have double value for us as well. They function as tools for the analysis of complex organizations (religious included), and they document the growing academic awareness of the organizational revolution. That is, they function both as secondary (interpretation) and primary (evidence). They analyze and document what Louis Galambos terms "The Emerging Organizational Synthesis in Modern American History." He contends:

> Our history no longer stressed liberal-conservative political struggles leading to pulses of progressive reform; instead, the primary processes of change involved organization building, both public and private, and the creation of new and elaborate networks of formal hierarchical structures of authority that gradually came to dominate our economy, polity, and culture. America's rendezvous was not with the liberal's good society. It was with bureaucracy.
>
> (1983, p. 471)

The contrast that Galambos draws between progressive and organizational values is, on the level of historiography, most instructive. On another level, as a depiction of the actual Progressive platform and action, it is somewhat misleading. For it was precisely the Progressives, the apparent enemies of economic concentration and corruption, the historians of the saga of liberty against privilege, who championed the use of scientific method, efficiency, expertise, order, organization, and professionalism—business methods—in governmental and voluntary associations. Ironically, then, the reformers who conceived history as the struggle between elites and the populace and who would be considered by history as anti-business, were the twentieth-century architects of the organizational society. This masking of their role has created the impression that the adoption of organizational culture outside the business sector derived from inadvertent, ill-advised, or unprincipled capitulation to corporate interests, an impression that colors some of the "discovery" of corporate-style organization in religion.

The truth is that religious institutions were quite deliberately modernized, by liberals (Social Gospel) who as leaders of denominational or interdenominational agencies self-consciously sought to appropriate modes of administration, specialization, communication, and organization from business. Inspired by this "ideology of organization" (Primer, 1979), they succeeded in refashioning the agencies and thereby institutionalized this gospel. Recent studies indicate that the correlation of bureaucracy and liberalism continues to prevail. This gospel also institutionalized itself in religious research divisions and seminary sociology departments, which functioned like research and development divisions for religious "management." So organization studies assumed tasks once left to the Holy Spirit—determining where to plant and sow, how to do so more efficiently, how to increase yield, and when to enlarge the field. By methods deemed scientific, quantitative, and behavioristic, this research spread and nurtured the seeds of organization. Eventually organizational research broke free from denominational control, sought greater academic neutrality, and founded professional societies to confirm its independence. But until then, organizational research was dedicated more to establishing the principles of organization than to studying it. For religion as for American society, organization study serves as evidence of the important changes for which it also provides interpretive theory.

A succession of distinguished statements exhibit the theoretical side of organization studies in religion: Douglass and Brunner (1935), Harrison (1959), Lee (1960), Gustafson (1961), Moberg (1962), Ehrenström and Muelder (1963), Winter (1968), Israel (1972), Beckford (1973), Schaller (1974), Fichter (1974), Primer (1979), Scherer (1980), Wood (1981), and King (1982). These studies take the premise that American religion can be profitably viewed through the conceptual lenses used for other complex organizations. The research has proceeded beyond the stage of proclaiming religious conformity with "iron laws" of association—inevitable institutionalization, minority rule, goal displacement, and goal succession. Current trends are illustrated by the open systems research described and exemplified by Beckford (1973) and Scherer (1980). In this framework, religious organization is depicted "as a huge transformation system, whereby its personnel procure resources (input), do something with and to them (throughput), and exchange the products (output) with other persons and organizations in the environment" (Scherer, 1980, p. 9). This model directs attention to the openness of systems to their environments; to the resources of ideas, people, materials, goals, and money requisite for survival or growth; to the processes of recruitment, nurture, socialization, and ordering by which the system operates; and to the structures through which the system coheres—including specialization, formalization, centralization, and authority configuration.

What are the principal findings about American religion by organization studies? The first and perhaps most important is, as we have indicated, implicit in its very existence and successful application. That is, twentieth-century religious institutions, however they may think of themselves, are complex organizations implicated in an organizational society.

Second, the theory has rather consistently exposed a relatively common failure on the part of American religions to acknowledge this complexity. Most penetratingly documented by Harrison (1959) in treating the American Baptists, this failure consisted in the Baptists' inability to comprehend functioning structures, processes, and leadership within formal polity. The theological or perspectival oversight (misperception) frustrated institutional oversight (accountability). Task-oriented agencies that were developed in the nineteenth century as voluntary endeavors on the society principle had stabilized themselves as bureaucratic power centers. They performed critical duties, exercised unchecked power, and possessed considerable resources. The Baptists' congregational polity (in the late nineteenth century) did not recognize the legitimacy of these agencies and could therefore not hold them accountable. Harrison's insights prompted investigation of other polities. Lee (1960) and Gustafson (1961) extended his findings to other Protestant bodies and Winter (1968) to Judaism and Roman Catholicism.

This work dramatically exposed the limited usefulness of the traditional (Christian) distinction of episcopal, presbyterial, and congregational for purposes of organizational analysis. Instead, most large-scale religious bodies (or at least those rooted in the Judeo-Christian tradition) typically possess dual, parallel structures. A pastoral structure derives from formal polity, though it has perhaps been adjusted (democratized) in important ways by the American experience. An agency structure exists in uneasy (but varied and complex) tension with this pastoral structure. Its resources and staff, which may be concentrated at national, regional, or state levels (or all three), carry on much of the vital work of the institution. Winter (1968) demonstrates that the relationships between the formal or pastoral and the agency or bureaucratic structures differ and that tradition and ethos contribute to the variance. Yet, in one form or another, the gap between authority and power analyzed by Harrison prevails. Whether uniformity will produce unity, as Lee (1960) once hypothesized, the comparable *structural* patterns within the diverse polities of Protestantism *and* in Judaism and Roman Catholicism are worth noting. Schaller (1974) underscores the similarity by suggesting that religious organization can be classified as congregational or connectional on a fiscal basis. Local bodies that are economically self-sufficient can function in a congregational (autonomous) mode, while those in various forms of dependency need connectional help.

The third finding relates to the emergence of the dual structure and complex organization of religious institutions. Incidentally, it also suggests limits to the historical range of organization studies: the significant growth, interconnection, and centralization of religious machinery occurred in the late nineteenth and early twentieth centuries. The tension between formal polities and the societies related to those polities also became acute at that time. To be sure, the societies had been seen as anomalous earlier by Old School Presbyterians, by the Christian and anti-mission movements, and by groups within many religious bodies. Yet if the problem was not new, the scale of it certainly was. As King

(1982) and Primer (1979) have shown, the borrowing of business methods of fund-raising and finance, enlargement and increased specialization of staffs, coordination of national machinery and tasks through departmentalization, and the increased complexity of communication and command—in short, the investment of time and money on administration—were to enhance religious mission and effectiveness. This openness to business culture in the late nineteenth and early twentieth centuries dramatically altered religious institutions.

Winter (1968) dramatizes the enormity of this transformation by terming it "The Other Protestant Schism," attempting thereby to suggest an importance comparable to the Reformation. He challenges the secondary status accorded societies, boards, and agencies by proposing that missions be thought primary and denominations called "paramissions." And he invokes Roman Catholic orders as providing precedent and legitimacy for these structures. While Winter intends by these proposals to argue for the normality of such structures in Christian history, they can also be used to underscore the fact and importance of the changes American religion underwent at the turn of this century. Organization study calls attention to those changes. In so doing it should but often fails to recognize that its own purview effectively begins there.

IDEAL TYPOLOGY

Ideal types as originally utilized by Max Weber might be thought of as extended definitions, as hypothetical-theoretical constructs based on empirical research but elaborated for their capacity to portray and relate variables critical to given phenomena, for their value in executing comparisons, and for their capacity to depict the role of the specific phenomena in overall societal transformation. Such tools permitted Weber to view religious leadership, membership, and structure in relation to the broad processes of change now loosely gathered under the rubric of secularization. The two religious institutional types advanced by Weber were the church and the sect, a dichotomy really, focused particularly on the character of membership.

Ideal typologies, by nature, diverge from concrete instances of religious organization. Nevertheless Weber's typology, like any, required revision as research sought to isolate other factors. Thus, it was perhaps inevitable that his typology was significantly altered as the sociology of religion matured into a discipline, developed new lines of inquiry, addressed itself to new societies, including the United States, and confronted changes in religious institutions. Some scholars (Eister, 1973; B. Wilson, 1982; Swatos, 1979) view the transformations in typology after Weber as so disastrous as to warrant a return to his foundations. For our purposes these critiques function to highlight how important the American scene has been in forcing reconceptualization of institutional types. Additional constructs, notably the denomination and the cult, were among a variety of elaborations introduced to make sense of the American institutional pattern.

Ernst Troeltsch represents the stage after Weber. In *The Social Teaching of the Christian Churches* (1912, 1931), Troeltsch adapted Weber's typology for historical-theological purposes, a history of Christian social ethics. His addition to the typology, a third type of mysticism, was to be of less importance for sociology and for analysis of American religion than two other contributions. First, in Troeltsch's hands, the typology became more a historical generalization than an ideal construct. Second, he introduced the term *compromise* as a judgment to be applied to the relation between ideals and their institutional embodiment.

In *The Social Sources of Denominationalism* (1929), H. Richard Niebuhr furthered the transformation of the typology from an ideal into a historical and ethical construct (reification). Its inclusion among the classics and subjection to rather severe criticism suggests its importance. The fact is that Niebuhr introduced the typology into American scholarship. His formulations influenced a generation of scholars, many of them directly, and found their way into the basic works in American sociology of religion (Eister, 1973). Surveying the American scene, Niebuhr added the denomination to the church and the sect and recognized it as the dominant institutional type. That contribution has seemed firm.

Further elements of his theory, less appreciated now by sociologists, should be seen as aspects of the theological reorientation captured by historical constructs like Neo-Orthodoxy,

ecumenism, and "the second disestablishment" (Handy, 1984). Niebuhr viewed religious institutions and their relation to culture from within the church—a church, he thought, threatened by enemies without and within, a "church which has made compromises with the enemy in thought, in organization, and in discipline" (1935, p. 1). This "question of the church" found expression in *Social Sources* as historical generalizations, laws really. For a period they guided sociological research but now would be recognized as more illuminating of Niebuhr than of history.

Placing religious institutions in a socioeconomic context, Niebuhr argued that the vital (Christian) religious spirit, ethic, and commitment emerged and took form in radical, lower-class, sectarian movements. These authentic expressions of the (Christian) religious impulse inevitably compromised themselves in their endeavor to conserve, embody, and transmit their vitality. That compromising transformation produced churches or denominations. The denomination or church came to terms with the dominant culture; and denominations further capitulated to class, caste, regional, national, and racial interests. To Niebuhr, denominations seemed to be about the most sinful creatures on the religious landscape—guilty of the sin of schism by their sanctification of division, guilty of a breech of brotherhood by their reinforcement of societal interests, and guilty of a betrayal of the Gospel by their exchange of its radical claims for a potage of middle-class culture.

Against the backdrop of the American experience, the notions that all religious movements originate among the dispossessed as sects, that sects inevitably metamorphose into denominations or churches, and that the process of institutionalization should be conceived as compromise made sense to Niebuhr and to many of his early readers. It did seem that in the American environment European sects (and churches, one should add) took denominational form, that their constituency typically became middle class, and that they institutionalized themselves in relation to the dominant trends and divisions of American society. American evidence generated Niebuhr's generic rules (his later typology in *Christ and Culture* [1951] is less provincial; while relevant to institutions its greater breadth does not permit its consideration here). For sociology, this national specificity severely limits the value of these rules. Few would now say with Niebuhr, as Becker once did, "Denominations are simply sects in an advanced stage of development and adjustment to each other and the secular world" (1951, p. 116). That point, and indeed Niebuhr's whole argument, might well be seen less as a sociological theorem and more as a reading (albeit an ethically evaluative one) of the prevalence of the denominational form at a point of its vulnerability in the early twentieth century.

While Niebuhr's subjection of ideal typology to historical and ethical constraints (and American ones at that) may seem in hindsight "unhelpful" (Beckford, 1973), he was among the many to recognize that the earlier typology misread the American scene. The churches of Europe— Roman Catholic, Lutheran, Reformed, Anglican —often found themselves, initially at least, in sectarian roles in American society. Their traditional place as world-embracing, universal, inclusive, objective institutions, meshed with the authority system of the state, integral with society and culture, enveloping the whole life of members, and effectively redeeming the individual and the world had been preempted by the collectivity of Anglo-Saxon denominations. And without the church to define itself against, the sectarian spirit—world-denying, voluntaristic, rejecting of church, society, and state, exclusive, antisacerdotal, intolerant, totalistic, morally rigorous—diffused itself vis-à-vis the denominational establishment. All bodies, at least since the nineteenth century, have shared the essential sectarian requisite, voluntarism, whether they played an establishment or dissenting role in American society. Hence, after Niebuhr, typologies and classificatory schemes oriented toward analysis of American institutions have featured the denomination.

The denomination has been seen as the American form of religious organization and its characteristics as strikingly American. Martin, for instance, offers this definition:

> The denomination does not claim that its institutional borders constitute the one ark of salvation. Its concept of unity is a unity of experience and its historical sense is likewise a unity of experience rather than an institutional succession. Its attitude to organization and to cultic forms tends to be pragmatic and instrumental, while its sacramental conceptions are subjective. This

subjectivity is related to a fundamental individualism. In the field of eschatology its conceptions are traditional and in the field of moral theory its conception of the relation of faith to works is dynamic but balanced.

> (1962, p. 11)

Johnson proposes a simpler conception, but one no less suggestive of the denomination's place in American society. The denomination, he suggests, is

> a religious organization that accepts the rules governing all voluntary associations in modern western society. The most important of these rules are the principle of voluntarism itself and respect for the rights of competing associations. . . . The first and most important test of whether an American body is sectarian is its attitude toward the rules.

> (1971, p. 133)

Swatos (1981) underscores the denominations' openness to and "at-homeness" in American society by terming them "the structural-functional forms that dominant religious traditions assume in a pluralistic society" (p. 222).

Sociological efforts to comprehend the dynamics of American religious institutions produced various classificatory/typological proposals, some quite elaborate. Becker (1932) suggested a continuum of cult, sect, denomination, and church. The continuum represented ever more elaborate structure, a scale of adjustment to the world, and stages in the life cycle of religious impulse. Becker, like Niebuhr, thought a religious movement might emerge as a cult, take sectarian form, consolidate itself as a denomination, and settle eventually into churchly status vis-à-vis its society. Yinger (1970) built an even more complex continuum—universal church, ecclesia, denomination, established sect, sect, cult—with subvarieties of churchly and sectarian types. His criteria for definition and categorization measured group inclusion of members of society, acceptance of "secular values and structures of society," and organizational complexity, professionalization, and bureaucracy.

In recent years much of the creative work on typology has concerned itself with the sect. Illustrative is B. Wilson, who though writing in a British context and increasingly moving beyond a Western orientation has applied his theory to

American institutions. In a succession of important works, he has elaborated quite intricate subcategories of sects, e.g., conversionist, revolutionist, introversionist, manipulationist, thaumaturgical, reformist, and utopian. His study of sectarianism, and particularly of permanent sects, renders highly problematic Niebuhr's notion that sects are ephemeral stages in the life cycle of religious movements that inevitably become denominations. Essential to the sect's nature and prospects is its relation to the world. Wilson discerns "world-denying, world-indifferent, and world-enhancing" responses (1982, p. 111).

These and similar refinements of sect theory and the typology are partially prompted by the effervescence of the so-called new religions, many of them new only to Americans, that do not fit neatly into existing institutional theory. So once again the religious fertility of the American soil promises as rich a yield of theory as of phenomena. Not only the new religions but also the rapidly growing nondenominational churches, the large-budget and high-visibility media evangelists, and the coalescing Christian Right call for typologies that make sense of the American scene. Are the existing schemes that reflect the earlier cultural dominance of the once mainstream denominations and feature the denomination as *the* American institution passé? Already Swatos (1981) has recast the category of denominationalism in the light of shifting patterns of religious institutionalization. Whether others will heed his call to reject classificatory schemes and return to Weber for ideal constructs we have yet to see.

What is clear is that despite such critiques by some users and dismissals by other theorists, ideal typology continues to direct scholarly attention to religious institutions. Part of its continuing appeal has to do with discussions internal to the sociology of religion. But its value both within and without the discipline derives also from the capacity of the typology to focus upon critical issues in the interpretation of religion. In particular, this approach, really alone of those surveyed here, takes seriously the institutional consequences of religion's claims to otherness, the holy, and God. Institutionalization of religious experience, what Weber termed the routinization of charisma, has proved an ambiguous enterprise. O'Dea (1970) appropriately describes these ambiguities as dilemmas and paradoxes. Office, symbols, administrative order, ethos, and authority never prove adequate bearers of the meanings that give rise to them. Typologies recognize, whether in the evaluative overtones of Troeltsch and Niebuhr's "compromise" or in O'Dea's dilemmas, that the finite strains to hold that which is experienced and viewed as infinite.

Oriented to the relation between the sacred and the world, typologies do greater justice to movements' self-conceptions and perceived missions than other approaches. However, it is often the initial world views, particularly sectarian ones, that typologies portray in sharpest outline. It should be no surprise that sect theory, rather than theory of denomination or church, has been most highly developed.

Typologies also make clearer than other theories that the transition from initial to subsequent leadership, with all that entails, differs from subsequent change. Perhaps Weber's notion of routinization is to be preferred to the life-cycle pattern of subsequent theorists. At the very least, much of typology theory focuses on the critical moment in the life of institutions. While that may not be the last thing to say about a religious body, it is not an unimportant insight.

ETHNIC STUDIES

"American religious denominations are ethnic groups" and America is a denominational society. So proclaimed Greeley (1972) in rejecting the notion that the denomination "is a compromise or halfway house between sect and church," in viewing it as "a unique and new social form of religion," and in portraying American pluralism in denominational terms (pp. 71, 108). Greeley's virtual equation of religious institutions and ethnicity represents an extreme. Yet it dramatically illustrates the dubious quality of the long-standing popular and academic expectation that ethnic particularism and religion disintegrate before the forces of modernity and secularization. As the titles of Michael Novak's *The Rise of the Unmeltable Ethnics* and Nathan Glazer and Daniel P. Moynihan's *Beyond the Melting Pot* indicate, the scholarly community awoke in the 1960s and 1970s to what seemed at times like a worldwide resurgence of ethnicity. Presumptions about the inevitable and imminent demise of religion and ethnicity seemed, at least, premature. With the larger dimensions of ethnicity and even the relation of religion and ethnicity we cannot here concern ourselves. Suffice it to say that they are now the domain of a sizable scholarly community, whose productivity has been termed an explosion and that communicates with itself through a dozen and more periodicals.

Two points that recur in this literature are of importance for understanding religious institutions. First, studies of immigration and ethnicity over the last several decades have revised our conceptions of the history and prospects of unity and diversity in American society and of the relation of group formation and institutionalization to American identity. Gleason (1980) isolates four distinct answers to the fundamental question "What does it mean to be an American?"— four models of how legitimacy is achieved. Two of these emphasize the unity essential to American well-being—Americanization, by stressing a requisite ideological minimum; Anglo-Saxon racialism, by demanding an exclusive form of American unity. The other two sanction diversity —the melting pot, by accepting diverse origins as productive of eventual cultural unity; and cultural pluralism, by envisioning a multiplicity of American identities (see Abramson, 1980, and Marty, 1972, for slightly variant models of unity and diversity, assimilation and pluralism). Obviously, it will be of great moment for our interpretation of institutions which of these proves most historically accurate. At a minimum, we need to be concerned with two interrelated questions. The first has to do with the relative unity or diversity in institutional patterns at any point in time and the degree to which *either* reflects ethnic factors. The second concerns the ethnic origins of our institutional patterns (whether relatively uniform or diverse).

To illustrate, we commonly assign the salient features of American institutional life to the Puritan/evangelical heritage and monitor Roman Catholic, Lutheran, Orthodox conformity as signs of Americanization (Anglo-conformity). However, recent studies by Dolan (1975, 1978) on Roman Catholicism and by T. Smith (1966, 1978) on a broad sampling of religious traditions insist that institutional patterns of leadership, promotion, piety, and life that were long thought

to be distinctively "American" derive from the respective traditions, not the host society. Catholic forms of revivalism, to take the most dramatic instance, can be seen as continuous with European parish missions and need not be read as signs of capitulation to Protestant practice. That may not make them less "American" but it does suggest that the origins of American institutional life may be more ethnically diverse than has often been supposed. And the fact that institutional traits taken to be distinctively "American" may derive from French or German Catholicism rather than New England Puritanism further suggests that it would be quite easy to overstate the degree of conformity and to underestimate the vitality of ethnicity in current institutional practice. Hence voluntary action research and organizational studies (and to a lesser extent denominational histories) that, in consensus fashion, employ societal models of organization to explain religious institutions may lack the lenses to see configurations derived from ethnic experience.

First, then, studies of ethnicity suggest plural origins of institutional patterns and more subtle transactions between immigrant bodies and the host culture than other more assimilationist models would suggest. Second, and ironically, ethnicity bids to be *the single* most important determinant of religious institutionalization. Here the accent falls not so much on the plurality of institutional traditions as upon the commonality of the immigrant and ethnic experience itself. These two points are not mutually exclusive, but the distinction and the irony still hold. Like the voluntarist pluralists, the ethnic pluralists at times seem to offer a single explanation for religious institutions—ethnicity.

We referred at the outset to one such instance, Greeley's functionalist estimation that in America religious institutions play ethnic or quasi-ethnic roles and that as gemeinschaft groups they are a central feature of American society as a whole. Even more ambitiously and quite subtly, T. Smith offers a general theory of religious institutions and their history with ethnicity as the controlling category (1966, 1968, 1978). As ethnicity appears to be the key factor in American institutional life, so also religion appears to be the major determinant of ethnicity. Migration, Smith suggests, "was often a theologizing experience" (1978, p. 1175). Migration disrupted relationships, shattered personal identity, and dismantled frameworks of meaning, what Berger has called "the sacred canopy." By necessity the immigrants became creators both of new social structures and of their meaning. The product of this creativity was peoplehood—new group and personal identity. The process began, Smith argues, at least for the immigrants of European origin, in the juxtaposition of peoples through commerce, warfare, and urbanization within Europe. It accelerated in America, in part because individuals receptive to such new alignments and groups in the process of formation were migration-prone. The role of religion in forging ethnic community and institutions was threefold (Smith does point out that other types of ideology have played this role).

First, religion marked out new boundaries of peoplehood, drawing upon prior traditions of language, nationality, association, and belief but reworking them in a significant manner. Those of a given linguistic, cultural, and national background often constituted not one but several peoples. The Germans and Magyars, for instance, clustered into Lutheran, Reformed, Catholic, and Jewish communities. And eventually, in addition to bodies that represented themselves as faithful to such inherited traditions, various other ethnic possibilities presented themselves—new movements, groups that had altered significantly in interaction with the dominant culture, and new constellations perhaps along confessional lines. Hence the individual's problem was not just whether to cross over into the community whose boundaries confronted him but which boundaries to cross. Ethnicity derived from the elaboration of and choice between religiously defined communities.

Religious institutions, first congregations, then successive layers of structure built to service congregations, defined, consolidated, and symbolized those new boundaries. The common patterns to be found in religious institutions derive from the common burdens that congregations and denominations were forced to bear. To them fell the tasks of order, nurture, meaning, and interpretation that had been the responsibility of village elders, authority (both civil and religious) at various levels, kin groups, and culture. It is, then, to ethnicity that the distinctive attributes of American religious institutional culture are to be

ascribed. And conversely, ethnicity has been largely defined in religious terms.

Secondly, the anxiety, grief, guilt, and loneliness produced by migration and the strangeness of the new customs in the new land prompted deep inner cravings for meaning and certainty. Such inner turmoil often found expression and release in religious commitment. This served, on the one hand, to reinforce the institutional commitment individuals made. On the other, it produced patterns of institutional or collective religious behavior thought to be typically American. These include the intense piety itself, a moralism that drew clean lines between what was acceptable and what was not, the notion that the people were in covenant with God, a biblicism establishing a clear and acceptable basis of authority, and the pragmatic or progressive orientation to adjust to new situations.

The third contribution of religion to ethnicity, according to Smith, was the belief, framed by Jewish messianism or Christian millennialism, that the peoplehood defined and the institutions created served the larger purpose of the unity of humanity. This catholic and purposive orientation—long thought to be the characteristic mark of the Anglo-Saxon Protestant establishment and the missionary and denominational institutions it created—Smith also ascribes to ethnicity. The forms of this universalism vary; the Hasidim, the Moravians, Eastern Orthodoxy, and black religion construe the hope for the human race in different fashion. They concur in asserting a catholic meaning to their particularity.

The close identification of religion with ethnicity posited by Smith and Greeley effectively illustrates this approach to institutionalization. Others (Thernstrom, 1980) stress the variety of factors formative of ethnic identity. Definitional issues are partly at stake. Isajiw (1974) examined twenty-seven definitions of ethnicity and isolated a dozen or so attributes. Religion figured in ten of the definitions, shared culture in eleven, national origin in twelve. Abramson (1980) proposes a threefold relation of religion and ethnicity: equation, with religion defining ethnicity in the manner suggested by Smith; centrifugal disengagement, with religion narrowing ethnic boundaries, perhaps through schisms; and centripetal convergence, with religion consolidating or enlarging ethnic borders, as perhaps in the triple melting pot popularized by Will Herberg. There is, as Abramson and virtually all students of ethnic religion indicate, an ethnic dimension to religion and a religious dimension to ethnicity. But studies of ethnicity worry, in a fashion not unlike the immigrants they study, over the tugs of both particularity and unity, of pluralism and assimilation. As far as religious institutions are concerned, the question finally is one of degree. How much of institutional life derived from the heritages imported or the exigencies of migration itself and how much from interaction with and appropriation of patterns elaborated by earlier and now dominant immigrants? That will doubtless remain an open question.

AN EVOLUTIONARY THEORY

As we have traced the emergence of the several theories of religious institutions, we have remarked, where appropriate, on the evidential character of the theories themselves. In particular, we noted that denominational history seems to mark an important stage in the evolution of institutional consciousness; that voluntary action research seemed especially apropos for the period in which it first appeared, namely the nineteenth century; and that organizational theory both evidences and interprets the dramatic changes of the late nineteenth and early twentieth centuries. We have also remarked on the different aspects of religious institutions that the theories bring into view. Here we would like to build on those two notes to suggest that the several theories do help us to understand what might best be termed the evolution of American institutional culture, and that they complement one another in important ways.

Chandler's observation about the radical dissimilarity between the business culture of different periods applies even more strikingly to religious institutions. A member of today's United Church of Christ would be more at home, we suggest, in contemporary United Methodism than in earlier phases of his own movement—in mid-nineteenth-century Congregational or Christian churches, in eighteenth-century Massachusetts parishes, or in seventeenth-century Puritanism. The institutional configurations on every level differ markedly from period to pe-

riod, a fact masked by the continuity of denominational identity, and more important, by the employment of the denominational language to cover successive and differing institutional realities. To be sure, language does define the religious system of a given body and the access to those meanings that denominational history provides is not insignificant.

Nevertheless, a religious institution existing at any given time seems to be shaped by three sometimes independent, often interactive dynamics: the institutional environment of the society as a whole, the level and character of its ethnic identity, and its orientation to both its own peculiar vision and the world. The latter two dynamics are recurrent possibilities, as the theories devoted to them (ethnic studies and typology) presume. That is to say, at any given point in American history, down to the present, either or both of those dynamics may be the primary determinants in institutional life. For instance, analysis of recent Hispanic developments in Roman Catholicism and Korean movements in Presbyterian, Methodist, and Baptist churches requires both typology and ethnic theory. However, it is not the case that the institutional configurations of Hispanic Catholicism or Korean Presbyterianism will appear through either ethnic or typological lenses to be identical to nineteenth-century versions of ethnic Catholicism or Presbyterianism. The successive phases of the organizational culture of American religion affect even quite particularistic movements. For that reason a few generalizations about major stages of American religious organization are in order.

Over the course of American history four distinctive configurations of religious community have emerged, assumed a certain prominence, even dominance, and then gradually found themselves not displaced, but subsumed in a successive communal form. The institutional expression of each closely resembled styles of community found elsewhere in the society. The first, represented by both the confessionally congregational Puritans and the more accidentally congregational Anglicans, ordered and legitimated local community. This institutionalized localism appeared in the seventeenth century but continues in places down to the present. Its aspiration for uniformity took varying temporal-spatial forms in the different regions. In New England, religious institutionalization completed the town; fittingly the meetinghouse defined the center of the community. In the Chesapeake, the parish was as much event as place; Anglicans established churches at places of convenience and sustained their community through a variety of ritual events. In the Middle Colonies religious institutionalization marked off neighborhood, thus legitimating pluralism. In each case the congregation was primary. Civil support, colonial clerical gatherings, and European religious authority ideally served the local institution. Access to this phase of institutional life through denominational history should be balanced by judicious use of perspectives drawn from typology (Swatos, 1979). For these institutions sought religious monopoly in the community to which they had access.

The second institutional stage appears most strikingly in mid-eighteenth-century Presbyterians and Lutherans. Ethnic voluntarism might name it best, for it betrayed that paradox identified by Timothy L. Smith of giving universal significance to ethnically limited endeavor. Modest paracongregational structure was elaborated, primarily clergy networks designed to support existing and new congregations among the target ethnic population. Denominational histories rather effectively retrieve this stage since, like most histories, they tend to feature beginnings and since denominational machinery elaborated during this stage constitutes an essential component of their narrative. But ethnic studies provide a needed balance, for the paracongregational or denominational structures served the ethnic functions outlined by Smith.

The third and fourth institutional stages have figured prominently in our discussion and can be more quickly sketched. Early-nineteenth-century Methodists exemplify the third stage, the era of expansive, purposive, national missionary denominational order, reinforced by voluntary societies, and oriented toward inclusive evangelization and the establishment of religious civilization. Experimental and pragmatic attitudes toward institutional machinery went hand in hand with a (limited) openness to other evangelical denominations. For all was deemed subservient to the common goal of the kingdom. While the local and ethnic forms of community lived on in this new order, community now increasingly defined itself in national terms, a voluntary community of evangelical cells knit by purpose and catholic Protestant belief into federation and confederation. This was the heyday of denominationalism. Yet, ironically, this stage belongs to voluntary action research. For this voluntarism had "established" itself in a Christian America.

In the fourth stage, denominational and ecumenical structures, increasingly centralized and bureaucratized, give shape to religious community. Within those structures, clergy define their own special community, a professional one like that now dominant in American society. Lacking the communal prominence of the local institutions of stage one, the ethnic universalism of stage two, and the national vision of stage three, twentieth-century denominations of the ecumenical variety at times peer nostalgically at the institutional formulae of earlier stages. They chafe as evangelical bodies and new religious groups profit by combining corporate and media culture with past visions. What the future holds for any of these bodies lies beyond the purview of this essay. What we can say is that organizational studies provide access to the various dimensions of this phase.

These four stages do not exhaust the saga of American religious institutions, but only outline the path charted by those movements that claimed dominance. To the degree that that dominance prevailed, the above patterns helped define one of the three dynamics in American religious institutionalization, the institutional environment of the society as a whole. The other two dynamics, the forces of ethnicity and the powerful appeal of new visions, brought ever new communities into being. At times the new communities seemed to replicate the four stages just described. But they also appropriated the styles of the day. And in many cases they invented or imported what they were thought to have pirated. The mainstream (represented by these four cycles) doubtless was more indebted to successful innovation at the margin, to new structures or procedures established by Catholics, black Protestants, or sectarian movements, than it has been willing to admit. Americans admired what worked. Hence the three dynamics interplayed to create new patterns of institutional life to fit the society of the day. To understand these complexities, we need all five of the theories here analyzed. We would also profit from significant dialogue between them.

BIBLIOGRAPHY

General Works

Thomas Bender, *Community and Social Change in America* (1978); Joseph L. Blau, *Judaism in America* (1976); Jay P. Dolan, *The Immigrant Church: New York's Irish and German Catholics, 1815–1865* (1975) and *Catholic Revivalism: The American Experience, 1830–1900* (1978); Robert T. Handy, *A Christian America* (1971; rev. 1984) and *A History of the Churches in the United States and Canada* (1976); James Hennesey, *American Catholics: A History of the Roman Catholic Community in the United States* (1981); William G. McLoughlin, *Revivals, Awakenings, and Reform* (1978); Martin E. Marty, *Righteous Empire* (1970) and *A Nation of Behavers* (1976); John M. Mulder and John F. Wilson, eds., *Religion in American History* (1978); Jacob Neusner, ed., *Understanding American Judaism*, 2 vols. (1975); Russell E. Richey, ed., *Denominationalism* (1977); Gregory H. Singleton, *Religion in the City of Angels: American Protestant Culture and Urbanization, Los Angeles, 1850–1930* (1979); Elwyn A. Smith, ed., *The Religion of the Republic* (1971); Robert H. Wiebe, *The Segmented Society* (1975).

Denominational History

Thomas Branagan, *A Concise View, of the Principal Religious Denominations, in the United States of America* (1811); Jon Butler, *Power, Authority, and the Origins of American Denominational Order: The English Churches in the Delaware Valley, 1680–1730* (1978); Peter D. Gorrie, *The Churches and Sects of the United States* (1850); J. Gordon Melton, *The Encyclopedia of American Religions*, 2 vols. (1978), and, with James V. Geisendorfer, *A Directory of Religious Bodies in the United States* (1977); Arthur C. Piepkorn, *Profiles in Belief: The Religious Bodies of the United States and Canada*, 4 vols. in 3 (1977–1979); I. Daniel Rupp, comp., *He Pasa Ekklesia: An Original History of the Religious Denominations at Present Existing in the United States* (1844); Philip Schaff et al., *The American Church History Series*, 13 vols. (1893–1897).

Voluntary Associations

Robert Baird, *Religion in America* (1844; abridged 1970); Joseph D. Ban and Paul R. Dekar, eds., *In the Great Tradition: In Honor of Winthrop S. Hudson* (1982); Keith R. Bridston, *Church Politics* (1969); James M. Gustafson, *Treasure in Earthen Vessels: The Church as a Human Community* (1961) and *The Church as Moral Decision-Maker* (1970); J. Roland Pennock and John W. Chapman, eds., *Voluntary Associations* (1969); Milton Powell, ed., *The Voluntary Church: American Religious Life (1740–1865) Seen Through the Eyes of European Visitors* (1967); D. B. Robertson, ed., *Voluntary Associations* (1966); Peter Romanofsky, ed., *Social Service Organizations*, 2 vols. (1977–1978); Philip Schaff, *America* (1855); Eva Schindler-Rainman and Ronald Lippitt, *The Volunteer Community* (1971); Gregory H. Singleton, "Protestant Voluntary Organizations and the Shaping of Victorian America," in *American Quarterly*, 27 (1975); Constance Smith and Anne Freedman, *Voluntary Associations: Perspectives on the Literature* (1972).

Religious Organization

James A. Beckford, "Religious Organization: A Trend Report and Bibliography," in *Current Sociology*, 21 (1973); H. Paul Douglass and Edmund de S. Brunner, *The Protestant Church as a Social Institution* (1935); Nils Ehrenström and Walter G. Muelder, eds., *Institutionalism and Church Unity* (1963); Joseph H. Fichter, *Organization Man in the Church* (1974); John R. Fry, *The Trivialization of the United Presbyterian Church* (1975); Paul M. Harrison, *Authority and Power in the Free Church Tradition* (1959); Jerry Israel, ed., *Building the Organizational Society* (1972); William M. King, "Denominational Modernization and Religious Identity," in *Methodist History*, 20 (1982); Robert Lee, *The Social Sources of Church Unity* (1960); Paul A. Mickey and Robert L. Wilson, *What New Creation? The Agony of Church Restructure* (1977); David Moberg, *The Church as a Social Institution* (1962); Ben Primer, *Protestants and American Business Methods* (1979); Lyle Schaller, *The Decision-Makers* (1974); Ross P. Scherer, ed., *American Denominational Organization: A Sociological View* (1980); Gibson Winter, *Religious Identity* (1968); James R. Wood, *Leadership in Voluntary Organizations: The Controversy over Social Action in Protestant Churches* (1981).

Organization Studies

Kenneth Boulding, *The Organizational Revolution* (1953); Alfred D. Chandler, Jr., *The Visible Hand: The Managerial Revolution in American Business* (1977); Louis Galambos, "The Emerging Organizational Synthesis in Modern American History," in *Business History Review*, 44 (1970), and "Technology, Political Economy, and Professionalization: Central Themes of the Organizational Synthesis," in *Business History Review*, 57 (1983); Robert Presthus, *The Organizational Society* (1962); David L. Sills, ed., *International Encyclopedia of the Social Sciences*, vol. 11 (1968); Robert H. Wiebe, *The Search for Order, 1877–1920* (1967) and *The Segmented Society* (1975).

Typology

Howard Becker, *Systematic Sociology* (1932); Allan W. Eister, "Toward a Radical Critique of Church-Sect Typologizing," in *Journal for the Scientific Study of Religion*, 6 (1967), and "H. Richard Niebuhr and the Paradox of Religious Organization: A Radical Critique," in Charles Y. Glock and Phillip E. Hammond eds., *Beyond the Classics?* (1973); Barbara Hargrove, *Sociology of Religion, Classical and Contemporary Approaches* (1979); Benton Johnson, "Church and Sect Revisited," in *Journal for the Scientific Study of Religion*, 10 (1971); D. A. Martin, "The Denomination," in *British Journal of Sociology*, 13 (1962), and *The Religious and the Secular* (1969); H. Richard Niebuhr, *The Social Sources of Denominationalism* (1929) and, with Wilhelm Pauck and Francis P. Miller, eds., *The Church Against the World* (1935); Thomas F. O'Dea, *Sociology and The Study of Religion* (1970); Liston Pope, *Millhands and Preachers* (1942); Rodney Stark and William S. Bainbridge, "Of Churches, Sects, and Cults," in *Journal for the Scientific Study* of Religion, 18 (1979); William H. Swatos, Jr., "Weber or Troeltsch? Methodology, Syndrome, and the Development of Church-Sect Theory," in *Journal for the Scientific Study of Religion*, 15 (1976), *Into Denominationalism: The Anglican Metamorphosis* (1979), and "Beyond Denominationalism: Community and Culture in American Religion," in *Journal for the Scientific Study of Religion*, 20 (1981); Max Weber, *From Max Weber: Essays in Sociology* (1946), *The Theory of Social and Economic Organization* (1947), and *The Sociology of Religion* (1963); Bryan R. Wilson, *Magic and the Millennium* (1973) and *Religion in Sociological Perspective* (1982); J. Milton Yinger, *The Scientific Study of Religion* (1970).

Ethnicity

Harold J. Abramson, "Assimilation and Pluralism" and "Religion," in Stephan Thernstrom, ed., *Harvard Encyclopedia of American Ethnic Groups* (1980); John D. Buenker et al., *Immigration and Ethnicity: A Guide to Information Services* (1977); Philip Gleason, "American Identity and Americanization," in Thernstrom (1980); Andrew Greeley, *The Denominational Society* (1972); John Higham, ed., *Ethnic Leadership in America* (1978); Wsevolod W. Isajiw, "Definitions of Ethnicity," in *Ethnicity*, 1 (1974); Richard Kilm, comp., *Bibliography of Ethnicity and Ethnic Groups* (1973); Ned Landsman, "Revivalism and Nativism in the Middle Colonies: The Great Awakening and the Scots Community in East New Jersey," in *American Quarterly*, 34 (1982); Martin E. Marty, "Ethnicity: The Skeleton of Religion in America," in *Church History*, 41 (1972); Wayne Charles Miller et al., *A Comprehensive Bibliography for the Study of American Minorities*, 2 vols. (1976); Timothy L. Smith, "Religious Denominations as Ethnic Communities," in *Church History*, 35 (1966), "Congregation, State, and Denomination: The Forming of the American Religious Structure," in *William and Mary Quarterly*, 25 (1968), and "Religion and Ethnicity in America," in *American Historical Review*, 83 (1978); Werner Sollors, "Theory of American Ethnicity," in *American Quarterly*, 33 (1981); Harry S. Stout, "Ethnicity: The Vital Center of Religion in America," in *Ethnicity*, 1 (1974).
[*See also* SOCIOLOGICAL STUDY OF AMERICAN RELIGION.]

THE PSYCHOLOGY OF
RELIGIOUS EXPERIENCE

Donald Capps

THROUGHOUT the twentieth century American religious life has been viewed through the lenses of the theologian, historian, sociologist, anthropologist, economist, political scientist, geographer, and psychologist. Each has made observations that the others did not see or make note of. Over the decades each has developed a keen eye for some facets of American religious experience and, at the same time, a certain myopia for others.

Psychologists have had greater difficulty than most professionals in determining where and how to focus their attention as far as American religious experience is concerned. Sociologists, probably the psychologists' closest counterpart, know that their central focus is American religious institutions and movements. They have been especially diligent in ensuring that their discipline takes a comprehensive view of these institutions—a view not limited to the mainline Protestant churches but including within its purview the evangelical, Pentecostal, and Fundamentalist traditions; the new religious movements (among many others, the Unification Church, the Hare Krishna Society, the Church of Scientology); the Catholic Church; Judaism; and Mormonism.

Psychologists have generally believed that it is their task to focus not on institutions but on religious experience. But what, after all, does "religious experience" mean? What does the psychologist see when he or she focuses on religious experience?

Many psychologists have been guided by William James's classic distinction between institutional and personal religion in *The Varieties of Religious Experience* (1902) and by his decision to limit his observations to the personal. As he puts it, the institutional branch of religion involves "the-ology and ceremony and ecclesiastical organization," while in the personal branch the center of interest is the individual's "inner dispositions," including "his conscience, his deserts, his helplessness, his incompleteness." *The Varieties of Religious Experience* was originally delivered as the Gifford Lectures on Natural Religion at the University of Edinburgh in 1901–1902, and James announced at the outset that he would attend exclusively to the personal branch of religion. Focusing on the "inner dispositions," he lectured on the experience of conversion, the characteristics of personal saintliness, the mystical experience, and prayer. He took as his primary data source the personal documents of self-acknowledged religious individuals, including autobiographies, memoirs, confessions, and journals, since these provided the most direct view of their inner life.

By differentiating the individual and institutional branches of religion and concentrating on the individual, James made clear that he was interested in the solitary religious experience that requires no social mediation. In such an experience "the individual transacts the business by himself alone, and the ecclesiastical organization, with its priests and sacraments and other go-betweens, sinks to an altogether secondary place. The relation goes direct from heart to heart, from soul to soul, between man and his maker." Given his special focus, James asks his audience to accept a specific definition of religion: "Religion . . . shall mean for us the feelings, acts, and experiences of individual men in their solitude, so far as they apprehend themselves to stand in relation to whatever they may consider the divine." While he recognizes that this definition has some inherent ambiguities, such as how the word "divine" is to be understood, he emphasizes that he has in mind the experience of a God who is conceived by the individual to have being and power and from whom there is ultimately no escape. This conception leads James, in turn, to stress that the individual's attitude in these religious experiences is solemn, which is appropriate for those who realize that they are apprehending a God who has ultimate control over them.

James's views on religious experience have evoked various responses. We can identify at least six different schools of psychologists who share his interest in the psychology of religious experience, but construe the enterprise as recognizably different from his and from each other's. For example, some psychologists have felt that James's focus on the solitary religious experience was too narrow. While agreeing that the psychologist's center of interest is not the institutional branch of religion, they disagree with James's decision to locate theology in the institutional branch if that means excluding religious beliefs of individuals from the psychologist's purview. In fact, James did consider the religious beliefs of the individuals whose personal documents he studied, recognizing that they were central to the individual's interpretation of his or her experiences. But he did not make religious beliefs as such the focus of his observations. Among the psychologists who argue that beliefs and belief systems should have greater importance are those influenced by Sigmund Freud, since he and members of his immediate circle were persuaded that an individual's religious beliefs have a decisive—and negative—effect on his or her psychological maturation. Paul Pruyser and Ana-Maria Rizzuto are examples of contemporary Freudians who give considerable attention to the psychology of religious belief.

Other psychologists believe that James's exclusion of the institutional branch led to the neglect of another feature of religious experience, religious myths. James has virtually nothing to say about religious myths, which he relegates to the institutional branch of religion. Psychologists who believe that religious myths should be given central consideration and not left to other scholarly disciplines do so on the grounds that such myths shape the inner lives of individuals, often in ways of which these individuals are not consciously aware. The most prominent advocates of this position have been the "depth" psy-

chologists identified with the traditions of Sigmund Freud, Carl Jung, and Otto Rank.

Another group of psychologists who believe that James's exclusion of the institutional branch was too severe are the social psychologists, who consider certain aspects of institutional religion itself to be appropriate for psychological investigation. While agreeing that the institutional structures and processes themselves are of greater interest to sociologists, they feel that certain, more specific features of the institutions are the legitimate focus of psychologists. One of these features is the clergy, specifically its personality characteristics and role expectations. Another is the social attitudes of religious people, with considerable emphasis given to religious, ethnic, and racial prejudice. A third feature is the motivation to affiliate with and participate in religious organizations, including the factors that aid, impede, or arrest such participation. Bernard P. Spilka and Merton P. Strommen, and their associates, are examples of contemporary social psychologists who have studied the impact of religious institutions on individual religious experience.

Some psychologists agree with James's emphasis on the solitary religious experiences of individuals but believe that his tendency to focus on discrete religious experiences is too restrictive. The Harvard psychologist Gordon Allport, for example, emphasizes that the religious "sentiment" of the individual has an intentional, directive, and integrative thrust. For Allport, a mature religious sentiment provides a greater sense of personal direction and purpose in life, helps individuals to recognize the complexity of their personal motivations, and provides a central core of meanings and values that are conducive to personal integration. Most important, Allport views the mature religious sentiment as forward-looking, contributing to future growth and enabling the individual to view life as an ongoing quest for meaning and purpose. James touches on these themes when he describes the "divided self" and its process of unification (integration), or the life of saintliness (intentional and directive). But his emphasis on discrete experiences such as conversion and his talk about various "states" and "conditions" of religious life are somewhat problematic for Allport, who wants to highlight movement, growth, process, quest, and becoming. He does not reject James's interest in "inner dispositions" but stresses the importance of "inner directions," the motivations that give the religious life a forward thrust and trajectory.

Allport underscores the directionality of the religious experience by discussing it in terms of developmental stages. In his classic *The Individual and His Religion* (1950) he compares the religious sentiment of the youth and the adult and contends that the religion of maturity is more consistently directive and more self-consciously intentional than the religious sentiment of the earlier years. By introducing a developmental factor into his discussion, Allport is no doubt only making explicit what James had left more or less implicit: that "inner dispositions" do not remain static or unchanged but evolve and undergo transformations throughout the course of life. Nonetheless, not until the 1950s did psychologists begin to observe religious experience through the lens of a variety of developmental theories, notably the life cycle theory of Erik Erikson and the cognitive development theory of Jean Piaget. (These will be discussed in greater detail below.)

Still other psychologists feel that the experiences treated by James do not reflect the depth and range of religious experience, especially as individuals in non-Western societies have apprehended the divine. They recognize and appreciate that James did not try to reduce the religious experience of individuals to a single disposition or to contend that the several dispositions he addressed could take only certain religious forms or expressions and not others. While they recognize that for his time James was unusually hospitable toward other faiths and made significant use of non-Christian and non-Western personal documents, still they argue that he selected forms of religious experience largely from the perspective of a twentieth-century Westerner with Christian affinities. His examples of conversion, a phenomenon in every world faith, not only are taken from Christian sources but reflect the introspective conscience of the Protestant tradition, with its emphasis on guilt and forgiveness, shame and remorse. His discussion of saintliness draws heavily on Christian sources, largely Catholic, and neglects forms of saintliness found among Muslims, Buddhists, Hindus, and Confucianists. Since the 1950s psychologists J. G. Arapura, S. K. Ramachandra Rao, and Gardner and Lois Murphy have empha-

sized the importance of a broader cultural perspective, with the result that Eastern forms of religious experience, especially meditational practices, have been given serious attention. This broadening of perspective has enabled American psychologists to recognize religious experiences of their own country and era that might have gone unnoticed but for their counterparts in other cultural and religious traditions.

One final group of psychologists for whom James's perspective is too restrictive argues that the issue is not whether the institutional branch of religion should be excluded but whether James has taken adequate account of historical events outside of the institutional branch of religion that often profoundly influence individual religious experience. Richard L. Rubenstein is a good example of this type of psychologist, as reflected in his writings on the Holocaust. Kenneth Earl Morris' study of Dietrich Bonhoeffer and Fred L. Downing's study of Martin Luther King, Jr., are also good illustrations of this psychological orientation. These psychologists do not disagree with James's emphasis on the religious experience of the individual but contend that the religion of the individual is shaped as much by historical events as by social institutions. Influenced by the psychohistorian Robert Jay Lifton and by Erik H. Erikson, they give particular attention to the way in which major historical events shape religious experience by confronting people with the need to reassess their perspectives on the world. The Holocaust, the bombing of Hiroshima, the assassination of President John F. Kennedy and of the Rev. Martin Luther King, Jr., and the Vietnam War have shaped the religious experience of many individuals since World War II, decisively affecting their "inner dispositions" far more than the institutional branch of religion has.

When James looked out on the American religious landscape, he saw varieties of religious experience. Looking back on the enterprise that he and other psychologists of his era inaugurated, it is possible to see varieties of psychologies of religious experience. The situation is highly pluralistic.

There is every reason to believe that this pluralism will continue and that each of the six schools identified above will play a significant role in the psychologies of religious experience. But three of these schools warrant further discussion here because they reflect the major theoretical as well as empirical thrusts in American psychology of religion since James. They are associated with the work of the major figures in the field, including Freud, Jung, Allport, and Erikson. These are the schools that emphasize belief, myth, and the developmental process. It can be argued that these three schools reflect greater theoretical continuity with James than do the other three schools.

THE PSYCHOLOGY OF RELIGIOUS CONVERSION

Of the variety of personal religious experiences that James took an interest in, the topic that he and his associates are best known for today is conversion. This type of experience fits James's special definition of religion well, for a critical element of any conversion experience is one's apprehension of oneself "in relation" to God. Moreover, conversion experiences are solemn, befitting the convert's awareness of the presence and power of God.

James and his associates felt that prayer should be the central focus of the psychology of religious experience. According to James, prayer is "the very soul and essence of religion," and George Albert Coe, a professor of religious education and psychology of religion at Union Theological Seminary in New York, claimed that "a history and psychology of prayer would be almost equivalent to a history and psychology of religion" (*The Psychology of Religion,* 1916). James and his associates also believed that their investigations of prayer would tell for or against the validity of religion. As Alexander Hodge points out in *Prayer and Its Psychology* (1931):

> Prayer is the center and soul of all religion, and upon the question of its validity depends the trustworthiness of religious experience in general. If psychology can invalidate prayer, it has succeeded in disproving the whole of religion. On the other hand, if prayer withstands the test of the new thought, then religion as a whole is vindicated.
>
> (p. x)

In similar fashion James notes that the "genuineness of religion is thus indissolubly bound up with the question whether the prayerful consciousness be or be not deceitful. The conviction that something is genuinely transacted in this consciousness is the very core of living religion."

Yet despite this emphasis on prayer, James devotes two long chapters of *The Varieties of Religious Experience* to conversion and relegates prayer to a few brief pages in an omnibus chapter on "other characteristics" of religion. The effect, whether intended or not, is that James and his associates are now clearly associated with conversion, and indeed it can be argued that some aspects of their work on conversion remain unsurpassed.

This work began in April 1896, when James Leuba, professor of psychology and pedagogy at Bryn Mawr College, published his doctoral thesis, a study of Christian conversion, in the *American Journal of Psychology*. This study, written under the guidance of G. Stanley Hall, president of Clark University, in Worcester, Massachusetts, focused on the role of conversion in overcoming obstacles to the unification of the person. Over the course of the next four decades, Leuba continued to write on the psychology of religious experience, gaining a reputation as the most agnostic psychologist of religion of his day and the most critical of religion's effects on the individual. One year later, Edwin D. Starbuck, assistant professor of education at Stanford University and, like Leuba, a former graduate student of G. Stanley Hall's, published two articles on conversion and religious growth in the same journal. Starbuck's articles, based on research he had carried out as a graduate student at Harvard, were later expanded into his extremely important book, *The Psychology of Religion* (1900).

Hall had been involved since the early 1880s in the study of the moral and religious training of children and subsequently published his own influential book, *Adolescence: Its Psychology and Its Relation to Physiology, Anthropology, Sociology, Sex, Crime, Religion and Education* (1904). Hall's book is credited with identifying the teen years as a decisive stage in human development, a stage accompanied by considerable storm and stress and radically discontinuous with the earlier childhood years. Starbuck's studies of conversion centered on adolescent conversions and lent support to Hall's views on this radical discontinuity.

Starbuck was also aided in his investigations

by James, to whom he first proposed his idea of studying conversion scientifically. In his preface to Starbuck's book James acknowledges that he had initially been less than enthusiastic about Starbuck's proposal but praises him for his patient labor in bringing compromise and conciliation into the long-standing feud between science and religion. Contrasting Starbuck with evangelical extremists and scientific sectaries, James praises him for seeing converson as "a perfectly normal psychologic crisis."

Providing the empirical foundation for much of James's own discussion of conversion in *The Varieties of Religious Experience*, Starbuck's studies include data consisting of autobiographical materials provided by a sample of 192 (120 females, 72 males) and questionnaire results from a sample of 1,265 (254 females, 1,011 males). He found that conversion experiences occur almost exclusively between ages ten and twenty-five. Age sixteen is the peak time for conversions, with a rapid decline from age sixteen to twenty, and a gradual decline after age twenty. He also found that conversion is linked to puberty, but not in a simple cause-effect manner. Contrary to the view that conversion experiences are the direct effect of physiological growth, Starbuck found that conversions are most likely to occur when physiological growth had temporarily slowed or abated, and less likely to occur when physiological growth was at its peak.

Starbuck identified two types of conversion experience. He found that some conversions center on the sense of sin and the desire for forgiveness. But the more frequent type is the spontaneous awakening, a spiritual illumination in which converts have a feeling of incompleteness and struggle after a "larger life." He contends that the latter type is the normal adolescent conversion and that it is largely positive, though accompanied by uncertainty and distress. The conversion involving a sense of sin is more typically effected through revivals, suggesting that the theology of revivalism, with its emphasis on themes of sin, guilt, and atonement, imposes an interpretation on the conversion that the adolescent would not likely come to on his own. What adolescents tend to experience is not guilt but a feeling of inadequacy and low self-esteem. The spontaneous awakening reflects the natural experiences of adolescents whereas the revival-induced conversion reflects what society

believes the adolescent ought to believe. Starbuck emphasizes that both conversions involve the perception of the old being replaced with the new, but the spontaneous awakening is more clearly an awakening to a "larger self." This enlargement of the self involves both greater self-awareness and a greater sense of harmony with the world in which one lives and to which one is accountable.

Starbuck was critical of revivalism because it produces the more negative escape-from-sin conversion rather than the more positive spontaneous-awakening conversion. In addition, he found that the main contribution of revivals is to accelerate a process that would otherwise have occurred more spontaneously later. He considers this a rather dubious benefit to the convert, for such acceleration may create unnecessary stress in adolescents who are already experiencing considerable loneliness and uncertainty. He also found that young Christians who did not experience conversions in adolescence were not less spiritual or less morally mature than converts when both groups were tested in their early twenties. He concludes that religious educators should be less concerned with inducing conversion experiences in adolescents and more attentive to the "importance of wisely anticipating the stages of growth and leading on [the adolescent] naturally and easily from one stage to the next."

Starbuck also notes that conversion experiences can be integral to the normal stages of growth if they are allowed to take the form of spontaneous awakenings. Such awakenings do not occur without stress and uncertainty, but they are ultimately consistent with the natural growth of the adolescent, which is first and foremost the enlargement of the self through its assimilation of the social world in which it exists. If such enlargement of the self involves greater self-awareness, this is not simply deeper insight into one's inner life, but greater clarity concerning one's vocation and purpose in the world.

The psychologist of religion who placed greatest emphasis on the social dimension of conversion was not Starbuck, however, but George Albert Coe. In *The Psychology of Religion*, Coe notes that "self-realization within a social medium has now been established as one important phase of the religious experience." He observes that adolescents experience a "strangeness of the self to itself" that "makes social support almost indispensable." Conversion is a step in the creation of a self, and it is generally, perhaps always, a step "in the creation of society."

> In conversion, the pronoun "my" acquires meaning that it did not have before; mere drifting, mere impulse, are checked; my conduct and attitudes attach to me more consciously; I stand out in a new way, judging myself and my world, and giving the loyalty of articulate purpose to the cause with which I identify myself.
>
> (p. 171)

Coe concludes that conversion "is a faith-creating process, specifically social faith." Previously the adolescent had knowledge *about* God, but now he experiences fellowship *with* God. The socius of other persons and God, their perceptible social reality and influence, has an immediacy that was not present before:

> Granted that his training has prepared him for the crisis, and that conversion puts him under the control of existing social standards and ideas of God, the fact remains that conversion makes these things real to the convert. . . . The world or God has meaning *for him* and makes response *now*.
>
> (p. 174)

In contrast to Coe, James pays little attention to the social dimension of the conversion experience and instead focuses almost exclusively on the internal processes involved in the experience. Noting with Starbuck that some conversions are gradual and others sudden and that some conversions involve the exercise of the will while others are characterized by submissiveness, James proposes that these differences are determined by internal processes. He introduces his theory of the mind to provide a theoretical explanation of these processes.

In his earlier work *The Principles of Psychology* (1890), James argues that the mind is not only productive of ideas but also permissive and transmissive, the carrier of ideas that have their origins outside the conscious mind. In his discussion of conversion in *The Varieties of Religious Experience* he introduces a distinction between the conscious and the subconscious mind. It is the subconscious that is most permissive and transmissive, allowing ideas to enter the mind without its awareness. James accounts for the difference

between gradual and sudden conversions by positing that in conversion ideas that have originally entered the subconscious make their way to the conscious mind. In gradual conversions the line between the subconscious and conscious mind is permeable, so that the ideas of the subconscious mind make their way to the conscious mind a few at a time. In sudden conversions the line is not permeable, so that the subconscious ideas are stored until they eventually burst into the conscious mind all at once.

If these two types of conversion are looked at to determine the role of the conscious mind in the conversion process, the gradual conversion appears to be more an exercise of the will, since the conscious mind appears more in control of the process and more able to assimilate subconscious ideas as they occur. Conversely, the sudden conversion appears to be more submissive a self-surrender, in that the conscious mind gives up any attempt to control the inrush of ideas. However, James resists making an easy correlation between volition and gradual conversion, or submission and sudden conversion, because he recognizes that the facts also lend themselves to precisely the opposite interpretation. It can be argued that the submissive, self-surrender conversion is possible precisely because the conscious mind exercised considerable willpower in keeping the subconscious ideas out of consciousness so long. Conversely, since in the gradual conversion the subconscious ideas were able to permeate the conscious mind more or less at will, the conscious mind may have been submissive by temperament or inclination.

James is not concerned to settle these issues. His primary interest is to identify the source of the unconscious ideas and to characterize the change that occurs once the conscious mind assimilates these ideas. As for the source of the unconscious ideas, he suggests that the subconscious has its nearer side, which contains ordinary sense data inattentively taken in and subconsciously remembered and combined, and its more distant side, which receives ideas that originate in "high spiritual agencies" and eventually make their way into the conscious mind. He contends that he arrives at this view strictly as a psychologist, not as an orthodox Christian. And while this recognition of higher spiritual agencies in the conversion process may appear to support orthodox interpretations of the experience, he warns that "the value of these forces would have to be determined by their effects, and the mere fact of their transcendency would of itself establish no presumption that they were more divine than diabolical."

Concerning the change that occurs once the conscious mind has assimilated the subconscious ideas, James proposes that the conscious mind be viewed as a field of forces whose energy center has shifted by the gradual infusion or sudden inrush of new ideas. The convert's perception of being wholly changed can be explained in terms of this major shift in the mind's center of energy. The psychological change effected by such a shift in the energy center is no less dramatic than, say, the changes that would occur in American political life if our nation's capital were moved from Washington, D.C., to Denver, Colorado. The effect is a total reorientation of all ideas and values relevant to the change in question.

James also suggests that his model explains why most conversions are permanent. Starbuck had found that conversion brings with it a changed attitude or disposition toward life that is fairly constant and permanent. Feelings or emotions might fluctuate (for example, there may be changes in mood, from happy to sad, or changes in the intensity of feelings), "accounting for the phenomenon of 'so-called' backsliding." But once the center of energy has changed, according to James, the mind reconstitutes itself around this new center. All significant ideas, values, and meanings are oriented to this new center, and thus the effect of a conversion is the recentering of the mind or conscious self. This model, moreover, explains why conversion is often depicted as an enlargement of the self, a sense of greater wholeness: not only has the field of forces been enlarged through the influx of new ideas, but there has also been a reconciliation of the conscious and the subconscious mind. Whether willingly or submissively, the conscious mind has accepted the ideas that emigrated from the subconscious region and is no longer expending its energy in a futile attempt to keep these foreign elements out.

James and his associates initiated what has proven to be a very long-lasting interest among psychologists in the conversion experience. As Lewis Rambo's excellent 1982 bibliography on current research on religious conversion shows, psychologists' interest continues una-

bated. Indeed, psychologists have long since been joined by anthropologists, sociologists, and historians in research on conversion. Further, James Scroggs and William Douglas have recently argued that psychologists have reached a broad consensus on the major research questions with respect to religious conversion, including the issues of definition, pathology, convertible type, ripe age, voluntarism, science versus religion, and appropriate conceptual scheme.

The *definition* issue concerns attempts to specify what constitutes a conversion experience. What allows us to say that a certain experience is or is not a conversion experience? And how does a conversion experience differ from other religious experiences? What makes it unique? The *pathology* issue asks whether conversions contribute to psychological health, as some have claimed, or whether they contribute to psychological illness or dysfunction, as others have claimed. The *convertible type* issue addresses the question of whether certain types of personalities are more likely candidates for conversion than other types and, if so, can these convertible types be identified? The *ripe age* issue concerns the generally accepted view that certain age groups are likely to experience more conversions than other age groups. Adolescents are generally considered to be more likely candidates for conversion than other age groups, but there is also considerable evidence to suggest that adults in their thirties and early forties are also at a "ripe age" for conversion. The *voluntarism* issue addresses the question of whether the convert has acted out of free will (i.e., made a conscious, voluntary decision) or whether he is being acted upon by forces beyond his control or awareness. The *science versus religion* issue addresses a number of concerns, including the problem of reductionism (i.e., does a psychological interpretation of conversion undermine or negate a religious or supernatural explanation?) and the problem of objective observance of a subjective experience (i.e., can a scientific study of conversion identify or take seriously the intrinsic meaning of a conversion experience?).

Among these issues, James and his associates will probably be remembered best for focusing on voluntarism: Is conversion the result of conscious striving and self-discipline, or does it happen to a person without his consciously willing it, or even against his will? Along with James's view that conversion experiences involve conscious striving and self-discipline or submission and self-surrender might be added that many conversion experiences are inherently conflictual, reflecting both tendencies. The early studies of James and his associates suggest that in the conversion experience individuals simultaneously abandon themselves to outside influences and, in so doing, assume greater control over their lives. While common sense would suggest that abandoning oneself to a higher power would result in a greater sense of being at the mercy of forces and influences outside oneself, the actual testimonies of converts suggest that the precise opposite occurs. By accepting or submitting to a higher power, the convert experiences himself to be less at the mercy of external influences and forces (especially forces in his social environment) and more in control of his daily existence. For the convert, the conversion experience is typically an empowering one. This theme of self-abandonment leading to increased self-control is relevant not only to conversion but also to virtually every form of religious experience that has attracted the interest of psychologists, including mystical experience, faith healing, prayer, and asceticism. Moreover, this theme of self-control versus self-abandonment runs through American religious life as a whole and constitutes a basic tension at the very heart of the American character.

THE PSYCHOLOGY OF RELIGIOUS BELIEF

Like James, Freud and his circle emphasized individual bases of religious experience, but also added a greater concern with the impact of beliefs, doctrines, and confessions of faith on such experiences. In *The Future of an Illusion* (1927) and *Civilization and Its Discontents* (1930) Freud addresses the effects of religious belief on psychological maturation. In the former book he argues that religious beliefs are created out of humanity's need to make its helplessness tolerable. Confronted by the superior powers of nature, the cruelty of fate, especially as it is shown in death, and the sufferings and privations of civilized life, individuals turn to religious beliefs to reduce the terrors of nature, reconcile themselves to fate, and compensate themselves for their sufferings and privations. Continuing this idea in *Civilization and Its Discontents,* Freud explains that the belief in a providential deity meets precisely these needs by assuring the "common man" that "a careful Providence will watch over his life and will compensate him in a future existence for any frustrations he suffers here."

Freud charges that this belief, despite its consoling effects, contributes to psychological atrophy because it encourages a childish view of reality. He suggests that the "common man cannot imagine this Providence otherwise than in the figure of an enormously exalted father. Only such a being can understand the needs of the children of men and be softened by their prayers and placated by the signs of their remorse." He maintains that "the whole thing is so patently infantile, so foreign to reality, that to anyone with a friendly attitude to humanity it is painful to think that the great majority of mortals will never be able to rise above this view of life." He takes the religious education of children to task for this unfortunate and painful situation because he believes that children, left to their own intellectual interests, would not trouble themselves about God and things of another world.

Freud's studies led to numerous other investigations of the interaction between religious beliefs and such emotional states as guilt, fear, rejection, and aggression. Among early Freudians an emphasis on these negative emotional states predominated. But a leading Freudian psychologist of religion in America today, Paul W. Pruyser, has been at pains to emphasize the interaction between more positive emotional states and religious belief. In *Between Belief and Unbelief* (1974) Pruyser explores the implications for religious belief of such processes as autonomy, productive fantasy, and reality testing, all processes with which Freud would not have associated religious belief. Pruyser's major contention, reasserted in his book *The Play of the Imagination* (1983), is that we live in not two but three worlds: the autistic world of untutored fantasy, omnipotent thinking, utter whimsicality, etc.; the realistic world of sense perception, reality testing, hard, undeniable facts, etc.; and the illusionistic world of tutored fantasy, adventurous thinking, orderly imagination, etc. He contends that Freudian thought has tended to set up a duality between the autistic and realistic worlds, and to argue for the necessity of renouncing the former and for making our peace with the latter. Instead, he argues for the illusionistic world that is intermediate between the other two and that, in his view, is the world in which religious belief ought to be most at home and is most true to itself. Unfortunately, institutional religion's emphasis on "plain truths" and "unarguable doctrines" is evidence of the "slippage of ideas from the illusionistic sphere in which they belong into the realistic sphere where they make a poor fit with the demands of ordinary reality testing." Thus, Pruyser accepts Freud's view that religious beliefs are illusions, but he rejects Freud's implication that they are therefore delusional or totally unrelated to what is occurring in the real world. Like visual art and music, religious ideas perceive the world in an imaginative way, as productive fantasy.

Another line of investigation prompted by the Freudians' emphasis on religious belief but no longer exclusively Freudian is the study of the cognitive orientations of religious persons. This work was originally stimulated by Milton Rokeach's *The Open and Closed Mind* (1960), in which he explores the relation between belief and cognitive processes, disbelief systems, and the dynamics of belief systems. Rokeach found two identifiable cognitive structures among his subjects, one of which reflected openness, tentativeness, and a tolerance of ambiguity, while the other reflected rigidity, dogmatism, and an intolerance for ambiguity. His work with various belief systems, including political ideologies, was furthered by Bernard Spilka and his associates in their research (1967) on committed versus consensual religion. These researchers identify two distinctive cognitive styles among religious persons—distinctive in the content, clarity, and complexity of their religious beliefs, in the flexibility with which they hold these beliefs, and in the importance they assign their religious beliefs.

The "committed" in this schema are those whose belief systems consist of concrete and imaginative content, exhibit a minimum of confused and nebulous thinking, recognize the inherent ambiguity and paradoxes of religious ideas, and reflect an openness to revision of their beliefs as new circumstances and experiences warrant or demand. In contrast, the "consensual" are those whose belief systems are abstract and simplistic, who view religion in primarily instrumental terms (i.e., not what it means but what it can do for me), and whose religious and ethical thinking is essentially bipolar (i.e., clear and absolute distinctions between right and wrong behavior, true and false belief). More recently, Spilka and his associates have adopted terms first introduced by Allport that distinguish between intrinsic and extrinsic religion. Spilka suggests that committed religion is virtually identical to intrinsic religion (as defined by Allport) and that consensual religion is virtually identical with extrinsic religion. Allport's distinction was based on the view that there are some individuals who truly live their religion (the intrinsics) while there are others for whom religion is a means to another end (the extrinsics). For Allport as well, the intrinsic versus extrinsic distinction applies not only to personality characteristics but also to cognitive orientations.

Psychologists have also evaluated Freud's view that most persons cannot imagine God as anything but an "enormously exalted father" by exploring the role that parental images play in religious beliefs. Recent cross-cultural studies by Antoine Vergote and Alvaro Tamayo indicate that believers find parental images appropriate for conceptualizing God, though for most of these believers representations of God combine paternal and maternal images. Significantly, images of God as providential include both maternal and paternal qualities. The divine attribute, "the one who is always there when needed," is typically assigned a maternal valence, while the attribute "guiding stimulus towards the future" is ordinarily given a paternal valence. These researchers find that among the various societies studied—including Belgium, Italy, India, and the United States—American subjects represented God in the most paternal terms.

Another study of God representations, based largely on clinical observation of children, is Ana-Maria Rizzuto's *The Birth of the Living God* (1979). This study recognizes, with the Vergote-Tamayo study, that the God representation may be composed of maternal as well as paternal imagos and may reflect either direct continuity between parental imagos and God representation, direct opposition between the two, or a combination of both. Rizzuto identifies four positions in relation to belief in God: those who have a God whose existence they do not doubt;

those who wonder whether or not to believe in a God they are not sure exists; those amazed, angered, or surprised to see others believing in a God who does not interest them; and those who struggle with a harsh, demanding God they would like to be rid of were they not convinced of His existence and power. Rizzuto concludes that Freud was correct in suggesting that God has origins in parental imagos, but whereas "Freud believes that only the father provides the imago for an 'exaltation' to Godhead," her study reveals that

> . . . either the father or the mother or both contribute their share. Other primary objects (grandparents, siblings) may also provide some representational components. The entire representational process occurs in a wider context of the family, social class, organized religion, and particular subcultures. All these experiences contribute a background to the shape, significance, potential use, and meaning which the child or the adult may bestow on their God representations.
>
> (p. 209)

Furthermore, Rizzuto disagrees with Freud's view that belief in God is "foreign to reality" and suggests that he creates an unnecessarily wide gulf between reality and illusion by failing to recognize that belief in God forms what D. W. Winnicott, an English psychoanalyst whose therapeutic work was centered primarily on children, calls the "transitional sphere" between illusion and reality. (Pruyser, too, makes considerable use of Winnicott's concepts of the transitional sphere and transitional objects to challenge Freud's separation of illusion and reality.) Rizzuto, however, continues to support without qualification Freud's view that religious beliefs grow out of emotional states. An individual's God representation will consequently develop in the course of life as emotional needs and desires change.

These views of God representations suggest that psychologists generally view conceptions and images of God as human projections. While this is true, it should also be noted that psychologists do not necessarily conclude that God is nothing but a human projection. Some psychologists subscribe to the view that projections are made upon a screen and that in this case the screen is God, who exists independently of human projections. This view was first proposed by Erwin Goodenough, a classics scholar at Yale who took interest in the psychology of religious experience. It allows for the contention that some or even many of man's religious ideas are projections from his own experience and yet at the same time preserves the traditional view that God exists independently. Others, like Erikson, take particular note of the self-revelatory quality of God and strongly imply that human images of God reflect divine self-revelation. On this basis it could be argued that parents are seen as images of various aspects of God, a view that does not preclude that the process may also take the opposite form of parental images projected onto God.

If the Jamesian perspective alerts us to the self-control versus self-abandonment theme in American religious life, the Freudians' concern for religious belief draws attention to the theme of divine providence. This theme, which is often expressed in terms of a tension between reliance on divine providence and dependence on human initiative and enterprise, is also deeply rooted in the American character. Richard Quinney points out that "providence is the wisdom of God expressed through time" and suggests that Americans have historically trusted in the providence of God. But the Civil War disabused the more thoughtful Americans of the belief that their enterprises and God's purposes for the world were necessarily mirror images. Commenting on the dilemma in his second inaugural address, Abraham Lincoln observed: "Men are not flattered by being shown that there has been a difference of purpose between the Almighty and them. To deny it, however, in this case, is to deny that there is a God governing the world."

THE PSYCHOLOGY OF RELIGIOUS MYTH

If the previous group faulted James and his associates for neglecting beliefs and belief systems, another group has the same concern with respect to religious myths and mythical systems. Because this concern for myths developed originally under Freudian auspices, there is considerable overlap in the membership of the two groups. Indeed, a major concern of Freudians, notably Theodor Reik, is the study of the psychological processes involved in the transition from myth to belief.

The psychological study of myth and mythological systems was imported from Europe. The only member of James's school who took any interest in religious myth was Leuba, and he was European by birth. American psychologists of religion shared traditional Protestantism's mistrust of the mythical, associating it with primitive forms of religion. For them, one sign that Christianity was an advanced religion was precisely that it had succeeded in divesting itself of the mythic impulse. They viewed Protestantism as a higher form of religion than Catholicism because Catholicism had not been as successful in ridding itself of the mythological. Thus, the psychological study of myth did not gain a foothold in America until well into the second decade of the twentieth century, when Freud's thought gained currency among American intellectuals.

For Freud and his followers, mythology is clearly an aspect of religion. In fact, for Freud, religion and myth are so deeply intertwined as to be nearly indistinguishable. In this, Freud reflects his own Jewish background and, more specifically, his appreciation of the fact that myths and legends comprise much of the Old Testament. Thus, whereas James and his associates considered religion and myth to be separable and even conflicting tendencies in the human psyche, Freud and his followers viewed them as functions of the same human needs and aspirations. Contemporary psychologists of religion in the Jamesian tradition, such as Allport and Spilka, continue to disregard the mythic impulse. They do not consider it an important feature of religion and thus give virtually no attention to it in their psychological investigations into religious experience.

Thus, in America, the Freudians initially took the lead in the psychological study of religious mythology. The Freudian journals *American Imago* and *Psychoanalytic Quarterly* have published numerous articles on the psychoanalytic interpretation of religious myths and legends. In addition to articles on Greek myths and mythical figures such as Oedipus, Orestes, and Electra, there are articles on biblical figures, many of them by Dorothy Zeligs, a Freudian analyst who has applied psychoanalytic concepts and theories to the narratives of virtually every major

figure in the Old Testament, among them Moses, David, Saul, Samson, and Jonah. There have also been psychological studies of significant figures in the history of Christianity. Perhaps the most notable are studies of figures like Judas and St. Nicholas, who were historical figures but around whom many myths and legends have developed.

The psychological study of myth was also fostered by Henry Murray, professor of psychology at Harvard University from the mid-1930s through the late 1950s. Murray is best known for the Thematic Apperception Test, a widely used projective instrument for personality assessment, that he and his collaborator, Christiana Morgan, developed. *Myth and Mythmaking,* published under his editorship in 1960, includes articles by a group of prominent mythologists in anthropology, folklore studies, history of religions, history, and social theory.

But the most prominent name in the psychology of myth is Carl Jung, to whose works Murray acknowledges a considerable debt. Jung's views on myth turn on his concept of the archetype, which he first introduced in 1919. Through his work on the interpretation of dreams, he became impressed with the recurrence of certain stereotypical figures of his own dream fantasies. Convinced that these recurrent symbols could not be explained by any experiences in his own life, Jung thought that they seemed to be aboriginal, innate, and inherited structures of the human mind, which he called archetypes. He subsequently distinguished between the archetype, or a latent structure within the human mind, and the archetypal image, or a specific cultural or personal rendition of the archetype.

Through Jung's own researches and those of his followers, a large number of archetypes and archetypal images have been identified and their characteristics delineated. Among the most prominent archetypal images are the hero, the trickster, the sage, the child, and the anima (a feminine archetype that takes various forms, including the Great Mother, the cruel mother, the lonely princess, the huntress, and the virgin).

In Jungian thought, Christ is a symbol of the inner self, itself an archetype, and of its transformation. Such symbols are important because, according to Jung, the existence of the archetypes themselves cannot be objectively proven. Rather, the evidence of their existence derives solely from our observation of the phenomena they serve to explain; namely, complex and powerful inner processes. But the archetypes reveal their presence through symbols, which are external or objective manifestations of the archetypes. One vital function of religion, therefore, is that it becomes the repository of symbols that disclose the existence of the archetypes. Thus, religious symbols, such as the symbol of Christ, have the power to initiate the transformation of the self. By interpreting these symbols in relation to an individual's immediate experience, we reveal the individual's basic psychological attitudes and motivations, and discover the manner in which these attitudes and motivations are undergoing or anticipating change. In effect, religious symbols provide insight into the workings of archetypes in the individual psyche.

In addition to archetypal images, Jung also identified archetypal processes, including the relationships between good and evil, death and rebirth, cosmos and history. Then there are archetypal numbers having special evocative powers, such as the famous 666 of the Book of Revelation, and archetypal shapes, among them the cross, the yin and the yang, the mandala, and the swastika.

In Jungian theory, archetypal images are to be found not only in individuals' dreams but also in the cultural products of given societies, including both high art and popular culture. Film, popular novels, dance, sports, mass media, advertising, and various other forms of entertainment are studied for their archetypal features. Such studies are considered to illuminate the psychological processes of the society, revealing its fears, tensions, aspirations, and zeitgeist. One of the most avidly studied cultural archetypes has been that of the hero, as it reveals the aspirations and perceived threats to these aspirations reflected in given societies.

The Jungian psychology of myth has achieved influence among certain Christian groups, particularly those that already have considerable appreciation for myth and for the development of the inner life. Thus, Jungian psychology has been most prominent among Catholics and Episcopalians, and most resisted by such Protestant groups as those in the Reformed tradition that are suspicious of myth and of systems, both religious and secular, claiming to understand the processes of inner transformation. While Jung-

ian psychology of myth has not achieved widespread acceptance among American religious groups in general, it has become a permanent feature of American psychology of religion. Yet its influence remains largely within the confines of the study of the individual. There has not as yet been much study of American religious history itself from the perspective of the psychology of myth. Major historical events and epochs in America, including its major wars, the Great Depression, and the counter-cultural movement of the 1960s, have not been studied from the perspective of the psychology of religious myth.

A potentially fruitful line of investigation in this regard is suggested by William Spengemann and L. R. Lundquist. Noting that the "American myth, in its most general form, describes human history as a pilgrimage from imperfection to perfection; from a dimly remembered union with the Divine to a re-establishment of that union," they proceed to show how American autobiographers account for their lives according to the expectations of this myth. In the process they identify the major cultural images that emerge out of these self-evaluations. Those that support the myth and function as insiders include the prophet (e.g., Cotton Mather), the hero (e.g., Benjamin Franklin), and the repenter (e.g., Charles Colson, the convicted Watergate conspirator who subsequently became a "born-again Christian"). The hypocrite (e.g., P. T. Barnum) wants to convince his readers that he supports the myth and deserves insider status. Those whose lives are not in concert with the myth and who function therefore as outsiders are the renegade (e.g., Mae West), the dissident (e.g., the feminist Mary Austin), and the exile (e.g., Whittaker Chambers, who during the McCarthy era claimed to have been a spy).

Spengemann and Lundquist's project could be developed further, with greater attention to the relationship between the lives of the autobiographers and their identification, whether conscious or unconscious, with the archetypal image. Most important, their work provides some support for the view that James's neglect of religious myth constitutes a serious lacuna in his psychology of religious experience, for it is noteworthy that the Spengemann and Lundquist study is, like James's, based on the investigation and interpretation of personal documents. Clearly, James and his associates did not pay any appreciable attention to the mythic features and dimensions of the personal documents they studied.

Another potentially valuable line of inquiry in the psychology of myth, with particular relevance to the American context, is suggested by Wayne G. Rollins' *Jung and the Bible.* The biblical tradition has received significant attention from Jungians, starting with Jung's own *Answer to Job* and including the Jungians' interest in the Christ archetypal image. But until Rollins' book appeared in 1983 there were no sustained discussions of Jungian thought and the Bible. Moreover, it has been the Freudians, with their deep investment in Jewish religious history, who have given greater attention to the psychological study of biblical figures. But even so, both schools of thought have drawn attention more to the religious mythology of the Greeks and Romans than to the mythology of the biblical tradition. As a result, the full potential of the psychology of religious mythology for the American context is as yet untapped, especially since in America the Bible has played an important role in the formation of personal and national character. Biblical narratives have had an especially important archetypal function in the lives of Americans, providing them with heroes and heroines with whom they may identify and with villains and fools whose lives and fates serve as negative examples to be resolutely avoided. A major hero is Abraham, whom many Americans during the Civil War saw personified in Abraham Lincoln. A major villain is Judas, as reflected in Americans' intense distaste for traitors and informers.

Identification, positive or negative, with biblical figures has been an important theme in Freudian studies, which frequently cite examples of patients in psychoanalysis who identify with Moses, Saul, Rebekah, David, Jesus, Judas, or Paul. But Freudians have not developed the implications of such identification as fully as have psychologists in the tradition of Hjalmar Sundén, professor of the psychology of religion at the University of Uppsala in Sweden. Sundén has adopted the important concept of "role-taking" generally ascribed to the American sociologist George Herbert Mead, who proposed that the social self is formed by means of the internalization of the roles of significant others. Sundén has elaborated Mead's notion of role-taking into a full-blown theory of religious role-taking. This theory proposes that individuals under stress take the "role" of a biblical figure confronted with a comparable stressful situation. In role-taking there is not only an identification with the biblical figure but also an anticipation that God will respond as he is reported to have responded in the biblical story. The Bible therefore provides not only a human role system but also a divine one, and in Sundén's view these two systems are comparable in importance to the other two major systems in the Bible, its belief and ethical systems.

Sundén's student and successor at Uppsala, Thorvald Källstad, has applied Sundén's theory to the life of John Wesley, the British founder of Methodism, showing that Wesley's sermons preached during his sojourn in Savannah, Georgia, reflect biblical role-taking. Sundén's theory has probably not been applied to American lives, either of famous Americans in earlier epochs or of ordinary believers today.

But there is evidence, both from sermon texts and from pastoral counseling verbatims, that indicates the widespread use of biblical role-taking. Sermons regularly invite parishioners to view their own problems and aspirations in light of the experiences of biblical figures. Through such invitations, sermons in effect instruct parishioners in methods and procedures for relating events in their own lives to the experiences recounted in biblical narratives. Transcripts of pastoral counseling sessions also reveal that parishioners frequently describe their difficulties in terms of various well-known biblical stories. A woman will confess to having a "Martha-complex" or a man will describe his relationship to his brother in terms of the Cain and Abel story, the Jacob and Esau story, or the story of the prodigal son and his envious elder brother. A common expression among members of the Unification Church is Caining, which refers to admonitions issued by one's spiritual brother or sister to foster spiritual growth. Thus, it is evident that many individuals consciously or unconsciously construct and interpret their lives according to the biographical pattern of a particular biblical figure.

The mythical perspective in the psychology of religious experience draws attention to another fundamental theme in American religious life, the theme of approval versus disapproval. As the Spengemann and Lundquist study shows, many

Americans have been able to remain cultural insiders by creating an approved self-image. Even those who fall outside the myth are able to return to the status of insiders (reapproved) if they are appropriately repentant or otherwise successful in their efforts at what Mordechai Rotenberg, professor in the school of social work at Hebrew University of Jerusalem, has called "biographical rehabilitation," a process by which individuals may reinterpret and lessen their past failures by identifying with biblical role models, like David and Solomon, who sinned but were subsequently acquitted by the Midrash (i.e., approved interpretations of biblical narratives). There are others who flaunt the American myth but do so in ways that do not threaten to subvert it: these are approved outsiders. One of the most dramatic and tragic instances of the role of biblical mythology in the process of social sanctioning is to be found in the verbatim account of the excommunication proceedings brought against Ann Hibbens by the First Church of Boston in 1640, nearly five decades before the witchcraft trials in Salem. Mrs. Hibbens was compared by her accusers to the biblical figure Miriam, who was Moses and Aaron's sister and, more important, a leper. Like the lepers of biblical times, Mrs. Hibbens was excommunicated from Christian fellowship, socially shunned, and, after her husband's death, tried as a common criminal, convicted, and hanged on the charge of witchcraft. Her story thus exemplifies involuntary role-taking, with biblical mythology employed as a means of negative social sanction. While many view the psychology of religious myth as the study of human liberation and transformation, religious myth is also implicated in the process of social sanctioning and contributes to religion's role in the approval versus disapproval dynamic in American society.

THE PSYCHOLOGY OF RELIGIOUS DEVELOPMENT

Early Jamesians were certainly aware of the relationship between religious experience and developmental stages. Starbuck, in fact, emphasized the importance of seeing conversion experiences as integral to the normal stages of growth. But the early Jamesians did not formulate their own general theory of development or, more specifically, a theory of religious develop-

ment. Allport, the major Jamesian in the post–World War II era, made significant distinctions between the religion of youth and the religion of maturity, but these analyses largely provide norms or criteria for determining what makes for a mature religious sentiment. He was not attempting to formulate a developmental theory as such.

But in 1950, the same year that Allport's *The Individual and His Religion* appeared, Erikson's *Childhood and Society* was published. This book, containing a chapter entitled the "Eight Ages of Man," offers a developmental theory that covers the whole life span, from infancy to death. The eight stages, which Erikson has slightly revised from time to time (see *Identity: Youth and Crisis,* 1968), now include: basic trust versus basic mistrust (infancy); autonomy versus shame and doubt (early childhood); initiative versus guilt (play age); industry versus inferiority (school age); identity versus identity confusion (adolescence); intimacy versus isolation (young adulthood); generativity versus stagnation (adulthood); and integrity versus despair (mature adulthood). This theory of the life cycle has enjoyed immense popularity among practical theologians and psychologists of religion, including such figures as LeRoy Aden, Thomas Droege, Don S. Browning, Peter Homans, and Walter Conn. These scholars have recognized that, while it is a general developmental theory, it provides an excellent foundation for a more specific theory of religious development. Or, if such a theory appeared too grandiose, Erikson's work offers at least the possibility of understanding religious experiences against the backdrop of a developmental perspective.

Erikson appeared to welcome the application of his life cycle theory to religion. In *Young Man Luther* (1958) he uses his life cycle theory to interpret Martin Luther's religious experiences as revealed in several critical events, beginning with his "thunderstorm experience" at twenty-two and culminating in his "tower experience" around age thirty. Erikson's essay "Human Strength and the Cycle of Generations," in *Insight and Responsibility* (1964), places the life cycle in a moral context by proposing a schedule of virtues corresponding to the eight developmental stages. These virtues, in order, include hope, will, purpose, competence, fidelity, love, care, and wisdom. Erikson's receptivity to the application of his life cycle theory to religion is further evidenced in *Toys and Reasons* (1976), in which he proposes a series of ritual stages corresponding to the eight stages and says that "of all institutions that of organized religion has the strongest claim to being in charge of the numinous," which is the first stage of ritualization. The ritual stages mediate between the developmental process and social structures. Individual societies have their own configurations of these rituals, but all must take account of the ritual elements themselves, which include the numinous, judicious, dramatic, methodological, convictional, affiliative, generational, and integral.

By the *numinous,* Erickson means personal recognition by the deity. By *judicious,* he means social mechanisms of approval and disapproval. By the *dramatic,* he means social manifestations of play, festival, fictive acts, and various forms of role-playing. By the *methodological,* he means a society's patterns of productive work. By the *convictional,* he means a society's most compelling ideologies and world views. By the *affiliative,* he means a society's patterns of interpersonal relationships, especially its family structures and friendship groups. By the *generational,* he means a society's methods for ensuring that its values and legacies are transmitted to the next generation and that, in turn, the next generation is cared for and prepared for future adult roles. By the *integral,* he means a society's ability to represent wisdom, especially as personified in its older adults. By taking these ritual elements seriously (i.e., making a place for them in the social process itself), societies provide their members a convincing orientation to life and enable them to cope with the inevitable disorienting experiences. On the other hand, each of these ritual elements can become excessive, as often occurs when a society places too much emphasis on one or another element and gives insufficient attention to others. The ritual excesses include, in order, idolism, legalism, moralism, formalism, totalism, elitism, authoritism, and dogmatism. In effect, these ritual excesses are forms of social pathology.

Various approaches have been recommended for relating Erikson's life cycle theory to religion. LeRoy Aden proposes that faith is itself a developmental phenomenon and suggests that "the dominant form that faith takes at any one time is determined in part by the particular developmental stage in which the individual is immersed." He proposes the following eight stages

of faith: trust, courage, obedience, assent, identity, self-surrender, unconditional caring, and unconditional acceptance. In each stage, the form of faith is a direct "antidote" to the specific form of estrangement from self, others, and God reflected in that stage. These forms of estrangement include mistrust, shame and doubt, guilt, dissent, confusion, self-seclusion, concupiscence, and despair.

It is possible to link Erikson's life cycle theory more directly to what might be called "mini-classics" of the Christian faith, among them such well-known expressions of Christian thought and life as the golden rule, the Lord's Prayer, the prayer attributed to St. Francis of Assisi ("Lord, Make me an instrument of thy peace"), and the parable of the Good Samaritan. First, Erikson's schedule of virtues might be augmented with a schedule of vices derived from the classical list of deadly sins. Prior to the fifth century of the Christian era, there were eight and not seven deadly sins; thus a sin or vice might correspond to each of the life cycle stages. They are, in order, gluttony, anger, greed, envy, pride, lust, indifference, and melancholy. As with Erikson's progression of virtues, each vice appears on schedule and then, having become part of an individual's attitudinal and behavioral repertoire, remains as a negative capacity or disposition for the rest of his or her life.

Second, following Erikson's recent article on the Galilean sayings of Jesus, the beatitudes of Jesus can be grounded in Erikson's life cycle theory. Since there are eight beatitudes in the Gospel of Matthew, a beatitude can be seen to correspond to each of the life cycle stages. They are, in order, purity of heart, meekness, hunger and thirst for righteousness, poorness in spirit, persecution for righteousness' sake, peacemaking, mercifulness, and mourning. The rationale for these proposed linkages between a beatitude and a life cycle stage is that the beatitude reflects the basic psychodynamics of the assigned stage. For example, "purity of heart" is a fundamental trust in God that has no other motive than the heartfelt desire to experience God's presence. This trust is dynamically similar to the trust that develops in infancy, as the infant perceives the presence of a caring person. The desire to experience the caring person for the sake of the experience itself contrasts with the attitude that underlies gluttony, in which the infant desires only what the caring person has to give and expresses this desire in a demanding and perhaps even hostile manner. In a similar way, the other seven beatitudes reflect the basic psychodynamics of their assigned stages and reflect a spirit or disposition that is diametrically opposite to that of the deadly sin of that stage.

Together these two proposals place the Christian tension between cursedness and blessedness in a developmental framework. This tension, reflected in Jesus' own use of both types of pronouncements, remains a permanent feature of the developmental process, from birth to death. Thus, this proposed model is congruent with the view that has been predominant in Christian theology at least since the time of Augustine, that the Christian life is not a simple progression from a sinful to a blessed state. Rather, the tension between sinfulness and blessedness continues throughout the life cycle.

Other authors have taken particular note of specific stages in Erikson's life cycle and have proposed that these are ethically normative (that is, a given stage sets forth Erikson's vision of what it means to be "a good person" or genuinely "responsible self"). In "Erikson and the Search for a Normative Image of Man" and in *Generative Man* (1972), Don S. Browning argues that in ethics the central stage for Erikson is the adult stage of generativity versus stagnation, with its corresponding virtue of care: "The end of man is care." Thus "seen from a normative perspective, all the earlier stages and virtues partially receive their meaning from what they contribute to the later stage of generativity and to the virtue of care." James W. Fowler, who has constructed his own developmental model of the formation of faith in the individual, echoes Browning's view that the generativity stage is ethically normative for Erikson. Furthermore, Fowler sees in Erikson's emphasis on generativity and care the basis of a vision of religious maturity. As he puts it in *Becoming Adult, Becoming Christian* (1984), "Erikson's vision is . . . religious in its clear suggestion that fulfillment in life derives from caring for the conditions that enable present and future generations to develop the full range of human virtues."

On the other hand, J. Eugene Wright disagrees with the proposal that the generativity stage is normative, either ethically or religiously. He suggests that if there were anything like an ethical normativeness in Erikson's thought, it

would center in a combination of the generativity stage and the intimacy stage, with its emphasis on the virtue of mutuality or love. But Wright is also uneasy with this suggestion because, like Browning's proposal, it neglects the final stage of life, with its virtue of wisdom. Even more important, as he points out in *Erikson: Identity and Religion* (1982), "the selection of any one emphasis in Erikson's scheme [does] a disservice to the remaining elements of an intricately and determinedly holistic system."

Erikson's life cycle theory was the first general developmental theory to be applied to religion and ethics and the only one applied with any degree of regularity. Jane Loevinger's theory of development has received only modest attention, and Daniel Levinson's theory of adult development is only now beginning to receive some attention from psychologists of religious experience.

Loevinger proposed a stage theory of human development that includes the following stages: the *presocial* and *symbiotic* stages of infancy; the *impulsive* and *self-protective* stages of childhood; the *conformist* stage of adolescence; the *conscientious-conformist* self-awareness transition; and the *conscientious* stage, *individualistic* transition, and *autonomous* and *integrated* stages of adulthood. Levinson offers a theory of human development that focuses on young and middle adulthood. His theory is best known for its emphasis on the mid-life crisis that typically occurs between ages forty and forty-five. His theory has attracted the interest of psychologists of religion because he recognizes that the mid-life crisis is, in a certain sense, a spiritual crisis. But these theories, promising as they may be for the psychology of religious development, have not received the attention accorded the "faith development" theory formulated by James W. Fowler and based on the moral development theory of Lawrence Kohlberg.

Kohlberg's theory has roots in the psychology of moral development, which began in the late 1920s with Hugh Hartshorne and Mark A. May's *Studies in Deceit,* an empirical investigation into the moral behavior of children (e.g., lying and cheating). But the more immediate influences on Kohlberg are Robert Havighurst, who in the 1950s was engaged in the study of moral character, and Jean Piaget, whose classic text, *The Moral Judgement of the Child* (1932), makes the case that the development of moral reasoning follows the same pattern as cognitive development. Kohlberg identifies six stages in the development of moral reasoning: moral judgment based on anticipated reward or punishment from an authority figure. The individual at this stage weighs the practical effects of wrongful action much more heavily than the motives involved; moral judgment based on instrumental exchange, which involves a concept of concrete reciprocity or fairness based on very specific face-to-face situations (e.g., a game or contest, the sharing of gifts or personal possessions, parental use of sanctions such as bedtime rules, eating between meals). The moral logic of this stage informs all theories of punishment and retribution of the type "an eye for an eye"; moral judgment based on social convention, involving mutual interpersonal expectations, relationships, and interpersonal conformity; moral judgment based on awareness of the social system and conscience, a stage in which society is perceived as a network of rules, roles, and relationships and adjudication of differences between persons is seen as involving consideration of rights, claims, desires, and promises; moral judgment based on social contract and individual rights, which involves recognition of certain inalienable rights that are not relative but must be upheld in any society regardless of majority opinion; and moral judgment based on universal ethical principles, a stage that focuses on principles of justice that claim universal validity and provide guidelines and tests by which particular actions, laws, or social policies may be made or evaluated.

Kohlberg has subsequently suggested a seventh stage, which he considers post-moral (in somewhat the same sense that stage one is pre-moral because it does not involve any internalization of values or consideration of personal motives). Individuals at stage seven address the fundamental question "Why be moral?" and rely on religion, among other things, for answers. This is not a moral stage because there is no higher way of moral judging than to judge in terms of the universal principles of justice of stage six. But, as F. Clark Power and Kohlberg point out, individuals are able at stage six "to differentiate moral from nonmoral concerns such that the limits of the moral domain become clarified, making the religious question inescapable."

Fowler's stages of faith development are based on Kohlberg's moral development stages and are therefore rooted structurally in Piaget's theory of cognitive development. However, some of the content of Fowler's faith stages is based on Erikson's life cycle theory. Like Kohlberg, Fowler first set forth a faith development theory involving six stages but has subsequently added a seventh. Unlike Kohlberg, Fowler added the seventh stage as the beginning one, not the end, and intended it to take into account Erikson's conviction that religious faith is initially mediated through the infant's benefactors or providers. Fowler's stages of faith are: primal (infancy); intuitive-projective (beginning at age two); mythic-literal (beginning at age six); synthetic-conventional (adolescence); individualistic-reflective (early adulthood); conjunctive (middle adulthood); and universalizing. (It should be noted that, unlike Erikson's stages, Fowler's are not irrevocably tied to chronological growth, and therefore the ages assigned to the stages indicate only when a faith stage is normally reached. For many adults, the fifth, sixth, and seventh stages are not reached at all.)

Fowler suggests that his model of faith development needs to have put to it the same questions he and others would put to Erikson's life cycle theory. What normative image of adulthood does it express? What vision of human wholeness and completion animates this research? Fowler acknowledges that his earlier discussions of the theory implied that the seventh, or universalizing faith, stage provides the normative standard of adult faith, and he notes that he has been criticized on this score because few persons achieve this stage. Sympathetic critics, such as Gabriel Moran, have proposed that conjunctive faith be taken as the normative end point of the faith development sequence. But Fowler argues instead in *Becoming Adult, Becoming Christian* that

Human development toward wholeness is, I believe, always the product of a certain *synergy* between human potentials, given in creation, and the presence and activity of Spirit as mediated through many channels. The most crucial factor differentiating the quality and movement of a person or group's development in faith, therefore, has to do with the conscious or unconscious availability of that person or group's potentials for partnership—for synergy—with Spirit.

He concludes that the goal is not for everyone to reach the stage of universalizing faith, but "for each person or group to open themselves—as radically as possible—within the structures of the present stage or transition—to synergy with Spirit." Thus, though the telos of the faith development process is universalizing faith, the norm is not universalizing faith but wholeness, understood as synergy with the spirit of God.

From Allport's *The Individual and His Religion* to Fowler's *Becoming Adult, Becoming Christian* the developmental approach to the psychology of religious experience has placed considerable emphasis on the issue of religious maturity. The broad consensus of nearly four decades of reflection on this issue is that religious maturity is not a set of personal characteristics or traits, nor a clearly definable goal, but a process of becoming. As William Bouwsma points out in "Christian Adulthood," "The essential element in the Christian idea of adulthood is . . . the capacity for growth, which is assumed to be a potentiality of any age of life."

But does this mean that there are no identifiable features of religious maturity besides that of capacity for growth? Recognizing that Christianity is composed of diverse groups and many competing theologies, Bouwsma nevertheless contends that Christianity has developed certain widely shared assumptions about religious maturity that at least characterize the process. One is that the person's experience as a child cannot be left behind but is the basis of the more mature personality. Indeed, Bouwsma points out that Christianity has tended to resist the notion that religious maturity is related to chronological age, and has therefore not been troubled or threatened by evidence that younger individuals may reflect greater religious maturity than older ones. Another is that growth involves the total personality as an undifferentiated unity and not only certain faculties or "higher" functions. A third is that growth occurs precisely where there is acknowledgment of personal limits and human contingency. A fourth is that the primary experiences through which the Christian grows are social experiences; the maturity of the individual is realized primarily through interaction with others. Admittedly, this is a Christian perspective on religious maturity and therefore reflects a partic-

ular perspective that is not universally shared. Yet the developmental theories of recent decades generally share the same assumptions as this Christian perspective does regarding growth and maturity.

Like the two previously discussed issues in the psychological study of religious experience—religious belief and religious myth—the issue of religious development focuses on a theme that is deeply rooted in the American experience, that of maturity versus innocence. Developmental psychologists emphasize the struggle involved in achieving maturity and the difficulties involved in determining what constitutes maturity. These emphases clearly suggest that maturity is problematic for Americans. But historians have also noted that Americans are deeply concerned with the issue of the maturity of the nation itself. Americans recognize that the nation has long since developed beyond the innocence of childhood and has assumed the responsibilities and obligations of adulthood, but not always with a clear understanding of what constitutes national maturity. Erikson's life cycle theory might be usefully employed in this regard, for there are indications that America as a nation has been passing through the same stages of development he ascribes to the individual. Thus, the identity versus identity confusion stage was reached at the beginning of American nationhood and continued into the early decades of the nineteenth century; intimacy versus isolation had focal importance in the latter half of the nineteenth century, especially during the Civil War, and continued through World War II; and generativity versus stagnation tensions characterized America during the 1960s and 1970s, as reflected in such national issues as the Vietnam War, the energy crisis, the abortion controversy, and the nuclear arms race. If, indeed, the most serious tests of American maturity today have ultimately to do with generativity issues, it is perhaps not surprising that the generativity versus stagnation stage has been proposed as ethically normative and as the heart of the religious vision of maturity.

In effect, historical events have forced Americans to come to terms with the question of what it would mean for America to become ethically and religiously mature. Through his concept of generativity, Erikson has suggested that the major sign of maturity among adults is the capacity to care for the younger generations, to make provision for the next generations' physical, emotional, and spiritual well-being. He also suggests that a corollary sign of adults' maturity is the capacity to limit productivity, especially the production of dangerous weapons, and, thereby demonstrate through actions that they recognize the difference between generativity and productivity. Such awareness is itself a sign of ethical and religious maturity. It would be fair to say that it is not yet clear whether America as a nation has acquired such maturity. Whether the next stage in American history is predominantly one of integrity or of despair depends to a considerable degree on whether America responds to the current challenge and takes significant steps toward becoming the ethically and religiously mature nation its Puritan forebears originally envisioned it to be.

THE AMERICAN RELIGIOUS CONTEXT

The six perspectives in the psychology of religious experience, in addition to the classical Jamesian perspective, did not emerge on the scene all at once. The study of religious belief emerged almost simultaneously with the Jamesian school. The study of institutional religion had its inception in the 1930s, when the Jamesian perspective was in eclipse, and came into its own in the 1950s and early 1960s, when clergy studies were very much in vogue. The study of religious myth and that of religious development go back to the early Freudian and Jamesian initiatives but did not develop fully until the 1960s and 1970s. The remaining two perspectives, those placing an emphasis on non-Western forms of religious experience and on larger historical events, were virtually unheard of prior to the mid-1950s but attracted substantial attention in the 1960s and 1970s.

The emergence of each new perspective was prompted, in part, by new developments in American religious experience. Like other professional observers, psychologists want to study what is immediately observable on the American religious landscape. The emergence of the two new perspectives in the 1960s is attributable in large measure to America's new interest in Eastern forms of religious experience, especially meditation, and to the divisive effects on American society of the unpopular war in Vietnam. New developments in American religious experience have also been responsible for the revival of older perspectives. The Jamesian school, for example, experienced an impressive rebirth in the 1960s and 1970s, owing in part to a revived interest in conversion and prayer—the former attributable to the resurgence of evangelicalism on college and university campuses and the new phenomenon of television evangelists, the latter attributable to the sudden manifestations of glossolalia (speaking in tongues) at major secular universities in the 1960s and developments within Catholicism, including Pentecostalism and renewed interest in the contemplative life.

In addition to these new developments in American religious experience, which can rarely be predicted or anticipated, there are other, more systemic features of American society that continue to interest psychologists and account in large measure for the discipline's stability and sense of continuity. Joseph F. Kett's *Rites of Passage: Adolescence in America, 1790 to the Present* (1977) demonstrates, for example, that prior to the twentieth century there was no clearly defined subgroup in America called adolescents. Once this subgroup was identified, and differentiated from children and adults, it became the focus of social concern and debate, being viewed as a particularly troubled and troublesome subgroup. We should therefore not be surprised that this particular age group has been of enduring interest to psychologists. Moreover, such systemic issues, reflecting deeply felt tensions within American society, have enabled psychologists of one perspective to make use of the work of psychologists of other perspectives, leading to significant integrated approaches, such as research suggesting that the adolescent religious conversion studied by Jamesians and the identity crisis studied by developmentalists are related experiences. (The relationship between religious conversion and the identity crisis was originally noted by Erikson himself, in *Young Man Luther.* Research by Joel Allison and by James E. Dittes has provided empirical support.)

The psychology of religious experience will undoubtedly continue to focus on these perennial features of the American religious landscape (e.g., religious conversion) while at the same time taking cognizance of new and unpredictable phenomena (e.g., glossolalia on college campuses). Given this dual outlook, the psychology of religious experience in America will both manifest certain continuities with the past and take novel directions. The perspectives discussed in detail here are undoubtedly weighted more toward continuity, but this does not mean that individual psychologists working within these perspectives have not been innovators. Indeed, if anything characterizes the discipline as a whole, it is that the psychology of religion, as a relatively young science, places a high value on innovation and rewards the independent and self-styled worker. Like the phenomenon it studies, it aspires to a settled maturity, but for this to occur it will probably have to develop a greater sense of community and shared outlook than it currently possesses. Its pluralism is both its greatest strength and greatest weakness.

BIBLIOGRAPHY

LeRoy Aden, "Faith and the Developmental Cycle," in *Pastoral Psychology*, 24 (1976); Russell O. Allen and Bernard Spilka, "Committed and Consensual Religion," in *Journal for the Scientific Study of Religion*, 6 (1967); Joel Allison, "Recent Empirical Studies of Religious Conversion Experience," in *Pastoral Psychology*, 14 (1966) and "Religious Conversion: Regression and Progression in an Adolescent Experience," in *Journal for the Scientific Study of Religion*, 8 (1969); J. G. Arapura, *Religion as Anxiety and Tranquility* (1972); William Bouwsma, "Christian Adulthood," in Erik H. Erikson, ed., *Adulthood* (1978); Don S. Browning, "Erikson and the Search for a Normative Image of Man," in Peter Homans, ed., *Childhood and Selfhood* (1978); Donald Capps, "Erikson's Life Cycle Theory and the Beatitudes," in *Pastoral Psychology*, 33 (1985), "The Psychology of Petitionary Prayer," in *Theology Today*, 39 (1982), and *Life Cycle Theory and Pastoral Care* (1983); John Donald Castelein, "Glossolalia and the Psychology of the Self and Narcissism," in *Journal of Religion and Health*, 23 (1984); Walter Conn, *Christian Conversion: A Developmental Interpretation of Autonomy and Surrender* (1986).

Adrianus D. de Groot, *Saint Nicholas: A Psychoanalytic Study of His History and Myth* (1965); James E. Dittes, "Continuities Between Life and Thought in Augustine," in *Journal for the Scientific Study of Religion*, 8 (1969); Fred L. Downing, *To See the Promised Land: The Faith Pilgrimage of Martin Luther King, Jr.* (1986); Thomas A. Droege, *Stages of Faith* (1981); Erik. H. Erikson, *Young Man Luther* (1958) and "The Galilean Sayings and the Sense of 'I'," in *Yale Review*, 70 (1981); James W. Fowler, *Stages of Faith* (1981) and *Becoming Adult, Becoming Christian: Adult Development and Christian Faith* (1984); Erwin R. Goodenough, *The Psychology of Religious Experiences* (1965); Hugh Hartshorne and M. A. May, *Studies in Deceit* (1928); Friedrich Heiler, *Prayer: A Study in the History and Psychology of Religion* (1932); Peter Homans, "The Significance of Erikson's Psychology for Modern Understandings of Religion,"

in Homans, ed., *Childhood and Selfhood* (1978); Richard A. Hutch, "The Personal Ritual of Glossolalia," in *Journal for the Scientific Study of Religion*, 19 (1980); C. G. Jung, *Answer to Job* (1954), *Psychology and Religion: East and West* (1958), and *The Archetypes and the Collective Unconscious* (1959); Thorvald Källstad, *John Wesley and the Bible: A Psychological Study* (1974); Robert Keaynes, "Proceedings of Excommunication Against Mistress Ann Hibbens of Boston (1640)," in John Demos, ed., *Remarkable Providences* (1972); Lawrence Kohlberg, *The Philosophy of Moral Development* (1981).

James N. Lapsley and John H. Simpson, "Speaking in Tongues," in *Pastoral Psychology*, 15 (1964); Daniel J. Levinson et al., *The Seasons of a Man's Life* (1978); Robert Jay Lifton, *Death in Life: Survivors of Hiroshima* (1967), *The Life of the Self* (1976), and *The Broken Connection* (1979); Jane Loevinger, *Ego Development: Conceptions and Theories* (1976); Adams Lovekin and H. Newton Malony, "Religious Glossolalia: A Longitudinal Study of Personality Changes," in *Journal for the Scientific Study of Religion*, 16 (1977); Kenneth Earl Morris, *Bonhoeffer's Ethic of Discipleship: A Study in Social Psychology, Political Thought, and Religion* (1986); Gardner Murphy and Lois Murphy, eds., *Asian Psychology* (1968); Albert Nicole, *Judas the Betrayer: A Psychological Study of Judas Iscariot* (1957); F. Clark Power and Lawrence Kohlberg, "Religion, Morality, and Ego Development," in Christiane Brusselmans, ed., *Toward Moral and Religious Maturity* (1980); Paul W. Pruyser, *The Play of the Imagination: Toward a Psychoanalysis of Culture* (1983); Richard Quinney, *Providence: The Reconstruction of Social and Moral Order* (1980).

Lewis R. Rambo, "Current Research on Religious Conversion," in *Religious Studies Review*, 8 (1982); Otto Rank, *The Myth of the Birth of the Hero* (1959); S. K. Ramachandra Rao, *Development of Psychological Thought in India* (1962); Norman Reiden, "Medieval Oedipal Legends about Judas," in *Psychoanalytic Quarterly*, 29 (1960); Theodor Reik, *Dogma and Compulsion* (1951); Ana-Maria Rizzuto, *The Birth of the Living God* (1979); Milton Rokeach, *The Open and Closed Mind* (1960); Mordechai Rotenberg, "The 'Midrash' and Biographic Rehabilitation," in *Journal for the Scientific Study of Religion*, 25 (1986); Richard L. Rubinstein, *The Religious Imagination: A Study in Psychoanalysis and Jewish Theology* (1968); David Schendler, "Judas, Oedipus and Various Saints," in *Psychoanalysis*, 2 (1954); James R. Scroggs and William G. T. Douglas, "Issues in the Psychology of Religious Conversion," in *Journal of Religion and Health*, 6 (1976); William C. Spengemann and L. R. Lundquist, "Autobiography and the American Myth," in *American Quarterly*, 17 (1965); Bernard Spilka et al., "A General Attribution Theory for the Psychology of Religion," in *Journal for the Psychology of Religion*, 24 (1985); Merton P. Strommen et al., *A Study of Generations* (1972); Hjalmar Sundén, "What Is the Next Step to Be Taken in the Study of Religious Life?" in *Harvard Theological Review*, 58 (1965) and *Die religion und die rollen* (1966); Sidney Tarachow, "Judas, the Beloved Executioner," in *Psychoanalytic Quarterly*, 29 (1960); Charles T. Tart, ed., *Altered States of Consciousness* (1969); Antoine Vergote and Alvaro Tamayo, *The Parental Figures and the Representation of God* (1980); D. W. Winnicott, *Collected Papers* (1958); Dorothy F. Zeligs, *Psychoanalysis and the Bible* (1974).
[*See also* Pastoral Care and Counseling.]

GEOGRAPHY AND DEMOGRAPHY
OF AMERICAN RELIGION

Edwin S. Gaustad

IT would seem to be a commonplace that religions are not to be understood apart from their natural environments nor apart from major population shifts over time. Yet scores of histories have been written without explicit attention to lakes or rivers, mountains or valleys, migrations or invasions. On occasion geography asserts itself with such force that it will not be denied: Mount Sinai for the ancient religion of the Hebrews, the Ganges River for ancient and modern Hindus, Mecca for all Muslims worldwide, and Jerusalem for Christians, Jews, and Muslims. Demography also sometimes cries aloud for attention, as when Siberian tribes made their way across a land bridge into North America, and then south across the Great Plains into Central and South America; or the restless migrations of Goths, Vandals, Teutons, Angles, Saxons, Jutes, and others that had such an effect upon the flavor and direction of medieval Christianity.

In folk religions, the habitations of the spirits or gods are directly related to major foci within the environment: sun, moon, river, mountain, spring, or mesa. Both totem and taboo may be related to population shifts; to a sense of foreignness, real or imagined; to tribal structures; or to a waning or waxing demographic profile. None would deny the centrality of the Nile River to ancient Egyptian religion, in its domineering presence as well as in its very ebb and flow across the landscape. Is it not fair, then, to ask what influence the Mississippi or Saint Lawrence rivers may have had upon religion in North America? Similarly, none would deny the influence of the Roman armies upon the remarkable spread of Mithraism from Persia into eastern Europe, then into western Europe and the British Isles. In the twentieth century, however, it is easy to overlook the influence of American armies in the South Seas generally and in the Hawaiian Islands specifically. Invading Huns will always receive notice; migrating Mennonites might not. As we turn, therefore, from a worldwide scene to an American one, we will attempt to see and understand the geographical and demographic influences on religion, not only on the grand scale but in subtler patterns as well.

COLONIAL PERIOD: ATLANTIC TO ALLEGHENIES

With voyages requiring anywhere from four weeks to three months, the ocean that separated the British colonies from European civilization constituted the major geographical factor for all of colonial history. The difficulties in communication and transportation, the extravagant and often tragic cost involved in such travel, the frustration as well as the opportunity presented by such isolation—all of these shaped the politics, economics, social developments, culture, and religious life of the seventeenth and eighteenth centuries. Religious bodies that valued their close connection to spiritual overlords abroad were notably hampered by that imposing, unyielding oceanic barrier. This was especially true of colonial Anglicanism, which did not have a complete ecclesiastical structure until after the American Revolution; young men wishing to be ordained in that church had no choice but to risk crossing the Atlantic twice and paying the expenses for both trips. Churches of a less hierarchical polity (e.g., Congregationalists and Baptists) found the absence of British overlords more a blessing than a bane. The uneven development of religious liberty in early America owed more to geography than to Parliament.

GEOGRAPHY AND DEMOGRAPHY OF AMERICAN RELIGION

The Atlantic seaboard presented a far more receptive shoreline to prospective explorers or settlers than did the Pacific coast. The former's great Chesapeake Bay and Gulf of Saint Lawrence seemed to extend welcoming arms, and their shores offered safe havens. Broad and navigable rivers—the Saint Lawrence, Connecticut, Hudson, Delaware, Potomac, James, and more—served for at least two centuries as the highways penetrating interior America. In Virginia, the Anglican intent was to establish small towns and congruent parishes, but the rivers dictated long, narrow plantations and hopelessly dispersed parishioners. In New York, a north-south river determined in which direction settlements and churches would move. And in New England, the pattern of town settlement was determined more by land and climate than by theology and polity.

Europeans had to adjust quickly to the stern demands of geography, whereas Native Americans had for generations found their survival dependent upon their gradual, if inevitable, acquiescence to those demands. The many religions of the Indians also reflected geography in more direct ways than either Judaism or Christianity did. But if the theology of these "higher" religions was relatively immune to geography, many other aspects of their corporate life were not. Freedom, for example, had much to do with the land. As Sidney E. Mead has pointed out in *The Lively Experiment* (1963), freedom for Americans through much of their history has meant a freedom to move on, to be done with "traditional boundaries of habit, class, custom and law." Ocean tides and valley floors gave direction to much colonial religion.

Despite some vigorous missionary efforts, European religions that were transplanted to the New World depended largely upon further immigration for their growth and prosperity. Some of that immigration was more political and commercial in motivation than religious, but a fair number of those leaving the Old World for the New World saw their migration in religious terms: pilgrimage, exodus, exile, errand, or promise. The best-known religious migration is that of Pilgrims and Puritans into Plymouth and Massachusetts bays. Especially with respect to the latter, the migration in the 1630s was of such homogeneity and number as to stamp the land with an enduring way of thinking, worshiping,

and behaving. New England (particularly the colonies of Massachusetts and Connecticut) was compact, was settled by persons of like mind religiously, and was able by a variety of means to maintain control of all the major institutions within: family, school, militia, church, and government. Puritanism (later, Congregationalism) afforded the best example in the colonial period of a happy coincidence of geography, demography, and religion. Such a generalization about New England must always make an exception for Rhode Island. Formed around the waters of still another bay (Narragansett), it was a refuge or cesspool—depending entirely on one's point of view—for religious dissent of many kinds. From the very beginning, the religious geography of Rhode Island was mixed, while its demographic flow was determined largely by those expelled from New York or New England.

Shortly after the Puritans began settling in Massachusetts, English Roman Catholics found a safe harbor in the Chesapeake Bay area. In the mid-1630s the colony of Maryland was launched under the proprietorship of the Catholic Calvert family. While some in England objected to the notion of "a Catholic colony," state interests indicated that between Virginia and New York (then controlled by the Dutch) it was better to have another English colony than to have a Spanish or French or Dutch one. Maryland was never exclusively Catholic, partly because of enlightened proprietary policy and partly because of takeovers and rebellions stemming from the surrounding lands. By the end of the colonial period, Maryland was nonetheless the major residence for Catholics in British America, the other colonies being, with few exceptions, inhospitable to all "papists."

In the second half of the seventeenth century, religious persecution goaded many Europeans into seeking a land less disposed to fine, whip, jail, maim, or destroy. With the restoration of the English monarchy in 1660, nonconformists in general, and Quakers in particular, felt the heavy hand of the state against them. In France, Louis XIV saw fit to revoke the Edict of Nantes in 1685, thereby driving large numbers of Huguenots away from French soil. And Mennonites, who found little acceptance anywhere in seventeenth-century Europe, except in Holland, also gazed with hope beyond that treacherous ocean. The most significant religious migration in this half-century was clearly that of the English Quakers. Begun well before William Penn secured a charter for his grand colony, that migration received a powerful boost when Pennsylvania officially opened its Philadelphia port in 1682. Eastern Pennsylvania quickly became Quaker territory, but because of Penn's steady policy of religious toleration, the "Quaker state" soon yielded its regional and political dominance to an ethnic and religious mixture that came to characterize this large and successful colony.

Jews, of course, knew persecution long before the seventeenth century. Driven from Spain in 1492, Jews found refuge in Portugal, Holland, or the overseas colonies of those countries. Jews migrated to North America only in small numbers in the colonial period; nonetheless, they managed a religious toehold in Newport, New York, Philadelphia, Charleston, and Savannah before the American Revolution.

Huguenots also arrived in modest numbers; their presence was felt especially in South Carolina (founded about the time of their exile from France) and in New York. And Mennonites hardly waited for the ink on Penn's charter to dry before settling near Philadelphia in a hamlet called Germantown. Not until early in the eighteenth century was that 1683 settlement augmented by other Mennonites who found land and freedom in the Conestoga and Pequea valleys of Lancaster County, as well as in other sparsely settled areas nearby.

The eighteenth century saw no end to either the persecution or the poverty that had driven earlier groups to America. From 1708 to 1710 Germans from the Palatinate, both Lutheran and German Reformed, made their way to the Hudson River valley, settling along both sides of that river as far north as the fur traders' much-used Mohawk River. In succeeding decades, the great Germanic immigration moved into Pennsylvania, where the farmlands and countryside of eastern Pennsylvania attest to that powerful population shift. Between 1730 and 1750 some 60,000 Lutherans arrived in the colony; when their first truly national leader, Henry Melchior Mühlenberg, arrived, he had no reason to hesitate in choosing his headquarters: Philadelphia. The German Reformed, like the Lutherans, found Penn's colony congenial and tempting, es-

pecially in those counties just west of the earliest settlements: Montgomery, Lehigh, Northampton, Lancaster, Berks, and York.

Some religious groups arriving in Philadelphia were pushed even farther west. There they found great valleys to the south, valleys that inhabitants of Virginia and the Carolinas had not moved into because of mountain barriers. From western Pennsylvania, however, no such barrier impeded the overland movements. Thus Presbyterians (Scotch-Irish), members of the Church of the Brethren (German), and others formed a back-country ethnic and religious community quite distinct from that of their fellow citizens closer to the coast. West Virginia was culturally separate from its eastern counterpart long before political boundaries established that fact.

One other distinct and recognizable colonial immigration must be noted: the Africans imported directly from Africa or from way stations scattered across the Caribbean. The only major immigration that was involuntary (although there were many convicts and indentured servants), the African population in North America in the eighteenth century was concentrated in Maryland, Virginia, South Carolina, and Georgia. Bringing many elements of African folk religion or even of Islam with them, the Africans soon lost much if not most of any tribal identity or culture. By the nineteenth century, these blacks tended to reflect the religious affiliations of the whites in the states noted above; that is, they became predominantly Baptist or Methodist. Concentrated in the Southeast, blacks constituted a major force within southern evangelical religion, so powerful both before and after the Civil War (Donald G. Mathews, *Religion in the Old South,* 1977).

In the colonial period, geography facilitated the entry into the North American continent of Anglicans, Congregationalists, Catholics, Quakers, Dutch and German Reformed, Lutherans, Presbyterians, Baptists, and, much later, Methodists, Jews, Huguenots, Mennonites, and many others. The geography of rivers and fall lines determined most early settlement patterns, while the mountains prevented an easy flow of population from east to west. Virginia's earliest settlements in and around Jamestown—sometimes referred to as a malarial swamp—made for a life expectancy in that colony far lower than that found in the generally healthier clime of New England. The officially encouraged religious migrations (such as those into New England, Pennsylvania, and Maryland) created a "religious geography" in colonial America.

THE NINETEENTH CENTURY: ATLANTIC TO PACIFIC

In American history, the nineteenth century is thought of as the period of immigration par excellence. And so it was. It was also, however, the period of enormous territorial acquisition, from shore to shore and beyond to Alaska, Hawaii, and the Philippines. It was a time of deliberate and sustained missionary activity, both within the United States and around the world. It was a time of denominational activism, cooperative voluntarism, new religions, utopian experiments, and local communes. Geography and demography played a primary role.

With respect first to immigration, four religious waves will be discussed. The earliest, the Irish and therefore Roman Catholic, began arriving in large numbers in the 1820s and continued for the next two decades to constitute a major population influx. By 1850 the Irish accounted for 43 percent of all foreign-born citizens in the United States. By that same year, the Roman Catholic church had become the largest single denomination in the land. If the Irish laity was strong, the Irish hierarchy throughout the nineteenth century and well into the twentieth appeared even stronger. Ethnicity and religion reinforced each other in those regions where to be Irish was to be Catholic and vice versa. The northeastern corner of the United States represented the major area of such geographical and numerical dominance.

While in 1850 the Irish accounted for 43 percent of the nation's foreign born, that percentage had by 1900 fallen to less than 16. Immigration accelerated, on the other hand, from such countries as Austria, Hungary, Italy, Russia, and Poland. Many of these immigrants were Roman Catholic as well, aggravating the cares of a church overwhelmed by the demands made upon its meager purse and by the ethnic strains and antagonisms that threatened to pull it apart. The church not only managed to hold itself together and keep its head above water, but grew by spectacular statistical leaps. Around the beginning of the nineteenth century, one estimate placed the number of Roman Catholics in America at around 50,000, with virtually half of them in the state of Maryland alone. By the end of the nineteenth century, Catholics numbered 12 million and could be found all across the continent.

By no means was all of the emigration from southern and eastern Europe by Roman Catholics. The second half of the nineteenth century was also the period of a great Jewish influx into the United States. At the beginning of the nineteenth century, there were fewer than four thousand Jews in America, but by the end of the century there were at least 1 million. In this period, settlement tended to be in the major eastern port cities, especially New York City; however, even before the Civil War, German Jews had migrated westward, founding their major center of learning (Hebrew Union College) in Cincinnati, Ohio, in 1875. Though the Jewish population is not the equivalent of the Jewish synagogue or temple membership, in 1900 there were more than one thousand synagogues. First-generation immigrants in particular clung to the liturgies and life-styles of their fathers and mothers, with the result that Judaism and the Jewish population were probably more nearly congruent in the nineteenth century than in the twentieth. This late-nineteenth-century Judaism, as will be noted later, divided into separate groups with ethnicity playing a major role, as it had threatened to do in Catholicism.

Ethnicity and religion joined forces once again in the latter half of the nineteenth century as Lutherans from Scandinavia arrived in impressive numbers. The growth was dramatic: from about one-quarter of a million at the beginning of the nineteenth century to about 2 million at the end. Most of that early one-quarter million in 1800 were found in Pennsylvania. Most of the 2 million in 1900, by contrast, were found in the upper Midwest: Wisconsin, Minnesota, and the Dakotas. Unlike Catholic and Jewish immigrants, between 1850 and 1900 the Lutherans tended to turn away from the overcrowded and overpriced cities to the rural frontiers, there to claim a territory that continues to be predominantly Lutheran. But if ethnicity in the broad Scandinavian sense reinforced the Lutheranism of this region, ethnicity in a narrower sense divided and weakened it. Swedish Lutherans settled and worshiped apart from Norwegian Lutherans; Danish from Finnish; Icelandic from Swiss and German. These quite separate communities continued well past 1900, often preventing Lutheranism from being either a visible or powerful force on the national scene. The twentieth century saw bold ecumenical endeavors designed to modify or eliminate most of these ethnic boundary lines.

In addition to nineteenth-century immigration, a second prominent feature of the American landscape was the frontier, or better, several frontiers. One thinks first of the trans-Appalachian frontier, across the Cumberland Gap, down the Ohio River, and into those states that were added soon after the original thirteen: Ohio, Indiana, Kentucky, Tennessee, and Alabama. This is the frontier of Daniel Boone and Davy Crockett, of most of the American mythology concerning those advancing outposts of civilization exported from the eastern United States. But there was also a Mississippi Valley frontier, heavily flavored by French Catholicism; a southwest frontier, permanently colored by Spanish Catholicism; and a Pacific frontier, infused with the religious traditions of the Far East.

The trans-Appalachian frontier presented an obvious and immediate challenge to those denominations long resident in America. Presbyterians and Congregationalists pooled their resources of money and personnel in their Plan of Union in 1801 to ensure that this newly settled region would be introduced, quickly, to both Christianity and the arts of civilization in general. Otherwise, it was widely assumed, the nation would find itself teetering on the edge of barbarism, unable to absorb large land masses and distant settlers. Lyman Beecher's eloquent *A Plea for the West* (1835) displayed both the apprehension and the optimism provoked by this first American "West." It was, however, the Baptists and the Methodists who most successfully infiltrated and tamed this territory. Methodists, utilizing the device of the circuit rider, and Baptists, resting on the talents and proximity of the farmer-preacher, divided much of this area between them. The recruitment techniques of frontier revivalism and camp meetings were used most effectively by these two denominations, though others participated in the "harvest" of converts.

Once westward travelers reached the Mississippi River—whether in its upper reaches in Minnesota, or at its midsection around Saint Louis, or near its mouth in New Orleans—it was evident to them that the French had not totally abandoned interior America. French Jesuits had been recalled from their long-standing mission stations in 1764, and the vast Louisiana Territory had been sold to the young United States in 1803, but France's Roman Catholicism continued to permeate the lifeline that joined the North of America to the South. It also gave the East a vital avenue of export via the Mississippi River. The French Catholicism of Quebec, Montreal, and the Great Lakes also joined with the French Catholicism of the South to form a ribbon of French culture and language that extended all the way from the Gulf of Saint Lawrence to the Gulf of Mexico; the survival of French place names along that ribbon is but one evidence of an influence never wholly eradicated. The scattering of Indians, traders, soldiers, and settlers had no priests' care when France made its official exit from the continent. America's only Roman Catholic bishop, John Carroll, back in Baltimore, made heroic efforts to meet the needs of those living in the Louisiana Territory, a region so vast that it virtually doubled the size of the United States in an instant.

When Protestant missionaries arrived in the Southwest, carrying the Bible along with their denominational credentials, they found that Spanish missionaries had preceded them by more than two hundred years. From the founding of Santa Fe in 1610, the fathers (chiefly Franciscan) maintained a visible presence in much of the Southwest. The famous chain of missions along the Pacific coast, established by Junípero Serra in the second half of the eighteenth century, was only one of the more visible and enduring symbols of Spain's (later Mexico's) indelible mark upon the land. When gold lured Americans from the East in great numbers around the middle of the nineteenth century, it appeared that the Anglo invasion might obliterate the Hispanic presence. Not only did this fail to happen, but the Hispanic and Catholic "sovereignty" over this corner of America has steadily intensified.

The final frontier was represented by America's move into Hawaii (annexation came in 1898) with its strong manifestation of Oriental religion, even as the ancient ways of Eastern faiths began making their presence felt on the

West Coast. For those Americans who in the nineteenth century continued to think of their land as a Christian nation, the incursion of Shinto, Buddhism, Hinduism, and even a bit of Confucianism sounded an alarm. For this and other reasons, immigration from the Orient was sharply curtailed in the 1880s. Chinese and Japanese populations remained heavily concentrated in Hawaii and California, with Buddhism proving in both places to be the most exportable and vigorous of all the Oriental religions.

In addition to the trans-Appalachian frontier (chiefly English), the Mississippi valley frontier (French), the Southwest frontier (Spanish), and the Pacific frontier (significantly Oriental), the nineteenth century saw a variety of new religions and new visions come into being, some with dramatic geographical or demographic effect. The opening of the first frontier, the excitement and optimism generated by a new nation flexing its muscles for the first time, the prevailing belief in progress, and the demonstrable reality of religious freedom—all of these combined to make the nineteenth century a time when men and women dreamed dreams, then proceeded to give those dreams concrete reality. If some of these dreams found no acceptance in the settled East, one simply transported that heavenly vision farther west where land was abundant, tradition absent, and unfettered daring ever present. In American religion, this was a time of adventure.

Of all the nineteenth-century experiments and visions, two left their mark permanently on the land. The first of these was Mormonism, officially the Church of Jesus Christ of Latter-day Saints. Originating in New York in 1830, the new church began moving westward almost immediately: to Ohio, Missouri, and Illinois. Arousing hostility and suspicion nearly everywhere because of its close-knit and separated community, its novel Scriptures, and the rumors of polygamy, the church found it necessary to keep moving westward. Not until the Mormons arrived in the Great Salt Lake Basin in 1847 did they achieve sufficient distance from non-Mormons (the "Gentiles") to put an end to their wandering. The basin became home, and the entire state of Utah, when finally admitted to the Union in 1896, was also home for Mormons from all across the nation as well as from many areas of Britain and continental Europe. This utopian experiment, as definitive in its success as so many

others were in their failure, not only made the desert bloom, but conquered the land in a religious sense as well, ultimately presenting the best example of geographical "control" to be found anywhere in the United States.

The Disciples of Christ frontier movement associated with Alexander Campbell, Barton Stone, and Walter Scott can best be understood in terms of the time and space of nineteenth-century America. As has been indicated, it was a time when the belief in "progress" ran high, even if progress took the form of turning backward. We prepare for a golden age by returning to an apostolic age; the Kingdom of God lies ahead of us, but we find the pattern and preparation for that Kingdom behind us—nineteen centuries behind. The frontier knew little in the way of authority, either civil or ecclesiastical. But one authority was appealed to over and over: the Bible. Thus the Disciples of Christ movement sought to restore the true church, Christ's church, by appealing over the heads of all existing denominations to the New Testament itself.

In the open spaces of the trans-Appalachian West, where no bishop resided, where no church was strong, where no heavy hand of tradition exercised sway, a new denomination was born, though the original idea was to rid the world of denominations and sectarian division. In western Pennsylvania, Indiana, Illinois, and other sparsely settled areas, separate movements joined together in the 1830s to create a frontier church whose voice often reached scattered settlements well ahead of that of the seaboard churches. The strength of the Disciples of Christ remained in these frontier areas throughout the nineteenth century, while that of the more conservative schism of the twentieth century, the Churches of Christ, grew in the border states and frontier South.

Mormons and Disciples represent only a small segment of the frontier's busy experimentation in religion, though these two experiments were the most successful geographically and demographically. Other experiments—for example, the Oneida community of John Humphrey Noyes and the Brook Farm venture of the Transcendentalists—were short-lived and modest in number. The Shakers, reaping converts from the camp meetings and frontier revivals, briefly made a mark upon the land in the mid-nineteenth century. Reaching their high membership level of around six thousand by 1850, Shakerism gradually declined thereafter, its demise foretold by its prohibition against marriage within the community. In upstate New York the adventist movement, associated with the name of William Miller, reached its zenith in the 1830s and 1840s, but then scattered both geographically and denominationally. The most successful offshoot, Seventh-day Adventism, grew powerful in and around Battle Creek, Michigan, then later made a major impact on a newer frontier: the Pacific coast.

RELIGIOUS GEOGRAPHY IN THE TWENTIETH CENTURY

By the time the twentieth century opened, the national land rush was over. Much assimilation remained, however, as territory that had been annexed or conquered had yet to participate more fully in the nation's culture. States were added to the Union in 1907 (Oklahoma), in 1912 (New Mexico and Arizona), and in 1959 (Alaska and Hawaii). With the exception of Alaska, the location of these states also indicated the direction of the country's population shift: to the West and to the Sun Belt. By the mid-1960s, California had replaced New York as the most populous state in the nation. The move from farm to factory, greatly increasing the urban population, continued from the second half of the nineteenth century through the first half of the twentieth. Not long after World War II, however, the shift from center city to suburbia intensified, especially in the North and East. Great and sprawling metropolitan areas, both urban and suburban, account for two-thirds of the total population in the 1980s.

The forces of American religion did not remain aloof from the pressures of urbanization and industrialization, but their participation or effectiveness in these new processes was uneven. The labor–capital division in the Northeast was often a Catholic–Protestant division as well, though this dichotomy did not prevail elsewhere in the country. Some denominations maintained a rural character far longer than others (Lutherans, Baptists, and Methodists), while others found the urban atmosphere more congenial or more challenging (e.g., Judaism, Catholicism [Irish and Italian], Episcopalianism, and the Salvation Army). Most of these identifications were sufficiently fluid so that a stable religious geography of rural versus urban or of labor versus capital was not possible. Even the familiar designation Bible Belt does not encompass an entire region but only pockets of territory or carefully selected categories of denominations.

A religious geography nonetheless remains, even in the final decades of the twentieth century. Such a geography is not primarily a function of size but of historical tenacity, ecclesiastical authority, and patterns of settlement. In the 1980s the ten largest Christian families in America are, in order of their size, as follows: Roman Catholics (52 million); Baptists (26); Methodists (13); Lutherans (8); Disciples and the whole Campbellite movement (4); Presbyterians and Mormons (both over 3); Episcopalians and Eastern Orthodox (less than 3); and the United Church of Christ (less than 2). Of these ten families only four manifest sufficient regionalism or geographical concentration to make a major cartographic impression: Catholics, Baptists, Lutherans, and Mormons. Catholics dominate the Northeast, the Southwest, and the Pacific West. Baptists (black and white) are the major cultural force throughout the Southeast, excepting only southern Louisiana and southern Florida. Much of the territory contiguous to Wisconsin, Iowa, Minnesota, and the Dakotas forms an identifiable Lutheran region. Mormons not only dominate the entire state of Utah but also adjoining counties in Wyoming, Colorado, Arizona, Nevada, and Idaho; indeed, the concentration of Mormons—which in some counties of Utah is to the exclusion of all other religious groups—far exceeds that of the preceding three "territorial religions."

Where these four territorial religions prevail, the line between sacred and secular grows faint as the church identifies closely with the entire life of a community. While no formal establishment prevails, few questions are raised about the easy and congenial relationships between local agencies, schools, and government on the one hand and the ecclesiastical membership or leadership on the other. Also, such churches more successfully retain their traditional membership even as they energetically add others to their rolls. Self-confidence and aggressiveness, not malaise, tend to characterize such churches.

But there are fewer Lutherans than Methodists, and almost as many Presbyterians as Mormons. What of the others in the "top ten" who cannot be rated as territorially dominant, at least as far as the macrocultures of the nation are concerned? Such groups as the Methodists, Presbyterians, and Episcopalians are certainly strong and influential churches; they are, however, national rather than regional, leaven throughout the large loaf rather than a separable section of that loaf. Influences come, of course, in many ways other than geography.

Apart from the Christian denominational families, Judaism is also reckoned among the major religious forces in America. The Jewish population in America is between 5 and 6 million in the mid-1980s, but synagogue or temple membership is probably about half that number. Religiously affiliated Jews, therefore, would constitute a religious force statistically comparable to the Episcopalians or Eastern Orthodox or Mormons. The Jewish population, like the black or Scandinavian, shows a concentration in specific areas rather than even dispersal across the land. The following eight states, listed in descending order, contain about 80 percent of the Jewish population in the 1980s: New York, California, Pennsylvania, Illinois, Florida, Massachusetts, metropolitan Washington, D.C., New Jersey, and Maryland.

Just as there are more Swedes in the United States than in Sweden, so there are almost twice the number of Jews in America as in the state of Israel. The United States, Israel, and the USSR have the heaviest concentrations of Jews, and together they account for about 80 percent of world Jewry. Religiously, America's Jews are divided among three denominational affiliations: Orthodox, Conservative, and Reform. A generation or two ago, it was widely assumed that Orthodoxy was the refuge of the uprooted, of the insecure and pogrom-bruised immigrant. When immigration declined, Orthodoxy would decline. This conventional wisdom has, however, been challenged by the tenacity of Orthodoxy long since the gates of Ellis Island closed. Small and intimate synagogues, buttressed by a strong and total community, have kept the ancient ways of life and worship lively and appealing.

Reform, the most liberal of the three groups, stresses a more intellectualized approach to Judaism, with much of the Torah, or Law, being understood in a figurative or culturally conditioned sense. Conservative, the halfway house between the Orthodox and Reform, is especially appealing in suburbia; it is, moreover, rapidly becoming "the favored religious self-designation of the American Jew" (Marshall Sklare, ed., *The Jewish Community in America,* 1974). Other experts on American Judaism, however, argue that these denominational divisions are less significant than the intense commitment of the nation's Jews to Israel, this commitment taking on the force and fervor of an overarching religion itself.

Curiously, some religious groups not found among the top ten, or even among the upper twenty, nonetheless have a religious geography; that is, they have an identifiable territory that they unmistakably shape or control. Such microcosms are notable, for example, among Mennonites and Hutterians who, while small in number, concentrate their membership and their energies in specific areas. The Mennonite mark on the land is particularly noticeable in southern Pennsylvania, then westward across Ohio, Indiana, Illinois, and Iowa. In Marion and Harvey counties in Kansas, Mennonites are the largest religious body. The same is true in Oscoda County in northern Michigan. Numbering only about 20,000 in all of North America, Hutterians are found in greater number north of the border with Canada. Where persecution and harassment do not intrude, the large communal farms of the Hutterians ensure their prosperity.

The Church of the Brethren (members are sometimes called German Baptists or Dunkers) has fewer than 200,000 members; yet, in the valleys along the West Virginia–Virginia border, these pacifists have settled in sufficient number to be a conspicuous presence. Unitarians and Universalists together also number fewer than 200,000; but their churches are visible forces in New England, the area of their early strength.

Quakers have separated into several small groups, but collectively their mark is evident, especially in the region of their colleges: Haverford, Swarthmore, and Bryn Mawr in southeastern Pennsylvania; Earlham in eastern Indiana; Guilford in central North Carolina; and Whittier in southern California. Quakers, even in the last quarter of the twentieth century, have scarcely penetrated most of the South, the upper Midwest, or the Great Plains.

Seventh-day Adventists (over one-half million members), a century after their organization in the mid-1800s, have congregations all across the continent (and well beyond), but have made their greatest impact along the Pacific coast. A group such as the Church of the Nazarene (about one-half million members) has been especially strong in the Ohio valley, in Oklahoma and Texas, and in the far West. The Charismatic Church of God in Christ (also about a half-million, with a predominantly black membership) has widened out from the lower Mississippi River valley to major urban centers from Buffalo to Houston, and from Saint Louis to Los Angeles.

The American Indian, as has been noted, has always adopted a special attitude toward the land, finding special sanctity and holiness in particular locales. And American Jews focus much attention and affection upon their Holy Land, Israel. Many smaller groups in the American past have resided or returned to private holy places: communal centers such as Amana, Iowa, New Harmony, Indiana, and Oneida, New York; to mountain or lakeside retreats where special revelations were given or spiritual ecstasies obtained; or to shrines or hallowed halls that stand as religious equivalents of national historic landmarks. Most of these holy places escape the notice of all but a few devotees or persistent historians. If a religious group has a special claim upon a small piece of land, no one is alarmed or anxious that the nation is in danger of being carved up along religious lines.

One group, however, did alarm with its stern territorial demands: the Black Muslims. Believing that the future of American blacks lay in separation more than in integration, the Black Nation of Islam called for land to be given to this religious group (numbering fewer than 100,000) on behalf of all America's blacks—over 26 million. Elijah Muhammad, an early leader of the Muslims, called for four or five states, at least one or two, to be set aside for those who could never become, would never become, full citizens in the United States. The Black Nation of Islam, if it was to be a nation, would have sovereignty over the land. "Why can't the Black Man in America have a piece of land," the charismatic spokesman Malcolm X asked, "with technical help and money to get his own nation established? What's so fantastic about that? We fought, died and helped to build this country, and since we can't be citizens here, then help us to build a nation of our own" (C. Eric Lincoln, *The Black Muslims in*

America, 1973). But "Black Zionism," as this perspective was sometimes called, found no wide response among the vast majority of Americans, either black or white.

The religions of the Orient have also made many anxious, especially when the children of Christian or Jewish parents seemed drawn to them and then wholly alienated from the parental environment. Such groups were charged with brainwashing, with involuntary confinement, and with an authoritarianism that destroyed all selfhood or individuality. Most of these groups made claims upon the land only for their places of worship and meditation: a Hare Krishna temple in West Virginia, a major Buddhist shrine in northern California, and Zen centers and Vedanta halls in major cities. One form of Shinto, the Church of Perfect Liberty, has shown a special affection for golf courses, and one form of personalized Hinduism, led by Bhagwan Shree Rajneesh, moved to Antelope Valley, Oregon. (In 1985 Rajneesh agreed to leave the country after being indicted for conducting sham marriages.) It was a homegrown cult, though, not an Oriental one, that terrified a whole citizenry with its power over the members of its closed and unquestioning religious society. James Warren Jones led his followers from California to South America and established his People's Temple in Guyana; the 1978 tragedy of "Jonestown" became a battle cry against all manipulative, seductive cult control.

RELIGIOUS DEMOGRAPHY IN THE TWENTIETH CENTURY

Immigration into the nation's eastern cities continued in a steady and ever enlarging stream for the first fifteen years of the twentieth century. World War I frustrated the efforts of many Europeans to leave for America, even as in America it accentuated concerns about what Woodrow Wilson uncharitably called "hyphenated Americans." In less than a decade after that war ended, the growing anti-immigration forces succeeded in passing legislation that effectively ended the nation's "open door policy" to the tired and the poor, the huddled masses, and the wretched refuse. With the adoption of the National Origins Act of 1924 a quota system favorable to immigrants from northern and western European countries remained the official policy for well over a generation. Since people from these areas were less often tired or poor, wretched or huddled, the stream of oceanic immigration was reduced to a trickle.

Other immigration, however, continued largely unchecked, even unnoticed, overland from Mexico as well as from Central and South America. The 1920s and 1960s were the decades when the number of Hispanics making their way to the United States rose sharply. They came by the thousands, to number in the millions (presently about 14 million). Puerto Rico's status as a territory since 1898 (and as a self-governing Commonwealth since 1952) exempted that island from the immigration quotas applied elsewhere; as a result, the Hispanic population in America has been sharply augmented by Puerto Ricans entering the country, notably in and around New York City.

The Hispanic increase represents a large source of new membership for the Roman Catholic church; current estimates suggest that about one-fourth of that church's membership is of Hispanic origin. Another religious group that has benefited from twentieth-century immigration is Eastern Orthodoxy. Russians and Greeks, who constitute the two largest ethnic groups within this ancient fellowship, both experienced new infusions of immigrant populations early in the twentieth century. Russian Orthodoxy made its initial entry into the American West: first into Alaska when it was still Russian territory, then southward as far as San Francisco. The immigration of the twentieth century, however, followed the more familiar pattern of Atlantic crossings into New York. In 1901 the Church of Saint Nicholas was erected in that city, and only four years later the official headquarters for Russian Orthodoxy was transferred from San Francisco to New York City. A membership of about 20,000 at that time grew to more than 1 million by 1980.

Greek immigration began in the final years of the nineteenth century, but continued apace well into the twentieth. By the beginning of World War I, over 100,000 Greek Orthodox inhabited the United States, that number increasing to more than 1 million soon after World War II. Their settlement pattern has been largely urban and eastern, with membership especially high in New York, Massachusetts, Pennsylvania, Ohio,

and Illinois. By 1980 the Greek Archdiocese of North and South America had grown to around 2 million members, the preponderance of these being in the United States. And while the Eastern Orthodoxy is counted among the top ten denominational groups, many Americans remain unaware of its presence. Still struggling with many internal differences and dissensions, as well as with an unfamiliar political and cultural environment, these Russians and Greeks have found ethnicity to be both barrier and bond. This has been more characteristic of Eastern Orthodoxy than of other religious groups simply because their immigration has been so largely in the twentieth century. It is also true that "Eastern" stands for a markedly different civilization from the Western, which has produced or at least shaped all others in the list of major denominations in America.

By and large, the twentieth century has been a time of steady progress for the nation's largest and oldest religious families. Church membership steadily increased from less than 40 percent at the beginning of the century to over 60 percent five decades later. Roman Catholics, who numbered around 15 million at the beginning of the century, increased about twofold by the 1950s. In that same time period, Baptists went from around 4 million to more than four times that number; Methodists from over 5 million to about 9; Lutherans from less than 2 to more than 4; Presbyterians from 1.5 to nearly 3 million; and so on. Mainline religion in America knew nothing but progress and growth: increased giving, attending, and joining.

Then, in the 1960s and 1970s something quite unexpected began to happen to mainline religion in America: growth lines on the church membership charts, which had angled upward decade after decade, now began to level out, sag, and even drop. If there was growth at all, it corresponded only to the modest increase in national population; at times, however, not even that comfort or encouragement could be found. Some denominations saw their numbers decline, while others that for years had flexed their muscles and raised their voices wondered where all the audience and all the clout had gone. What went wrong?

That question proved both tantalizing and difficult to answer. In 1972 Dean M. Kelley (*Why Conservative Churches Are Growing*) attempted to respond. Kelley argued that those churches that found their membership dwindling should give themselves a rigorous and totally honest self-examination. They should inquire into their theological understanding, their moral discipline, their intellectual certainties, and their evangelical zeal. These were the very things that Kelley found missing from so many of the mainline churches. His response to that situation was blunt: such churches decline because they deserve to. On the other hand, churches of strict demands, both theological and moral, churches of visible zeal, and churches that know who they are and where they are headed—these churches grow ever stronger because they deserve to.

In 1979, Dean R. Hoge and David A. Roozen edited *Understanding Church Growth and Decline, 1950-1978* and took a much broader view of the situation. They inquired into such contextual factors as national birthrates and youthful rebellions, as well as local population shifts and economic reversals. They also examined institutional factors: the local church, as Kelley had done, and the entire denomination to which that church belonged, as Kelley had not done. Reasons why some churches grow are much more complex than most suppose, the editors wrote, with the external or contextual factors being somewhat stronger than the institutional ones. The editors allowed themselves to be argued against, even within their own book. Kelley himself, as well as others, averred that theology was far and away the most important factor in church growth or decline. The editors also recognized that more research was called for. This was especially true since their time line was quite brief (if one thinks of the whole history of Christianity) and since they studied only mainline Protestantism, not fringe Protestantism or other religions, to determine both weaknesses and sources of strength. In any event, the ruddy-cheeked optimism of much of American religion was severely shaken by demographic evidence that no longer lined up to show faithful support of all the churches.

If mainline Protestantism appeared to be on the skids, other, often newer religions looked amazingly vigorous and began to flourish. The 1960s and 1970s were also a period of cultic flowering, of novel and unsettling challenges to the familiar ways of worship. The Orient, once thought to be confined to Hawaii or to graduate centers where world religions were quietly discussed, now confronted one in the airports (the International Society for Krishna Consciousness), in the public schools (Transcendental Meditation), in the streets (Zen Buddhists on their *kinhin,* or "walking meditation"), and most intimately of all in the family (the Unification Church, among many others). Demographically all of these groups were negligible; in their impact upon the public consciousness, however, they were seen as powerful threats to traditional patterns. They aggravated the insecurities already created by declining church membership, declining church influence, and declining church support. Such great world religions as Buddhism and Hinduism were no longer distant objects for investigation and study; they were lively options to be embraced, or fearful and competing strangers to be eschewed.

Competition with the "mainliners" was by no means limited to imports from abroad. Much nearer to home, indeed spawned at home, were dozens of zealous sects that appeared to know nothing of declining birthrates, disaffected youth, urban blight, or galloping secularism. These churches, defying all national trends, were growing at phenomenal rates, burying last year's records under a mass of new adherents, new buildings, and new lands to conquer. The Holiness and Pentecostal movements reflected this demographic surge. Statistics were not always solid, especially in the short range, but few would deny the surprising strength manifest over a half-century—well into the 1980s—of such groups as the Church of God (both the Anderson, Indiana, and the Cleveland, Tennessee, denominations), the Assemblies of God, the United Pentecostal Church International, the Pentecostal Church of God, and many, many others. One feature of Pentecostalism, the speaking in tongues under the direct inspiration of the Holy Spirit, spread far beyond the ranks of denominations officially called Pentecostal. The charismatic movement invaded even the mainline churches in the 1960s and 1970s, strengthening and reviving some, weakening and dividing others. But by the 1980s the charismatic movement as a pervading element in American religious life appeared to have lost much of its steam.

While the Holiness' emphasis on perfection is as old as "Be ye therefore perfect, even as your

Father which is in heaven is perfect'' (Matt. 5:48) and the Pentecostal emphasis on glossolalia as old as that day described in the second chapter of the Book of Acts, other demographic marvels owe much to the modern world. The "Electronic Church," a phenomenon of the television age, implies more than religious programs available on a Sunday morning: it points to entire cable systems, powerful broadcasting networks, stations owned by religious organizations, and a viewing audience of impressive proportions. Though many argue that the size of that audience is grossly exaggerated by the television performers and programmers themselves, the financial receipts demonstrate that the size of the sympathetic audience is large. Estimates range as high as $1 billion received annually by the ministry of this elusive but powerful church, with such widely known figures as Oral Roberts, Marion G. (Pat) Robertson, Jim Bakker, and Jerry Falwell heading the list of the most financially favored.

In the 1980s, public attention is focused with new intensity upon such religious programming, for much of it has become overtly political and socially involved. Traditional Fundamentalism in America had, for the most part, been withdrawn from the world, alienated from the major social and educational institutions of the culture. But the new Fundamentalism, especially in its electronic mode, began to endorse candidates and platforms, to address the concerns not simply of a congregation but of a nation, and to call for not a millennial return of Christ but a political return to a Christian America. The "radical Christian right," as it was quickly named, had unmistakably found its voice. What the long-term effects of that stentorian voice would be on the local congregation and its membership was not clear. The electronic ministry is remote: How can it heed? The viewer is alone: How can he or she serve? The fellowship of the people of God gathered together may yet prove more powerful than all the kilowatts combined.

TRENDS

In 1760 Ezra Stiles, Congregationalist minister and sometime college president, predicted (*Discourse on Christian Union*) that a century later the number of his co-religionists would be 7 million. In fact, the number amounted in 1860 to a mere one-quarter million. Stiles was no fanciful guesser riding some wild hunch. He was a careful statistician (insofar as the eighteenth century could boast of any), a keen and tireless observer, and he possessed a cool, rational head. He estimated that the nation's population would double every twenty-five years, which was an excellent guess. Stiles further estimated that the Congregationalist population, very significant in 1760, would also double every twenty-five years. That turned out to be a bad guess, and hindsight helps us to see why. For one thing, Congregationalism remained—even after the American Revolution—a prominent feature only of New England, never moving with any strength into the Middle Atlantic or southern states. When it did move westward, it lagged far behind such frontier competitors as the Methodists and Baptists in breaking out of its colonial mode. As late as 1830, nine-tenths of all Congregationalist churches were still to be found in the New England states alone. The miscalculation of the astute Stiles merely warns all trend predictors of the dangers and tricks of history that await them: population shifts, immigration floods, unforeseen competition or unimagined indifference, birthrate fluctuations, emigrations, and so on.

The temptation to try to say where American religion is headed is nevertheless virtually irresistible. In the 1950s, as has been noted, the growth rates for all major denominations seemed permanently set; in the 1980s, not so. In the 1950s, the ecumenical movement had so much momentum that predictions were commonplace that there would be only three or four major denominations in America by the end of the century. While ecumenism is not wholly moribund in the 1980s, the National Council of Churches has suffered severe setbacks and the once headlined Consultation on Church Union speaks in a voice that few hear.

An additional difficulty besetting predictions in religion is that one does not begin with a solid data base. Religious statistics are notoriously suspect and will remain so as long as one must depend almost exclusively upon denominational reports, estimates, and hopes. The U.S. Bureau of the Census has not attempted a systematic survey of the nation's religion since 1936, and even that effort was seriously flawed. Apart from a few population sample surveys, the bureau has left all questions of religious membership and strength to the churches themselves. Inevitably, some denominations are much better record keepers than others; some do not bother to report; others on principle oppose the reporting; and still others, too new and busy, and too concerned with matters beyond this earth, are simply ignored by all those doing the counting.

Into this vacuum where no consistent, reliable, methodologically sound data are to be found, private research centers and university scholars have moved. The periodic *Gallup Reports* on "Religion in America" (May 1985) are not only the best-known products of such polling and surveying but probably the most useful as well. For nearly half a century, church and synagogue attendance figures in America have been remarkably consistent and, compared with most European nations, remarkably high. In the decade 1973 to 1983, variation from a prevailing 40 percent was minimal. Attendance was highest among Roman Catholics (52 percent), though that figure represented a sharp drop from pre-Vatican II days; average among Protestants (only slightly under the 40 percent noted above); and lowest among Jews (32 percent). The relative stability of these figures suggests that church and synagogue attendance in America will continue through the twentieth century to involve two-fifths or more of the national population.

Church membership in America has been even higher in the 1980s than church attendance, a reversal of the colonial pattern where the "auditory" regularly exceeded the number who were full members. Denominational reports themselves tally up to a collective membership of over 60 percent, while the Gallup method of individual interrogations places that percentage at nearly 70 percent. Regionally, church membership is highest in the Midwest (though church attendance there, curiously, is lowest) and lowest in the far West. It is true, of course, that denominations determine membership according to varying standards; people who classify themselves as members presumably also have differing criteria in mind. The long-term trend in America, nonetheless, suggests that church and synagogue membership, however that status is arrived at in individual instances, has steadily increased. In the 1860s and 1870s, membership stood at around 25 to 30 percent; in the 1960s and 1970s, the figure was around 60 to 65 percent. When mainline denominations decline, newer and smaller movements take up the statistical slack. For the remainder of the twentieth century, therefore, while two-fifths of the population will be found attending weekly religious services, three-fifths or more will be found on the institutional rolls.

Higher still than church attendance or church membership in the 1980s has been a sense of kinship with or loyalty to some religious tradition. In Census Bureau samples, well over 90 percent of the population identified themselves as Protestant, Catholic, or Jewish. A 1983 Gallup poll supported this general finding, with the following percentages indicated for the three large divisions: Protestant, 56 percent; Catholic, 29 percent; and Jewish, 2 percent. The percentage of the population that declined to state any religious preference had increased from 5 percent in 1972 to 9 percent in 1983. One cannot place great weight upon vague loyalties or dimly recalled traditions, except to note the obvious: being "religious" in the America of the late twentieth century is to risk no social stigma, no cultural ostracism, no political liability. In fact, when it comes to running for office in the United States, representatives, senators, governors, and presidents all find it appropriate if not essential to indicate some religious identification. For the remainder of the century at least, one can safely predict that, for the vast majority of the citizens, being American and being religious will imply no contradiction. Two-fifths will be in attendance, three-fifths as members; well over four-fifths somehow and in some way will be sympathetically identified with religion.

Religion in America presents to observers from abroad a picture of such complexity as to provoke often a sense of despair or defeat in any attempt to comprehend the whole. Geography and historical demography cannot erase all of that complexity, but they can reduce it. It is essential that the scholar of American religion keep both the temporal and spatial dimensions in mind. When speaking of the Dutch Reformed adherents, for example, one must carefully distinguish between those of New York and those of Michigan, those of the seventeenth century and those of the nineteenth. The Roman Catholicism of colonial Maryland cannot be simply fused with the Catholicism of contemporary Rhode Island or New Mexico without losing virtually all precision in such an amalgamation. Patterns of immigration and migration, though now centuries old, still help to explain or at least clarify that rich and colorful mixture known as "religion in America." The frontier by its resistance to or removal from ecclesiastical authority, as well as by its freedom from fixed behavior patterns and strong precedent, invited experimentation and novelty. Religion in Hawaii is inseparable from its geography, and the proximity of Mexico to the continental United States has shaped religion here more than the proximity of Canada has. Much that seems obscure, ambiguous, or hopelessly entangled in this nation's religion becomes less so as we fasten our attention upon space, time, and motion.

BIBLIOGRAPHY

Religious Geography

Lester J. Cappon, *Atlas of Early American History* (1976); Jackson W. Carroll et al., *Religion in America, 1950 to the Present* (1979); Edwin S. Gaustad, *Historical Atlas of Religion in America* (1962; rev. 1976); Peter L. Halvorson and William M. Newman, *Atlas of Religious Change in America, 1952–1971* (1978); Charles O. Paullin, *Atlas of the Historical Geography of the United States* (1932); Wilbur Zelinsky, "An Approach to the Religious Geography of the United States," in *Annals of the Association of American Geographers*, 51 (1961).

Religious Demography

Conveniently, summarized data on membership, churches, finances, and other items may be found in the annual *Yearbook of American and Canadian Churches*, published under the auspices of the National Council of Churches of Christ in the U.S.A. That council, now in cooperation with the Glenmary Research Center, has also issued decennial reports entitled *Churches and Church Membership in the United States*, the most recent report being in 1982. The *Gallup Reports*, now issued by the Princeton Religion Research Center, offer data drawn directly from the public rather than from the denominations; the most recent report, #236, was issued in May 1985. The most recent U.S. Bureau of the Census systematic survey of religion in America is *Religious Bodies: 1936* (1941). Demographic analysis is provided in Dean R. Hoge and David A. Roozen, eds., *Understanding Church Growth and Decline, 1950–1978* (1979).

[*See also* RELIGION IN THE SPANISH EMPIRE; RELIGION IN HISPANIC AMERICA SINCE THE ERA OF INDEPENDENCE; *and* FRENCH CATHOLICISM IN THE NEW WORLD.]

FOLKLORE AND THE STUDY
OF AMERICAN RELIGION

Donald E. Byrne, Jr.

UNTIL recently, the study of historical and contemporary American religion was dominated by approaches that concentrated on the institutional and rationally articulated expressions of religious life. Although the achievements of such scholarship cannot be minimized, it was as if the story of American religion could be told adequately only by focusing on those phenomena with a certain kind of social identity, such as denominations, sects, and cults; or propositional identity, such as creeds, platforms, theologies, and biographies. Implicit in this approach was a narrow and restrictive definition of religion; religion was presumed to exist primarily in concentrated institutional forms, not at all in widely diffused cultural forms. Implicit as well was the assumption that only written sources, to the exclusion of song, symbol, ritual, custom, story, and art, counted in describing American religion. Since relatively few practitioners of religion had found their way into print, however, one encountered the curious and parochial situation of an intellectual elite telling the story of another intellectual elite as if it were the story of the whole.

Recent studies of civil religion and popular religion (among others), by noting religiosity outside ecclesial boundaries, have attempted to balance the traditional preoccupation with institutional religion. Relatively meager attention, however, has been devoted to nonwritten sources, in part because phenomena such as symbols, rituals, art, and festivals are larger than words and yield only grudgingly to rationalistic analysis. For example, it is one thing to understand the chapter on "Eschatology" in the seminary theology textbook, but quite another to comprehend a mute slab of granite shaped like a weeping willow. It may be easy to know what

the hymn "Now Thank We All Our God" says, but more difficult to express what its singing says. The official Roman Catholic position on ecumenism may be lucidly stated by the Second Vatican Council, but what does one make of the Roman Catholic manager at the office party telling a joke that begins "There was this priest, minister, and rabbi in a boat . . ."?

Folklore (commonly used to refer both to a discipline and to its subject matter) invites students of American religion to investigate nonwritten sources seriously. Folklore deals with elements of group culture, such as play, ritual, song, and story, that are transmitted informally, most often orally or by example (one person showing another some traditional skill, such as quilt-making or cooking), in a variety of communicative processes. Far from being the exclusive possession of marginal groups, folklore transcends dichotomies between high culture and popular culture: professors as well as peasants, monks as well as mountain men have folklore. And far from being quaint marginalia, folk data disclose the vital innards of living groups. Religious folk, like others, come alive when they are talking their talk, telling their stories, playing their games, and singing their songs with others like them. Indeed, the study of folklore can lead students of American religion not only to neglected sources but also to a renewed humanism that takes informal religious culture as seriously as formal religious culture.

The study of folklore also suggests fresh ways to grasp the mutual diffusion of religion and culture. For one thing, the history of American religion unfolds in dynamic interaction with a culture most tellingly delineated by its folk art, legend, humor, and heroes. More directly, much apparently "secular" folklore is covertly religious. Frontier heroes embody metaphysical ideals or invert conventional norms; folk songs and jokes attack accepted morals; supernatural legends teach world views. Further, in a variety of symbiotic ways, folklore has insinuated itself into institutional religion, and religion, from its side, has generated folklore. All three of these phenomena—the covert religiosity of secular folklore, the folk dimensions of institutional religion, and the overt religious dimensions of folklore—point to American folk religion, a subject matter that bridges folklore and religion. For students of American religion, recognition and study of folk religion can help redress the imbalance caused by the preoccupation of traditional scholarship with institutional forms of religion and academic sources.

As with many interdisciplinary fields, folk religion is not easy to define precisely. Part of the problem stems from the fact that both terms, folklore and folk religion, are used loosely in popular and scholarly parlance. The first step in defining folk religion, therefore, is to define folklore precisely (or at least as precisely as folklorists have defined it) and then to build a definition of folk religion.

DEFINING FOLKLORE

Once a stepchild of anthropology and English literature, folklore has achieved disciplinary autonomy in American academe. Although this coming-of-age is directly related to clarifications of folklore's subject matter, unanimity remains an elusive goal; appropriate items for the folklore of folklorists are the oft-repeated, somewhat frustrated observations that folklore is what folklorists study and that a folk group is any group that possesses folklore. Nevertheless, an emerging, if tentative, consensus is available. At issue are both halves of the word: What is the lore, and who are the folk?

The "lore" of folklore has several distinctive marks that, taken together, distinguish it from other aspects of culture. First, it must be traditional; that is, passed from one generation to the next, rather than ephemeral (as is popular culture). Many cultural items, however, such as language or legal processes, are traditional, but are not considered folklore. Together with tradition, therefore, a second distinguishing mark of folklore is its mode of transmission. Folklore is traditional culture passed on orally or by example or, in general, informally. Folklore may originate from print (as with sayings from Shakespeare), or may gravitate toward print (as with sermon exempla in devotional magazines), or may exist simultaneously in print and oral tradition (as with folk hymns such as "I Am a Poor Wayfaring Stranger"), but in order to qualify as folklore, it must at one time have circulated orally or by example. Cultural material passed off as folklore without ever having enjoyed oral circulation (such as the saga of Paul Bunyan) is dubbed by folklorists "fakelore."

The third mark of folklore, variation, generally follows from the mode of transmission. Whereas cultural items transmitted by print, such as religious creeds or decrees, are fixed and invariable, folklore, shaped by individuals to suit the needs of the occasion, exhibits fluidity within relatively fixed forms. For example, within days of the election of Pope John Paul II, freely circulating Polish jokes were adapted to make the new pontiff the butt of the humor.

As a mark of folklore, variation exists in dynamic tension with the fourth defining characteristic: formularization. Relatively fixed formulas —whether simple phrases or entire narratives, standard gestures, patterns, tunes, styles, designs, or the like—provide ongoing structure for folk data. Thus, while the procession with the statue of the heavenly patron may take place at varying times during an Italian religious festival, it is a fixed element without which the festival would lose its fundamental structure.

The fifth and final mark of folklore is anonymity of origin. This is not to say that the origin of some folk items is unknown or undiscoverable (although this is true for most folklore), but only to observe that when folklore is functioning as folklore, its source, even if mentioned, is unexamined. Such anonymity contributes to the authority of folklore. The ethical weight of a proverb such as "Look before you leap" is enhanced, rather than diminished, by the fact that it presents itself as the wisdom of many, not one.

On the basis of these criteria, folklorists have isolated a number of folk genres. Oral folklore includes folk speech, proverbs, riddles, rhymes, narratives (including myths, legends, and folktales), and folk songs. Customary folklore, with both verbal and nonverbal elements, includes folk beliefs, customs, festivals, dances, dramas, gestures, and games. Finally, material folklore refers to folk architecture, crafts, arts, costumes, and foods.

As useful as these classificatory tools are, contemporary folklorists contend that they give a distorted picture without additional considerations that focus on the dynamic process that transmits folklore. Folklore is therefore understood as an event, performance, or communication. For example, analysis of a religious joke must take into account not only the text of the joke, but also the telling of the joke, including gestures, facial expressions, and audience reaction. In addition, context is important for understanding folklore: Who is telling the joke, to whom, when, and for what purpose? Collecting texts is no longer enough; one must also collect contexts.

The second major question in the definition of folklore is: Who are the folk? Popular understanding of the term burdens it with fallacious conceptions derived in part from early folklorists' preoccupation with peasant and primitive societies. Such misconceptions include the ideas that the folk are rural, that they are dying out, that they are quaint, odd, or exotic, that they are noble savages and their lore is innocent and pure, and that the folk are "the people": in short, that the "folk" of folklore are not compatible with the denizens of modern, literate, technological society. Contemporary folklorists, however, see folk groups wherever common factors such as occupation, age, geographical location, ethnic and racial affiliation, religion, education, sex, hobby, neighborhood, or even family are present. Persons may belong to more than one folk group at once, but not all members of a particular group have the same relationship to its lore.

On the basis of such considerations, folklore may be defined as "those materials in culture that circulate traditionally among members of any group in different versions, whether in oral form or by means of customary example, as well as the processes of traditional performance and communication" (Brunvand).

DEFINING FOLK RELIGION

American folk religion should not be understood as the religion of "the people": it is not the same as popular religion. Like folklore, folk religion refers to the informal culture of specific groups, not "the masses."

Folk religion is not solely the religion of old-timers, country bumpkins, or rednecks, although such groups (if they do exist) certainly have folk religion. Urban, educated, and sophisticated persons also have folk religion.

Nor is folk religion the exclusive property of Appalachian Fundamentalists, exotic snake handlers, fringe cultists, or nineteenth-century communitarians. Folk religion flourishes in mainstream denominations and nonreligious folk groups as well.

Another mistaken notion is that folk religion is simply survivals from Greek, Roman, Celtic, Teutonic, or West African religions, or their syncretistic combinations, along with culturally dominant religions; and that it is breathing its last under the chokehold of modernity. Rather, it is traditional, informal religious culture, sometimes involving survivals or syncretism, endlessly adapted to new situations.

Again, folk religion is not automatically false or stupid, simply because it is folk religion. It may be unorthodox by prevailing religious or cultural standards, but it is rational by its own standards. It may also be orthodox, if assimilated by an organized religious group.

Finally, folk religion is not the pristine religion of the Noble Savage, uncontaminated by modernity. Some informal religious culture is blasphemous, obscene, or scatological—which is why it remains informal.

American folk religion results from the symbiosis of religion and folk culture. As long as careful definitions of the "folk" and "lore" of folklore are maintained, and a flexible definition of religion is allowed, folk religion can be easily understood as the folk dimensions of religion and the religious dimensions of folklore. Put another way, folk religion is the folk culture of religious groups and the religious culture of folk groups.

The mutual diffusion of religion and folklore takes on a variety of forms. Institutional religion may absorb and transform folklore, incorporating it into its belief and practice. Prime examples are the Bible, which abounds with material originally folkloric, and festivals such as Christmas and Passover. Sometimes folklore and religion reinforce each other; for example, when both religious rituals and folk customs mark passages such as birth, marriage, sickness, and death. Institutional religion often generates its own lore or provides occasions for borrowing from folklore, as when legends or jokes cluster around saints and sinners. Conversely, folk culture generates religious lore, particularly to fill gaps unaddressed by institutional religion; for example, folk beliefs connected with healing. Some nonreligious lore is covertly religious; proverbs, for example, although not taught by any church, express a comprehensive, informally maintained ethical system. Institutional religion may merely tolerate some kinds of folklore, such as magic, or may actively condemn others, such as witchcraft, even though such practices derive validation, in part, through appeal to orthodox beliefs and practices.

Examination of various folk genres, religious folk groups, historical periods, and geographical regions suggests a number of themes particularly useful for understanding American folk religion. These themes include religious folk speech, play, story, morality, ritual and belief, and music.

RELIGIOUS FOLK SPEECH

Folk speech, the most basic form of verbal folklore, refers to "the traditional word, expression, usage, or name that is current in a folk group or in a particular region" (Brunvand). Folk speech has affinities with other departures from standard usage, such as slang and jargon, but when such expressions become traditional, rather than remaining ephemeral or technical, they are considered folk speech. The presence of folk speech is the most obvious mark of the existence of a folk group.

In folk religion, as in folklore, folk speech has several functions. Brief verbal formulas may serve as derogatory epithets, as when Roman Catholics are referred to as "mackerel snappers." Some religious groups, in fact, derive their names from such uncomplimentary descriptions: Methodists, Shakers, and Quakers, for example.

Formulaic units of folk speech may also serve as vehicles for the expression of belief, as esoteric signals to distinguish insiders from outsiders, or as intriguing verbal come-ons in witnessing. The language of born-again Christians, for

example, is peppered with formulas such as "Amen, brother," "Praise the Lord" (or simply "P.T.L.," parodied as "Pass the Lettuce" among insiders and "Pass the Loot" by outsiders), "Take it to the Lord in prayer," "Jesus as my personal Savior," and so on. Some formulas are accompanied by gestures, such as the "One Way" sign (the index finger pointing upward), or become written slogans on bumper stickers or T-shirts: "Honk if you love Jesus" and "In the event of the Rapture, this T-shirt will be empty" (observed on the T-shirt of a buxom coed).

Isolated formulas may cluster into larger units, such as graces, benedictions, invocations, hymns, and "spontaneous" prayers. Such verbal expressions are often accompanied by an altered tone of voice (sometimes negatively described as "preacher's whine") and regular, metric phrasing close to chanting. Altered intonation and chanting are even more apparent in still larger verbal units, such as sermons and personal testimonies, particularly in conservative evangelical churches. Contemporary black preachers, like epic storytellers of many cultures, utilize traditional topics, chanted deliveries, and repetitive verbal formulas (as mnemonic and transitional devices) to build compelling sermons. Among white Pentecostals, traditional verbal units, variously arranged and often without any novelty, structure personal testifying during religious services. Such testimonies powerfully embody shared community values, particularly when effectively performed. For female members of the congregation, testifying sometimes serves to perpetuate their traditionally subservient status and at the same time to provide breathing space in an otherwise stifling social hierarchy. Traditional verbal formulas can also be observed in the sermons of television evangelists and in healing performances.

Depending on its context, religious folk speech says who you are, what you believe, and how you are different from others. In traditional ways, it maintains group traditions and social control. Investigation of the folk speech of groups other than conservative Christians is a fertile field for future research.

PLAY: HUMOR AND FESTIVITY

A recurrent interest of religious scholarship has been the theological significance of play in human culture and religion. Folklore investigates informal play, such as riddles, jokes, parodies, graffiti, customs, and festivals. Since religious persons, beliefs, and practices are often the objects of humor, and since many customs and festivals are either overtly or covertly religious, folklore can illuminate the American religious experience by showing how and why religious people, among others, play, and what fun they have with and in religion.

Riddling jokes (a subclass of riddle), jokes (a subclass of folktale), and humorous anecdotes (a subclass of legend) are the most common expressions of folk humor. Even informal fieldwork suggests that hundreds of jokes and anecdotes circulate informally in religious and secular folk groups, and that not even the most sacred subjects—God, Jesus, the Virgin Mary, the Bible, heaven, and the sacraments, for example—are exempt from attention. Although many jokes and anecdotes are innocent (humorous stories about Pope John XXIII), others are obscene (jokes about celibates), blasphemous (sick Jesus riddles), or scatological (sick biblical riddles).

Religious jokes and humorous anecdotes are told in a wide variety of situations: at the cocktail party, around the supper table, during the sermon, in the dormitory, among clergy gathered for a meeting. The situation, in fact, helps to determine both the propriety and function of the joke. An "off-color" riddle told among a group of ministers would be inappropriate for a Sunday school class. Mormon jokes told among Mormons might relieve tension and build camaraderie; told among non-Mormons, the same jokes might express ridicule and antagonism. A complete analysis of the meaning of religious folk humor depends as much on the intention and performance of the joke teller and on the situation as it does on the words of the joke.

From one point of view, humor exists simply for entertainment, and nothing seems so ill-humored as attempts to analyze it. From another point of view, however, humor has profound social, psychological, historical, and theological implications.

On a social level, the most obvious function of humor is to reinforce communal bonds. Jokes and anecdotes, like those told among frontier Methodist itinerants or contemporary Baptist ministers, release tension, ease frustration, and lighten the burden of an often overwhelmingly serious enterprise. In such circumstances, shared laughter does not erase common problems, but rather makes them more tolerable by assuring participants that the problems are shared. The fact that the humor is obvious only to "insiders" reinforces the bonding function of the laughter.

Closely related to the community-building function of humor is its role in conflict resolution. A joke about birth control might help Roman Catholic laity deal with the conflict between church teaching and their consciences. The same joke, told by a Protestant to a Catholic, could express hostility. But the shared laughter could also create a bond that transcends the anxiety each feels about the other. Among college students of different faiths, or between "competing" religious groups such as Dominicans and Jesuits or Baptists and Methodists, trading humorous insults may even become a kind of game that ritualizes antagonism—thereby rendering the antagonism socially manageable, even a form of cooperation.

Humor, of course, also functions as a form of moral protest against discrimination and exploitation—for example, nineteenth-century master-slave jokes in which the slave plays the role of the sly trickster. Some jokes—such as the sick riddle fads about Auschwitz, Jesus, dead babies, Helen Keller, lepers, or starving Ethiopians—may even have a cathartic and healing effect; they objectify deeply rooted personal or cultural ambivalence and insecurity.

Historically, religious folk humor can be seen as part of a larger current of cultural behavior that took distinctive shape during the nineteenth century. Yankee nonconformity, frontier exaggeration, and democratic windiness contributed to a generally irreverent spirit that debunked convention and pretension wherever they were found. Constance Rourke has noted both the pervasiveness and the purpose of this national trait:

> Humor has been a fashioning instrument in America, cleaving its way through the national life, holding tenaciously to the spread elements of that life. Its mode has often been swift and coarse and ruthless, beyond art and beyond established civilization. It has engaged in warfare against the established heritage, against the bonds of pioneer existence. Its objective—the unconscious objective of a disunited people—has seemed to be that of creating fresh bonds,

a new unity, the semblance of a society and the rounded completion of an American type.

Americans take religion seriously. But to judge from the undercurrent of guffaws (if not chorus of catcalls), they are also laughing up their sleeves. The gravity of formal religion and the levity of religious humor need not be understood as a kind of schizophrenia, however; the latter is a necessary corrective to the former (and, as Rourke suggests, even an instrument of unity). Humor illustrates the folly of all seriousness by pointing out the incongruity and pretentiousness of human efforts in light of the twofold certainties of death and divine transcendence. Humor debunks stuffy idols, insisting that humans—including popes, rabbis, ministers, and saints—have feet of clay and that human religion—including dogmas, commandments, scriptures, theologies, and institutions—is at best a faltering approximation of the absolute. Both in its historical and contemporary manifestations, folk religious humor is a heuristic device that opens transcendent perspectives by inverting and relativizing conventionally serious religion.

Despite laments over the alleged decline of festivity in a technological era, celebrative play flourishes in informal culture. Within the family, for example, folk customs and rituals celebrate passages such as birth, birthdays, baptism, circumcision, first communion, confirmation, bar and bas mitzvah, graduation, courtship, engagement, marriage, anniversaries, changes of occupation and retirement, reunions, and death.

When such activity involves a larger community, it is called a festival. Folk festivals involve celebrations by groups as diverse as extended families, ethnic, racial, or religious communities, local, regional, or national groups, occupational and fraternal organizations, and their combinations. Such larger communities not only join hands with families in rituals of passage, but also furnish the stimulus for celebrating a great number of holidays linked to the traditional Judeo-Christian liturgical calendar (Passover, the Assumption of Mary, Advent, St. Lucia's Day, Three Kings' Day, Mardi Gras), to survivals of primitive religions (Halloween, May Day), or to events of national historical significance (Independence Day, Thanksgiving).

While it is not always easy to distinguish customs from mores or manners, or true folk customs and festivals from re-created folk and commercially sponsored holidays or celebrations, or folk elements from other cultural elements in a given festival, most festivals are sustained, at least in part, by informal culture; that is, few festivals have written plans. They are simply done a certain way—learned informally by organizers and expected by participants. In addition, not all customs and festivals need to be "religious" in order to be religiously significant, if it is true that play as such has theological implications. Secular festivity, including such typically American celebrations as the rodeo, county or state fair, church bazaar, town carnival, local circus, tent show, parade, prom, homecoming game, and a staggering array of parties, all bespeak a level of celebrative intensity that transcends tidy categories.

Folk festivity typically involves other folk genres, such as traditional music, ritual, drama, food, costume, belief, story, game, dance, art, artifact, and gesture. For example, at Italian religious festivals in the anthracite region of Pennsylvania, one might march in procession behind a statue of the Virgin bedecked with ribbons on which money is pinned, sing folk hymns in honor of the patron, and consume gnocchi, calzone, or linguine under an outdoor tent next to a carnival. Later, one might dance to the music of an Italian band, wear elaborate medieval costumes, tell children of miracles wrought through the patron's intercession, and celebrate with one's family at an ancestral house with an exterior or interior shrine. In a real sense, the festival is a microcosm of folk religion.

Like humor, customs and festivals are forms of play. Both have serious dimensions: passages such as birth and death are fraught with danger, while holidays are essential for communal continuity. To play at such times, however, is not to escape what is serious but to put it into perspective. Play snatches humankind, if only for the moment, from its seemingly inexorable march toward personal and communal extinction by suggesting another dimension in which all are perpetually children. Seriousness is not the last word: the comic transcends the tragic.

Play is significant both for its presence and its absence in American religion. Protestantism, particularly in the culturally dominant form of ascetic Calvinism, has been accused of banishing fiddle music from folk song and play from religion. If so, American Christianity has been narrowed to its sober, morally earnest, dead-serious manifestations, while play, not to be denied, works its magic only in the exterior darkness. The scenario of a split between religion and fun in American culture needs careful investigation; perhaps much religious play goes unnoticed simply because it is the antithesis of sober, morally earnest scholarship.

STORY IN FOLK RELIGION

Recent theological interest in storytelling as a form of theology is joined from the side of folklore by a fertile, endlessly malleable supply of traditional prose narratives. Many of the stories used as exempla in contemporary sermons, testimonies, devotional literature, or as "strange, but true" episodes in tabloid newspapers are simply updated versions of stories that have been told for centuries. Narratives cross not only times and oceans, but genres as well; the joke about absurd reliance on divine providence heard on Wednesday may serve as sermon illustration on Sunday.

Myths (traditional prose narratives set in the remote, sacred past, understood as true by the community that recounts them), legends (traditional prose narratives set in a less remote and usually secular past, understood as true by the community that recounts them), and folktales (traditional prose narratives told primarily for entertainment, understood as fictional by the community that recounts them) are the most complex forms of verbal folklore. If folktales are the short stories of informal culture, myths and legends are its history. In a folkloristic sense, the American people have no myths, simply because the "myths" of the Judeo-Christian tradition are written in the Bible and formally maintained. The only true American myths are Amerindian myths. Nevertheless, some historians and folklorists speak of national cultural myths, including America as the new Eden or Promised Land, although these motifs have not, generally speaking, entered oral tradition as prose narratives.

If impoverished in informal myth, American culture is rich in legend. The term *legend* originally referred to the lives of the saints, or hagiography, which were read for the devotional enrichment of Christians. In medieval times, vast storehouses of such material, richly embellished with mythic and legendary material from oral tradition, were collected into works such as Jacob de Voragine's *Golden Legend;* until recently, the less extravagant *Roman Martyrology* was read aloud daily in Roman Catholic seminaries. Indeed, despite the recent official demythologization of Saint Christopher, Saint Philomena, and other saints, devotion to heavenly beings flourishes in folk Catholicism. National and home shrines, devotional objects such as holy cards, statues, rosaries, and medals, and devotions like novenas and pilgrimages are the focal points for hagiographic lore. Stories of miraculous cures by Saint Anne, lost objects found through Saint Anthony's intercession, hopeless causes transformed by Saint Jude, and remarkable conversions and deliverances at the hands of the Virgin Mary circulate freely at retreats, novenas, cursillos, and in devotional literature. Apparitions, particularly of Mary, but also of images of Christ or of weeping, bleeding statues, recur in the United States, despite selective opposition by official Catholicism. Local legends about wonder-working holy priests and nuns are also current.

The hagiographic vacuum left by Protestantism's demythologization of Roman Catholic lore was quickly filled by an alternative tradition. John Foxe's *Book of Martyrs* and the seventeenth-century Anabaptist *The Martyr's Mirror,* which recount the heroic exploits of crypto-Protestants from the time of the early church, culminating with the martyrs of the Reformation, embody a Protestant folk history that not only powerfully shaped positive self-conceptions and negative attitudes toward Catholicism, but also continued traditional legends under a new guise. The focal theme of this folk history, God's providential guidance of the Protestant enterprise, flourished in the New World at the hands of seventeenth- and eighteenth-century Puritan divines, particularly Increase and Cotton Mather. In *Magnalia Christi Americana* (1702), for example, Cotton Mather recorded countless remarkable providences, including conversions, deliverances, judgments upon unbelievers, answered prayers, omens, and portents as evidence that God smiled especially on the Puritan mission.

As unaware as Mather that much of the evidence was traditional lore, nineteenth-century frontier preachers followed in his footsteps. In their autobiographies, Methodist itinerants, among others, continued the tradition of recording traditional providences as fresh signs of God's favor on their work. With the demise of the frontier, which had spawned a vast body of secular folk material generally supportive of the idea that America was a likely place for a new start in the divine plan, stories of remarkable providences moved with religion into the city, where they adjusted to new forums such as the Sunday school, missionary relations, and direct mail solicitations, along with traditional uses in preaching, evangelizing, and devotional literature. Ripe with the hope that God's providence was especially apparent in their genesis, new initiatives such as revivalism, Mormonism, millennialism, the temperance, Holiness, and Pentecostal movements, communitarian societies, Fundamentalism, the Jesus movement, and Neo-Pentecostalism provided fertile soil for continuance of the tradition. In fact, the vitality of biblical literalism appears to encourage remarkable providences; when contemporary preachers assert that AIDS is God's punishment for the sin of homosexuality, they stand at the forefront of a long tradition.

Another kind of religious legend in Protestantism focuses on seminal figures and great leaders. Edifying stories, replete with legendary embellishment, recount the miraculous, heroic, and sometimes humorous deeds of European founders like Martin Luther and John Wesley, and American giants like Francis Asbury and Peter Cartwright (Methodist), George Whitefield, Charles Finney, and Billy Sunday (revivalist), Joseph Smith and Brigham Young (Mormon), Franz Pieper (Missouri Synod Lutheran), and many others. Such stories, rooted in the folk history of Protestantism, can illuminate the religious aspirations of groups and historical periods more vividly than can conventional sources.

Along with religious and personal legends, folklorists note supernatural legends. These coexist less comfortably with official religion than other legends do, although they appear to feed upon the supernaturalistic world view sanctioned by the Judeo-Christian tradition and certainly reinforce it in substance, if not in detail. Yet the animism and polytheism of such legends take them beyond orthodoxy into a widely diffused undercurrent of supernaturalism. To be sure, the trolls, fairies, werewolves, elves, brownies, ghouls, and vampires of European folklore do not figure prominently in American oral tradition (although they do flourish in children's literature, fantasy, and television cartoons). But stories about ghosts, haunted houses, witches, devils, demonic possession (including demonic messages on records), exorcisms, vanishing hitchhikers, visitors from outer space, "scientific" verification of biblical miracles, letters from heaven, the Bermuda Triangle, cosmic portents, parapsychological phenomena, premonitory or prophetic dreams, and miraculous cures have a lively currency in informal culture. This supernaturalist substratum sometimes erupts into official religion, as with the tragic witchcraft episode in seventeenth-century Salem, and sometimes it coalesces into movements or sects, such as the Satanic Church. Closely related to such supernatural legends are stories of the grotesque and macabre—legends about wilderness and lovers' lane maniacs, death cars, mysterious murders, suicides, accidents, buried treasures, Sasquatch, and the like.

Like other forms of folklore, the meaning of supernatural legends depends on performance and context. The story of an insane ax murderer loose in the woods is certainly more believable when told at camp around a flickering fire, especially if performed effectively. Yet the adult narrator values the story only as a means of social control, whereas youthful listeners will be appropriately frightened. The presence of religious and supernatural legends does not necessarily imply literal belief.

Nevertheless, the persistence of such material in modern times should at least qualify generalizations about the historical triumph of the scientific world view and, even more, about the demise of the supernatural. Naturalism and supernaturalism seem to coexist in contemporary society; for many moderns, God has not died, in part because a world view that sustains him lives in informal culture.

FOLK MORALITY

Although other folk genres clearly have ethical implications, none teaches ethics so pointedly as proverbs. A true proverb, as distinguished from other fixed forms of traditional speech, such as proverbial phrases ("to raise the roof") and proverbial comparisons ("as long as the pope's nose"), is defined as "a popular *saying* in a relatively *fixed form* which is, or has been, in *oral circulation*" (Brunvand). Proverbs abound in historical documents, in literature, and in common speech; even haphazard collecting uncovers dozens of such sayings. Some proverbs are specific to groups and regions; many, however, circulate across cultural and national boundaries.

Although biblical religion canonized proverbial lore in the Book of Proverbs, relatively little of that wisdom has become "proverbial," except for a few sayings such as "Spare the rod and spoil the child." Instead, an alternate body of empirically tested wisdom has prevailed and goes generally unnoticed by official religion. This proverbial lore constitutes a ghost ethic, parallel to the moral teaching of the churches. It is not always easy to discern whether this ghost ethic reinforces church teaching or contradicts it. When someone asserts "Pride goeth before a fall," biblical injunctions against hubris quickly come to mind. On the other hand, the Pelagian tone of the proverb "God helps those who help themselves" (which is thought by many to be a Bible verse) clearly contradicts Pauline teachings about justification by grace. In general, the self-interested prudentialism characteristic of proverbial wisdom seems to involve a more restricted ethical commitment than that demanded by Judaism and Christianity.

The relation between the moral teaching of official religion and of proverbs is clarified by noting that the two operate at different levels. Whereas the moral norms of official religion derive from a universal, transcendent reference point, proverbs derive from experience and are concrete in orientation, if not in formulation. They give concise advice for dealing with mundane domestic, social, or economic situations that Christianity is reluctant to address for fear of legalism. To parody a proverb, one might say that proverbs rush in where religion fears to tread, without the implication, of course, that proverbial lore is foolish.

The empirical context of proverbs helps to explain why they are sometimes contradictory. The saying "Haste makes waste" appears to be at odds with "He who hesitates is lost." However, different situations, such as whether to marry after one date or after ten years of courtship, validate the wisdom of both proverbs.

Similarly, the empirical orientation of proverbs makes general statements about their moral message tenuous. Many seem to extol enlightened self-interest ("The early bird catches the worm"), self-reliance ("If you want something done right, do it yourself"), or even Machiavellianism ("Why buy the cow if you already get the milk free?"). Others, however, encourage socially useful virtues, among them honesty ("Honesty is the best policy"), diligence ("Practice makes perfect"), humility ("Pride goeth before a fall"), self-control ("Loose lips sink ships"), responsibility ("You make your bed, you lie in it"), cooperation ("Two heads are better than one"), decency ("Cleanliness is next to godliness"), and thrift ("A penny saved is a penny earned"). Many proverbs enjoin prudent assessment of persons ("If you lie down with dogs, you will get up with fleas"), situations ("A good garden may have some weeds"), or opportunities ("Don't count your chickens before they hatch"). Others put painful dilemmas in perspective ("Don't make a mountain out of a molehill") or advocate stoic endurance in the face of difficulty ("If you've got the devil in your boat, you must row him to shore" or, better, "You have to kiss a lot of frogs to find the prince").

Apart from their perceived usefulness (useless moral advice would not become proverbial), proverbs derive their authority from two factors. First, even though the sources of some proverbs may be traced by scholars, they present themselves anonymously and therefore appear to embody timeless wisdom. By fitting an individual's particular moral dilemma into a larger context, the proverb says, in effect: "You are not alone; others have experienced the same problem and have approached it in this way." Second, proverbs are frequently used in informal counseling by authority figures, particularly parents, to sum up, resolve, or dismiss ethical dilemmas.

The question should at least be raised whether many people, without being aware of it, rely more strongly on informal morality than on official religious morality. One often encounters the notion that the church is fine in its place, but that it is too theoretical and has little to do with people's lives. Proverbs, partly because of their pithy, easily remembered structure, partly because they offer down-to-earth solutions to everyday problems, and partly because American culture is predisposed to common sense and hardheaded realism, may appear more reliable than what is regarded as the preacher's lofty moralizing.

A balanced assessment of this question will depend on careful attention to the sociocultural context in which proverbs are used. Considered abstractly, proverbs and institutional religion may be at odds. As employed by individuals, however, proverbial morality may simply be one element in a larger, syncretized system.

Another issue involving folk morality has to do with the relation of folklore to bigotry. Many kinds of informal culture are important for the self-definition and self-expression of religious groups. But sometimes folklore turns ugly, perpetuating prejudice and encouraging persecution. Epithets, legends, jokes, and songs attack Jews, Mormons, Roman Catholics, various Protestant denominations, blacks, Amerindians, women, unbelievers, clergy, and religion as such. Thus, initiatives in American religion toward unity, tolerance, and cooperation, such as the ecumenical, interfaith, interracial, and equal rights movements, are counterbalanced by informal traditions that encourage division, jingoism, and hatred. Such folklore starkly contradicts the fundamental moral orientation of the Judeo-Christian tradition toward the unity of the human family under God.

Many religious legends exemplify this point. Nineteenth-century Methodist itinerants routinely attacked their frontier competitors, such as Baptists, Deists, Campbellites, Episcopalians, and "infidels," with stories recounting God's vengeful judgments on those who resisted Methodism. A story, dating from the fifth century, about Jews ritually torturing and murdering a Christian child continues to circulate, sometimes with Mexicans or blacks as protagonists. Anti-Catholic lore, focusing on the alleged sexual congress of priests and nuns and horror stories about the murder or enslavement of their illegitimate offspring, or accounts of Jesuit-directed conspiracies for world domination, are also part of this lore. Polemical material about Mormons, Fundamentalists, cult groups, liberals, and other religious groups has circulated at various times. Often delivered with documentation as to time and place in sermons and devotional literature, such stories seem authoritative to credulous ears.

Folk humor can be another vehicle for big-

otry. It is difficult to think of any religious, racial, or ethnic group, or any belief, practice, or calling that has not at some time been the butt of somebody's joke, dialect story, sick riddle, parody, or song. Of course, not all such material expresses bigotry. Sometimes the humor is intentionally self-deflating, as when a Jew tells a Yiddish dialect story to another Jew. Jokes about the beliefs and practices of others may even defuse potentially destructive aggression in a socially acceptable manner. But when humor is used to foster bigotry, as it sometimes is, it renders prejudice seductive and disarming. By coating crude and bitter sentiments with the sugar of laughter, jokes make prejudice more palatable.

FOLK RITUAL AND FOLK BELIEF

Broadly understood, rituals are regular, prescribed enactments of belief. Although ritual is an important part of institutional religion, it is by no means confined to churches; anthropologists and sociologists, for example, study cultural and social rituals. Secular ritual in fraternal organizations or sports may sometimes function as a surrogate for religious ritual. In informal culture, ritual behavior is particularly apparent in folk belief, custom, festival, dance, drama, and game, and it sometimes involves other folk genres such as stories, songs, and artifacts.

Some kinds of religious folk ritual, such as drama, are not widespread in the American folk tradition. Exceptions occur in the Spanish-American Southwest, where *Los Pastores,* a shepherds' Christmas play, and reenactments of the Passion by a cult known as the Penitentes have been studied. Mardi Gras and mummers' festivities, although once folk plays celebrating pre-Lent and Christmastide, are now officially maintained by civic organizations. But traditional Negro religious plays, such as *Heaven Bound* and *Ship of Zion,* are still performed in rural and urban black churches.

Other kinds of folk ritual, however, are widely prevalent, particularly in association with customs, festivals, and folk belief (pejoratively denoted in popular speech as "superstition"). Ritual enactments of folk belief offer people traditionally prescribed and trustworthy ways of dealing with the critical times of everyday life. Successful negotiation of potentially disastrous passages such as birth, marriage, travel, sickness, and death are crucial to human well-being. But potential danger lurks in ordinary activities as well. Domestic activities, social relationships, and economic pursuits often seem to be controlled more by blind chance and fitful luck than by transcendent rhyme or reason. For no apparent reason, a cake falls, lightning strikes, a crop fails, a child sickens, a relationship curdles. Folk belief struggles to explain the inexplicable and sometimes provides strategies for dealing with it by prescribing ritual. Like proverbial lore, folk belief fits individual experience into a larger context, but it also links activities to beliefs. And like proverbs, folk belief addresses practical concerns often neglected by institutional religion.

Many folk beliefs are expressed or conceived in a causal form, describing signs or causes in the conditional clause ("If you see a ring around the moon . . .") and results or effects in the consequent clause ("it will rain"). Whoever knows or performs the conditional gains predictive or causal control over the consequence. Whereas the Judeo-Christian tradition yields ultimate control of individual lives to inscrutable divine providence, folk belief takes charge, offering people a small measure of apparent control over, or at least foreknowledge of, present and future imponderables.

Thousands of folk beliefs exist in informal culture. Folklorists have classified them under four categories: the cycle of human life, the supernatural, cosmology and the natural world, and miscellaneous. Not all folk beliefs are necessarily believed by those who know them. Yet people often have ambivalent attitudes toward beliefs they claim not to take seriously. Those who disavow the unlucky significance of numbers might feel acutely uncomfortable if they were to stay on the thirteenth floor of a hotel (and, because of the folk belief, hotels do not number a thirteenth floor). The comeback of the two-dollar bill was short-lived because it was believed to be unlucky. While dismissing notions about good or bad luck, persons will avoid walking under ladders or will carry a rabbit's foot "just in case." Athletes and students make fetishes of articles of clothing used during successful games or examinations. Actors are reluctant to wish a fellow performer "Good luck!"; they wish the opposite: "Break a leg!"

Folk beliefs are continually updated and appear to thrive at every level of society. In the 1940s, proximity to radar installations was believed to cause sterility; current lore attributes the same effect to color TVs and microwave ovens. If once it was believed that an apple a day kept the doctor away, today megadoses of vitamins, particularly vitamin C, keep him at bay. Attitudes of folk belief clearly underlie some people's practice of religion as well. When batters cross themselves at the plate, when people use rosaries, medals, relics, or candles at critical times, or when they finger a random passage of Scripture for guidance, the attitude involved, if not always the practice, may be unorthodox. Typically, most people with folk beliefs do not believe they have folk beliefs; only others do.

Of particular interest to students of American religion is the massive body of folk belief having to do with healing. In Roman Catholicism, institutional support, such as the sacraments of penance and anointing of the sick, approved shrines, and charismatic healing, has generally kept healing within institutional bounds. The Protestant Reformation, however, moved ritual in general and healing in particular out of official religion. Left on its own, healing either surfaced in sectarian form, such as Christian Science, or flourished informally as folk medicine.

Folk medicine involves folk food and nutrition, a pharmacopoeia of preventive and curative medicines, ritual practices and objects, designated healers, and attitudes toward health, sickness, and death. Unlike orthodox medicine, it is holistic in orientation, and treatment involves not only the body but the patient's psyche and community as well. It is eclectic when it is linked to popular medical practice such as chiropractic or reflexology, and syncretic when healing is combined with millenarian beliefs, with convictions about alleged international conspiracies, and with moral concerns about modern technology and education. Although folk healing is unorthodox by prevailing medical standards, it is not irrational. Rather, it is solidly empirical, rational by its own standards, and frequently efficacious, whether for scientific or other reasons.

Despite attempts to explain, and to explain away, folk healing in particular and folk belief in general as false reasoning, magic, primitivism, or some other kind of nonscientific thinking, folk belief and attitudes have not gone away. The question, then, is not whether folk belief is true or false, but what its presence says about American culture and religion. This can only be answered by attention to the contexts that give it meaning.

RELIGIOUS FOLK MUSIC

Like other forms of folklore, folk music is traditional, is transmitted informally, and generates variants. It differs from popular and art music, which are transmitted in fixed form, and from "commercial folk" music (as in the folk revival of the 1950s and 1960s), which transforms traditional music into fixed, commercially useful forms.

Folk music that is not overtly religious may have much to say about religion in American history. Outlaw ballads such as "Jesse James" invert accepted moral and social codes, and social protest songs as sung by the IWW ("Wobblies") during the early union movement, by Woody Guthrie during the Depression, and by the Weavers after World War II express moral outrage. Such music takes a prophetic stance, often vis-à-vis the moral complacency of institutional religion. In fact, some songs are explicit parodies of hymns, as in the Wobbly version of "In the Sweet By and By": "Work and pray, live on hay, you'll get pie in the sky, bye and bye." Other songs of social protest have supported the civil rights, anti–Vietnam War, and antinuclear movements.

In addition to secular folk music, there is a large body of religious folk music. Paralleling official denominational hymnody (often maintained in disdainful distance from folk music), religious folk music has left marks at every significant period of American history. The "Singing School" movement, originating in Puritan New England, for example, developed into a full-blown musical idiom involving an unconventional system of music notation, called shape notes, particularly apt for teaching sight singing. Camp meeting revivalism generated an extensive body of spiritual songs, or simply "spirituals," which, after the heyday of the camp meeting, continued to develop among both blacks and whites. Urban revivalism, with its emphasis on solo vocalists such as Ira David Sankey, brought gospel music to the city. Similar observations might be made about the Holiness and

Pentecostal movements, the temperance crusade, Fundamentalism, and countercultural religious movements of the 1960s. Today, black and white gospel music is a well-defined, commercially established (and thereby distanced from its folk roots) musical tradition maintained independently from both country music and the institutional church.

Not only historical periods but also religious groups have generated distinctive bodies of religious folk music. Among the Pennsylvania Dutch, for example, the Old Order Amish use the *Ausbund,* a hymnal without tunes; traditional melodies dating to pre-Reformation times are "lined out" by the song leader, or *Vorsänger.* Mormon folk songs celebrate their epic past or laugh about polygamy. During the Shaker revival in the 1840s, hundreds of hymns were written under the influence of the spirit by Shaker believers. The "bush-meeting" Dutch, or Pennsylvania German, Methodists still sing dialect spirituals set to folk tunes. Other groups, such as Schwenkfelders, Moravians, Adventists, Jews, Amerindians, the Salvation Army, and rural Fundamentalists, have put their unique stamp on religious folk song and style.

Religious folk music involves both texts and tunes. Both have been studied, the former by church historians as illuminating historical documents, the latter by folklorists as examples of folk music. Texts, of course, tell a great deal about those singing them; studies of the words of Negro spirituals, of camp meeting songs, and of urban revival, Holiness, and Pentecostal music have made important contributions to knowledge of specific periods.

Increasingly, however, folklorists studying religious folk music are attending to the broad theological, historical, and institutional context that gives meaning to religious folk music as religious. From the side of the study of American religion, much more attention needs to be given to the folk and musical dimensions of the texts. This is not to suggest that a degree in ethnomusicology is necessary to understand the material, but to say that the text is only part of the evidence. What kind of experience is involved in the singing of the song or listening to it? What role do tradition, emotion, and imagination play in the unique kind of bonding effected by music? Answers to such questions will involve careful attention to the details of performance, such as instrumentation, vocal timbre, and the relationship of musicians to congregation. The performance, in turn, must be understood in the larger context it at once expresses and reinforces.

The themes in American folk religion noted to this point—religious folk speech, play, story, morality, ritual and belief, and music—are by no means exhaustive. Historical and contemporary religious folk art, for example, expressed in a variety of forms ranging from paintings to shrines, attests to the ubiquity of the aesthetic impulse in American religion. Or studying (and tasting) traditional foods connected with religious feasts and festivals might well be the most satisfying way to approach folk religion.

A second way to approach American folk religion—and to appreciate the relation of religion to folklore—is to study readily identified religious folk groups. In this approach, themes and folk genres will be found to have been shaped by the interests and needs of particular groups.

RELIGIOUS FOLK GROUPS

Denominations, sects, and cults are the most obvious examples of religious folk groups, although the informal culture of relatively few has been investigated. Some attention has been devoted to Roman Catholic lore, particularly in its ethnic variations, to Methodist lore, and to a number of Fundamentalist groups. Jewish folklore, including dialect and immigrant stories, religious legends and folktales, and customs and festivals, has been more carefully documented.

Considerable attention has focused on the Mormons, whose relatively recent origin makes them a good case study of the evolution of informal culture. Although the earliest Mormon lore was anti-Mormon, subsequent experience generated legend-cycles about the two founders, Joseph Smith, Jr., and Brigham Young; songs celebrating the hegira from Nauvoo to the State of Deseret; humorous dialect stories involving Scandinavian converts who settled in southern Utah; and jokes about polygamy and folk heroes such as J. Golden Kimball, a church leader whose own transgressions of rules against "cussing" spawned a series of spicy anecdotes. In addition, legends about the miraculous interventions of heavenly visitors known as the Three Nephites began circulating after 1855 and continue unabated to the present day. Rooted in the larger Protestant tradition of recording remarkable providences as evidence of chosenness, such stories chronicle remarkable conversions, deliverances, and judgments, particularly for the benefit of struggling Mormon missionaries.

Communitarian societies, such as the Shakers, Harmonists, and Hutterians, typically conserve or generate folk culture. Although now all but defunct, the Shakers produced a rich body of religious folk song and folk narrative during the nineteenth century. Shaker art, crafts, and architecture, rooted in and expressive of the society's religious vision, remain famous for simple, elegant beauty.

Regional groups provide another window into American folk religion. In southeastern Pennsylvania, the German peasant culture of seventeenth- and eighteenth-century immigrants provided a cohesive bond for a wide variety of religions, ranging from the Old Order Amish to Mennonite, Moravian, Lutheran, Reformed, and German Methodist groups. Bound together by the Pennsylvania Dutch dialect, such groups also found common expression in proverbs, folk beliefs, folk healing, religious and secular songs, jokes, stories, legends, folk heroes, and what is perhaps the richest example of decorative art and handicraft in American culture. Another regional group, strikingly different from the Pennsylvania Dutch, emerged in the American South-West from the interplay of Hispanic, Mexican, Indian, and Catholic traditions. The Ozarks, a third region, reflects a full range of Anglo-American folk traditions in its folk religion.

Another kind of folk group is the ethnic community. One need not look very long to notice the persistence, even resurgence, of ethnic pluralism in modern America, or to observe the pivotal role that religion plays in shaping ethnic identity and that ethnicity plays in shaping religion. Thus one notes significant differences between Scandinavian and German Lutherans; Irish, Puerto Rican, and Italian Catholics; and German and Russian Jews. Among other factors, religious folk traditions play an important role in accounting for such distinctiveness.

Racial groups also have informal religious culture. For example, until recently, Amerindian culture seemed to be disappearing; its remnants were studied by anthropologists, purchased by tourists, and ridiculed in popular media. The "red power" movement of the 1960s, however, rekindled interest in Amerindian myth, legend, art, song, and festival. Such materials stimulated cultural renewal in many tribes and helped historians understand the tragic conflict between red and white cultures. Similarly, interest in Oriental-American folk cultures, renewed first by countercultural searching in the 1960s and then by the influx of immigrants from Southeast Asia, has led to greater appreciation of non-Western folk religion.

Most attention, however, has been devoted to black folk religion. In the crucible of slavery and segregation, Afro-Americans forged a unique religiosity out of a blend of West African and American Protestant traditions. Spirituals, originally shared with whites at camp meetings, and black gospel music, developed in conjunction with later urban revivalism, expressed a style and a piety at variance with those of the dominant white religious culture. The antiphonal, rhythmic distinctiveness of such music found expression as well in chanted sermons of rural and urban preachers, who shaped traditional themes and phrases into outcries against injustice. Stories and jokes with traditional trickster motifs portrayed the roguish slave outwitting his master and subtly embodied the same moral revulsion. At the periphery of the black church, lively supernaturalism and animism flourished, as well as stories that recount possessions, haunts, ghosts, cures, and prophetic visions.

Yet another kind of religious folk group is the occupational group. Clergy in all denominations are bound by a common lore; for example, nineteenth-century Methodist itinerants, particularly at gatherings like annual conferences, shared stories of preaching mishaps, the perils of wilderness traveling, and triumphant encounters with sinners. Among immersionist preachers, humorous stories of bungled baptisms circulate. Priests, nuns, ministers, and rabbis have an esoteric lore, as do seminarians and church bureaucrats of all denominations. In Roman Catholicism, different orders of clergy, such as Franciscans, Jesuits, or Benedictines, are distinguished by customs, festivals, narratives, and jokes (often at each other's expense). Enterprises tangentially connected with religion, such as funeral homes and the religious press, also have distinctive folklore.

In addition, the lore of many secular groups has religious content. Among aficionados of rock music, for example, supernatural legends circulate about the deaths of famous stars such as Buddy Holly and the "Big Bopper," fatefully occurring at ages that are multiples of three. Sightings of the deceased Jim Morrison recur regularly. Fraternal and civic organizations, such as the Masons, Knights of Columbus, Rotary, and Lions, perpetuate traditional ritual, as do Boy and Girl Scouts and college fraternities and sororities. In many corporations, founding fathers are granted informal canonization; miners, steelworkers, sailors, and soldiers, among many others, share lore with an often supernaturalistic content.

Finally, the family, insofar as it has any appreciable cohesion, is a religious folk group. Despite the assaults of modernity, the family often functions as more than a haven in a heartless world; it is a womb where religious, metaphysical, and ethical attitudes are nurtured. Not all family culture is folklore, nor is all family folklore overtly religious. Yet much family behavior falls into ritual patterns, follows traditional structures, is transmitted informally, and shapes world views. Stories about family ancestors and contemporary relatives, including "black sheep," not only entertain but enjoin appropriate behavior. Anecdotes about significant family events, including sicknesses, accidents, deaths, dreams, omens, and portents, express attitudes toward the transcendent. Such stories stick in the mind and heart; children particularly relish them and object vigorously if the parental performance lacks traditional detail. The kind of jokes permitted in a family shapes attitudes toward others; if a white Christian family privately jests about blacks and Jews while maintaining a facade of tolerance, both hypocrisy and intolerance may result. Parental proverbs sum up family morality, and folk beliefs guide activities such as cooking, cleaning, travel, and the maintenance of health. Family celebration of birthdays, anniversaries, and holidays almost always includes traditional ritual and implicitly teaches the difference between everyday and extraordinary time.

CONCLUSION

The study of folklore suggests a number of intriguing approaches to the study of religion and religious history in America.

First, it opens a window to the emotional and

imaginative core of religion. To know what the Mormons are like, read the *Book of Mormon;* better yet, laugh with them at the comic failings of J. Golden Kimball, listen to "The Handcart Song," or hear how a Nephite miraculously saved a young missionary. To understand historical change in the black church, read institutional chronicles; to appreciate it, listen to the difference between Vera Hall and Mahalia Jackson singing the same gospel hymn.

Second, the study of folklore reveals the emotional and imaginative soul of American history, which has developed in dialectical interplay with institutional religion. The mutual interaction of sacred and profane idealism is only partly understood without attention to the pivotal role informal culture plays in the secular realm.

Third, folklore suggests that history, and the history of religion, is not simply linear but is also cyclical. There was only one Half-Way Covenant, one Bishop Asbury, and one Second Vatican Council, but every year there are Christmas, Passover, and Saint Patrick's Day. Every year seasonal and national cycles turn. And there are wheels within the yearly wheels, even if only dimly felt by moderns: every month, a new moon; every week, a new Sabbath or Sunday; every day, a new sun. In counterpoint, each human life turns a circle of passages from birth to death. These multiple loops of cyclical time, in contrapuntal rhythm to the time line from Creation to the Last Judgment, link individuals to meanings and communities that transcend historical particularity. To understand Judaism in America, study the Torah, or Isaac M. Wise; better yet, eat matzoth and maror at a seder. The story of religion, in short, is only partially told if it remembers events that occurred but once; "once upon a time" experience needs to be remembered as well and is not forgotten by folk religion.

Fourth, whereas Western religion tends to demythologize, folk religion remythologizes. Divine providential intervention is alive and well in religious folk legends; the "other world" of ghosts, haunts, possessions, visions, and premonitions is sustained by supernatural legend. Liturgical, seasonal, and individual celebrations presuppose meanings that transcend time. The world of folk belief embodies a fatalistic supernaturalism. Although religious themes have all but disappeared in secular art, they thrive in religious folk art. Even jokes about heaven and hell perpetuate the picture of a triple-decker universe, replete with pearly gates, angels, harps, and clouds at the one extreme and demons with tails and pitchforks at the other. As noted above, generalizations about the triumph of secularism need to be weighed carefully against such evidence.

Fifth, folklore helps illuminate the proclivity of the American people to fuse elements from disparate belief systems into personally satisfying world views. Conservative Pennsylvania Dutch Christians may center their beliefs simultaneously around the Bible, chiropractic, and reflexology, preventive medicine through exercise and organic nutrition, and proverbial wisdom, fashioning an integrated system that appears to contradict high cultural norms of coherence. Roman Catholics who remain devoted to Saint Anne, Saint Anthony, or Saint Jude may otherwise embrace the Christological focus of the Second Vatican Council. Rural Fundamentalists who acknowledge the providential guidance of God in all things may plant their crops only under the most favorable astrological signs. A balanced account of religion in America should note that alternative belief systems do not exist in isolation from the practices of institutional churchgoers. Tendencies toward syncretism should be recognized by scholars, but even more by pastors, who may otherwise be preaching to and counseling a congregation that exists more in their textbooks than in the pews.

Sixth, the study of folklore shows how religion in America transcends not only institutional boundaries and elite sources but also the dominant religious culture. That is, folklore highlights the pluralism of American religion. At the level of popular culture, the "melting pot" may well be working toward homogeneity. Informal culture, however, particularly in its ethnic and regional variations, tenaciously guards heterogeneity with distinctive folk practice. The face of American religion is black, yellow, and red, southern and eastern European, Near Eastern and Russian, as well as Anglo-Saxon Protestant.

Religion in America smells and tastes, dances, laughs, dresses up, and plays. It makes pictures, icons, and stories of itself and delights in rituals of all kinds. It traffics in the bazaar, the homecoming game, and neighborly conversation as well as in the synod, parsonage, or seminary classroom. Nurtured in the family, it mirrors itself in the common culture. Confined to the church, it bursts out in a profusion of forms. Where institutional religion falters, religion in America fills the gaps, zealously surrounding everyday life with meaning, power, and grace from the storehouse of folk tradition.

BIBLIOGRAPHY

Dickson D. Bruce, *And They All Sang Hallelujah: Plain-folk Camp-Meeting Religion, 1800–1845* (1974); Jan H. Brunvand, *The Study of American Folklore* (1968; rev. 1978); Donald E. Byrne, Jr., *No Foot of Land: Folklore of American Methodist Itinerants* (1975); William M. Clements, "The Folk Church: Institution, Event, Performance," in *Handbook of American Folklore*, Richard M. Dorson, ed. (1983); C. Kurt Dewhurst, Betty MacDowell, and Marsha MacDowell, *Religious Folk Art in America: Reflections of Faith* (1983); Richard M. Dorson, *American Folklore* (1959); Alan Dundes, *The Study of Folklore* (1965) and *Interpreting Folklore* (1980); Lydia Fish, "Folklore in the Church" (1979; a cassette available from everett/edwards, inc., P.O. Box 1060, Deland, Fla. 32720); Cathleen C. Flanagan and John T. Flanagan, *American Folklore: A Bibliography, 1950–74* (1977).

Charles Haywood, *A Bibliography of North American Folklore and Folksong* (1951; rev. 1961); David J. Hufford, *The Terror That Comes in the Night: An Experience-Centered Study of Supernatural Assault-Traditions* (1982) and "The Supernatural and the Sociology of Knowledge: Explaining Academic Belief," in *New York Folklore*, 9 (1983); Elaine J. Lawless, "Shouting for the Lord: The Power of Women's Speech in the Pentecostal Religious Service," in *Journal of American Folklore*, 96 (1983); C. Grant Loomis, *White Magic: An Introduction to the Folklore of Christian Legend* (1948); John Messenger, "Folk Religion," in *Folklore and Folklife, An Introduction*, Richard M. Dorson, ed. (1972); Venetia Newall, *An Egg at Easter: A Folklore Study* (1971); Américo Paredes and Richard Bauman, eds., *Toward New Perspectives in Folklore* (1972).

Constance Rourke, *American Humor: A Study of the National Character* (1931); Barre Toelken, *The Dynamics of Folklore* (1979); Francis X. Weiser, *Handbook of Christian Feasts and Customs: The Year of the Lord in Liturgy and Folklore* (1958); Peter W. Williams, *Popular Religion in America: Symbolic Change and the Modernization Process in Historical Perspective* (1980); Don Yoder, "Official Religion versus Folk Religion," in *Pennsylvania Folklife*, 15 (1965–66), "Toward a Definition of Folk Religion," in *Western Folklore*, 33 (1974), "Introductory Bibliography on Folk Religion," in *Western Folklore*, 33 (1974), and, as ed., *American Folklife* (1976); Steven J. Zeitlin, Amy J. Kotkin, and Holly Cutting-Baker, *A Celebration of American Family Folklore* (1982).

[*See also* POPULAR CULTURE.]

THEOLOGICAL INTERPRETATIONS AND CRITIQUES OF AMERICAN SOCIETY AND CULTURE

James H. Moorhead

IN 1854, Philip Schaff, a Swiss-born and German-educated historian and theologian who had spent the previous decade as a seminary professor in Pennsylvania, returned to Germany. Speaking in Frankfurt on 20 September, he offered this assessment of his adopted country:

> In short, if anywhere in the wide world a new page of universal history has been unfolded and a new fountain opened, fraught with incalculable curses or blessings for future generations, it is in the Republic of the United States with her star-spangled banner. Either humanity has no earthly future and everything is tending to destruction, or this future lies—I say not exclusively, but mainly—in America, according to the victorious march of history, with the sun from east to west.
>
> (*America*, Perry Miller, ed., 1961, p. 212)

America would bless or curse the world, but either way it held the key to the future.

This view has typified the vast majority of theological interpretations of America from the colonial era to the present. With relatively few dissenting voices until the twentieth century, analysts of the American experience have presupposed their culture's extraordinary status in the divine economy; often extolling the nation's glories, sometimes damning its faults, they have seldom questioned that America is the locus of a drama whose outcome carries universal significance.

The first intimations of America's uniqueness appeared when colonists had scarcely set foot on these shores. The discovery of the New World elicited two conflicting images in the minds of Europeans—paradise and wilderness—and the two would long play against one another as symbols of America's meaning.

According to many sixteenth- and seventeenth-century writers, the New World exhibited nature in its original untainted form; and this happy environment nurtured an American Adam and Eve. Often pictured disporting in the nude and showing little concern for the European obsession with private property, the aborigines displayed a generosity and simplicity far removed from the effete civilizations of the Old World. "We found the people," wrote an early English visitor to Roanoke Island, off the Carolinas, "most gentle, loving, and faithful, void of all guile and treason, and such as live after the manner of the golden age" (quoted in Mumford Jones, p. 19).

America, in short, was a new Eden untouched by the ravages of the Fall. It presented Europeans with an opportunity to slough off the past and start life anew like Adam at the dawn of creation. A characteristic of the New World, said the Italian cleric Peter Martyr in 1511, was that "each day it creates without ceasing." It is little wonder, then, that Sir Thomas More set his vision of *Utopia* (1516) somewhere to the west of Europe and that Francis Bacon placed his ideal society, *The New Atlantis* (1627), in the same region.

Yet America also cast shadows. If its pristine character suggested escape from civilized decadence, it also represented untamed power threatening the precarious good humankind had achieved. This darker Eden—Eden after the Fall—appeared almost as soon as the Arcadian image of innocence. Travelers reported cannibalism and other atrocities committed by the native American Adam. These accounts evoked another vision of nature long present in the Christian tradition—the wilderness whose ferocious creatures and inhospitable environment made it a fitting symbol of sin and the curse of God. According to this interpretation, the New World was something to be feared and subdued or was at best a place of spiritual catharsis where one would fight, as did Jesus, the temptations of the devil.

These two visions existed side by side, often in the work of a single author. Thus Amerigo Vespucci, in a letter to Lorenzo de Medici (1503), claimed that the New World afforded a temperate environment enabling its denizens to live 150 years, and he opined that the "terrestrial paradise" might lie in that region. Yet Vespucci simultaneously averred that America contained "horrible creatures and deformed beasts" and that its inhabitants "mutually kill with great cruelty." This awkward conjunction of images left the meaning of the new land problematic. Was America an Eden to be celebrated or a wilderness to be subdued? Did the American Adam and Eve live before or after the Fall? Perhaps in those unanswered questions lay one of the roots of the perennial ambivalence toward the Indian, sometimes portrayed as a noble primitive like James Fenimore Cooper's Chingachgook, but more frequently depicted as a savage to be exterminated or at least confined to the reservation for the betterment of civilization. Perhaps here also was a premonition of America's propensity to sentimentalize scenes of unspoiled nature even as it built the factories, cities, and automobiles that destroyed those vistas.

Of all the early theological interpretations of American culture, none was more significant than that of the English Puritans who swarmed to Massachusetts and its environs after 1630. While critics have sometimes complained of the disproportionate attention lavished on New England Puritanism, the fact remains that few, if any, religious traditions have exercised a comparably decisive influence in shaping Americans' understanding of themselves.

The Puritans immigrated with the sense of a divinely appointed mission. They were to be a New Israel, a new chosen people. Governor John Winthrop of the Massachusetts Bay colony reminded his people that they were engaged in the establishment of a Christian commonwealth des-

tined to serve as a model for the Old World. "We shall find that the God of Israel is among us," said Winthrop; ". . . we must consider that we shall be a city upon a hill, the eyes of all people are upon us" (*A Modell of Christian Charity*, in *The Founding of Massachusetts*, Edmund S. Morgan, ed., 1964, p. 203). The colonists undertook this exemplary task at a propitious moment, for the signs of the age indicated that the Apocalypse was about to be fulfilled. After centuries of "popish" darkness, the Roman Catholic church—the whore of Babylon—teetered on the verge of collapse, and the long-promised millennium of Revelation, chapter 20, might soon come to pass. In this drama, New Englanders would play a crucial role by providing an example of thoroughgoing reform to Europeans still struggling to escape the dark night of superstition. "For your full assurance," Edward Johnson reminded colonists in 1654, "know this is the place where the Lord will create a new Heaven and a new Earth . . . , new Churches and a new Commonwealth together" (*Wonder-Working Providence*, J. Franklin Jameson, ed., 1910, p. 35). New England's errand, in short, was to renew Christendom in preparation for the latter days. In America, history might discover its proper end by recovering its lost beginning. The wilderness, emblematic of sin, might become the restored Eden and, in fulfillment of eschatological promise, blossom as the rose.

A different future, however, might betray those intoxicating dreams. Because much had been given to the people of New England, much would be expected of them. Having entered into solemn covenant with God, the colonists would suffer divine punishment if recreant to their obligations. Or, in John Winthrop's words, "the Lord will surely break out in wrath against us, [and] be revenged of such a perjured people." The Puritan clergy institutionalized this threat in a sermonic form known as the jeremiad (so named after the Hebrew prophet Jeremiah). Whenever moral declension—real or imagined—occurred, the clergy fulminated that God was about to voice his wrath or had in fact already thundered his displeasure in some disaster. Indian attacks, epidemics, and squabbles with the Crown over the Massachusetts charter were among the evidence that God disagreed with his people. Through the jeremiad, an elect community engaged in criticism of itself.

Self-exaltation and self-abasement were not mutually exclusive conclusions that the colonists could deduce from the fact of a special mission. These conclusions presupposed each other and in fact were alternating modes in a single process defining New England's election. The very extravagance of condemnatory rhetoric testified to the special status of New England. Moreover, the clergy couched its words of judgment in language implying that God's wrath was corrective rather than punitive, and in this way confirmed that the colonists were indeed a chosen people. Through the jeremiad, the clergy elicited anxiety and self-criticism as a means of rededication to the community's holy errand. As Sacvan Bercovitch has demonstrated, the jeremiad, though later transmuted into forms that the Puritans would not have recognized and transferred to the entire United States, has remained one of the most enduring rituals of cultural consensus. Celebrations of the nation's grandeur, interspersed with fervent denunciations of its betrayal of that trust, have tended to reinforce Americans' conviction that they are a people set apart. While this process has made American self-understanding remarkably adaptive to criticism, it has also tended to remove the sting from protest by forcing the dissenter to frame objections in terms that tacitly assume American exceptionalism. Dissent has, as it were, been encouraged and then co-opted into the prevailing national consensus.

Yet its legacies to subsequent generations notwithstanding, the Puritan vision of the New World did not go unchallenged. Although they set in motion far-reaching changes, most New England Puritans still harbored medieval views about the nature of church, state, and society—a fact that dissenters such as Roger Williams, Anne Hutchinson, and the Quakers learned to their sorrow. Between the late 1600s and the antebellum era, at least four major developments challenged the assumptions of the first Puritans: (1) increased religious pluralism (albeit still largely Protestant in character), accompanied by eventual disestablishment of churches and by religious toleration; (2) the Enlightenment; (3) a widespread "democritization of mind," as Gordon Wood calls it, which became manifest in the Revolution and its aftermath; and (4) the evangelical revivals that began with the First Great Awakening and then recurred more

systematically in the Second Great Awakening. These trends helped to make America more thoroughly novel than even the most radical of the first Puritan settlers could have imagined. In this context, many people found themselves searching for updated theological answers to Michel Guillaume Jean de Crèvecoeur's famous question in *Letters from an American Farmer* (1782): "What then is the American, this new man?"

According to those who most fully imbibed the spirit of the Enlightenment, the answer was that the American lived in nature's nation. *Nature* did not mean, as it later did for many romantics, a reality transcending human understanding and best grasped by intuition or imagination. It denoted instead an orderly universe governed by laws that could be discerned through patient observation. Freeing themselves from the superstition of the past, Americans would accept as truths only those ideas or practices that rational investigation supported. One can see this mentality in diverse manifestations: in the scientific experiments of Benjamin Franklin; in Thomas Jefferson's appeal to the laws of nature and of nature's God for support of revolution; and in the confidence of the makers of the federal Constitution that a compact, framed in accordance with the observed facts of human nature, could establish an effective political order. In all spheres, Americans were throwing off ignorance and adjusting themselves to the pre-established harmony of nature. Or as Delaware lawyer Caesar Rodney wrote to Jefferson in an assessment of the Age of Enlightenment and Revolution: "Every door is now open to the Sons of Genius and Science to inquire after Truth. Hence we may expect the darkening clouds of error will vanish fast before the light of reason; and that the period is fast arriving when the Truth will enlighten the whole world" (quoted in May, p. 164).

Taken to its logical conclusion, the Enlightenment's definition of America might have been a prescription for a nation of freethinkers; and there were such individuals. Franklin, Jefferson, and Washington typified a discreet deism popular among many educated Americans in the late eighteenth century. After the Revolution, this heterodox impulse flamed openly, if briefly, in the writings of men—such as Thomas Paine, Elihu Palmer, and Ethan Allen—who sought to expunge the vestiges of traditional Christianity from America's self-understanding. Yet these individuals were relatively few in number and were soon overwhelmed by an evangelical crusade to reaffirm the specifically Christian character of American culture.

Reinvigorated by the Second Great Awakening (often dated from the 1790s to the 1830s), Protestantism offered its own definition of the meaning of America. While in some respects a repudiation of the Enlightenment's idea of the United States as an empire of reason and a reaffirmation of older Puritan themes, the evangelical crusade did not merely revert to an earlier ideal. It revitalized that ideal in light of the Revolution, the Enlightenment, and religious pluralism. It created a new cultural consensus about the meaning of America.

According to evangelicals, America was God's country because it united Protestant religion with a republican-democratic political order. To secure that fortunate combination, God had providentially hidden the New World from settlement until after the Reformation and the first stirrings of freedom in Europe. Had God done otherwise, immigrants would have perpetuated in America a decadent Catholicism and the remnants of feudal civilization. In averting that catastrophe, the Lord had signaled his intention to raise up in the New World an ideal nation, one that wedded true religion to libertarian social principles. Constituted on this happy basis, America would enjoy material as well as moral progress and would serve as a model for the renovation of the world. Protestants often described this destiny in an eschatological symbolism that cast the United States as a redeemer nation preparing the way for the Kingdom of God on earth. By the early 1800s, many Protestants were boldly declaring what Jonathan Edwards had ventured only cautiously during the First Great Awakening; namely, that the millennium might begin in America. This confidence usually assumed a postmillennial form; that is, it was predicated on the belief that Christ would return after the millennium and that Christians would in the interim build the Kingdom of God on earth.

Thus antebellum Protestants maintained the Puritan vision of America as revivifier of Christendom and harbinger of the millennium, but they infused those dreams with libertarian, democratic meaning. They spoke, in the words of the *Ladies' Repository,* a Methodist publication, in 1850, of "civilization, republicanism, and Christianity" as interdependent elements. In the gentle atmosphere of freedom, the churches prospered, demonstrating what one speaker to the American Home Missionary Society called in 1848 "the power of an untrammeled Gospel" (Rev. Erskine Mason, *An Evangelical Ministry,* p. 23). Liberated from coercive efforts by the civil authorities to suppress their activity and likewise from the stultifying effects of state aid, the churches were thrown back on persuasion to effect their goals, and therein they discovered an extraordinary power.

Advocates of this voluntary principle seldom tired of contrasting its superior efficacy to the system of state-supported churches in Europe. Thus Robert Baird in his classic *Religion in America* (1844), which was originally written to explain American Christianity to Europeans, boasted of the number of churches created, religious schools founded, Bibles distributed, and social evils combated by the free association of devoted believers. Yet if freedom benefited the churches, democracy had an even greater need for the Christian faith. Religion had to make democracy safe for itself. Given the inherent sinfulness of human nature, liberty naturally tended toward lawlessness and anarchy. The only effectual restraints against this degeneration lay in persuading people, through the power of the Gospel, to exercise freedom in an orderly and self-disciplined fashion. As Baird put the matter: "Nothing but the Bible can make men the willing subjects of law; they must first acquiesce with submission in the government of God before they can yield a willing obedience to the requirements of human governments" (1970 abridgement, Henry Wainer Bowden, ed., p. 153). Or as Schaff summed up, the inner meaning of America was that "the impulse towards freedom and the sense of law and order are inseparably united, and both rest on a moral basis" (p. 47).

Religious pluralism was a potential obstacle to this vision of a people united by their loyalty to God. With the churches having accepted the principle of disestablishment and with a multiplicity of religious bodies scattered across the nation, even wildly partisan denominationalists could no longer imagine that their particular churches would eventually displace all rivals. At what point on this fragmented religious landscape would Americans find the common values and purpose enabling their culture to be a single Christian civilization? The answer lay in what Perry Miller called "the concordance of dissent." It was assumed that beneath denominational imbroglios over such issues as the proper mode of baptism, church government, or free will lay a core of shared values: though they fought one another over tangential matters, the individual churches were establishing a cultural consensus about essential issues of faith and morals. This assumption governed Baird's assessment of American church life, for he emphasized those areas in which religious bodies cooperated and ignored those where they differed. A similar conviction enlivened Schaff's faith that America was destined "to be the Phenix grave" of old loyalties and "that out of the mutual conflict of all something wholly new will gradually arise" (pp. 80–81).

Most theologians took for granted that this unifying perspective would be essentially Protestant. In spite of their acceptance of disestablishment, most church people did not unreservedly accede to pluralism. They remained as committed as their Puritan ancestors to an America whose mores and ethos would lie under Protestant dominion. Only the tactics for attaining that goal had changed. While relatively few people engaged in the uglier excesses of anti-immigrant or nativist crusading, most would have agreed with the Presbyterian minister who declared in 1867: "This is a Christian Republic, our Christianity being of the Protestant type. . . . As for this land, we [Protestants] have taken possession of it in the name of the Lord Jesus Christ; and, if he will give us grace to do it, we mean to hold it for him till he come" (S. M. Campbell, in *American and Theological Review,* July 1867, 390–391). Before the Civil War, the first surge of non-Protestant immigration was already preparing the conditions that would eventually challenge this vision of America. But in the early nineteenth century—nativist fears notwithstanding—the evangelical dream still seemed attainable. America would be simultaneously democratic and Protestant, an evangelical empire flourishing under religious toleration; for the millennium was in the offing.

Different but equally exuberant descriptions of nineteenth-century America's destiny came from outside the churches. Literature, which increasingly exhibited an American self-consciousness in the antebellum period, likewise celebrated the promise of the United States, often in symbols richly suggestive of religious meaning. No one exemplified this outlook better than the former Unitarian minister turned writer and lecturer Ralph Waldo Emerson. Perhaps the fundamental dictum of his thought was a call to each person to sustain "an original relation to the universe." In his Phi Beta Kappa oration of 1837, Emerson applied that prescription to the nation as a whole. "We have listened too long," he complained, "to the courtly muses of Europe"; but he predicted: "We will [henceforth] walk on our own feet. . . . A nation of men will for the first time exist, because each believes himself inspired by the Divine Soul which also inspires all men."

Motivating Emerson's confidence was his belief that the United States could indeed be nature's nation, albeit in a sense different than the one proposed by the Enlightenment thinkers of the previous century. Emerson viewed nature with eyes trained by Romanticism and Idealism. For him nature was a mystic spiritual harmony disclosing God, and all people could directly intuit that harmony because God was in every soul. This metaphysics justified America's revolt against the past, provided a religious charter for democracy, and affirmed the boundless potential for American self-expression.

Other literary figures, perhaps most notably Walt Whitman, explored the dynamism of that self-expression. In "Song of Myself," Whitman apotheosized the self—a quintessentially *American* self—that could virtually re-create the world out of consciousness. That restless energy propelled Americans westward to fulfill their Manifest Destiny of transcontinental empire, and Whitman gloried in the result. In "Pioneers! O Pioneers!" he exulted: "All the past we leave behind; / We debouch upon a newer, mightier world." In the process, "Never was average man, his soul, more energetic, more like a god."

Likewise, James Fenimore Cooper, in spite of growing reservations about the course of American democracy, created a classic image of an emerging new world. In his Leatherstocking series, he began with an aged protagonist and in succeeding books traced him back to his youth. Fenimore Cooper depicted a hero who, in tune with nature's rhythms, seemed capable of perpetual renewal; and this artistic strategy yielded what D. H. Lawrence later called "the true myth of America. She starts old. . . . And there is a gradual sloughing off of the old skin, towards a new youth." In a similar fashion, George Bancroft, whose *History of the United States of America* was one of the nineteenth century's most celebrated pieces of research, premised his multivolume chronicle on the idea that the United States represented a new beginning: America came into being when God willed for "humanity to make for itself a new existence."

In these and other literary figures, one discerns themes analogous to ideas preached to the masses from Protestant pulpits across the land. Like the ministers, the men of letters gloried in America's exceptional status, marveled at its opportunity to begin history anew, and expected from it a golden age of democratic felicity.

Beyond the mainstream of both literary and ecclesiastical culture, various sectarian and communitarian groups adumbrated their own visions of America's extraordinary place in the divine economy. Of these bodies, the most notable—certainly the most durable—was the Church of Jesus Christ of Latter-day Saints, better known as the Mormon church. Founded in 1830 by Joseph Smith, the Latter-day Saints claimed a new Scripture, *The Book of Mormon,* which purportedly chronicled America's civilization long before the age of Christopher Columbus; and they also believed that they were receiving continuing revelations through their prophet-president Smith. With a New World Scripture supplemented by New World revelations, the Mormons constructed one of the most theologically explicit analyses of American uniqueness to emerge from any religious community.

According to Smith, America was literally the beginning and end of God's plan. The Garden of Eden had been located in the New World; and after their expulsion from paradise, Adam and Eve dwelt at Adam-ondi-Ahman, not far from Independence, Missouri. In the fullness of time when God wished to restore the primitive purity of the church and bring his purpose to eschatological fulfillment, he chose the land where creation had begun. To secure its safety amid democratic institutions, he reestablished the church (Mormonism) and commissioned it with the task of building the Kingdom of God on earth, beginning in the United States. Never were the

Adamic and millennial myths so prevalent in American culture more literally espoused. By comparison to Joseph Smith's vision, the glorification of America in Whitman, Emerson, or the evangelical pulpit appeared almost pallid. That the Mormons were teaching fundamental myths of the culture became apparent when, once they had renounced their tribalism and the institution of polygyny, many of their fellow citizens hailed them as representatives of archetypal American values.

Despite these varied celebrations, antebellum Americans were not without inklings that the nation's future might hold something other than millennial glory and an Eden restored. Nathaniel Hawthorne used his fiction—for example, *The Scarlet Letter* and *The House of the Seven Gables*—to probe the darkness in the human soul and to suggest that overly optimistic efforts to evade this shadow would only compound tragedy. Likewise, Herman Melville—at least in some of his works—appeared to question whether any cultural myth could fully correspond to the terrors and enigmas of ultimate reality; and, with Hawthorne, he implied that aspirations in that direction might prove demonic. In *Pierre* (1852), one of his characters, Plotinus Plinlimmon, remarks: The person who believes "that he must, while on earth, aim at heaven, and attain it, too, in all his earthly acts . . . is too apt to run clean away into all manner of moral abandonment, self-deceit, and hypocrisy." Melville illustrated that principle most forcefully in *Moby-Dick* (1851), where Captain Ahab's Promethean quest to harpoon the white whale destroys him and his crew. Yet however profound their message, it was not from such works that the majority of Americans gained knowledge of the moral ambiguities of their national life. That awareness came from a more immediate source: slavery and the fratricidal war it produced.

More than any other dilemma in the nineteenth century, the issue of slavery disclosed the moral evasions of the American experience and brought into focus divergent interpretations of the nation's meaning. Those differing views in large measure turned on a crucial distinction: Did the meaning of America reside in a completed system to be protected or in a set of values to be advanced? Was America a sacred polity to be preserved or a sacred principle still in the process of realization? Many Americans viewed the federal Union as an object of transcendent worth because it embodied a nearly perfect political order and because it carried the hopes of the world. Therefore the Union had to be maintained at all costs. As the Methodist bishop Leonidas Hamline declared in 1841: "No government excels our own. Its prominent features are so nearly what one might desire that there is small chance for improvement. . . . Our office is to preserve, not to create" (*Works*, F. G. Hibbard, ed., pp. 399–400). As invoked by unionists such as Daniel Webster, this preservationist rhetoric served as a call for sectional compromise and mutual forbearance in the face of the divisive question of human bondage.

After the 1830s, a small but growing antislavery vanguard grew restive with this conservatism. Believing the sacredness of the nation to reside in its democratic principles, they called on the United States to proclaim liberty for the captives, even at peril to the Union. While relatively few were willing to accept the extreme position of William Lloyd Garrison that the Constitution was a pact with the devil, many did feel that the mere survival of the United States intact did not constitute a patriotism lofty enough to command respect. For them the fulfillment of American election required self-criticism and repentance for the sin of slavery. Moreover, at least some antislavery crusaders—most notably Garrison and his circle—also added items such as nonresistance and women's rights to the reform agenda and insisted that the nation must address these issues as well if it were to fulfill its mission of liberty. Although only a handful of northerners became full-blown abolitionists, growing numbers did believe, after the 1840s, that further expansion of the "Slave Power" had to be stopped if the nation were to maintain its integrity. It was on such a platform of nonextension that the Republican party won its first presidential contest in 1860.

In the antebellum South, the vision of America was complex. Especially in the border states, and even in the deep South until the secession crisis, strong unionist sentiment existed. Increasingly, however, southerners emphasized that their culture embodied a distinct way of life superior to that of the Yankees. Historians have attributed this sense of difference to the South's peculiar institution, its predominantly agrarian character, and its identification with the cavalier myth and the code of chivalry. Yet it was evangelical Protestantism, more than any other force, that shaped these elements into a distinctive southern identity. Southerners gloried that theirs was a Bible-based culture and that they, more than their neighbors above the Mason-Dixon Line, embodied the evangelical ideal. That boast became more shrill after the 1830s when abolitionist attacks and Nat Turner's slave revolt (1831) threw the South on the defensive. Unlike Yankee rabble-rousers who played fast and loose with the Scriptures to support abolition, the people of the South claimed to adhere to the literal meaning of the Bible, as their acceptance of slavery's divine sanction testified. While northerners might prostitute religion in the service of radical political causes, southerners preserved what the Presbyterian James H. Thornwell called the spirituality of the church. In a word, the clergy progressively identified the sacred element in American culture with the *southern* way of life.

When war came in 1861, both sections were armed with appropriate theological rationales. For the South, the struggle was a holy one to repel Yankee aggression. Dixie stood for a sacred amalgam of states' rights, agrarianism, and biblical religion, uncorrupted by "infidel" abolitionists or would-be tyrants of the North. For Yankees, the battle was to preserve the redeemer nation and to guarantee that the light of freedom would remain lit, not only for America but for the entire world. In successfully putting down the rebellion, northerners would demonstrate the viability of republican government and provide an object lesson for the world.

The Civil War thus assumed universal significance, and many people drew on eschatological imagery to suggest that the struggle was an apocalyptic war to fulfill biblical prediction and bring in the Kingdom of God. On the hot summer night when Julia Ward Howe penned her lines describing the "coming of the Lord" in the "watch-fires of a hundred circling camps," she gave utterance to a widespread faith. Undoubtedly, Confederates could also have sung her "Battle Hymn of the Republic" with equal fervor, though with a different view of whose army was responsible for the advent.

The war would inaugurate a new era by cleansing the sins of the nation in a baptism of blood. Depending on their political and religious persuasions, theologians differed about the nature of the transgression for which atonement was required. Many named slavery as the great offense, while others believed the excesses of unbridled democratic individualism had called forth retribution. In both instances, the sin would be bled away and Americans would be reborn, in the words of Baptist preacher Henry Clay Fish, as a "God-fearing, liberty-loving" people "bound together in one tender and beautiful brotherhood" (*The Valley of Achor,* 1863, p. 22). The Congregational theologian-pastor Horace Bushnell developed the theme of moral rebirth with particular power (*Reverses Needed,* 1861). Prior to the war, he said, Americans lacked an authentic common life. Rather than constituting a single folk, they had existed only as an aggregation of individuals recognizing no higher loyalty or shared moral purpose. But out of terrible suffering—"tears in the houses, as well as blood in the field"—America would become a regenerated and united nation.

No one expressed a theological interpretation of the war with greater eloquence than the sixteenth president of the United States, and his death at the moment of victory subsequently endowed his words with hagiographic significance. Abraham Lincoln voiced the common northern faith that the Union was "the last, best hope of earth" and that the war was thus a crucial test of republicanism everywhere. Yet his understanding of the conflict transcended a mere chauvinistic certainty that God was on the northern side, and his profundity was perhaps most apparent in his Second Inaugural Address. Alluding to the fact that the war had come in spite of the wishes of North and South, that it had endured long past their expectations, and that it had surprised both by destroying slavery, Lincoln concluded: "The prayers of both could not be answered; that of neither has been answered fully. The Almighty has His own purposes." And what were those purposes? The president suspected that God willed the conflict to "continue, until all the wealth piled by the bond-man's two hundred and fifty years of unrequited toil shall be sunk, and until every drop of blood drawn with the lash, shall be repaid with another drawn with the sword."

Yet having speculated about the divine plan, Lincoln then returned to the immediate duty incumbent upon America: "With malice toward none; with charity for all . . . to bind up the nation's wounds." Lincoln's great achievement was that he tempered his faith in the justice of the Union's cause with an awareness of the inscrutability of divine providence, and he saw the appropriate fruits of America's bloody ordeal to be charity and justice rather than self-righteousness and vindictiveness.

Unfortunately, subsequent views of the war often lacked Lincoln's sensitivity. Whether it was ex-Confederates lamenting the Lost Cause or Union veterans gathering in the Grand Army of the Republic to wave the "bloody shirt," many Victorian Americans viewed the conflict through the lens of unreflective partisanship. In the North, wartime success bred smug self-righteousness; in the South defeat brought a nostalgic glorification of the nation that had died and cast an aura of moonlight and magnolias over the lost world of the antebellum plantation. In both instances, the deeper moral issues over which Americans had fought were trivialized or obscured. To the extent that ideological reunification of the nation occurred, Afro-Americans paid the price, for victor and vanquished soon tacitly agreed to end Reconstruction without securing the political and social rights of the former slaves.

The failure of the war to issue in Lincoln's "new birth of freedom" did not, however, dim faith in America's providential mission. The foreign missionary enterprise surged to new prominence after the late 1880s, and a major premise of that movement was America's cultural superiority and concomitant responsibility to uplift less favored peoples. New outpourings of blood again became religious causes, first in the Spanish-American War of 1898 and again in the crusade to "make the world safe for democracy" in 1917.

Yet despite these continued paeans to the redeemer nation, evidence accumulated that the meaning of America needed to be rethought amid a new set of social and intellectual realities. The "new immigration" deepened the pluralism of America, as ever larger numbers of non-Protestants poured through Ellis Island. Rapid urban growth eroded older social patterns. Burgeoning industries and giant corporations undercut the ideal of the United States as a nation of independent workers, farmers, and owners of small businesses. A culture of professional and managerial expertise gradually gained ascendancy. Moreover, the rise of biblical criticism and Darwinian theory posed serious questions about evangelical beliefs long basic to the self-understanding of many Americans.

One effort to adapt Christianity—and by implication the vision of America—to this new milieu was Protestant liberalism. A diverse religious phenomenon that achieved the status of a movement by the 1880s, liberalism insisted, in the words of William Hutchison, "that theology must adopt a sympathetic attitude toward secular culture and must consciously strive to come to terms with it" (*American Protestant Thought*, 1985). That conviction was nurtured by the liberals' faith in the indwelling presence of the divine within modern culture and by their confidence that this immanent God was moving history in a desirable direction. Thus liberals could trust themselves to modern culture—whether manifest in the discoveries of Darwin, the biblical critics, or inventors—because God spoke in those places. While not oblivious to the faults of the age, liberals remained confident that its basic currents were carrying the world toward the Kingdom of God. They assumed that this process, though worldwide, had reached its furthest advance in the Western nations, especially in the United States. Analyzed as a cultural phenomenon, liberalism was in part a way for traditional faith in the religious character and destiny of America to express itself amid the realities of a postbellum world.

If liberalism at its worst tended toward an uncritical acceptance of American culture, at its best it promoted a serious encounter with modernity and led to a reappraisal of American values. This aspect of liberalism was nowhere more apparent than in the Social Gospel, which was largely a submovement within liberalism. The Social Gospel continued under a new guise the old Protestant dream of a Christian America, but the movement recognized that a basic retooling of social ethics was imperative if that goal were to be attained in an urban-industrial world.

In accord with liberalism in general, Social Gospelers argued that the central motif of Christianity was the Kingdom of God—an ideal they understood to emphasize the collective and this-worldly character of Christianity. As Walter Rauschenbusch, chief theologian of the Social Gospel, asserted in *Christianity and the Social Crisis* (1907, p. 31): Establishing the kingdom "is not a matter of saving human atoms, but of saving the social organism. It is not a matter of getting individuals to heaven, but of transforming the life on earth into the harmony of heaven." The Kingdom of God thus stood as a rebuke to all individualistic interpretations of Christianity and to the laissez-faire economics then enshrined as orthodoxy. The message of the kingdom was a summons to displace the present competitive capitalism—with its terrible disparities of wealth—with a more cooperative and equitable social order.

Although Social Gospelers often spoke vaguely about the precise nature of that order, its central quality was clear. Most expected the establishment by evolutionary (rather than revolutionary) means of some sort of non-Marxist democratic socialism or at least of a regulated capitalism. Like the political Progressives whom they supported, advocates of the Social Gospel shared a faith in the deliberate management of the socioeconomic order; and together both movements represented an effort to wed an old-fashioned moralistic view of society with the new ethos of professional expertise, bureaucratic organization, and rational planning. In short, the Social Gospel, despite its often trenchant criticism of existing social structures, was a restatement rather than a repudiation of American exceptionalism. In the tradition of the Puritan jeremiad, the movement sought to purge the United States of its defects and then to send it forward revitalized in pursuit of its unique errand.

A different understanding of America's meaning took shape in a nascent Fundamentalism. In the process of formation at least from the 1870s, this movement was in reality not a single entity but rather a congeries of ideas and persons united solely by a commitment to traditional Protestant evangelicalism (or at least their conception of it) and a determination to prevent its erosion by the acids of modernity. Within this emerging movement was ample room for diverse interpretations of American culture. Proto-fundamentalism included old-fashioned postmillennialists (such as William Jennings Bryan) who, in the tradition of Robert Baird, looked toward the gradual perfecting of America as an evangelical empire; but the movement also counted within its ranks militant premillennialists—that is, those who expected the return of Jesus before the millennium—and these persons often portrayed all existing nations, including the United States, as part of a decadent order sliding to an inevitable doom.

During World War I and shortly thereafter, these disparate elements coalesced in a crusade to purge the churches of liberalism and to save the public schools from the virus of evolution. The fierceness of the effort to protect the public schools testified to the significant role that those institutions had long played in transmitting religious interpretations of American culture. Throughout the nineteenth century, schoolchildren had read lessons extolling the nation's glory and attributing its greatness to Christianity. When evolution invaded the public schools, it thus symbolized for many an attack on one of the major bastions of evangelical hegemony. Conservative anxieties were augmented by a sense of cultural crisis in the wake of the Great War—a crisis fueled by rapid demobilization, the fear of bolshevism, labor unrest, and a vaguely focused sense that old moral landmarks had fallen.

William Jennings Bryan's prominence in the movement notwithstanding, Fundamentalism as a whole took on an increasingly strident premillennial tone as critics espied everywhere the signs of America's terrifying moral decline. Yet that rhetoric of impending doom must not be accepted at face value. Even if the logic of the premillennial position might seem to indicate that apostasy was inevitable and America's doom sealed, Fundamentalists strove mightily, as if under the impression that decline could be reversed. No more than their modernist opponents had the Fundamentalists given up the ideal of American uniqueness. The Fundamentalists differed only about what constituted that exceptional status: their ideal was a supposed mid-nineteenth-century evangelical dominance of American life.

While liberals attempted to revitalize the vision of America by adapting it to new social and intellectual realities, Fundamentalists tried to recover an older cultural consensus. Though defeated in the 1920s, the Fundamentalist dream of a golden age from which America has declined and which, despite the logic of premillennialism, it might yet recapture, has continued to be a powerful minority current in national life.

Another kind of ambivalence about the meaning of America had long been common outside the ranks of white Protestantism. Catholics, Jews, and blacks occupied an uncertain place in a nation whose ethos was mostly Anglo-Saxon Protestant. Stigmatized as different by faith, race, ethnicity, or immigrant status, such people wondered whether they had a share in the nation's meaning. Their theological evaluations of America were in large measure an attempt to answer that question.

For Roman Catholics, the assessment of America was complicated by the fact that the church espoused teachings seemingly incompatible with national values. Besieged by the forces of nationalism and liberalism after the French Revolution, the Roman See issued pronouncements condemning democracy, the separation of church and state, and religious toleration. Although these strictures were aimed more at anti-clericalism in Europe than at the relatively benign liberalism of America, they did suggest that the spirit of Catholicism was perhaps too medieval to permit a wholehearted embrace of American ideals. (When apologists for the faith tried to forget this fact, Protestant nativists were more than willing to remind them.) Yet most American Catholics, while loyal to Rome, did embrace America sincerely. Catholics were, in short, simultaneously insiders and outsiders in American culture.

From that dual experience emerged a theological ambivalence oscillating between affirmations of the nation's promise and suspicions of its peril. Orestes Brownson, a convert who made his way to the church via a circuitous route, argued that America offered Catholicism a congenial atmosphere and that the faith was in turn vital to the success of America's providential mission. "The Catholic religion," he declared in 1856, (*Brownson's Quarterly Review*), "is at home in the American breast, [and is] . . . more American than the greater part of the Americans themselves." It "is just what is needed to complete and consecrate the American character." A free, democratic society permitted Catholicism to flourish; but that order could not endure unless undergirded by Catholic moral principles and freed from the vagaries of Protestant sectarianism. "Catholicity is here," he concluded, "to perfect our civilization and to make ours the land of the future." Arguing for a similar congruence of

American ideals and Catholicism, Archbishop John Ireland declared in 1884: "There is no conflict between the Catholic Church and America. . . . Republic of America, receive from me the tribute of my love and my loyalty. . . . *Esto perpetua.* Thou bearest in thy hands the hopes of the human race" (*The Church and Modern Society,* vol. 1, pp. 28, 64). Persons of Brownson and Ireland's sympathies generally called on the church to shed the ethnic heritage of its immigrants and to assimilate to American culture.

Other Catholics, however, viewed the United States less favorably. Witnessing the prevalence of Protestantism in American life, the periodic outbursts of nativism, and the dissonance between the church's teaching and American pluralism, they concluded with Cincinnati's Anton Walburg that America was "impervious to the spirit and claims of the Catholic religion" (*The Question of Nationality . . . ,* 1889). Since America, as another conservative (C. B. Pallen, *What Is Liberalism?,* 1889) put it, "exhales an atmosphere filled with germs poisonous and fatal," the church had no choice but to isolate its members from the contagion. Through parochial schools and the maintenance of the immigrants' original languages and customs—in short, through a ghetto mentality—Catholics might preserve the purity of their faith. Pope Leo XIII's ambiguous condemnation of the so-called "Americanist heresy" in 1899 gave apparent support to the conservatives without definitively refuting the liberals and thus left the debated issues unresolved. Well into the twentieth century, American Catholicism remained an enigma. For the most part intensely patriotic and increasingly accepted by other Americans, Catholics still had no explicit theological rationale for their pluralistic nation. Not until the Second Vatican Council's *Declaration on Religious Freedom,* whose logic owed much to the American Jesuit John Courtney Murray, did Catholics in the United States officially gain this rationale.

Unlike Roman Catholics, who came chiefly from nations where their church had a special relation with the government or was numerically dominant, American Jews had enjoyed no such prior dominance. Since the political destruction of their homeland near the beginning of the common era, they had lived scattered throughout a largely Christian or Muslim world. The Dispersion was not merely a demographic real-

ity; it was also a spiritual fact of profound significance to Jewish self-understanding. Separated from the land of promise, Jews waited in *galut* (exile) for the Messiah to return them home. Although they experienced moments of freedom and even grandeur in the Dispersion, prejudice and the possibility of persecution usually remained close enough to remind Jews that they were aliens. The pluralistic American environment, which, despite anti-Semitic elements, was remarkably free of the restrictions previously imposed on Jews, represented a relatively novel situation. Perhaps here the Jewish people could lose their wayfaring status. Maybe America could be more than a provisional home in *galut.*

The most cogent theological expression of that hope emerged from Reform Judaism. A product of the German Jewish migration in the early to mid-1800s, Reform owed much to European rabbis exposed to the Enlightenment, but probably even more to the extraordinary mobility of the mass of German Jews who attained middle-class status more quickly and thoroughly than virtually any other immigrant group in America. The Reform program espoused assimilation unabashedly. Whether in worship or culture, Jews were asked to cast off much of their ethnic distinctiveness—their Jewishness—and to become merely one American denomination among others. According to the advocates of Reform, *galut* had ended, for as the Pittsburgh Platform declared in 1885: "We consider ourselves no longer a nation but a religious community, and therefore . . . expect . . . [no] return to Palestine" (quoted in Glazer, 1957, p. 152). Or as Oscar and Mary Handlin have summarized, Reform Jews "proclaimed 'America is our Zion'" (quoted in Joseph L. Blau, *Judaism in America,* 1976, p. 86). Washington, D.C., it was said of a leading rabbi, became his Jerusalem. There were, however, soon to be countervailing tendencies. A resurgence of nativism reinforced the Jewish sense of difference, a massive influx of eastern European Jews between 1880 and 1920 tilted American Judaism (at least temporarily) back toward more traditional ethnic patterns, and the emergence of a nascent Zionism served as a reminder that Jews might still harbor aspirations that could not be fully realized in America. In the twentieth century, most Jews from all three branches of the faith—Reform, Conservative, and Orthodox—have managed to become quite at home in the United States; but few have been able, after Hitler and the creation of the state of Israel, to invest all their hopes in the American republic.

Few citizens had greater reason than Afro-Americans to question the assumption that the United States was an elect nation. If those in the white majority styled themselves a new Israel exemplifying liberty, blacks often perceived America as a modern Egypt oppressing God's children. David Walker, a free black whose *Appeal to the Coloured Citizens of the World* (1829) constituted one of the most trenchant pieces of antebellum protest, captured this irony succinctly. "The condition of the Israelites was better under the Egyptians than ours is under the whites," he declared, adding that this mistreatment was perpetrated by a people "who are, notwithstanding, looking for the Millennial day." Echoing Walker's criticism, Frederick Douglass mocked the notion of a righteous America and spoke instead of a country where "the slave prison and the church stand near each other" (*Narrative of the Life of Frederick Douglass,* Benjamin Quarles, ed., p. 157).

Perhaps the most sublime inversions of the national myth were the black folk songs, or spirituals. When slaves sang, "Go down, Moses, way down in Egypt land, / Tell ole Pharaoh to let my people go," they testified with the simple eloquence of the illiterate that they had not been gulled by the rhetoric of America as a new Israel. Yet that rhetoric could not be completely shaken off, for the national vision of liberty and equality spoke profoundly to black longings no matter how grievously America had betrayed those ideals. Perhaps then the national myth was not in error but rather the whites who had failed to extend its promise to others. Near the end of the Civil War, the Reverend Henry Highland Garnet, a frequent advocate of slave resistance, gave utterance to this hope in the first address by a black clergyman to the House of Representatives. With slavery ended, he dared to believe that "the nation has begun its exodus from worse than Egyptian bondage" and might at last "give to the world the form of a model Republic" (quoted in Earl Ofari, *"Let Your Motto Be Resistance": The Life and Thought of Henry Highland Garnet*, pp. 201, 203).

Garnet's hopes were not to be realized during the post–Civil War years, a period some historians call America's nadir. Southern states soon passed Jim Crow laws, the Supreme Court gutted civil rights legislation, and northern politicians wearied of the effort to enforce the claims of justice. Under a new form of vassalage, blacks thus continued to gaze upon the nation with profound ambivalence. They were Americans drawn to the culture's prevailing myths, and yet they were simultaneously outsiders. As W. E. B. Du Bois wrote in his classic *The Souls of Black Folk* (1903):

> One ever feels his two-ness,—an American, a Negro; two souls, two thoughts, two unreconciled strivings; two warring ideals in one dark body, whose dogged strength alone keeps it from being torn asunder. . . . The Nation has not yet found peace from its sins; the freedman has not yet found in freedom his promised land.

In the twentieth century, misgivings about the "promised land" spread beyond ethnic or religious minorities and Fundamentalist Protestants to invade the mainstream of literary and theological culture. Although writers such as Melville and Hawthorne had probed the dark side of American existence, their criticisms had often been oblique and were often ignored or misunderstood by the masses. At most their works constituted a minority report on the American Dream. No one, however, could miss the massive repudiation of American exceptionalism implicit in many disaffected writers of the 1920s and 1930s. H. L. Mencken lampooned the anti-intellectualism and mediocrity of the nation's "booboisie." Sinclair Lewis described the hypocrisies of Protestantism in *Elmer Gantry* and *Main Street.* Joseph Wood Krutch portrayed a decadent civilization whose science had destroyed belief in a transcendent order of meaning and had brought the "inevitable realization that living is merely a physiological process" (*The Modern Temper,* 1929). Ernest Hemingway in *A Farewell to Arms* voiced the disillusionment of a generation chastened by World War I—a generation that "had seen nothing sacred," only sacrifices comparable to those in "the stockyards of Chicago," where "nothing was done to the meat except to bury it." Even authors such as T. S. Eliot and William Faulkner, whose works employ religious symbolism of sin and redemption, depicted present culture as hollow and decaying.

In theological circles, this disenchantment took the form of Neo-Orthodoxy. Usually traced to the European theologian Karl Barth, Neo-Orthodoxy was a variegated intellectual movement. Its adherents, however, did share a common somber assessment of Western civilization's prospects—an appraisal rooted in a sense of cultural crisis and sustained by an appreciation of classic Protestantism's emphasis on human sinfulness. Although many people contributed to American Neo-Orthodoxy—including emigrés like Paul Tillich—its theological interpretation of America is perhaps best exemplified in the writings of Reinhold and H. Richard Niebuhr.

During a career that took him from a pastorate in Detroit to a professorship at New York's Union Theological Seminary, Reinhold Niebuhr was successively a pacifist, a democratic Marxist, an early advocate of military action against Nazi Germany, a proponent of nuclear deterrence against the Soviet Union, and at the end of his life a vehement critic of U.S. policy in Vietnam. Yet amid his shifting positions ran a constant theme. "There is no purely moral solution for the ultimate moral issues of life," he declared in *The Irony of American History* (1952), "but neither is there a viable solution which disregards the moral factors." Americans, in a word, could not build the Kingdom of God on earth; but they could strive for imperfect, proximate goals dimly mirroring the transcendent ideal. Niebuhr believed that the illusion of American innocence was a major obstacle to responsible national action. That fantasy led, he observed in 1943, to vacillation "between ascetic withdrawal from the world 'power politics' and a too simple identification of the nation's purpose with the divine Will" (quoted in Cherry, p. 307). On occasion Niebuhr could speak of America's significant, even providential, role in world history; but he steadfastly attacked any notion of the United States as a redeemer nation. That idea betrayed an "inability to comprehend the depths of evil to which individuals and communities may sink, particularly when they try to play the role of God to history."

H. Richard Niebuhr, though by no means a carbon copy of his brother, voiced similar criticisms of American culture and religion from his post at Yale after 1931. Convinced that Western civilization, with its excesses of nationalism and capitalism, had reached a moment of reckoning, Niebuhr charged the churches with abetting the crisis by equating a middle-class faith in gradual progress with the Christian hope. The churches and the nation alike had been seduced by a "romantic conception of the kingdom of God [which] involved no discontinuities, no crises, no tragedies, or sacrifices." Renewal of culture was possible—Niebuhr adhered to a view that can best be described, in his own phrase, as "Christ the transformer of culture"—but there could be no return to a nineteenth-century vision of America gradually becoming the Kingdom of God. No effort to particularize the kingdom was legitimate, for all such expressions were at best partial; and even the highest cultural attainment needed to be tempered by what Niebuhr called Jonathan Edwards' "intense awareness of the precariousness of life's poise."

Despite its influence in major seminaries down to the 1960s, Neo-Orthodoxy seldom made a complete transition from academe to the pew. The popular mood, though more chastened than nineteenth-century optimism, was not attuned to Neo-Orthodoxy's somber realism and its love of paradox. Most Americans continued to hold more hopeful religious assessments of their culture. In World War II, the churches, while generally avoiding the quasi-millennial rhetoric with which they sent soldiers to Europe in 1917, usually endorsed President Roosevelt's idealistic interpretation of the struggle.

The postwar revival, reaching its peak in the 1950s, also affirmed a positive vision of America. The tokens of the so-called Eisenhower revival—increased religious affiliation, a building boom in church construction, a surge of interest in inspirational books, the addition of the phrase "under God" to the Pledge of Allegiance, and the elevation to celebrity status of such religious leaders as Fulton J. Sheen and Billy Graham—fit into a larger pattern of patriotic religiosity spawned in part by the Cold War. "Being a church member and speaking favorably of religion," Sydney Ahlstrom has written, "became a means of affirming the 'American way of life,' especially since the USSR and its Communist allies were formally committed to atheism." Critics charged that the revival was an unreflective attempt to reduce religion to a mere instrument of patriotism and personal self-fulfillment; and they decried the revival's blandness and theological vacuity—its "faith in faith."

Will Herberg provided the classic analysis of the postwar revival in *Protestant–Catholic–Jew* (1955). He concluded that America had become a "triple-melting pot" in which each of the three major religious groups functioned as a means of affirming loyalty to American ideals. "To be a Protestant, a Catholic, or a Jew," he wrote, "are today alternate ways of being an American." That Herberg could advance this thesis was a tribute to a maturing religious tolerance and also a testimony to the success of Catholics and Jews in resolving the issue of their identity with the American Dream. (It was also, one must note, a commentary on the times that Afro-Americans did not figure significantly in Herberg's scheme.) While appreciative of the virtues of the triple-melting pot, Herberg feared that it had made religion little more than a pious and uncritical gloss on the American way of life.

The 1960s forced a sobering reappraisal of America's religious meaning. The election of John F. Kennedy as the first Roman Catholic president eliminated any vestigial evidence that America was a Protestant nation. Two Supreme Court decisions in 1962 and 1963 struck down mandatory prayers and Bible reading in the public schools—decisions that some hailed as a mature recognition of pluralism and others damned as evidence of creeping secularism. The escalation of the conflict in Vietnam undermined traditional religious understandings of America. To a degree unprecedented, large numbers of citizens contended that the United States was waging an unjust war. Far from being the redeemer nation, the United States had become a purveyor of destruction. The civil rights struggle evoked similar questions about the righteousness of the city set on a hill. Initially black protest represented an attempt to revivify traditional American myths and values. As Martin Luther King, Jr., attested in a moving address before a massive audience in Washington, D.C., during the summer of 1963, black demonstrations did not aim at the subversion of the national ideals but rather their fulfillment. In a nearly millennial vision, King foretold a day when "all God's children will be able to sing with new meaning, 'My country, 'tis of thee,

sweet land of liberty, of thee I sing' "; and he summoned the United States to "rise up and live out the true meaning of its creed."

Yet even King, increasingly embittered by the Vietnam War and growing more aware of the deeply entrenched nature of injustice in America, gradually moved toward a more thoroughgoing critique of the nation. The year before his assassination in 1968, King was calling for a radical reformation of national values as the only hope for the United States. Other protesters began raising the chant of "Black Power," flirted with revolutionary ideologies, and appeared to reject the American Dream entirely. Taking a cue from black radicals, various theologies of liberation—feminist and Third World, for example— soon began portraying America as an oppressor. Even some Jews, belatedly trying to understand the horrendous fact of the Holocaust and contemplating Israel's terrible isolation in the Six Day War of 1967, experienced a new sense of separateness in their American Zion.

It was a mark of the times that some thinkers tried to make a virtue of America's loss of traditional religious meaning. Self-styled Death-of-God theologians, for example, argued that all language about God had ceased to have meaning and that culture should be understood in entirely secular terms. Though not a part of that movement, Harvey Cox shared its enthusiasm for secularity. His *Secular City* (1965) gloried in the fact that culture and society could now be understood as human artifices requiring no religious sanction. Instead of fighting a rearguard action against this reality, Christians should abandon the effort to find some ultimate meaning in culture or politics and instead should concentrate on facilitating solutions to the specific problems of creating a more humane urban civilization. Advocating a practical rather than a metaphysical stance, Cox's analysis took the cool pragmatism of John F. Kennedy as its model.

Although this brief sketch can only hint at the complexities of a decade whose meaning historians have just begun to fathom, it does suggest that the 1960s fragmented the received interpretations of America's meaning. What remained of former schemes was a series of diverse, often contradictory, images; and it was uncertain when —or how—the pieces could be reassembled.

During the 1970s, the nation witnessed efforts to recover a religious sense of American purpose. In 1967, the sociologist Robert Bellah wrote of a civil religion that supposedly existed alongside the fissiparous denominational faiths and that might yet provide a transcendent unitive purpose for America. Even Harvey Cox lost much of his enthusiasm for secularity and began looking to Eastern religion, cultic movements, and Third World theologies in search of a religious revitalization of the culture. New sectarian movements thrived in part because they promised to fill this need; and the most notable of these groups—the Reverend Sun Myung Moon's Unification Church—unashamedly sang praises to America's preeminent role in God's plan. Jerry Falwell's Moral Majority along with kindred groups of the New Right sought a reactionary renewal. These organizations wish to restore America as God's nation through school prayer, a ban on abortion, opposition to homosexuality, and other conservative policies. Although the Moral Majority and its allies form only a controversial minority within the electorate, they express a more widespread yearning for a return to traditional religious symbols embodying American purpose. In *The Naked Public Square* (1984), Richard John Neuhaus has given cogent expression to this longing. Criticizing secularists who wish to banish religious symbols from the public domain, Neuhaus contends that this policy has impoverished civic life and that Americans must recover a common vocabulary of spiritual and moral values.

At this writing—at the end of 1985—Neuhaus' prayer appears, at least in part, to have been answered. Religious images have returned to the naked public square with a vengeance. Republican oratory about America as a "shining city" has summoned up the shade of Winthrop; and Democratic rhetoric has, with appropriate partisan modifications, followed suit. Whether these invocations of traditional images can shape a consensus that will successfully cope with the threat of nuclear war, revolution abroad, persisting inequities at home, and the reality of pluralism remains problematic. To date recent popular theological visions of America resemble an exer-

cise in nostalgia as much as they do a summons to look ahead. But a definitive evaluation must await a future historian.

BIBLIOGRAPHY

Aaron I. Abell, ed., *American Catholic Thought on Social Questions* (1968); Sydney E. Ahlstrom, *A Religious History of the American People* (1972); Sacvan Bercovitch, *The American Jeremiad* (1978); C. Conrad Cherry, ed., *God's New Israel: Religious Interpretations of American Destiny* (1971); James H. Cone, *Black Theology: A Documentary History* (1979); Nathan Glazer, *American Judaism* (1957; rev. 1972); Giles Gunn, ed., *New World Metaphysics: Readings on the Religious Meaning of the American Experience* (1981).

Robert T. Handy, *A Christian America: Protestant Hopes and Historical Realities* (1971; rev. 1984); Klaus J. Hansen, *Mormonism and the American Experience* (1981); Nathan A. Hatch, *The Sacred Cause of Liberty: Republican Thought and the Millennium in Revolutionary New England* (1977); James Hennesey, *American Catholics: A History of the Roman Catholic Community in the United States* (1981); Will Herberg, *Protestant–Catholic–Jew: An Essay in American Religious Sociology* (1955); Winthrop S. Hudson, ed., *Nationalism and Religion in America: Concepts of American Identity and Mission* (1970); William R. Hutchinson, *The Modernist Impulse in American Protestantism* (1976).

Howard Mumford Jones, *O Strange New World; American Culture: The Formative Years* (1964); D. H. Lawrence, *Studies in Classic American Literature* (1923); R. W. B. Lewis, *The American Adam: Innocence, Tragedy, and Tradition in the Nineteenth Century* (1955); George M. Marsden, *Fundamentalism and American Culture: The Shaping of Twentieth-Century Evangelicalism, 1870–1925* (1980); Leo Marx, *The Machine in the Garden: Technology and the Pastoral Ideal in America* (1964); Henry F. May, *The Enlightenment in America* (1976); Sidney E. Mead, *The Nation with the Soul of a Church* (1975); James H. Moorhead, *American Apocalypse: Yankee Protestants and the Civil War, 1860–1869* (1978); Roderick Nash, *Wilderness and the American Mind* (1967); H. Richard Niebuhr, *The Kingdom of God in America* (1937); Albert J. Raboteau, *Slave Religion* (1978).

Elwyn A. Smith, ed., *The Religion of the Republic* (1971); Henry Nash Smith, *Virgin Land: The American West as Symbol and Myth* (1950; rev. 1970); Cushing Strout, *The New Heavens and New Earth: Political Religion in America* (1974); Ernest Lee Tuveson, *Redeemer Nation: The Idea of America's Millennial Role* (1968); G. H. Williams, *Wilderness and Paradise in Christian Thought* (1962); Charles Reagan Wilson, *Baptized in Blood: The Religion of the Lost Cause, 1865–1920* (1980).

[*See also* BIBLE IN AMERICAN CULTURE; CIVIL AND PUBLIC RELIGION; *and* IMPACT OF PURITANISM ON AMERICAN CULTURE.]

Part II
NORTH AMERICA:
CONTEXTS AND BACKGROUNDS

RELIGIONS OF MESOAMERICA

Wayne Elzey

THE cultural area of Mesoamerica was first defined by Paul Kirchoff in 1943. Geographically, Mesoamerica encompasses the region extending roughly from the Pánuco River in Mexico to parts of Honduras and Costa Rica, and includes all of Guatemala, Belize, and El Salvador. Some fourteen language families have been isolated in the area with upwards of twenty-five Maya languages currently spoken. A number of cultural groups, most of them still poorly understood, had long been established in Mesoamerica by the time of the Spanish Conquest in the sixteenth century. Among the most important were the Zapotecs in the eastern part of the Mexican state of Oaxaca and the Mixtecs in the west; the Tarascans in Michoacán; the Huaxtecs and Totonacs in northern Veracruz; various Maya groups in the Yucatán Peninsula and in the highlands of Guatemala; the Otomí to the north of the Valley of Mexico; and the Náhuatl speakers around the lakes of the valley and in Tlaxcala.

Chronologically, Mesoamerica is divided into periods and/or cultural stages, with the dates varying somewhat according to region: the Formative or Preclassic period, 1500 B.C.–A.D. 300; the Classic period, 300–900; and the Postclassic period, 900–1519. As the terminology indicates, the focus of attention has been on the rise and, in some senses, the decline of high civilizations. During the Formative period, several key Mesoamerican cultural traits emerged, including the establishment of elite religious and administrative centers, settled agricultural villages, monumental sculpture, hieroglyphic writing, distinctive systems for counting time, and professional classes of priests and religious specialists.

The Classic or Theocratic period, the golden age of Mesoamerica, saw the development of massive architecture and stepped-pyramid temples; the emergence of cities in some areas and perhaps of loosely federated empires; the Long Count system for measuring time in the Maya area; and large-scale trade. The Postclassic or Militaristic period customarily has been viewed as a time when some of the dominant traits of the Classic were exaggerated (e.g., human sacrifice) and others secularized (e.g., rule by military leaders instead of priests). The major Classic ceremonial centers were abandoned or replaced by others at the end of the Classic period, and cities and city-states entered a period of contention for sovereignty that lasted until the Spanish Conquest.

The bulk of the written evidence concerning the religions of Mesoamerica at the time of the conquest comes from two areas, that of the Náhuatl speakers in central Mexico and, to a far lesser extent, that of the Maya in the Yucatán and the highlands of Guatemala. The focus of the following pages will be on the former.

Pre-Hispanic Maya cultures were located in a region encompassing the Yucatán Peninsula, Belize, the eastern part of the state of Chiapas, and most of Guatemala. The region is divided culturally into southern, central, and northern areas, with the central area, a jungle rain forest, witnessing the greatest florescence of Maya civilization during the Classic period. More than 100 ceremonial centers with hieroglyphic writing on stelae, dating from the third to the ninth centuries, are known to have existed. These sites were not cities but elite religious centers peopled by religious specialists, and they served also as markets and administrative centers for surrounding villages. The largest of the Maya ceremonial centers, Tikal, in the central region, covered one square mile in the center itself during Classic times. It contained temples, dwellings, and six pyramid temples, the largest of which reached nearly 230 feet in height; its attached population was estimated at more than 10,000. For reasons not understood, the ceremonial centers were abandoned during the ninth century. Written evidence concerning the religious life of the Maya, even at the time of the conquest, is scanty. Three screenfold books (with pages folded accordion-like) in the native pictorial writing tradition have survived, along with a few post-conquest books in European script dealing with prophecies, tribal histories, medical formulas, incantations, and creation myths.

Outside the Maya region, ceremonial centers with ritual burials, pyramids, and other religious structures existed from at least the ninth century B.C. in the so-called Olmec civilization on the Gulf Coast, thought to be the mother culture of the high civilizations in Mesoamerica. The largest of the Olmec centers, La Venta, in the state of Tabasco, was located on a swampy island and contained a clay pyramid, massive sculpted heads, and baby-faced figurines carved in the form of a were-jaguar (a sort of werewolf; but feline, not canine). Burials of serpentine blocks formed what is believed to be a stylized jaguar mask, resembling later representations of Tláloc, god of the mountains and the rains. Excavations at Tlatilco in the Valley of Mexico, a settlement that once covered approximately 160 acres, disclosed Olmec influence during the Formative period. They also yielded a number of figurines that depict individuals in a dualistic or monstrous fashion, with two faces, three eyes, two mouths, or split faces.

Important centers during the Classic period were those of the Zapotecs at Monte Albán in the Valley of Oaxaca, at Xochicalco near modern Cuernavaca, El Tajín in northern Veracruz, Cholula in Puebla, and, most importantly, at Teotihuacán in central Mexico. According to the Nahua myths, Teotihuacán was the City of the Gods, where the gods were sacrificed and where the present cycle of the universe began. With its temples, palaces, Pyramids of the Sun and the Moon, and residential quarters, Teotihuacán was perhaps the first true city in Mesoamerica. At its height during the fourth to the mid-seventh centuries, it covered an area of seven square miles, with a population estimated to be as great as 120,000. The influence of Teotihuacán, through trade or conquest, spread through much of Mesoamerica, extending to an outpost at Kaminaljuyú in the highlands of Guatemala, nearly 700 miles to the south, where a miniature replica of the city was constructed.

The religion of the inhabitants of Teotihuacán, and indeed of the peoples of the Classic period through much of Mesoamerica, has been viewed as a theocracy managed by an elite class of priests. Prominently represented in the sculptures and frescoes of Teotihuacán are the god Tláloc (and his consort, Chalchiuhtlícue), the culture hero Quetzalcóatl (Feathered Serpent), and Xipe Totec (Our Lord the Flayed One). The most famous of the frescoes, that of the palace of Tepantitla, is thought to depict the otherworldly paradise of Tlalocan, in later times a place reserved for those who died by drowning, lightning, or by some other agency of Tláloc.

As a major center, Teotihuacán was destroyed in the seventh century. Legendary histories gradually add to the archaeological evidence, telling of the establishment of the Toltec capital of Tollan, sometime during the ninth century, near the contemporary town of Tula in Hidalgo. By the time of the arrival of the Spaniards, the term *Toltec* was synonymous with "culture," and aspiring groups took pains to establish their Toltec lineage. Strong Toltec influences are evident in the northern Yucatán, especially at Chichén-Itzá, where Kukulcán (a Maya equivalent of the Nahua god Quetzalcóatl) was said to have founded the city prior to departing to the east.

After the collapse and destruction of the Toltec capital in the mid-twelfth century, nomadic tribes from the north, the so-called Chichimecs, came into the Valley of Mexico, adopted Toltec or Nahua culture, and were caught up in the struggles for supremacy that marked the next two and one-half centuries. Refugees from Tula established themselves in a number of cities and city-states near the lakes in the valley, one of the most important being Culhuacán, regarded as the authentic center of transmission of Toltec civilization.

The last of the wandering tribes to arrive were the people now popularly known as the Aztecs (or *mexica, culhua-mexica, tenocha*: Mexicans). Originally "little more than squatters," as Michael Coe (*Mexico,* 1962) puts it, in less than two centuries after establishing themselves at Tenochtitlán (modern Mexico City) in 1325, the Aztecs had defeated the dominant city-state of the Tepenecs at Azcalpotzalco. They had formed a triple alliance with the neighboring cities of Texcoco and Tlacopan, destroyed previous records, rewritten history to reflect their own centrality in the cosmos, and built a loose federation or empire of thirty-eight tributary provinces, extending to both coasts. By the time of the conquest, the population of Tenochtitlán may have numbered as many as one-quarter of a million people, with perhaps 5 million or more under the direct influence of the Aztec ruler.

Most descriptions of the religions of Mesoamerica stress the existence of a common tradition but allow for significant variations according to region and period. With some notable exceptions, the religions of ancient Mesoamerica have attracted comparatively little modern scholarly attention apart from that of the specialist. In *The History of America* (1777), William Robertson consigned the Aztecs to the cultural stage of barbarism, midway between savagery and civilization, where they remained for the next century and a half. The high cultures of Mesoamerica were too complex and differentiated to be of much interest to those seeking the essence of religion in its primitive origins. At the same time, given the Aztecs' religiously motivated warfare, human sacrifice, and cannibalism, they were of little interest to scholars of comparative religion like A. Eustace Hayden, who sought to trace in the religions of the world "the quest for the values of the noblest ideal of living" (*The Quest of the Ages,* 1929). Nonetheless, in the second half of the nineteenth century, two of the first European chairs in comparative religion were held by scholars of Mesoamerica, J. G. Müller in Basel and Albert Réville in Paris. Wilhelm Schmidt and Raffaele Pettazzoni contributed valuable comparative studies of high gods and rituals of confession. A masterful and synthetic survey of the place of central Mexican cultures and religions in European and American scholarship and literature can be found in Benjamin Keen's *The Aztec Image* (1971).

Knowledge of the religions of late Postclassic Mesoamerica derives from several kinds of sources. The native sources are of three sorts: pictorial, those written in the European script, and archaeological or monumental. Directly and indirectly, the most important and as yet incompletely understood are the pictorial codices, screenfold books containing hieroglyphic writing, color painting, and standardized sets of symbols, which were to be "read" accompanied by an oral commentary. Several of the written descriptions of religious life in central Mexico derive from commentaries on the codices.

Sixteen of the screenfold books (or copies) are thought to be pre-conquest and eight others have survived that were produced after the conquest. Two of the sixteen books (*Codex Borbonicus, Tonalámatl de Aubin*) are from the Valley of Mexico; three are from the lowland Maya area (codices *Dresden, Madrid, Paris*); five are thought to be from Puebla-Tlaxcala-Oaxaca (codices *Borgia, Cospi, Fejérváry-Mayer, Laud, Vaticanus B*); and the remaining six are from the region of western Oaxaca (codices *Becker no. 1, Bodley, Colombino, Nuttall, Vienna,* and *Aubin Manuscript no. 20*).

The first ten of the codices deal with ritual and calendrical matters, listing sequences of deities such as the thirteen and nine Lords of the Day and the Night, and served as *tonalámatls,* handbooks for divination and prognostication. The remaining six, the Mixtec codices from western Oaxaca, deal in genealogical and historical narratives extending back to the end of the seventh century. In addition to the screenfold books, several narrative accounts were written shortly after the conquest. Although Christian, European, and extraregional influences are present, the texts contain a wealth of indigenous material. The anonymous *Popol Vuh* is the sole unitary book containing narrative myth and tribal history, this from the Quiché Maya in the Guatemalan highlands. Among the other important Maya texts are the eighteen books of *Chilam Balam* and the *Ritual of the Bacabs,* containing useful lore about divinatory practices, myths, and prophecies. Several Indian and mestizo authors also left valuable accounts of religion in the region of central Mexico, including those of Diego Muñoz Camargo, Fernando Alvarado Tezozómoc, and Fernando de Alva Ixtlilxóchitl. Important collections of Náhuatl poetry are the *Romances de los Señores de la Nueva España* and *Cantares Mexicanos.*

The most detailed and systematic descriptions of pre-Hispanic religions are the accounts of the Franciscan and Dominican missionaries working in Mexico in the sixteenth and early seventeenth centuries. For the region of central Mexico, the best-known and most systematic account is found in the corpus of texts from the pen of the Franciscan friar Bernardino de Sahagún, first recorded in Náhuatl from his questioning of native informants, later expanded in his *Historia general de las cosas de Nueva España.* Sahagún and other missionary ethnographers left a detailed record of native religions, but it is a record that is indelibly marked by the purposes for which it was compiled.

The meeting in central Mexico between the greatest empires in the Old World and the New confronted both sides with realities difficult to assimilate into their respective religious visions of the world. The Mexican emissaries sent by the Aztec emperor Moctezuma Xocoyotzin to investigate the arrival of the Spaniards reported that creatures with very light skin, long beards, and short hair had come on mountains floating in the water. Dressed in iron, these men or "gods" (*teteo*) rode on deer as tall as a house and brought with them large tubes whose entrails disgorged fire, a ball of stone, and smoke smelling like rotten mud.

To the Christian missionaries, the religious beliefs and practices they encountered seemed hardly less strange. Here were religions with complicated notions of sin and the sacrament of confession but with little or no sense that one's sins were in any way connected with destiny after death. An incipient monotheism existed alongside a pantheon estimated by Fray Juan de Torquemada to number more than 30,000. To the most perceptive of the missionaries, the native religions were problematic, but not because they seemed unique. Many of the deities of the New World found their parallels in the paganism of antiquity. Sahagún equated Tezcatlipoca (Smoking Mirror) with Jupiter; the Aztec tribal god Huitzilopochtli (Hummingbird on the Left) with Mars and Hercules; Tlazoltéotl (Filth Goddess) with Venus; Tláloc with Neptune; and Xiuhtecuhtli (Fire Lord) with Vulcan.

But it was the parallels between the native religions and Christianity that proved most troublesome, the former often looking like some counterfeit version of the latter. The Dominican friar Diego Durán catalogued a Mexican Adam and Eve, a Mexican version of Noah, the ark and the flood story, several of the sacraments, holy days, bishops, relics, a holy Ark carried by priests during an exodus to a promised land, a conception of the Trinity, and in all more than a hundred correspondences between the native and biblical religions.

Not unlike the scholars who followed, the missionaries tended to see the religions at the time of the conquest as veering toward opposite extremes, neither of which logically could be brought into harmony with the other. The sentiments so pervasive in some of the surviving poetry and the ritual speeches—that life on earth is only an illusion, a trick played on men by the gods, or a dream—existed alongside barbarism of the worst sort. Durán reported that Tlacaélel, chief adviser to the Aztec king Ahuízotl and to several other Aztec rulers during the last half of the fifteenth century, dedicated the great temple in Tenochtitlán to the tribal god Huitzilopochtli, saying, "Our god will not be made to wait until new wars arrive. He will find a way, a marketplace where he will go to buy victims, men for him to eat. They will be in his sight like maize cakes hot from the griddle" (Durán, *The Aztecs*). Sahagún was told of the fate of traveling merchants who sometimes doubled as spies. If they "came to an evil pass, if they were discovered, then [the foe] slew them in ambush; they served them up with chili sauce." Probably nowhere have the contradictory images of the "melancholy" and the "savage" Indian been so closely intertwined as in the descriptions of Aztec religion.

The perception of a different sort of religious mentality added to the bewilderment of the missionaries. "One clearly sees," wrote Sahagún,

> that they did not hold as sinful those things they did while drunk, even though they might be grave sins, for it was reasoned with some logic that they got drunk in order to do what they wished, and that therefore they should not be blamed and should be released from punishment.
>
> (*Historia generale,* Acosta Saignes, ed., vol. 1)

In addition to the casuistry, the native religious mind seemed prone to couple a deep religiousness with a childlike credulity. Sahagún doubted "that there are any idolaters in the world more religious." So eager were the natives for conversion, reported Gerónimo de Mendieta, that the friars were unable to generate enough saliva to baptize them. One of the original group of twelve Franciscans to arrive in Mexico, Fray Toribio de Benevente, known as "Motolinía," depicted the would-be converts as "hungry dogs tracking down food."

But it was the seeming credulousness of the Indians that struck the missionaries as especially peculiar. Durán found something very different in New Spain from the blend of ignorance and religious fanaticism he took to be typical of the Spanish peasant. In the provinces of Spain,

> where men's minds are extraordinarily brutish and rude (especially in matters of religious instruction), [a person will] allow himself to be torn to pieces defending a single article of the Faith. If you ask him, "Why is God One and also a Trinity?" he will answer, "Because that is the way it is." And if you ask him, "Why are there Three Persons in the Trinity and not four?" he will answer, "Why not?"
>
> (p. 52)

In New Spain, on the other hand, "if a thousand dogmas were preached, they would believe all of them." Motolinía concurred. Before their conversion to Christianity, the natives worshiped a hundred gods. Now they worshiped one hundred and one.

The great civic feasts held throughout the year were not exempt from the same judgment. To the missionaries, the most impressive of the festivals was that held during the fifth of the native months, *Tóxcatl* (Dry Thing). With its processions, communal meals, and the voluntary death of a perfect man it was, said Durán, "one of the most ostentatious and imposing known to the Indians." Sahagún thought that "this feast was the most important of all the feasts. It was like Easter, and fell near Easter Sunday." An impersonator of Tezcatlipoca, one of the central Nahua gods, had been selected during the feast the previous year, a young man "without flaw, who had no defects," and he lived for a year as the god, honored and "acknowledged as our lord." As the day of the major ritual approached, the impersonator of Tezcatlipoca was ceremonially married to impersonators of the goddesses Xilonen, Huixtocíhuatl, Atlatonan, and Xochiquetzal. He was borne on a litter over a ground strewn with maguey leaves, a communal meal was prepared, and the impersonator of the god was abandoned by his wives. According to Durán's summary description:

> The meal having ended, the people of the city gathered once more in the courtyard of the temple to observe and celebrate the end of the feast . . . and then he was delivered to the sacrificers who appeared at the same time. . . . Four of the sacrificers seized the victim by the feet and the hands while the priest opened his chest and extracted his heart, raising it with his hand as high

as he could, offering its steam to the sun. After a moment . . . the heart was thrown towards the idol, and the cadaver was rolled down the steps.

(pp. 106–107)

According to Sahagún's informants, the ceremony illustrated that "none come to an end here upon earth with happiness, riches, wealth."

The challenge the missionaries saw themselves increasingly facing was to determine if the conversions were authentic. Even though the idols had been overturned, the temples demolished, the great civic feasts suppressed, and the hierarchy of priests dissolved, the suspicion was that the native religions continued to be practiced in ways the untrained could not see. Fray Francisco de Burgoa, working in the region of Oaxaca, questioned the wisdom of performing a Mass for the dead when the onlookers saw the wine and the wafer as food provided for the dead on their journey through the underworlds. Satan was still at work, cunningly disguising the old religions in the trappings of the new.

Thus the friars sensed an atmosphere of urgency. As much as possible had to be learned about the deceptions if the true faith were to take root. The missionaries had to be familiar with the languages, customs, laws, social institutions, the ceremonies, the codices, the calendars, auguries, and native gods. The missionary was to serve, in Sahagún's words, as "a doctor of the soul," and the doctor "cannot use his medicine with any certainty without first knowing the nature and cause of the illness." Precise and detailed knowledge of the spiritual illnesses of the Mexicans and their neighbors was needed for a correct diagnosis and, more importantly, as a means of distinguishing the cure from the symptoms of the disease, which so often resembled the cure.

Required was a body of information that was accurate and encyclopedic in scope. Sahagún, relying on the form of the medieval encyclopedia, traced the native traditions according to the great chain of being, beginning in book 1 with the gods and concluding in book 11 with the names of animals, birds, snakes, stones, minerals, and grains. While none of the other missionary writers was as systematic as Sahagún in this respect, they did compile dictionaries, grammars, chronicles, and histories of native life. In some instances, notably with Sahagún, Durán, and Fray Andrés de Olmos, they formulated questionnaires (none of which have survived) and, in the case of Sahagún, systematically set about obtaining and cross-checking information and commentaries on the codices by employing trilingual students from the nobility who had been educated in the mission schools.

The result, especially from the region of central Mexico, was a remarkably detailed description of native religion as it existed at the time of the conquest. There are major gaps, nonetheless. To say of Sahagún's work, as Walter Krickeberg did, that it "was written from the native point of view," badly misstates the case. At best, the native point of view was refracted, limited, and distorted by the missionaries' questions and concerns.

The friars showed little interest in history, apart from that of their own orders and of the significance of the conquest in the broad context of Christian salvation history. They tended to slight questions concerning myth and cosmology in favor of those about the calendar, omens, and the civic festivals. Their record perhaps overemphasizes the importance of religion in native life. Eight of the twelve books in Sahagún's encyclopedia deal substantially with religious matters. While purportedly aiming at writing a comprehensive study of native life and culture, Sahagún dealt with religious matters to the exclusion of things like science, trade, and history. Moreover, the missionaries were most attentive to the public cult and the role of the elite. Too often, as Durán recognized, they tended to overlook the ways in which idolatries continued to pervade everyday life. "Heathenism and idolatry are present everywhere," he observed, "in sowing, in reaping, in storing grain, even in plowing the earth and in building houses, in wakes and funerals, in weddings and births." But given the distortions, the gaps, the Christian biases, and the regional and chronological limitations, the missionary chronicles remain an invaluable record of religion in late Postclassic central Mexico.

A number of ancient gods, most of whom play no major role in the surviving myths, were prominent throughout much of Mesoamerica. Among the most important was an eternally existing bisexual deity, invoked as "Our Father, Our Mother," who originated creation from the summit of the universe and sent down souls of infants into the wombs of their mothers. An identical or closely related high god, known to Náhuatl and Maya speakers as "the true god," had little prominence in cult or religious art but may have been important among priestly and philosophical elites.

Widespread throughout Mesoamerica was a deity associated with the mountains and the rains (Tláloc, Tajín, Cocijo, Muy'e), along with his small ministers or assistants who parceled out the rains and the weather from the four corners of the universe. A young maize god (the Nahua male/female divinity Cintéotl) is found among several groups. Also important were gods and goddesses associated with the fire and the hearth (Xiuhtecuhtli, Huehuetéotl, Otontecuhtli, Chantico), a (sometimes) male/female deity of the dead residing in the lowest of the underworlds (Mictlantecuhtli, Pitao Pezela, Ah Puch, Cizin), and a goddess closely linked with childbirth, weaving, sexual misconduct, curing, and confession (the Nahua and Huaxtec Tlazoltéotl, Ixchel among the Maya, the Tarascan goddess Xaratanga).

Numerous regional variations of the *altepeyollotl* (heart of the community) were considered patrons and/or legendary founders of the centers and cities. Hours, days, and larger units of time had their special patron deities, as did occupations and offices. Historical figures and cultic offices sometimes took their titles from and represented specific gods, according to a pattern Alfredo López Austin has called *Hombre-Dios*. The most famous example is the god, the historical ruler(s), and the priestly offices all known among the Nahuas as Quetzalcóatl.

Many of the gods appeared in various aspects or manifestations. Widespread borrowings occurred, at least in Postclassic times. As Jacques Soustelle noted:

> The tendency of the Aztec mind to syncretism is illustrated by their pantheon, which at the time of the Spanish conquest included the Otomí fire god Otontecuhtli, the Huaxtec love goddess Tlazoltéotl, the Yopi god "Our Lord the Flayed One" [Xipe Totec], the earth goddess of the northern steppes Itzpapalotl, and the deity of anointments and medicine Tzapotlatenan from the Zapotec area.
>
> ("Aztec Religion," *New Encyclopaedia Britannica*, 1977)

The ethnohistorian Henry B. Nicholson recently proposed an ambitious scheme for cataloguing the Nahua gods under three major cult themes and twelve major subthemes or "deity complexes." With no thought of being exhaustive, Nicholson listed more than 130 gods and goddesses from the central Mexican region alone. Many of the Mesoamerican deities are known only by name and others only through isolated pictorial representations.

Other dimensions of Mesoamerican religion are even less well understood. Moreover, because of the dearth of documentary sources for most of the high cultures of Mesoamerica, general treatments of Mesoamerican religions tend to be restricted in their scope. As Ronald Spores noted,

> the Zapotecs, Mixtecs, Mixes, Mazatecs, Huaves, Chinantecs, Tlapanecs, Totonacs, Tarascans, Otomis, and Huastecs, to name but a few, were groups of considerable size and importance that have received only passing attention from historians and anthropologists. Gross misconceptions have resulted from attempts to project Aztec or Maya patterns onto other cultures.
> (*The Mixtec Kings and Their Peoples*, 1967)

Much the same could be said with respect to tendencies to project late Postclassic beliefs and practices onto earlier periods. Significant changes in religious life clearly took place from the Classic to the Postclassic, for example, and the extent to which the late Postclassic myths, priestly organizations, ceremonial patterns, and migration legends existed in earlier times is open to question. The same might be said of the temptation to read twentieth-century non-Catholic beliefs and practices as pre-Hispanic "survivals."

Underlying the Mesoamerican world view was a sense of being properly situated or centered in time and space and of having to bear the responsibility of serving as a representative or "impersonator" (*ixiptla*) of the gods on the earth. One of the poems in *Romances de los Señores de la Nueva España* speaks of "the navel of the earth" (*tlalxico*) and of "the navel of fire" (*tlexico*) and of how the high god Ipalnemoani (He Through Whom We Live) "revolves around the sacred fire, sending his commands in the four directions." Scholars of Aztec religion have frequently emphasized the self-conception of the Aztecs as a chosen people—to use Alfonso Caso's phrase, "the people of the sun"—with a cosmic duty to maintain the order of the universe and dominated by the idea that they were "collaborators of the gods."

The historian of religions Mircea Eliade noted "a certain connection between the predominance of sun religions and what I may call 'historic' destinies. It could be said that where 'history is on the march,' thanks to kings, heroes or empires, the sun is supreme" (*Patterns in Comparative Religion*, 1958). Eliade observed that a strong apocalyptic strain often accompanies the dominance of solar symbolism, along with a singular role for an elite. "It *is* worth underlining the close connection between solar theology and the elite—whether of kings, initiates, heroes or philosophers. Unlike other nature hierophanies, sun hierophanies tend to become the privilege of a closed circle, of a minority of the elect."

Although other groups in Mesoamerica may not have carried the sense of historical consciousness and cosmic responsibility to the political and religious lengths reached by the Aztecs, there is evidence that the idea of taking on the burden of the gods, coupled with a recognition that one is neither worthy nor capable of carrying it, antedates the rise of the Aztecs. Sahagún recorded an extensive body of some sixty native speeches, orations, prayers, exhortations, ritual formulas, and invocations in book 6 of his history, a part of which was given the name *Huehuetlatolli*, "speeches of the elders" or "ancient discourses." These ritualized speeches, according to Sahagún, described how "they made formal conversation through which they displayed rhetoric and moral philosophy." The speeches represent, in microcosm, several of the major themes of central Mexican religions.

Sahagún divided his material, collected shortly before the middle of the sixteenth century, into four major sections: prayers and speeches delivered during times of civic crisis, such as drought, famine, the death of a ruler, an evil ruler; conversations between parents and children; speeches marking critical moments in the life cycle at the times of marriage, pregnancy, childbirth, naming, cradling, and entrance into the native schools; and proverbs, riddles, and metaphors. The speeches characteristically warn of dangers and provide injunctions about the proper role of human beings in relation to the gods.

In a majority of instances, the deity invoked was Tezcatlipoca, a quasi-omnipotent and omniscient sorcerer. The newly installed king (*tlatoani*) addressed Tezcatlipoca, saying:

Perhaps thou hast mistaken me for another, I who am a commoner; I who am a laborer. In excrement, in filth hath my lifetime been—I who am unreliable; I who am of filth, of vice. And I am an imbecile. . . . And here my real desert, my real merit, my real gift is blindness, paralysis, rottenness. . . . However, thou hast determined it; thou art provided with laughter on earth.

(*Florentine Codex*, bk. 6, p. 41)

The same sentiment—that the individual is unworthy but has been singled out by the gods—pervades many of the other speeches and ceremonials. Characteristically, the participant is charged with having covered himself with "filth and excrement" and with being undeserving to bear the "burden" or the "bundle" or the "carrying frame" handed down by the gods and the ancestors. Such is the case with the newly installed ruler, a child about to enter the *calmecac* or priestly schools, the new mother, or those about to assume the privileges and freedoms coming with the elevation to the status of the aged. One was to serve as a "replacement" and representative of the gods. "I am thy backrest, I am thy flute," confesses the new ruler. "I am thy lips, I am thy jaw, I am thy eyes, I am thy ears. And me, a commoner, a laborer, thou hast made thy teeth, thy fingernails. Insert, place within me a little of thy spirit, of thy word" (*Florentine Codex*, bk. 6, p. 45).

Human existence, individually and collectively, was due to the gods. "Thou wert good, thou wert fine when thou wert sent here," the confessor addresses the penitent, "when thy mother, thy father Quetzalcóatl made thee, created thee." Yet typically, the ceremonial speeches refer to the individual as having been polluted by some form of bodily waste (urine, excrement, saliva, spittle) or residual matter (chaff, straw, dirt, refuse, rags, tatters). Alonso de Zorita recorded the verbal and physical abuse of new rulers during enthronement ceremonies in Tlaxcala, Huexotzinco, and Cholula. According to Mendieta, charges and confessions of sins also held an important place in medical practice, serving as a means of expelling a foreign substance from the soul for the health of the body.

The rituals of elevation were accompanied by a ceremonial humbling of the participant. A noblewoman counseled her daughter on reaching discretion: "Although we are the parents, and although thou art born of goodly parents, thou art not to overesteem it; thou wilt offend our lord. For that he will pelt thee with dust, refuse, debauchery." Pride, arrogance, and brazenness were signs of a refusal to recognize that everything from the office of emperor to the newborn child to life itself is only on loan from the gods. Tempered by humility, the duty of men and women was to serve and to represent the gods while on the earth. The midwife addressed the gathered elders as "gods" and as the primordial first couple, Oxomoco and Cipactonal, after which she exhorted the new mother, "Thou hast exerted thyself, thou hast encountered, imitated our mother, Cihuacóatl, Quilaztli. . . . Thou hast returned exhausted from battle, my beloved maiden, brave woman; be welcome." A prayer advised the new ruler, "Take yet, grasp yet, arrive yet at the truth, for it is said and it is true, thou art the replacement, thou art the image of the lord of the near, of the nigh [Tloque Nahuaque]."

But while the principal gods (Tezcatlipoca, Tloque Nahuaque, Ometéotl, Quetzalcóatl) were invoked as residing at the navel of the earth and were "the knowers of men, seers into men's hearts and men's thoughts," the native idiom "No one is a navel on earth" meant that no one could presume with certainty to judge another. The role of humans, the *macehualli* or "obligated ones," was to assume and carry out the tasks of the gods while recognizing the unworthiness and even the futility of all human effort. The midwife advises the new mother to rear her child in service to the gods, "for our lord can only be helped, can only be aided [by what we do]." But, she concluded, "what we do is only [like] fanning flies away."

Especially dangerous were marginal times such as eclipses, midnight, and pregnancy. If special caution were not exercised during these periods, transformations and mutations were expected to occur. The midwife warned the expectant woman that if she engaged in excessive intercourse, the baby would be born feeble, or with lamed toes or fingers, or would become stuck in the womb. If she slept during the day, the infant would have large eyelids. If she chewed chicle, the baby would be unable to suckle. Were she to look on anything red, she would suffer a breech birth, and were she to eat chalk or earth, the baby would be born restless. "For what the mother drank, what she ate, that also the baby absorbed." Similar warnings marked other marginal and dangerous times. Living at the center demanded caution and moderation. "On earth we live, we travel along a mountain peak. Over here there is an abyss, over there is an abyss. . . . Only in the middle doth one go, doth one live."

This picture of living at the center of the earth as crisis, passage, struggle, and danger, with human beings singled out to represent the gods and to serve as their images, while recognizing that all things are only borrowed for a brief time, was mirrored in the stories of creation and in the cosmology. One key myth, found in various forms throughout Mesoamerica, describes how the present universe and its inhabitants were preceded by other worlds and other peoples, and how, as with the previous worlds, the present universe, too, will come to an abrupt and catastrophic end. The most detailed evidence comes from the Valley of Mexico, where more than twenty variants and fragments of the myth, some monumental and pictorial, have survived. The most extensive versions of the myth are recorded in a number of anonymous sixteenth-century documents, the *Histoyre du Mechique*, the *Anales de Cuauhtitlán*, the *Leyenda de los Soles*, and the *Historia de los Mexicanos por sus pinturas*. The last may be summarized briefly.

Prior to the existence of the world and the gods, an uncreated dual high god, Tonacatecuhtli–Tonacacíhuatl (Lord of Our Sustenance–Lady of Our Sustenance), existed alone at the summit of the universe in the highest of the thirteen heavens. The deity gave birth to four sons, in this version the Red Tezcatlipoca (identified with Camaxtli), the Black Tezcatlipoca, Quetzalcóatl, and Huitzilopochtli. For six hundred years the gods were inactive. Then the sons convened to determine what order should prevail. Quetzalcóatl and Huitzilopochtli were commissioned, and the cycles of creation began. They created fire, a half sun that lit the world poorly, and a primordial human couple, Oxomoco and Cipactónal, who were commanded to work the earth and weave and spin. The gods provided them with the arts of curing, the knowledge of divination with maize kernels, and a system for measuring time. The gods of death and the underworld, Mictlantecuhtli–Mictecacíhuatl, were created, along with the vertical levels of the universe, and these were populated with their appropriate deities. Then came the waters and in the waters a *cipactli* or alligator. The gods reconvened and tore the *cipactli* in half to form the sky and the earth.

The sun illuminated only poorly. The four primary gods or their representatives, in sequence, then assumed the role of the sun. The periods during which each of the gods held supremacy were called "Suns" and each Sun began and ended as one god overthrew another. According to the *Anales de Cuauhtitlán*, the first Sun (4 Water) ended in a flood and the inhabitants were turned into fish; the second (4 Ocelot) was inhabited by a race of giants and ended as the skies collapsed on the earth and the people were devoured by savage animals; the third (4 Rain) ended in a rain of fire and boulders; the fourth (4 Wind) ended in a tempest that carried away all the inhabitants, transforming them into monkeys.

Two periods in this cosmic history are especially significant and creative: the period following the birth of the four sons of the high god and the period following the fourth Sun. The calendar, the other gods, the earth, sky, and space were created in the first of these periods. They were re-created in the second. Two kinds of mythic themes predominate, that of the trickster-transformer and culture hero (Quetzalcóatl or Xólotl), and that of deities from whose bodies spring elements of the universe. In the first, Quetzalcóatl (or Xólotl) journeys to the underworld in search of the bones of the earlier inhabitants from which to create a new race. By means of magic, trickery, and theft, he secures the bones from Mictlan, accidentally breaks them, and carries them to Tamoanchan, where they are ground up by the goddess Quilaztli or Cihuacóatl. Quetzalcóatl then draws blood from his penis and mixes it with the bones, creating the present human race.

In another myth, Quetzalcóatl searches for maize hidden in Tonacatepetl (Sustenance Mountain) after changing himself into a black ant. He obtains some of the maize, it is chewed by the gods, and later, with the assistance of Nanahuatl or Nanahuatzin (Little Pimply One), Quetzalcóatl carries away the maize, providing the human race with its food.

These cycles of hero myths were complemented by creation stories in which elements of the creation come from the body of a slain and/

or buried deity. In one account (*Histoyre du Mechique*), Quetzalcóatl and Tezcatlipoca tear an earth monster in half, one part forming the sky and the other the earth, while from the remains come flowers, caves, trees, plants, mountains, and rivers. The same text tells how a variety of food plants came from the buried body of Cintéotl (Maize God), and how the intoxicating drink *octli* came from the buried bones of the goddess Mayahuel.

The fifth or present age of the world, *nahui ollin tonatiuh* (Four Motion Sun), began as a result of the gods again gathering to hold council, this time in Teotihuacán. Sahagún, who recorded nothing of the lore concerning the earlier ages, here provides the best account. For four nights the gods sacrificed to determine who among them would be selected to assume the role of the sun. Tecciztécatl and Nanahuatzin were chosen, the second depicted as a poor and humble figure, suffering from diseases of the skin and with nothing to offer other than his blood and scabs from his sores. Four times the wealthy god Tecciztécatl attempted to throw himself into the fire, but four times he drew back. Nanahuatzin then entered the fire and emerged as the sun, with Tecciztécatl becoming the moon after he entered the ashes. In *Historia de los Mexicanos por sus pinturas*, the sons of Quetzalcóatl and Tláloc play similar roles.

Still the sun did not move. The gods then sacrificed themselves, with the exception of Xólotl, who, fleeing the sacrifice, transformed materials he encountered (fish, ears of maize) into twins or doubles before finally being sacrificed. With the death of the gods, the present age began. It, too, would be destroyed, this time in an earthquake, and the sources are silent about the existence of any future ages.

In the myth, a preexistent primordial unity is broken with the birth of the first gods. After further creations and conflicts, another kind of unity is established, more tenuous than the first, and one that has to be periodically renewed at the end of calendrical cycles in the present age. Paul Westheim's observation about Aztec art fits equally well the Aztec conception of cosmic history: "There is never a harmonious flow. There is a struggle of elements, an interruption of the course of the movement, a brusque change of direction, a new advance, a new defeat, birth and death" (*The Art of Ancient Mexico*, 1965).

The world that eventuated from the sacrifices of the gods was conceived as a large disc floating on the water. Thirteen, or sometimes nine, vertical tiers or levels extend upward to Omeyocan and nine levels beneath to Mictlan (the place of the dead). In the Mexican, Mixtec, and Maya pictorial representations, world trees support the sky at the four quarters; in the Maya versions, a sacred ceiba tree extends through the middle of the heavens from the center of the earth. Horizontally, the earth is divided into four quadrants, east, north, west, and south. Each of the quadrants, in turn, possesses its own associated colors, qualities, sexual connotations, divinities, birds, and powers, with considerable regional variation.

A similar pattern underlay the time-counting systems, which were made up throughout most of Mesoamerica of two independent calendars. The preoccupation with time and with recurring cycles of time is one of the distinctive features of Mesoamerican religions. According to J. Eric S. Thompson, during the Classic period, "Maya astronomers at Palenque were recording calculations which sweep more than 1,250,000 years into the past, and then forward to dates over four millennia in the future. At about the same time, in another Maya city, there was recorded a computation which in all probability spans over 400,000,000 years" (*Maya Hieroglyphic Writing: An Introduction*, 1960).

"The Maya conceived of the divisions of time as burdens which were carried through all eternity by relays of bearers," Thompson observed. "This imagery differs strikingly from any picture of time our civilization has produced. For time was not portrayed as the journey of one bearer and his load, but of many bearers, each with his own division of time on his back." While the vast majority of peoples in Mesoamerica did not amplify the cycles of time to the dimensions of the Classic Maya, the attention to cycles and periods, each under the control of complexes of superhuman powers, is a significant part of the central Mexican myths, rituals, and calendars.

The first of the calendars, the *tonalpohualli* (Count of the Fates), was a divinatory and ritual calendar consisting of the permutation of the numerals 1 to 13 with twenty named days, signified by glyphs, resulting in a complete cycle of 260 days. The calendar was organized in such a way that each of the days was allotted to one of the four horizontal quadrants of the universe in the sequence, east, north, west, south, east, etc.

Each of the twenty thirteen-day periods, when the numeral *1* recurred, was believed to be under the influence of the day name and associated powers with which it began, and followed the same sequence of spatial relations, connecting the passage of time to the colors, trees, birds, and deities associated with each of the four quadrants.

The second calendar consisted of eighteen named "months" of twenty days each, plus five anomalous days at the end of the 365-day year called *nemontemi* by the Nahuas and *uayeb* by the Maya. Each of these months was marked by one or more great civic festivals. The two calendars were brought into relation with one another in such a way that the 365-day count could begin with only four of the day names; in central Mexico, the days were Reed, Flint, House, and Rabbit, days associated with the same sequence of horizontal quadrants. The same day names, the so-called year bearers, also marked out four periods of thirteen years each in the same directional sequence, each period being under the dominance of the name with which it began.

The calendars—or compasses or cosmographs—functioned to define cycles of time from four-day to thirteen-year periods, each period recapitulating the horizontal universe. As Clifford Geertz said of the Balinese calendars, "They don't tell you what time it is; they tell what kind of time it is"; and the *tonalpouhque* (calendar priests) employed the native codices as *tonalámatls* (Books of the Fates) to determine auspicious and inauspicious times, depending on the balance of the forces dominant in the cosmos.

Time and space were thus linked in discrete "moment-loci," as Soustelle called them, which "follow one another cyclically in an abrupt, total change according to a determinate rhythm, in conformity with an everlasting order. When the Duality decrees that a man shall be born or 'come down' (*temo*) he consequently finds himself inserted automatically into this order and in the grasp of the omnipotent machine." The present world age, the Fifth Sun (4 Motion), mirrored the quadripartite structure of the calendars. This "age of the center," as it is depicted on the famous Aztec Calendar Stone, was structured as the continuous recapitulation of the struggles of the gods, which began and ended the earlier Suns. As Miguel León-Portilla has pointed out, competition for supremacy caused the four Suns to pass, one after the other, until

a new kind of harmony was achieved by the death of the gods at Teotihuacán. "But to keep the sun in motion, constantly moving, a concession had been necessary. . . . To each of the four directions, a specified period of time within the Fifth Age was allotted for domination and subordination. . . . In abstract terms, motion appeared as a consequence of the spatialization of time and of the orientation of the years and days towards the four directions." Human time, in the cycles of the present age of the world, continuously repeated the pattern of divine time in the previous four ages of the world. Periodically, the universe faced dissolution and chaos if the structure established by the death of the gods at Teotihuacán could not be reestablished.

Places, too, were repeated and synthesized, the cosmic places of the horizontal world and those traversed during birth and death, and also the mythical places of the establishment and fall of sovereignty and civilization. In a recent intriguing study of the figure of Quetzalcóatl (*Quetzalcóatl and the Irony*, 1982), Davíd Carrasco argued that the mythical paradigmatic city, Tollan, did not refer to just one historical city, the Toltec capital at Tula, "but to an archetypal kingdom that contained the buildings, heroes, achievements, and memories of several illustrious sacred spaces." Similarly, the civilizing hero Quetzalcóatl was at once a divine being, several historical personages, a priestly office, and a paradigm of legitimate authority, the founder of the city "through which later people had to pass as pedestrians enriched socially and cultically, or as members of genealogies invigorated by Toltec blood," in order to be accepted as civilized leaders, founders, and rulers of their own Tollan.

The cycle of myths and tales surrounding Quetzalcóatl are the most famous in all of Mesoamerican legend. They span the time from the first of the creations to the meeting between Hernán Cortés and the Aztec emperor. In the collection of quasi-historical tales describing the establishment and fall of the Toltec capital, Quetzalcóatl was said to have been born in the year *ce ácatl* (One Reed), after his mother, Chimalman, had swallowed a green stone or had been impregnated by the god Mixcóatl. Quetzalcóatl fought with his father against the *centzon mimixcoa* (Four Hundred Ones of the Clouds), and his father was slain. Quetzalcóatl recovered and buried the bones, avenged his father's death, then ruled Tollan as the model priest Ce Ácatl Topiltzin Quetzalcóatl (Our Prince One Reed Quetzalcóatl), forbidding human sacrifice and establishing civilization.

According to the legends, the sorcerer Tezcatlipoca visited the city and sought out Quetzalcóatl, who had become ill. After prophesying the ruler's departure, Tezcatlipoca persuaded him to take an intoxicating drink as a remedy. Drunken, the chaste priest slept with his sister Quetzalpetatl and, shamed, abandoned Tollan. Tezcatlipoca, through disguise, magic, and sorcery, destroyed the Toltecs. Appearing as a naked peddler of chili peppers, he inflamed the desires of the daughter of the ruler Huemac, married her, and provoked a rebellion. He made the infant Huitzilopochtli dance magically on his hand in the marketplace, and in the crush to witness the miracle, many of the Toltecs died. He held a feast and, in the course of the dancing, people fell into a ravine and were changed into rocks. He transformed himself into a tiger, provoking panic and destruction.

After fleeing Tollan, Quetzalcóatl journeyed toward the south and the east, stopping at several places (notably Cholula), leaving behind knowledge of the civilizing arts. He then sailed off on a raft formed of serpents, or immolated himself and rose as the morning star, after promising to return and reclaim the throne he had left behind. Quetzalcóatl was described as "a white man, with a large body, broad forehead, large eyes and a long full beard." Cortés landed in Mexico in the year *ce ácatl,* 1519. Sahagún's informants said of the emperor Moctezuma,

> thus he thought, thus it was thought that this was Topiltzin Quetzalcóatl who had come to land. For it was in their hearts that he would come, that he would come to land, just to find his mat, his seat [throne]. For he had travelled there [eastward] when he had departed. And [Moctezuma] sent five emissaries to go and meet him, to go give him gifts.
>
> (Cited in Carrasco, p. 195)

The miraculous birth of Quetzalcóatl (legends record similar stories about Huitzilopochtli and the emperor Moctezuma Ilhuicamina), his battles, civilizing role, founding of the city, and his subsequent defeat and departure highlight the tenuous character of sovereignty gained, en-

joyed, and then inevitably lost. Durán recorded a cycle of legends telling how the tribal god Huitzilopochtli set out on a pilgrimage to guide the Aztecs and settle them in Tenochtitlán. But afterward, the god prophesies, the conquered "will turn against me, they will pick up my feet and throw me headfirst onto the floor."

The establishment of order and its periodic dissolution were reflected in the renewal rites common throughout Mesoamerica, usually involving sweeping, cleaning, and the lighting of new fires. Fray Diego de Landa, bishop of the Yucatán, described the rituals of the first day of the first month, Pop.

> They renewed on this day all the objects which they made use of, such as plates, vessels, stools, mats, and old clothes and the stuffs with which they wrapped up their idols. They swept out houses, and the sweepings and the old utensils they threw out on the waste heap outside the town; and no one, even were he in need of it, touched it.
>
> (p. 151)

In central Mexico the end of the great cycle of fifty-two years was marked by the ceremonial Binding of the Years, initiating a new cycle of time. According to Sahagún, all fires were extinguished, domestic icons and statues of the gods were thrown into the water, along with the hearthstones used for cooking, "and everywhere there was much sweeping—there was sweeping very clean. Rubbish was thrown out; none lay in any of the houses." He added in another place that "they had a prophecy or oracle of the devil that at [the end of] one of these periods the world would come to an end." Thus, at the end of the fifty-two-year period, the events through which the present age of the world had begun were ritually enacted. A new fire was drawn on the chest of a sacrificial victim on the hill Huixachtecatl and then carried to the temple of Huitzilopochtli, the *calmécac,* to the other temples, the *telpochcalli,* into the neighborhood temples and then into the homes, as the people threw themselves at the fire, blistering themselves. Rituals of sweeping and cleaning and the laying of new fires also marked the dedication of temples and preparation for battle.

"It is difficult to find in the history of religious cults one more complicated and ostentatious than that of the Ancient Mexicans," wrote the great Náhuatl scholar Ángel María Garibay K. In addition to the Binding of the Years, the ceremonies of enthronement, and those of the life cycle, Sahagún listed nineteen "moveable feasts" determined by the *tonalpohualli.* Besides these, each of the eighteen months saw the performance of one or more great civic ceremonies, to which the missionaries devoted considerable attention. The rituals were complex and defy brief summary. Though all of them had a major cultic theme linked with phases of the agricultural cycle, the rains, or the *gesta* of the gods, many also incorporated special rituals for patron deities of various occupations or rituals of healing, curing, or confession. In a monthly ceremony of preparation of the fields for planting, for example, a cycle of rites for the initiation of warriors began; in a harvest ceremonial, the ritual purification of women who had given birth took place. There was evidently considerable regional variation in the ceremonies but, as with other aspects of Mesoamerican religions, information is sparse outside the Náhuatl-speaking groups of central Mexico.

In six of the monthly festivals (those of the first, third, sixth, thirteenth, and sixteenth months) Tláloc played a central role; four of the monthly feasts (the second, fourth, eighth, and eleventh) centered on the maize cycle, from seedtime to harvest; in two (the tenth and eighteenth) Xiuhtecuhtli (Fire Lord) held a major role; one (the fourteenth) involved hunting rites and the god Mixcóatl; the seventh was celebrated in honor of Huixtocíhuatl (Salt Lady); in three of the festivals (the fifth, ninth, and fifteenth) Huitzilopochtli and Tezcatlipoca had major roles; the twelfth witnessed the return of all the gods; the seventeenth honored Llamatecuhtli (Old Lady), patroness of the *cihuateteo,* the women goddesses who became escorts of the sun after dying in childbirth.

Preparations for the rituals began sometimes as far as a year in advance and overlapped into the subsequent months. Ritual offerings (rubber, paper, beheaded quail, food, clothing, incense), ritual dancing and singing, processions, insults, and mock skirmishes were common. In the majority of the feasts, one or more impersonators of the gods was slain and in some, priests or other functionaries assumed anew the role of the gods following the sacrifice. Distinctive forms of ritual

killing were a central part of the ceremonies and reached massive proportions in the late Postclassic period, especially among the Aztecs. Estimates of the victims sacrificed at the completion and dedication of the great temple of Huitzilopochtli range from 100 (Bartolomé de Las Casas) to 80,000 (Torquemada). Ritual warfare, the *xochiyáotl* (Flowery War), between the Mexicans and groups such as the Tlaxcalans whom they had not conquered, was instituted to provide victims for the sacrifices. The native gloss on the sacrifices seems to have been that the sun needed human lives, hearts, and blood to continue living. Children were sacrificed to Tláloc by drowning or shutting in caves. Flaying and beheading and ritual dancing in the skins of the victims marked the inauguration and end of the yearly maize cycles. Ritual burnings took place in the tenth month, Xocotlhuetzi, in honor of Xiuhtecuhtli/Otontecuhtli.

Several of the monthly feasts included a dramatic portrayal of historic legendary events. In one Aztec myth, the goddess Coatlicue (Serpent Skirt) was sweeping on Coatépec (Serpent Mountain) when a ball of cotton fell from the sky, which she placed in her skirt. She became pregnant, angering her daughter and her sons, the *centzon huitznáhuac* (Four Hundred Ones of the South), who advanced to kill her. Huitzilopochtli was born fully armed, beheaded his sister with his weapon, the *xiuhcóatl* (Fire Serpent), and chased the four hundred around Coatepec before killing them. The great German scholar Eduard Seler, who set the standards for the modern interpretation of the Mexican codices and texts, noted that the fifteenth month, Panquetzaliztli (Raising of Banners), celebrated the mythic event. Captives were ritually bathed and an image of Paynal, described as the lieutenant of Huitzilopochtli, was carried rapidly to several locations near the capital, where captives were slain. Ritual skirmishes took place between the bathed ones and others called *huitznauhac.* At the temple of Huitzilopochtli, a priest lit sacrificial papers with a ritual *xiuhcóatl,* and when the god arrived at the base of the temple, also called Coatepec, the captives were beheaded.

Other ceremonies drew in part on the dramatic battles through which the universe had passed. The annual agricultural cycle began with the second of the monthly feasts, Tlacaxipehualiztli (The Feast of the Flaying of Men).

According to Durán, this was "a most solemn, festive, bloody ceremony, which cost so many human lives that no other rivaled it . . . and was the most popular of all the solemnities." Forty days before the feast, captives were bathed and dressed to honor Xipe Totec and were engaged in ritual skirmishes. Then began the gladiatorial sacrifice (*Tlahuahuanaliztli*) in which a captive was tied by the ankle to the center of a sacrificial stone and attacked by four warriors in succession, two "eagles" and two "ocelots." If he survived, a fifth warrior, "The Left-Handed One," killed him. The victim's heart was removed and the body flayed, the skin being worn in ritual begging before being buried the following month.

The maize rites continued during the fourth month, and in the eighth month an impersonator of the goddess of the young maize, Xilonen, was decapitated on the back of a priest; seed corn (*cintéotl*) was prepared for the following year, and ceremonies were performed for midwives and curers. The cycle of maize rites concluded one-half year after it began, in the eleventh-month festival, Ochpaniztli (The Sweeping of the Way), held at harvest. A woman was selected to be the image of Teteo Innan or Toci (Our Grandmother) and provided with a retinue of older women who engaged in ritual battles for a four-day period, after which either real or symbolic intercourse with the emperor took place and the young maize god, Cintéotl, was born. The impersonator of Toci was decapitated and flayed, and a male priest wearing her skin ran through the city until he reached the temple of Huitzilopochtli, where "she" met her son, Cintéotl, wearing a mask made from the thigh skin of the victim, after which "she" was ritually driven from the city.

At the conclusion of the monthly ceremonies, the five-day period *nemontemi* began, a time hedged by warnings and cautions. Whatever happened during this period was thought to have a lasting effect. "Neither might one sleep during the day. If so, it was said: 'So shalt thou always.'"

The ceremonies and the managing and maintenance of the temples and other religious structures involved a large-scale priesthood, both full- and part-time, and great numbers of assistants. Torquemada reported that nearly 5,000 persons were subject to service in the temple of Huitzilopochtli. The first modern historian of ancient Mexico, Francisco Javier Clavijero, estimated that 1 million priests were in service throughout the empire. Sahagún listed thirty-eight types of priests in one section of his *Historia* and nearly eighty temples and other sites of major ritual activity in and around the capital. "To the priests they gave the name *teopixque*," Clavijero wrote, "which is the same as guardian or official of God." Another term, *tlamacazqui*, was applied both to the young Nahua priests and to the gods.

The political role of the priesthood varied. In some instances the cities were under the control of a dual priesthood (as in Postclassic Cholula). In others (Tenochtitlán) the priesthood was separate from the secular king, although the highest of the priests allegedly served as elector(s) of the emperor. Among the Aztecs, the two highest priests were the *quetzalcoa*, dedicated to the service of the gods Tláloc and Huitzilopochtli. Under them was the *mexícatl teohuatzin*, "the Mexican in charge of the gods," who, according to Sahagún, "controlled other, less important priests, somewhat like bishops, and he saw to it that everything to do with divine worship in all places and provinces was carried out diligently and perfectly. . . . He controlled all matters concerning the worship of the gods in the provinces subject to Mexico."

The male and female priests served a wide variety of functions. They supervised and saw to the maintenance of the temples, collected tribute for the temples, managed the civic feasts, served as singers, dancers, temple guardians, overseers, treasurers, advisers, electors, and warriors. Alongside their more explicitly ceremonial functions, the priests also supervised education in the *calmécac*, where the children of the nobility were prepared for the priesthood or for posts in government. In addition to the state-associated priests, there were evidently large numbers of diviners, soothsayers, readers of the *tonalámatl*, astrologers, shamans, diviners with maize kernels, illusionists, curers, confessors, and midwives, most of whose roles the missionary ethnographers did not describe in detail and which, in some cases, persisted after the conquest.

León-Portilla has stressed the importance of the priestly philosopher, the *tlamatinime* (He

Who Knows Things), metaphorically portrayed in one of Sahagún's texts as "a stout torch that does not smoke." Among the surviving Náhuatl poems is a genre of poetry called *icnocuícatl* (Songs of Orphanhood). Several of these poems, along with the ritual speeches, bring to the fore a dimension of the cosmogony and cosmology somewhat different from the demand to uphold order and serve as the representative of the gods.

In the poems, the top of the universe, *Omeyocan* (Two Place or The Place of Duality), is pictured as the primordial source from which all creation proceeded and from which souls descended into the wombs of their mothers at conception. In the poems of orphanhood, birth and creation are regarded as moments of estrangement and separation. Life on the earth is but a dream and an illusion. "No one matters to the giver of life," states one of the poems, and according to another, "Thou mockest us, we are nothing, in nothing you hold us, you are destroying us, you are destroying us here"; and still another, "In vain am I born, in vain I descended from the house of the god to the earth. I am an orphan."

The view that things on the earth are only on loan for a short time found its expression in the judgment that "this is the inevitable outcome of all powers, empires, and domains; transitory are they and unstable. The time of life is borrowed, in an instant it must be left behind." According to one of Sahagún's informants:

> Our lord, the lord of the near, of the nigh, is made to laugh. He is arbitrary, he is capricious, he mocketh. He willeth in the manner he desireth. He is placing us in the palm of his hand; he is making us round. We roll; we become as pellets. We make him laugh; he is making a mockery of us.
>
> (*Florentine Codex*, bk. 6, p. 51)

From such a perspective, the purpose of life is less to preserve the order of the world by impersonating the deeds and the deaths of the gods than to recover the primordial unity, ruptured at the moment of birth and creation, and to return to the highest of the heavens, "where there is happiness, where one lives and there is joy," and where "it is unceasing, the song which vanishes our tears and our sadness. It is where one lives, it is one's home."

These contrasting outlooks, correlating roughly with the respective dominance of the horizontal and vertical orders of the cosmos, indicate the breadth of the Nahua world view. It was a view in which a conviction of a special historic and cosmic destiny coexisted with a sense of the impermanence of earthly existence. Pride in being heir to a distinctive Toltec cultural legacy was matched by the tendency to easily assimilate and adopt the religious beliefs and practices of other groups, both native and Christian.

The result, according to many of the missionaries, was that Christianity and paganism were blended and transformed in such a way that in religious matters the natives were, in Durán's words, "neither one nor the other" (*neutros*) and the religion that emerged was a "salad." Three centuries later, a pioneer of modern anthropology, Edward Burnett Tylor, reached much the same conclusion. Following a journey to Mexico in 1856, Tylor wrote that

> practically, there is not much difference between the old heathenism and the new Christianity. . . . They had just received the Immaculate conception, as they had received many mysteries before it; and they were not a little delighted to have a new occasion for decorating themselves and their churches with flowers, marching in processions, dancing, beating drums and letting off rockets as their custom is. The real essence of both religions is the same to them.
>
> (*Anahuac*, 1861)

The issue of what Tylor called "survivals" (the persistence of earlier customs) is a complicated one. Pre-Hispanic folk traditions and popular cults are documented less extensively in the sources than are the public state cults, making it difficult to trace the origins of many non-Christian customs. Moreover, not all non-Christian customs are pre-Hispanic, nor is it likely that every modern practice for which a pre-Hispanic parallel can be cited is genuinely pre-Hispanic. Some may have developed independently; others may have derived from Spanish folk religion.

A brief illustration, taken from Elsie Clews

133

Parsons' *Mitla: Town of Souls* (1936), will suffice to illustrate some of the complexities, in this instance limited to the issue of witchcraft, in a few twentieth-century Zapotecan communities.

> On the whole I think there is a much greater measure of Spanish than of Indian in the whole complex of Spanish-Indian witchcraft, but until we have a thorough study of witchcraft in Spain the analysis in America must be guesswork. At Mitla, my guess is that the concept of the witch who "blows" is Indian, and the concept of the doll representative or image of the victim is Spanish; that the most prevalent concept of sickness as something deleterious sent by a witch into the body is Indian; that sucking out the *chizo* is outstandingly Indian, and treatment of bewitchment by egg, outstandingly Spanish. Blowing or spraying alcohol (medicine) is Indian. The belief in *ojo*, evil eye, is, of course, Spanish, but the belief that infants are peculiarly subject to witchcraft, necessitating, for example, anti-witch fumigation—this belief may be Indian as well as Spanish. . . . The concept of *aire* as a cause of sickness appears to be Indian . . . although it may have been confirmed together with the attitude in general toward evil winds by the early European fear of fresh air, particularly night air, which is linguistically recorded in our term "malaria."
>
> (pp. 493–494)

Various substitutions have taken place as well, the most famous being the building of a Christian shrine on the spot of an ancient pilgrimage site at Tepeyac, north of Mexico City. "Now that the Church of Our Lady of Guadalupe has been built there, they call her Tonantzin too," Sahagún wrote, referring to the substitution of the mother of Jesus for the native earth goddess, Tonantzin (Our Mother). The practice of sacrificing impersonators of the gods occasionally led to crucifixions. The cults of the Christian saints (including the several Christs and Virgins) seem to have replaced and transformed some of the ancient gods.

Closely allied to the cult of the saints are the *santo-cargo* and *mayordomía* ritual systems, requiring men of the village to assume the burden (*cargo*) of sponsoring, through the course of the year, the ritual activities and masses celebrated in honor of one of the *santos*, thereby gaining prestige and the opportunity to hold political office in the community. In *Sons of the Shaking Earth* (1959), Eric Wolf observed that although it has Spanish prototypes (the *cofradías* or brotherhoods), the core of the system seems to be pre-Hispanic. He cited Motolinía's comment that

> there were some who labored two or three years and acquired as much as possible for the purpose of honoring the demon with a feast. On such a feast they not only spent all that they possessed, but even went into debt, so that they would have to do service for a year and sometimes two years in order to get out of debt. . . .
>
> Each year, a different group of men undertakes to carry out the tasks of religious office; each year a different group of men makes itself responsible for the purchase and ritual disposal of food, liquor, candles, incense, fireworks, and for all other attendant expenditures. A tour of religious duty may leave a man impoverished for several years, yet in the eyes of his fellow citizens he has added greatly to his prestige. . . . Each year, religious participation wipes out considerable sums of goods and money; each year part of the surplus of the community is consumed in offerings or exploded in fireworks to please the saints.
>
> (pp. 215–216)

In Zinacantan, a Maya village in the highlands of Chiapas, Evon Z. Vogt noted over fifty-five saints and a waiting list of twenty-two years for the assumption of ritual sponsorship. Vogt speculated that "the cargoholders are the contemporary equivalents of the ancient Maya Year Bearers. Each carries the burden of office for a year before passing it along to his successor." He also suggested that some similar rotational priesthood may have been in existence at the Classic Maya ceremonial centers.

The cycle of creation stories and lore of the ages of the world also persist in some areas. In *Maya History* (1970), Thompson summarized a number of contemporary Maya creation stories, three of which may serve as examples. In a Mam account, the first inhabitants of the world were monkeys who were destroyed by burning pitch; in the second, the inhabitants were gophers who were destroyed in a flood. In the third creation, the first couple, Mary and Joseph, appeared. Since it was dark, Joseph made the sun, the moon, and the earth. Jesus was born and said to his father, "Do not be troubled, father, for I am going to make another world and you will be able to help me." Then Jesus began to make the mountains, valleys, and canyons, making the moon less bright than the sun so people could sleep at night.

According to a Tzotzil story, in an earlier age Lucibel (Lucifer?) had been the sun, but the sun lighted the world poorly and gave off little heat. The child Jesus then assumed the role of the sun, ascending to heaven with his mother, who became the moon. "In present-day Santo Tomás Chichicastenango," Thompson noted, "it is told that when Jesus was crucified, He miraculously turned, exposing his back. From it came white, yellow, and black maize, beans, potatoes, and all other food plants. Then He died. This legend may have arisen from Jesus' words, 'I am the bread of life.' "

The cults and traditions of ancient Mesoamerica and their transformations constitute an important chapter in the history of religions. The dualisms and the contradictions many scholars have noted in late Nahua religion reveal the tensions inherent in Aztec culture, but also the richness and complexity of the Nahua world view, according to which human existence was judged to be purposeful and real, yet illusory. The goal of life, as the texts so often intimate, was to accept periodically the privileged responsibility of imitating the gods and ancestors and assuming their burdens. They, in turn, frequently through their deaths, had assumed the roles of the elements of creation, upholding for a time the tenuous order of the universe. At the same time, a significant number of the formal speeches and poems give expression to the sense, quite literal, of living on borrowed time. Birth, as descent from Ometeotl, was estrangement, passage into a transitory realm of orphanhood, deception, and futility. "We come only to sleep," said one of the poets. "We come only to dream. It is not true, it is not true that we come to live on the earth."

BIBLIOGRAPHY

Alfonso Caso, *The Aztecs: People of the Sun* (1958); Francisco Javier Clavijero, *The History of Mexico, Collected from Spanish and Mexican Historians, from Manuscripts and Ancient Paintings of the Indians* (1806); Diego Durán, *The Aztecs: The History of the Indians of New Spain* (1964) and *Book of the Gods and Rites and the Ancient Calendar,* Fernando Horcasitas and Dario Heyden, trans. and eds. (1971); Ángel María Garibay K., *Historia de la literatura Náhuatl,* 2 vols. (1964–1965); Benjamin Keen, *The Aztec Image in Western Thought* (1971); Walter Krickeberg, "Mesoamerica," in *Pre-Columbian American Religions,* Stanley Davis, trans. (1968).

Diego de Landa, *Relación de las Cosas de Yucatán,* Alfred M. Tozzer, trans. and ed. (1941); Miguel León-Portilla, *Aztec Thought and Culture: A Study of the Ancient Náhuatl Mind,* Jack Emory Davis, trans. (1963); Alfredo López-Austin, *Hombre-Dios: Religión y política en el Mundo Náhuatl* (1973); Gerónimo de Mendieta, *Historia Eclesiástica Indiana: Obra escrita a fines del siglo XVI* (1971); Toribio de Benevente o Motolinía, *Memoriales* (1903); Henry B. Nicholson, "Religion in Pre-Hispanic Central Mexico," in *Handbook of Middle American Indians,* Robert Wauchope, ed., vol. 10, pt. 1 (1971).

Bernardino de Sahagún, *The Florentine Codex: General History of the Things of New Spain,* 12 vols., Arthur J. O. Anderson and Charles E. Dibble, trans. (1950–1976); Eduard Seler, *Gesammelte Abhundlungen zur Amerikanischen Sprach- und Altertumskunde,* 5 vols. (1902–1923); Jacques Soustelle, *Daily Life of the Aztecs on the Eve of the Spanish Conquest,* Patrick O'Brian, trans. (1961); Juan de Torquemada, *Los veintiún libros rituales y monarquía indiana,* 3 vols. (1969); Juan Adolfo Vázquez, "The Religions of Mexico and of Central and South America," in *A Reader's Guide to the Great Religions,* Charles J. Adams, ed. (1977); Evon Z. Vogt, *Tortillas for the Gods: A Symbolic Analysis of Zinacanteco Rituals* (1976).

[See also Native American Religions; Religion in Hispanic America Since the Era of Independence; and Religion in the Spanish Empire.]

NATIVE AMERICAN RELIGIONS

Sam D. Gill

IN the journal of his 1492 voyage, Christopher Columbus wrote the following about the religion of the peoples he called *los indios:*

> They should be good servants and very intelligent, for I have observed that they soon repeat anything that is said to them, and I believe that they would easily be made Christians, for they appear to me to have no religion.

AN OBSCURING PRIMITIVISM

Columbus' identification of religion with Christianity is that of virtually every student of American religious history. Indians have been a part of American religious history only insofar as they have been subjects of the Christianization of America. If anything of their native ways could be called religion it was always a "primitive religion," and from the point of view of an historical study, primitive religion is scarcely religion at all.

Columbus held that the land he encountered was Asia. Though by the early sixteenth century the land had already gained a new identity—America—Native Americans have continued to be called Indians, and it is still widely held that they have no religion. Why have our perceptions of the land changed and grown, while our perceptions of the people have not? As Edmundo O'Gorman has shown in *The Invention of America* (1961), America exists for us as "America" because, after Columbus' death, Europeans came to recognize an incongruity between the observations of Columbus and other travelers and what they knew of the geography of the world at the time. The beginning of the resolution of this incongruity was the invention of the idea of a new continent, a place that came to be called

America. American history may be seen as the working out, over time, of the identity of this idea, expressed through images of the landscape and through actions of peoples within this landscape. American history has been made and written in the process of responding to and resolving the incongruities that have existed between our experience in America and the expectations that stem from our images of America.

Against the background of the unfolding of American history, we may consider the character and history of the encounter with the peoples native to the Americas. In the time of Columbus no incongruity was recognized between the images and expectations held for *los indios* and the actual peoples encountered, even though many elements of this incongruity were present. More important, no such incongruity has ever been recognized. As Columbus believed that he had found a trade route to Asia, we have persisted in the belief that we know "the Indians." The voyages of Columbus became significant only when it was recognized that the observations he made did not correspond to the maps he was using. Yet we persist in believing that "the Indians" we observe conform to our preconceptions. American history documents this fact.

Government policy has always assumed that "we" know what "they" want and need more than they do, even when they openly express opposing views. At best this has been a policy of paternalism that commonly has been supplanted by one of killing and/or moving entire peoples to meet the exigencies of the advancement of American and Christian interests. It was public policy from the late nineteenth century to nearly the mid-twentieth century to prohibit dances and feasts—that is, the public religious practices—of native peoples, and Native Americans were not granted the religious freedom guaranteed to all Americans until passage of the American Indian Religious Freedom Act of 1978.

Throughout American history "the Indians" have been seen as "primitive peoples," and this prejudice has commonly yielded either the image of the "noble savage"—that is, a pristine natural people untainted by history and civilization—or a contrasting image of the ignoble savage—a wretched, dull, illiterate, dirty, nearly inhuman race unable either to express itself or to care for itself. Neither image allows for what we call religion as understood in terms of the history, institutions, Scriptures, and doctrine that have characterized Christianity. The history of our encounters with Native Americans has been almost wholly shaped by the images held of them. There is a blinding tyranny in these images.

We, like Columbus before us, inevitably find what we set out to find, see what we want to see. Like Columbus before us, we have expressed through public action, if not always through clear statement, that these native peoples "have no religion." We remain deaf to their insistence that we have not understood them, that we have not seen them, and that our policies, as well as our studies, radically transform, even violate, them.

In the presentation of Native American religions we must recognize the incongruity between our images of these peoples and their religions, images we may identify by the term *the Indian,* and the actual people themselves, whom we may call *Native Americans.* We must reject all the implications of terms like *primitive religions, primitive peoples,* and *preliterate peoples.* We must see that Native American religions not only provide a context and background for the history of American Christianity, but are also true religions sharing the landscape with American Christianity. Indeed, these native religious traditions have roots that run more deeply into the soil than those of Christianity in America.

TRIBAL TRADITIONS

Shape of Native American Religions. The most fundamental fact to begin with is that there is no such thing as "the Native American religion"—that is, a single, consistent religious practice, set of beliefs, institution, and history that exists throughout the Americas, or even just North America. There is no such thing as the Indian language, the Indian culture, or the Indian way. Diversity, variety, and complexity characterize the shape of Native American religions. A brief outline of the cultural and language diversities will help establish this point as well as provide the necessary context in which to present Native American religions.

The length of time the Americas have had human inhabitants is a subject of continuing controversy, yet it is incontestable that it has been thousands of years. During that time peoples spread throughout the Western Hemisphere and developed a wide variety of cultures. In the study of North American cultures a number of methods have been used to analyze and present this complex array. The most common among them is the designation of culture and language phyla. Culture-area designations are delimited geographically on the basis of the consistency of cultural patterns. Signal among the factors distinguishing a culture area, beyond geography, is the mode of subsistence, which, in turn, is reflected throughout the cultural patterns, particularly through the shaping of material culture (houses, tools, artworks). For North America nine language phyla are described, in which hundreds of distinct languages are classified. Language classification provides one line of evidence, complementing the archaeological, for discerning the long history of tribal cultures. As yet there is no system for classifying native religions in North America other than designating the culture area and subsistence mode.

In spite of the common insistence on the singularity and commonality of "the Indian religion," the shape of Native American religions can best be characterized by the term *diversity.* We can appreciate this in a variety of frames. For example, while it is commonly held that subsistence patterns—simplified as hunting and agriculture—correlate with modes of religion, a review of religions among cultures with similar subsistence patterns reveals considerable variety. Bear ceremonialism, for example, has been understood as a core feature of hunting cultures with religious practices throughout the sub-Arctic regions, maintaining a continuity with religious practices from great antiquity. There is certainly a basis for this position, for throughout the region one can find the belief in a master/mistress of the animals, a magico-religious character to the practice of hunting, and special treatment of the bones or other physical parts of the killed game. Despite these common features, it must be remembered that the geographic area for hunting bears is enormous, extending from the Labrador Peninsula to western Canada and Alaska. The religious and cultural diversity is great even around this common subsistence practice. In some of these tribes, hunting is linked with individual and shamanistic activities, while in others it is a community activity involving elaborate ceremonies, including dance and drama.

Generally, almost all tribes in North America gain a portion of their subsistence from hunting. Even the Pueblo tribes of the American Southwest, identified so strongly with agriculture and a sedentary life-style, depend seasonally upon hunting. The Pueblo hunt in a ritually prescribed manner. Hunting and animals are prominent subjects in a huge body of Pueblo oral traditions. Likewise, religious and cultural diversity occurs among cultivators who reside in North America in latitudes from southern Canada south.

At this early stage in the study of the religions of Native American cultures, it is essential to appreciate the diversity of religious beliefs and practices throughout North America and, further, to understand the inadequacy of ecology, geography, language, and the principal source of sustenance as the basis for classifying the religions. Though all of these factors are important, they do not give enough information in themselves for a satisfactory classification of religions.

Opacity of Native American Theology. The great bulk of research into the spiritual and theological conceptions of the tribal peoples of North America has been directed toward the search for evidence to establish theories about the evolution of religion. Some scholars have sought the prevalence of a high god and monotheism in North America to demonstrate an original monotheism among all peoples. Others have held that the high god is a product of human evolution culminating in Christianity and have thus attempted to show that such figures did not occur among the peoples of North America. What we must acknowledge is that these theories

of Native American theology are products of European (predominantly Christian) thought that have drawn a veil over native conceptions of the spiritual world.

Even fundamental questions about the presence of Native American categories of the spiritual, supernatural, and theological have not been adequately raised, much less extensively dealt with. In a provocative article entitled "Ojibwa Ontology, Behavior, and World View," A. Irving Hallowell, upon considering the Ojibwa language and world view, demonstrates that the natural-supernatural dichotomy appears to be alien to the Ojibwa. There should be no question that, given the diversity and complexity of the tribal religions in North America, no single set of theological terms is adequate and explicit and, further, that the common theological terminology derived from Western religious traditions (including such words as *god, deity, spirit,* and *supernatural*) is inadequate. Such terminology makes it likely that native religious conceptions will be misrepresented. Given these cautions and admitting the inadequacy of our available terminology, we may make some tentative remarks about Native American spiritual conceptions.

Some, but certainly not all, native cultures in North America name and otherwise identify at least one major figure that is spiritual in character. Both male and female figures appear in this role. There may or may not be a cosmic creator. It is unusual for there to be a highly developed story tradition associated with those figures designated as creators. Some are removed from the human world and are never addressed in prayer or through ritual, while others are close at hand and approachable by human beings.

For some tribes a pervasive spiritual power has been identified and discussed—for example, *orenda* for the Iroquois, *manitou* for the Algonquian, and *wakan* for the Dakota (or Sioux). This power not only pervades all existence but can also be conceived of in a personified form, such as Gitchi Manitou and Wakan Tanka.

In recent times many tribal peoples have referred to a major spiritual figure by the English term *Great Spirit.* A variety of views have been expressed regarding the history and identity of this being, but it seems clear that from a tribal perspective this figure corresponds to a number of beings identified in tribal history by specific tribal names. The "Great Spirit," while perhaps common in modern pan-tribalism, was in earlier times not a single figure believed in by many tribes, but rather a common term for a number of beings with various identities. Doubtless the development of the "Great Spirit" has been influenced by the theological conceptions of Christianity, which is a monotheistic and male-dominant religion.

Apart from spiritual presences of extraordinary power and prominence, beings of almost untold variety exist in the oral and ritual traditions of Native Americans. These figures may be referred to as mythological and must certainly be considered evidence of native theological conceptions. Mythological figures commonly are animated aspects of the natural world: waters, winds, celestial phenomena, animals, insects, plants, and so on. Other mythological figures have no physical counterpart in the human natural world. Because these beings are so extensively developed in story, and because storytelling is so central to many Native American tribal peoples, these mythological figures are central to our comprehension of Native American spiritual and theological conceptions.

Throughout North America the native peoples do not see and encounter their world in merely physical and banal terms. Every plant, animal, object, and point of orientation is the subject of a story in which personal, moral, and spiritual dimensions are drawn that shape the way human beings live every day with these elements of the world.

Through the ritual dimensions of Native American life we can discern another dimension of their spiritual conceptions. (There is an overlap here with the mythological dimension.) Native Americans express their theological conceptions through ritual personification in masked and dramatic presentations, through acts of prayer, through vision and guardian spirit quests, through shamanistic performances, through hunting and planting rites, and through totemic acts. Here we find a variety of entities conceived by Native Americans, none of which we are likely to understand as clearly as they do.

Religious Symbolism. Native American languages are exclusively oral. Until recently at least, Native American languages were not written; there are no alphabetic counterparts to the spoken words. Exclusive orality greatly shapes the forms of expression, the religious practices and symbols, and even the modes of thought.

We customarily center descriptions of religious traditions on their history, scriptures, doctrine, and expressions of thought. All of these depend upon writing. Native Americans do not have written histories, written scriptures, statements of doctrine, or second-order traditions of critical and interpretive thought presented in writing. We must look to artifacts, actions, and stories as the religious principles of these symbols, from which we may discern the shape, character, and fundamental principles of these religious traditions. We must consider expressions of the landscape, shapes of houses and other architectural forms, costumes, dances, masks, medicine bundles, and the oral forms of song, prayer, and story.

Native American religious symbols are commonly displayed in museums and in publications, intermingled with artifacts shown for their cultural and aesthetic values. While there is often a correlation between the religious importance of symbolic objects and their aesthetic value, this is certainly not always the case in Native American cultures. For example, a Crow medicine bundle might contain feathers, bird and animal skins, animal and human bones, teeth, herbs, pigments, and minerals. If the bundle's contents were simply displayed, it would appear to outsiders, and perhaps even to many Crow people, as an assortment of apparently valueless objects— that is, as junk. But this would be to greatly misunderstand the symbolic character of these objects. Such bundles contain the history, the power, and the authority of a community of people; they are carefully and privately held by the most trustworthy members of a community; and they are rarely opened for display even by members of the group, and then according to ritual procedure. While such objects are not likely to be considered art, their religious importance may be misunderstood because they have little apparent aesthetic appeal.

On the occasion of transitions in the calendrical cycle, transitions in the life cycle, the onset of an illness, or the needs of the community, religious actions are performed by tribes throughout North America. Such actions are often of a highly symbolic character. We tend to consider symbols primarily in terms of their referential values; in other words, we ask what they represent. For example, in considering the grand performance of the Sun Dance, which is still practiced by many Plains cultures, we tend to ask what the central pole stands for, what the elements of costuming stand for, and why certain rites and songs are sung. These are, without a doubt, important considerations, but they do not lead to an adequate or complete understanding of the event.

The holding of such an event is inseparable from its being enacted; that is, from its effects, including the evocative and emotive ones that are inseparable from performance and observation. Such effects occur on many levels, from the transmission of culture from one generation to another, to the reaffirmation of the many positions and interrelationships in the social structure, to the highest level of re-creating or reaffirming the cosmic order, the order of the world. It is in religious performance and action that we must seek the fullest meaning of Native American religious symbolism; unfortunately, however, these very dimensions are often ignored in the published records of Native American religions.

Native Americans widely utilize symbolic reversals in an effective manner. Performances of clowns are widespread. Through their performance a community shares the experience of foolish action, of actions proceeding from human needs gone out of control, of actions that are forbidden and even unspeakable. In the widespread stories of trickster figures—such as the coyote, raven, mink, and raccoon—the reversals and the extremes of the ordered human world are explored. The trickster figure is not a deity but rather a utopian figure who resists the rules of order and their accompanying restrictions. Nonetheless, through his defiance and reversal of the expected order of things, and through the shared experience of his foolishness and suffering, order is reaffirmed. Trickster and clown figures in Native American religions participate in the ongoing creative religious process. Their acts serve to transform and fix the world, and their enactments of symbolic reversals serve to reaffirm the order of the created world.

In many if not all Native American cultures there are dominant symbols or symbolic relationships. Such dominant symbols are found replicated in many ways at many levels, from the simplest level of material culture to cosmology. Many, especially Plains tribes, have described and interpreted the importance of the circumscribed cross whose arms correspond with the cardinal or semicardinal directions.

The complexity and pervasiveness of a dominant symbolic pattern of the Tewa village of San Juan, located north of Santa Fe, New Mexico, is carefully described by Alfonso Ortiz in *The Tewa World* (1969). The pattern, which is one of a complexly mediated duality, can be found replicated in physical and mythological geographies, in calendrical and seasonal distinctions, in social and ceremonial organizations, in economic and sustenance activities, and in village and house structures.

In many cultures a dominant symbolic complex may center on a single object that has manifold uses and interpretations. Objects commonly found in North America that serve as dominant symbols are corn (and corn meal and corn pollen), tobacco (and also the pipe and the smoke), and other plants such as squash, beans, and cacti. Many animals serve as dominant symbols—the eagle, bear, and wolf.

In the Navajo culture of the American Southwest a physical representation of a dominant symbol is the open circle. The ideas it incorporates may be found replicated in cosmology, ritual patterns and procedures, craft and material objects, house structures, and cultural practices. The symbolic motif is related to motion, interdependent relationships, and the imminence of closure—that is, the constriction and confinement of being encircled.

Religion and the Landscape. Presently, non–Native Americans often express their admiration for "the Indian" spiritual relationship with the land, its plants, and its animals—a relationship seen as a harmonious, holistic, and spiritual ecology. This view of "the Indian" is more the product of a European-American disenchantment with Western lifeways and modernity than the result of careful study of Native American cultures and histories. It needs to be tested. These expectations of ecological and spiritual purity pressure Native Americans to act accordingly or to suffer frustration when they cannot. While well intended, such expectations may have the effect of once more manipulating Native Americans and predetermining who they are and how they can acceptably act. Native Americans' humanity will in some ways be denied until their cultures and religions are considered more openly, thoroughly, and even critically; and until Native Americans are permitted the possibility of a spirituality that manipulates and alters the landscape, even to the extent of having a negative ecological impact upon the land, as well as the possibility of a spirituality that correlates with current understandings of proper ecology.

For Native Americans the landscape is the site upon which is projected and through which is concretized a gradient of values, a set of categories and distinctions that comprise their religious world views. To be attentive to these fundamental categories and distinctions is the first key to understanding Native Americans and their religions, particularly in light of their exclusive orality.

There are many ways the landscape gives form to religious ideas. Fundamentally, Native Americans see their landscapes as bound spaces; that is, as territories. This conception of territory is expressed in both temporal and spatial dimensions. The limits of a territory are defined by the physical extent of the domain of the culture. It is the land of the people of the culture and is usually termed as such. The home territory or land of a culture is coextensive with the world of order and meaning. Many tribes delimit their territories by distinctive features of the land—mountains, rivers, lakes, and forests mark the center, the perimeter, and the principles of human orientation.

The landscape gives expression to intent and value by serving as the setting for the journey along the road of life. For the Hopi the orientation of life, goodness, health, and happiness is toward the east. For the Oglala the orientation is toward the south. Many Native American cultures designate cardinal or semicardinal directions (sometimes in combination with the zenith, nadir, and world center) and bestow these directions or sectors with values and attributes. Prayers are offered with regard to direction. Houses are oriented with regard to direction, and most architectural forms have cosmological significance. Ritual processes are conducted constantly with an eye to orientation. Pilgrimages, of both body and mind, have directional orientations, usually expressed as journeys through a landscape.

The extent of a culture's territory is pragmati-

cally defined by the physical movements and places of occupancy of its people. The religious character of the land is often reflected in these practical activities. For example, hunting involves a religious relationship between human beings and animals, a relationship that takes form in spatial terms. Hunters live in human homes in the human world, while the game live in dwellings that are usually inaccessible to human beings, under the guidance of a protector of animals. The preparation for the hunt is one of spiritual communion with the game or the master/mistress of the game. The hunt is a journey by both hunters and animals into a mediating landscape—the hunting grounds—where hunter plays host to game that in turn, upon being killed, plays host to the hunter.

The landscape also gives language to the religions of Native Americans in the form of story traditions, the stories of the creation and history of the world. Native Americans generally do not have creation stories in which the physical world is made from nothing. Their stories commonly tell of the primordial or ancestral designation, transformation, and orientation that resulted in the present landscape. Native American stories often tell how the world was found, how its shape gained its significance, and how human beings should orient themselves within this landscape; these stories tell how life not only became possible but also came to have meaning.

There are major creator figures who bring order to the world, such as the Winnebago Earthmaker and the Laguna Thought Woman, but commonly there are many other figures who contribute in a variety of ways to the origin and primordial ordering of the world. For example, in the widespread earth-diver story, many animals and birds make the effort to obtain, from the bottom of the primordial sea, a bit of soil for creating the world. In western North America creation stories often involve the theft of something essential to life, such as fire or light, that has been secreted away by some mythological figure. In other regions, the character of the world and of human life is attributed to mythological siblings who fought and counteracted one another's efforts to establish the world. Trickster figures are commonly ascribed the roles of creators and transformers. Elsewhere in Native American oral traditions there is an abundance of stories of magical flights to spiritual worlds, of long migrations in search of a livable place, and of major catastrophic events that transformed the world. For all these stories the result is the world, the land imprinted with a gradient of values that are observed by the people who live within it. Thus the religious dimensions of the culture are made concrete in the landscape.

The landscape is also the arena of history. Features in the land serve as reminders of history, from points on the migration routes of mythic ancestors to points on historical journeys, such as the many trails of tears. There are physical reminders of wars, of great personal achievements, of former residences, and of revelations and visions. For Native Americans, history is told in stories that are read from the features in the landscape.

American history has seen the progressive displacement of Native Americans from their land, from the territories that have been their sources of meaning. Of necessity, these displacements have resulted in radical transformations and innovations. Displaced peoples have had to redefine themselves and re-create their worlds in new, often unfamiliar lands, in the confines of reservations, and in cities where there was no land for a tribal culture. An appreciation of the importance of land to cultural and religious identity and continuity is essential to understanding the impact of American history on Native Americans and to begin comprehending their tenacity and creativity in having survived and maintained their identities and bases for meaningful lives.

Religion and Health. Health and healing are religious concerns throughout much of native North America. The English term *medicine* is commonly used to refer to a magico-religious power or object of power. Religious specialists are often referred to as "medicine persons." This dimension of Native American religions is widely misunderstood, principally because it is considered in terms of modern Western medical science; that is, in physical and impersonal terms, rather than in personal and religious ones. Native healing practices have tended to be defended and respected only to the extent that they have contributed to or complied with scientific medical practice. While some pharmacological and therapeutic contributions made by native peoples can be identified, this fact almost wholly obscures and ignores the greater sophistication and importance of religion and health.

In native conceptions, physical and psychological health often stands as a sign of the status of the social, cultural, and spiritual aspects of the world in which one lives. In this view, the individual is integral to a complex web of interrelationships and interdependences, the disturbance of which, even if remote from the individual, has an impact upon that person, an impact that may be signaled by symptoms and feelings of illness. Consequently, and quite logically, curing techniques often focus not directly on the symptoms but on the causal factors. The restorative, rectifying, re-creative actions are commonly identified primarily as healing processes. It is quite possible for these actions to be performed successfully without an accompanying change in the symptoms of the illness. Thus the success of the treatment must be considered in terms derived from specific tribal conceptions. We have done very little to comprehend Native American understandings of the human body, of health, and of techniques of healing. Without a doubt there are often significant physical and psychological effects to Native American curing practices, but these are quite often secondary to the intent: to give an illness meaning, to rectify and repair relationships at a human or spiritual level, to place an individual and a community in a context where life and death may have meaning.

Shamanism, the common term by which certain forms of healing practices are identified, has a Siberian origin, and while the term has come to be used to refer to phenomena found throughout the world, the Siberian examples stand as prototypes. Consequently, shamanism is most commonly seen as a magico-religious process of curing and divination whereby a practitioner engages in techniques of ecstasy (entrancement) to achieve an other-than-ordinary psychic and spiritual status. Particularly since the publication of Mircea Eliade's classic study, *Shamanism* (1964), ecstasy has been a common definitional criterion for shamanism.

In North America ecstatic techniques are not widely used beyond sub-Arctic regions (by the Eskimo) or the Pacific Northwest coast (the Kwakiutl, for example). Consequently, some have doubted the antiquity or authenticity of practices that in some way resemble shamanism in North America, dubbing them "pseudo-shamanism" or else ignoring them altogether. Nonetheless, the enormous ethnographic record of the tribal cultures of the area documents many forms of religious practice that, while not always ecstatic, must still be considered in the context of the studies of shamanism worldwide. These forms offer a major enrichment to such studies.

While not defined by any particular set of traits, shamanism in North America is commonly distinguished by some of the following features. Shamans invariably have extraordinary spiritual power so that they may influence the world through spiritual forces. The spiritual power of a shaman is identified in a variety of forms: from animals and natural forms to ghosts and mythological beings. Individuals gain access to spiritual power by means of a power quest, inheritance, election, or purchase. Hallucinogenic drugs are not commonly used in North America. Initiatory experiences are common, although they do not often involve strong imagery of skeletonization (being stripped of flesh), spirit flights, or death.

The most widespread function of the shaman in North America is healing, and two disease theories and conjoined curing techniques are most common. First, illness may be attributed to either the loss or theft of life's vitality, or soul. The associated cure is to determine the cause of the loss and the location of the departed life form, and to rescue and restore the life form to the suffering person. The techniques may include magical flight and rescue missions, ritually dramatized. Second, illness may be attributed to some object of malevolence that has penetrated the body of the sufferer. Also, the object of intrusion may simply be the objectification of the felt pain. The accompanying curing technique is to remove the object by various means, most commonly by sucking, but also by blowing, singing, and using formulas. Other common shamanistic functions are associated with divination serving hunting and agricultural needs and, in former times, serving war activities.

Practices that correspond to a majority of these traits are to be found in every culture area in North America and in practically every tribe. Most commonly shamans practice as individuals in their communities, but there are also shamanistic societies reaching even the grand proportions of the *midéwiwin,* or Grand Medicine Societies, of the central Algonquian tribes in the Great Lakes region.

Religion: The Individual and Society. One might suspect that in small tribal societies the customs, procedures, and structures of the society would bring great pressures to bear on the individual, thus constraining him or her, with the result that little personal freedom and creativity are enjoyed and personhood is not fully developed. Without a doubt most, if not all, Native American cultures have a very strong influence on the actions, views, and characters of individuals, but the conclusion that the individual suffers a loss of personhood and freedom does not necessarily follow.

There are many institutions and structures through which a culture shapes individuals and demands conformity. The system of kinship is a major basis for structuring interrelationships and activities, from marital to occupational, ceremonial, and religious responsibilities. Ancestry, clan, and family roles are often defined and given religious significance by oral traditions, which establish the origins of these societal orders and their responsibilities and characters. For example, for the Zuni there is a correlation between clan, direction, occupation, ceremonial, and ritual responsibilities and a set of natural elements (birds, plants, landscape features) and character values. In many cultures sex distinctions determine and limit a whole range of activities, from work to religion; yet there is usually a balance in the division of activities between males and females, and some of the assumed exclusions do not exist—women as well as men are leaders, respected elders, owners of property, and religious practitioners (including shamans).

Age is another factor that often determines roles and responsibilities in Native American societies. Most Native American cultures have some form of initiation of the young. This often corresponds to the initiation of religious awareness and the acceptance of religious responsibilities. This transition is commonly effected through a formal religious rite of passage. Age sets—that is, groups formed around a common age proximity—are occasionally a formal base for societal distinctions and exist everywhere, even if informally. Widespread, but not without exceptions, is a correlation between the advancement of wisdom, knowledge, and respectability and the advancement of age.

Many Native American cultures have formal religious societies into which individuals may be initiated. These societies—such as the Crow Tobacco Society, the Winnebago *midéwiwin,* and the Tewa "Made People"—correspond to the structure of political and religious authority of the culture. Members bear enormous responsibilities for the community. There are war societies, medicine bundle societies, ritual and religious orders, priesthoods, curing and medicine societies, and, arising in this century, tribal councils, governing societies, and singing and dancing societies. The Native American church, or the peyote religion, is a strong social and religious society in many present-day communities.

In these many cultural forms it is clear that individuals must conform to highly, and often very narrowly, defined roles as they become full members of their cultures. The alternatives, until very recently, have been practically nonexistent; for it is not at all easy for a Native American simply to reject his or her culture and survive, much less live a meaningful life. Until recently, one's life virtually depended on maintaining a good standing in society.

Despite these enormous pressures for conformity, it is quite clear that many Native Americans develop distinctive personalities and experience considerable individuality. Quite often the status and accomplishment of the individual who takes one of the various roles are measured by the distinctiveness and innovativeness with which he or she performs. We may see this in a variety of ways. Warriors in many societies would proclaim their abilities and accomplishments in war by public pronouncements. For example, the Dakota warrior would report his accomplishments in battle by striking a pole with each statement, in an act called "counting coups." Likewise, hunters may publicly recall and proclaim their hunting feats. Agriculturists tell how plentiful and fine their crops are. Food preparers are known for the delight of their food. Potters and weavers are distinguished by the fineness, beauty, and usefulness of their works. Shamans and medicine people often display their spiritual powers, performing publicly, by eating live coals, plunging their arms into boiling water, and deeply cutting their flesh only to be healed instantly. They also tell of their successes in curing, finding lost objects, and performing many other tasks. While roles, occupations, and certain limitations are set by Native American cultures, these structures become the vehicle by which individuals develop their personalities and enjoy their freedom. Fortunately, in this century

a good many biographies and autobiographies have been collected and written, giving a new perspective from which to view people within Native American cultures.

There may also be an assumption that Native Americans never doubt their religious beliefs or are skeptical about the religious performances and practices of their culture. Certainly, without written accounts, and with ethnographic attention focused more on the group—the collective—rather than on the individual, this aspect of Native American individuality is not easy to examine. However, a review of a number of accounts of Native American religions in which individuals are permitted free expression reveals considerable evidence that some Native Americans are critical and skeptical about their own religions, at least at some stages of their religious lives.

Perhaps the balance between the forces of conformity to society and of freedom to develop individuality is most clearly seen in many of the rites of passage. In most Native American cultures, for a child to become an adult and be recognized as such with the privileges and responsibilities of adulthood, he or she must undergo a rite of passage. Here there is little choice for the individual, and the manner in which that ritual process is performed is usually closely monitored and directed in a strongly conservative manner by the elders of the society. Still, the very structure of the ritual process is often centered upon the individual undergoing the initiatory experience and gaining distinctiveness and personhood. In the widely practiced rite of passage that involves vision questing, for both male and female initiates, the experience of the vision quest and the content of the vision itself are owned by the individual. The vision becomes the very vehicle toward individuality and personal distinctiveness.

In general, Native American creativity, freedom, and personhood are found more in the exercise and perpetuation of long-established societal forms rather than in the transformation and transcendence of these forms. Freedom is won through tradition. Personhood and individuality are achieved as a dimension of societal structures that require conformity.

Religion and Authority. Because of the exclusive orality—that is, nonliteracy—of Native Americans, the character of religious authority is different from religious traditions that have writing. In cultures without writing, tradition and continuity are always virtually on the brink of extinction, since all history, experience, knowledge, and wisdom must be borne in the minds of the living. With good reason Native Americans recognize a close connection between religious responsibility, knowledge, experience, and authority. Age is honored and is often the basis for authority because one gains knowledge and experience and the accompanying wisdom over time. Authority, especially religious authority, is commonly vested in the elders of Native American communities. At present it is a widespread practice to describe the religious authorities of Native American cultures by the simple term *elders.*

While authority is ultimately a human attribute, there are a number of forms in which authority is exercised. Some authority is exercised through the structures of religious and ritual societies, religious offices and occupations. Notable among these are the storytellers and the story elements by which authority is proclaimed. Also, among the great variety of stories told by Native Americans, levels of authority may be discerned. Stories set in the primordium—in the beginning, in mythological times, at the time when human beings and animals spoke the same language—assert their claim to authority in their very setting and form. These temporal settings are not to be confused with the effort to establish an historical precedent or line of historical development. The setting is a statement of authority, proclaiming that there is no precedent to the events and knowledge revealed in the stories. The setting of these stories is equivalent in some ways to the canon in literate traditions. Furthermore, especially when compared with many other forms of tales and legends, stories with a mythological or primordial setting are more commonly accompanied by a strict prohibition against changing or altering the stories when told or transmitted from generation to generation. In some cultures where the same creation story has been recorded on different occasions, with a time lapse of generations between recordings, a remarkable stability has often been demonstrated.

In Zuni oral traditions, an individual is designated to be Kyaklo, the mythical figure responsible for the very extensive creation story cycle. Once each four or eight years Kyaklo comes to Zuni village to tell the story. No Zuni ever hears his story in total on one occasion, yet many Zuni storytellers retell parts of this long tradition, but in a manner that interprets these parts as they recount them. In this situation the second renderings, by their very form and situation, hold the story telling of Kyaklo to be "canon," and they amount to an exegetical exercise based upon this canon. Such forms of authority related to oral traditions vary widely among Native American cultures, but have yet to undergo extensive study.

Religion and History. Native American religions are frequently described in the past tense. When they take their place in discussions of American religious history or the history of world religions, they are placed in sections establishing a context, the usual implication being that they are of the past, bygones. This suggests not only that the present-day practice of Christianity and the Native American church cannot be considered Native American religions, but also that neither can the tribal religious traditions that are still practiced. In the case of the latter, the implication is that those presently practiced traditions cannot but have been influenced, and thus corrupted, by nearly half a millennium of European-American influence.

These perspectives stem from the notion that Native Americans, in contrast to Europeans and their American descendants, are not historical beings. Thus, while Eastern and Western religious traditions are presented in terms of history, Native American religions are presented as collapsed not only into a common "Indian religion" but also into a timeless past. There is an implication that this presentation of "Indian religion" seeks to capture the tradition as it existed in a golden age prior to European influence.

In one sense, Native Americans have not been interested in history because they have not produced a written record of the past. But in nearly every other sense Native Americans have been as much historical beings as any others in human history. Their traditions and religious institutions have been the instrument of development, change, and encounter with outsiders—European-American or from other tribes. These traditions have also been the defense against pressures to change, to acculturate, and to undergo radical transformation.

In the first place, it must be recognized that although a lack of written records makes it difficult to discern Native American religious history, Native American religions do have histories. A simple example demonstrates this point. While sun worship is as usual a stereotypical depiction of "the Indian religion" as the northern Plains warrior is of the popular image of "the Indian," the Sun Dance, practiced by the peoples across the northern Plains, has a complex history spanning the last several centuries. The Sioux tribes, most widely associated with the Sun Dance, were not Plains tribes until early in the eighteenth century, when they were displaced from the woodland and lake regions surrounding the Great Lakes by other tribes responding to the waves of westward expansion of European-Americans. Arriving on the Plains and taking advantage of their new access to horses introduced earlier by the Spanish, the Sioux became hunters and warriors. Their strength was in their capacity to change and adapt their historical situation to their advantage. Drawing influence from the sedentary agriculturists who lived along the Missouri and Mississippi rivers and their tributaries, as well as from the nomadic hunters who lived in small bands along the eastern side of the Rocky Mountains, these newcomers developed new religious forms. The Sun Dance was one development that soon came to be practiced by many tribes across the Plains. The Sun Dance was outlawed by a Bureau of Indian Affairs directive in the late nineteenth century but has been revived in the mid-twentieth century and is presently practiced.

Secondly, it is important to understand that Native American peoples have strong interests in history. Common are stories an individual tells of important events occurring early in his or her lifetime, or frequently even well before that lifetime. A major portion of oral tradition is based on the maintenance and use of history without the convenience of writing. Winter count records were kept by some tribes, in which a graphic image served as a reminder of the significant events that occurred during the year. Major natural events, floods, earthquakes, and eclipses often serve as markers by which to orient historical events. Scott Momaday, in *The Way to Rainy Mountain* (1969), shows how significant the major meteor shower that occurred in 1832 was to his people, the Kiowa. Referring to this event as "the night the stars fell," the Kiowa connected this natural, seemingly cataclysmic event with

their own history and interpreted it as an ominous event coinciding, and likely connected, with their decline as a people.

Finally, while Christian and European-American influence is usually thought to coincide with the date of initial contact, there is considerable evidence that this influence may have had an effect long before. Deward Walker's studies of the Nez Percé and other tribes in the plateau region of the northwestern United States indicate that these tribes had for some time heard about and adopted some of the patterns of Christianity years earlier than their actual contact with Christians. He describes this as "mediate influence" and believes that it greatly exceeds commonly held expectations about influence. Since contact in this region did not occur until the early nineteenth century, it is easier to document than elsewhere, but in principle the importance of mediate influence on Native American religions must be both long and extensive.

NATIVE RELIGIOUS RESPONSES TO "AMERICANIZATION"

The European presence in America initiated a process. The landscape became an arena in which the idea of America was made concrete: trees were cut down; rivers were bridged and dammed; roads were built; and "the Indians," conceived as part of the landscape, were treated likewise. They were removed, displaced, or assimilated; that is, they were Americanized. The conquest of Mexico, the establishment of Jamestown, the westward expansion, the Indian wars, the Dawes Severalty Act (and many other legislative directives), the prohibition of "Indian dances" and other religious activities—all of these contributed to the pressure on Native Americans to become more "American." Clearly, from the native and tribal point of view, such acts threatened the total destruction of their culture; often they succeeded in this destruction.

As a threat to identity, meaning, and existence, the Americanization of "the Indians" fostered a variety of responses from Native Americans. Many of these responses were religious in character. Examination of several examples will illustrate the variety of these religious responses.

One common response to the suffering of oppression in North America has been the rise of prophets who have directed attention toward a hopeful future. In a several-century history of Delaware prophecy, a clear correlation can be shown between prophetic activity and the pressure of oppression. Although it is likely that prophecy was a dimension of at least some tribal traditions before the European presence, as in the strain of prophecy in Hopi traditions, there is nonetheless a very clear correlation with encounter and oppression.

At the turn of the nineteenth century a Shawnee, Tenskwatawa, brother to Tecumseh, was an active prophet. His message was strongly nativistic and separatist in character, yet it was a message that bore the seeds of a pan-tribal commonality and identity. He encouraged the peoples of all native tribes to avoid European-American ways, including clothing, schooling, Christianity, alcohol, and the English language. He granted that these things were appropriate for European-Americans, but claimed they were dangerous to Native Americans.

About the same time a Seneca, Handsome Lake, whose personal history reflected the state of decay and degradation suffered by his people, arose as a prophet and founded a new religion. Handsome Lake was an alcoholic. He had a miserable existence, not fitting in a world so radically and rapidly changed because of the European-American presence. During an illness he "died," and during this experience he had a vision in which he was escorted to heaven, where he encountered spiritual figures of wisdom. They revealed a new road for the people to follow, which contrasted with Christianity yet incorporated and built upon both tribal traditions and elements of Christianity. With this revelation, Handsome Lake proclaimed the *giawiio* (good news), the basis for the establishment of the Handsome Lake religion.

Many of these prophetic movements were millenarian in character, and a great many of them arose in the northwestern United States during the nineteenth century. Among these was the Ghost Dance, the most widespread and well known of new native religious movements. A Paiute man by the name of Wovoka, with a Christian and native tribal religious background, experienced a revelation during the winter of 1888–1889. On the authority of his vision Wovoka preached a message of hope and a prescribed course of action. The message predicted

that the degradations and changes of the world would be destroyed in a major cataclysmic event, but that the world would be restored to its pristine condition, with the European-Americans removed. The many native peoples who had died would be restored to life. The animals and territories of the tribal peoples would be wholly restored; that is, restored for those who faithfully followed the mandates of the Ghost Dance prophecy.

The prophecy included a number of ethical directives. People were not to lie, to steal, or to fight or harm anyone. It also established a course of ritual action, the Ghost Dance. This dance was to be performed regularly and involved a circle and a center pole around which the dancers would increase their dancing fervor to the point of attaining ecstasy; thus, they themselves might experience visions in which they could communicate with their deceased relatives. Commonly their ecstatic experiences envisioned a march of the dead toward the world of the living. The visionary would be encouraged to persist in the practice of the Ghost Dance until the imminent millennial event. The major thrust of the Ghost Dance movement was foiled in the massacre of many Sioux people at Wounded Knee Creek in December 1890, but ghost dancing has persisted as an established religiosocial practice among some Plains and western tribes.

Many native religious movements have been spawned by the oppressive effects of American history and its pressures of Americanization. Indeed, this dimension of the experience cannot help but have deeply influenced the character of all we know of Native American tribal traditions.

ENCOUNTER WITH CHRISTIANITY

It is often inadvisable to use the word *religion* when discussing native tribal traditions with Native Americans, for in their experience with European-Americans religion has been synonymous with Christianity. For many tribes, their first contact with European-Americans was with missionaries. And certainly missionaries have maintained a constant presence among native peoples. Missionaries have often learned native languages—for many tribal languages missionaries have been the principal linguists, writing the only grammars and dictionaries.

Missionaries commonly established the first

schools among native communities to teach reading and writing so that the scriptures might be read, a civilizing element seen to be necessary in Christianizing "the Indians." Native practices that competed with Christianity were commonly suppressed and discouraged. Such practices were seen as barbaric, savage, and pagan. While the ethnographic and anthropological interest in Native American religions was not motivated by the mission to Christianize, clearly the understanding of religion as a human phenomenon was most heavily shaped by Western religious traditions. Thus when ethnographers asked native peoples about their religion, it must have sounded very much as if they were asking about their Christianity.

This equation of religion with Christianity seems alien to the modern academic study of religion, but it is strongly evidenced in the field of American religious history, which has included Native Americans only insofar as they have entered American mission history; that is, only insofar as they have encountered Christianity. The Native American encounter with Christianity seems to be a rather one-sided affair, one in which native religions have not only been ignored, but also suppressed; one in which Christianity has been the measure and the only acceptable religious presence. It has been a history of oppression, insensitivity, arrogance, and misunderstanding. Certainly from the native point of view, the encounter with Christianity has often been unhappy and frustrating.

It has become popular to center on this encounter to demonstrate the evils of Christianity and the glories of "the Indian religion." Both Native Americans and European-Americans have engaged in this polemic. Although there is a basis for such a position, it is far too superficial, leading to a misunderstanding of both Christian mission history and native religious traditions. There are two areas that should illustrate something of the richer character of this encounter.

First, many missionaries to "the Indians" were profoundly interested in tribal religions, far beyond the knowledge necessary to Christianize them better. For example, Father Berard Haile served as a Franciscan missionary to the Navajos at St. Michael's near Window Rock, Arizona, throughout much of his adult life. He never participated in Navajo ceremonials, but he was deeply knowledgeable about their ritual practices, oral traditions, and language. His legacy

amounts to thousands of pages of information, carefully written in Navajo and translated in a nearly literal fashion. His translations and writings burgeon with notations in which he reports Navajo responses to questions he had about the stories and ceremonials he recorded.

One cannot read these materials, so carefully collected and presented, without realizing the great appreciation and admiration that Father Berard had for the Navajo people and their religious traditions. Yet, as a missionary to the Navajo people, Father Berard remained firm in his Christian faith. One can only begin to glimpse the complexity of this kind of encounter. It is a human encounter of persons from vastly different cultural, historical, and religious backgrounds, yet an encounter characterized by mutual respect and integrity. Certainly many other missionaries to "the Indians" have been party to comparable experiences. This area remains among the least pursued, but most highly interesting, topics in American religious history.

Second, many Native Americans have become Christians as a result of the missions. From one point of view this is a victory; from another, a failure. Unfortunately, from either point of view this has usually marked the end of the story. In a sense it should be the beginning of one. We have been far too narrow-minded in appreciating the important influence of Christianity on Native American cultures and religions, preferring to see the acceptance of Christianity as synonymous with the loss of native tradition.

A few examples may suggest the importance of viewing the Christian influence in a new light. An Apache Christian community sings Christian hymns during their worship service; however, they sing in the Apache language, accompanied by music sounding more Apache than European-American. The Yaqui people of Arizona perform a dramatization of the events of Easter that involves a sizable portion of the community for most of the time during Holy Week. Many are involved throughout the entire period of Lent. The Yaqui encounter with Christianity dates from the early seventeenth century. Christian churches are the dominant architectural feature in most Pueblo villages. Not only are these churches attended for the celebration of Mass, but dances and other tribal religious performances may take place in them. At Zuni life-size depictions of Zuni religious figures are painted on the walls of the Catholic mission church. Such murals date from the nineteenth century. A Comanche eagle doctor in Oklahoma uses the Bible to describe her doctoring practice. Jesus is commonly prayed to in peyote meetings.

Such examples begin to suggest the adaptability and creativity of Native American religions. They suggest that the Native American encounter with Christianity has in some sense been one in which tribal traditions have eagerly taken elements of Christianity to develop and enrich their own religious traditions.

NATIVE AMERICANS DISCOVER THEIR "INDIANNESS"

Before the American experience, it seems clear that tribal identity was most basic to Native Americans. Language and tradition defined one's identity, in contrast to those who spoke other languages and practiced other traditions; that is, to those of other tribes. Conflict, war, trade, and alliance doubtless occurred among tribes. No evidence suggests that any common identity was recognized among all these peoples. Many tribes referred to themselves by a term that translates as "the people," or "the human beings," sometimes with the clear implication that other tribes did not belong in this category.

From the time of Columbus the tribal peoples of the Americas were called "the Indians," but Native Americans did not recognize such an identity until much more recently. "Indianness" was discovered as a product of the realization among tribal peoples of their common experience and plight; namely, oppression at the hands of European-Americans. Thus in appropriating the term "Indian," native peoples identified themselves at a level superseding tribal, religious, and language distinctions. Such an identity was forged to facilitate a political alliance, and the roots of this movement date at least to the turn of the nineteenth century, if not earlier. This identity has gained its fullest development only in recent decades, through the formation of a number of significant pan-tribal organizations used by Native Americans to discover and express their "Indianness." Notably, the "Indian" identity has distinguished itself more socially and politically than religiously. Still, some religious developments relate to this recent discovery of "Indianness."

Christianity among Native Americans has served as a basis for establishing an "Indian" identity without violating a tribal identity. Through native Christian ministries, through religious publications, and through charitable work projects, Native American Christians have found an arena in which to consider the continuity between their tribal traditions and their practice of Christianity, and between their practice of Christianity and the European-American or "white" practice of Christianity.

Peyote religion—a development from the late nineteenth century, now legally established as the Native American church—has been widely recognized among its practitioners as an "Indian religion." Peyote religion is performed as an all-night singing, praying, and drumming ceremony directed toward the health, happiness, and welfare of its members. Peyote, a type of cactus and a hallucinogen, is consumed during the meeting, but it is eaten for its medicinal value and to promote communal bonds rather than for individual ecstatic experiences. The Native American church has also been effective in treating alcohol and drug abuse and in resolving a variety of social problems. It may incorporate Christian elements, it may even have an occasional non-native participant, and it is largely practiced by local communities, but peyote religion is "Indian" in character and functions importantly as a way of reinforcing and supporting "Indian" identity.

Recent developments of the powwow have provided a social form in which people from many tribes participate. Powwows have a religious dimension as well as a strong dimension of American patriotism. The religious dimension is expressed through prayers offered during the event, and the continuity through dance as a tribal form of religious expression. The decorum and attitudes maintained by many powwow participants can scarcely be separated from a form of religious attitude.

While little of a pan-tribal, or "Indian," religious tradition has developed, perhaps the most characteristic one is the stated belief in Father Sky and Mother Earth. The history of this belief is very complex and a good deal shorter than might be expected. Such a belief most effectively expresses the Native American sense of separate and superior identity when compared with European-Americans. It has as its base a relationship to the land, a religious ecology. Importantly, the relationship is spiritual in character. With this general, pervasive base the "Indian" identity has developed around a strongly mystical, spiritual, and religious character.

BIBLIOGRAPHY

Peggy V. Beck and A. L. Walters, *The Sacred: Ways of Knowledge, Sources of Life* (1977); Joseph Epes Brown, *The Spiritual Legacy of the American Indian* (1982); Harold Driver, *Indians of North America*, rev. ed. (1969); Sam D. Gill, *Native American Religions: An Introduction* (1981) and *Native American Traditions: Sources and Interpretations* (1983).

A. Irving Hallowell, "Ojibwa Ontology, Behavior, and World View," in Stanley Diamond, ed., *Culture in History: Essays in Honor of Paul Radin* (1960); Charles Haywood, *A Bibliography of North American Folklore and Folksong*, 2nd rev. ed. (1961); Hazel W. Hertzberg, *The Search for an American Indian Identity: Modern Pan-Indian Movements* (1971); Frederick W. Hodge, ed., *Handbook of American Indians North of Mexico* (1959); Ake Hultkrantz, *The Religions of the American Indians* (1979) and *The Study of American Indian Religions* (1983); Dell Hymes, "In Vain I Tried to Tell You," in *Essays in Native American Ethnopoetics* (1981).

Karl Kroeber, ed., *Traditional Literatures of the American Indian: Texts and Interpretations* (1981); Weston La Barre, *The Peyote Cult*, rev. ed. (1969); Robert S. Michaelson, "The Significance of the American Indian Religious Freedom Act of 1978," in *Journal of the American Academy of Religion*, 52, 1 (1984); James Mooney, *The Ghost Dance Religion and the Sioux Outbreak of 1890* (1896); George P. Murdock, *Ethnographic Bibliography of North America*, rev. ed. (1975); Alfonso Ortiz, *The Tewa World: Space, Time, Being, and Becoming in a Pueblo Society* (1969).

Edward H. Spicer, ed., *Perspectives in American Indian Culture Change* (1975); William C. Sturtevant, ed., *Handbook of North American Indians* (1967–); Stith Thompson, *Tales of the North American Indians* (1929); Harold W. Turner, *Bibliography of New Religious Movements in Primal Societies*, vol. 2: *North America* (1978); Deward E. Walker, ed., *The Emergent Native Americans: A Reader in Culture Contact* (1972); Bryan R. Wilson, *Magic and the Millennium: A Sociological Study of Religious Movements of Protest Among Tribal and Third-World Peoples* (1973).

[*See also* NORTH AMERICAN INDIAN MISSIONS; CALIFORNIA AND THE SOUTHWEST; DIVERSITY AND PLURALISM IN CANADIAN RELIGION; MILLENIALISM AND ADVENTISM; *and* RELIGION IN MESOAMERICA.]

THE ROMAN CATHOLIC HERITAGE

Mary Jo Weaver

ONE way to understand Roman Catholicism might be to read *The Divine Comedy* as an adventure story. The cosmic quest that begins with Dante in despair on the lip of Hell ends in the highest recesses of Heaven with "the poet's will and desire moving in perfect co-ordination with the love of God" (*Paradise,* Dorothy Sayers and Barbara Reynolds, trans., 1962, p. 348). In the last stanza of his epic work, Dante relates what he can of his vision of God: the ineffable nature of the experience makes this rendition nearly impossible and he says repeatedly that he can neither recall nor express what he has seen. Nevertheless, his joy is infectious as he expresses in poetic language the experience of transforming union and the bedazzlement of divine light. Up to the Second Vatican Council (1962–1965), some version of that vision sustained Catholics all over the world.

Until fairly recent times Catholicism shared a view of religion similar to the one that characterized the Middle Ages: religion was not something one did along with other things; it was all-absorbing and primary, intertwined with the legal, emotional, artistic, intellectual, and physical aspects of one's life. Whatever ethnic particularities different groups of Catholics brought with them to America, they all acted out their lives as if religion, politics, theology, and daily life were ineluctably united. They might not have understood or agreed with the specific images of Dante's *Comedy,* but they would have shared with him the nagging urgency of the religious quest, the almost epic proportions of personal salvation and the mixing of religion and life.

The Divine Comedy can be read for its politics, history, poetry, or spiritual insights: so can Roman Catholicism. The *Comedy* is intensely personal, yet cosmic; obsessed with papal politics and abstruse theological discussions, yet generalizable to common human experience: so is Catholicism. Most importantly, in the *Comedy* one has a profound sense of journey—it is neither advisable nor permitted to stay too long in one place—and of the necessity for maintaining the readiness of a pilgrim. The Roman Catholic heritage, at its best, has that same sense of adventure about it; the most troublesome times in the history of the Catholic church have been times in which it forgot to keep moving.

GENERAL CHARACTERISTICS

Roman Catholicism, as distinct from other Christianities, has one exceptional feature, the belief that the papacy is an integral part of its ecclesiastical structure. Beyond that, Catholicism shares many of its components with other Christian groups, though its particular cluster of characteristics is unique. Catholicism is an ancient form of Christianity with a long political history and an imposing set of traditions. Its theological framework, characterized from the beginning by a drive toward rational understanding, embraces many diverse schools and is open to almost endless permutation and development; yet it is grounded on Scripture, indebted to ancient spiritual insights, and bound by certain dogmatic definitions.

Catholics have a sacramental view of life, believing that one encounters God through material realities. They would agree that God can be met by way of a direct, mystical experience or by way of inward consciousness, but most often, Catholics believe, the divine presence is available through concrete, visible, historical events or things. Accordingly, there is a reverence for sym-

153

THE ROMAN CATHOLIC HERITAGE

bols and sacraments as well as for the church itself as the locus of divine-human interaction. In theological terms, as the Word of God is made flesh, Jesus Christ becomes "the sacrament of the encounter with God" (Schillebeeckx), the material reality through which one meets the invisible God. As one approaches God through Christ, one approaches Christ through the church, which becomes, by extension, the sacrament of the encounter with Christ: participation in divine life (grace) is mediated to Catholics by Christ and by the church. Roman Catholicism reflects its history, theological adaptability, and sacramentality; and it manifests a high tolerance for fallible humanity. "Consequently, the love of life, the appreciation of the body and the senses, of joy and celebration, the tolerance of the sinner, these natural, worldly and 'human' virtues are far more clearly and universally embodied in Catholics and Catholicism than in Protestants and Protestantism" (Gilkey).

Catholicism aims to be universal in its diverse embodiments of Christian belief and practice. Like humanity itself, Christianity is a mixture of the divine and the human, the graced reality of the image of God existing in consistently sinful people. The Roman Catholic church, as an institution with a long history, has had graceful moments and lapses into insidious corruption. Read with an eye to its sinfulness, Catholic history is a horror story of persecution, megalomania, inquisitorial strategies, arid, repressive dogmatism, and a stubborn refusal to take its critics seriously. Read with an eye to its gracefulness, Catholic history is a magnificent example of adaptability, civilizing influence, thriving spirituality, creative, heroic reform, and an admirable ability to outlast its critics and to endure.

From whichever direction one reads this story, it must be admitted that Roman Catholicism is and usually has been catholic—i.e., universally embracing. From its beginnings as a small Palestinian sect to its late-twentieth-century self-understanding as a pluralistic, modern, ecumenical, and universal church, Roman Catholicism has drawn strength from every group and situation it has encountered. The challenge in reading its history, assessing its theology, and describing its patterns of worship and spirituality is to see the myriad ways in which it has responded to the vicissitudes of the world it found itself in, taking new contexts as occasions to define and redefine itself.

HISTORY AND POLITICS

Roman Catholic history begins with a sense of missionary journey and reaches its modern peak expression at the Second Vatican Council with the assertion that the church is a "pilgrim people," a community on the move. The nearly two thousand years between these two self-understandings are filled with combinations of genius and folly that have shaped and continue to shape Roman Catholic relations with secular governments and ecclesiastical polity and to provide the immediate context for theology, spirituality, and ethics. Although this long time span cannot be summarized here, it can be characterized by the struggle between adaptation and atrophy: Catholicism usually flourished when it expanded to receive new ideas, and it withered when it took on postures of rigidity and condemnation.

Roman Catholicism has never been exclusively rigid or totally expansive and welcoming of new ideas; it has often fought for its independence, but has also been willing to enter into partnerships in which that freedom was circumscribed. It has been extraordinarily adaptable throughout the years, willing to build on and use institutional structures, philosophical systems, scientific explanations, and religious insights from a variety of other places. It has sometimes condemned an idea in one century to embrace it in the next. Most of all, through a combination of inspired decisions, recuperative powers, good fortune, and the amalgamated energies of its people, it has endured and continues to be an important religious and political entity.

Young Catholicism was not particularly "Roman." Early in the fourth century Christians comprised probably less than 10 percent of the Latin-speaking population of the West and not more than 35 percent of the Greek-speaking East. But with the support of the state, its ascendancy as the dominant religion of the Roman Empire was ensured and Christianity became the universal religion of the Mediterranean. With the signing of the Edict of Milan (313) the Christian church won imperial support but virtually lost its independence. The emperor Constantine I and his successors took specific interest in endowing, protecting, and controlling the church; the Eastern Orthodox system of church-state relations was designed by the emperor to ensure a strong political-cultural unity. Seeing themselves as "new Romans," Orthodox Christians in Constantinople supported Constantine's dream of restoring the empire and renewing the world, especially since that restoration was to be fueled by Christian theology and practice. Rome, on the other hand, was quickly becoming a faded outpost of its former luster. Free from the emperor's direct control, it therefore was a better place for the Christian church to work out its own political identity.

"Roman" is not just a geographical adjective: imperial Rome in its zenith was a highly organized, universal empire able to ensure peace throughout the world. Its military genius and legal sagacity were legendary, and it also projected a glorious image supported by the moral strength of its people. This "idea of Rome" long outlived the empire itself and inspired development in Eastern and Western Christianity in different ways. In Constantinople, *emperors* pursued the Roman dream while seeking the support of the Christian movement; in Rome, on the other hand, *popes* sought Roman greatness while seeking the support of kings. In the Eastern system the dominant force was imperial, while in the West it was ecclesiastical: the rivalry between the two shaped the controversial questions of church-state relations that continue to the present day.

In becoming the "Roman" Catholic church, Christianity in the West had predictable problems, not unlike those faced by the empire itself. Questions of political succession, legitimate authority, and balances of power tended to dominate Roman Catholicism during much of its history. These problems, however, need to be assessed in terms of the church's goal of spreading the Gospel throughout the world: in order to be effective and true to its mission, Western Christianity believed it needed its independence. Early popes, especially Leo I (440–461) and Gregory I (590–604), advanced a theory of papal supremacy in which they argued that the church could not and would not be subordinated to any government, army, or civilization. The church, they argued, exists in its own realm and, like its founder, is both master and servant. The theories of papal primacy devised by Leo and Gregory took nearly five hundred years to become the foundation of medieval Catholicism. In the meantime, the Western church encountered a series of challenges that called forth its adaptability.

If the church-state arrangement of the Ortho-dox East stifled some of the church's independence, it also provided the security and leisure in which the church could define doctrine in precise philosophical language, develop and pursue a hunger for beauty in the creation of astonishing icons and mosaics, and spread the Gospel in a well-financed missionary movement. The Roman church, by contrast, had a more modest and more dangerous mission: it had to survive. On the verge of decay in the third century, the Western half of the Roman Empire fell in 476. Into this collapsing system came the nomadic peoples, fierce, but probably not more so than the Romans themselves. As their legal codes have shown, the so-called barbarians were not savages bent on destruction but a people capable of bringing energy, daring, and ingenuity into a demoralized situation.

When these tribes invaded the Roman Empire, they encountered the church in various ways. First, they met territorial administrators (bishops), who acted as religious and civil leaders. Second, they heard about the pope, politically independent, financially stable, and recognized throughout the broad territory of the Western empire as a moral leader. Last, they encountered monastic life.

Christian monasticism began in the East as a life in which one could combine asceticism, mysticism, and discipline in search of both a direct experience and a reasoned appreciation of God. In the West, monasticism was intended to draw people to a contemplative life, but circumstances demanded that monks be highly involved with the world around them. Monasteries were islands of learning, and monks quickly were recruited to educate barbarian chieftains and their children. As tutors, advisers, administrators, and diplomats for barbarian kings, bishops and monks were able to see that the church in the West did more than survive: the church civilized and Christianized the West through church-state alliances and eventually achieved an enormous amount of control over civil and religious life.

One of the most vexing problems of these alliances did not become clear until the ninth century. For a variety of complicated reasons, Pope Leo III crowned the Frankish king, Charlemagne, emperor in 800—a disastrous political move for two reasons. By assuming the power to "create" an emperor, Leo said, in effect, that emperors are not born but are made by the power of God operative through the pope. The effect of his claim was to make the papacy a pawn in a dirty game of Italian politics that lasted for about two hundred years. The effect of Charlemagne's acceptance of the coronation was the insinuation of "sacred kingship" into Western Christianity: Charlemagne thought of himself as the "new David" anointed by God and he began to act the part, by protecting and controlling the church.

From the collapse of the Carolingian empire in the mid-ninth century until the early years of the new millennium, the Catholic church and the West itself were immersed in political conflicts. The papacy had been disgraced by intrigue, murder, and conspiracy, and spiritual life seemed moribund. New life emerged in the tenth century when Otto I revived the imperial claims of the Frankish empire and used his power to reform the papacy. At the same time, the reforming monastery of Cluny began to flourish and to revitalize the institutional church. Diligent eleventh-century popes (Leo IX, Nicholas II) began to reestablish ecclesiastical strength and supremacy. Their successor, Gregory VII, was able to recall the old claims of papal primacy and make startling new ones with power to enforce them. Solidly aware of the church's sorry history in the past two hundred years, hoping to extinguish secular claims to divine kingship, and convinced that the road to ecclesiastical independence and moral reform lay in dominating strength, Gregory VII asserted old doctrines of papal primacy, protected them with elaborate legal justifications, and projected them onto the civil sphere. His pontificate marks the high point of a long reform movement and the beginning of the medieval papacy, when the Roman Catholic church became prolific and, toward the end, corrupt.

If the pontificate of Gregory VII strengthened the papacy for its role as supreme leader of all Christendom, subsequent popes extended papal power by means of crusades, councils, and concordats, showing themselves capable of military, doctrinal, and diplomatic leadership. The church in the High Middle Ages was the setting of great drama and breathtaking achievement: religious orders flourished, universities grew, theological understanding deepened, and majestic cathedrals were built. It is little wonder that the medieval church took hold of the human imagination and often after appeared as part of a golden age, a graced time and space in which the mystical body of Christ could gather in unity and confidence.

On the other hand, it was during the medieval period that the adaptability that had characterized Roman Catholicism in its first thousand years began to disappear. The institutional church used its energy to standardize its practice, universalize its ecclesiastical discipline, and extend its power. Although these projects were successful, they led to serious problems. As John Emerich Edward Dalberg-Acton, Lord Acton, observed in the nineteenth century, "Power tends to corrupt, and absolute power corrupts absolutely." The medieval church seeking absolute power precipitated much of the decay and corruption in the fourteenth-century church.

The fifteenth century can be seen as the beginning of the modern world. Geographical and theological boundaries began to shift, a new economic and military order became increasingly visible, and an urge for ecclesiastical and doctrinal reformation grew strong. Renaissance popes were usually more interested in military and artistic endeavors than they were in the internal, spiritual life of the church. Learning that they could not control the secular rulers of Europe, they attempted to compete with them by making Rome the cultural capital of the world and by making sure that the papal states—the central third of the Italian peninsula, claimed for hundreds of years by the popes as the rightful territory of the church—were well defended. In this setting, the breakup of Christendom may have been inevitable. The criticism and demands of reformers, who would become Protestant leaders, would be met by the Roman Catholic church, but not for another four hundred years; in the meantime, Protestants developed their own vision of Christianity and Catholicism clarified its self-understanding at the Council of Trent (1545–1563).

The Catholic reformation at Trent clarified questions of doctrine, discipline, and education that had been plaguing the church for many years. It established a clearly definable Catholicism, giving ordinary people the means for satisfying their deepest impulses through ritual, images, symbols, and new examples of sanctity. Trent was not merely a reforming council; by the end of the sixteenth century its doctrines and regulations had become normative for Catholicism and by the twentieth century most Catholics had forgotten that there had ever been any other form of Catholicism.

The liabilities of Trent's vision were rigidity and a siege mentality: the church, from the sixteenth century on, did not operate as a pilgrim people, but as a fortified castle, its members hiding behind spiked palisades of anathema and retreat. Attempting to guard what it perceived as eternal truth, Roman Catholicism tried to become an unchanging church in a changing world. To its adherents it offered a secure and ancient system of ecclesiastical polity and uniformity in doctrine and worship, even in liturgical language. In providing this kind of haven for believers, however, it had to live an isolated life and to become, in some ways, a world unto itself.

The state of siege that characterized Roman Catholicism from the sixteenth to the twentieth centuries was, in some ways, a natural legacy of the medieval church. Having reached an apex of power in the thirteenth century, Catholicism did not respond graciously to secular challenges to its authority or to the insistent urgings of religious reformers.

The Council of Trent provided an impressive embodiment of the ideals of the Catholic reformation, but it did very little to give Catholicism the flexibility to respond to the momentous changes in the world around it. The seventeenth and eighteenth centuries brought radically new forms of politics, scientific inquiry, and religious life. The old order that the Catholic church had helped to build and with which it identified was threatened on all sides. Whereas medieval science had always bowed to the church, to what it understood to be a divinely established teaching authority, the new scientific method questioned the authority of tradition and developed a new set of evaluative criteria quite apart from religion. Where, in the old order of church-state relations, the church could, more often than not, assert itself as the primary source of spiritual and temporal authority, the new world had no room for theocracies, and the church was in real danger of becoming a department of state under the thumb of enlightened despots. Where the medieval world rested its intellectual claims on supernatural religion, new intellectual life was skeptical of such religion and was based on a rationalism inimical to the supernatural realm. Last, where the old order, sure that its doctrines

were the only possible version of religious truth, had little trouble justifying the persecution of "heretics" or enforcing religious belief, the new idea of religious toleration finally freed people to believe what they wanted, even when they began to believe that there was no God.

The legacy of the seventeenth- and eighteenth-century Enlightenment took centuries to change long-established patterns of thought. Freedom of conscience, religious toleration, separation of church and state, and the consistent use of a free scientific method—all were worked out over a period of several hundred years.

An astonishing change in Roman Catholicism in the modern period can be illustrated with two pictures. In the first (ca. 1870) Pope Pius IX, the "prisoner of the Vatican," sits, bereft of the papal states and armed only with the doctrine of papal infallibility. In the second (ca. 1962) Pope John XXIII stands at an open window in the Vatican, arms extended to the world. The context for both pictures is the modern world in which there is separation of church and state and personal freedom of conscience. Pius IX shows the reaction of the first modern pope to those realities: he is remembered for resistance and condemnation and for presiding over the First Vatican Council (1869–1870), which defined papal infallibility. John XXIII was more accustomed to modernity: he is remembered for ecumenical outreach and openness, and for calling the Second Vatican Council, which embraced a more collegial form of church government, welcomed dialogue with non-Catholic and non-Christian religions, updated church discipline and practice, and incorporated a specifically American contribution to Roman Catholicism, *The Declaration on Religious Freedom*.

Roman Catholic history has been characterized by expansiveness and rigidity. In its early years, Roman Catholicism fought for and won a costly political ascendancy that it used during the period of the "barbarian invasions" to create a remarkably inventive and adaptable form of Christianity. In the medieval period, Catholicism was splendidly fruitful, taking to itself the transformative insights of Aristotle and witnessing a proliferation of religious orders and other manifestations of spiritual energy. At the same time, papal claims to be the supreme authority in the world were dangerous and ultimately corrupting: the state of the church during the Renaissance and Reformation was dismal. While the Catholic reformation—at Trent and beyond—was regenerative and helpful, Catholicism from the sixteenth to the twentieth centuries was characterized by rigidity; the church feared dialogue with the Protestant or secular world. In its contemporary years (since the Second Vatican Council), the Catholic church has taken on a new life in dialogue with other religions, and is self-defined as a "pilgrim church" in vital contact with the world around it.

THEOLOGICAL FRAMEWORK

Roman Catholic theology, like its history, is complex and stretches over a long time period. It is distinct from Protestant theology in its claim to be in possession of a continuous, historical tradition stretching back to apostolic times; Protestant theology, on the other hand, usually bases itself on the Bible as interpreted by the principles of the Reformation. Theology is the study of God; that is to say, a reflection on divine self-disclosure or revelation. The sources of revelation, therefore, are important clues to the theological enterprise. Whereas both Protestants and Catholics regard the Holy Spirit as the internal source of revelation, Protestants have typically identified the external source of revelation as Scripture; in the parlance of the Reformation era, their position was captured with the words *sola scriptura,* Scripture alone being their font of God's word. Catholics, on the other hand, have always proceeded on the assumption that there are two external sources of revelation, Scripture and tradition, a parallel, extrabiblical, interpretation of divine truth that has genuine and binding religious authority. Although the entire theological framework of the Roman Catholic church cannot be sketched out here, it can generally be described in terms of four major themes: the definition of theology, its operating principles, its history, and some of its contemporary questions.

When Anselm of Canterbury (1033–1109) described his own work as *fides quaerens intellectum* (faith seeking understanding), he meant to make faith an integral part of theology, a claim some modern interpreters might deny. While Anselm's definition is not the end of the discussion,

it is the usual starting point: theology, as the science of God, is a faith-illumined, rational investigation of the contents of belief. Theologians hear, study, and reflect upon the implications of God's word, which they find in the church in three important ways: Scripture, tradition, and the magisterium.

Scripture speaks for itself as a source of divine revelation: it is the historical disclosure of the divine will and personality in written form, possessing the highest authority, since it is inspired and guaranteed by God. *Tradition* is a historical process of interpreting and transmitting Scripture. Because people often expand a concrete communication beyond its original scope, tradition adds something new by explicitly enlarging upon the written words. Accordingly, human ingenuity is a factor in the development of tradition, and arguments against it have usually claimed that the human factor is too dominant, that tradition is innovative and has no roots in Scripture at all. Nevertheless, Catholics believe that since tradition is a specific interpretation of Scripture elaborated within the believing community, it is ultimately guaranteed by the text. The *magisterium* is, for Catholics, the divinely empowered teaching authority of the church and is infallible in this sense: the church, as a whole, cannot make a mistake harmful to the salvation of believers. The magisterium, therefore, not only instructs believers; it also has an obligation to consult them. The judgment of the magisterium is based on tradition and needs to be ascertained with reference to the believing community. It is not an arbitrary definer of doctrine, but rather the collective expertise of the church that demands obedience. Arguments within Catholicism have not been whether there is such a power within the church, but where that power is located: in the pope, in the collective leadership of the church, or in the whole church.

All theology begins with revelation, but revealed truths are not the esoteric property of theologians; they are meant to be heard and understood by ordinary people. Since human beings are shaped by their own contexts and their backgrounds, theologians must use whatever knowledge their period gives them when trying to articulate the implications of revelation. Theology, in other words, always bears the hallmarks of its time, sometimes paradoxically. In periods of ambiguity, theologians have often stressed the rational clarity of God's word, while in highly rational times they have focused on divine unintelligibility. Part of the theological task is to keep the proper tension between transcendence and immanence, to assess and maintain the balance between the human power to know and God's enigmatic elusiveness.

Roman Catholic theology, like Dante in the *Comedy,* is continually in search of fuller explanations of God's interactions in human life. In the earliest controversies of the Christian church, certain principles were established that continue to guide the theological enterprise: theologians read and reflect on the word of God, particularly as manifested in the life and work of Jesus; they deepen this reflection in light of their own spiritual journey and make it practically available to the community; they are expected to consult one another and to search out past "answers" in order to see if the ancient church came to any consensus on disputed questions; and they consult with and advise church leaders, especially when those leaders meet in local synods or international councils for the express purpose of defining doctrine.

In the earliest times, the church's theologians were usually those leaders who were deeply involved in the daily life of particular communities: from Paul to Augustine one has a sense of profound theological questions being worked out in the context of local controversies. At the same time, the church has always revered its corporate wisdom, believing, as the apostles did (Acts 15), that formal gatherings of church leaders work in special partnership with the Holy Spirit. The great councils in the history of Christianity have been ecumenical, meetings that include bishops from the whole, universal church: Catholics recognize the dogmatic decrees of ecumenical councils as truly authoritative, authentic interpretations of the Gospel because they represent the mind of the whole church.

Because revelation is heard and interpreted historically, one can expect genuine development of doctrine and a variety of interpretive approaches in Roman Catholic theology. The Catholic church has never identified itself with any one particular theological school—though in the nineteenth century it came close to doing so in highly, almost exclusively, recommending the system of Thomas Aquinas—because, in order to be true to its own principles, it must be open to its whole interpretive history and to new insights.

Theological schools testify to the historically conditioned ways in which believers and theologians have heard and understood revelation. The existence of different schools of theology within Catholicism also underscores the importance of historical context in theology: different theologies are reflections of the times and places in which they were devised. The Alexandrian school, for example, took a mystical-Platonic approach to the interpretation of Scripture: its second- and third-century theologians looked for the mystery symbolically present in the written word and formulated their questions in the light of spiritual reality. The Antiochene school, on the other hand, was indebted to Aristotle and so interpreted Scripture historically and literally: its theologians asked what the writers actually meant, and its questions were presented against the background of material reality. These two early schools shaped the great Christological debates of the fourth- and fifth-century ecumenical councils, showing, perhaps, that schools and councils, theologians and bishops function best when operating dialectically, moving together toward deeper understanding.

The relationship among the various kinds of theologians, and between them and ecclesiastical authorities, has not always been smooth. Additionally, the tensions between the authority of ecumenical councils and papal authority have consistently been problematic in Roman Catholicism and underlie, to a great degree, the discord between Orthodox Christianity and Roman Catholicism. In former times, theologians were usually bishops, priests, or monks (sometimes nuns), all of whom operated within the system and so were subject to its disciplinary actions. Nowadays, however, theologians are often lay persons, removed from the immediate juridical power of the church. Furthermore, modern theology is increasingly interested in incorporating insights from Protestant Christianity and from non-Christian religions. What this will all mean to hierarchical authorities remains to be seen, but it will no doubt have an important effect on the definition and operation of the magisterium, whose function it is to judge theological speculations in light of the ancient Catholic ideal, "one truth, one faith, one church."

Theology began as a process of continuity and defense: believers handed on what they had learned about Jesus and those who spoke for the church used rhetoric, philosophy, and law to explain Christian teachings to incredulous Jews, supercilious pagans, and hostile emperors. To forestall misleading doctrinal interpretations, councils formulated carefully crafted statements of Christian doctrine and theologians made that doctrine philosophically precise and spiritually accessible. Even as third- and fourth-century theologians challenged the hegemony of Greek philosophy, they used its vocabulary to develop Christology and Trinitarian theology. Not surprisingly, Eastern and Western theology differed in emphasis: Orthodox Christianity tended to be more mystical and liturgical in its preoccupations while Roman Catholicism was more legalistic in its approaches to church and to sacraments. Whatever differences exist between these two ancient Christianities, however, Roman Catholicism embraced Eastern theology as its own: the Catholic church owes as much to Origen Adamantius, Basil, and Gregory of Nyssa as it does to Cyprian, Ambrose, and Augustine.

The golden age of early Christian literature in the West reached its peak in the work of Augustine (354–430), whose influence on subsequent theological thinking is legendary. His conversion is one of the great "romantic" stories of Christian history (Brown), and his theology was worked out in the last few years of the Roman Empire. As bishop of Hippo, in northern Africa, Augustine was passionately interested in the daily care of his community, and his philosophically sophisticated positions were, first of all, attempts to answer practical questions posed by three important religious controversies. In response to Manichaean dualism Augustine argued for the essential goodness of the created order and so postulated the reality and function of free will as the explanation for evil in the world. Against Donatist rigorism, he worked out theories of grace and sacramental life that explained how the church can be one and holy in spite of sinful ministers and wrenching controversy. In opposition to the Pelagian belief that human beings can move toward salvation on their own, without the help of grace, Augustine devised a theological anthropology and theory of

predestination, both of which had an enormous impact on the development of Catholic and Protestant theology. His *City of God,* written as Rome fell to the Visigoths, contrasted Christianity and "the world," becoming the first philosophy of Christian history.

During the Middle Ages, up to the eleventh century, theology was mainly taken up with collecting and preserving the great heritage of early Christianity. It was not a period of creative thought, because of the transitional and missionary nature of the church's life, but it did manage to keep the ancient tradition alive, accurately copied, and safe. Just as the eleventh century began "the great thaw" in Christian art and architecture (Clark), so it saw the beginnings of a new, systematic theology: scholasticism. Starting with the intellectually independent work of Peter Abelard (1079–1142), whose dialectical principles had a major effect on theological method, and culminating in the magisterial work of Thomas Aquinas (1225–1274), John Duns Scotus (1265–1308), and others, scholastic theology was philosophical, synthetic, embracing, and methodical.

Scholastic theology combined the monastic inheritance of Bible *lectio* (reading) with the Carolingian inheritance of *disputatio* (a pedagogical method based on argumentation). Early medieval Bibles were often "glossed": a scriptural text was surrounded by various ancient commentaries upon it. By the twelfth century theologians attempted to arrange the glosses under specific headings: the "Sentences" of Peter Lombard were composed of four books devoted to specific theological questions (e.g., the Trinity) culled from the glosses. At the end of the compilation, Lombard inserted his own opinions. Once university students and teachers had the Bible, the opinions of ancient writers, and Lombard's "Sentences," a series of "disputed questions" arose and days were set aside so that theologians could argue about them. These sessions came to be organized in a specific way: the theologian stated the question, listed various opinions on it, responded with arguments and sources, repeated the opinions, and then gave the answers. A "master theologian," who had participated in these debates and organized his notes, often wrote a "Summa." The most remarkable organization, and hence the most enduring and remarkable "Summa," was that of Aquinas. The extent of his writings is immense, and their substance brilliant. Little wonder that the nineteenth-century Catholic church, looking for a nearly perfect expression of Roman Catholicism, chose to extol Thomism.

Apologetical theology was the inheritance of the Reformation: sixteenth-century Catholicism defined itself in opposition to the reformers and concentrated on the teaching authority of the church. Theology became defensive and controversial, seeking to expose and ridicule the doctrines of Roman Catholic opponents. If theologians sometimes searched opposing viewpoints in order to "understand" them, their more accommodating approach was usually aimed at apologetic acuity, at being better able to vanquish Protestants and draw unbelievers into the safe haven of the "one, true church." For all its systematic rigor and constructive energy, however, Trent's theology was essentially geared to respond to a state of siege. The philosophical challenges of the eighteenth-century Enlightenment, far from drawing Catholic theology into creative dialogue, made Catholicism more defensive and effectively stagnant; when Catholicism did emerge somewhat from its fortress to address the modern world, it did so by looking backward, into the high achievements and unsurpassable triumphs of the medieval period.

In the nineteenth century, a rift between theologians and the institutional church grew perilous. In an attempt to address Enlightenment challenges, theologians of the early nineteenth century made some creative and careful moves. Their work, however, was virtually ignored within the church: neither the nonscholastic style of the Tübingen school nor the impressive arguments of John Henry Newman (1801–1890) had much impact on Catholic theology until the middle of the twentieth century.

The failure of the church in the early part of the nineteenth century to come to terms with some critical questions led late-century scholars into the nexus of controversial events known as modernism. The work of the modernists—some of it brilliantly suggestive, some of it decidedly quirky—and its scathing condemnation by church officials disclosed the painful distance between the needs of the time and the actual state of theology. Ignoring or condemning new directions was an official defense against modernity based partially on an enthrallment with medieval Catholicism. The romantic movement, which swept through nineteenth-century literature and art, stirred the Roman Catholic church to remember its past glory. By removing itself to the medieval period, the church could disguise the siege mentality of the Counter-Reformation and escape the frightening challenges of the modern world: it could offer its believers a vision of itself as the dominant spiritual and cultural force of Europe. Roman Catholicism returned to the medieval period for aesthetic excellence, an alternative social model, and systematic theology.

Heralded by Leo XIII's encyclical *Aeterni Patris* (1879), Roman Catholic theology from the late nineteenth century until the mid-twentieth century was known as neoscholasticism and was essentially Thomistic; it brought Catholic enthusiasm for the medieval period to a climax and also gave it a clearly Roman Catholic identity. In America, Catholic journals were devoted to neoscholastic theology and the religious curriculum of Catholic colleges was defined by it. One of the reasons the American Catholic bishops at the Second Vatican Council were dubbed by the press "the silent contingent" was the total immersion of American theological education in the neoscholastic system; in Europe, on the other hand, the stage had been set for modern Catholic theology several decades before the council.

Contemporary theological questions must be placed both in the context of preconciliar European theology and post–Second Vatican Council experience: the former leads to political and liberation theologies while the latter situates some of the hostile discontent in present-day Catholicism. European theology before the council was fed by several disparate streams of thought. Inspired by Pierre Teilhard de Chardin (1881–1955), theologians began to talk about God as a being "in process" rather than ultimately "finished," a God related to and crucially involved in the world. From the existential philosophy of Martin Heidegger (1889–1976) and the Thomistic theology of Joseph Maréchal (1878–1944), Karl Rahner (1904–1984), the most influential Catholic theologian of the twentieth century, devised his category of the "supernatural existential." According to Rahner, questions about God are also questions of human existence; the cognitive processes and actions of human life are revelatory in the most profoundly religious sense of that word. Rahner's student Johannes Baptist Metz, influenced by an increasingly rich ecumenical dialogue, developed "political theology," arguing that God is intimately present in political life; the Gospel is necessarily bound up with the here and now.

One of the most creative trends in the last few years has been "liberation theology," a specifically Third World brand of political theology associated with Gustavo Gutiérrez. Classically, Roman Catholic theology has always asserted that the revealed word of God is found in the church, particularly in Scripture, tradition, and the teaching of the magisterium. Liberation theologians argue that God is revealed in the historical praxis of liberation as well; one must look to Scripture, tradition, and the magisterium, but one finds God's word expressly revealed today in the lives of the poor.

Liberation theology is not a branch of theology, but a dimension of all theology; traditional theological questions, according to liberation theologians, must be reformulated in the light of specifically liberationist insights. The need for revisioning theological questions in pursuit of new answers is also evident in the work of Roman Catholic feminist theologians: Rosemary Radford Ruether, Elisabeth Schüssler Fiorenza, and Mary Daly bring a bold challenge to traditional theology to incorporate women's experience into its categories and explanations.

Ironically, feminist theologians may be the ones to rediscover the power of Mary as a religious symbol. As they reclaim the feminine dimensions of the divine and recover the powers of the ancient mother goddess, feminists may present a new dimension of Mary to the Catholic church. Gospel writers and early Christian theologians, building on scanty historical information, developed a theology of Mary that gave rise to a number of doctrines: she was the ever-virgin "Mother of God," more powerful than the saints as an object of intercessory prayer, "assumed" into heaven and crowned there as its queen. Theologians explained her as the mother of all Christians, a type of the church, and the firstborn of redeemed humanity. In the overblown Marian piety of the nineteenth century, some Catholics wanted her declared as the "mediatrix of all graces" and "co-redemptress" of the human race: Pius IX proclaimed her Immaculate Conception (her freedom of original sin from the moment of her conception) in 1854. By the Second Vatican Council, however, "Mariology" had toned down considerably. The council fathers were remarkably restrained in their Marian doctrines: they refused to write a separate document on Mary and instead appended a chapter about her onto the Constitution of the church.

The post–Second Vatican Council Catholic experience has raised yet another set of contemporary questions. "Traditional Catholicism" as defined by the Council of Trent and the First Vatican Council presented a powerful symbol system to Catholics. The Dantean vision, enormously reenforced by the romantic return to medieval Catholicism in the nineteenth century, wrapped the spiritual strength of Roman Catholicism in poetic language. The Roman Catholic ideal was universal, had its own language and music, was ruled by a pope who stood in a consecutive line from Peter, and had a brilliant theological system in the writings of Aquinas.

For all these wonders, however, traditional Catholicism tended to stand dangerously still, and it perceived reality dualistically: Catholics were accustomed to think that the church was a "perfect society" and had always been as it was now and need never change; they conceptualized reality in terms of opposing pairs: church and world, the secular and the sacred, clergy and laity. Catholics took it for granted that those who were really serious about personal salvation had to "leave the world" in order to pursue evangelical perfection.

Most American Catholics, including bishops and priests, did not question these assumptions; but European Catholicism had, for decades, attempted to come to terms with what critics perceived as the intellectual and cultural doublethink that Catholicism required. The Second Vatican Council, therefore, was partly a search for and recovery of a rich tradition, an attempt to define Catholicism in terms far broader and more mobile than the Council of Trent's version of "traditional" Catholicism.

Revisionary movements usually have destructive and constructive sides. In disabusing Catholics of the notion that "traditional" Catholicism was all there was to Catholicism, the Second Vatican Council was superbly destructive. When Latin was replaced with the vernacular, traditionalists argued that Catholicism would die and some interpreters concluded that renewal was no more than accommodation. The constructive work of reshaping Catholicism so that its ancient sacramental sensibility can permeate the political realities of its universal extension is just beginning.

In redefining itself as a "pilgrim church" (as opposed to a "perfect society") the Second Vatican Council upset long-cherished notions of "traditional" Catholicism; it is no surprise, therefore, that present-day Catholicism is contentious within itself. At the same time, by defining Catholicism as a moving, growing tradition, open to ecumenical dialogue, the church has, in a way, stated its profound confidence in its theological stability. The arguments of today incorporate insights from newly vocal centers: Third World theologians, feminists, Protestants, and non-Christian religious leaders all widen the context in which Roman Catholic theology is defined. If it is true to form, the Catholic church will learn how to adapt itself to these new challenges and emerge, as it has before in controversial times, stronger and richer for the conflict.

ROMAN CATHOLIC WORSHIP

The core of the Catholic experience has always been repentance and conversion, then nurture in new life with celebrations of renewal and revitalization. For Catholics, as for most religious groups, the believing community is the locus of identity and religious intimacy: worship is a public manifestation of belief rather than a private devotion. Catholic worship has usually included preaching, prayer, sacraments, and singing; its weekly celebration of the Eucharist is called the Mass. The accents of Catholic worship —sacramentals, devotional life, and spiritual disciplines—reflect the context in which they were developed and show, to some extent, how grassroots practice intersects with and interprets larger theological questions.

Primitive peoples believed that there were especially holy times and places when and where the gods were more accessible and more likely to hear their prayers. Although that consciousness is considerably diluted in the modern era, it has not fully disappeared; Catholics consider their places of worship to be sacred and divide their years into holy liturgical seasons. Because they are a sacramental people, Catholics, more easily than other Christian groups, attach the word "holy" to things: it is not unusual for them to talk about holy days, or cards, or water. The accoutrements of their piety can be seen, tasted, touched, heard, and smelled, which makes Catholic worship significantly more sensual than the worship experienced in other Christian communities. Indeed, non-Catholic critics have often identified the "smells and bells" aspects of Catholic worship with medieval superstition. While post–Second Vatican Council worship has eliminated some of the sounds and odors associated with Catholicism, it has not really changed the essential sacramental character of it: Catholics still believe that God is most clearly accessible to the community through concrete, visible, historical events or things.

Prayer, which is the explicit response to God as the source of life and love, has been defined by the old catechism as a "lifting of the mind and heart to God." Many Catholics grew up summarizing the reasons for prayer in the acronym ACTS: one prayed for purposes of Adoration, Contrition, Thanksgiving, and Supplication. Following the example of Jesus in the New Testament, Catholics pray both privately and publicly. A myriad of private devotional practices within Catholicism may reflect radically different historical circumstances, but they also testify to the basic motivation for prayer, a hunger to be in touch with the divine.

Catholics, typically, do not think of themselves as alone in their quest for God: they not only have the example of the saints; they have, in some way, their company. Doctrinally conceptualized as the "mystical body of Christ," the Catholic church has never limited itself to its worldly embodiment, but has embraced its members in all aspects of their spiritual journeys. In the pre–Second Vatican Council church Catholics talked about the church as "militant" (working its salvation out on earth), "suffering" (paying for its sins in Purgatory), and "triumphant" (in the presence of God in heaven), a tripartite division inspired by the theology of the Middle Ages and sustained by its poetry and devotion.

This vision was supported by the cult of the saints—belief in and devotion to Catholic heroes publicly acknowledged to be "in heaven," able to intercede for those on earth. The saints were canonized because they exhibited heroic sanctity in their lives; but they were also demonstrably human, and their lives had often been scandalous before they heard and responded to God's call to them. As such, saints were able to understand common human experience, to serve as role models and as powerful "friends" in the heavenly court. Pious Catholics often undertook pilgrimages to the hometowns or shrines of certain saints, finding in those places some touch of the divine, which makes earthly space sacred. In this medieval model, the emphasis was on the word *mystical;* one's prayer life could easily become privatized and separated from life "in the world."

In much contemporary Catholicism, at least in its American expression, mystical body theology has become demystified: prayer and spiritual life often take place in the world and one's actions on behalf of other members of the "body" are as important as—probably more important than—private devotions. "Saints" in this contemporary model may not be canonized or even Catholic. Heroic sanctity is now understood in terms of the New Testament interlocking of the two great commandments; it is simply impossible to love God unless one loves one's neighbor. American Catholics looking for saints might feel as moved by Mahatma Gandhi as by Francis of Assisi, more inspired by Martin Luther King than by Martin de Porres. Accordingly, one is not urged to lose the self in a lone spiritual quest, but to find God in situations of oppression and liberation. Prayer in this situation may look and feel far removed from medieval devotion to the saints. Yet, looking at what those saints did in their own times—responding with charity and goodwill in extreme or dangerous situations—one can see more continuity than disruption.

Preaching, in the early church, was the proclamation of the Gospel, usually aimed at repentance and conversion: New Testament sermons, full of urgency and persuasiveness, were usually aimed at unbelievers. As stories of Jesus developed into the New Testament and patterns of worship took on consistency, preaching became part of community celebration. Ancient collections of sermons show that early preachers usually gave extended commentary on Scripture readings. Preaching, therefore, became a method of teaching and deepening faith in Jesus.

It is not hard to imagine that sermons in the richly endowed Constantinian church were magnificent. John Chrysostom (347–407), the great Orthodox theologian, was nicknamed "golden tongued" precisely because of his extraordinary abilities as a preacher. Similarly, one can suspect that preaching in the West, especially after the fall of Rome, was dismal at best. The newly anointed Charlemagne managed to inspire a small ninth-century renascence that underscored the importance of preaching by commanding it to be done in the vernacular; but there were not many good preachers around, and what we know of the period indicates that its preaching was not of high quality.

In the twelfth century, with the rise of scholasticism, preaching was done in universities and was, often, expository. Also, flowerings of mystical devotion produced great spiritual preachers like Bernard of Clairvaux (1090–1153); but the sad conclusion of church officials at the Fourth Lateran Council (1215) was that most parish priests were illiterate and that preaching was abysmal. Into this vacuum came two new groups of eager preachers: lay movements like the Waldenses, twelfth-century followers of Peter Waldo, were condemned by the church, while new religious movements like the Dominicans, named for Saint Dominic (1170–1221), were given official sanction and supported by the church. Together, however, they led to a rebirth of interest in preaching.

By the sixteenth century, it had become increasingly clear that although there was regular preaching, it was not focused on the Gospel: rather, preachers spun apocalyptic visions, sold indulgences, interpreted mystical experiences, and entertained their listeners. Reformers—both Catholic and Protestant—were eager to restore preaching as exposition of the word of God. The Council of Trent instructed all parish priests to preach each Sunday, and seminary education was strengthened so that priests would learn to do it well. Still, even in its reformed state, Roman Catholic preaching tended to focus on doctrine, morals, and explanations of the orthodox theses of the faith rather than on the Gospels. When Protestants accused Catholics of knowing virtually nothing about the Bible, they were right: it was only when the Second Vatican Council stressed the link between preaching and the proclamation of the biblical word of God that Catholics started to change their preaching style and center their worship much more clearly on Scripture.

Earliest Christian practice included the sacraments of baptism and the Communion, initiation into the celebration of the life, death, and resurrection of Jesus. Catholics believe that sacraments are visible signs given to the church by Christ to draw the community of believers into a more intimate relationship with God. Sacraments can be seen, touched, or consumed, yet they are not just things: they are symbols of divine power, ritual actions celebrated in a special way because Jesus instructed his followers to do so. Catholics differ from Protestants both in the number of sacraments they accept and in what they understand sacraments to do. While most Protestants find baptism and the Lord's Supper clearly mandated in the New Testament, they do not agree that other sacraments are found there. Similarly, while Roman Catholics believe that sacraments "give grace" to those who receive them with the right intention, Protestants believe that sacraments are either channels of grace or nontransmitting symbols of grace.

Roman Catholics and Orthodox Christians observe seven sacraments, not just two. Part of the reason for this difference lies in the longer historical tradition of these churches and their association with the medieval desire to make religion all-embracing by periodizing the phases of life and making lists that specify the ways God relates to the world. For Catholics, besides baptism and the Eucharist, the sacraments are confirmation, penance (or reconciliation), holy orders (whereby a man is ordained to the priesthood), matrimony (which consecrates marriage), and the anointing of the sick. All these ritual celebrations have a long history and some New Testament context (Jesus' presence at the wedding feast at Cana, for example, and his words about the permanence of marriage), though none of them is as clearly mandated by Jesus as baptism and Communion. Catholic belief in the presence of the Holy Spirit in the church and the authority of tradition is perhaps more of a basis for these "other" sacraments than is the New Testament itself.

Acceptance of seven sacraments in the Middle Ages was considered to be a conservative step— some theologians thought there were more than thirty and some Orthodox Christians insisted there were hundreds—but by the twelfth century and again at the councils of Florence (1439) and Trent the Catholic church affirmed its belief in seven sacraments. Not surprisingly, given the Aristotelian proclivities of medieval theology,

Catholic theologians specified the necessary elements of a sacrament: it had to have the right *matter* (water in the case of baptism), the proper *form* (the words "I baptize you in the name of the Father and of the Son and of the Holy Spirit"), and the right *intention* on the part of the priest (to do what the church did in the sacrament; to forgive all sin and admit the person to church membership). The person receiving the sacrament had to be rightly *disposed* (to have faith and, in the case of baptism, repentance: Catholics baptize babies on the theory that the faith and repentance of the church can be extended to them through their godparents until they have faith and repentance of their own).

After the Council of Trent, the assertion of objective sacramental efficacy against what was regarded as Protestant subjectivism resulted in a period of atrophy in which sacramental understanding declined. Some sacramental practices lost touch with their roots and either became mechanical or took on fanciful or constricted explanations. The sacrament of penance, for example, lost its role as a guided step in one's spiritual life and became automatic: rather than celebrating the sacrament as a means of reconciliation and moral improvement, many used it as a kind of weekly cleanup.

Sacraments are meant to be unique visitations of the divine, moments in which God communicates with believers. They also reflect an understanding of the church as community bound together in the life of Christ. Sacraments bind individual believers to God through Christ, but they also link individuals to one another in one body of Christ. In traditional Catholic theology, sharp distinctions between natural and supernatural are somewhat softened by sacramental understandings of the world: extensions of divine life are to be found in many dimensions of human existence.

Early Christians sang psalms and used singing in other parts of their worship, but congregational singing did not survive through the Middle Ages in Western Christianity. It was reintroduced into Protestant worship during the Reformation both as a means of worship and as a way of teaching doctrine, but Catholics did not use congregational singing again until after the Second Vatican Council, a fact that may account for their relatively poor showing as congregational singers. Because the Catholic church celebrated its liturgy in Latin, it relied on trained choirs using medieval Gregorian chant: congregational singing was not encouraged except in devotions such as prayer services, holy hours, and Lenten exercises.

What has most distinguished Catholic worship, however, has been the Mass, the particular way in which Catholics celebrate the Eucharist. For Catholics, time is sacred; the year is divided into liturgical "seasons" beginning in the four weeks before Christmas (Advent) and climaxing in the sacred Triduum, the three holy days celebrated at the end of the penetential (Lenten) season: Holy Thursday, Good Friday, and Easter. Since each season of the year has distinctive readings, prayers, practices, and even colors —celebrants wear special liturgical clothes called vestments, modeled on ancient tunics, with different colors specified for different seasons— Catholic liturgical life is rich and varied.

It is also controversial. The celebration of the Eucharist, up until the Second Vatican Council called "the sacrifice of the Mass," was understood as an unbloody re-presentation of Christ's sacrifice on the cross. In order to make its theology accessible to people, various parts of the Mass were explained as symbols or images of Jesus' last hours on earth: the priest washing his hands, for example, was related to Pontius Pilate washing his hands.

In the fifty years before the Second Vatican Council, liturgical scholars began to rediscover the lush tapestry of the Catholic tradition and began to explain the Mass in terms of its roots in Jewish ritual meal ceremonies. The washing of the hands, in this more embracing and historically accurate accounting, was related to ritual purification. The Mass, which had taken on characteristics of sacrifice and, in the baroque period, the trappings of opera (Bouyer), came to be understood as a meal. The private expressions of devotion during Mass were eschewed after the council in favor of a more participatory, community-centered model. Many older Catholics, trained in their youth to see the Mass as a time for special, private prayer in hushed, mysterious space, were shocked and confused when they experienced noisy festivity in church and were told that private prayer was inappropriate during a "community celebration."

Roman Catholic worship, like its history and theology, has changed dramatically in the last twenty years. The changes were not precipitous:

solid liturgical renewal began in the nineteenth century and the contribution of the American Catholic church through liturgical centers like St. John's Abbey in Collegeville, Minnesota, was outstanding. In the present climate of ecumenism and social justice, Catholics are learning about their roots in Jewish practice and their similarities to and differences from traditional Protestantism. Non-Christian religions have widened Catholic understandings of prayer, and conservative, Pentecostal Christians have enriched Catholic experience by their witness to the power of the Holy Spirit in daily Christian life. Many of the new hymns used during worship emphasize a deepening social awareness on the part of Catholics and show the connection between worship and belief. Since worship touches virtually all Catholics, it sometimes appears to be more problematic than it is: the most urgent and divisive arguments usually occur over liturgical practice. Underneath the arguments and real differences in form, however, Catholics continue to affirm the importance of prayer, biblically based preaching, sacramental encounters with God, liturgical festivity, sacred time and space, and regular participation in the celebration of the Eucharist.

SPIRITUALITY

Spirituality is faith made explicit in life. Like Dante's *Comedy,* it is an adventure motivated by a desire for union with God. In more ordinary terms, it describes ways in which Catholics live in the world knowing that death is not the end of their story. Because Roman Catholic spirituality has its roots in the ascetic traditions of the ancient Greeks, it has too often been understood as the province of a few heroic souls aiming at perfection. The Second Vatican Council, however, reaffirmed the more orthodox view that sanctity is for everyone: "all the faithful, whatever their condition or state, are called by the Lord . . . to perfect holiness" (*Dogmatic Constitution on the Church*).

Roman Catholic spirituality is predicated on the belief that it is possible and desirable to have a deeply intimate relationship with God. In the early church, such a relationship often seemed to require the obliteration of the self: one left the world, disciplined the body, and mastered the

THE ROMAN CATHOLIC HERITAGE

self in order to be ready for union with the divine. In contemporary Catholicism, spirituality is characterized by an openness both to the self and to God: as Karl Rahner says, "the experience of self *and* the experience of God . . . constitute a unity" (*Theological Investigations,* 1975, vol. 13, pp. 122–132).

In some ways these two spiritualities reflect different understandings of God; in the first, God is utterly transcendent, unknowable, and unapproachable, while in the second God is more clearly involved with the world, evident in events and accessible. An ancient Christian writer, trying to summarize a similar opposition, said, "This neither is Thou, this also is Thou," meaning that no experience really manifested the divine since God was beyond all expression; yet each image of goodness or charity encountered in one's daily life was, in fact, a manifestation of God, abundantly present in the created order. Roman Catholic spirituality has resonated between these two insights: the first finds its classical expression in the *via negativa* represented by Dionysius the Areopagite (ca. 500) or Walter Hilton's *Cloud of Unknowing* (fourteenth century); the second, the way of affirmation, can be imaged by the creation-centered spirituality of Meister Eckhart (1260–1327) or the poetic mysticism of Dante.

From another perspective these opposing spiritualities have been reflected in two different modes of "religious" life within Catholicism: the contemplative life, centered on prayer and mysticism, and the active life, directed toward good works. Contemplatives usually argue that one must leave the world in order to have time and space for prayer: their goal, direct union with God in mystical experience, has had various embodiments throughout the history of the church. Active spirituality, on the other hand, argues that one finds God in the needs of the poor or the sick or the dying: its goal, following Jesus' commands to love and care for the "neighbor," has also had a number of different expressions in Roman Catholic history. In modern American Catholicism there have been significant attempts to bridge these two traditions, especially in the active spirituality of the contemplative Thomas Merton (1915–1968) and the deeply prayerful life of the activist Dorothy Day (1898–1981).

Before describing these embodiments of Roman Catholic spirituality, a word must be said about another division within Catholicism: laity and "religious." From ancient times there has always been a distinction in Catholicism between clerics and nonclerics. The clergy are those ordained and designated to be the official leaders in the church—priests, deacons, bishops—and the laity are "the people," those served by the clergy. Together these two constitute the church, all sharing in "priestly prophetic and royal offices of Christ" (Second Vatican Council, *Constitution on the Sacred Liturgy*), and each having some special gift in building up the body of Christ.

In the early church, antagonisms between clergy and laity were usually over matters of discipline or interpretation, not over the supposed superiority of one group over the other. In time, however, climaxing in the High Middle Ages, the clerical state came to be considered superior, sometimes far superior, to the laity: clericalism at its worst appropriated the church for the clergy so that the church *was* the pope, bishops, priests, and deacons, while the laity supported the church and was served by it. The post–Second Vatican Council slogan of the laity—"We are the church"—expresses both a surge of power felt by the laity in the 1960's and a reaction against the ecclesiological model that identified the church with the clergy.

The laity, encompassing, as it does, all nonordained persons, did not originally support internal distinctions of merit even though it was apparent that some Christians were more dedicated, more heroic under torture during times of persecution, and more given to prayer, fasting, and almsgiving than others. Gradually, however, especially in the context of persecution when heroism and cowardice were particularly visible, a distinction between ordinary and extraordinary Christians began to emerge. Those who withstood torture without apostatizing were considered to be powerful and holy. When the persecutions ended, those searching for new ways to demonstrate their total dedication to God interpreted Jesus' words in Mark 9:29 as a mandate: they fled to the desert in order to confront intractable demons.

As a literature began to build up around the eremetical life, interpreters remembered a second-century penetential text by the ancient Christian writer Hermas, which said that good works beyond the commands of Jesus win more

167

glory. Since one interpretation of the Gospel admits that Jesus demanded total surrender to God, it may be hard to imagine what good works were possible beyond that command; still, within a short time, a distinction was made in the requirements for a Christian life that separated "commands" from "counsels." The former applied to all Christians, while only those seeking "perfection" were called to observe the latter. These so-called counsels of perfection—total renunciation of property (poverty), abstinence from sexual expression (chastity), and complete submission of the will (obedience)—formed the basis of "religious life" in the church, a state existing somewhere between the laity and the clergy, yet above them both since neither clergy nor laity was vowed to follow the counsels of perfection.

As the eremetical life developed into monasticism, rules were formulated—by Basil (329–379) in the East, Benedict (480?–547?) in the West—to make "religious life" possible within a community context. Neoplatonic philosophy provided this new life with an intellectual basis, so that the classical expression of early Catholic spirituality became known as the *via negativa*. One could have an immediate experience of God by way of mystical experience, but only by abstraction: everything specifically human had to be abandoned so that God alone remained. "This neither is Thou": all experience is rejected until nothing is left but the soul and God, until progressive divinization is complete. Dionysius the Areopagite gave this tradition its classical expression, describing the process in terms of purgation (the obliteration of bad habits and repentance for sins), illumination (a cleansing from attachments and enlightenment as to spiritual realities), and union (deeply intimate union with God and habitual practice of virtues).

Roman Catholic spirituality has been enriched by a continual reinterpretation of this tradition: Gregory of Nyssa (ca. 330–ca. 395); Bonaventure (1217–1274); Bernard of Clairvaux (1090–1153), founder of the Cistercians; Juliana of Norwich (ca. 1342–ca. 1413); Teresa of Avila (1515–1582); and John of the Cross (1542–1591) are only some of the more illustrious saints developing this kind of spirituality. The contemplative ideal continues to be a significant part of the Roman Catholic tradition in a variety of religious orders founded specifically to enhance mystical life (the Carmelites, for example), in experimental contemplative groups (like the Spiritual Life Institute in Sedona, Arizona), and in its extension to other members of the church by way of directed retreats and literature.

While monastic life in the East has always been dedicated predominantly to prayer and contemplation, it has often been more active in the West. Monks may well have spent themselves in pursuit of mystical union, but they were also the guardians of the Christian heritage and the mainstays of civilization in the Christian West for a considerable period of time. Religious life in the West, therefore, had from its inception an active possibility built into it. "This also is Thou": pains and needs are embraced so that in seeing Christ in the wretched, one becomes like Christ. Religious orders proliferated to respond to urgent needs: Dominicans, founded by St. Dominic (1170–1221), were trained to be preachers at a time when preaching had reached perhaps its lowest ebb; Franciscans, named for Francis of Assisi (1181–1226), embraced poverty as rich Christians became increasingly fascinated with wealth. When the church needed teachers or groups to work with the poor, the Vincentians (seventeenth century) and the Salesians of Don Giovanni Bosco (nineteenth century) were founded. The most famous religious order, whose representatives are found today both on Wall Street and in Third World slums, is the Society of Jesus (the Jesuits), established during the Catholic Reformation by Ignatius of Loyola (1495–1556): they have distinguished themselves as missionaries, spiritual directors, intellectuals, and diplomats, and their services to the pope have been a special part of their mission.

The most dramatic aspect of the story of religious orders relates to women. Nuns had been part of the eremetical tradition from its inception, distinguished for holiness as they had been honored for heroism in times of persecution. The Roman Catholic tradition has always had a long list of female saints, most of whom were canonized for the same reasons men were: for holiness, heroic practice of virtue, martyrdom, spiritual wisdom, and service to the church.

For a number of reasons, both cultural and political, male church leaders were especially energetic in their attempts to control and contain women, culminating in Boniface VIII's bull *Periculoso* (1298), which specified that "all and sundry nuns shall remain perpetually enclosed." Female religious life, distinct from that experienced by males, was to be lived in a cloister: nuns were not permitted to go out, to have any contact with the world, or to respond to any of the active needs of the church. Those who attempted to lead a noncloistered, pious community life—the Beguines, for example—were denounced, discouraged, and persecuted. Not until 1633, when Vincent de Paul and Louise de Marillac founded the Sisters of Charity, was there a nonenclosed religious order of women dedicated to working with the poor.

The proliferation of male and female religious orders, especially in the nineteenth century, extended the spiritual life to active groups: the quest for God could no longer be understood as the exclusive pursuit of contemplatives. Still, spirituality was based on an old dualism that saw reality in terms of the secular and the sacred. The laity, especially married people, was not generally included in understandings of spirituality since it was, almost by definition, the province of those in "religious life." Not until the Second Vatican Council did Roman Catholicism make explicit a universal call to holiness, showing the influence of Pierre Teilhard de Chardin, whose "spiritual attachment to the universe" was meant to be a new, "positive mysticism" contrasting with what he understood to be the negative detachment of John of the Cross. The Second Vatican Council documents—reflective of twentieth-century theological development and contemporary spiritual insights—blurred, if not obliterated, the antagonistic distinctions between the secular and the sacred: God was to be found in the world, in one's work, and in one's self.

The more embracing spirituality of modern Catholicism has led to enrichment of both active and contemplative religious orders. Contemplatives, who probably always conceptualized their vocation as praying "for the world," now take more responsibility for knowing what is going on in the world. Having been given charge of the ancient modes of spirituality, contemplatives are now much more willing to share them with others, and they have developed ways to extend their prayer to the troubling events in the world. Active religious orders, for their part, have become more involved with the laity and also more conscious of their own quasi-contemplative

roots. All sorts of Catholics—the laity and members of religious orders—are deeply involved in a number of different retreat movements and strategies: the universal call to holiness sounded at the Second Vatican Council has inspired a new burgeoning of prayer forms enriched by dialogue with non-Christian religions and by a revisionary look at the roots of ancient spirituality.

Two modern American Catholics whose lives have deeply influenced spirituality are Dorothy Day and Thomas Merton. Day, the founder of the Catholic Worker Movement (1933), was noted for her untiring work for the poor in the slums of major American cities: her radical poverty, persistent pacifism, and steady support of the downtrodden have had a major impact on American Catholicism. In some ways she embodies the epitome of modern Catholic spirituality, deeply rooted in the traditions, committed to care for the poor, and profoundly prayerful. Day was never "just an activist"; she struggled to maintain a balance between active Christianity and searching prayerfulness.

Merton spent most of his life in a Trappist monastery in Kentucky and is remembered for his incisive spiritual writings. Yet some of the most radical activists in the American Catholic church (Daniel J. Berrigan, for example) attribute much of their inspiration to Merton's encouragement and insight. In his own life Merton bridged the gulf between the active and the contemplative life but, more importantly for the history of spirituality, he welcomed the insights of Buddhist spirituality into the Catholic tradition. With him, Roman Catholic spirituality reached a new moment, ecumenically embracing, deeply contemplative, yet fully committed to the needs of the world, to social justice and peace.

Roman Catholic spirituality, therefore, is a dynamic blend of ancient asceticism, medieval expressions of religious experience—the metaphors of Catholic spirituality were particularly rich during the Middle Ages—and modern social ecumenical consciousness. Holiness is not the path of a few, but a call to all within the Catholic tradition. In responding to that call, Catholics have an enormous range of spiritual options from which to choose. New prayer forms (often, now indebted to the Buddhist or Orthodox tradition), modern applications of older modes of spiritual direction, and contemporary retreat centers make the "spiritual life" accessible to all.

"Religious life," still traditional in some ways, has also changed dramatically in the last twenty years. The modern American sister is usually not found in a convent, and contemporary American saints might well resemble the four women killed in El Salvador in 1981: by all accounts they were prayerful women, idealistic, determined to seek God by serving the poor in a desperate situation. What will become of "religious life" in the next two or three decades is not clear; but it is a safe prediction that Roman Catholic spirituality will survive and become both more contemplative and more active.

CONCLUSION

Since the Roman Catholic heritage emanates from the past, Dante is perhaps its best poet: much of what can be said about *The Divine Comedy* can be said about Catholicism. It is grounded in Rome as an ancient symbol of universal unification; its vision is cosmic and poetic, yet mortifyingly real in its scandals and mistakes; at its center one finds the mystery of the Incarnation, a perspective that honors the individual as well as calls that person into communion with the divine; its sacramental character is evident in its language, imagery, literature, and practice; it is self-involved, yet communal, intended for everyone while sometimes able to be especially ap-

pealing to a few. Most of all, it unfolds as a good story, still, after all this time, capable of astonishing even itself.

BIBLIOGRAPHY

Geoffrey Barraclough, *The Medieval Papacy* (1968); Ernest Benz, *The Eastern Orthodox Church* (1963); Louis Bouyer, *Liturgical Piety* (1955); Peter Brown, *Augustine of Hippo: A Biography* (1967); Kenneth Clark, *Civilisation* (1969); Bernard J. Cooke, *Ministry to Word and Sacraments* (1976); Christopher Henry Dawson, *Religion and the Rise of Western Culture* (1958); Avery Dulles, *Models of the Church* (1974).

Matthew Fox, ed., *Western Spirituality: Historical Roots, Ecumenical Routes* (1981); Langdon Gilkey, *Catholicism Confronts Modernity: A Protestant View* (1975); Philip Gleason, "Mass and Maypole Revisited: American Catholics and the Middle Ages," in *The Catholic Historical Review*, 57 (July 1971), 249–274; E. E. Y. Hales, *The Catholic Church in the Modern World* (1958); J. Derek Holmes and Bernard W. Bickers, *A Short History of the Catholic Church* (1984); Hans Küng, *The Church* (1967); Henri de Lubac, *Catholicism* (1950).

Richard P. McBrien, *Catholicism*, 2 vols. (1980); Arthur Mirgeler, *Mutations of Western Christianity* (1974); Leo J. O'Donovan, ed., *A World of Grace: An Introduction to the Themes and Foundations of Karl Rahner's Theology* (1980); Edward Schillebeeckx, *Christ: The Sacrament of the Encounter with God* (1963); Mary Jo Weaver, *Introduction to Christianity* (1983).

[*See also* AMERICAN CATHOLIC THOUGHT; CATHOLICISM FROM INDEPENDENCE TO WORLD WAR I; CATHOLICISM IN THE ENGLISH COLONIES; CATHOLICISM SINCE WORLD WAR I; ETHNICITY AND RELIGION; FRENCH CATHOLICISM IN THE NEW WORLD; *and* RELIGIOUS ARCHITECTURE AND LANDSCAPE.]

THE AFRICAN HERITAGE IN CARIBBEAN AND NORTH AMERICAN RELIGIONS

Leonard E. Barrett

MOST Europeans came to the Americas in search of fortune or freedom. Africans were brought as slaves and sold in bondage for life. The Europeans who came to the Americas brought with them a written religious tradition: some groups saw themselves as pioneering missionaries, establishing the religions of Europe in the Americas, while those who had been oppressed for nonconformity sought a place where they could develop their own brand of Christianity, free from the priestly scrutiny of Europe. The Africans who were brought to the Americas came from societies with no written traditions. They adhered to oral traditions, where religion was a way of life.

All religious practices were prohibited among Africans because the idea that they could have a viable religion was inconceivable in the sixteenth and seventeenth centuries. It took another century before it became evident that the slave ships carried not only men, women, and children but also systems of beliefs and practices, and a highly developed pantheon of gods and spirits—all supported by oral myths. The Africans' various ethnic beliefs and practices were later to undergo modifications as many traditions fused into one in various parts of the New World, both as a resistance to forced conversion and as an alternative religion to Christianity.

Slavery, one of the oldest human institutions, had the blessings of the Christian church. Some rationale had to be worked out in order to place the most brutal elements of the system in a broader perspective. It was therefore the rationalization of the church that the slaves were being brought to the New World to be Christianized. Proselytism was the motivation of the church. Both Spain and France developed instruments for the forced conversions of African slaves in their colonies. The Edict of March 1685, commonly known as the Code Noir, signed by His Christian Majesty the King of France, demanded that all slaves living in the islands were to be instructed and baptized in the Apostolic and Roman Catholic religion, and that public practice of any other religions be prohibited.

Laws are never created in a vacuum; they are generally established to correct what threatens the status quo. As early as the seventeenth century, African slaves had introduced their ancient religion in the islands despite the opposition of the masters. One can imagine the emotional states of the Africans on their initial entry into the New World as they were confronted with unexpected violence to person and belief. Torn from their ancestral communities, separated from members of their "tribes," clans, and families, and suddenly reduced to chattel, Africans were subjected to a disaster that could create dizziness or even delirium. Even worse, they were forced to repudiate their religion, customs, and languages and were required to replace these with a foreign culture that was alien, threatening, inhuman, and outrageously cruel. Africans, caught in the plantation system without an alternative, thought it easier to assume the facade of conversion and the rudimentary instructions of the established church rather than suffer pain or even death.

Despite all this, the Africans' fundamental beliefs were never shaken, and their consciousness was basically unchanged. It is important to understand that traditional African religions were

171

not based on creedal formulas that could be unlearned; rather, they were a way of life.

The number of African slaves and their places of origin have occupied students of the social sciences for over one hundred years. Various estimates have been attempted, but accurate statistics are hardly possible due to the secrecy of ships' captains, the forging of documents, and the widespread clandestine traffic in Africans that occurred during and even after the slave trade was abolished. The overcautious estimate of 9 to 12 million suggested by Philip D. Curtin (*The Atlantic Slave Trade: A Census,* 1969) has been widely accepted by Western scholars, but even this estimate is a staggering figure when one considers that for every African entering the New World, three had lost their lives either in the capture, in the march to the sea, or in the middle passage. When all the Africans who lost their lives in the slave trade are counted, the total approaches 40 million people, mostly between the ages of sixteen and thirty-five. Contrary to the reports of some slave propagandists that only the weak and the lazy were captured in the slave trade, planters in the New World often boasted that the "cream of African manhood" was delivered in slavery (Gilberto Freyre, *The Master and the Slaves,* 1953).

The same controversy that surrounded the numbers of Africans brought to the New World also surrounded their place of origin. Early writers believed that all of Africa shared equally in providing the slaves for the New World, but recent scholars such as Melville J. Herskovits give them a West African provenance. It is now broadly accepted that the majority of the slaves came from the Guinea coast, primarily from the Gambia to the Congo, but it is clear that toward the end of the slave trade small numbers of Africans were taken from as far as Mozambique.

Not only were West Africans the largest number of slaves in the New World, they were also the culture bearers and religious innovators. Dominant among them were the Yoruba of Nigeria, whose language, religion, and folklore found roots in many parts of the New World, especially in Cuba and Brazil; the Fon-speaking people of Dahomey, whose religion and customs were preserved in Haiti; and the Ashanti-Fanti people of the Gold Coast (present-day Ghana), whose religion and culture dominated most of the early English Caribbean, especially Jamaica.

The reasons for the dominance of these three cultures are still unknown. In many cases their numbers were minuscule when compared with the hundreds of "tribal groupings" found in the New World. Slave literature shows that leaders among the Maroons, leaders in rebellions, and leaders of religious cults nearly always turned out to be from one of these three groups.

British North America received only one-sixth of the African slaves who were taken to the islands of the Caribbean, an area about two-thirds the size of the Pennsylvania colony. The Caribbean islands are therefore a most important case study of African reaction to slavery. It was there that most organized resistance to slavery was staged by Maroon communities, and it is in these communities that the purest kind of African culture was retained. Unlike British North America, where the master class dominated the social and economic environment, the Caribbean was primarily made up of slave colonies. In these environments, Europe ruled, but Africa reigned. Despite laws governing the practices of African customs, the proximity of African peoples from the Guinea coast soon resulted in a breaking down of tribal barriers and generated a feeling of solidarity of the oppressed against the oppressors. One of the first institutions to emerge was African religion. Assemblies began as little more than secret societies, but in time they formed an island-wide network of communication. Sometimes religious expressions were disguised in a dance form filled with African symbols unknown to the masters. The leader of these secret societies, the head dancer of a troupe, would usually be a religious functionary, a man or woman possessed by the gods of the ancient tradition.

Little or nothing of the religious behavior of the Africans in the early slave period has been recorded. Many of the slave records were compiled after the system was well established. Much was written on slave rebellion, the Maroon wars, and runaway slaves, but very little on the psychological effects of slavery on Africans' lives. In addition, very few of the writers on the slave period were interested in religious behavior; they used stereotypic expressions of the day, such as "dark superstition." Several islands had learned writers, but their writings were geared to their class. Those official writers, who disdained the culture of the common people, included Edward Long and Bryan Edwards of Jamaica, writing in 1714 and 1793, respectively; Moreau de Saint Mery of Haiti, 1797; and Ulrich Bonnell Phillips, 1918, of the North American colonies.

European writers of the seventeenth and eighteenth centuries all agreed that Africans were inferior to Europeans; that they were the most primitive of the human race and were therefore without a recognizable culture; and that their entrance into the New World was providential. Through this contact with civilized Europeans, the Africans would receive the blessings of European civilization. Nineteenth-century Darwinism gave scientific respectability to these early writers; it remained the intellectual monitor of pulpit and podium until well into the twentieth century. By this time the Africans had become Afro-Americans, and in the Caribbean there were several generations of people of African descent. Joseph R. Washington, Jr., has summarized the Africans' plight in the Americas in one short sentence: "Born in slavery, weaned in segregation, and reared in discrimination." Despite many changes, the descendants of Africa were still an unassimilated ethnic entity in the United States and elsewhere in the New World. Afro-Americans had come a long way, from slavery through emancipation; they had contributed intellectually, economically, and culturally to the New World.

After centuries of benign neglect, scholarly knowledge about the black community was urgently sought. How much of their African heritage still existed in their community? How should they be treated in the broader society? Such questions prompted the Carnegie Corporation of New York to undertake a monumental study, to be carried out by Dr. Gunnar Myrdal of the University of Stockholm in Sweden. Along with this brilliant sociologist were several other specialists in their various fields.

One of the earliest anthropological studies to emerge from this project was Herskovits' *The Myth of the Negro Past* (1938). The official study of Dr. Myrdal, *An American Dilemma* (1944), created far less controversy than Herskovits' book. The author was a student of the American Negro long before the corporation made its announcement; the corporation only gave him a broader sphere of interest. As a cultural anthropologist he made a thorough study of Afro-Americans, West Indians, South Americans, and West Africans. Herskovits was interested not only in the descen-

dants of Africans in the New World, but sought firsthand information about cultural institutions in Africa as well.

The Myth of the Negro Past attempted to destroy the five myths surrounding Africans in the New World. First, "Negroes are naturally of childlike character, and adjust easily to the most unsatisfactory social situations, which they accept readily and even happily . . ." (p. 293). Using copious documentation, Herskovits dismissed this myth with overwhelming evidence. According to Herskovits, Africans under New World conditions were capable of assessing their situations and adapting to their conditions with sophisticated subtleties. This was not a childlike attitude, but rather a keen psychological sense based upon the ancient teachings of Africa. Besides, contrary to commonly accepted beliefs, the Africans in the New World were never content with their servile conditions, because not a year passed without some serious rebellions.

Second, "only the poorer stock of Africa was enslaved, the more intelligent members of the African communities raided, having been clever enough to elude the slavers' net" (pp. 293–294). In answer, Herskovits had only to cite the fact that the slave trade was not selective. Every class of African society was included: priests and paupers, royalty and prisoners.

Third, "Negroes were brought from all parts of the African continent, spoke divers languages, represented greatly differing bodies of customs, and, as a matter of policy, were distributed in the New World, so as to lose their tribal identity, no least common denominator of understanding or behavior could have possibly been worked out by them" (p. 294). Herskovits was well acquainted with the demography of Africa and so was fully capable of showing that the Africans brought to the New World were mostly coastal people who had interacted with each other for centuries. Despite their language differences, slaves in the New World were better able to communicate with each other as they learned the languages of their masters. European words were translated into African molds, allowing for an interpretation of African customs in European languages.

Fourth, "the cultures of Africa were so savage and relatively so low in the scale of human civilization that the apparent superiority of European customs as observed in the behavior of the masters would have caused and actually did cause them to give up such aboriginal traditions as they may otherwise have desired to preserve." On this point Herskovits states that the African civilization of the sixteenth and seventeenth centuries was neither savage nor low in comparison with that of Europe. Africans were not merely passive recipients of European acculturation; acculturation was a two-way process. Africans in the United States were exposed to a more intense acculturation due to the ratio of whites to blacks. In the Caribbean an inverse ratio prevailed; hence, a greater number of Africanisms were nurtured.

Fifth, if the first four myths are true, the Negro is a man without a past. Herskovits insisted that the Negro does have a past culture and history, which makes him as distinctive a participant on the American scene as the Swedish, German, and Irish immigrants.

The Myth of the Negro Past was probably the first serious anthropological study of Afro-Americans on a cross-cultural perspective. The work of Herskovits was suspect for two reasons: first, he was not an Afro-American; second, the Afro-American elite saw behind his study a hidden public policy agenda contrary to the dreams and aspirations of the black leaders of the period. After four hundred years, few Afro-Americans could appreciate the idea that any trace of African culture remained in their lives. Such a suggestion was seen as an attempt to undo all the efforts made toward total assimilation in the American mainstream.

There were many great black writers in America from 1755 to 1930. The first were the preachers of the eighteenth and nineteenth centuries, culminating in the eminent historian Carter G. Woodson (1875–1950); philosopher-sociologist W.E.B. Du Bois (1868–1963), by far the greatest black scholar of his day; and Edward Franklin Frazier, a contemporary of Melville Herskovits. Frazier, an eminent sociologist at Howard University, became the foremost dissenter from Herskovits' views. He vigorously denied that African culture could have survived the conditions of slavery within the borders of the United States. He did admit, however, that African cultural elements were to be found in other parts of the New World. Frazier's rejection of the conclusions of Herskovits was based on emotions, not on scholarly research. This recriminatory debate still goes on among Afro-American scholars, but

a calm observation of the evidence amassed by this anthropologist is still the stronger argument. Culture is the preserve of the anthropologist, not the sociologist.

Culture may be interpreted as varied systems developed by human societies as media for adaptation to the environments in which the members live. In its totality a cultural system constitutes the means through which the group achieves and organizes society. Cultural systems may be simple or complex, exhibiting a wide range of differences in form and content. When speaking of culture, we generally have two kinds of ingredients in mind: the material and the nonmaterial. Material culture consists of tools, techniques, fashions, and so on, while the nonmaterial culture consists of such ideas as social consciousness, kinship systems, marriage customs, government, religion, customs, and languages. Africans who were brought to the New World were torn from their material cultural patterns, with the consequent loss of many common points of reference. But the nonmaterial aspect of their culture was a part of their values and emotions.

Culture exists on several levels. The first can be called the technical-industrial. The Africans were known agriculturalists. It was this cultural patterning of hard work and technical-industrial skill that appealed to New World planters. Africans easily adapted themselves to the techniques and tools of their new environments. Africans' negative reaction to slavery was not simply a reaction to hard work, but the consciousness of their predicament of serving not only as human tools or beasts of burden but also as both labor and capital for the masters. Most of all, they were destined to a system of exploitation without recompense for the duration of their lives.

The second level of culture, the domestic-technical, operates on slightly deeper levels of consciousness. On this level, Africans recalled aspects of their past lives by reflecting on lore, proverbs, religion, nurturing, and the cuisine of their past life. From this level, elements of African traditions were handed down to generations born in the New World. At this level of conscious reflection, Africans grappled with the pressures of forced acculturations that attempted to rid them of their being African.

A third, ethical level of culture, the level of values, is the most resilient one, where choices

174

are made and actions are taken. This is the level on which overt and covert behavior are executed. The history of slavery is the record of a people who resisted their servile conditions in unexpectedly creative ways. Africans proved that they knew the difference between slavery and freedom, and many died in search of this freedom.

The foregoing confirms that Africans were culture bearers, freedom fighters, art inspirers, and religious innovators. A brief review of the African heritage from which the dominant culture bearers originated will aid in understanding the African heritage brought to the New World.

THE AFRICAN HERITAGE

The entire west coast of Africa contributed to the slave trade. Among the dominant people brought to the New World were the Ashanti-Fanti of the Gold Coast, the Yoruba of Nigeria, and the Fon-speaking people of Dahomey. The number of tribal communities involved in the slave trade has never been researched; Roger Bastide has suggested that the list is virtually endless. The history of the dominant people of the Guinea coast has been extensively documented, but African history and culture are yet unknown to all but a very few. Despite the volumes of work available to the American audience, Africa is still the "dark continent." To Herskovits, this was an "irony of history."

Few Westerners are aware that the Africans who were brought to the New World as slaves came from those West African regions where the higher and most complex civilizations were found and continued to flourish, even at the time Europeans made their so-called discovery of the American continent. To cite only a few examples: when European contact began, West Africa was far advanced in smelting iron and bronze. It had developed a highly technical, polyrhythmic style of music that still baffles students of ethnomusicology. The folk philosophy manifested in African tales and proverbs has such subtleties that the tales and proverbs have been compared with the "wisdom literature" of the ancient world by Marcel Griaule (*Conversation with Ogotemelli*, 1948). African sculpture in its classical versions has exercised the minds of art students from the time of Picasso to the present. The

African Customary Laws were of such sophistication that even the colonizing nations were reluctant to supersede them. Today African Customary Laws are taught in American law schools. African traditional medicine, especially the knowledge of herbs, has made great advances in curing, and in the field of holistic medicine African healers were far advanced.

Western writers have done their most creative work in the study of West African religions. These scholars range from the early-nineteenth-century evolutionary anthropologists to the present indigenous Africans. Traditional African religions are now widely studied on a comparative basis from the pre-Christian era to the present. Dr. Christian Gaba of the University of Ghana has said that to understand African culture one must study its religion. Religion is still the source of meaning in every aspect of African life. Dr. Kofi A. Opoku put it this way:

> The phenomenon of religion is so pervasive in the life of the Akan (the people of the Gold Coast) and inextricably bound up with their culture, that it is not easy to isolate what is purely religious from other aspects of life. It may be said, without fear of exaggeration, that in the life of the Akan, a thorough knowledge of his religion is imperative.
>
> ("Aspects of Akan Worship," in Lincoln)

The sentiments of Professor Opoku of West Africa are confirmed by Professor John S. Mbiti of East Africa:

> Traditional religions permeate all the departments of life, there is no formal distinction between the religious and the non-religious, between the spiritual and the material areas of life. Wherever the African is, there is his religion. . . . Although many African languages do not have a word for religion as such, it nevertheless accompanies the individual from long before his birth to long after his death. . . . African peoples do not know how to exist without religion.
>
> (*African Religion and Philosophy*, 1969, pp. 2–3)

The African theological systems that have survived in the New World are continuations of religious traditions, beliefs, and ritual systems that predated the slave trade—and even Christianity. Leading scholars in the area of African religions transplanted to the New World (Melville J. Herskovits, George Eaton Simpson, and Roger Bastide) have suggested that various religious sentiments of the African slaves were incorporated under the rubric of a few dominant cultures in the New World.

What were the important features of the ancient way? The African world view is best described as a vision of a cosmic harmony in which people and animate and inanimate beings exist in vital interaction. The world of beings and things is not just an abstraction but a field of forces in which all the parts interact. At the apex of this field of force is God, the Creator, who upholds and sustains creation. Below the Creator are the lesser divinities—the manifestations of the power of God, whose functions are to see that the different departments of the universe obey the divine principle. Below the divinities are the ancestors—the progenitors of the human family—who are venerated, and who have become intercessors between humans and God. They are exemplars of moral virtues to their descendants. The African world includes both animate and inanimate objects—all of these can be conduits for God's revelation. Every tree, every stone, Mother Earth, mountains, and animals may become manifestations of God.

Sources for the Study of African Religions. Books on African religions below the Sahara have been published for well over one hundred years, but most are now out of date. A few volumes written before 1960 were the work of ethnologists steeped in the tradition of Darwin, with a modicum of field research techniques; some were by speculative philosophers who sought ideas from the so-called primitives to support their alien philosophies. They were the typical armchair anthropologists—long on ideas but short on facts. Most of these writers depended on the observations of missionaries whose basic philosophy conveyed two modes of comparison: we are not like them and they are not like us.

To most nineteenth-century scholars, African religions were classified as religions of the "primitives," an elementary form based on mystical participation or mere illusions. It was not until the second half of the twentieth century that objective observations on African traditions began to be published; and not until native-born African scholars began to do research on their native traditions was it possible to do serious comparative studies on African religions.

The Ashanti-Fanti Heritage. Within the British slave system, the most dominant cultural influence from Africa was that of the Ashanti-Fanti. These two tribes were the largest in the Akan nation of the Gold Coast in West Africa. The classic study was carried out by the anthropologist-administrator Captain R. S. Rattray, a linguistic expert on the Akan language who both studied Akan history and became the authority on their religion. Rattray concluded that the Akan conception of the Supreme Being emerged in the West African mind before the advent of Greece, Rome, and Christianity, and that this Supreme Being was none other than the God who was revealed to the Hebrews. Rattray believed that the concept of the Supreme Being was not the legacy of the Hebrews only but of ancient Africa also.

Another authority on the Ashanti-Fanti religion was the native-born lawyer-philosopher J. B. Danquah, author of *Akan Doctrine of God* (1944). Danquah explained the belief system of the Akan people. The power of sacred inanimate objects of the universe, which were thought to contain spirits, affected popular beliefs and folklore. Above these belief systems were the beliefs in the "lesser divinities"—the Abosom, or animate powers, the sons of God. These were tutelar deities whose main function was to protect the towns, villages, and the state. Shrines were built in their honor, and they were worshiped individually and collectively. The third level of belief centered on the veneration of approved ancestors, including important rulers and founding fathers and leaders of the communities whose lives were examined after death and found to have been exemplars of life and godliness. Once judged to be an example of godliness, a symbol of reverence was preserved in a "chair" or a "stool" for the individual. This practice eventually expanded into a long line of approved ancestors who became the center of national veneration. This religious sentiment, uniquely African, was found in most West African nations, and became a part of the traditions brought to the New World.

At the pinnacle of the Akan pantheon is the Supreme Being. The Akan names for the Supreme Being were Onyame and Nyankopon; he was the creator of all things, the source of all wisdom, and had to be worshiped unconditionally. According to J. G. Christaller (*Dictionary of Asante and Fanti Language Called Tshi* [*Twi*], 1881;

rev. 1983), the word *onyame* means "the shining, bright, illustrious, glorious, majestic, graceful and beautiful one."

The solar aspect of God is as old as creation. The sun as symbol can be found in almost all African words for the Supreme Being. According to Danquah, Akan thinkers, philosophers, and theologians were convinced that the heavens proclaimed the glory of God and that he was behind the firmament; and they rightly concluded that this Being was Onyame—the person of brightness, of splendor, of glory, "the Shining One."

The second name, Nyankopon, was the shortened form of Nyame-koropon, meaning "God who alone is great." (This idea would recur in the New World.) Another name for the Supreme Being was Odomankomo, the creator or inventor, the originator.

Danquah compared African theology with that of the ancient Hebrews. According to the latter, God made man from the dust of the earth, and woman from the rib of man, whereas in the former, both were direct offspring of God.

From this sketch of Akan theology, a religion existing millennia before European contact with West Africa, one cannot but regret that African theology has been ignored in the "God talk" of Western nations, because it presumably had nothing to contribute to Western scholarship. Theology in its totality acknowledges the uniqueness of divine revelations in every culture, but Western theologians have, until recently, ignored this revelation in West Africa.

The Yoruba of Nigeria. The second dominant cultural influence from Africa was that of the Yoruba of Nigeria. The Yoruba were made up of many ethnic groups bound by language, customs, and religion. Olumide Lucas, in *The Religion of the Yoruba* (1948), sees a linguistic and ritual connection between the Yoruba and the ancient Egyptians. E. B. Idowu, in *Olodumare: God in Yoruba Belief* (1962), informs us that the names of the Supreme Being in western Nigeria were Olodumare and Olorun. Olodumare was the Creator, the king, the omnipotent, and the final judge—a covenantal god. He was known in popular speech as Olorun, the ruler of the heavens.

The religion of the Yoruba, like that of the Gold Coast people, was a state institution. Religion, like the state, was hierarchical. The Supreme Being presided over a large pantheon of intermediary divinities even though the *oba,* the king, was at the head of the religious institution. In his position as sacred king, the *oba* presided over the yearly religious festivals. Because of his sacred office, his subjects, as a rule, could only approach him through intermediaries. The earthly order was a mirror of the heavenly. The intermediary divinities were the channels between humanity and God.

The numerous intermediary divinities in the Yoruba tradition were called *orishas* (powers). They were emanations of the Supreme Being. First among these powers was Obatala, the *orisha* of *orishas.* Yoruba mythology ascribed to him a close relationship with Olodumare. Obatala received the duty to shape the earth for humans and other living things; he shaped humans, while God gave them life.

A second *orisha* of great importance, Orunmilla, was the god of oracles, the embodiment of wisdom, knowledge, and understanding. He understood all languages and was a symbol of revelation. He was the patron god of the Ifa oracle, the system of divining well known among the Yoruba. The ministers of the cult of Ifa were called *babalawo,* a name also familiar in Nigeria and the New World. These priests were brought to the New World, and their fame after four hundred years is still strong in Cuba and parts of South America.

A third *orisha,* Ogun, was the god of war, warriors, and artisans. The tutelary spirit of smithies, engineers, and engines, Ogun also presided over contracts and oaths. He was invoked in traditional courts by the kissing of a piece of iron, a practice similar to the kissing of the Bible in Western law courts.

A fourth *orisha* was Shango, the god of lightning and thunder. The priests of the Shango cult were traditionally called to minister to anyone struck by lightning. Tradition states that Shango was one of the ancient rulers of the province of Oyo, the largest province of modern-day Nigeria. Shango, it is said, took his life because of internecine struggles with his neighbors. Before his death he vowed to visit his enemies with thunder and lightning, and his faithful followers remembered him in the frequent violence of thunder and lightning. Other traditions, however, say that the Shango myth was a later interpretation of an older myth of Jakuta, the hurler of stones and god of wrath. The Shango cult was transported to the New World and remains one of the strongest cults in Cuba, Trinidad, and Brazil.

The last of these *orishas* was Esu, a divinity who had his counterpart in most West African religions. He was called Legba by the Fon and Anansi by the Akan. (These gods are known as "tricksters" in scholarly literature because of their unpredictable nature.) Esu was the tester of sincerity in worship and in human relationships. He was the god of mishaps and errors, similar to the Satan of the Book of Job.

In all there were more than a thousand *orishas.* Elaborate myths surrounded their various functions in the religious life of the Yoruba. The *orishas* were complex manifestations of the Supreme Being: some were pure spirits of nature; others, deified aspects of historical figures. But Yoruba religion was not unlike most other religious systems in belief and practice.

The Fon of Dahomey. Anyone acquainted with the religion of Dahomey is aware of the prominent role it played in New World black culture, both in Haiti and more recently in the United States. The Supreme Being of the Fon people, Mawu-Lisa, was often presented as an androgynous, three-dimensional figure: one side was Lisa, the male, representing the sun and symbolizing strength and energy; on the other was Mawu, the female, representing the moon and symbolizing coolness, wisdom, and mystery. Together, the divine pair represented the dialectical rhythm of life, an idea evocative of the ancient Chinese concept of Yin and Yang, the combinations of opposites that maintain the equilibrium of the world. In Chinese thought, this interaction was known as "the way" of the universe, operating through the medium of complementary opposites. Mawu-Lisa represented a similar idea, called Da—the manifest power of God symbolized in the "holy serpent," *da ayido hwedo.* This serpentine symbol dominated religious symbolism in both Dahomey and Haiti, and became a popular theme in the artwork of the Haitian people.

As with all West African traditional religions, the will of God was implemented in the world by intermediary divinities who oversaw the smooth functioning of humankind and nature. This work was done by the voduns, or *loa,* who were emanations of the Supreme Being. The voduns were spirits and powers who manifested themselves in rivers, mountains, oceans, iron, fire, and war.

The greater voduns ruled land and sea; the lesser occupied themselves with everyday human life. Humans had to placate them with prayers, libations, and sacrifices. Shrines were built in their honor, and special days dedicated to their worship. Elaborate systems of mythologies grew around each of them, as with those of Nigeria, since in historical times there was a close interaction between Dahomey and southern Nigeria; thus, Gu, the god of iron, compares with Ogun of Nigeria, and Fa of Dahomey with Ifa of Nigeria.

AFRICAN HERITAGE IN THE CARIBBEAN

That Africans transported their religious traditions to the New World is obvious to any tourist who visits the Caribbean or South America. Afro-Americans manifest religious behavior that is radically different from what the European-American is familiar with in his own church or synagogue. Although most Africans assimilated the alien culture of their new environment and retained little of their African heritage, traces of that past still persist in some segments of America in language and religious beliefs.

American scholars who wrote on African customs during the period of slavery often commented on African forms of worship, but few were able to place them in historical perspective. Scholars saw these practices as phenomena that would vanish with the work of missionaries and exposure to "civilization." A study of cultural continuities had to await the genius of anthropologists such as Herskovits who became interested in New World Africans.

The propensity to hold on to the ancient religion appears to be common to all people who are forcibly transported from their cultural communities to a foreign environment. One classical example is the ancient Jews in Babylon. Their religion was the only point around which life could be reorganized. Africans also found themselves in an entirely new environment devoid of sacred borders, and they had to introduce their spiritual cosmology in order for life to continue. This process took time, but we are now more aware of how it came about.

The indiscriminate capturing of Africans brought to the New World numerous members of the priestly classes, whose influence prepared the environment for a reestablishment of their traditional religion. Although the priests operated in secret throughout the period of slavery, their influence was felt by those who operated the slave system. The multitude of laws passed by the various parliaments of the Caribbean islands against the beating of drums, witchcraft, slave meetings, and secret societies all attest to the fact that African slaves were organized. From the second half of the seventeenth century on, serious rebellions were led by charismatic leaders against the system, a fact that became troublesome to the plantocracy.

The Jamaican journalist Herbert G. De Lisser observed, "Both witches and wizards, priests and priestesses were brought to Jamaica in the slave trade, and the slaves recognized the distinction between the former and the latter" (*Twentieth-Century Jamaica*, 1923, p. 108). Between the African slaves and these religious functionaries a conspiracy of secrecy developed into a thriving underground religion, outside the purview of the slavemasters. To this day, secrecy is still prevalent in some African cults in the rural areas of the Caribbean. De Lisser's observation holds true not only for Jamaica but also for most New World slave communities—whether British, Spanish, or French.

In the Latin American system, where the Africans were forced to convert to Christianity, most slaves simply went through the motions in order to avoid punishment, at the same time holding onto their time-honored African traditions. Jean Price-Mars, the eminent Haitian physician, folklorist, and statesman, wrote that the slaves devised ways of having themselves baptized more than once, "so that they could have several opportunities for fun." He continued, "It is obvious merely through this fact that the religious state of the slave was only a facade; that his fundamental beliefs were only slightly shaken by official conversion and remained all the more mysterious in order to withstand the pressures of the law and his human surroundings" (*So Spoke the Uncle*, 1983 trans. of 1928 ed., p. 44).

While the Catholic priests were going through the motions of converting the Africans in Haiti, traditional priests from Africa were busy operating and blending the various slave communities into a new solidarity, which we now know as Haitian Vodun. Throughout the New World, clandestine African assemblies were organized with a blending of the various African beliefs and practices. Some were political, while others were religious. These were "new" religions because they were unique. For the first time in African history, there was a synthesis of the various religious sentiments under one strong cultural dominance. This new structure was developed in Jamaica, Haiti, and in the United States.

Cumina of Jamaica. The Ashanti-Fanti people of the Gold Coast became the most dominant people in British Caribbean slavery from the seventeenth through the eighteenth centuries. Every slave rebellion was under their leadership. It was this group that organized the Maroon communities in the islands; it was they who fought the Maroon War against the British from 1653 to 1738, finally gaining their freedom in the 1830s. It was, therefore, to this group that all the tribes brought to Jamaica looked for leadership and guidance in the beginning. It was in the Ashanti-Fanti religious cult of ancestral reverence that the slaves of Jamaica found satisfying alternatives in which to express their religious and political sentiments.

Ancestral reverence is known today as cumina, derived from two words in the Twi language of Ghana: *akom* (possession) and *Ana* (ancestor). Cumina existed in secret, although it surfaced in the form of dance from time to time, dance being the manifestation of deep religious sentiment in African tradition. Cumina appears to have had a large following. By the eighteenth century, the *okomfo* (Ashanti-Fanti priests and priestesses) united the slaves of various plantations under the old religious rite disguised in what is now known as the Myal dance. Priests and priestesses became known as Myal-men and Myal-women. (The origin of the word *Myal* is still uncertain.)

These Ashanti-Fanti functionaries, disguised as leaders of the dance, became the healers of the sick, the interpreters of hidden things, the comforters of the suffering, and the secret instigators of resistance to slavery. Cumina was to be the only religious alternative for Jamaican slaves for nearly 300 years. Ignored by the Christian church, the slaves continued in their African-derived religion until the emergence of nonconformist sects in Jamaica during the last decades of the eighteenth century. It was not until then that the Church of England was forced to consider the state of religion among the slaves. Yet no action was taken to missionize the African slaves; in fact, it was not until the Emancipation of 1834 that the Church of England extended membership to the African community of Jamaica. It was the Methodists with their "dark and dangerous fanaticism" who became the champions of the African slaves, and it was the Baptist members of the slave community who forced the British to proclaim the Emancipation after the Baptist war of 1831.

Cumina, then, was one of those pure African religious cults in the Caribbean, and elements still remain in the rural communities of Jamaica. In times of rebellion, it was a society that protected its members from the white man's bullets; the member possessed by the spirit of the ancestors would undergo an agitated dance and would not recover from "altered states of consciousness" until awakened from the trance state. The individual would be entirely ignorant of anything that had transpired. This possession trance is still found in all the African-derived religions of the Caribbean and would later be incorporated into the Christian-synchretized sects of Pukumina, Revivalism, and Holiness of both the Caribbean and the United States.

Haitian Vodun (Voodoo). Hispaniola, the second largest Caribbean island between Cuba and Puerto Rico, was divided into two republics. The Dominican Republic (Spanish) occupies the eastern two-thirds of the island, and Haiti (French) the western third. Haiti has generated an abundance of scholarly material, not only because of its importance as a valuable French outpost but also because of its creative slave population. Their superior organizing genius helped them to defeat the French and become the first slave colony in the Caribbean to gain its independence, in 1804. The Haitian struggle for independence sent a shock wave throughout the nineteenth-century slaveholding nations. At the center of the Haitian struggle was a religious sentiment, nurtured in the deep forests, away from the probing eyes of the Catholic priests and the slave police. This religion was handed down from generation to generation and is known to us as Haitian Vodun.

An impressive body of literature is available to students of Haitian history and culture from the colonial period to the present. Moreau de Saint Mery considered Jean Price-Mars's two-volume bibliography (1787–1798) the most reliable source on the slavery period. Some of the most interesting works on Haitian Vodun were written after 1804 by Haitian-born scholars, among them *Ainsi parla L'oncle* (1928) by Price-Mars. Two twentieth-century studies by non-Haitian scholars are *The Haitian People* by James G. Leyburn and *Voodoo in Haiti* by Alfred Metreaux.

Vodun is an all-embracing religion of the Haitian peasant. It has touched the lives of everyone regardless of class. It is the ancient creed that has nurtured all the African ancestors of present-day Haiti. It emerged as a reaction to forced conversion to Christianity and was nurtured by the brutality of the slavemasters. Under the penalty provided by the Code Noir, the state and the church joined in the attempted conversion of all the Africans entering the colony. Although the law was usually ignored in the rural areas, masters in the urban centers, who were under the eyes of the priests, obeyed in a halfhearted way. The duplicity of the slave system, with its utter disrespect for the humanity of the slaves on the one hand and the false piety of forced conversion on the other, inspired rage in the slave population. To a newly arrived African, frightened of the surroundings, knowing nothing of the church or its ways, let alone of Latin, the whole exercise was confusing and frightening. The slaves had developed a more satisfying alternative—Vodun.

James G. Leyburn has suggested four stages in the development of Vodun. The first period, 1730–1790, was one of gestation. As the slaves became more numerous, so did the laws that governed them. As disenfranchisement of the slaves became complete, millenarianism swept the slave communities, and secret meetings, led by charismatic Maroon leaders such as Boukman, became more prevalent. The Afro-Haitians rallied to the ancient African creed, and an ethnic religious syncretism under the rubric of Dahomean Vodun was achieved. Price-Mars believed that Moreau de Saint Mery was the first to identify the movement by name in 1790.

The second period, 1790–1800, was that of expansion and self-assertion. Buffeted by an unrelenting system of oppression and depersonalization, the Haitians decided to overthrow the oppressive regime. Such an undertaking needed total solidarity, arms, and leadership to fight against the formidable armed forces of the French republic. Millenarian movements had to rely on the supernatural; for Vodun, this meant the gods of Africa. On the memorable night of 14 August 1791 a group of slaves assembled at Bois-Caiman, near the Red Mountain, to swear an oath of fidelity to the leadership of Boukman. It was a night of rain, thunder, lightning, and wind. After the sacrifice of a boar, whose blood was used to seal the oath, Boukman, according to Haitian tradition, offered the following prayer:

> The God who created the sun which gives us light, who rouses the waves and rules the storm, though hidden in the clouds, he watches us. He sees all what the white man does. The God of the white man inspires him to crime, but our God calls upon us to do good works. Our God who is good to us orders us to revenge our wrongs. He will direct our arms and aid us. Throw away the symbols of the God of the whites who has often caused us to weep, and listen to the voice of liberty, which speaks in the hearts of us all.
>
> (C.L.R. James, *Black Jacobins,* 1963, p. 87)

The oral tradition that has conveyed this incident no doubt has been exaggerated, but to the descendants of these freedom fighters the story captured the flavor of those frightening days. A "blood pact" had been the traditional means of uniting African warriors against dangerous situations—from Dahomey to Kenya. It encouraged solidarity, magical confidence, and, most of all, secrecy. A few days after the oath of Bois-Caiman, the first blows of insurrection were struck: several Frenchmen were killed, and many sugar plantations were reduced to ashes. What started as a local rebellion soon escalated into a bloody slave revolution that lasted for the next twelve years.

The third period, 1800–1815, was one of subtle transformation. After the revolution, the African creed that had united the Haitian people against the might of France was gradually abandoned. In 1801, Jean-Jacques Dessalines, inspector general of culture for the department of Northern Haiti, had moved rapidly to suppress Vodun, and in the new Charter of Haiti the Catholic church was declared the official religion of Haiti. Vodun was outlawed by the state, though it remained the sentiment of the peasants.

The fourth period, 1815–1850, was that of diffusion. Vodun quietly diffused among the poorer class in the villages and towns as an unorthodox African cult. It was despised by the elite in public, but earnestly sought after in times of psychological stress. It was not until the reign of physician-ethnologist François Duvalier (1957–1971) that Vodun was rehabilitated. Today, it can even be found in the major cities of the United States, especially in New York and Miami, brought there by Haitian immigrants. In these cities Vodun priests and priestesses operate their age-old religion.

Haitian Vodun is a ritual syncretism that incorporates the rites of several African ethnic groups into one kaleidoscopic religious drama. The beliefs and practices vary significantly, depending on the ethnic composition of the various sects. Arada, Nago, Congo, and Petro Vodun each represent slightly different practices. Arada is predominantly Dahomey; Nago, Yoruba; Congo, the ethnic practices of slaves from the Congo regions; Petro, predominantly Creole. These divisions, though obvious to scholars, are not conscious sectarian divisions among the devotees; they are merely liturgical.

Three practices common to all sects of Vodun are liturgical dances, trance possession, and sacrifices. A Vodun service is primarily a dance in honor of the gods, who at certain peak periods may come down to possess the devotees with supernatural powers that disgorge human reason. The devotee falls into a trance and becomes the mouthpiece of the god. Sacrifice is a common religious practice of all traditional African religions, not only Vodun. It may be anything from pouring a simple libation to the bloody sacrifice of an animal.

But Vodun as a religion is even more complex than the three practices would suggest. It has historical roots in the traditions of Africa and psychological roots in its New World emergence. It has developed its own folk theology about the world, humanity, and destiny. Though African, Vodun is a new formulation, a new cultural reality, that must be studied in the light of its own significance.

Jean Price-Mars, using the "minimal definition" of religion suggested by Émile Durkheim, concluded that Vodun was a religion because all its adherents believed in the existence of spiritual beings who live everywhere in the universe and dominate human activities. Vodun is a religion because the cult requires a hierarchical priestly body, a society of the faithful, temples, altars, ceremonies, and an oral tradition, which is handed down in its essential elements, although in an altered form. According to Price-Mars, "Vodun is a religion because a theology can be discerned, a theology upon which the hybrid Catholicism of Haiti rests."

The Supreme Being of traditional African religion played a minor role in the New World. In Haiti, as in other places in the New World, worship was reserved for God's manifestations. In Haitian Vodun these powers were given the name loa. Price-Mars observed: "The Haitian people are preoccupied with the 'Loa' or the mystère of Voodoo to an indescribable degree." These divinities control biological functions such as fertility, births, and deaths; and they control natural functions such as wind, rain, thunder, agriculture, and the ocean. The loa permeate every aspect of the waking life of the vodunsi (one who is married to a vodun).

Despite the fact that Catholicism and Vodun have occupied the same island for centuries, they remain two separate and distinct entities. The juxtaposition of Catholicism and Vodun has yielded some fascinating coincidences. Whereas a true Catholic, one who is trained in the mysteries of the Catholic church, will have nothing to do with Vodun, a true vodun will declare that he or she is a member of the Catholic church. It is believed that one cannot be a vodunsi unless he or she is a Catholic. This hybrid Catholicism has its historical roots in the forced conversions during the years of slavery.

Today, most of the Catholic saints have been appropriated as African loa in the minds of the Haitian peasants. Thus Legba, the Vodun god of communications, is also the Catholic Saint Peter, the one who holds the key—the one who opens barriers to communication between God and humans. His symbol is a cross, which, for the vodunsi, represents the crossroads; to the Catholic, the cross of Jesus. Damballah-Wedo, the serpent deity of Dahomey, is associated with Saint Patrick—the saint who walked on the snakes. Shango, the god of lightning and thunder, is Saint John the Baptist, who, according to tradition, controls the storm clouds. To the vodun, Ogun is the god of iron and thus the god of war; he is closely associated with Saint James the Elder, who is portrayed as a knight in steel-plated armor by the Catholic church. These are only a few of the subtle borrowings or one-dimensional syncretisms that have operated whenever African religions confront other religions. Unlike Catholicism's inflexible dogma, African religion is protean, always adding to its form selective aspects of other religions without endangering its function.

The priestly class in Haitian Vodun consists of men and women who have gained the respect of their communities for their leadership qualities, their knowledge of African lore, and their supernatural insight. At the pinnacle of the priestly class are the *hungan,* the male, or the *mambo,* the female. The term *hungan* is probably of Haitian peasant origin. *Hu* in the Fon language is the word for divinity, while *nganga* is derived from a Congo word meaning "he who deals with occult forces." *Hungan* may be translated as "the one who is possessed with divinity." Price-Mars speculated that the earliest name for the priest was *vodoun-non*—he who possesses the spirit. According to Price-Mars, he is the high priest and principal sacrificer, the supreme depository of the wishes of the divinity. He is always connected to the temple and is the teacher of the esoteric language derived from early Dahomey.

The priestly class is not an organized clerical system. Priests and priestesses have authority only in their communities, but theirs is a ranking of prestige from the rural to the urban communities, and some of these religious functionaries have even gained national acclaim. This priestly class has historically been the guardian of an African tradition to which the masses could relate.

Vodun in Haiti is one of the strongest of the African religions transported to the New World. Despite the pressure of the slave environment and the Catholic church, it found acceptance among the peasants. Vodun and Catholicism exist in a symbiotic relationship that has resulted in a very close parallelism between their respective religious calendars. The feast days of the Catholic saints often coincide with those of Vodun religious celebrations of their loa, so that an outsider cannot easily separate what is Christian from what is African.

Santeria of Cuba. The island of Cuba was the largest of the Spanish Caribbean slave colonies. The total number of African slaves in Cuba up to the year 1853 is estimated at 644,000, and importation continued even after that date. Numerous tribal groups were transported from the

Guinea coast and from as far as Mozambique to satisfy the insatiable demands of the Cuban cane colonies.

Compared to the English system of slavery, where slaves were entirely at the mercy of the slave masters, and the French system, as in Haiti, where slaves were coerced to convert to Christianity, the Spanish system in Cuba was more humane. That is not to say that Cuban slavery was unoppressive, but that both the church and the crown gave close official oversight to the system.

The Catholic missionaries in Cuba preceded the colonialists, dedicated themselves to the conversion of the Indians, and quickly added the Africans to their program when the Indian population declined. The Spanish Crown was in constant communication with the church and the landlords, directing them to guard the welfare of the slaves. This surveillance resulted in official benignity to the Africans and their customs.

The policy facilitated close contact between African religions and the Catholic church in Cuba. Although the Africans accepted Catholicism nominally, the sacramental efficacy of the church was not enough to turn them from their ancient customs. In addition, the ratio of clergy to laity made thorough conversion almost impossible. Given the minimal contact of the Catholic clergy and that nominal conversion was attained, the slaves' needs were not fulfilled in a spiritual way; thus the Africans sought religious fulfillment in their ancient religions.

Unlike most of the other Caribbean islands, where African customs were suspect, in Cuba the Catholic church was tolerant of ethnic traditions and even allowed various African groups to create their own "clubs," which became known as the Cabildos. The Cabildos were not only ethnic clubs but also religious organizations under the secret leadership of the *babalawo*—the religious functionary whose patron divinity was Orunmilla, the oracle divinity of the Yoruba. The contact between African religion and Catholicism in Cuba yielded a synthesis known as Santeria.

As already mentioned, there was a strong symbiosis between the Catholic sacramental system and that of traditional African religion. Under the Yoruba *babalawo,* the Catholic calendar was wisely utilized for the veneration of African saints. The word *santeria* itself means veneration of the saints. Thus out of the Cabildos of slavery arose a second religious system in Cuba, whose

core is unmistakably African. Roger Bastide claims that "of all the African religions that have been preserved in America . . . it is undoubtedly that of the Yoruba which has remained most faithful to ancestral traditions."

What is Santeria? A complex of divination, spirit possession, and sacrifice, with the Yoruba tradition as its core. One becomes a member through initiation into its mystères. The principal ceremony of initiation is the *asiento* (seating of the divinity in the initiant). At the center of Santeria is the *babalawo.* He is seen as the diviner of the future, as the one who seeks the causes of sicknesses both in the past and the present. He knows the secret of the Ifa oracle, and he is able to determine the causes of events, their nature, and what to do about them. He is not only the prescriber of herbal medicine, baths, and potions, but of the kinds of sacrifices needed to appease the gods for serious moral breaches. He is the officiating priest at initiations, which culminate in the possession of the saints or the gods who are to be the spiritual director of the believers. Like the Vodun *hungan,* the *babalawo* in Cuba was persecuted by the official religion. For decades he existed in secrecy, presenting himself as an underground alternative to the Catholic priest.

The African-derived Santeria has become the legitimate "folk religion" rooted in the lives of the Cuban peasants, mostly of African origin, but its membership also includes a large segment of the Spanish population. Here and there one can find a few *babalawos* of Spanish ancestry. Santeria is therefore an Africanization of Christianity and a Christianization of African religion, in which both the African gods and the Christian saints hold reciprocal relationships.

Santeria shops, commonly called botanicas, can be found in many of the large cities on the eastern seaboard of the United States, especially in cities where Cubans have migrated and settled. These shops sell spiritual art objects, candles, and herbs used by members of Santeria now living in the United States.

AFRICAN HERITAGE IN THE UNITED STATES

The Africans who were brought to British North America were taken from the same cultural communities as those brought to Barbados and Jamaica in the Caribbean. Unlike the French and Spanish, the British had no tradition of slavery. There was no protection from the Church of England similar to that given by the Catholic church in the Latin American colonies. Under the English representative system, constitutional recognition was given to the European minorities in each colony, who, in turn, legislated whatever laws were necessary to control the natives or the slaves of the colony.

Virginia was the first to receive Africans, in 1619; the slave population grew to millions by the first half of the nineteenth century. The colony also set the legal precedent for the handling of Africans in 1668. They were denied personal property and every amenity due civilized people. The master–slave relationship was established by law: "If any slave resists his master (or other by his master's correcting him) and by the extremity of the correction should chance to die, that his death shall not be accounted a felony."

Laws are always made in view of a problem in the society. The law of 1668 was instituted because the relationship between masters and slaves had gone awry. This adverse relationship was perhaps anticipated in the following: "If any negro or slave shall presume to lift up his hand in opposition against any Christian, shall for every offense . . . have and receive thirty lashes on his bare back well laid on" (*The Statutes at Large . . . All the Laws of Virginia from the first session of the Legislature in the year 1619*, vol. 2, p. 270).

English colonial assemblies, operating thousands of miles from England, devised ad hoc slave laws for every real or anticipated misdemeanor and to repress the Africans. Most of these laws later failed to gain royal consent, but their effects were to continue despite their nullification. In British North America, African slaves became chattel to be used and abused at the will of their owners; they were excluded from the Christian religion despite the official declaration that the reason for transporting them to the New World was to rid them of ignorance, animalism, and savagery, and to expose them to Christian civilization. When the Church of England brought pressure on the American colonies to instruct the Africans in the Christian religion, laws were instituted with severe penalties against the teaching of the art of reading to slaves, in order that they might be catechized. Despite the work of missionaries sent out by the Church of England in 1701, at the close of the English colonial period in North America only a handful of slaves had been introduced to Christianity.

Speaking to this point of neglect on the part of colonial America, Charles C. Jones lamented:

> The Africans who were brought over and bought by us for servants, and who wore out their lives as such enriching thousands from Massachusetts to Georgia and were members of our households, never received from the colonists themselves a solitary missionary exclusively devoted to their good; nor was there ever a single society established within the colonies, that we know of, with the express design of promoting religious instruction.
>
> (*Religious Instruction of the Negroes,* 1842, p. 48)

Jones, a white missionary to the African-Americans about two decades before the Civil War, looked on the cruelty of American slavery and reflected on the old argument of providential design. Seeing the weakness of it all, he concluded: "And thus, those who advocated the slave trade on the grounds that it introduced Negroes to the blessings of civilization and the Gospel, saw their favorite argument losing its force in a great measure from year to year."

Albert J. Raboteau, in his excellent book *Slave Religion: The "Invisible Institution" in the Antebellum South,* discussed at length the African influence on black religion in the United States from early slave days to the close of the Civil War. After discussing the debate between Frazier and Herskovits, he took the middle ground and concluded: "While it is true that Africa influenced black culture in the United States, including black religion, it is also true that African theology and African ritual did not endure to the extent that they did in Cuba, Haiti, and Brazil. In the United States the gods of Africa died."

Raboteau suggested various reasons why the gods of Africa did not survive in the United States. First was the religious context that existed in America. Countries that were dominated by the influence of the Catholic church were more conducive to the survival of African religion than those dominated by Puritan Protestantism. The rituals and customs of Catholicism in the French, Spanish, and Portuguese colonies were nearer to those practiced by the Africans; thus, various ethnic beliefs were nurtured or even encouraged. Catholic devotion to the Virgin Mary and the saints offered a rich context for syncretism of African gods and Catholic saints. The sacramentals (blessed objects such as statues, pictures, candles, incense, holy water, rosaries, and relics) were all familiar to African piety. Most of these elements were lacking in Puritan America, which held such practices to be idolatrous. African religious ideas confronted Puritan America in a period of utter callousness to any form of worship other than that concocted within its own narrow limits.

A second factor working against African retention in Puritan America was demographics. As mentioned earlier, the number of Africans brought to North America, when compared with the number brought to the Caribbean and Latin America, was exceedingly small. The black slaves were, therefore, in very close contact with the white masters. Such contact demanded a change in customs, language, and religion.

A further factor working against retention was geography. Africans were distributed throughout the colonies, thus inhibiting ethnic groupings necessary to sustain cultural solidarity. C. Vann Woodward summed up this fact in the following statement: "The Islands of the Greater Antilles . . . with an area roughly one third that of Texas, imported nearly six times the slaves landed in the entire territory of the United States. . . . In fact, Cuba took in more (Africans) after 1808, than the United States received in all" (*Slaves in the New World,* 1971, p. 82). If these statistics are correct, the majority of Africans in the United States would have been native-born, and the languages of Africa would have begun to lose their force on the imagination of the youth as English became the language of communication. But this process took years, and the majority of the original slaves who were brought over and continued in their African ways of life were the repository of a heritage that was handed down to their descendants. The slaves never accepted the doctrine of God projected to them by official Christianity. Even after blacks accepted Christianity, black theologians' interpretation of God was radically different from that of white theologians.

By the second half of the eighteenth century,

African descendants in the United States had adopted the Christian religion despite the numerous obstacles placed in their way. What began as a small stream gradually grew into a mighty river. W.E.B. Du Bois saw black acceptance of Christianity as a "terrific social revolution" in which traces of former group life were retained. The chief trace was the medicine man, who functioned as healer, comforter, and interpreter of the unknown. Du Bois concluded: "Thus, as a bard, physician, judge, and priest, within the narrow limits allowed by the slave system, rose the Negro preacher, and under him the first Institution, the Negro Church."

Christian piety was nothing new to the Africans. The idea of the Supreme Being, the creator of the world of humanity, was a common belief of all. The gods of Africa did not die when Africans accepted Christianity; if anything, Africans enriched Christian theology with their unique concept of deity. The divine sonship ascribed to Jesus was also not strange to African beliefs. All Africans believed that God became various divinities to human beings. The spirits and powers of Christianity closely paralleled African beliefs. And the idea of an afterlife was equally accepted by the Africans, who saw their communities as composed of the living and the dead. The notion of human depravity was most offensive to African theology.

Prayers and adoration were an indispensable part of African piety. African conversion to Christianity was not a radical conversion but an adaptation to a newer system of the old. Africans were not Christianized, but, to a great extent, Christianity was Africanized.

The African heritage in the New World is an undeniable fact. It can be observed in language patterns of the Caribbean, speech patterns of African descendants in the United States, proverbs and dance rhythms of the New World, Christianity of the masses, and various other forms wherever the sons and daughters of Africa are found in large numbers. Dr. Henry Mitchell, speaking of the African cultural heritage, states: "Whether by means of a Jungian 'collective unconscious' or the 'primitive' transmission system known as 'the mother's milk,' no folk culture, world-view, or religion, can be stamped out unless its bearers are massacred *in toto* or denied all forms of associations, including the rearing of children" (*Review and Expositor,* 1973).

THE AFRICAN HERITAGE

BIBLIOGRAPHY

Africa

Joseph Boakye Danquah, *Akan Doctrine of God: A Fragment of Gold Coast Ethics and Religion* (1944; rev. 1968); Cyril Daryll Forde, ed., *African Worlds: Studies in the Cosmological Ideas and Social Values of African Peoples* (1954; rev. 1968); Marcel Griaule, *Conversation with Ogotemelli: An Introduction to Dogon Religious Ideas* (1948; rev. 1975); Melville J. Herskovits, *Dahomey* (1938); E. Bolaji Idowu, *Olodumare: God in Yoruba Belief* (1962; rev. 1966) and *African Traditional Religion: A Definition* (1973).

John S. Mbiti, *African Religion and Philosophy* (1969; rev. 1970) and *Concepts of God in Africa* (1970; rev. 1972); Malcolm J. McVeigh, *God in Africa: Conceptions of God in African Traditional Religion and Christianity* (1974); Geoffrey Parrinder, *West African Religion* (1961); R. S. Rattray, *Religion and Art in Ashanti* (1927; rev. 1967); Aylward Shorter, *Prayer in the Religious Traditions of Africa* (1973; rev. 1976); John Vernon Taylor, *The Primal Vision: Christian Presence Amid African Religion* (1963).

Jamaica

Roger D. Abrahams and John F. Szwed, *After Africa: Extracts from British Travel Accounts and Journals of the Seventeenth, Eighteenth and Nineteenth Centuries Concerning the Slaves, Their Manners, and Customs in the British West Indies* (1983); Leonard E. Barrett, *The Sun and the Drum: African Roots in Jamaican Folk Tradition* (1976); Roger Bastide, *African Civilizations in the New World* (1971); Herbert G. De Lisser, *Twentieth Century Jamaica* (1913; rev. 1923); Bryan Edwards, *The History, Civil and Commercial, of the British Colonies in the West Indies* (1793); William James Gardner, *A History of Jamaica from its Discovery by Columbus to the Year 1872* (1909); Edward Long, *The History of Jamaica* (1774); Joseph John Williams, *Psychic Phenomena of Jamaica* (1934).

Haiti

Harold Courlander, *The Drum and The Hoe: Life and Lore of the Haitian* (1960); Maya Deren, *Divine Horsemen: The Living Gods of Haiti* (1953; rev. 1984); Melville J. Herskovits, *Life in a Haitian Valley* (1937; rev. 1975); James G. Leyburn, *The Haitian People* (1941; rev. 1966); Médéric L. E. Moreau de Saint Mery, *Description of Saint Dominique*, 2 vols. (1792); Alfred Metreaux, *Voodoo in Haiti* (1959; rev. 1972); Jean Price-Mars, *So Spoke the Uncle*, Magdaline W. Shannon, trans. (1983; originally *Ainsi parla L'oncle*, 1928); George Eaton Simpson, *Religious Cults of the Caribbean: Trinidad, Jamaica, and Haiti* (1970).

Cuba

William R. Bascom, "Two Forms of Afro-Cuban Divination," in *Acculturation in the Americas*, vol. 2, Sol Tax, ed. (1949); Migene Gonzales-Whippler, *Santeria* (1972); Herbert S. Klein, *Slavery in the Americas: A Comparative Study of Virginia and Cuba* (1967); Frank Tannenbaum, *Slave & Citizen* (1946).

United States of America

Catherine L. Albanese, *America: Religions and Religion* (1981); Leonard E. Barrett, *Soul-Force: African Heritage in Afro-American Religion* (1974); Edward Franklin Frazier, *The Negro Church in America* (1964); Vincent Harding, *There Is a River: The Black Struggle for Freedom in America* (1981; rev. 1983); Melville J. Herskovits, *The Myth of the Negro Past* (1938; rev. 1969).

C. Eric Lincoln, ed., *The Black Experience in Religion* (1974); Albert J. Raboteau, *Slave Religion: The "Invisible Institution" in the Antebellum South* (1978); Joseph S. Rouček and Thomas Kiernan, eds., *The Negro Impact on Western Civilization* (1970); Kenneth M. Stampp, *The Peculiar Institution: Slavery in the Ante-Bellum South* (1956); Gayraud S. Wilmore, *Black Religion and Black Radicalism: An Examination of the Black Religious Experience in Religion* (1972).

[*See also* BLACK CHRISTIANITY IN NORTH AMERICA; BLACK MILITANT AND SEPARATIST MOVEMENTS; *and* BLACK RELIGIOUS THOUGHT.]

RELIGION IN THE SPANISH EMPIRE

Lino Gómez Canedo

THE religious institutions of Spanish America were basically those that already existed on the Iberian Peninsula, most of which stemmed from the Catholic church. It could not be otherwise, since Catholicism was the official religion of Spain, and at that time religious tolerance, as we understand it today, was not known. Although Spanish-American Catholicism did eventually exhibit its own unique characteristics, these were of an incidental nature; in general its features were drawn from those of Spanish Catholicism. These characteristics, therefore, are the important ones to point out here.

Religion was without a doubt one of the great forces that moved Spanish society in the fifteenth century, at the time of the discovery of America. The people were deeply religious, and their leaders shared the same faith, beginning with the king and queen, Ferdinand and Isabella. They understood the importance of religion as a way of maintaining the recently attained national unity and made use of religion to increase their political and economic power; but there is no reason to question the sincerity of their beliefs.

Theirs was a militant and proselytizing form of Catholicism, primarily sustained by the prolonged struggle against the Muslims. The conquest of Granada in January 1492 ended the conflict in Spain itself, but the king and queen thought of taking it to other parts: hence the enterprises in North Africa and the ideal of freeing the Holy Sepulcher from the Turks. But the final goal of Spanish domestic policy at that time was to achieve the religious unity of the kingdom as a complement to political unity. Thus in March 1492, banishment was decreed for those Jews who refused to be baptized. This was the culmination of a series of measures against the Jews—among them the Inquisition, which had been at work since 1481.

These measures, the Inquisition included, were brought to America, where as in Spain they perhaps helped maintain unity and preserve customs but sadly poisoned the social life as well.

MISSIONARIES AND CONQUISTADORES

Luckily, the Inquisition had little effect on evangelical work, which was already in a very advanced stage when the Inquisition was established in Mexico in 1571. As for missionary work, it had been started the year following discovery, that is to say, in 1493. The crown promoted missionary work even more vigorously than did the church itself, and Christopher Columbus had already expressed the intention of seeing it through in his introductory letter to his diary of the first voyage (1492).

Several clergymen and religious, headed by the vicar apostolic Bernardo Buil, arrived in the Antilles as part of Columbus' second voyage in 1493. Five more Franciscans were sent in 1500 and another seventeen in 1502. With these and a few more that came in the following years, the Franciscans founded in Hispaniola (the island that today is made up of Haiti and the Dominican Republic) a province of their order; from there they took their apostolate to the rest of the Greater Antilles (Jamaica, Puerto Rico, and Cuba) and to the eastern coasts of Venezuela and Panama. The Dominicans arrived in Hispaniola around 1510–1511 and progressed along the same routes as the Franciscans. Meanwhile,

Queen Isabella had reaffirmed the Crown's missionary policy in the following paragraph of her will (1504):

> Our principal goal was to obtain, to influence, and to attract the peoples of the Indies in order to convert them to our holy Catholic faith, and to send to those islands and mainlands prelates and monks, clergymen and other learned, God-fearing people to instruct the inhabitants and neighbors of those lands in the Catholic faith and to show them new customs.

This solemn declaration was incorporated into the *Cedulario* (1595) of Diego de Encinas and later in the *Recopilación de las leyes de las Indias* (1680).

The crown's missionary goals were largely accomplished. In 1523–1524 the evangelization of Mexico was started by a notable group of Franciscans, who rapidly extended their influence throughout the country. In 1526 the Dominicans arrived and in 1533 the Augustinians. The Jesuits, having arrived in 1572, did their missionary work mostly in the northwest.

From Mexico and the Caribbean the missionaries spread out toward the south—Central America, Peru, and the rest of South America. In 1538 they could be found in Paraguay, in 1550 in Colombia, and, before the sixteenth century came to an end, in Venezuela. According to recent studies by Pedro Borges Morán, some 15,585 missionaries came from Spain to America between 1493 and 1820. During the same period, about an equal number probably entered the various religious orders to dedicate themselves partly to missionary work. All of these missionaries came from Spain and traveled through America at the expense of the royal treasury, which supplied the necessities for the maintenance of the missions.

The relations between missionaries and conquistadors, if not always cordial, were usually respectful, on the latter's part. The reasons for this were that, first of all, the conquistadors, even the harshest ones, were men of faith; and secondly, the crown protected the missionaries. On the other hand, the need for the intervention of conquistadors in the missionary work came about because of the missionaries themselves. At first, in the Antilles, it seems that the missionaries—two Franciscans who arrived in 1493 and the hermit Ramón Pené, about whom little is known—acted independently of the conquistadors and relied solely on the goodwill of the natives. Also, in the 1514–1522 missionary attempt of the Dominicans and Franciscans along the coast of Cumaná (Venezuela), the presence of all soldiers and settlers was expressly prohibited by the missionaries. The Venezuelan attempt ended in tragedy; that on the Antilles brought short-lived results.

Thus, to protect both the missionaries and the natives, certain rules were established for new conquests and missions—the first of which were proclaimed in Granada in November 1526. According to them, every discovery expedition or conquest had to be accompanied by two priests, who were to intervene in everything concerning the treatment of the Indians; contact with and conversion of the Indians were to be brought about through peaceful, nonviolent means. This legislation was reinforced in 1543 by the so-called *leyes nuevas* (new laws), but not even these left everyone satisfied; and thus in 1549 the crown ordered the temporary suspension of all expeditions of conquest. The matter was examined again in *juntas,* or conferences, at Valladolid (1550–1551), led by Bartolomé de Las Casas and Juan Ginés de Sepúlveda, but they did not produce any practical results. Armed conquests remained suspended until 1556, when the Council of the Indies reauthorized them, though with many stipulations aimed at avoiding all violence that was not entirely defensive or indispensable.

Nevertheless, the discussion continued between those who supported peaceful *entradas* (inroads) and those who preferred to have them carried out with some protection from the army or the settlers. It is noteworthy that during these years some missionary expeditions had been accomplished by peaceful means: that of the Dominicans in Florida in 1549 (which ended with almost everyone being killed); the successful one of the Franciscans Rodrigo de la Cruz and Bernardino de Alcalá, to the northwest of Mexico (1550); that of Andrés de Olmos, to the north of Tampico (1556); and that of Juan de Tapia, from Jalisco up to Nueva Vizcaya (1558–1559). These expeditions produced good, but not lasting, results. In 1558 the Dominicans' provincial in Mexico voiced opposition to this kind of mission, and in 1562 the bishop of Guadalajara, Pedro de Ayala, also advised against it. In light of the opinions expressed and problems experienced, in 1573 King Philip II proclaimed new ordinances for "discoveries and new settlements," which Don Juan de Ovando, president of the Council of the Indies, had prepared. They reiterated the principal missionary purpose of these settlements, with precise rules about their peaceful nature and the primary role of the missionaries. Future missions adapted to these ordinances.

THE RELIGIOUS ORDERS

As has already been indicated, the evangelization of America was almost exclusively the work of the religious orders. The secular (diocesan) clergy had a small part in the period of evangelization itself; their role was not important until after the converts' baptism, when religious instruction was meant to consolidate the gains already achieved. This had traditionally been the clergy's role in the Roman Catholic church and remained thus in America.

As we saw, the first religious contact with the natives took place on the Antilles in 1493 through members of religious orders: two Franciscans and one Benedictine. Even the official representative of the pope was a monk: Bernardo Buil. From the beginning an attempt was made to organize the church according to the prevailing principles of the Old World: bishops, clergymen, and friars. When the first vicar apostolic left his position, the Franciscan Juan de Trasierra, having scarcely arrived from Spain, sought the appointment of a substitute for Buil, who had returned to Spain in 1500, even seeking for him the concession of tithes, "thus to provide the necessities for the churches as well as the provisions for the religious," but this only *while a prelate is brought . . . to plant the Church in these lands."*

This same goal of establishing the church with its traditional structure was expressed by some other Franciscans of that second group who had arrived in Hispaniola. In fact, the church was established there by Pope Julius II in 1504 with the creation of one archbishopric and two bishoprics; but this didn't go into effect until 1511, with limitations imposed by a recently granted royal patronage but still covering the same boundaries assigned to them. Also, the bishop of Santo Domingo set up two parishes. The friars, how-

ever, are not mentioned at all in these decrees, though they probably were almost the only priests on the island at that time. Their official role was different.

The situation changed for them with the conquest of Mexico in 1521, which became the site of the most famous apostolate of all America. Two Franciscans, among the most noteworthy of their order, offered to join the new mission: they were none other than Juan Glapión, native of Flanders and the former father-confessor of Emperor Charles V; and Francisco de Quiñones, later to become a cardinal. With the papal bull of 25 April 1521, Pope Leo X gave them considerable authority for accomplishing their tasks. Among their new powers included all rights pertaining to pastors and even some pertaining to the episcopate (when no bishop was available), such as consecrating altars, granting dispensations, and administering the tonsure and the minor orders. These concessions were confirmed and extended to all friars of the mendicant orders (who did not have an income and lived by alms) by a papal bull of Pope Adrian VI (Zaragoza, 13 May 1522). In this way, the friars, who were already free from the bishops' authority by common law, were left to practice the various functions that had generally been entrusted to the secular clergy. This measure allowed for a labor force that the secular clergy would not have been able to gather, even if they had attempted to do so. The need for having these pontifical concessions had already been seen by the promoter of the Dominican and Franciscan missionary work in Cumaná, Pedro de Córdoba, who had applied for them in 1513.

The religious orders took advantage of this opportunity to bring about what is probably an unparalleled effort in the history of the Catholic church. It is enough to mention the case of Mexico, where the Franciscans organized four autonomous "provinces," or districts, in the sixteenth century and two more in the first years of the seventeenth, with several independent groups dedicated especially to the native missions; the Dominicans had two provinces and the Augustinians another two. Although the Jesuits organized themselves in only one province, they were strong in the number of religious. The same can be said, more or less, of all Spanish America. By virtue of pontifical authority, the religious were engaged not only in converting Indians but also in seeing to their religious needs after they had been Christianized. Until the middle of the eighteenth century a great majority of the *doctrinas* (parishes for the Indians) were run by Franciscans, Dominicans, and Augustinians, and in some places also by the Mercedarians.

METHODS AND MEANS OF EVANGELIZATION

America was the site of a new apostolate, for whose Christianization no specific model could exist. It had been a long time since the church had evangelized so exclusively non-Christian a people, of such numbers and of such a culture. The methods used with the Jews and the Muslims would not work here, nor would those recently tried with the Tartars and the Chinese. Some of the Franciscan missionaries who had arrived in Mexico did have some knowledge of the conversion of the Moors from the kingdom of Granada, and other missionaries may have known of the work done on the Canary Islands, but it does not seem that these two cases had much in common with the situation in America. In fact, it is not clear whether the missionaries had arrived from Europe with specific rules for their new evangelical work, aside from the general ones concerning the obligation to preach the gospel, train the natives, and show them new customs.

The Franciscans who arrived in Mexico in 1524—the famed twelve—brought a noteworthy set of guidelines: *Instrucción,* with directions for their missionary work; and *Obediencia,* which laid down rules of order and government. Both documents came from the then minister-general of the order, Francisco de Quiñones, a very talented man, who restricted himself to generalities, waiting to know the situation in better detail later. Thus, those first missionaries had great freedom, which was probably the cause of their extraordinary success. They also brought instructions prepared by two pious advisers to Charles V, the brothers Antonio and Luis Coronel, who were Parisian doctors, admirers of Erasmus, "very famous men of letters," according to Gerónimo Mendieta. It is not clear whether other missionaries brought similar guidelines with them, but eventually everyone either received some or developed their own.

Among the methods used for conversion, the following were prominent: learning the native tongue, which allowed missionaries to prepare grammars, dictionaries, and catechisms and have them printed (printing had been introduced in Mexico by Bishop Zumárraga in 1539); schools to teach the Indians how to read and write; boarding schools for the children of caciques and other chiefs, as had been done before in the Antilles and continued afterward in Mexico and other parts of the continent; the use of music (song and instrumental) that the natives liked, which helped make them so fond of the grand liturgical ceremonies; and the religious theater and the arts in general (architecture, sculpture, painting, gold and silver work) at which the natives were adept. From the start an attempt was made to have discussions among the missionaries, caciques, and native priests. This endeavor and its results are known by a curious book that has survived, though in a mutilated form: *Coloquios y doctrina cristiana con que los frailes de San Francisco . . . convertieron a los indios de la Nueva España.*

Likewise, an attempt was made to give the Indians in Mexico a superior education, for which the Franciscans founded the College of Santa Cruz de Tlatelolco in Mexico City. At the *colegio,* the level of teaching was above that of an elementary school; the humanities were taught, and for a while, philosophy, theology, and even medicine. The school of San José de los Naturales taught the arts and trades; Indian painters and sculptors had to be approved by this school before they could ply their crafts.

THE ORGANIZATION OF THE CHURCH

The missionary work was, of course, the labor of the church since it was being carried out under the express instructions of the pope; but during the first stages of evangelization, the missions could not yet rely on a definitive ecclesiastical structure. Nevertheless, we have already seen that such structures began to be established, or designed, from the very beginning: dioceses, cathedral chapters, parishes.

The ecclesiastical hierarchy spread to all of Spanish America before the end of the sixteenth century and was almost completely established by the first half of the seventeenth. By 1620, thirty-seven dioceses had been erected; four were established in the eighteenth century; and three more in the nineteenth, before the period of Spanish rule came to an end. Their internal organization was subject to general ecclesiastical law, as modified by the patronage the popes had granted to the kings of Spain. This patronage was the distinctive trait of the ecclesiastical organization of the church in Spanish America.

The intrusion of the state in the affairs of the church was nothing new. It had been increasing since the start of the fourteenth century, due mainly to the confusion caused by the great Western Schism (1378–1417). In the Council of Constance, which sought to put an end to the schism, the phenomenon of "nations" with which the new pope, Martin V, had to deal via concordats arose. The concordat with the Spanish "nation" (13 May 1418) allowed the pope to fill the Spanish vacancies that took place in the Roman curia, but the remainder would be provided by means of "canonical elections," which the pope would confirm or reject.

Very soon, however, the kings of Castilla obtained the authority to intervene in these elections by claiming an age-old custom. Ferdinand and Isabella succeeded in limiting the electoral faculty of the chapters in favor of the crown, not of the pope. In 1486, they obtained the patronage of the kingdom of Granada, the Canary Islands, and the town of Puerto Real (next to Cádiz), which had just been settled; this patronage included the right to present to the pope the candidates for the major offices (dioceses and abbeys), sinecures, prebends, and parishes. This was only the beginning for the kings: they sought the same concessions for all their dominions. In 1508 they obtained them for America; this became known as the Royal Indian Patronage. (The general patronage for all the Spanish dominions would be granted in the mid-eighteenth century.)

These concessions were already contained in the papal bull *Inter cetera* of Pope Alexander VI (Rome, 4 May 1493), in which the pontiff specifically ordered King Ferdinand and Queen Isabella to send to the newly discovered islands and territories "the virtuous and God fearing, the learned and experienced to teach the natives and inhabitants there the Catholic faith and acquaint them with our customs." But the king and queen wanted a more explicit statement, and they obtained it. Afterward, the jurists serving the Crown tried to widen the interpretations of these concessions, many times successfully; while the Roman curia attempted, with less success, to restrict them. But in general, their differences did not extend beyond the juridical domain. As a whole, it can be said that church-state relations were peaceful and mutually beneficial. The state did profoundly intervene in the life of the church —sometimes in an annoying way—but the church did not lose its freedom or the ability to fulfill its role. In return, the church took advantage of many resources that it would not have had without the crown's help. Not even in the appointment of bishops—the designates were generally sound and in many cases excellent— did the crown commit any greater errors than Rome would have.

THE INQUISITION

The use of corporal punishment against heretics is very old, and it was the civil authorities who first established it. The state considered heresy a crime against society. At the beginning, the church opposed these measures, or at least tried to temper the harshness of the civil courts. Little by little, the church began to yield to this opposition, and in 1231 Pope Gregory IX formally organized the ecclesiastical inquisition, adopting for it several decrees of Emperor Frederick II. This inquisition acted mainly in Germany and in France; although in the year it was instituted, it made inroads into the kingdom of Aragón, it was not then accepted in the rest of Spain. The position of inquisitor was generally filled by the respective bishop, although in some cases the inquisitors were designated by special legates of the pope. Therefore, the ecclesiastical inquisition was an episcopal or papal institution.

Ferdinand and Isabella extended the Inquisition to the rest of Spain in 1481, by virtue of the papal bull of Pope Sixtus IV (1478), which authorized them to appoint inquisitors. This measure was directed against the Jews, who were accused of deception in their conversion to Catholicism. The Jews had enjoyed great freedom in Spain during the Middle Ages, but their situation had changed drastically in the first half of the fifteenth century. Popular riots against them, religious dissent within the Jewish community, the Catholic goal of achieving religious unity, and other factors (more economic and social than religious) contributed to a change in official policy. Even some renowned Jewish converts helped to turn public opinion against their former kinsmen.

During its first years, inquisitorial persecution was very stiff, but it had subsided to a great degree by the time the colonization of America started. Bartolomé de Las Casas was the first person that we know of who sought the Inquisition for the New World. In his *Memorial de los remedios,* addressed to Cardinal-Regent Jiménez de Cisneros, he wrote:

> I beg your most reverend lordship by God . . . to order the Inquisition to those islands and to the Indies, for which I believe there is a great need; for when the faith is to be newly planted, as in those lands, there may be no one there to sow any of the awful discord of heresy, since two heretics have been caught and burned there, and perhaps more than fourteen remain. For it could be that many heretics have fled this kingdom and, in thinking of saving themselves, have gone to those lands.

Cisneros, who was inquisitor general in Spain, did not judge it useful to establish the Inquisition in America at that time. He preferred to issue a general mandate to the bishops; some religious superiors were also delegated as inquisitors.

The first bishop of Mexico, Juan de Zumárraga, acted as inquisitor in his capacity as bishop; in 1535 he received special authority from the inquisitor general, which he exercised until 1543. During this period, he indicted approximately 150 people: sixty-six for blasphemy, twenty-three for witchcraft and superstition, twenty for bigamy, nineteen for observing the Jewish faith, fourteen for idolatry, eight for heresy, five for suspicion of Protestantism, five clergymen for immorality, and the rest for different offenses against orthodoxy. Zumárraga's successor (from 1554 to 1569), Alonso de Montúfar, undertook a lot of inquisitorial activity—especially against those suspected of Protestantism—but he did so only as bishop, apparently without special appointment as inquisitor.

In 1569, the first two tribunals of the Inquisition were established in America: one in Lima, the other in Mexico. Proceedings in Lima began in 1570; in Mexico, in 1571. A third was established in 1608 in Cartagena Colombia de Indias. Each of these tribunals had deputies in key parts of their districts. The jurisdiction of the district of Mexico was extended to also include the Philippines. As for their proceedings, these tribunals probably pursued more cases of immorality and witchcraft than of heresy.

EDUCATIONAL WORK, CHARITY WORK, AND OTHER ENDEAVORS

Education. The first task of the church in America was, naturally, evangelization and Christianization. Catechesis, the administration of the sacraments, and everything associated with public worship formed the basic activities. But the church also contributed to cultural development (education, writing, and the promotion of the arts) and was probably the institution that played the most important role in public welfare and social advancement.

At the time of the discovery of America, education was still controlled mostly by the clergy. This explains, perhaps, why the instructions for Nicolás de Ovando, first governor of the Indies, ordered him to establish a school in every settlement and have it run by a chaplain; this 1503 order was reiterated to Diego Colón in 1509. Around the same time the Franciscans started their boarding schools for the sons of caciques and high-ranking people; these were firmly established by 1511, the same year the Franciscans were told to start similar schools in Puerto Rico. The Franciscans also established some on the coast of Cumaná as part of the previously mentioned attempt at "peaceful conquest."

Before 1513, the clergyman Hernán Suárez, having received his baccalaureate degree, had begun teaching grammar to some of the Indians of Hispaniola who had been educated by the Franciscans; we know that grammar was still being taught around 1525–1527, probably to Indians and Spaniards. The same system was taken to Mexico by the first missionaries in 1523; one result was the school of San José de los Naturales, near the Convent of San Francisco de México. It was directed by Pedro de Gante until his death. Before 1533, a study of Latin grammar was started for selected groups of natives; this curriculum passed on to the College of Santa Cruz de Tlatelolco in 1536, where a whole program in the humanities was taught, and for a time even university courses. One of its renowned professors was Bernardino de Sahagún, who was helped by some of his students who were knowledgeable in Latin, Spanish, and Nahuatl in the preparation of his magnum opus, *Historia de las cosas de la Nueva España,* and other writings that are essential today for an understanding of pre-Spanish Mexico.

This effort in the education of the Indians was mainly the labor of the Franciscans. Before 1529, they had established schools for Indian girls and later collaborated with Bishop Zumárraga to reorganize them with the help of schoolmistresses brought from Spain around 1530. In 1551 the Franciscans proposed establishing an instructorship in grammar for the natives in Mérida (Yucatán), which we know was begun the following year and remained for many years hence. Something similar was planned seven years later for Jalisco.

The Franciscans, like Zumárraga, were very interested in the teaching of trades. The Augustinians did the same in their college at Tiripitío (Michoacán); furthermore, in 1537 they established a college of higher education in Mexico City, to which the Indians also had access. In 1547 the College of San Juan de Letrán was also founded in the capital city and was intended for mestizos. Likewise, there were similar kinds of schools throughout America, and it is clear that the example of Mexico was very influential for Colombia, Ecuador, and perhaps Peru.

The centers of education for Spaniards and Creoles were also in the hands of the church; that control continued until well into the eighteenth century. The Jesuits held the lead in this activity. It is enough to note the origin of Spanish-American universities: a considerable number had arisen from a college belonging to the Society of Jesus (which was expelled from the Spanish dominions in 1767). Some universities emerged out of grammar schools, most of which were of ecclesiastical origin, while others stemmed from diocesan seminaries. Ecclesiastical intervention in the establishment of the three oldest universities (at Santo Domingo, Mexico, and Lima) was significant, and so continued to be its contribution in teachers and students to these and other universities during colonial times.

A list of some of the universities that were in the hands of the church from their inception speaks for itself: Bogotá, Colombia—Santo Tomás (founded in 1580 by the Dominicans) and Javeriana (1605, by the Jesuits); Quito, Ecuador —San Fulgencio (1603, by the Augustinians), San Gregorio Magno (1591, by the Jesuits), and Santo Tomás (1688, by the Dominicans); Cuzco, Peru—San Ignacio (in the 1650s, by the Jesuits). The one in Charcas, Bolivia, was requested in 1552 by the city's first bishop, Tomás de San Martín, while another bishop sought to found it in 1600; the Jesuits finally established it in 1621. The one in Córdoba, Argentina, begun in 1613 by a Franciscan Creole, Fernando Trejo y Sanabria, was managed by the Jesuits until their 1767 expulsion and afterward by the Franciscans. Other universities include two in Santiago de Chile—San Felipe (the request for which had come from the first bishop of La Imperial [Chile], Antonio de San Miguel, though it was not established until 1747) and Nuestra Señora del Rosario (1622, by the Dominicans); one in Buenos Aires—the request for which came from the city's learned bishop, Pedro de Carranza, in 1622, though it was not established until 1731 by the Jesuits; and one in Guadalajara, Mexico— endowed by its bishop, Antonio Alcalde, in 1792.

The church also established large ecclesiastical libraries in America. Their origin dates from the coming of the first missionaries: books were part of their equipage as early as 1502. The first bishop of Mexico, Juan de Zumárraga (1527– 1548), brought a remarkable library, whose remnants are kept in several libraries today. The bibliographer Juan José Eguiara, in his *Biblioteca Mexicana* (1755), mentioned several libraries of his time that equaled or surpassed—according to official data—other famous libraries in Europe. The stock of many national libraries of Spanish America today came from monasteries. The Palafoxiana de Puebla (founded by the famous Bishop Palafox) is still a source of admiration. In Argentina, the most important library was that of the University of Córdoba, the university's origin being Franciscan and Jesuit; in Venezuela those of San Francisco de Caracas and the Jesuit school at Mérida were outstanding.

The introduction of printing to Spanish America is also due to Bishop Zumárraga, who after 1539 promoted the printing of many books in Spanish and Nahuatl. Printing was introduced to Lima by a protégé of both Zumárraga and the Jesuits, Alonso Fernández de Bonilla, future archbishop-elect of Mexico. It was introduced in Guatemala by its bishop, Payo Enríquez de Rivera; in Bogotá and Quito, by the Jesuits. The clergy were likewise the main clients of the presses, as we can see from the vast publications of José Toribio Medina on printing in Spanish America. His works show the great quantity of writing the clergy did, though the figures should be complemented by his *Biblioteca hispanoamericana* (1898–1917), which records the books by Spanish Americans in Europe.

The clergy, especially those of religious orders, not only dominated the study of Indian linguistics, philosophy and theology, mysticism, sacred oratory (homiletics), and missionary and monastic historiography; they also wrote nearly everything that has come to us about the pre-Spanish past. We would be ignorant about Mexico's past in almost its entirety without the writings of such clergymen as Andrés de Olmos, Toribio de Motolinía, Bernardino de Sahagún, Diego Durán, Juan de Tovar, Diego de Landa, and Juan de Torquemada. The Franciscans Pedro de Aguado and Pedro Simón were the first historians of Colombia and Venezuela, as the Jesuits Alonso de Ovalle and Diego Rosales were of Chile. The *Crónica miscelánea* (1891) of Antonio Tello constitutes the main source for the history of Jalisco. Missionaries also left accounts, and even maps, of noteworthy importance for geographical studies.

Charitable Work. Hospital work accounted for a majority of the charitable work done in Spanish America. From the first distribution of tithes in the New World (1512), one part was allotted to hospitals. Years before, Alonso de Espinar, the superior of the Franciscans, collaborated on the establishment of the first hospital in the city of Santo Domingo. In Mexico, hospitals were promoted especially by the Augustinians and Franciscans to provide assistance for the natives; in some regions no Franciscan monastery could be found without one. The bishops did the same. Zumárraga established a large one, Amor de Dios, and helped with the foundation of others. The bishops Domingo de Alzola in Guadalajara (1583–1590), Don Vasco de Quiroga, and Juan de Medina Rincón in Morelia (1575–1588) also did the same. In 1543 the Hospital of San Andrés was founded in Lima by clergyman Francisco

Molina, and in 1549, Archbishop Jerónimo de Loaisa established the Santa Ana for the Indians. In Cuzco another hospital was built around 1556 on the initiative of the local Franciscan superior, Antonio de San Miguel, future bishop of La Imperial. There are many similar cases throughout Spanish America.

Several religious orders devoted themselves especially to hospital work. The most important one was that of San Juan de Dios, or the Juaninos, founded in Granada, Spain, for the care of the most destitute of the sick. The Juaninos began work in America in the early seventeenth century. The viceroy of Mexico, Marqués de Montesclaros, gave them the administration of the Hospital of Nuestra Señora de los Desamparados. Later, they took charge of the hospitals at Colima, Zacatecas, Durango, San Luis Potosí, Orizaba, Puebla, Toluca, Aguascalientes, Guadalajara, Mérida, and other Mexican towns. They also established hospitals in other countries of Spanish America: Guatemala, Nicaragua, Cuba, Venezuela, Colombia, Peru, and Chile. Their hospitals included some of the most competent doctors and surgeons and generally were among the best at the time.

Two religious orders were begun in Spanish America with the purpose of working in hospitals. The first was in Mexico, started in the sixteenth century, under the name of the Brothers of Charity. They principally cared for the insane and the convalescent poor and had the Hospital of San Hipólito in Mexico City under their auspices. They also founded hospitals in other parts of Mexico: Oaxtepec (for the terminally ill; the ruins of this hospital can still be seen), Veracruz, Acapulco, Perote, and Puebla.

The second group, the Order of the Bethlehemites, was founded in Guatemala in the mid-seventeenth century by Friar Pedro Betancurt; its first hospital was named Our Lady of Bethlehem, hence the name of the order. When Bishop Payo Enríquez de Rivera became archbishop of Mexico in 1668, he brought the Bethlehemites with him, and they branched out throughout the country. From there they went to Peru, where they founded several hospitals; they also established themselves in Potosí (Bolivia), Quito, and Havana.

As one can see, the presence of religion was far-reaching in all facets of life. The outward forms of religiosity were overwhelming. The new architectural style could have been a mere product of European influences, but the austerity or the ornate quality of the temples had to affect the attitude of the faithful toward public worship. Processions and sermons attracted large crowds. The number of confraternities and other religious associations was also very large. This can still be seen in many places, in spite of the new trends that time and circumstance are bringing about.

Mexico is, perhaps, the best place to see this, for it was, after all, the most Christianized country in Spanish America. The influence of Mexico could also explain the force of evangelical expansion that took the church to vast regions belonging today to the United States: New Mexico, Texas, Arizona, and California (Florida, which had contact with Mexico, gravitated directly toward Spain or indirectly through Cuba). Because the influence in New Mexico has been the most prolonged—since the arrival of the first missionaries in the late sixteenth century—that state shows the greatest traces of that influence. Hispanic religious traces and vestiges are also visible today in Texas, New Mexico, and California but stem more from the present Spanish-American culture than the Spanish colonial past. I mean, of course, the religious customs and practices of today and not the churches and missions.

It is useful to remember, however, that religious customs and practices, forms of worship, and other aspects of Christianity were already changing during the period of Spanish rule. Catholicism could be considered as monolithic only in its fundamental dogma, but nothing more. Its "accommodation" to the times has been constant. There were changes in the liturgy, new devotional practices were popularized, and the worshipers' attitudes changed in many aspects of Christian life. And the most modern was not always the best. The simple and austere spirituality of the first missionaries can be considered superior to the baroque style of the seventeenth and eighteenth centuries, which style expressed itself as much in architecture as in the manifestations of public worship. Not even the period of the "Enlightenment" by itself brought the decadence of religious fervor; it was rather a change in tastes.

Erasmus, the Dutch cleric who died in 1536, inspired a reform movement that some of his followers interpreted in various (even contradic-

tory) ways. Others judged him in a more critical vein—accepting, rejecting, or suspending some of his opinions. That Cisneros or Zumárraga accepted some of Erasmus' doctrines does not mean that they accepted all. At times it was a question of ideas renewed by the spirit of Erasmus, though perhaps ideas not so new to the church—in which case such notions were perfectly acceptable. The pretended Erasmism of the first missionaries and of Bishop Zumárraga may have been of this sort. And if they really absorbed the works of Erasmus—as seems possible, since at least Zumárraga had these writings at his disposal—there would still have been no problem: generally the works of Erasmus contain orthodox doctrines and in any case have never been condemned by the church.

As for the Enlightenment, one first needs to define the term well, since the word itself does not convey the pejorative sense that many have given it. In Spanish America, at least, many of the "enlightened" belonged to the clergy or were Catholics above reproach—and perhaps constituted a majority. Thus, in Mexico we find Díaz de Gamarra, Clavijero, Alzate, León y Gama, and Pérez Calama; in Guatemala, José Antonio Goicoechea; in Colombia, Archbishop Caballero y Góngora and José Celestino Mutis; in Peru, Rodríguez de Mendoza and Bishop Martínez Compañon; in Bolivia and Mexico, Bishop Moxó; and in Argentina, the canon Maciel and the dean Funes. For these men there was no contradiction between "enlightened" doctrines and religion. They were orthodox reformers.

However, there were other "enlightened" doctrines that made their way to America, coming principally from France and basically of an anticlerical or antireligious nature. Although the Inquisition tried to stem this influence—perhaps for political, rather than religious, reasons—it thrived as an underground movement. The results of this effort would clearly be seen in the nineteenth century, after independence. The movement did not influence the masses but did affect the ruling class. Such antireligious—or at least anti-Catholic—"enlightened" propaganda was helped by other forces: Freemasonry and a growing desire for change that touched religion as much as it did politics.

These and other similar forces worked toward the goal of a secular society, in which the church and religion would lose their dominant role.

This campaign was furthered by the regalist tendencies the state under the Bourbon dynasty imposed on the church from 1700 on. Under the Austrian dynasty the royal patronage over the church had been treated as a concession granted by the popes to the Spanish rulers. Since the middle of the seventeenth century jurists currying favor with the crown had been developing the theory of *regalias:* that one of the attributes of royalty was its right of patronage on ecclesiastical matters. Although many royalists—perhaps the majority—were men of faith and practicing Catholics, the abusive incursions of the Crown into ecclesiastical matters discredited the church and confused the faithful.

Naturally, there were repercussions in Spanish America that created a favorable milieu for the development of laicism. On the other hand, the church, being a strongly conservative institution, was not about to abandon its privileges and its traditional place of action. This attitude, though not the only cause, could have contributed to both anticlericalism and a typical phenomenon in Spanish America: a person who believed in God and his church but not in its ministers.

Anticlericalism had had a long history, going all the way back to Spain. According to Domínguez Ortiz, to appreciate the Spanish religiosity of the sixteenth century, one must distinguish between the hierarchical church, an object of severe criticism, and the religious sentiment of the people, who could separate the hierarchy from the adherence due church doctrine and the respect and veneration due its ministers. Thus it remained, according to Ortiz, until after the Tridentine age and clearly showed itself in the seventeenth century, "with its intellectual cowardice, its timid piety and its inability to separate the essential in religion from the contingent."

Since the theme of religion in the Spanish Empire is so vast as to be impossible to adequately treat here. In view of this, I have preferred to highlight the fundamental or representative, instead of hazarding opinion and reflection. One could touch on many important points; for example, the church's social work—building towns, aqueducts, bridges, roads, and *montes de piedad* (money-lending institutions for the poor); bringing new agricultural techniques; and providing other forms of social advancement and help for the needy. Similarly, one could discuss

catechesis, preaching, public worship, and the formation of the clergy; but lack of space precludes it. Nevertheless, I would like to briefly refer to the clergy's participation in civil government.

In general, the Crown was wary of granting both civil and ecclesiastical authority to one person. Occasionally, though, clerics were given assignments of a political nature. Sebastián Ramírez de Fuenleal, the bishop of Santo Domingo, was named president of the second Audienca (a judicial body with some legislative functions) of Mexico (1530–1535), and his successor in the episcopate, Alonso de Fuenmayor, also presided in the Santo Domingan Audiencia. In 1516 three monks of the Order of Saint Jerome were entrusted with an important mission to the Antilles. A very important appointment was that of the cleric, later bishop, Pedro de la Gasca, who put an end to the civil war that was provoked by the enactment of the *leyes nuevas* of 1542–1543; the establishment of these same laws in Mexico was given to another cleric, Francisco Tello de Sandoval.

Other commissions to clergymen include that of Alonso Fernández de Bonilla, archbishop-elect of Mexico, to the viceroyalty of Peru in the last years of the sixteenth century; that of Juan de Mañosca to the Audiencia of Quito in 1521; and that of the famous bishop of Puebla, Palafox y Mendoza, to Mexico. The governing of this important Mexican viceroyalty was carried out pro tempore by several prelates: Pedro Moya de Contreras (1583–1585), Francisco García Guerra (1611–1612), Payo Enríquez de Rivera (1672–1680), Juan Ortega y Montañes (1701–1702), Juan Antonio de Vizarrón (1734–1740), Alonso Núñez de Haro (1787), and Francisco Javier Lizana (1809–1810)—all archbishops of Mexico. In addition, these churchmen were viceroys of Mexico: the bishop of Yucatán, Marcos de Torres (1647–1649), and the bishop of Puebla, Diego de Escobar y Llamas (1664). Peru's viceroyalty was governed by three of its bishops; Colombia's by Antonio Caballero y Góngora (1782–1788), during one of the most fertile and productive periods in that country's history.

These commissions were even more frequent in Spain and concerned major areas of government. In either case, these commissions show the close ties between church and state, as well as the prestige that bishops, and clergymen in general, garnered. Those assigned had to have a good academic background, generally in juridical matters. The majority of those chosen for civil posts in Spanish America proved to have talent as leaders.

SPANISH MISSIONS

An allusion was made earlier to the Spanish missions in territories that now form part of the United States, from Florida to California. Something more needs to be added. All of these missions, except for Florida's, had Mexico as their starting point, and all of them had Mexican antecedents and a certain dependence on Mexico itself.

Florida. After various setbacks (1527, 1539, and 1549) the Jesuits started the first of Florida's missions in 1566, but they did not succeed in keeping it, since they were obliged to abandon it in 1572. The following year the mission was entrusted to the Franciscans, who remained there until 1763, when Florida was ceded to the British.

In 1615 missionary work was done in the provinces of Apalache, Latama, Machagua, and Santa Elena—about thirty missionaries distributed among seven missions. In 1609 these missions, along with the monasteries in Cuba, had formed the *custodia* (a region somewhat smaller than a province) of Santa Elena. Though the *custodia* (later raised to province) came to include a large number of personnel, missionary work always remained difficult; in 1597 five Franciscans had been martyred there.

New Mexico. Similar difficulties were encountered in the Texas and New Mexico missions, primarily due to the disposition of the inhabitants, though in the case of New Mexico also to the barrenness of the land. New Mexico's first mission had been planned ever since 1539 as a result of the account—a bit fanciful, it seems—that the Franciscan Marcos de Niza gave of his visit to the famous "cities of Cibola." Indeed, this enterprise had to be accomplished without an armed conquest, hence

> keeping to the conditions and limitations set by theologians and canonists, and in this way the Gospel would be preached under conditions similar to those of the apostles of the early

Church, and sermons to the pagans would be delivered accordingly.

> (Mendieta, 1971)

Such an attempt was tried, first in 1540, then again in 1582–1583, but the first Spanish town was not established until 1598. The city of Santa Fe was founded in 1610. According to a report dated 1629, some thirty thousand Indians had been baptized, a count probably too low, since a memorandum written the following year lists the population of all the missions as forty-five (with a detailed account given of all the residents of the twenty-seven missionary posts).

A revolt in 1680 destroyed all that had been attained up to that point. The territory was reclaimed in 1693, and again in 1696 after another insurrection. In 1706, the twenty-seven missions were reestablished, and in the same year Santa Fe and the town of Galisteo were refounded. In 1748 the Franciscans had under their care 17,176 Christian Indians and 4,395 Spaniards. According to a detailed visitation in 1776, the twenty-seven missions had a total of 18,261 Indians. In the same year, the friars Francisco Atanasio Domínguez and Silvestre Vélez de Escalante reached Utah Lake in search of a passage between Santa Fe and Monterey. (Monterey, capital of the California missions, was home for both the civil and religious authorities.)

Texas. The first attempts at evangelistic work in Texas date back to 1674 and were started from the Mexican state of Coahuila, where the Franciscans had established their missions. Almost immediately, the Spanish authorities began to worry about the rumored French scheme of infiltrating, from Louisiana, the Spanish territories. When in 1688 definite proof of a French presence in Texas was obtained, a decision was made to fend it off by the settlement of the region.

A mission seemed the most convenient means, and in 1690 Mission San Francisco de los Tejas was established near the eastern border of Texas. Four Franciscans, escorted by three soldiers, began their missionary work there. A plan for eight missions and towns was quickly put into effect, in accordance with instructions (Mexico, 23 January 1691) that

> neither to royal allegiance nor domination, nor to the Catholic religion, nor to acceptance of

missionaries should these nations be compelled . . . by force or hostility, but rather through reason, kindness, and charitable and gentle means, and arms are not to be used, except out of the necessity of self-defense or aid to Indians who are our friends and have pledged themselves to the Royal Crown.

(Gómez Canedo, 1968)

As one can see, it was a plan of peaceful conquest and conversion, whose success depended entirely on the Indians themselves. The plan failed, however, not so much because of the hostility of the Indians, but from other causes (among them, the difficulty of supplying provisions to the colonists). In 1694, missionaries and settlers were forced to leave Texas.

Still, the Franciscans did not forget about Texas. In 1698 they began their evangelistic work in the border region of the Rio Grande, and from there renewed their contact with the Tejas Indians. In 1716 they were able to establish once and for all the Texas missions, first in the eastern part of the state and later in the vicinity of the San Antonio River. These missions were maintained until the end of Spanish rule in 1821, and to some extent under Mexican rule. Of their first years there is abundant information in the *Crónica* of Espinosa, who was both witness to and participant in the events described; the works of Castañeda also give a detailed account of the entire missionary period.

California. Although the missions in California were established late in the period of Spanish rule in America, they were quite successful. When the Jesuits were expelled from the Spanish dominions in 1767, their missions in Baja California, which they had run for more than fifty years, were handed over to the Franciscans.

The Franciscans took charge in 1768, but their tenure was shortened, for immediately afterward the proposal to settle and Christianize Alta California went into effect, and they were assigned to establish new missions there. Even though they retained provisional control of the missions in Baja California until 1772, a group of Franciscans embarked northward in 1769. On 16 July 1769, Mission San Diego was established by Junípero Serra—the first of twenty-one missions founded by the Franciscans between 1769 and 1823 (the last one being Mission Sonoma, north of San Francisco).

There is no doubt that California relied on some extraordinary missionaries. Serra had associates of comparable stature: such men as Francisco Palou, Fermín Francisco de Lasuén, and Juan Crespi. Taking them into account, it is easier to explain the rapid and constant progress of the missions, both spiritually and physically. It is interesting to compare Serra's report, dated 10 December 1773, to one from 1788. The 491 christened in 1773 had become 10,752 in 1788; the 205 head of cattle had become 13,291; the 94 sheep, 13,104; and so forth. The 17,842 bushels of grain in 1788 had become 23,290 in 1790.

Arizona. From the state of Sonora, Spanish missions, first under the Jesuits and afterward under the Franciscans, were established in Arizona. The magnificent Mission San Xavier del Bac and the city of Tucson are testimony to the Spanish presence. There the Jesuit Eusebio Francisco Kino and the Franciscan Francisco Garcés distinguished themselves.

All of the Spanish missions had much in common with regard to their organization. All were established according to the rules contained in the ordinances proclaimed by Philip II in 1573. What was prescribed may be termed a system of reduction. Evangelistic work was combined with colonization, while the use of force was kept to a minimum (solely for defense and limited to protecting the missionaries or the Christianized Indians).

I previously referred to the instructions given in 1691 for the Texas missions: they reflected a missionary policy, a program that became part of the *Recopilación de las leyes de las Indias.* The opinion of the Franciscan Isidro Félix de Espinosa (*Crónica,* ch. 19), one of the great missionaries of Texas, is noteworthy:

The missionaries of Texas did not ask for the assistance of soldiers for fear of their lives, since they wandered alone from place to place in search of the dying, rather for the purpose of encouraging and persuading [the Indians], through a show of arms, to assemble, and that the Priests and soldiers should help them, by example, to clear a field, to transport water from a stream for irrigation, and for all to help in building one another's dwellings; none of this goes against, but rather conforms to, what the laws of the Indies have arranged. . . . [T]o make war in order to convert, that was never considered.

RELIGION IN THE SPANISH EMPIRE

BIBLIOGRAPHY

Spanish Antecedents

Antonio Domínguez Ortiz, *Estudios de historia social de España,* vol. III (1956); Albert A. Sicroff, *Les controverses des statuts de "pureté de sang" en Espagne du quinzième au dix-septième siecle* (1960).

Missionaries and Conquistadors

Pedro Borges Morán, *El envío de misioneros a América durante la época española* (1977); Martín Fernández de Navarrete, *Colección de los viajes y descubrimientos,* vol. I (1825; rev. 1945); Frederick A. Kirkpatrick, *The Spanish Conquistadores* (1934).

Religious Orders and Evangelization

Lino Gómez Canedo, *Evangelización y conquista* (1977); Robert Ricard, *The Spiritual Conquest of Mexico* (1966).

The Organization of the Church

John Lloyd Mecham, *Church and State in Latin America: A History of Politico-Ecclesiastical Relations* (1934; rev. 1966); William Eugene Shiels, *King and Church: The Rise and Fall of the Patronato Real* (1961).

The Inquisition

Richard Greenleaf, *Zumárraga and the Mexican Inquisition, 1536–1543* (1961); Henry Kamen, *The Spanish Inquisition* (1965).

Education, Charity, and Other Fields

Germán Cardozo Galué, *Michoacán en el siglo de las luces* (1944; rev. 1973); Juan José Eguiara, *Biblioteca mexicana,* vol. I (1755); Lino Gómez Canedo, *La educación de los marginados durante la época colonial* (1982); Mario Góngora, "The Enlightenment, Enlightened Despotism and the Ideological Crisis in the Colonies," in *Studies in the Colonial History of Spanish America* (1975); Josefina Muriel de la Torre, *Hospitales de la Nueva España,* 2 vols. (1956–1960); Juan Manuel Pacheco, *La ilustración en el nuevo reino* (1975); Agueda María Rodríguez Cruz, *Historia de las universidades hispanoamericanas,* 2 vols. (1973); Carl Schmitt, "The Clergy and the Enlightenment in Latin America: An Analysis," in *The Americas,* 15 (1959).

Spanish Missions

Carlos E. Castañeda, *Our Catholic Heritage in Texas, 1519–1936,* 7 vols. (1936–1958); Isidro Félix de Espinosa, *Crónica de los colegios de propaganda fide de la Nueva España* (1746; rev. 1964); Lino Gómez Canedo, ed., *Primeras exploraciones y poblamiento de Texas, 1686–1694* (1968); Oakah L. Jones, Jr., *Los Paisanos: Spanish Settlers on the Northern Frontier of New Spain* (1979); Gerónimo de Mendieta, *Historia eclesiastica indiana* (1870; facs. ed., 1971); Andrew F. Rolle, *California: A History* (1963).

[*See also* RELIGION IN HISPANIC AMERICA SINCE THE ERA OF INDEPENDENCE.]

RELIGION IN HISPANIC AMERICA SINCE THE ERA OF INDEPENDENCE

Edwin E. Sylvest, Jr.

RELIGIOUS values and institutions have been vital to Hispanic America from its inception. The New World was conquered and colonized with ecclesial sanction as a Christian missionary enterprise; colonial society depended upon the church to satisfy its need for education, health care, and economic development. Christian symbols and concepts provided a matrix within which the traditions of Spain were mingled with the diverse cultures of the Americas and Africa to form new cultures and new peoples. The Crown provided political unity; Castilian Spanish, a common means of communication. The Christian faith, in its endeavor to embrace everyone, so permeated the fabric of individual and communal life that it forged an identity which survived the vicissitudes of time and circumstance and which continues as a powerful social force in the present.

Catholic Christianity was the glue binding together persons of all ethnic and cultural backgrounds, as well as of socioeconomic class and status. Relations between ecclesial and secular institutions, always problematic, became even more so after the 1808–1825 struggle for independence, but Catholic faith was everywhere affirmed as the symbolic center of society. Post-independence challenges to ecclesial authority and privilege were understood to be political rather than theological, although political challenges were rooted in certain unexamined theological presuppositions. Religious struggle continues as an element in national life in the Hispanic American republics. Political revolution and social transformation in the region have always had to respond to the religious dimensions of human interaction. The revolutions of Mexico, Cuba, and Nicaragua all illustrate that point in various ways.

The territory of the old viceroyalty of New Spain provides an appropriate context within which to examine religious developments in Hispanic America. That region, embracing the islands of the Caribbean, much of the North American mainland from Florida to the Pacific Ocean and from the Straits of Juan de Fuca to the isthmus of Panama, has been longest in the cultural orbit of Spain: it includes Cuba, Puerto Rico, and Hispaniola (the island that makes up Haiti and the Dominican Republic), insular societies that did not achieve independence in the upheavals of 1808–1825; and, in Mexico, Cuba, and Nicaragua, it also encompasses the three genuine revolutions that have occurred in Hispanic America.

Religion in Hispanic America is a complex phenomenon. Spanish Catholicism, forged as it was in the encounter with alien traditions and Christian heterodoxy, was not simple. Inquisitors labored to protect orthodoxy, but there was considerable theological diversity within the church, especially within and among the orders. Franciscans, Dominicans, Augustinians, Jesuits all held the faith and taught it in their distinctive ways. Secular priests, who did not belong to religious orders, and bishops envisioned a church different from that of the friars. All, lay and cleric alike, engaged in forms of pious devotion that stretched the limits of right faith and practice. The decrees of the Second Vatican Council and the 1968 Conference of the Latin American Episcopal Conference accentuated old differences and introduced new tensions into the Catholic community.

The combination of the council's emphases on the missional nature of the church, laity and clergy alike, as the people of God in the world, episcopal collegiality, and vernacular liturgies, among other things, and the conference's call for the church to identify with the struggles of the poor were threatening to all, both within and without the church, who had vested interests in the status quo. The church hierarchy was frightened lest it lose control of the institution. Secular politicians feared that the church was becoming subversive and an instrument of instability as opposed to its accustomed role of sustaining the prevailing order. Radical adherence to the enactments of the Second Vatican Council and the Episcopal Conference would be nothing less than revolutionary. Conservative elements, traditional allies of the church, found themselves increasingly at odds with it. Traditional liberals were also anxious lest the new modes of political activism result in new forms of clericalism or the reestablishment of ecclesial dominance in the political process. Liberals and conservatives alike were disturbed over the openness to socialistic solutions to economic problems.

Protestant Christianity entered Hispanic America after independence in 1825, at first to serve the needs of foreign entrepreneurs and technicians; later, with the approval of reforming governments desirous of curbing the power and influence of the Catholic church, to seek converts. Protestant schools and social agencies provided needed services in nations whose resources were stretched thin and that sought alternatives to Catholic schools and philosophies of service. New ideals and behavioral patterns challenged ancient mores. In the nineteenth century, churches of the continental and English reformations predominated among the Protestants; in the twentieth century, Fundamentalist and charismatic groups.

Among the masses, important elements of indigenous traditions survived, often through assimilation to Christian faith traditions. Those remnants of the past challenge the institutional interests and orthodoxy of Catholic and Protestant churches alike. In addition to the indigenous religions of the Americas, important elements of African traditional religion survive on the islands of the Caribbean and in certain areas of Mexico and Central America. Small Jewish communities and, in urban centers like Mexico City, religions of Asia have their adherents as well.

Secular alternatives to religious faith present the churches with their most serious challenge and are viewed by many with alarm and suspi-

cion. The fear of Marxism, in particular, occasions great controversy both inside and outside the churches. The radical secularity of the Mexican and Cuban revolutions and the cooperation between Christians and Marxists in the Nicaraguan revolution have been especially problematic for the churches.

THE CHURCH AND BOURBON REFORM

In an event that had far-reaching consequences for the Spanish empire, Charles of Ghent, son of Ferdinand and Isabella's daughter Juana and Archduke Philip of Austria, became king of Spain on the death of Ferdinand in 1516. Charles' mother, Juana, had been adjudged mentally incompetent; Ferdinand and Isabella's other children, Juan and Isabella, had also died. Thus it was that the Habsburgs of Austria came to occupy the Spanish throne until the beginning of the eighteenth century; thus it was that Spain became embroiled in the conflictive politics of the Holy Roman Empire. Her king, Charles I of Spain, was elected Holy Roman Emperor Charles V in 1519. This involvement with European affairs contributed to a style of colonial administration in Hispanic America that provided a significant degree of actual autonomy in the colonies, while exacting a heavy cost in drawing off wealth that could have been used in New Spain.

Although never tension free, the union of church and state and the conjunction of interests prevailed throughout the colonial period in New Spain. Under the Habsburgs in the sixteenth and seventeenth centuries the Catholic church provided powerful institutional and spiritual support for the monarchy. In many remote areas priests and friars were the sole representatives of Spanish interests. In addition to its evangelizing task, the church provided sacramental ministry and nurture for its new converts as well as for Spanish Christians; its schools educated the realm, in however limited a degree; its hospitals provided health care; its wealth financed economic development. Beyond these services to the people, the church also served the Crown directly in the collection of taxes, the maintenance of order (especially through the Inquisition), and in providing basic information concerning life in the colonies. As Habsburg political power declined, the church grew relatively stronger and its importance as an instrument of colonial control increased. Royal patronage notwithstanding, the church enjoyed significant autonomy under the Habsburgs.

Along with the exercise of great power, the church enjoyed important privileges. Litigation involving clerics could not be heard in civil courts but rather had to be considered in church courts.

Over time the church came to hold great wealth, not only from the tithe that was collected by the Crown as a tax, but from bequests. Religious orders, especially, were the recipients of much real property and many capital assets as the result of testamentary provisions. These bequests, given as tokens of devotion to support chaplaincies and pious works, were held in perpetuity for the designated purposes. Rents and other income produced through the use of such assets provided important support for the church and gave it the means to serve as banker to the colonial society in New Spain.

With the accession of Philip of Anjou to the Spanish throne in 1700, and the resolution of the war of succession (1701–1714) in his favor, a new dynasty with different perspectives undertook to govern Spain and her empire. The Bourbons centralized the administration of the realm so as to improve its efficiency and to subject it more consistently to the royal will. The full impact of this transition was not felt until the reign of Charles III (1759–1788). Indeed, that there was no effort to separate from Spain during the war of succession is testimony to the general sense of satisfaction with the status quo. With Charles III, however, there began a transformation so radical as to merit the sobriquet "the second conquest of America."

In the case of the church, great effort was invested by the royal administration in reducing the autonomy that had come to prevail. Even before the reign of Charles III, steps were taken to that end. The number of regular clergy was reduced in favor of secular; the number and size of convents was limited; missions were secularized where possible; the number of *cofradías* (lay societies formed to support popular devotions to the saints) was limited; and the administration of community funds was removed from church control and placed in the hands of civil bureaucrats.

A significant result of such activity was that control of Indian labor and protection of Indian health and well-being were taken from the church and placed in the hands of the civil bureaucracy.

One of the most notorious and far-reaching actions taken by Charles III was the expulsion of the Jesuits in 1767. The motives were complex and not exclusively a function of Bourbon interests in the American colonies. Bound by vow to be obedient to the pope, the Jesuits were viewed by some European governments as a threatening alien force. They were expelled from Portugal in 1759 and from France in 1764. Likewise, the expulsion from the American colonies illustrates the extent of the Spanish monarchy's concern to assert its authority against the relative autonomy of the religious establishment. The Jesuits controlled great wealth, were engaged in extensive and productive economic enterprises, and enjoyed significant influence and control over indigenous populations. In all of these areas the monarchy was concerned to assert its power more directly.

Perhaps as important as any other consideration in the suppression of the Jesuits was the evident desire to check the growing influence and power of the Creoles (Europeans born in the New World). Although there were stringent regulations restricting the involvement of Creoles in civic and ecclesiastical administration under the Habsburgs, they had become a strong and influential element in colonial society. Almost two-thirds of the Jesuits expelled from New Spain were Creoles. That fact alone would prove to be critical in the public reaction to the expulsion and to the development of patriotic sentiment in a highly articulate exile community. Such patriotic sentiment played an important role in the formation of Hispanic American national consciousness and became a factor in the struggle for independence.

The Bourbons limited ecclesiastical privilege as well as power. They restricted clerical immunity from prosecution in secular courts. That privilege, jealously guarded by the church, was of particular importance to many parish clergy who had little wealth or other social advantage, and its reduction occasioned vigorous negative reaction, another factor that influenced clerical attitudes in the independence struggle.

Church wealth was of considerable interest to

the royal administration. The philosophy that land held by religious institutions could be developed better if placed in private hands influenced policy. Steps were taken to deprive the church of its inherited wealth, especially real estate, a process actually completed not by the monarchy and its agents but in the liberal reforms after independence.

Notwithstanding these efforts to limit ecclesial power and privilege, the church, especially the hierarchy, continued to be regalist in its sentiment. In certain aspects the royal objectives were consistent with the interests of bishops, who had long sought to restrict the influence and semiautonomy of religious orders and to gain more direct control over the administration and pastoral practice of local parishes. Many bishops were actually pleased with the expulsion of the Jesuits. Of course, the hierarchy was almost entirely European, but that alone is not a sufficient explanation for their loyalty. There was a coincidence of political and ecclesial interest as well.

Attitudes, ideas, values, and devotion were as important in the religious situation as were institutional considerations. At two diverse points the church was instrumental in shaping those nonmaterial elements of religious culture in ways that profoundly affected the development of the entire society in New Spain. On the one hand, evangelistic activity among the indigenous resulted in syncretistic forms of Christian faith that are evident in the festival and drama associated with saints' day observances, which served to integrate native populations into new systems imposed by the conquerors, while still allowing for the preservation of many aspects of their ancient traditions. The church itself nurtured, even among the conquerors, forms of popular devotion, such as the cults of the saints, that were imported from the peninsula but were not totally dissimilar to those developing in the indigenous and mestizo communities. On the other hand, the church also provided through its schools and universities educational opportunities for European and Creole elites that introduced and nurtured ideas and methods of critical inquiry apparently antithetical to its institutional interests and problematic for the majority of its constituency.

Devotion to Mary and the saints was particularly widespread, not only among indigenous and mestizo (ethnically mixed) groups but among Creoles and peninsulars as well. The *cofradías* formed to support such devotion were often wealthy and powerful organizations throughout colonial society, from the humblest village to the sophisticated urban center. In the Creole and European communities, popular devotion continued according to the traditions of Spain, but in the mestizo and indigenous communities there was such a high degree of syncretism that the clerical establishment, whether religious or secular, found difficulty in accepting it. In any case, the *cofradías* were lay societies and were self-sufficient except for sacramental ministries, for which they depended upon the clergy. That self-sufficiency, coupled with the reality that popular religion was more closely associated with the common life and more nearly represented the symbolic center of personal and group identity, led to tension and conflict with the institutional church and relativized the importance of the institution within the general populace.

The cultus and devotion associated with Our Lady of Guadalupe of Tepeyac are characteristic popular phenomena. Ten years after the devastating siege and conquest of the Aztec capital, Tenochtitlán, by Hernán Cortés in 1521, an indigenous man by the name of Juan Diego is said to have appeared before the bishop-elect of Mexico, Juan de Zumarraga, reporting that the Virgin Mary had appeared to him at the hill of Tepeyac and sent him with a message. It was the desire of the Virgin, who identified herself as the Lady of Guadalupe, that a church be built at Tepeyac as a sign of her presence with the suffering people of Mexico. According to the tradition, Zumarraga sent Juan Diego away, but over the period of 9–12 December 1531 the Virgin appeared to her messenger four times and healed his ailing uncle, Juan Bernardino. As validation of her appearance and request she directed Juan Diego to pick some roses growing on the hillside and to take them in his *tilma* (cloak) to the bishop. When Juan Diego reached the bishop he opened the *tilma* to display the roses. As the flowers fell to the ground an image of the Immaculate Conception was seen imprinted upon the maguey fiber garment. That image was placed in a shrine erected at the site of the apparition and became the center of a popular devotion. An image reputed to be the one given to Juan Diego hangs to this day in a magnificent modern basilica built at Tepeyac, the site of daily pilgrimages by groups and individuals from all over Mexico and beyond.

In the sixteenth century, as devotion to Our Lady of Guadalupe grew in the indigenous and mestizo communities, the hierarchy and even the Franciscans, the religious order most closely related to the early evangelization of the Valley of Mexico, were strongly opposed to its development. It was feared that devotion to Mary under the appellation of Guadalupe and in association with the hill of Tepeyac where the Aztec mother of the gods, Tonantzin, had been worshiped would be confusing at best, and a perpetuation of past idolatry at worst. Controversy continued.

On the feast of the Nativity of the Virgin, 8 September 1556, Franciscan friar Francisco de Bustamante preached a sermon in which he disputed the authenticity of the image, calling it a painting, and questioned the appropriateness of using the name of Guadalupe. He, like many other of his confreres, argued that the cult was idolatrous, perpetuating an indigenous devotion to Tonantzin. Notwithstanding such objection by the Franciscans, in the same year that Bustamante preached his sermon, only twenty-five years after the reported apparition in 1531, an official investigation vindicated the cult, and the first chapel was erected at Tepeyac with the approval of Archbishop Alonso de Montúfar, a Dominican. By the time of the wars of independence, Our Lady of Guadalupe was so identified with Mexico that she became the focal symbol of the struggle and the emblem of the new nation.

That a mass devotion should have become identified with Creole consciousness—and also a symbol of an essentially conservative reaction that led finally to Mexican independence—is testimony to the power of religious sentiment and symbol in Hispanic America and in the ideological foundations of the movement toward liberation. The expulsion of the Jesuits was a key element in the process leading to that identification, for it was the writing of expatriate Jesuits such as Francisco Javier Clavijero that grounded the *American* identity of the Creoles in the traditions and symbol systems of Mexico and especially that of Guadalupe.

Not only did the writing of exiled Jesuits articulate a developing consciousness within the Creole establishment of New Spain, but it also created for Mexico a sense of national identity in the consciousness of Enlightenment Europe. Our Lady of Guadalupe of Tepeyac, formed in the union of traditions of Estremadura and ancient Mesoamerica, symbolized the new nation. She was a figure intimately related to the Hispanic tradition, but with the transformations of time and association, thoroughly Mexican. At the symbolic level, in their mutual embrace of the Virgin, conqueror and conquered embraced each other and the two became something new.

The Jesuits played a key role in that transformation. Through their simultaneous concern for the masses and their education of the Creole elites they formed a bridge between the cultures and traditions of the Iberian Peninsula and the colony. Of course, they were not alone in that role, but their efforts were singular in scope and effectiveness. Before their expulsion Jesuits had been instrumental in introducing the ideals and methods of Enlightenment scholarship into the universities and schools of New Spain, but it was after their departure that those values had their greatest impact. The anticlericalism of France was muted in America. Religious and secular clergy alike were among the advocates of the new ideas. They were most enthusiastic in accepting the critical methods of Cartesian philosophy and the experimental science of Bacon and Newton. The Franciscan José Antonio Goicoechea at the Guatemalan University of San Carlos exemplifies the role of clergy in promoting Enlightenment ideas. Goicoechea contributed to the *Gaceta de Guatemala* (published weekly during the years 1729–1731; 1793–1816), an important medium for the communication of those ideas. He was also a sponsor of the Sociedad Económica de Amigos del País de Guatemala, founded in 1794, one of many such societies that emerged throughout New Spain as an arena for intellectual activity and for the advocacy of practical steps that might lead to the development of stronger and more productive national economies.

There were traditionalists who insisted upon teaching Aristotelian physics and who continued to assert the preeminence of ancient authority over that of reason. But the point of greatest tension was in the conflict between two Enlightenment philosophies that were themselves contradictory: the "enlightened despotism" of the Bourbons and the constitutionalism rooted in the thought of Rousseau, Locke, Hobbes, Jefferson, and Franklin. But tendencies toward popular sovereignty were not alien to the Hispanic tradition itself, as evidenced by the councils of Toledo, the constitutional patterns of the Crown of Aragón, and the political philosophy of Francisco Suárez, preeminent Jesuit theologian whose *De Legibus* (1612) ranks with the *Relecciones* (1527–1540) of Francisco de Vitoria as a foundation for modern international law. Contrary to Bourbon absolutism, each of these Spanish traditions understood sovereignty in some way to belong to the people and not to the monarch except at the sufferance of the people. Higher clergy, at least until the usurpation of the Spanish throne by the Bonapartes in 1808, joined royal bureaucrats and some Creole aristocrats in support of the monarchy, notwithstanding the limit placed upon ecclesial privilege and power. Lesser clergy and religious whose work placed them in closer contact with those less privileged tended to resist "enlightened despotism."

As for the general populace, the implications of Enlightenment political and economic thought were lost to most. Poor Creole farmers, mestizo and mulatto laborers, and the indigenous, although required to render tribute and personal and public service, had little appreciation for the new ideas and tended to remain loyal to the authority of the monarchy and the church.

Indeed, there was advantage to those of low degree in Bourbon policies concerning social mobility. Freed blacks and mulattoes were entitled to purchase certificates of whiteness and to enjoy the legal privileges associated with that status. Mestizos eagerly sought documentation of their identity in order that they not be considered indigenous and be required to pay tribute or render involuntary service. Baptismal records were important to such proceedings, and churches kept separate registers for each group. Many whites refused to go to church for baptism but held private ceremonies so as not to be associated with those who sought to improve their status by such means. While this policy improved the legal situation of persons on the bottom of the social scale, it also hardened the attitudes of the privileged and, in the case of the insular society of Cuba, which had large black and mulatto populations, diminished enthusiasm for separation from Spain.

None of these factors was a sufficient cause for the eventual revolt against Spanish rule, but all were important. There was no revolt against the church, nor were the motives for revolt against Spanish rule ostensibly religious. When the decisive rupture did come to New Spain it was primarily the result of Creole anxiety that the liberal Spanish constitution of 1812 might be implemented to the detriment of their privilege. The role of ideology was subordinate to pragmatic considerations in the independence of New Spain, although ideas and political philosophies did matter in the struggle, and care was taken to assert the value placed upon the Catholic faith as the religious center of the society.

THE CHURCH AND INDEPENDENCE

If the struggle for independence came to fruition as the conservative reaction of Creole aristocrats, it began as a genuine social revolution. Events on the Iberian Peninsula provided the occasion for revolt. In March 1808 popular resentment against the dictatorial government of Manuel de Godoy, prime minister to the ineffectual Charles IV, and lover of the queen, erupted in a demonstration that resulted in the king's abdication in favor of his son, Ferdinand VII. Napoleon took advantage of the situation, forced Ferdinand to abdicate along with his father, and installed Joseph Bonaparte as king of Spain. In June 1808 a popular rebellion against the French established a provisional government that claimed authority to rule as regent for the deposed Ferdinand VII. In 1810, with the convocation of the Cortes (parliament) at Cádiz and the enactment of the constitution of 1812, the principle of national sovereignty was asserted as the grounds for legitimate political authority and freedom of speech, the press, and the right to assembly were guaranteed. From 1808 to 1814 there were two governments in Spain, that of Joseph Bonaparte, and the Cortes of Cádiz (actually, from 1808 to 1810 the Supreme Central Junta preceded the Cortes).

In 1814 Napoleon's ill-fated peninsular campaign ended and Ferdinand VII was restored as king of Spain. But there were deep political divisions in the nation. The masses seeking fundamental social transformation had emerged as a significant factor in the equation. Among the supporters of monarchy there were absolutists and constitutionalists. Some liberals were constitutional monarchists, others republicans. There was controversy concerning the proper relationship of the state to the religious establishment, some preferring the traditional pattern, others a separation and secularization of the state. Just as there was factionalism on the peninsula, so in New Spain.

As Creoles argued among themselves and with peninsular Spaniards about appropriate action in the face of political upheavals in Spain, Miguel Hidalgo y Costilla, himself a Creole priest, and a group of conspirators, also Creoles, plotted to overthrow the Spanish vice-regal administration in Mexico City in 1810. Hidalgo, who served in an important mining and agricultural area, knew the plight of the indigenous and resolved that a primary objective of the movement must be justice for them. His views were tolerated by his co-conspirators because they needed the indigenous to bear arms in the conflict, but when the undisciplined ferocity of indigenous anger against all who had participated in their oppression was unleashed, all but a few Creoles abandoned the fray.

Hidalgo's social agenda included the abolition of indigenous tribute and slavery as well as the seizure and redistribution of European property. With a real sense of the religiosity of the masses and their devotion to Our Lady of Guadalupe of Tepeyac, he took her banner and used it as the emblem of the revolution.

Not all the masses were responsive to Hidalgo's leadership. Many of the more conservative and land-bound indigenous in Puebla and southern Mexico were cool to the struggle. Even reformist elements in the church hierarchy were repulsed by the violence of the movement and repudiated Hidalgo, who was finally excommunicated and executed by Spanish troops in 1811.

The revolution did not die with Hidalgo. Several of the military leaders allied with him continued guerrilla actions throughout the country and the mantle of leadership passed to yet another priest, José María Morelos y Pavón, a mestizo. Morelos was a passionate nationalist who understood the religious center of Mexican identity. He was devoted to Our Lady of Guadalupe and recognized her as the sign of God's special favor for Mexico as well as the national symbol. The struggle for independence was a holy war, and in the program proposed to the Congress of Chilpancingo in 1813, Morelos advocated support for the Catholic religion through the payment of the tithe.

Unlike Hidalgo, Morelos displayed a cooperative attitude toward the Creole elites and sought to enlist their support. His social program, however, was not different from that of Hidalgo's. Indeed, he sought to establish a legal framework that would abolish all distinctions among the castes. His program was too liberal for most Creoles; and his understanding of Christian faith as a demand for social justice was too much for the vested interests of the institutional church.

With the restoration of Ferdinand VII to the Spanish throne in 1814, royalist elements in Mexico were strengthened in their resolve and their ability to put down the rebellion. In 1815 Morelos was defeated and executed. For the moment Mexico was saved for Spain, preserved by royalist Creoles.

The church emerged from the struggle as the most conservative and effective political institution in New Spain. The division between hierarchy, lesser clergy, and the devoted masses of peasants was profound, but ecclesial structures were intact and privilege secure. Hidalgo's and Morelos' visions of a church committed to social justice and revolution appeared dead.

Yet another change in the volatile politics of the peninsula frightened the conservative Creoles and drove them to complete the process of separation from the mother country. In 1820 a liberal revolt in Spain resulted in the restoration of the constitution of 1812 and the reconvening of the Cortes. Actions were taken that sharply limited ecclesial power and privilege: prohibitions against the establishment of new chapels and pious foundations were enacted; the Inquisition was abolished; all religious orders were suppressed; clerical immunity from prosecution by civil authority in criminal cases was abolished; property of those opposed to the constitution was confiscated; freedom of the press was established. The Cortes also acted against the privileges enjoyed by the military and other secular interests. In the colonies suffrage was extended to the indigenous and the castes. The cumulative effect was to persuade the Creole aristocracy of Mexico that it must declare its independence in order to preserve its heritage and way of life.

In 1821 an opportunistic Creole professional soldier, Agustín de Iturbide, negotiated secretly for the support of the rebel leader Vicente Guerrero, persuaded his own troops to abandon the royalist cause, and formulated his Plan of Iguala as the basis for an independent nation. The plan's three guarantees were that Mexico was to be Catholic, a constitutional monarchy, and united—all inhabitants of the nation were equally to share the benefits of citizenship. By 1822 Mexico's congress had adopted the plan and elected Iturbide Agustín I, constitutional emperor of Mexico. The revolution had been stymied, but Mexico was independent.

The kingdom of Guatemala, which encompassed the present-day Central American nations of Guatemala, El Salvador, Honduras, Nicaragua, and Costa Rica, had been in turmoil throughout the colonial era, especially during the period of Bourbon rule in the eighteenth century. Creoles were divided among themselves concerning issues of trade and political organization. Factional and regional disputes among the provinces fed the sense of ambivalence with which the oligarchy greeted Mexican independence. Guatemalan merchants, liberal in their advocacy of free trade but conservative in their valuing of the traditions of Spain and in their desire to protect the hegemony of Guatemala, led the nation into union with Iturbide's conservative Mexican empire and independence from then liberal Spain. More liberal elements that favored a federal republic gave reluctant support to the Mexican union in order to stave off a threatened invasion by Spanish imperial troops. San Salvador, which did resist incorporation into the empire, was occupied, first by Guatemalan forces, then by Mexican, and was compelled to become a part of the Mexican empire.

The Guatemalan hierarchy, like the Mexican, recognized the threat to ecclesial privilege in the efforts of Spanish liberals to enact the provisions of the constitution of 1812 and supported the decision to align the nation with Catholic Mexico.

Iturbide's reign was short-lived. Within ten months of his accession, he was forced to abdicate. Congress resisted his royal pretensions and refused to provide the finances necessary to support them. In 1824 new constitutions in Mexico and Guatemala established the separate federal republics of Mexico and the United Provinces of Central America.

Each of the new republics entered a period of inner turmoil as rival factions sought to assert their interests. Conflict developed along the lines of the old liberal and conservative splits that had characterized the Bourbon century. Conservatives, generally the Creole aristocrats and the higher clergy, supported programs designed to preserve old patterns of privilege and position. Liberals, a less-well-defined anticlerical group of merchants advocating free trade and intellectuals enamored of the republican experiments in the United States and France, tended to continue the reforms initiated by the Bourbons. The constitutions of 1824 were essentially liberal documents, but neither party in either of the new nations was strong enough actually to gain control and maintain itself in power.

The church as an institution was profoundly affected by independence. Its fortunes fluctuated with the ebb and flow of political power. When conservative governments were in power, it enjoyed privilege and respect, but when liberal governments presided, it experienced severe limitation. But regardless of the party in power, the church would not again hold the status it did even in the Bourbon regime. Even conservative governments felt it necessary to lay claim upon church wealth in an effort to solve the overwhelming economic problems confronting the new states, and in the prolonged struggle over the rights of patronage the church lost institutional strength while sees remained vacant and parishes were left without adequate pastoral attention.

The Mexican and Central American constitutions both provided that the Roman Catholic faith should be the religion of the nation, but neither was regarded as adequate by the church. The Mexican constitution guaranteed ecclesial privilege in judicial proceedings but reserved to the state the right to enter into concordats, to give permission for the promulgation of papal decrees, and to exercise the rights of patronage. The church was deprived of exclusive control over education. Beyond establishing the Roman Catholic faith as the state religion, the Central American constitution said nothing else about religion; but that produced a situation in which there was considerable dispute between the federal government and the provinces over patronage. Both nations clearly intended to control the church.

In Central America the liberals' assault on the church contributed not only to their loss of power but to the destruction of the federal union. Francisco Morazán, elected federal president in 1829, undertook a vindictive campaign against the church in retaliation for its support of the conservative government of the previous four years. That government had reinstituted privileges the church had enjoyed in the colonial period. Morazán revoked those privileges, sent anti-liberal clerics, including the archbishop, into exile, suppressed the monastic orders, established religious freedom in the nation, and encouraged the provinces to institute their own repressive measures. Church correspondence was censured; celebration of feast days was prohibited; church property and funds were seized; the state ceased to collect the tithe; civil marriage was authorized and divorce legalized; education was secularized.

Not only did that program arouse the clergy, but it also offended the indigenous and ladino (mestizo) masses, who entrusted to their priests political as well as religious leadership. Peasant rebellions that erupted in the highlands of Guatemala received the support of the priests. Rafael Carrera became the leader of the revolt as it became a more general conflict and eventually succeeded in defeating Morazán. By 1840 the United Provinces of Central America had disintegrated into the five independent nations of Guatemala, El Salvador, Honduras, Nicaragua, and Costa Rica that presently exist. Though varying in intensity, the conservative reaction against the liberal agenda extended throughout Central America. Guatemala, traditionally the most conservative province, went furthest in restoring the institutions and ideals of the colonial past, but in every state a restoration occurred. Although that was to change again as liberals gained ascendancy in the latter third of the nineteenth century, a significant social transformation resulted from the struggle: ladinos were accepted in leadership roles by the aristocrats. Never again would political power be monopolized by Creole elites.

The church was not responsible for that transformation, but it was associated with it. The social programs implemented through the church under the aegis of the conservative governments were paternalistic in their approach to the masses, but they did represent a concern that had been lacking and, in a sense, manifested a respect for the value of indigenous traditions that the liberals in their zeal for assimilation and acculturation did not have.

Ironically, the reestablishment of the University of San Carlos (1843) and the opening of new universities in Costa Rica (1843), El Salvador (1847), and Honduras (1847) provided a setting within which a new liberal leadership was formed. The restored Hispanic Catholic cultural matrix nourished intellectual developments and political vision that resulted in a liberal restoration which endures to the present.

With the ascendancy of the liberals, the privilege and power of the church were once again reduced. Clerics were restricted from wearing their garb except in the performance of their religious duties; religious processions were banned; civil marriage was made compulsory; religious toleration was instituted; Protestants were encouraged to immigrate and to pursue their missionary interests. Limitations were placed upon the number of clergy permitted to serve in many areas. In short, the church was thoroughly subjected to the power and authority of the state. As an institution, it appeared to have lost its role as a significant actor in political and social life.

As the struggle went on in Central America, Mexico, too, experienced great difficulty in maintaining its unity and integrity as a nation. Separatist movements in Texas and the Yucatán threatened the federal union. Texas, with its aggressive Anglo population, gained independence in 1836; and war with the United States (1846–1848) resulted in the loss of half the national territory. Internally, liberal and conservative elements vied for power. Those sectors of the society that had been suppressed in the independence struggle, primarily the indigenous and mestizos, sought advantage in a system that continued to be oppressive for them.

Gen. Antonio López de Santa Anna, originally a supporter of the Iturbide government, in 1823 led an opportunistic rebellion that resulted in the fall of that government in 1824. From that moment until his self-imposed exile in 1855, Santa Anna was able to exploit the conflicts between liberals and conservatives, between the indigenous and mestizo masses and the Creole elites, to his personal advantage. It was he who lost Texas to the republic in 1836. With the end of his political domination, a new order emerged in Mexico. A mestizo revolution under an indigenous leader, Benito Juárez, began.

The reform did not alter the oppressive circumstances of the indigenous masses, but it did bring to power a new mestizo leadership. In that way it was like the struggle that brought ladinos into the national political arena in Central America; but the reform was unlike the Central American situation in that it sought the repression of the old colonial institutions, especially the church. The Mexican program corresponded to the liberal agenda for the neighboring republics to the south.

Juárez, as minister of justice in the new liberal government, took the first step to limit the autonomy of the church by abolishing clerical immunities from civil justice. The next step was to limit the wealth of the church. In 1856 Miguel Lerdo de Tejada promulgated the *Ley Lerdo* (Lerdo Law), which decreed the sale of all property directly owned by the church. Tenants had priority, but anyone who followed proper procedure could "denounce" the property and purchase it. The objective of the law was not to strip the church of wealth but to change its form. The state itself received little direct economic benefit, only 5 percent on the transfer of possession. It was believed that depriving the church of its real estate would create a new class of owners loyal to the liberal government, and that property would be put to more productive use if placed in private hands.

In an effort at evenhandedness, the *Ley Lerdo* decreed that no estate could be held by any corporation, but only by individuals. The *ejidos*, lands held in common by towns and by indigenous groups, were ordered sold. Despite an effort to divide the indigenous *ejidos* among individual peasants, it was impossible to prevent exploitation by those who by unscrupulous means bought up large tracts of land. Indigenous peoples were thus deprived of their means of support, and the church's real property was converted into liquid assets. With the landholdings going to wealthy capitalists, foreign and national, the result was that a new group of *hacendados* (hacienda owners) became influential in Mexican politics.

Resistance by the indigenous in the provinces was widespread. They and the conservatives represented a potential alliance that threatened the government and its reforms. Response within the church was not uniform. Some especially secular clergy took advantage of the law to purchase property themselves.

Religious resisted and refused to abandon their haciendas. In retaliation for their participation in an alleged conspiracy, Ignacio Comonfort, president of the republic, ordered the Franciscan monastery in Mexico City destroyed in 1856. The property was large, centrally located, and valuable. A new street bisecting the convent was constructed. By this action, an important colonial monument was ruined, a popular symbol of the religious heart of Mexico defaced.

Earlier in the same year, the government put down a reactionary revolt in Puebla. The bishop was banished, but rebellion occurred again. There was resistance in San Luis Potosí, Querétaro, Michoacán, Tlaxcala, and Vera Cruz. For the moment, the government succeeded in quelling the disturbances, but the tranquillity was soon to be disrupted by a violent civil war.

A new constitution gave permanence to the *Lerdo* prohibitions against corporate ownership of land; clerical immunity was abolished; and religious were guaranteed the legal right to renounce their vows. Clerical resistance was strong and direct: any public official who swore an oath of allegiance to the constitution was to be excommunicated. At Easter 1857, President Comonfort and his cabinet were denied entry to the metropolitan cathedral. A reactionary coup ousted the president, who, after belated resistance, was forced into exile.

A reactionary government under the leadership of Félix Zuloaga was installed in Mexico City. His government rescinded the *Ley Lerdo*. But in the provinces there remained support for the constitution of 1857 and the reforming laws. After Comonfort's departure, Benito Juárez, who had been elected president of the supreme court under the new constitution, succeeded to the office. Mexico had its first, and only, indigenous president.

Juárez was forced to govern from Vera Cruz, but he was not deterred in his efforts to liberalize the regime. In 1859 an even more restrictive set of laws against the church was promulgated. The new laws of reform brought about the confiscation, without compensation, of all church property except the actual buildings; all monasteries were immediately closed; convents of nuns were to be closed as members of the communities died; cemeteries were nationalized; civil marriage was instituted.

Juárez's forces prevailed on the field of battle so that he was able to return to Mexico City in January 1860. But once again he would be forced to flee. The conservatives had been scheming with European powers, especially the French, who with Spain and England had determined that it would be necessary to intervene militarily in Mexico in order to recover financial losses incurred by their lending institutions. The intervention began in 1862. Spain and England could not support the ultimate designs of Napoleon III, so they withdrew, leaving France to assist in the effort to reestablish conservative rule in Mexico. That effort eventually led to the imposition of the Habsburg prince Maximilian upon another Mexican throne. But the unpopular enterprise came to a tragic end in 1867.

The church had supported the intervention and the imperial experiment, but it was sorely disappointed. Maximilian, a man of liberal tendencies, refused to restore church properties and proposed to institute freedom of religion. He resisted pressures from the Vatican to restore ecclesial privilege and finally died before a firing squad in Querétaro in 1867 after his pathetically ill consort, Carlotta, tried without success to persuade the pope to intervene.

A major consequence of the imperial interlude was that reform came to be identified, at least symbolically, with national independence. The church as an institution was apparently thoroughly discredited. Juárez returned to Mexico and was reelected president of the republic. Conservatism and clerical privilege were apparently dead. But it was not so.

Juárez died in 1872, after successfully subduing dissident elements that would have subverted his government and the reform. Sebastian Lerdo de Tejada succeeded him but governed so ineffectually that Porfirio Díaz, the ambitious and jealous mestizo general who had participated in the Mexican victory over the French invaders at Puebla on 5 May 1862, declared against him and assumed the presidency in 1876.

The crude but crafty Díaz maintained control of the Mexican presidency until 1910. Key to that control was his skillful accommodation with the church. He did not rescind the laws of reform; he simply left their enforcement to local officials.

The church once again began to acquire wealth through bequests and a "voluntarily" collected tithe. New schools were opened as the church recovered its preeminent role in education. Religious orders were restored and new convents for men and women were opened throughout the republic. Public spectacle on religious feast days became commonplace. Five new archiepiscopal sees and eight new dioceses were established during the Porfiriato (the period of the Díaz regime), more than at any time since the reign of Philip II. Although he refused to resume official diplomatic relations with the Vatican, Díaz maintained close relationships with apostolic delegates to Mexico and enjoyed cordial relations with Rome.

Such a policy was not merely an acknowledgment of the power of the institutional church; it was a recognition of the power of the people's devotion. Notwithstanding the church's persistence in identifying itself with the conservative political tradition that had been so oppressive of the masses throughout the history of the nation, its power as a symbol of faith that sustained, and its sacraments, were fundamental to the self-understanding and well-being of the people. Although severely limited by legal restraints, the church was powerful because it expressed something essential in the national life. Part of Díaz's genius was his recognition, however intuitively, of that fact.

If the Roman Catholic church flourished anew during the Porfiriato, Protestant churches also enjoyed a period of significant growth. Gabino Barreda, a physician entrusted by Benito Juárez with the task of educational reform, had studied in Paris under Auguste Comte. In Mexico City Barreda established the National Preparatory School, where a curriculum based upon positivist principles of intellectual inquiry formed a generation of Mexican intellectuals, the *científicos,* who led the bureaucracy of the Díaz regime. These *científicos* sought to govern on progressive scientific principles, ordering social and economic activity toward the achievement of that stage of human evolution envisioned by Comte in which the myths of theology and the abstractions of metaphysics were abandoned in favor of knowledge based upon concrete observation and experience.

Protestantism, with its rejection of Catholic scholasticism and popular piety, its perceived openness to scientific enquiry, its emphasis on lay education and lay religious vocation to work in secular society, seemed a natural ally in the efforts at reform. Benito Juárez and the reformers had expressed interest in Protestantism and encouraged its growth in Mexico. Part of the attraction was Protestant support for education for indigenous peoples. It was felt that Protestant missionaries were interested in improving their lot rather than in manipulating them for the sake of an institution. In the opinion of some, Mexico needed the influence of the work ethic as a means to the general improvement of the society, and, in purely pragmatic terms, a strong Protestant community would be a religious balance for the Roman Catholic church. Díaz was forthright in acknowledging the latter concern.

The first Mexican Protestant church grew out of efforts to create a national reformed church independent of Rome, but Catholic in tradition. That action, begun in 1859, led to the formation of a Mexican church in 1861 with parishes in Tamaulipas and Mexico City. By 1869 the church had affiliated with the Episcopal church in the United States, which sent its first missionary to Mexico in the same year.

In the 1870s the Methodists, Presbyterians, and Baptists began churches in Mexico. Their activity tended to follow the development of mining and the railroads, partly because the foreign technicians who assisted in those operations were often Protestant, and partly because of a genuine concern for the workers in those industries.

Government support and encouragement did not translate into a popular welcome, and many Protestants were persecuted at the behest of priests and others who felt threatened by the new movement. William Butler, bishop of the Methodist church in Mexico, reported that in the years 1873–1892, fifty-eight Protestants were killed. Of that number, only one was a North American missionary.

In spite of opposition, the new churches took root and grew not only in Mexico, but also in Central America. Although in many places they did not become a statistically significant proportion of the population, their presence and influence were important. By the 1980s their numbers were substantial, especially in Guatemala, where they represented approximately 20 per-

cent of the population. (In Mexico a bit less than 4 percent are Protestant.)

Indeed, in the case of Guatemala and the rest of Central America, Protestant Christianity has become a significant factor in the struggle for justice. Protestant groups are affiliated with both the forces of reaction and of revolutionary change. In either case, evangelical Christians, as they style themselves, cannot be ignored in twentieth-century Hispanic America.

Inevitably, the growth of Protestantism is associated with the extension of U.S. influence and economic domination of the region. The two developments were coincident and, to an extent, interrelated. The organic unity that obtained between the Roman Catholic church and other Spanish institutions in the colonial period in Hispanic America was not characteristic of the relationship between Protestant missionary activity and the growth of U.S. economic power and political influence. But, beginning with the Mexican Revolution in 1911, growth of the latter was accompanied by significant Protestant growth as well as involvement by the U.S. government and Catholic hierarchy in the affairs of the Roman Catholic church in Hispanic America.

By the end of the nineteenth century all of the former viceroyalty of New Spain had become independent of Spain. The island of Hispaniola, site of the first Spanish settlement in the New World in 1492, had been torn by conflict among the competing colonial powers of Spain, France, and England. It was eventually divided by the Treaty of Ryswick (1697) between France and Spain. Spain held the eastern portion of the island, which eventually freed itself from colonial rule in 1865 and became the Dominican Republic.

The western end of the island, Haiti, achieved independence in 1804 and, after continued conflict with Spain and France, was recognized by France in 1825. The success of Haiti's former black slaves was a factor in the political conservatism of Puerto Rico and Cuba, which did not gain independence until Spain was defeated in the Spanish-American War of 1898. Cuba became an independent nation, though until the revolution of 1959 it was in continual conflict with the United States over the exercise of full sovereignty. Puerto Rico was a U.S. colony until

1952, when it became a commonwealth, a free and associated state, of the United States.

In Cuba and Puerto Rico, one of the principal impediments to earlier independence was the attitude of the clergy, especially the hierarchy. In both cases the majority of priests and bishops were Spaniards. The few Creole clergy were Hispanicized and loyal to the Crown. That loyalty was as much a function of class affiliation and racial prejudice as of philosophical or theological conviction. The specter of black revolution of the sort that had occurred in Haiti tended to ensure loyalty to the monarchy as the guarantee of stability and protection of the status quo.

Even after independence, the Cuban and Puerto Rican clergy maintained their allegiance to Spain and the Hispanic tradition. Most priests continued to be Spanish either in national identity or by education. Many harbored the dream that Spain would return to reincorporate the islands into the realm. Such attitudes, coupled with the reality that the church had never really penetrated the countryside, meant that the church's influence was essentially limited to the urban elites. The rural masses, primarily peasant farmers and field hands, found meaning in popular religiosity rooted in Hispanic and African traditions. They had little need for, or appreciation of, the institutional church.

Those elites who were involved in the independence struggle found support in Masonic lodges, not in the church, and while they were not hostile to the church, they found it to be fundamentally irrelevant. Freemasonry had been introduced into Cuba during the brief English occupation of the island in 1762–1763. The lodges established there, and elsewhere in Hispanic America in the early nineteenth century, became important centers for the dissemination of liberal ideas and the development of relationships among men of influence. Most Hispanic American lodges developed out of Spanish, not English, roots, though in Spain itself English and French Masonry came into conflict during the Napoleonic period, 1808–1814, and the succeeding struggle to define the nature of the reestablished Bourbon monarchy. Many Spanish liberals, some of them Masons, who had advocated constitutional government went into exile in Hispanic America and established lodges. Other lodges were established by Spanish troops sent to put down the rebellions that marked the beginning of the wars for independence.

Masonry in Hispanic America reflected its complex origins. Not all lodges were supportive of independence. Some, especially of the Scottish Rite in Mexico, were sympathetic to Spain and were advocates of the monarchy; others were republican and loyalist; others, advocates of independence. But whatever their vision of the ideal state, all the lodges provided a space free from the clerical authority of the church within which to pursue ideas and to consider political, economic, and social issues of importance to the nation.

By the beginning of the twentieth century the old Bourbon program of limiting the power and influence of the church had been accomplished. Although Roman Catholicism enjoyed a constitutionally privileged place in most of the successor states to the viceroyalty, it did not have the institutional means to capitalize on that privilege. Protestantism had become a factor everywhere in the region. Many supporters of Cuban independence went into exile in the United States, where they were influenced by Protestant Christianity and became instrumental in introducing non-Catholic churches to the island.

The religious center of the culture continued to be people's deep devotion to those elements of the Catholic tradition that they understood and appropriated as their own. There was great residual power in the church, but it was a power essentially unrecognized by the institution. When that power did manifest itself, revolutionary transformations occurred.

THE CHURCH AND REVOLUTION

Mexico was the first of the new Hispanic-American republics to experience social revolution. The incipient movement that had been suppressed by the Creole reaction during the wars of independence erupted again in the violent conflicts of 1910–1929. If liberalism and conservatism had been in conflict in the nineteenth-century reform, now liberalism became the new conservatism.

The church as institution benefited greatly from its tacit alliance with Porfirio Díaz. There was no enthusiasm in the hierarchy for the revolution of Francisco Madero. Madero himself was an improbable revolutionary. Scion of a wealthy Creole family from Coahuila, he was an unimposing person who, unlike the rest of his family, was given to altruistic treatment of the workers on the cotton plantation that he managed. Altruism notwithstanding, Madero seemed not to understand the seriousness of the economic and social problems confronting his country, but he did sense the political sentiment of the times. In 1908 he published a little book, *The Presidential Succession of 1910,* that argued for the open election of a vice president in the presidential election of 1910 as a step toward breaking the dictatorial control Díaz exercised over the electoral process. The book sparked a nationwide response and Madero found himself something of a hero, touring the republic making speeches and organizing clubs dedicated to the principle that Mexican presidents should be ineligible for reelection, the position that Porfirio Díaz himself had advocated in 1876, the year of his first election. In 1910 the no-reelection movement held a national convention and nominated Madero as its candidate for the presidency.

Díaz was unprepared for the popular response to Madero's candidacy. After a mass rally of no-reelectionists in front of the National Palace, he had Madero arrested and imprisoned on the charge of planning an armed rebellion. Díaz proceeded with the election and won yet another term as president. Meanwhile, Madero had been released on bond and from his refuge in San Antonio, Texas, declared himself provisional president on the grounds that the election was invalid. Response was slow, but before the end of the year 1910 Pascual Orozco, a storekeeper, and Francisco "Pancho" Villa, who as a young man had escaped debt peonage and had established a reputation by rustling cattle from the hacienda of the principal landholding family of the region, began a revolutionary movement in the state of Chihuahua. Emiliano Zapata, a peasant sugar worker, had done the same in the state of Morelos. These two movements represented, in a way that Madero's no-reelection campaign did not, the deeply experienced frustration and oppression felt by the campesino masses of Mexico. They expressed the hope for a real revolution that would transform the social order. Zapata's slogan, *Tierra y Libertad* (Land and Liberty), reflected a more far-reaching vision than

the desire merely to establish free and open elections. By the spring of 1911 guerrilla activity was widespread throughout the nation.

In the negotiations that ended the uprising it was agreed that Díaz would resign and that a provisional president would serve until a new election could be held. In November 1911 Madero was finally elected president of the Republic of Mexico. Zapata and Villa were quiet for a while, but not for long.

Madero had no real appreciation of the social forces that had been mobilized to elect him. Although he had spoken of the need to restore lands taken from indigenous villages, his program amounted to little more than a reassertion of the positions of the reform under Juarez. That made him unpopular with the church hierarchy, whose tacit alliance with the Díaz regime had greatly benefited the institution. In 1912 Zapata began again the struggle for land reform. Yet another group, the incipient Social Action movement, took advantage of the new openness to pursue its objectives, but it was not supportive of Madero either.

Catholic Social Action had begun in Europe as a movement of lay persons who were concerned that the church respond to the social consequences of industrial capitalism. The movement shared the negative judgment upon liberalism and socialism that had been expressed in the *Syllabus of Errors* issued by Pius IX in 1864. Without disputing the position taken by the pope, Social Action sought a positive "Catholic" solution to the problems that liberalism and socialism addressed from their secular perspectives. In 1891 Pope Leo XIII issued his landmark encyclical *Rerum Novarum* in part as a magisterial statement of the concern that had been expressed in the Social Action movement. That action at once gave sanction to the movement and established the authority of the church's hierarchy over it.

Rerum Novarum offered a "third way" between liberal and socialistic responses to the problems of industrializing societies. It emphasized the family as the basis of society and private property as a natural right necessary for the support of the family. It advocated a just wage sufficient to support a "frugal and well-behaved worker." The right of workers as well as employers to form associations and to bargain collectively for wages was affirmed, though syndicalism was rejected. The church itself was the institutional context within which such groups were to function. If it was the duty of the church to respond to the moral demands of the society, the duty of the state was to ensure justice. Further to support the centrality of the family in society, the encyclical maintained that the natural place of women was in the home and enjoined child labor until such time as their "bodies and minds are sufficiently developed."

In precise accord with papal teaching, the Social Action movement began in Mexico with the organization of the unions of Catholic men and Catholic women that met in the Catholic congresses of 1903, 1904, 1906, and 1909. The concepts of family and private property were its governing principles. Workers were encouraged to consider themselves a family and were urged to shun labor unions in favor of workers' associations within the embrace of the church. In the process of negotiation, the rights of property owners were to be considered along with those of the workers. Accommodations were to be made so as to avoid class conflict and to preserve the social fabric.

The fundamental changes necessary to produce a more just distribution of resources in a society like Mexico's would be slow in coming under such a system. Most workers in Mexico were rural, while the Social Action program was governed by the ideals of the more highly urban and industrialized societies of Europe. The proposed redistribution of land among the peasants provided no mechanism by which the workers might acquire the means to purchase their family plots. Expropriation and redistribution by the state, as envisioned by Emiliano Zapata, were not an option.

Notwithstanding the shortcomings of Social Action, a Catholic party was formed and offered candidates in the national elections of 1911 and the congressional elections of 1912. Although the Roman Catholic hierarchy disavowed any official relationship, the party platform was clearly the Social Action program, and bishops in their pastoral counsel urged the faithful to consider seriously the church's teachings as they voted. The national campaign was unsuccessful, but members of the Catholic party were elected to the congress, and in the state of Jalisco the party prevailed.

Events moved too quickly for the Social Action movement to sustain its efforts. Madero was overthrown and assassinated, and the devious Victoriano Huerta emerged as chief of state. Huerta was a drug user, an alcoholic, but also an effective military commander. In 1901 he had subjugated the last of the Maya in the Yucatán and in 1912 put down rebellions against Madero in Chihuahua and Morelos. It was on the occasion of another rebellion in Mexico City that Maderos was forced reluctantly to place Huerta in command of the troops at the National Palace. From that vantage point he subjected the city to ten days of terror, 9–18 February 1912, as he exchanged cannon fire with the rebels who had taken refuge about a mile away in the Ciudadela. Huerta used that episode as an occasion to manuever himself into position to assume the presidency upon Madero's death. Vicious and ruthless though he was, the church hierarchy was delighted. The liberals were defeated, and Huerta was strong enough to withstand the resistance of the radical "socialist" *zapatistas.*

If the hierarchy saw in Huerta a new champion, the revolutionaries did not. New figures who were to become important to the revolution joined the struggle, Venustiano Carranza, Álvaro Obregón, and Plutarco Elías Calles among them. Carranza, a landowner and the governor of Coahuila, had been a senator during the Díaz regime. He had joined Madero in 1911 and, with a small force that he had at his disposal, determined to overthrow Huerta. Carranza proclaimed himself First Chief of the Constitutionalist Army. Obregón, a young Sonoran rancher who had assisted in putting down the 1911 rebellion in Chihuahua, responded to Carranza's initiative and was placed in command of the Army of the Northwest. Calles, part of a cadre of young leaders in alliance with Obregon, became commander of the forces in the state of Sonora. Villa commanded the Army of the North. These leaders styled themselves Constitutionalists, claiming to defend the constitution of 1857. In a vicious and bloody military campaign, the Constitutionalists prevailed and succeeded in installing Carranza as provisional president of the republic.

Partly in retaliation for the support given by clergy to Huerta, Constitutionalist forces, especially Villa's, subjected priests and religious, men and women alike, to persecution and demeaning treatment. The propaganda generated out of that circumstance led Catholics in the

United States into an antirevolutionary stance and caused them to place heavy pressure on the administration of Woodrow Wilson to intervene in Mexico and to refuse recognition to Carranza. Beyond that, Villa and Zapata were regarded as socialists who were, by all means, to be resisted.

Indeed, within Mexico, fear of socialism among those in Social Action contributed to their support for Huerta and to their, and the hierarchy's, eventual refusal to support any revolutionary leader. That refusal surely contributed to the severity of the actions against the church authorized in the constitution of 1917.

The reform laws of 1859 had placed strict limits on the privileges of the clergy and deprived the church of its property, but the constitution of 1917 subjected the church utterly to the control of the state. The anticlerical provisions of the laws of reform were reaffirmed and extended. Not only was the clergy prohibited from owning property, but church buildings themselves were declared the property of the state. Priests could not organize political parties or control primary schools; they were required to register with the state; each state had the authority to limit the number of clergy permitted to function within its jurisdiction; foreign priests were prohibited.

Carranza did little to enforce the religious provisions of the constitution, but his successors, Obregón and Calles, were determined in their efforts to limit the power and influence of the church. There were many points of conflict. Priests encouraged peasants to reject the land they were offered in the redistribution program, and laborers were encouraged to affiliate with church-sponsored organizations rather than those offered by the government. In short, Social Action was presented as the alternative to the new constitution. Antagonism erupted into open, violent conflict in 1926, when Calles decided to enforce the constitutional provisions requiring the registration of clergy and the prohibitions against foreign priests and religious. The bishops of Mexico responded by announcing that after 31 July 1926 religious services requiring priestly function would be suspended. Mexicans were encouraged to join an economic boycott that had been announced by the Liga Nacional Defensora de la Libertad Religiosa, a lay group formed for the defense of church interests.

The church strike lasted for three years, and Mexico was subjected to yet another civil war as restless generals seized upon the opportunity to militarize the conflict. Leaders of the Liga Nacional, despairing of success through the boycott, decided that armed resistance was necessary. They formed a War Committee to coordinate the effort to overthrow the Calles government. The National Army of Liberation was established and young men were enlisted as soldiers of Cristo Rey (Christ the King), or *cristeros*. Their slogan, "Viva Cristo Rey!" rallied many to the cause. The conflict was violent and divisive, but in some respects it was more a Creole movement against government policy than a mass protest. The impoverished masses were generally content with their popular devotions to the saints and other forms of religious practice that did not require the services of priests, though they, too, were disturbed by the government's assault on the clergy.

Once again, Catholics in the United States were alarmed and urged action in support of their beleaguered sisters and brothers. In 1929 Ambassador Dwight Morrow was instrumental in negotiating a peaceful settlement to the conflict and achieving a modus vivendi by which the church and the state have been able to function until the present moment. Although the constitutional provisions affecting the church would remain intact, clergy would comply with the requirement to register and the state would register no one not approved by proper religious authority. Religious education was permitted in church buildings. Many church schools operated openly under the official cover of a civil society in which was vested ownership of the property.

It appeared in 1930 that the accommodations achieved in church-state relations would provide Mexico a period of peace and domestic tranquillity. That was not to be. The one element of the revolutionary program pursued with real vigor was the effort to limit the power and influence of the clergy. With the *cristero* settlement the national government ceased its harassment of the church, but the constitution gave the states of the republic the authority to limit the number of clergy permitted to serve within their boundaries. Consequently several states, Tabasco notable among them, in 1931–1932 enacted severe anticlerical legislation. Tomás Garrido Canabal, dictatorial governor of Tabasco, organized a Red Shirt group to harass the clergy and enacted legislation that permitted only married clergy to serve within the state. Other states either limited or prohibited the presence of clergy. By 1933 only 197 priests were active in the entire nation.

Circumstances changed with the election of Lázaro Cárdenas to the presidency in 1934. A former cabinet minister and governor of Michoacán, Cárdenas had developed a reputation as an effective and honest leader in his military and political careers. He began the process of adopting a six-year plan at the beginning of the presidential term. Though he was regarded by many as a socialist, his main agenda was simply to enact the revolutionary program of land reform and to support labor in its struggle for justice. Cárdenas gained in respect and popularity with the nationalization of the petroleum industry in 1939. The new archbishop of Mexico, Luis M. Martínez, installed in 1937, reflected the growing support among some clergy when he endorsed Cárdenas' action.

By 1940 church-state relations had improved to such an extent that an active Catholic layman, Miguel Ávila Camacho, was elected to the presidency. Under Camacho the accommodation of 1929 was restored. Anticlerical provisions of the constitution were not repealed, but were rarely enforced. For its part, the church professed an apolitical stance. Finally acknowledging the revolution and determined to live within the limitations it imposed, the hierarchy declared that the consequence was actually beneficial to the spiritual well-being of the church. Certainly the people's devotion continues with great vigor and there is amazingly vital parish life evident as liturgical renewal, new emphases on the role and status of laity, and collegiality among bishops and clergy and between clergy and laity prevail in the post–Vatican II environment.

The Roman Catholic church in Mexico is in some ways stronger than ever. The faith and devotion of the people, not institutional privilege, sustain it in a radically secular state.

Mexican Protestants actively supported the Constitutionalists in the revolution. Many had favored Madero and found little difficulty in aligning themselves with the programs of Carranza, Obregón, and Calles. They found themselves in positions of responsibility within the revolutionary army and the propaganda campaigns of the carrancistas, and played significant roles in developing the postrevolutionary educa-

tional system of Mexico. As the constitution of 1917 limited Roman Catholic clergy, so also it limited Protestant clergy and placed the same restraints on institutional privilege as it had upon the Roman Catholic church. However, the anticlericalism of the regime resonated with the anti-Catholicism of the Protestants to create a mutuality of interest. Protestants felt themselves protected in the revolutionary program precisely because the power and privilege of the Roman Catholic church were attacked.

The alliance with the revolutionary regime was a generally happy one until the administration of Lázaro Cárdenas. Under Cárdenas, the "socialistic" curriculum of public schools required by the constitutional amendment of 1934 was put into effect in a way that compromised the ability of Protestant groups to sustain the schools that they regarded as principal instruments of their evangelistic program. Protestants began defensively to protest their allegiance to the revolution but also to launch an attack on Marxism.

Some Protestants, a minority, were in sympathy with the radical agenda of the populist Cárdenas administration. They formed the Unity and Progress movement, which allied itself with the government's program. That movement evidenced a class division within the Protestant community. Middle-class Protestants oriented toward the value systems of mainline North American churches were more comfortable with the Constitutionalists' program, but lower-class railroad and mine workers, and the growing population of workers migrating to the cities, found Pentecostalism to be a more satisfying form of religious expression and the more radical populist politics a better response to their perceived needs.

Despite the growth of marginated population in Mexico, and the increased size and influence of Pentecostalism in that population, the earlier affinity for the political activism of a Cárdenas has waned, and those groups have become passive supporters of the status quo.

Minority groups within the Roman Catholic and Protestant churches have responded positively to the revolutionary stance taken by the Latin American Episcopal Conference at Medellín, Colombia in 1968, where it was determined that the church should ally itself with the poor in their struggle for justice. An important out-

217

growth of the bishop's decision was a pastoral strategy that promoted the organization of Ecclesial Communities of the Base (Comunidades Ecclesiales de la Base), small neighborhood gatherings of lay people, often without the direct involvement of clergy, for the purpose of studying the Bible and reflecting upon the implications of the Scriptures for the situation in which they live. In these Ecclesial Communities, a process of consciousness-raising developed that led people to understand themselves as agents of their own destiny and competent to act against an oppressive system. As people understood the political implications of their faith, they sought changes that would lead to a more just social order. Governmental authorities tended to view these groups with suspicion as centers of subversion and began to harass them and the church leadership they believed to be responsible for promoting revolution. There are active Ecclesial Communities of the Base in Mexico, but on the whole neither the Roman Catholic nor the Protestant institutions have risked serious encounter with the government, partly out of fear that constitutional restrictions on the churches would be invoked and the modus vivendi destroyed.

If the Mexican revolution was the first real social revolution in Hispanic America, the Cuban revolution of 1959 was the first socialist one in the region. Although not avowedly Marxist at the outset, Fidel Castro's 26th of July movement resulted in the overthrow of the unpopular government of Fulgencio Batista and the creation of a Marxist regime with the sponsorship of the Soviet Union. The turn to communism was the consequence of a complex set of pragmatic and ideological considerations, not of a preconceived design to establish such a regime.

Independent Cuba had been controlled by U.S. political and economic interests and was governed by persons who cooperated in the protection of those interests. Even before independence from Spain, the United States had become the chief consumer of Cuban sugar, so that afterward the bonds of economic dependence became even more important. Most of Cuba's agricultural land was devoted to sugar production; it was necessary to import food; manufacturing was almost exclusively sugar refining. The demand for labor was seasonal, which meant that most Cubans, certainly in rural areas, were unemployed for significant periods of the year;

and wages were inadequate when there was employment. Prices were controlled by demand in the United States. Reciprocal trade agreements that bound the United States and Cuban economies even more tightly were negotiated in 1903. The benefits from such arrangements reached only a privileged elite and, to an extent, the urban middle class.

Politically, the Cuban constitution of 1901 incorporated terms imposed by the U.S. government as a condition of ending the military occupation of the island. The Platt Amendment provided, among other things, that the United States should be permitted to maintain two military installations and that it should have the right to intervene "for the preservation of Cuban independence, the maintenance of a government adequate to the protection of life, property, and individual liberty." This serious limitation upon sovereignty for the new nation fed the nationalistic sentiments of all Cubans and stirred resentment even in those sectors of the society that benefited from the arrangement.

In 1933 a nationalistic revolt led by students of the national university, intellectuals, labor, and enlisted personnel in the army, with the complicity of the U.S. government, forced the resignation of President Gerardo Machado because of dissatisfaction with his dictatorial control of the government and Cuban society. When the clique of political and military leaders that had provided the power base for the Machado government installed one of their own in the presidency, there was renewed protest. A barracks revolt led by Sgt. Fulgencio Batista, a self-made man of humble Cuban-Chinese ancestry, led to the overthrow of the government and the installation of a well-meaning but ineffectual university professor, Ramón Grau San Martín, as provisional president. Grau, though popular with the students, was not acceptable to the United States. Sumner Welles, special envoy sent by President Franklin D. Roosevelt to help resolve the crisis of the Machado regime, encouraged Batista to stage a coup. This began an alliance between Batista, the Cuban army, and the United States that resulted in Batista's emergence as the dominant figure in Cuban politics from 1934 to 1959. With Batista in control, the United States abrogated the Platt Amendment in 1936, but retained the Guantánamo naval installation.

During the Batista years there was prosperity for some Cubans who benefited from the sugar industry, but for most the situation became increasingly difficult. Outside the cities there was little or no health care or educational opportunity. The situation of the laborer was no better than it had been in the nineteenth century. To maintain his position, Batista governed in the interest of the United States–dominated sugar industry, suspending the constitution in 1957 in the effort to control growing unrest and to put down the guerrilla movement led by Fidel Castro. Finally on 1 January 1959 the government collapsed and Batista and his family fled to the Dominican Republic.

For Hispanic America the Cuban revolution was important not because Cuba became Marxist but because the revolution represented the first successful effort of a Latin American nation to free itself from economic and political domination by the United States. Cuba became a symbol of the hope cherished by many that a new order in which Hispanic Americans might determine their own destiny was on the horizon. Cuba was dependent upon the economic support of the Soviets, but it had undertaken a social transformation that was distinctively its own.

One aspect of that distinctiveness was the attitude of Castro toward religion as a factor in the revolutionary struggle. Although the Catholic church emerged after independence as an ineffectual foreign institution, it did provide critical services for the nation. Catholic schools did much to shape the attitudes of young people and to provide an arena within which to develop value systems that would undergird the society. Castro was the product of those schools. His revolutionary program was not anticlerical. Indeed, Roman Catholic priests and lay people were part of the movement from the outset.

Catholic Social Action and many of the lesser clergy, especially secular priests, had been active in their resistance to the Batista dictatorship as it was reestablished by the 1952 coup. The hierarchy was divided, though not uncritical of the regime. Monseñor Pérez Serantes, archbishop of Santiago, had intervened personally with the military authorities to secure the guarantee of a trial for Castro and his conspirators after the abortive raid on the Moncada barracks in 1953. That intervention saved the fugitives from being shot on sight and helped to facilitate their amnesty after sentencing. When the guerrilla band returned from Mexico in 1956, Serantes was among those who were supportive of their efforts. In fact, there was widespread support for the 26th of July movement from all sectors of the population.

Sympathy for the revolution began to cool within the church in the face of the executions of 1959, the threat to private schools, and agrarian reform laws that evidenced communist tendencies. The Catholic congress of November 1959, with Castro and President Osvaldo Dórticos and the cabinet in attendance, turned into a public rally for a "Catholic Cuba." Other confrontations, including the participation of Catholic clergy, along with at least one Methodist pastor, in the abortive Bay of Pigs invasion of April 1961 widened the gulf between the revolutionary government and the church. Then, in May 1961, Cuba was declared a socialist republic and all private schools were confiscated. A great exodus of priests and religious ensued, although very few were actually sent into exile. Even Archbishop Serantes had become an outspoken opponent of the regime.

Withal, diplomatic relations between the Cuban government and the Vatican were maintained. During the years 1962–1965 tensions eased, and an accommodation between the church and the government was developing. The government proclaimed its commitment to the free exercise of religion within constraints not unlike those imposed by the Mexican laws of reform and established by the constitution of 1917. Church activity was restricted to church grounds and facilities.

Suspicion and distrust developed again in 1965 when a young Cuban priest, ordained in the United States, was admitted to Cuba. His intention to collaborate with the U.S. Central Intelligence Agency came to light and interrupted the movement toward a modus vivendi.

During the interval of reduced tension the influential Second Vatican Council began a redefinition of the Roman Catholic church in its relations to the modern world. Two documents, "The Pastoral Constitution of the Church in the Modern World" (*Gaudium et Spes*), adopted by the council in 1965, and the encyclical of Pope Paul VI, "The Progress of Peoples," issued in 1967, were particularly important in opening new horizons for the church in Latin America.

They defined a stance for the church that, in its elaboration by the bishops of Latin America at their 1968 conference at Medellín, would revolutionize historic attitudes concerning the interests of the church. Fundamentally, the church was called on to be less concerned for its privilege and position as an institution and to identify itself with the struggles of the oppressed in Latin America. The institution was to be placed at the service of the people, its power to be understood in terms of its participation in God's activity in human history to achieve justice and to sustain the worth and dignity of all peoples, not in terms of its affiliation with governing authority or of its wealth.

The Cuban hierarchy and some priests participated in the events at Medellín. New perspectives were formed. In 1969 the Cuban bishops issued a pastoral letter to be read in all the churches. It was a landmark document. The Roman Catholic church in Cuba associated itself, not uncritically, with the aims of the revolutionary government to secure justice and well-being for all Cubans. Beyond that, the bishops took the politically daring step of denouncing the economic blockade that had been encouraged by the United States.

Protestant churches on the island took advantage of the pastoral letter to voice their own concerns and to call into question those forces challenging the revolution and its ultimate objectives for the Cuban people.

For his part Castro, at the Intercultural Conference in Havana in January 1968, had articulated a redefinition of the Marxist-Leninist attitude toward religion. He was especially concerned to acknowledge the revolutionary role of certain sectors of the Christian community and to challenge his comrades to abandon their dogmatic prejudices toward religion in the revolutionary process. Camilo Torres, the revolutionary priest in Colombia who had met his death as a guerrilla fighting the Colombian government, was honored by the Cuban regime, his works published. Dom Helder Cámara, archbishop of Recife, Brazil, and an advocate of nonviolent action, was similarly regarded as an exemplar of Christian commitment to revolutionary transformation.

These developments, especially the bishops' pastoral letter, were not well received by everyone, particularly by Catholics in exile, but they marked a turning point in church-state relations in Cuba and indicate the potential for cooperation between Christians and Marxists in the continuing struggle for social and economic justice in Hispanic America.

Just such cooperation is at issue in Central America, for the Nicaraguan revolution of 1979 evidenced an even closer association of Marxists and Christians in the overthrow of Anastasio Somoza Debayle's government and the establishment of a new regime. The Somoza family had been in control of Nicaraguan affairs ever since 1932, when Somoza Debayle's father, Anastasio Somoza García, was placed in command of the National Guard that had been established as an internal police force to replace the U.S. marines that had been withdrawn after over twenty years of occupation. The elder Somoza, sole candidate for the presidency in 1936, was elected and served until he was assassinated in 1956. He was succeeded by his son Luis, who served until 1963, when a Somoza supporter, René Schick Gutiérrez, was elected. When Schick died in 1967 Anastasio Somoza Debayle became president.

During the years of Somoza rule the family acquired vast landholdings and control over much of the nation's commercial enterprise. When an earthquake devastated Managua in 1972, Somoza manipulated much of the aid given to relieve victims of the disaster to his own advantage. He was already unpopular among laborers and students, but then people in the middle class and business leaders began also to be disaffected. In January 1978 Pedro Joaquín Chamorro, editor of *La Prensa,* the country's leading newspaper, was assassinated, apparently at the direction of Somoza's son, who was angered at the paper's exposé of the family's involvement in Plasmaferesis, a company that exported blood. The murder of Chamorro produced a massive protest and helped to galvanize opposition to the government in all sectors of the society.

The opposition, eventually including the church hierarchy as well as the priests and laity involved with the Ecclesial Communities of the Base, found a focus in the activity of the Sandinista National Liberation Front (FSLN), a militant Marxist group organized in 1961 to undertake guerrilla action against the government, to educate peasant workers, and to organize opposition to the regime. In 1979 the FSLN provided the most viable organization around which to coalesce a national revolutionary consensus. Significantly, the movement included many more non-Marxists and was joined by the Roman Catholic church and many Protestant churches as well. After a bitter struggle, with much loss of life, the revolution prevailed. Not only had priests and lay people participated in the Sandinista army, but four priests retained key roles in the cabinet of the revolutionary government, despite the disapproval of the Vatican and their own national hierarchy.

While it is in Nicaragua that the struggle has come to fruition in a new political and social order, the movement is of regional dimensions. Events in El Salvador and Guatemala, though not coordinated with those in Nicaragua, do reflect a common effort to overcome similar situations that have resulted in the marginalization and continued subjugation of peasants, workers, and indigenous peoples especially. A conservative church allied itself with the resistance of such people to the programs of the liberals in the nineteenth century. At that time it sought to regain the privileged position it had enjoyed in the colonial period. In the twentieth century the church, not without considerable ambivalence, champions the cause of such people as a function of its commitment at Medellín to identify itself with the struggles of the poor.

The pastoral efforts of the Roman Catholic and some Protestant churches have been significant in creating the consciousness and sustaining the revolutionary commitment of many engaged in the Central American conflict. Base communities like the one established by Father Ernesto Cardenal on the island of Solentiname in Lake Nicaragua developed throughout the region as a result of the Medellín conference of 1968. The consequence has been the development of a network of committed church people who understand themselves to be involved in a common cause, God's activity in human history to establish justice.

The strength of the movement was such that when the Latin American Episcopal Conference met again in 1979, in Puebla, Mexico, to assess the state of the church in Latin America and to reconsider the position taken a decade earlier at Medellín, it was impossible to retreat from the decision to place the church in solidarity with the poor. Considerable effort had been invested by the bureaucracy of the conference to ensure a different result, but the vitality of the people's conviction would not permit it. Indeed, Puebla

resulted in an even sharper affirmation of the "preferential option for the poor."

The efforts to produce fundamental change in El Salvador were undergirded by such a process. It was Archbishop Oscar Romero's encouragement of and participation in that process which brought him into conflict with his government and ultimately resulted in his assassination in March 1980. Delegates of the Word, lay people trained to lead Ecclesial Communities of the Base in their study of the Scriptures, were abused and murdered throughout the area. In Guatemala the Bible came to be regarded as a subversive book.

While the success of the Nicaraguan revolution is not simply a function of this pastoral activity of the Roman Catholic church, there can be little doubt that it was a critical element in creating the revolution and in sustaining it. The Nicaraguan hierarchy was ambivalent toward the Sandinistas and gave support to the enterprise only after it became evident that many sectors of the society were able to join together in the final stages of the campaign to oust Somoza.

Once the regime was in place, the church hierarchy became outspokenly critical of it, especially of its Marxist affiliations. The government, for its part, has undertaken to maintain its promise to guarantee religious freedom, though it has imposed limitations on the hierarchy's access to and use of public communications media.

Protestant groups have been divided in their attitudes toward the revolution. Groups like the Protestant Committee for Aid and Development have been active in support of the regime. On the other hand, mission groups associated with the Miskitos in eastern Nicaragua have reacted negatively to the interventions of the government. Historically the Miskitos lived relatively free of control by either the Spanish colonial government or the republican governments of Nicaragua. Their territory, the Atlantic coastal region, isolated beyond the mountain ranges separating the Pacific coastal area where Spanish settlement had concentrated, actually was effectively under the control of British commercial interests throughout the eighteenth and nineteenth centuries and on into the twentieth. English is spoken, and Protestant missionaries, especially the Moravians, have developed a significant ministry among the native peoples. As the revolutionary government of Nicaragua has established its control over the eastern half of the country, and especially as it has moved Miskitos away from the Honduran border in the effort to create a protective buffer against invasion, many Miskitos have resisted, and some have joined the effort to overthrow the government.

The eventual outcome of the revolution is difficult to predict. The hierarchy and the majority of the clergy tend increasingly to support counterrevolutionary movements while much of the laity, particularly those who were disadvantaged under the Somoza rule, tend to support the government. It is clear that religious institutions and values continue to play a significant role in the process.

Finally, the growing importance of conservative Protestantism in Central America, with support from parent groups in the United States, must be noted. As the prolonged struggle for justice continues increasingly to be identified with an international communist conspiracy, much support for reactionary movements and governments is engendered. The Ríos-Montt government of Guatemala, although short-lived, partly because of its open promotion of a variety of "born again" Christianity, is an example of this phenomenon.

But not all Protestant groups are caught up in the efforts to see conflict in Central America as a manifestation of an East-West struggle. The Protestant Committee for Aid and Development has been noted as a group committed to the revolution in Nicaragua. The Biblical Seminary of Latin America of San José, Costa Rica, exemplifies a group that began under conservative evangelical auspices but now functions as an autonomous indigenous center for theological education. The faculty and student body of that school risked conflict with their sustaining bodies by declaring their commitment to justice for the oppressed of Central America.

The situation of the churches in the twentieth-century revolutions of Hispanic America illustrates the intrinsic relationship of religious values and institutions to the cultural life of the region. Notwithstanding efforts that began during the period of the Bourbon monarchy to limit the power of the church, it remains a factor to be considered, not only as an institution, but more importantly as a movement of peoples whose faith, however naive or sophisticated, is an essential element in their personal and communal identities. Even in those regimes that would seem to be most antithetical to religion, accommodations have been found, and religious institutions are reinvigorated as significant actors in national life.

BIBLIOGRAPHY

General

Enrique D. Dusell, *A History of the Church in Latin America: Colonialism to Liberation, 1492–1979* (1981); John Lynch, *The Spanish-American Revolutions, 1808–1826* (1973); J. Lloyd Mecham, *Church and State in Latin America* (1934; rev. 1966); Hans-Jürgen Prien, *Die Geschichte des Christentums in Lateinamerika* (1978); Arthur P. Whitaker, ed., *Latin America and the Enlightenment* (1942; 2nd ed., 1961).

Mexico

David C. Bailey, *Viva Cristo Rey! The Cristero Rebellion and the Church-State Conflict in Mexico* (1974); Jean-Pierre Bastian, *Protestantismo y sociedad en México* (1983); Jan Bazant, *Alienation of Church Wealth in Mexico: Social and Economic Aspects of the Liberal Revolution, 1856–1875* (1971); G. Baez Camargo and Kenneth G. Grubb, *Religion in the Republic of Mexico* (1935); Michael P. Costeloe, *Church Wealth in Mexico: A Study of the "Juzgado de Capellanías" of Mexico, 1800–1856* (1967); Jacques Lafaye, *Quetzalcoatl and Guadalupe: The Formation of Mexican National Consciousness, 1531–1813* (1976); Jean A. Meyer, *The Cristero Rebellion: The Mexican People Between Church and State, 1926–1929* (1976); Henry Bamford Parkes, *A History of Mexico* (1969); Robert E. Quirk, *The Mexican Revolution and the Catholic Church, 1910–1929* (1973).

Cuba

J. Merle Davis, *The Cuban Church in a Sugar Economy* (1942); Leslie Dewart, *Christianity and Revolution: The Lesson of Cuba* (1963); Justo L. González, *The Development of Christianity in the Latin Caribbean* (1969); Alice L. Hageman and Philip E. Wheaton, eds., *Religion in Cuba Today: A New Church in a New Society* (1971); Ramón Eduardo Ruiz, *Cuba: The Making of a Revolution* (1968).

Central America

Humberto Belli, *Nicaragua: Christians Under Fire* (n.d.); Philip Berryman, *The Religious Roots of Rebellion: Christians in Central American Revolutions* (1984); James R. Brockman, *The Word Remains: A Life of Oscar Romero* (1982); Penny Lernoux, *Cry of the People: United States Involvement in the Rise of Fascism, Torture, and Murder and the Persecution of the Catholic Church in Latin America* (1980); Pablo Richard and Guillermo Meléndez, eds., *La ilesia de los pobres en América Central* (1982); Ralph Lee Woodward, Jr., *Central America: A Nation Divided* (1976; 2nd ed., 1985); Miles L. Wortman, *Government and Society in Central America, 1680–1840* (1982).
[See also RELIGION IN THE SPANISH EMPIRE.]

FRENCH CATHOLICISM
IN THE NEW WORLD

J. E. Robert Choquette

CATHOLICISM in North America has largely been created and significantly influenced by Frenchmen and their descendants. In late-twentieth-century North America, French Catholicism is primarily found in Canada, especially in the province of Quebec. This should not allow us to forget the pioneering role French Catholics have played since the seventeenth century, not only in all parts of Canada, but in the State of Maine, in the area of the Great Lakes, throughout the valley of the Mississippi River, and in the Caribbean islands.

SEVENTEENTH-CENTURY CATHOLICISM IN FRANCE

Catholicism in France has undergone important changes since the second half of the twelfth century, when popes granted French royalty the title *roi Très Chrétien* (very Christian king), a title that would be given real substance during the reign of Louis IX. This time (the thirteenth century) was also that of the fragmenting of Christendom and of the rise of nation states, leading to the centralized rule of kings who exchanged their roles as suzerains for those of absolute monarchs. Absolutism in France was not, however, despotism. His Most Christian Majesty acknowledged his duties toward God from the day of his anointing, when along with the religious character stamped upon his soul, he swore to defend the church and to "exterminate" heresy in his realm. Royal edicts served as constant reminders of this vocation.

This combination of a royal religious calling and of a French national identity would later be called Gallicanism. By the seventeenth century it consisted of an awareness of the centuries-old rights of the church of France, and not of the growing centralization (ultramontanism) that came to the fore in Roman Catholic theology after the Council of Trent (1545–1563).

The Council of Trent undertook the reformation of the Roman Catholic church in response to the growing dissatisfaction among sixteenth-century Catholics and in reaction to the Protestant Reformation. French Catholics, however, believed that the authority of an ecumenical council was greater than that of the pope, for such a principle safeguarded the prerogatives of their national church. They also believed that their king was sovereign and answered to no man on earth. These principles were reflected in the Concordat of Bologna (1516), signed by King Francis I and Pope Leo X, the document that defined church-state relations in France. This concordat gave His Most Christian Majesty the right to nominate the candidates who would occupy major benefices in the realm—some 100 bishoprics and 500 abbeys by the seventeenth century. Upon receiving the nomination, the pope would issue bulls to the chosen bishops and abbots, who would thereupon swear an oath of allegiance to their king, thereby gaining the civil rights to their ecclesiastical properties. The concordat of 1516 did away with the previous policy of diocesan chapters (or councils of canons) electing bishops; the authority of both the pope and the king was thus reinforced.

In order to be binding, church decisions needed to be promulgated in France, and this required royal consent. Because of its strong Gallican orientation, the church of France never promulgated the texts of the Council of Trent. The latter never became legally binding; the texts were simply "received" by the Assembly of the French clergy.

FRENCH CATHOLICISM IN THE NEW WORLD

Before 1682, the rights of the church of France had not been defined or codified, but were generally understood to include many "autonomous" customs. In addition to the king's prerogatives of controlling church properties and of nominating to major benefices, the royal treasury sometimes seized the revenues of vacant sees; and in 1673 Louis XIV claimed the right of appointing to certain benefices within dioceses whose see was vacant. Gallican sentiment was thus growing in intensity during the seventeenth century, reinforced by the teachings of Edmond Richer and culminating in the Four Gallican Articles (1682), issued by the Assembly of the French clergy (30 October 1681–9 May 1682). These articles claimed that infallibility belongs to the church, and not personally to the pope, and that the church should speak through general councils. The pope was to share his divine authority with bishops, and each national church had the right to dispose of its own revenues. The pope was acknowledged as having the primary honor and jurisdiction within the church, but his authority was neither absolute nor separate and had to be exercised within the framework of traditional church rights and customs.

In spite of its importance, Gallicanism and its related Erastianism were but two of the major factors affecting the church of France in the seventeenth century. (Erastianism, named for the sixteenth-century Swiss theologian Thomas Erastus, held that in a state professing a single religion, civil authorities had exclusive jurisdiction in matters both civil and ecclesiastical.) Another factor that would determine the course of events in North America was the moral, disciplinary, theological, and spiritual renewal of seventeenth-century French Catholicism. Jansenism would prove just as important for one and a half centuries after 1640 but would affect North American affairs only indirectly. Jansenism, named for Cornelius Jansen, author of the *Augustinus* (1640), held that man could not perform God's commandments without special divine assistance and that the operation of this divine grace was irresistible, thus determining man's destiny and denying his freedom. This led to theological pessimism and a strong rigorist tendency in matters of morality and church discipline. Jansenists became the foremost opponents of the Society of Jesus (the Jesuits).

Le grand siècle (as the time of the reign of Louis XIV was called) of French Catholicism was set in the troubled context that followed the Council of Trent and the Wars of Religion (1562–1598), four decades of bloody internal strife in France. The Edict of Nantes, issued by King Henry IV in 1598, marked the beginning of the official religious toleration of the Protestant (Huguenot) minority, a policy that would in effect come to an end under Cardinal Armand Jean du Plessis de Richelieu, who was cardinal from 1622 to 1642, although the edict would be officially revoked by Louis XIV only in 1685.

The Thirty Years War (1618–1648) also raged in Europe, intensifying the insecurity and threats hanging over French people's daily lives. This fearfully horrible war witnessed mercenaries raping and scorching the land while peasants sustained themselves by eating grass, the bark of trees, dead dogs, or even their own children. With a 50 percent rate of infant mortality and the average life span reduced to twenty years of age, massive depopulation ensued in a country whose population stood at 18 million in the early seventeenth century. The stage was set for deep-seated emotional disturbances, neuroses, and feverish spiritual and religious concerns, for in despairing of man, one turns to God.

The French school of spirituality was rooted in the apostolate of Philip Neri in Rome and the work of Teresa of Ávila in Spain, two leading sixteenth-century forerunners of Catholic renewal. While Teresa, in cooperation with John of the Cross, undertook the reform of her Carmelite nuns, Philip Neri bore witness to the Christian meaning of poverty and service. Francis of Sales, who in 1602 would become the bishop of Geneva, persuaded more than commanded French aristocrats of the value of the imitation of Christ. Pierre de Bérulle founded the Congregation of the Oratory in France, a community of priests modeled on Philip Neri's work in Rome. With the Incarnate Word of God at the center of his spirituality, he understood that the holiness of the church and its priests was the *sine qua non* of church renewal. Charles de Condren succeeded him as superior general of the Oratory, and Jean-Jacques Olier assisted Condren until Olier founded a seminary at Saint-Sulpice in Paris, the first of a series of seminaries that would also emerge in North America. John Eudes also left the Oratorians to establish another congregation of priests dedicated to the pastoral training of candidates for the priesthood. Finally, Vincent de Paul set his stamp upon this renewed French Catholicism of the seventeenth century, his name becoming synonymous with the apostolate in favor of the poor and the sick. A revolution was at work in the church of France.

Numerous religious congregations led the French missionary endeavors in the New World: some were orders revitalized, such as the Franciscans (from the thirteenth century) and the Jesuits (from the sixteenth century), others were newly created congregations, such as the Sulpicians, the Vincentians (or Lazarists), the Eudists, and the Ursulines (or the Sisters of Notre Dame). Some, such as the Sulpicians, shared in the Gallican persuasion of most French clerics. Others, particularly the Jesuits, were of the ultramontane school and thus sought to reinforce Roman, as opposed to French, authority. This ecclesiological bent, when coupled with the usual institutional and personal rivalries in the church, would lead to many episodes of clerical trench warfare in the North American missions.

Thus it was a revitalized Gallican church of France that would serve the needs of French explorers and colonizers, as well as to evangelize an amazing variety of native peoples, none of whom were even remotely aware of European civilization. Religious orders, particularly the Society of Jesus, would usually be entrusted with missionary endeavors, while a variety of clerics, regular and secular, would minister to the needs of white settlers.

NORTH AMERICAN BEGINNINGS: THE CARIBBEAN AND ACADIA

In the wake of the discoveries of America by Christopher Columbus and Giovanni da Verrazano, many European states turned inquiring and interested eyes toward the New World. While fishermen continued to ply the waters of the Grand Banks of Newfoundland and pirates raided the Spanish galleons of the Caribbean, during the sixteenth century France endeavored to establish colonies: first on the Saint Lawrence River, between 1534 and 1542, under the leadership of Jacques Cartier, and then in Florida, under the Huguenot leader Admiral Gaspard de Coligny. Fort Caroline, on the Saint John River,

was destroyed within three years (1562–1565) by the Spaniards.

The first permanent French settlement on North American soil would have to await the efforts of Samuel de Champlain in the valley of the Saint Lawrence from 1608 on. While its northern colony developed slowly, France also established a permanent foothold in the Caribbean, an area that had been a Spanish monopoly since the first voyage of Columbus in 1492.

By 1550 the diseases imported by Europeans, coupled with the systematic butchering of native peoples by some Spanish commanders, left the Caribbean's original Arawak, Carib, and Chibcha tribes decimated. African slaves were soon imported into many islands, a practice that grew in importance throughout the seventeenth and eighteenth centuries, the latter century being the slave trade's "golden age"—when English, Portuguese, French, Dutch, and Danish authorities strove to outdo each other in this lucrative business. (Such vast numbers of slaves were imported into the West Indies that the region's history since the seventeenth century rests primarily on this phenomenon.) The United States joined the ranks of slavers in the late eighteenth century.

France established permanent colonies in the Caribbean after 1626. The initial settlement on the island of Saint Christopher was followed in 1635 by others on the islands of Guadeloupe and Martinique. Within fifty years seven more islands in the West Indies were French, most of them controlled by the larger Guadeloupe and Martinique. Catholic priests of course participated in these new settlements from the outset, as was the case in the Spanish possessions. Capuchins, Dominicans, Jesuits, Carmelites, and secular priests were responsible for most of the seventeenth and eighteenth centuries' clerical story in the French West Indies. Early in the nineteenth century, priests from the Seminary of the Holy Spirit in Paris became more and more numerous in the area. Clerical bickering and squabbling frequently cast a shadow over the church's record in these French islands.

French religious orders, along with the rest of white society, benefited from the financial advantages of slavery until its abolition in the nineteenth century. While several missionaries denounced the abuses of the institution and recommended generous treatment for slaves, few churchmen campaigned to overthrow this system of Negro slavery, which had become widespread since the fifteenth century. These clerics were not known as emancipators on islands whose populations were overwhelmingly of slave origin.

One French Jesuit, Antoine de La Valette, working in the French West Indies in the mid-eighteenth century, became famous throughout the Western world. He indulged in commercial and real estate transactions on a grand scale, allegedly in order to finance his missions. Burdened with large debts, in 1755 he lost two shiploads of his goods to the English and was driven into bankruptcy. European creditors held the already unpopular Society of Jesus responsible for La Valette's misadventures, a position upheld by the French courts and parliaments in 1761. The latter also decreed the closure of all Jesuit colleges and ordered the dissolution of the Society of Jesus in the realm in 1762, a decision that meant the end of Jesuit activities not only in the West Indies but throughout North America, for in 1773 the pope ordered the Jesuits throughout the world to disband.

While missionaries were all too frequently quarreling in the French West Indies, they were writing a far nobler, indeed a heroic, story in Canada. Acadia, an area that in addition to the state of Maine included Canada's maritime provinces, was the first target of French settlement. Before 1667, when it became a royal colony, Acadia was granted by royal charter to various commercial entrepreneurs who undertook not only to make money but also to start settlements and provide for the evangelization of both natives and Europeans. Priests therefore accompanied French settlers from the outset, first at Sainte-Croix Island (1604) and Port Royal (1605), on the Bay of Fundy, and subsequently throughout various white settlements and Indian villages. Father Jesse Fléché developed a dubious reputation for having baptized more than one hundred Indians within weeks of his initial contact with them (1610), when they did not even speak French or have the least inkling of Christian doctrine. In May 1611, the first Jesuits arrived in Acadia. Pierre Biard and Ennemond Massé planned to establish a mission at Saint-Sauveur (near Bangor, Maine) but before realizing their project were taken prisoner on Mount Desert Island (1613) by Captain Samuel Argall.

For more than a century afterward, Catholic missions suffered the same uneven and weak development as did all of Acadia. From 1608 to 1750 the population of the American colonies grew from 100 to 1,200,000; that of New France went from 28 to 55,000; while that of Acadia grew only from 10 to 8,000. While some 115 priests worked in Acadia during the seventeenth and eighteenth centuries, Friars Minor in the form of Capuchins and Récollets were especially active in the area between 1632 and 1755, while Jesuits became more evident after the 1680s, the work of Sebastian Rale (or Rasle) among the Abenaki Indians being prominent. Secular priests supervised by the bishop of Quebec were also active, the better known being the controversial Jean-Louis Le Loutre, accused of treason by the English, and the accommodating Pierre-Antoine Maillard, who obtained a priest's salary from the same English government of Nova Scotia that had outlawed Catholic priests. Indeed, the church history of Acadia (1604–1713) and Nova Scotia (from 1713 on) initially proved as unstable as that of the Acadian colony as a whole.

NEW FRANCE

While the Acadian colony floundered, in 1608 Samuel de Champlain established a colony at Quebec on the Saint Lawrence River. Upon a return voyage to France in 1612, Champlain obtained the services of four Récollet friars, who arrived in the summer of 1615. Their superior, Father Denys Jamet, celebrated the feast of Saint Jean-Baptiste, the first Mass in the colony of New France, on June 24, thus establishing the patronal feast of French Canada. The Récollets ventured out to evangelize the diverse Indian tribes of the southerly Iroquoian or northern Algonquian linguistic families. Joseph Le Caron in fact preceded Champlain (1615) on the more than 500-mile voyage up the Ottawa and down the French rivers into the Huron country around Lake Simcoe, where he in turn celebrated the first Mass on Ontario soil.

Aware of the tremendous distances involved in evangelizing North American Indians, the Récollet friars asked for the assistance of the powerful Society of Jesus, whose resources in men, money, and influence far surpassed their own. Six Black Robes, including Charles Lalemant, Ennemond Massé, and Jean de Brébeuf, arrived in Quebec in 1625. From this Quebec base, the Jesuits fanned out through most of North America, including Acadia, the Great Lakes and Illinois regions, and the Mississippi River valley. While other secular and regular clergy shared in this missionary adventure, the Society of Jesus dominated the missionary life of New France in the seventeenth and eighteenth centuries.

The capture of Quebec by the English in 1629 and its subsequent restitution to France by the Treaty of Saint Germain-en-Laye (1632) brought a new beginning to the settlement and missions. While residence in the colony was reserved for Catholics by the charter of the ruling Company of One Hundred Associates (1627), France's powerful Cardinal Richelieu decided to entrust New France's missions to a single religious order; the Jesuits were chosen, and between 1633 and 1657 they ruled unchallenged in New France. The disciples of Saint Ignatius were simultaneously involved in ministering to white settlers and evangelizing Indians. In this latter capacity, their activity between 1634 and 1649 among the Huron of Lake Simcoe and the Five-Nations Iroquois of upper New York State became legendary. Their mission station at Sainte Marie, in the midst of Huron territory, was at the center of the Five-Nations' attack on the Huron throughout the late 1640s. Several missionaries lost their lives, many of whom were subsequently declared saints by the Roman Catholic church on 29 June 1930; they were Jean de Brébeuf, Gabriel Lalemant, Antoine Daniel, Charles Garnier, and Noël Chabanel—all five died in Huronia. In addition, Father Isaac Jogues and lay missionary workers René Goupil and Jean de La Lande died among the Iroquois of northern New York State. The church of New France now had the blood of martyrs to nourish its soul.

Meanwhile, although the colony on the Saint Lawrence was developing in a more "civilized" way, the decades 1633–1663 were nevertheless a time of perfervid religiosity and of the founding of several religious institutions of lasting importance.

Within three years of their return to Quebec, the Jesuits founded a college (Collèges des Jésuites) (1635) for the education of young men, thus preempting Harvard College (1636). They favored the arrival of the teaching Ursulines (1639), who, with their great mystic, Marie de l'Incarnation, opened a convent school in Quebec for French and Indian girls, while three nuns from an Augustinian convent in Dieppe established Quebec's Hôtel Dieu Hospital in 1639.

France's religiosity also expressed itself in the founding of Montreal. In France, Jérôme Le Royer de la Dauversière felt a supernatural calling to establish a hospital on the island of Montreal, while Jean Jacques Olier responded to a divine directive to found a seminary there. The two inspired men thereupon jointly created a company whose mandate was to supervise the building of the new colony. The appointed governor, Paul de Chomédy de Maisonneuve, stepped ashore on Quebec in August 1641 and in May 1642 began the building of Montreal. Jeanne Mance was also of the party; she established a hospital in Montreal. Her Hôtel Dieu Hospital (unrelated to the Hôtel Dieu of Quebec) was in operation by September 1642 and developed under Mance's able leadership until her death in 1673.

Montreal's early evangelical enthusiasm was also due to Marguerite Bourgeoys, the founder of the congregation of Notre Dame of Montreal. She arrived from France in 1653 intent on opening a school. Her school opened on 30 April 1658, the first of dozens that would dot the North American landscape down to the present. Bourgeoys was beatified by Pope Pius XII in 1950 and declared a saint in 1983.

New France's thirty-year religious epoch closed with the arrival of the Sulpician fathers and Bishop François de Laval, and with the establishment of the Quebec Seminary. Gabriel de Queylus led the trio of Sulpician fathers who settled in Montreal in 1657, thereby breaking the long-standing monopoly of the Jesuits in the ecclesiastical affairs of New France. The Society of Saint-Sulpice became the legal owner of the island of Montreal and its arrival marked the beginning of clerical quarreling over ecclesiastical control of the colony. Indeed, the Roman-leaning Jesuits tangled with the French-leaning Sulpicians on the question of selecting Quebec's first bishop. The Jesuits won the day when one of their former students, François de Laval, was appointed first bishop of the newly erected (1658) vicariate of New France. He arrived in Quebec in 1659 and soon took over effective leadership of the colony's church.

In addition to establishing his authority in both church and state and in trying to control the brandy trade with the Indians, one of Laval's major accomplishments was the founding of the Quebec Seminary in 1663. Besides providing training of secular priests, his seminary served as the headquarters of all Quebec secular priests. The seminary collected parish revenues, governed all clerical affairs, and served as a refuge for priests in need. Laval himself governed the seminary. The new bishop also saw to the enactment, in civil and ecclesiastical law, of tithes (1663), whereby one twenty-sixth of the settlers' crops were payable to the church. This powerful bishop tangled with various government officials, most notably the intendant (1665–1668, 1670–1672) Jean Talon and Louis de Buade de Frontenac, the governor of New France (1672–1682, 1689–1698).

Having obtained the elevation of his vicariate to the rank of diocese in 1674, the sixty-year-old churchman was feeling the weight of his years by the early 1680s, after returning from another of many pastoral visitations. He obtained the canonical erection of his diocesan chapter in 1684 and his resignation was accepted by the French court that same year. The retiring bishop's chosen successor was appointed in 1685, Laval agreeing to remain in office as long as necessary. On 6 May 1708 this episcopal giant died in Quebec, where he had lived in retirement for more than twenty years.

Jean-Baptiste de la Croix de Saint-Vallier first came to Quebec as bishop-elect in 1685 and immediately tried to undo many of Laval's accomplishments. He reduced the Quebec Seminary to the rank of an ordinary seminary, reinforced the Gallican and Erastian tendencies in his diocese, and managed to quarrel with most clerics and many civil government officials—all this in spite of prolonged absences from his episcopal see, including one continuous absence from 1700 to 1713.

Saint-Vallier's misadventures were the harbinger of New France's episcopal floundering, which would last until 1741. Indeed, his successor, Louis-François Duplessis de Mornay, always refused to set foot in Canada, while de Mornay's successor, Pierre-Herman Dosquet, administered the diocese of Quebec from 1729 until his resignation in 1739, although officially the bishop of Quebec for only part of that decade. Like Saint-Vallier, Dosquet managed to alienate most clerics and faithful. Discouraged, he sailed back to France in 1735, never to return to the shores of the Saint Lawrence. He submitted his resignation only after the French court had guaranteed him an adequate pension. His successor was François-Louis de Pourroy de Lauberivière, who died twelve days after his arrival in Quebec.

This series of ineffective bishops came to an end with the appointment of Henri-Marie Dubreil de Pontbriand. Consecrated on 7 April 1741, the sixth bishop of Quebec occupied his see by 30 August 1741. Full of goodwill but determined to be in control of his diocese, Pontbriand managed to stay on good terms with most of his regular and secular clergy. Although caught up in the caldron of civil and military strife culminating in the Seven Years War (1756–1763), he kept his church on an even keel through most of his term as bishop. In 1755 he approved the official founding of the Sisters of Charity of Montreal, whose members had already been entrusted with the management of the Montreal General Hospital in 1747. This group of dedicated women, led by Marie-Marguerite Dufrost, better known as Madame d'Youville, developed into one of North America's largest congregations of nursing and teaching sisters.

Like his predecessors, Pontbriand swore an oath of allegiance to the king of France, for all bishops had to be loyal subjects. This policy continued under British monarchs until the midnineteenth century. Pontbriand's church was thus very dependent on the French crown for grants, privileges, and legislative protection. This last bishop of New France died on 8 June 1760, having witnessed the fall of Quebec to the English and anticipated the capitulation of Montreal and Canada that would follow in September 1760.

The death of Pontbriand and the conquest of Canada marked the onset of difficult years for the church of Quebec. Six years passed before the appointment of another bishop, during which the legalities involved in appointing a French Catholic bishop in an English Protestant province appeared insurmountable. Ultimately the persistence of the Quebec clergy, the common sense of Governor James Murray, and the reasonableness of Rome and of London's Colonial Office overcame the technical imbroglio. Jean-Olivier Briand, former confidant and vicar general of Pontbriand, was elected on Murray's recommendation.

The seventh bishop of Quebec needed to rebuild a church whose clergy stood reduced in numbers from 180 in 1758 to 138 in 1766 under a British government that forbade the recruitment of Frenchmen (aliens) as secular clergy and did not allow male religious orders to recruit. The Jesuits and Récollets thus disappeared from the colony by the end of the century; only the Sulpicians managed to maintain themselves, largely due to the sudden influx of French royalist clergy fleeing revolutionary France during the 1790s. Religious congregations of women fared better, however, the conqueror having soon noted the indispensable services they rendered society.

Briand also faced the challenge of rebuilding a number of churches and religious institutions either demolished or damaged during the siege of Quebec in 1759. He successfully rose to these challenges by simultaneously showing unalloyed loyalty to the new crown—for he firmly believed that all legitimate authority came from God—and insisting politely but firmly on the rights of his church. British governors, for their part, soon realized that they needed the cooperation of Quebec's native clergy in order to govern effectively in a predominantly French and Catholic country.

The revolution brewing in the Atlantic seaboard's thirteen colonies also facilitated the emancipation of the province of Quebec's church. Indeed the British government, prompted by Governor Guy Carleton, chose to emancipate Canada's Catholics in 1763 in order to ensure their loyalty during the forthcoming rebellion. The Quebec Act was adopted by the British parliament in 1774. Among other things, the official policy of anglicization of Quebec was set aside, French civil law was recognized as valid, Catholics were permitted to hold public office, and the ordinary rights and customs of the church of Rome were acknowledged. Briand was jubilant, for Catholics thereby obtained emancipation in Quebec fifty-five years before they did so in England. His loyalty would never waver thereafter.

THE UPPER GREAT LAKES, THE ILLINOIS COUNTRY, AND LOUISIANA

With the exception of the English colonies east of the Appalachians and some Spanish posts on the Gulf of Mexico, most of today's United States and Canada was claimed, explored, evan-

gelized, and partially settled by the French. The main springboard for this activity was the Saint Lawrence River colony, although France also sent expeditions toward the Gulf of Mexico.

The protection from Iroquois attacks provided by the arrival in Quebec of the régiment de Carignan (1665) once again allowed French authorities to send far-ranging expeditions into the hinterland. Jean Nicollet de Belleborne had explored Lake Michigan as far as Green Bay, Wisconsin in 1634, but the route to China still eluded the French. In order to establish the authority of the crown over North America's vast frontier, Jean Talon sent Jean-Baptiste Daumont de Saint-Lusson in 1671 to take possession of the upper Great Lakes. Four Jesuits attended the grandiose ceremony held in the wilds for the benefit of the fourteen Indian nations represented at this meeting at Sault Sainte Marie. The Jesuits were indeed becoming very active in missionary endeavors in the area, for many of their men, most notably Claude Allouez, were building mission stations and evangelizing several Indian nations in today's northern Ontario and the states of Wisconsin, Michigan, and Illinois. In order to check this growing Jesuit influence, colonial authorities invited Récollets back into the colony in 1670 and hoped to use them as well as the Sulpicians as spoilers; it was with this same intention that Saint-Lusson and Robert Cavelier de la Salle were chosen as leading explorers.

Still intent on finding the route to the southern sea and thus to China, French authorities sent the Canadian Louis Jolliet to explore in a southwesterly direction. Accompanied by the Jesuit Jacques Marquette, the two-canoe expedition discovered the Mississippi in the summer of 1673; the adventurers descended the river as far as the mouth of the Arkansas and concluded that the river emptied into the Gulf of Mexico. During the journey Marquette had made contact with the Kaskaskia Indians in Illinois, thus opening a field of missionary endeavor that the Jesuits would nurture for close to a century.

La Salle led, in his usual bungling fashion, an expedition (between 1679 and 1680) to the Illinois country, then another down to the mouth of the Mississippi (in 1682), on which occasion he named the new territory Louisiana in honor of King Louis XIV. Having returned to France, in 1684 he embarked with four ships on the last of his journeys of exploration. This viceroy of North America was accompanied by three Franciscan and three Sulpician priests. The ill-fated expedition to the Gulf of Mexico resulted in the murder of La Salle by one of his men (19 March 1687) and the massacre of the colony's survivors by Indians in 1689. The first attempt at French settlement in Louisiana had failed.

A decade later permanent ecclesiastical development began on both the upper and lower reaches of the Mississippi. The Jesuits had established three mission stations in the Illinois country, and one of these, the mission to the Tamaroas on the Mississippi, became a bone of contention between rival missionaries. Indeed, in 1698 Bishop Saint-Vallier had granted ecclesiastical authority in the mission to the priests from the Quebec Seminary, an institution that had been affiliated since 1665 with the Seminary of Foreign Missions in Paris. The Tamaroa Indian village located on the site of today's East Saint Louis, came to be designated Cahokia, the name of another tribe in the area. Seminary priests labored there and in the surrounding country until the 1770s, while an uneasy truce existed between them and the Jesuit missionaries from 1702 on, the latter's main center being the neighboring Kaskaskia River.

Military command of the Illinois country was located at Fort de Chartres on the Mississippi, with satellite posts at Fort Arkansas (1686) on the Arkansas River, Fort Orleans (1723) on the Missouri River, and Fort Vincennes (1732) on the Wabash River some 240 miles east of the village of Cahokia. When the British took over in 1763, there were only some 1,000 blacks and whites in the area, in addition to the Indians. Franciscan friars ministered to the garrison at Detroit from its beginning in 1701 until 1782.

On the southern reaches of the Mississippi, Louisiana welcomed its first permanent French settlement in 1699. Fort Maurepas on Biloxi Bay was established by the Canadian Pierre Lemoyne d'Iberville, one of New France's most renowned explorers and adventurers. In 1702 the unsuccessful settlement moved to Fort Louis on Mobile Bay (Mobile, Alabama), which became the capital of the colony in 1710. Twelve years later, the capital was transferred to New Orleans, founded in 1718 by Jean Baptiste Lemoyne de Bienville, d'Iberville's brother. The new capital was located 150 miles southwest of Mobile and 110 miles from the mouth of the Mississippi.

The troubled civil administration of the French colony of Louisiana (1699–1766) was compounded by constant bickering and rivalry among its secular, Jesuit, Carmelite, Capuchin, and other clergy. Negro slaves had been imported into the colony since 1717. They were employed by the clergy as well as by others, for while the Roman Catholic church had frequently condemned the slave trade, it had not condemned slavery itself. The Society of Jesus, here as elsewhere, proved most active in Indian missions, and had just as little to show for its efforts.

Finally, the British expulsion of the Acadians from Nova Scotia resulted in the arrival in Louisiana beginning in 1755 and continuing over the subsequent thirty years, of more than 1,500 Acadians, the Cajuns of later years. Saint Martinville came to be acknowledged as their principal center. Meanwhile the Spanish takeover of Louisiana in 1769 added only a few Spanish priests to a land that was sold to the United States in 1803. At the time of the Treaty of Paris (1763) it is estimated that some 10,000 French subjects inhabited the Louisiana and Illinois countries.

BRIAND'S SUCCESSION

The British conquest of Canada, the Quebec Act, and the American War of Independence led to the arrival of more than 30,000 Loyalists in Canada, refugees from the new American republic. Given the English-speaking and largely Protestant affiliations of the newcomers, Canada's political circumstances were bound to change dramatically. Not only did Nova Scotia and the new province of New Brunswick (formed in 1784) become resolutely British and Protestant, but the British Parliament divided the vast province of Quebec, which extended to the Ohio and Mississippi rivers. In 1791 the Saint Lawrence colony was divided into Lower Canada and Upper Canada, the former roughly corresponding to a smaller version of today's province of Quebec and the latter to a similarly reduced contemporary Ontario. This constitutional framework lasted for fifty years.

Until the erection of the diocese of Baltimore in 1789, the bishop of Quebec was responsible for the ecclesiastical administration of all North American Roman Catholic affairs, with the exception of those pertaining to Spanish possessions. Although the diocese of Baltimore and the purchase of Louisiana by the United States reduced his area of jurisdiction, the bishop of Quebec still needed assistance. Briand had managed to obtain (in 1772) the right to appoint a coadjutor bishop, thereby ensuring episcopal succession on the see of Quebec. This did not divide the vast territory under his charge, however. It is to this issue that his successors turned.

When Briand resigned in 1784 the Saint Lawrence colony—with its towns of Quebec, Trois-Rivières, and Montreal—included 100,000 Catholics in 118 parishes, served by ninety-nine pastors. Given the British government's sustained, albeit uneven, efforts to anglicize its new subjects and convert them to Protestantism, the Catholic church was gradually becoming the guardian of the colony's "Canadian" identity.

Upon Briand's resignation, the seventy-four-year-old coadjutor Louis-Philippe Mariaucheau d'Esgly automatically became bishop of Quebec and immediately sought a dynamic and able coadjutor. He chose Jean-François Hubert, who proved a worthy successor to Briand, for Hubert in effect administered the diocese for twelve years, three as coadjutor and nine as resident bishop. Due in part to the hostile maneuvering of an ill-chosen coadjutor (Charles-François Bailly de Messein), Hubert decided to forgo his plans for dividing his vast diocese. The death of Hubert ensured the promotion of his coadjutor, Pierre Denaut. The latter administered his diocese for nine years (1797–1806), one of his more notable accomplishments being his choice of Joseph-Octave Plessis as coadjutor and successor.

Plessis stands along with Laval and Briand as one of the great bishops of Quebec. Indeed, this skillful and determined bishop not only managed to check the hostile intentions of Governor James Henry Craig toward French Canadians and the Catholic church, but he also showed unalloyed loyalty to the crown during the War of 1812 against the United States; he was rewarded accordingly, for the British government increased the stipend it had been paying the bishop of Quebec since 1772. When this stipend was discontinued in 1850, it stood at 3,000 pounds sterling.

Also, Plessis finally succeeded in obtaining the division of his diocese by Roman authorities, with the consent of the British government. Indeed the vicariate of Nova Scotia was erected in 1817, that of New Brunswick and Prince Edward Island in 1819, and the diocese of Kingston, Upper Canada, in 1826. At the same time, the town of Saint Boniface on Manitoba's Red River became an ecclesiastical district in 1820, headed by Bishop Joseph-Norbert Provencher, while Montreal (1820), Kingston (1818), and Charlottetown experienced the same administrative changes. Therefore, beginning in the 1820s six consecrated bishops administered the territory formerly governed by the bishop of Quebec alone. Plessis had overcome another major obstacle to Roman Catholic development in Canada.

This turnabout in church fortunes was helped along by the arrival in Canada of forty-five French émigré priests and seminarians between 1791 and 1802. These clerics of royalist persuasion had fled to England, then set sail for Canada. Not only did they reinvigorate the moribund Sulpicians, but they also helped infuse Canadian Catholicism with a perfervid antirevolutionary conviction that the French Revolution and its assorted dogmas were the work of the devil. Such an ideology meshed with the ultramontanism of nineteenth-century Catholicism.

THE NINETEENTH-CENTURY CHURCH IN THE VALLEY OF THE SAINT LAWRENCE

The sudden development in administrative structures was accompanied by serious difficulties within the church. During the 1820s and 1830s the most notable problem was the refusal by Montreal's Sulpicians to allow their confrère Jean-Jacques Lartigue, the duly consecrated auxiliary bishop entrusted with the district of Montreal, to assume effective command of his territory. Indeed the Society of Saint-Sulpice had held legal title to the island of Montreal since the seventeenth century and was not about to allow other churchmen, bishops or otherwise, to meddle in what it considered its civil and ecclesiastical fiefdom. Lartigue managed to have his district raised to the rank of diocese of Montreal in 1836, but it would be left to his successor, Ignace Bourget, to settle, once and for all, during his prolonged episcopate (1840–1876), the thorny question of the respective ecclesiastical rights of the diocese of Montreal and the Society.

During the first half of the nineteenth century,

however, the greatest challenges to the church came from the political quarter, with the emergence of a new socioeconomic class composed of lawyers, notaries, doctors, and small merchants. Spokesmen for this group challenged the authoritarian rule of the *clique du château* (a clique of influential aristocrats who tended to monopolize power) and demanded representative government, indeed responsible government. British authorities opposed the rising agitation, which culminated in the rebellion of 1837–1838 in Lower Canada, led by Louis Joseph Papineau. His *Parti Canadien* stood at the center of the political turmoil that haunted Lower Canada during the first half of the nineteenth century. After a similar rebellion occurred in Upper Canada, under the leadership of William Lyon Mackenzie, the British Colonial Office appointed a new governor of its North American colonies. John George Lambton, first earl of Durham, was asked to study the situation and suggest ways of solving the colony's problems. His 1839 report recommended the anglicization of French-Canadians and their conversion to Protestantism, in addition to the union of Upper and Lower Canada. Britain followed his advice and created the province of Canada in 1841.

The Catholic church, whose bishops had proven most loyal to both the French and British crowns, discovered in 1834 that the *Patriotes* were steering a course different from their own. Disenchantment and outright opposition developed, a situation that would again serve the church well after British troops had crushed the rebellion, whose inept leaders had fled to the United States. The British government, however, proved equally inept in decreeing the Union of the Canadas, with its obvious policies of anglicization and Protestantism not to mention the act's manifest injustices in the matters of unequal political representation for French-Canadians and an unjust debt load forced on Lower Canada.

The net result was to drive the church and *Patriotes* together, for both were threatened. A distinct chapter of the history of French-Canadian nationalism began; for more than a century afterward, a French-Canadian cleric was also a French-Canadian nationalist, and the lay nationalist could not do otherwise than be a practicing Roman Catholic. By the same token the clergy led and dominated French-Canadian nationalism until the "quiet revolution" of the 1960s.

The 1840s thus proved to be a decade of radical political reorientation, as well as a period of intense religious revival in Canada's church. The accession of Ignace Bourget to the see of Montreal in 1840 marked the beginning of a revival in the Catholicism of French Canada. Bourget began the publication of his *Mélanges Religieux* (*Religious Miscellany*, 1840), a religious newspaper that would prove important in revitalizing the faith of the diocese of Montreal's 186,000 faithful. Bourget saw to the importation of external religious resources, beginning with the preaching tour of the French bishop Charles de Forbin-Janson between 1840 and 1842.

Seeking ecclesiastical personnel to staff his present and projected parishes, colleges, convents, hospitals, and missions, Bourget journeyed to Europe many times and obtained the services of a growing number of religious congregations of men and women. They arrived in Montreal over the next several decades, thus providing additional clergy at a most opportune moment. This was also the case for the Oblates of Mary Immaculate (1841), the Society of Jesus (1842), the Sisters of Charity of the Good Shepherd (1844), the Holy Cross Fathers (1847), and the Clerics of Saint-Viateur (1847)—all imported from a France that did not encourage the multiplication of religious congregations on its soil.

Moreover, during the same decade the bishop of Montreal created his own native religious congregations; namely, the Sisters of Charity of Providence (1843), the Sisters of the Holy Names of Jesus and Mary (1843), the Sisters of Mercy (1848), and the Sisters of Saint Anne (1850). In all, between 1837 and 1867, twenty-two new congregations appeared in French Canada; between 1867 and 1914 there were another fifty-seven; between 1915 and 1939, another forty-one; and between 1940 and 1970, twenty-two more. Many of the members of these congregations were French religious encouraged to leave France during the 1830s and 1840s and again between 1903 and 1908.

Having also seen to the development of numerous temperance societies, Bourget was not about to allow heretical, atheistic, or immoral ideas into his diocese. In 1844, the *Institut Canadien*, an association of young intellectuals concerned with all areas of social concern, was founded in Montreal. During the 1850s the *Institut*'s leadership appeared to the bishop to be moving further and further toward the left in the heated political and ideological battles of the day. Indeed the *Institut*'s reading room welcomed publications reflecting all shades of political and religious opinion, European as well as Canadian, much to the displeasure of the bishop, who hoped to ban access to all "bad" literature. Bourget intervened in an attempt to bring the *Institut* to heel, which led to a protracted struggle (lasting until 1875) centering on the primacy of civil rights, as opposed to ecclesiastical rights, in Canada.

In the wake of the increasingly polarized European scene after 1850, Roman Catholics closed ranks in the face of the Protestant hostility provoked by the reestablishment of the Catholic hierarchy in England (1850). Developing atheistic and/or secular ideologies such as Marxism, social Darwinism, evolutionism, and positivism threatened the premodern understanding most Catholic churchmen had of church-state relations. In 1864 the pope responded with the encyclical *Quanta Cura* and its companion *Syllabus of Errors,* before seeing to the adoption in 1870 by the First Vatican Council of a declaration of papal infallibility in matters of faith and morals. Henceforth the modern world was anathema to Roman Catholics.

Nourished by the writings of the French journalist Louis François Veuillot and by the strictures of Roman officials, French Canada's clergy launched a crusade against liberalism in Canada, frequently not realizing that their political circumstances were much different from those in Europe. Canadian ultramontanism went hand in hand with both conservative feelings and strong convictions regarding the nefarious effects of the French Revolution. Freedom and democracy became synonymous with the revolutionary; conservatism and authoritarian rule with "Catholic" values. In rejecting the modern world as a whole, ultramontane Catholics were in the long run bound to lose their battle. Their strategy proved very effective, however, until the 1950s.

One instance of this fear of modernity was the hostile attitude of some Quebec bishops to the Knights of Labor, an American labor union that moved into Canada during the 1880s. Known as a secret society, due to the refusal by American industrialists to acknowledge the principle of un-ionized labor, the Knights were reputed to number some 2 million members in the early 1880s, including large numbers of Catholics. Implicitly approved by the Catholic church in the United States, beginning in 1883 the Knights faced a series of condemnations by Archbishop Elzéar-Alexandre Taschereau of Quebec, who also managed to obtain their condemnation by the Holy See on 27 August 1884 and again on 27 June 1886. The Knights were considered a secret society, thus falling under the general ban of the latter by Rome. They were also suspected of being a Masonic front.

When James Cardinal Gibbons of Baltimore entered the fray in 1886, the debate took a new turn. In successive reports to Rome, Gibbons argued in defense of the Knights and underlined their beneficial work in favor of workers. Gibbons was to emerge victorious, Taschereau being directed by Rome to suspend his condemnation of the Knights. The Archbishop of Quebec did so, although continuing to advise against joining the union, in spite of a Roman directive of 29 August 1888 which stated that the membership of Catholics could be tolerated.

In addition to being a period of dramatic political and religious change, the 1840s witnessed the arrival of an increasing number of immigrants in North America, culminating in the Irish famine migration of 1847, when 90,000 Irish people came to Canada alone. This wave of immigrants coincided with the onset of economic depression provoked by the temporary collapse of the lumber trade due to Great Britain's abolition of preferential tariffs on Canadian wood. Responding to the new challenge, Canada's bishops began in 1848 to organize colonization societies. Their purpose was to divert the growing number of French-Canadians headed for the United States toward Canadian vacant lands instead.

THE FRENCH-CANADIAN DIASPORA IN NORTH AMERICA

Half of the 90,367 Americans of French stock reported in the U.S. Census of 1790 were probably of Canadian origin. In the following 150 years, such large numbers of French-Canadians would migrate to the United States, particularly to New England, that it is estimated there are now more Franco-Americans of Canadian origin in the United States than there are French-Canadians in Canada.

The Catholic church usually accompanied these immigrants. Indeed, between 1791 and 1802, twenty-nine French émigré clerics came to the United States, including the initial seven Sulpicians who established Saint Mary's Seminary in Baltimore. Six of these refugee priests became bishops in early-nineteenth-century America; namely, Benedict Joseph Flaget (Bardstown and Louisville), Jean Louis Lefebvre de Cheverus (Boston), Louis William Valentine Dubourg (New Orleans), Ambrose Maréchal (Baltimore), John Dubois (New York), and John Baptist David (Bardstown and Louisville). Their presence fueled the nationalistic agitation that troubled the period's American church.

Most French-Canadians arrived from Quebec beginning in the 1840s, when a prolonged economic depression settled in Canada; it lasted, with few interruptions, for nearly half a century. Lumber and copper booms drew some French-Canadians to Minnesota, Michigan, and Wisconsin in the 1840s, while the 1849 gold rush drew others to California. The largest number settled in New England, where steady employment was available in brickyards and textile factories. After some 20,000 had joined the Union Army during the Civil War, the number of immigrant French-Canadians rose anew after 1865. It is estimated that in 1873, when more than a quarter of Quebec's farmlands lay uncultivated, 400,000 French-Canadians resided in the United States. Another 1 million arrived before 1929, causing the emergence of "little Canadas" throughout New England.

Messianic zeal had dominated the Canadian church since the 1840s, a conviction that God had chosen these people to serve as a beacon of truth and light in a continent dominated by gross Anglo-American positivism and materialism. Before 1869, spokesmen for this messianic school dismissed their emigrant brothers as lost apostates condemned to be the hewers of wood and drawers of water for corrupt Americans. Beginning in 1869, however, the massive southward movement of French-Canadians began to be understood as resulting from God's providence. This lost tribe was called upon to form a fifth column for the evangelization of the United States. Some even predicted the eventual domination of the eastern United States by French-Canadians, thereby consecrating a new nation built on a common language and faith.

During the second phase of this messianic phantasm, Catholic church activity became prominent. Whereas the first French-Canadian parishes in New England were established in the 1850s, by 1890 eighty-six French-language parishes existed in the eastern United States alongside fifty bilingual schools. In 1910 there were 202 such parishes and 101 missions served by 432 priests of French-Canadian origin. More than 2,000 teaching sisters and brothers directed the schooling of 55,000 pupils, while 3,500 Franco-Americans studied in the classical colleges of the province of Quebec.

By 1930 this dream of a new Quebec came crashing down because of serious opposition from American nativist spokesmen, dwindling migration from Quebec, and increasing pressures to assimilate into the American mainstream. Also, Irish-American bishops, supported by the Vatican, contributed to the repression of French-Canadian Catholics, who were perceived as un-American.

The vast prairies, mountains, and tundra of northwestern Canada also proved to be an area of evangelization for the church of French Canada. At the request of Thomas Douglas, Lord Selkirk, missionaries had been sent by Bishop Plessis to the Red River in the early nineteenth century. Bishop Joseph-Norbert Provencher spent more than thirty years struggling, with limited resources, to develop his infant church. His Northwestern District became a vicariate in 1844, a diocese in 1847, and ultimately the archdiocese of Saint Boniface in 1871, the oldest see in Canada's Northwest. Beginning in the second half of the nineteenth century, it was subdivided, eventually giving rise to the twenty dioceses and vicariates of today. The majority of missionaries in Canada's Northwest were oblates of Mary Immaculate. One of the first oblates sent into the area (in 1845) was Alexandre-Antonin Taché, who became famous not only as the bishop of Saint-Boniface but as a middleman between the government of Canada and Louis Riel, the leader of two Métis uprisings in western Canada between 1869 and 1870, and again in 1885.

In 1890, the province of Manitoba legislated

FRENCH CATHOLICISM IN THE NEW WORLD

the abolition of confessional schools and the use of the French language in its legislature and courts. Taché's church met the challenge by launching two appeals to the courts against the abolition of Catholic schools. Although these appeals proved unsuccessful, the Manitoba schools question polarized state and church opinion throughout Canada, and contributed to the defeat of Canada's Conservative government (1896) and the emergence of the Liberal party that was destined to dominate Canadian politics until the present.

Until 1913, all Roman Catholic bishops in western Canada were French-speaking, a fact that occasioned much bickering and squabbling, particularly among rival Irish-Canadian and French-Canadian clerics. By the turn of the century, however, the majority of the faithful were increasingly English-speaking, for with few exceptions immigrants of whatever linguistic origin chose to assimilate into the majority English-speaking community. This ethnolinguistic quarrel would poison western Canadian church affairs until World War II.

Except for New England, the French-Canadian diaspora in North America was primarily found in the province of Ontario. Quebec's neighboring province had been part of New France, indeed of the province of Quebec (1774–1791), before becoming Upper Canada (1791–1841), then Canada East (1841–1867), and finally Ontario (1867). Its oldest permanent white settlement (1749) on the south shore of the Detroit River still stands as an island of French culture, its parish of L'Assomption being the oldest on Ontario soil. The vast numbers of American and British immigrants after 1783 resulted, by 1850, in the reduction of the number of Franco-Ontarians to a tiny minority (26,417, or 2.8 percent) of the population. The same economic factors that were driving French-Canadians into New England were also, however, driving them into Ontario, although in lesser numbers. Thus by 1881, Franco-Ontarians numbered 102,743 (or 5.3 percent of the population), and in 1921 they numbered 248,275 (or 8.5 percent of the population). This "tidal wave" of French-Canadian immigration intensified fears among the "native" English-speaking majority of Ontarians, fears for their continued domination of Ontario life. The widespread racism and bigotry of the period helped things along.

Until 1860, Ontario's Catholic church depended largely on the mother church in Quebec. Indeed the first missionary voyages into Ontario by Catholic priests during the 1790s signaled the ecclesiastical development that would subsequently accompany accelerated settlement during the nineteenth century. The bishops of Quebec and Montreal provided many of Upper Canada's ecclesiastical resources for several decades. The place of origin of the clergy, aided by the mediocre quality of many Irish immigrant clerics before 1850, resulted in the domination of Upper Canada's hierarchy by French-speaking bishops. Thus, in 1856, four of Upper Canada's five dioceses were governed by French-speaking bishops—namely, Armand-François Marie de Charbonnel in Toronto, Joseph-Eugène-Bruno Guigues in Ottawa, Pierre-Adolphe Pinsoneault in London, and Remigius Gaulin in Kingston. In the latter instance, Bishop Patrick Phelan was the official administrator of the see, the only other English-speaking prelate being the newly appointed John Farrell in Hamilton.

English-speaking—that is to say, Irish—clergy began to gain their place in the sun particularly after the appointment of John Lynch as third bishop of Toronto in 1860. While campaigning to obtain better representation in the ranks of the hierarchy, Ontario's English-speaking bishops also endeavored to bring all of Ontario's territory under their ecclesiastical sway. Indeed the sections of eastern and northern Ontario that were part of the diocese of Ottawa, since the election in 1847, had thereby been incorporated into the ecclesiastical province of Quebec, established in 1844; and the bishop of Ottawa insisted on retaining his allegiance to Quebec when the ecclesiastical province of Toronto was erected in 1870. Rejecting this state of affairs, Ontario's English-speaking bishops campaigned to obtain from Roman authorities the appropriate boundary changes. Canada's French-speaking bishops managed to keep their fellow English-speaking bishops in check for close to a century. The reason for this persistence by Ontario's English-speaking bishops was their ethnocentric conviction that French-Canadian bishops just did not measure up to their own standards.

This ethnocentrism went hand in hand with

the increased migration of French-Canadians into Ontario noted above. French-Canadian bishops such as Guigues and Joseph Thomas Duhamel made every effort to encourage colonization societies within their diocese, thereby suggesting that the hierarchy was leading a well-orchestrated campaign by French-Canadians to "invade" English Ontario.

When English Ontario's white Anglo-Saxon Protestant nativism and bigotry came to the fore in the 1880s, English-speaking Catholics began to fear for the existence of their separate schools, for New Brunswick (in 1871) and Manitoba (in 1890) had abolished their confessional schools. These Catholics felt trapped between the upper millstone of French-Canadian nationalism and the lower millstone of Protestant bigotry. They chose to join the side of the linguistic and cultural majority, thereby rejecting their French-speaking coreligionists. Meanwhile, the government of Ontario's campaign to impose English and restrict French in its schools also pushed Franco-Ontarians out of public schools and into the separate school system, a situation that has prevailed until the present.

By the turn of the twentieth century, Ontario's French-speaking Catholics were growing rapidly in numbers, and while gradually becoming aware of their new strength, they had to cope with growing opposition on the part of an English-speaking majority that felt threatened in its continued domination of Canada's perfervidly British citadel. The French-Canadian clergy proved the armature of Franco-Ontarian identity and *survivance* (cultural survival) until the 1960s.

Similar developments occurred in Canada's maritime provinces, where Acadians had gradually drifted back home in the aftermath of the expulsion that began in 1755. While Catholic administrative structures developed in step with those of the rest of Canada during the nineteenth century, Acadians wallowed in a deep-seated inferiority complex, having become accustomed to submitting to the English-speaking majority. Five dioceses existed in maritime Canada: Halifax (1818), Charlottetown (1829), Arichat (1844), New Brunswick (1842), and Chatham (1860). These sees were held by prelates of Irish or Scottish origin, while Acadians represented two out of every three Catholics in 1900.

The lethargic Acadians of old started to give way to dynamic and determined militants at the dawn of the twentieth century. In addition to the National Association of the Assumption and a bank, Acadians had created a college and had representatives elected or appointed to most levels of government. They also undertook to obtain Acadian episcopal appointments and had to overcome the opposition of racist Irish prelates. Victory came to the beleaguered Acadians in 1912 with the appointment of Bishop Édouard Le Blanc to the see of Saint John, New Brunswick.

By the early twentieth century, French Catholicism in North America was so strong and disciplined, it embarked on a crusade to evangelize North America, for this was the will of God. Churchmen firmly believed that providence had designated French Catholics for the task. Why else would they have been granted spiritual superiority? This crusading conviction was tied to a linguistic and cultural sense of superiority, all of which collided not only with Irish-Catholic culture but also with Protestant evangelicalism and its assorted dogmas of evolutionism, progressivism, and Anglo-Saxonism. The conflicts that ensued and continued well into the twentieth century were numerous.

THE TWENTIETH CENTURY

Notable developments in twentieth-century North American French Catholicism have pertained primarily to Canada. Acadians have consolidated their position within the Catholic church, controlling three of the four episcopal sees in the ecclesiastical province of Moncton (formed in 1936), one of the four in the ecclesiastical province of Halifax (formed in 1852), and none of the three in Newfoundland, where the number of Acadians has always been negligible. In western Canada the proportion of French-speaking Catholics has constantly diminished, so that the church has put on a decidedly English face.

In Ontario one-sixth of the 3 million Catholics in 1981 were French-speaking. With the leadership and support of the church these Franco-Ontarians overcame the most serious challenge to their existence between 1912 and 1927, when the government of Ontario, supported by public opinion and the province's Irish-Catholic clergy, endeavored to abolish French schooling in Ontario. After fifteen years of frequently bitter fighting and civil disobedience, the government amended its infamous Regulation 17, ensuring thereafter the development of French schools. Today a full network of French schools exists from kindergarten to the university level. Five of Ontario's fourteen dioceses and vicariates are headed by French-speaking bishops and another two have French-speaking coadjutor bishops. The Franco-Ontarian church can indeed be proud of its achievement.

During the first sixty years of the twentieth century, the Catholic church in Quebec basked in the glow of its triumphant social and political status. This church of the majority (some 90 percent) of the province's population controlled most, if not all, schools and hospitals and held a dominant position in Quebec society. A phenomenal birthrate ensured the growth of French Canada's population, which had been doubling every twenty-five years since 1760. The number of priests in Quebec had grown from 225 in 1830 to 2,102 in 1850, ensuring that there was one priest for every 510 Catholics, a proportion that would not change significantly until 1960. During the period 1850–1960 the number of men and women in Quebec-based religious congregations grew from 1,034 to 59,558. There was one religious man or woman for every eighty-seven Catholics in 1941, an army of religious brothers and sisters spread out among 133 female and 63 male congregations (as of 1969). Two-thirds of them were working in the field of education. No government dared oppose these powerful interests. Thus when various popes spoke out against socialism, liberalism, or Freemasonry, or when churchmen expressed a dislike of Sunday cinema, the government of Quebec rushed to ensure conformity with Catholic social doctrine.

At a time when the European church had long since adjusted to working-class disenchantment with Catholicism, the church of French Canada drew into its numerous churches and shrines the overwhelming majority of Catholics. Indeed socioeconomic penalties were usually associated with delinquency in church attendance. While rural Catholics erected crosses by the wayside, the seventeenth-century shrine of Sainte Anne de Beaupré, the nineteenth-century shrine of Cap-de-la-Madeleine, and the twentieth-century's Oratoire Saint-Joseph continued to draw increasing numbers of pilgrims from the North American continent—the Oratoire's famous miracle worker, Brother André, transforming Montreal into an international center for pilgrims. Between 1850 and 1960 the church held an unchallenged sway over the consciences of French Canada's Catholics.

This era of triumphant Catholicism, symbolized by the International Marian Congress held in Ottawa in 1947, came to an abrupt end with the onset of Quebec's "quiet revolution" during the 1960s. While international Catholicism was busy writing its charter for a rejuvenated church at the Second Vatican Council (1962–1965), in Quebec church attendance plummeted to formerly unimaginable depths, while disenchanted priests, nuns, and brothers created bottlenecks in exiting from their ministries. During these years of confusion, many of the faithful began for the first time to question seriously many of the disciplinary and moral tenets of their church. While the church gracefully withdrew from its monopolistic position in educational and health services, Catholics in Quebec became aware, frequently for the first time, of other belief and value systems.

By the late 1970s the storm had spent itself and Quebec's Catholic leaders began to emerge from their fifteen-year silence, assessing their newfound social and political poverty and evangelical freedom. In 1985, many, and frequently most, social activists and reformers in Quebec society can be shown to have strong Christian motivations and attachments, although this does not appear obvious at first sight. The difference from the pre-1960 era is that this engagement results from strong personal commitments that are reflected in diversified, flexible, and varied institutional attachments. Cassocks and crosses no longer cover Quebec, which has put on a secular face, although faith still dwells in the hearts of many *Québécois.* The providential mission to the Philistines of English North America has become a sincere commitment to bear witness to the Gospel in all quarters.

BIBLIOGRAPHY

Robert Choquette, *Language and Religion* (1975) and *L'Eglise catholique dans l'Ontario français du XIXe siècle* (1984); Glenn Conrad, ed., *The Cajuns: Essays on Their History and*

Culture (1978); Jean Daigle, ed., *Les Acadiens des Maritimes: études thématiques* (1980); M. Devèze, *Antilles, Guyanes, la mer des Caraibes de 1492 à 1789* (1977); Micheline Dumont-Johnson, *Apôtres ou agitateurs: La France missionnaire en Acadie* (1970); John Tracy Ellis, *Catholics in Colonial America* (1965); Naomi E. S. Griffiths, *The Acadians: Creation of a People* (1973); Benoît Lacroix and Jean Simard, eds., *Religion populaire religion de clercs?* (1984); A. Latreille et al., *Histoire du catholicisme en France*, vol. 2 (1957).

John S. Moir, *The Church in the British Era* (1972); A. G. Morice, *History of the Catholic Church in Western Canada*, 2 vols. (1910); Hermann Plante, *L'Eglise catholique au Canada (de 1604 à 1886)* (1970); J. Rennard, *L'Histoire religieuse des Antilles françaises, des origines à 1914* (1954); L. J. Rogier et al., *Nouvelle histoire de l'église: vol. 3, Réforme et contre réforme* (1968); Joseph Henry Schlarman, *From Quebec to New Orleans: The Story of the French in America* (1930); André Sénécal, "La thèse messianique et les Franco-Américains," in *Revue d'histoire de l'Amérique française*, 34, 4 (March 1981); Jean Simard, ed., *Un patrimoine méprisé: La religion populaire des Québécois* (1979); Martin S. Spigelman, "Race et religion: Les Acadiens et la hiérarchie catholique irlandaise du Nouveau-Brunswick," in *Revue d'histoire de l'Amérique française*, 29, 1 (June 1975).

René Taveneaux, *Le catholicisme dans la France classique 1610–1715*, 2 vols. (1980); Nive Voisine, *Histoire de l'église catholique au Québec 1608–1970* (1971) and, as ed., *Histoire du catholicisme québécois*, 2 vols. (1984) and *Les ultramontains canadiens-français* (1985); Mason Wade, "French and French Canadians in the U.S.," in *New Catholic Encyclopedia*, vol. 6, 143–148; Eric Williams, *From Columbus to Castro: The History of the Caribbean, 1492–1969* (1970).

[*See also* CATHOLICISM IN THE ENGLISH COLONIES; DIVERSITY AND PLURALISM IN CANADIAN RELIGION; *and* PROTESTANTISM AND SOCIETY IN CANADA.]

PROTESTANTISM AND SOCIETY
IN CANADA

John Webster Grant

ON 18 June 1597, Charles Leigh sailed the *Hopewell* into Basque Harbor with the intention of founding a Puritan settlement on the bleak Magdalen Islands in the Gulf of Saint Lawrence. He discovered the French already in possession, and the proposed colony soon evaporated in bitter theological dissension among its sponsors. Despite its ignominious failure, Gov. William Bradford later acknowledged it as the precursor of his colony at Plymouth.

Among early Protestant forays into what was to become Canada, this was the one most obviously motivated by religion; however, it was by no means the first. Jean-François de La Rocque de Roberval, a Huguenot who led a French expedition to the Saint Lawrence in 1542, was murdered for his faith in 1560. In the years from 1576 to 1578, Sir Martin Frobisher made three attempts to discover a northwest passage to Asia; in the course of the third of these voyages, the first known Anglican eucharist in Canada was celebrated. In 1604 the first permanent French settlement, in Acadia (now Nova Scotia), was established under the Huguenot leadership of Pierre du Gua de Monts, who carried with him not only two Roman Catholic priests but a Protestant minister. Over the next twenty years, Huguenot merchants largely dominated the commerce of New France. In 1628, however, a monopoly of trade was granted to the Company of One Hundred Associates, who were pledged to the support of Roman Catholic missions. Thereafter, Huguenots were not excluded from New France as rigorously as has sometimes been supposed, but clearly the colony was not destined to be Protestant.

Continuous Protestant influence thus began only under British sovereignty. In Newfoundland, Church of England clergymen accompanied the first colonizing expeditions, but during the rest of the seventeenth century, no religious services were provided for fishing families who had settled on the island without official sanction. Elsewhere, Protestant opportunity depended on French cessions of territory: peninsular Nova Scotia by the Peace of Utrecht in 1713, the rest of New France by the Treaty of Paris in 1763. Almost from the outset, the colonies attracted settlers from all of the British Isles as well as from the Rhine valley. Except for Newfoundland, however, they drew their first substantial Protestant population from the colonies to the south. New Englanders took up lands vacated by the Acadians after their expulsion in 1755 or set up fishing stages along the coast. In the wake of the American Revolution, United Empire Loyalists swelled their numbers and founded the provinces of New Brunswick and Upper Canada (now Ontario). Those who settled in the Maritime Provinces were mainly New Englanders; those who opened Upper Canada were predominantly from the Hudson and Mohawk valleys. The latter were followed by others, mostly from New England and the middle states, who had changed their minds about the Revolution or who merely felt the attraction of cheap, fertile land. Except in Lower Canada (Quebec) and perhaps Newfoundland, which provided a haven for many Roman Catholic Irish, Protestants constituted a large majority of the population.

The Protestant colonization of Canada, after the failure of Leigh's ill-starred effort, was determined largely by secular motives. Colonists might be political refugees, land-hungry frontier folk, tenants squeezed out by exorbitant rents, fortune seekers, or fishers in long-familiar waters, but they were seldom sufferers from religious persecution or seekers of a religious utopia. Their affiliations reflected, in most cases, the religious composition of the regions from which they had come. Early Newfoundlanders from the west country belonged to the Church of England, while later ones may have been in contact with the Methodist revival. Highland Scots were Roman Catholics or members of the established Church of Scotland, which was Presbyterian. The first wave of New Englanders was Congregationalist, with a sprinkling of Baptists. The circumstances of the American Revolution ensured that a large proportion of Maritime Loyalists would be Episcopalian. Those who settled Upper Canada, however, reflected the religious pluralism of upstate New York, and later arrivals broadened the spectrum further. They included Presbyterians, Congregationalists, Methodists, Lutherans, Quakers, Mennonites, Baptists, and the Episcopalians, whose number has been very variously estimated.

Missionary zeal, a notable feature of English-speaking Protestantism in the nineteenth century, was little in evidence in the early days of Canadian settlement. The government-assisted Society for the Propagation of the Gospel provided stipends for ministers of the Church of England, as was fitting in provinces peopled largely by Loyalists, but it attracted few beyond refugee clergy, and its ministrations were by no means universally acceptable. Settlers of other denominations had to secure ministers where they could, depending on such uncertain factors as the willingness of ministers to serve in an unattractive backwater, the willingness of home churches to spare them, and the settlers' own ability and willingness to support them. Best off were groups such as Quakers and Mennonites who maintained close ties with the communities from which they had come. Those without this cohesion, such as Presbyterians and Lutherans, often had to put up with drunkards, incompetents, and ministers who had fallen into disgrace at home. Some of the more zealous missionaries were supplied by Scottish groups that had seceded from the established church and by American bodies that had been affected by the revivalist tradition. In many communities something of a spiritual vacuum existed, and two movements of revival that helped to fill it were to prove especially significant in the shaping of Canadian Protestantism.

In 1775, Henry Alline, a farm boy who lived on the edge of Nova Scotia's Annapolis valley, had the first of a series of mystical experiences that left him dissatisfied with the sober Calvinism taught by neighboring Congregational ministers. He soon felt a call to preach, in defiance of Puritan inhibitions against the assumption of ministerial authority by the unlearned. In succeeding years he took his message of "new light" to all of the New England settlements of the region, extending his mission to Maine shortly before his death from tuberculosis in 1784. His preaching, which called for strict moral living, placed an extreme emphasis on the priority of gospel over law that imperiled the morals of some of his followers and left behind a ferment of ecstasy that lasted for some years. When the excitement cooled, most of Alline's leading followers embraced Baptist principles and they gradually restored the New England settlers to Calvinist orthodoxy. The tone thus set has characterized the region ever since, although sufficient residue of Alline's influence has remained to impart a certain unpredictability to its religious behavior.

The most dynamic religious movement to affect the inland provinces of Upper and Lower Canada, by contrast, was introduced directly from the United States. In 1791 a group of Methodist itinerants under the leadership of Freeborn Garrettson were engaged in carving out new circuits in upstate New York. One of Garrettson's lieutenants, William Losee, carried the spark to Upper Canada, where settlers had already organized two unofficial Methodist classes. The movement was promoted with typical efficiency by the Methodist Episcopal Church of the United States, which treated it as part of its internal operations and annually sent a steadily increasing number of itinerants across the border. By the outbreak of the War of 1812, Methodism had spread to almost every settled community and was well situated for further growth. It made its way as noisily as Alline's revival, but with a much firmer discipline. During the same period, Wesleyan Methodist missionaries from England were achieving similar results in the outports (fishing villages) of Newfoundland, while competing less successfully with "New Lights" and Baptists in the Maritime Provinces. Thus in all English-speaking areas there now existed more volatile alternatives to the types of Protestantism that most of the settlers had originally professed.

240

PROTESTANTISM AND SOCIETY IN CANADA

By the early years of the nineteenth century, the demographic and denominational pattern of the Atlantic provinces was largely set, although continued emigration from the Scottish Highlands would eventually make Presbyterians more numerous than either Anglicans or Baptists in Nova Scotia and Prince Edward Island. In Upper Canada, however, the War of 1812 ushered in radical changes. American influence was now suspect in religious as in other matters, and in the wake of the Napoleonic wars a massive influx of immigrants from the British Isles rapidly overlaid the earlier, largely American-oriented population. During the famine years Irish immigrants predominated and, through the attraction of the imperial tie, a much larger proportion of them than in the United States were Protestants from both north and south. By mid-century, Upper Canada was unequivocally a British province. It had become a well-settled community: log cabins were by then long forgotten except in the newest settlements, and the railways were the coming means of transportation.

During the early years of the nineteenth century, European churches were at last becoming aroused to mission, and those of Britain were eager to reach expatriates in Canada. After the War of 1812, the Church of England multiplied its clerical force. The formation of the Glasgow Colonial Society in 1825 goaded the Church of Scotland into action, and shortly thereafter the United Secession (later United Presbyterian) Church of Scotland extended its operations into Upper Canada. In 1828 the Methodists of Upper Canada, embarrassed by accusations of disloyalty, were granted autonomy by the American General Conference. Thereupon the Wesleyan Methodists of Britain, who had agreed to leave the province to the Americans, considered themselves free to send missionaries, and during the next decade several dissident English Methodist bodies also established small branches in Canada. Meanwhile, opportunities for extension did not go unnoticed in the United States. The American Home Missionary Society sponsored Presbyterian missionaries in both Lower and Upper Canada; Baptist associations in New York and New England sent a series of missionary delegations to organize churches; and during the 1830s and early 1840s, emissaries of Mormonism, Millerism, and of other novel doctrines swarmed across the Niagara River.

Except among the Baptists, who resisted attempts by immigrant Montreal businessmen to assert denominational leadership, it was the British influence that largely prevailed. Scottish immigrants were repelled by the revivalist methods of American Presbyterians, while many pioneer Presbyterian ministers of various origins ultimately joined the Church of Scotland. Upper Canadian Methodists accepted British leadership in 1833, and although this move led immediately to a secession of continuing Methodist Episcopals and seven years later to a temporary breach between Canadian and British Wesleyans, the connection ultimately held for the larger body of Canadian Methodists. Newer sectarian movements from the United States proved too exotic to leave a lasting residue. Meanwhile, the British orientation of Methodists and Presbyterians in the Atlantic provinces was never in question, and despite increasingly friendly relations with American Episcopalians, the Church of England remained throughout an important link in the imperial connection.

By the middle of the nineteenth century, Canadian Protestantism had set a denominational pattern that would endure practically until the 1980's, modified from time to time by divisions and unions but never disturbed by large-scale transfers of allegiance or by the appearance of major new denominations. Its denominational constituents were all ones that Canada shared with the United States, but their balance and general orientation differed significantly from the situation south of the border. Denominations holding closely to European traditions bulked much larger than in the United States, and movements of American origin had great difficulty in establishing themselves. The Church of England claimed a much larger proportion of the population than its American equivalent, while the Baptists, despite continuing strength in the Maritime Provinces, made a much smaller showing. Disciples of Christ and Mormons, major denominations in the United States, never came close to attaining that status in Canada. Congregationalists, after their brief period of ascendancy among the New England settlers of Nova Scotia, were able to establish few strong churches in Canada and were mainly successful among English immigrants. Especially striking, in comparison with the United States, was the narrowness of the Canadian denominational spectrum. Anglicans,

241

Presbyterians, and Methodists accounted for the great bulk of the Protestant population; among the rest, only the Baptists could claim more than local followings.

The gradual coalescence of pioneer congregations into coherent denominations raised with increasing urgency the question of their public status. The British colonial authorities had their own ideas on the matter, which they applied in varying ways in each province. Every state should have a religion, they reasoned, and logic decreed that the Church of England, as the national church of the homeland, should be similarly established in British possessions overseas. In 1758 the first assembly of Nova Scotia dutifully granted the Church of England this status; although, in an effort to attract settlers from New England, it assured full liberty of conscience to dissenters. Roman Catholics for a time remained outside the bounds of toleration, and priests at first had virtually to be smuggled into Newfoundland. But even this exclusion became untenable when the surrender of Quebec introduced a large Roman Catholic population, and complete religious freedom was gradually extended to all provinces.

The authorities still considered the Church of England to be entitled to privileged status; the outcome of the American Revolution confirmed them in this view and made implementation seem more urgent than ever. Colonists had lost their loyalty, the theory went, because they had never experienced the full working of the British constitution. Now, therefore, there would be a more consistent effort to export the entire system, including a secular aristocracy and an ecclesiastical hierarchy. For the church, this meant financial aid that usually included stipends for the clergy and grants of land, although imperial stinginess prevented the appointment of the number of bishops implied in such a policy. The Church of England was also given a privileged position in educational administration, and its clergy were at first the only Protestant ministers authorized to perform marriages. Since the necessary revenues were drawn not from tithes or other taxes on the colonists but rather came from sources at the disposal of the crown, it was reasoned that no one could validly object.

As might have been expected, some people did object. Anglicans constituted a minority of the population in every province, with the possible exception of Newfoundland, and in many rural communities their clergy were never seen. To colonists, especially those of American background, the Church of England was merely one church among others, and not one that had justified its claim to privileged status by superior energy in reaching out to scattered settlers. In the eyes of British North Americans, moreover, the land was their patrimony and not a resource that a distant imperial government was entitled to parcel out at will. Little was made of such grievances so long as settlers were preoccupied with the pioneer tasks of clearing land and establishing rudimentary communications. Once a sizable proportion of the population was roused to political consciousness, however, ecclesiastical inequality became a major source of contention. Discontent was exacerbated by the close connection between some leading members of the Anglican clergy and the official cliques, or "family compacts," with which British governors regularly surrounded themselves. In economic terms, the impact of subsidies to the Church of England was scarcely comparable with that of giveaways to friends of the government, but under the circumstances the two were not always easily distinguished.

Since British politicians were keenly aware that serious alienation of British North American opinion might lead to the loss of the provinces, Anglican privilege could scarcely have survived long if its enemies had been able to agree on an alternative. Baptists and Congregationalists, along with American and United Presbyterians and the smaller Methodist bodies, held high the flag of "voluntarism" (complete dependence by churches on voluntary givings). The Church of Scotland or "Auld Kirk," as the national church of a part of the United Kingdom, was more interested in enforcing its claim to co-establishment with the Church of England. Other Presbyterian ministers of varied origin found their parishioners so poor or so niggardly as to make the prospect of government bounty very attractive; hope of sharing in such bounty was almost the sole motive that induced a number of them to throw in their lot with the Kirk. The Wesleyan Methodists of the Maritime Provinces were too suspicious of worldly involvements to play much part in the contest, although those of Newfoundland entered into an alliance of expediency with Roman Catholics to limit Anglican dominance.

In Upper Canada, the sentiment of the main body was generally resentful of claims to privilege on the part of a church that seemed to them to have been less effective than their own in spreading the gospel, and a young preacher named Egerton Ryerson was one of the first to bring the issue into public discussion. The British Wesleyans were successful in securing a government grant for Indian missions, however, and when the Canadians accepted union with them, Ryerson was chiefly responsible for inducing reluctant colleagues to overlook this dilution of their voluntarism. Always, to be sure, Methodist itinerants insisted that they were accepting money only for the missions and never for themselves. The existence or projected foundation of denominational colleges was another fertile source of ambiguity, for it could be claimed that such colleges existed for general education rather than for denominational indoctrination. Even the ultravoluntarist Baptists of Upper Canada were shocked by the disclosure that their Maritime colleagues were accepting government aid for Acadia University in Nova Scotia.

Instead of a quick termination of the quasi-establishment of the Church of England, therefore, a protracted struggle ensued that took a different form in each province. Controversy ranged widely around such issues as rights to the solemnization of marriage, burial in church plots, and the place of the Church of England in the governance and staffing of provincial universities that still existed largely on paper. The most contentious issue in Upper Canada was a provision of the Constitutional Act of 1791 that set aside one-seventh of all land granted in the province for the support of a "Protestant clergy." The Church of England claimed these "clergy reserves" as its by right. Radical reformers called for the complete separation of church and state, while others would have been content with a more equitable—or at least extended—distribution of government bounty. By 1840 it seemed likely that the struggle would end in compromises that would satisfy no one but would placate all but the most intransigent voluntarists.

Then two significant external factors intervened. One was the growing influence of the Oxford Movement, which led many Anglicans to revive medieval concepts and practices and virtually to unchurch nonepiscopal bodies. An immediate result in Canada was an awakened fear that continued state support for the Church of England would not merely perpetuate an injustice but would subsidize perversion of Protestant principles. The other disturbing event was the secession from the mother Church of Scotland in 1843 of the bulk of its dominant evangelical wing. Their protest was against the denial by the civil courts of the church's right to set up new parishes or to limit the power of lay "patrons" to install ministers of their choice, regardless of congregational wishes. Local counterparts of the resulting Free Church, which quickly sprang up in almost every province, soon proved a potent political force. Although in principle they favored a close connection between church and state, their intense opposition to government support for "false" religion and their hostility to all catholicizing tendencies made them in practice the most strident of voluntarists. They quickly reactivated a largely dormant controversy, with the result that earlier compromises were swept aside in favor of the complete religious neutrality of the state. In Upper Canada, where controversy was most prolonged, the secularization of King's College, Toronto, in 1849 and of the clergy reserves in 1854 brought an end to Anglican dreams of special status.

During the same period, similar struggles for the equality of churches before the law were waged in many American states. To all appearances, results on both sides of the line were much the same: the disappearance of the last vestiges of European-style establishment. There were, however, significant differences in detail between the Canadian and the American experiences. British respect for vested property rights ensured that compensation would be granted for the loss of pledged sources of revenue, with the result that the future endowments not only of the Church of England but of several other denominations included funds that had come originally from the government. Moreover, earlier suggestions that government aid to the churches might appropriately be given so long as it was shared equitably have always retained a certain appeal, especially with regard to the financing of denominational colleges. Per capita government grants for theological students today recall this long-standing Canadian tradition. Thus, while Canadians have come to insist as a matter of principle on the necessity of maintaining a wall of separation between church and state, they have been prepared to allow chinks in it that most Americans would regard as unthinkable.

The issue of church and state was raised not only by the claim of one church to special status but by the demands of minorities for special treatment. Once Anglicans had abandoned their hope of controlling public education, some of their leaders asked that they be allowed to use their portion of tax money for their own schools. The same request was made, even more insistently, by members of the Roman Catholic hierarchy. Anglicans were too divided on the issue to be taken seriously by Canadian politicians, but Roman Catholics were able to enforce their claim. Events proceeded differently in each province, resulting in a bewildering variety of devices for satisfying the wishes of particular groups. Quebec set up two separate systems, Roman Catholic and Protestant. In Newfoundland, all schools came under denominational control. Other provinces, except British Columbia, made some provision for Roman Catholic—and, less frequently, Protestant—separate schools. Even in Nova Scotia, where the law is silent on the matter, tradition has long recognized certain schools as Catholic and appropriately served by nuns.

While Protestants almost without exception deplored separate schools and resisted all attempts to expand their operations, the necessity of coming to terms with their existence affected their own attitudes toward educational institutions. They seldom thought of public schools as Protestant, but they found it natural to regard them as their own. Religious exercises of a distinctly Protestant pattern seemed an appropriate way to begin the school day. Access to the schools and even the offering of religious courses in them seemed logical prerogatives for the Protestant clergy, especially since priests enjoyed similar privileges in publicly supported Roman Catholic schools. In Upper Canada, Protestants actually took the initiative in injecting the religious issue into education, for it was their insistence on making a place for the King James version of the Bible that prompted Roman Catholic demands for schools of their own. More often, Protestants have been reluctant to press claims that might provoke Roman Catholic counterdemands, although from time to time zealous ministers have taken advantage of statutory provisions for religious instruction.

The problem of dealing fairly with minorities has also been posed by individuals and groups who have conscientious scruples against conforming to some of the requirements of the state. Canadian governments have typically dealt with them, not in the American way of laying down general principles, but in accordance with the European monarchical custom of providing exemptions in particular cases. This was the method followed in early days with peace groups such as Quakers and Mennonites, who were excused from bearing arms but were required during the War of 1812 to render noncombatant service. This precedent has made it possible in more recent times for Canada to offer generous terms of immigration to Doukhobors and Hutterites as well as to Mennonites. It has also worked at times to the disadvantage of groups, such as the Jehovah's Witnesses, that governments have been unwilling to recognize as pacifist denominations, as well as of individual conscientious objectors unable to cite denominational principles sustaining their choices. In this matter, as in others, Canadians have shown a disposition to approach issues of church and state somewhat pragmatically.

Whatever its other effects, this reluctance to admit a rigid separation has encouraged the churches to envisage themselves as having a significant public role. Although no formal establishment of religion would be tolerated, Canada's major denominations have assumed some of the functions of national churches. An Anglican sense of imperial responsibility has been the most obvious expression of this attitude, but of comparable importance have been the Free Church's assertion of the lordship of Christ over national life and the aggressive Canadian consciousness that Methodism carried over from the days of its pioneer missions.

To churches thus oriented, the confederation of most of the British North American provinces in 1867 presented a major challenge, especially since Canada began its career as a nation without a coherent ideology. The motives that inspired confederation were essentially utilitarian, ranging from internal communications to national defense. The British North America Act, which served until 1982 as a national constitution, contains no ringing declarations but confines itself for the most part to a delineation of areas of responsibility between the federal government and the provinces. Sir Samuel Tilley, one of the fathers of confederation, is reputed to have suggested the national motto from Psalm 72, "He shall have dominion also from sea to sea, and from the river unto the ends of the earth," but politicians considered only its geographical implications to be their business. It was left to such church leaders as Robert Murray, editor of the *Presbyterian Witness* of Halifax and a prolific hymn writer, to express the hope that "fired with true devotion enkindled by thy word, from ocean unto ocean our land shall own thee Lord" (*The Hymn Book*, 1971).

Since no major Protestant denomination had anything like a national organization in 1867, the first necessity for implementing this vision was consolidation into effective units. In 1875 the Presbyterians crowned a series of earlier unions by bringing together their four remaining segments. Methodists achieved the same result through successive unions in 1874 and 1884. Anglicans, although untroubled by sectarian division within their ranks, were in practice fragmented by pride in diocesan autonomy and by mutual suspicion between their Anglo-Catholic and evangelical wings. In 1861 the formation of the ecclesiastical province of Canada brought most eastern dioceses within a loose federation, but only in 1893 was it possible to organize a general synod with jurisdiction from sea to sea. Baptists had even greater difficulty in getting together. At the time of confederation, there were several competing conventions in the Maritime Provinces, while the central Canadian body had had relatively little success in inducing individual congregations to join it. The Baptist Federation of Canada, embracing only one segment of the denomination and dependent largely on agreement among regional conventions, came into existence only in 1944. Lutherans, in 1867 still concentrated within a few areas of German settlement, looked to various American synods for support.

The decades immediately after confederation were marked not by gradual development along lines already familiar but rather by change and challenge. In 1870 the purchase of Rupert's Land from the Hudson's Bay Company and the formation of the province of Manitoba extended the new nation to the Rocky Mountains, and in the following year the admission of British Columbia fulfilled the dream of "dominion from

sea to sea." There was no immediate inrush of settlers comparable to that which created almost instant American states, but the frontier of settlement crept gradually westward through Manitoba and then, as the Canadian Pacific Railway moved toward completion in 1885, leaped hundreds of miles as newcomers occupied strategic sites along its line.

Despite its slow pace, settlement was beginning to submerge the native population of the West, to which Anglicans had been ministering since 1820, Methodists since 1840, and Presbyterians since 1866. Around the turn of the twentieth century, the prairies at last began to fulfill Canadian expectations, attracting 2 million settlers in the first decade. The more attractive American frontier had been closed, and new strains of wheat made northern farming at last profitable. Most immigrants were from Britain and the United States, but more conspicuous in what had been essentially a bilingual country were many from central and eastern Europe.

Unlike the American West, which presented no serious problems of access, the Canadian prairies were separated from populous eastern cities by a thousand miles of Precambrian rock. Reaching settlers there imposed a formidable problem of church extension that had to be approached with careful planning and substantial resources. Large denominations with national organizations that could readily be expanded— a condition that only Presbyterians and Methodists could meet—had distinct advantages, but even they had to evolve new techniques, such as mission superintendencies. Smaller groups, especially those with decentralized polities, found the task too large; indeed, the challenge of the West was an important factor in hastening Presbyterian and Methodist consolidation. The Baptists, although accounted a major denomination, were unable to develop a centralized missionary organization that would enable them to hold their own. Even the Church of England was too late in consolidating its national resources to move with the necessary speed. Its Indian missions were sponsored by the London-based Church Missionary Society, and English initiative was long instrumental in supplying clergy to the West. Eastern Canadian Anglicans gradually began to assume responsibility, but only when the great immigration had passed its peak.

While the prairies were attracting a substantially rural population, a few cities were beginning to approach metropolitan dimensions. Montreal and Toronto experienced rapid growth during the 1850s and 1860s, and before the end of the century Winnipeg, Vancouver, and Hamilton were becoming significant urban centers. At first, the cities seemed mainly to offer the churches opportunities for growth. They were able to erect cathedral-like sanctuaries, mount ambitious parish programs of Christian education and fellowship, and insist on more extensive preparation for the ministry. Incipient bureaucracies began to appear, and before the turn of the century the Methodist Publishing House was producing Canadian materials for Sunday schools. With the rise of cities, however, there also came into existence spreading slums and unchurched classes. Canadians were forewarned of the problems inherent in urbanization by experience in Britain and the United States, and churches and concerned individuals established city missions and put into place new programs designed to appeal to migrants from rural areas. Good results were achieved in many cases, but difficulties in reaching the masses seemed to outrun remedies.

Along with urbanization, there arrived a number of new ideas that were disturbing Protestants elsewhere: Charles Darwin's theory of evolution; the Higher Criticism of the Bible; Victorian doubts about eternal punishment; and various forms of German idealism. Although two heresy trials and several dismissals from theological faculties resulted, the general response in Canada reflected the moderation that is supposed to be a national characteristic. Theological professors gradually accepted evolution while remaining skeptical of natural selection, and they sifted "assured results" of biblical criticism from extreme views that could not easily be assimilated. Some others were more dubious. Sir J. William Dawson, an outstanding geologist who was principal of McGill University in Montreal, held to the traditional cosmology without attempting to retain a literal interpretation of the six days of creation. Even greater unease was reflected in the Niagara Bible Conferences, held on Canadian soil from 1883, and a few influential lay persons dissented vocally from the liberalism of their ministers. Most people in the pews were largely unaffected, in part because ministers were careful not to share all they knew. Probably

the most significant intellectual change, however, was not the impact of scientific scholarship but the influence of German idealism. In one form or another it largely replaced William Paley's confident search in nature for evidence of a divine design and the belief in innate ideas pointing inexorably to the recognition of a divine economy that characterized Scottish common-sense philosophy. Conservatives, sensing the loss of stable bases for logical deductions from Scripture, directed most of their wrath against more visible enemies, such as Darwin and the Higher Critics.

Despite some loss of support on the margins, Canadian Protestants felt strong enough not only to occupy their own West but to take their share in the missionary thrust of Christianity. Although Maritime Baptists and Presbyterians had missionaries overseas by the 1840's, the chief impetus to Canadian participation was provided by the Student Volunteer Movement in the 1880s. One result of this timing was a considerable concentration of Canadian effort in the Far East, which seemed to offer the greatest opportunities. Another was fairly general acceptance of the rounded programs of evangelism, education, and medicine that were then gaining favor. Canadians also took the lead in the formation of the Sudan Interior Mission, one of the largest Protestant faith missions. Missionaries preceded both traders and diplomats as representatives of Canada in almost every country to which they went, with the result that missionary visits and the study programs of women's auxiliaries were major factors in shaping Canadian consciousness of the Third World. Despite considerable diversity in doctrinal position and philosophy of mission, the influence of Canadian Protestant missionaries in the twentieth century has on the whole been a liberalizing one, both theologically and politically. Canada's situation as a former colony has also made its churches readier than most to respond to the desires of indigenous churches for autonomy and for participation in the life of the world church.

In a country that seemed in such need of a sense of national purpose, Protestants had to be interested in social transformation as well as in individual conversion and the foundation of churches. In content, nineteenth-century Canadian Protestant thought about society was largely derivative. Methodists and Presbyterians borrowed the functionalism of the American Social Gospel, while Anglicans preferred the more organic approach of Frederick D. Maurice's Christian socialism. Even before external influences had much effect, however, Canadian Protestants had assumed responsibility for promoting national righteousness. Moralism was thus a paramount interest and long remained so. Even the most radical representatives of the Social Gospel during its heyday in the early twentieth century were as dedicated to such causes as Prohibition, the observance of the Lord's day, and the suppression of prostitution as their predecessors had been. Purity was not a virtue cultivated only in Canada, but to Canadians the northern air seemed peculiarly favorable to it.

Conspicuous for their dedication to educational efficiency, hospitality to contemporary thought, missionary outreach, and moral and social reform were Methodists and Presbyterians, who were also more centrally organized than any other Canadian denominations and thus better equipped to direct resources to various regions and enterprises. Congregationalists, although few in Canada, shared the same general outlook and contributed leadership to causes of the day out of proportion to their numbers. The union of these three denominations, which took place in 1925 to form the United Church of Canada, was in many ways a culmination of the Protestant dream for a Christian Canada. Significantly, planning for it was essentially complete before the World Missionary Conference at Edinburgh in 1910, from which the rise of modern ecumenism is usually dated. Only in 1977, with the formation of the Uniting Church of Australia, did a comparable union take place outside the Third World.

The inspiration behind the union, as of many Canadian projects, was largely external. The circumstances that made it possible were specifically Canadian: the expense of serving the religious needs of a large area with a small population; the weight of Catholic French Canada, adding urgency to Protestant solidarity; the failure of politicians to provide an ideological framework for the nation. Wider union was already in the air at the time of the Presbyterian and Methodist internal unions, and it became the object of a conference, held at Anglican initiative, in 1889. An economic upturn around the turn of the century generated expansive hopes,

while the mingling of many ethnic groups was perceived as a threat to Victorian values that called for a unified response by the church. Local mergers took place in advance of union in many rural areas, and a number of western congregations banded together on the basis of the proposed constitution of the United Church. The union was clouded, however, by the decision of at least one-third of the Presbyterians to remain aloof as a continuing Presbyterian Church in Canada.

By the time the United Church was inaugurated, the utopian dreams that had inspired its formation had largely dissipated. Optimism had never been more evident than in the years preceding World War I, culminating in a great display of solidarity at a Social Service Congress in 1914. The war itself, while contradicting the pacifism to which many Protestants were cautiously moving, roused expectations of an outcome favorable to Social Gospel ideals. The prohibition of beverage alcohol in every province, although essentially a wartime measure, seemed a good omen. The disillusionment that followed the war was not peculiar to Canada and may not even have been as severe as in Europe or the United States. Certainly there was no collapse of Protestant hopes for the evangelization of the world, such as Robert T. Handy has noted for the United States, and denominational forward movements just after the war exceeded their financial targets. During the 1920s, however, the repeal of Prohibition in one province after another blasted the hopes of Social Gospelers. The churches were marking time at best, and processes of secularization that had long affected older countries were now unmistakably evident in Canada.

Closely associated with this loss of momentum was the disintegration of a consensus that had increasingly characterized the major Protestant denominations since the late nineteenth century and had helped make church union possible. The most spectacular expression of a new belligerency was an attack by T. T. Shields on theological teaching at McMaster University, which culminated in 1927 in a split within the Baptist Convention of Ontario and Quebec and created an atmosphere of mistrust that led to further schisms. Shields, pastor of the leading Baptist church of his convention, was well known in Fundamentalist circles in both Canada and the

United States. His ability to gain support rested in large measure on the discontent with theological liberalism that had been simmering for many years, and this same discontent was certainly an important factor in stimulating opposition among Presbyterians to church union. Yet Fundamentalism has had even less success in Canada than in the United States in dislodging liberal and neo-orthodox leaders from the major churches, including the Presbyterian. Until recently their chief strength has been in splinter groups and newer denominations.

During the last half-century, Canadian Protestantism has been subject to trends evident throughout North America and beyond. The Depression was felt with unusual severity in a country that relied heavily on foreign trade, and it coincided with a series of disastrous crop failures in the prairie provinces. One of its effects was to reactivate interest in social reconstruction. In 1934 radicals within the United Church organized the Fellowship for a Christian Social Order, which eventually broadened to include members of other denominations, while the Montreal-based Anglican Fellowship for Social Action increasingly drew inspiration from the Christian Marxism of Frederic Hastings Smyth. Resolutions against war or capitalism came to be regular features of ecclesiastical assemblies, especially those of the United Church, although they usually drew greater support at the regional than at the national level. In other circles, there were repeated calls for the revitalization of personal religion. They seemed to be answered when Frank Buchman's Oxford Group, later renamed Moral Re-Armament, toured Canada in 1932 and again in 1934. Pressing the familiar appeal for conversion at house parties designed to attract the well-to-do, the group became known chiefly for its call to commitment to the four moral absolutes of honesty, purity, unselfishness, and love, as well as for its encouragement of the practice of sharing guilty secrets with others who had been spiritually reborn. It vanished as quickly as it had arrived, although the influence of individuals affected by it can be traced in some later movements of conservative renewal. Despite such activities on the left and the right, the general mood of the 1930s was one of surviving and maintaining basic services.

Morale recovered slowly, at first almost imperceptibly. World War II, which seemed to most Protestants a painful necessity despite the recent popularity of pacifist sentiment, evoked from them neither enthusiastic advocacy nor widely sustained protest. Largely depersonalized by mechanization, the war encouraged no flocking to the churches for prayer. By way of compensation for the apparent failure of the war to stimulate a revival of religion, there was little inclination afterward to blame the churches for complicity in wartime propaganda. The speedy achievement of the kingdom of God no longer seemed a realistic goal, however, and in disillusionment many Protestants turned to the Christian realism of Reinhold Niebuhr or to the neo-supernaturalism of C. S. Lewis as more suited to the time. Others, less theologically inclined, were content to urge the grounding of society in rather vaguely defined spiritual values. Even so, there were still few signs in the late 1940s of an approaching revival of religion.

Then, in the 1950s, Canadian Protestant leaders were treated to a series of pleasant surprises: a sudden and spectacular increase in attendance at Sunday schools; the willingness of young parents, who for the most part were saddled with heavy mortgages, to erect and pay for expanded Christian education facilities; their willingness then to follow their children to church and to build sanctuaries for unaccustomed crowds of worshipers. In retrospect, it has become clear that the high wartime birthrate did much to set the stage for ecclesiastical recovery and that the growth of suburban congregations was at the expense of others in rural and downtown areas. There can be no doubt, however, that many Canadians of all religious persuasions who had become lukewarm toward their churches renewed their commitment during the 1950s, participating in religious activities with a zest that had not been evident for many years. Explaining this sudden return to religion is still not easy. Fear of communism and of nuclear war doubtless contributed to it, although cold war hysteria was distinctly muted in Canada. The centrality of the maintenance of family life in both Protestant and Roman Catholic programs suggests that the most significant single factor may have been a vague sense that traditional concepts of marriage were under strain and that the churches might offer the best prospect of reinforcing them.

The 1960s at first showed great promise, although a falling off in response to programs for young people might have warned of trouble ahead. Seeing a need for deepening the faith of enthusiastic but often poorly instructed new members, and finding that many of them had difficulty responding to traditional language and approaches, most Protestant churches began to prepare new Sunday school curricula, youth programs, prayer or service books, and hymnals. In order to rouse interest in these projects, they also encouraged members to ask questions about current practice and to participate in planning. Congregations began to experiment with new forms of worship and parish organization, and guitars began to be heard in church. All churches were greatly affected by the Second Vatican Council, which not only sweetened the ecclesiastical atmosphere but encouraged Protestants to accelerate the updating of their own programs. The council was exceptionally well received in Canada, where Roman Catholic bishops almost without exception espoused progressive positions in council debates, and Canadian Protestants responded by seeming to shed their traditional suspicions of Roman Catholicism almost overnight.

The most ambitious ecumenical project of the period was a serious attempt to extend the process of church union. In 1943 the Anglican general synod had invited other communions to engage in conversations that might lead to greater unity, and the United Church responded positively. But the years of postwar expansion were more conducive to competition than to cooperation, and the negotiations inspired little enthusiasm. When the Second Vatican Council stimulated renewed interest in ecumenism, the conversations took on a new urgency. In 1965 a joint committee found it possible to issue *Principles of Union* in which agreements on the touchier issues dividing the two churches were proposed, and in 1967 commissions were appointed to work out details in various areas. In 1969 the two original partners were joined by the Christian Church (Disciples of Christ). This was relatively a much smaller body than its American counterpart but it offered a distinct perspective that could open up possibilities of even wider union. In 1972 the General Commission on Church Union unanimously endorsed a document entitled *Plan of Union* and sent it to the churches for study and action.

Developments that excited some Protestants disturbed others, while failing to convince a number of activists that they promised significant change. Instead of advance all along the line, the decade brought on a wave of hostile criticism, initiated innocently by the Anglican Church of Canada when it commissioned a popular historian, Pierre Berton, to write his impressions of Canadian religious life. The furor caused by the publication of *The Comfortable Pew* in 1965 continued as lay people, women, and youth demanded a larger place in the decision-making processes of the churches. Religious institutions were under a cloud even when they sought to be ecumenical, and in 1975 union discussions were terminated as the result of the rejection of *Plan of Union* by the Anglican house of bishops and then by the general synod. Anglicans had specific objections to the plan; but more apparent than its deficiencies was a general lack of enthusiasm for union on all sides. Meanwhile, church membership and attendance were declining, most dramatically in the largest Protestant churches, and many elaborate new facilities for Christian education went almost unused. Revolt against institutions was a phenomenon by no means limited to Canada, but the Canadian institutions thus affected had previously been characterized by unusual stability.

In 1969 a survey commissioned by the United Church indicated that a continuation of current trends would result in zero membership in metropolitan Toronto within fifteen years. This and similar dire predictions have not been fulfilled. About 1972 a stabilizing trend became evident, and since that time membership and other indicators have shown little change. Ministerial vocations, after declining to less than half of their previous number, have risen well beyond earlier records. Desertions from the pastorate, which took place at an alarming rate in the 1960's, are now less worrisome than is the prospect of a shortage of available postings. Morale has recovered sufficiently that the Anglican and United churches have engaged in successful financial campaigns. While church membership has remained static, however, the population has increased significantly. Constituencies are aging, and there has been no notable inrush of young people.

Amid the confusion of these roller-coaster swings, some more permanent trends can be discerned. Clearly Protestantism has lost the ascendancy it had once enjoyed in Canada. After confederation, Protestants constituted slightly more than half of the Canadian population, although their majority tended to decline marginally from census to census. In the census of 1981, however, out of a population of 24 million, slightly less than 10 million reported themselves as Protestants, compared with more than 11 million Roman Catholics. The United Church of Canada, with 3¾ million adherents, is well ahead of any other Protestant church. Anglicans (many of whom would not be comfortable with the term *Protestant*) come second, with almost 2½ million. Far behind are Presbyterians, Lutherans, and Baptists, with eight, seven, and six hundred thousand respectively. Even the United Church seems a pygmy beside the Roman Catholic population, although the heavy concentration of the latter in Quebec makes the disproportion less evident elsewhere.

Within Canadian Protestantism, moreover, the hegemony of the major churches is being challenged for the first time since the rise of Methodists and Baptists in pioneer days. To be sure, the figures in themselves do not suggest dramatic changes. The five largest denominations still constitute more than 80 percent of the Protestant population. Pentecostals, the sixth largest, have only a little more than half the following of the Baptists; the Mennonites, who come next, are neither new nor rapidly expanding. Census totals, however, do not tell the whole story. Members of charismatic and conservative evangelical groups tend to be much more regular in attendance and generous in giving than others. In many communities, especially in western Canada, they outstrip the more traditional churches in attendance and can credibly claim to represent the religious orientation of a majority of the population. Nor does this spectacular growth represent merely a temporary enthusiasm, like the meteoric rise of the Salvation Army in the late nineteenth century; for more than fifty years they have been growing in something like geometrical progression.

Even more significant than the decline in numbers of the major Protestant denominations in relation to other religious bodies has been the fading of their influence on those who have never claimed any other allegiance. The most dramatic trend disclosed by census figures is the increase in those who express no religious preference. As late as 1961, such persons were rare. In 1981 they numbered almost 2 million, and one can safely assume that the bulk of them were of Protestant background. How much this increase has been due to the relaxation of pressure to state a preference and how much represents a real change is impossible to determine. What is certain is that the major Protestant churches no longer serve as Canada's moral arbiters as they were once accustomed to do. Ironically, this role largely dropped away during the prosperous 1950's rather than in the tumultuous years that followed. In the postwar period, James R. Mutchmor, the secretary of the United Church's Board of Evangelism and Social Service, assumed the role of moral censor. Working tirelessly to prevent the proliferation of liquor outlets and to keep salacious literature out of circulation, he was able, despite widespread unpopularity, to keep his efforts before the public and to gain the ear of government officials. But even during his tenure, church members were losing interest in these traditional moral causes, and no one has attempted to assume his mantle. It should be noted that Mutchmor promoted the extension of social welfare programs with equal zeal, if not with equal notoriety.

This loss of public stature has not inclined Protestant leaders to retreat to the private sector. On the contrary, they have become more active than ever in seeking social change. They have, however, shifted their emphases and modified their methods. Under the impact of movements of anticolonialism and liberation, they have largely dropped their attempts to enforce traditional taboos and have concentrated on the cause of the poor and oppressed. They still pass resolutions, but they also organize boycotts and attempt to influence financial institutions by speaking up as shareholders at annual meetings. Notably, also, the Anglicans, under the leadership of Edward W. Scott as primate, have moved from their traditional position as "the Conservative party at prayer" to vie with the United Church in social and political activism.

In making this shift, the churches have risked the alienation of influential sections of their constituencies. Organized resistance to denominational social programs has been a latecomer to Canada, but in 1977 the Confederation of Church and Business People was formed to challenge what its members regard as naive and irresponsible positions adopted by Protestant leaders. Expressions of sympathy for anticolonial movements are received with special touchiness, and the 1983 assembly of the World Council of Churches at Vancouver provided a ready-made opportunity for unfavorable publicity directed at its Program to Combat Racism. As yet, however, such criticisms have had little apparent effect on church policies.

Meanwhile ecumenism, not long ago rejected in the form of church union, is alive and well in other enterprises. Cooperation in theological education has developed to the point where the great majority of students of the larger Protestant denominations are brought into daily contact with other traditions. The Toronto School of Theology, a federation of three Roman Catholic, two Anglican, and single United Church and Presbyterian seminaries or faculties of divinity, is one of the largest theological consortia in North America and has been unusually successful because of its ability to persuade constituent schools to agree to a single timetable and schedule of courses. At Vancouver and Halifax, there have been complete amalgamations of denominational theological colleges, in the latter case with direct Roman Catholic participation. The typical Canadian approach to social issues, such as poverty and the effects of northern development on the native peoples, is now through interdenominational coalitions in which the participation of the Roman Catholic church is regarded as essential. The Canadian Council of Churches, a federation of Protestant and Orthodox bodies that has had an up-and-down existence since its formation in 1944, now appears insufficiently inclusive to do justice to the current ecumenical situation; negotiations are proceeding for its replacement or, more likely, enlargement.

Cooperation at the parish level is less frequently evident, and some promising Anglican–United Church enterprises have not regained the momentum lost with the sudden cessation of union talks. Nevertheless, while local inter-church events have lost some of the appeal of novelty, they continue to take place with considerable regularity and with general acquiescence, if not always enthusiasm. Relations with Jewish and other religious communities outside the Christian circle have also been cultivated to some extent, and for the first time Protestants are seriously attempting to appreciate the religious traditions of the native peoples.

There are still limits to the range of ecumenical interaction. Polarization between Roman Catholics and Protestants, which has been a primal fact of Canadian life almost from the outset, is scarcely discernible today. That Canada had four Roman Catholic prime ministers in succession representing both major parties—Pierre-Elliott Trudeau, Joseph R. Clark, John N. Turner, and Brian Mulroney—has attracted virtually no comment in the press. There has been no such easing of relations between "liberal" and "conservative" Protestant denominations. Roman Catholic priests now fit easily into local ministerial associations, but Protestants of conservative temper usually hold themselves aloof. The participation of the latter in formal ecumenical organizations remains almost unthinkable. Apparent readiness on both sides to join in sponsoring a national program of religious television may indicate some willingness at least to narrow the breach, although clearly this projected rapprochement has come about only because of the difficulty of obtaining official approval for such a program on any other basis.

To complicate the picture further, relations within denominations are often more difficult than relations among them. Fundamentalists, who hitherto had little influence within major denominations, became increasingly militant in the 1970s and stimulated renewed debate on issues of scriptural authority that had been considered closed. "Born again" Christians joining the traditional churches in increasing numbers have not readily found themselves at home among members of longer standing. Charismatic movements have proved both stimulating and divisive in all major denominations, while demands for more direct and aggressive evangelism have collided with efforts to enter into dialogue with members of other faith communities.

Issues of personal morality have also come to the fore again, with the definition of acceptable sexual behavior a particularly thorny topic. Both Anglican and United churches have at various times urged governments to relax their requirements for divorce, birth control, and abortion; a report on human sexuality being considered by the United Church in the mid-1980s seeks to establish guidelines of behavior that will take into account changing social mores. Members of more conservative convictions, especially in rural areas, see such initiatives as evidence of increasing conformity to the world, or even of apostasy. Emotions on either side are readily stirred, especially over such issues as the ordination of practicing homosexuals. On the other hand, theological and political conservatism no longer correspond as neatly as they did in the 1950s, and many conservative evangelicals now vigorously support the social action programs of their denominations.

The situation of Canadian Protestantism in the mid-1980s suggests to many a need for sober reassessment. More worrisome than losses in numbers and influence, or even than internal tensions, is a nagging suspicion that Protestants are no longer sure that they have a distinctive witness to offer. Most Protestants are confident that the activities in which they are engaged are meaningful and, in some cases, of urgent importance; they are less certain of the basis of these actions in Scripture and in the traditions of the church. Frequent emphasis on action at the expense of reflection is a natural consequence of this ambiguity. There are signs, however, that the preoccupation with the present that marked the 1960s and early 1970s is giving way to a conviction that a viable future will depend on a selective reaffirmation of the past. The United Church, which more than any other has been accused of accepting uncritically each successive trend in theological and methodological fashion, has recently launched an intensive study of the roots of its faith. Such a return to basics may presage a renewal of Protestant consciousness in Canada as a significant component of an ecumenical Christian witness.

BIBLIOGRAPHY

Richard Allen, *The Social Passion* (1971); Maurice W. Armstrong, *The Great Awakening in Nova Scotia, 1776–1809* (1948); Philip Carrington, *The Anglican Church in Canada* (1963); S. Delbert Clark, *Church and Sect in Canada* (1948); C. R. Cronmiller, *A History of the Lutheran Church in Canada* (1961); Stewart Crysdale and Les Wheatcroft, eds., *Religion in Canadian Society* (1976); G. S. French, *Parsons and Politics* (1962) and "The Evangelical Creed in Canada," in *The Shield of Achilles*, W. L. Morton, ed. (1968); John W. Grant, *The Canadian Experience of Church Union* (1967), *The Church in the Canadian Era* (1972), and, as ed., *The Churches and the Canadian Experience* (1963); Robert T. Handy, *A Christian America* (1971) and *A History of the Churches in the United States and Canada* (1977); *The Hymn Book of the Anglican Church of Canada and the United Church of Canada* (1971).

A. B. McKillop, *A Disciplined Intelligence: Critical Inquiry and Canadian Thought in the Victorian Era* (1979); D. C. Masters, *Protestant Church Colleges in Canada* (1966); John S. Moir, *Church and State in Canada West* (1958), *The Church in the British Era* (1972), *Enduring Witness* (1974), and *A History of Biblical Studies in Canada: A Sense of Proportion* (1982); Claris Edwin Silcox, *Church Union in Canada: Its Causes and Consequences* (1933); C. B. Sissons, *Church and State in Canadian Education* (1959); Peter Slater, ed., *Religion and Culture in Canada/Religion et Culture au Canada* (1977); Henry H. Walsh, *The Christian Church in Canada* (1956).

[See also DIVERSITY AND PLURALISM IN CANADIAN RELIGION; and FRENCH CATHOLICISM IN THE NEW WORLD.]

DIVERSITY AND PLURALISM
IN CANADIAN RELIGION

Earle H. Waugh

VISITORS from the United States to English-speaking Canada often remark that there is little difference between the two countries and point with good reason to the many common religious and cultural institutions as proof. Even in the area of scholarship, similar concepts have been utilized to evaluate socioreligious phenomena; for example, Edmund H. Oliver's use of frontier theory in his *Winning of the Frontier.* But such comments are not always welcomed by Canadians, and their responses reside as much in religious attitudes as in secular nationalism.

This is not to say that Canadian concern for religion is more "European," since Canadians join with their American confreres in churches and religious organizations in roughly the same proportion. The Canadian Institute of Public Opinion reported in 1974 that 39 percent of Canadian adults attended church weekly, a figure that compares favorably with 42 percent of American adults. The 1972 Gallup poll, which provided the American figure, also indicated that this percentage was higher than in Switzerland, Greece, and Germany, and significantly higher than in the Scandinavian countries. Judging from the 1981 statistics, Canadians are a religious people; only 1.37 percent of the population consider themselves to be nonreligious (Statistics Canada, 1981 Census).

Religion thus enjoys the support of a sizable portion of the citizens of both countries. Moreover, both Canada and the United States are considered denominational societies, since neither can be characterized as having an established church with a variety of sectarian protestors, and both are voluntaristic regarding institutional religion and law and taxation. Finally, both countries are clearly pluralistic, in the sense that over 90 percent of believers are either Protestant, Catholic, or Jewish.

Despite these common elements, there are many differences that can be traced to the way in which Canada has developed and the role that religion, both institutional and otherwise, has played in its cultural formation. The first is that, although Canadian institutional religion is pluralistic, it is not as diverse as her neighbor's. The combined total of the United, Anglican, and Presbyterian churches' adherents represents 70.7 percent of Protestants, admittedly a drop from the previous totals (in excess of 85 percent in 1971; Statistics Canada 1974), but far ahead of the twenty-one churches required to produce the same percentages in the United States. Canadian church polity reflects the centralizing tendencies: none of the major institutions is congregational, and the United Church of Canada, while it is the country's largest Protestant denomination and itself formed by corporate union, is far more centralized than, for example, either the Methodist or the Baptist church in the United States. Until recently, the Anglican and United churches were seriously discussing merger, an action that would have little credence in the United States.

The second difference is that the church has always played a key role in immigration, through either providing whole groups for homesteading or taking charge of ministry to the frontier even before the immigrants arrived. This radiation from center to periphery has continued to exercise a restraining influence on schisms, with smaller groups following the model of centralized bureaucracy so evident in the larger institutions. Moreover, the need to survive in a harsh environment with few people to assist required more from those structures that were in place, and right from the founding of Canada the church was present. Thus it has taken on the hue of an establishment organization without the formal requisites necessary to make it so.

In a peculiar way, the conflicts between the French and English have assured an establishment mentality in Canada. When the company of New France was granted the charter in 1627, all colonists were required to be Roman Catholic, even though France had a sizable religious minority in the Huguenots. It was partially this traditional homogeneity in New France that allowed the Roman Catholic hierarchy to support confederation, as one way of preventing a feared annexation to the United States, and the creation of provinces (including the two most populous, Ontario and Quebec) was a tacit recognition of the counterbalance of Catholic Quebec and Protestant Ontario. The autonomy in cultural and educational matters in Quebec granted to the Roman Catholic hierarchy in exchange for its support for confederation has guaranteed a self-confident church, which in turn has allowed it to influence public policy and initiate debate across denominational and provincial lines.

While this balance of religious forces might have provided Canada with positive elements for discourse in the early decades, this did not occur. Instead a tone of rancor and competition prevailed and played a role in the mission enterprises and immigration reactions of the churches in the developing West. Protestants looked to it as an arena to extend the Reformation heritage, and Catholics saw it as the logical extension of the church in Quebec. The French hierarchy supported the French language and culture as a means of maintaining the hegemony of the Catholic vision in Canada, while Protestant groups labored vigorously so that their dreams would not take second place. The one positive result not immediately evident was that settlement on the prairies was intimately tied to the "national" church, in direct contrast with the situation in the United States, where individuals and sects looked to western settlement for religious and personal freedom. Because of these characteristics, it must be recognized that organized religion asserted far more than a voluntary role in the shaping of the Canadian experience.

The third difference is a cluster of ideological concerns with religious dimensions. Some of these concerns were connected with the mission of the church to the masses of immigrants. More than one church official saw the Christianizing of the nation as a necessary ingredient in civilizing it. The church, whether Catholic or Protestant, developed energetic mission programs, at the heart of which was the conviction that moral fiber and strong character were essential in building up the kingdom of God. The mission was to blossom mightily during the nineteenth century, when Catholic orders and Protestant mission groups set their sights on continuing the great values of Christian tradition in the new nation of Canada. These two religious orientations differed significantly in the definition of the mission —the ultramontanists of Quebec would look to a strong hierarchy, almost medieval in ideal, from the local parish through the archbishops to the Holy Father in Rome, while the most aggressive Protestants, the Methodists and the Baptists, would brandish millennial visions and actively fight against alcohol and other social vices in their effort to bring about the morally upright Canada of their hopes. Yet both Catholics and Protestants wanted legislation to reflect their concepts, and in many cases it did. Government was shaped by their concerns. Ultimately social activism embodied in legislation was to secularize the mission legacy of the churches, giving Canadian governments the appearance of liberalism and community sensitivity. Especially among Protestants, the moral responsibility built into missions would translate into the material and cultural development of the nation when the original message had withered and died.

This focus on community over the individual has made the Canadian experience far less schismatic and particularist than the American experience; Canada's wild West was very dull indeed compared with that of its southern neighbor. The Northwest Mounted Police were already there before the settlers arrived, and the sense of extending tradition in a hostile environment applied not only to religion but also to law. Since some of the greatest conflicts were between groups within a religious tradition, the law mediated for them. Since law was held to embody the moral dimensions of society, it came to be a kind of supra-value-system for all. Respect for law remains one of the chief traits on which

DIVERSITY AND PLURALISM IN CANADIAN RELIGION

Canadians pride themselves, and this is demonstrated by a markedly lower per capita crime rate than in the United States.

Loyalties to community and law have had their impact in turn on the religious life. No authentically Canadian religious group has sprung up. A number of movements and revivals have influenced the whole, and they will be surveyed below, but no new group has appeared as a genuinely Canadian religion. Canada's best-known evangelist, Aimee Semple McPherson, did not remain in her homeland but found her success in Los Angeles. Individual initiative in a number of areas always seemed to run counter to the prevailing spirit of the country, with the result that Canada is lauded for its stability and conservatism while being chastised for its reluctance to risk and its resistance to difference. Conversion to a new or radical group is not effectively salable in Canada—only fifty-odd groups comprise the identifiable Christian diversity in the census figures. In contrast, the United States must have several hundred by now.

Fourth, religion has not sparked any equivalent of "manifest destiny." No religious group has linked its identity with Canada as a nation, and religionists have been far less concerned with the fact of Canada's existence than with its character. Since the inculcated values were the finest from the past, Canada was no "lively experiment." The spiritual patriotism that marks the church in the United States is absent in Canada, and the messianic mythology underlying the Union is exclusive to that domain. The church in Canada has been excited by national achievements, such as construction of the national railway system, but it has scarcely presented the country with a definite answer to whether Canada has any destiny, let alone one clear and manifest. The result is that participation in a local religious organization does not provide the average Canadian with an entrée into national identity and seldom links him with fellow Canadians in a common national symbol-system. The qualifier *seldom* is deliberate. The Catholic church may for some Canadians represent that system, and for others it is the United Church. By acknowledging its pluralism legally, however, and by firmly holding to ethnic and racial differences, Canada has effectively moved religion out of the national identity business.

This does not mean that there are no religious dimensions to Canadian identity, but that they are of a diffuse and ambiguous nature. Canadians have rarely speculated upon religious dimensions, even in the academy, and they are more likely to be found in the arts and literature than in quantifiable studies. Nevertheless, religious dimensions do present a kind of civil religion.

CANADIAN "CIVIL RELIGION"

The most evident example of Canadian civil religion is in the province of Quebec. Quebec society has so embodied a messianic vision of French culture in North America and has given it form and substance through state festivals, legendary heroes, and popular epics that elements of a grand destiny appear. This collective direction has continued to play an effective role, even when the province became far more ethnically divided and certainly more secular than in the ultramontane days of New France. It has continued to shape public opinion in the conflict between Quebec and the federal government and the other provinces, ultimately giving birth to the Parti Québécois and its separatist agenda.

If, as some have contended, Protestant civic piety is one meaning of civil religion, then the other provinces have had their own form. Even when immigration has brought non-Christian traditions, the mores and customs take on this Protestant civic coloring. Some provinces, like Alberta, mindful of the serious problems that prejudice and lack of communication between various social groups can have, have instituted major curriculum reforms with a view to incorporating more values in the educational diet. The very will to do this indicates a transorganizational ethic and a certain concept of what Canadians "should be" that harks back to the nation-building images of the missionaries of an earlier time. It also reflects a Canadian identity transcending sectarian consciousness.

If Canadians live in isolated communities strung out along the U.S. border, and if they relate primarily through local group consciousness, they are held together by a collective response to their natural environment. A very contemporary picture is embraced by F. R. Scott in his meditation:

Hidden in wonder and snow, or sudden with
    summer,
This land stares at the sun in a huge silence.
Endlessly articulating something we cannot
    hear.

The corporate image of the land is not always depicted as so alien. Jacques Cartier went to great lengths to describe it as a "new earth," deliberately drawing on Christian allusions. The prolific writings of the Jesuits present a land of natural paradisal dimensions. It is impossible, then, on the basis of the artistic and literary traditions, to talk of being Canadian without noting the connectedness of identity with the land.

If the land is so multivalent and even foreign, the human response posed by experiencing its history is fairly simple and straightforward: one is lost. George Grant's *Lament for a Nation: The Defeat of Canadian Nationalism* is famous for the description of what happens to loyalty to Canada in the wake of a liberalism bent on fulfilling its individual entrepreneurial goals regardless of the cost. The result is a book moving for its sense of loss.

Other writers have attributed the loss not so much to the awesomeness of an unforgiving land or to the inability to relate to its first inhabitants, but to slavish attention to U.S. values, culture, and influence. The ambiguity for identity is obvious. Some of Canada's best writers, like Margaret Atwood, use losing and victimization as unifying themes in their writing. It is too facile to regard this literature of deprivation as Canada's reaction to living next door to success. The United States throws a long shadow, and existing at a time of nearly universal doubt and alienation surely helps, but the trait goes back to the way people have looked upon their history. Some see it as a profound expression of the Canadian soul.

THE RELIGIONS OF THE FIRST PEOPLE: INDIAN AND INUIT

The people whose culture has been most associated with the land and who best have a reason for "being lost" are the people who were there when white people came. Even among them, there are great differences, both in habitat and in custom. The Eskimos, or Inuit ("the people") as they prefer to be called, have physical features distinct from those of the Indians, and they are largely coastal; that is, they live near and make their living from the sea. This distinction is not absolute, however, because the Northwest Coast people also derive their livelihood from the sea, as most likely did the now extinct Beothuks of Newfoundland.

The Inuit are not the only people who live in the Arctic. There are subarctic Indians, some of whom live above the Arctic Circle, stretching from Alaska to Hudson Bay. One of the largest groups is the Kutchin (whose neighbors are the Inuit), concentrated in the northwestern corner of Canada and in eastern Alaska; they have been little influenced by the fur trade of Pacific Coast "totem pole" traditions. Despite their locale, the Kutchin are inland Indians, dependent on the woodland caribou for their livelihood. They are joined in the eastern subarctic by the Loucheux, or Canadian Kutchin.

Northern people traditionally have linked themselves together in small groups, normally called bands, that united them according to kinship structures, linguistic commonality, and culture. Much of their yearly cycle was spent in hunting groups, however, with the entire assembly coming together during the off-season. At the time of first contact, some Inuit maintained permanent settlements in Greenland and Alaska, but the Canadian Inuit are known chiefly as the snowhouse and tent-dwelling people.

Most non-natives think of Indians as buffalo hunters, totem-pole carvers, corn-raisers, and birch-bark-canoe makers. The one correct assumption behind this is that most Indians live in the temperate part of the continent, where such activities can be carried on. In Canada there are six cultural areas inhabited by distinctive peoples: Algonkian, Iroquoian, Mackenzie River, Plains, Plateau, and Pacific Coast. But a cultural area may not belong to a common linguistic family. There are now ten such families, known as Algonkian, Athapaskan, Haida, Iroquoian, Kootenayan, Salishan, Siouan, Tlingit, Tsimshian, and Wakashan; yet, for example, the Algonkian, Athapaskan, and Siouan languages are all spoken in the Plains region. To this complexity are added several qualifiers: linguistic families are made up of a number of subgroups, speaking languages related to each other or dialects; some linguistic families are very distant from each other (e.g., the Blackfoot of the Plains are Algonkian, as are the Micmacs of the Maritimes); some but not all Indians share both a linguistic heritage and a cultural heritage; some groups were forced by circumstances to adopt a kind of cultural dualism (the Kootenayans were originally Plains but were forced into the Plateau region of British Columbia). Hence these people demonstrated within themselves a pluralism that belies our term "Indian." It follows that they are religiously diverse as well.

Inuit Religion. Initial studies by whites of the Inuit stressed their superstitious nature. For example, a visitor was surrounded by ritual forms from the time he entered their presence until he left, giving him the impression that these rites were based on strange superstitions, and even someone as sensitive as the Danish explorer Knud Rasmussen was excited by the Inuit's apparent fear of spirits. But much of this early evaluation was culturally bound; Europeans had a singular idea about what was religion and what was not, and many of the tales told derive from that myopia. This makes it difficult to describe Inuit traditions with complete confidence.

It is better to begin with rituals rather than with gods and deities. The traditional Inuit saw and lived life as a continuous cycle that represented the system of nature as they understood it. As such, they had a deliberate "religious" policy of defining normalcy according to their own cultural dictates. Normalcy, however, was being constantly challenged by the circumstances of their environment—the game was scarce, or sickness threatened, or storms raged, making life-as-usual impossible. When normalcy was upset, procedures were begun to restore the balance and stability that characterized life when everything was "normal." The Inuit believed that they were an integral part of the natural order and indeed that their actions and reactions could have a direct impact on the forces that made up their environment. They did not hold that they created the environment, but they believed that the way in which that environment interacted with them was directly related to their attitude toward it. This conviction was so profound that even a storm evoked a ritual response that would serve to control the elements and reestablish equilibrium. The arrival of a stranger was a similar situation, requiring a ritual response. Whether the white man understood or not, his presence had to be regularized or the community

might be faced with extensive disruption. This sensitivity to the environment was expressed through myriad ritual gestures and taboos that left the white visitor impressed with their "superstition."

The Inuit shared with his Indian brethren the common conviction that the natural environment was empowered; that is, expressed life forces. Sometimes these forces were obvious, as, for example, unusual outcroppings, bays, or islands; sometimes they were not obvious, like the spirits that inhabited strange territories. They had to be recognized and honored or they potentially could harm. Hence offerings of animal parts or gifts were given as recognition of the special character of the locale, lest the lack of proper propitiation bring about malevolence and disruption of normalcy. It was this "spirit territory" that set one people's land off from that of another, and one would hardly transgress the boundaries unless, like a shaman, one had extraordinary powers of self-protection. This belief also explains the almost paralytic fear the Inuit had about being transported to the white man's hospitals. In short, the territory housed spirits and souls, as well as animals and humans; there was a direct connection between the former and the latter.

It was also a triangle. Humans could kill animals for food, but in doing so they had to be aware of the animals' souls. Rasmussen noted that a small piece of salmon was placed underneath the floor skin of a snowhouse by the Netsilik Inuit as a sign of respect for its soul, and chants to a dead bird or animal were common. Since the animal would be reincarnated, proper respect would ensure the animal's compliance to being killed the next time. On the other hand, improper respect could turn the animal into a Tornait, or evil spirit, whose wrath would be visited upon the hunter and his community.

Humans too had souls; in fact, they had two kinds of souls. They shared the immortal nature of soul with the animal and could be reincarnated, but they also had a "natural" soul. This "natural" soul was the soul of the ordinary human being, probably close to the notion of personal integrity and well-being. A human who was sick had some problem with this soul; the shaman, or angakok, would address the individual, try to elicit certain telltale signs from him, and pronounce the means of cure. If there were foreign substances like worms or bones, he would drive them out. If the problem arose from the violation of a taboo, he heard confession and helped put things right. If a significant evil broke out in the community, such as an epidemic or a prolonged hunting drought, the collective "soul" of the whole group would undergo rituals of identification and purification, once more under the guidance of the shaman. Rasmussen has some dramatic descriptions of these seances, which required the shaman to journey to the land of Narssuk, the Moon Spirit, to mollify him in the face of the tremendous storm he had unleashed upon the people. While there, the shaman would find out what his people had done to deserve this treatment and would return to the community for confession and repentance. The collective "soul" of the group having been returned to normal, the environment followed suit.

The Inuit also associate strong power with an individual's name, seeing this as a way of maintaining the individual's positive influence after death. The collection of good qualities embodied in the name is held to reappear in the person of a just-born infant. Sometimes that name is given to a child as a kind of guardian spirit to aid him until his own *nappan* (human soul) is strong enough to carry him. As the child matures he takes on his own personality, with the name of the ancestor diminishing in power before his own power. The human soul, with the potential for disruption if the taboos or ritual prescriptions are broken, also dies at death, save for his name power, and his immortal soul is sent off to the land of the dead.

Death, particularly of a mature member of the group, is a major disruption and must be treated with full ritual precautions. The body is sometimes taken through a window to deliberately confuse it. Since death is polluting, the dead person's igloo must be abandoned, and even the deceased's name may not be mentioned until it is pronounced at the birth of a child held to inherit it. A shallow grave or rocks piled on the body are all the burial required, although special care is taken among some groups as to the direction in which the body is placed. Some stories tell of the abandonment of those too old to move with the group or to be helpful, and Rasmussen related that babies born of someone regarded as accursed could be killed.

The immortal soul may go directly to heaven in the sky or, among some peoples, go to a world where it moves through progressively happier lands in four stages until it comes to the happiest. In this sacred territory there are never modifications of normalcy, so game is plentiful, feasting is constant, and the sun never sets.

The shaman is the most powerful religious specialist. It is he who weighs the happenings of the environment and of the community and understands specifically and accurately what factors have led to disruption. He is the master of the normal, since he also has keen insight into the chaos around it. Most of his knowledge is gained from personal wrestlings with sacred powers beyond the ken of the ordinary person, although some may be apprenticed to family members of the shaman or his associates. In any case, the shaman's life is not an easy one, since he must undergo long fasts, extreme suffering, and prolonged separation from his people, in addition to his struggles with spiritual forces. He is always feared in the community, even as the group recognizes his special gifts to them.

The shaman's role in community maintenance can hardly be overemphasized. In a religious system as intricately balanced as that of the Inuit, he must not only know every individual personally and thoroughly, but also understand that individual's role in the group. Personal illness must be judged in the light of that knowledge with a keen eye to the community's view of the shaman and his power. He must also understand the limits to frenzy and must internalize the community's disintegration so that it may eventually be healed. This ability to lead the group into emotional agony and then transform that turmoil into community integration demonstrates a capacity that few religious specialists enjoy.

The shaman deals not only with human problems but also particularly with those that arise from the interaction between the deities and humans. The deities are associated with the mysteries of life—where things come from, why they are like they are, and how one relates to them. Sedna, the mistress of animals, lived under the sea, and the myth tells of her father's attempt to throw her overboard during a gale. He succeeds only in getting her over the side, where she clings to the edge. Finally he chops her fingers off at the first and second joints. The first joint pieces become whales, the second joint pieces become seals. Then he loosens her by knocking out her eye, whereupon she descends to the depths to control the animals of the hunt. It is to Sedna that the shaman must journey, sometimes to clean and stroke her hair, which has become filthy with the people's breaking of taboos. Moody, she must be won by him lest the people die.

The deities are not universally the same; shamans in the West journey to Narssuk, while in the East a male deity is honored. But the critical aspect of their being is that the deities are identified with certain personalities, have groups of myths associated with them, and control the environment from which humans must draw their sustenance. Deities do not function like the gods of Western tradition, but then the religion of the Inuit does not focus on gods or goddesses. It is far more a system of controlling chaos and restoring and preserving normalcy in a meaningful, religiously satisfying manner.

Contemporary Inuit culture has been modified significantly under white influence; both Catholic and Anglican missions now dominate the religious views of the Inuit. Southern development has altered the style of life in the North; with permanent sites scattered throughout Inuit territory, many Inuit no longer travel out for hunting and whaling, relying instead on the largess and odd jobs of the white community for survival. The result has been a profound alteration of the Inuit world view. Christianity has changed the assumptions and reoriented the Inuit in their environment. The delicate balance between man, nature, and the master of animals has been replaced by the creedal and liturgical focus of the churches. Vestiges remain, however, and small pockets of Inuit still retain the old ways.

INDIAN RELIGIONS

Any discussion of Indian religions must acknowledge two critical factors: the limitations of our understanding and the artificiality of our boundaries. On the first issue, we must now admit that much of the data and its interpretation, even by objective scholars, is skewed away from the religious intentions of the practitioners. In short, would the people who acted and believed the way we say they did recognize themselves in what we have written? It is doubtful. On the second issue, our categories of delineation come out of our scholarly tradition, based on our assumptions. Many of these are inappropriate. A pertinent example is our category of a cultural area.

What follows is a capsule comment, built from one group within each of the six cultural areas normally identified in Canada: the Naskapi for the Algonkian, the Blackfoot for the Plains, the Tlingit for the Plateau, the Kwakiutl for the Pacific Coast, the Chipewyan of the Mackenzie River, and the Iroquois of the Iroquoian.

The Algonkian. The Naskapi, like all the natives under this heading, inhabit an area within the woodlands of the eastern and central section of Canada. They reach as far north as the subarctic, and hence some of them impinge on the Inuit. They developed excellent means of transportation for their migratory hunting life-style—canoes, snowshoes, toboggans, and dog teams. Their chief livelihood is bush game, supplemented by fish, birds, and wild berries.

One helpful way of describing Naskapi religion is to say that hunting is a sacred responsibility. Taking animals is a religious act that makes the hunter into a priest of the living world. The living world includes primarily the animals, but also encompasses the spirits and powers in the nonhuman realm. The Naskapi's power to manipulate the world comes about because he is ever-attentive to correct behavior in light of the fact that careless acts, disregard for taboos, or foolish ignorance of the spirits of the animals will surely affect his family and his hunting success. In order to carry out his ordained task, the Naskapi must not only obey rules handed down from his ancestors but also weigh the influence of Mistapeo in his own inner life. Mistapeo is an inner force that represents a superego of the soul. Mistapeo is the life force that moves and directs the meaning of the individual, but he retains a distinction from the self of the person and is held to direct that person. Mistapeo is also the seat of moral expression, since he finds generosity, helping others, and kindness to humans and animals praiseworthy; at the same time, he interacts with the inner soul by providing dreams and revelations that lead directly to game. Without Mistapeo, the Naskapi would not be human.

But humanness is hardly a category that concerns the Naskapi, for animals and humans are not essentially different in nature or construction. Personal awareness of some slight or mal-treatment that goes unrepented leads to disruption in humans. It also affects animals. The spirit dynamic of all living things is intimately and personally known through the life force of the hunter. In effect, then, the animal allows itself to be taken by the hunter because there is an inner solidarity between them, a spiritual link that allows the hunter to control the animal's Mistapeo, providing that the life force has been and will be properly respected.

A number of elements of Naskapi religion follow from this: taboos must be scrupulously observed, a shaman must repair any great rent in the spiritual fabric, ceremonial life surrounds the taking of life and eating, and mythology is intimately tied up with this relationship to the life force. For the Naskapi, Atikwanabeo (or Caribou Man), who lives on a high mountain, is the master of the animals. No Indian would dare visit the area unless he be a shaman in a vision, and then only on very special occasions. Caribou Man releases only 'so many caribou for humans to kill; hence the Indian belief that an animal that becomes available for killing must be taken or relationships will be disrupted. The Naskapi show great reverence for the bear, even though bears are rarely seen. In this they appear to have been influenced by a bear ceremonial that straddles the circumpolar region, for the Naskapi often take seal but show little reverence or concern for taboos in their killing. Even the caribou is somewhat less important ritually than the bear, even though it is far more the animal of sustenance.

Divination is a critical part of this religious world. Since the rules by which one may hunt are defined by this life force, any number of means might be used by that force to reveal its will. The hunter becomes a priestly interpreter of the elements, reflecting the inner dynamic. Scapulimancy, or scorching an animal's shoulder blade and reading the cracks and spots, is practiced, as are various forms of drumming, singing, and rattling. Charms are a necessary part of hunting paraphernalia, and natural phenomena, like the sun bursting through a heavy cloud-cover, are given omen value.

Finally, souls that represent the true identity of an animal are transformed into stars until such time as they are reincarnated. Babies are said to come from the clouds, and Tsekabec, the trick-ster figure, is transformed into either the sun or the moon. The Milky Way is the road traveled by souls who as the northern lights periodically gather for a great dance in the night skies.

Development in the North appears to have had a more potent impact on the Naskapi than Christianity. Flooding from Hudson Bay Hydro projects has inundated some of their lands, leaving them without hunting grounds. A sedentary life has destroyed the sacred hunting ideology, leaving little in its place. For those affected, this has been a tragedy. For those still able to hunt, the religious traditions of their ancestors sit side by side with those of their Christian priests or ministers (and sometimes both), apparently without overt conflict.

Plains Traditions. The Blackfoot Plains traditions developed to their classical extent with the adoption of the horse. The increased mobility seems to have had a creative effect on the cultural life, providing the impetus for reformulation and revision. Out of this reformulation came one of the most distinctive religious practices—the Sun Dance.

The Sun Dance incorporated most of the central ideas present in previous traditions, but it seems to have brought them together in a macrocosm-microcosm structure. Thus the Sun Dance is really not a sun rite at all, but a dance reflecting the renewal and reconstruction of the cosmos. The Sun Dance is performed in a specially constructed building called the lodge. The lodge is built of poplar and willow, both of which have abundant new growth at the time they are cut, and so it retains a connection with new vegetation and the revivification of the earth.

Among the Blackfoot, the Sun Dance may involve a torture rite in which a participant pierces the skin of his chest with pegs and dances with strings tied to the center pole until he breaks loose. The dance is not primarily for a personal trance, although this may occur, but rather is a gift of oneself in exchange for a renewed spiritual and physical world. Since this ceremony traditionally took place at the new year, the potential for individual and corporate renewal is very evident. The ceremony takes place over four days and is sponsored by a holy woman, an elder of great respect in the tribe, assisted by the leading "grandfather." It incorporates the repetitive recital and dancing of various cycles of songs according to the same pattern of four, along with sweat and pipe ceremonies, healing prayers, consecration of the prayer flags, ritual gift-giving, and secret society meetings. So powerful a ritual was the Sun Dance that the missionaries appealed to have it outlawed and the federal government complied.

Another important element of Blackfoot religion was the vision quest, a rite of discipline, fasting, prayers, and self-mortification that often led to a personal trance in which a guardian spirit appeared, giving the devotee a new name, new songs, and a new status in the group. Out of this rite young men became medicine men or acknowledged hunters and warriors. It was thus the key to personal identity within the group, and it sealed the nature and spiritual makeup of the young man for the tribe's well-being. Some of the inner life of the young man was centered upon the dream, which operated in the same way as a vision, except that its recurrence was held to be the guarantee that the spirit world was communicating with him. Weapons, shields, and special amulets could be the subject of these dreams, providing the accoutrements for a complex magical and spiritual power. It was this same dreaming power that provided the format for the secret societies and the power of the medicine bundles.

Both Catholic and Protestant missionaries set up churches and schools on Blackfoot reservations. Most Blackfoot Indians who converted became Christians in some meaningful way, accepting that the cosmic religion they had practiced was part of a tradition they could not regain. However, Sun Dances are still held throughout Alberta every summer, and loyalties among those who attend are clearly with the old ways. The Canadian government's change of heart concerning the rites has removed the interference of the Mounties, and it remains for the elders to inspire a new generation to rediscover the rich heritage. At the same time, Indian young people are moving to cities in unprecedented numbers. Still the potential for rediscovery is there. Some look to it for help; many do not.

Plateau Religion. The Tlingit, the Plateau people, live in the inner areas of British Columbia and the Yukon. They are well known for their salmon-fishing expertise, although they also hunt and gather wild plants and berries. Because of their proximity to the Pacific Coast traditions, they demonstrate some ritual elements drawn from that quarter, although they did not incorporate massive totem carving into their religious life as one would have expected had they been deeply influenced. Interior house posts and screens are much more important to them.

Totemic beliefs dominate the Tlingit world. The people are divided according to two prime totemic figures, Raven and Wolf. These mythological and symbolic creatures serve as the focus of all official ritual. Tlingit religious sensitivity centers on the house as a ceremonial and spatial representation of a sacred space. Little ceremony deals with food supply, so the difference from their northern neighbors is obvious.

Tlingit religion concerns the preservation of the clan ideology, and that ideology is represented in the construction of the house. The house is a holy place, dwelt in by the most recent expression of the ancestor, the *yitsati.* Hence the house is always a male domain, and a wife may not even know what meanings are attached to the carvings within. Childbirth is a secular act, or at least not of the same order of sacredness as the house. For this reason, a little house is built behind the main lodging when a wife is expecting a child, and she stays in it until the child is born.

The *yitsati,* or keeper of the house, is a ceremonial leader and a priest of the house group. He should not labor in anything but ritual activities. Consequently, slaves were an accepted part of Tlingit social order. The *yitsati* sleeps behind the clan screen at the back of the house, and he is responsible for the clan symbols that he keeps there. On ceremonial occasions, he comes out through the center hole in the screen and speaks, as it were, with the voice of the ancestor. The strong emphasis on house group identity is reflected in the strength of kinship organization.

Of equal importance is the shaman, who plays a far greater role among the Tlingit than in any other group. Called *ichta,* he provides a direct contrast to the well-manicured *yitsati*—his hair is wild, dirty, and never touched by a comb or brush. He has a repertoire of masks, each of which represents a particular spirit and attracts that spirit. He is paid well for his services, which include going into a trance and dancing animal-style in a wild contortionist manner. Like the Inuit shaman, his power depends upon his ability to control the spirits and to bring benefit to the people. These are not ancestral spirits. They are spirits of animals and mythical beings that form part of his religious scenery. Many stories are told of the combat between powerful shamans. In fact, war seems to have been one of the shaman's chief measures of power. Traditionally he had a powerful role in defining religion in the group.

Missions were early accepted as part of the interaction with whites, and acculturation has proceeded, but the ability to maintain some sense of distance from the white man, especially by the more remote groups, has guaranteed some survival of the old ways.

Pacific Coast Religion. The Kwakiutl appear to have no myth of creation. There is a good reason for this: they believe they are responsible for making and maintaining the world as a reasonable human place. Otherwise, who knows what state the universe would be in? Before the trickster-transformer Q!anequelaku there was chaos and hunger; after his powers, the world had ritual order and the potential to supply food. One of his first acts was to kill the beast *sisiutl,* a monster with three heads for devouring but with no anus. He did nothing but devour the world, and he had to be stopped. By finding food, the hunter, like the ancestral transformer, demonstrates that the re-creative powers of the world are still alive, and by killing he is transforming the animal into a form from which it can be reborn. The animals he kills are also intimately involved with the hunter, since he in effect becomes them through eating. In addition, humans have a direct relationship to the spirit world, since by their moral life and sensitivity to the true values of the universe they encourage the life force to multiply, especially in twin births.

This characteristic is most evident in the perceptions of the salmon—who is like man in every possible way. Since salmon live in villages at the bottom of the sea, they perform the same kinds of winter rites as mankind. Their race upstream in the spring mimics man, who expends himself for his offspring, only to die and pass on the name and power he has marshaled throughout. Likewise, each of the animals represented in the Kwakiutl pantheon elicits some honorable quality or characteristic that is necessary for maintaining proper relationships among the world, humans, and spirits. Humans reciprocate with the spirits in maintaining the proper balance and harmony in the universe, and it is the goal of Kwakiutl religion to provide the means—

through myths, rituals, social order, and ceremonies—of constantly creating the world in its proper order. Humans are absolutely necessary, but they are only spirits with a different form than others, so they have no absolute position in the spiritual order.

Totem poles are family statements, but not statements of extravagance. They record visually the mythological history of the house, identifying it with those creatures that reflect both community honor and house honor. Placed outdoors, they signal to the spirits where their owners are, so that solidarity between the spirit world and the human world may remain controlled and settled.

Similarly, the shaman is not operating out of his own abilities when performing a rite, even if it clearly is sleight of hand. He is providing a medium through which the spirit forces can appear to the onlooker. He needs to demonstrate that he has a controlled wildness so that, while chaos is present, it is delimited by his performance. The spirits are reflected in this drama, and they respond to a good performance by giving glimpses of themselves. Thus, the shaman is dependent upon the spirit to validate his performance, and the spirit needs the shaman to provide a revelatory vehicle. Subordination to the spirit world is reflected in the shaman's assumptions about his performance, just as assumptions about subordination are built into the Kwakiutl social structure and emerge in the potlatch and in the size of the totem pole.

Kwakiutl religion still retains some force, even though the great totem ways are now secularized and spirits are not the inspiration of the carvers. Shamans have disappeared, and the winter rituals have decayed. Potlatches, however, are still carried on, as are the social traditions of lineage and kinship. The church, including the more fundamentalist groups, is the official religious activity of the communities, but the art of the Pacific Coast people has become a valuable asset, greatly prized by whites.

Mackenzie River Religion. Of the eight groups in the area known as the Arctic drainage lowlands, the Chipewyan are the most widespread; they lay claim to the largest territory of any native group in Canada. The Chipewyan speak an Athapaskan language and thus have linguistic features common to many groups in the northern part of Canada and Alberta and in the United States. They developed the narrowing enclosure to trap the caribou (their favorite animal) and used snares to hamper the animals while they killed them. They also drove the animals into water, where they became easy prey. Moose were also hunted, but less because the moose live in woodland and scrub areas, while the Chipewyan dominate the barrens.

These people are inveterate storytellers, and their rich mythological resources indicate that they have interacted culturally with coastal and Inuit areas. Both humans and animals come from the same source and share common elements, such as souls. They strongly believe in the reincarnation of the soul, and some stories relate a Chipewyan's reluctance to die until a suitable woman is pregnant. They show the same close connection with the animals of the kill noted among the Woodlands people, but they maintain that Raven and other trickster figures were instrumental in the creation process, as did the Plateau people. In effect, such a rich mythological culture allows the individual Chipewyan to piece together his own structured understanding of the important religious occurrences, and great diversity can exist between or within groups.

The Chipewyan give an important place to *nakhani*, a supernatural being sometimes called Bush Man. He roams in the bush hoping to bring evil upon the unwary, and he is greatly feared. Mothers threaten their children with him, and unusual noises are attributed to his presence. Terrifying experiences of the forest are universally laid at his feet, and he becomes the personification of the dangers and fears of the forest hunter. Besides Bush Man, the entire environment can be alive with spirits and supernatural beings, and the cautious traveler will be aware of the powers he will face and take precautionary measures. Hence the popularity of amulets, spells, and taboos.

The best way to catch animals was not with traps; traps could catch nothing if the animals would not give themselves up. Some groups held that the animals were people who had already died, so the relationship was intimate and intricate. In addition, dreams provided power to lure the animals to the traps or to allow the hunter to get close enough to kill them. Boys especially were encouraged to seek such powers, and they often were associated with a particular animal that became the guardian of their prowess. The most important characteristic was to learn the best way to approach the spirits of the animals.

This was not something that could be learned by stalking an animal. Inevitably, as among the Woodlands and the Inuit, special care had to be taken not to offend the animals. Scarcity is linked directly to unbridled offense against them.

Chipewyan shamans were powerful people, and though usually men, some women could wield enormous control. Shamanic healing was very important, especially the use of sucking and blowing, but the trance was also part of the shaman's repertoire. Any cure necessitated a payment. However, no payment was made when a shaman played a role in divination for game or in war expeditions.

Chipewyan religion has had its share of nativistic movements, usually focused on the amazing powers of curing or prophet-like activities. These show the impact of Christian tradition, which reached the Chipewyan people during the last half of the eighteenth century under the influence of the Hudson's Bay Company. The most effective missionary work was undertaken by the Oblates, who began proselytizing among the Chipewyan in 1847; it is largely because of their vigor that most Chipewyan regard themselves as Roman Catholic today. They were little influenced by the Russian Orthodox church, which had begun work among their Athapaskan brothers, the Tanaina, in 1794. Most Chipewyan are nominally Christian, although some retain attitudes drawn from the old ways. It is not unusual for both religious ideologies to sit side by side among them, perhaps because the region has always been religiously heterodox. Their individuality, religiously, is their most unusual distinguishing characteristic.

Iroquoian Religion. The Iroquoian live in southeastern Ontario, the area where the impact of the early explorers was felt. At the time of the first contact, they had a highly developed political and religious system. Their first agriculture was advanced, cultivating such staples as corn, beans, squash, and tobacco. With agriculture came a sedentary life-style, and they built gabled houses.

Two factors in Iroquoian culture spring immediately to mind, the master orators and the longhouse, but these are the elements given emphasis by white students, and the Iroquoian find the categorization by whites totally artificial. Even such notations as sacred and secular would sound strange to Iroquoian ears, who would see a treaty discussion as no less sacred than a myth-speaking ceremony. Nevertheless, for our purposes, oratory and longhouses are adequate places to begin.

Oratory takes place in the longhouse, the original of which was a rectangular bark house large enough to accommodate comfortably the two moieties, or "sides of the fire," that make up the Six Nations Confederacy. Each speaker is answered by an opposite from the moiety on the other side, but it is not the formalized style that is significant. Rather, both speakers are actually debating before the Creator, the pinnacle figure in the hierarchy of spirit forces recognized in the rites. The Creator lives "on the other side of the sky," and descriptions suggest an influence of Christian ideology in contemporary performances. The Creator, for example, loves the people and responds when they repent. The ritual activities are seen as beneficial in keeping the way to the Sky World open and free of obstacles, and the oratory rites are ways of maintaining that route. In actual belief, there are three distinctive levels to Iroquoian spirit hierarchy—spirit forces beyond the sky, in the sky, and on earth. In the first, standing above the others, is the Creator. Closely related in the first are the Four Beings (of the four cardinal directions) and Handsome Lake (the prophet). In the second stand equally the Wind, Thunderers, Sun, Moon, and Stars. In the third equally represented are People, Earth, Grasses, Fruit, Trees, Water, Animals, Birds, and Our Sustenance (corn, squash, etc.). Rituals must recognize each of these spirit forces in its proper place.

Words are crucial because of the myth that established order between people and the highest level. According to this myth, a powerful chief lived in a primal village on the other side of the sky. He had a dream that gave him a special word, but he wanted someone to tell him what it was. He called all the village to him, asking them to give him the secret word. They paraded by in ritual attempts, a most diversified group: the Sun, the Moon, the Stars, the Trees, the Bushes, the Grasses, the Animals and Birds, the Springs of Waters and all the Flowing Waters, the Light, the Clouds, the Corn and Squash, the Tobacco, the Night and the Day, the Thunderers and the Meteor, the Blue Sky, and the Air. None could tell the word. Angry and full of despair, the chief banished them all from the sky. That is why they ended up on earth.

The Iroquoian must keep the path to that other world open, not only by appealing to the Creator (not perceived as the old chief), but by eliciting the power of each of the spirit forces as they move from one level to another. It follows that the only language that can be used is the ritual language of the five northern Iroquoian people. It also explains why the first whites to witness their ceremonies came to regard the Iroquoian as fine orators. The cultural content required that this talent be developed. From the Iroquoian perspective, each orator was a gift who had experienced a crisis, becoming an orator in response to that crisis. His gift was a community asset in the largest meaning of that term, although the orator was not necessarily held to be a mystic or a shaman.

Longhouse oratory is oriented to a religious purpose, and through it the whole community is reunited with the world of the primal village from which all spirits originated. While it no longer retains the active myth-speaking it once had, perhaps because of the reforms instituted by the prophet Handsome Lake, the original cosmology of the Iroquoian people is retained, as is the unifying theme derived from the Hiawatha stories. Certainly the distinctives of each tribe are submerged beneath usage and dual moiety organization.

PAN-INDIAN AND RECENT MOVEMENTS

Messianic movements have influenced Canadian Indians since the seventeenth century. The Ghost Dance religion and the various nativistic movements are examples. More recently, the Native American Church, with its focus on peyote rituals, has had an impact, especially among the Plains people. This religion has succeeded in overthrowing many of the old ways still practiced by these tribes, notably in Saskatchewan as late as 1982.

Of a different order is the almost universal standing that elders have even when they are in a completely different cultural area. Young educated Indians are attracted to this sophisticated elder, who is able to represent to them the old ways, but in a manner that stresses the broad unifying elements. Especially attractive is the herbalist and healer, who combines many of the characteristics associated with white doctors, but in a more holistic vein. Powerful healers are visited by believers regardless of which religion they espouse.

Reservations, for all the segregation and loss of status that they imply to their inhabitants, have kept some areas relatively isolated from white prying, allowing some rituals to be carried on. Unfortunately, young Indians leaving the reservations have negative feelings toward them, and the elders are often included in those feelings. The result is that the young have rejected both Christianity and the old ways. Some have turned to atheism or agnosticism. With few skills in an urban society, they have become a disillusioned generation. In some areas of the prairies, the majority of the prison population is native, and alcohol and drug abuse is commonplace.

Canadian willingness to accept some form of collective representation of aboriginal nations in Parliament might aid Indian identity in a way that would encourage a revival of traditional ways and, since aboriginal rights are guaranteed in the new Canadian Constitution, the Indians' special place in the makeup of the country is basically established. The role their religions will play is a question that has not been faced, but the Indians' fundamental religious connection with the land may have long-term impact should Canadians define their identity in its terms.

IMMIGRANT RELIGION

George Étienne Cartier, one of the fathers of Confederation, expressed the basis of religion for Canadian history as a unity of diversity:

> If we unite we will form a political nationality independent of the national origin and religion of individuals. As to the objection that we cannot form a great nation because Lower Canada is chiefly French and Catholic, Upper Canada English and Protestant, and the Maritime provinces mixed it is completely futile. . . . In our confederation there will be Catholics and Protestants, English and French, Irish and Scotch, and each by its efforts and success will add to the prosperity, the might, and the glory of the new federation.

The fruit of this policy was to accept religion as establishment, but without formally acknowledging any one type as favored. Influencing government policy for social concerns, spurring

Canada on to moral decisions, and striving for a more just national character have been some of the nobler sentiments churchmen have urged. Their interests have not been brought about by the direct power of an establishment church, but through pressure on government or through officials sensitive to religious ideology.

The nature of Canadian immigration has been directly influenced by the national churches: in the early days a majority of the people came to Canada from or through their organizations. The result was that the number of immigrants with little church affiliation was small. Especially when the prairies opened up and the flood to the West began, arrangements for immigration that respected certain "values" allowed churches (for example, the Mennonites) to sanction the movements of whole communities of people onto the land. The result has been churches of national and ethnic consciousness.

The policy was carried out through the active participation of the governments of central Canada for their own reasons. It was, on the one hand, a colonization policy, designed to carry on Canadian national destiny by peopling the prairies. Part of this was motivated by a concern that if Canada did not populate the West, the United States would. Immigrants were part of national establishment policy. In addition, the prospect of a West that required the manufacturing capabilities of eastern Canada was attractive to Toronto and Montreal. But there was also Canadian ideology behind this move; a vast unpopulated land lay open to developing British conceptions of law, justice, and ultimately a distinctive sense of freedom.

Immigrant ethnic and religious diversity was the price the eastern governments were willing to pay, since it not only offset the dreams of the French Catholics, but guaranteed a grateful and submissive foreign contingent. All this took place in a remarkably short period of time, between 1870 and 1920, a factor that made continuity all the more important.

The manner in which traditional forms of religion came to dominate the West can be gauged by a look at the Orthodox church. Orthodoxy derives from peoples of Eastern Europe, Africa, the eastern Mediterranean, and Asia; the distinction from the Roman Catholic church is usually identified with the schism of 1054, when the Eastern church broke away from Rome. On occasion, Orthodoxy is known as the Eastern or Byzantine rite, to parallel it to the Western rite of Roman Catholicism.

The use of rite is significant, because for these Eastern churches it is the ritual commonality that unites, not the administrative and authoritative jurisdiction. This is demonstrated by the fact that there are believers in Canada who may owe allegiance to the ancient patriarchates of Constantinople, Alexandria, Antioch, or Jerusalem; they may also belong to one of the so-called national churches of Russia, Serbia, Romania, Bulgaria, Cyprus, Greece, Albania, Poland, or Czechoslovakia; they could adhere to the autonomous churches of Sinai or Finland or Japan; or they could have recently joined a daughter church formed from one of the aforementioned national churches in Canada and the United States. There is also a small group of believers who do not adhere to this "Byzantine" Orthodoxy, but rather follow the non-Chalcedonian doctrine of Christ's nature. (This doctrine places emphasis on the divine in the person of Christ, with the human element reduced to an impersonal humanity.) These Oriental Orthodox—the Armenian, Coptic, Syrian, Ethiopian, and South Indian Orthodox churches—are rejected as noncanonical by the Byzantines.

Probably the largest group practicing the Byzantine rite is the Ukrainian Orthodox church in Canada, numbering in excess of 140,000. Their ancestors came to Canada at the turn of the century in the immigration flood, and most of them were from peasant stock; they have been joined recently by post–World War II immigrants who settled not on the prairies but in the eastern manufacturing centers. They came principally from Galicia in the Ukraine. The first church was established at Gardenton, Manitoba, which is still the scene of an annual pilgrimage. They are not regarded as canonically Orthodox by the other Byzantine rite churches, because Galicia was traditionally under the jurisdiction of the Roman Catholic church and used the Ruthenian rite. The Galicians have a married clergy, however, and the Church of Rome wished to dispense with that right. They also had used the Ukrainian language in the liturgy. By 1918 a protective organization called the Ukrainian Greek Brotherhood evolved, and many of its adherents joined the Orthodox church through its auspices.

Also of interest is the single church of the African Orthodox Church, founded in Sydney, Nova Scotia. The church came out of a growing awareness of black solidarity at the turn of the century, and the resulting organization, founded in 1921, follows Orthodox liturgical practice and accepts the seven ecumenical councils. It is also significant that Orthodoxy first came to North America not through immigration but through Russian Orthodox missionary activity among the Aleut in Alaska. The diocese was established in 1799 and by 1905 had an archdiocese in New York. Most of the Orthodox organizations have a North American rather than a Canadian focus.

An entirely different genre of church is associated with the Doukhobors. A pietistic group, the Doukhobors originated in Russia in the eighteenth century. They rejected both the Russian Orthodox church and the state. It was this conflict that led them to Canada in 1899. Indeed, they were opposed to all the trappings of church, dispensing with priests, liturgies, sections of the Bible, and church edifices, and they resisted any education that would lead them away from the immediacy of the oral tradition and spiritual enlightenment. Their life in the Crimea had centered on communal living and total nonviolence; the latter concept was close to that of the Quakers. When the czar moved to conscript the young men into his army, they resisted. News of the resulting bloodshed reached sympathetic ears in Canada, where Clifford Sifton was looking for strong farm workers, like the Mennonites who had come earlier. By June 1899 over 7,500 Doukhobors had come to Canada, the largest group migration to the prairies. They immediately moved to communal farms in Saskatchewan, where they faced strong resistance from other immigrants who envied the huge tracts of land they had been given. Ultimately they had to abandon their communal living and principles of universal peace and brotherhood. Required to give an oath of loyalty before they could get land, some simply "affirmed" and received land; many refused on grounds of religious conviction. This group, the largest, became known as the Orthodox Doukhobors and was led by the mystical Peter V. Verigin. They purchased private land in British Columbia and became quite successful. A third group, seeking a totally untrammeled existence, began a trek across the West to British Columbia and became known as the Sons of Freedom. Utilizing the shock tactic of burning buildings while they stood in the nude before them as a protest to affluence and injustice, they became notorious very quickly. The negative publicity applied to all Doukhobors indiscriminately, and the members in British Columbia were twice banned from voting in federal elections.

Despite the extraordinary nature of their religious convictions and the difficulties in transplanting them to Canada, the Doukhobors have persevered and today represent a Russian group that maintains an almost mystical belief in the homeland and in the principles of communal and nonviolent living.

The Mennonites are another group who arrived on the prairies, but with an entirely different story. Originally an urban people, the Mennonites had been forced to live in rural areas because of their nonviolent and independent church conceptions. They became very productive farmers, achieving their most extensive holdings in Russia, where they enjoyed almost autonomous self-government. The successors of Alexander I withdrew their privileges, however, and they moved to the Canadian prairies, where the government gave them large tracts of land together and made concessions about military service and their own schools. Early in the 1920s thousands of Mennonites flocked onto the land, displaced by the Russian Revolution. The magnitude of the group meant conflict with other Canadians and splits within the group over policy. Their goal of living an isolated life evaporated under the strain of realities in the Canadian West. Their Christian separation of church from state, the kingdom of God from that of man, and distinctive ways of life were all blurred under the pressure of living with others from all over the world.

DIVERGENT RELIGIONS

No discussion of Canada's diversity would be complete without some mention of traditions of an entirely different nature—Judaism, Islam, and Buddhism. All have played a role in the development of Canada's religious environment.

Jewish immigrants came to Nova Scotia from New England in the mid-1750s, and Sephardim from England journeyed to Montreal about the same time. By 1768 they had formed a group called Shearith Israel, similar to one in New York. Nine years later they had built a synagogue. Their numbers were small—the Census

of 1901 reported 16,400 Jews—but a dramatic change came in the next decade when the western Jewish population increased more than fourfold. This shift to the prairies came about through Jewish societies in the East, such as the Colonization Committee of the Young Men's Hebrew Benevolent Society of Montreal, which sponsored the oldest Jewish farm community, in Oxbow, Saskatchewan, in 1892. Farming communities were also established in Alberta and Manitoba. In 1905 many responded to Prime Minister Wilfrid Laurier's speech on the occasion of the condemnation of the Russian pogrom against the Jews of Kishinev, when he promised a "hearty welcome" to Jews who came to Canada. Following World War I, however, Jewish immigration slowed to a trickle, and in the face of the Nazi peril in Europe, Canada virtually shut the door on the problem. Meanwhile, believers moved from farming communities to towns and cities as they sought the social and religious advantages that numbers provided. Today there are synagogues in only two centers outside major cities—Prince Albert, Saskatchewan, and Lethbridge, Alberta.

Most of the first Muslims came to Canada from Lebanon, and they set to work not as farmers but as peddlers. A nucleus made Edmonton, Alberta, its departure point for selling routes to the North. These early families were finally able to construct a mosque, completed in 1938 with the help of a few Christian friends and much sacrifice. After World War II the much less restrictive immigration laws opened the way for additional Muslim immigrants, most of whom were from Pakistan and India. Today the largest contingent of Muslims in Canada, they are centered in urban areas, notably Toronto and Montreal. A most unusual town in Alberta, Lac La Biche, has a sizable Muslim population, all of whom are Arab, and a mosque that is one of the main sights in town. Edmonton now boasts the only Arabic-English bilingual program in Canada in its public school system, with classes scheduled to progress to the sixth grade.

The earliest Muslim immigrants were Sunnis, and the preponderance of Muslims in Canada belong to that tradition, but lately, largely through the racist policies of Idi Amin, significant numbers of Isma'ilis have settled in the western provinces, particularly in the main cities of Edmonton, Calgary, and Vancouver.

The Canadian West is also the site of Buddhist

congregations. The earliest immigrants came to southern Alberta and the coastal regions of British Columbia from Japan around the turn of the century. Some worked on the railways, some came to work in the coal mines or to begin farming. A number of the latter settled in Raymond, Alberta. They banded together in 1929 and established Raymond Buddhist Church, the first in the province. They purchased a former Mormon church and today have one of the finest shrines in North America.

When World War II began, the Japanese were rounded up and sent to internment camps in Alberta and in the interior of British Columbia. Their forced evacuation from the coast spurred the building of churches, and new congregations sprang up in Taber, Picture Butte, Coaldale, and Rosemary, with Lethbridge, the largest town, as the center of Japanese activities. After the war, the Alberta churches organized into the Alberta *Kyoku,* or ministerial jurisdiction, as part of four *Kyokus* in Canada: British Columbia, Alberta, Manitoba, and the East. Despite a split and the formation of the Honpa Buddhist Church of Alberta, the Buddhists of the West have maintained an ongoing congregation. Regular and special services of the True Pure Land Buddhist tradition are conducted by resident ministers, one of whom is currently a Caucasian woman from California.

The federal government's multicultural policy has encouraged the various ethnic and religious groups to preserve their traditions, and Canada now has congregations of religions as disparate as the Rastafarians, Sikhs, and Hindus, as well as the traditional ancestor worship of the Chinese. This plethora of cultures is most noticeable in western Canada, where summer festivals of ethnic heritage are very popular. While the Canadians support the contributions these various people make to the country, some worry privately that they are challenging the essentially Christian character of Canada.

RELIGIOUS MOVEMENTS

The face of religion in Canada has been decisively changed through a number of movements. Few lasting ones have been native to Canada; some have increased sectarianism, others have affected the established churches and Canada's social outlook. In the main, the impetus for these movements has come from the United States, and only two of significance, the Salvation Army and the Plymouth Bretheren, have European origins. Canada has been impressed deeply by the religious ferment of its southern neighbor.

Some of this religious ferment was brought by Americans themselves. Before the War of 1812, eight out of ten residents of Ontario were Americans; most of the Icelandic, Norwegian, Swedish, and Danish Lutherans who settled on the Canadian prairies came from the Dakotas; early Congregationalists in Nova Scotia influenced the religious development of that province; the Mormons came directly to southern Alberta to establish a thriving community. But much of it was a conscious adaptation of American religious forms to Canada.

Not all are as dramatic as the New Light movement among the Baptists of the Maritimes or the camp meeting movement among the Methodists. Anglicans molded their structures according to Episcopal innovations in the United States, and Canadian sectarian congregations used liturgical forms drawn from American evangelism. Strategies for winning converts, such as the huge religious forums of Billy Graham, were first tried in the United States and found an acceptance among Canada's evangelicals. Some groups, like the Canadian Pentecostals, preferred the boisterous and dramatic evangelists of the United States, and Catholic charismatics found adherents there before trying similar forms in Canada.

Despite this close connection, Canada has not always responded to these movements as the United States has. The revivalism that swept the eastern seaboard of the United States under Jonathan Edwards in the mid-eighteenth century had an impact in Canada, but not as broadly nor as deeply. America's repeated revivalist history has not found similar expression in Canada.

The church in Canada responded, too, to its own agenda. Most notable is the Church Union movement, the most impressive achievement of which was the union of Presbyterian, Congregational, and Methodist churches in 1925, but which periodically took place between Baptists, Lutherans, and others throughout Canada's history. Canada thus had an ecumenical movement of its own kind and flavor before it became popular in other countries of the world.

But the movement that has flowered in Canadian religion has been the Social Gospel movement. The Anglican, Methodist, and Presbyterian churches were most inspired by the need to make the Gospel relevant to the everyday concerns of humans, although their motivations arose not from conditions that they saw as unique to Canada but as part of a movement that embraced the Western world. The ways they responded may well not have come from the United States. In fact, the institutional structures, like the brotherhoods, the settlements, and the labor churches, were of British derivation rather than American, but many of the themes had American counterparts. Even the anti-alcohol crusade, well known in the United States, can be seen as an attempt to apply Gospel interpretations to social problems.

The center of the Canadian Social Gospel movement was not in the Maritimes or in Ontario but in Winnipeg, at Wesleyan College, where staff and students responded to the depression of the 1890s that saw farmers inundated with unsold grain. Railway rates, tariffs, and a host of related issues became matters on which Christians had to take a stand. When Salem Bland arrived at Wesleyan in 1903, he found fertile ground for his social perspectives, and Methodists in particular dominated the progressive wing of the movement. The best-known Social Gospel clergyman, J. S. Woodsworth, was a Methodist, even though he later resigned from the church. The movement built rapidly. From 1890 to 1914 it dramatically increased its impact on church and labor organizations, but its very success spelled its doom: its impact fostered groups, institutions, and responses that outgrew its religious sources and spread its attitudes through church, labor, and social networks in such a way that by 1928 the movement had given over its formulation to labor and political forces. With the crash of 1929, it was no longer effective. Nevertheless, it has left an important legacy in Canadian society, and its ideas flow with regularity close to the surface of church discussion of issues.

Mention should be made of the Métis movement, led by Louis Riel. (The Métis were communities formed by the mixed marriage of native people and early French trappers.) It is a measure of how controversial this man is that even in the twentieth century he is not recognized as a father of the nation, although his opposition to the federal government is little different from that lauded by provincial premiers today. Riel was born in 1844 to a settled Métis family who represented well the combination of Indian and French blood. A devout Catholic, he believed that Providence wanted the western lands to stay under the domination of the people who lived on them, and he fought with messianic vision to resist federal encroachment on Métis land. He often did this in the name of French-Canadian and Catholic culture. His sense of destiny for the West ended with his execution for treason in 1885 by the federal government, but his dream of regional power and the rights of French Catholics is as alive as ever in western Canada.

NEW RELIGIONS

Of the welter of religions that have sprung up in Canada, several seem to have been more successful than others. The Baha'is have built a national organization and have succeeded in attracting middle-class youth and educated Canadians alike. The Church of Scientology recruited aggressively in the 1970s and established groups across the country, as did the Reverend Moon's Unification Church. Edmonton has had a continuing Dharmadhatu congregation, and that group has also decided to establish a permanent base in Halifax because, as one devotee put it, Canadians are stable about religion. Mantra meditation was taught earlier in Canada by Transcendental Meditation and still has adherents.

Various self-improvement groups operate in Canada, including Silva mind control and the New Light, which are based upon certain religious views of the individual. And while Hare Krishna and Divine Light people are not as prevalent as they used to be, those groups have attracted a wide range of converts. Sri Chinmoy adherents are found across Canada, as are Tai Chi Chu'an participants. While not new, spiritualist groups and the Unity Church appeal to some Canadians. Sometimes the charismatics are considered a new religion, although their message is hardly different from that of the Pentecostals, and speaking in tongues is also advocated by Subud.

Almost all these religions require or promote a split from former relationships and traditions. The Charismatic Renewal movement is the only one that acknowledges the presence of another religious dimension in adherents' lives, and it is the closest to traditional Christian inspiration. While little factual data is available, group-hopping seems to be less prevalent in Canada than in the United States, and worried parents and relatives hire deprogrammers to offset the impact that cults have on individuals. Canadian animosity to cults is largely inspired by media reports about non-Canadian groups, such as the Jonestown cult in Guyana, and about kidnapping and deprogramming of adherents. No government in Canada has enacted restraining laws, with the exception of some municipal jurisdictions for the control of street harassment. The groups have free rein in attracting secular or disillusioned persons to their organizations.

Some people regard the television evangelists as cultic in that much of the impact of their message derives from personal appeal. Canada has a long and vigorous evangelical tradition, however, and the strong support evangelists receive from Canadians may only reflect that sympathy. The most important fact about all this diversity is that it is derived from American sources, re-flecting the continuous interaction between American and Canadian culture and religion.

BIBLIOGRAPHY

S. D. Clark, *Church and Sect in Canada* (1949); Harold Coward and Leslie Kawamura, eds., *Religion and Ethnicity* (1978); Michael K. Foster, "From the Earth to Beyond the Sky: An Ethnographic Approach to Four Longhouse Iroquois Speech Events," in National Museum of Man Mercury Series, no. 20 (1974); George M. Grant, *Lament for a Nation: The Defeat of Canadian Nationalism* (1982); John Webster Grant, ed., *The Churches and the Canadian Experience* (1966); Åke Hultkrantz, *Belief and Worship in Native North America* (1981).

Aurel Krause, *The Tlingit Indians* (1956); Hans Mol, "Religion and Eskimo Identity in Canada," in *Studies in Religion*, 2, no. 2 (1982); Knud Rasmussen, *Intellectual Culture of the Iglulik Eskimos* (1929); Peter Slater, ed., *Religion and Culture in Canada* (1977); Frank G. Speck, *Naskapi: The Savage Hunters of the Labrador Peninsula* (1977); James W. Van Stone, *Athapaskan Adaptations: Hunters and Fishermen of the Subarctic Forests* (1974); Stanley Walens, *Feasting with Cannibals: An Essay on Kwakiutl Cosmology* (1981); Henry H. Walsh, *The Christian Church in Canada* (1956).
[*See also* FRENCH CATHOLICISM IN THE NEW WORLD; NATIVE AMERICAN RELIGIONS; *and* PROTESTANTISM AND SOCIETY IN CANADA.]

Part III
JEWISH AND CHRISTIAN TRADITIONS

THE EMERGENCE OF AN
AMERICAN JUDAISM

Abraham J. Karp

TWO distinctive features characterize American Jewry: its tripartite division into Orthodox–Conservative–Reform and the centrality of the synagogue in Jewish life and activity. Religious denominationalism, to be sure, exists in other Jewish communities, and the synagogue has played and continues to play a central role in Jewish life worldwide, but nowhere to the extent and degree to which these obtain in America. Both of these features have their roots in American realities and are the result of wedding Jewish needs to American possibilities. In Europe, unlike America, the Jews had a legally defined corporate identity. Denominationalism would have splintered the community, an act inimical to the welfare of the Jews and frowned upon by the state and the established church. In America, where there was neither a legally defined Jewish identity nor an established church, religious denominationalism was accepted. Indeed, the religious diversity in American Protestantism invited a similar development in American Judaism.

In Europe, Jewish identity was established by birth; in America, through a voluntary act of affiliation or association. From the beginning, American Jews chose the synagogue to serve that function—the transmission and expression of Jewish identity.

A TRIPARTITE COMMUNITY

European Antecedents. The European Jewish historic experience in the nineteenth century was largely that of Emancipation and Enlightenment. The promise of the French Revolution of *liberté, égalité, fraternité* was carried by Napoleon's conquering armies throughout Europe. Grudgingly, but increasingly, civic and political rights were extended to the Jew. The period of reaction that followed the Congress of Vienna in 1815 and the abortive revolutions of 1848 erased many hard-won rights, but not all. The Jew's usefulness to an expanding economy opened for him heretofore closed doors. He entered these with alacrity. He sensed that the price of admission was a lessening of his Jewish national identity and aspirations, and a casting off of the ways that made him different. These sentiments were fortified by his experience with Enlightenment. Both in its Western European form of *Jüdische Wissenschaft* and in its Eastern European expression, *haskalah,* it led to a loosening of ancestral ties, a broadening of cultural and spiritual experimentation, and a restructuring of communal forms and religious usage.

Emancipation and Enlightenment made the soil fertile for the sprouting and growth of Reform Judaism, which undertook a restatement of religious views and values as well as a program of changes in synagogue and home ritual and in the personal and public life of the Jew. Orthodoxy proclaimed Reform heretical and dangerous, urging the full retention of the traditional way of life. Radical aspects of the Reform program caused a leading participant, Zacharias Frankel, to turn away from it to formulate a "positive historical Judaism," loyal to the traditions of Judaism yet recognizing and accepting their ongoing evolutionary development and change—the forerunner of American Conservative Judaism. An Orthodox response to Emancipation and Enlightenment was Samson Raphael Hirsch's Neo-Orthodoxy, calling for the observance of Jewish laws and rituals in their entirety while urging participation in the cultural and social life of the larger society—a formulation of traditional Judaism that became a major influence in modern American Orthodoxy.

In Colonial America. Judaism—still purely Orthodox, though the term wasn't yet used—arrived in America in the summer of 1654, brought by twenty-three refugees from Portuguese Brazil seeking a haven in New Amsterdam. Within the year of their arrival, the Jews of New Amsterdam had already joined together for their common religious needs, the first of which was a consecrated ground for burial. Less than two years after their arrival, Governor Peter Stuyvesant complained that "the Jews . . . have many times requested of us free and public exercise of their abominable religion."

By the end of the colonial period, congregations had been established in New York City; Newport, Rhode Island; Philadelphia and Lancaster, Pennsylvania; Richmond, Virginia; Charleston, South Carolina; and Savannah, Georgia. Religious functionaries were imported, trained, and supported. Kosher meat was provided, marriages were solemnized, boys were circumcised, and burial grounds were consecrated.

All things considered, there was a flourishing organized religious life in colonial America. In 1761 the first English translation of any part of the Jewish liturgy appeared, a fifty-two-page booklet of the evening services of the New Year and the Day of Atonement. Five years later a translation of Sabbath and High Holy Day liturgy was published. Although colonial Jewry probably numbered about a thousand people—at most fifteen hundred—and the Jewish community of England was tenfold in size, it was in colonial New York, rather than in metropolitan London, that the first translation of the prayer book was published. The introduction to the volume explains that Hebrew "being imperfectly understood by many, by some not at all, it has been necessary to translate our Prayers in the Language of the Country wherein it has pleased the divine Providence to appoint our Lot." Primarily because of the small size of the Jewish community in the New World, linguistic acculturation had proceeded at a far more rapid pace than in England.

Jewish religious life in colonial America faced serious dangers. One was the imported division between Ashkenazic (Jews from central and eastern Europe) and Sephardic (descendants of Jews from the Iberian Peninsula) Jews. The Reverend S. Quincy reported in 1738 that in Savannah, Georgia, "they want to build a synagogue, but the Spanish and German Jews cannot come to terms. The Spanish and Portuguese Jews are not so strict insofar as eating is concerned. They eat, for instance, the beef that comes from the warehouse. The German Jews, on the other hand, would rather starve than eat meat they do not slaughter themselves." Another danger was the small size of the Jewish community and its dispersion throughout the colonies, which made intermarriage with non-Jews, though officially condemned, a recognized reality in the frontier society. Formal adherence to religion was the public posture of the colonial Jews, but personal religious observance often fell victim to the free atmosphere of the frontier. Many intermarried Jews remained practicing, participating Jews during their lifetime, but their children entered the majority society as Protestants.

Synagogues and Rabbis. The early nineteenth century was marked by a great religious revival throughout America. Churches were built and filled; laws were enacted to preserve the sanctity of Sunday as the Sabbath; and the clergy was highly esteemed. Religious concerns such as salvation, the state of man's soul, the power of grace, and the need for baptism were topics of conversation and controversy.

The Jews could not help but be influenced by this atmosphere. Pious Jews founded congregations and erected synagogues for their own spiritual needs; Jewish nonbelievers helped maintain them because it was the American thing to do. In city after city, a small group of Jews would establish the Jewish community by organizing a congregation. The consecration of a synagogue was an event of public celebration. The *Savannah Republican* of 21 April 1820 reported that the Masonic "Grand Lodge of Georgia assembled for the purpose of making the necessary arrangements for the laying of the cornerstone of a Hebrew Synagogue, about to be erected in this city."

The nascent awareness of the singular needs of a native-born generation of American Jews became apparent as early as 1824. In that year, forty-seven members of Congregation Beth Elohim in Charleston presented a "Memorial" to the community's leadership asking that the service be abridged, that portions be repeated in English, and that a sermon in English become part of the service. The petition was rejected, and the dissenters founded a new congregation, the Reformed Society of Israelites. Isaac Harby, the moving spirit of the society, described its goals as the establishment of "order and decency in worship, harmony and beauty in chanting, the inculcation of morality and charitable sentiments upon individuals, and the promotion of piety toward the Deity. In these things, the Society believes, consist religion, virtue and happiness; in these, the salvation of every rational and immortal being." This initial native American attempt to establish Reform Judaism, though brief in duration, laid the groundwork for the later, viable venture imported from Germany, which found a hospitable environment in America and flourished on its adopted soil as nowhere else in the world.

Jewish religious life in nineteenth-century America was shaped by the labors of a few dedicated, creative individuals. Whereas in Europe the rabbi was a product of the community, in America the community was the product of the rabbi. Even a cursory glance at the early history of any American Jewish community discloses the vast influence exerted upon it by its pioneer rabbis. The organizations and institutions of the Philadelphia and Cincinnati Jewish communities of the last century, for example, were in large measure the legacy of Rabbis Isaac Leeser and Isaac Mayer Wise. The mid-nineteenth-century American Jewish communities challenged the energies, initiative, and abilities of dedicated and courageous spiritual leaders.

The rabbi became a multipurpose functionary: a teacher of the young, a preacher to the elders, an organizer of Jewish institutions to serve community needs, and a representative of the congregation to the larger community as a participant in civic enterprises and interests. The multiplicity of function demanded of the rabbi, as his role evolved in America, required a scope of ability and interests far broader than that traditionally associated with the rabbinic role. Isaac M. Wise, writing to a young American studying for the rabbinate in Europe in 1859, advised: "You know that a Rabbi here must have more universal knowledge than one in Europe, he being closer connected with the world at large and being placed in a juxtaposition with the whole community."

Traditionalists and Reformers. Leeser, a German immigrant who served as *hazan*-minister of Sephardic congregations in Philadelphia, was a traditionalist who had faith that America would be hospitable to a traditionally religious and cultured Jewish community. Wise, who was to become the architect of the Reform movement in America, believed that Judaism would in time become the religion of enlightened modern man. First, however, it had to be modernized and democratized or, better still, "Americanized." He entered upon a rabbinic career and became the exponent of a moderate, pragmatic Reform Judaism, responsive to the practical necessities of contemporary democratic living. Thus, for example, the prayer book that he prepared and vigorously promoted was a modified traditional order of services with Hebrew text and facing German or English translations. Modernity necessitated the elimination of prayers for the restoration of sacrifices, while references to a Messiah and return to a homeland were omitted because America was Zion, and "Washington our Jerusalem." Appropriately, Wise entitled his 1857 prayer book *Minhag America* ("The American Rite").

Overriding individual ritual differences and liturgical preferences was the conviction that American Jewry needed to erase differences and establish a unifying religious mode, an *American* Judaism. To do so Reform and traditionalist elements joined together in a conference convened in Cleveland in 1855. The rabbis recognized that unity demanded compromise. Leeser's compromise consisted in attending a conference planned and dominated by Reform Jews; Wise's in accepting the Talmud (the compendium of Jewish law and lore, compiled in the second to fifth centuries A.D.) as the authoritative interpretation of the Bible.

But the conference did not lead to unity. Instead, it strengthened division and led to further subdivision. Leeser and Wise dissolved their "partnership" with recriminations that grew progressively harsher as the years went on. A group of Reform rabbis from the East, led by David Einhorn of Baltimore, attacked the Cleveland conference. Declaring that its platform would "condemn Judaism to a perpetual stagnation," it rejected the Reform of Wise as puerile and retrogressive, and branded its chief proponent as opportunistic. The rift between the moderate, practical Wise and the radical, ideological Einhorn, and their disciples, was to divide the Reform movement for three decades. On the traditionalist side, whatever chance Leeser had of exerting influence on the Orthodox was greatly dissipated by his having consorted with the enemy, Reform.

In Philadelphia in the late 1860s, Reform and Traditionalist groups undertook enterprises that would foster their individual interests. Isaac Leeser, supported by the Board of Delegates of American Israelites, organized and served as provost of Maimonides College, the first Jewish seminary in America. It opened its doors to four students in 1867 but closed for lack of support four years later. A rabbinic conference was convened in Philadelphia in 1869 in an attempt to heal the rift in Reform Jewry. The convener and leading spirit of the conference was David Einhorn. The resolutions adopted reflected his ideology, denying Jewish nationality and separateness, and proclaiming the Jewish Diaspora as a divinely ordained opportunity for the Jews to fulfill "their high priestly task to lead the nations in the true knowledge and worship of God." The one "practical" resolution declared that because Hebrew has become "incomprehensible for the overwhelming majority of our present-day coreligionists . . . in the act of prayer Hebrew must take second place behind a language which the worshippers can understand."

Isaac M. Wise was not prepared to follow Einhorn's extreme ideology; he viewed radical Reform as a divisive force. Wise's essential commitment was to a united American Judaism. Gifted organizer that he was, he understood that congregations could be united through participation in a project rather than through agreement on resolutions. A "Jewish Theological Institute" was the vehicle he chose as a rallying center for a "Union of American Hebrew Congregations" that would provide room for Jewish groups of all religious viewpoints. Wise was able to attract to his enterprise such traditionalists as Sabato Morais (1823–1897), *hazan*-minister of Congregation Mikveh Israel in Philadelphia. In 1880, the dream of a united American Jewish religious community not only looked attainable but seemed well on the road to fulfillment. The dream did not last long.

Tripartite Division. The Union of American Hebrew Congregations, established in Philadelphia in 1873, and its Hebrew Union College, founded two years later, were intended to serve all of American Jewry. But the issues that divided American Jewry were stronger than the wish to establish an American Judaism. Which prayer

book was to be accepted for "American Judaism" —the traditional, the moderate Reform *Minhag America* of Wise, or the radical *Olat Tamid* (1858) of Einhorn? Some leading congregations were holding their main religious service of the week on Sunday morning; others denounced this as rank apostasy. There were those who were most meticulous in their observance of *kashruth* (the Jewish dietary laws); others termed it a remnant of an ancient cult and poked fun at "kitchen Judaism."

The conflict came to a dramatic head in 1883, at the banquet celebrating the first commencement of Hebrew Union College. The first course (and three others) was the religiously prohibited shellfish, causing the observant Jews present to leave the dinner and the movement. Visible insult had now been added to the long-standing verbal attack on Jewish traditional practices, which could lead only to a split within American Jewry.

The break was, of course, long in the making. For three decades reformers and traditionalists had been engaged in battle, attack and counterattack, filling the pages of the contemporary Jewish press. After the death of Leeser in 1868, which left the traditionalist forces without an effective leader, the field was open for the spread of Reform, and spread it did. Virtually all the leading congregation and rabbinic personalities were to be found in its camp. Ironically, the ever-increasing immigration of Eastern European Jews, a community far removed from Reform ideology and practices, helped bring unity to the Reform movement. The radical and moderate elements found a reason for rapprochement in their desire to remain separate and apart from the new immigrants. It has been suggested that radical Reform gained the victory over moderate Reform because the "native" Jew was convinced that its more extreme form of religious life and worship would keep the new immigrant out of his temple.

All the elements of Reform Judaism joined in a conference held in Pittsburgh in November 1885 "for the purpose of discussing the present state of American Judaism . . . and of uniting upon . . . plans and practical measures." Nineteen rabbis deliberated for three days. Wise presided, but the leading spirit was Kaufmann Kohler, a son-in-law of Einhorn's, whose radical Reform dominated the proceedings. The eight-point platform was a forthright and succinct statement of an extreme Reform viewpoint on God, the Bible, *kashruth*, the priesthood, the nature of Jewish identity, immortality, and social justice:

> Such mosaic and Rabbinical laws as regulate diet, priestly purity and dress . . . their observance in our days is apt . . . to obstruct . . . modern spiritual elevation. . . . We consider ourselves no longer a nation but a religious community, and therefore expect neither a return to Palestine . . . nor the restoration of the laws concerning the Jewish state.

Though never formally adopted as the official Reform position, it remained the most authoritative statement of Reform Judaism for the next half century.

The radical Pittsburgh platform met with immediate opposition and denunciation, and roused its critics to concrete counteraction. Morais denounced the platform for its "unwarrantable antagonism to the five holy books" (the Pentateuch); and his fellow Sephardic minister Henry Pereira Mendes declared: "They may give up . . . the doctrine of a restoration in Palestine if they like. But I prefer His voice to the voices of these ministers." The action they jointly undertook was to establish the Jewish Theological Seminary of America in New York in 1886, laying the foundation for Conservative Judaism.

Like many religious movements, Conservative Judaism had its beginnings in protest: the incident at the Hebrew Union College banquet roused the ire of traditional elements in American Jewry, while the tone of the Pittsburgh platform fed the misgivings of a group of moderate Reform rabbis who felt that American Reform had become too extreme. They found common ground in the founding of a seminary whose purpose would be to assure "the preservation in America of the knowledge and practice of historical Judaism as ordained in the Law of Moses and expounded by the prophets and sages of Israel."

The ideologists of the Conservative philosophy institutionalized in the Jewish Theological Seminary varied in their views. Morais, the seminary's first president, and Mendes were the spiritual leaders of Sephardic congregations in Philadelphia and New York. Coworker Bernard Drachman was rabbi of an Orthodox congregation in the Western European style. All three were formally Orthodox. Cofounders Alexander Kohut, Marcus Jastrow, and Benjamin Szold were rabbis of moderate Reform congregations, and were ideologically committed to the "positive historical" view of Judaism of Zacharias Frankel, principal of the Jewish Theological Seminary of Breslau.

"Positive historical Judaism," which became the philosophical cornerstone of Conservative ideology, viewed Judaism as the product of historical development. It called for a positive attitude of reverence and understanding toward traditional Judaism. The complex of traditional Jewish values, practices, and ideals was not to be lightly surrendered for the sake of convenience, conformity, or material advantage. The specifically Jewish elements in Judaism—for example, the Hebrew language—were considered essential to the preservation of its character and vitality. But Judaism, it maintained, was formed and would continue to be re-formed through an ordered process of change inherent in the Jewish legal system.

The leaders of the seminary looked to the rapidly growing Eastern European Jewish community in America as a source of students and of congregations for its graduates. But the Eastern European Orthodox community did not respond with support for the seminary. Its members would not seek religious leadership from a Sephardic *hazan* like Morais, nor from a moderate reformer like Kohut. It had a plan and a project of its own. In 1887 the Association of American Hebrew Congregations was formed to seek a chief rabbi, who would "be the leader in the battle which must be waged to keep the next generation faithful to Judaism in spite of the educational, social, and business influences which in America are so powerful as to make our sons and daughters forget their duty to [their] religion."

A Call, issued in April 1888, described the purpose, the project, and the hope:

> In this land, where we are at liberty to observe our religion, to study, teach, observe, perform and establish our Law, we find that our religion is neglected and our Law held in light esteem.
>
> Rouse yourselves and let not the mistake be repeated and continued by which Orthodox Judaism has lost so many who should be enlisted under its banner. Congregations have united in

order to create an intelligent orthodoxy, and to prove that also in America can be combined honor, enlightenment and culture, with a proper observance of religious duty.

Rabbi Jacob Joseph of Vilna came as chief rabbi to a community fired with great hopes and high enthusiasm, but the venture proved to be ill-fated. Poorly conceived and mismanaged, the project aroused antagonisms and rivalries in the community, and it brought personal tragedy to the rabbi. But it also marked the emergence of Orthodoxy in America as an independent, self-conscious religious force, jealous of its place and zealous for its prerogatives.

Within a brief span of four years (1885–1888), the division of American religious Jewry into Orthodox, Reform, and Conservative movements had been concretized. Each group decided to strike out on its own and undertook a project that emphasized the nature of its philosophy. Reform Judaism, which had rejected the binding authority of a received tradition, recognized that it nonetheless required a declaration of commonly accepted principles and adopted a platform stating its ideological position and commitment. Orthodoxy, accepting the authority of the received legal tradition, sought a rabbinic figure of stature to transmit and enforce that authority. Conservative Judaism, committed to the relevance of the entire Jewish religious experience, established a rabbinic school to educate young American men in the tradition and train them to expound it in a contemporary fashion.

By 1890, the pattern was set for American Judaism. Reform was armed with an ideology. Conservative Judaism had its struggling seminary. Orthodoxy, having flexed its organizational muscles, looked to an ever-increasing immigration to bring it new adherents.

In the last two decades of the nineteenth century, some six hundred thousand Jews came to the United States. Three times that number arrived in the first two decades of the twentieth. Some 95 percent of the immigrants came from Eastern Europe; they added to the largely Western European, German-speaking, religiously Reform, and rapidly assimilating American Jewish community a vital Yiddish-speaking, Orthodox (or militantly antireligious), culturally creative component. Orthodoxy was given a new vitality by this mass immigration. The children of the

Eastern European immigrants seeking religious affiliation turned in the main to Conservative Judaism and made it the most rapidly growing religious movement.

The tripartite division of the American Jewish religious community became institutionally concretized in the twentieth century. Each group maintained a rabbinic seminary and established its own congregational and rabbinic organizations. American Judaism was being fashioned at conferences, in the seminaries, and through rabbinic pronouncements. In the main, however, it was shaped in the locus where all religious forces and influences—the received traditions, the ideological reactions and the practical applications, rabbinic demands, and lay needs—met and interacted, in the emerging American synagogue.

THE SYNAGOGUE

From the beginning of Jewish communal life in America, the synagogue has been the central institution for establishing and enhancing Jewish association, for the transmission of Jewish knowledge, and for the retention and the fostering of Jewish loyalties. For many, the synagogue was not only an institution that served their religious needs as Jews but also a component of the larger American religious landscape, standing side by side with the churches of the community. For those who had seen synagogues merely tolerated in the lands of their birth, the freedom and respect accorded all religions in America became a mandate to establish congregations and build synagogues. In an address at the consecration of the newly built synagogue of Congregation Mikveh Israel of Savannah, Georgia, on 21 June 1820, Dr. Jacob De La Motta said: "Were we not influenced by religious zeal, a decent respect to the custom of the community, in which we live, should actuate us to observe public worship."

In Colonial America. In colonial America, synagogue and community were synonymous. The synagogue alone provided for the basic needs of the recently arrived or native Jew: companionship with fellow Jews; a place to worship when piety or other sentiments demanded it; circumcision for a son and a wedding service for a daughter; kosher meat for the table and a proper burial in consecrated ground; the opportunity to give or to receive charity. The chief religious functionary was the *hazan*, who led the services, officiated at the religious ceremonies (though permission to officiate at a marriage had to be granted by the lay leaders), and on occasion would be permitted to preach. The governance of the congregation in all its aspects was in the hands of the lay leaders.

For the immigrant, the synagogue provided the comforting continuity of familiar liturgy and ritual and the security of the company of fellow Jews who would care and provide for one's family in time of need or loss. To his stereotypic identity, the synagogue added a spiritual dimension. In a society that was splintering into a religious pluralism, the synagogue was becoming part of the religious landscape, its adherents clothed with an identity coherent and acceptable to the host community. Ezra Stiles reports that when Rabbi Haim Isaac Carigal, emissary from Hebron, preached in the Newport synagogue on Shavuot, 1773, the twenty-five Jewish families were joined at the service by Governor Wantan and Judges Oliver and Auchmuty. The dedication of a new synagogue in Charleston on 19 September 1774 was attended by Governor William Moultrie and officers of both the state and city.

No more than a half dozen congregations served colonial Jewry. Although small and far apart—almost one hundred miles separated the nearest two, New York's Shearith Israel and Philadelphia's Mikveh Israel—they were united not only by their shared Jewish identity and a similar synagogue rite, but also by the high mobility of the community. One congregation could freely turn to another in time of need, whether it was for aid in building a synagogue, for the loan of a Torah or other ritual objects, or for guidance in religious matters. This unity found symbolic expression when the synagogues of Philadelphia, New York, Richmond, and Charleston united in a congratulatory "Address to the President of the United States," George Washington, in 1790. Only the most northern congregation, in Newport, and the most southern, in Savannah, framed their own letters. The Jewish communities spoke through their synagogues, which were the sole communal institutions.

The small size of the Jewish communities in colonial America permitted only single congregations, all following Sephardic rite. The prevalence of established churches in the colonies made for identity of community and congregation. Functionally the total needs of Jewish life were provided for by the congregation, which in turn exerted considerable discipline over its membership. The synagogue as an institution of religion afforded the immigrant community an accepted and respected vehicle for its integration into the larger society.

In the Early Republic. During the first half of the nineteenth century, while the world Jewish population doubled in size, the Jewish population of the United States increased twenty-five-fold, from some two thousand to fifty thousand. Migration from Central and Western Europe provided the numbers and made for the diversification of the rapidly growing network of Ashkenazic synagogues. By midcentury the ten synagogues of the early 1800s had grown to almost ninety. New York City alone could boast of twenty; Philadelphia, five. Their diversity of rite (*minhag*) was based on country of origin. In 1853, New York's synagogues ranged from one following the Portuguese *minhag*, Shearith Israel, to seven following the Polish *minhag*, seven the German, one the Bohemian, and one described as a Dutch congregation; the rites of Philadelphia's five synagogues were Portuguese, German (two), Polish, and Dutch.

Factors external and internal to Jewish life made for the proliferation and diversification of synagogues. In the 1830s Francis Grund noted that "the Americans look upon religion as a promoter of civil and political liberty; and have, therefore, transferred to it a large portion of the affection which they cherish for the institutions of their country."

The immigrant Jew quickly perceived that religion and religious institutions were highly esteemed in America, and that those associated with them were respected as "good citizens." Religious diversity was viewed as a mandate of democracy. As Thomas Jefferson stated to Jacob De La Motta: in religion the maxim is reversed to "divided we stand, united, we fall." Hence, to build and maintain synagogues was in response to the American as well as to the Jewish call to duty. Wherever Jewish and American interests fortified each other, American Jews responded with great enthusiasm.

American church bodies, whether Episcopalian, Presbyterian, Lutheran, Methodist, or Baptist, reflected not only differences in religious ideology but also their differing European national origins. The synagogues did the same: they afforded the immigrant the needed comfort and security of the known, the habitual. Continuity of ritual and familiar liturgical melodies sung by *landsleit* (from the same European town or region) eased the trauma of migration and resettlement.

In 1825, fifteen members of New York's Shearith Israel founded a new congregation that they called B'nai Jeshurun, explaining: "We have a large portion of our brethren who have been educated in the German and Polish minhag, who find it difficult to accustom themselves to what is commonly called the Portuguese minhag." Once begun, the process continued, aided by growing immigration. In 1828, a group of German, Dutch, and Polish Jews left B'nai Jeshurun, which styled itself as an English synagogue, to found Ansche Chesed. Eleven years later, a group of Polish Jews left both synagogues to form Shaarey Zedek, which in turn was abandoned by a group of its congregants who organized Beth Israel in 1843.

Most separations were acrimonious, occasioned by disagreement on ritual or liturgical usage as well as on social distinctions, ethnic loyalties, or personal peeves. What made possible this volatility was the congregationalism that marked American religious life, legitimizing the right to secede, and a constantly increasing immigration that was growing more diverse in countries of origin.

Isaac Leeser described Jewish religious life in 1844:

> We have no ecclesiastical authorities in America, other than the congregations themselves. Each congregation makes its own rules for its government and elects its own minister, who is appointed without any ordination, induction in office being made through his election. . . . As yet we have no colleges or public schools of any kind, with the exception of one in New York . . . one in Baltimore and another in Cincinnati, and Sunday schools in New York, Philadelphia, Richmond, Charleston, Columbia, S.C., Savannah, and Cincinnati. . . . In all our congregations where the necessity demands it, there are ample provisions made for the support of the poor.

In the smaller communities one congregation served the needs of all. Since the very great majority of the Jews in these cities were immigrants from Germany, the congregational articles of incorporation often provided that the "Divine . . . services shall be held according to the German Ritual (Minhag) and not be changed," as did those, for example, of Congregation Beth El in Detroit. But acculturation was proceeding at so rapid a pace that its constitution, adopted in 1856, indicates the inroads of moderate Reform and an allegiance to an American Judaism:

> The congregation shall, in all its religious institutions, pay due attention to the progress of the age, and maintain the respect due to customs or laws handed down to us by our pious fathers. In case of innovation, this congregation shall attempt to remain in unity with the majority of the American congregations, and shall always attempt to produce uniformity in the American synagogue.

In the second half of the nineteenth century Reform began to make serious inroads. Within three decades it had enlisted the great majority of the leading congregations and grew ever more radical with each new triumph.

Reform Temple and Orthodox Shul. "The number of reform congregations prior to the Civil War was small," Leon A. Jick notes, but "by 1870, there were few congregations in America in which substantial reforms had *not* been introduced and in which an accelerating program of radical revision was *not* in process." The war had brought to a virtual end the large-scale immigration from Germany, which had trebled the Jewish population from fifty thousand in 1850 to one hundred fifty thousand in 1860. Few immigrants "who might have reinforced the ranks of traditionalism" arrived in the 1860s and 1870s; those who had arrived earlier were caught up in an assimilatory process of Americanization, which the "nationalist fervor generated by the war" accelerated and which expressed itself through religious reform. "Respectability and Americanization were the goals; decorum, reform of ritual, and English were the means." Reform as a product of the Americanization process had already been noted by Joseph Krauskopf in 1887. "From the moment that the American-born element began to make itself felt," he wrote, "it could not reconcile its mode of thought and its higher aspirations with the musty ghetto religious practices which had outlived their time and usefulness."

The virtual cessation of Jewish immigration during the first two decades of the nineteenth century (the huge influx occurred in the next three decades) had made for a highly acculturated, homogeneous Jewish population in America. In its largest community, Charleston, a very large portion were American born. In 1825, members of Congregation Beth Elohim founded the Reformed Society of Israelites, adopted articles of faith, and worshiped from their own prayer book, with heads uncovered, to the accompaniment of instrumental music. The society lasted only eight years, but the tendency for Reform remained. When Beth Elohim built a new synagogue, it voted to grant a petition "that an organ be erected in the Synagogue to assist in the vocal parts of the service." At the synagogue's dedication, the Reverend Gustav Poznanski proclaimed: "This synagogue is our *temple*, this city our *Jerusalem*, this happy land our *Palestine*, and as our fathers defended with their lives *that* temple, *that* city and *that* land, so will their sons defend *this* temple, *this* city, and *this* land."

The Charleston experience of the 1820s and 1830s—the founding of a Reform congregation and the religious reformation of an existing synagogue—was replicated in the decades that followed in community after community. In 1842 in Baltimore, a group of German immigrants, influenced by the Hamburg Reform Temple, protested the Orthodoxy of the existing congregation and formed the Har Sinai Verein, "the first American synagogue founded *ab initio* on a Reform basis." The new congregation used the Hamburg Temple prayer book at its Rosh Hashanah services, singing hymns from its hymnal to the accompaniment of a parlor organ.

Two and a half years after its organization in 1845, having purchased a church building, New York's Temple Emanu-El began its program of Reform: an organ to accompany the choir, the triennial cycle of Torah reading, confirmation service for boys and girls; and "old-fashioned, useless ceremonies, such as reading a portion of the Law by a so-called Bar Mitzvah boy, making a *Mi-scheberach* [blessing] for one called to hear the Law read, and eventually the calling up to the reading of the Law, were abolished." The week-day elementary school was replaced by a religious school meeting on Saturday and Sunday.

Har Sinai and Emanu-El had been founded as Reform congregations. More typical was the reformation of a traditional congregation, as was the case with Congregation Berith Kodesh in Rochester, New York. Founded in 1848 by German Jews mainly from Bavaria, it remained fully traditional until 1862, when an organ and choir music were introduced into its services. Family pews followed in 1869, and a year later the minister of the Unitarian church was invited to lecture at the temple. In 1873, the lecturer, Dr. N. M. Mann, and Rabbi Max Landsberg brought their congregations together for a Union Thanksgiving service. In 1882, the temple introduced a new ritual "which practically excluded the use of Hebrew from the services, the English language being substituted." Its chronicler boasted that it was the first Jewish congregation in the United States, and probably in the world, to take this step.

The service of worship of the Reform temple was rabbi centered, but the governance as well as the authority were in lay hands. Thus, for example, Chicago's Congregation Sinai presented in 1885 questions on such matters as the rite of circumcision and the language of prayer to its rabbi, Dr. Emil G. Hirsch, for his opinions. These obtained, they were circulated to the congregants, who thereupon decided by vote what the policy would be. The rabbi voiced his view; the power of decision was in the hands of the laity.

The Reform temple served its congregants as their bond to Judaism and their portal to America. Beyond that, its leaders saw its purpose as the creation of a new Judaism, suitable to the new age and their new homeland. As the president of Congregation Sinai expressed it: "We have discarded many obsolete rites. . . . [But] our work will not be completed until we have removed every unnecessary vestige, until we have built on the old foundation a new structure."

In the last decades of the nineteenth century, while the great majority of American synagogues were turning to Reform, a new kind of congregation was being introduced to the American scene, the Eastern European Orthodox *shul* (synagogue). The first "Russian-American Jewish Congregation," Beth Hamedrash, was organized in New York in 1852 by Eastern European immigrants and "several non-Russian Jews who were dissatisfied with the reform movement." Open all day for study, its activities included daily services, morning and evening; every evening "a portion of the law is expounded publicly and there are persons who study the law for themselves, either in pairs or singly; on Sabbaths and festivals the house is full to overflowing." The immigrant congregants in need of the known and the accustomed felt impelled to transplant religious usage as they had known it in the Old World. The mass immigration permitted diversification, and Jews from Russia, Poland, Romania, Hungary, Lithuania, Galicia, and Bohemia formed their own distinct *landsmanschaft* (place of origin) congregations.

Moshe Weinberger in his *Jews and Judaism in New York* (1887) estimates the number of Orthodox congregations on the Lower East Side in 1887 to be 130 and describes their function as "to gather twice daily, or on the Sabbath to worship together, to visit the sick, to provide a proper and honorable burial for the dead, and to help a brother member in time of need. But the highest ambition is to build an imposing synagogue edifice."

The constitution of New York's Beth Hamedrash Hagadol, adopted in 1887, provides that the ritual of the congregation shall be conducted in accordance with the "Shulchan Aruch" (Jewish Code of Law); that "Nussach Ashkenaz" be the only prayer book used for services; and that one who openly violates the Sabbath is ineligible for membership, as is one who is married "otherwise than in accordance with the law of Moses and Israel." Enumerated are the congregation's obligations to a member in case of sickness or death. If taken ill, the member will be visited daily by two brother members; if deathly ill, a person will be sent "to watch at the death bed, and to perform the religious rites." In case of the death of a member, his wife, or any of his children, the congregation will not only defray all funeral expenses but provide ten members to accompany the funeral to the cemetery, four of whom shall perform the burial ceremonies and rites; it will send a *minyan* (the quorum of ten adult males needed for public worship) to the house of mourning, and a committee of five will "call and tender the sympathy of themselves and in behalf of the congregation." In the absence of the extended family, the greatest benefits the congregation could provide its immigrant constituency were brotherly concern and care in case of sickness or death.

Although the salaried officers listed are "Rabbi, Chazan [cantor], Sexton and Secretary," there is a description of the duties of only the last three. The rabbi was considered a communal, not a congregational, functionary, following the usage in European communities. The later, more Americanized Orthodox *shul* incorporated the rabbi as a congregational functionary. The constitution of sister congregation Kahal Adas Jeshurun, adopted in 1913, makes provision for a congregational rabbi, stipulating that "no Rabbi can be accepted by this Congregation, who is not in possession of bona fide certificates [*smichot*] of at least three celebrated authorities on theology of Russia and Poland."

Among the chief characteristics of the Orthodox *shul* in the early twentieth century were the use of Yiddish in the pulpit and at meetings, and the *landsmanschaft* composition of the membership. Both of these came in for criticism by the younger generation, undergoing Americanization. The exclusion of English from services and governance, it was pointed out, excluded the sons of immigrants from participation in synagogal affairs and discouraged their attendance at services.

The *landsmanschaft* designation marked the *shul* as an Old World institution to a generation of young Jews seeking acceptance by the New. A solution was attempted by members of that generation—the Young Israel movement. Organized in 1912 by a group of young men on New York's Lower East Side, it had as its aim the transformation of the *shul* into an Americanized synagogue offering decorous services conducted by its members, and a program of educational, cultural, and social activities using the English language, yet remaining fully Orthodox. What the Young Israel movement announced was that the days of the transplanted Eastern European *shul* were coming to an end and that America's Jews, even the Orthodox, were in need of a new type of synagogue that would be responsive to traditional Jewish needs but would not ignore the realities of American life.

Synagogue-Center. Mordecai M. Kaplan, who helped found the Young Israel movement, viewed with alarm the condition of the synagogue in 1918. Noting that it owed its existence "more to the momentum of the past, than to any new forces created in this country," he warned that only the concentration of "all possible material and moral resources" might save "the synagogue from impending doom." He proposed the creation of a new type of synagogue, a synagogue-center, which would provide its members activities of a "social, intellectual and spiritual character." He was founder and rabbi of the Jewish Center (on the West Side of Manhattan), which incorporated a synagogue, an assembly hall, a gymnasium, a swimming pool, meeting rooms, and classrooms. The evolution of the synagogue from a worship-centered institution, as were both the Reform temple and the Orthodox *shul*, into a multifaceted entity serving the social, cultural, and spiritual needs of the community was in process in the years after the Civil War. The change was due in part to the new needs of a rapidly Americanizing community; in part to response to a new conceptualization of America and the role of a minority culture within it; and in part to forces that brought about a similar development in American Protestantism, the *institutional church.*

The redefinition of Judaism into a cultural and ethnic rather than a solely religious identity, creating a formulation appropriate and desirable in America, was the work of secularists Chaim Zhitlowsky and Horace Kallen and religionists Bernhard Felsenthal and Israel Friedlaender. In the first decades of the twentieth century they rejected the melting-pot concept of America as being inimical to both America and its component minorities, and propounded a new image of America, which came to be called cultural pluralism. Kaplan translated their ideological stance into practical application.

Both the temple of radical Reform and the *shul* of insular Orthodoxy were responses to a melting-pot America—the former altering its house of worship in response to what it perceived to be the assimilatory demands of such an America; the latter reacting to such perceived demands by withdrawing from the influences of the American environment into self-imposed isolation. The synagogue-center drew its ideological justification as an American institution from cultural pluralism, which argued that a minority group had both the right and the duty to retain and develop its culture. Indeed, such adherence and creativity

were not only in the best interests of the individual and his group, but were also a singular contribution to the strengthening of democracy and the flourishing of American civilization. A synagogue so conceived and so fashioned had great appeal to a generation of American Jews, the children of the Eastern European immigrants, desirous of maintaining a Jewish identity while intent on the fullest integration into the American scene.

In 1915, a group of younger members of Rochester's pioneer Orthodox Congregation Beth Israel issued a call and solicited participation: "Recognizing that it is our duty as Jews to bear witness to the truths of our Faith in our days and generation as our Fathers did in theirs . . . we hereby constitute ourselves a Jewish congregation for the purpose of conserving Judaism." Their fathers had established an Orthodox *shul*; now they in response to their views and their needs were organizing a Conservative synagogue (which they later called Beth El) that would provide family pews for men and women; prayers in Hebrew and English, conducted by the rabbi, cantor, and choir; congregational singing and music with organ, the choir composed of Jews and the congregation to wear hat and tallith (prayer shawl); daily services, with special services on Friday evening, Saturday morning, and holidays; and a daily and Sunday school to be supported by the congregation.

The Rochester congregation placed special emphasis on education. The rabbi was to "supervise the Sunday School and Hebrew School" and "establish classes for adolescents and study circles of adults," in addition to attending all services and officiating at "all religious ceremonies." The rabbi was established as the central congregational functionary, the cantor his associate and assistant. By 1922 the synagogue could boast the largest congregational school in the community. And in the 1920s and 1930s its Sisterhood, Men's Club, junior congregation, Boy Scout troop, youth clubs, and athletic teams made it "respected as an established coequal" of the old-established German Jewish Temple B'rith Kodesh.

Rabbi Ralph Simon reports on the transformation of Rodef Sholom (Johnstown, Pennsylvania), which had been established in 1885 as an Orthodox synagogue. In the 1930s, fearing that unless the synagogue was modernized the next generation would join the Reform temple, the board invited him to serve as its first Conservative rabbi:

> Very few changes [were made] in the Sabbath and holidays Synagogue service. It was only in Friday evening late service that changes could be made ... sermons in English ... decorum and interpretation of the liturgy. The major area of change was in the cultural and social programs. All the activities envisioned in the synagogue-center program of Dr. Kaplan were introduced. Adult education classes were organized. A good Hebrew school was conducted. There was an active Men's Club, Sisterhood and Youth Group. There were frequent programs of music, a new choir, dramatic presentations and guest speakers.

Across the state in Scranton, Temple Israel was proud to report what a newly established synagogue could accomplish in but a year and a half: a Hebrew school of over one hundred children attending daily, and a religious school meeting every Sunday morning; a Boy Scout troop, the second leading troop in the city; a Girl Scout troop, which carried away all the prizes for scout work; a musical glee club for the junior congregation; the *Zadik-Zadik* club of the junior auxiliary, which looked after the social programs; the Junior Menorah Society for high school boys and girls, meeting weekly for discussion; and the Progress Club, consisting of older sons and daughters of members. For the adult membership there were services, twice daily, Sabbaths, and holidays; and "visiting speakers from New York who were delighted to find such a large turn-out at the late Friday night Services, considering the location of the Temple, being in the non-Jewish section of the city."

The synagogue-center characterized its function as threefold, a *beth hatefillah* (house of worship), a *beth hamidrash* (house of study), and a *beth hakenesseth* (house of assembly). Initially descriptive of the Conservative synagogues, this definition applied to a growing number of Orthodox and Reform congregations as well.

Centrality of the Synagogue. In the years between the world wars, the synagogue-center replaced the classic Reform temple and the insular Orthodox *shul* as the prototypical American synagogue. In post–World War II America, the synagogue's central position in the Jewish community was confirmed.

During the 1920s and 1930s the growth in the number of synagogues had been dramatic. While the Jewish population had grown by some 40 percent, the number of synagogues had almost doubled, rising from 1,901 in 1917 to 3,738 in 1937. What makes this growth all the more noteworthy is that the 1930s were the years of economic depression, a time of great difficulty for religious institutions.

The war years witnessed an upsurge in the general influence of religion and the status of its institutions, which continued in postwar America. The suburbanization of America after 1945 affected the Jews, the most urbanized Americans, more than any other group. The need for the new "suburban immigrants" to secure their status made for the establishment of congregations and the erection of synagogues. The Jews became part of their new community through their religious institution, which was accepted by the "natives" as part of the suburban landscape.

All three religious movements were directing resources to the new suburban communities. The Union of Orthodox Jewish Congregations launched a $300,000 campaign for a program to establish Orthodox congregations in the suburbs. The New York Federation of Reform Synagogues placed a pre–High Holy Days ad in New York newspapers listing its congregations in the metropolitan area, thirty-three in suburban Nassau and Westchester counties, where 200,000 Jews lived, fourteen to serve the 1,345,000 Jews in the Bronx and Brooklyn. The architectural consultant for the Conservative United Synagogue claimed that in 1954–1955 alone 150 Conservative synagogues were being planned or constructed.

Each movement claimed rapidly growing numbers of affiliated synagogues, and all suburban synagogues boasted increasing membership. Most telling of all about the growth of synagogues and their status in the community was their dominance in the area of education. Jewish religious-school enrollment more than doubled in the first postwar decade, rising from 231,028 in 1946 to 488,432 in 1956. Of that number, over 85 percent were in schools under congregational auspices.

The upsurge of Jewish religious life made the synagogue "suburbia's nuclear and most important Jewish institution." Like its neighboring Protestant church, it emphasized "the ethical, moral and social values associated with religion, and the needs of living people." Albert I. Gordon in his study *Jews in Suburbia* (1959) attributed the preeminence of the synagogue in suburbia in the mid-1950s not so much to its being a religious institution as to its being "usually the first organized body to provide a physical structure in which Jews can meet as Jews within the community . . . because it provides for the formal Jewish education of the children . . . and because it helps Jews 'feel' Jewish even when there is little Jewish symbolism in the home."

The process of founding a suburban synagogue begins with the need for fellowship felt by the young couples newly arrived in a suburb who also seek an institution that will provide for their children's religious needs. They soon find that the rabbi is available to counsel them in the many personal problems that dislocation from expanded family and integration into a new community may bring. They also find that the same rabbi who has become counselor and friend is the recognized leader of the Jewish community and its accepted representative to the general community.

The American Jew in the early postwar decades had chosen to live a largely secular life, free of religious discipline, but at the same time he demanded that American Jewry maintain a communal religious identity. This for him was the American way of life—to esteem established religion and its institutions, but to live free of their restraints. The synagogue-center was the institution that served him well in this choice. To the world outside, it was a synagogue, a religious institution; for him, it was a center for Jewish fellowship, with religious services and cultural activities playing a secondary role.

In the postwar years, America accepted Will Herberg's image of America as the Land of the Three Great Faiths—Protestant, Catholic, Jewish. Such a formulation lifted American Jewry from the status of one of many minority groups to that of one-third of America. This was expressed symbolically in a whole network of interfaith activities in which synagogue and rabbi were equal partners with church and minister. When, on such occasions, priest and minister spoke of the Judeo-Christian tradition, the Jew heard his faith accorded parity with the majority faith. It was satisfying and rewarding for the Jew to maintain a religious posture in an America in which religion was esteemed and its influence growing, as a Gallup Poll conducted in 1957 indicated. Only 14 percent thought that the influence of religion was decreasing, while 69 percent believed that it was increasing.

The Contemporary Synagogue. The change in the cultural climate and the status of organized religions that took place in the late 1960s was as precipitous as it was dramatic. Americans turned their attention and concern from societal betterment to personal satisfaction. The church as savior of society gave way to churches as servants of their communicants. The mainline Protestant denominations that had been in the forefront of civil rights activities suffered a hemorrhaging of membership and influence. The privatization of religion caused an erosion in its influence. In 1970 a Gallup Poll asked the same question as it had in 1957, and now found 14 percent responded "increasing," while 75 percent stated "decreasing."

The synagogue, which had benefited from its association with the church in the "glory days" of American organized religion in the early postwar decades, now was affected by the decline in status and influence of mainline Protestantism. But to a degree unmatched by the major church denominations, the synagogues were able to retain their membership by becoming "service synagogues," ready to provide, as called upon, specific, discrete services: education; life passage rites for birth, bar and bat mitzvah (confirmation services at age thirteen), wedding ceremonies and celebrations, burial, mourning, and *yahrzeit* (anniversary of death); and ministration of the realm of spiritual social work.

The synagogue of the 1970s and 1980s, "decades of the ethnics," has continued in its primacy because it has continued to provide spiritual and cultural nourishment to its constituency, which lives ethnically, but under a religious identity. The synagogue has retained its ability to adopt and adapt. In this era in which pluralism and diversity have been highly esteemed as being in the best interest of the individual and the nation, the synagogue has diversified itself into a mosaic of distinct and differing congregations, and individual congregations have effected inner diversification.

A wide variety of synagogues serve a widely varied constituency. They range from the ultra-Orthodox Hasidic *shtibl* (prayer room) in Brooklyn's Williamsburg or Boro Park, presided over by a dynastic *rebbe* (Hasidic rabbi), to the Reform Stephen S. Wise Temple across the continent in

Los Angeles with its staff of rabbis, cantors, educators, social workers, and executives administering day-care centers, schools, social service bureaus, and a fleet of buses.

Congregations grown large in the 1960s attempt to answer needs of the 1980s for the humanization and "personalization" of the synagogue. The *havurah*, a product of the Jewish students' counterculture movement, has been seized upon by a large number of synagogues. Rabbi Harold M. Schulweis, who pioneered with *havurot* in his Congregation Valley Beth Shalom (Encino, California), reported on his experience in 1973:

> In our congregation, a *havurah* is [composed] of a minyan of families who have agreed to meet together at least once a month to learn together, to celebrate together and hopefully to form some surrogate for the eroded extended family.
>
> There was a death in the *havurah*. The widow had few members of the family around her. I saw who was at the funeral, who took care of the children during the black week of the *shivah*. The *havurah* offers the synagogue member a community small enough to enable personal relationships to develop. It enables families to express their Jewishness. Hopefully the synagogue itself will gradually be transformed into a Jewish assembly [of] *havurot*. My grandfather came to the synagogue because he was a Jew. His grandchildren come to the synagogue to become Jewish.

The American synagogue, coextensive with the entire historic experience of the Jews in America, has been remarkably sensitive to the changing needs of America's Jews and has responded by reordering its priorities and programs to meet these needs. It continues to retain its resilience and adaptability, but the problems besetting it are substantial. The local Jewish community federations have grown in power because of the vast sums that campaigns for overseas needs place in their hands to allocate. More than half these sums are now apportioned for national and local needs, and as a general rule, federations have chosen the Jewish community centers as their institutional counterparts in the community and allocate increasing subsidies to them. In the 1970s and 1980s, when synagogue-building has all but ceased, multimillion-dollar centers continue to go up. Their new facilities

and communal subventions enable them to compete successfully with the synagogues in cultural and fellowship activities—activities generally of lesser Jewish content than those provided by the synagogues.

The great majority of American Jews, however, choose to express their Jewish identity through affiliation or association with the synagogue. It continues to be the preeminent institution in American Jewish life, in large measure because there is wide agreement with the view of Mordecai M. Kaplan that:

> In this country, the synagogue is the principal means of keeping alive the Jewish consciousness. . . . [It] is the only institution which can define our aims to a world that would otherwise be at a loss to understand why we persist in retaining our corporate individuality.

New Forces in American Judaism. The postwar years also saw the emergence of religious groups at both ends of the religious spectrum. Among the survivors of the Holocaust who found a haven in the United States was a remnant of the pietistic religious movement Hasidism, which had its origins in Eastern Europe in the latter part of the eighteenth century. It emphasized personal piety, prayer, the joyous worship of God through religiously focused common deeds of life, and the centrality of the zaddik or rebbe, the charismatic (later, dynastic) leader of each of the communities of the faithful.

The newly arrived Hasidim established self-contained communities in the Williamsburg, East New York, and Boro Park sections of Brooklyn and in suburban areas of New York, where they built networks of institutions: synagogues, schools, ritualiriums (ritual baths), and social agencies. Their way of life, extending from a particular mode of dress and diet to the use of Yiddish as the common language, sets them apart from the mainline Jewish community. Hasidism incorporates both the insular and self-isolated anti-Zionist (they deem Israel a "creation of Satan") followers of the rebbe of Satmar and the Habad or Lubavitch sect, which utilizes the media and the most contemporary form of public relations in an outreach program to win fellow Jews to piety. A high birthrate and success in retaining the loyalty of its children and in attracting small but highly publicized groups of young

Jews to its way of life have made Hasidism a growing force in Jewish life. It influences the wider religious and intellectual scene through the works of its interpreters and popularizers, notably Martin Buber, Abraham Joshua Heschel, and Elie Wiesel.

The radical theology of Mordecai M. Kaplan, his rejection of supernaturalism, his depersonalization of God, and his emphasis on the historical-cultural rather than the purely "religious"— that is, the Jewish way of life as historic folkways rather than God-given laws—won him a body of adherents who, under his leadership, established Reconstructionism. It took its name from its announced purpose: to reconstruct Judaism, ideologically and practically. For almost four decades, from the 1920s through the 1950s, it constituted the left wing of Conservative Judaism. In the postwar decades it began to move toward an independent posture, and in the 1960s it assumed its denominational identity, proclaiming itself the fourth component of the American Jewish religious establishment. Prayer books reflecting Reconstructionist theology were the first step toward denominationalism, followed by the organization of rabbinic and congregational fellowships. Full denominational independence was concretized by the establishment of the Reconstructionist Rabbinical College in 1968. Devoutly Zionist, committed to the overarching unity of the Jewish people and to Jewish cultural expression in all its varieties, Reconstructionism exerts influence in the non-Orthodox community, but it has remained limited in numbers of congregations and active adherents.

The 1960s saw a rise in Jewish theological writing and interest. Jewish thought became a central concern of a small but influential group of Jewish scholars. The existentialist mood was evidenced in the popularity of the writings of Martin Buber, Franz Rosenzweig, and Abraham Joshua Heschel, and in renewed interest in the ways of Hasidism. On the campus, "radical" Jewish students were seeking a new view of God, world, and self, and a new way of life within the Jewish tradition. It is significant that a good portion of the creative theological thinking and writing, and innovative institutional experimentation, took place outside the religious establishment, without organizational sponsorship or support.

In the waning years of the 1960s and in the early 1970s there was a perceptible weakening in organized Jewish religious life, reflecting, in part, the general crisis in organized religious life in America. Church membership and attendance had declined. Aspects of Catholic life were in disarray. The mainline Protestant bodies were experiencing a serious diminution in adherents, support, and influence. Only the fundamentalist, evangelical churches were healthy and growing. In the Jewish community the number of synagogues was declining. Some closed down because of neighborhood changes; others amalgamated. Synagogue membership dropped, while the median age of members rose. Only fundamentalist Orthodoxy seemed to be on the increase. Traditionalism was reemphasized even among Orthodox groups that sought to grapple with the implications and demands of modern American society. Right-wing Orthodox groups in the large urban centers increased in number, through accretion from the outside and a high birthrate. Some Hasidic groups carried on successful educational campaigns in communities and on campuses, gaining "converts" among noncommitted Jewish youth.

THE RELIGIOUS ESTABLISHMENT

The tripartite division of the American Jewish community continues, but each of the groups, Reform, Conservative, and Orthodox, has undergone and continues to undergo significant change.

During the first two decades of the century, Reform had continued its drift away from tradition. A return to traditionalism then began, at first hardly perceptible, then developing slowly, and finally bursting into great activity in the years following World War II. An increasing number of rabbis ordained by the Reform seminary, Hebrew Union College, came from an Eastern European traditionalist background, and a significant number came under the influence of Zionism, which refocused their interest on Jewish peoplehood and Jewish culture.

The Columbus platform, adopted by the Central Conference of American Rabbis (CCAR) in 1937, which redefined Judaism from the credal formulation of the 1885 Pittsburgh platform to the historical religious experience of the Jewish people, affirmed "the obligation of all Jewry to aid in [Palestine's] upbuilding as a Jewish homeland" and called for "the preservation of the Sabbath, festivals and Holy Days, the retention and development of . . . customs, symbols and ceremonies . . . and the use of the Hebrew Language in our worship and instruction."

A mass influx of sons and daughters of Eastern European immigrants into the Reform congregations stimulated return to traditional forms in the temple and reintroduction of ritual into the home. Use of Hebrew in the liturgy increased. Bar and bat mitzvah, *kiddush* (the prayer of sanctification of the Sabbath), and even *habdalah* (the synagogue and home ceremony at the conclusion of the Sabbath) became part of Reform practice. In 1976 the CCAR reassessed the "spiritual state of Reform Judaism," calling for a renewal of obligation to Jewish religious practice and to the survival of the Jewish people.

The turn to traditional forms has evoked resistance by a group of rabbis advocating the retention of classic Reform "verities" in ideology and practice. The phenomenon of Reform rabbis co-officiating with priests and ministers at mixed marriages has led to organized criticism by colleagues. Yet the number of Reform rabbis who perform such religious ministration is growing, as is the number of those who are turning to the *halakah* (the Jewish religious legal system) for guidance. Similar trends are evident in the laity. How institutional unity will be able to encompass such growing polarity is a major challenge facing organized Reform Jewry.

In the era (1902–1915) of the Jewish Theological Seminary's charismatic president Solomon Schechter, Conservative Judaism was an ideological reaction to Reform. It was a reaffirmation of the authority of *halakah* as a living albeit changing system of law, custom, and traditions. It emphasized the total historical religious experience of the Jewish people, and held precious all Jewish cultural and spiritual creations. Later, Conservative Judaism came into competitive confrontation with Orthodoxy. Many Orthodox congregations turned Conservative in the hope of retaining the interest and loyalty of the new generation. Graduates of the Jewish Theological Seminary founded Conservative congregations that drew their membership from the Orthodox camp.

The Conservative emphasis on family worship and the congregational school, and the stress on Zionism and Jewish culture, attracted the children of the immigrants. The movement adopted Mordecai M. Kaplan's definition of Judaism as "an evolving religious civilization" as its ideological stance, and turned Conservative synagogues into cultural, spiritual, and social centers that embraced Jewish culture in its totality—language, literature, music, and art.

Marshall Sklare, who published his study *Conservative Judaism* in 1955, took another look in 1970 and reported "a notable increase in the number of Conservative synagogues, as well as a sharp rise in membership." He observed that the movement had achieved "primacy on the American Jewish religious scene" and that its synagogues have emerged "as the leading congregations in their communities." Yet, he notes, "the morale of the Conservative movement is on the decline."

This erosion in morale Sklare attributes in part to Conservative Judaism's misreading of the future of Orthodoxy in America. It expected Orthodoxy's strength and influence to wane, when they in fact have risen. Another cause for the crisis in morale, especially among the rabbis, is what Sklare termed "Conservatism's defeat on the ritual front which can be demonstrated in almost every area of Jewish observance."

An issue agitating Conservative Judaism in the 1980s has been the division between the rabbinate, the laity, and the Jewish Theological Seminary faculty on the ordination of women. (Women had been ordained at the Reform Hebrew Union College since 1972. The ordination of women is universally opposed in Orthodoxy.) A vote of the faculty in October 1983 to accept women into the Rabbinical School resulted in the formation of the Union for Traditional Conservative Judaism, a body of rabbis and laymen opposing "revolutionary change." Conservative Judaism, like Reform, seems to be facing a growing polarization.

The era of mass migration from Eastern Europe (1880s–1920s) had been religiously calamitous for the Orthodox immigrant. Although the transplanted Old World synagogal forms satisfied the immigrant's spiritual needs, they did not win the interest or allegiance of his children. The Orthodox reaction was to withdraw into self-contained communities, and spiritual and cultural isolation. Forward-looking leaders, taking their example from the mid-nineteenth-century Neo-Orthodoxy of Samson Raphael Hirsch of Frankfurt-am-Main, launched an attempt in the 1920s at making the traditional faith at home in the modern world. Their efforts took the form of a yeshiva-university, where young men would receive modern high school and college training while studying the sacred texts in the traditional manner, all in an Orthodox religious atmosphere. Yeshiva University and its Rabbi Isaac Elchanan Theological Seminary graduated rabbis, teachers, and lay leaders who have given renewed vitality to Orthodoxy. Orthodox congregations have taken on new life, though the price has sometimes been the adoption of new forms borrowed from more liberal coreligionists.

In the post–World War II years, there has been a growth of fundamentalist traditionalism in Orthodoxy, largely occasioned by the immigration of Hasidim from Central Europe, and a new militancy on the part of some native-born Orthodox leaders critical of Yeshiva University's religious liberalism.

Orthodoxy, for all its increasing visibility, constitutes a diminishing percentage of American Jewry. Splintered by ideological and *halakic* differences, which now and again flare up into political conflict, Orthodoxy is moving away from the mainline community into a self-imposed isolation, which may insulate it against corrosive influences but in turn vitiates its influence on the Jewish community at large.

For reasons both Jewish and American, American Jewry defines itself as a religious community. The synagogue is its most enduring and pervasive institution; Jewishness is expressed through religious celebrations and observance, which are viewed as simultaneously cultural and national. This is not to say that the community is defined by piety. Though there are pious Jews in America, those who are less pious consider themselves no less Jewish. Whether less or more devout, American Jews have found that ritual observance and liturgy add dimension to their Jewish identity and being. For some, ritual observance of the Sabbath, the festivals, and the High Holy Days marks the rhythm of life; for others it offers meaning and uplift; for nearly all, it serves as a bond with the Jewish people, past and present.

In 1984, Orthodox rabbi Shlomo Riskin raised the alarm of "the scourge of assimilation" that threatens the American Jewish community with a Holocaust-like devastation. He lists as its signals here, an intermarriage rate "approaching 47 percent"; that "82 percent of our children do not attend synagogue"; and the "declining figures for congregational affiliation, Hebrew school enrollment, and membership in Jewish communal organizations." A year earlier Charles E. Silberman, "after four and a half years of research," concluded that "the overwhelming majority of American Jews are choosing to remain Jews" and saw "the early stages of a major revitalization of Jewish religious, intellectual and cultural life."

Both Riskin and Silberman are describing the same community, and both are describing it correctly. The rabbi judges it against the standards of what ought to be (piety, learning) and bewails what it has not become; the social scientist sees it as it is (positive identity, cultural awareness) and hails what it seems to be becoming. The American Jewish scene offers ample documentation for both the fear of Riskin and the faith of Silberman. But most American Jews are optimistic that the demonstrated will to survive and virtuosity at adaptation of American Jewry will enable it to continue the enterprise of creative Jewish living in the free and open society that is America.

BIBLIOGRAPHY

Jews and Judaism in America

Naomi W. Cohen, *Encounter with Emancipation: The German Jews in the United States, 1830–1940* (1984); Moshe Davis, "Jewish Religious Life and Institutions in America," in Louis Finkelstein, ed., *The Jews*, vol. I (1949); Nathan Glazer, *American Judaism* (1957; rev. 1972); Leon A. Jick, *The Americanization of the Synagogue, 1820–1870* (1976); Abraham J. Karp, *Haven and Home: A History of the Jews in America* (1985); Jacob R. Marcus, *The Colonial American Jew, 1492–1776*, 3 vols. (1970); Jacob Neusner, ed., *Understanding American Judaism*, 2 vols. (1975); Charles E. Silberman, *A Certain People* (1985).

Reform Judaism

Joseph L. Blau, ed., *Reform Judaism: A Historical Perspective. Essays from the Yearbook of the Central Conference of American Rabbis* (1973); Samuel E. Karff, ed., *Hebrew Union College–Jewish Institute of Religion at One Hundred Years* (1976); David Philipson, *The Reform Movement in Judaism* (1907; rev. 1931; rep.

1967); W. Gunther Plaut, *The Growth of Reform Judaism: American and European Sources Until 1948* (1965); David Polish, "The Changing and Constant in the Reform Rabbinate," in *American Jewish Archives*, 35 (1983); Sefton D. Temkin, "A Century of Reform Judaism in America," in *American Jewish Yearbook*, 74 (1973).

Conservative Judaism

Moshe Davis, *The Emergence of Conservative Judaism* (1963); Abraham J. Karp, *A History of the United Synagogue of America, 1913–1963* (1964) and "The Conservative Rabbi—'Dissatisfied but Not Unhappy,'" in *American Jewish Archives*, 35 (1983); Herbert Parzen, *Architects of Conservative Judaism* (1964); Marshall Sklare, *Conservative Judaism* (1955; rev. 1972); Mordecai Waxman, ed., *Tradition and Change: The Development of Conservative Judaism* (1958).

Orthodox Judaism

Jeffrey S. Gurock, "Resisters and Accommodators: Varieties of Orthodox Rabbis in America, 1886–1983," in *American Jewish Archives*, 35 (1983); Samuel C. Heilman, *Synagogue Life: A Study in Symbolic Interaction* (1976); Gilbert Klaperman, *The Story of Yeshiva University: The First Jewish University in America* (1969); George Kranzler, *Williamsburg: A Jewish Community in Transition. A Study of the Factors and Patterns of Change in the Organization and Structure of a Community in Transition* (1961); Charles S. Liebman, "Orthodoxy in American Jewish Life," in *American Jewish Yearbook*, 66 (1965).
[*See also* RELIGIOUS ARCHITECTURE; JEWISH LITERATURE AND RELIGIOUS THOUGHT; JUDAISM IN CONTEMPORARY AMERICA; LITURGY AND WORSHIP; RELIGIOUS ARCHITECTURE; RELIGIOUS PREJUDICE AND NATIVISM; *and* SOCIAL HISTORY OF AMERICAN JUDAISM.]

SOCIAL HISTORY OF
AMERICAN JUDAISM

Deborah Dash Moore

THE process of immigration that brought Jews from different European nations to the shores of North America created an American Jewish community culturally diverse and organizationally complex. Since 1654 continuous immigration has renewed the relevance of this experience. Even in the last half of the twentieth century the arrival of thousands of Jewish immigrants has prompted changes in established institutions and the introduction of new ones. The self-selection of Jews for migration brought individuals motivated and equipped for the task of community building. The American Jewish community that emerged was woven out of the fabric of these immigrants' experience.

The Jews who came to the New World shared characteristics that decisively affected the type of communities they built. Generally the immigrants were young, ambitious, and single, albeit with close family ties often expressed through the financing of the subsequent migration of other family members. Almost all were poor and unaccomplished, making up in energy what they lacked in training and wealth. The majority came from urban milieus, a reflection of the dominant Jewish situation in Europe. When they arrived in America, most Jews lived among other immigrants in an enclave composed largely of young adults. Without elders or parents present, and often without the responsibilities of children, immigrant Jews discovered far fewer constraints in America than they had known in Europe. This peer group environment encouraged them to create communities founded upon shared values, activities, and culture. Consequently these communities lacked much social differentiation, hierarchy, and deference. They were largely indifferent to tradition, religious authority, and history, the usual sources of Jewish solidarity.

Jewish immigrants instead relied upon a common experiential reality and economic interdependence to produce bonds among rough equals and to nourish a pragmatic Jewish identity.

The character of the peer group communities received significant form from the American milieu in which they were rooted. The American Jewish communities' strengths appear in their innovation, energy, and flexibility. The relative openness of American society, the high rates of social and physical mobility, the absence of received tradition and centralized authority, the emphasis on the importance of experience and segmented, voluntarist activity, and the rampant denominationalism all provided a congenial environment for these aspects of American Jewish life. By contrast, when immigrant Jews desired to preserve traditional religious practices, to maintain close ties with the European Jewish world, to pass on a rich historical heritage, and to sustain patterns of deference to an acknowledged rabbinical elite, they faced an inhospitable milieu. Nevertheless, American Jews succeeded in supporting some traditionalist aspects of Jewish communal life due to the saliency of pluralism, a value produced in the heterogeneous reality of America. Pluralism particularly sustained American Zionism, providing Jews with an American rationale for their support of Jewish nationalism and the state of Israel.

The source of Jewish immigrants shifted with the pace of modernization in Europe as the character of American society changed with the growth of the nation. The periodization of American Jews' social history derives from a rough intersection of these two aspects of social change. European modernization compelled Jews to leave their homes and to seek new occu-

291

pational opportunities. Concurrently, developing European states, beginning with France in 1791, granted political rights and citizenship to Jews as individuals. The changing legal status of European Jewry weakened Jewish communal bonds, especially the formal obligations of the *kehillah* (community), thus loosening the hold of tradition. Liberal and Enlightenment ideas challenged the religious elite and fostered a secular intelligentsia. The Jewish masses experienced the pervasive effects of modernity on a life cycle structured according to religious norms. Jewish family patterns changed in response to the new conditions. In eastern Europe the decline in infant mortality and the lengthening of life expectancy produced a population explosion: from 1.5 million Jews in 1800 to 6.8 million by the end of the century. In western Europe Jews quickly began to limit their family size, responding to the economic and social demands of an upwardly mobile urban group.

In the seventeenth and eighteenth centuries, modernization had touched only the western fringes of European Jewish society. As a result, small numbers of Jews came to North America from western Europe during the colonial period. A substantial percentage of these immigrants were Sephardic Jews, whose religious and cultural traditions had been shaped by the medieval Mediterranean world, especially the flourishing Jewish community of Spain. This community's existence had come to an abrupt end in 1492, the year of Columbus' fateful journey, with the expulsion from Spain of all Jews who refused to convert to Christianity (Portugal followed suit in 1496). Of the 150,000 who chose exile, a minority settled in the Netherlands, then a Spanish possession, and spread from there to other parts of western Europe, including France, England (which Jews entered again as unofficial residents during the Glorious Revolution of 1689), and some German states. A few immigrated even farther, settling during the late seventeenth century in the port cities of North America.

During the period of United States westward expansion, particularly the two decades preceding the Civil War, Jewish immigrants came largely from the German states and the Austro-Hungarian empire; they were part of a mass migration of Germans to the United States. German Jews, like their Christian countrymen, settled along the rapidly expanding American frontier as well as in the burgeoning cities. They brought with them Ashkenazic traditions that had developed over the course of 1,000 years in central and eastern Europe, flourishing especially in Poland in the sixteenth century. The migration of German Jews westward also signaled a reversal in previous eastward European patterns of Jewish migration, following the disastrous attacks of cossacks on Polish Jews in 1648 and the dismantling of Poland at the end of the eighteenth century. In the mid-nineteenth century, as modernization reached the heartland of Polish Jews, now largely under Russian rule, they became the main source of Jewish immigration.

Migration from Germany, especially the former Poznan district annexed by Prussia, and from eastern sections of Austria-Hungary, which included the previously Polish province of Galicia and the previously Ottoman province of Bukovina, continued throughout the nineteenth century. However, the outbreak of fierce pogroms against Russian Jews in 1881 and 1882 following the assassination of the czar drove such large numbers to settle in the United States —2.3 million between 1882 and 1924—that they rapidly eclipsed the 250,000 Jews of German origin. The arrival of these eastern European Jews, as well as a large number of Rumanian Jews after 1900, coincided with the surge of industrialization that transformed American economic and social life in the years after the Civil War. Because eastern European Jews suffered the dislocation of a modernizing society, aggravated by severe persecution and violence—a situation not shared with their Gentile countrymen—their immigration assumed unique attributes and proportions. The distinctive Jewish culture of *yiddishkeit*, embracing both secular and sacred spheres and rooted in the Yiddish language, contributed to the singular character of this mass immigration.

World War I disrupted Jewish immigration from eastern Europe, then the imposition of drastic quotas by the immigration acts of 1921 and 1924 reduced it to a trickle. But lack of hospitable countries ready to accept them did not curtail the desire of many Jews to leave eastern Europe. Since World War I political persecution more than modernization has pushed Jews out of their native lands. Because of the political motivation for their immigration, these immigrants usually have been classed as refugees. When Adolf Hitler and the Nazi party gained power in January 1933, they imposed the first legislation discriminating against Jews turning Germany again into a source of Jewish immigrants. However, until Nazi attacks on Jews escalated into widespread violence in 1937–1938, few Jews were admitted to the United States. The severity of the economic depression, the bitter competition for scarce jobs, and widespread anti-Semitism reinforced Americans' reluctance to return to a liberal immigration policy, even to assist the victims of racist persecution.

Jews with widely divergent traditions fled the Nazi Holocaust that eventually claimed the lives of six million Jews. Approximately 250,000 found refuge in America. These refugees and survivors included several groups of Hasidim, pious ultraorthodox sectarians devoted to their *rebbe,* or spiritual leader, as well as modern orthodox German and Hungarian Jews, and a small but significant number of left-wing European Jewish intellectuals. Because of the bias of American immigration legislation and the devastating effect of the Nazi Holocaust, a larger proportion of the Jewish religious and intellectual elite came to America than had in previous eras. Although many of these individuals succeeded in reestablishing their careers or reconstituting their sects, they often experienced a double alienation—from both American society and the American Jewish community. By 1940 the children of the east European migration had molded Jewish collective activity into patterns that bore only faint resemblance to European Jewish cultures.

Recent Jewish immigrants—estimates range from 350,000 to 500,000—from the Soviet Union, Iran, South Africa, South America, and Israel have entered a postindustrial, suburban America eager to partake of its economic opportunities. Israelis, who come from their own sovereign Jewish state, resemble non-Jewish immigrants in their ability and expressed desire to return home more than do earlier or contemporary Jewish immigrants. The other recent migrants have left the lands of their birth because of political difficulties, revolutions, or a threatening anti-Semitism. Like many of the refugees of the Hitler era, they often come from bourgeois, highly educated, or privileged sections of society with advanced industrial and commercial skills but relatively meager Jewish traditions. Those Jews more closely tied to Judaism or to an ethnic Jewish identity often choose to immigrate to Israel, rather than to the United States. Yet the migrants' experience of modernization as Jews in their native lands differs from the American Jewish version of collective and individual adaptation. Visible and cohesive minorities in American cities, they contribute to the established Jewish community a measure of ethnic diversity.

The cultural resources Jews brought with them influenced their economic, political, and religious behavior. Within a society they experienced as modern—that is, nontraditional, nonhierarchical, democratic, capitalist, and individualist—Jews shaped communal institutions to accommodate their cultural baggage, their ambitions, their needs, and the demands of their neighbors.

During each period different communal forms dominated Jewish group life. In the colonial era the social structure established by Sephardic Jews centered communal life around the congregation. German Jews destroyed this pattern during the period of westward expansion and created multiple foci of community that competed with the synagogue. These included fraternal orders, philanthropic institutions, and recreational organizations. But fragmentation spurred efforts to coordinate Jewish activity on a national scale leading to nascent political organization. During the Progressive era east European Jews multiplied varieties of communal activity, from intimate social fellowships of *landsmanshaften* (mutual benefit societies based on town of origin) to industrial unionism. National and international political groups appeared on the American Jewish scene. The intellectual migration of the 1930s strengthened the ranks of the American Jewish intelligentsia and loosened their ties to Jewish communal organizations while other refugees speeded the trend toward the professionalization of Jewish community life. The postwar survivors introduced varieties of orthodoxy, especially modern Hasidism, to American Jewry and enhanced the influence of this segment of the Jewish community through the establishment of educational institutions, from parochial day schools through yeshivas for advanced study of sacred texts. The most recent immigrants of the 1960s and 1970s have contributed to the international focus of Jewish national organizations and enriched their political culture.

The impact of immigration and of internal migration in creating the structural basis of American Jewish life appears most vividly in the population figures for American Jewry (see Table 1). From a tiny fraction during the colonial era, the number of American Jews increased by 2,400 percent by the eve of the Civil War. The mass migration of eastern European Jews boosted the population of American Jewry by a substantial 1,256 percent by 1920. While the influx of refugees and survivors stimulated a growth of almost 60 percent over the post–World War I population, American Jews reached their peak as a fraction of the American population in 1940. However, the concentrated character of Jewish population distribution in the United States has assured much greater Jewish visibility in America and ensured the viability of Jewish collective life.

A comparative examination of Jewish geographic distribution over the century from 1877 to 1983 reveals that Jews have consistently congregated in urban centers, but, with the exception of New York, the major five cities have changed dramatically (see Table 2). In 1877 the top five cities that included almost half of the total American Jewish population were: New York, San Francisco, Philadelphia, Chicago, and Baltimore. By 1905 New York City alone accounted for more than half of the American Jewish population. But the influence of the eastern European migration also appeared in the prominence of the following four: Chicago, Philadelphia, Boston, and St. Louis. By 1927 the major industrial cities dominated American Jewish life with New York retaining its position as the premier city of American Jewry and Cleveland replacing St. Louis among the top five. The impact of suburbanization and internal migration registered by 1955 with the growth of Los Angeles, which attracted both internal migrants and immi-

grants. In 1983 Los Angeles continued to expand, especially into surrounding suburban counties, eclipsing Chicago as the "second city" of American Jewry.

But the most distinctive impact of internal migration appears in the rapid, dramatic growth of Miami. Before World War II some 8,000 Jews lived in Miami. The war economy doubled the number of Jews in the Florida city, and by 1950 it was home to 55,000 Jews. This population doubled again in five years with the number of Jews reaching six figures. By 1960 Miami had become a major Jewish community of 140,000, and by 1970 with 230,000 Jews it was among the top centers of Jewish population. In 1983 it ranked fourth after Philadelphia. Miami's impressive growth in thirty years from 8,000 to 230,000 Jews illustrates the power of chain migration to amplify an initial trend sparked by a booming economy. It also suggests how Jews transform dispersal into concentration, thus reproducing distinctive demographic patterns of integrative dissipation. This urban penchant, coupled with the need and desire to live close to other Jews, appears even in the beginning of Jewish history in North America.

The first American Jews settled in New Amsterdam. A small group of twenty-three men, women, and children, who had fled Dutch Recife, Brazil after the city fell to the Portuguese, arrived at the port in 1654. The irascible governor, Peter Stuyvesant, did not welcome the addition of poverty-stricken individuals to his already heterogeneous city population, and he immediately wrote to his superiors in Amsterdam for permission to eject the "deceitful race." But the board of the Dutch West India Company concurred with the arguments of the Amsterdam Jewish community. Persuaded by the posture of the wealthy Jewish shareholders of the company, it directed Stuyvesant to permit Jews to trade, albeit denying them the right to work as mechanics. The board also insisted that Jews live close to each other, guaranteed that they could "exercise in all quietness their religion within their houses," and stipulated that the Jewish poor "be supported by their own nation." These limitations resembled those faced by Jews in Holland but were more restrictive than conditions had been in Dutch Brazil. The Jewish foothold in New Amsterdam survived the transition to English rule but the community remained small and transient until the eighteenth century.

TABLE 1   Estimated Jewish Population in the United States

Year	Number	Percentage of Total Population
1790	1,500	.05
1830	6,000	.05
1860	150,000	.47
1880	250,000	.50
1900	1,058,000	1.39
1920	3,390,000	3.18
1940	4,770,000	3.61
1960	5,367,000	2.99
1980	5,500,000	2.42

TABLE 2   Top Five Cities in Jewish Population

City	Population	City	Population	City	Population
1877		*1905*		*1927*	
1. New York City	73,000	1. New York City	772,000	1. New York City	1,765,000
2. San Francisco	16,000	2. Chicago	80,000	2. Chicago	325,000
3. Philadelphia	12,000	3. Philadelphia	75,000	3. Philadelphia	270,000
4. Chicago	10,000	4. Boston	45,000	4. Boston	90,000
5. Baltimore	10,000	5. St. Louis	40,000	5. Cleveland	85,000
		1955		*1983*	
		1. New York City	2,050,000	1. New York City	1,734,000
		2. Los Angeles	325,000	2. Los Angeles	500,000
		3. Chicago	262,000	3. Philadelphia	295,000
		4. Philadelphia	245,000	4. Miami	253,000
		5. Boston	140,000	5. Chicago	248,000

Sources: *The Jewish Encyclopedia*, 1877 and 1905; *American Jewish Year Book*, 1927, 1955, 1983.

In the decades prior to the American Revolution, Jewish merchants and their families settled in five colonial seaport cities—Philadelphia, Charleston, Savannah, Newport, as well as New York—with mixed populations and mercantile economies. Most of the Jewish breadwinners engaged in trade. Some used contacts with relations overseas to participate in the trans-Atlantic traffic of raw materials in exchange for finished products while others dealt in local commerce with the burgeoning farming hinterland. Unlike in Europe, legal recognition and political acceptance accompanied Jewish integration into the city economy of colonial America.

In 1740 an Act of Parliament granted foreign-born Jewish colonials citizenship rights by exempting them from taking a Christian oath required of Jews resident in England. Under the Naturalization Act, colonial Jews who possessed sufficient property acquired the franchise. Inspired by the success of naturalization of foreign-born Jews in the colonies, sympathetic members of Parliament introduced a comparable "Jew Bill" in 1753 for England, only to withdraw it in the face of virulent anti-Jewish agitation. The discrepancy in favor of foreign-born colonial Jews, giving them rights only native-born English Jews had, continued until the American Revolution. The relative openness of urban colonial society by midcentury encouraged a variety of Jewish-Gentile contacts. Jews turned to Gentiles to witness their wills; in the years from 1690 to 1806, of forty-one extant wills thirty-five are witnessed by Gentiles. By the time of the

Revolution, most Jews in North America were no longer a separate segregated element of the population but interacted socially with their Christian peers. A Hessian officer observed that Newport Jews "are not distinguishable by their beards and attire . . . while their women wear the same French finery as the women of other faiths" (Goren).

This social integration of the Jewish population coexisted with a distinct religious and cultural life organized around the congregation. Although public worship did not begin until 1692 in New York City, Jewish congregations were founded in New York (1656), Newport (1677), Savannah (1733), Philadelphia (1745), and Charleston (1750). The congregations provided as many of the communal services as they could muster though only New York and Newport had synagogue buildings. Jewish children went to school under congregational auspices, widows and orphans received support from the congregation, guests found meals and lodging through its good offices, the poor obtained assistance, and the dead were buried in the congregation's cemetery. To fund these activities the congregation taxed its members, sold the honor of participating in the Sabbath Torah service, supervised the provision of kosher meat, and charged modest fees for such life-cycle events as weddings. Given the small size of each community, members appealed for aid from abroad, especially to London's Jews, when they contemplated expensive projects like building a synagogue. London Jews also provided a model of congregational structure for their colonial contemporaries and a source of reference when seeking authoritative religious advice.

The leadership of the American congregations remained in the hands of a male elite, including educated laymen and occasionally *hazanim* (cantors) who could also preach and teach (and often slaughter animals according to ritual). Not trained as rabbis, they did not have sufficient command over the religious texts to answer questions of Jewish law. Where American Jews diverged from accepted norms, they did so largely due to their relative isolation on the western outpost of Jewish settlement—the first rabbis did not arrive until the nineteenth century—and to the influence of the mobile colonial society.

The American Revolution disrupted the commercial activities of Jewish colonials and split the community into patriots and Tories. The majority fell into the former category to such an extent that they abandoned their homes in the wake of the British occupation of New York City. Many fled a second time when the British conquered Philadelphia. Jewish sentiments favored the concepts of liberty and equality articulated in Thomas Jefferson's Declaration of Independence. Jews joined the colonials' cause, some contributing their financial means and others their military skill. Their participation in the Revolution was a measure of both their integration into colonial society and their espousal of liberal ideals embodying the hope of even greater equality. Jews understood the expansion of democracy to mean the removal of all disabilities based upon religious distinctions that hindered full Jewish political participation in the new republic. Philadelphia's Mikveh Israel congregation petitioned both the Commonwealth of Pennsylvania and the Constitutional Convention to eliminate religious restrictions on holding office. After the debate over ratification of the Constitution, Newport's Jewish congregation expressed in a letter of congratulation to George Washington their dream that the United States would "give to bigotry no sanction, to persecution no assistance."

Although Washington's reply echoed their words, the reality of political equality in the new nation depended upon the individual states. In Maryland Jews waged a rigorous battle in the 1820s to be admitted to the state legislature and to have its Christian oath of office removed from the state constitution. Although successful in Maryland in 1828, Jews did not acquire such rights in North Carolina and New Hampshire until after the Civil War. By contrast, in New York the Jacksonian revolution opening the franchise to all white males allowed Jews not only to enter party politics but to rise to positions of leadership. In the 1820s and 1830s Mordecai Manuel Noah served as a sachem of Tammany Hall. His political vision included a proto-Zionist dream of saving European Jewry from persecution and discrimination and he unabashedly used his position to promote Jewish immigration to an upstate island—which he named Ararat—where he hoped to found in 1825 a "city of refuge for the Jews." Yet despite federal commitment to the new and untried principle of separation of church and state, Jews found themselves disadvantaged in states where the religious revivals of the 1830s and 1840s led to legislation banning commerce on Sunday. The bitter dispute among Christians over public education also involved Jews, who welcomed free elementary schooling while protesting against its overt nondenominational, evangelical Protestant character. But as public schools spread in the decades before the Civil War, Jews abandoned their congregational Jewish schools, in the process developing a strong ideological commitment to public education in a democratic society.

Given the marginality of the American Jewish community relative to world Jewry and its integration into the economic, social, and political life of the new nation, it is unlikely that it could have survived as a separate religious group organized around the synagogue had the immigration of Germans to America not brought also thousands of German Jews. From 1830 to 1860 the Jewish population of the United States jumped from a mere 6,000 (.05 percent of the total population) to 150,000 (.47 percent). But the immediate effect of the new immigration was to disrupt established Jewish communal life rather than to strengthen it.

Ill at ease among bourgeois English-speaking Jews, German Jewish immigrants left the synagogue and, as a result, the constituted community—as soon as they had sufficient numbers to form their own congregation. Among their own kind they could comfortably disperse and receive both charity and honors, pray in Yiddish or German according to accustomed melodies, and maintain some ties to the lands of their nativity. In western and southern frontier cities Jewish immigrants banded together first to form burial societies to provide for those who succumbed to the hardships of pioneering and then to create congregations to give religious expression to their Jewish lives. But these congregations failed to emerge as the central focus of the entire growing community, serving instead groups of *landsleit*—fellow immigrants from the same province or town—as their home away from home. As early as the 1840s dissension among the members of several New York City congregations and discomfort with the biased character of many Gentile fraternal orders prompted a dozen German Jews to found a modern Jewish fellowship. The establishment of the B'nai B'rith (Sons of the Covenant) in 1843, the first Jewish fraternal order, contributed to the dissolution of a unified Jewish community. But it also revealed German Jewish immigrants' creative energies and innovative approach to Jewish institutional life.

The heady experience of political equality in the context of a frontier society propelled German Jews, recent arrivals to American shores, to experiment with communal forms. Native-born American Jews looked to the American Protestant denominations when they introduced new institutions into Jewish life. The list of firsts includes the Jewish newspaper the *Occident* (1843), published in English by Isaac Leeser, the minister of Philadelphia's Mikveh Israel; Jewish Sunday schools, pioneered in 1838 in Philadelphia by Rebecca Gratz, daughter of a distinguished colonial family, as part of an antimissionary endeavor against Protestant efforts to convert Jews; a Jewish publication society (which later folded and was reestablished in 1888); Gratz College, founded in 1897 by a provision in Hyman Gratz's will forty years earlier for the education of Jews living in Philadelphia, and a Jewish orphan asylum, established in Charleston in 1801. But German Jewish immigrants found models in the ethnic organizations established by Christian German immigrants. In addition to Jewish fraternal orders (the B'nai B'rith was followed by other organizations) that provided insurance benefits in case of sickness or death, and the first women's organization (National Council of Jewish Women, 1893), German Jews introduced Jewish social clubs, literary societies, hospitals—the first two opened in Cincinnati and New York

in 1850 and 1852, respectively, as did the first libraries—and in the 1870s Young Men's Hebrew Associations (YMHAs).

Because of the class and ethnic differences between the immigrant and native-born Jews, the groups within the orbit of the synagogue that ministered to those in need discovered that they would be more effective as independent bodies. As congregations proliferated, so did charitable organizations with increasingly specialized tasks. The arrival of so many young and poor German Jews in the 1850s strained the resources of established congregations and prodded the earlier arrivals to seek new ways to fulfill their traditional obligations to fellow Jews in distress. The result by the eve of the Civil War was a voluntary community bursting with energy but lacking coordination or cooperation.

The process of chain migration carried German Jews throughout the breadth of the United States, forming the modern map of Jewish communities. The sibling family and occasionally the town formed a migration unit. Often brothers brought over their unmarried siblings, building business relationships along family lines. Chain migration also channeled former neighbors, creating clusters of Jews from different German states in varied American cities. Cincinnati and Cleveland attracted Bavarians; Boston, Poseners; Atlanta, Jews from southern Germany, especially Hesse and Württemberg, while Milwaukee drew evenly from Austria-Hungary and Germany. These formed the nucleus of an American Jewish community, influencing its emerging character. Subsequent settlers less frequently came directly to the cities but served a critical apprenticeship in the rural areas. For several years they worked as peddlers, returning once or twice a month to their city boardinghouses to restock supplies. On the road the new immigrants absorbed American values, learned English, and discarded many Jewish customs. The more successful peddlers—and many eventually fell into that category—gradually moved up to a small dry-goods store at a rural crossroads, often relying on other family members whom they brought from abroad to take over the peddling routes.

The enormous expansion of American society, its physical dispersal, and its extraordinary economic growth offered a wide field for supplying isolated farming settlements with merchandise. As the economy matured, Jewish immigrants transformed their peddling careers into wholesale and retail trade, the most successful moving to the regional centers. Thus when many Jews entered the cities of the South and Midwest, they did so with years of trade experience and with established familial and business networks behind them. In fact, the anti-Semitic bias of credit agencies forced Jews to develop their own reliable sources. This situation in turn helped a handful of Jews make the transition from trade to banking. But the *embourgeoisement* of the German Jewish immigrants really came after the Civil War, when those who had accumulated capital discovered opportunities to invest in such fields as manufacturing and banking and to introduce new retailing methods, including department stores and mail-order services.

German Jews' economic achievement rested upon a firm social foundation. The early arrival of Jews in American frontier cities allowed them to prosper with the city and as part of it. In San Francisco, where Jews not only were among the city's founders, arriving in 1849, but constituted a significant minority of the population (by the mid-1850s, there were 4,000 Jews in the city), distinctions based on religion or ethnicity carried little weight. Jews integrated into the rough equality of city society, and as class differences appeared they were counted within the upper as well as other classes. Jews participated in civic endeavors, becoming town boosters along with other Americans. In some cities Jews shared in the city's social life through the German immigrant community, joining its organizations and identifying as German. The reality of integration found ideological expression at the dedication of the new building of congregation Beth Elohim of Charleston in 1841 when the rabbi declared: "This synagogue is our temple, this city our Jerusalem, this happy land our Palestine" (Naomi W. Cohen, *Encounter with Emancipation*). Yet acceptance also encouraged Jews to assert their separate identity. In Chicago during the Civil War, Jews contributed a company of Jewish soldiers and sponsored their own booth at the Sanitary Fair to raise money to help the wounded. Whether expressing their particularism or their universalism, Jews sought the goal of true equality.

Whereas colonial Jews had turned to the patriots' cause to further their political liberty, and subsequently many embraced the party of Jefferson and Jackson, in the 1850s German Jews committed to Enlightenment ideals of freedom most often adopted the Republican party's platform. For immigrants fleeing Germany after the abortive revolution of 1848, among them a number of well-educated men, the Republican position of free labor, free soil, and free men promised a liberal democratic social order they hoped would liberate all men, Jews included. During the Civil War many Jews in the North adopted the Union cause out of prudence, if not conviction, but others remained loyal to the Democratic party. In the South, Jews supported the Confederacy and one, Judah P. Benjamin, the "brains" of the Confederacy, achieved cabinet status. The Civil War drove Jews into opposing, but not bitter, camps since—unlike the Protestant national denominations torn asunder by the impending conflict—Jews had only fragile national organizations and a corresponding weak sense of a national American Jewish identity. Having migrated from a nation divided into small, competing states, German Jews found it relatively easy to identify with their locality or their state as the means of expressing an American loyalty.

The lack of a national American Jewish perspective disturbed aspiring leaders of American Jewry. In the post–Civil War decades they forged instruments of national Jewish unity to express the opinions of American Jews, even on such divisive issues as politics and religion. Isaac Mayer Wise, among the first rabbis to come to America in the 1840s, from his pulpit in Cincinnati helped create the Union of American Hebrew Congregations (UAHC) in 1873, which shared his religious perspective, adopted the prayerbook he compiled, *Minhag America* (1857), and supported a school to train American rabbis (Hebrew Union College, 1875). These institutions strengthened the position of Reform Judaism, a rationalist and optimistic modification of Jewish religion that emphasized the centrality of ethics and denied the binding validity of *halakah* (law). Reformers also introduced into the synagogue decorum, organ music and mixed choirs, prayers in the vernacular (English), mixed seating of men and women, and other departures from tradition that they justified as vital to modernize Judaism.

Rabbis Isaac Leeser and Sabato Morais in Philadelphia remained outside of Wise's Reform consensus. They tried instead to further traditional Judaism in the United States and to build a common congregational platform on the defense of Jewish rights at home and abroad. In 1859 they established the Board of Delegates of American Israelites on the British model. During the Civil War, the board succeeded in overturning Gen. Ulysses S. Grant's discriminatory order of 1862 that banned "Jews as a class" from the area controlled by his Union army. Later, during Grant's term as president, the U.S. formally protested Rumania's mistreatment of its Jewish residents, a conciliatory presidential gesture prompted by the board's petitions. But some prominent Jews objected to the board, especially after it was absorbed into the UAHC. Philanthropists like Jacob Schiff, who immigrated to New York City in 1875 to join the German Jewish banking firm of Kuhn, Loeb & Co., advocated a secular rather than a religious framework to unify Jews, urging the viability of the burgeoning YMHA movement as such a vehicle. Even the fraternal orders' leadership looked beyond insurance and fellowship to a united American Jewry.

The postwar prosperity and the birth of a second generation, children of the German Jewish immigrants, lent an increasing homogeneity to American Jewry. By 1880 a collective portrait of American Jews could be drawn with some accuracy. Comprising 250,000 people (.5 percent of the total population), largely middle- or upper-class, American Jews lived in cities throughout the United States, spoke English, and sent their children to public schools. Most Jewish men worked in trade, manufacturing, or banking; in 1890, 15 percent were bankers, brokers, and wholesalers, 35 percent were retailers, 17 percent accountants, bookkeepers, and clerks, and 12 percent salesmen. Their wives, who were younger by an average of seven to ten years, devoted their time to childcare, housework, and volunteer activity. The average household contained 5.5 persons, and two-thirds employed at least one servant. Jews married later than the general population—men between the ages of 25 to 35, women between 20 and 30—and their rate of marriage, 7.4 per 1,000, was significantly lower than that of most Americans (8.9). These patterns accounted for fewer children, an average of 4.6. Approximately 250 congregations—or one per 1,000 Jews—with modernized religious services placing them in the Reform camp offered a religious community for those wishing to affiliate. A substantial minority belonged to a fraternal order and many supported an impressive network of charitable agencies. In 1887 one estimate suggested that Jews spent $1.3 million annually on philanthropy, about $20 per capita, excluding contributions to non-Jewish causes and congregational expenses. Although still on the fringes of world Jewry, American Jewry's representations increasingly were heard in Europe. American Jews even exported their innovations, establishing the first branch of the B'nai B'rith in Germany in 1882. When the first pogroms exploded in Russia in 1881, American Jews demonstrated their self-confidence as Americans and as Jews by participating as regular partners with representatives of British, French, and German Jews, in meetings to protest the violence and organize relief and rescue.

East European Jews entered the United States as industrialization and urbanization were changing the face of the nation. Since the majority were skilled workmen, they more often turned to light industries—especially the burgeoning ready-made clothing industry—than to trade to find an economic foothold. This employment drew them to the cities instead of dispersing them throughout the country. As the numbers of immigrants snowballed, reaching a peak in 1906, when 152,000 Jews arrived, visible and concentrated settlements of Yiddish-speaking Jews appeared in the nation's industrializing cities. Preeminent among these was the major port of entry itself: New York. In the former German neighborhoods, close to the garment shops, east European Jews settled by the thousands, crowding into the tenement houses and creating a density of 700 persons per acre by 1900. Though they lived under unsanitary, miserable conditions, their mortality statistics were low. By 1892 the Lower East Side held 75 percent of New York's Jews or approximately 135,000, of whom 60,313 were children, the total making up over one-third of American Jewry. When World War I interrupted immigration, eastern European Jews had established New York as the center of American Jewish life, home to roughly half of American Jews.

Like their German Jewish predecessors, eastern European Jews followed a process of chain migration. However, the links were as often forged through marriage as through sibling relationships. The immigration of eastern European Jews has been characterized as a family migration not because the family traveled as a unit—in fact, the opposite was usually the case, with the husband preceding his wife and children by several years—but because so many children under the age of 14 (26 percent for the years of mass migration, 1880–1920) arrived with their mothers. In New York, by 1910 women exceeded men among Hungarian and Rumanian Jews and were almost half of the Russian Jews.

The relatively rapid reconstitution of the two-generation family unit put severe economic strains on the primary breadwinner and encouraged the participation of women and children in the family economy. Married women assisted by doing piecework at home, helping with the store or pushcart, or taking in boarders. Unmarried teenage sons and daughters alike went into the garment factories or worked in the tenement sweatshops. But gender distinctions rapidly emerged, with women dominating in the production of underwear, dresses, and shirtwaists. *Landsleit* also channeled migration not only to localities, but to specific occupations. In New York men's tailors often hailed from Poland's Suvałki province, furriers from Puchevitz, pursemakers from Warsaw, while 90 percent of the pants makers in the 1890s were Rumanians.

Opportunities to escape the poorly paid seasonal labor of the garment trades lay in becoming a "boss," a capitalist, a manufacturer or jobber, or on the lowest rungs, a "sweater" of relatives and *landsleit* as well as oneself. Others moved up by entering the slum economy as tradesmen, providing the restaurants, bakeries, butcher shops, dry-goods stores, groceries, and candy stores the neighborhood needed, while a substantial minority worked in the building trades as craftsmen: carpenters, locksmiths, glaziers, plumbers. Later, those who succeeded bought real estate, very often his or her own tenement or apartment building.

Within a decade of their arrival the immigrants had organized a vibrant communal life that built upon the rich tradition of collective solidarity and self-reliance Jews had known in eastern Europe. Although the legally constituted Jewish community, the *kehillah,* had been shorn of its rights, a strong voluntary community continued to care for most Jewish social and religious needs, including education, worship, burial, and charity. The increasing inability of the community to solve the problems of extreme poverty and degradation led to a revolt against the *kehillah* and its authority by young Jews imbued with a desire to correct the world's injustices. Some among the early immigrants in the 1880s belonged to these radical idealistic groups, others were merely young adventurers seeking their fortune in the *goldene medina* (golden land), while many immigrated out of a mingled sense of desperation and hope. After the first bewildering years in America, those who got a foothold immediately sought to succor the less fortunate newcomers. Jewish immigrants adopted the principles of American voluntarism to fashion their community and drew upon their rich experience in eastern Europe, which had taught them how to hold meetings, write constitutions, and run an organization. They established a wide array of organizations in the fields of religion, politics, social welfare, and culture, divided along ideological, class, and regional lines.

Immigrant social welfare activity flourished in the intimate *landsmanshaften*, mutual aid societies that provided health insurance and death benefits to members who came from the same town in Europe. Unlike the early Jewish fraternal orders, some *landsmanshaften* embraced socialism and affiliated with the Workmen's Circle brotherhood (founded in 1900) while others pledged themselves to the Zionist Jewish National Workers Alliance (1912). The majority remained independent until the crisis of World War I prodded them to pool their resources to help their relatives and *landsleit* overseas. Several large federations of *landsmanshaften*, such as the Federation of Galician and Bukovinan Jews (1903), remained active in local Jewish communal life as well as coordinating rehabilitation and rescue efforts during the interwar decades.

Other social welfare organizations looked exclusively to the needs of immigrant Jews in the United States. In New York City eastern European Jews established first the Hebrew Sheltering Society (1890), modeled on the traditional hostel, then the Hebrew Immigrant Aid Society (1902), finally merging them to form an expanded HIAS (1909) to shelter and guide newcomers. Women set up day nurseries to assist mothers who had to work outside the home. Immigrants also founded hospitals that served kosher food and respected Jewish religious tradition, unlike the Jewish medical facilities supported by the German Jews. The disruption of family life caused by immigration and poverty produced innovative responses to Jewish criminal behavior that drew upon the joint resources of American and immigrant Jews. Facing a common communal crisis, Jews joined hands to establish such novel institutions as reformatories for young men (Hawthorne School, 1906), homes for unwed mothers (Lakeview Home, 1908), a big brother association to help juvenile delinquents (Jewish Big Brother Association, 1909), and a national service to trace husbands who abandoned their wives (National Desertion Bureau, 1911). Finally, immigrants transported from the Old World the free loan society (Hebrew Free Loan Society, 1892) to assist the ambitious but poor and the desperate but deserving with cash grants free of interest.

Seeking protection from the evils of an unregulated and exploitive capitalist system, Jewish immigrants turned as well to collective action in the labor marketplace. As early as the 1880s Jews tried to organize the various trades, establishing the United Hebrew Trades (1888) on the German model. But lasting success came only in 1909 with "the uprising of the twenty thousand," the spontaneous strike of teenage female shirtwaist workers, followed in 1910 by "the great revolt," the planned general strike of 60,000 largely male cloak makers. The union president watching the thousands of workers jamming the streets of the garment district observed: "In my mind I could only picture to myself such a scene taking place when the Jews were led out of Egypt" (Howe). Both strikes produced substantial victories for the union locals and established the International Ladies Garment Workers Union (1902) on a firm footing. Subsequently, in a dispute over policy and tactics, socialist Jewish workers in the men's garment industry walked out of the American Federation of Labor to form the Amalgamated Clothing Workers of America (1914). These large Jewish unions, together with diverse, smaller ones of fur workers, bakers, printers, waiters, actors, and musicians, did not confine themselves to improving wages, hours, and working conditions. Committed to a socialist vision of a cooperative commonwealth, the unions pioneered in offering medical and later dental benefits, vacation resorts, adult education programs, and cooperative housing to make a better life for the working man and woman. Labor's participation in the New Deal introduced some of these immigrant Jewish values to other American workers.

The proliferation of immigrant organizations accompanied a renaissance of Yiddish culture on the stage and printed page. The large concentrations of immigrant Jews in New York City provided an eager audience for the Yiddish theater and avid readers of the Yiddish press. During the peak years of immigration before World War I, New York City boasted four Yiddish dailies—two Socialist, one religious, and one nationalist—with a combined circulation of over 455,000. The papers gave not only news, especially of Jewish events abroad, but also advice on how to cope with American society. At the turn of the century Yiddish theaters on the Lower East Side and Second Avenue catered to an audience of 2 million with 1,100 performances annually. Cities with smaller Jewish populations supported fewer cultural institutions but all of the major cities had at least one Yiddish paper and theater. The diverse origins of Jewish immigrants also appeared in their foreign-language press, which included periodicals in Ladino, Russian, Hungarian, and German. The Hebrew press reflected the influence of the Jewish Enlightenment and the Zionist movement. Book publishing—fiction, nonfiction, and poetry—flourished in such a milieu. Music of all sorts, from popular songs to classical compositions, similarly thrived among Jewish immigrants. These media often educated their followers to American tastes, preparing some of the most talented to contribute to American English-speaking culture in subsequent years.

This self-contained immigrant Jewish world both challenged and threatened native-born Jews of German descent. American Jews felt called upon to Americanize the newcomers and assist their adjustment to the New World. But the immigrants also seemed to spark anti-Semitism through their foreignness, poverty, and visibility. Native-born Jews responded to the flood of immigrants with sympathy and fear: a desire to help fellow Jews coupled with concern for their own status. Their ambivalent emotions also reflected a sensitivity to the increased respectability of anti-Semitism among the upper classes that led to the exclusion of Jews from resorts and clubs that they had previously frequented. Richard Gottheil, a Semitics scholar, recalled that in the 1880s "private schools began to be closed to Jewish children" (Moore, *B'nai B'rith*). The rapidity with which the new immigrants overwhelmed the established community in terms of sheer numbers—the 13,000 who arrived in the single year of 1882 accounted for almost half the number of the preceding decade—and the alteration of the whole character of American Jewry —by 1890 the American Jews of German background formed a distinct and privileged minority —also help to explain the ambivalent reaction to the newcomers. Furthermore, the immigrants' employment in the clothing factories owned by American Jews hardly enhanced a sense of rapport. But the anti-immigrant sentiment that swept through Congress in the 1890s spurred American Jews to conceal their misgivings and to aid their persecuted coreligionists.

American Jews turned to the task of assisting eastern European immigrants with vigor and imagination. Established Jews spoke out on behalf of free immigration, defended Jewish immigrants threatened with deportation, spread information on current conditions in the United States to prospective migrants, helped new arrivals to find jobs and housing, and developed novel methods of Americanizing the newcomers. The latter included trade and night schools to teach English and civics along with industrial skills, settlement houses with lectures and libraries, clinics with cheap milk and free advice on how to cook food, raise children, and run a household. In their efforts to promote the integration of eastern European Jews, the American Jews even hit upon a scheme to disperse immigrants throughout the country to reduce the visible concentration in New York's Lower East Side. Responding in 1901 to a fresh flood of Rumanian Jewish immigrants fleeing persecution, a group of Jewish leaders implemented the Galveston plan and Immigrant Removal Office. The former took Jews from Europe directly to the Texan port of Galveston and from there sent them into the interior while the latter paid the transportation and other expenses of selected Jewish men to cities in the South and West that were ready to receive and employ them. In response to the male bias of Jewish communal life, Jewish women organized themselves for the first time in 1893 into a national federated body of women's clubs. The National Council of Jewish Women adopted the teenage immigrant girl who traveled alone as its special concern, trying to protect her from unscrupulous men who sought to trick the naive and innocent into prostitution.

But differences in class, language, education, politics, and background were too great to be bridged by goodwill and a measure of Jewish solidarity alone. As succeeding decades brought ever more immigrants, the gulf between the two groups widened until they were seen as two camps: the American Jews of German descent, assimilated, bourgeois, English speaking, Reform, and Republican, living in nice "uptown" neighborhoods; versus the eastern European Jewish immigrants, unassimilated, proletarian, Yiddish speaking, Orthodox or secular, and socialist (though many voted for Republican presidents and Democratic congressmen), living in the crowded immigrant slums "downtown." Only as eastern European Jews achieved a measure of upward mobility did a basis emerge for cooperation.

The upward mobility of eastern European Jews was slow in comparison with their German Jewish predecessors, albeit rapid in comparison with other immigrants arriving at the same time. After twenty-five years in New York City, over half could point to progress up the economic ladder, usually rising from blue- to white-collar work. But it took the second generation to parlay the modest success of their immigrant parents into firm footing in the middle class as manufacturers and builders, as salesmen and retailers, and as professionals: doctors, lawyers, dentists, teachers, accountants, and, with the expansion of government under the New Deal, civil servants. Many succeeded by combining a Jewish occupational penchant for the self-employed professionals—a way of avoiding anti-Semitic discrimination—with the potential provided by free public education to acquire skills and American values. Encouraged by German Jews to send their children to public schools, eastern European immigrants absorbed the American ethos of public education despite the strident Americanization programs, denigration of Yiddish working-class culture, and Christian bias of most public schools. Jews relegated almost the entire structure of Jewish education that had been developed in eastern Europe, primary and secondary, to a supplementary position in the United States with classes held in the afternoons at the end of the public-school day.

The social mobility of Jewish immigrants and their children was mirrored in their residential mobility and dispersal. By 1916 the Lower East Side held only 25 percent of the city's Jewish population. As early as 1900 immigrant Jews had moved across the river to Brooklyn, settling in Brownsville and Williamsburg; others journeyed up to Harlem and a few went as far as the Bronx. In the 1920s this intracity migration involved hundreds of thousands who dispersed themselves in the more suburban boroughs of Brooklyn and the Bronx. A similar pattern appeared among the other half of American Jewry living outside of New York who abandoned the immigrant slums of Chicago and Philadelphia, Cleveland and Detroit to move to middle-class neighborhoods away from the city's core. As Jews exchanged a tenement dwelling for a modern apartment they acquired new neighbors, American born, English speaking, and Christian. Within this social setting American Jews created anew a basis for unity, a form of American Judaism and a sense of Jewish identity that combined their immigrant heritage with the traditions of German Jews in the United States.

The first example of effective eastern European–German Jewish cooperation appeared in the religious sphere. While most immigrant congregations remained wedded to the *landsmanshaft*, providing an important link with the old country, eastern European Jews created two alternatives to Reform Judaism. Both adapted Judaism to the American scene while maintaining a greater commitment to tradition than characterized Reform. Conservative Judaism emerged with the reorganization of the Jewish Theological Seminary (1902), a school to train American rabbis, under the leadership of the Rumanian-born British scholar Solomon Schecter. The school's financial sponsors came from the ranks of the uptown philanthropists who sought to promote a Judaism acceptable to the immigrants' children and thus combat the dangers of Orthodox fanaticism, rampant secularism, and demoralizing Americanization. Modern American Orthodoxy also grew with two New York City schools that were joined together in the establishment of the future Yeshiva University (1925) under the guidance of Bernard Revel, an immigrant Talmudist. The Rabbi Isaac Elchanan Theological Seminary (1896) encouraged future rabbis and laymen alike to pursue advanced Talmudic study, while the Teachers Institute (1917) embraced a religious Zionist perspective in its training of Hebrew teachers. As an American-born generation came of age, it formed the congregations that employed the young rabbinical graduates and eventually supported the two schools financially. Congregational and rabbinical unions helped to give a sense of identity to each new religious movement.

The rise of Zionism on the world Jewish scene after 1897 introduced both a source of contention and a bridge of understanding between the two segments of American Jewry. Zionism emphasized the struggle to rebuild the Jewish homeland and revive Hebrew culture, arguing that the Jews were a nation as well as a religious group. Some of those who championed Jewish nationalism combined their vision with socialism, some brought a religious perspective, while others argued that Zionism expressed the best of American idealism. The latter group included such native-born Jews as Louis Brandeis and Henrietta Szold. Brandeis led the American Zionist movement in the tumultuous years of World War I but left official Zionist politics shortly after his accession to the Supreme Court. Henrietta Szold founded Hadassah (1912), a women's organization devoted to providing health care for the residents of Palestine. Hadassah, which means myrtle, is the Hebrew name of Esther, the Jewish queen who saved her people from destruction, according to the biblical account. Szold's Zionist study circle adopted the name at their meeting on the night of Purim when they organized a national women's Zionist association. Two years later the national Daughters of Zion, at its first and last convention, decided to call itself Hadassah, taking the name from its leading New York City branch.

Though few immigrant women initially had the means to join Hadassah in its early years, it became the most popular Zionist enterprise in America after World War I. As Jews acquired increasing affluence, Hadassah enrolled more members than any other Jewish organization. Zionism also served as the vehicle for the proponents of democracy in the Jewish community, those who rejected a communal leadership based upon an elite of wealthy or learned men. The movement appealed to the downtown masses more successfully than to the uptown Jews, who preferred to focus their political energies on defending Jews against anti-Semitism and promoting their right to equal treatment under the law.

The wealthy elite feared that a Jewish homeland in Palestine would threaten the security of Jews happily living in the United States. Both the American Jewish Committee (AJC, 1906) and the Anti-Defamation League of the B'nai B'rith (ADL, 1913) entered the arena of Jewish politics from such a perspective. Zionism brought a handful of uptown leaders into genuine rapport with their downtown allies; similarly anti-Zionism encouraged some socialists to cross class lines in alliance with capitalists.

The vigorous cultural life of the immigrants, the proliferation of social welfare activities, and the bitterness of ideological political disputes challenged aspiring leaders of American Jewry. New means of uniting a fragmented and partisan community had to be found, for the old organizations were unequal to the task. In 1895 the federated charities movement appeared among Jews in Boston and thereafter spread rapidly to other communities. Jewish federations united philanthropic organizations by combining their fund-raising into one joint annual appeal. Although only the most successful eastern European Jews and a handful of their organizations were included in the early federations, during the interwar years federations helped to bridge the gulf between uptown and downtown, at least among the wealthy. With the establishment of the Council of Jewish Federations and Welfare Funds (CJFWF) in 1932 as the national coordinating body of the federations, they moved to assert their centrality as the secular arm of the American Jewish community. The financial success of the local federations had encouraged Jews to adopt a similar strategy during World War I. In 1914 several fund-raising organizations had united by establishing a single distributing agent of funds, the American Jewish Joint Distribution Committee (JDC). Created to cope with the unparalleled needs produced by the devastation of World War I, the JDC continued to assist Jews during the interwar years and performed its most valuable service after World War II. The apparent power of joint fund-raising convinced the Zionist organizations to pool their drives and establish the United Palestine Appeal (UPA) in 1925.

Participation of local Jewish federations in Community Chest or United Way appeals in the 1920s led many Jewish communities to establish welfare funds. These provided monies for national and international Jewish organizations that were inappropriate to fund out of United Way appeals. In 1939, on the eve of war, the two largest bodies raising money to help Jews overseas combined into the United Jewish Appeal (UJA), but not without ongoing dissension between the Zionist part (UPA) and the assimilationist part (JDC) over the division of the funds. (UJA also included the HIAS and the New York Association for New Americans, serving Jewish immigrants to the United States.)

While fund-raising and philanthropy forged one link to unify a fragmented community, before World War I Jewish spiritual leaders preferred to unite Jews along more democratic lines. In New York and Philadelphia Jews tried to reestablish the *kehillah* within a democratic, voluntarist framework. The advocates of this form of communal cooperation envisioned the participation of Jews of all classes and ideologies eager to tackle the enormous educational, religious, social, and economic problems facing Jews. But despite good records in regulating *kashruth* (the supervision of kosher meat), developing new curricula and model Jewish supplementary schools, arbitrating labor disputes, collecting vital data on Jewish activities, and fighting crime, the New York Kehillah (1909–1918) succumbed to ideological dispute. The Philadelphia Kehillah (1912–1916) similarly could not contain the antagonisms on the common ground of cooperative endeavor.

Jewish socialists rejected all such forms of class collaboration. Even those working within the Yiddish-speaking world saw the ultimate goal as integration in a socialist America, not the maintenance of a separate Jewish group life and distinctive Jewish identity. This position led them to clash with Jewish nationalists, a group that included both Yiddishists, who saw the language as a vehicle of Jewish national culture, and Zionists, who supported an American Jewish Congress to unite American Jews. Although Jewish socialist leaders and the American Jewish Committee failed to prevent a democratically elected congress from convening in 1918, they limited its scope to preparing a delegation to the postwar peace conference to represent American Jews. Given the diverse and volatile character of American Jewry, the deep divisions over politics ranging from pacifism and bolshevism at one extreme to jingoism and Republicanism at the other, the reality of class, ethnic, and religious differences, the agreement reached in the American Jewish Congress to support Jewish minority rights in eastern Europe and a Jewish homeland in Palestine represents a major accomplishment.

In the 1920s and 1930s the national organizations of American Jewry grew and prospered because the class and ethnic distinctions among American Jews narrowed. During the war the National Jewish Welfare Board (1917) had provided services for American Jewish soldiers. Subsequently it expanded to help plan programs for the recreational organizations, the Ys and Jewish community centers. The burgeoning philanthropic federations founded the Council of Jewish Federations and Welfare Funds (1932) to exchange information and assist in planning. Jewish educators and their supporters established the American Association for Jewish Education (1939) to promote Jewish education throughout the United States. With increasing anti-Semitism, symbolized by the publication of the notorious forgery *The Protocols of the Learned Elders of Zion* in Henry Ford's *Dearborn Independent,* came concern that the Jewish defense agencies were wastefully duplicating efforts to fight hostility toward Jews. Although reluctant to give up any measure of independence, the agencies yielded to enormous pressure from communal leaders during a period of crisis and created a coordinating committee, the National Community Relations Advisory Council (NCRAC, 1944), later renamed the National Jewish Community Relations Advisory Council. The ADL, the American Jewish Committee, a modified American Jewish Congress under the leadership of Rabbi Stephen S. Wise, and the Jewish Labor Committee (JLC, 1934), a voice for the unions and socialists on Jewish and antifascist issues, joined the NCRAC, as did the local community relations councils created in the interwar years to combat anti-Semitism. Despite cooperation, each organization maintained its independence and no overarching institutional unity developed.

Instead, Jews found themselves increasingly sharing common political values, those of liberal, New Deal Democrats committed to collective security and a policy of internationalism. Only a small number of Communists deviated from this consensus. Yet agreement on American politics did not lead to agreement on how to respond to Hitler. Many, but not all, favored the anti-Nazi boycott movement (1933). A few pressed Congress and President Franklin Delano Roosevelt to modify restrictive immigration laws and processes. Zionists urged immigration to Palestine as an answer and they attracted increasing numbers to their banners as the hopelessness of the European situation was revealed. In 1937 the Reform rabbinical association's Central Conference of American Rabbis (CCAR, 1889), one of the last strongholds of anti-Zionism, reversed itself and affirmed the concept of Jewish peoplehood and the significance of Zion for American Jews. Thus the CCAR modified the Reform platform adopted in Pittsburgh in 1885, which had denied that the Jews were a people as well as a religious group and had disclaimed any belief in a return to the land of Israel. Increasingly recruited from the ranks of the children of eastern European Jews, Reform rabbis were not the only ones to incline toward Zionism in the face of impending catastrophe in Europe.

But even Zionists did not agree on political methods to help European Jewry. Debate raged also over techniques of political behavior—e.g., the usefulness of rallies and demonstrations versus the effectiveness of quiet intercession with the president. Finally, in 1942 the Zionists at their Biltmore conference accepted David Ben-Gurion's proposal that statehood for Palestine be adopted as an immediate postwar goal. The following year the American Jewish Conference, called to produce a plan of rescue for European Jewry that would unite American Jews, overwhelmingly endorsed a resolution calling for a Jewish commonwealth in Palestine. Shattering the hoped for unity, the American Jewish Committee and the Jewish Labor Committee walked out, albeit for different reasons. The AJC held fast to its anti-Zionist position, fearing that a Jewish commonwealth would threaten American Jewry's security, while the JLC objected to the conference's refusal to support a call for the U.S. to open a second front in Europe.

American Jewry's trauma when the destruction of six million Jews and the entire cultural world of *yiddishkeit* was revealed turned almost all American Jews to the Zionist solution of the political dilemma of how to help the surviving remnants of European Jewry. Most of the survivors, too, turned to Palestine as their only hope. Between 1933 and 1941, 100,000 Jewish refugees had entered the United States, among them a substantial number of intellectuals and rabbis. From 1945 to 1952, 137,000 more arrived in America, but the DP (Displaced Person) legislation passed by Congress in 1948 admitting 200,000 discriminated against Jews. The law specified categories of DPs to be admitted, including farmers and ethnic Germans, that deliberately excluded Jews. An article in *The Reconstructionist*, a magazine that reflected the philosophy of Rabbi Mordecai M. Kaplan and the newly created Reconstructionist religious movement (1936), attacked the legislation under the headline: "Admitting Pogromists and Excluding Their Victims." The bitter experience with the DP legislation—Congressman Emanuel Celler, a New York City Democrat, later said, "It wasn't 'half a loaf'; it wasn't even half a slice"—underscored the reality of persistent anti-Semitism despite Nazi excesses.

While a minority pressed to have Jewish DPs enter the U.S., the majority of American Jews lobbied Congress, pressured the State Department, and petitioned President Harry S. Truman to secure active American support for a Jewish state despite British opposition. They argued that the state would welcome the DPs and rehabilitate them most effectively. In November 1947, when the United Nations, including the United States and the Soviet Union, voted for the partition of Palestine, statehood seemed assured. Yet the difficulties threatening the Jewish settlement in Palestine from unabated Arab hostility and British callousness called forth an enormous outpouring of aid and sympathy from American Jews. The UJA set record highs in funds raised to help and continued to do so for several years after the state of Israel was born.

American Jews' Zionist consensus when it finally emerged carried with it a heavy overlay of spirituality. Few American Jews agreed that they had no future in America, a land of exile, and few planned to immigrate to the Jewish state—two cardinal doctrines of political Zionism. Most affirmed the centrality of Israel to the Jewish people, a traditional religious value, and the spiritual significance of a Jewish state after the death of millions in the Nazi gas chambers. Few saw any contradiction between their American citizenship and Jewish loyalty since American ideals favored national self-determination and applauded the establishment of democratic states. The creation of the Conference of Presidents of Major American Jewish Organizations (1955) expressed the pro-Israel consensus of organized American Jewry. Only the Jewish Communist left dissented, as did a fringe group of Reform rabbis and wealthy descendants of German Jews who had founded the American Council for Judaism in 1942. But the furor surrounding the trial of Julius and Ethel Rosenberg as spies in 1951, their subsequent execution in 1953, and the anti-Communist hysteria promoted by Sen. Joseph McCarthy largely silenced the voices of Jewish radicals. Their organizations—including the popular International Workers Order with its network of Yiddish supplementary schools—were declared subversive and forced by national and state legislation to disband.

In truth, Communism ill fitted a community composed of middle-class suburbanites. Taking advantage of the G.I. Bill, American Jews, like their Christian countrymen, began the trek to the suburbs and home ownership. Following a pattern similar to that of their parents, second- and third-generation Jews scattered into an even wider number of settlements. A growing handful traveled farther afield to the cities of the South and West they had discovered as servicemen during World War II. Even elderly immigrants began to leave the crowded, dangerous city neighborhoods for the final incarnation of the American dream: a home where the sun always shines. The pioneers moved first to popular vacation spots like Miami Beach; in the 1960s and 1970s others went as well to the Southwest and West Coast.

In the suburbs Jews built lavish synagogues with complete recreational and educational facilities. They also transplanted the active organizational life of their parents, leaving behind only the *landsmanshaften*, the Socialist clubs, and the Yiddish language—institutions associated indelibly with the immigrant working-class world. Women's organizations, however, including Hadassah, National Council of Jewish Women, and a relative newcomer devoted to providing trade education for Jews throughout the world, the women's branch of the Organization for Rehabilitation through Training that was originally established in Russia (Women's

American ORT), flourished in the suburban bedroom communities as did social and charitable groups.

The integration of Jews into the suburban way of life led Will Herberg, the labor leader who abandoned Marxism for Judaism in the 1940s, to observe that Judaism had become one of the three major American religions. Certainly the rapid drop in popular anti-Semitism (polls showed 34 percent held anti-Semitic views in 1955) and the legislation and court rulings invalidating discrimination in higher education, employment, and housing encouraged Jews to feel part of the American mainstream. New job opportunities in previously closed fields like engineering and college teaching changed the economic profile of the grandchildren of the eastern European immigrants. With a greater sense of assurance, Jews continued the legal and educational fight to dismantle existing barriers of prejudice, to uphold the sanctity of separation of church and state, to remove the evangelical Protestant bias of public schools, and to protect the civil liberties of those who chose to be different.

These included the small groups of Hasidic Jews who had escaped the Holocaust with their *rebbes* (spiritual leaders) and reconstituted themselves in the old neighborhoods of several American cities. The Hasidim (pious ones) revitalized Orthodox institutions by replicating the European network of Jewish education, including advanced yeshiva study, on American soil. Their distinctive dress, conservative politics, and rejection of most of American culture as immoral added a vigorous right wing to American Jewish religious life. Their presence encouraged more Jews to display their Jewishness openly, further fragmented the regulation of *kashruth* by creating a new category, *glatt* (very) kosher, and tested the limits of American Jewish pluralism.

Less religious Holocaust survivors and refugees from Hitler chose not to stand apart from American society, though they found it difficult to integrate into the established Jewish community. The German culture of the refugees, their bitter experience of uprooting, and their downward mobility in middle age upon arrival in the United States led most to live in separate enclaves in the large cities. Holocaust survivors also found it easier to live among their own because of their common suffering and the burden of guilt they carried for having survived. Until

the trial of Adolf Eichmann in 1961 brought the issue of responsibility for the Holocaust into public discussion, American Jews viewed the survivors with some misgivings. In addition, their foreignness and accented English separated them from a community of second- and third-generation American Jews. But the survivors' children also appeared to follow American Jewish social patterns despite the burning questions they held regarding their parents' past. Like the children of the refugees they went to American schools and many rose directly into the ranks of the upper middle class as professionals. These two new groups of second generation American Jews, the children of the refugees and Holocaust survivors, greatly enhanced the secular accomplishments of American Jewry. In the case of the refugee intellectuals, the first generation itself, which included such figures as Albert Einstein and Hannah Arendt, contributed important human resources to the world of American learning in science, philosophy, the arts, and social sciences.

Ironically, the security that American Jews acquired during the Eisenhower era, their high occupational achievements and residential integration, failed to sustain a social and political consensus during the 1960s. The emergence of a New Left stimulated the participation of many young Jews in radical politics. In turning to radicalism, Jewish youth forsook and derided their parents' liberalism. As members of Students for a Democratic Society (SDS), as participants in the freedom rides and voter registration drives, and as protesters of the Vietnam War, many young Jews criticized the values of internationalism and New Deal domestic policy that had been the cornerstones of Jewish political participation. The high rate of college attendance among Jews of the postwar baby-boom generation also contributed to widespread Jewish involvement in the civil rights movement, antiwar demonstrations, and the youth counterculture. More "Jewishly" conscious Jews rallied to protest the Soviet government's refusal to let Soviet Jewry emigrate or live active Jewish lives in the USSR. A handful expressed their survivalist commitment by holding sit-ins at the offices of the Boston and New York federations for Jewish philanthropies for increased funding of Jewish education in America.

Dedication to the ideals of democratic equality and the absence of significant social segregation encouraged young Jews to ignore religious injunctions regarding marriage. Prior to World War II, barely 3 percent of American Jewish marriages had been intermarriages. Even in the 1950s Jews had maintained a pattern of endogamy that resembled interracial marriage rates: only 6 percent of Jewish marriages were intermarriages. But from 1961 to 1965 the intermarriage rate rose to 17 percent, and from 1966 to 1972 the rate of intermarriage leaped to 32 percent and did not decline.

Other Jewish family patterns also changed. In the decade of the 1970s, American Jews experienced a 74 percent increase in single-person households. The number of Jews separated, divorced, and living alone rose by 122 percent for men and 79 percent for women (more women lived with their children than did men). Despite the rising Jewish divorce rates, Jews maintained the same ratio of divorce to Protestants—Jews divorced half as frequently as Protestants—and to Catholics—Jews divorced two-thirds as frequently as Catholics. By 1978, 10 percent of Jews had been divorced at least once. The decline in the opprobrium of divorce and expanding economic opportunities for women contributed to the changing family patterns. Many married middle- and upper-class Jewish women also returned to the work force and became members and leaders of the burgeoning feminist movement.

The social integration of Jews into American society also narrowed the gap between pathological behaviors of Jews and Gentiles. In the postwar period Jewish criminals had largely disappeared from the scene of organized crime, marking such behavior as characteristic only of the first and second generations. But new forms of deviant behavior appeared among Jews, including alcoholism, a problem conspicuously absent in immigrant and second generation communities.

As Jews grew more similar to other Americans of the same class and region, they also evinced a revived interest in their past. From a distance of two decades Jews were able to return to the traumatic event of recent Jewish history and explore the meaning of the Holocaust. Two or three generations removed from the immigrant experience, many American Jews sought to understand the world that had been. The threat of Israel's annihilation in 1967 accelerated this revivalism and forced many to realize how vital the Jewish

state was for their continued existence as Jews. Many felt that without Israel, Judaism would not survive; American Jews would be unable to bear the crushing burden of two catastrophes in one century. A few recognized that Israel had become the single most powerful religious symbol for most American Jews. The Six-Day War also introduced a new, powerful image of the Jew as hero that appealed to many Americans. Despite the manifold opportunities to assimilate and abandon their Jewish identity, American Jews remained committed to Jewish survival if not to Jewish distinctiveness.

These trends blossomed in the 1970s as a fourth generation came of age. The center of Jewish residential distribution shifted westward while New York City's importance for American Jewry declined. Upper-middle-class salaried professionals began to take their places next to the successful businessmen in Jewish communal affairs. Small, informal congregational fellowships of *havurot* mushroomed along with a Jewish counterculture. Created by young Jews, this counterculture protested against the undemocratic character of the religious, communal, and political institutions of American Jewish life, favoring instead a spontaneity and intimacy of association, eclectic and experimental religious practices, and a blend of radical politics with a Jewish conscience.

By the late 1970s many elements of the counterculture had themselves become institutionalized. The *havurot,* some independent and some synagogue-affiliated, had grown sufficiently numerous and self-conscious to band together to form the National Havurah Committee (NHC). Committed to egalitarianism and pluralism, the NHC sponsored its first annual conference in 1980 to share ideas and fellowship. Another organizational expression of the Jewish counterculture appeared in the Coalition for Alternatives in Jewish Education (CAJE; 1975). CAJE served as a resource and network stimulating innovative approaches to Jewish education from preschool to adult. Although the Jewish feminist movement began as part of the counterculture, by the 1980s Jewish women had achieved sufficient acceptance as rabbis, cantors, communal leaders, and educators to be considered in the American Jewish mainstream. Only *Breira* (Alternative), founded in the wake of the Yom Kippur War of 1973 to promote dialogue between Israel and its Arab neighbors, failed to attract enough support to become accepted by the American Jewish community.

The return to religious fundamentalism that swept the world also touched young Jews who joined the swelling ranks of the *baalei teshuva* (those who return) movement. Committed to a traditionalist style of life, these seekers rejected both the innovative eclecticism of the Jewish counterculture and the culture of organizations of the established American Jewish community. Dissatisfaction with American modernity often accompanied a messianic mysticism, giving a political dimension to Jewish religious revivalism focused on Israel. More secular Jews placed Israel at the center of their experience of Jewishness. The philanthropic organizations cultivated this sanctification of Israel in order to raise funds to help the growing state solve its social problems. By the end of the decade one-third of American Jews had visited Israel at least once. The secular pilgrimage to experience Israel acquired critical importance for anyone aspiring to a position of leadership within the Jewish community. Israel also increasingly served as the touchstone of American Jewish politics, eclipsing other domestic issues. With the election of Richard M. Nixon in 1972, a substantial minority of Jews dropped their traditional allegiance to the Democratic party. Ronald Reagan in 1980 and 1984 also succeeded in attracting a substantial minority of Jews to the Republican party. Since 1928, American Jews had seen in liberalism the politics of group integration. By the 1970s and 1980s, Jews had achieved integration and entered the American mainstream, which was decidedly more conservative. Other constraints, including Jewish religious traditionalism and a concern for group-interest politics (especially Israel), also weakened Jewish commitment to political liberalism.

Despite the immigration of several hundred thousand Jews to the United States from the Soviet Union, Iran, South Africa, and South America—with the largest single contingent arriving from Israel—the demographic profile of American Jewry by 1980 characterized an aging group. The consistently low birthrates of American Jews for two decades reduced natural increase to zero population growth, thus steadily shrinking the percentage Jews constituted of the American population. The larger numbers of children of the small Orthodox minority did not appreciably influence the dominant trends that reflected the

high degree of urbanization and education of American Jewry as well as their privileged socioeconomic position. Conspicuous pockets of poor Jews, many of them elderly living in decaying inner-city slums, contrasted sharply with the general picture of suburban affluence. A lack of emphasis on intergenerational family life accompanied a high valuation on self-fulfillment and stimulated the creation of peer-group family surrogates. These values meshed with the process of physical mobility that hastened the dispersal of American Jews, speeding their integration into American society.

Ongoing Jewish immigration has continuously renewed the presence of first- and second-generation Jews and has assured the pluralistic character of the American Jewish community. In the 1980s approximately 5 to 10 percent of American Jews were recent immigrants. Thus the European and immigrant experience has remained an important element of American Jewish consciousness, contributing a sense of the willed character of their American identity and enhancing their solidarity with world Jewry and especially the state of Israel. The flexibility required of immigrants and the constant need to adjust to newcomers has strengthened the fluid nature of American Jewish communal life. In the 1970s, for the first time in modern Jewish history, significant numbers of Gentiles chose to convert to Judaism, many prompted by marriage to a Jew. In a sense, converts in the 1980s emerged as the new "immigrants" to Judaism. Unlike immigrants from overseas, these Jews by choice have had to adapt to Jewish society, not American values. The established community has perceived them—as it has previous newcomers—as a challenge and a threat.

In the 1980s the issue of survival reached the top of the agenda of American Jewry. In earlier decades as immigrants, Jews had pursued acculturation and adjustment; subsequently, native-born generations had rallied to fight anti-Semitism at home and abroad while seeking integration into American society. By the 1980s delegates to the annual conventions of the CJFWF, perhaps the single most important meeting-place of American Jewish leaders, debated how to promote Jewish survival in the United States as a distinct, if not necessarily distinctive, group. Most American Jews saw their survival in a free and open society inextricably linked to the survival of Israel as a democratic state. Sharing in the sense of national self-confidence that returned during the Reagan presidency, American Jews even sought to assert their position as co-partner with Israel on issues affecting world Jewry.

The changing status of Jewish women and the rapid growth of Jewish studies on university campuses also contributed to a feeling of pride in Jewish accomplishments in America. In 1972 the Hebrew Union College ordained the first woman rabbi, and by 1985 the Reconstructionist Rabbinical College (founded in 1969) and the Jewish Theological Seminary had accepted women as rabbis, leaving only the Orthodox outside of what appeared to be an emerging new consensus. These palpable signs of successful innovation coexisted with demographic trends and associational patterns that suggested the loosening of the group boundaries defining American Jews and the disintegration of a collective way of life that had assured survival in previous decades. Weighing the conflicting evidence, a number of articulate Jews worried aloud whether American Jewry could survive without embracing a measure of both separateness and distinctiveness from American society and its values. Yet despite the opportunities to disappear as a group into American society, most American Jews still desire to survive as Jews, to maintain links—however tenuous—with their non-American past, to foster their Jewish identity—however vague—with others. As they have done before, American Jews continue to refashion their community, remodeling its rooms to house a diverse and pluralistic Jewry.

BIBLIOGRAPHY

Bibliographies

American Jewish Year Book (1899–); William Brickman, ed. *The Jewish Community in America: An Annotated and Classified Bibliographical Guide* (1977); Jeffrey Gurock, *American Jewish History: A Bibliographical Guide* (1983); Jacob Rader Marcus, ed., *An Index to Scientific Articles on American Jewish History* (1971).

General Accounts

Lucy Davidowicz, *On Equal Terms: Jews in America 1881–1981* (1982); Henry Feingold, *Zion in America: The Jewish Experience from Colonial Times to the Present* (1974); Arthur A. Goren, *The American Jews* (1982); Marshall Sklare, *America's Jews* (1971); Chaim I. Waxman, *America's Jews in Transition* (1983).

Social Historical Studies

Charlotte Baum, Paula Hyman, and Sonya Michel, *The Jewish Woman in America* (1976); Naomi W. Cohen, *Not Free to Desist: The American Jewish Committee, 1906–1966* (1972) and *Encounter with Emancipation: The German Jews in the United States* (1984); Steven M. Cohen, *American Modernity and Jewish Identity* (1983); Leonard Dinnerstein, *America and the Survivors of the Holocaust* (1982); Arnold Eisen, *The Chosen People in America: a Study in Jewish Religious Ideology* (1983); Daniel Elazar, *Community and Polity: The Organizational Dynamics of American Jewry* (1976); Henry Feingold, *The Politics of Rescue: The Roosevelt Administration and the Holocaust, 1938–1945* (1970).

Lloyd Gartner, *The History of the Jews of Cleveland* (1978); Arthur A. Goren, *New York Jews and the Quest for Community: The Kehillah Experiment, 1908–1922* (1970; repr. 1979); Jeffrey Gurock, *When Harlem Was Jewish, 1870–1930* (1979); Ben Halpern, *The American Jew: A Zionist Analysis* (1956; repr. 1983); Irving Howe with Kenneth Libo, *World of Our Fathers* (1976); Paula Hyman, "Culture and Gender: Women in the Immigrant Jewish Community," in David Berger, ed., *The Legacy of Jewish Migration: 1881 and Its Impact* (1983); Jenna Weissman Joselit, *Our Gang: Jewish Crime and the New York Jewish Community, 1900–1940* (1983); Abraham J. Karp, *To Give Life: The UJA in the Shaping of the American Jewish Community* (1980); Thomas Kessner, *The Golden Door: Italian and Jewish Immigrant Mobility in New York City, 1880–1915* (1977).

Arthur Liebman, *Jews and the Left* (1979); Charles S. Liebman, *The Ambivalent American Jew: Politics, Religion and Family in American Jewish Life* (1973); Jacob Rader Marcus, "The Periodization of American Jewish History," in *Publications of the American Jewish Historical Society* (March 1958); Deborah Dash Moore, *At Home in America: Second Generation New York Jews* (1981) and *B'nai B'rith and the Challenge of Ethnic Leadership* (1981); Moses Rischin, *The Promised City: New York's Jews, 1870–1914* (1962); Melvin Urofsky, *American Zionism from Herzl to the Holocaust* (1975) and *We Are One! American Jewry and Israel* (1978); David Wyman, *The Abandonment of the Jews: America and the Holocaust, 1941–1945* (1984).

Biographies of Jewish Leaders

Joan Dash, *Summoned to Jerusalem: The Life of Henrietta Szold* (1979); Allon Gal, *Brandeis of Boston* (1980); Jonathan Sarna, *Jacksonian Jew: The Two Worlds of Mordecai Noah* (1980).

[*See also* EMERGENCE OF AN AMERICAN JUDAISM; ETHNICITY AND RELIGION; JEWISH LITERATURE AND RELIGIOUS THOUGHT; and RELIGIOUS PREJUDICE AND NATIVISM.]

JUDAISM IN CONTEMPORARY AMERICA

Jacob Neusner

IN America Judaism faces the challenge, and the opportunity, of addressing Jews in a free society. For the long centuries in which Jews lived as a separate and (usually) protected minority, Judaism constructed a way of life and expressed a worldview for a social group whose persistence seldom was called into question. Christianity and Islam recognized the legitimacy of Judaism, which Jews took to be self-evident. To be sure, Jews found their lives and property threatened. But Judaism could explain that fact and so find even reinforcement in it. Persecution confirmed Jews' acute self-consciousness and underlined their desire for the Messiah, who, at the end of time, will give Israel the just reward. More important, memories of times of stress flowed together with the experience of a world in which Jews found themselves living mainly among other Jews, by both mutual consent and political constraint.

In America, by contrast, the life of Jews as a distinctive group has come to depend mainly upon inner assent, through decisions by individuals to value their religious/cultural origins. Less and less, as time passes, has being Jewish resulted from external compulsion. The reason is that in the open and free American society, Jews did not find themselves much different from others. The distinguishing traits—whether imposed or voluntary—of a Jewish language, Jewish clothing, and Jewish occupations and places of residence had marked the Jews of Central and Eastern Europe; but in America these differences were absent from the very beginning. Consequently, Jews, and therefore Judaism, found themselves in a circumstance hitherto not common in their history.

The condition of freedom overtook the Jews slowly, and then only through successive genera-

tions. The immigrants of the late nineteenth and early twentieth centuries (from 1880 to 1920 more than 3.5 million Jews came to the United States from Russia, Poland, Rumania, Hungary, and Austria) retained the use of Yiddish in their daily lives. They pursued a limited range of occupations and lived mainly in crowded Jewish neighborhoods in a few large cities. Language, occupation, and location reinforced separateness. But it was Judaism that explained it. In the same period other immigrant groups, together with their churches, also formed tight enclaves reminiscent of the old country in the new. How much freedom of choice a Yiddish-speaking Jewish immigrant from Poland actually exercised, or would have wanted to recognize, surely was limited.

The children of the immigrants, who were born in America and are counted as the second generation—the immigrants being the first generation in America—along these same lines adopted the American language and American ways of life. But they grew up in a period of severe anti-Semitism at home and in Europe. While trying to forget the immigrant heritage, the second generation found the world a school for Jewish consciousness, but it was one of a distinctly negative sort. Coming to maturity during the Great Depression and World War II, the second generation did not have to decide whether or not to be Jewish. The society at large made that decision for them. Anti-Semitism and segregation of Jews in their own neighborhoods dictated that Jews would be Jewish.

That set of decisions, amounting to the framing of a situation of genuine free choice, awaited the third generation, reaching its maturity after World War II. That generation found little psychological pressure, such as had faced its prede-

311

cessors, in favor of being Jewish. Surveys of anti-Semitic opinion turned up progressively diminishing levels of hatred. More important, while the second generation had strong memories of Yiddish-speaking parents and lives of a distinctively Jewish character, the third generation in the main did not. For in line with Hanson's law, the second generation made a vigorous effort to forget what they knew. The third generation had to make the decision to learn what they did not know. The parents had made little effort to pass along to the children a rich knowledge of what it meant to be Jewish. American Judaism as we know it today is the creation of that third generation, the result of its conscientious effort to remember what their parents equally deliberately forgot. The decision was made in a free society and represented free and uncoerced choice. So the third generation forms the first generation of Judaism in a very long sequence of centuries to have the right to decide in an open society whether or not to be Jewish. More interesting, it is the first generation to define for itself what being Jewish would consist of, and how Judaism, as an inherited and received religious tradition, would be taken over as part of this definition.

To understand how the third generation of American Jews defined for itself a distinctive and fresh Judaic system—that is, a world view and a way of life serving a distinct social group or class —we have to effect a striking contrast. It is between the state of Judaism at the point at which the second generation had defined matters, with the equivalent condition of Judaism thirty years later, hence the Judaism of the 1940s and 1950s with the Judaism of the 1970s and 1980s.

Beginning, for purposes of comparison and contrast, with the latter period, we find a vast network of educational activities in Judaism, both formal and informal. There are, for example, camps devoted to the use of the Hebrew language in both prayer and everyday activities; youth groups; and programs of Judaic interest in Jewish community centers. A system of Judaic schooling based on afternoon and Sunday sessions now competes with the more intensive all-day schooling of Jewish parochial schools, under Orthodox or Conservative auspices. The organized Jewish community in its philanthropic activities invests sizable sums of money in Judaic activities, youth programs, camps, and formal schooling. The religious observances of classical Judaism in both Orthodox, Conservative, Reform, and Reconstructionist modes reach beyond the synagogue into the home, on the one side, and into formal community programs, on the other. Important historical events, such as the destruction of the Jews of Europe (the Holocaust, in English; *Shoah*, in Hebrew), are the focuses for community attention and commemoration. Even for a program of quasi-religious pilgrimage, in the form of study trips to the Holy Land, the state of Israel draws strong participation from the American Jewish community, old and young. Jewish organizations of non-religious orientation (it is difficult to regard them as wholly secular) undertake travel programs, generally imparting to them a strong religious-educational aspect. These same supposedly secular organizations include in their programs study sessions of a decidedly religious character, in which the Hebrew Scriptures and other Judaic texts or events of sacred history play an important role. Surveys of religious observance confirm a fairly broad level of popular participation in at least some Judaic rites, for example, the Passover Seder, though many other rites have become mere curiosities.

Finally, we note that alongside the neo-Judaic activism of the third generation comes the foundation, in the American Jewish community, of a quite distinct generation. Now a new first generation takes root, this one made up of survivors of the European catastrophe who came to the United States in the late 1940s and early 1950s, with yet more recent immigrants from the State of Israel and oriental countries, on the one side, and the Soviet Union, on the other. The new first generation, beginning its own history, has founded a broad range of vigorously Orthodox institutions and created a quite separate life for itself, in which Judaism as a classical religion defines the affairs of culture and society in every detail. The new first generation has had a deep impact on the orthodoxy of the third generation. It must be said that by the late 1980s, therefore, a distinctively American expression of Judaism has come to full realization. What this means is that a set of Judaic systems has come to definition in this country and that those who have defined it clearly have found effective ways of transmitting, to a fourth, fifth, and sixth generation, a rooted and ongoing Judaism made in America.

Why that fact is noteworthy has now to be

spelled out. The first generation, completing its migration and settling down in the 1920s, took for granted that its ways would not continue. The Yiddish language within the first generation gave way to English, and with it much else that had seemed definitively Jewish in Central and Eastern European settings. With the notion that Jews (like other immigrants) must become American, the immigrant generation tended to accept, not always benignly to be sure, what it perceived as the de-Judaization of its children. The parents kept the dietary taboos, the children did not. The parents practiced distinctively Jewish occupations, dominating some few fields and absent in most others. The children spread out, so far as they could in the prevailing climate of anti-Semitism and exclusion. It follows, therefore, that the founding generation of the sequence at hand did not define a system of Judaism, let alone a set of such systems, that it imagined it could transmit to the next generation. It contributed in rich and important ways to what the coming generation would inherit and utilize. But it defined nothing, except by negative example: the second generation wanted to be American, therefore not Jewish. Judaism as an inherited religious tradition with rich theological perspectives and a demanding, enduring way of life bore little relevance to the American children of those Europeans who had walked on that path to God and lived by that mode of sanctification. And the immigrants took that fact for granted.

The second generation, for its part, accepted more from the founders than it planned. For while explicitly opting for "America" and against "Judaism," that generation implicitly defined life as a set of contrasts. One was Jewish or something else—and the given, for Jews, was that they were Jews. Being Jewish was what defined existence for the second generation. That fact of life was so pervasive as not to demand articulation, let alone specific and concrete expression. The upshot was that the second generation would organize bowling leagues and athletic clubs, rather than prayer circles and study groups. But everyone in the bowling league would be Jewish, and they also would be neighbors and friends. The cultural distinctiveness that had characterized the first generation gave way to a Jewishness by association for the second. The associations, whether political or recreational or philanthropic, took for granted that the goal was non-

sectarian. Little that proved definitively Jewish would mark the group's collective life. But how nonsectarian could an association be, when its members lived in the same neighborhood, pursued the same lines of work, and came from Yiddish-speaking parents? In fact, the community life constructed on the basis of associationism characteristic of the second generation constituted a deeply Jewish mode. It took for granted exactly what the first generation had handed on; that is, the basic and definitive characteristic of being Jewish, whatever, for the new generation, that might come to mean.

The second generation did little to found camps, youth programs, schools beyond a perfunctory sort. The institutions of the second generation did not make explicit, through either substantive or symbolic means, their Jewish character. There were few Jewish parochial schools. Jewish community centers regarded themselves as nonsectarian "community agencies." Jewish philanthropic agencies maintained a high wall of separation between church and state. The result was that very little Jewish philanthropy was directed to Judaic activities of any kind. However, a great deal was spent on fighting anti-Semitism and maintaining nonsectarian hospitals. Proof of these contrasting modes of Judaic life comes readily to hand. Nearly all of the Judaizing programs and activities of the third generation, now received as the norm and permanent, date back only to the decades after World War II. Most of the earliest summer camps of Judaic character come from that period, especially camps under religious auspices (as distinct from Zionist and Hebraist ones). The several youth movements got under way in the late 1940s. The Jewish federations and welfare funds in the 1960s fought the battle for a policy of sectarian investment in distinctively Jewish programs and activities. They undertook to treat as stylish anything markedly Judaic only from the 1970s. These and equivalent facts point to the passage from the second to the third generation as the age of decisive redefinition.

The factors that account for the shifts in generations begin in one simple, negative fact. The second generation did not need schools or youth groups in order to explain what being Jewish meant. Why not? Because they could rely on two more effective educational instruments: memory and experience. The second generation remembered things that the third generation could scarcely imagine: genuinely pious parents, for example. But, as we noted earlier, the second generation also came to maturity in an age in which America turned against the newest Americans. Universities open to Jews before World War I imposed rigid quotas against them afterward. More important, entire industries declared themselves off-limits to Jewish employment. The climate of bigotry and exclusion affected others just as much as the Jews. Blacks (then called Negroes), Catholics, various ethnic groups in different parts of the country all suffered in a prevailing attitude of intolerance of difference. Race riots in Detroit and New York, the absolute exclusion of Catholics from secular university faculties, the isolation of diverse racial and ethnic groups not by choice but by policy—these testify to the prevailing climate.

Far more profound than the experience of personal exclusion was the impact of the rise of political, organized anti-Semitism as an instrument of national policy in Germany, Poland, and other European countries, with its extension and counterpart in the Western democracies. What this meant was that the exclusion from a country club or an executive suite took on a still more ominous character, as the world at large took up the war against the Jews. Jewish immigration was barred when people sought to flee for their lives. In such a setting Jews scarcely needed to find reasons to associate with one another; the world forced them together. They did not lack lessons on how and why to be Jewish, or what being Jewish meant. The world defined and taught those lessons with stern and tragic effect. All of the instrumentalities for explaining and propagating Jewishness, created for the third generation, and, in time, by the third generation, would earlier have proved superfluous.

The contrast, then, between the second and the third generations sets up the encounter with a hostile and threatening world, against the experience of an essentially neutral and benign one. Yet that contrast proves somewhat misleading. For three other factors contributed to the renaissance of articulated and self-conscious Jewishness, along with a renewed search for Judaism, among third-generation Americans of Jewish descent. The first was the rise of the State of Israel. The second was the discovery not of the murder of nearly 6 million Jews in Europe but of "the Holocaust." The third was the re-ethnicization of American life; that is, the resurgence of ethnic identification among the grandchildren of the immigrant generations and among blacks and other excluded groups that long ago had become American by force. Just as the Jewish third generation tried to remember what the second generation had wanted to forget, so the same pattern was exhibited elsewhere. Just as black students demanded what they deemed ethnically characteristic food, so Jewish students discovered they wanted kosher food too.

All three factors, among the Jews, reinforced one another. The rise of the State of Israel to constitute a critical component of American Jewish consciousness today appears perfectly routine. But in the 1940s and 1950s American Jewry had yet to translate its deep sympathy for the Jewish state into political activity and the shaping element for local cultural activity and sentiment. So too the memory of the destruction of European Jewry did not right away become the Holocaust, as a formative event in contemporary Jewish consciousness. In fact, the re-ethnicization of the Jews could not have taken the form that it did—a powerful identification with the State of Israel as the answer to the question to the Holocaust—without a single, catalytic event.

That event was the 1967 war between the State of Israel and its Arab neighbors. When on 5 June 1967, after a long period of threat, the dreaded war of "all against one" began, American Jews feared the worst. Six days later they confronted an unimagined outcome, with the State of Israel standing on the Jordan River, the Nile, and the outskirts of Damascus. The trauma of the weeks preceding the war, when the Arabs promised to drive the Jews into the sea and no other power intervened or promised help, renewed for the third generation the nightmare of the second. Once more the streets and newspapers became the school for being Jewish. The world again ignored Jewish suffering, and a new holocaust impended. But now the outcome was quite different. The entire history of the twentieth century came under a new light.

The third generation had found its memory and its hope. It now could confront the murder of the Jews of Europe, along with its parents' (and, for not a few, its own) experience of exclusion and bigotry. No longer was it necessary to avoid painful, intolerable memories. Now what had happened had to be remembered, because it bore within itself the entire message of the new day in Judaism. That is to say, putting together the murder of nearly 6 million Jews of Europe with the creation of the State of Israel transformed both events. One became the Holocaust, the purest statement of evil in all of human history. The other became salvation in the form of "the first appearance of our redemption" (as the language of the Jewish prayer for the State of Israel has it). Accordingly, a moment of stark epiphany captured the entire experience of the age and imparted to it that meaning and order that a religious system has the power to express and make self-evident. The self-evident system of American Judaism, then, for the third generation encompassed a salvific myth deeply and personally relevant to the devotees. That myth made sense equally and at a single instant of both the world and the self, of what the newspapers had to say and what the individual understood in personal life.

The distinctively American form of Judaism under description here clearly connects to classical Judaism. But it is not continuous with it. American Judaism draws upon some of the received religious tradition and claims to take up the whole of it. But in its stress upon the realization, in the here and the now, of ultimate evil and salvation, and in its mythicization of contemporary history, American Judaism offers a distinctively American, therefore a new and unprecedented, reading of the received tradition. This is by definition. For when Jews have come to speak of fully realized salvation and an end of history, the result has commonly proved to be a new religion, connected to, but not continuous with, the received religion of Judaism. That is very much the case even in the late twentieth century.

The ambiguity of American Judaism lies in sorting out what is old from what is new, in discovering, in the continuation of the familiar, what has changed, and in determining, in what appears to be new, what turns out to be entirely familiar and well-attested for centuries. In order to accomplish this work of analysis, we proceed to consider each of the primary categories of the received version of Judaism. When we allow the Judaism brought from Europe to tell us how to organize our data, we must speak of the categories out of which that system for a social group had constructed its world view and expressed that world view through a distinctive way of life. The simple categories, each beyond reduction to any more general or encompassing one, are these: way of life (including everyday mode of social organization and types of religious leadership) and world view (spatial, in terms of location, and theological). These, then, in detail, allow us to speak of holy way of life, holy man, holy people, and holy land. Our task is now to describe that distinctive system of Judaism produced in America, in particular by the third generation for the fourth and fifth generations, in terms of the categories just now defined.

Holy way of life. In archaic Judaism the holy life—the things one did to conform to the will of God or, in secular terms, the behavior patterns imposed by the Judaic tradition—was personal and participative. Every man, woman, and child had a myriad of deeds to do because he or she was a Jew. No one was exempt from following the holy way of living. Everyone expected to share in it equally. One did not speak of how others should keep the Sabbath. One kept the Sabbath, along with everyone else in the community. People individually said their own prayers, advanced their own education in the tradition, did good deeds on their own part. Prayer, study, and the practice of good deeds were personal and universal. To be a Jew meant to do a hundred *mitzvot,* holy actions, every day.

In modern America to be a Jew means to join an organization. It may be a synagogue, or a Zionist group, or a Jewish community center. People join synagogues but attend services only a few times a year; they deem their membership important. That points to a gap between joining and doing, and suggests that when people join, it is to support the organization, not necessarily to do the things, themselves, that the organization is meant to carry out. The formation of large organizations, characteristic of modern life, tends to obliterate the effective role of the individual. In the Judaic situation, however, even the synagogue, with its substantial budget and massive membership, its professional leadership and surrogate religiosity, follows the pattern. If to be a Jew now means to take an active part in the Jewish community, then the holy life is lived chiefly by paying one's part of the budget of the organizations that call themselves the community.

People join organizations because they have been convinced that that is what "Judaism" expects of them. They think this primarily because of the patterns established, or already imposed, by others. The result is the concentration of power in the hands of the few who actually determine what organizations do. These few are not democratically elected, but generally come up out of an oligarchy of wealthy and influential men (only a few women are included). But even these men do not actually effect the work of the community. They raise the funds and allocate them, but local funds are in fact spent by, and chiefly upon the salaries of, the professional bureaucrats trained to administer the functioning of an organization. In general their work is to keep the organizations alive and prosperous.

What has all this to do with being Jewish? Ordinarily people provide an account of what "Jews believe" or what "Judaism teaches." But what concerns us in describing American Judaism is what Jews believe being Jewish means and requires of them. We have a clear picture of what most Jews do and do not do. They keep some rites and not others; for example, rites of passage and of family are almost universally observed, by upwards of 80 to 90 percent of the community in most surveys, while rites of the corporate community, public prayer for instance, attract far smaller proportions of the whole. It is estimated that 500,000 Jews in America keep the dietary laws (concerning suitable, or kosher, food). That means approximately 1 in 10 or 11. The other 90 percent then do not regard those rules as applicable. Excluding small circles of American Jews, identified as Orthodox, we cannot describe the life and religion of American Jews simply by opening the books that describe the Judaism of the authoritative sources.

Since we ask what it means to be a Jew in America, the first thing we want to know is: What do people do because they are Jewish? And the answer is: They join organizations and give money. In this respect, what makes a person Jewish in American society primarily depends on which organization he or she joins and to what worthy cause he or she gives money.

That the holy way should have become the "culture of organizations" tells us that modernity has overtaken the Jews. What characterizes group life in modern times is the development of specialists for various tasks, the organization of society for the accomplishment of tasks once performed individually and in an amateur way, the growth of professionalism, the reliance upon large institutions. What modern humanity gains in greater efficiency and higher levels of competence cannot be given up because of nostalgia for a way of life few now living in a traditional society would want to preserve. But as everyone recognizes, the cost of "progress" is impersonality and depersonalization. The real question is not whether to return to a more primitive way of living, but how to regain the humanity, personality, individual self-respect, and self-reliance necessarily lost along the way.

Holy man. The "professional Jews" who run the Jewish institutions and organizations that constitute for the ordinary folk the holy way are anonymous, faceless, and wholly secular. People relate to them no differently from the way they do to other bureaucrats, in government offices, public schools, and department stores. However, there is one Jewish functionary whom the common people continue to regard as quintessentially "Jewish," important, and formative of values, and that is the least powerful and least effective figure—the rabbi. For nearly twenty centuries the rabbi was the holy man of Judaic tradition. He became a rabbi through study of Torah, which comprised not only the Hebrew Scriptures, but also the Oral Torah, believed to have been handed on in Mosaic revelation and eventually recorded in the pages of the Babylonian Talmud and related literature. The rabbi was a holy man consecrated not by prayer, though he prayed, nor by asceticism, though he assumed taxing disciplines, but by study and knowledge of Torah. That knowledge made him not merely learned or wise, but a saint; and it endowed him with not only information, but also insight into the workings of the universe. Consequently, in earlier times rabbis were believed to have more than commonplace merits, therefore more than ordinary power over the world; and some of them, especially qualified by learning and piety, were seen as being able to pray more effectively than common people and to accomplish miracles.

Today rabbis (now both women and men) are essentially peripheral figures in organized Jewish life, outside of the framework of the synagogue. Dropping the rabbi out of the decision-making circles of the Jewish community merely took account of the rabbi's profoundly different role. Formerly judge, administrator, holy man, scholar, and saint, the rabbi in American Judaism at first served as a rather secular leader of a rather secular community, spokesman for Jews to Gentiles, representative of his synagogue to the larger Jewish group, agent of Zionist propaganda, and certifier of the values of the upper-class Jews who employed him. But as time has passed, these roles and tasks have been given to others who are better equipped for them because of community position, economic power, and public acceptance. The rabbi is left to preside at circumcisions, weddings, and funerals, to "conduct" religious worship, which in traditional synagogues means to announce pages and tell people when to stand up and sit down, to counsel the troubled, and to teach the children.

But that is not the whole story. With the decline of the effectiveness of education, for the third and fourth generations, the rabbi, who normally was nearly the only one who could read Hebrew and intelligently comprehend a Jewish book, by the 1970s and 1980s stood forth for the same reason as in classical times—because of his learning. So far as access to Judaic tradition and capacity to comprehend Judaic thinking proved important, the rabbi continued to hold the key to the mind and intellect of Judaism. Second, and still more important, while the rabbi could be made into a pathetic remnant of the ancient glories of his office, he remained the rabbi. The title and the role persisted in setting the rabbi apart from others, in making him a kind of holy man. In psychological terms, he continued to function as a surrogate father and God. Secularity did not, could not in the end, deprive him of his role as a religious figure, even leader. The holy man remained just that, even to the most secular people, by the late 1980s.

Today the rabbi serves primarily his congregation. In a sense he has become a more religious figure than earlier. That means, to be sure, he has less power in Jewish communal affairs. But it is likely that he now enjoys more influence than before, and influence in shaping the ideas and purposes of others represents significant power to achieve concrete ends. The rabbi does not stand at the head of organizations or of community bureaus. But he stands behind those who do, for Jewish leaders nearly universally belong to synagogues and rely upon religious rites at least at the time of life crises—birth, puberty, marriage, and death.

Above all, they are under the spell of the rabbi as a holy man, in a way in which the passing generation was not. To be sure, lay people are as well-educated as the rabbi in many ways. But in respect to the knowledge of Judaism, standards of literacy have so fallen that the rabbi now predominates in precisely the one area appropriate to his calling. So far as people remain Jews, they depend more than ever upon rabbis to explain to them what Judaism should mean. At the same time, one should underline that the commitment to being Jewish seems likely to continue to flourish. It is an inchoate, amorphous commitment. But it moves people to do things they otherwise would not do. And it is the rabbi who retains the prestige and the learning to fill that empty commitment with purpose and meaning. That is so even though secular leaders accomplish more practical tasks.

The real foundations for the rabbinical position are the convictions people retain from archaic times about holy men, set aside for God and sanctified by sacred disciplines. In archaic times the rabbi was a holy man because of his mastery of Torah. Today the rabbi remains a holy man for that reason. Thus far we have seen the sociological side of that holiness: the rabbi continues functionally to dominate because of his knowledge of Torah. With women now included, the rabbi has new opportunities for effective contemporary service.

Holy people. The holy people in archaic times certainly knew who they were and confidently defined their relationship with Gentiles. Jews saw themselves as "Israel," the people to whom Torah had been revealed, now living in exile from their homeland. Israel was a nation within other nations. But eventually Israel would return to the holy land, with the coming of the Messiah. Gentiles were outsiders, strangers to be respected but feared, honored but avoided, except when necessary.

Modern times are different. Since the nineteenth century Western European Jews have consciously entered the societies of the nations among which they have lived for generations. They have become German, French, and British citizens, ceased to form separate communities, and sought normal relationships both with Gentiles and with their culture.

For the immigrants to America the nineteenth-century Western European experience repeated itself. At first the Jews formed separate, Yiddish-speaking enclaves in large cities; but as time passed they and their children moved to less uniformly Jewish neighborhoods, entered less characteristically Jewish occupations, wholeheartedly adopted the language and culture of the America they had chosen. The assimilation of Jews into American culture continued apace in the second generation, and by the third it was virtually complete.

After World War II, survivors of the European war emerged from the death camps to immigrate to America. That group of immigrants overall chose to form self-segregated communities and to retain the Yiddish language and the holy way of life without compromise. These immigrants did not wish to join a Gentile world, since their experience of the Gentile world had proved negative. They wished to live only or mainly among Jews, so far as possible. The pattern of assimilation did not repeat itself. Nor did American society expect immigrants to erase difference, in the way in which former generations of immigrants found it necessary to conform. Consequently a decision to segregate themselves on the part of the immigrants, some of them members of a mystical branch of Judaism called Hasidism, led to a different form of Judaism for some. But for the vast majority of American Jews, self-segregation bore slight appeal. And the paramount questions for them became, and now remain, these: What is a Jew? Who is Israel? What makes a person into a Jew? Are the Jews a religious group? Are they a people? Are they a nation? The Jews have entered a lingering crisis of group identity. They are not certain who they are or what is asked of them because of what they claim to be. And individual Jews face a severe dilemma of personal identity as well: Why should I be a Jew? What does it mean, if anything, that I am born of Jewish parents?

One important measure of modernity is the loss of the old certainties about who one is. The sense of a crisis of identity is a condition of being a modern person. Formerly, people suppose, men and women were confident of their place in the life of the community and certain of the definition of that community in the history of mankind. To be a Jew not only imposed social and economic roles, but it also conveyed a considerable supernatural story. Israel was the people of the Lord, bearer of revelation, engaged in a pilgrimage through history, en route to the promised land at the end of time. To be a Jew was to know not only who one was, but also what that meant in the economy of universal history.

To identify oneself as a Jew was a privilege and a responsibility, but it was not a problem. The world posed problems to the Jew. Judaism and being Jewish, not separated from one another, solved those problems, explained events, interpreted everyday reality in terms of a grand and encompassing vision of human history and destiny. "We are Israel, children of Abraham, Isaac, and Jacob, loyal sons of the Torah of Moses at Sinai, faithfully awaiting the anointed of God." What difference did it make that Gentiles treated Jews contemptuously, despised them, maligned their religion? In the end everyone would know the truth. Before the eyes of all the living would God redeem Israel and vindicate the patience and loyal faithfulness of its disagreeable experience in history among men.

What strikingly characterizes the imagination of the archaic Jew is the centrality of Israel, the Jewish people, in human history; the certainty that being a Jew is the most important thing about oneself; and Jewishness, meaning Judaism, being the dominant aspect of one's consciousness. The "holy people" today has disintegrated in its classical formulation. How so? First, Jews are no longer certain just what makes them into a people. Second, they see themselves as anything but holy; they interpret in a negative way the things that make them Jewish and different from others; and above all they introduce into their assessment of themselves the opinions of the Gentiles.

It is easy enough to draw invidious contrasts between the virtues of the archaic world and the shortcomings of modernity. But since the old certainties and securities are mostly gone, one might observe that not only necessity but choice moved Jews away from them. When Jews in Eastern Europe began to feel the birth pangs of modernity, all the more so when the immigrants came to America and plunged into the modern condition; they scarcely looked backward. Whatever virtues they had known did not restrain them. Something in the traditional life seemed to them to have failed, for in their thirst for whatever was new and contemporary they demonstrated that the old had not fulfilled their aspirations.

It did not have to be so, and for some it was not. Both the immigrants of the 1890s and those who came after World War II, as noted above, included considerable numbers of Jews who remained loyal to the tradition in a wholly traditional way. The appeal of modernity was lost on them. Still others entered the modern situation and quickly turned their backs on tradition. The return to religion in the decades after World War II saw considerable strengthening of Orthodox commitment and conviction in American Judaism, and renascent Orthodoxy did not take the modern form of surrogate religiosity, large synagogues, and impersonal professionalism, but the entirely traditional forms of personal commitment and maximum individual participation. Whether traditional Orthodox Judaism in America is traditional and orthodox in the same ways as in Eastern European Judaism hardly matters. The fact is that the classical Judaic perspective remains a completely acceptable choice for substantial numbers of American Jews. Those Jews who fully live the traditional life and adhere to the traditional way of faith seem to me to have made a negative judgment on modernity and its values. It becomes all the more striking that larger numbers—the vast majority of American Jewry—came to an affirmative opinion.

But in affirming the modern and accepting its dilemmas, American Jews continued in important modes to interpret themselves in the archaic ways. Most important, they continued to see themselves as Jews, to regard that fact as central to their very being, and to persist in that choice. That fact cannot be taken for granted. The Jews are not simply an ethnic group characterized by primarily external, wholly unarticulated, and un-self-conscious qualities. They are Jewish not merely because they happen to have inherited quaint customs, unimportant remnants of an old heritage rapidly falling away. On the contrary, they hold very strong convictions about how they will continue to be Jews. Most of them hope their children will marry within the Jewish community. Most of them join synagogues and do so because they want their children to grow up as Jews. Above all, most of them regard the fact that they are Jewish as bearing great significance.

These convictions conflict with the earlier characterization of the practiced religion as checkbook Judaism. They point toward a more complex world view than suggested above. What we may surmise is that enduring human problems, affecting home and family, precipitated by passage through life, present problems that cannot be set aside. At those turning points, Jews look toward Judaism not as a matter of cultural identity or social group alone, but also for solace and hope. Just as Catholics return to the church in their late twenties and thirties, as they settle down and begin to raise families, so Jews do the same. And for both groups—and many others—religion (in this case, Judaism) finds a new hearing, and one in its own terms and for its own purposes.

Jews see everyday life in terms different from their Gentile neighbors, beginning with the fact that to them, if not to their neighbors, their being Jewish seems an immensely important fact of life. The words they use to explain that fact, the symbols by which they express it, are quite different from those of archaic or classical Judaism. They speak of Jewishness, not Torah. They are obsessed with a crisis of identity, rather than with the tasks and responsibilities of "Israel." They are deeply concerned about the opinions of Gentiles.

In all, they are eager to be Jewish—but not too much so, not so much that they cannot also take their place within the undifferentiated humanity of which they fantasize. They confront a crisis not merely of identity but of commitment, for they do not choose to resolve the dilemma of separateness within an open society. In preferring separateness, they seem entirely within the archaic realm; in dreaming of an open society, they evidently aspire to a true accomplishment of the early promise of modernity. But if that truly open society should come to realization, one wonders whether the Jews would want to enter it. But the Jew clearly continues to take with utmost seriousness the fact of his being Jewish, indeed to speak, precisely as did those in the classical tradition, of Israel.

Holy land. Archaic religions usually focus upon a holy place where God and man come together, the focus for the sacred upon earth. In classical Judaism, Palestine ("the Land of Israel") was not merely the place where Jews lived, but the holy land. It could never legitimately be governed by pagans—thus, the continuing efforts of Jews to drive pagan rulers out of the land. There the Temple was built, the nexus of the God-man relationship. The mountains of the land were the highest in the earth. The land was the center of the world, of the universe. Jerusalem was most beautiful, most holy.

No element of the classical myth at the turn of the twentieth century could have seemed more remote from the likely preferences of nascent American Judaism. When the immigrants left Russia, they could have gone southward, to Palestine, and a few of them did. But most went west, and of these the largest number came to the United States. Since Zionism was even then an important option in Eastern European Judaism, one can hardly regard the immigrants as Zionists. A few stayed in the United States only a short while, then departed for Palestine. The vast majority came and settled down.

Now, nearly ninety years later, the vast majority of third-, fourth-, and fifth-generation American Jews support the State of Israel, and whether they are called Zionists hardly matters. The sole commitment shared by nearly all, uniquely capable of producing common action, is that the State of Israel must live. Zionism accounts for the predominance of the welfare funds. To American Jews, "never again"—referring to the slaughter of nearly 6 million European Jews—means that the State of Israel must not be permitted to perish. But there is a second, less often articulated fact about American Jewry. Alongside the nearly universal concern for the State of Israel is, by definition, the quite unanimous Jewish commitment to the United States and to remaining Americans. Immigration to the State of Israel since 1948 has been negligible. Indeed, until the present time more Israelis have settled in America than American Jews in Israel.

Clearly, Zionism, with its focus on the State of Israel, solves problems for American Jews. How does it do so, and why, then, do American Jews in the vast majority find Zionism so critical to their sense of themselves as a holy people?

Zionism provides a reconstruction of Jewish identity, for it reaffirms the nationhood of Israel in the face of the disintegration of the religious bases of a Jewish peoplehood. If in times past the Jews saw themselves as a people because they were the children of the promise, the children of Abraham, Isaac, and Jacob, called together at Sinai, instructed by God through prophets, led by rabbis guided by the whole Torah—written and oral—of Sinai, then with the end of a singu-

larly religious self-consciousness, the people lost its understanding of itself. The fact is that the people remained a community of fate but, until the flourishing of Zionism, the facts of its continued existence were deprived of a heuristic foundation. Jews continued as a group, but could not persuasively say why or what this meant. Zionism provided the explanation: the Jews indeed remain a people, but the foundation of their peoplehood lies in the unity of their concern for Zion, devotion to rebuilding the land and establishing Jewish sovereignty in it. The realities of continuing emotional and social commitment to Jewish grouphood or separateness thus made sense. Mere secular difference, once seen to be destiny—in the words of the *Alenu*-Prayer, "who has not made us like the nations" —once again stood forth as destiny.

Herein lies the ambiguity of Zionism. It was supposedly a secular movement yet, in reinterpreting the classic mythic structures of Judaism, it compromised its secularity and exposed its fundamental unity with the received Judaism. Groups with like attributes do not necessarily represent "peoples" or "nations." The primary conviction of Zionism constitutes an extraordinary reaffirmation of the primary element in the classical mythic structure: salvation. What has happened in Zionism is that the old has been in one instant destroyed and resurrected. The holy people are no more, the nation people take their place. The allegedly secular successor-continuator has not only preserved the essential perspective of the tradition, but done so in the tradition's own symbols and language.

Nor should it be supposed that to the Jews' crisis of identity the Zionist is a merely theological or ideological figure. We cannot ignore the practical result of Zionist success in conquering the Jewish community. For the middle and older generations, the Zionist enterprise provided the primary vehicle for Jewish identity. The Reform solution to the identity problem—we are Americans by nationality, Jews by religion—was hardly congruent with the profound Jewish passion of the immigrant generations and their children. The former generations were *not* merely Jewish by religion. Religion was the least important aspect of their Jewishness. They deeply felt themselves Jewish and did not feel so marginal as Jews to need to affirm either their Americanness or their Judaism at all. Rather they participated in a reality; they were in a situation so real and intimate as to make unnecessary an uncomfortable, defensive affirmation. They did not doubt they were Americans. They did not need to explain what being Jewish had to do with it. Zionism was congruent with these realities; and because of that fact, being Jewish and being Zionist were inextricably joined together.

But Zionism also constitutes a problem for Judaism. The mythic insufficiency of Zionism renders its success a dilemma for contemporary American Jews, and for Israeli ones as well. Let us begin with the obvious. How can American Jews focus their spiritual lives solely on a land in which they do not live? It is one thing for that land to be in heaven, at the end of time. It is quite another to dream of a faraway place where everything is good, but where one may go if he wants. The realized eschaton (end of history) is insufficient for a rich and interesting fantasy life; moreover, in worldly terms it is hypocritical. It means American Jews live off the capital of Israeli culture. The "enlandisement" (land-centeredness) of American Judaism—the focusing of its imaginative, inner life upon the land and State of Israel—therefore imposes an ersatz spiritual dimension: "We live here *as if* we lived there—but do not choose to migrate."

It furthermore diverts American Judaism from the concrete mythic issues it has yet to solve: Why should anyone be a *Jew* anywhere, in the United States or in Israel? That question is not answered by the recommendation to participate in the spiritual adventures of people in a quite different situation. Since the primary *mitzvot* (commandments) of American Judaism concern supplying funds, encouragement, and support for Israel, one wonders whether one must be a Jew at all in order to believe in and practice that form of Judaism. What is being Jewish now supposed to mean?

The underlying problem, which faces both Israeli and American Jews, is understanding what the ambiguous adjective "Jewish" is supposed to mean when the noun "Judaism" has been abandoned. To be sure, for some Israelis and American Jews to be a Jew is to be a citizen of the State of Israel; but that definition hardly serves when Israeli Moslems and Christians are taken into account. If one ignores the exceptions, the rule is still wanting. If to be a Jew is to be—or to dream of being—an Israeli, then the Israeli who chooses to settle in a foreign country ceases to be a Jew when he gives up Israeli citizenship. If all

Jews are on the road to Zion, then those who either do not get there, or, once there, choose another way are to be abandoned. That makes Jewishness depend upon quite worldly issues: this one cannot make his living in Tel Aviv; that one does not like the climate of Affula; the other is frustrated by the bureaucracy of Jerusalem. Are they then supposed to give up their share in the God of Israel?

American Jews half a century ago would not have claimed "religious" as an appropriate adjective for their community. Today they insist upon it. The moralists' criticism of religion will always render ever more remote what is meant by true religion, so we need not be detained by carping questions. But can there be religion with so minimal a quotient of supernatural experience, theological conviction, and evocative ritual, including prayer, as is revealed in American Judaism? If one draws the dividing line between belief in a supernatural God and atheism, then much of American Jewry, also much of American Judaism, may stand on the far side of that line. If the dividing line is, in the words of Krister Stendahl, "between the closed mind and spiritual sensibility and imagination," then American Jews and American Judaism may stand within the frontier of the religious and the sacred.

Let us consider again the substitution of organizations and group activity for a holy way of life lived by each individual. What the Jews have done in their revision of the holy way is to conform to—in their own way to embody—the American talent for actually accomplishing things. Americans organize. They do so not to keep themselves busy, but to accomplish efficiently and with an economy of effort a great many commendable goals. They hire professionals to do well what most individuals cannot do at all: heal the sick, care for the needy, tend the distressed at home and far away. In modern society people are not supposed to keep guns in their homes for self-protection. They have police. Nations do not rely upon the uncertain response of well-meaning volunteers. They form armies. The things American Jews seek to accomplish through their vast organizational life derive from their tradition: they want to educate the young and old, to contribute to the building of the ancient land, to see to it that prayers are said and holidays observed. Hiring a religious virtuoso may seem less commendable than saying one's own prayers, but it is merely an extension of the specialization people take for granted elsewhere.

In archaic times people believed that salvation depended upon keeping to the holy way; so it was done, each person being sufficiently expert to know how to carry out the law. Today few believe that supernatural salvation inheres in prayers, dietary taboos, and Sabbath observance. It is therefore curious that the Jews nonetheless want to preserve the old salvific forms and symbols, as they certainly do. Few pray. Fewer still believe in prayer. It is astonishing that the synagogues persist in focusing their collective life upon liturgical functions. Perhaps the best analogy is to a museum, in which old art is preserved and displayed, though people do not paint that way anymore, may not even comprehend what the painter did or the technical obstacles he overcame. The synagogue is a living museum and preserves the liturgical and ritual life of the old tradition. Why should Jews choose this way, when earlier in their American experience they seemed to move in a different direction? Is it nostalgia for a remembered, but unavailable experience of the sacred? Is the religious self-definition they have adopted merely an accommodation to American expectations? Or do they hope the archaic and the supernatural may continue to speak to them?

The figure of the rabbi calls forth the same wonderment. Why call oneself rabbi at all, if one is not a saint, a scholar, a judge? Given the ultimate mark of secularization—the complaint that rabbis no longer reach high places in the Jewish community—should we not ask what is still sacred in the rabbi and his learning, calling, leadership? The answer would be, nothing whatsoever, were it not for people's relationships to the rabbi, their fantastic expectations of him or her. The rabbi, unsure of his or her role, at once self-isolated and complaining at his or her loneliness—whatever he is, he is the rabbi. He knows it. The people know it. They look to him as a kind of holy man. No nostalgia here: the rabbi is a completely American adaptation of the ancient rabbinic role. But American society never imposed the peculiar, mainly secular definition of "Jewish clergyman" upon the modern rabbi. For two hundred years American Jewry had no rabbis at all. And the rabbis they now have are not merely Judaic versions of Protestant ministers or Roman Catholic priests, but uniquely Judaic as as well as exceptionally American. The remembrance of rabbis of past times—of the saints, scholars, and holy men of Europe—hardly persists into the fourth generation and beyond. The rabbi, profane and secular, is the only holy man or woman they will ever know. So onto him or her they fix their natural, human fantasies about men and women set apart by and for God.

The holy people, Israel, of times past has become "the American Jewish community," uncertain what is Jewish about itself, still more unsure of what Jewish ought to mean at all. Surely the lingering crisis of self-definition, characteristic of modern men and women in many situations, marks the Jew as utterly modern and secular. Add to that the second component of the holy people's self-understanding: concern for what the Gentiles think of Jews, readiness to admit that negative opinion into the Jewish assessment of the Jews. This submission to universal opinions and values hardly characterizes a holy people, set apart from all others. Frail and uncomfortable, hating those "Jewish traits" in oneself that set Jews apart from everyone else, and wanting to be Jewish but not too much, not so much that they cannot also be undifferentiated Americans—is this the holy people that traversed thirty-five centuries of human history, proud, tenacious, alone? Can they claim their collectivity to be holy, separate, and apart? Surely in the passage from the sacred to the secular, the holy people has disintegrated, become a random group of discrete, scarcely similar individuals. Yet while that may seem to be so, the one point Jews affirm is that they shall be Jews. This they have in common.

The very vigor of their activity together and the commonalities of a quite discrete folk suggest that the group, once a people, is still a people. The secular separateness of the Jews, their inner awareness of being a group, their outward view of themselves as in some ways apart from others, that separateness is probably all modern man can hope for socially to approximate the holy. The archaic holy people has passed from the scene. In its place stands something different in all respects but the most important: its manifest and correct claim to continue as Jews, a different, separate group, and the claim that that difference is destiny.

The relationship between secular Zionism and sacred messianism, modern nation building and the myth of the return to Zion at the end of time, is complex. It seems clear that the pattern recurs, perhaps most vividly, in the modern and secular modulation of the myth of the holy land.

Let us end with attention to doctrine, Torah in the mythic language of Judaism. We may ask three questions: What of the religious life of American Jews? What of the study of Torah? And what of the theological enterprise? The first question produces an uninteresting answer, the second, an obvious one. But the third is consequential: the grandchildren of Jews who would not have understood what theologians do, but persisted in an episodic, aphoristic expression of a folk faith as theology enough, not only write theology, but correctly claim it to be Judaic. This is the decisive evidence that something new has been created out of something old. Contemporary American Judaism, for all its distance from the classic forms of the past, its unbelief and secularity, constitutes a fundamentally new and autonomous development, not merely the last stages in the demise of something decadent. American Judaism calls forth, in the task of formulating a systematic account of its faith, the talents of philosophical sophistication and religious conviction, able to speak in the name, even in the words, of the classic tradition, but in a languauge alien to that tradition. To be sure, the Jews' response to Judaic theology thus far is routine and inconsequential. The best books reach a tiny audience, the worst only a slightly larger one. The finest theological journals are read chiefly by those who write for them, or aspire to. So the theological movement must stand by itself, as evidence of the modernity and secularity of the theologians, on the one side, but of their participation in the traditional sacred values and in the archaic texts, on the other.

American Judaism constitutes something more than the lingering end of old ways and myths. It is the effort of modern men and women to make use of archaic ways and myths for the formation of a religious way of living appropriate to an unreligious time and community. Spiritual sensibility and, even more, the remnants of the archaic imagination are the sources for the unarticulated but evident decision of American Jews to reconstruct out of the remnants of an evocative but incongruous heritage the materials of a humanly viable, meaningful community life. To have attempted the reconstitution of traditional villages in the metropolis and of archaic ways of seeing the world in the center of modernity would have been to deny the human value and pertinence of the tradition itself. But few wanted even to try. In the end the effort would have had no meaning. The Jews had the courage to insist that their life together must have more than ordinary meaning. In American Judaism they embarked upon the uncertain quest to find, if necessary to invent, and build that meaning. Despite their failures, the gross, grotesque form they have imposed upon the old tradition, that uncommon, courageous effort seems to testify to whatever is good and enduring in modernity. But whether good or not, abiding or ephemeral, all that modern men and women have, and all that they shall ever have, is the mature hope to persist in that quest.

BIBLIOGRAPHY

Steven M. Cohan, *American Modernity and Jewish Identity* (1983); Daniel J. Elazar, *Community and Polity: The Organizational Dynamics of American Jewry* (1976); Nathan Glazer, *American Judaism* (1957), and with Daniel Patrick Moynihan, *Beyond the Melting Pot: The Negroes, Puerto Ricans, Jews, Italians, and Irish of New York City* (1963); Hillel Halkin, *Letters to an American Jewish Friend: A Zionist's Polemic* (1977); Ben Halpern, *The American Jew* (1956); Oscar Handlin, *The Uprooted* (1951; 2nd ed., 1973) and *Children of the Uprooted* (1968); Samuel C. Heilman, *Synagogue Life: A Study in Symbolic Interaction* (1973; rev. 1976) and *The People of the Book: Drama, Fellowship, and Religion* (1983); William B. Helmreich, *The World of the Yeshiva: An Intimate Portrait of Orthodox Jewry* (1982); John Higham, *Send These to Me: Jews and Other Immigrants in Urban America* (1975); Charles S. Liebman, *The Ambivalent American Jew: Politics, Religion, and Family in American Jewish Life* (1973); Jacob R. Marcus, ed., *The American Rabbinate: A Centennial View* (*American Jewish Archives*, 1983, vol. 35).

Jacob Neusner, *American Judaism: Adventure in Modernity* (1973; rev. 1978), *Stranger at Home: "The Holocaust," Zionism, and American Judaism* (1981), *Jewish War Against the Jews* (1984), *From Words to Worlds: Enchantment and Transformation in Judaism* (1987), and as ed., *Understanding American Judaism*, 2 vols. (1975); Yonathan Shapiro, *The Leadership of the American Zionist Organization, 1897–1930* (1971); Marshall Sklare, *Conservative Judaism: An American Religious Movement* (1955, 1972), and with Joseph Greenblum, *Jewish Identity on the Suburban Frontier: A Study of Group Survival in the Open Society* (2nd ed., 1979); Stephen Steinberg, *The Ethnic Myth: Race, Ethnicity, and Class in America* (1981); Chaim I. Waxman, *America's Jews in Transition* (1983).

[See also EMERGENCE OF AN AMERICAN JUDAISM; ETHNICITY AND RELIGION; JEWISH LITERATURE AND RELIGIOUS THOUGHT; RELIGIOUS PREJUDICE AND NATIVISM; and SOCIAL HISTORY OF AMERICAN JUDAISM.]

EASTERN CHRISTIANITY

Paul D. Garrett

W HERE the traditions of the Christian East are known at all in the West, they tend to be regarded as exotic remnants of foreign cultures: picturesque and anachronistic, introverted and rather anarchistic. This is especially the case with the Eastern churches in America. In a necessarily limited discussion of the historical road and beliefs of Eastern Christianity, we will concentrate on showing how this view developed— and why it is an unfortunate misperception.

ORIGINS OF EASTERN ECCLESIASTICAL GROUPS

The distinctive doctrines, liturgies, and ethos of Eastern Christianity are rooted in a history largely removed from that of the Christian West, although the beginnings of Christianity were common throughout the Roman Empire. It is essential to note the unity before the differences. Forged in the catacombs, freed by the emperor Constantine in the early fourth century, and transformed into a new state religion that declined in zeal even as it grew in numbers, Eastern Christianity everywhere responded in two ways. First, monks fled the new Christian city for the deserts to proclaim the good news of a kingdom not of this world, even as the martyrs before them had borne supreme witness to the reality of Christ's victory over death. As monasticism spread and crystallized into an institution, it influenced the local liturgies and structures of the universal church.

Second, a dogmatic and canonical tradition developed in the still-infant church, not out of idle speculation, but of necessity whenever dangerous interpretations and customs threatened the mystery of salvation. In the era of the church

fathers and the seven ecumenical councils (325– 787), "orthodoxy" (correct faith) and "heresy" (false opinion) were differentiated regarding the Trinity and the Incarnation, while, on a more mundane level, appropriate bounds of Christian behavior were addressed.

With the exception of the writings of Irenaeus of Lyons, Augustine of Hippo, Cyrian, and Tertullian, the literature of the early Christian West was primarily one of translation; the theologically creative work of the period was done in the East, where most of the major heresies also originated. With some notable exceptions, the West accepted the Eastern definitions without discerning the gravity of the conflicts that produced them. By the beginning of the Middle Ages, however, these roles had reversed. Under the pressure of events, the deep well of Eastern creativity dried up and its primitive materials fossilized, leaving a heritage that remains highly venerated, indeed normative, to our own day. The West, however, continued to evolve intellectually and dogmatically.

Because opposing sides fought zealously to protect the salvation proclaimed in the Gospel from corruption or distortion, the ecumenical councils were rarely peaceful or unanimous. Arius' refutation of the divinity of Christ disappeared without a trace after a long and painful dispute following the councils of Nicaea (325) and Constantinople I (381); but the equally intense christological disputes that followed the definitions of Chalcedon (451) and Constantinople II (553) left permanent divisions. These are all the more lamentable as they occurred less for theological reasons than because of political (ultimately racial) tensions between the Greek elite and the other nationalities inhabiting the fringes of the Byzantine Empire. To this day most non-

Greeks of the East belong to one of two theological camps: the East Syrians are Nestorians, maintaining that in Christ the human and divine persons were not hypostatically (or personally) joined, as the Chalcedonians hold, but merely coexisted in Christ autonomously. Their West Syrian brethren, the Jacobites, together with the Armenians and Copts, reacting violently to that perceived error, maintain that there is but one nature *(mia physis)* in Christ, a fusion of God and man. Once termed Monophysites, these Christians now prefer to be referred to as Oriental Orthodox.

Today most theologians concede that the strictly theological divisions between these churches and the Chalcedonian (Eastern) Orthodox can be overcome. In fact, the divisions may well simply reflect two semantic approaches to a commonly understood reality, blown out of proportion by polemics. The real barrier to Eastern reunion is the psychological effect of long-term separation and mutual enmity; how does one proceed when each side's most beloved saints are the other's anathematized heresiarchs? Because there was little contact between these groups and the Chalcedonian Orthodox in America, we will discuss them separately.

Cultural divergence from the Latin West began virtually as soon as the empire was divided into two administrative halves, late in the fourth century. Byzantium, rediscovering its Hellenic past, increasingly looked eastward to the strategic regions of Georgia, Armenia, and Persia, then northward to the Balkans, where Byzantiums-in-miniature were created in Bulgaria and Serbia. Rome, at the same time, began abandoning the Greek language in favor of Latin and was overrun by barbarian hordes with whom it had to make its own cultural peace. As the ground of common heritage eroded, each side developed in isolation from the other; deepening differences went long unnoticed. Only the mission to the Slavs led by Sts. Cyril and Methodius in the ninth century caught the interest of both Old and New Rome, the latter ultimately the victor.

When the final estrangement did occur half a millennium later, it was every bit as passionate as the earlier Eastern schisms. Cessation of sacramental communion occurred a number of times over a variety of issues before the break, and 1054 (the customarily accepted date of the final schism) in reality marked just another minor rit-

ual dispute that had become overinflated. Most scholars today date the irrevocable division from 1204, the year of the infamous sacking of Constantinople during the Fourth Crusade. This betrayal by the papacy left in the Greek people a profound hatred for Rome that has little to do with theology.

The concrete differences that separate Rome from the Orthodox East were and are: (1) the Western addition of the *Filioque* ("and from the Son") to the Nicene-Constantinopolitan Creed, a phrase symptomatic of a mechanistic and scholastic approach to triadology (the doctrine of the Trinity) substantially different from the Eastern fathers' approach that emphasized concrete relationships among the three Divine Persons; (2) papal primacy, which developed very early but came to be insisted upon in the Middle Ages and dogmatized as infallibility only in 1870; it is symptomatic of an administratively centralized ecclesiology radically different from the decentralization policies of the East; (3) Purgatory, a doctrine reflecting an essentially pessimistic and Augustinian view of humanity and a mechanistic view of salvation that is radically different from the East's optimism in the face of divine grace; and (4) the twin Mariological dogmas of the Immaculate Conception (1854) and Assumption (1950), which also bear on basic anthropology (the doctrine of human nature) and soteriology (the means by which fallen nature was redeemed).

Lesser points of dispute have often proved even more divisive. The Roman imposition on Eastern-rite clerics in America of the distinctively Western requirement of celibacy for all clerical orders brought sharp reactions. While never denigrating celibacy as a vocation, the East since the eighth century has required it only of candidates for the episcopacy, reasoning that the bishop's task demands total dedication. Presbyters and deacons remain free to marry once before ordination and are even encouraged to do so because of the nature of their ministry.

Indeed, while many outward forms, such as the threefold ministry, seven sacraments, and a well-developed cult of Mary and the saints, have been preserved in both East and West since antiquity—facilitating modern ecumenical discussions—the content and understanding of those forms, indeed, the very ethos of the two communions, differ fundamentally. The long-standing questions concerning papal primacy and corporate reunion remain topics central to the history of the Eastern churches in America.

The ecumenical councils responded to the tremendous geographical growth of the church by redrawing ecclesiastical boundaries to parallel the secular and by ranking the episcopates according to the commercial and political importance of their sees. For organization's sake, a system of appellate and conciliar structures was established above the local bishop, without abrogating his sole responsibility for the spiritual life of his flock. The exalted titles of metropolitan, patriarch, and pope imparted to their holders a primacy of honor (primus inter pares) within their districts and at councils but invested no juridical authority in them, thus creating the characteristic decentralization of the Eastern churches.

Nonetheless, there were difficulties. The Council of Chalcedon (in its canon 28) responded to a new political reality by advancing the bishop of the upstart Eastern capital of Constantinople to a position ahead of Alexandria's pope and Antioch's patriarch. The resulting outcry can hardly be compared with that which echoed across the East when the Eternal City evolved an independent conception of primacy as universal jurisdiction and tried to exert it outside its traditional sphere of influence.

Over the centuries Rome in its concern for reuniting the separated, schismatic Eastern-rite Christians has insisted on their accepting this juridical primacy and the essential dogmas noted above. In return, according to the canons of the councils of Lyons (1274) and Florence (1438–1439), Uniate churches (those reuniting with Rome—hence the term Unia and its adjectival form Uniate; Uniate is used interchangeably with Eastern-rite Catholic and the preferred term Byzantine Catholic) would be allowed to retain their distinctive ritual practices. Large corporate unions have proved unfeasible, but the Maronites of present-day Lebanon (who in the fifth century followed the monk Maron into Monothelitism, a more radical form of Monophysitism, wherein the single nature of Christ [physis] had but a single, united will [thelema]) united with Rome in 1182; the Monophysite Armenians of Syria followed suit in 1198, the Nestorian Chaldeans in 1552, certain Orthodox Slavs over the sixteenth and seventeenth centuries (chiefly at the councils of Brest-Litovsk in 1596 and Uzhhorod in 1649),

and the Arab-speaking Chalcedonian-Orthodox Melkites of Lebanon in 1729.

SPREAD OF CHALCEDONIAN CHRISTIANITY

The "Easternness" of Chalcedonian Christianity was finally sealed with the fall of Constantinople to the Seljuk Turks in 1453. Byzantium's satellites in the Balkans yielded by the end of the century, and almost half a millennium of oppressive Ottoman rule began; theologically and culturally, it crippled the Eastern church from the Euphrates to the Danube. Sultans used the church, particularly the Ecumenical See, as an agency of secular rule. The patriarch became the millet pasha, and his moral prestige diminished even as his temporal power grew. Although all Christians were heavily taxed and arbitrarily maltreated—the Turks referred to them as rayah (cattle)—the Greeks' financial prowess won them a place in the administration of the Ottoman Empire, and from their quarter in Istanbul, the Phanar, their regime spread Grecophobia across the Balkans. To some degree, however, it can be said that the subject peoples were united by their faith, which came largely to be equated with and limited to sumptuous liturgical rites. Even as it sustained them, it fanned their hopes for national renewal.

In the wake of the Reformation and Counter-Reformation in the West, conditions worsened across the East as mutually hostile bands of missionaries vied for support among politically vulnerable hierarchs, proselytizing the masses of people and scholasticizing Orthodox theology itself. Large-scale Uniate movements developed in Polish- and Hungarian-controlled territories of eastern Europe and in the Middle East, embittering the masses further against everything foreign.

To the north, however, beyond Ottoman borders, the seeds of Christianity planted in the twilight of Byzantium flourished. Cyril and Methodius' work in the Balkans may not have long outlived them locally (being subverted by hostile German princes), but in 988 Kievan Rus' was converted and embraced the high traditions of the imperial court, its splendor and aesthetics in particular. Monasticism also flourished and produced missionaries who pushed north and eastward across Siberia toward the Arctic and, more important, to the Pacific. After a period of slavery to the Tatars not unlike the Ottoman oppression, the principality of Muscovy emerged as a "Third Rome," uniting the Russian lands. In 1448 Moscow unilaterally proclaimed its ecclesiastical independence (autocephaly) from besieged Constantinople; this was belatedly formalized in 1589 with the crowning of the first Patriarch of All Rus'. Patriarchal Moscow nurtured the morally ambiguous Byzantine concept of a "symphony" between church and state (usually to the former's detriment) until Peter the Great in 1721 swept it away in favor of a Western-style secular state in which the church formed but one "department." A Holy Ruling Synod, and its lay president, the *Ober Procurator,* replaced the patriarch.

Shortly afterward, French-inspired nationalism broke what little sense of unity had prevailed among the minority Christians in the multiethnic Balkan peninsula. A bewildering patchwork of autocephalous churches arose in often feuding territories. There, too, began World War I, whose revolutionary aftermath returned most of the Orthodox East to the age of the catacombs, renewed in the blood of the neo-martyrs, but forced as never before to sit silently and outwardly divided. Only in America were the churches completely free.

THEOLOGY AND LITURGY

The Eastern approach to all things is best summed up in the words of the Nicene Creed, "for us men and for our salvation." In distinction to the scholastic West, the East has never viewed Christianity as a subject for speculation; dogmas, often very bold ones, were promulgated only when some essential element of the faith was under attack. It is characteristic that even when forced to define an article of faith, the East preferred to take a negative *(apophatic)* approach. Thus, any positive statement about God is prefaced by a confession that human reasoning and language are radically incapable of expressing the fullness of God's nature or any of His attributes. For instance, God cannot be said to be good by our limited understanding of goodness; grasping, however, that He transcends goodness, we can boldly state that He is indeed good.

It is worthy of note at this point that the final challenge to such mysticism, the rise of humanism in the West, provoked the Greeks in the fourteenth century to their last great theological rally. St. Gregory Palamas risked charges of pantheism to defend the essential doctrine of hesychasm: that God does not remain isolated within His divine nature, but makes himself tangibly present to believers through the uncreated energies of His grace.

The universal and binding Tradition *(paradō-sis)* that Orthodoxy venerates thus represents the church's coming to understand with increasing profundity, and to steward with greater responsibility, the faith "once delivered unto the saints" (3 Jude). Although in late Byzantium, under the Turkish yoke, and in the Russian synodal period (1721–1917), an uncritical acceptance of established traditions was officially encouraged, the authentic Orthodox Tradition was by then a glorious and carefully wrought one.

Orthodoxy worships one God as He has chosen to reveal Himself in history: as three distinct yet equal persons, one of whom—the Son—is the Messiah looked for by the Jews and the *Logos* (word or reasoning) anticipated by the Greeks. He put on human nature in the womb of a virgin who is termed "Theotokos" (God-bearer), rather than simply "Christotokos" (Christ-bearer) as Nestorius insisted. Her glory is perfectly to "hear the word of God and keep it," and, in the words of the definition of Chalcedon, her Son is "one and the same Christ, Son, Lord, the Only-Begotten, in two natures without confusion, without change, without division, without separation." Her title thus safeguards His position as unique mediator between God and humankind.

Similarly, the Seventh Ecumenical Council in 787 warned that to worship *(latreuein)* icons is idolatry, yet boldly defended their relative veneration *(proskynēsis)*. This was not for aesthetic reasons, but because when God put on human nature in Jesus Christ, He accepted everything that pertains to that nature, including being depictable. To refuse to venerate an icon is, in the Eastern Orthodox view, to deny the concrete reality of the Incarnation and thus to endanger one's salvation.

The East views Christ's death and resurrection as returning creation to its proper relationship with God the Father; the Spirit He sent into the world from the Father continues the work of bringing it to perfection, or deification *(theōsis).* This daring use of an ancient Greek concept has never been fully understood or accepted in the West. The Christian's goal is not simply to escape God's juridical wrath (as Augustinian and later Thomistic theology, which defined Purgatory, contends), but to live in perfect unity with Him, beginning in this world.

This goal is effected through regular prayer and fasting, founded on and sustained primarily by the reception of the mysteries (sacraments in Western terminology) of baptismal regeneration and the "mystery of mysteries," Holy Communion. In chrismation, the newly baptized are granted the "seal of the gift of the Holy Spirit"; in confession (or penance), sinners are reconciled to the church; in marriage, ordination, and the anointing of the sick, God is perceived to be at work reinforcing the Christian life. In addition, a large number of rites sanctify individuals and the church at large throughout the year; they are excluded from the list of sacraments only because of the late influence of Western scholasticism. Most prominent among these is monastic tonsure, wherein a man or woman abandons this world for a celibate life consecrated to intensified prayer and fasting on behalf of all.

The East views the church as the Body of Christ, realized locally in the Eucharist presided over by the bishop. It interprets St. Cyprian of Carthage's *cathedra Petri* (seat of Peter) as being occupied by every bishop and believes that catholicity results from his representing his local community in the larger gatherings of all the bishops. Necessity has everywhere dictated that local communities be presided over by presbyters as the bishop's representatives, and the practice of true conciliarity has for centuries proved impossible in the East. Only now is it slowly, sometimes fitfully, reviving. The hierarchical principle of government has always been tempered by the requirement that the people accept all proclamations. A broad, though juridically undefined, responsibility of the laity for the preservation of the Orthodox faith lies at the base of the famous *Reply of the Eastern Orthodox Patriarchs* to Pope Pius IX in 1848.

Liturgy is what most Westerners think of when they hear of the Eastern church. It is verbally and ritually florid yet theologically sober. For successive centuries strong Hellenistic and monastic washes were applied over a Hebraic base until the liturgy achieved its present essential shape in the early ninth century. All strata have been overlaid, impasto-like, by interpretations that have tended to heighten the aura of mystery by making every ritual detail symbolic of something biblical or heavenly, often to the detriment of the original sense. Over adverse centuries, and in the Soviet bloc today, the liturgy has borne the full weight of Christian witness and life in a way few Westerners can imagine. As a result, it has grown conservative to the point of rigidity. A particular case can be seen in the evolution of what was once a spoken language into fossilized, hieratic forms that today vitiate the pastoral usefulness of celebrating in the vernacular.

Chalcedonians utilize two full divine liturgies, traditionally (but uncritically) ascribed to Sts. John Chrysostom and Basil the Great. During Lent, weekday communion is also distributed at a vesperal liturgy known as the Liturgy of the PreSanctified Gifts, attributed to Pope Gregory Dialogus. This represents quite a thinning of the original variety of Eastern eucharistic prayers, and it is fortunate for scholars and enriching for them that the Oriental Orthodox have preserved many of these. As in the Latin West all of the Eastern churches have a daily office consisting of vespers, compline, nocturns, matins, and the first, third, sixth, and ninth hours. Rarely are these performed outside of monasteries, however.

The great events of salvation history are celebrated liturgically throughout the year, some of the feasts falling on set dates, others depending on the movable date of the Christian Passover (in Greek *Pascha*—Easter), the Feast of Feasts. Fasting is more frequent and intense throughout the East than in the West, with four extended periods, led by the forty-seven days of Great Lent and Holy Week. Lesser events and individuals (often locally venerated) are also celebrated. These, together with regular Wednesday and Friday fasts, ideally give shape to the "time of our salvation," although secular society has lessened their influence.

The pre-Christian Julian calendar is still in effect in much of the Orthodox East; introduction of the "papist" Gregorian reckoning was staunchly resisted until the twentieth century, when business contacts made a change expedient for the governments of Orthodox nations.

The so-called Revised Julian calendar adopted by many Orthodox churches since 1923 coincides with the secular reckoning for the solar year but preserves its own rules for establishing the date of Easter.

Although the essential outlines of the Byzantine rite are the same everywhere, two monastic *typika* (books of rubrical prescriptions)—the Sabbite (553) and the Studite (789)—produce notably variant usages; in addition, the Ecumenical Patriarchate in this century has authorized a much-needed parish *typikon*. Ad hoc abbreviations and condensations are also widespread. In each nation that celebrates it, the Byzantine liturgy has taken on a unique temperament; this is clear in the rich variety of music and ritual practices that eventually made their way to America. At home, in isolation, these variants caused few problems; but abroad, ranging as they do from the severity of Turkish-influenced neo-Byzantine chants to florid polyphonic Russian compositions (influenced by Italian and German romanticism), they have proved divisive. Another example of localisms in conflict can be seen in the Latinisms that crept into the Byzantine rite among the Uniates. Such non-Eastern practices as bination (a cleric's celebrating several liturgies on a given day), confirmation by a bishop rather than chrismation by a priest, and obligatory clerical celibacy have caused consternation and conflict in America.

The essential unity of the Orthodox church, in spite of conflicts and paradoxes, is still evolving. But if unity comes and the false accretions finally fall away, it will be in America, for only here is Orthodoxy free.

EARLY PROGRESS OF ORTHODOXY IN AMERICA

Eastern Orthodoxy's initial contact with America brought minimal shock and disruption; it occurred in the far North Pacific under conditions very much like those of its traditional past. Although individual Orthodox Christians of various nationalities made their way to America in colonial times (and an organized Greek colony existed briefly at New Smyrna near St. Augustine, Florida, in 1768), no organized ecclesiastical work preceded the Russians' arrival on Alaskan shores. The Eastern church, unique among Christian bodies in America, proceeded from west to east.

As they had in the conquest of Siberia, Russian churchmen swept up the Aleutian Island chain in the wake of rapacious fur companies, which since 1743 had been regularly deployed in Alaskan waters. The first Eastern Orthodox liturgy in the Western hemisphere was served by naval chaplains on 20 July 1737. With rare exceptions, the initial contacts were tragic. Taking advantage of the laissez faire attitude prevailing in St. Petersburg, the *promyshlenniki* (hunter-adventurers, frontiersmen) profited greatly at the expense of the Native Americans. Some *promyshlenniki* used Christianity as a lever to gain loyalty; a few of the better-educated sincerely shared their ancestral faith, which quickly put down roots that proved to be tenacious throughout the islands.

In 1784 the merchant Gregory Shelikhov founded the town of Kodiak; ten years later he succeeded in convincing Empress Catherine and Metropolitan Gabriel Petrov of Novgorod and St. Petersburg that the civilization of the region could best be advanced by dispatching an ecclesiastical mission. Its ten monks were chosen from the Valamo and Konev missionary monasteries, which were famous for their strict asceticism. They arrived on 24 September 1794.

The monks' success was severely limited by natural hardships and personality clashes with the imperious but commercially invaluable governor, Alexander Baranov. They registered an impressive 6,740 baptisms in the first year but could do little to further Christianize the flock. The chief fruits of the Kodiak mission lie in the personal sanctity of the recluse monk Herman, who in 1970 was canonized as the first Orthodox saint in North America. Another member, Hieromonk (a monk ordained to the priesthood) Juvenaly Govorukhin, suffered the first martyrdom while penetrating inland. The mission's leader, Ioasaf Bolotov, returned to Russia for advancement to the episcopacy in 1799. When he tragically drowned during the return voyage to Kodiak, the work of the already foundering mission effectively ceased.

Evangelism did not resume until the 1820s, when it was undertaken by better-seasoned missionaries whose labors flourished. Preeminent among them was John Veniaminov. A true "Renaissance man," Veniaminov traveled widely for fifteen years in Unalaska and Sitka, personally helped the people build churches, mastered their languages (translating and writing in Aleut), and provided the first detailed scientific description of the region. In 1840 he was consecrated bishop of Kamchatka and the Kurile and Aleutian Islands, with his see in Sitka, and assumed the monastic name of Innocent. (In renouncing this world, monastics give up their surnames. And bishops are often referred to by their first names in Orthodox literature.) After another twenty-eight years of tireless ministry to the people of Alaska and the expanding Russian holdings in East Asia, he was elevated to the see of Moscow; there he founded the Russian Imperial Missionary Society. This organization supported the work in Alaska and the rest of North America until 1917. Innocent was canonized in 1978 in Moscow as the "Enlightener of the Aleuts and Apostle to America."

Under Innocent's guidance, and with co-workers like the first Creole priest, Iakov Netsvetov, the rudiments of Christianity were carried in diverse tongues to most of the Eskaleutian tribes and to some of the Indians inhabiting the islands and near hinterlands of Alaska, chiefly the Kenai Peninsula and the Kuskokwim and Nushagak river systems. A small outpost, Fort Ross, briefly challenged the Spaniards north of San Francisco from 1812 to 1844. A seminary was founded in Sitka in 1841 to foster a Native American clergy.

In 1867 Alaska was sold to the United States, and two decades of sharp institutional decline began for the church. Virtually all Russian subjects fled the territory. Support from Russia, which had always been limited, paled in the face of the systematic corruption that entered the territory with the American administration. Other factors were the well-organized and well-financed Protestant activities supervised by Sheldon Jackson and a determined policy of Americanization, which in reality amounted to little more than crude de-Russification.

An independent Diocese of Alaska and the Aleutian Islands was created on 10 June 1870, but a consistent hierarchical presence never developed. John Mitropolsky, who ruled it until 1876, felt drawn to San Francisco; his return to Russia for health reasons resulted in a destructive three-year interregnum. The arrival of Bishop Nestor Zakkis in 1879 brought zeal and

hope, but his drowning in the Bering Sea in 1882 initiated a second, six-year lapse. After 1888, when Bishop Vladimir Sokolovskii arrived, Alaska was increasingly neglected. Nevertheless, as a result of improved education and continued indigenization of the faith, combined with a well-rooted tradition of lay initiative for its preservation, almost all the Eskaleutians today are Russian Orthodox. After 1904 Alaska was administered as a special vicarate, served most illustriously for the first five years by Bishop Innocent Pustynsky.

The Alaskan church provided the ideological foundation of mission to all the peoples of the North American continent in their own tongues, including English. This concept, clearly enunciated by St. Innocent and practiced by his co-workers, is very much at odds with the decidedly non-missionary path Eastern Christianity subsequently followed.

With few exceptions the Eastern churches in the "Lower 48" and Canada have been preoccupied with caring for people from their respective homelands rather than with reaching out to strangers. For the Orthodox, this can be partly explained by an innate reluctance to return proselytism for proselytism; in large measure, however, it was forced upon them by the flood of immigrants that began in the 1880s, crested immediately before World War I, and subsided only with the passage of restrictive immigration laws in the 1920s.

In the earliest years parishes were formed in the ports of New Orleans (1864), San Francisco (1868), and New York (1870); they catered to all isolated Orthodox Christians in those localities, regardless of national origin. The cultured Bishop Vladimir Sokolovsky, in fact, widely encouraged the use of English and patronized the first translations by Nicholas V. Orloff of London. As numbers swelled toward the turn of the century, however, small ethnic ghettos turned into viable communities, and separation into closed ethnic parishes became the rule.

A few generalities apply to all the Eastern immigrants. They were poor but not desperately so; they were semiliterate but enamored of the word; they were drawn to the United States by the promise of quick riches, but political and religious oppression at times were an added incentive. The vast majority were young, male, and unattached. They came from the countryside but found work only in the cities. They arrived with little consciousness of nationality; ties of family, village, and region either drew them together or set them apart. Only as they grieved in isolation in America did they coalesce as larger entities. Knowing little English, their customary passion for arguing politics was displaced to religion. In some cases, diverging languages and cultures united people who differed over dogma (chiefly, the papacy); in others, those dogmatically united were torn apart.

For virtually all, New York was their port of entry and served as their major population center. Individuals then fanned out in search of relatives and employment in the coal, steel, and mill towns, primarily of Pennsylvania and Ohio, but also along the eastern seaboard, in New England, and in the Midwest. Chicago became a second major center.

The Greeks were less inclined than the Slavs and Rumanians to accept work requiring heavy manual labor; as petty merchants they climbed the economic ladder more quickly. The Arabs tended to become peddlers, spreading out far more thinly across the continent and assimilating more rapidly than any other Eastern immigrants.

Parish formation followed a common pattern. The oppressed masses in urban ghettos would congregate in their ethnic rooming houses, saloons, and coffeehouses, first to form mutual aid societies, then to organize a parish. They would either save to purchase land, build, and furnish a church, or they would buy an existing edifice from some already upwardly mobile group. Only then would they petition an Old Country bishop for a priest. The first such Eastern cleric was the Galician-born Byzantine Catholic (Uniate) Father John Volansky, summoned to Shenandoah, Pennsylvania, in 1884.

Although this lay initiative facilitated the building of churches and communities, it was destined to evolve into trusteeism, a variant of the American phenomenon of congregationalism, which challenged the very meaning of priestly ordination. It reduced the clergy to the status of hirelings and caused them decades of untold grief. By the time bishops began being regularly assigned to America, it was too late for the church—Orthodox or Byzantine Catholic— to return to its correct hierarchical polity. The clergy were further frustrated by the fact that the industrial workweek left no room for the traditional liturgical cycles that sustained the people.

This made the new arrivals easier prey than ever to the Protestants, who were willing to use any tactics to enlarge their own flocks.

Only the Russians had bishops in America from the start of the immigration, but after 1867 they were largely hierarchs without a flock since most early immigrants from imperial Russia were Jews or atheistic radicals. The situation began to change in the 1880s in a rather remarkable way.

The earliest Eastern Christians to emigrate en masse were Rusyns, Byzantine-rite Catholics (Uniates) from the Carpathian Mountains. They were primarily fleeing economic hardship, but political and religious oppression were also factors in Hungary after the revolution of 1867. Arriving here they found themselves looked down upon by both Protestants and Catholics, the latter's leaders even refusing to allow them to practice their Eastern rite. In the next three decades, frustration over this situation led some 400,000 of them to flee the Roman church in favor of their ancestral faith.

With very limited concern for the missionary significance of the shift, the Russians transferred their episcopal see from Sitka to San Francisco in 1872. There they were in a position to react to the plight of the Byzantine-Catholic Rusyn clergy, led by the fiery priest Alexis G. Toth. Toth had been assigned to the Minneapolis parish by the bishop of Prešov (now in Czechoslovakia), but as a married man he was refused authorization to serve as a priest by the Roman Catholic Archbishop John Ireland.

Though Orthodoxy in general eschews proselytism, it has always looked upon the Uniates as sheep led astray, and has endeavored to win them back from "Latin deception." The Holy Ruling Synod in St. Petersburg, through Bishop Vladimir Sokolovsky, was happy to receive the Minneapolis community in 1891. Thereafter a steadily growing number of other Rusyns converted (or defected) under Vladimir's successors, Nicholas Ziorov, Tikhon Bellavin, and Archbishop Platon Rozhdestvensky. The Vatican's inept handling of the Rusyns' demands for the appointment of a bishop and its failure to respect their legitimate traditions accelerated this movement. The culmination came in the 1907 publication of the bull *Ea semper,* which officially demanded celibacy of Uniate clergy in America, and the appointment of the sharply impolitic Bishop Soter Ortinsky. On both sides the years 1907 to 1917 were marked by increasingly vitriolic propaganda and by physical violence.

Massive growth required that the Russian mission shift its priorities. Bishop Nicholas recruited some remarkable people for the mission: Father Alexander Hotovitzky, dean of the New York Cathedral and editor of the diocesan newspaper, the *Russian-American Orthodox Messenger;* Archimandrite Raphael Hawaweeny, dean (later, bishop) of the Syro-Arab mission and editor of *al-Kalimat (The Word);* and Father Leonid (later, Leonty) Turkevich.

Tikhon, the most revered of the early bishops, surpassed his predecessor while continuing his policies. He placed full trust in these mission workers and utilized their talents and the mission's modest resources to the fullest. In 1905, to be nearer to the bulk of his flock, he transferred his see to New York, then established St. Tikhon's Monastery in South Canaan, Pennsylvania, and a seminary in Minneapolis. On the eve of his departure for a new assignment in Russia, Tikhon crowned his American career by returning the diocese to a conciliar form of government. This was a radically new departure in the postpatristic Orthodox world, but in keeping with the spirit of both American democracy and the traditional canonical understanding of the Eastern church. Tikhon presided at the first All-American Council held in Mayfield, Pennsylvania, in 1907. Composed of both clergy and laity, its immediate fruits may have been meager, but it established a tradition that spread to the other ethnic groups in America—and to the mother Russian church. At a council held ten years later in Moscow and closely modeled on the American experience, Tikhon was elected to the reestablished Patriarchate of Moscow.

Tikhon was also bold in advocating the establishment of a territorial Orthodox church in America, ethnically diverse yet jurisdictionally united. To this end, in 1904 he consecrated Raphael Hawaweeny as bishop for the Syro-Arabs, the first such consecration performed in America. Raphael was a remarkable man of great energy, patience, and tact, and his administration reflected the Tikhonian plan in an exemplary way. Candidates were similarly advanced, though not immediately consecrated, for the Serbs and the Albanians.

Although turn-of-the-century statistics are unreliable, Eastern Christians appear to have affiliated themselves as follows in North America:

Galicians and Rusyns: 250,000 Byzantine-Catholic, 12,900 Orthodox; Greeks: 50,000 Orthodox (Tikhon's 1905 report showed only 460 had affiliated with the Russian jurisdiction); Syro-Arabs: 38,300 Maronite Catholic, 20,000 Orthodox, 13,600 Melkite Catholic; Eskimos, Aleuts, Indians, and Creoles (in Alaska): 28,000 Orthodox, 1,260 Protestant, 170 Roman Catholic; Rumanians and Bukovinians: 8,000 Byzantine-Catholic, 6,000 Orthodox; Serbs and assorted Slavs: 11,000 Orthodox; Russians from the empire: 2,700 Orthodox; other nationalities (Estonians, Americans, Japanese, etc.): 128 Orthodox.

Most of the early Slavs and Rumanians came from Austria-Hungary; emigration from integral Orthodox lands (the Old Kingdom of Rumania, Serbia, Bulgaria, and Russia) began after World War I. Most of the Galicians (from Austrian-controlled lands) and Rusyns (from Hungarian-controlled lands) were born in the Unia.

Under Archbishop Platon the Russian mission's focus turned to social action, and an Immigrant Home and Orphanage were established. Platon's recall in 1914 was mourned throughout the diocese, but the arrival of Evdokim Meshchersky, who was pious as well as an activist, brought further growth. His arrival, however, was delayed by events stemming from the assassination of Archduke Franz Ferdinand in Sarajevo, Bosnia. World War I would radically change Eastern Christianity on the North American continent. Emigration from Europe and the Levant quickly grew impossible, and Americanist sentiment began to rise. In 1921 restrictive barriers became so tight that the Orthodox population was virtually frozen. Substantial growth resumed only after World War II.

One noteworthy trend in the period from Tikhon to Evdokim was the development of cordial relations with the Episcopal church. Sharing with Orthodoxy an aversion to both Roman and Protestant proselytism, Episcopalians helped the immigrant Orthodox in many ways. Their sponsorship of the New York Cathedral choir won for the Russians a rare favorable press and contact with persons of note in American religious and governmental circles. In turn, Russian choirs stimulated an interest in a cappella music in American Protestant churches. Among Orthodoxy's best friends in this period was Isabel F. Hapgood, translator of the *Service Book of the Holy Orthodox-Catholic Apostolic Church* (1906). Revised in 1922, it remained the essential book for English-speaking Orthodox until the 1970s.

BETWEEN THE WARS

The true watershed in the life of the Orthodox church in America came at the time of the Russian revolutions of February and November 1917. Subsidies were abruptly cut off and chaos ensued, not so much because of economic hardship but because the church was deprived of effective leadership. (That the 89,930 rubles received annually since 1897 was clearly insufficient for the 300,000-strong, 328-parish diocese is shown by Evdokim's 1916 request that the subsidy be raised to a million rubles.) Evdokim chose to remain in Russia after attending the Moscow Church Council of 1917–1918, leaving his well-meaning but weak vicar, Alexander Nemolovsky, in charge from 1918 to 1921. Four decades of progressive growth were crushed.

The non-Russian Orthodox had already begun to be alienated by Evdokim's rabidly nationalistic policies, but nothing had come of their appeals overseas. Now, faced with complete hierarchical collapse, their renewed pleas for protection to their respective Old World mother churches began to receive a hearing. Prior to the war, no overseas Orthodox church had seriously challenged the Russian jurisdiction in America, while some had shown remarkable indifference to the cries from across the Atlantic for pastors and bishops. Action, now clearly essential, could have but one result: the establishment of parallel ethnic jurisdictions, a clear violation of the basic territorial rule of Orthodox canon law requiring "one bishop in one city" (1 Nicaea: 8). Nevertheless, the 150,000 Serbs, organized into thirty-six communities, received a charter from the Belgrade hierarchy in 1921; their first bishop was Mardarije Uskokovich, named in 1927. From 1920 to 1921 their administrative leader had been the remarkable educator and spiritual author Bishop Nikolaj Velimirovich.

The Rumanians, with some forty parishes, were chartered in 1930 but received their first bishop from Bucharest, Polycarp Morusca, only in 1935; he ruled through 1939, when he was permanently marooned in Europe by the outbreak of war. In 1932 the Albanians, numbering 30,000 with three parishes, received their charter and a bishop, Fan Noli, who had returned after a short political venture as president of Albania. The Bulgarians, 1,000 strong with five parishes, were chartered by Sofia in 1938 under Bishop Andrey Velichky.

It was the separation of the 18,000 Syrians, however, that most clearly shows the tragedy of the breakup. Under the leadership of Archbishop Raphael they had been the showcase of the united American church. After Raphael's death in 1915, the visiting metropolitan Germanos Shehadi of Zahle in the patriarchate of Antioch illegally sought to succeed him. His followers, the so-called Antacky (pro-Antiochians), began to clash with the "Russy," led by Raphael's assistant, Aftimios Ofiesh. In 1917 the Russian synod authorized the consecration of Aftimios, but the able, over-idealistic bishop ruled only until 1933, when he married and was deposed. His administration was marred by open schism. Germanos' faction, which was publicly disavowed by the Antiochian patriarchate, was still able to hold eighteen parishes to Aftimios' thirty. There was also an abortive attempt at forming an autocephalous church backed by Platon, who meantime had been elevated to the rank of metropolitan in Russia and had returned to America. In 1922 the patriarch of Antioch dispatched first an official observer, Metropolitan Gerasimos Messara, then an official legate, Metropolitan Zacharias, who in 1924 consecrated Victor Abo-Assaley as the first archbishop of the Antiochian Orthodox Archdiocese of North America. Vicar Bishop Emmanuel Abo-Hatab succeeded Aftimios on the other side.

In 1934 hopes for reunion rose as all the principals died. These hopes were dashed, however, in 1936, when two groups of Russians, each without the knowledge of their metropolitan, simultaneously consecrated Antony Bashir in New York and his rival, Samuel David, in Toledo, Ohio. A chastened Russian hierarchy soon granted all groups their canonical release to Antioch, whose synod proved incapable of effecting a reconciliation.

The most important new foundation of the era was a hierarchy for the numerous and relatively affluent Greeks. Church growth had begun with the immigration to New York of Archimandrite Paisios Pheretinos in 1891. By 1900 the Greeks had only five parishes across the continent; subsequently, they grew briskly, with 57 in 1910 and 166 by 1921. Few parishes enjoyed regular ecclesial relations with the Russian hierarchy. Rather, as independent, lay-run communities, they hired and ruled priests sent over from Athens or Istanbul. In 1908 the Ecumenical Patriarchate, under Turkish pressure, relinquished all control over the Greek diaspora in favor of Athens, but that synod failed to respond to increasingly insistent calls for a bishop. It was 1918 before action was taken, and it came in the shrewd and enigmatic person of Meletios Metaxakēs.

Meletios, founder of the Greek Orthodox Archdiocese of North and South America, shared Tikhon's vision of a united American church, which he saw as having vast missionary potential, encompassing as it would some 2 million members. The two differed, however, on the question of who would lead this united church. Meletios wished to see it under the jurisdiction of Constantinople; he cited canon 28 of the Council of Chalcedon, which assigns to the Ecumenical See all "barbarian" lands lying outside the boundaries of an established autocephalous church. No other American Orthodox group was by this point willing to accept either Russian or Greek hegemony. Though weakened, the Russians challenged the move canonically, citing their priority on this continent.

In 1918 Meletios headed a commission sent to evaluate the American situation firsthand. He departed after establishing a synodal trusteeship, presided over by his vicar, Alexander Demoglou, bishop of Rhodostolou. In February 1921 Meletios returned to America, a political exile from his Athenian see; then on 25 November, he was surprisingly elected ecumenical patriarch. Before departing for Istanbul, he convened the first clergy/laity convention, established a short-lived theological school, and legally incorporated the archdiocese on 19 September. On 1 March 1922 he issued the patriarchal and synodal decree transferring jurisdiction over the diaspora to Constantinople. In 1923 two very able ruling bishops were consecrated to form an American synod: Philaretos Ioannides for Chicago, and Ioakeim Alexopoulos for Boston.

The mass of Greek-Americans, however, proved unable to unite behind Alexander. Meletios' political enemies in Athens (called Royalists because they supported King Constantine against his rebellious prime minister, Eleutherios Venizelos) set up a parallel exarchate headed by the noted preacher Metropolitan Ger-

manos Troianos; when the latter finally accepted recall in 1922, Vasileios Komvopoulos filled the vacuum among the Royalists, proclaiming himself for seven years the Unattached Metropolitan of America and Canada. Conflicts smoldered until a new generation emerged, disgusted with overseas political feuds. Providentially this communal change of heart coincided with the assignment of the dynamic and personable Archbishop Athenagoras Spirou in 1930 and the removal to Greece of all the feuding hierarchs.

Athenagoras' long American archpastorate, from 1930 to 1949, began with determined policies aimed at centralizing the archdiocesan administration. The other dioceses were demoted to the status of vicarates, church finances were regularized, and the priests' status in the parishes was notably elevated. These achievements came only at the personal cost of exhausting travel and long legal battles with schismatics led by Christophor Kontogeorge of Lowell, Massachusetts.

Athenagoras was also successful in promoting strong educational and philanthropic programs, at rallying Greek-Americans around their Hellenic heritage, and at elevating the prestige of Orthodoxy in American society. In this, the American Hellenic Educational Progressive Association (AHEPA; founded in 1922) led the way. A sign of Greek Orthodoxy's coming of age was Athenagoras' flight to Istanbul on President Harry Truman's private plane following his election to the ecumenical throne in 1949. He was, after Tikhon, the second American bishop to ascend a patriarchal throne.

With varying degrees of success the remaining Eastern churches followed these same lines in consolidating themselves between the wars. Early bishops moved to found monastic diocesan centers—the Serbian St. Sava Monastery in Libertyville, Illinois, in 1923, and the Rumanian Vatra Romaneasca in Grass Lake, Michigan, in 1937—and to use tireless travel and the written word to unite and enlighten their flocks. The conciliar principle was widely adopted, but it met with disdain or hostility in the Old Country when clergy and laity dared to nominate candidates to the episcopacy.

A general interest in professional clerical training reemerged in 1937–1938. The Russian St. Platon's Seminary in Tenafly, New Jersey, had failed after the Revolution, and an early Greek attempt in New York, St. Athanasios' Seminary, never won broad support. Again, no united effort was made. The Greeks entrusted to the learned Bishop Athenagoras Cavadas the founding of the Holy Cross Greek Orthodox School of Theology in Pomfret Center, Connecticut (moved in 1947 to Brookline, Massachusetts); the Russians, unable even to agree upon what level of education would best suit parishioners' needs, founded St. Vladimir's Theological Seminary (Academy) as a graduate school in New York City (moved in 1966 to Crestwood, New York) and attached a less ambitious pastoral school to St. Tikhon's Monastery in South Canaan, Pennsylvania. Parochial education and philanthropies in all these groups lagged far behind the efforts of the more affluent and organized Greeks.

In the 1930s two new waves of American Slavic Uniates returning to Orthodoxy resulted in the first advancement of Constantinople's jurisdiction beyond its Greek constituency. Both were rebelling against enforced celibacy and the abrogation of traditional ritualistic practices, set forth in Pius XI's bull *Cum data fuerit.*

The first group were Ukrainians, who in 1929 renounced the Unia and the next year elected Joseph A. Zuk as their bishop at a congress attended by Greek Vicar Bishop Kallistos Papageorgakopoulos. Kallistos subsequently arranged for a return of the Ukrainians to their pre-seventeenth-century status within the jurisdiction of the Ecumenical Patriarchate. Zuk was consecrated to the episcopacy in 1932 and endured a difficult two-year ministry, attempting to unify the Ukrainian diaspora.

His task was formidable, indeed, for a fiercely independent Ukrainian church had existed in Canada since 1918, serving half a million immigrants. Most had arrived as Greek Catholics, but a good number converted to Orthodoxy under the Russian mission, only to endure bitter neglect. Orthodox and Uniate alike fell prey to the unscrupulous followers of the usurper "metropolitan" Serafim (Stefan Ustvol'skyi) at the turn of the century. The first Uniate bishop, Nykyta Budka, from 1912 until 1927 encountered problems with his flock similar to those of Soter Ortinsky in the United States. Ultimately, however, it was revolution in the homeland that determined the future of the Ukrainian church in Canada.

Exceedingly strong renovationist and auto-

cephalist movements rocked the Ukraine following the Bolshevik victory in 1921. Loyalties were divided between canonical principles and ethnic unity when, deprived of bishops by the Moscow Patriarchate, one faction, led by Vasyl Lipkivs'kyi, resorted to the canonically invalid Alexandrian method of consecrating bishops (presbyters laying on hands). They were promptly cut off from the body of world Orthodoxy. John Teodorovich, one of the self-consecrated *(samosviaty),* was dispatched by this faction in 1924 to North America. He found numerous compatriots who had withdrawn from the Russian mission in 1919. He headed both the Canadian and American churches until 1949, when he relinquished Canada, where sentiments ran high against his submitting to "reconsecration" in a vain attempt to regularize his status. The bishops he recruited to perform the rite, coupled with his refusal to disavow the principle of presybterial consecration or to reordain his clergy, left the clergy suspect, and they are still not in communion with other canonical Orthodox bodies.

The second group to leave the Unia in this period were Rusyns (Carpatho-Russians) led by the priest Orestes Chornock. He, too, refused to lead his flock into the Russian archdiocese, which he justly charged with the cultural absorption of the Rusyns it had earlier accepted. Turning instead to the ecumenical throne, Chornock was consecrated there in 1938. His American Carpatho-Russian Orthodox Greek Catholic Diocese in the U.S.A. was granted broad autonomy. It founded its own seminary, Christ the Saviour, in Johnstown, Pennsylvania, in 1951.

Constantinople's hegemony was further extended in the post–World War II era when the Russians' experience of political division became common to all Americans from eastern Europe. A group of Albanian-Americans was accepted in 1950, their homeland having been declared the first totally atheistic state in the world and their hierarchy destroyed; a year later the Byelorussian Council of Orthodox Churches in North America was received. The Russian churches here were too weak to make more than feeble, unsuccessful overtures to these Slavs to abandon Constantinople.

The old Russian missionary archdiocese had, since 1905, called itself the Russian Orthodox Greek Catholic Church of America, reflecting the fact that 60 percent of its constituency were former Byzantine-Catholics. It came to be known as the Metropolia when Platon Rozhdestvensky, then metropolitan of Kherson and Odessa and one of the most respected of Russian hierarchs, returned to America in 1921. Acquiescing to calls that he take up the slack reins from Archbishop Alexander, he was acclaimed metropolitan of All-America and Canada at the extraordinary Third All-American Council in Pittsburgh in 1922. Platon's second American administration, from 1922 to 1936, faced economic disaster from the start, but even this crisis paled before substantial challenges stemming from the canonical irregularity of his second appointment.

The first challenge came from his vicar for the Rusyns, Stephen Dzubay, who led a vitriolic but brief rebellion in 1922. This particular rift was healed, but Dzubay himself returned to the Unia. Archbishop Adam Philippovsky, in concert with Moscow, continued to lead strong Rusyn opposition to the Metropolia.

A second battle had its roots in Bolshevik Russia. There a group of clergy split from Patriarch Tikhon, declared him deposed, and proceeded to introduce a number of liturgical and canonical innovations, among them the consecration of married men to the episcopate. This group soon fragmented into a number of movements and sects, commonly referred to as the Living Church. One faction was led in Moscow by America's former archbishop, Evdokim. In 1923 the Living Church dispatched a married metropolitan to America, the renegade and formally suspended and excommunicated mission priest John Kedrovsky. He enjoyed marked success in obtaining from American courtrooms title to the 115 Russian parishes founded before 1917. Platon's followers then changed their incorporation papers to exclude the central church authority, thus strengthening the already rampant congregational principle. Only a generation of tough-minded priests kept the Russian church alive in this period.

Little respite came when the Living Church movement collapsed in the 1930s, for the Moscow patriarchate, under its substitute *locum tenens*, Metropolitan Sergii Stragorodsky, had survived the Bolshevik terror only at the price of moral compromise. It began to press Platon to accept its jurisdiction. He and most of his followers refused to enter communion with an authority they perceived to be a puppet of the godless Bolshevik powers, and they proclaimed temporary autonomy at the Fourth All-American Council in Detroit (1924). Sergii retaliated by interdicting them and establishing in 1933 a parallel Patriarchal Exarchate of the Aleutian Islands and North America under Archbishop (later Metropolitan) Benjamin Fedchenkov. Undaunted, subsequent All-American Councils of the Metropolia confirmed this temporary autonomy in 1935 (Cleveland), 1937 (New York), 1946 (Cleveland), 1950, and 1955 (both in New York).

Nor was Moscow the sole, or even the chief, source of trouble for Platon. A group of Russian hierarchs forced by the Bolsheviks to flee their sees in southern Russia gained sanction from the Ecumenical Patriarchate to care for their compatriots in Istanbul. When they sought to extend their authority beyond this tiny constituency, however, they were rebuffed and forced to accept the only sanctuary offered them: by the patriarch of Serbia. From headquarters in Sremski Karlovci, Yugoslavia, they proclaimed themselves a Russian Orthodox Church Outside of Russia (commonly abbreviated as the Synod in Exile). Led by the renowned archconservative theologian Metropolitan Anthony Khrapovitsky, they fought to preserve the unity of the entire Russian diaspora from Manchuria to North America, pending what they saw as the inevitable fall of the usurper Bolshevik regime. This plan disregarded the reality of a well-established (if presently impoverished) American church possessed of a history, practices, and destiny of its own. Platon's initial cooperation with the Karlovci hierarchs proved his undoing, for they interpreted it as juridical subjection, and his withdrawal from the council in 1923 resulted in the final establishment of yet another Russian hierarchy in North America, the Synod in Exile, which was led from 1926 until his death in 1933 by Platon's former vicar, Apollinary Koshevoy.

The key to the bewildering Russian situation in these years lies in the preparations the church felt obliged to make at the Moscow Council of 1917–1918 in order to protect itself against Bolshevik attack. First, secrecy was invoked in a complex plan to render the central administration of the church invulnerable to liquidation through a succession of *locum tenentes* to the patriarchal throne. Second, provisions for decentralization—radical even by Orthodox standards—were countenanced in November 1920 in Tikhon's famous Ukase No. 362. He ordered bishops cut off from the central church administration to organize temporary organs of local conciliar government. While Tikhon was imprisoned, the *locum tenens* Agafangel broadened this order further to allow temporary autocephalies in areas unlikely to restore communications with Moscow. After Patriarch Tikhon's death in 1925 *locum tenens* Sergii advanced the suggestion that Russians in heterodox lands ally with Orthodox of other ethnic backgrounds to form local churches. Together, these two opposing approaches saw the Russian church through to relatively better days, but confusion was virtually ensured.

Tikhon was determined to preserve the viability and autonomy of the American church. He accepted the popular will first by confirming Alexander's election as archbishop of North America by the Second All-American Council in Cleveland (1919). Then, when Alexander's leadership proved inadequate and Platon was elected metropolitan, the patriarch relieved Platon of his duties in Kherson and Odessa in order to free him for a second administration in America. By 1922, however, the Bolsheviks' tactics had isolated Tikhon from the outside world, and confirmation of Platon's election had to be transmitted through the irregular (but not unprecedented) method of oral communication via reliable channels. Someone in Metropolia circles, however, did Platon a great disservice by trying to assist the process by forging an official ukase. This forgery was skillfully exploited by Dzubay, Kedrovsky, and the synod in Karlovci.

Tikhon and the church inside the Soviet Union found themselves consistently endangered by the anti-Bolshevik statements made by emigré churchmen. Eventually the patriarch sincerely wished to eschew political involvement, and he ordered the radical Karlovci administration disbanded. Following Tikhon's death in 1925, his most moderate followers, led by Metropolitan Sergii, sought to advance their position by further appeasement of the regime. They were afforded just enough freedom to claim with some credibility that communications with Moscow were once again possible and, therefore, that all temporary arrangements were annulled. Though virtually no Russian-Americans wanted to break with their mother church, very few found it possible to accept the loyalty to the Soviet state as demanded in Sergii's infamous 1927 *Declaration.* Platon and the Karlovci bishops found themselves among the rebels and were duly interdicted.

In 1935 the shared anti-communism of Platon's and Apollinary's followers allowed them to overcome their competition briefly following their leaders' deaths within a few months of each other. Platon was succeeded as metropolitan by one of the "old missionaries," Theophilus Pashkovsky. This more malleable hierarch signed a temporary statute of agreement with Karlovci. The Metropolia's rank and file consistently understood this agreement as merely a loose federation in which they would retain full autonomy. From 1936 until the agreement was canceled in 1946, a single episcopal synod under Theophilus (and incorporating Apollinary's dual successors, Archbishop Vitaly Maksimenko in New York and Tikhon Troitsky in San Francisco) governed the American church, although at the parish level jurisdictional conflicts continued. In fact, the small Karlovci faction in America took advantage of the peace to consolidate itself, founding in 1935 the Holy Trinity Monastery in Jordanville, New York. In 1947 the monastery became the home of the St. Job of Pochaev Press, which had enjoyed great success in anti-Uniate apologetics in the Carpathian Mountains. To this day it remains one of the world's premier publishers of Russian religious materials. A theological seminary was added to the monastery in 1948.

In 1946 relations ruptured between the Metropolia and the Synod in Exile. While the Karlovci hierarchs (transferred to Munich during the war) remained adamantly opposed to any discussions with the Bolshevik-controlled Moscow Patriarchate, the Metropolia had taken advantage of the ostensibly legal patriarchal elections in Moscow to make new overtures to the mother church. These proved premature, and visits from the Soviet Union by Archbishop Aleksey of Yaroslavl in 1945 and Metropolitan Gregory of Leningrad in 1947 failed to bring the Metropolia back into the fold. Suspicions (particularly of Gregory) still ran high among the emigrés, although Sergii's impossible political demands had by then been officially dropped.

The Metropolia remained the largest Russian

jurisdiction, with some 750,000 faithful organized in 220 parishes. Five diocesan bishops oversaw an essentially Tikhonian plan of conciliar government. The Patriarchal Exarchate had some 50,000 adherents, organized in 40 parishes. The Synod in Exile attracted fewer members still. Court battles between the Metropolia and the Synod over individual parishes were frequent.

POST–WORLD WAR II

The Soviet-American wartime alliance, augmented by Stalin's utilitarian relaxation of restrictions on the Russian church, brought a surge of enthusiasm to Russian-Americans. The Exarchate rode this mood successfully in the postwar years, claiming a number of clergy and parishes from both the Metropolia and the Synod. In 1950, led by Metropolitan Anastasy Gribanovsky, the post-Karlovci Synod, which had spent the war years in Munich, moved its headquarters to New York. Here it attracted a number of displaced persons who had suffered under communism and who found the Metropolia parishes too Americanized for their tastes.

Theophilus' death in 1950 brought to the metropolitan see the already aged Leonty Turkevich. He had been one of the workhorses of the early church in America, first dean of the Minneapolis seminary, a renowned educator and publicist, and architect of the autonomy arrangement. Despite the fact that a number of conservative bishops and clergy accepted his jurisdiction and partially re-Russianized the Metropolia, the years of his primacy generally prepared the way for a permanent autocephaly. In 1965 Philaret Voznesensky succeeded Anastasy as metropolitan of the Russian Synod in Exile.

Under Philaret this jurisdiction has adopted an increasingly strident stance in opposition to the Moscow Patriarchate, the Gregorian calendar, the ecumenical movement, and "modernism" in general. At present it enjoys regular relations with no other Orthodox church in America. In 1986 Philaret was succeeded by the equally conservative Vitaly Ustinov.

The 1950s brought a new influx of highly political, virulently anti-Communist displaced persons from all over eastern Europe. Charges of Communist control of the hierarchies at home were met by countercharges of canonical insubordination and formal interdictions, long commonplace among the hapless Russians. The postwar era has been marked, first of all, by the growth of parallel political jurisdictions.

The majority of Rumanian-Americans, bishopless since the forced detention of Bishop Polycarp in Rumania after 1939, and frustrated in attempts to elect Bishop Antim Nica as successor, unilaterally proclaimed full autonomy for their diocese in 1950. A minority faction, however, elected and obtained patriarchal consecration for Andrei Moldovan as their bishop.

A church council the following year formally rejected Moldovan, together with all administrative ties to the mother country, and elected as their bishop an energetic immigrant theologian/journalist, Valerian D. Trifa. In the face of opposition from Bucharest, Valerian had to seek consecration in 1952 from the uncanonical Teodorovich faction. In 1960 he regularized his situation by accepting the then still dubious canonical protection of the Russian Orthodox Greek Catholic Church in America. His Romanian Orthodox Episcopate of America has grown to be one of the most stable and progressive church structures in the Western hemisphere. Opposition has come from the Romanian Orthodox Missionary Archdiocese in America and Canada, headed since 1966 by Victorin Ursache. There have also been persistent—and ultimately successful—media attacks and legal proceedings against Archbishop Valerian based on charges that he was involved in Rumanian fascism before and during World War II. The Ecumenical Patriarchate, on strictly legal grounds, favored the minority Bucharest faction, and the head of the Greek Orthodox archdiocese, Archbishop Iakovos, presided at Victorin's consecration. In 1985 Valerian was succeeded by an American-born bishop, Nathaniel Popp.

The Bulgarian Bishop Andrey was somewhat more fortunate than Rumania's Polycarp. He returned to America in 1945 as a metropolitan and incorporated the Bulgarian Eastern Orthodox Diocese of America, Canada, and Australia in 1947. At the same time an assembly broke administrative ties with Sofia, and the Bulgarian exarchate predictably suspended Andrey. His followers as predictably ignored the order, and peace was restored only in 1962. A year later this reconciliation sparked an anti-Communist rebellion by half the parishes, led by Archimandrite Kyrill Yonchev. He was consecrated in 1964 by the Russian Synod in Exile, remaining in opposition to Andrey and Sofia. In 1976 he led his parishes into the autocephalous Orthodox Church in America, which had meanwhile been established by agreement between Moscow and the Russian Metropolia.

Authentic tragedy befell the Serbian-Americans in 1963, when the Holy Synod in Belgrade summarily suspended its vicar here, Dionisije Milivojevich, and created three geographic dioceses on the North American continent. Dionisije declared the action uncanonical and prejudiced, and proceeded to form a parallel Free Serbian Orthodox Diocese. Lawsuits over properties cost millions of dollars and created the most intense antagonisms that exist among Orthodox Christians today. The U.S. Supreme Court in 1976 finally decided in favor of the authentic Orthodox hierarchical principle adopted by the Belgrade majority.

Dionisije has at times been allied with Teodorovich's Ukrainians and with Greek dissidents, and he was briefly accepted into the Alexandrian patriarchate. The Russian Synod in Exile's lingering gratitude to the Belgrade patriarchate for providing its long refuge in Karlovci has, ironically, prevented the unity of these ideologically identical groups.

This same synod of Belgrade in 1960 initiated a mission among Macedonian-Americans who had previously attended Bulgarian churches. In 1963 Archbishop Dositei emigrated from Ohrid, and in 1967 was named their metropolitan. Fan Noli's Albanian Orthodox Archdiocese in America similarly split in 1950, some remaining loyal to him and the mother church, while others followed Constantinople's Bishop Mark I. Lipa. Noli had long been a pioneer for English and pan-Orthodox unity, and in 1971 his personally chosen successor, Stephen V. Lasko, brought his diocese into the new Orthodox Church in America.

Two postwar emigré bodies also arrived en masse to further complicate Ukrainian matters: the Ukrainian Autocephalous Orthodox Church in the United States, under Archbishop Hrihoriy Osiychuk, in 1950, and the Holy Ukrainian Autocephalic Orthodox Church in Exile, under Metropolitan Polycarp Sikorsky, in 1954. After

World War II, the Moscow Patriarchate made an unsuccessful bid to wrest from Constantinople the followers of Bishop Zuk's successor, Bishop Bohdan T. Shpilka, who had been consecrated by the Ecumenical Patriarchate in 1937. Under Shpilka's leadership the flock quadrupled in size; in 1966 he was succeeded by Andrey Kuschak.

The Teodorovich Ukrainians, meanwhile, were moving further to establish themselves. Metropolitan Mstyslaw Skrypnyk and the renowned scholar Ilarion Ohienko provided stable leadership and made overtures to the Ecumenical Patriarchate for rapprochement. Among the most notable efforts of the Canadian group was the founding in 1955 of St. Andrew's Theological College in Winnipeg, long the only Ukrainian Orthodox seminary for the training of clergy in the diaspora.

Similar is the case of the Byelorussians, who began emigrating in very small numbers only in 1950. They, too, were led by men of strong autocephalist and nationalist leanings, and their hierarchies proved unstable. Autocephaly was proclaimed in Byelorussia in 1925, but the hierarchs were deported to Siberia two years later. Only under German occupation did the church revive, and it seceded from the Moscow Patriarchate in 1946. Archbishop Sergii Okhotsenko formed a synod in exile in Konstanz, Germany, in 1948. In 1951 Bishop Vasily Tamashchyk immigrated to America to head the European-American diocese. Finally, four scattered Byelorussian parishes with immigration experiences differing from the rest have sought refuge in the Ecumenical Patriarchate.

Greece and the Middle East, though threatened, were spared a Communist takeover, so their American flocks should have weathered the postwar storm of division. The Greeks for the most part did. Some Old Calendarist and anti-Athenagoras schisms stemming from the 1920s persisted, but feebly. The Greek archdiocese moved into the forefront of American Orthodoxy under the dynamic Archbishop Athenagoras, his successor in 1949, the cultured and spiritual Michael Constantinides, and the present archbishop, Iakovos Coucouzes. Youth work was promoted under Michael with the publication of the first serious Sunday School materials and the formation of a national organization, the Greek Orthodox Youth of America (GOYA). Holy Cross School of Theology began to flourish. English began to be introduced, though against the Patriarchate's expressed will. Iakovos was granted the additional title of Patriarchal Exarch Plenipotentiary, and in 1978 the archdiocese was granted a new decentralized charter by the Patriarchate. The archbishop now heads a synod of seven bishops ruling geographically authentic dioceses. This marks a return to the canonical appearance of a local territorial church, which the Greeks enjoyed prior to 1930, but true autonomy such as Alexander had sought —and largely enjoyed—was strictly avoided.

Antiochian loyalties remained divided between Antony Bashir and Samuel David. When the latter died in 1958, the Patriarchate, over Bashir's strenuous objections, consecrated Michael Shaheen to succeed him in the see of Toledo. Bashir, who stabilized his archdiocese, lived to see it acclaimed the most progressive branch of American Orthodoxy, uniquely devoted to missionary endeavors and youth education with its own Syrian Orthodox Youth Organizations (SOYO). He was succeeded in 1966 by Philip Saliba, who continued and built on the Bashir legacy. In 1975 Philip negotiated the reunion of the two factions as the Antiochian Orthodox Christian Archdiocese of North America. Archbishop Philip has been one of the most consistent and insistent spokesmen for a strong and united American Orthodoxy.

Fortunately, the postwar period has not been entirely one of creeping disunity for the Eastern Orthodox. In the late 1950s and 1960s Antony Bashir, Iakovos, and Metropolitan Leonty succeeded in resurrecting the Tikhon/Meletios vision of a united American Orthodoxy. The realization that equal religious rights for Eastern Orthodox servicemen had been gained during the war only through a united effort provided practical incentive. Although the cry of "fourth major faith" represented a perversion of basic Orthodox ecclesiology, clergy and laity had succeeded in gaining such recognition in most states and by the federal government. In 1957 Archbishop Michael became the first Orthodox hierarch to be invited to offer prayers at a presidential inaugural.

On a more profound level, in 1960 the Standing Conference of Canonical Orthodox Bishops in the Americas (SCOBA) was founded. Jurisdictional rivalries marred its early years, and the fact that it was never taken seriously by most of the

mother churches prevented its evolving organically into the local synod hoped for. Nevertheless, its practical subcommittees, most notably the Campus Commission and the Orthodox Christian Education Commission (OCEC), have made remarkable advances. In 1968 SCOBA officially petitioned the Inter-Orthodox Committee meeting in Chambésy, Switzerland, to consider the irregular and counterproductive condition of Orthodoxy in the diaspora but was sharply rebuffed.

The Russian Metropolia, meanwhile, finding itself at odds within SCOBA and the rest of world Orthodoxy over its continued schism with Moscow, in 1968 under Metropolitan Ireney Bekish opened direct negotiations with the Patriarchate for autocephaly. An agreement was struck on 12 April 1970, and the Orthodox Church in America (OCA) came into being. Its canonicity was violently challenged by Patriarch Athenagoras in Constantinople and the other ancient patriarchates, and to this day it enjoys, at best, only tacit acceptance by world Orthodoxy. The *Tomos* (decree) of autocephaly, recognizing that long-standing antagonisms could not quickly be overcome, made provisions for exarchal parishes to remain temporarily under Moscow's canonical protection through a vicar bishop resident in New York. The Patriarchal Exarchate, however, was officially dissolved. The Synod in Exile rejected the move absolutely and succeeded in winning the allegiance of several Metropolia parishes.

At the Fifth All-American Council of the Orthodox Church in America in 1977, Metropolitan Ireney retired, and Orthodoxy's first American-born primate, Theodosius Lazor, was elected to succeed him. In 1980 his see was transferred to Washington, D.C., the capital of the country. In 1981 bilateral discussions on unity were initiated between the Orthodox Church in America and the Antiochian archdiocese, the two jurisdictions most clearly sharing a missionary outlook.

The presence of autonomous Rumanian, Albanian, and Bulgarian archdioceses in this jurisdiction; and of non-Greek bodies (Ukrainian, Carpatho-Russian, and Albanian) under Constantinople; and even of a few non-Russians (Rumanians, Greeks, and for a while Bulgarians) finding refuge from modernism in the Russian Synod in Exile—all point to the feasibility of the early plan of unity. Additional support is given by the postwar expansion of the Russian St. Vladimir's Seminary into a pioneer pan-Orthodox institution under deans Georges Florovsky and Alexander Schmemann, the pan-Orthodox Orthodox Theological Society of America (OTSA), and the Orthodox Inter-Seminary Movement (OISM). Pan-Orthodox gatherings on the first Sunday of Great Lent have become a thriving American tradition.

Most would agree today that while canonical unity is necessary, concerns over the mechanics of achieving it while preserving cherished ethnic diversity loom over the current scene. In this regard, some attention should be given to the abortive attempt at autocephaly made in the 1930s by Archbishop Aftimios Ofiesh, backed initially by Metropolitan Platon. Although roundly repudiated at the time by everyone except the Syrians, Ofiesh's *Constitution of the Holy Eastern Orthodox Catholic and Apostolic Church in North America* (1928) is a measured and reasonable document that warrants careful consideration sixty years later.

CURRENT DISTRIBUTION OF EASTERN CHRISTIANS

Today some 3.5 million Orthodox Christians reside in North America, divided into the following jurisdictions: (1) the Greek Orthodox Archdiocese of North and South America with 2 million nominal members organized in 579 parishes. Its mother church, the Ecumenical Patriarchate, through its exarch in America, also cares for the American Carpatho-Russian Orthodox Greek Catholic Church (100,000 members in 70 parishes), the Albanian Orthodox Diocese of America (6,000 members in 7 parishes), and the Ukrainian Orthodox Church of America (30,000 members in 23 parishes); (2) the autocephalous Orthodox Church in America with 1 million nominal members in 440 parishes; it bears canonical responsibility for three so-called ethnic archdioceses: Archbishop Valerian's Rumanians (50,000 members in 44 parishes), Archbishop Fan Noli's Albanians (40,000 members in 15 parishes), and Bishop Kyrill's Bulgarians (105,000 members in 18 parishes); (3) the Antiochian Orthodox Christian Archdiocese of New York and North America with 250,000 mem-

bers in 125 parishes; (4) the Serbian Eastern Orthodox Church with 50,000 members in 72 parishes.

Parallel with these groups are: (5) the Bulgarian Eastern Orthodox Church, loyal to the patriarch in Belgrade (105,000 members in 18 parishes); (6) the Patriarchal Parishes of the Russian Orthodox Church in the U.S.A., formerly the Exarchate (61,000 members in 65 parishes); (7) the Romanian Orthodox Episcopate of America under Bucharest (40,000 members in 34 parishes).

In addition, there exist a number of bodies not in communion with SCOBA, accounting for some 445,000 members. Largest among these are the Ukrainian Orthodox Church of the United States of America (100,000 members in 105 parishes), the Russian Orthodox Church Outside of Russia (Synod in Exile) (86,000 members in 138 parishes), the Free Serbian Diocese (75,000 members in 55 parishes), and, by far the largest Orthodox church in Canada, the Ukrainian Greek-Orthodox Church in Canada (150,000 members).

Relations between these churches and those of Eastern-rite Catholicism (or Byzantine-Catholic or Uniate) in North America are, in the wake of Vatican II, less strained than in the early days —although worldwide the Orthodox continue to take offense at and challenge the very raison d'être of the Unia. Rome, on the contrary, views it as a potential bridge to the East, and has grown more considerate in respecting the integrity of the various rites and sensibilities of the peoples. The most notable exception is that the Uniate churches are still forbidden a married clergy in America. For all nationalities, conversions back and forth are now mostly individual decisions and stir little rancor. There are today some 800,000 Eastern-rite Catholics in the United States and 220,000 in Canada. Roman discipline has largely prevented the kind of political fragmentation among them that we have seen among the Orthodox, although jurisdictionally they are divided along strictly ethnic lines into eleven groups, five having their own ordinaries (ruling bishops).

The 23,000 Melkites have 28 parishes. The first was founded in 1896 in Lowell, Massachusetts; most of the rest date from 1910 to 1930. Metropolitan Maximos Sayegh visited America in 1921 as the first of many patriarchal delegates, but opposition from the Latin hierarchy prevented his staying. At the end of Sayegh's own patriarchate in 1966, the first permanent Melkite exarch was appointed, Justin A. Najmy. Upon his death in 1968 there was some controversy between Damascus and the Congregation for the Eastern Churches in Rome before the principles of succession were worked out and the present exarch, Joseph Tawil, was appointed archbishop in 1969. Relations among the Arabs, Orthodox and Melkite, are closer than in any other ethnic group. The Maronites, now 30,000 in 50 parishes, also received their first exarch, Francis M. Zayek, in 1966.

Because the early history of the Eastern Slavs, Orthodox and Catholic, was so closely intertwined, we have dealt with them together. Following the death of Soter Ortinsky, Rome sought to eliminate ethnic tensions between Galicians (or Ukrainians, as they came increasingly to call themselves) and the Rusyns by dividing them into two dioceses. Constantine Bohachevsky led the Ukrainians, and Basil Takach the Rusyns. Today the Uniate Ukrainian province of Philadelphia, some 285,000 members in 240 parishes, is divided into three eparchies. Another Ukrainian diocese, in Canada, enjoys jurisdiction over all other Eastern bodies there; total membership is 240,000 in 240 parishes. The Ruthenian province of Munhall, Pennsylvania, counts 281,000 (incorporating the Slovaks, Hungarians, and Croatians) in 255 parishes; since 1983 it has been divided into four eparchies. Finally, 10,000 Catholic Armenians in 6 parishes have since 1981 been headed by their own exarch, Nerses Mikael Setian.

Other Eastern-Catholic bodies—Chaldeans, Italo-Albanians, Rumanians, Russians, Syrians, and Byelorussians—totaling some 10,000 faithful in 10 parishes, find themselves under the jurisdiction of local Latin ordinaries.

Contact between the 140,000 non-Chalcedonian Eastern Christians living in North America and the Orthodox and Catholic Byzantines has been slight. Of them all, the Armenians shared the closest cultural ties with Byzantium, and their tragic development in the New World closely parallels that of their Chalcedonian brethren.

Armenians began arriving in the United States in the 1880s, but growth was most rapid following the Turkish massacres of 1895–1896, 1909,

and 1914–1915. Their first priest was sent over in 1888. Housep Sarajian was subsequently appointed their first bishop as well; he ruled here from 1898 until 1906. Sharp factionalism led to his resignation, and a progression of *locum tenentes* attempted to cope with accelerated parish growth.

Incorporation of Armenia into the Soviet state in 1921 led to familiar political splits here. The largely autonomous Armenian Church in America was founded by the Catholicos (Patriarch) of Etchmiadzin in 1931 and headed by the unpolitic Archbishop Ghewont Tourian. In 1933 a formal split occurred, with Tourian defrocking some anti-Soviet nationalist clergy; shortly afterward he was assassinated in his cathedral. The nationalists formed the Armenian Apostolic Church of America, which had to wait until 1956 to receive recognition from the emigré Catholicos of Cilicia in Lebanon. Now headed by Archbishop Torkom Manoogian, the Etchmiadzin jurisdiction is about twice as large as the other, under Bishop Karekin Sarkissian. Together they have some 300,000 adherents in 96 parishes.

Syrian Jacobite immigration also began in earnest following the Turkish persecutions of 1893. Their first priest, Hanna Koorie, was elevated to the episcopacy in 1924 and founded the Archdiocese of the Syrian Church of Antioch. He was succeeded by Mar Athanasius Y. Samuel, who presides over 13 parishes with 30,000 members. The related Syrian Orthodox Church of Malabar (India) has a tiny, scattered membership here.

Coptic immigration is largely a post–World War II phenomenon, resulting from a rise in Muslim fundamentalism in Egypt. A Coptic Association of America was founded in 1962, and three years later a Diocese of North America was established; however, no bishop has yet been assigned. The widely dispersed Copts number some 2,000 adults. Two tiny, quarreling Ethiopian churches also came to the United States in the postwar era.

America is also home to some 25,000 Nestorian Christians, whose immigration dates to the 1890s. Organization was achieved only in 1940 with the move of the patriarch himself, Mar Eshai Shimun XXIII, to San Francisco.

Relations among the various Eastern Christian churches worldwide are much improved in modern times, and in this country affinities between the Orthodox and the Copts in particular are marked.

The Eastern churches, whose history in America form a crazy quilt that defies simple telling, seem to have passed their adolescent growth. Only a few groups still experience active immigration to any marked degree and have thus to deal with the passions and conflicts that we have seen this bring. For most, reality is a steady Americanization that can be fought, with the inevitable loss of future generations, or welcomed as the means to meeting a call to mission now more than a century and a half old.

The choice of response to mission will require that Orthodox theology once again be accepted as an eternal truth and not just one of many cultural expressions. St. Innocent understood and championed this radical perspective. With the immigrant chapter of its history written, Orthodoxy can survive and flourish only by taking its place in American life outside the ethnic ghetto and challenging it with a message that in ages past transformed the alien cultures that bore it to a New World.

BIBLIOGRAPHY

Gregory Afonsky, *A History of the Orthodox Church in Alaska (1794–1917)* (1977); Donald Attwater, *The Catholic Eastern Churches* (1935; rev. 1937) and *The Christian Churches of the East: Churches Not in Communion With Rome* (1937; rev. 1948); *Autocephaly: The Orthodox Church in America* (1971); Gerald J. Bobango, *The Romanian Orthodox Episcopate of America* (1979); Aleksandr A. Bogolepov, *Towards an American Orthodox Church: The Establishment of an Autocephalous Orthodox Church* (1963); Demetrios J. Constantelos, *Understanding the Greek Orthodox Church: Its Faith, History, and Practice* (1982); *Does Chalcedon Divide or Unite?* (1981); Keith P. Dyrud, Michael Novak, and Rudolph J. Vecoli, eds., *The Other Catholics* (1978).

Eastern Christianity: A Bibliography Selected from the ATLA Database (1982); Paul D. Garrett, *St. Innocent, Apostle to America* (1979); Edward J. Kilmartin, *Toward Reunion: The Roman Catholic and the Orthodox Churches* (1979); Paul Robert Magocsi, *The Shaping of a National Identity: Subcarpathian Rus', 1848–1948* (1978); John (Jean) Meyendorff, *The Orthodox Church, Its Past and Its Role in the World Today* (1962, rev. 1981); George Papaioannou, *From Mars Hill to Manhattan: The Greek Orthodox in America Under Athenagoras I* (1976); Henry R. Percival, ed., *The Seven Ecumenical Councils of the Undivided Church, Their Canons and Dogmatic Decrees* (1889; rev. 1971); Arthur Carl Piepkorn, *Profiles in Belief: The Religious Bodies of the United States and Canada* (1977); Dimitry Pospielovsky, *The Russian Church under the Soviet Regime, 1917–1982* (1984).

Mario Rinvolucri, *Anatomy of a Church: Greek Orthodoxy Today* (1966); *Russian Autocephaly and Orthodoxy in America: An Appraisal with Decisions and Formal Opinions* (1972); Alexander Schmemann, *The Historical Road of Eastern Orthodoxy*, trans. by Lydia W. Kesich (1963; rev. 1977); John Slivka, *Historical Mirror: Sources of the Rusin and Hungarian Greek Rite Catholics in the United States of America, 1884–1963* (1978); Barbara S. Smith, *Russian Orthodoxy in Alaska* (1980); James Ward Smith and A. Leland Jamison, eds., *Religion in American Life:* vol. 4, *A Critical Bibliography of Religion in America,* Nelson R. Burr, ed. (1961); Serafim Surrency, *The Quest for Orthodox Unity in America* (1973); Constance J. Tarasar and John H. Erickson, eds., *Orthodox America, 1794–1976: Development of the Orthodox Church in America* (1975); Timothy (Father Kallistos) Ware, *The Orthodox Church* (1963; rev. 1964).

[*See also* ETHNICITY AND RELIGION *and* LITURGY AND WORSHIP.]

CATHOLICISM IN THE

ENGLISH COLONIES

James Hennesey

LEGENDS and half-truths surround the earliest coming of Catholics to the New World: from exciting tales of Brendan the Navigator, the sixth-century monk from Tralee, and of tenth-century Norse adventurers on the northern ocean, down to fifteenth-century Portuguese, French, and Spanish visitors and the three voyages of 1496–1498 by John Cabot, born Giovanni Caboto, who explored the western Atlantic under license from Henry VII of England. Two Catholic knights, George Peckham and Thomas Gerard, thought of founding a Catholic colony in connection with Sir Humphrey Gilbert's 1583 expedition. But permanent English settlement on the North American mainland began at Jamestown in 1607, with the Reformation firmly established in Britain and James I on the throne.

Earlier in James's reign there had been a Catholic colonial prelude. Catholic hopes of toleration at the hands of Mary Stuart's son were shaken by a royal proclamation in February 1604 giving priests three weeks to "depart out of the realm" and by reenactment in James's first parliament of Elizabethan penal laws. Papists were banned from crown service, socially ostracized, and penalized for religious nonconformity with fines, imprisonment, and the ultimate threat of hanging, drawing, and quartering at Tyburn. No great rush of Catholics to foreign parts ensued, but this was the climate when, in March 1605, the Protestant Henry Wriothesley, third earl of Southampton, and his Catholic relative Sir Thomas Arundell of Wardour sent out the *Archangel,* under Captain George Weymouth, which explored Nantucket and the Maine coast as possible venues for Catholic emigrants. Jesuit propagandist Robert Persons discouraged the venture as politically impractical, counterproductive to the Catholic interest in England, and

possibly threatening to Spanish monopolistic claims on "the Indyes." No Catholic colony came of it, but James Rosier's *Relation* of the voyage fueled interest, which led in 1605 and 1606 to the London and Plymouth companies and to English mainland colonies.

The first English possession where Roman Catholics might practice their religion in peace was Sir George Calvert's settlement at Ferryland on Newfoundland's Avalon peninsula. Calvert, a state secretary to James I, was a top-ranking mercantilist with interests in the East India, Virginia, and New England companies, the silk trade, and Irish plantations. His Avalon and later Maryland ventures were not primarily designed to provide sanctuary for Catholic coreligionists. In fact, the 1621 Avalon colonists were all Anglicans, as was Calvert himself at the time. He did not become a Roman Catholic until about 1624. The change of religion did not erase his entrepreneurial bent. He did want to make it possible for Roman Catholics to share in colonization and he understood that this was feasible in England's Protestant empire only in the context of broad religious toleration for all, whether Protestant dissenters, Anglicans, or Catholics. The notion was not uncongenial to him. As David Lloyd described him in 1670, Calvert was "a man of great judgment, yet not obstinate in his sentiments, but taking as great pleasure in hearing others' opinions, as in delivering his own."

What developed in Calvert's two colonial enterprises was not unlike the process that Ralph Barton Perry described of another group of dissenters from the Church of England, the Puritan Separatists: "The first and in the long run the strongest force for religious tolerance is the desire to be tolerated." Conscience, not civil authority, became the highest norm. Faith and worship were not matters for governmental coercion, but exercises in human freedom, as the Baltimore pamphlet *Objections Answered Touching Maryland* (1633) explained with a characteristically pragmatic twist: "Conversion in matter of religion, if it bee forced, should give little satisfaction to a wise State of the fidelity of such convertites, for those who for worldly respects will break their faith with God doubtlesse will doe it, upon a fit occasion, much sooner with men" (Hughes, 1907–1917).

Avalon's charter was broad enough to allow for Catholics, requiring only that "no interpretation bee admitted thereof whereby God's holy and true Christian Religion, or the allegiance due unto us, our heires and Successors may in any thing suffer any prejudice or diminution" (Lahey, 1977). The oath of supremacy went unmentioned. In 1625 Calvert, by then first Baron Baltimore, named a Catholic, Sir Arthur Aston, governor. Fifteen Catholics were to go out with him to Avalon. Whether they did so is unclear. Carmelite friar Simon Stock Doughty told Rome that they were "to preach the Gospel to the heathens living there, and to thwart the English heretics who have already reached the said Island, lest they infect the people of those parts with heresy" (Lahey). He also dreamed of a Northwest Passage, with Newfoundland as a way station to already established missions in the Far East.

Baltimore had other concerns. He had spent the summer of 1624 in the colony "to settle it in better order" (Hughes). Two secular priests, Thomas Longville and Anthony Pole (known in Avalon as Smith), accompanied him. When Baltimore returned to London, Pole stayed as English America's first resident pastor. In June 1626 the proprietor was back with his wife and children, a priest named Hacket, and forty Catholics, bringing the colony's population to about 100, a majority of whom were still Protestant. The two religious groups were expected to live together peaceably, a novel notion in the seventeenth century. Erasmus Stourton, soon to be dismissed as Protestant parson of Ferryland, complained that "the sayd Hacket and Smith every Sunday say Masse and doe profess all other ceremonies of the Church of Rome in the ample manner as tis used in Spayne," while at his listening post in Brussels Pope Urban VIII's nuncio was shocked that "under the same roof of Calvert, in one area

Mass was had according to the Catholic rite, while in another the heretics carried out their own" (Lahey).

By summer's end 1629, Baltimore had had his fill of the "crosses and miseryes" of Newfoundland life. With his wife and children and forty Catholics, he sailed to Virginia, only to be denied admission for refusing the oath of supremacy. No Catholics remained in Avalon. Back in London, Baltimore made two applications, to King Charles I for land lying north of Virginia and to the provincial superior of the English Jesuits for priests to go there. Seeking to honor Queen Henrietta Maria, the king suggested calling the colony "Mariana," which "his lordship excepted against as being the name of a Jesuite that wrote against monarchy," so they agreed on *"Terra Mariae,* Mary-land" (Hughes). George Lord Baltimore died on 15 April 1632, before the Maryland charter passed under the great seal of England. The grant was made on 20 June to his son Cecilius.

Four documents helped set Maryland's religious tone: the Maryland charter; the *Account of the Colony* (1633) drawn up by the Jesuit Andrew White and containing the first conditions for the establishment of the plantation; the pamphlet *Objections Answered;* and the *Instructions* to the proprietor's brother, Governor Leonard Calvert, and commissioners Jerome Hawley and Thomas Cornwaleys.

James Anderson has complained of the "disingenuousness" pervading the charter, as if the proprietor belonged to the state church, while in fact the proprietor, the governor and commissioners, and the gentry among the original party that sailed on the *Ark* and *Dove* on 13 November 1633 were Roman Catholics. Under the charter, Baltimore controlled all churches. He was to erect and found churches, chapels, and places of worship and have them dedicated according to the ecclesiastical laws of England. The proprietor substituted for the king as source of all property titles. The laws of mortmain (dealing with ownership of land by religious corporations) did not apply and neither did the penal statutes, which in England burdened religious dissenters. Laws made for Maryland were to be consonant to and not repugnant or contrary to "but (so far as conveniently may be) agreeable to" English laws, statutes, and rights (Commager, 1963).

The *Account of the Colony* listed spiritual and

temporal advantages in the venture. Stress was laid on converting the Native Americans to Christianity. *Objections Answered* handled five topics, three dealing with the possible loss of crown revenues and two with Protestant scruples. The pamphleteer met squarely the toleration of popery that Baltimore's scheme involved, noting that Catholics were exchanging "a pleasant, plentiful and . . . native country" for a "wildernesse among salvages and wild beasts," and arguing the inconsistency of denying them the right to live in peace while tolerating in the king's dominions the Native Americans, "who are undoubted idolators," and in England itself allowing foreign diplomats free exercise of their Catholicism (Hughes). If the argument was tortuous, it left no doubt that toleration for Roman Catholics was intended in Maryland.

According to the *Instructions,* officials were to preserve unity and peace in the ships' company, and it was on the score of religion that Baltimore feared trouble. No scandal or offense should be given Protestants. Catholic religious practice was to be private; Catholics were to avoid religious debate. The governor and commissioners must treat Protestants "with as much mildness and favor as Justice will permit" (Ellis, 1967). The same policies were to apply after landing. Overtures to Virginia's governor and to Captain William Claiborne, the Virginian who occupied Kent Island, should be delegated to Anglican emissaries. A final religious note ordered erection of a chapel, no denomination specified.

The party on the *Ark* and *Dove* included the proprietor's brothers Leonard and George, "with very nearly twenty other gentlemen of very good fashion" and an undetermined number of working people (Hughes). Baltimore's count was 300; others have since calculated the number at half that. There was no clergyman from the Church of England, and none came to Maryland until 1650, but there were three Jesuits, the priests Andrew White and John Altham (also called Gravener) and lay brother Thomas Gervase. The Baltimores enlisted Jesuits for Maryland for the sake of the English colonists and also to work for the conversion of the Native Americans. No subsidy was offered. They came on the same terms as other "gentlemen adventurers." For every £100 paid for transport of five men to the colony, they would receive 400 acres and a share in colonial trade. The Jesuits paid for thirty

men; fourteen were assigned to their credit by other gentlemen. Thomas Copley, later the organizer of the Jesuit mission, boasted that "in peopling and planting this place, I am sure that none have donne neere soe much as we; nor endeed are lykly to do soe much" (Hughes). Among those credited to Andrew White was Maryland's first black person, "Mathias Sousa, Molato," who in later records appears as a freeman in attendance at the assembly of 1641–1642 (Hughes).

White's *Relatio itineris in Marylandiam* (*A Brief Relation of the Voyage unto Maryland*) describes the trip and the first day in the colony. The *Ark* and *Dove* sailed up the Potomac, the passengers parceling out saints' names to promontories they sighted and calling the river itself the St. Gregory. They anchored off an island they called St. Clement's, where,

> on the day of the Annunciation of the Most Holy Virgin Mary [March 25] in the year 1634 we celebrated mass for the first time on this island. This had never been done before in this part of the world. After we had completed the sacrifice, we took upon our shoulders a great cross, which we had hewn out of a tree, and advancing in order to the appointed place, with the assistance of the Governor and his associates and the other Catholics, we erected a trophy to Christ the Saviour, humbly reciting, on bended knees, the Litanies of the Sacred Cross, with great emotion.
>
> (Ellis, 1967)

Catholic religious practice was somewhat less private than the proprietor had envisioned.

Dropping back down the Potomac, the colonists laid out the town of St. Marys on land purchased from the Yaocomicos. White and his companions were assigned a cabin, Maryland's first chapel. They took up town land and 3,400 nearby acres as the initial installment of what was due them under the conditions of plantation. By 1638 they had a new brick chapel, and Thomas Copley, White's successor as head of the Jesuit band, made his first report on religious practice.

Reception of the sacraments matched that in Europe, catechism lessons and feast-day sermons were regular, and special lectures were available to the more advanced. Mass was offered daily, and both Catholics and Protestants attended. Priests assisted the sick and the dying.

Although settlers were moving off at a distance, none had died without the last sacraments. Among the victims of a yellow-fever epidemic were Brother Gervase and a young priest only two months in Maryland. Jesuit effectives were reduced to three, none of whom was as yet among the Native Americans. Copley recorded religious conversions: Protestant servants who became Catholics, and Frenchmen, possibly in Virginia, reclaimed for Catholicism. The Jesuits bought two indentured servants in Virginia. "Nor was the money ill-spent, for both showed themselves good Christians; one, indeed, surpasses the ordinary standard" (Ellis, 1967). Catholic lay people imitated the priests and more Catholic bondmen were redeemed. Colonial leaders made the "Spiritual Exercises," the program of meditation and prayer outlined by the Jesuit's founder, St. Ignatius Loyola. One was Jerome Hawley, who had left Maryland to become treasurer of Virginia. He died soon after, as did his wife, Eleanor, praised as a model of prayer, charity, and domestic virtues.

"Occasions of dissension" were not wanting, but Copley neglected to mention religion's role. Protestant servants completed their indenture and as freemen challenged Catholic dominance in the assembly. Bondmen on the Jesuits' St. Inigoes farm argued religious issues with overseer William Lewis, who was fined. Copley criticized Lewis for the slanging match and agreed that he should be punished. One other such incident is recorded, when Councillor Thomas Gerard was fined in 1641 for locking the "Protestant Catholics" out of his manor chapel (Hughes). The fine was held in escrow for support of a Protestant minister when he should arrive.

Ferdinand Poulton, Jesuit superior in 1639, reported expansion. Copley remained at St. Marys, Father Altham had gone to Kent Island, and Poulton was at Mattapany on the Patuxent, mission property given by a chief named Maquacomen. White was at Piscataway on the Potomac, where on Pentecost Sunday 1640 he baptized Chief Kittamaquund with his wife and child. Governor Leonard Calvert and his colonial secretary attended the ceremony. That afternoon the couple were married and the Native American and English chiefs raised a large cross to mark the event. This mission later moved to Potupaco to escape the attentions of Susquehannock raiders. Prospects looked good all around.

The priests' annual report for 1640 claimed that "the Catholics who live in the colony are not inferior in piety to those of other countries. But in urbanity of manners, according to the judgment of persons who have visited other colonies, they take the lead of settlers elsewhere" (Hughes).

Conflict simmered over a law code. John Lewger, secretary of the colony since 1637, represented Baltimore. They had been fellow students at Oxford, and Lewger, a one-time Anglican rector, had converted to Catholicism. Facing the novel situation of a Catholic-controlled colony in a Protestant empire, they devised a system that prescinded from canon law and made no special provision for clergy or church. Priests were quietly excused from the assembly to avoid their political involvement and free them from sitting in judgment in capital cases, but other concessions were refused.

In a set of "Cases," Lewger argued that Catholicism was not "publicly" allowed in Maryland. Copley knew the problems, but held that "while the government is Catholique," priests should enjoy traditional privileges. His argument was backed by hints of excommunication for the recalcitrant. Clerical grievances were spelled out: contacts with Native Americans were restricted; priests were taxed and their servants subject to arrest; no exemption was given from militia duty or military levies; the corn laws favored monopolists; restrictions were proposed on manorial holdings; and unmarried women had to forfeit landholdings after seven years.

Complications multiplied. The Mattapany mission was seized for having been illegally accepted from an Indian chief, when all property was controlled by the proprietor. Although Jesuits in Maryland did not constitute a legal body, the new conditions of plantation included retrospective introduction of mortmain. Land gifts to church corporations were banned; so was holding property in trust for them. Copley had in 1641 placed Jesuit lands in the vicinity of St. Marys with a lay trustee, Cuthbert Fenwick.

Negotiations were carried on between Jesuits in Maryland and London, Lord Baltimore, and Roman officials. Two secular priests sent out by the proprietor went over to the Jesuits' side. The latter claimed support from a majority of the Catholic laity, among them Captain Cornwaleys, who announced: "I will rather sacrifice myself and all I have in defence of God's honor and his Churches right, then willingly consent toe anything that may not stand with the good contiens [conscience] of a real Catholic" (Hughes). Baltimore stood firm. Henry More, the English Jesuit provincial, worried about the prudence and judgment of the Maryland Jesuits, and the Jesuit general commented from Rome: "I should be sorry indeed to see the first fruits, which are so beautifully developing in the Lord, nipped in their growth by the frost of cupidity" (Hughes).

The dispute eventually died down. The mission was supported through the colonial period by income from more than 20,000 acres claimed under the conditions of plantation, along with tracts inherited by individual American-born Jesuits and, in the eighteenth century, several bequests from lay benefactors. Property was either held by lay trustees or passed by legacy from one Jesuit to another. The controversy demonstrated that religious liberty, Maryland style, meant not only free exercise of religion, but also nonestablishment of anyone's church, the proprietor's included.

While Jesuits battled Baltimore, such Catholics as Cornwaleys, Fulk and Giles Brent, and Thomas Greene were prominent in the assembly that on 13 March 1639 legislated that the "Holy Churches [sic] within this province shall have all her rights, liberties, and immunities, safe, whole, and inviolable in all things" (Hughes). Whatever the disputes about the extent of "rights, liberties, and immunities," historians know from the appeal to this act in the unsuccessful 1661 prosecution of Jesuit Francis Fitzherbert that all Christian churches were meant. "Her" was an obsolete form of "their." Consistent practice since 1634 was now law.

Maryland grew slowly. By 1641 there were fewer than 400 English colonists, 100 of them Catholics. In his *Journal,* John Winthrop noted Baltimore's invitation through Major General Edward Gibbons to Massachusetts Puritans, promising them "free liberty of religion and all the privileges which the place afforded," if they moved south (Hughes). Relations with the Native Americans remained chancy. While Baltimore authorized Kent Islanders to shoot them on sight should they venture there, among the Patuxents on the opposite side of the Chesapeake Jesuit Roger Rigby shared their life, learning their language and writing a catechism in it.

The English Civil War came to the colony in 1645. The missions were plundered and Fathers White and Copley were sent in chains to England. There, they were tried for their lives for being priests who had been ordained abroad and had illegally entered the kingdom. They pleaded successfully that their visit was involuntary, but nevertheless they were exiled. By 1646 three other Jesuits had died from disease, Rigby among them. Of fourteen who had come since 1634, four stayed only briefly, eight died in America, and two were in exile.

With help from some Maryland Protestants, Virginia Puritans took over. While in England plans were discussed to exile English Catholics to Maryland and send Maryland Catholics to the Spanish West Indies, Protestants sympathetic to Parliament flooded the province and replaced Catholics in public office. Leonard Calvert died in June 1647. His Catholic successor as governor, Thomas Greene, was replaced by a moderate Protestant, William Stone, whose oath, as a sign of the changing times, included a promise not to hinder Catholics' free exercise of religion. Leonard Calvert's personal affairs were put in the charge of Margaret Brent, whose handling of mutinous soldiers won from the freemen the accolade, "It was better for the collonys safety at that time in her hands then in any mans else in the whole Province." But she failed in her demand for voice and two votes in the Assembly, one as proprietor's attorney and the other in her own right as landholder (Hughes).

Catholics probably had a slight majority in the 1649 assembly, which adopted an act concerning religion complete with elaborate sanctions for violation. Like the governor's new oath, this act signaled a mood different from what the colony had known in earlier days. Its harsher phrases echoed current acts of Parliament such as that of 2 May 1648 against heresies and blasphemies. The old order was changing. With Puritans in control (1655–1657), toleration was denied to both "Popery and prelacy."

The Jesuits, who had returned in 1648, fled again to Virginia in 1655, when St. Inigoes Manor was ransacked, the booty including "consecrated ware . . . pictures, crucifixes, and rows of beads, with great store of relics and trash they [the Jesuits] trusted in" (Hughes). Peace came in 1657, but Catholics were a declining minority, identified with an upper social stratum and the feudal ways of an increasingly unpopular proprietary party. This was particularly true from 1661 to 1684, the years that Cecilius' son Charles, third Baron Baltimore, spent in the province. The population changed as Protestant dissenters poured in. By 1677 Baltimore judged Quakers to be the largest single denomination, followed by Presbyterians, Independents, and Anabaptists. Catholics came last.

Between 1672 and 1720 Franciscans joined the Jesuits in two or threes. Living on farms worked by slaves, the priests exercised an itinerant ministry by boat and on horseback. The more settled nature of the times was reflected in the opening of Ralph Crouch's school on the Jesuits' Newtown Manor in the 1650s. It admitted both Protestants and Catholics. Edward Cotton was the school's first benefactor with the bequest of "a horse and mare, the stock and all its increase forever" (Hennesey, 1981). Closed in 1659, the Newtown school reopened in 1677. Four years later the first alumni graduated to the emigré English Jesuit college at St. Omer in France.

Maryland Catholic links with the tiny but well-to-do English Catholic community were strengthened. A steady flow of boys and girls to continental schools began, seasoning Maryland Catholicism with a well-educated laity at a time when schooling in the province was notably poor and contributing to the gap between Catholics and the vocal and influential populist element. Native Catholics also began to enter the clergy. Nearly half of the forty-nine Americans who became seminarians returned as priests, while others worked in England. Thirty-three colonial women became nuns in European convents, although none of them came home until a Carmelite monastery was founded in 1790.

In the wake of the Glorious Revolution of 1688 (which replaced Catholic King James II with his Protestant daughter Mary II and her Dutch husband, William of Orange), Catholics were charged with Jacobite and French sympathies. Jack Coode's 1689 rebellion scattered the priests. Maryland became a royal colony and the Church of England was established. John Seymour, governor from 1704 to 1709, understood that he was to tolerate "all but Papists." An act to prevent the growth of popery forbade Catholic baptism of any but the children of Catholic parents, the saying of Mass, proselytizing, and the running of schools under Catholic auspices.

Robert Brooke, the first American-born priest, was prosecuted and let off with a warning for saying Mass at St. Marys City. The Newtown school was closed once again. But a suspending law confirmed by Queen Anne in 1706 allowed private celebration of Mass. The third Baron Baltimore, barred by his religion from government of the province, supported the Catholic mission with an annual £5 grant for each priest, which was accompanied by a caution against aggressive proselytism. A test act demanding denial of transubstantiation excluded Catholics from public office. In 1718 Catholics were disfranchised.

Only weeks before the 1689 coup a young Irish lawyer, Charles Carroll, had arrived in Maryland with a commission from Baltimore as attorney general. His tenure was brief, but he became the proprietor's private agent. In twenty years as a merchant-importer, moneylender, and planter he founded what was by the American Revolution the greatest fortune in the colonies. The Carrolls married into the network of older Catholic families like the Brookes, Sewalls of Mattapany, Diggeses and Darnalls, Neales and Fenwicks. Across the Potomac were the Brents, who had left Maryland in 1651 for Virginia's northern neck.

By 1707, Catholics, including slaves and indentured servants, numbered 2,974 in a population of 33,883. They were sailors, oystermen, laborers, and mechanics or substantial farmers like the Coles. A lone Dutch Catholic, Arnold Livers, arrived a bondman and died owning indentured servants. Irish immigrant Daniel Carroll parlayed a canny business sense into a general store and import operation and a country estate. Marriage to a Darnall tied him to the "attorney general" Carrolls. His daughters married Brents, one son signed the federal Constitution, and another became first archbishop of Baltimore.

The Baltimore heir, Benedict Leonard Calvert, conformed in November 1713 to the established church. Seven weeks after succeeding as fourth baron in February 1720 he was dead, and it was to his son, Charles Calvert, that George I restored the government of the province, where a population explosion resulted in 80,000 inhabitants by 1719, 25,000 of them slaves. Protestant dissenters predominated, while the Church of England, plagued by inept clergy, grew slowly. Catholics were made scapegoats. "The whole province smells of popish superstitions," one clergyman wrote. Although in 1725, Maryland had only twelve priests and four brothers, he blamed the "vast number of Jesuits . . . so numerous that their name is Legion." Another clergyman complained in 1734 of "Romish pamphlets diligently dispersed up and down" (Hughes). The Newtown circulating library may have been his target. It was stocked with Douai-Rheims Bibles and a variety of spiritual, controversial, and historical works.

In 1704 the Catholic mission had expanded to the head of the Chesapeake in an area where Catholics numbered less than 25 in 1,000. But George Talbot was inviting Irish immigrants to his 55,000 acres, and Charles Carroll had a similar scheme. In 1741 a classical and commercial school opened on the Jesuit farm popularly called Bohemia Manor. "Latinists" paid forty shillings and others thirty to support a lay master. Students included John Carroll, the future archbishop, and Charles Carroll III, later "of Carrollton," who in 1776 signed the Declaration of Independence. Other missions sprang up at Whitemarsh, Prince George's County, where James Carroll, a cousin of Charles Carroll II "of Annapolis," had donated a valuable 2,000 acres and, in the 1760s, in Baltimore, until then a town of few Catholics, apart from Acadian refugees.

The early 1750s saw renewed anti-Catholic activity, fueled by the 1745 Jacobite uprising in Scotland and the continuing wars with France and its Native American allies. In 1755, 900 Acadians landed and had to be supported by private charity. Double taxation was imposed on Catholics. Two priests were arrested, one for being "a clerk and priest of the Church of Rome" and for reclaiming for Catholicism an Irish Quaker woman, the other for treasonous communication with the French. Neither was convicted, but a law was proposed to control the Catholic clergy. The regular convoys of students to schools in Europe provoked a scheme to deny property ownership to those educated on the Continent.

Agitation was particularly severe in the lower house of the Assembly, but Catholic family and social connections in the council exercised a moderating influence. This did not prevent the choleric and wealthy Charles Carroll of Annapolis from venting his frustration in a protest nailed to the statehouse door, while he also framed petitions for relief to the proprietor, governor, and council. In 1759, London "merchants trading to Maryland" petitioned the king on behalf of their trading partners. They feared they would decamp to French or Spanish territory and there build a rival tobacco trade. Charles Carroll II considered doing just that and inquired about land on the Arkansas River. But his son, arriving home in 1765 after sixteen years of education abroad, preferred to stay in Maryland, where he was soon aligned with the patriots' cause.

Maryland Catholicism included the plantations in Virginia, where in 1687 George Brent had secured an ephemeral grant of religious toleration to assist Huguenot immigration, but the only other colony with an organized Catholic community was Quaker Pennsylvania. An Anglican missionary reported in 1708 that "Mass is set up and read publicly in Philadelphia" (Ellis, 1965). Priests rode from Bohemia Manor, center also for excursions to Delaware and Maryland's Eastern Shore. Sometime in 1733–1734 Joseph Greaton, S.J., and forty parishioners began St. Joseph's Church in Philadelphia, the first urban Catholic parish in the English colonies and the first church financed by regular congregational support. German, English, and Irish tradespeople, laborers, sailors, and servants mingled with Acadian exiles, Senecas, and other western Indians in town on business with the provincial government and prosperous international traders like the Meades and Moylans. Thomas FitzSimons, later a signer of the federal Constitution, was a parishioner, along with Continental Navy hero John Barry.

Rural missions at Lancaster, Conewago, Goshenhoppen, and Reading served Catholic Rhinelanders and Palatines among the "Pennsylvania Dutch" and Marylanders led by John Digges, to whom Lord Baltimore granted 10,000 acres of what the Mason-Dixon Line would determine was Pennsylvania land. The country missions were supported by Jesuit farms worked by tenants and by two funds of English origin, one the gift of Sir John James, the other from the patrimony of a Jesuit, Gilbert Talbot, thirteenth earl of Shrewsbury. A 1757 census counted among Pennsylvania's half-million inhabitants 692 male and 673 female Catholics over age twelve, 70 percent German speaking. Germans outnumbered all others in the Philadelphia parish, 228 to 150. By 1765 the Catholic population was estimated at 6,000, half of them children. English and German Jesuits staffed the mission, among them Theodor Schneider, one-time rector of Heidelberg University, and Ferdinand Farmer, who from 1756 to 1786 was pastor in Philadelphia and itinerant missionary in the Jerseys and in New York's Hudson Valley. Pennsylvania Catholics benefited from the tolerant 1701 charter of privileges, although they were barred from public office by a required declaration against transubstantiation. The 1757 militia act forbade them arms and exacted of them the same twenty-shilling tax imposed on conscientious objectors.

Missionaries from Pennsylvania attended stations in West Jersey such as that at the Salem glass works, and Farmer's travels took him to West Jersey. Nothing had come of Sir Edmund Plowden's palatinate of New Albion (established in 1634 on the Jersey side of the Delaware), where a grant of religious liberty was planned, but individual Catholics appeared in the 1680s. Bergen elected William Douglas to the 1680 East Jersey assembly, but he was excluded upon declaring himself a Roman Catholic. John Tatham, an obscure figure who held several West Jersey posts, seems to have briefly been acting governor of both Jerseys. He died in 1700, leaving a 500-book library rich with works reflecting the Benedictine tradition of Catholic spirituality.

The later canonized martyr Isaac Jogues, S.J., visited New Amsterdam in 1643 after the Dutch assisted his escape from Mohawk captivity. He found but two Catholics in the town. The number increased after 1672 under the proprietorship of James Duke of York. Anthony Brockholls was Sir Edmund Andros' chief lieutenant and, from 1680 to 1683, acting governor. Jarvis Baxter was commander at Albany. Governor Thomas Dongan brought with him in 1683 Jesuits Thomas Harvey and Charles Gage. Sixty pounds annually was allocated for their support. They had a chapel in Fort James and a school, like that at Newtown open to Protestants and Catholics, on the King's Farm (now Trinity Church property). Dongan's master plan for the frontier envisioned them replacing French Jesuits among the Iroquois. Their own superiors in London saw New York as an American headquarters from which priests would attend the "adjoining" Maryland colony. A charter of liberties and privileges affirmed free exercise of religion, although allowing church establishment where, as in Puritan Long Island, two-thirds of the inhabitants wanted it. Dongan welcomed Huguenot refugees, and Sephardic Jews were enrolled as freemen and granted trading rights.

Although James II annulled the charter in 1686, the religious clauses stood until Jacob Leisler's 1689 revolt. The Jesuits fled, but Harvey returned in 1690 and remained until he "incurred the fury of the wife of the new governor" in 1693 and left for good. In 1691 Catholics lost the free exercise of their religion. That same year Governor Lord Bellomont offered the Iroquois 100 pieces of eight for every "popish priest or Jesuit" taken prisoner. The cosmopolitan city of New York continued to attract Catholics of several nationalities, but only with the American Revolution, and then with the help of the foreign consuls, was a parish organized. The colony's lone organized Catholic community was that of the 300 Scots from the western Highlands who in 1773 settled under Sir William Johnson's protection in the Mohawk Valley. With their priest, John MacKenna, they moved to Canada during the war, many of the men serving in loyalist regiments.

In colonies such as the Carolinas and Georgia popular anti-papist sentiment and restrictive laws inhibited Catholic settlement. New England saw only the occasional visitor. Jesuit Gabriel Druillettes came on a Canadian trade mission in 1650–1651. He offered Mass privately in the Boston home of Edward Gibbons, whom Lord Baltimore had earlier approached about Puritan settlers and who was prominent in coastal trade with Maryland. The priest visited Salem, Plymouth, and New Haven and was hosted at Roxbury by John Eliot. In 1674 Jean Pierron, S.J., traveled from Acadia to Maryland and back. He caused a stir in Boston by appearing in apparently transparent disguise to dispute with local ministers.

Boston also executed the only colonial Catholic whose death had religious overtones: Ann Glover, hanged as a witch on the common in 1688. But New Englanders had their own martyrology of suffering at Catholic hands, recorded in the "captivity narratives," harrowing yet inspirational tales of pillage and looting on the frontier, of death and destruction, and of the firm Puritan faith of women and children held captive in the wilderness or taken to Canada (Hambrick-Stowe, 1982). John Adams expressed the common feeling when he boasted of his hometown of Braintree that papists there were as rare as a comet or an earthquake.

Maine contributed a separate chapter. Border skirmishes with the French were common. At Norridgewock in 1724 Massachusetts troops scalped Jesuit Sebastien Rasle. His Abenaki dictionary still lies as war booty in Harvard's Houghton Library. Negotiating with the Massachusetts governor, who in 1759 took possession of the Penobscot Bay area, the Abenaki complained they had no priest, "by which the old men forgot their religion, the young men could learn none, nor have proper marriages and christenings, by which it was not in their power to live as Christian people ought to do." Five years later, they pleaded for "a Father to baptize our Children and marry us, and administer the Sacrament to us, and confess us, and shew us the way to Heaven" (Leger, 1929). The Abenaki pressed their demand as a condition of alliance with the Massachusetts congress in 1776, and a French naval chaplain was finally sent to them in 1779.

Between 65,000 and 70,000 French and Huron Catholics along the St. Lawrence passed to British control in 1763. They had 196 priests and six communities of nursing and teaching sisters in parishes, hospitals, and schools. It was the one time in British North America that Great Britain faced Catholicism's full institutional panoply. Governor James Murray was impressed by the hospital nuns but hoped that the Canadians would in time forsake Catholicism. The Hurons, he wrote, were "all Roman Catholics and a decent well-behaved people," whose conduct at divine worship showed "a punctuality and decorum worthy of imitation by more enlightened people" (Usherwood, 1979). The Quebec diocese lacked a bishop, but in 1766 Joseph-Olivier Briand was consecrated and recognized as "overseer of the Roman Church." Dreams of Anglican establishment faded, and the 1774 Quebec Act guaranteed civil and religious liberty, tithes for the Catholic church, and a special oath permitting Catholics to hold office without contemning their religion. For the *bostonnais* to the south the act was an infringement on their liberties. It won Briand's support for the Crown and

sparked Canadian indifference to American pleas for help in the Revolution.

Newfoundland's fishing grounds attracted a handful of French and Irish Catholics in the seventeenth century, but significant immigration, largely from Ireland's County Waterford, came late in the eighteenth century. In 1784 an Irish Franciscan became prefect apostolic, a preliminary to diocesan organization. Irish immigrants continued to arrive and were by the 1830s about half the island's population.

Despite the Acadians' declared neutrality in the British-French struggle, Governor Charles Lawrence began in 1755 eight years of deportations that scattered 14,000 of them among the seaboard colonies, many to make their way eventually to Louisiana's Cajun country. About 2,000 remained, and more found their way back. By the century's end, 40 percent of the region's Catholics were Acadians. The Abenaki remained Catholic, and Lawrence provided priests for them, including Acadian-born Joseph-Mathurin Bourg. A few Irish Catholics were among the 2,500 people who settled Halifax in 1749. The Church of England was established in Nova Scotia in 1758, and Catholics were denied the vote and admission to the local legislature. Priests were banned. The final quarter of the century saw increasing immigration of Gaelic-speaking Irish and Scots Catholics, the latter often arriving in groups such as the 200 from South Uist in the Outer Hebrides who in 1772 came with John Macdonald of Glenaladale to his 40,000 acres on Isle St. John (Prince Edward Island).

Middle-class Irish merchants in Halifax gained religious toleration in 1783, but priests were lacking. The Maritimes had only a Scots priest on Isle St. John and Mathurin Bourg, who lived on the Gaspé Peninsula. An Irish Capuchin friar brought in by the Halifax community became superior of the mission under the bishop of Quebec in 1787, and a separate vicariate apostolic, or missionary diocese, was set up at Halifax in 1817.

British America was overall unattractive, either as refuge or opportunity, for Catholics. By 1776 they were about 1 percent of the population, concentrated in Maryland, Pennsylvania, and the Maritimes. The bishop of Quebec's authority encompassed the Maritimes, but he was

CATHOLICISM IN THE ENGLISH COLONIES

hard-pressed to find priests. In Maryland and Pennsylvania, two dozen ex-Jesuits (their religious order was suppressed in 1773 by Pope Clement XIV) labored under the jurisdiction of the vicar apostolic of the London district, but de facto authority was loosely exercised by the last Jesuit superior, John Lewis. A proposal for a resident bishop drew in 1765 a protest against "so fatal a measure" from 256 laymen headed by Charles Carroll of Annapolis. When a visit from the bishop of Quebec was proposed, Ferdinand Farmer explained in 1773 that "it is incredible how hateful to non-Catholics in all parts of America is the very name of Bishop, even to such as should be members of the Church which is called Anglican" (Ellis, 1967). Only with John Carroll's 1784 appointment as superior of the mission and 1789 election as bishop of Baltimore was normal church organization begun.

Maryland Catholics were English, Irish, and African. They ran the gamut from slaves and indentured servants to gentry whose political influence was increasingly diminished and indirect but who managed to maintain a respectable economic and social standing. Identification with the Baltimores' proprietary interests and the growing influx of dissenting Protestants, coupled with anti-papist legislation, marginalized them and drove them to isolation in the province's southern counties. The relatively small size of the English Catholic community from which Maryland Catholics sprang also precluded major growth. The best estimate places the number of English Catholics at 60,000 in 1641 and 80,000 by 1770 (Bossy, 1976). Only in the nineteenth century, when a wider base for immigration developed, did the American Catholic community really grow.

Poverty characterized the Pennsylvania German farmers, while in Philadelphia the parish modeled the style of future Catholic growth. It was multinational, straddled socioeconomic classes, and was congregationally supported. Less prophetic of the future was the strong say the laity had in church affairs, a situation that lasted into the early nineteenth century but was then reversed. Lay power was also a fact in Halifax, as it was with transplanted lairds throughout the Maritimes. With no effective episcopal government for 150 years, colonial Catholicism everywhere developed independent ways, which in the postcolonial era would be accommodated to more traditional church polity with difficulty.

Conscious of the imperative nature of religious toleration if they were to prosper peaceably in a hostile environment, colonial Catholics were its consistent advocates in early Avalon and Maryland, in Edmund Plowden's dreams for New Albion, on Virginia's northern neck, and in Dongan's New York. They accepted it from Pennsylvania Quakers and pressed for it in Nova Scotia. It was for them a matter of realistic, practical logic, which they promoted everywhere. But in a British America hemmed in by Spaniards on the south and French on the north, and where memories of the Fires of Smithfield still burned bright, theirs was a tiny, lonely voice.

BIBLIOGRAPHY

J. M. S. Anderson, *The History of the Church of England in the Colonies and Foreign Dependencies of the British Empire*, 3 vols. (1845–1856); *Archives of Maryland*, 72 vols. (1883–1972); Edwin W. Beitzell, *The Jesuit Missions of St. Mary's County, Maryland* (1960; rev. 1976); John Bossy, *The English Catholic Community 1570–1850* (1976); J. M. Bumsted, "Highland Emigration to the Island of St. John and the Scottish Catholic Church, 1769–1774," in *Dalhousie Review*, 58 (1978); Henry Steele Commager, ed., *Documents of American History* (7th ed., 1963); John Tracy Ellis, *Catholics in Colonial America* (rev. ed., 1965) and, as ed., *Documents of American Catholic History* (2nd ed., 1967); Henry Foley, ed., *Records of the English Province of the Society of Jesus*, 8 vols. (1877–1883).

Martin I. J. Griffin, *American Catholic Historical Researches*, 29 vols. (1884–1912); Charles E. Hambrick-Stowe, *The Practice of Piety: Puritan Devotional Disciplines in Seventeenth-Century New England* (1982); Thoman O'Brien Hanley, *Their Rights and Liberties* (1959); James Hennesey, *American Catholics: A History of the Roman Catholic Community in the United States* (1981); Michael F. Hennessey, ed., *The Catholic Church in Prince Edward Island* (1979); Thomas A. Hughes, *The History of the Society of Jesus in North America: Colonial and Federal*, 4 vols. (1907–1917); John D. Krugler, "'With Promise of Liberty in Religion': The Catholic Lords Baltimore and Toleration in Seventeenth-Century Maryland, 1634–1692," in *Maryland Historical Magazine*, 79 (1984); Raymond J. Lahey, "The Role of Religion in Lord Baltimore's Colonial Enterprise," in *Maryland Historical Magazine*, 72 (1977); Mary Celeste Leger, *The Catholic Indian Missions in Maine (1611–1820)* (1929); David Lloyd, *State Worthies, or, the Statesmen and Favourites of England, from the Reformation to the Revolution* (1670; 2nd ed., 1679).

Richard K. MacMaster, "Parish in Arms: A Study of Father John Mackenna and the Mohawk Valley Loyalists, 1773–1778," in *Historical Records and Studies*, 45 (1957); *Maryland Historical Society Fund Publications*, 7 (1874; supplement,

1877), 28 (1894), 34 (1895), 35 (1899); Terrence Murphy, "The Emergence of Maritime Catholicism 1781–1830," in *Acadiensis,* 13 (1984); Ralph Barton Perry, *Puritanism and Democracy* (rev. ed., 1964); John Gilmary Shea, *The History of the Catholic Church in the United States,* vol. 1 (1886); Bruce E. Steiner, "The Catholic Brents of Virginia: An Instance of Political Toleration," in *The Virginia Magazine of History and Biography* 70 (1962); Stephen Usherwood, "Conquered Canada: General James Murray's Impressions, 1762," in *History Today,* 29 (1979).

[*See also* AMERICAN CATHOLIC THOUGHT; CATHOLICISM FROM INDEPENDENCE TO WORLD WAR I; CATHOLICISM SINCE WORLD WAR I; ETHNICITY AND RELIGION; FRENCH CATHOLOCISM IN THE NEW WORLD; *and* RELIGIOUS PREJUDICE AND NATIVISM.]

CATHOLICISM FROM INDEPENDENCE TO WORLD WAR I

Debra Campbell

IT is anachronistic to refer to the Catholic church in colonial America. It is far more accurate to speak of the Catholic community, a collection of scattered congregations formed at the initiative of the local laity and suffering from a chronic shortage of priests. Outnumbered and isolated, members of these scattered Catholic congregations confronted legal disabilities stemming from a deep-seated English tradition of anti-Catholicism brought to the New World by the first Puritans, nurtured by the Puritans' reverence for Foxe's *Book of Martyrs* and their penchant for celebrating Pope Day (Guy Fawkes Day), and transmitted to subsequent generations in the pages of the *New England Primer*.

This dilemma forced subsequent generations of American Catholics not only to formulate rebuttals to nativist charges but also to try to resolve a profound identity crisis rooted in the "mixed marriage" of Roman Catholicism and Protestant America. The tenuous relationship between the Catholic community and their non-Catholic neighbors influenced the policies of the bishops and clergy who sought to maintain a delicate balance between the demands of Rome and the needs of their self-consciously American constituency. From the 1780s onward, the relationship between the Catholic faith and American (Protestant) ideals became increasingly complex, undergoing numerous permutations in the final quarter of the nineteenth century, until it attracted the attention of the Vatican. Just at this point a new generation of American bishops educated in Rome took the helm and sought to establish uniformity and consensus within the American Catholic community. Beneath the surface, however, many of the laity, clergy, and religious remained irrepressibly American, and the

conflict between American and Catholic ideals, first aired by the patriots before the American Revolution, lived on into the twentieth century.

The decades spanning the two Treaties of Paris (1763–1783) witnessed the birth pangs of the American Catholic church and of the nation. The British succeeded in expelling France from North America in 1763, but they did not remove the French Catholics from Quebec or from the region between the Appalachians and the Mississippi River. Instead, the Treaty of Paris (1763) had granted religious freedom to Catholics in the former French colonies, much to the despair of their British Protestant counterparts, and with the Quebec Act of 22 June 1774 the former French colonists gained further concessions, including tithes for the support of Catholic clergy and exemption from the traditional oath of loyalty to the British crown. Thus the Quebec Act became a rallying cry for the patriots and the occasion for outbreaks of anti-Catholic bigotry along the eastern seaboard. Nevertheless, the Revolution won the support of colonial Catholics, who were anxious to escape not only taxation without representation but also the harsh penal codes that restricted the civil rights and public worship of British Catholics. Thus the Revolution, launched with a strong protest against popery, ushered in a new age of toleration for Catholics, an age in which the church would grow in size and strength under the protection of the First Amendment.

Although Catholics numbered only 20,000 to 25,000, about 1 percent of the population in the thirteen colonies, they played prominent roles in the Revolution. One Catholic, Charles Carroll of Carrollton, who in 1773 skirmished with the Tory Daniel Dulany, Jr., in the *Maryland Gazette*

357

over the colonial governor's right to extract fees from citizens, later served on committees of correspondence and signed the Declaration of Independence. Another Catholic, Colonel John Fitzgerald, served as Washington's aide-de-camp, and his fellow colonels Francis Vigo, Joseph Cauffmann, and Timothy Murphy were also Catholics. Regiments from the Catholic strongholds of Charles and St. Mary's counties in Maryland contained an especially high proportion of Catholics. Not all Catholics joined the patriots, however. The men from one community of over two hundred Catholic Scottish Highlanders in the Mohawk Valley of New York and their priest, John MacKenna, lent their support to the Loyalists. Philadelphia Catholics formed their own Loyalist regiment, the Roman Catholic Volunteers. The contributions of prominent European Catholics who fought on the patriot side, such as Lafayette, Friedrich Wilhelm von Steuben of Prussia, and the Poles Thaddeus Kosciusko and Casimer Pulaski, coupled with the alliance with France in 1778, did much to temper colonial hostility to Catholics.

Even after the peace treaty of 1783, Catholics continued to suffer under state constitutions, in the case of Massachusetts until 1833. On the national level, however, the Catholic church witnessed a dramatic change in its status and prospects when it was suddenly legalized by the Constitution and even protected by the First Amendment.

In 1776 there were two dozen priests in the thirteen colonies; except for MacKenna in New York, they all lived in Maryland and Pennsylvania and all were former members of the Society of Jesus, which had been dissolved by Pope Clement XIV in 1773. Two French priests, Sébastian Meurin and Pierre Gibault, served as pastors to the French Catholics on the western frontier. Technically speaking, colonial Catholic priests remained under the jurisdiction of the vicar apostolic of the London district; however, the relations between the priests in Maryland and Pennsylvania and ecclesiastical authorities in London had been less than cordial for decades before the Revolution complicated matters even further.

The idea of an American bishop remained controversial. Protests against episcopacy had mingled with other revolutionary slogans during the recent conflict. Although the absence of a bishop meant that two sacraments (confirmation and holy orders) could not be administered in America, the Jesuits of Pennsylvania and Maryland assembled at Whitemarsh, Maryland, in October 1784 still agreed unanimously that the appointment of an American bishop was untimely, possibly even dangerous to the safety of Catholics in general and to the status and property of the American Jesuits in particular. The same year American Episcopalians faced the same question and chose to consecrate their own bishops. Leonardo Cardinal Antonelli, prefect of the Sacred Congregation for the Propagation of the Faith, proposed a compromise. On 9 June 1784, after considering recommendations made by the papal nuncio in Paris and by Benjamin Franklin, American minister to France, Antonelli appointed John Carroll not bishop but prefect Apostolic and superior of the missions in the United States.

Thus Carroll, scion of a prominent Maryland Catholic family, became the first in a long line of American Catholic ecclesiastical leaders to meet the challenge of finding solutions approved by Rome for the unprecedented problems faced by the Catholic church in the American environment. Carroll envisioned an elected hierarchy in democratic America rather than one appointed by Rome, a preference shared by his fellow priests. After petitioning Pope Pius VI for permission to elect a bishop, the assembled American clergy chose Carroll on 18 May 1789 and the pontiff responded with the brief *Ex hac apostolicae* (6 November 1789), which confirmed the election and erected the first American diocese in Baltimore. Carroll's preference was honored only twice, however: once in the selection of his coadjutor bishops, and again in the choice of the first four suffragan bishops. After 1808, despite protests from America, bishops were nominated in Rome.

With the appointment of four suffragans to the new dioceses of Boston, New York, Philadelphia, and Bardstown, Kentucky, in 1808, the organizational structure of the Catholic church in the United States began to conform more closely to the pattern set in Europe. As early as 1791, however, when the first American diocesan synod met in Baltimore to lay the groundwork for ecclesiastical administration, it was already apparent that conformity to European organizational structures would not be achieved without a struggle. One of the most serious challenges

Carroll confronted was trusteeism, a widespread pattern of lay administration in local congregations. In the colonial era, the shortage of priests, the lack of a bishop, the legal strictures placed upon the church, and the pervasive Protestant models combined with the growing popularity of democratic ideals to recommend the congregational pattern of church government to the American Catholic laity. Thus Carroll faced considerable resistance on the local level when he tried to organize the American Catholic church in conformity with canon law into a network of parishes under the jurisdiction of bishops.

As early as 1785 Carroll became embroiled in a conflict at Saint Peter's Church, a privately incorporated New York City parish, over which of two Irish Capuchins should serve as pastor. The crisis revealed a basic disagreement between Carroll, representative of the Roman hierarchy, and the American lay trustees regarding who had the authority to appoint and dismiss a local pastor. (The lay trustees of Saint Peter's engaged in sporadic conflict with ecclesiastical authorities for four decades before they finally succumbed to Bishop John Hughes's demands and to the growing economic burdens of a burgeoning immigrant congregation.) Carroll witnessed other outbreaks of conflict over trusteeism in Charleston, Baltimore, and Philadelphia.

The trustee question illuminates two aspects of the ongoing struggle over the compatibility of American and Catholic ideals. The first, the recurring attempt on the part of a vocal minority of the laity to assert their rights as citizens of the church, surfaced in the controversy at Saint Peter's and later in Philadelphia (the "Hogan Schism" of 1820–1824) and Norfolk, Virginia (1815–1820). In Norfolk, lay trustees led by Dr. John Oliveira Fernandez affirmed their right, as administrators of the temporal property of their parish, to reject priests appointed by the bishop. Although the trustees' preference for Irish clergy over those of other ethnic groups remained a point of contention in their struggles with Archbishops Leonard Neale and Ambrose Maréchal of Baltimore, the Norfolk controversy revolved around the issue of the rights of the laity, which trustees perceived were being abrogated by an undemocratic, clerically dominated system of church government centered in Rome. A second aspect of the conflict between American and Catholic ideals surfaced in the trustee

controversy which exploded in 1787 at Holy Trinity, a privately incorporated German parish in Philadelphia. The protracted conflict between Bishop Carroll and Holy Trinity trustees led by James Oellers, sustained for almost two decades until 1806, represents an early instance of the nationalistic conflicts that became increasingly common in the American Catholic community in the nineteenth century.

Ethnic tensions extended beyond the squabbles between lay trustees and bishops to the hierarchy itself. After the Revolution a small number of educated upper-class English Catholic families in Maryland assumed the leadership of the scattered Catholic flock composed chiefly of Pennsylvania farmers, French mechanics, and ordinary laborers in the small towns and growing cities along the eastern seaboard. During the century following the Declaration of Independence these Maryland Catholics and others of English descent virtually monopolized the metropolitan see of Baltimore: from Archbishop John Carroll (1789–1815) to Archbishops Leonard Neale (1815–1817), James Whitfield (1828–1834), Samuel Eccleston (1834–1851), Martin John Spalding (1864–1872), and James Roosevelt Bayley (1872–1877). The only exceptions to this pattern were Ambrose Maréchal (1817–1828), a Frenchman, and an Irishman, Francis Patrick Kenrick (1851–1863). The arrival of twenty-seven exiled French priests in the wake of the Civil Constitution of the clergy (July 1790) almost doubled the number of priests in the United States, but it also aggravated ethnic tensions within the Catholic community. In the early decades of the nineteenth century, lay representatives of German and Irish immigrants voiced strong preferences for their own clergy over French priests, and Irish-Americans even accused Maréchal of purposely excluding talented Irish priests from the hierarchy. Recurring waves of immigration further increased ethnic tensions.

In 1829, the year America entered the Jacksonian age and England witnessed the passage of the Catholic Emancipation Act, the American hierarchy met on 4 October in Baltimore to convene the First Provincial Council. The bishops sought to solidify their authority by placing priests belonging to religious orders under the jurisdiction of local bishops, by requiring incardination of all priests in a diocese, and by upholding the sole right of bishops to hold the deed to church property. In an immigrant church in which sacramental rituals varied according to national customs, and abuses had crept in due to ignorance and poor supervision, the bishops sought to establish uniformity in the administration of the sacraments and required parishes to keep records of baptisms, confirmations, marriages, and burials. They also expressed the need for Catholic schools and a new catechism. The American hierarchy was especially scrupulous in obeying the Tridentine decree stating that provincial councils should meet every three years. Between 1829 and 1849 they convened seven such councils. American bishops of the antebellum period also responded dutifully to the drive for uniformity and centralized authority in the church led by an increasingly important ultramontane faction in Rome under Pope Pius IX (1846–1878) and his immediate successors.

When Archbishop Cajetan Bedini, papal nuncio to Brazil, visited the United States in 1853 to investigate certain disputes and determine America's readiness for a nuncio, he noted that American bishops had absolute authority; the hierarchy had taken the first steps in the remodeling of their church, with its early congregationalist tendencies, in the image of Rome. Even in 1853, however, the trustee problem lingered on. Bedini, publicly assailed by the ex-priest Alessandro Gavassi and threatened by mobs in Pittsburgh, Cincinnati, and Wheeling, West Virginia, failed to resolve the dispute between Bishop John Timon and the trustees of Saint Louis' parish in Buffalo over Timon's right to the title deed of the church property. A decade later, with the passage of the Church Trustee Law by the New York State Legislature, Timon's claims were vindicated and the sixteen-year struggle with Saint Louis' parish drew to a close.

Between 1790 and 1850 the western boundary of the United States moved from the Allegheny Mountains to the Pacific Ocean and the Catholic church followed the receding frontier. In the late eighteenth century Maryland Catholics had settled in western Pennsylvania and in Kentucky, where such prominent Maryland families as the Spaldings, Wathens, Coomes, Haydens, Clements, and Mattinglys contributed to the swift institutional growth of the diocese of Bardstown. In 1803, with the Louisiana Purchase, the United States annexed an area equal to its own size with French roots dating back to 1699. Carroll became bishop of Louisiana and the Two Floridas in 1805. In the Northwest Territory, French Catholic roots ran deep and early-nineteenth-century missionaries in Green Bay, Mackinac, Detroit, and Saint Joseph, as well as in Vincennes, South Bend, and Fort Wayne, faced the task of reviving long-neglected French Catholic communities.

Catholicism in the Midwest witnessed significant growth during the antebellum years. Detroit and Vincennes became separate dioceses in 1833 and 1834. Beginning in 1837 the diocese of Dubuque, Iowa, served as the headquarters for Catholic missions in what later became Iowa, Minnesota, and the Dakotas. In 1843 and 1850 the dioceses of Wisconsin and Minnesota were established, destined to serve a burgeoning German immigrant population in the upcoming decades.

The 1840s also witnessed the annexation of Texas and part of the Oregon Territory previously owned jointly with England. In 1846 Walla Walla in the Oregon Territory became the second metropolitan see in the United States. New Mexico came under the jurisdiction of the hierarchy in 1850. In 1853 Jean-Baptiste Lamy, immortalized in Willa Cather's *Death Comes for the Archbishop* (1927), took the helm in the new diocese of Santa Fe, where he fought an uphill battle to impose his French concept of Catholicism upon a church richly infused with Mexican, Spanish, and Indian influences. Not all segments of the Catholic community succumbed to Lamy's efforts to remodel the church, however. From the Catholic Pueblo Indians to the flagellants of the Penitente brotherhoods, reminders of seventeenth-century Spanish Franciscan influences persist into the present. In Arizona, where the Catholic community also suffered from isolation and neglect when the Franciscans left in 1828, some vestiges of the work of Jesuit missionaries of the previous century survived among the Yaqui and Sonora Catholics, whose religion represents a fusion of eighteenth-century Catholicism and their own Indian traditions.

The spiritual legacy of the Spanish Franciscans in Florida and California is less tangible. Soon after Florida passed into American hands in 1821, Protestant Christianity overshadowed Catholic influences everywhere but in the old Catholic strongholds of St. Augustine and Pensacola. Catholicism in California, rooted in twenty-one Spanish Franciscan missions, settlements feverishly built in the late eighteenth century and secularized between 1831 and 1845, had suffered decades of not-so-benign neglect before the Diocese of the Two Californias was established in 1840. Moreover, the church in California witnessed a crisis of leadership after the Mexican War, the Gold Rush, and the death of its first bishop in 1846; this crisis did not abate until the appointment of Joseph S. Alemany as bishop of Monterrey in 1850. The period between the Gold Rush and the Civil War was a troubled time for California's Catholic community, shaken by "race wars" (Mexicans against Yankees) from within and by nativism from without.

Between 1790 and 1820 the American Catholic population grew from 35,000 to 195,000. Between 1830 and 1860 it skyrocketed from 318,000 to 3,103,000. In both cases the major cause of the increase was immigration, generally into the larger cities. Only about 15,000 Catholics became Americans with the Louisiana Purchase and another 26,000 were added to the American Catholic community after the war with Mexico in 1848.

By the middle of the nineteenth century many foreigners had contributed heavily to the advancement of Catholic evangelization in America. Among the French émigrés were Sulpicians who came to establish Saint Mary's Seminary in Baltimore, but even in the early 1790s some Sulpicians, including Benedict-Joseph Flaget, Gabriel Richard, and Michael Levadoux, set out as frontier pastors in Vincennes and the Illinois country. During the second half of the eighteenth century the Swabian Jesuit Ferdinand Steinmeyer (Ferdinand Farmer) cared for the spiritual needs of German and Irish Catholics in Philadelphia, New York, and East and West Jersey. The Belgian Jesuit Pierre-Jean De Smet established Catholic outposts in the Northwest Territory during the third quarter of the nineteenth century and traveled over 180,000 miles in Europe and America begging for money for the evangelization of American Indians.

Catholic efforts to convert American Indians were sporadic. Seventeenth-century French Jesuits had made some progress in the East as well as around the Great Lakes and in the Mississippi Valley. During the Revolution, Catholic Penob-

scots in Maine asked the colonial government in Massachusetts for help in finding a priest. As early as 1832 Bishop Edward Fenwick of Cincinnati sent two American Indians, William Maccodabinasse, son of Blackbird, a Catholic Ottawa chief, and August Hamelin, future chief of the Ottawa and Chippewa, to Rome to study for the priesthood, but illness terminated both men's studies. During the 1830s Bishop Simon Bruté of Vincennes failed in his attempt to intervene on behalf of the Catholic Potawatomi in Indiana and Michigan, who were compelled to move to Sugar Creek, Kansas, in compliance with Jackson's new Indian policy. Sugar Creek became a Catholic Indian community, complete with schools for boys and girls run by the Jesuits and the Religious of the Sacred Heart and subsidized by the federal government. Evangelization of the Indians was severely hampered, however, by the eighteenth-century Vatican pronouncements condemning previous efforts by missionaries in India and China to accommodate indigenous beliefs and rituals. This meant that nineteenth-century Catholic missionaries had to employ the same approach as their Protestant counterparts who tried to obliterate the religion and culture of the Indians and replace it with an American (or European) Christian substitute.

European organizations backed individual missionary efforts. The Society for the Propagation of the Faith (1822), a French lay organization in Lyon, launched many early Catholic forays into the American frontier. The Leopoldine Foundation (1829) and Ludwig's Mission Society (1838) bear witness to the missionary zeal of Austrian and Bavarian Catholics. Missionaries from Europe also brought the parish mission to America. Although missions had originated in sixteenth-century Europe, they met the needs of nineteenth-century American Catholics both in the established parishes and in outposts on the frontier. These periodic attempts to increase observance of the sacraments of Penance and the Eucharist through intense paraliturgical services and fiery sermons by itinerant preachers represent the Catholic equivalent of the revivals that formed the backbone of American Protestant religion in the nineteenth century. American Catholic missions dated back to the late eighteenth century, but they gained new prominence during the jubilee year 1825. Seven years later German Redemptorist mission specialists began their work in America, aided by Jesuits and (later) Paulists, and also by Franciscans and Holy Cross Fathers.

The growing Catholic population on the frontier during the antebellum period caused deep concern within the Protestant community. In *Democracy in America* (1835), Alexis de Tocqueville rejected the widespread stereotype of Catholicism as the enemy of democracy, but this did not decrease the public appeal of Lyman Beecher's exposé of the papal plot to win the frontier in *Plea for the West,* which appeared the same year. Although Beecher persuaded many Protestants, others thought the real battle with popery was in the eastern cities, the ports of entry where growing numbers of Catholic immigrants lived in increasingly congested conditions.

During the 1820s, 50,724 Irish people arrived in the United States, fleeing the effects of the potato blight of 1821; this number rose to 780,719 during the decade of the Great Famine (1845–1847) and to 914,119 in the following decade. In all, 4.5 million Irish emigrated to America between the end of the eighteenth century and the 1920s. Six million Germans arrived during the same period.

After the Civil War the United States witnessed a major influx of German immigrants and the rapid expansion of the German-American Catholic community. Bismarck's tax increases and his enforcement of universal conscription laws lessened the prospects of small landowners and shopkeepers seeking economic advancement and stimulated German emigration to the United States. Meanwhile, *Kulturkampf,* Bismarck's attempt to subordinate the Catholic church to the German government, added another incentive for German Catholics to leave their homeland. Although some Germans settled with the Irish in the East—40,000 to 50,000 German Catholics occupied eight national parishes in New York City in the late 1860's—large numbers had the funds and farming skills to move directly to the Midwest and buy land. They settled in the "German Triangle" between Cincinnati, Milwaukee, and St. Louis.

By 1865 the Catholic church had become the largest American denomination, with 3.5 million members. In crowded urban parishes this rapid growth in the Catholic community required a new style of clerical leadership epitomized by the "brick and mortar priest," who, in addition to administering the sacraments and serving as spiritual adviser, became a professional fundraiser and supervised the construction of new churches and schools to meet the needs of a burgeoning "immigrant church."

The growing Irish and German Catholic populations added diversity to a church long dominated by English and French traditions. Germans brought with them special veneration for certain patron saints (Saint Joachim, Saint Anne, and Saint Alphonsus), a strong preference for pomp and splendor, a tradition of parish confraternities and organizations (even military societies) for the laity, and an inclination toward lay administration of church property. Their chosen slogan, "Language Saves Faith," explains the rationale behind the strenuous efforts of German-American Catholics to preserve their language, religion, and customs by maintaining separate national parishes and parochial schools, sometimes even separate cemeteries.

Irish Catholics brought with them a tradition of mixing religion and politics and a certain political savvy, which served them well both in the American hierarchy and in urban politics in the second half of the nineteenth century. They also carried with them the legacy of the "Devotional Revolution," which blossomed in Ireland from 1850 to 1875. Like their counterparts back home, American Irish Catholics began to receive the sacraments of Penance and the Eucharist with increasing frequency, rather than merely fulfilling the annual "Easter Duty." They participated enthusiastically in the "new devotions" —the rosary, forty hours, novenas, stations of the cross, benediction, and special devotions to the Sacred Heart of Jesus and the Immaculate Heart of Mary—as well as in processions and pilgrimages.

Although, in the nineteenth century, Catholics throughout the world displayed doctrinal uniformity, devotional and liturgical styles and trappings varied from culture to culture. This became evident in the contrast between Irish and German Catholic life in America. While the Germans exhibited a strong attachment to sacred music, including bells and bell ringers, parish orchestras, and choirs singing German hymns, the Irish preferred simple, low-key liturgies. Especially important to German Catholics were first communions and weddings celebrated with solemn processions and musical extravaganzas.

Among the most distinctive Irish paraliturgical practices were "wakes" held at home to commemorate the dead; wakes long remained more significant to mourning Irish Catholic families than the funerals held in parish churches. However, the piety of mid-nineteenth-century Catholic immigrants must not be exaggerated. During the 1860s somewhere between 40 and 60 percent of the Catholics in New York City worshiped regularly on Sundays. Although Catholic churches were attracting a larger percentage of their urban constituency than their Protestant counterparts, this did not mitigate the growing anxieties of Catholic bishops and clergy concerning the leakage of Catholic immigrants from the fold.

For many Protestants, the strange beliefs and religious practices of the Catholic immigrant were far less unsettling than the cost of feeding, housing, and incarcerating members of the ever-growing immigrant population. In 1852 the New York Association for Improving the Condition of the Poor reported that half of the needy they had assisted that year had been Irish and three-fourths of them Catholic. Such assistance remained a crucial supplement to the heroic efforts of individual pastors and religious orders to care for the throngs of sick, poor, and uneducated peasants from rural Ireland and Germany who came to New York or Boston totally unprepared to compete for work in the urban-industrial environment. Individual priests devoted their lives to the care of the immigrant poor: from the Cuban aristocrat Felix Varela, pastor to Irish immigrants in New York at the beginning of the nineteenth century, to Edward McGlynn, who sought at the end of the century to help Catholic immigrants in the same city through political means. However, female religious remained the major source of Catholic aid for the poor, sick, orphaned, and displaced. Among the first lay organizations were benevolence societies, such as the Ladies' Society of Charity in Transfiguration parish in New York in the 1830s and branches of international groups such as the Saint Vincent de Paul Society, which had spread to America by 1845.

During the first half of the nineteenth century the American Catholic approach to poverty remained confined to exhortations to practice the corporal works of mercy (feed the hungry, shelter the homeless, clothe the naked, and so on).

The Sisters of Charity grew rapidly, establishing six foundations between 1809 and 1870; their work in hospitals, orphanages, sanitoriums, hospices, and schools not only met the pressing needs of the immigrant poor but also epitomized the solution to poverty preferred by the majority of American Catholics. Other significant efforts to aid the immigrant poor included the trade schools established by the Brothers and Sisters of the Holy Cross in cities across the country during the antebellum years and the "houses of protection" for young single working women first launched by the Irish Sisters of Mercy in Pittsburgh in 1843 and soon duplicated in other cities. Only toward the end of the nineteenth century did a tiny minority within the church propose social reforms that struck at the socio-economic roots of urban poverty rather than those that merely bathed its wounds, but this group found itself on the wrong side of the church's official position on socialism.

Non-Catholic Americans resented the Catholic immigrants because their poverty placed a burden upon the community and because they represented unwelcome competition in the job market in an age of economic turbulence. Moreover, these immigrants, even the English-speaking Irish, were vivid reminders that the Catholic church was a church of foreigners, who were the subjects of a monarch in Rome. The emergence of Protestant newspapers and periodicals during the Second Great Awakening (1800–1830) created a new forum for the anti-Catholic sentiments previously aired in sermons and lectures. In fact, the escalation of anti-Catholic sentiments during the first third of the nineteenth century proved to be a boon to the growth of both Catholic and Protestant journalism in America. The anti-Catholic tirades of the *Boston Recorder* (1816), the *Christian Watchman* (1819), and the *New York Observer* (1823) gave birth to the *United States Catholic Miscellany* (1822), the nation's first Catholic newspaper, founded by John England, bishop of Charleston; the *Truth Teller* (1825) in New York; and the *Jesuit* (1829) in Boston.

Unfortunately the religious conflicts of the antebellum years were not confined to the arena of journalism. On 11 August 1834 an angry mob burned the Ursuline Convent in Charleston, Massachusetts, causing the sisters and their (predominantly Unitarian) charges to flee for their lives. Afterward a group of Bostonians published *Six Months in a Convent* (1835), an account of life at the Ursuline convent purportedly written by Rebecca Reed, an escaped nun. The following year another allegedly autobiographical exposé, Maria Monk's *Awful Disclosures of the Hôtel Dieu Nunnery in Montreal,* won instant popularity in nativist circles. Monk, dressed in a habit and carrying an infant, went on the lecture circuit and even produced a sequel, *Further Disclosures* (1837). Ex-nun lecturers presenting exposés of convent life continued to appeal to some segments of the American population throughout the nineteenth century and even into the opening decades of the twentieth century.

Nor was the incident in Charlestown the last outbreak of public violence. In 1844 the Philadelphia suburbs of Kensington and Southwark witnessed a series of riots sparked by hostility between Irish Catholic and Protestant laborers. The threat of similar riots in New York City quieted down only after Bishop Hughes arranged for armed Catholic men to guard each Catholic church in the city. Between 1854 and 1856, nativism attracted national attention with the rise of the American or Know-Nothing party on the political scene. Before its crashing demise in 1856, when it was upstaged by the slavery debate, the nativist American party managed to monopolize the Massachusetts state government and send seventy-five congressmen from across the nation to Washington in 1854.

Nativist tensions in the East and news of opportunities in the West stimulated a drive for the relocation of poor urban Irish Catholics. The chief promoters of Irish colonization, Bishop Loras of Dubuque and Irish-American journalists Thomas D'Arcy McGee and Patrick Donahoe, sponsored an immigrant aid convention held in Buffalo, New York, on 12 to 15 February 1856. Although Bishop Hughes of New York vigorously opposed the project, after the bishop's death in 1864 John Lancaster Spalding, bishop of Peoria, championed the cause. Spalding lent his full support to the Irish Catholic Colonization Association founded in 1879. Nevertheless, the response of the Irish to colonization and to the rural version of the American dream remained halfhearted at best.

Thus by the end of the antebellum period the American Catholic church was closely identified with the German and Irish immigrant population. Not all of the immigrants from Catholic backgrounds remained Catholic in Protestant America, however. As early as 1836 Bishop John England had estimated a "leakage" of 3.75 million Catholics during the previous half-century. By the 1840s German and Irish converts from Catholicism had become successful hawkers of Protestant books, tracts, and Bibles, especially among lukewarm Catholics from their own ethnic groups.

Meanwhile, just as the foreign element in the church began to increase dramatically, the number of Catholic converts rose. Approximately 48,000 Americans converted to Catholicism during the 1840s and 1850s, the heyday of nativism, and the ranks of the converts continued to increase as the century progressed. Between 1840 and 1860 the American Catholic church witnessed a full-scale influx of prominent, educated American converts, which has evoked comparisons with the Oxford Movement under way in England at the same time. Ironically, most American converts came from what might be considered the two opposite poles of American Protestantism: the Unitarian and the Episcopal churches.

In 1840 James Roosevelt Bayley, a New York Episcopal pastor who was related to an earlier convert, Elizabeth Seton, converted to Catholicism; he later became archbishop of Baltimore. Other prominent converts of the period included James A. McMaster, future editor of the *New York Freeman's Journal;* Levi Silliman Ives, Episcopal bishop of North Carolina; Columbia University professor William Henry Anderson; and West Point general William Rosecrans. Famous female converts included poet and essayist Eliza Allen Starr and Cornelia Connelly, founder of the Sisters of the Holy Child Jesus in England in 1846, who had successfully opposed her former husband's efforts to sue for a restoration of his conjugal rights.

Considerable scholarly attention has been focused upon Isaac Hecker and Orestes Brownson, two converts of the antebellum period who made major contributions to the ongoing debate on the compatibility of American ideals and Catholic religion. Both men came to the church from the Transcendentalist movement, on the left flank of Unitarianism. Following his conversion in 1844, Brownson served as editor of *Brownson's Quarterly Review* and fought off critics both inside and outside the church as he first affirmed and later denied that American democracy and Catholic faith were fundamentally compatible. Although Brownson influenced Hecker's decision to become a Catholic, the two men joined two different Catholic churches, Brownson the church of the European Catholic philosophers and Hecker the church of the common people. After his conversion in 1844 Hecker became a Redemptorist mission preacher. By 1858 he had received permission from Rome to establish the Congregation of the Missionary Priests of Saint Paul the Apostle, the Paulists, who, from Hecker's time onward, sought to develop new methods of evangelization especially suited to the American environment.

The turbulent 1850's, which witnessed nativist strife, the birth of the Irish colonization effort, and the rise of the Paulists, also saw a shift in the American hierarchy. In 1851 Francis P. Kenrick became the first Irish-born prelate to be consecrated archbishop of Baltimore. Kenrick convened the First Plenary Council at Baltimore, at which the American hierarchy presided for the first time over a church that stretched from coast to coast. The council began on 9 May 1852 with a procession of the hierarchy, six archbishops and twenty-six bishops, into the Baltimore cathedral. None of the archbishops and only eight of the bishops had been born in the United States. They met to discuss the needs of the expanding Catholic community of 1.6 million members and to formulate a uniform system of church discipline, a task complicated by the variety of customs and practices introduced by the growing immigrant population. They also urged that Catholic schools be built in every diocese, reaffirming a papal encyclical on the subject dated 21 November 1851.

During the opening decades of the nineteenth century, when Protestants of the Second Great Awakening had set forth ambitiously to establish a string of denominational colleges on the frontier, Catholics, with similar motivations, had done the same. Considerable progress had already been made in the area of Catholic education by the time of the First Plenary. The two pioneering American Catholic institutions, Georgetown Academy and Saint Mary's Seminary, Baltimore, had accepted their first students in the fall of 1791. By 1840 a number of small Catholic colleges had sprung up across the nation: Mount Saint James (later Holy Cross) in Worcester, Massachusetts; Saint Philip's University in Detroit; the College of Vincennes; Saint Mary's College at the Barrens and Saint Louis University (both in Missouri); Saint Charles College at Grand Coteau, Louisiana; the College of Spring Hill in Alabama; Saint Joseph's College, Bardstown; and Saint Mary's College, Kentucky. In 1842 the Congregation of the Holy Cross established Notre Dame.

Meanwhile, important strides had been made in Catholic women's education. Although the Ursulines had been teaching young women in French Louisiana since 1727, seven decades passed before the first Catholic women's academy was founded in Philadelphia in 1797 by an Irish immigrant, Alice Lalor. Lalor later moved the school to Georgetown, where she founded the first American Visitation Convent in 1816. Elizabeth Bayley Seton, a convert from the Episcopal church, established the Sisters of Charity in Emmitsburg, Maryland, in 1803. (Seton, canonized in 1975, became the first saint born in the United States.) Seton's followers did pioneering work in women's education during the antebellum period, but they did not work alone. The Loretto Sisters of Kentucky (1812), the first order of women religious established in America, educated young women, including American Indians, in Kentucky, Missouri, and New Mexico, and later Arkansas, Colorado, Texas, and Nebraska. In 1818 Mother Philippine Duchesne and four other members of the French Religious of the Sacred Heart established the first free school for girls west of the Mississippi in Saint Charles, Missouri. By mid-century the order had opened schools in Louisiana, New York, Pennsylvania, and Kansas, as well as in Montreal and Halifax in Canada. Among these early foundations were two schools for young Potawatomi women in Sugar Creek and Saint Mary's, Kansas. Third Order Dominicans, also active in women's education, had established nine foundations in Kentucky, Ohio, Wisconsin, New York, Louisiana, and Tennessee by the Civil War.

In areas where priests were scarce, women religious provided more than education for children and care for the poor and sick. They functioned as the abiding Catholic presence during the long intervals between the visits of itinerant priests and nurtured the faith of tiny Catholic communities surrounded on all sides by Protestants. Between 1790 and 1859 fifty-one communities of female religious were established in the United States. Sixteen of these originated on American soil; the others had European roots. Between 1860 and 1870 eight new communities of women religious, all with European roots, were launched. By the year 1900, fifty-nine more sprang up, thirty-nine of which were founded by European sisters.

All new religious communities faced serious challenges: financial duress, internal conflicts regarding the rule of enclosure, power struggles with bishops and priest-advisers, the hostility of non-Catholics, and the limits placed upon women's activities in the public sector. In addition, the European religious themselves had to weather culture shock and language problems and acclimate themselves to the American environment. The statistics attest to the stamina of the sisters. During the nineteenth century, their numbers rose from less than 40 to over 40,000; by 1900 they taught in 663 academies for young women and virtually all of America's 3,811 parochial schools.

In many places the parochial schools served as the focal point in debates concerning the compatibility of American and Catholic ideals. Before the common school movement began in the 1830's, elementary education remained in the hands of the various denominations. The proliferation of public schools prompted mixed reactions. Many non-Catholics believed that public schools both symbolized and transmitted the values underlying American democracy. Catholics protested that public schools propagated Protestant values and threatened the Catholic students' faith. By the mid-nineteenth century the situation was further complicated by financial considerations. Some local school systems offered funding to religious schools, while others withheld it.

When, in 1840, New York's Bishop Hughes requested public school funds for the city's Catholic schools, this sparked a heated conflict between Hughes and the New York Public School Society. Hughes turned the 1841 elections for the state legislature into a referendum on the school issue. Although the independent candidates backed by Hughes failed to win seats in the legislature, they dramatized the power of the Catholic voting bloc and paved the way for the demise of the Public School Society. Hughes

failed to win public support for parochial schools, however; it became apparent that Catholics in New York and across the nation would have to rely upon their own resources to build and maintain Catholic schools.

Thus the bishops at the First Plenary Council in 1852 urged Catholic Americans to support parochial over public education and to make the sacrifices necessary to educate their children in a religious environment. (This paved the way for the goal set by their counterparts at the Third Plenary Council in 1884: a Catholic education for every Catholic child.) Although the bishops spoke confidently and univocally on the issue of parochial education, they remained silent on slavery, the most controversial topic of the 1850s. The Catholic community had its deepest roots in the slave states of Louisiana and Maryland. Southern Catholics—clergy, laity, and religious—were as dependent upon the slave system as their Protestant neighbors. The Jesuits in Maryland had owned slaves from the turn of the eighteenth century until 1838, when they sold virtually all of their slaves in a single year. From John Carroll in 1785 to Augustin Verot, bishop of Saint Augustine in the 1860s, southern Catholic bishops assailed abuses of the system and the neglect of the slaves' souls, but they did not question the morality of slavery itself. Of similar mind, Pope Gregory XVI condemned the slave trade in 1839 but failed to speak out against slavery as an institution.

While Methodists and Presbyterians divided their churches over the question of slavery, the American Catholic hierarchy maintained an official silence, which allowed unity and variety within the church. Geography, rather than doctrine, determined the attitudes of individual Catholics on slavery. The views of the hierarchy ran the gamut from Charleston's Bishop John England's defense of slavery in his *Letters to the Hon. John Forsythe on the Subject of Domestic Slavery* (1844) to Cincinnati's Archbishop John Purcell's public support for emancipation, as early as August 1862, reinforced by the *Catholic Telegraph,* edited by Purcell's brother, Edward.

Other factors complicated the attitudes Catholic lay people held on the issues of slavery and emancipation. Recent Irish immigrants competed with blacks (free and slave) in expanding southern cities such as Charleston and New Orleans before the Civil War. Violence had broken out between Irish immigrants and free blacks in Cincinnati in 1829 and in New York in 1863. Irish-American Catholics remained alienated from the abolition movement even after Irish celebrities such as Daniel O'Connell and Father Theobald Matthew, the temperance advocate, had endorsed it. Meanwhile, in the North in the 1850's, especially in Massachusetts, the rolls of the Know-Nothings contained the names of numerous abolitionists.

Like the Revolutionary War and unlike the war with Mexico, the Civil War had a positive impact upon relations between Catholics and Protestants. The 640 sisters who served as nurses in military hospitals did much to counteract the negative image of female religious popularized by Maria Monk. Given the shortage of official Catholic chaplains, the sisters frequently functioned as surrogate pastors, performing numerous baptisms and preparing soldiers for death and for the sacraments. Meanwhile, the 84 official Catholic chaplains played a more prominent role than they had in previous conflicts, reflecting recent gains in Catholic numbers. Public affirmations of faith, such as the general absolution given by Father William Corby of Notre Dame on the Gettysburg battlefield, foreshadowed a new confidence and visibility in the church.

The Civil War and Reconstruction focused attention on another challenge faced by the American hierarchy: the apostolate to the 4 million emancipated blacks, 100,000 of whom were Catholics. When on 19 March 1866 Archbishop Martin J. Spalding of Baltimore called for the Second Plenary Council to be held later in the same year, he added an urgent appeal to his fellow bishops to take advantage of the "golden opportunity" to evangelize the former slaves. Nonetheless, the council closed before specific plans to reach out to the former slaves had been made.

The hierarchy and clergy of the church turned their attention to the European immigrants rather than the freed blacks and thus lost a large portion of formerly Catholic slaves (slaves of Catholic masters) to the emerging black Protestant churches. One can point to only a handful of exceptions that prove the rule. The Louisiana *creoles de couleur,* of mixed black and French (or Spanish) ancestry, formed a distinct caste with abiding ties to the Catholic faith. One community founded by Nicholas Augustin Metoyer, a Creole of color, in Isle Brevêlle, Natchitoches parish, in northern Louisiana, has retained its separate religious and ethnic identity for over 200 years. Other exceptions include the Oblate Sisters of Providence, a congregation of black religious established in Baltimore in 1829 to educate black children, and the Sisters of the Holy Family, another black order, founded in New Orleans in 1842 to care for orphans and elderly blacks.

A third apostolate to black Americans, the Society of Saint Joseph (Josephites), was launched in 1866 in England by Father Herbert Vaughan. In 1871 Vaughan and four priests arrived in Baltimore. On Vaughan's subsequent tour through the South, with stops in Savannah, Vicksburg, Natchez, Charleston, and New Orleans, he discovered a thoroughly segregated American Catholic church: separate and inferior seating for blacks, separate celebrations of black and white First Communions, even an incident in which a white priest withheld the Eucharist from a black man. Despite adverse conditions, the Josephites persevered. In December 1891 Charles Uncles, a Josephite, became the first black ordained priest in the United States. Three years before, Augustine Tolton, raised a slave in Missouri, had been ordained in Rome for a pioneering ministry to his own black people in Illinois. The first black American priest, James Augustine Healy, son of a Georgia plantation owner and his mulatto wife, was ordained in Paris in 1854 and went on to become bishop of Portland, Maine, in 1875. Healy's brother Patrick, a Jesuit, served as president of Georgetown College from 1873 to 1882.

After the Civil War other concerns detracted from the apostolate to the blacks, among them the escalating rate of immigration into the United States and the increasing identification of the American Catholic church with the nascent American labor movement. Between 1871 and 1880, years punctuated by the Panic of 1873 and the violence among the Pennsylvania coal miners in 1877, the Catholic population in America rose from 4,504,000 to 6,259,000. By 1896 the "new immigrants" from Southern and Eastern Europe outnumbered those from Northern and Western Europe, a shift that added to the Polish and Italian Catholic communities and to the diversity of the church. When the American Catholic population reached 16,363,000, in 1910, this represented an increase of 12 million since 1870.

Just as the newcomers appeared to share the bottom rungs of the social ladder with the newly emancipated blacks, the descendants of the earlier Catholic immigrants experienced a long-awaited rise in status and power. By the 1870s the Irish had found their niche in the police and fire departments in Massachusetts, where the Know-Nothings had held such a firm grip only two decades before. In 1884 Hugh O'Brien became the first Irish Catholic mayor of Boston. Three years later in Clinton, Iowa, mounting fears concerning the expanding Catholic immigrant voting bloc gave birth to the American Protective Association (A.P.A.). Before it declined in the late 1890s, the A.P.A. had attracted half a million members who had made a solemn promise never to vote for a Catholic, go on strike with a Catholic, or hire a Catholic if a non-Catholic was available.

By the second half of the nineteenth century Catholics had assumed prominent positions in the labor movement. Two aspects of organized labor raised objections from the American hierarchy, however. First, most early labor unions required an oath of secrecy to protect members from the reprisals of their employers. The Catholic church had consistently condemned secret societies ever since Clement XII's negative ruling on Catholic membership in the Freemasons was issued in 1783. Second, the labor movement was connected in the public mind to socialism and violence. The goal of the Knights of Labor, to abolish the wage system and replace it with a system based upon cooperation, invited comparisons with socialism. When members of a secret union, the Molly Maguires, were found responsible for violence and deaths among the Pennsylvania anthracite coal miners in 1877, this confirmed the worst fears of those who opposed organized labor. Three years before the incident, Archbishop James Roosevelt Bayley of Baltimore had publicly attacked labor unions for their communistic leanings. Bayley's condemnation of socialism followed the precedent set by Pope Pius IX in 1846 in his encyclical *Qui Pluribus* and anticipated Pope Leo XIII's statements in *Quod Apostolici Muneris* in 1878.

While Archbishop Bayley might have been able to dismiss labor unions as ideologically and spiritually unsafe, American Catholic laborers with more practical concerns recognized the positive side of unionization. Terence Powderly, a Catholic who served as grand master of the Knights of Labor during the eventful 1870s and 1880s, persuaded the Knights to discontinue their oath of secrecy in 1881; nevertheless, some members of the hierarchy, notably Archbishop Michael Corrigan of New York and Bishop James A. Healy of Portland, remained vehemently opposed to Catholic membership in the Knights. Ironically, the American Federation of Labor had already begun to overshadow the Knights of Labor by the time the archbishops met in Baltimore on 28 October 1886 to discuss whether Catholics could belong to the Knights. The archbishops favored the Knights in a ten-to-two vote. The following February, James Cardinal Gibbons of Baltimore carried to Rome a memorial on behalf of the Knights, which was drafted by himself and fellow bishops John Ireland of Saint Paul and John Keane of Richmond. The following year the Vatican announced its toleration of Catholic membership in the Knights of Labor and the American hierarchy openly supported labor's right to organize.

Starting in the 1880s Catholic lay people, including two women, Mary Harris ("Mother") Jones and Mary Kenney O'Sullivan, served as prominent labor reformers and reinforced the increasing identification of the church with the cause of working people. There were still limits placed upon Catholic support of social and economic reform, however, as the case of Father Edward McGlynn illustrates. When McGlynn openly supported the "single tax" platform of Henry George in the 1886 mayoral election in New York City, Archbishop Corrigan suspended his powers. When this failed to hamper McGlynn's public speaking, Corrigan declared attendance at McGlynn's lectures a mortal sin and finally had the priest excommunicated. McGlynn was exonerated in 1892.

The Catholic laity of the late nineteenth century became increasingly involved in religious as well as labor organizations. Previously, when antebellum Protestants had volunteered enthusiastically to support numerous religious, moral, and social reform movements, there were few parallel efforts among Catholics. The organization of the Catholic laity hinged upon the full support of the bishops, which was not forthcoming until after World War I. Nevertheless, the need to provide alternative insurance and fraternal organizations for a church composed largely of immigrants and workers caused bishops to encourage the formation of certain kinds of lay societies. Thus by the late 1830s Irish immigrants were joining the Ancient Order of Hibernians, an American variant of an Irish organization called the Saint Patrick's Funeral Benefit Society. In 1855 many of the local German-American mutual aid societies, which had sprung up since the 1830s, converged to form the German Catholic Central Verein. Other lay societies of wide scope included the Irish Catholic Benevolent Union (1869), the Catholic Total Abstinence Union (1872), the Catholic Young Men's National Union (1875), and the Knights of Columbus (1882). At the same time Catholic lay people were also organizing on the parish level into such groups as the Rosary, Sacred Heart of Mary, and Scapular Confraternities, and the Sodality of Our Lady.

The efforts of American lay people to follow the examples set by their coreligionists at lay congresses in Mainz (1848) and Malines, Belgium (1893), culminated in two lay congresses held in Baltimore (1889) and Chicago (1893) organized by the emerging lay leaders Henry F. Brownson, William Onahan, Henry Spaunhorst, and Peter Foy. At the Baltimore congress, part of a protracted celebration of the American centennial, Archbishop John Ireland delivered a sermon entitled "The Mission of Catholics in America," which urged lay people to dedicate themselves to making America Catholic and establishing, once and for all, the profound compatibility of American and Catholic ideals. Lay representatives at Baltimore discussed a wide array of topics from education and charities to journalism, labor organizations, and lay activities. At the second congress, held in conjunction with the World's Columbian Exposition in Chicago in 1893, Catholic women took an active role and defended their responsibility to do so. This theme was addressed by Nathaniel Hawthorne's daughter Rose Hawthorne Lathrop, a convert who, seven years later, took the vows of the Dominican Third Order and launched her own religious community, the Servants of Relief for Incurable Cancer. Other speakers at the Chicago congress criticized American Catholic failure to reach out to blacks and Indians, spoke out in opposition to the arms race, and affirmed the

right of the laity to speak out in the church. Black Catholics held the first Colored Catholic Congress in Washington, D.C., in 1889; four more congresses followed, ending in 1894.

Another important development paved the way for the lay congresses: the growing popularity of local Catholic reading circles during the final quarter of the nineteenth century. In 1889 the Columbian Reading Union was established to coordinate the activities of the many smaller groups, and reports and reading lists appeared in the Paulist magazine the *Catholic World.* Other outgrowths of the reading circle movement include the Catholic summer schools founded in New London, Connecticut (1892), and Madison, Wisconsin (1895), along with a winter session in New Orleans (1896). The reading circles and summer schools, which were especially popular with Catholic women, reached their peak at the turn of the century and died out during the opening decades of the twentieth century.

Because it witnessed the emergence of a new, articulate, and confident breed of lay leaders with a vision for the future, the period between 1885 and 1893 has been called the "lay renaissance." By the middle of the 1890s, however, the lay renaissance had foundered, in part because other issues had deflected the attention of the hierarchy. Perhaps the most prominent issue at the end of the nineteenth century was the polarization of the hierarchy on the question of how American the church could become without succumbing to secularization or Protestantization. This question had surfaced in the disputes over the Knights of Labor and Father McGlynn's support of Henry George, as well as in the controversy over parochial schools and the Catholic University of America, established in 1889. It had occupied center stage in the debates between German trustees of national parishes and the hierarchy.

Two incidents that occurred during the final decades of the nineteenth century exacerbated the existing tensions within the church. In 1886 Peter Abbelen, a Milwaukee priest, delivered a petition to Rome requesting that the Vatican protect German national churches from attempts by the Irish-American hierarchy to force them to assimilate into an English-speaking geographical parish system. In 1891, Peter Paul Cahensly, a member of the Prussian Diet and a founder of the Saint Raphael's Society, a German immigrant aid society with branches on both sides of the Atlantic, issued a memorial to Pope Leo XIII charging that millions of Catholic immigrants were leaving the church. Cahensly suggested that national parishes and perhaps national bishops would be able to stop the leakage of Catholic immigrants.

The protests prompted by Cahensly's memorial called attention to the polarization of the American hierarchy on the pivotal issue of Americanization. Leaders of the liberal group included Denis O'Connell, rector of the American College in Rome from 1885 to 1895; John Keane, rector of the newly established Catholic University of America from 1889 to 1896; and John Ireland, archbishop of Saint Paul. In this same period a substantial minority of other American archbishops leaned in the liberal direction, notably Patrick Feehan of Chicago, William Gross of Oregon City, Peter Kenrick and John Kain of St. Louis, Patrick Riorden of San Francisco, and James Gibbons of Baltimore. Nevertheless, the greater portion of the laity, priests (minus the Paulists and Sulpicians), and bishops appear to have sympathized with the conservative flank, which placed a high value upon tradition and considered unnecessary innovation a compromise with the Protestant environment. Archbishop Michael Corrigan of New York and Bishop Bernard McQuaid of Rochester, the most vocal conservatives, enjoyed the strong support of the midwestern German bishops.

During this period punctuated by internal conflicts within the hierarchy, James Gibbons, cardinal of Baltimore (1877–1921), a prudent, diplomatic man with liberal sympathies, performed a delicate balancing act in order to maintain cordial relations with Rome and relative peace at home. At the helm of a church composed largely of immigrant laborers intent upon assimilation into the American mainstream, Gibbons fought for the rights of Catholics to join labor unions, despite the strong protests of conservatives. On the other hand, Gibbons quietly withheld his support when liberal members of the laity were planning the Lay Congress of 1893 and then proceeded to watch the lay renaissance die a natural death. Although concerned about the leakage of immigrants from the fold, Gibbons nevertheless opposed the efforts of German bishops and clergy to establish nation-al dioceses and parishes and German-speaking schools on a permanent basis.

While Gibbons favored parochial schools, he lent his support to the Faribault-Stillwater plan launched in 1891 under the jurisdiction of Archbishop Ireland. This controversial program, which allowed school boards to lease parochial schools and hire sisters to teach in them with the stipulation that religion classes take place outside school hours, resembled a similar arrangement in effect in Poughkeepsie, New York. Both plans came under attack by Protestants and conservative Catholics and were discontinued during the 1890s. Turn-of-the-century Catholics steered away from released-time plans that allowed public school students to receive religious education elsewhere during official school hours. Protestants had been experimenting with these plans for decades before Catholics followed suit during the second quarter of the twentieth century.

Since an important point of contention between liberals and conservatives concerned the appropriateness of Vatican displays of authority and intervention in American Catholic affairs, it is significant that American bishops did not divide into two sharply opposing camps at Vatican I (1869–1870) on the issue of papal infallibility. Twenty-five Americans, Gibbons included, voted in favor of the schema on infallibility, three left Rome before the balloting to avoid opposing it, and one, Edward Fitzgerald of Little Rock, cast one of the two negative votes. Increasing immigration intensified polarization in the American church. By the 1890s the liberals appeared to be riding the crest. In 1892, at the bidding of Pope Leo XIII, John Ireland explained church-state relations in America to French audiences in an effort to bolster French Catholic loyalty to the Third Republic. Two years later, Keane told delegates at the Third International Catholic Science Congress in Brussels what American Catholics had learned about the value of interdenominational dialogue.

Meanwhile, harbingers of change had appeared on the horizon. Leo XIII's appointment of Francesco Satolli as apostolic delegate to the United States on 1 January 1893 showed that Rome intended to keep American Catholics under closer supervision. Leo XIII's negative verdict on Catholic participation in interdenominational parliaments of religion was announced in 1895 and came as a slap in the face to Catholics who had spoken in Chicago two years before. Also in 1895 Leo XIII issued the encyclical *Longinqua Oceani*, addressed specifically to American Catholics, a document that praised the zeal and accomplishments of the Catholic church in the United States but warned against idealizing the American separation of church and state. That same eventful year Denis O'Connell was dismissed from his post as rector of the American College in Rome and was replaced by ultramontane William Henry O'Connell, future bishop of Boston. Keane's dismissal from the rectorship of the Catholic University of America occurred the following year.

By the mid-1890s the question of the compatibility of American and Catholic ideals had ceased to be an intramural issue. In 1897, a translation of Walter Elliott's biography of Father Isaac Hecker appeared in France and acted as a bombshell in a French Catholic church already divided on the question of the compatibility of democracy and Catholicism. Especially incendiary was translator Abbé Félix Klein's suggestion in his preface that Hecker's individualism and activism represented a new model for the priesthood, superseding the old ideals of submissive obedience and inner spiritual discipline. The Spanish-American War further aggravated European suspicions concerning American Catholic orthodoxy, as had the controversial *Evolution and Dogma* (1896) by Father John A. Zahm, banned by the Sacred Congregation of the Index in a decree dated 10 September 1898.

The debate reached a climax on 22 January 1899 with the publication of Leo XIII's encyclical *Testem Benevolentiae*, a document that called attention to certain doctrinal errors allegedly embraced by American as well as European Catholics. The errors condemned included claims that apologists for the church can abrogate religious vows and even change doctrines of the church in order to win converts and assertions that individual judgment and initiative take precedence over dutiful obedience to ecclesiastical authorities. American Catholic liberals denied the existence of the "phantom heresy" of Americanism as strongly as conservatives expressed their gratitude for Rome's intervention on behalf of orthodoxy in America. On 17 March 1899 Gibbons of Baltimore wrote to Leo XIII to assure the pontiff that the so-called doctrines described in the encyclical bore no resemblance to American Catholic beliefs.

The rise of Pope Pius X (1903–1914) represents the sequel to the international ecclesiastical drama that had led to *Longinqua Oceani* and *Testem Benevolentiae*. During the Modernist controversy, which exploded in the first decade of the twentieth century, the liberals Keane, Ireland, and Denis O'Connell openly sided with Rome against the so-called Modernists, who were European proponents of the "new apologetics," which followed "Protestant" trends in biblical scholarship and emphasized the historicity of Catholic doctrines. When Modernism was condemned in the syllabus *Lamentabili* (3 July 1907), and the encyclical *Pascendi Dominici Gregis* (8 September 1907), American Catholics, who had remained isolated from the theological ferment underway in Europe, could rightly wonder whether they had any Modernists in their midst. After the condemnations, any theological innovations that had appeared in the *Ecclesiastical Review*, the *Catholic Quarterly*, and the *New York Review* stopped summarily. For half a century American Catholics abandoned all hopes for a theological bridge between Catholic theology and the American situation.

With the recession of the last remnants of liberalism came a change in leadership epitomized by the rise of William Henry O'Connell, archbishop of Boston from 1907 to 1944. Educated in Rome and dedicated to a new streamlined corporate model of ecclesiastical leadership, O'Connell emphasized the compatibility of Catholic doctrinal orthodoxy, including a strictly hierarchical concept of authority, with a patriotic devotion to American democracy. He spoke out strongly against socialism during the decade before World War I when the Socialist party of America reached the peak of its power. For, despite the church's long-standing condemnation, socialism attracted a vocal minority, including the socialist priests Thomas McGrady of Bellevue, Kentucky, Thomas Hagerty, who served parishes in Texas and New Mexico, and the members of the Catholic Socialist Society, established in Chicago in 1909. To guard against the spread of Catholic socialism, O'Connell and the national leadership of the Catholic Central Verein and the Knights of Columbus sponsored lectures on the perils of socialism, delivered by the former socialist turned Catholic David Goldstein. Socialism held little appeal for the expanding segment of the church with middle-class aspirations and a desire to see Leo XIII's recent encyclical, *Rerum Novarum* (1891), as a defense of private property rather than as an indictment of the oppression of American workers.

While liberals, including Hecker and John Lancaster Spalding, had championed the cause of women's education, women's suffrage remained a stickier issue for Catholics, with female pioneers like Mother Jones supporting the opposition. Nevertheless, a few ardent Catholic suffragists, including Margaret Foley, who organized Boston Catholic women into the Margaret Brent Suffrage Guild, helped spread support for the cause among Catholic women. After the Nineteenth Amendment was passed, even former opponents, notably Cardinal Gibbons, urged Catholic women to vote to offset the votes of female radicals intent upon restructuring the American family. Although some nineteenth-century Catholic women—the poet Mary Elizabeth Blake, the suffragist Lucy Burns, and the lawyer-reformer Hortense Ward—were feminists, most Catholic lay women preferred the activism of patriotic and charitable organizations such as the Catholic Daughters of America, established in 1903.

In 1908 the American Catholic church came of age and became a national hierarchy in its own right, leaving its mission status behind. The years between the dawn of the twentieth century and World War I brought new confidence and visibility. These years witnessed the rise of the short-lived American Federation of Catholic Societies in 1901 and its demise, due to a lack of support from the hierarchy, by 1917; they also witnessed growing pluralism due to an increase in Italian and Polish Catholics. With pluralism came fragmentation. As early as 1897 Chicago Poles under Anton Kozlowski had formed a separate Polish Catholic church. By 1907 Kozlowski's group and the Polish Catholic Independent Church, founded in Buffalo in 1898 by Stephan Kaminski, became part of the Polish National Catholic church established in Scranton in 1900.

While Poles worried about the dangers of assimilation and domination by a non-Polish hierarchy, they, like the rest of their coreligionists, sought acceptance as middle-class Americans. World War I gave Catholics the opportunity to dramatize the compatibility of American and Catholic ideals. On 17 April 1917 Supreme Knight James Flaherty promised President Wilson the support of 400,000 Knights of Columbus in the upcoming war. American bishops made similar public professions of Catholic support for the war, as did their Protestant counterparts. A million Catholic soldiers went off to war and only four of the almost four thousand conscientious objectors were Catholics. The war, like the elevation of the American Catholic church from mission status nine years before, represented a turning point for a Catholic community already assured of the compatibility of its patriotism with its faith. The aftermath of the war would show that not all Americans accepted this premise and that even within the Catholic community the relationship between America and Catholicism had yet to be resolved.

BIBLIOGRAPHY

Aaron I. Abell, *American Catholicism and Social Action: A Search for Social Justice 1865–1950* (1960) and, as ed., *American Catholic Thought on Social Questions* (1968); Ray Allen Billington, *The Protestant Crusade, 1800–1860: A Study of the Origins of American Nativism* (1938; reissued 1964); Daniel J. Callahan, *The Mind of the Catholic Layman* (1963); Robert D. Cross, *The Emergence of Liberal Catholicism in America* (1958); Robert Emmett Curran, *Michael Augustine Corrigan and the Shaping of Conservative Catholicism in America, 1878–1902* (1978); Jay P. Dolan, *The Immigrant Church: New York's Irish and German Catholics, 1815–1865* (1975) and *Catholic Revivalism: The American Experience, 1830–1900* (1978); Keith P. Dyrud, Michael Novak, and Rudolph Vecoli, eds., *The Other Catholics* (1978).

John Tracy Ellis, *American Catholicism* (1956; rev. 1969) and, as ed., *Documents of American Catholic History* (1962); John Tracy Ellis and Robert Trisco, eds., *A Guide to American Catholic History* (1982); Mary Ewens, *The Role of the Nun in Nineteenth-Century America* (1978); Albert S. Foley, *God's Men of Color: The Colored Catholic Priests of the United States, 1854–1954* (1970); Philip Gleason, *The Conservative Reformers: German-American Catholics and the Social Order* (1968) and, as ed., *Catholicism in America* (1970); Peter Guilday, ed., *The National Pastorals of the American Hierarchy (1792–1919)* (1954); James Hennesey, *The First Council of the Vatican: The American Experience* (1963) and *American Catholics: A History of the Roman Catholic Community in the United States* (1981); Dan Herr and Joel Wells, eds., *Through Other Eyes: Some Impressions of American Catholicism by Foreign Visitors from 1777 to the Present* (1965); John Higham, *Strangers in the Land: Patterns of American Nativism, 1860–1925* (1955; rev. 1963).

Christopher J. Kauffman, *Faith and Fraternalism: The History of the Knights of Columbus, 1882–1982* (1982); James J. Kenneally, "Catholicism and Woman Suffrage in Massachusetts," in *Catholic Historical Review*, 53 (1967) and "Eve, Mary and the Historians: American Catholicism and Women," in *Horizons*, 3 (1976); Emmet Larkin, "The Devotional Revolution in Ireland, 1850–75," in *American Historical Review*, 77 (1972); Richard M. Linkh, *American Catholicism and European Immigrants, 1900–1924* (1975); Thomas T. McAvoy, *The Americanist Heresy in Roman Catholicism, 1895–1900* (1963), and *A History of the Catholic Church in the United States* (1969); John J. Meng, "Growing Pains in the American Catholic Church 1880–1908," in U.S. Catholic Historical Society, *His-*torical Records and Studies, 36 (1947); Donna Merwick, *Boston Priests 1848–1910: A Study of Social and Intellectual Change* (1973); Randall M. Miller and Jon L. Wakelyn, eds., *Catholicism in the Old South* (1983); James Edmund Roohan, *American Catholics and the Social Question, 1865–1900* (1976); Gerald Shaughnessy, *Has the Immigrant Kept the Faith? A Study of Immigration and Catholic Growth in the United States, 1790–1920* (1925).

[*See also* RELIGIOUS EDUCATION.]

CATHOLICISM SINCE WORLD WAR I

Peter W. Williams

A S World War I came to an end, the Roman Catholic church in the United States was a complex, changing religious community situated in a country that was itself experiencing intense change and contradiction. The church's increasingly cohesive leadership found itself having to deal with issues raised by at least three significant sources. First, the international focus of Roman Catholicism, the Vatican, was still embroiled in coping with the perceived threat of Modernism from within as well as with the convolutions of European and Italian political and social upheaval. Second, the often allied forces of nativism and Evangelical Protestantism presented a major challenge on the domestic front, since they themselves were forced to deal with rapid and perplexing social and technological change. Finally, in the years preceding the war internal ethnic and ideological disunity within the American Catholic community had been an endless source of contention and still raised questions needing resolution.

Before examining each of these three broad areas in detail, it is important to note that by 1902 it was becoming increasingly possible to speak of the American Catholic church as a unity in some significant respects. To be sure, a religious community of such size and diversity of membership has never been completely united in any absolute sense. However, since the Third Plenary Council of Baltimore in 1884 the hierarchical leadership of the American Catholic church was increasingly seeing itself as a united force whose goal was an ever-increasing uniformity of organization and practice within its domain. The conflict over "Americanization" had been resolved in part by Pope Leo XIII's encyclical *Testem Benevolentiae* of 1899, and sharp divergence of opinion and strategy within the

ranks of the hierarchy did not become a significant factor again in American affairs for decades. A united front to achieve common goals through a tightly organized and disciplined governance structure—a model becoming increasingly popular in education, industry, government, and other segments of American society during these years—was the norm for the American church until the changes that were brought about by Vatican II long afterwards.

Although the situation in Rome was still beclouded by the impasse between the Vatican and the Italian government, a conflict that had arisen in 1870 and was not resolved until the concordat with Mussolini in 1929, the influence that the pope and his assistant congregations exerted on the American church was by no means negligible. Encyclicals on "Americanism" (*Testem Benevolentiae,* 1899) and Modernism (*Pascendi Dominici Gregis,* 1907) had had a definitive dampening effect on theological and social experimentation on this side of the Atlantic, and it was by then substantially clear that the American church was very much a part of the *Roman* Catholic church. The creation of the North American College in Rome for the training of talented young clergy in 1859 helped further to strengthen these international linkages, and the existence of the college helped to ensure that the leadership of the American church in future generations would be thoroughly imbued with the spirit of *Romanità,* a sympathy with the traditional ways of the Vatican and an implicit allegiance to them.

On the domestic front the 1920s were a time of great turmoil in American life in general and in the relations between Catholics and "other Americans" in particular. The Catholic presence in America had come increasingly to be an urban one, and the specter of the newly dominant city in American society fueled a reaction in the form of resurgent nativism, Fundamentalism, and the Ku Klux Klan. Fundamentalists feared Catholicism almost as much as they did Protestant "Modernists" (whose doctrines, ironically, had been roundly condemned by Catholics), and the Fundamentalists' implicit alliance with the newly revived Klan in the South and Midwest put Catholics in the company of Jews and blacks as putative enemies of the traditional American rural Protestant order.

For the nativists of the 1920s the symbolic role of the Catholic church had a number of related sources and aspects. Although many of the immigrants from southern and eastern Europe who had flooded into this country from 1870 through the war years were Jews, Eastern Orthodox, and even socialists, a vast number were Roman (or Uniate) Catholics who were often poor, unskilled, undereducated, and not able to speak English. They tended to aggregate in the newly populous urban areas of the East and upper Midwest, where jobs in mines and factories were abundant if only marginally rewarding, and their presence in homogeneous urban enclaves generated not only Catholic parishes but the other features of immigrant society as well: saloons, political machines, and various forms of vice (particularly drink) that were not always perceived by the Catholic church as unmitigated evils. Two of the major legislative achievements of the postwar era—Prohibition and immigration restriction—were both aimed more or less directly at, among other things, Catholic immigrants, their mores, and the church that supported or at least tolerated them.

The church, in return, made its opposition to these challenges known. Hierarchical spokesmen almost unanimously opposed the Eighteenth Amendment, even though they may have been supportive of temperance on a voluntary basis. (The proverbial Irish problem with drink had led to vigorous campaigns to "take the pledge" by and among Irish-American Catholics during the nineteenth century.) Although wine for sacramental purposes was generally procurable, interference with its supply occasionally arose and was not wrongly interpreted as a form of anti-Catholic harassment. Severe immigration restriction in some ways may have eased the task of the institutional church by giving it breathing space to deal with the already massive challenge

of meeting the social and economic as well as the religious needs of previous newcomers, but the use of quotas based on a period of American history when the Catholic presence was relatively small to favor Protestants from northwestern Europe was also interpreted as sending a distinctively nativist message.

Still other political and legal issues calling for a Catholic response to not very subtle forms of opposition arose during the "Jazz Age." The issue of women's suffrage was not in any way directly connected with nativism or anti-Catholicism, but many Catholic leaders perceived it as a repudiation of traditional Catholic attitudes toward the role of women in society. After it became national law, however, James Cardinal Gibbons and others urged women to educate themselves on contemporary issues and vote, since no fundamental teaching of the church was at stake and since Catholic interests had to be defended through the democratic process. An initiative in Michigan in 1924 that would have eliminated parochial schools, for example, was solidly defeated at the polls, while in less strongly Catholic Oregon a state law requiring universal attendance at public schools was finally struck down by a series of judicial decisions culminating in a major Catholic victory at the Supreme Court the following year (*Pierce* v. *Society of the Sisters*, 1925).

The major symbolic confrontation between the nativists and American Catholics was the presidential election of 1928, in which Al Smith, the Irish Catholic Democratic governor of New York, was defeated by the Republican Herbert Hoover, who had achieved a distinguished record for humanitarian relief in postwar Catholic Europe. Although Hoover was not guilty of nativist agitation, Smith's combination of urban ethnic values and manners, opposition to Prohibition, and Catholic affiliation made him a natural target for a conservative Protestant attack, which found its major strength in the same "Solid South" that had for decades been a major source of national Democratic strength. It is doubtful, however, that any Democrat could have defeated Hoover at a time when many believed that America had attained a "permanent high plateau of prosperity," and the burden of the subsequent debacle of the Crash and the Depression was probably seen by Smith and his allies in retrospect as something he was fortunate to have missed. In any case, the willingness of a major political party to nominate a Catholic and the outpouring of organized anti-Catholic sentiment and activity that the nomination evoked were both important signs of the problematic but rapidly changing role of Catholics in the public life of the nation.

The third arena in which major developments in American Catholicism were played out during these years was internal to the Catholic community itself. Since at least 1890 major ethnic enclaves within the American church had been organizing themselves to resist assimilation into the broader stream of American society and culture and were vocal in their insistence that the church not abet the process of pouring them willy-nilly into the "melting pot." Although the more aggressive forms of Americanization promoted by Archbishop John Ireland and his colleagues had been put to rest by Vatican edict, the predominantly German and Polish demands for the perpetuation of their traditional languages and cultures through the instrumentality of religious worship and education could not prevail against an increasingly uniform policy of the dominant Irish-American hierarchy to make the English language and the territorial (as opposed to the national) parish normative for the entire nation. Polish demands for *rownouprawnienie*—representation in the hierarchy in numbers roughly proportional to their strength—were somewhat more successful (Paul Rhode, a second-generation Polish-American, was appointed auxiliary bishop of Chicago in 1908), but never on the scale that the Polish-American leadership thought proper. Nativist sentiment for the elimination of German, and by extension all foreign languages, from the schools in this case played into the hands of the hierarchy against their ethnic antagonists, and parochial schools ceased to be vehicles for the perpetuation of German and Polish language and culture with American involvement in the war.

Education proved to be a vehicle for furthering the policy of standardization and Americanization in other ways. From the time of the Third Plenary Council of Baltimore the American church was committed to a program of parochial elementary education for all Catholic children (at least in theory), since the public schools were viewed as a vehicle for the inculcation of, at first, Protestant and, later, secular values. Even if they could be made free from overt and covert proselytizing, however, the public schools would still lack positive instruction in religion and a Catholic perspective in areas such as literature, history, and even biology, where moral or philosophical issues might be raised. Schools were even to take priority over churches in new parishes, since the instilling of Catholic knowledge and values in the young was seen as crucial to keeping the Catholic presence in America alive and uncontaminated.

After World War I many Americans, including Catholics, were no longer content to have their children's education cease after the primary grades had been completed. Previously, secondary education for Catholics had been largely provided (when it was available at all) by religious orders that were in considerable measure independent of diocesan control, and the cost of such education made it inaccessible to many poorer Catholics even if their children were free from the demands of income-producing activity. As Catholics slowly began the process of integration into American middle-class society, increasing social demands for education and vocational training led many Catholic dioceses to expand their educational plants to the secondary level and beyond. Since high schools served a larger geographical area than elementary schools, coordination at a higher level became a necessity.

The general result of this expansion and coordination of Catholic education inevitably resulted in increased uniformity and centralization. Diocesan school superintendents and school boards were appointed, beginning in the early 1900s; religious orders were pressured into loosening their exclusive control over their schools, and teaching sisters of various orders were often mixed when given secondary assignments; curricula were standardized, with texts uniformly in English; sisters were required to receive certification, mandated by increasingly strict state laws; central purchasing made possible economies of scale. Although instruction at the collegiate level and beyond, which was also growing rapidly during the 1920s, remained almost solely in the hands of Jesuits, Dominicans, Holy Cross Fathers, and the like, the education received by most Catholics in parochial schools (by no means a large majority of Catholics at any time) was regulated by a set of hierarchical structures that inevitably culminated with the bishop or archbishop.

Other forces moving the church toward uniformity and centralization were appearing at a variety of levels. Many bishops, for example, made a policy of systematically assigning clergy from one ethnic background to parishes where the congregation was largely of another, so that English became the only possible mode of communication. (In unusual cases, such as the assignment of Italian parishes to the ministry of the Scalabrini Fathers, the ethnic parish was perpetuated, but these exceptions were increasingly rare. Italians, in any case, seldom made troublesome nationalistic demands.) Diocesan newspapers, formerly extremely varied in form and content (for a considerable time the Boston *Pilot,* for instance, was a model of literacy and professionalism, while many others were not), began to draw increasingly on the same sort of syndicated press materials that secular papers were employing. A Catholic News Service paralleled the AP and UPI, and chains such as the Denver *Register* group similarly provided standardized materials to participants. Catholic journals of a wide variety began to proliferate from early in the century, and Catholics of a literary or intellectual bent across the country could participate in the community of readership of the Jesuit-edited *America* (1909), the lay-staffed *Commonweal* (1924), and others. Catholic book clubs, including one founded by the *America* staff, made works of Catholic interest readily available to a broad public as an alternative to the secular Book-of-the-Month Club's selections. Professional societies for Catholic academics, including historians, sociologists, and educationists, also were organized on bases similar to those of their secular counterparts and, like the latter, began to issue journals on their respective subjects. Some, like the *Catholic Historical Review,* eventually achieved a very high quality of contributions. The diversity occasioned by differences in wealth, sophistication, region, language, theological perspective, and other factors was being displaced by a uniformity of organization and outlook, although *Commonweal* and a few other lay-run journals frequently took an independent course not universally popular with the hierarchy and clergy.

Associational life was another area in which nationwide organization became increasingly effective. Since Catholics were precluded from membership in such secret societies as the Masons, both by the anti-Catholic character of some of them and by church policy, Catholics were not slow to create their own fraternal counterparts to fill the need for benevolent societies (which provided insurance, burial, and other benefits for the members and their families) and more general social and recreational opportunities in the days before mass entertainment. The Knights of Columbus rapidly emerged as the largest and most successful of these organizations and gained a reputation beyond Catholic circles by providing recreation for troops abroad during the war. The Knights also offered the usual fraternal benefits and in addition attracted attention by an extensive campaign of providing information about the Catholic church to prospective converts or otherwise interested non-Catholics through advertising in secular periodicals the availability of their pamphlets by mail. The massive, modern towers that house the Knights' headquarters in New Haven, Connecticut, are an impressive architectural testimony to their success. The activities of such nationally based organizations, which were generally very supportive of the policies of the hierarchy, added a further dimension to the increasing uniformity of American Catholic life during these decades. Other groups, such as the Catholic Youth Organization, the National Council of Catholic Men (and Women), Newman clubs at non-Catholic colleges, and a whole host of other movements and organizations came into being to meet both religious and social needs for every conceivable cohort of lay Catholics, involving them in a "lay apostolate" while insulating them from too direct contact with those of other religious persuasions.

The onset of the Depression naturally had a severe impact on those in the Catholic community, many of whom were still among the poorer strata of American society. The massive building programs of the 1920s were curtailed to some degree in response to diminished resources and the need for relief efforts, but the general momentum of institutional expansion was slowed rather than halted. The political results of the Depression also had major and more positive implications for Catholics, since Franklin Roosevelt brought the Democratic party back to power through his adroit fashioning of a coalition of minorities including blacks, Southerners, Jews, and ethnic urban Catholics. After his election Roosevelt moved to restore the economy, to repeal the Eighteenth Amendment, which most Catholics had found obnoxious, and to appoint more Catholics to the Cabinet and other high positions in the government than had ever been the case previously. In addition, a number of Catholic priests such as John A. Ryan and Francis J. Haas were engaged as public servants to help implement New Deal policies. As head of the Social Action Department of the National Catholic Welfare Council (later Conference) from 1928 until his death in 1945 and previously as the primary author of the "Bishops' Program on Social Reconstruction" of 1919, Ryan especially came into prominence over an extended period as a vigorous advocate of reform in the sphere of labor in the spirit of the social encyclicals of Pope Leo XIII. An impressive number of the causes that he helped to advocate were enacted into national law.

The Depression evoked other Catholic responses of a less "establishment" character as well. Charles Coughlin, a Canadian-born cleric who gained a national reputation as Detroit's "radio priest," at first supported Roosevelt and the New Deal but later turned against him to venture into independent politics of an increasingly right-wing, populist sort; he also helped to launch the Union party, which proved to be only a minor diversion in the 1936 presidential election. The anti-Semitism and general virulence of Coughlin's magazine, *Social Justice* (1936–1942), eventually lost him episcopal protection, and he spent the remainder of his long life as the rector of the Shrine of the Little Flower in Royal Oak, Michigan.

An even more radical and, in many ways, more successful response to the social problems of the era was the Catholic Worker movement, of which the redoubtable laywoman Dorothy Day was the moving spirit, together with her friend Peter Maurin, the anarchist philosopher. The Worker movement attacked the capitalist economic order as unchristian, advocated pacifism and nonviolent resistance to unjust laws, and translated its ethical impetus into the active relief of suffering through the establishment of houses of hospitality in which the poor could find refuge. Although the movement was often highly critical of the American political and social system in the pages of its publication, the *Catholic Worker* (first published in 1933), and Day and her followers often found themselves in jail for civil disobedience, they never directly challenged ecclesiastical authority and were seldom harassed even by the most conservative episcopal leadership.

Foreign policy and relations also became a matter that was increasingly of concern to many Catholics. From the time of the Spanish-American War in 1898 American Catholics kept a wary eye on the trouble spots of the world in which the fortunes of the church were involved and tried to influence the American government to be protective of those interests. The war with Catholic Spain raised the question of the fate of Catholics and particularly of the clergy in Cuba and the Philippines, and Catholics were perhaps rightly suspicious that a then predominantly Protestant occupying nation would be less than delicate in its recognition of traditional church rights. The Mexican Revolution a few years later unleashed militant anticlerical legislation and violent action against the clergy of that country, and Catholics lobbied intensively (though not very successfully) for the American government to intervene on their behalf, a campaign that lasted into the 1930s. The major squaring off against official policy, however, came to a head late in the 1930s when the Spanish Civil War polarized American opinion between sympathizers with the leftist Loyalists and the right-wing pro-clerical forces of General Francisco Franco. With the exceptions of *Commonweal* and the *Catholic Worker* the American Catholic press urged active support for Franco's Falangists at a time when non-Catholic liberals were rushing to participate in the Loyalist cause in an aura of romantic glory. Again, the Catholic effort was unsuccessful in its immediate objectives. The result was a hardening of what had become, since the days of the Russian Revolution, an increasingly militant anti-Communist stand on the part of the leadership of the American church, a stand that reasserted itself in the aftermath of World War II.

While World War I had divided Catholic opinion until American entry due to the pro-German and anti-English sentiment of many German- and Irish-American Catholics, World War II was far less controversial, since Pope Pius XI had been denouncing the German and Italian governments with increasing vehemence as outrages against the church had mounted during the 1930s. Although Catholic suspicion of the Russian alliance never abated, young Catholics enlisted or were inducted into the armed services in vast numbers, chaplains and relief workers participated with equal dedication, and New York's Archbishop Francis Joseph Spellman became a firm supporter of Roosevelt's war policies. Where World War I had proved internally divisive because of the nativist hostility to foreign-born Americans, Catholics, mostly of the second or third generations, encountered little nativist sentiment in this new and greater conflict. Wartime films stressed the solidarity of the American people by emphasizing the ethnically mixed character of military units, and Japanese Americans, few of whom were Catholic, were the only major group to encounter serious injustice. (The Catholic press, in fact, seemed more circumspect than its secular counterpart in the "Jap-baiting" of the times.)

During the postwar years Catholic concern with public policy had two foci. On the international front Communist takeovers in much of heavily Catholic eastern Europe and the persecution of such Catholic leaders as Hungary's József Cardinal Mindszenty aroused considerable anxiety and hostility in the American church, and anti-Communism and Catholicism became even more closely equated in this country. On the domestic scene the increasing attention of the federal government to the realm of education was of concern. On the one hand, vast numbers of former Catholic servicemen benefited from the "GI Bill" of 1944, which not only made higher education possible for many Catholics of a working-class background but also helped to expand Catholic educational facilities at the collegiate level and beyond. On the other hand, attempts by Congress to enact legislation providing aid to public schools from which Catholics were to be excluded (e.g., the Barden Bill of 1949) provoked Catholic cries of discrimination and injustice and raised serious questions about the proper relationship between church and state. The public dispute that ensued between Cardinal Spellman and Eleanor Roosevelt over this issue added further heat, which added to the doubts that many Protestants entertained about Catholic political intentions.

Catholics during these years were influenced not only by overtly political issues but also by the social, demographic, and technological changes affecting all Americans in subtle but profound ways. Educational horizons were expanding rapidly at this time, and higher education was becoming an option for most if not all Americans. Academia was also changing from the preserve of a largely Protestant elite to a meritocracy, in which Catholics and especially Jews were becoming increasingly represented, although many Catholics still preferred to study and teach

at institutions connected with the church. Discrimination against those with conspicuously "foreign" (mainly Italian and eastern European) surnames persisted in many of the higher social and economic circles of society, but the long-term trends favored assimilation and acceptance.

During the postwar years the impact of the mass media, especially television, on American life also promoted assimilation by raising several Catholics to national celebrity status. In earlier years sports and entertainment figures such as Babe Ruth and Bing Crosby had come into the spotlight, but they were later joined by specifically clerical figures such as Father Coughlin, whose message was more political than religious, and finally Francis Cardinal Spellman of New York and Monsignor (later Bishop) Fulton J. Sheen. Spellman had early established friendly personal relations with the Roosevelt family but came into the news after Roosevelt's death through his public controversy with Eleanor Roosevelt on the issue of federal aid to parochial schools. Sheen was less a controversialist and attracted vast audiences through his enormously popular television series, "Life Is Worth Living," through which he conveyed an appealing Catholic interpretation of current events and cultural topics in an extraordinarily skillful use of the medium. Although Catholics were still conspicuously "different" from "other Americans," both through choice and circumstance, they were becoming increasingly accepted as an integral part of what sociologist Will Herberg calls the "triple melting pot" in which virtually all Americans were divided into the religious communities of "Protestant, Catholic, Jew."

Television also played a prominent role in still another major controversy of the early 1950s in which Catholics were necessarily involved. Joseph McCarthy, the Catholic and Republican junior Senator from Wisconsin, generated furious controversy with his accusations that significant numbers of government officials were abetting the Communist cause through conscious subversion or as puppets in a Soviet attempt to undermine the nation. Catholic opinion was by no means unified in support of McCarthy, but such prominent figures as Cardinal Spellman attempted to put an unofficial ecclesiastical cachet on his activity. The Jesuit weekly *America*, which had frequently identified itself with anti-Communist causes in the past, opposed McCarthy vigorously but was eventually forbidden to engage in further controversy on the subject after its editorials began to polarize members of the order. Other traditionally conservative Catholic publications such as *Our Sunday Visitor,* the *Catholic World,* and the *Brooklyn Tablet* supported McCarthy, while not surprisingly, the progressive *Commonweal* joined the opposition. It was also in this context that William F. Buckley, a wealthy and sophisticated Catholic Yale alumnus and founder of the ultraconservative *National Review,* began to defend McCarthy and attack his own alma mater as antireligious and insufficiently attuned to the Communist danger.

The vigorous Catholic program of growth and expansion that had been characteristic of earlier decades may have been slowed by the Depression and diverted by the war but began to move into higher gear again during the "postwar baby boom" and the general atmosphere of prosperity of the 1950s. Vast numbers of Catholics joined the exodus to the suburbs, and new churches, schools, and parish plants were erected to accommodate their needs. Education at all levels flourished, and universities such as Notre Dame, Georgetown, and Fordham began to emerge as centers of recognized scholarship as well as athletic prowess. Curricular materials for Catholic schools, developed in part at Catholic University in Washington, also came to resemble their secular counterparts, although distinctively Catholic themes were introduced to show that Catholics were both fully American but religiously set apart in symbolically important ways.

The mass media, which flourished during the 1950s as never before and which had helped elevate Catholic spokesmen to national prominence, were still regarded by Catholics as mixed blessings. Cardinal Spellman again came into the national spotlight through his denunciation of such films as *The Miracle* (1951) and *Baby Doll* (1956) but church-supported attempts at public censorship did not meet very favorable receptions in the courts. The National Legion of Decency, a national Catholic organization founded in 1934 to guide Catholics in their choice of film entertainment, regularly published listings rating movies according to moral suitability but seemed to have little impact on the fare presented to the general public. The combination of anti-Communism and moral rectitude, however,

helped to establish a generally conservative image of the church among the public at large. The shift in allegiance of many Catholics to the Republican party, especially in support of the popular President Dwight D. Eisenhower, indicated a drift toward economic conservatism as well, a major departure from the strongly pro-labor stance of much of the institutional church during the previous decades.

Although the major part of Catholic effort during the middle decades of the century was devoted to meeting the needs of an upwardly mobile and heavily urban (later suburban) and Americanized people, other developments pointed in the direction of diversity. The National Catholic Rural Life Conference, founded by Father Edwin V. O'Hara in 1921, attempted to provide religious support for Catholics engaged in farming and even to encourage a "back to the soil" movement as a counterforce to urban pressures. The Grail, an international movement founded in Holland in 1921 and established in America in 1940, was dedicated to the development of Catholic spirituality and culture among women. Although hardly feminist in the modern political sense, it nevertheless recognized that women had a distinctive and vital role to play in the development of both religion and civilization. Although most Catholic public pronouncements generally encouraged women to pursue traditional roles as wives and mothers or else to enter female religious orders, Catholic women's colleges were quietly paralleling the Grail's work in preparing women for roles of leadership that eventually began to open for them, however slowly and problematically, at a later time. In yet another realm a new interest in monasticism was sparked by Thomas Merton's enormously successful autobiography, *The Seven Storey Mountain* (1948), which led to a significant influx of young people into such contemplative orders as the Trappists.

Another major source of potential change was the liturgical movement, which found its center in the work of the Benedictine order and especially in the leadership of Dom Virgil Michel, O.S.B. Much Catholic piety of the nineteenth and earlier twentieth centuries had been devotional and individualistic in focus, and the Rosary, the cults of the Sacred Hearts, and the visions at Fatima often occupied a greater place in the popular Catholic consciousness than the mass itself. Criticism of clerical carelessness in the celebration of the liturgy and of poor homiletics gradually began to attain momentum, and the derivative character of much church architecture and devotional art also became a sore point for those who thought that Christian life should focus on a dignified liturgy in which clergy and laity participated together. Increased knowledge of church history and new attention to Scripture encouraged by cautious papal endorsement of contemporary critical methods of study also helped to put liturgy into a sharper focus, and the modern architectural experiments of Europeans such as Rudolf Schwartz increasingly attracted American attention. The journal *Liturgical Arts* (1931–1972) and the Catholic Art Association (1937–1970) also helped to lay the foundations for this new consciousness, the consequences of which reached fruition with the impetus of Vatican II. The implication of these developments transcended the aesthetic, moreover, since they were based on an incarnational theology that emphasized the communal nature of human existence and the resultant obligation of Christians to rise above individual greed and selfishness.

Diversity and dissent in the realm of thought and letters also began to arise during the 1950s, which was perhaps an indication of a new maturity of an American Catholic community, now numbering over thirty-five million, that no longer felt obliged to present a conservative and monolithic front to itself and the outside world. Little of an original character in the realm of theology had emerged thus far in America, but the work of European thinkers such as Jacques Maritain, Jean Danielou, Louis Bouyer, and Pierre Teilhard de Chardin began to make American Catholics aware of a depth of cultural heritage and contemporary intellectual possibility that transcended the derivative Neo-Thomism that had for several decades formed the core of theological and philosophical instruction. In 1955 John Tracy Ellis, perhaps the foremost American Catholic church historian of the century, raised the then dramatic question as to whether American Catholic intellectual life might be not only uncreative but also actively hindered by the ethos that had been until that time prevalent in Catholic academic circles. He was soon joined by Thomas F. O'Dea, a lay sociologist of religion, and many others who were

calling for a reappraisal of American Catholic attitudes toward intellectual life. Original American Catholic thought soon began to appear in the work of the Jesuit John Courtney Murray, who defended the compatibility of American institutions with Catholic teaching in his highly influential *We Hold These Truths* (1960), as well as in the work of Gustave Weigel and others of similar caliber. The phrase "ghetto Catholicism" evoked the spirit of deliberate isolation, derivative intellectual culture, and a defensiveness that may have proven useful as a way to shield unsophisticated immigrants from an aggressively Protestant or secular society but was no longer appropriate for a mature and independent laity.

Similar though perhaps less dramatic developments were taking place in the realm of literature as well. Much American Catholic fiction and poetry until this time had been part of the "genteel tradition," in which modernist form had been avoided and happy endings reinforcing moral orthodoxy prevailed. Some major American writers of the pre–World War II era such as F. Scott Fitzgerald, James T. Farrell, and Eugene O'Neill came from Irish-Catholic backgrounds, but all dropped any formal ties with the church in maturity. Although Ernest Hemingway was a convert to Catholicism, his erratic personal life, culminating in suicide, and his lack of any intimate connection with the quotidian realities of the American church rendered him a rule-proving exception. By the 1950s, however, the increasing popularity of British and Continental Catholic writers such as Evelyn Waugh, Graham Greene, Sigrid Undset, and François Mauriac helped to raise levels of American literary consciousness, and a few Catholic writers of the first rank began to emerge on native grounds. Foremost among them was Flannery O'Connor of Milledgeville, Georgia, who used some of the conventions of "Southern Gothic" to create stories and short novels at once informed by Catholic symbolism and sensibility while avoiding any traces of conventional piety in their starkness. J. F. Powers went about his craft of storytelling more quietly and produced a novel, *Morte D'Urban* (1962), and several collections of stories in which he satirized the foibles of Midwestern priests and bishops who had become too comfortable in the fleshpots of rectory culture. Edwin O'Connor's novels—e.g., *The Last Hurrah* (1956) and *The Edge of Sadness* (1961)—were more in the popular mode but did successfully evoke the cultural and religious milieu of Irish Boston.

The decade of the 1960s was crucial for the American Catholic community, as it was to be in radically different ways for American blacks. The 1960 presidential election was the first since 1928 in which a Catholic received the nomination of a major party, and Massachusetts senator John F. Kennedy directly addressed the questions of possible divided loyalty with which he was confronted by such diverse sources as the Houston Ministerial Conference and the Reverend Norman Vincent Peale. Questions about the proper relationship between the American government and the Vatican had surfaced periodically since World War II, as when President Truman had attempted to send Mark Clark as ambassador to Rome in 1951 and was forced to withdraw the appointment in the face of hostile popular reaction. (It was not until 1984 that President Reagan succeeded in establishing an American diplomatic presence at the Holy See.) Paul Blanshard, the author of *American Freedom and Catholic Power* (1949), and the POAU (Protestants and Other Americans United for the Separation of Church and State) had kept up a steady drumfire of criticism of Catholic efforts to secure governmental aid to education, and Cardinal Spellman's efforts to regulate aspects of public morality also aroused fears that the church sought extensive political influence. Kennedy successfully dissociated himself from accusations that he would be deferential to the pope in decisions affecting foreign and domestic policy in which church teachings or interests were at stake, and he in fact angered many Catholic leaders after his election by turning a cold shoulder to plans for federal aid to Catholic schools. His victory over Richard Nixon, precarious as it was, put an effective end to anti-Catholicism as a force in national politics, and a number of Catholics have subsequently been nominated for or appointed to high office without attracting the slightest attention because of their religious affiliations. Among these have been vice presidential candidates Sargent Shriver, William Miller, and Edmund Muskie and Secretaries of State Muskie and Alexander Haig.

The brief Kennedy era also pointed to other transformations in the American Catholic social experience. Kennedy himself was the grandson of a Boston Irish political boss and the son of an extremely wealthy and politically influential financier. Educated at Harvard, he easily bridged the gaps among the "lace curtain" Irish constituency that had formed his early political base, the realm of national Democratic politics in which Catholics had played influential but subordinate roles since the time of the New Deal, and the literary and intellectual world of New York and Cambridge for which he served as a patron and on which he drew for policy advice. The juxtaposition of the aging poet Robert Frost and the feisty Richard Cardinal Cushing at the Kennedy inauguration symbolized an increasing symbiosis, if not fusion, of the worlds in which at least some American Catholics could move and function with comfort.

The other major event of the early 1960s that affected American Catholicism even more directly was the convening of the Second Vatican Council by Pope John XXIII in 1962. Angelo Roncalli, the patriarch of Venice, was himself a startling contrast to his predecessor, the austere, intellectual, and militantly anti-Communist Pius XII. In his role as Pope John, Roncalli, short, heavyset, and genial, charmed all who came into contact with him by his simplicity and good humor. Although hardly a radical by temperament, Pope John proceeded during what many viewed as a potentially brief, "care-taking" pontificate to unleash forces within the international and American church the implications of which are still by no means resolved.

Vatican II was so styled because it was conceived as a continuation of the First Vatican Council (1869–1870), which had declared papal infallibility to be a binding dogma and then had been dispersed by invading troops before it could complete its agenda. The question of the role of bishops in the church and, by implication, that of the clergy and laity as well had not been addressed. The theme of "collegiality" thus emerged as a major focus of the second council, and the ecclesiology that began to emerge from its documents stressed not papal supremacy but rather the mutual relations of the episcopate, clergy, and, most radically, the laity. The heavily clerical character of what became known as "pre-Vatican" Catholicism, in which the church was supposed to subsist in the clergy, who in turn regarded the laity as passive adjuncts, was undermined at the highest levels of theory and authority. In addition, the dominant metaphor for the church as a whole was no longer that of a militant body aiming at final triumph but rather that of "the Pilgrim People of God" making their way through the uncertainties of a fallen world in humility but ultimate faith and trust.

One of the specific changes in attitude brought about by the council that most affected Americans came about in considerable measure through American initiative. The "Declaration on Religious Freedom" of 1965 put an end to the traditional attitude that the ideal relationship of church and state was one in which the Catholic church enjoyed a position of official preeminence and in which other religious groups were at best tolerated. American Catholics had been divided for decades on the issue of whether, as the social justice advocate John A. Ryan surprisingly had advocated in his jointly authored work, *The State and the Church* (1922), the American system of separation was only to be tolerated out of necessity or whether, as "Americanizers" from Archbishop Ireland to President Kennedy had declared, legally enforced religious freedom and its resultant pluralism was not only tolerable but actively to be preferred. John Courtney Murray, the author of the seminal work *We Hold These Truths,* who attended the council as *peritus* (theological expert) on the request of the often relentlessly conservative Cardinal Spellman, provided much of the intellectual groundwork that made a new affirmation of normative religious freedom possible. The triumph of these new ideas over the objections of Alfredo Cardinal Ottaviani and other confirmed traditionalists came about through the efforts of Spellman and other American delegates. The era inaugurated by *Testem Benevolentiae* was at a definitive end.

Other consequences issued from the Council's pursuit of *aggiornamento,* Pope John's word for bringing the church "up to date." A new openness to dialogue with Protestants, Eastern Orthodox, and even Marxists and Buddhists replaced the former stance that Roman Catholicism claimed a monopoly on Christian or, more broadly, religious truth; also, the anti-Semitism that had existed for centuries as an unofficial but potent attitude among many Catholics was denounced and repudiated. Worship in the vernacular was now mandated in place of the universal Latin, thus giving a new impetus to the liturgical movement. The collective result of these and other changes and redefinitions of traditional practice was for many an exhilarating sense that the Catholic church was no longer a clerically dominated monolith that took a posture of aggressive defiance of contemporary society and culture but rather a human agency, still based on divine sanction, though one in which all members had a vital role and which acknowledged the presence of truth and goodness beyond the boundaries of the institutional church. For others, however, in America as elsewhere, doubt bordering on despair about the church's future arose, since the seemingly eternal verities preserved in an archaic language were now open to what only a few years earlier had seemed unthinkable questioning and reformulation. A "Catholic Traditionalist Movement" dedicated to the preservation of the Latin liturgy was founded by Gommar A. DePauw in 1965, and similar leadership was provided in Europe by French archbishop Marcel Lefebvre. Since the council these rearguard actions have precariously balanced on the border of schism, but to date no major overt defections have taken place.

Although the mandate for collegiality and renewal that emerged from the council seemed clear enough in its general outlines, its implementation in detail was more problematic. The Catholic church in its institutional aspects had not been accustomed to rapid change, and the disparity perceived by some between ecumenical ideal and quotidian reality led to works of protest such as James Kavanaugh's *A Modern Priest Looks at His Outdated Church* (1967), as well as sometimes rather puerile satirical fiction on the excesses of "ghetto" culture. Although the response of the conservative laity was more often one of confusion than defection, many priests and sisters began to reflect critically on their vocations and to leave the religious life, with or without formal approval, to marry and pursue careers in the secular world. Enrollment in seminaries, which had reached unprecedented numbers during the previous decade, rapidly declined, so that the vast physical plants maintained by most dioceses for the training of priests began to empty, their spaces only partly refilled by increasing numbers of women seeking theological education with, for some, a hope of eventual priestly ordination.

Since the 1960s the role of women in the church has remained one of its most acute and unresolved problems. Women religious, such as graphic artist Corita Kent and college president Jacqueline Grennan, left their religious orders, at times in the context of irresolvable conflict with local bishops, and pursued their careers in secular contexts. During the 1980s at least two prominent women religious left their orders in order to hold or seek public office after they had been forbidden to do so. Women religious determined to remain within their vocational structures began to organize on the national level, and some even confronted Pope John Paul II directly on the question of women's ordination during his visit to the United States in 1979. Many sisters and nuns had accepted a passive and subordinate posture during the previous decades; others, lacking public support for open defiance and consequently any hope of success, managed to maintain certain measures of free action without provoking confrontations, especially after certain freedoms of initiative they had enjoyed prior to World War I had been inhibited by the consolidation of episcopal power that characterized the ensuing decades. What was happening, then, was not entirely novel, but its open character and such radical demands as access to ordination were something new indeed.

The whole character of ecclesiastical and especially episcopal authority has been one of the most important underlying issues in the American church since Vatican II. An authoritarian style had become characteristic of many of the powerful "builder bishops" of the "ghetto era" and was certainly part of the public mystique projected by such figures as New York's Francis Spellman, Boston's William O'Connell, Los Angeles's James Francis McIntyre, Cincinnati's John McNicholas, and Chicago's George Mundelein and John Cody. Most of these men were elevated to the cardinalate, and all ruled supreme in their archdioceses, secure from any challenges within and confident of their role as unimpeachable public spokesmen where Catholic interests were concerned. After the council, however, new governance structures began to be mandated at every level of polity, and bishops heretofore accustomed to speaking only after whatever consultation may have pleased them now faced diocesan councils of priests who sometimes confronted them on issues in a context in which neither side was ultimately sure where final authority (if not power) resided.

Similarly, pastors used to governing their parishes autocratically, however benevolently paternal their rule may have been, now had to deal with parish councils composed of a laity free, and even encouraged, openly to speak its mind. In addition, the growing shortage of priests meant that religious women and lay people were being given organizational and leadership tasks in parishes where priests were unavailable or overworked, further complicating the question of exactly who was in charge of what.

The celebration of the liturgy was also the occasion of complication and uncertainty, though perhaps not as drastic. Until this time liturgical revival had focused on the restoration of the allegedly glorious past of the Middle Ages, and dignified Latin and Gregorian chant were usually regarded as the focus of Eucharistic-centered liturgy in which the congregation would follow actively in its missal rather than attending to private devotions. In the wake of the council's endorsement of liturgy in the vernacular, however, no traditional norms were available, and considerable confusion attended frantic efforts to translate Latin into English (and sometimes back again into Latin) while adapting folk and popular songs to religious purposes. The use of "altar girls" and female lectors also injected the question of the role of women in the liturgical arena, especially during the pontificate of the more conservative Pope John Paul II. A somewhat less confusing aspect of worship lay in the lifting of traditional Catholic prohibitions on participation in non-Catholic or interfaith services. As a result, a spirit of cooperation and openness in special liturgical events and on ecumenical discussion of theological questions, especially with liturgically oriented Lutherans and Episcopalians, emerged, however inconclusive the results of initial hopes for Christian reunion at an institutional level may have been.

Closely connected with both worship and Protestantism was the emergence of a charismatic movement within the American Catholic community beginning at Duquesne University in Pittsburgh in 1966. Previously, Catholic devotionalism had focused on Jesus, Mary, and the saints, but now the Holy Spirit became the center of a quest for personal religious experience. Speaking in tongues, healing, and the other gifts of the Holy Spirit, which had for decades been associated with conservative Protestantism in the

United States, found a wide and appreciative audience of American Catholics all across the socio-economic and geographical spectrum, although both Catholic and secular campuses such as Duquesne, Notre Dame, and Michigan served as focal points. Since the movement was biblically based, did not contradict any official teachings, and served as a stimulus for personal and collective religious renewal, it was not condemned for its novelty and was eagerly embraced by a number of clergy as well as laity. On the other hand, its individualistic base and potential for the disruption of regular structures caused considerable unease among other priests and bishops, and its place within the American Catholic community remained problematic.

One of the most unsettling areas of questioning of traditional authority during the postconciliar years was in the realm of sexual ethics. Until the 1960s Catholic teaching on the permissibility of artificial contraception had been uncompromisingly negative, even after "the pill" had introduced a new measure of pharmaceutical security into the process. Pope John's successor, Paul VI (the former Cardinal Montini), issued an unequivocal condemnation of any artificial interference into the sexual act in his encyclical *Humanae Vitae* (1968), a condemnation that opinion surveys, such as those conducted by the priest and sociologist Andrew Greeley, showed to be disregarded completely by a very high percentage of American Catholic women of childbearing age. Surveys also showed that many American priests similarly rejected papal teaching on the matter and did not attempt to implement such Vatican directives in the confessional (a device that had also come into increasing disuse or substantial modification). In one extremely crucial area of everyday life, it appeared that ecclesiastical authority of the highest level was simply and quietly rejected by laity and clergy alike, a disregard blamed by some on a postconciliar spirit of "permissiveness."

Other areas involving human sexuality were also problematic in these later years, though not in such dramatic fashion. Most American Catholics supported the traditional prohibition on abortion and often aligned themselves with politically conservative causes to work to reverse the general social and legal tendencies toward making the practice widely available. This reemergence of a conservative position on moral issues converged during the late 1970s with an increased distancing of many Catholics from the social and economic liberalism that had characterized the then largely working-class Catholic community of the New Deal years and was thought by many to have helped contribute to the election of Ronald Reagan in the 1980 presidential elections. Catholic attitudes, "official" and popular, toward homosexuality also underwent some reappraisal, and groups of Catholic "gays" such as Dignity began to advocate recognition of homosexuality as a permissible lifestyle within the church. Although some measures of tolerance may have been gained, no fundamental reversal of traditional attitudes seemed imminent by the mid-1980s. Divorce, on the other hand, had become a personal reality for such vast numbers of Catholics that momentum for recognition seemed to have considerably greater chances for eventual success, if only at the informal level.

The issue of abortion emerged as a polarizing force among American Catholics again during the presidential election of 1984. Geraldine Ferraro, a Catholic of Italian descent and member of Congress from New York City, was chosen by Democratic presidential nominee Walter Mondale as the first woman to run as a major party's candidate for vice president. Ferraro, like many liberal Catholics, distanced herself from a personal endorsement of abortion but firmly maintained that such questions of public policy were best left to individual decision. This stand, shared by Massachusetts senator Edward M. Kennedy and other prominent Democratic leaders, drew Ferraro into at times heated conflict with conservative New York archbishop John J. O'Connor and other members of the American hierarchy. In addition, a number of prominent Catholic clergy, sisters, and laity publicly asserted that American Catholic attitudes toward the question of governmental policy on abortion was by no means monolithic, a stance that elicited a strong negative response from the Vatican. Although it is doubtful that this conflict played any decisive role in Reagan's subsequent overwhelming electoral victory, it nevertheless highlighted the increasingly conservative stance of many Americans, Catholic and otherwise, on such questions of social morality.

The issue of ecclesiastical authority was by no means confined to the realm of sexual morality.

The questioning of the 1950s and the ferment of the Vatican II era brought into the open the thorny question of the nature of Catholic higher education and research activity and the possibilities of free and original enquiry in realms where final truth had for long been thought to have been irrevocably and unquestionably achieved. Catholic University in Washington, D.C., which had been founded late in the nineteenth century as a national center for Catholic higher education, perhaps appropriately became a focus for these questions of academic freedom in 1963, when its administration placed a ban on student-sponsored lectures by such eminent but controversial theologians as John Courtney Murray, Gustave Weigel, and Hans Küng, allegedly at the urging of the apostolic delegate. The ban stood at the time without successful challenge, but four years later an aroused student body, backed by a supportive faculty, brought about a reversal of a negative tenure decision for moral theologian Charles E. Curran through a boycott of classes. Other controversies at the University of Dayton and St. John's University in Jamaica, New York, demonstrated that an institutional heritage of traditionalism was not to be reversed overnight.

Still another area in which the authority of church leaders was at stake in a very different way was that of the civil rights movement, which gained momentum in the South during the late 1950s and which within a few years resulted in major changes in national laws and attitudes after a long and occasionally violent struggle. Historically, few blacks, except for those in traditionally Catholic southern Louisiana, had been Catholics, and the church had often been content to follow local mores on the issue of race relations. John La Farge, S.J., who served for a time as editor of *America,* was a conspicuous exception to this attitude through his involvement in the Catholic Interracial Council, as was, perhaps surprisingly, the usually conservative Cardinal Spellman. When integration became a matter of public policy and law, however, the Catholic hierarchy put its weight behind it as normative for parochial schools, as exemplified in the leadership of Joseph Cardinal Glennon of St. Louis during the late 1940s. The most dramatic defiance of this new attitude in the Deep South took place in Louisiana in 1962, when Leander Perez and other Catholic politicians proclaimed their refusal to comply and were subsequently excommunicated. Other incidents involving Catholics, such as the disturbances in heavily Irish South Boston in the 1970s, did not involve the parochial schools directly, but did call attention to deeply ingrained racial attitudes in many enclaves of ethnic Catholicism even in the North. Hostile reaction by Catholic laity to extensive participation by priests and women religious in the civil rights marches of the early 1960s in both the North and South was a further indication of a polarized community.

The entire question of the parochial schools was another major issue of the 1960s and beyond. Many Catholic parishes were located in neighborhoods deep within urban areas from which ethnic Catholics were moving to suburbs and their places being taken by blacks and others, most of them non-Catholic. Many upwardly mobile black parents, however, chose to send their children to the academically superior and more disciplined parochial schools, a factor precipitating a debate about what exactly the purpose of Catholic education was to be since an increasing percentage of its clientele was non-Catholic. Some, such as Mary Perkins Ryan, argued publicly in her book *Are Parochial Schools the Answer?* (1963) that the parochial system had served its purpose and ought to be phased out. Others, such as Andrew Greeley, defended the accomplishment of the schools, using statistical data to demonstrate that they were effective in ensuring continued active participation in the church. The precipitous decrease in the number of teaching sisters, which began during the 1960s, also necessitated the increasing utilization of lay instructors, with a corresponding increase in expense for salaries. Federal aid to Catholic education also continued to be a sensitive political issue, and none of these questions had been definitively resolved by the mid-1980s.

Another minority group that was heavily Catholic was the Hispanic population of the United States, which constituted one of the major sources of non-native population increase during the decades following World War II. The first major wave of migrants came from Puerto Rico, which was legally part of the nation and which many chose to leave to seek their fortunes in the continental states, especially in New York City. Spanish Harlem and the South Bronx rapidly became major areas of extreme poverty and social disorganization, and many immigrants of Catholic background soon joined Pentecostal and other conservative Protestant groups. Ministry to this natural but problematic constituency was a major challenge to the New York dioceses and one that has never been satisfactorily dealt with.

Cuban immigration to southern Florida by middle-class Catholics following Fidel Castro's revolution in 1959 created major Catholic enclaves in an area where the Catholic presence had never been especially strong. Although the challenges to ministry were also intense in this case, the desire and ability of Cubans, many of them possessing professional skills, to learn English and assimilate into American society produced a situation different in character from that farther north. (This, however, was not the case with the impoverished Haitian refugees who later thronged into the Miami area, there to encounter a hostile reception from immigration authorities.) Where both the Cuban and Puerto Rican populations on the east coast were intensely concentrated, however, the ongoing flow of Mexicans and other Spanish-speaking people into the Southwest, from Texas to California, was a situation of a wholly different magnitude. On the one hand, cultural tensions between the Irish-American hierarchy and the Spanish-speaking practitioners of what was frequently a syncretistic folk religion impeded the establishment of an effective institutional outreach to the migrants. On the other hand, the organizing efforts of the intensely religious Cesar Chavez on behalf of Mexican farm workers helped to create a more immediate and positive presence, though often evoking cries of outrage from Catholic employers.

During the 1970s the flood of Mexican migrants seeking economic opportunity was further augmented by Spanish-speaking people seeking political refuge from increasingly violent and repressive conditions in Central America. The murder of four Catholic missionaries in El Salvador in 1980 brought the situation home to many Americans otherwise unaware of its gravity, and Catholics joined with other religious groups in providing sanctuary for refugees who were refused legal admission by immigration officials. The increasing tendency of the Latin American clergy and hierarchy to sympathize with the victims of oppressive social structures, especially after the assassination of Salvadoran

archbishop Romero in 1980, was a dramatic contrast with previous church-state relations in that part of the hemisphere and aroused considerable interest and sympathy in the American Catholic community.

Another major political question that took changing forms from the mid-1960s onward was that of war and its legitimacy. The official Catholic attitude toward both World War II and Korea had been primarily supportive, and Cardinal Spellman, as national military vicar, was a familiar figure at American armed forces bases at home and abroad. Spellman continued in this posture as American troops became increasingly involved in the conflict in Vietnam during the late 1960s, but he by no means reflected a uniform Catholic endorsement of the war. Collective statements by the episcopate began with support but, as the conflict continued, notes of unsureness about the morality of the means employed in the struggle and its legitimacy as a "just war" began to be articulated. More dramatic and visceral protests came from the "Catholic Left," a movement inspired directly by antiwar teachings of such older Catholic radicals as Dorothy Day and, from a very different background, the paradoxically articulate Trappist monk Thomas Merton.

In 1964 Jesuit poet Daniel Berrigan and his brother Philip, a Josephite priest, were instrumental in founding the Catholic Peace Fellowship and soon came in for widespread attention. The following year, as American involvement in Southeast Asia escalated, David Miller, a young member of the Catholic Worker movement, became the first American to violate a new law that prohibited the burning of draft cards. His gesture was soon followed by that of a fellow member of the movement, Roger LaPorte, who doused himself with gasoline and immolated himself in imitation of Asian Buddhist monks who had been employing similar tactics of protest. Individual action soon gave way to that by groups such as the Baltimore Four, including Philip Berrigan, who in November of 1967 poured a mixture of human (their own) and animal blood over draft files seized at the Baltimore customs house. While out on bail, Berrigan was joined by his brother Daniel and seven others at Catonsville, Maryland, where they proceeded to burn other draft records with homemade napalm. The subsequent trial of the Catonsville

Nine resulted in widespread publicity for the movement and in jail sentences for its perpetrators, although Daniel Berrigan went into hiding for several months until he was captured on Block Island by the FBI (an organization whose membership included considerable numbers of Catholics).

Catholic division over the war came to include laity, clergy, and hierarchy alike. Eugene McCarthy, a Catholic senator from Wisconsin, helped to mobilize antiwar sentiment through his vigorous campaign for the Democratic nomination for president in 1968; together with momentum generated by the similarly liberal and Catholic Robert F. Kennedy, who was assassinated at the height of his campaign popularity that same year, McCarthy's movement helped to bring about President Johnson's decision not to seek reelection. In addition, selective conscientious objection, which had never been a very live option for young men in the eyes of the American hierarchy, was endorsed the same year in a national pastoral letter by the bishops.

Roughly a decade after the Vietnam War had ended, a new and official initiative added a further development to the evolution of American Catholic attitudes toward war and peace. Individual members of the hierarchy, such as Detroit's auxiliary bishop Thomas Gumbleton, had long been involved in the Pax Christi movement, and Seattle's Bishop Raymond G. Hunthausen publicly declared his unwillingness to pay taxes in support of nuclear weapons. In 1983 the National Conference of Catholic Bishops, with Chicago's irenic Joseph Cardinal Bernardin as their spokesman, issued a vigorous and carefully prepared condemnation of the morality of nuclear warfare, a stance criticized by politically conservative Catholics in the Reagan administration as harmful to American efforts to contain the spread of Communist aggression, which the institutional church had for so long seen as a greater menace than the threat of war.

The pilgrimage of American Catholics from the era of World War I to that of the 1980s was in some ways one of diversity through an apparent unity to another sort of diversity. The question of ethnic pluralism, for example, which had been hotly debated and then seemingly definitively solved in favor of assimilation by the 1970s, now emerged again as a de facto reality with the flood of Hispanic immigrants and smaller numbers of Asian and Middle Eastern Catholics during the 1970s and 1980s. Questions of the morality of racial segregation, nuclear war, and sexual issues also brought an end to what for several decades had seemed like a monolithic Catholic posture on public issues. New journals such as the *National Catholic Reporter,* which had begun publication during the social and theological ferment of the early 1960s, also added alternative voices to the generally more cautious postures of diocesan "house organs"; even in many of the latter, however, it was clear that a new spirit of inquiry and social concern was being manifested. Although, presumably, a reasonable number of disgruntled Catholics had joined other religious groups or simply "drifted off" during these years, no major schism took place, and a broad institutional unity was preserved. Major questions of authority remained, though, as the differing attitudes of many American clergy and laity confronted during the 1980s the "hard line" of Karol Wojtyla, the cardinal archbishop of Krakow who had, to the surprise of many, become the first non-Italian in centuries to be elevated to the papacy. Whether the emphasis on obedience to authority enunciated by John Paul II, an attitude developed in the context of a church in constant tension with a hostile Communist government, could be reconciled to the new American Catholic exuberance in diversity, remained a major question as the 1980s began to run their course.

BIBLIOGRAPHY

John Cogley, *Catholic America* (1973); Donald F. Crosby, S.J., *God, Church, and Flag: Senator Joseph R. McCarthy and the Catholic Church, 1950–1957* (1978); Dorothy Day, *The Long Loneliness: The Autobiography of Dorothy Day* (1952); John Tracy Ellis, *American Catholicism* (1956; rev. 1969); John Whitney Evans, *The Newman Movement: Roman Catholics in American Higher Education, 1883–1971* (1980); Robert I. Gannon, *The Cardinal Spellman Story* (1962); Philip Gleason, "A Browser's Guide to American Catholicism, 1950–1980," in *Theology Today* 38 (1981), ed., *Catholicism in America* (1970); Francine du Plessix Gray, *Divine Disobedience: Profiles in Catholic Radicalism* (1970); Andrew M. Greeley, *The American Catholic: A Social Portrait* (1977), and with Peter H. Rossi, *The Education of Catholic Americans* (1966).

William M. Halsey, *The Survival of American Innocence* (1980); Oscar Handlin, *Al Smith and His America* (1958); James Hennesey, S.J., *American Catholics: A History of the Roman Catholic Community in the United States* (1981); Edward R. Kantowicz,

Corporation Sole: Cardinal Mundelein and Chicago Catholicism (1983); James Kavanaugh, *A Modern Priest Looks at His Outdated Church* (1967); John La Farge, S.J., *The Manner Is Ordinary* (1957); Thomas T. McAvoy, C.S.C., *A History of the Catholic Church in the United States* (1969), ed., *Roman Catholicism and the American Way of Life* (1960); Meredith B. McGuire, *Pentecostal Catholics: Power, Charisma, and Order in a Religious Movement* (1982); Theodore Maynard, *The Catholic Church and the American Idea* (1953); Thomas Merton, *The Seven Storey Mountain* (1948); William D. Miller, *A Harsh and Dreadful Love: Dorothy Day and the Catholic Worker Movement* (1973); Philip J. Murnion, *The Catholic Priest and the Changing Structure of Pastoral Ministry* (1978); John Courtney Murray, S.J., *We Hold These Truths* (1960).

David J. O'Brien, *American Catholics and Social Reform: The New Deal Years* (1968); Mary Perkins Ryan, *Are Parochial Schools the Answer? Catholic Education in Light of the Council* (1964); James W. Sanders, *The Education of an Urban Minority: Catholics in Chicago, 1833–1965* (1977); Fulton J. Sheen, *Treasure in Clay: The Autobiography of Fulton J. Sheen* (1982); Charles J. Tull, *Father Coughlin and the New Deal* (1965); Rodger Van Allen, *The Commonweal and American Catholicism: The Magazine, the Movement, the Meaning* (1974); Gary Wills, *Bare Ruined Choirs: Doubt, Prophecy, and Radical Religion* (1972).

[*See also* American Catholic Thought; Catholicism from Independence to World War I; Catholicism in the English Colonies; Ethnicity and Religion; *and* Religious Prejudice and Nativism.]

THE ANGLICAN TRADITION AND THE EPISCOPAL CHURCH

David L. Holmes

THE Anglican Reformation was the most complex, contradictory, and conservative of all the movements that broke from Roman Catholicism in the sixteenth century. On the European continent, theologians precipitated the Reformation; in England, though Protestant teachings had been present since the time of John Wycliffe and the Lollards, the Reformation emerged from the concern of King Henry VIII for a papal annulment of his marriage to Katharine of Aragon. Since she was the widow of his elder brother, Arthur, Henry had been required to obtain a dispensation from Pope Julius II before marrying her in 1509.

Such annulments of long-standing royal marriages had been granted before. The monarch's reasons for seeking one and Pope Clement VII's unwillingness to declare one are far more complex than popular history indicates. Failing to secure any ruling from the pope, Henry initiated in 1529 a series of acts that resulted in the establishment of the Church of England, independent of papal control. Since the number of Protestants influenced by Lutheranism, Zwinglianism, Calvinism, and Anabaptism steadily increased in England year by year, the question remained what form the national church would take.

The reigns of the Tudor and Stuart monarchs through 1689 witnessed a pendulum swing of Anglicanism in terms of confessional loyalty. Under Henry VIII the church was a kind of autocephalous Catholicism, independent of Rome, like Eastern Orthodoxy or the apparently indigenous British Catholicism of the earliest Christian centuries. But Henry entrusted the education of his son, Edward VI, to Protestants, and during Edward's reign (1547–1553) Anglicanism moved closer theologically to Calvinism. Although Mary Tudor (ruled 1553–1558) returned the country to Roman Catholicism, the majority of English citizens by then opposed papal control. Desirous of national unity and confronted by religious factions, Elizabeth I (ruled 1558–1603) secured the "Elizabethan settlement," in which the Church of England attempted to blend Catholic and Protestant elements and to exist as a middle way between theological extremes.

The period of the Stuart sovereigns that followed was one of civil and ecclesiastical turmoil. High church policies forced out large numbers of Calvinists; two monarchs (Charles II and James II) converted to Roman Catholicism; and Puritans ruled during the Commonwealth period. But Elizabeth's long reign had placed an indelible stamp on the national church's life and worship. Since the time of William and Mary (ruled 1689–1702) and Anne (ruled 1702–1714), all monarchs of England have remained Anglicans, and the Church of England has become increasingly open to a wider latitude of belief and practice.

In the sixteenth century the Church of England continued the threefold ministry of bishops, priests, and deacons and claimed to have kept the apostolic succession. Unlike Lutheranism and Calvinism, it produced only one doctrinal statement, the Thirty-nine Articles of Religion (1571). Though reflecting the early Calvinist influence on the English Reformation, the articles display the common Anglican fear that overprecision in doctrinal definition would only prove divisive. With the exception of members of Oxford and Cambridge universities, the articles have never been required of laity in England or the United States. Their authority among the clergy in both countries has steadily declined since the nineteenth century, though many Evangelicals have continued to view them as a summation of Anglican belief.

THE ANGLICAN TRADITION AND THE EPISCOPAL CHURCH

Today the American Book of Common Prayer places the Thirty-nine Articles in the section entitled "Historical Documents of the Church." The Apostles' and Nicene creeds (which "may be proved by most certain warrants of Holy Scripture," in the words of the Thirty-nine Articles) remain the church's principal doctrinal symbols. Upon ordination Episcopal clergy must affirm that they "believe the Holy Scripture of the Old and New Testaments to be the Word of God, and to contain all things necessary to salvation."

If the Anglican reformers very early gave up on enforcing common theological belief upon England, they emphasized in its place the unity Christians could attain through common prayer. Thus the church's official service book, the Book of Common Prayer (first issued in 1549, subsequently revised several times in England and America), has served as a principal standard of doctrine for Anglicanism. Writings of the early church fathers and aspects of the Roman Catholic, Eastern Orthodox, and Lutheran liturgies were revised to conform in doctrine to what Anglicans considered biblical teaching. The Book of Common Prayer witnesses to the Anglican belief that the highest privilege of the Christian is worship.

From the time of Elizabeth I on, an unwillingness to accept theological inclusiveness led to the emergence within Anglicanism of church parties, each of which tried to move the church to its own interpretation of "true Christianity." The defining question has been whether the Elizabethan settlement diverged too far from medieval Catholicism, failed to go far enough toward continental Protestantism, or struck precisely the right balance.

The high church party has placed a "high" estimate upon the ministry and sacraments. Asserting that Anglicanism is a true representative of Catholic Christianity, its supporters declare that it has maintained the apostolic succession, sacramental system, and creeds of ancient and early medieval Christianity.

While firmly believing that they continue in the teachings of the early church fathers, the low church party has emphasized the Protestant element in Anglicanism. Stressing the primacy not only of Scripture over the church, but also of the primitive over the medieval church, it places a comparatively "low" value upon the episcopate, priesthood, and sacraments, and makes less use of symbolic acts in worship. The Puritans, for example, were initially low churchmen who believed that Anglicanism had insufficiently purified itself of medieval "accretions."

The central church party (a term used more commonly in England than in the United States) has continued the tradition of the Elizabethan settlement. Claiming that Anglicanism incorporates the best from both traditions, it typically stands (to quote a frequently used definition that may go back to the sixteenth-century English theologian Richard Hooker) in the posture of "Catholic for every truth of God, Protestant for every error of man." Since Anglicanism is more homogeneous than it appears, the majority of Anglicans undoubtedly fall into this category. (Additional parties within Anglicanism—Evangelical, Anglo-Catholic, and broad church—will be discussed in the appropriate places.)

Though the existence of such parties has often given Anglicanism the appearance of a warring household, its vitality has seemed to spring precisely from their mutually enriching contributions. Anglicanism claims to be a body that is both truly Catholic and fully Protestant, both loyal to the past in creed and polity yet gladly open to reform and change in conformance with Scripture and modern thought. Although tensions persist, they are contained within a broader loyalty.

If Anglicanism has a genius, it lies in this attempted synthesis of Scripture, tradition, and reason. For the last one hundred years its apologetic has claimed that the Catholic tradition alone can lead to narrowness, bigotry, and fear of new information; that the Evangelical tradition alone can lead to loss of the living tradition from which the Gospel emerged; and that the humanist tradition alone can lead to a secular faith that views Christianity as an ethical system only. Thus in place of the former high church and low church arguments about whether Anglicanism is a form of Protestantism or Catholicism, the recent self-understanding of Anglicanism has stressed the church's distinctiveness and comprehensiveness. In ecumenical discussions other churches have increasingly recognized that Anglicanism represents a different way of being Christian than Protestantism, Roman Catholicism, or Eastern Orthodoxy.

THE ANGLICAN TRADITION AND THE EPISCOPAL CHURCH

THE COLONIAL AND REVOLUTIONARY PERIODS

The Church of England was the first denomination to come permanently to the original thirteen colonies. Though Anglican services were held in the seventeenth century on the coasts of California and North Carolina, the settlement of Jamestown in 1607 by the London Company (after 1609, the Virginia Company) marked the permanent beginnings of the Church of England in America. Led by Anglican Puritans, the Virginia colony enforced mandatory attendance at worship. Captain John Smith wrote of the first church at Jamestown:

> Wee did hang an awning (which is an old saile) to three or foure trees . . . our seats unhewed trees, our Pulpit a bar of wood nailed to two neighboring trees. . . . This was our Church, till wee built a homely thing like a barne. . . . Wee had daily Common Prayer morning and evening, every Sunday two Sermons, and every three moneths the holy Communion. . . .
> (Edward Arber, ed., *Travels and Works of Captain John Smith*, 1910, pp. 957–958)

Almost as frequent as morning and evening prayer in Virginia during the difficult early years was the office for the burial of the dead. Commercial purposes were primary for the Virginia colony, though the charter also expressed a concern for the evangelization of the American Indians. From Virginia came the most famous Indian convert to Anglicanism, Pocahontas.

Anglicans also settled steadily in other colonies in the seventeenth century. By 1700 the Church of England was second only to Congregationalism in number of churches. More than one hundred Anglican churches were scattered from Massachusetts to South Carolina, with 80 percent concentrated in Virginia and Maryland. Many of the parishes lacked clergy, however, and membership was becoming increasingly nominal.

Established by law in Virginia in 1619 or 1624 and in the lower four counties of New York in 1693, the Church of England gradually became the established church in all of the southern colonies—in North Carolina in a series of acts beginning in 1701; in Maryland in 1702; in South Carolina in 1706; and in Georgia in 1758. South Carolina was perhaps the most vital of the Anglican establishments. Only in Virginia, and perhaps Maryland, did Anglicans ever outnumber other denominations. The Puritanism of the earliest years of the century changed to a moderate Arminianism, or emphasis on the human role in redemption (as opposed to the Calvinist emphasis on predestination), that became increasingly influenced by the Enlightenment. Leading clerical figures in the church's first century in America were James Blair of Virginia, founder in 1693 of the College of William and Mary, and Thomas Bray of Maryland, founder in 1701 of the London-based Society for the Propagation of the Gospel in Foreign Parts (SPG), whose purpose was to advance Anglicanism among the settlers, Indians, and slaves in the English colonies.

To the SPG is owed much of the credit for the expansion of Anglicanism outside Virginia and Maryland. A high church organization of relatively high devotional and moral standards, the "venerable society" dispatched more than three hundred missionaries to the American colonies from 1701 until 1783. On their salaries and on the erection of Anglican churches it spent the equivalent of over $1 million. New England received more than eighty missionaries; New York and South Carolina more than fifty each; both Pennsylvania and New Jersey more than forty; and North Carolina over thirty. Only Virginia and Maryland failed to require substantial aid from the society.

Led by SPG missionaries such as George Keith, a former Quaker, Anglicanism gained converts in the Middle Colonies. Under aggressive SPG leadership the Church of England also made great gains in the eighteenth century in Congregationalist New England, especially in the Puritan citadels of Massachusetts and Connecticut. Symbolic was the conversion to Anglicanism, on the "dark day" of 13 September 1722, of the rector and sole faculty member of Congregationalist Yale College, along with five Yale-trained Congregationalist ministers in neighboring towns. Most famous of the SPG missionaries to America was John Wesley, future founder of Methodism. Then a legalistic high churchman, Wesley served as a missionary in Georgia from 1735 to 1737.

The ship that carried Wesley back to England passed that carrying his successor, George Whitefield, to Georgia. In England, following his Aldersgate Experience, Wesley founded the

Methodist societies and sparked the Evangelical Revival. In America, Whitefield made seven preaching tours of the colonies and spread the parallel revival known as the Great Awakening.

The Anglican churches of the colonies gained little from the Great Awakening, though it permanently changed the course of American Protestantism. With the notable exception of parsons such as Virginia's Devereux Jarratt, Anglican clergy resisted—often bitterly—the conversion-centered, experiential religion of the Great Awakening. Although Anglican laypeople proved more open to the message of the Awakening, those who accepted its emotionalism and teachings tended to leave for New Light denominations; the Methodist societies, for example, ceased being an evangelical college of piety within the Episcopal Church and formed a separate denomination in 1784. Though an antirevivalist backlash caused numbers of the rural poor to convert to Anglicanism in New England, elsewhere the Church of England in America lost the ordinary people and became the church of the educated and wealthier classes.

The legacy of the Awakening remained in the Evangelical party, a conversion-centered and pietistic form of low churchmanship that revived classical Reformation teachings about sin and judgment. Though loyal to the prayer book, Evangelicals emphasized preaching, classes for religious study, and lay participation. Toward worldly amusements they were as stern as the Methodists and Baptists. The Evangelical party experienced its greatest period in America in the early decades of the nineteenth century.

Though it suffered in transit, English practice was continued in America. In colonies such as Virginia and Maryland, where Anglicanism was established, the legislature divided settled areas into parishes. In Virginia the average parish was twenty miles long and included 150 families and two or three churches. Subject to the acts of the legislature and the theoretical spiritual control of the bishop of London, groups of economically and socially privileged laymen called "vestries" ran the affairs of each parish.

After 1688, the colonies received leading clergymen, called commissaries, to provide liaison with the bishop of London. Clergy lived on tracts of farmland called glebes; assisted by lay readers called clerks, they rotated their services among their parish's churches. Throughout the colonial period the majority of Anglican clergy were of British birth, though the number of American-born clergy in Anglican pulpits increased as the eighteenth century went on. The lack of a bishop in America required Americans seeking ordination to take an expensive and dangerous 6,000-mile round trip across the Atlantic. SPG agitation for an American episcopate in the 1760s and 1770s may properly be seen as one of the contributing causes of the American war for independence. Among Congregationalists, Presbyterians, and others, the new aggressiveness of Anglicanism aroused old memories of repressive laws in England against dissenters and of lordly bishops who were officers of state.

Although writers have long tied Anglicanism to Loyalism, recent scholarship has shown that some 45 percent of Anglican clergy (most of whom came from Virginia or South Carolina) and a solid majority of Anglican laity supported the American side actively or passively in the American Revolution. Washington, Hamilton, Franklin, Madison, Monroe, Marshall, Jay, Mason, Robert Morris, Francis Hopkinson, John Randolph, Patrick Henry, and more than half of the signers of the Declaration of Independence were Anglicans.

The Loyalist clergy (some of whom may actually have favored an American victory) believed they had to remain true to the solemn oaths they had sworn to God upon ordination. These oaths bound them to remain loyal to the king and to perform public worship without change from the Book of Common Prayer (which included prayers for the king, royal family, and Parliament). Their suffering and courage were great. The strength of the patriotic clergy lay in their realization that oaths, liturgies, and governments are subordinate to the commission of Christ and that Anglicanism (as American history has amply borne out) can exist without formal connection to any government.

Saddled with the politics of imperialism, the Anglican church was disestablished in all southern colonies during the Revolution. In Virginia full disestablishment took until 1784. The losses to Anglicanism in clergy, lay membership, buildings, and parish life were great; they were increased when the Methodist societies (which had existed as an Evangelical yeast within Anglicanism since the 1730s) broke off and became a separate denomination in 1784. Having had little communication with each other prior to the revolutionary war, the Anglican churches began after the war to organize themselves in each state and to seek a national unity.

The state of war that existed between the colonies and England and the rise of nationalistic consciousness in America made the continued use of the title "Church of England" or "Anglican" unwise. The newly independent parishes therefore had to search for a new church name. "Episcopal" was an old title, dating to the struggles with the Puritans in seventeenth-century England, when it described persons who believed that true church order involved a ministry of three distinct orders and government by bishops. In New England and elsewhere during the colonial period, the Church of England had occasionally been referred to as "the Episcopal Church."

The first use of the title "Protestant Episcopal" occurred at a convention of clergy and laity in Maryland in 1780. In the usage of the time, the name meant that the church differed from Roman Catholic episcopalians because it was Protestant and from other Protestant churches because it was episcopal, or governed by bishops; the title was not intended to deny that the church was Catholic, for both in England and in New England "Catholic" was frequently used as synonymous with "Anglican."

Gradually the new name "Protestant Episcopal" spread to other states. The General Convention of 1789, which met in Philadelphia, adopted "A General Constitution of the Protestant Episcopal Church in the United States of America"—the name by which the denomination was officially known until 1967, when the General Convention made the word "Protestant" optional. From the start both Episcopalians and members of other American churches used the shorter "Episcopal Church" as another name for the denomination.

American Episcopalians continued to use the name "Anglican," especially after the middle of the nineteenth century, to describe the worldwide communion of churches holding to the faith and order of the Church of England. Thus they would speak of Lutheranism, Calvinism, Roman Catholicism, Anglicanism, and similar interpretations of Christianity. This article occasionally uses the word "Anglican" in that manner.

The scattered churches took the first steps toward forming a national organization even before the Revolution was over. In 1782 the Reverend William White, rector of Christ Church, Philadelphia, and former chaplain of the Continental Congress, wrote *The Case of the Episcopal Churches in the United States Considered.* White's *Case* proposed several principles, which eventually became the basis of the Episcopal Church: that the church was to be independent not only of foreign but also of American civil powers; that the church desired and acknowledged three historic orders in the ministry—deacons, priests, and bishops; and that the church was to be democratically operated, with not only clergy but also laity participating in all church councils.

In 1783 conventions of the churches in Maryland and Pennsylvania affirmed these principles. They added another that White had implied—that the worship of the church was to conform as much as possible to the worship of the Church of England. In 1784 additional meetings of Episcopalians representing various states occurred in New Brunswick, New Jersey, and in New York City.

Episcopacy—or the governing of the churches by bishops—proved the greatest stumbling block to unity. Most of the state churches believed that the forming of a national church structure should precede the consecration of bishops. In addition, some of the southern states, where laity had long controlled ecclesiastical affairs, felt no need for a bishop. In the *Case*, White—who can best be described as a low churchman of the eighteenth-century type—had proposed a temporary system of presbyterian ordination. Until bishops could be consecrated, three clergymen would lay hands upon ordinands. This proposal shocked the high churchmen of Connecticut.

Convinced that an Episcopal Church without episcopacy was a contradiction in terms, ten of Connecticut's clergy met secretly at the village of Woodbury in 1783. For their bishop they elected Samuel Seabury, a former SPG missionary in New York who had published several pamphlets supporting the British during the Revolution. The doctrine of apostolic succession required that Seabury receive consecration from a minimum of three bishops of the Church of England. But when Seabury sought consecration, the English bishops refused to cooperate. Above all, the bishops believed they lacked the power to consecrate anyone who could not take the required oath of loyalty to the Crown.

Disappointed, Seabury went to Scotland, where he was consecrated by three non-juring bishops (the successors of those English clergy who refused to forswear their oath of loyalty to James II when William and Mary assumed the throne in 1689). Returning to the United States in 1785, the new bishop began to organize the Episcopal Church of Connecticut. He ordained the first twenty-six Episcopal clergy of the new nation, many of whom came from states other than Connecticut.

For the other Episcopal churches in the United States, the situation was awkward in the extreme. Unity with the Connecticut church seemed unlikely, since it refused to accept the principle of lay participation in councils. In addition, the Loyalist Seabury (who was still on half-pay from England for services rendered during the war) not only was disliked by most American clergymen but was also in disfavor with the English bishops because of his Scottish consecration. The state churches wanted national unity, but they also had to appease the English bishops, from whom they hoped to receive consecration of their bishops.

Nevertheless, in 1785 lay and clerical delegates from seven of the nine states south of Connecticut (the Episcopal churches of North Carolina and Georgia were too weak to send delegates) met in Philadelphia in the first general convention. There they established a constitution, drafted an American version of the Book of Common Prayer, and devised a plan to obtain English consecration for American bishops. Meeting in Philadelphia and Wilmington in 1786, the second general convention adopted measures that allowed White and Samuel Provoost, rector of Trinity parish, New York, to go to England for consecration later in the year. In the meantime, Parliament had passed an act permitting the English bishops to consecrate American bishops without requiring the loyalty oath.

Although these conventions were important, the 1789 general convention, which met in Philadelphia in two sessions, was critical. Still at odds with the southern churches over the questions of lay participation and the validity of Seabury's episcopal orders, the churches in Connecticut (joined by those in Massachusetts) sent no delegates to the first session. This session declared

Seabury's consecration valid and removed the requirement that compelled all state churches to send lay representatives to the general convention. It also created a house of bishops over which the senior bishop in date of consecration (called the presiding bishop) would preside. This upper house would have veto power over the house of clerical and lay deputies.

Appeased, the delegates from Connecticut and Massachusetts joined the second session. That session completed the constitution, established a system of canon law, and adopted in final form an American Book of Common Prayer—all of which was at last acceptable to the whole church. When the convention adjourned on 16 October 1789, the fragmented state churches (later known as dioceses) had finally united.

The constitution, the canons, and the Book of Common Prayer of 1789 laid the basis on which the Episcopal Church operates today. Three clerical orders exist—bishops, priests, and deacons; the church has consecrated its own bishops since 1792. Consisting of an upper house of bishops with all bishops as members and a lower house of deputies with an equal number of clerical and lay delegates elected by the various dioceses as members, the general convention meets every three years and in special sessions. The house of bishops usually meets at least once between general conventions. The convention has the power to amend the canons and to alter the constitution after the proposed alteration has been approved by individual dioceses.

Although the Book of Common Prayer of 1789 has undergone three revisions (1892, 1928, and 1979), it has formed the pattern of worship used in the church ever since. Known officially since 1789 as the Protestant Episcopal Church in the United States of America, the denomination is also known as the Episcopal Church—an alternate official title permitted since 1967 by the general convention and now more generally used. Members are known as Episcopalians.

MISSIONARY WORK

Largely because of the legacy of the revolutionary war, the church grew slowly in the twenty years after 1789. The turn of the nineteenth century saw bishops in seven of the fifteen states. Episcopal work had been organized in five additional states. Everywhere else in the United States the Episcopal Church was either without representation, unorganized, or in danger of extinction. The general convention had the names of approximately two hundred clergy, though some were of superannuated priests ordained during the colonial period. Fewer than one in four hundred citizens of the new nation were Episcopal communicants. Fears of "prelacy" hampered the work of the bishops.

Assessments about whether the first twenty years of the church's united existence represent a period of suspended animation or of quiet revival vary. But 1811 is generally considered a turning point in the church's history. That year saw the consecrations of John Henry Hobart as assistant bishop of New York and of Alexander Viets Griswold as bishop of the eastern diocese. The year also witnessed the ordination of two future leaders in the denomination, William Meade and Jackson Kemper. After 1811 the church revived in the wake of the Second Great Awakening.

Vigorous, contentious, and efficient, Hobart was in charge of his 45,000-square-mile diocese from the first, since the elderly bishop of New York, Benjamin Moore, was partially paralyzed. A high churchman in the tradition of Lancelot Andrewes, William Laud, and other Caroline divines who flourished during the reigns of Charles I and II, Hobart believed the episcopate, the priesthood, the sacraments, and the visible church to be the appointed channels for God's grace. Under his aggressive nineteen-year leadership, the Episcopal Church in New York expanded from 25 clergy, 40 churches, and 2,300 communicants to 133 clergy, 165 congregations, and 6,700 communicants. Hobart's influence extended far beyond the confines of his diocese and life.

Griswold and Meade were both Evangelicals. A man of plainer cloth than most of his contemporaries in the episcopate, Griswold increased the number of parishes in his diocese (a temporary one that brought together all of the New England dioceses except Connecticut) fivefold by the time of his death in 1843. Like Hobart, he confirmed over 1,000 persons on an early tour of his diocese.

Ordained at a time when the general convention feared for the future of the Episcopal Church of Virginia, the ascetic, single-minded Meade quickly attracted fellow Evangelicals to Virginia. In 1814 the Evangelical Richard Channing Moore of New York was consecrated as bishop of Virginia. Using such methods as circuit riding, preaching that aimed at conversion, and strict discipline, Moore and his clergy revived the Anglican tradition in Virginia. By 1835, Virginia was the fourth-largest diocese in communicant membership. Elected assistant bishop of Virginia in 1829, Meade succeeded Moore as bishop in 1841.

Kemper's ministry is tied up with the formation of the Domestic and Foreign Missionary Society, which in turn is tied up with the story of Episcopal expansion in areas west of the Alleghenies and south of the Ohio River. As early as 1792, the general convention considered a proposal to send Episcopal missionaries to the frontiers of the United States. From 1796 on, the individual dioceses formed missionary societies. Though the general convention had asked them to send missionaries west, the societies, with very few exceptions, limited their work to the boundaries of their own states.

Thus when Episcopal clergy went into western areas prior to 1835, they went either as freelancers or in response to a call from a group of laypeople. The general convention consecrated bishops for developing areas of the United States only when the Episcopalians who lived there had voluntarily formed dioceses and elected a bishop. Not until 1821—a year in which Indiana, Illinois, Tennessee, Mississippi, Louisiana, Missouri, Michigan, and Arkansas combined had more than half a million residents but only two Episcopal clergy—did the general convention form the Domestic and Foreign Missionary Society. The voluntary character of the society—members paid annual dues—and its discouraging lack of results soon forced the church to another strategy.

In 1835, using the New Testament for its model, the general convention decided that missions should not be a subsidiary committee but rather a responsibility of the entire church. A tacit agreement (regretted by the Evangelicals, who subsequently formed their own domestic missionary society) gave the responsibility for foreign missions to the Evangelicals and for missions in the new areas of America to the high church party. A second innovation was the general convention's decision to create missionary districts in those new areas and to send missionary bishops to them even before any Episcopal work had been started.

A forty-five-year-old graduate of Columbia University and a high churchman, Kemper was the first missionary bishop sent west. That the nineteenth century was more than one-third over before he was sent illustrates the first of four reasons the Episcopal Church lagged behind other denominations in western membership. First, when Kemper and other bishops made the first tours of their missionary districts, they found that the Baptists, Methodists, and Presbyterians had already established churches. The churchgoing population among the settlers, including many of Episcopal background, had been swallowed up.

Dioceses of unmanageable size represented the second reason. Even when the general convention divided the West and New South into missionary districts, it generally made them too large for any one bishop to supervise efficiently. Kemper had responsibility for the areas that are now Indiana, Wisconsin, Minnesota, Iowa, Missouri, Kansas, and Nebraska. To visit his district, Leonidas Polk, consecrated missionary bishop of Arkansas in 1838 with jurisdiction in adjoining states, had to travel 5,000 miles a year; the district soon grew to include all lands between Missouri, the Gulf of Mexico, California, and Florida. The missionary district of Joseph C. Talbot (consecrated in 1860 as missionary bishop of the Northwest) covered one million square miles; Talbot described himself as "the bishop of all outdoors." Salt Lake City was the seat of Bishop Daniel S. Tuttle (consecrated 1867), but he carried the title of "Bishop of Montana, with Jurisdiction in Idaho and Utah." All of this undercut the church's growth on the frontier. Missionary bishops spent more time on travel than they did preaching, encouraging scattered and often dispirited clergy and congregations, or establishing new Episcopal churches.

A third hindrance for the missionary bishops stemmed from a lack of financial support. Missionaries required salaries; congregations required buildings. As late as 1862, however, less than half of the parishes of the Episcopal Church contributed to the Domestic and Foreign Missionary Society. The average contribution for missions per Episcopal communicant approximated one dollar a year. In 1876 the church

spent $4,000 for missionary work in Kansas, a state in which hundreds of thousands of persons lived. That amount was one-seventh what the Presbyterians spent, one-eighth what the Congregationalists spent, and one-fifteenth of the Methodist expenditures. From the start of his episcopate, the tireless Kemper lamented what he could not accomplish simply because of lack of funds.

Finally, a shortage of missionaries continually handicapped Episcopal missionary work. After the first tour of his district, Kemper reported that he could immediately employ one hundred clergy; seven years later, he had been able to attract a total of only thirty-one. By 1840 the Baptists had almost as many clergy at work in Missouri as the Episcopal Church had in all of the states and territories west of the Alleghenies combined.

The shortage of clergy stemmed from more than lack of funding. Most Episcopal clergy came from reasonably comfortable backgrounds; the frontier mission field held relatively little appeal for them. Missionaries who went west could anticipate low salaries, isolation, danger, substantially lowered life-styles, and unremitting work. Bishop Alexander Garrett of north Texas said that he needed clergy who could "ride like a cow-boy, pray like a saint, preach like an apostle, and having food and raiment be therewith content" (C. B. Goodykoontz, *Home Missions on the American Frontier,* 1939). The denominations that had the most success in evangelizing the New South and West—the Baptists and Methodists—had such ministers. But Episcopal seminaries produced relatively few such men.

These four obstacles were largely of the church's own making. That it faced other obstacles not of its own making in the new areas cannot be denied. Though Episcopal missionaries attempted to appeal to all settlers, the churches they established generally attracted the more prosperous and educated people. In the Deep South, for example, the Episcopal Church largely became the church of the wealthier planters. The result was that people of lower economic and educational levels felt out of place. Protestants accustomed to emotional sermons, extemporaneous worship, and an opposition to card playing and dancing often found Anglicanism too formal and too worldly.

In addition, crop failures, epidemics, and the

usual obstacles of mountains, rivers, forests, and hostile Indians hindered growth, as did the constant attraction of new land; western missionaries of the Episcopal Church frequently complained that the congregations they had so painstakingly gathered were continually moving. The serious economic depressions of the nineteenth century and the disruptions of the Civil War affected missions everywhere. In the later years of the Victorian era, materialism, Darwinism, biblical criticism, the migration of rural people into the cities, the emergence of the trolley car and automobile, and the rise of secular amusements brought a decrease in membership and attendance in Episcopal churches in all areas of America.

Yet what some persons considered handicaps, others saw as attractions in the nineteenth century. Americans were moving west at the precise time that the revolt from Calvinist orthodoxy was accelerating. The Arminian theology, intellectuality, and sensibility of the Episcopal Church inevitably appealed to many settlers of Congregationalist, Presbyterian, or Reformed background. Some of the greatest leaders of the church in the nineteenth century were reared in Calvinist denominations.

The dignity and beauty of Episcopal worship also attracted many Americans, especially in an era of romanticism. Reading the Book of Common Prayer caused persons raised in other denominations to become Episcopalians; their number included Philander Chase, later bishop of Ohio, and James Hervey Otey, subsequently bishop of Tennessee. The church's episcopal polity and claims of antiquity called it to the attention of other Christians. In frontier areas social respectability could also prove an advantage, for Episcopal churches provided a sense of civilization and a means of escaping the crudities of daily life. When an Episcopal church was established, many western towns believed they had "arrived."

To a lesser degree, the church also benefited during the period of western settlement from the reaction against emotionalism in the Methodist and other denominations, from the decline of Quakerism, and from the resistance to German-language services in Lutheranism. In areas of the South and West where they found no churches of their own, Roman Catholics often opted for the Episcopal Church. Christians seeking to escape

narrower backgrounds also responded to the church's toleration of alcohol, dancing, Masonic membership, and many shades of theological opinion. Even the observance by Episcopalians of Yuletide traditions and Christmas services—rare among Protestant denominations of English origin until after the Civil War—served as an attraction.

To form a congregation in new areas, Episcopal missionaries would frequently comb the countryside for persons who had been brought up as Episcopalians or who were thought to be friendly to the Episcopal Church. Often they would preach in a new community and begin a congregation with persons who responded favorably. Occasionally Episcopalians in new settlements would take the initiative and ask for a clergyman. Until churches were built, the missionaries used homes, courthouses, schools, stores, and the churches of other denominations as places for Episcopal services.

To found and establish parishes, missionaries distributed Bibles, Episcopal tracts, devotional works, and copies of the Book of Common Prayer. Some missionaries established parish libraries and reading rooms. Sunday schools, which initially taught children not only religious education but also reading and writing, provided a means of carrying Christian influence into unchurched homes. As in other denominations, primary and secondary schools proved an important means of nurturing youth in church teaching. Most bishops also established hospitals. Most of the colleges and theological seminaries started by the bishops ultimately failed, but Kenyon College (founded by Bishop Chase in 1824 in Gambier, Ohio) and its theological seminary, Bexley Hall (which moved to Rochester, New York, in the 1970s), stand as examples of what most western bishops hoped to do.

Methods of evangelization used by Episcopal missionaries included itinerancy, in which one missionary served a number of preaching stations and parishes. In North Dakota, Bishop William D. Walker fitted a 60-foot railroad car as a traveling chapel and took services to remote settlements. In rural areas of the South, "associations," in which a number of clergy converged on a point of missionary interest and held several services a day for several days in a row, built up parishes. In the later years of the nineteenth century, "parish missions" in city churches featured a noted preacher who held intensive public meetings for up to two weeks. Widely publicized in frontier areas, Episcopal visitations provided a major opportunity not only for encouragement of a congregation but also for evangelization of the unchurched. Often all of the residents of a frontier town would turn out to see and to hear "the bishop."

Relatively few settlers of the New South and the West seem to have come from Anglican backgrounds. But since the majority of settlers came from British or German stock for much of the nineteenth century, the Episcopal Church should not have found the West and New South alien ground. Historically, it could claim to be the mother church of all British Protestants; liturgically, it was similar to Lutheranism. That it failed to become a major presence in most parts of the Deep South and the West stemmed largely from its slowness to seize opportunities.

The effects have been long-lasting. On the eve of World War II, the ratio of communicants to population in the diocese of Virginia was one to thirty-four; in Alabama, it was one to 243. In the mid-1980s, approximately 140,000 baptized Episcopalians live in Massachusetts. To reach the same number in the West, one has to combine all of the baptized Episcopalians in the states of Iowa, Missouri, Kansas, Oklahoma, Arkansas, and Mississippi. In the Far West states, Episcopal membership is higher in ratio to population, for the church's missionary organization was largely in place by the time those states began to receive significant numbers of settlers.

The history of the church's work with the Indians is largely unflattering. It is a record not of an overall effort to bring the Christian faith to the native Americans, but rather of the efforts of a small number of committed individuals. Although the Church of England was the only established church in the southern colonies, missionary work there was generally ignored. A British benefactor's bequest caused Virginia's Anglicans to found an Indian school at the College of William and Mary for the purpose of Christianizing the Indians, but the school was unsuccessful and closed during the Revolution.

In the North the fear of Indian allegiance to the French and the impulse to convert the heathen combined to encourage the SPG to evangelize tribes of the Iroquois nation, especially the Mohawks. The SPG provided them with missionaries, chapels, and Mohawk versions of several books of the Bible and the Book of Common Prayer. After the revolutionary war, the Episcopal Church continued the work in New York under Bishop Hobart—a popular figure among the Indians—by establishing a mission to the Oneidas. Under the leadership of Eleazar Williams, a missionary of mixed Indian and white parentage, many New York Indians moved to Green Bay, Wisconsin, in the 1820s, where the church founded another mission.

While the Green Bay mission prospered, the church also established a mission to the Chippewas in Minnesota. These two missions, however, were the only signs of Episcopal activity among the Indians before the Civil War. The great surge in missionary work to the Indians began in the 1870s. In response to pleas from Bishop Henry B. Whipple of Minnesota and William Welsh (an Episcopalian who headed the congressional Board of Indian Commissioners), the church formed the Indian Commission under its board of missions. The commission chose the Reverend William Hobart Hare (grandson of John Henry Hobart) to be the bishop of the Niobrara missionary district, which encompassed the western half of present-day South Dakota.

Although whites lived in the area, Hare's primary responsibility was to Christianize the Indians of the Great Plains. "The Apostle to the Sioux" became the leading figure in the church's work among the Indians. After more than thirty years of crossing South Dakota by wagon and camping out on the plains, Hare had confirmed over 7,000 Indians. By 1909, the year of his death, 10,000 of the estimated 20,000 Indians of South Dakota were baptized members of the Episcopal Church. To this day, the diocese of South Dakota claims a sizable Indian membership. The first American Indian to become a bishop, Harold Jones, was the suffragan of South Dakota from 1971 to 1976. (Suffragans are bishops who exercise authority delegated by the diocesan bishop but have no right to succeed him.)

The last great expansion in missionary work came among Indians, Eskimos, and white settlers in Alaska after the turn of the century under Bishop Peter Trimble Rowe. A man of immense stamina who covered vast distances by boat, dog sled, and eventually airplane, Rowe established missions, schools, and hospitals all over Alaska. Assisted by the courageous Archdeacon Hudson Struck, he served as bishop of Alaska for forty-seven years. By the time Rowe died in 1942, he had made Episcopalians across the nation concerned with the church's work in Alaska. More recently, the church has created a mission and a bishopric among the Navajos of New Mexico, Arizona, and Utah.

Among the many obstacles confronting Episcopal missions to the Indians were the staggering number of dialects, the shortage of missionaries, the scattered settlements, and the migrations forced upon the Indians by the U.S. government. The church not only established many schools to educate Indian young, but also trained Indians to become clergy among their own people. Today clergy in the diocese of South Dakota have such names as Two Bulls, Brokenleg, and Two Hawk.

Despite this impressive record, from the colonial period on, the majority of Episcopalians remained indifferent to missionary work among the Indians. The overall effort of the church was minor.

The first Episcopal missionary sent overseas by the Domestic and Foreign Missionary Society went to Greece in 1828. Before the Civil War, the society had established missions in Turkey, Liberia, China, and Japan, all of which received American bishops. Among the colleges established by the church were St. John's College, Shanghai, and St. Paul's College, Tokyo.

By the turn of the century, missions had been founded in Haiti, Mexico, Puerto Rico, and the Philippines. The black nationalist leader James T. Holly served as the first bishop of the Haitian church. The first bishop to take up residence in Manila was the influential Charles Henry Brent.

Today, the Episcopal Church is represented throughout Central and South America and the Caribbean; it has also extended its missionary work to Taiwan. Several of the missions have developed into independent national churches. The church operates theological seminaries in Mexico City and the Philippines and supports colleges in Liberia and the Philippines. From the Victorian period on, the Episcopal Church has established self-supporting parishes for American residents and travelers in the major cities of

Europe. The total number of overseas communicants stood at 79,701 in 1984.

THE OXFORD MOVEMENT

The issues raised in the 1830s and 1840s by the Oxford movement formed a central tension that has colored the Episcopal Church's activities ever since. Begun in England by Anglican clergymen John Keble, E. B. Pusey, and John Henry Newman—all three were Oxford dons, hence the term "Oxford movement"—the cause was initially spread by a series of pamphlets called *The Tracts for the Times* (starting in 1833). The movement taught a high doctrine of the church, ministry, and sacraments, emphasizing especially the apostolic succession, the real presence, and baptismal regeneration. Its sources lay in Henrician Catholicism, in the patristics-oriented high church movement of the Carolinian period, in the emphasis on personal religion of Anglican Evangelicalism, and in the veneration of the medieval by the romantic revival. In the 1830s the movement spread to the United States, where it built upon the tradition of Hobartian high churchmanship.

The second phase of the movement, called "ritualism" (because its adherents used medieval or post-Reformation Roman Catholic ceremony and symbolism in worship), or "Anglo-Catholicism" (because its adherents emphasized the continuity of the Church of England with the Catholicism of the patristic and medieval periods), became especially prominent in America following the Civil War. In it the revival of medieval theology expressed itself in medieval forms. In architecture, the movement replaced Georgian and classical revival churches with gothic and romanesque churches. It replaced plain church windows with stained-glass windows and pulpit-centered churches with altar-centered churches. Episcopal churches now also began to employ crosses in their interiors and on their exteriors.

In liturgy, the movement emphasized the Eucharist, the observance of saints' days, voluntary private confession and priestly absolution, and prayers and requiems for the dead. In ceremonial, the movement tried to express the *mysterium tremendum* through the use of incense, bowing or genuflection, Eucharistic vestments, copes and mitres, and processions and recessions of clergy with surpliced choirs and lights, music, and crucifers.

In addition to returning medieval worship to Anglicanism, Anglo-Catholicism restored monastic orders for men and women. As exemplified by the career of the Reverend James O. S. Huntington, founder of the monastic Order of the Holy Cross—who lived and worked in the slums of the Lower East Side of Manhattan and founded the influential Church Association for the Advancement of the Interests of Labor—it also displayed a great concern for the problems of society. As indicated by the title of Ferdinand C. Ewer's *Catholicity in Its Relationship to Protestantism and Romanism* (1878), the movement liked to contrast real Catholicism (which it claimed to possess) with "Romanism."

The earliest manifestations of Anglo-Catholicism in America centered around the semi-monastic community formed in the 1840s by James Lloyd Breck in Wisconsin. In later years bishops and clergy such as Ewer, Charles C. Grafton, and James De Koven, architects such as Ralph Adams Cram, dioceses such as Fond du Lac and Milwaukee in Wisconsin, and churches such as Advent in Boston and St. Ignatius and Saint Mary the Virgin in Manhattan became its leading representatives in America. Like all movements, Anglo-Catholicism had wings. By the later years of the Victorian period, Episcopalians could tell the altitude of a parish's churchmanship by such things as whether it used the word "Eucharist" or "Mass," whether its clergy were celibate or married, whether it prayed to the Blessed Virgin Mary, and whether it held such services as Benediction of the Blessed Sacrament.

Anglo-Catholic interpretations of faith and worship were not espoused in Episcopal parishes without opposition. In older dioceses, the opposition not only from Evangelicals but also from traditional high churchmen was vigorous, long lasting, and frequently bitter. Churchmen of both parties believed that the movement denied the Reformation heritage of Anglicanism. That a number of Anglo-Catholics adopted Roman Catholic practices in their parishes and later converted to Rome amid great publicity only confirmed suspicions.

Critics often overlooked the fact that Anglo-Catholicism quietly attracted even larger numbers of Christians of Protestant, Roman Catholic, and Eastern Orthodox backgrounds than the Episcopal Church lost to Roman Catholicism. By 1900 Anglo-Catholicism was strong in the "Biretta Belt" dioceses of the Midwest (the six dioceses in Wisconsin and Illinois plus several in adjoining states—so named because many of the Episcopal clergy in those dioceses wore the same kind of cap with tassel, or biretta, favored by Roman Catholic clergy) and in certain parishes and dioceses in the East and West. Episcopalians raised in low church dioceses, however, could still be baptized, confirmed, married, and buried without smelling incense or seeing an Episcopal monk or nun.

The Oxford movement and Anglo-Catholicism challenged the eighteenth- and early-nineteenth-century belief that Anglicanism was simply another form of Protestantism. Positively, the movement reversed the centuries-old process by which Anglicanism had been impoverishing itself by casting out its nonconformists. It enriched the denomination by recalling its Catholic heritage. Henceforth Anglicanism would be a more comprehensive church than it had been since the Elizabethan period. Not only the movement's concern for higher standards of worship but also many of its "innovations"—colored stoles, vested choirs, chanted psalms, processions and recessions, frequent holy communion—subsequently became widely accepted not only in the Episcopal Church but also in other denominations.

Negatively, the movement's warmth and color may have attracted many persons whose interests lay more in aesthetics than in Christianity. It may also have attracted more people of a combative temperament than entered other aspects of the Episcopal Church's life. The image of the church as a circus of ecclesiastical gladiators clearly kept many potential converts from it. Though the original battle of Anglo-Catholicism in the 1830s and 1840s was for a life of prayer, discipline, and devotion, its stormy petrels in later decades often battled for candles, titles, and ecclesiastical millinery. Slavery, child labor, twelve-hour workdays, and impoverished lives were just outside the doors of Episcopal churches. But for many years questions about ecclesiastical garb, church ornaments, and flowers or candles on the Lord's table dominated the concerns of Episcopalians.

BLACK EPISCOPALIANS

Since slavery was centered in the South, where the Church of England was the established church during the colonial period, Anglicanism had a head start in the evangelization of blacks. From its founding until the American Revolution, the SPG also devoted part of its ministry to the religious instruction of slaves. In the antebellum period, Episcopal Evangelicals in the South maintained an active ministry to slaves.

Institutions employed in missionary work among southern blacks included Sunday schools, catechetical schools, and plantation chapels. Household servants of Episcopal families often attended white churches, sitting in slave galleries or in special sections in the back or sides. In town churches, Episcopal parishes occasionally formed black congregations led by white clergy and supervised by white laity.

The total number of black Episcopalians in the antebellum South was approximately 35,000. Missionary work was most successful in South Carolina, where an estimated 14,000 blacks were Episcopalians at the time of the Civil War. In the North, beginning in 1794 with St. Thomas Church, Philadelphia, a small number of Episcopal churches were formed among free blacks. The pastor of St. Thomas, Absalom Jones, was the first of twenty-five blacks ordained to the Episcopal ministry in the North prior to 1865.

These numbers were small; Baptist and Methodist membership among blacks was substantially larger. Reasons cited for the failure of the Episcopal Church to evangelize the blacks, despite its head start, are many. The church was slow in establishing a presence in the Cotton Belt, where the majority of slaves eventually lived. When it did establish parishes, relatively few slaveowners were attracted. Everywhere in the South the British model of ordination and worship kept the Episcopal Church from adapting to the religious needs and emotional expressions of the slaves. Identified with the gentry, the church had a great difficulty establishing a link with the lower classes.

Unlike other denominations, the Episcopal Church was not formally divided over the issue of slavery. Fearing schism above all else, and realizing that resolutions on slavery would inevitably bring disputes, the church avoided an official stand on human bondage. Anglican habits of compromise were partially responsible for this neutrality. In keeping with their emphasis on personal religion, many Evangelicals and high churchmen also felt that slavery was a purely political issue and therefore outside the concerns of the church. Those Episcopalians who knew southern planters from college or from fashionable summer resorts also seem to have been repelled by the characterization of slaveowners given in abolitionist publications.

As individuals, however, a number of Episcopal laity and clergy became involved in the slavery controversies. In the South, Episcopalians who published defenses of slavery included Bishop George Washington Freeman and Thomas Roderick Dew, president of the College of William and Mary. Three northern clergy—Bishop John Henry Hopkins of Vermont, Samuel Seabury (grandson of the bishop), and N. S. Wheaton—published similar defenses based on biblical literalism and political conservatism.

In the North, William Jay and his son, John Jay, were active abolitionists. Three Episcopal clergymen—Evan Johnson, John P. Lundy, and Thomas Atkins—published tracts supporting abolition. E. M. P. Wells, a Boston rector, served as a vice president of the American Anti-Slavery Society. Northern Episcopalians who accepted the lawfulness of slavery but opposed its extension included Bishop William R. Whittingham of Maryland, Bishop Alonzo Potter of Pennsylvania, and Free-Soil leaders William H. Seward and Salmon P. Chase. But of the more than 2,000 Episcopal clergy and almost 150,000 laity in America at the time of the Civil War, relatively few left any permanent statement against human servitude.

In both the North and South, Episcopalians supported the American Colonization Society and its goal of returning free blacks to Africa. Many in the laity were among the founders of the society; Bishop William Meade of Virginia served as its first national agent. Beginning in 1835, the denomination sent missionaries to the society's colony of Liberia. In 1850 the general convention elected John Payne, a white graduate of mission-centered Virginia Theological Seminary, as the first bishop for Africa. Though the venture in colonization was not a success, some Episcopal congregations were still sending funds to it at the time of the outbreak of the Civil War.

Given the Anglican tradition of independent national churches, the formation by the eleven southern dioceses of an independent Protestant Episcopal Church in the Confederate States of America was inevitable. The new church's constitution, canon law, and prayer book were all patterned closely upon those of the parent church. Jefferson Davis and Robert E. Lee were among its leading laymen; two graduates of West Point—Bishop Leonidas Polk of Louisiana (who owned several hundred slaves) and the Reverend William N. Pendleton of Virginia—served in the Confederate army as generals. The Confederate church's major act was to consecrate Richard Hooker Wilmer as bishop of Alabama in 1862, a consecration the northern dioceses ratified following Lee's surrender. The first pastoral letter issued by the Confederate bishops declared that the South's slaves were "a sacred trust."

The war not only disrupted parish life but also destroyed many Episcopal churches. During the northern occupation of Louisiana and Virginia, the canonical obligation to pray for the president of the Confederacy rather than the president of the United States caused the arrest of some Episcopal clergy. In Alabama, northern military authorities at one point suspended all Episcopal services.

But Episcopalians emerged from the war less divided than might have been expected. Because so many of the southern and northern bishops were friends, because the northern church refused to accept the schism as permanent and still began the roll call with Alabama at its general conventions, and because the presiding bishop of the northern church was the south sympathizer John Henry Hopkins, reconciliation occurred with remarkable smoothness. By 186_ all of the southern dioceses had returned to the Protestant Episcopal Church in the United States of America.

Following the Civil War, many blacks in the South left the slave galleries of the Episcopal Church, preferring the more spontaneous worship of the Baptists and Methodists to the formal services of the Book of Common Prayer. At the

general convention of 1868, the southern dioceses reported major losses of black communicants, with South Carolina reporting the departure of over 90 percent.

Southern blacks who remained in the Episcopal Church soon discovered that they lacked the status and freedom that came with membership in denominations founded and controlled by blacks. The black Baptist, the African Methodist Episcopal, and the African Methodist Episcopal Zion churches had black clergy and black bishops. But white pastors generally led black congregations in the Episcopal Church. Because of lay opposition, most southern dioceses also refused to grant full membership to black congregations. From 1875 to 1889, for example, the diocese of South Carolina was racked over the request of St. Mark's Church, Charleston (a self-supporting black congregation with a white rector), to be admitted to the diocese.

The ultimate solution of South Carolina, like that of most southern dioceses, was to impose a color line. All black congregations were segregated into a separate diocesan organization under the direction and authority of the bishop and assisted by a black archdeacon. Many southern bishops and clergy initially supported full rights for black congregations. The general convention, however, took no action, preferring to leave racial matters to the individual dioceses. Not until the 1950s did every diocese of the Episcopal Church grant blacks equal voting representation.

What little work the Episcopal Church did for its remaining black members in the South revolved around societies like the Freedman's Commission and the American Church Institute, which promoted black welfare in education. Schools for blacks founded under Episcopal auspices after the Civil War include St. Augustine's College (1867), Raleigh, North Carolina; St. Paul's College (1889), Lawrenceville, Virginia; Voorhees College (1922), Denmark, South Carolina; and a number of secondary and vocational schools. The request of a black layman in Virginia for ordination prompted the incorporation of the Bishop Payne Divinity School in Petersburg, Virginia, in 1884. A branch of Virginia Theological Seminary, it was named for the first missionary bishop sent to Africa by the American church. Its faculty was originally composed entirely of whites.

THE ANGLICAN TRADITION AND THE EPISCOPAL CHURCH

The years between 1874 and 1940 also saw repeatedly unsuccessful attempts in the general convention to create missionary districts in the United States for blacks headed by black bishops. The proposal was blocked primarily by northern dioceses, on the grounds that it would make segregation a permanent feature of national Episcopal church life.

In 1910 the general convention established suffragan bishops, who are barred from diocesan succession. In part the canon was a response to the desires of dioceses in the West and Northeast for bishops who could supervise expanding missionary work. Though it mentioned neither race nor color, the canon opened the way for blacks to become bishops, for no diocese at the time would have elected a black who might become a diocesan. Suffragans lacked a vote in the house of bishops; it was also understood that no black suffragan would exercise episcopal oversight of white congregations. Thomas Demby became the first black bishop when he was consecrated suffragan bishop of Arkansas in 1918; in the next year, a graduate of St. Augustine's College, Henry Delany, was consecrated suffragan bishop of North Carolina. The first black bishop to have jurisdiction over white congregations, John M. Burgess, was consecrated suffragan bishop of Massachusetts in 1962. Eight years later Burgess became the first black diocesan bishop when he became bishop of Massachusetts.

In the North and West, the situation for black Episcopalians differed. Prior to the Civil War large congregations of black Episcopalians had existed in Philadelphia, New York City, New Haven, and elsewhere. After the war influential congregations emerged in Newark, Buffalo, Detroit, Chicago, St. Louis, and other cities. Though some had white rectors, most were founded by black clergy. In these dioceses lack of equal accommodations at meetings and lack of representation in positions of leadership, rather than denial of diocesan membership, represented the major problems. Though a number of the northern bishops were outspoken integrationists, these marks of a color line generally were not removed until the 1950s and 1960s.

Since some blacks were communicants of predominantly white churches outside the South, membership figures for black Episcopalians during the period can only be approximate. George F. Bragg's *History of the Afro-American Group of the Episcopal Church* lists, as of 1922, 288 exclusively black congregations in 58 dioceses with two bishops, 176 clergy, and about 32,000 communicants. Total Episcopal membership in the same year was about 1.1 million, with some 6,000 clergy. St. Philip's Church, New York City, was the largest black congregation. Besides Bishops Demby and Delany, Alexander Crummell and Bishop James T. Holly were among the leading black clergy.

IMMIGRANTS AND THE CHURCH

The Episcopal Church benefited little from the massive immigration that began in the 1830s and continued through World War I. The obstacles were many, though some were of the church's own making rather than inevitable.

The national clannishness of the immigrant groups, their lack of prior knowledge of Anglicanism, the atmosphere of rented pews, cushions, and carpets, the Anglo-American background of so many Episcopal clergy and laity, the requirement for English literacy built into the prayer book worship, the lack of experience of the immigrants with the voluntary principle, and the emphasis in so many Episcopal churches on non-sacramental services of morning prayer with sermon (rather than on the Eucharist)—all tended to discourage immigrants from joining Episcopal churches. In addition, some eastern dioceses believed that immigrants should quickly adjust to Anglo-Saxon Episcopalianism rather than have the church temporarily adjust to the ways of foreigners.

From English immigrants the church inevitably gained its greatest numbers. The percentage of Anglicans among the English and Anglo-Irish immigrants is unknown, but a sufficient number clearly remained loyal to the established church of their homeland. New Episcopal churches sprang up wherever the English settled in the nineteenth century—in the mill towns of New England, the mining districts of Illinois, the farming communities of the plains states, and the orange groves of land-boom Florida. To assist Anglican emigrants, the Episcopal Church established the Anglo-American Church Emigrant's Aid Society in 1855. Emigrants who had converted to Mormonism in England became some of the early Episcopalian converts of Bishop Tuttle and his clergy in Utah. As early as 1875, blacks from the British colonies in the West Indies had formed an Episcopal parish in Florida.

For a time, Episcopalianism also found promising ground among Swedish-Americans. Beginning in 1845, a group of Swedish-American clergy led by Gustaf Unonius argued that the Episcopal Church better represented the high church Lutheranism of Sweden than did the pietistic Augustana Synod, the principal Swedish church in America. Calling themselves the "national church of Sweden" and using its liturgy, they established more than a dozen Episcopal parishes among Swedish immigrants along the East Coast and in the Midwest. In 1866 Bishop Henry J. Whitehouse of Chicago returned from a meeting with the Lutheran bishops of Sweden with an agreement (later revoked following protests from the Augustana Synod) that clergy in Sweden would recommend that members of their parishes who emigrated to America join Episcopal congregations when no Lutheran churches existed in their area. The Episcopal mission to the Swedes cannot be called a success. More Swedish-Americans subsequently became Episcopalians through the normal process of assimilation than through evangelism.

With several other immigrant groups the Episcopal Church encountered some success. Though attempts to evangelize German immigrants failed in many places, German Lutherans felt a kinship with the Episcopal liturgy and tended to be open to the Episcopal Church when Lutheran services were not available. From 1874 on, the Book of Common Prayer was available in German. The church German Society, also formed in 1874, which had its center in chapels established by English-speaking parishes in New York City, attempted to train German-speaking Episcopal clergy. Episcopal parishes abandoned separate work with Germans when the American-born generations assimilated into regular parish structures and demanded services in English.

Initially, Italian immigrants seemed to present a special opportunity for evangelism by the Episcopal Church. Some Italians arrived in the United States already disaffected with Roman Catholicism because of its opposition to the unification of Italy and to the Italian kingdom that had incorporated the former papal states. Others stopped attending church when they experienced the Irish domination of American Roman Catholicism, which could extend even to Irish priests staffing Italian parishes.

Using an Italian translation of the Book of Common Prayer and tracts in Italian such as one entitled *Return to the Faith of Your Forefathers*, dioceses from Connecticut to Chicago established missions to unchurched Italians. The Episcopal churches in Italian neighborhoods bore such names as La Chiesa dell' Annunziata or La Chiesa della L'Emmanuello; former Roman Catholic priests of Italian birth often staffed them. In Hackensack, New Jersey, and in Youngstown, Ohio, groups of Italians and their clergy left the Roman Catholic for the Episcopal Church. On the Lower East Side of Manhattan, an Italian congregation of several hundred worshiped in Grace Chapel each Sunday. By the 1920s the church's department of missions and church extension could report twenty-two missions to Italians, most ministered to by Episcopal priests of Italian birth. More than half were in New York. Given the immigration of 4 million Italians to the United States in the forty years prior to the report, the yield was small.

The church also had some success with Jewish immigrants (several of whom—like the scholarly Samuel Isaac Joseph Schereschewsky—became bishops), with the Hungarians in Indiana and New Jersey, with the Czechs (many of whom were estranged from Roman Catholicism), and with the Chinese and Japanese on the West Coast, in New York City, and elsewhere. Some Cubans who came to work in the tobacco fields and new industries of Florida also became Episcopalians. Among the Poles, for whom nationalism and Roman Catholicism were interlinked, the church was able to establish only a few missions. Episcopalians attempted virtually no missionary work among the Roman Catholic Irish, for whom religion, nationalism, and dislike of things English were combined.

Though Episcopalians sponsored some missions to immigrants of Eastern Orthodox background, Anglo-Catholic influence caused the church increasingly to seek fellowship and intercommunion with these churches. In the diocese of Fond du Lac an attempt in the 1870s to form an Old Catholic movement among Belgian immigrants who had become disaffected with Roman Catholicism created far more problems than it did new parishes.

THE ANGLICAN TRADITION AND THE EPISCOPAL CHURCH

Victorian immigration to America caused the rapid growth of Roman Catholicism, Lutheranism, and Judaism, and radically changed the composition of many American states. Many of the immigrants were open to evangelization, as World War I chaplains discovered when large numbers reported no religious affiliation. But for a variety of reasons—lack of representatives to meet ships, delayed translations of the prayer book into foreign languages, failure to establish a "foreign-born division" in its Domestic and Foreign Missionary Society until 1920, and, above all, lack of vision—the Episcopal Church was slow to seize its opportunities.

That Episcopalianism did benefit to some extent from the immigration was indicated by a census of one parish in the 1940s, which revealed more than thirty national strains. The impact of immigration is also seen in the current *Episcopal Clerical Directory,* where clergy with names such as Carlozzi, Jensen, Olubowicz, O'Shaughnessy, De Chambeau, Likowski, Kontos, Orozco, Giovangelo, Berdahl, Desroisers, Kitagawa, O'Brien, and Valdes-Perez are listed side by side with names of distinctly English origin.

NEW INTELLECTUAL INFLUENCES

In the latter half of the nineteenth century, the Episcopal Church had to confront evolution, the Higher Criticism of the Bible, and other intellectual currents of the Victorian era. The Higher Criticism involved the scientific investigation of the sources, date, authorship, and form (and hence accuracy and reliability) of the biblical books.

As in England, the adaptation of Episcopalians to the revolution in religious thought was gradual. The American house of bishops condemned the controversial *Essays and Reviews* (1860), in which seven Anglican writers accepted the methodology of the Higher Criticism and called into question some formulations of Christian doctrine and the authorship of the Pentateuch.

But *Essays and Reviews,* like the earlier *Tracts for the Times,* heralded a new movement in Anglicanism. In response to the challenges, Anglicans concerned with a quest for truth from all sources gradually came together in England and America in the broad church movement. Broad church-

men tried to assimilate the new scientific knowledge and critical approach to the Scriptures into a positive, confident Christian world view.

Though theirs was an intellectual movement rather than a churchmanship party, their wide sympathies and sense of comprehensiveness caused broad churchmen initially to be more congenial with the low church party than with the emerging Anglo-Catholic party. Leading figures in the movement in America were Phillips Brooks, rector of Trinity Church, Boston, William R. Huntington, rector of Grace Church, New York, and Bishops Henry C. Potter of New York and Thomas M. Clark of Rhode Island. Church congresses, forums of Episcopalians that cut across party lines, represented the principal means by which the movement brought major intellectual issues before the consideration of the church. The Episcopal Theological School in Cambridge, Massachusetts, was the movement's intellectual center.

For several decades, the broad churchmen were the only figures in the Episcopal Church to insist that the church could not ignore the new intellectual currents. In 1889, however, English members of the Anglo-Catholic party produced *Lux Mundi,* a series of essays that attempted "to put the Catholic faith into its right relation to modern intellectual and moral problems." Although many Anglicans attacked *Lux Mundi* as heretical, the book showed that even conservative parties in the church were beginning to accept the methods of the Higher Criticism and the new scientific points of view. For a time the Anglo-Catholic party in America was slower to adapt than its counterpart in England, and much of the early opposition to the broad church movement in America came from Anglo-Catholics.

To a large extent, the Episcopal Church avoided public controversy in the course of debating the intellectual challenges facing it. In the most famous case, Bishop Potter aroused vigorous protest when he ordained Charles A. Briggs in 1899. An otherwise theologically conservative professor of biblical theology at Union Theological Seminary in New York, Briggs had left the Presbyterian church after being charged with heresy for questioning the Mosaic authorship of the Pentateuch. Other church trials receiving national publicity were the depositions in 1891 of Howard McQueary, rector of St. Paul's

407

Church, Canton, Ohio, and in 1905 of Algernon S. Crapsey, a highly respected Rochester priest of Anglo-Catholic background. The records of their trials indicate that both men remained strongly oriented toward the person and social teachings of Jesus Christ. At a time when many in America and elsewhere believed that science was undercutting the entire dogmatic system of the Christian faith, both McQueary and Crapsey had become convinced that Christianity must broaden the definition of some of its doctrines or lose thinking people to unbelief.

Unlike most Protestant denominations, the Episcopal Church gradually assimilated the revolutionary intellectual trends with little trauma. Beginning in the 1870s with the Episcopal Theological School (later named Episcopal Divinity School) of Cambridge, Massachusetts, which quickly became the center for the new intellectual forces among Episcopalians, the church's seminaries "fell" one by one to the Higher Criticism. Following the lead of the Lambeth Conference of Anglican bishops, the house of bishops formally declared in 1899 that the reverent critical study of the Bible was necessary not only to maintain the Christian faith but also to protect it. By World War I the majority of Episcopal clergy had accepted evolution and the methods (if not all the conclusions) of the Higher Criticism.

That Anglicanism was able to accept these changes with relative ease stemmed from its conception of comprehensiveness and from the expression of its faith in terms of the historic creeds and the prayer book rather than through an official doctrine of the literal inerrancy of Scripture. The low church emphasis on the right of private judgment and the Anglo-Catholic emphasis on the guidance of the Holy Spirit when the church interprets Scripture also contributed. Finally, the Episcopal Church's emphasis on reason, which it inherited from the English intellectual tradition, enabled it to adapt to the new intellectual challenges.

THE SOCIAL GOSPEL

The medieval belief that a Christian social ethic must permeate society informed the codes of the colonial Anglican establishments. From 1785 until the rise of the Social Gospel in the high Victorian period, the social witness of the Episcopal Church was generally limited to parish charities, to participation in such movements as prison reform, and to the support of institutions for the destitute, widowed, orphaned, or handicapped. The separation of church and state, the emphasis not only of Evangelicals but also of traditional high churchmen on "personal religion," and the nation's economic dogma of laissez-faire combined to discourage Episcopal social concern. When William Paret was called in 1876 to the rectorship of the important Church of the Epiphany in Washington, D.C., and asked its vestry the extent of their work with the poor, "the answer was that the parish had no poor; every pew was let" (William Paret, *Reminiscences,* 1911).

Yet the middle- and upper-class Episcopal Church was one of the first denominations in America to welcome the Social Gospel's critique of industrial society and to urge the improvement of wages, working and living conditions, and the rights of working men and women. Scholars generally explain this paradox by pointing to the medieval heritage of Anglicanism and the rise of Anglo-Catholicism, the spreading influence among Episcopalians of the Christian Socialist movement (founded in 1848) of the Church of England, the leadership of committed bishops, and the concentration of church membership in cities, where social and political problems were obvious. The majority of Episcopalians undoubtedly remained conservative on economic and social issues and continued to believe that the church's duty was to inspire individuals who as Christians would then improve society. But general conventions from the 1890s on began to concern themselves with questions of social justice.

The earliest organizational expressions of the Social Gospel in America emerged from the Episcopal Church. Among the most important were the Church Association for the Advancement of the Interests of Labor (founded 1887, with almost fifty bishops among its members) and the Christian Social Union (founded 1891). When the church established permanent committees and departments to deal with the problems of American society, these voluntary organizations disbanded. After 1919 their witness was continued by the Church League for Industrial Democracy (later called the Episcopal League for Social Action), which counted more than one thousand members by the Depression.

Clergy who provided early leadership in the

Social Gospel included William S. Rainsford, Philo W. Sprague, R. Heber Newton, W.D.P. Bliss, George Hodges, James O. S. Huntington, and his father, Frederick Dan Huntington, bishop of Central New York. Laymen included Richard T. Ely, founder of the American Economics Association. Henry George, author of *Progress and Poverty* (1877–1879), was attracted to the Episcopal Church because of its social statements. Bishops such as Henry Codman Potter of New York, Charles D. Williams of Michigan, Franklin S. Spalding and Paul Jones of Utah, and William Scarlett of Missouri, clergy such as Bernard Iddings Bell and Edgar Gardner Murphy, and laity such as Professor Vida Scudder of Wellesley College and U.S. Secretary of Labor Frances Perkins carried on the movement in the twentieth century. Williams, whose see was in Detroit, was a persistent critic of the ethics of the emerging automobile industry, as was Spalding of the mining companies in the West. Mrs. Perkins was responsible for many of the reforms of Franklin D. Roosevelt's New Deal. The social activism of the Episcopal Church during the presiding episcopate (1964–1973) of Bishop John E. Hines (who as a young priest was influenced by Scarlett) must be seen in the context of the denomination's earlier role as a pioneer in the Social Gospel.

CHURCH PARTIES, ECUMENISM, AND PACIFISM

Tensions between church parties have characterized ecumenical relations in the Episcopal Church in the same way that conservative-liberal tensions have in other denominations. While some Episcopalians have looked for unity toward the Eastern Orthodox, Roman Catholic, and Old Catholic churches, others have looked first toward Protestant denominations.

The Episcopal Church's relations with other denominations were generally distant and occasionally antagonistic during the colonial period. In the nineteenth century, under the leadership of the Evangelical party, the church began to cooperate with such interdenominational societies as the American Bible Society, the American Sunday School Union, the American Tract Society, and the Evangelical Alliance. The high church party, however, opposed such cooperation. In the West, Episcopalians of all parties

generally maintained cordial relations with denominations other than the Latter-day Saints. After the 1830s the rapid growth of the Roman Catholic church and the "Romanizing" influences of the Oxford and Ritualist movements revived Reformation memories and ushered in a long period of hostility among most Episcopalians toward Roman Catholicism.

As for relations with Protestant denominations, the Muhlenberg Memorial, presented to the house of bishops in 1853 by William Augustus Muhlenberg and others, urged that Episcopal bishops contribute to a wider unity by ordaining qualified Protestant clergy and allowing them to continue to minister in their denominations. The memorial failed, but did cause the creation of the Commission on Church Unity (now the Standing Committee on Ecumenical Relations), which has remained perhaps the most active ecumenical agency in any denomination. More systematic was the Chicago-Lambeth Quadrilateral of 1888. The quadrilateral, which is still the official ecumenical platform of the Episcopal Church, listed four essentials to church unity: the Scriptures, the Apostles' and Nicene Creeds, the two dominical sacraments of baptism and the Lord's Supper (held to be clearly instituted by Jesus in the New Testament and not added in later centuries by the church), and the historic episcopate. On that basis the Episcopal Church held unity discussions with the Lutherans and Presbyterians in the years prior to World War I.

Additional ecumenical relationships with Protestantism prior to 1917 include the "open pulpit" canon of 1907, which permitted non-Episcopal clergy and laity to speak in Episcopal churches, and a cooperative relationship with the Federal Council of Churches without actual membership. Overtures in the direction of the Catholic churches included closer relations with Eastern Orthodoxy, the Old Catholic Church, the Polish National Catholic Church, and the Church of Sweden.

As might be expected of a church of British heritage, virtually all Episcopalians seem to have supported America's entrance into World War I. Prior to the declaration of war, clerical leaders such as Bishop Brent and William Manning had openly opposed neutrality. The house of bishops opposed isolation in 1916 and pledged complete cooperation when America entered the war in 1917.

The few pacifists in Episcopal churches after

1917 generally came from the ranks of clergy who had been influenced by the Social Gospel. Bishop David Greer of New York opposed America's involvement throughout the war; Bishop Jones of Utah resigned his episcopate because of opposition to his pacifism. More typical were jihadistic clergy such as Randolph H. McKim, rector to the Church of the Epiphany in Washington, D.C., who described the war in sermons as "a Crusade. The greatest in History—the holiest. . . . a Holy War" (*God's Call to America*, 1917). The church's war commission and other agencies supplied Episcopal military personnel with crosses to be worn with dog tags; they also sent Bibles, prayer books, and hymnals. More than two hundred Episcopal clergy became military chaplains. World War I also saw the first regular use of the American flag in Episcopal churches. Since 1940, the year of its adoption, the red, white, and light blue Episcopal Church flag has joined it in processions and chancels.

Following the Treaty of Versailles, the general convention of 1919, along with many Episcopal clergy and journals, endorsed the League of Nations—though the principal opponent of the league, Henry Cabot Lodge, was himself an Episcopal layman. By 1924 disillusionment about the war had changed attitudes so greatly that antiwar sentiment, whether caused by pacifism or isolationism, continued to be strong among Episcopalians through the 1930s.

THE CHURCH AFTER WORLD WAR I

In 1919 the Episcopal Church attempted to create greater efficiency and corporate consciousness by centralizing its previously uncoordinated denominational boards in New York City. Chaired by the presiding bishop (who was now elected for a set term), a twenty-four-member "national council" consisting of elected bishops, priests, and laity was given the responsibility for carrying on the work of the denomination between sessions of the general convention. Building on experience gained from successful fund-raising for the establishment two years earlier of a pension fund for clergy, the general convention of 1919 also established a "nationwide campaign" directed at identifying the needs of the church and increasing its financial support. Remarkably successful, the campaign made

pledge envelopes and the annual Every Member Canvass a regular part of Episcopalian life.

Ecumenical advances during the 1920s included a seldom-used concordat patterned upon the Muhlenberg Memorial. It allowed Episcopal bishops to ordain Congregational and other ministers without requiring them to leave their denomination's ministry. The landmark World Conference on Faith and Order, which met in 1927 in Lausanne, Switzerland, owed much to the vision of Bishop Brent and more to the years of preparatory work by layman Robert H. Gardiner of Maine, secretary of the Episcopal Church commission charged with assembling the conference. At Lausanne four hundred representatives from more than one hundred Protestant, Eastern Orthodox, and Old Catholic churches met to discuss Christian unity.

Theologically, the controversy over Fundamentalism and evolution had few ramifications in the Episcopal Church. Most Episcopalians had accepted Darwinism and the need for biblical criticism by the 1920s. In 1923 the house of bishops declared that Episcopal clergy and laity must believe in the literal interpretation of the virgin birth and the physical resurrection of Jesus. The resulting dispute between "modernist" and traditional factions in the church subsided more quickly than did similar controversies in other denominations. An extreme form of modernism appeared in such clergy as Bishop William Montgomery Brown of Arkansas (who was deposed from the episcopate in 1924 after publicly denying many traditional tenets of Christianity), but extreme modernism found fewer advocates in the Episcopal Church than in the Church of England.

In the 1920s the majority of Episcopalians clearly found prohibition a failure, though many seem to have desired modification instead of complete repeal. The Church Temperance Society, which had first urged prohibition during World War I, reversed its position following six years of experience with the Volstead Act. The general convention deprecated the Ku Klux Klan, a group that found little support among Episcopalians, but took no official action on the red scare or the Sacco-Vanzetti case, over which Episcopal opinion divided.

New evangelistic methods included the use of advertising and the introduction from England of the Church Army, a society of lay evangelists.

The shortage of clergy continued, but the heavy emigration from non-British countries meant that the rate of growth from 1900 to 1930 was the smallest since the establishment of the Domestic and Foreign Missionary Society in 1820.

The denomination suffered seriously from the economic collapse of the Depression. In some parishes, virtually the entire congregation was unemployed. Churches reduced staff and salaries. Young men graduating from seminary found few positions. Churches that had embarked on major building programs during the 1920s encountered difficulty in making mortgage payments. Contributions to missions declined from $2.25 per capita in 1930 to 96¢ in 1940.

While the Protestant adoption of business techniques and outlook that some church historians have titled "the Babbittonian captivity of the church" had failed to engulf the Episcopal Church in the 1920s, only a small minority of its clergy and laity had remained actively involved in the concerns of the Social Gospel. During the Depression, the majority of Episcopalians probably continued to vote Republican; the leading Republican challengers to Franklin Delano Roosevelt—Wendell Wilkie, Thomas Dewey, Robert Taft—were Episcopalians. One survey has shown that the majority of Episcopal clergy seem to have viewed the New Deal favorably but were somewhat less favorable toward it than the general clergy population of America.

A significant minority of the denomination, however, swung to the left in social and economic thought. Both Franklin and Eleanor Roosevelt were Episcopalians, as were two of the most influential members of Roosevelt's cabinet, Frances Perkins and Henry A. Wallace. Several Episcopal periodicals and unofficial organizations took strong pro-labor stances, as did the general convention of 1934.

One hundred years after the start of the Oxford movement, the often bitter controversies it created in the Episcopal Church had declined but not entirely ceased. Resolutions to drop the name "Protestant" from the church's official title became routine in the triennial general conventions. By the 1930s liberal Evangelicalism and liberal Catholicism—twentieth-century descendants of the Evangelical and Oxford movements that accepted the insights of biblical criticism and modern scientific thought—were dominant;

the two parties increasingly learned from each other. The remaining tensions between church parties did not prevent Episcopalians from opening negotiations for organic unity with the Presbyterian Church in the U.S.A. in 1937 and from finally voting full membership in the Federal Council of Churches in 1940.

Three diverse theological movements of the first decades of the twentieth century found expression in the Episcopal Church. The reemphasis on Reformation theology and reaction from theological liberalism called Barthianism, or Neo-Orthodoxy, found some disciples in the Episcopal Church, but fewer than in churches tied more tightly to the doctrinal formulae of the sixteenth century. Faith healing entered the Episcopal Church through Elwood Worcester's Emmanuel movement, which combined modern science with biblical religion; the movement was named for the church of which he was rector in Mary Baker Eddy's Boston. Partially because it adapted its evangelistic methods to the life-style of the upper class and partially because it maintained its headquarters until 1941 in the parish house of Manhattan's Calvary Episcopal Church, Frank Buchman's Oxford Group movement (named Moral Re-Armament after 1939) gained more support from Episcopalians than from the members of any other American denomination.

THE CHURCH AFTER WORLD WAR II

On the eve of World War II, the majority of Episcopalians, like the majority of Americans, seem to have wished to stay out of another European war; on Armistice Day, 1939, the Episcopal Pacifist Fellowship was founded. Two years later the Japanese attack on Pearl Harbor not only created a national consensus but also neutralized most theological opposition; Christians could now view World War II as a defensive (and hence just) war. More than five hundred Episcopal clergy served in the war as chaplains, creating a shortage of civilian clergy. The war devastated Episcopal missionary work in countries such as Japan and China. In the Philippines the two American bishops and virtually every other American Episcopal missionary were imprisoned.

Unlike most wars in American history, World War II was followed by a nationwide religious revival. Critics questioned the theological depth of the revival, but the Episcopal Church benefited greatly in terms of sheer numbers. By 1960 the number of baptized Episcopalians had risen to 3,444,000. The ratio of Episcopal communicants to the general population increased from 1 to 102 in 1900, to 1 to 92 in 1950, to 1 to 86 in 1960. As veterans and converts packed the denomination's seminaries, candidates for the ministry doubled. The postwar increase in membership prompted not only the construction of a new headquarters building in New York City but also the founding of the denomination's first official publishing house, the Seabury Press, which remained under church ownership until 1984.

Growth in the mushrooming suburbs following World War II raised questions (such as those covered in 1961 by Episcopalian Gibson Winter in *The Suburban Captivity of the Churches*) about the denomination's role in urban areas. When Puerto Rican and other new immigrant groups began to appear in the 1940s, missions among them were pioneered by such inner-city parishes as Grace Church, Jersey City. If the Episcopal Church had a figure to rival Norman Vincent Peale, Fulton Sheen, and Billy Graham during the postwar resurgence of religion, it was the maverick James A. Pike. Pike's ministry, which was initially orthodox but became increasingly controversial as he called for the reformulation of certain Christian beliefs and became highly visible in the social causes of the 1960s, began in the 1940s on the eastern seaboard but ended in the 1960s in California. During the same period the center of Episcopal Church membership began to move westward from the old eastern dioceses as well.

The 1960s ushered in a period of ferment and change in the church. The decade began in the confident spirit of the 1950s, with a call by Presbyterian Eugene Carson Blake in San Francisco's Grace Episcopal Cathedral for a united church that would be "truly catholic, truly reformed, and truly evangelical." Out of the proposal came the Consultation on Church Union, in which the Episcopal Church and other major denominations in America continue to participate as discussants or observers.

The open, positive spirit of Pope John XXIII and the reforms of the Second Vatican Council (1962–1965) also had a major impact. Vatican II's concern with such issues as the role of the laity in parish work, the church as a community

rather than an institution, and the challenges of the modern world intensified the examination of the same topics in Anglicanism. Vatican II's revision of the Roman Catholic liturgy encouraged the general convention of 1964 to authorize a revision of the Book of Common Prayer. The irenic, liberal, and ecumenical spirit of the council also brought the Roman Catholic and Episcopal churches much closer; pulpit exchanges, consecrations of Episcopal bishops in Roman Catholic cathedrals, shared theological seminaries and churches, and a continuing ecumenical dialogue were signs of that change. A new spirit of self-examination and openness to Protestants and to other schools of Anglicanism also developed among many American Anglo-Catholics.

During this period the Episcopal Church was involved in the struggle for social justice. In 1957 the presiding bishop, Henry Knox Sherrill of Massachusetts, transferred the general convention to multiracial Honolulu when the scheduled city, Houston, could not live up to its desire to provide equal accommodations. In 1959 clergy and laity organized the Episcopal Society for Cultural and Racial Unity. In the early 1960s Episcopal clergy and laity participated in sit-ins and marched with Martin Luther King, Jr. In 1964 the general convention banned the exclusion of worshipers from Episcopal churches on racial grounds. Finally, in 1967 the general convention, under the leadership of presiding bishop John E. Hines, announced a special program to "help the poor and disenfranchised gain social, political, and economic power." The program included channeling $3 million during each of the next three years to black, Indian, and Chicano organizations.

A reaction among conservatives and traditionalists soon occurred. In 1963 a North Carolina rector renounced his ordination and established the Anglican Orthodox Church. In 1964 an all-white parish in Georgia left the Episcopal Church. The dissidence increased during the social and political revolution that swept America from approximately 1965 through 1973. Contributing to the conflict were the financial support by the General Convention Special Program of minority empowerment groups (a few of whose leaders had committed violence) and the activism of some bishops and clergy during the Vietnam War. Also important were the liberalization during the period of Episcopal teaching about divorce (now fully and clearly acknowledged), remarriage (now permitted with fewer restrictions), and abortion (now permitted under certain circumstances).

In reaction, conservative and traditionalist Episcopalians began to withhold financial support from their dioceses, which in turn (approvingly or otherwise) withheld it from the national church. In protest of the general convention's support of a militant Hispanic group, the bishop of New Mexico cut the contributions of his diocese to the national church from $80,000 to $1. By 1970 diocesan support for the national church had fallen $3.5 million short of needs. The decline caused the staff at the Episcopal Center in New York to be reduced and reduced again.

In addition to social activism, the three issues that caused the most controversy were the ordination of women, the rights of homosexuals, and the revision of the Book of Common Prayer.

Although women historically formed the majority of communicants of the Episcopal Church, both the canons of the Church and the customs of American society kept them until recently from playing more than subordinate roles. Traditionally, women served the church through such activities as Bible and tract societies, sewing circles, altar guilds, and Sunday schools. The wives of clergy took an active role in parish charities. Women's auxiliaries raised money for missions and for parish needs. All of these activities fell into the ecclesiastical category called "women's work." Mary Sudman Donovan's *A Different Call* (1986), the first major work to display the significant role women have played in the Episcopal Church, appeared too late for inclusion in this article.

With the coming of Anglo-Catholicism, women were able to enter monastic orders. Their roles moved closer to the ordained ministry when the general convention of 1889 created the office of deaconess. An unmarried or widowed woman could now be appointed (though not ordained) by a bishop to care for the sick, to teach, to baptize infants, to read services in the absence of a priest, and generally to "carry out Church work to women and children." Eighty years passed before the general convention of 1970 authorized women to serve in the house of deputies and to be ordained to the diaconate.

The controversy over women's ordination to the priesthood began in the 1960s. Supporters argued that God could call women as well as men to the ministry. Jesus Christ was fully human, the proponents asserted. His priesthood is an office of his humanity. To deny women the priesthood would be to deny their humanness. Just as the Christian priesthood changed from orthodox Jews to Gentiles, so it could now incorporate women as well as men. Proponents argued that the Episcopal Church was running the risk of denying the Holy Spirit and of alienating large numbers of women who were current or potential communicants.

The opponents based their arguments on the maleness of Jesus. Just as the priest represents Christ at the altar, so a woman by definition could not be a priest; the apostles were male, so the apostolic succession must remain male. Women's ordination, their argument continued, would break with more than four hundred years of Anglican tradition and almost two thousand years of Christian tradition. Practical reasons cited by opponents included the fear of schism, the collapse of ecumenical discussions with the Eastern Orthodox and Roman Catholic churches, and the creation of a surplus of clergy.

In 1970 the house of deputies defeated a proposal authorizing the ordination of women to the priesthood. The defeated proposal did not reach the upper house of bishops, but unofficial votes in 1972 and 1974 indicated that a majority of bishops favored women's ordination. When the resolution was presented again to the house of deputies in 1973, it received more ayes than nays but was again defeated because of a rule that counted tie votes in any diocesan delegation as negatives.

Nevertheless, in the summer of 1974, in Philadelphia's Church of the Advocate, eleven women deacons were ordained to the priesthood by three Episcopal bishops. Two of the bishops were retired; the third had resigned as bishop of Pennsylvania earlier in the year. Neither the bishops, nor the deacons, nor the parish had authorization for the ordinations. In an emergency session, the house of bishops declared the ordinations invalid and rebuked the ordainers.

Following two more years of conflict, the general convention approved the ordination of women to the priesthood in 1976. A conscience clause has allowed bishops to refuse ordination to women if they so choose. John M. Allin of

Mississippi, who became presiding bishop in 1974, was among those who so chose, but Edmond L. Browning, who succeeded Allin in 1986, supports the right of women to be ordained not only to the priesthood but also to the episcopate.

Browning's election by the house of bishops indicated the degree of support for women's ordination among bishops. By 1986 American bishops had ordained over six hundred women to the priesthood. Fewer than a dozen dioceses still refused to ordain women to the priesthood. That dioceses frequently elected bishops who supported women's ordination to succeed opponents who were retiring also indicates the degree of support among laity and clergy. Women priests continued to encounter difficulty securing parish rectorates (rather than assistantships), but polls indicated that an increasing majority of Episcopalians felt comfortable with women clergy.

The maleness of Jesus and the apostles, the inevitability of the election of women bishops, and the effect of women's ordination upon reunion with the Eastern Orthodox and Roman Catholic churches dominated the concerns of Episcopalians who continued to oppose women clergy. As in the 1960s and 1970s, talk of schism was in the air. The Anglo-Catholic wing of the Episcopal Church provided the largest number of opponents of women's ordination. But support for their ordination was also found among Anglo-Catholic bishops and clergy, and some of the women priests considered themselves Anglo-Catholics.

In 1975 the standing committee of the diocese of New York, composed of clergy and laity, approved the ordination to the diaconate of a seminary graduate who acknowledged her lesbian orientation. The committee reasoned that it would be hypocritical to deny ordination for an honest answer when they and other standing committees had approved homosexuals for ordination in the past after dishonest answers. When Bishop Paul Moore, Jr., of New York ordained the candidate to the priesthood in 1977, the church was again engulfed in publicity and controversy. The ordination underlined the loss of confidence in the church's leadership. It also called into question the doctrine and discipline of the church.

Although the house of bishops declined by a vote of sixty-two to forty-eight to censure Bishop Moore in its next meeting, the bishops declared their opposition to the ordination or marriage of practicing homosexuals. Two years later the general convention adopted a statement that recognized "marital fidelity and sexual chastity" as Christian norms. After differentiating between homosexual orientation and homosexual practice, the statement declared that "practicing homosexuals, or any person who is engaged in heterosexual relations outside of marriage," should not be ordained to the Episcopal ministry. Succeeding general conventions have not changed these guidelines. That the question will not easily go away is indicated by the determination of Integrity, Inc., a gay and lesbian organization of Episcopalians formed in 1974, to eliminate all barriers to full homosexual participation in the life and work of the Episcopal Church.

After approving a new standard Book of Common Prayer in 1928, the general convention established a standing liturgical commission of clergy and laity to prepare for future revisions. In 1964, following the major liturgical reforms of the Second Vatican Council, the general convention directed the commission to begin the process for a new revision. From 1967 to 1976 the commission submitted a series of rites for trial use and discussion by Episcopal congregations. The process allowed parishes not only to experiment with the new services but also to respond with comments and suggestions. During the process the liturgical commission remained in close communication with the liturgical committees of other denominations, in order that the new prayer book might serve as an instrument of unity.

In 1976 the general convention approved the full report of the commission (entitled *Draft Proposed Book of Common Prayer*) by an impressive majority. At the 1979 general convention, the proposed book was adopted as the new, standard Book of Common Prayer. Based upon Scripture, the church fathers, and the historic Christian liturgies, the 1979 prayer book incorporates the teachings of the liturgical movement that emerged in Christianity following World War I. It keeps many of the forms of the 1928 Book of Common Prayer, but uses contemporary language and new material.

Although opposition had greeted the revisions of 1892 and 1928, it was minor compared to the outcry that attended the process of revision in the 1960s and 1970s. For some Episcopalians, revision of the familiar prayer book and its "incomparable English" during an era of social turmoil was the last straw. For older Episcopalians, the changes in inherited worship habits were unsettling. For conservatives and traditionalists, the gender-free language and the addition of prayers for social concerns were disturbing. The revision seemed to show that the same liberals who had led the church into social action and women's ordination were now forcing their views on its worship life. Through lobbying, mailings, and organized protests, the well-funded Society for the Preservation of the Book of Common Prayer attempted to stop the process of revision. After the general convention adopted the new book, those members of the society who remained within the Episcopal Church worked unsuccessfully for the retention of the 1928 prayer book as an alternate rite.

Schism was not a new experience for the Episcopal Church. In 1873 Assistant Bishop George D. Cummins of Kentucky, a leading Evangelical, and more than twenty other Evangelical clergy and laity organized the Reformed Episcopal Church. A protest against the "de-Protestantizing" of Episcopalianism after the rise of Anglo-Catholicism and Ritualism, the new denomination hoped to attract other Evangelical Episcopalians and to serve as a center for the union of all Evangelical Protestants. Its high hopes went unrealized. Since the time of its founding, its membership has steadily declined and today approximates 7,000.

It is too early to say what the future holds for the Anglican churches that emerged out of disaffection with the Episcopal Church in the 1960s and 1970s. The American Episcopal Church, the Anglican Catholic Church, the Anglican Rite Jurisdiction of the Americas, the Diocese of Christ the King, and the United Episcopal Church of America—all have bishops, claims of apostolic succession, and active parishioners. Some have theological seminaries. Most profess deep devotion to the 1928 Book of Common Prayer. Many represent conservative political views. In churchmanship, the new groups range from extreme low churchmanship to an Anglo-Catholicism that seeks uniate status with Roman Catholicism. After a series of protest meetings following the approval of women's ordination by the general convention, one leader of the disaffected Episcopalians declared that half a million clergy and laity would secede from the Episcopal Church. The total who have affiliated with the schismatic groups may not exceed 5 percent of that figure. The record seems to indicate that these new Anglican churches will follow the pattern of the Reformed Episcopal Church.

Another development in the church in recent decades has been an oversupply of clergy. Membership declined from the mid-1960s through the early 1980s. At the same time, partially because of the ordination of women, the number of clergy increased. A surplus of clergy and a shortage of positions resulted. The church still lacks a central authority to control the number of ordinations.

From the 1960s on, the church also witnessed the emergence of new revival movements. Led by such clergy as Dennis J. Bennet of Seattle and Terry Fullam of Darien, Connecticut, the Episcopal charismatic movement spread to many dioceses and created some of the largest parishes in the church. Evangelicalism—which had remained strong in the Church of England but muted in the Episcopal Church since approximately 1900—reappeared as a force. Both movements added to the vitality and comprehensiveness of the church.

From the parsons' academies of the colonial period to the preparatory schools of late Victorian America, the Episcopal Church has been second among mainline denominations in America only to the Roman Catholic church in primary and secondary education. Though many of the Episcopal schools developed into fashionable academies, the original purpose of most was to nurture young people in the Anglican faith and to direct many of the males into the ministry.

The College of William and Mary, Williamsburg, Virginia, established in 1693 for the dual purpose of converting the Indians and training young men for the ministry, was the first Anglican college in America. King's College (1754, now Columbia University) in New York City was also Anglican. While unaffiliated with any denomination, the College of Philadelphia (1751, now the University of Pennsylvania) had strong Episcopal influences. Other colleges founded by the church but no longer operated under its auspices include St. John's College (1784), Annapolis, Maryland; the College of Charleston (1785),

Charleston, South Carolina; Washington College (1823, now Trinity College), Hartford, Connecticut; and Lehigh University (1865), Bethlehem, Pennsylvania.

Throughout the nineteenth century, Episcopal dioceses established additional colleges, often for the purpose of giving a college and then a theological education to young men intending to join the clergy of their diocese. Like similar colleges established by other denominations, many proved short-lived. Four remain Episcopal colleges today—Hobart College (1822), Geneva, New York; Kenyon College (1824), Gambier, Ohio; the University of the South (1857), Sewanee, Tennessee; and Bard College (1860), Annandale, New York. Following the Civil War the church also founded the several black colleges already mentioned.

During the colonial period, young men who wished to enter the Anglican ministry in the American colonies normally attended a college such as William and Mary, which had a faculty of theology. After studying for the ordination examinations of the Church of England, they traveled to England; if successful in the exams, they were ordained deacon and priest by the bishop of London. Converts from other denominations and Anglicans who had attended non-Anglican colleges read for orders under the direction of a local rector, often living in his parsonage and assisting him in the work of the parish. In the absence of theological seminaries, the apprenticeship system continued after the revolutionary war, with American bishops ordaining qualified candidates.

In 1817 the general convention established the General Theological Seminary in New York City as the official or "general" seminary for the entire Episcopal Church. The seminary's distance from other dioceses and its distinctively high-church tone quickly caused the creation of additional seminaries.

The theological and liturgical changes of the 1960s and 1970s render generalizations tenuous. Of the seminaries that survive today, however, Nashotah House (1840), Nashotah, Wisconsin, has traditionally represented Anglo-Catholicism; Virginia Theological Seminary (1824), Alexandria, Virginia, has been the principal Evangelical seminary; and Episcopal Divinity School (established in 1867 in Cambridge, Massachusetts, as the Episcopal Theological Seminary, but merged in 1967 with the 105-year-old Philadelphia Divinity School) has represented the broad-church point of view. While incorporating all of the emphases of Anglicanism, General Seminary has remained in the high-church tradition.

Other seminaries for the Episcopal Church are located in Sewanee, Tennessee; New Haven, Connecticut; Rochester, New York; Evanston, Illinois; Berkeley, California; Austin, Texas; and Ambridge, Pennsylvania. Numerous Episcopal clergy have also attended such interdenominational seminaries as Chicago, Yale, and Union Theological Seminary in New York. By canon law, bishops have the power to decide which seminaries their candidates may attend. Clergy of other denominations who wish to become Episcopal clergy often spend a year in an Episcopal seminary prior to ordination.

Although their origin lay in the Anglican parsons' academies of early America, Episcopal boarding schools date from the late nineteenth and early twentieth centuries. Patterned upon Eton, Harrow, and other public schools of England, boys' preparatory schools such as St. Paul's in New Hampshire, Groton, St. Mark's, and Middlesex in Massachusetts, St. George's in Rhode Island, and other institutions of the church stretched as far west as Hawaii. Led by headmasters such as Groton's Endicott Peabody, the schools concerned themselves not only with inculcating Christianity and the beginnings of a liberal education but also with teaching discipline, morality, manners, dress, and what the Victorians called "manliness." Over the years these Episcopal schools, especially those in New England, played a major role in preparing graduates for the Ivy League and in grooming the economic, political, and social leadership of America. Numerous graduates also became Episcopal vestrymen, priests, and bishops.

Weaker in endowments and mystique than the boys' schools, Episcopal boarding schools for girls included St. Margaret's in Connecticut, St. Agnes' in New York, St. Mary's in New Jersey, St. Timothy's in Maryland, Stuart Hall and Chatham Hall in Virginia, and Annie Wright in Washington. Critics of Episcopal boarding schools (including some graduates) deplored their Social Register atmosphere and the homogeneity and snobbery of their students. Critics and supporters alike viewed them as groomers of a new

American aristocracy. The 1960s and early 1970s witnessed changes that included coeducation, minority recruitment, and emphasis on academic excellence.

The Episcopal Church is the sixth-largest Christian denomination in the United States, behind the Roman Catholics, Baptists, Methodists, Lutherans, and Presbyterians. According to the 1980 figures, the number of communicants (active, confirmed adult members) stood at 1,933,080, slightly less than 1 percent of the population. The Gallup religion in America survey of 1981, however, reports that 2 percent of all Americans say they are Episcopalians; active membership and denominational loyalty are two different things. As it did in most mainline denominations, membership in the Episcopal Church began to decline in the mid-1960s. In 1970, roughly one of every 90 citizens were Episcopal communicants. In 1980 the ratio had dropped to one in 124. This trend may be changing, however, for the church reported an increase in U.S. membership in 1984 (2,773,082 baptized members; 1,895,970 communicants).

According to Gallup, the Episcopal Church is numerically strongest in the East and in urban areas, while weakest in the Midwest and rural areas. Fifty-eight percent of Episcopalians received a college education; 50 percent earn over $20,000 in income (by far the highest percentages of any denomination). Politically, more Episcopalians are Republicans than Democrats. Forty-six percent of church members are over fifty years of age, 55 percent are women, and 95 percent are white. In annual giving, Episcopalians contributed $507 million to the church in 1980, a total of $262 per capita.

Episcopalians have long played leading roles in American society. Such diverse figures as Fiorello La Guardia, Oliver Hazard Perry, Margaret Mead, John Jacob Astor, George Gallup, Richard Upjohn, Nicholas Murray Butler, George Marshall, and J. Pierpont Morgan have been Episcopal laity. In literature the denomination has been represented by such authors as William Byrd, Washington Irving, James Fenimore Cooper, Clement Clarke Moore, Francis Scott Key, Thomas Nelson Page, Willa Cather, John Dos Passos, John Cheever, and Louis Auchincloss. Harriet Beecher Stowe, Henry Clay, Daniel Webster, Richard Henry Dana, John Cog-

ley, and Mortimer Adler are among the many Americans who entered the church during their later years.

Ten presidents of the United States were Episcopalians. Thirty-three of 106 Supreme Court justices and seven of the chief justices of the Supreme Court have been Episcopalians. In the Ninety-ninth Congress (1985–1986), 20 percent of the Senate and 10 percent of the House of Representatives were members of the Episcopal Church. Families such as the du Ponts, Vanderbilts, Whitneys, Roosevelts, Astors, Mellons, Harrimans, and Morgans have been Episcopalians. In 1976 *Fortune* magazine reported that Episcopalians headed 20 percent of the Fortune 500 companies. Although only sixth in terms of numbers in the United States, the Episcopal Church may be second to none in terms of power and influence.

BIBLIOGRAPHY

James T. Addison, *The Episcopal Church in the United States, 1789–1931* (1951); G. W. O. Addleshaw and Frederick Etchells, *The Architectural Setting of Anglican Worship* (1948); Raymond W. Albright, *A History of the Protestant Episcopal Church* (1964); Alexander V. G. Allen, *Life and Letters of Phillips Brooks* (1900–1901); *Anglican and Episcopal History* (1987–); *Anglican Theological Review* (1918–); Anne Ayres, *The Life and Work of William Augustus Muhlenberg* (1880); *Book of Common Prayer* (1789, 1892, 1928, 1979); George F. Bragg, *History of the Afro-American Group of the Episcopal Church* (1922); Edward C. Chorley, *Men and Movements in the American Episcopal Church* (1946); George E. De Mille, *The Catholic Movement in the American Episcopal Church* (1940; rev. 1950) and *The Episcopal Church Since 1900* (1955); Mary Sudman Donovan, *A Different Call* (1986); Julia C. Emery, *A Century of Endeavor, 1821–1921* (1921); *Episcopal Church Annual* (formerly *The Living Church Annual*) (1892–).

Charles C. Grafton, *A Journey Godward* (1910); Marion Hatchett, *Commentary on the American Prayer Book* (1981); Charles R. Henery, ed., *Beyond the Horizon* (1986); *Historical Magazine of the Protestant Episcopal Church* (1932–1986); George Hodges and Powell M. Dawley, *A Short History of the Episcopal Church* (1967); Mark A. De Wolfe Howe, *The Life and Labors of Bishop Hare* (1911); William Lawrence, *Memories of a Happy Life* (1926); *Journals of the General Conventions of the Protestant Episcopal Church* (published triennially); Clara O. Loveland, *The Critical Years* (1956); William W. Manross, *The Episcopal Church in the United States, 1800–1840* (1938) and *A History of the American Episcopal Church* (1935; rev. 1950); John Howard Melish, *Franklin Spencer Spalding* (1917); Paul Moore, Jr., *Take a Bishop Like Me* (1979); Robert Bruce Mullin, *Episcopal Vision/American Reality: High Church Theology and Social Thought in Evangelical America* (1986).

THE ANGLICAN TRADITION AND THE EPISCOPAL CHURCH

William S. Perry, *The History of the American Episcopal Church, 1587–1883* (1885); William S. Rainsford, *A Preacher's Story of His Work* (1904) and *The Story of a Varied Life* (1922); Henry Knox Sherrill, *Among Friends* (1962); Robert W. Shoemaker, *The Origin and Meaning of the Name "Protestant Episcopal"* (1959); Virginia Driving Hawk Sneve, *That They May Have Life* (1977); William B. Sprague, *Annals of the American Pulpit,* vol. V (1859, 1969); Bruce Steiner, *Samuel Seabury* (1962); Greenough White, *An Apostle of the Western Church* (1899); Edwin A. White and Jackson A. Dyckman, *Annotated Constitution and Canons* (1954); William White, *Memoirs of the Protestant Episcopal Church in the United States of America* (1820, 1836, 1880); John F. Woolverton, *Colonial Anglicanism in North America, 1607–1776* (1984); Alexander C. Zabriskie, ed., *Anglican Evangelicalism* (1943).

[*See also* RELIGIOUS ARCHITECTURE AND LANDSCAPE.]

LUTHERAN HERITAGE

Jaroslav Pelikan

LIKE many other religious groups in America —and perhaps more than most of them— Lutheranism has been shaped by the heritage it brought from the churches of Europe. Indeed, its attitude and relations to those churches must be seen as a central and continuing theme in its history to the present day—a theme that has often seemed to demand greater attention than have its relations with and attitudes toward other churches in America itself. Confessional affinity has mattered far more than geographical proximity.

Although the Lutheran heritage is the product of several centuries extending back to the Reformation of the sixteenth century (and even earlier), a chronological account of that history would not do justice to the way it has been appropriated, and sometimes reappropriated, in the development of American Lutheranism itself. For although it is accurate, roughly speaking, to characterize the sixteenth century as the age of Luther and the Reformation, the seventeenth century as the age of Confessional Orthodoxy, and the eighteenth century as the age of Pietism, it is no less correct to assert, again roughly speaking, that the Lutheran churches of America have taken possession of those specific components of their heritage in reverse order. Almost all of them initially brought to the New World an understanding of Lutheran Christianity that had been decisively affected by the Pietist movement. Most of them went on, particularly in the nineteenth century, to modify that Pietism in the direction of classical Lutheran Orthodoxy, or of what they believed to be Orthodoxy, on the basis of a particular understanding of the Lutheran Confessions. And it was only in the twentieth century that American Lutheranism, in its piety, ethics, and theology, began to come to terms with Martin Luther himself, as his thought and work came to be understood and interpreted with new vigor in the "Luther Renaissance" of Germany and Scandinavia, in which American Lutheran scholarship would also eventually play an increasing part.

Appropriate and necessary though a chronological survey of Lutheran history since the Reformation may be for other purposes, therefore, that was not how the Lutheran immigrants to America arranged the books they had carried in their trunks across the Atlantic. Nor is it how the Lutheran heritage has shaped—and been shaped by—the American experience. For our purposes here, moreover, that heritage needs to be seen in the fullness of its expression, rather than only in its conventional forms. For it is this fullness of expression that formed the raw material of the Lutheran heritage in America, whether amplified, reworked, or rejected (or any combination of these).

THE STRUCTURE OF LUTHERANISM

Although it is as *Lutherans* that the followers of this tradition are generally known today, that was not always what they had been called before they came to the New World, nor what they called themselves upon arriving. Since the sixteenth century, *Evangelical* (*evangelisch*) had been a standard term in German-speaking lands to designate those who adhered to one or more of the Reformation confessions, whether the Augsburg Confession or one or another of the Reformed standards such as the Belgic Confession, the two Helvetic Confessions, and the Heidelberg Catechism. That nomenclature was to become significant in the ecumenical history of American Protestantism with the organization in 1846 of the Evangelical Alliance in London. Through the leadership of such American Lutheran churchmen as S. S. Schmucker, the program of Evangelical (and anti–Roman Catholic) Christianity espoused by the Evangelical Alliance became a force soon after its formation, even though the American branch of the Evangelical Alliance did not exist as an organization until 1867. The title *Evangelical* was to become even more confusing in North America (and consequently less useful to Lutherans) with the creation of two distinct American Protestant denominations that incorporated it into their official names: the Evangelical Church ("Albright Methodists"), early in the nineteenth century, and the Evangelical Union in 1840, which became the German Evangelical Synod of North America, then merged with the (German) Reformed Church in 1934 to form the Evangelical and Reformed Church. Because of this American usage and confusion and because of their own confessionalism, the Evangelical Lutherans in America, while continuing to claim that they were authentically Evangelical as well as authentically Lutheran, have, therefore, tended to prefer the second of those appellations —despite Martin Luther's own disavowal of the practice of labeling his followers with his name, since they had been baptized into the name of Christ and not into that of Luther.

Significantly, however, Luther was the only one of the major sixteenth-century Reformers who became the eponymous founder of a denomination. *Calvinists,* by contrast, have generally avoided using that title for themselves, preferring to be known by other designations, of which the predominantly European name *Reformed* has gained increasing favor as Continental, British, and American churches of this tradition have grown together. Lutheranism found, and still finds, much of its genius in the figure of Luther, his struggle for faith, and his eventual discovery and declaration of that faith.

The Festival of the Reformation, commemorating Luther's posting of the ninety-five theses on 31 October 1517, became a part of the church calendar upon the centenary of that event in 1617. The tercentenary, in 1817, provided Klaus Harms in Kiel with the occasion for publishing *The Ninety-five Theses or Propositions for Disputation by Dr. Luther of Blessed Memory, Reprinted with Another Ninety-five Theses as a Translation from the Year 1517 to the Year 1817.* In his new theses Harms called for the recovery of what he believed to be normative Lutheran confessionalism specifically within the Lutheranism of Germany, but his thought and work also had widespread impact on much of Lutheranism in America throughout the nineteenth century.

Beginning in the sixteenth century and continuing into the twentieth, successive editions of the works of Luther, in whole or in part, including several published in America, have sought to assure and enshrine the special place he holds in the piety, theology, and folklore of his spiritual descendants. Portraits (of which the Lutherhalle in Wittenberg has more than 2,400), monuments, and statues of Luther (the most familiar of which is that in Worms, with several copies in the United States) are a celebration of his unique place. His hymns, especially "A Mighty Fortress Is Our God," though not absent from the service books of most other denominations, have been central to Lutheran hymnals. Orthodox Lutheran books of dogmatics in the seventeenth century even had a special chapter bearing the caption "On Luther's Call," defending the legitimacy of his reformatory work and his divine call against the polemical accusation of Roman Catholics that he had acted as a headstrong and disobedient individual who refused to heed the voice of the church. Perhaps, above all, Luther's translation of the Bible into German, which was of great importance for the development and stabilization of literary German, also permeated the language and life of German Lutheranism. It has been estimated that more scholarly literature is published about Luther each year than about any other figure in the history of Western civilization except Jesus Christ. Accurate or not, that estimate does give some indication of the preoccupation with Luther, which has seemed sometimes to grow into an obsession, throughout the five centuries since his birth.

Strictly speaking, however, it has not been by Luther's own thought and writings as such that the Lutheran heritage has officially defined itself, but by the Lutheran Confessions. These sixteenth-century statements of faith (only three of them by Luther himself) were assembled into *The Book of Concord* (1580) and are, significantly, spoken of by Lutherans simply as the Confessions.

The confessionalism of the Lutheran churches,

in their European homelands and then even more explicitly in America, has distinguished Lutheranism in both its nomenclature and self-definition. More than either *Evangelical* or *Lutheran,* the title Church of the Augsburg Confession (and, after efforts by Calvin and his later followers to claim loyalty to the Augsburg Confession "as its author [Philip Melanchthon] interpreted it," even Church of the Unaltered Augsburg Confession) has been the way Lutheranism has differentiated itself from Roman Catholicism as well as from other Protestant groups.

Anglo-Saxon Protestantism in Great Britain and in America has tended to identify churches by their structure and polity—Congregational, Presbyterian, Episcopalian, Baptist. But Lutheranism has used its Confessions to identify itself. It has sought, therefore, to employ the same principle in identifying and describing other groups. *Comparative symbolics* (*Konfessionskunde*) is the standard term in the Lutheran theological curriculum for the comparative study of the various churches and denominations, and *confession* is preferred to *denomination* as the generic term. The inappropriateness of such a criterion for understanding other traditions—which, it was believed, ought to be confessional even though they were not—gradually became clear, principally, it would seem, through historical study.

The Lutheran Confessions. The three so-called ecumenical creeds—the Apostles', the Nicene, and the Athanasian—stand first in *The Book of Concord,* both as a statement of what it holds in common with all of orthodox Christianity and as a foundation for the particular confessions that follow. Primary among these is the Augsburg Confession, written by Philip Melanchthon on the basis of earlier confessions (some of them by Luther), in the name of the Lutheran churches, princes, and free cities and presented in both German and Latin to the Diet of the Holy Roman Empire at Augsburg in 1530. A Roman Catholic reply at Augsburg by Johann Eck and others, known somewhat mistakenly as the Papal Confutation, evoked, in turn, the Apology of the Augsburg Confession, likewise composed by Melanchthon, which stands as the authoritative commentary on the Augsburg Confession.

The three confessional books from Luther's own hand are the Enchiridion or Small Catechism, the Large Catechism (both 1529), and the Smalcald Articles (1537), which he prepared in response to the prospect of a general church council summoned by the Pope for assembly at Mantua in 1537 (but, in the event, postponed until the convoking of the Council of Trent in 1545, just before Luther's death). The last of the confessions in *The Book of Concord* was the Formula of Concord of 1577. Unlike the Augsburg Confession and its Apology, which had been addressed to a Roman Catholic audience in defense of the Reformation, the Formula was directed principally to resolving conflicts that had arisen within German Lutheranism itself (with some additional references to other Protestant groups).

Outside Germany, therefore, the Formula of Concord did not achieve universal status as a norm of Lutheran teaching—a difference that was to become critical when Lutheran churches of varying national (and thus confessional) backgrounds confronted one another in North America. They found themselves able to agree on the principle that one can be a true Lutheran without the Formula of Concord, but not against the Formula of Concord. More fundamental still throughout most of the history of the Lutheran churches in America were the hereditary differences over the status, and the enforcement, of subscription to the Lutheran Confessions—by individual congregations, by total church bodies and synods, by clergy as a precondition of ordination, and by theological professors as a standard of doctrinal orthodoxy—as the definition of what was normatively Lutheran. In the light of the Reformation's own insistence on the sole authority of Scripture, some (in Europe, and then in America) have defined such subscription to the Confessions as pertaining to them only insofar as (*quatenus*) they were in agreement with Scripture; but strict confessionalists, charging that one could accept the Koran with a *quatenus* subscription, insisted that the oath of confessional fidelity stipulate an acceptance of the Confessions because (*quia*) they were in harmony with Scriptures.

Even the strictest of the confessionalists have recognized, however, that the Augsburg Confession holds pride of place within *The Book of Concord,* and that the other Confessions, as various formulas of ordination also indicate, derive their standing from it as faithful exhibitions of its doctrine. Among the Lutheran Confessions, moreover, Luther's Small Catechism also occupies a unique place. It is an official confessional document of the Lutheran Church; it is the manual of instruction for preparing young "catechumens" (or "confirmands," to use a term that, according to H. L. Mencken's *The American Language,* was contributed to American usage by English-speaking Lutherans of German origin) for confirmation; it has been expanded, by means of exposition with proof texts, into comprehensive volumes of systematic theology, some running to hundreds of pages; it has been the basis for many series of sermons (*Katechismus-Predigten*); it has even been set to music several times in hymns. Taking its name from Augustine's *Enchiridion,* which was also entitled *Faith, Hope, and Charity,* it was based on medieval prototypes of "faith, hope, and charity" (Apostles' Creed, Lord's Prayer, and Decalogue, in various sequences). To these it added one section each on the sacraments of baptism and the Lord's Supper, and (eventually) one on "The Power of the Keys," or absolution, which Luther had sometimes, though not consistently, listed as a third sacrament.

In each of these chief parts, even in its explanation of the Ten Commandments, the Small Catechism placed primary emphasis on correct doctrine, from which correct and moral life would then flow. This was in keeping with the central concern for doctrine that has been characteristic of Lutheranism from the beginning. "Our churches *teach* with great unanimity" are the opening words of the Latin text of Article I of the Augsburg Confession.

The compass of this article precludes a minidogmatics that would recite, doctrine by doctrine, the principal teachings of Lutheranism. But it is necessary to point out that it shares with orthodox Christendom, Eastern and Western, the doctrinal consensus on the Trinity and person of Christ, as formulated by the councils of Nicaea (325) and Chalcedon (451). It shares with orthodox Western Christendom the major emphases of Augustine's schema of nature and grace, in particular the Augustinian doctrine of original sin, to which Luther in his doctrine of the bondage of the human will gave an even more unequivocal formulation than did the Roman Catholicism against which he was contending. In keeping with that doctrine, Luther and his followers have, together with the mainstream of the Reformed tradition, insisted on the primacy of divine grace over human merit in the restoration of a right relation with God; the

human role in the achievement of salvation is restricted to the acceptance of the divine gift ("justification by faith"). On the other hand, this insistence did not lead Lutheranism, as it did other forms of Protestantism, to affirm a doctrine of double predestination (despite occasional tendencies in that direction in Luther's own thought) or to reject the doctrines of baptismal regeneration and the real presence of the body and blood of Christ in the Eucharist. Lutheran rejection of the claims of papal primacy and infallibility is accompanied by affirmation of the one, holy, catholic, and apostolic church and of its continuity—not as institution, but as the people of God, among whom "the gospel is rightly preached and the sacraments are administered in accordance with the institution of Christ."

Clearly, then, it has been characteristic of the Lutheran heritage to make doctrinal questions decisive both for internal, confessional identification and for external relations. Studies of Lutheran homiletical manuals have shown that throughout the changes in theological opinion over the centuries there has remained a concern with the use of the pulpit to instruct the faithful in Christian doctrine. As the Augsburg Confession repeatedly insisted, this concern with doctrine was seen to stand in continuity with the creedal orthodoxy of the ancient church. Like Roman Catholicism and Eastern Orthodoxy, therefore, Lutheranism has insisted, for example, that a correct doctrine of the church and of the Lord's Supper must precede any sharing in the sacrament. And it has regularly justified both its separation from other denominations and its own repeated internal schisms on doctrinal grounds, regardless of the personal and political factors that may in fact have been responsible. But Roman Catholicism has embedded its emphasis on right doctrine within its demand for acceptance of the authority of the church and the papacy, and Eastern Orthodoxy has been especially articulate in stressing the inseparable connection between right doctrine and right worship (the "Feast of Orthodoxy" celebrates the restoration of the icons, not the promulgation of the creed). Lutheranism, on the other hand, has subordinated both church authority and right worship to right doctrine.

Relations with Other Communions. This concentration on the primacy of doctrine has also marked Lutheran relations with other communions. Where there was doctrinal agreement, there could be church unity, regardless of differences over church polity, liturgical observance, political affiliation, or moral discipline. And where such doctrinal agreement had not yet been achieved, all other shared values and needs —including the need for a common front against a common enemy, political or ecclesiastical— could not serve as a substitute for it. Thus at the Colloquy of Marburg in 1529, Luther, although affirming common ground with Martin Bucer, Huldreich Zwingli, and others on fourteen fundamental articles of faith, refused to overlook their differences over the real presence in the Eucharist and declared: "You have a different spirit from ours." That uncompromising stand has often been invoked, also and perhaps especially in America, as a precedent to justify Lutheran separation from other denominations, and sometimes even from other Lutherans; but it would be a mistake to ignore the continued and repeated affirmation of the ecumenical imperative that is no less a part of the Lutheran heritage. Among the European expressions of that imperative, perhaps the one most often invoked, though usually as a cautionary tale rather than as an example, was the "Prussian Union," which was also set forth as a celebration of the tercentenary of the Reformation in 1817 and which sought to replace the distinctively Lutheran and Reformed doctrines with the Evangelical doctrines shared by both sides and by their confessional books.

It was with a conscious sense of the positive as well as the negative outcome of the Lutheran Reformation that in the ecumenical movements of the twentieth century, Lutheran theologians and churchmen, above all perhaps the archbishop of Uppsala and primate of the (Lutheran) Church of Sweden, Nathan Söderblom, have taken such a decisive and leading part. And at the Synod of Barmen in 1934, Lutheran theologians, including some who were uncompromisingly confessional, joined with Reformed theologians in a common declaration against National Socialism and the so-called German Christians.

THE ETHOS OF LUTHERANISM

The participation and the nonparticipation by Lutheran churches in various ecumenical enterprises has sometimes been related to their status as national churches (or "folk churches," as they are better known in the Scandinavian languages). An examination of the confessional map of Europe on the eve of the Thirty Years War in 1618, and thus on the eve of the earliest significant Lutheran emigrations to the New World, reveals that Lutheranism was concentrated almost (but never quite) exclusively in lands that spoke one or another Germanic tongue, while the string of localities with a Reformed identification reached from Switzerland, the Palatinate, and the Low Countries to England and Scotland (and soon to North America) on the west and all the way to Hungary and Bohemia on the east.

Lutherans and Reformed could both claim to be international communions, but in quite different ways. The role of this ethnic factor, and of the language question to which it gave rise, is almost impossible to exaggerate in the history of American Lutheranism. The perpetuation in North America of patterns of worship, religious education, social life, and also of doctrine that had developed in the folk churches of northern Europe is what has given American Lutheranism much of its distinctive character. Even when a new generation in Minnesota or Pennsylvania could no longer speak the language of its immigrant grandparents, what it expressed in English was a set of cultural values still redolent of these origins. And the process of learning to express them in English, as a special chapter in the history of "the uprooted," has imprinted on these new generations an identity that sometimes sets them apart not only from their fellow Americans, but also from their fellow Lutherans, even when they are not aware of it. Only in the twentieth century has there been a permanent crossing of ethnic boundaries in the reorganization of Lutheran church bodies in America.

The area in which observers of American Lutheranism, both inside and outside, have most often sought to mark such identity and difference has been the political. Although Luther had hoped for the creation of a free church, the political outcome of his Reformation was an arrangement in which secular princes took over, as emergency bishops (*Notbischöfe*), many of the functions and the authority previously exercised by bishops. Some of these functions, to be sure, had been taken over by the bishops from secular princes in the Middle Ages and thus were now being restored rather than usurped. To the Scandinavian countries it is possible, *mutatis mu-*

tandis, to apply the celebrated—and often controverted—topic sentence of Sir Maurice Powicke's *The Reformation in England* (1941): "The one definite thing which can be said about the Reformation . . . is that it was an act of State." Lutheranism has therefore often been characterized as politically conservative or even "quietistic," and Luther's doctrine of the two kingdoms (*Regimente*) has been taken to imply an indifference to the task of changing the social and political order. This attitude stands in contrast with the tendency of Reformed and Puritan thought, just as often characterized as "theocratic," to strive for what Walter Rauschenbusch called Christianizing the social order (the title of his 1912 book).

Perhaps because the principal enemy of the United States in the two world wars of the twentieth century has been Germany, the complex relation between *Deutschtum* and *Luthertum* has provided almost irresistible fascination. Kaiser Wilhelm II represented himself as a guardian and authoritative interpreter of the Lutheran tradition, and an American political scientist, William McGovern, even published a book entitled *From Luther to Hitler.* Most oversimplifications of the relation, including the highly sophisticated oversimplifications of Ernst Troeltsch, have preferred to ignore the political pluralism of the Lutheran churches in various countries. In nineteenth-century Hungary, for example, the conventional wisdom about conservative Lutheranism versus more radical Calvinism was in fact reversed, so that the Magyar Reformed churches turned out to be the conservative protectors of a monarchist and feudal status quo, while the Slovak Lutheran churches were attacked as hotbeds of social radicalism and political revolution. More successfully than either Reformed or Roman Catholic or Eastern Orthodox societies have, the monolithically Lutheran kingdoms of Scandinavia have evolved "the third way" of a social democracy that goes beyond both capitalism and Marxism. There would, then, appear to be as much (or, more likely, as little) justification in drawing a line "from Luther to Swedish Socialism" as "from Luther to Hitler."

The several national churches that emerged from the Lutheran Reformation differed from one another not only in political orientation, but in ecclesiastical organization itself. As it is noteworthy that the first World Conference on Faith and Order held at Lausanne in 1927 coordinated doctrine and polity in its official title, so it is also characteristic of Anglo-Saxon Protestantism that so many of its major divisions, in the British Isles and particularly in North America, have had their origin, or at any rate their justification, in the area of church polity. As mentioned earlier, that origin is reflected in the nomenclature of denominations: Congregational, Presbyterian, Episcopalian. (Even Roman Catholic, for that matter, pertains to polity rather than only to doctrine.) In most of these cases, moreover, the assumption was that the New Testament had prescribed, certainly as preferable (so John Calvin) but probably as normative (so some later Presbyterians, Congregationalists, and Baptists), a specific way of organizing and administering the church.

It was frequently over the competing claims of various such ways of organizing the church, rather than over what Lutherans have tended to define as doctrine, that controversy raged within Anglo-Saxon Protestantism. That attention to doctrine and its definition, as described earlier, seems to have had as its consequence a relative indifference on the part of Lutherans to the normative questions of polity, and it was as much the political circumstances of the Reformation in a particular principality as any such normative question that decided the outcome of the question of polity there. Thus the Lutheran Church of Sweden retained the historic episcopate and a form of apostolic succession that is acknowledged, by the criteria of canon law, as possessing a species of legitimacy. On the other hand, Luther himself was prepared to designate bishops "without their being smeared" (*ohne Schmier*), and he frequently spoke as though the local congregation (*Gemeine* or *Gemeinde,* later to be called *Ortsgemeinde*) was the only divinely instituted structure in the church.

In much of Lutheran Germany after the Reformation, the "consistory," made up of higher clergy, functioned as the fundamental administrative unit, taking a form that bears many similarities to the Presbyterian, although the twentieth century was to see the reappropriation of the title "bishop" for the central administrative functionary of these "presbyterian" Lutheran churches. These systems of polity existed side by side within European Lutheranism, and except for an occasional partisan of one or another of them no one denied the name Lutheran to the adherent of another polity simply on that ground. In the New World, the problems of polity were often to become more troublesome than they had been in the Old World, at least partly because the church no longer had (or wanted) the patronage of the state, but also because the Protestant neighbors and competitors of the Lutheran bodies made questions of polity unavoidable to them, often for the first time.

Nor was it only to the issues of polity that Lutheran confessionalism appeared to be indifferent because of its primary concentration on purity of doctrine. A more widespread and more far-reaching accusation against it was that it had lost the concern for piety, stressing theology at the expense of ethics, dogmatic orthodoxy at the expense of moral obedience, and polemics at the expense of charity. The publication in 1675 of the *Pia Desideria* of Philipp Jakob Spener is usually identified as the beginning of the Pietist movement, which sought to correct conditions in the Lutheran Church (and beyond) by an emphasis on six major aims: the devotional study of the Scriptures, lay piety, practical service rather than merely the intellectual understanding of doctrine, moderation and love in theological polemics, the reform of the theological faculties of the universities, and the recovery of a way of preaching that would reach the heart and not only the head. From that modest and relatively conservative set of "simple recommendations," Pietism became an international, and an interconfessional, movement.

In the present context, however, Pietism should be seen as initially a continuation and eventually a fundamental revision of tendencies that had been present in the Lutheran tradition from the beginning. The Pietist emphasis on genuine repentance and changed life as the necessary precondition for being Christian could, and did, lay claim to the first of Luther's ninety-five theses of 1517—"When our Lord and Master Jesus Christ said, 'Repent,' he willed the entire life of believers to be one of repentance" —with which Lutheranism had begun. The insistence on the authority of the Bible over tradition, even over the tradition represented by the Lutheran Confessions, was set forth as a recovery and a correction of Reformation teaching. The demand that the pulpit and the pew both take more seriously the moral imperatives of the Gospel presented itself as the necessary counterpart to the emphasis of orthodoxy on the doctrinal imperatives. The critique of the state churches for their indifference to the missionary impulse came as the extension to foreign fields of the proto-Lutheran emphasis on the proclamation of the word of God. And the organization, within the state churches, of small groups (*ecclesiolae in ecclesia*) devoted to Bible-reading, prayer, and mutual edification appealed to what appeared to have been the religious intention, though it had not turned out to be the ecclesiastical outcome, of Luther's work.

Nevertheless, Pietism evoked vigorous criticism on grounds of self-righteousness, emotionalism, and doctrinal indifference; and there were continuing controversies between "Pietist" and "Orthodox" as well as between "Pietist" and "Rationalist" throughout the eighteenth century. On the other hand, it is important, especially for the development of Lutheranism in America, to remember Ernst Troeltsch's generalization:

> Pietism remained within the Church; indeed, at the time of the Enlightenment it bound itself very closely with the relics of the old dogmatic ecclesiastical system, and from its reawakening at the beginning of the nineteenth century there arose the great renewal of orthodoxy in this century, through which, however, the Church life of the present day has been impregnated with a mass of Pietist explosive material.

That was, in most instances, the brand of Pietism (and, for that matter, the brand of orthodoxy) that Lutherans brought to America.

One of the consequences of the Pietist controversies was the appearance, within various Lutheran churches of Europe, of more rigorous styles of piety and stricter rules of morality than were thought to characterize the average level of the Christian life, among both clergy and laity, in the established churches. These moralizing emphases, too, tended to manifest themselves in more exaggerated forms under the conditions of American life. The sexual morality of Pietism, for example, directed itself against the laxity of Lutheran attitudes toward marriage, including the double standard, and it sometimes went on to condemn not only overt acts of adultery and promiscuity, but "indecent" fashions in women's clothing and various kinds of mixed dancing. (C. F. W. Walther, founding father of Missouri Synod Lutheranism in America, wrote a small but uncompromising book called *Dancing and Theatergoing* [*Tanz und Theaterbesuch*].) Scandinavian Lutheranism appears, from recent studies, to have been especially hospitable to Pietist attacks on card playing as a form of idleness, even where gambling for money was not involved. In Scandinavia, too, the temperance movements of the eighteenth and nineteenth centuries received extensive support, and many Swedish and Norwegian Lutherans, both in the Old World and in the New, took a leading part in the crusade for total abstinence. Such moral concerns as these would also mean, in the New World, that, regardless of supposed confessional differences, Pietists who happened to be Lutherans and Pietists who happened to belong to other denominations would often tend to find common ground.

Whatever negative implications there may have been in some of these more moralistic expressions of the Pietist spirit within Lutheranism, they were the obverse side of positive strengths in the Lutheran ethos. At the center of that ethos, beginning already with Luther himself, was the family. Luther frequently identified as one of his major accomplishments the rehabilitation of marriage and the family, rather than asceticism and celibacy, as the noblest form of the Christian life, for clergy and laity alike. In Werner Elert's judgment, "The 'profanation' of marriage which seems to be found in Luther's denial of its sacramental character is in fact the exclusive grounding of marriage in the very will and institution of the Creator himself." That helps to explain the puzzle that, by contrast with its refusal to elaborate a full-scale political theory, based on supposedly theological foundations, Lutheranism did devote extensive attention—in theological literature, church law, preaching, and practice, even in poetry and novels—to the family as the primary unit of society.

Luther spoke glowingly and often about the blessings of marriage and family as a divine gift. Although his attitude to marriage in the abstract and, concretely, his own marriage were the very antithesis of the romantic definition of love, he did find in his life with his wife, Catherine, and their children a source of great joy, as well as a kind of laboratory for faith, hope, and charity—and for forgiveness. Luther's marriage became an exemplar for the Lutheran tradition: Lutherans would hang pictures of the Luther family on the walls of their homes, and the Reformation doctrine of the universal priesthood of believers was seen as having found its fullest expression in the Lutheran home. A corollary of this stress on the centrality of the monogamous family was an opposition to divorce that was in many ways even more unequivocal than that of Roman Catholicism, because Lutheranism took over from medieval canon law only selected portions of the system of annulment.

LUTHERANISM AS A CULTURE

As the considerations of the theological structure and of the ethos of Lutheranism have already made evident, the heritage of the Lutheran churches in America was far more than what Lutherans call "doctrine," more even than what they call "doctrine and life." Uniting itself as it did with the class structure, the education, and the national aspirations of the peoples among whom it took root, Lutheranism became a total culture, in fact a series of total cultures. In the formula of Wilhelm Dilthey, "The spirituality [*Religiosität*] of Lutheranism cannot be fully recognized from its books of dogmatics alone; but its documents are the writings of Luther, its hymns, the religious music of Bach and Handel, and the shape of life in the church."

One of the principal nurseries of that culture was the Lutheran parsonage. By his rejection of clerical celibacy and by his own marriage, Luther not only affirmed the exaltation of marriage over lifelong virginity as the proper expression of the Christian life; he thereby also introduced into the cultural and intellectual life of Europe and America a new and powerful force: the Protestant manse. This acquired a form that had not been known before in Christian history, even in Eastern Orthodox cultures, where parish clergy were indeed married, but where the seats of cultural and intellectual life were principally either lay or monastic.

The nearest analogy in Western culture to the quasi-dynastic role of the ministerial family within Lutheran and other Protestant groups would probably be the rabbinical family, which has played a similar part in preserving and transmitting substantial elements of both religion and culture. As statistical and demographic studies of *das evangelische Pfarrhaus* have repeatedly shown, the literature and scholarship, the art and public life, of Lutheran lands (as well as of Anglican and Reformed lands) owe a disproportionate amount to clerical homes, which, wealthy in everything but money, passed on to successive generations the faith and culture—or at any rate, in a significant number of instances, at least the culture—of the Lutheran heritage. In the conditions of the New World and in the setting of immigrant society, the Lutheran parsonage as a cultural and ethos-bearing force assumed an even more influential place, because of the loss of continuity with other such forces, including the schools, theaters, and courts of the Old World.

Among the several components of European high culture, it was predominantly literature, philosophy, and music, rather than art and architecture, that Lutheranism fostered. It is, however, far too easy to allow the impression created by such massive figures as Bach and Handel in music, or Kant and Hegel in philosophy, or Goethe and Grundtvig in literature, to lead to an exaggeration of that difference. Thus in church architecture, the Lutheran Reformation had initially taken over the existing buildings of the medieval church and of the (Northern) Renaissance, whatever their style. But as necessity (particularly the ravages of the Thirty Years War) and opportunity (above all, of course, the move to America) required, the design and building of churches manifested a continuing creativity. Especially significant was the effort to give architectural form to the Lutheran coordination of word and sacrament as means of grace, which made both the design of the Roman Catholic church, intended for watching the sacrifice of the Mass, and the pattern of the Protestant meeting house unacceptable.

In painting and graphics likewise, beginning with Luther's friend and personal portraitist, Lucas Cranach, the Lutheran tradition had always been hospitable not only to "secular" art, but likewise to ecclesiastical art and even to liturgical iconography. In the Reformed tradition, by contrast, as studies of Rembrandt by W. A. Visser 't Hooft and others have shown, the principal intention and primary inspiration of Christian art was not specifically the liturgy, but more broadly the profoundly evangelical faith and piety of the painter as a believer and as a member of the believing community.

It is, nevertheless, as the words quoted earlier from Dilthey also suggest, in "the religious music of Bach and Handel" (both of them born in 1685) that the heritage of Lutheranism as a culture found perhaps its most profound expression. Handel's oratorios, among which *Messiah* (1742) has become (especially in Britain and in America) a folk institution as well as a religious affirmation, adapted to Christian purposes much of the form and method involved as well in the evolution of secular opera. (The name *oratorio* itself seems, however, to have been coined in the Roman Catholic Counter-Reformation, deriving from the Oratory established by Philip Neri in Rome at the end of the sixteenth century, out of which this form of religious music sprang.) Both in their origin and in their subsequent use to the present day, however, the oratorios of Handel are probably at least as much Anglican or generally Protestant as they are Lutheran.

On the other hand, the church music of Johann Sebastian Bach, which must certainly be regarded as the principal single cultural monument of the Lutheran heritage, is much more unmistakably Lutheran, as was he himself both in his piety and in his theology. The structure of his collection of chorale preludes, the *Orgelbuchlein*, is the liturgical year, as this was adopted (and adapted) by the Lutheran Church during and after the Reformation. His cantatas, of which he composed perhaps as many as five series in whole or in part, were likewise appointed for the Sundays of the church year and were related both to the succession of the liturgical seasons and often to the readings from Scripture (and thus the sermons) on those Sundays. Bach's *Passion of Our Lord According to Saint John* and the later *Passion of Our Lord According to Saint Matthew* expanded the cantata form, with its use of the Lutheran chorale, combining it with the oratorio, with its use of aria and recitative, into a form intended for the setting of the worshiping congregation, which often joined the chorus in the singing of the chorales. A special case is his *Mass in B Minor,* which was assembled from various discrete components, only some of which had been intended for Lutheran church services; it is probable, in any case, that Bach himself never heard the entire *Mass* performed as a unit.

As its use in the cantatas and *Passions* of Bach

indicates, the Lutheran chorale must be regarded as one of the most distinctive components of Lutheranism as culture. Unhampered from the beginning by any anxiety over the free composition of verse texts for worship or over the creation and adaptation of musical settings—as Luther said, there was no reason why the devil should have all the pretty tunes—the Lutheran church, beginning as has been noted already with Luther himself, continued, but deepened and expanded, the hymnology of the medieval church and has continued to do so into the twentieth century. Among the many authors of hymns, Paul Gerhardt deserves specific mention. A stoutly confessional Lutheran in his doctrinal hostility both to Roman Catholic and to Reformed tendencies in the church, he nevertheless incorporated into his chorales whatever seemed to him appropriate also from those traditions, as well as from the nascent Pietism of his time. And amid the ravages brought on by the Thirty Years War he gave voice to the Lutheran understanding of faith, of hope, and of charity in hymns that have become the common possession of all Christendom—and, through their central position in the music of Bach, of an even larger community.

The heritage of the chorale was continued especially in the age of Pietism with the composition of many thousands of new hymns. Although many of them must be regarded, because of the subjectivity of the piety and because of the almost rococo quality of their imagery, as inferior in both their literary quality and their theology to the hymns of Luther or Gerhardt, they did speak to the people and for the people of the Lutheran churches in Germany and Scandinavia in fresh and relevant ways. The needs of the American immigrant communities, first for hymnals in their mother tongues and then increasingly for service books that would translate European songs and add some from British and American sources, have been responsible for the proliferation of hymnals, and the publication of competing hymnals, within American Lutheranism.

Those American service books simultaneously reflected the continued vitalities and the unresolved tensions of the Lutheran liturgy. Both of these characteristics can be seen already in Luther's own efforts at liturgical reform. For while his *Formula of the Mass* (*Formula missae et communionis*) of 1523, as its Latin title indicates,

represented an attempt to adapt the liturgy of the (pre-Tridentine) Mass to Evangelical use by expurgating objectionable elements such as the Canon, the *German Mass* (*Deutsche Messe und Ordnung des Gottesdiensts*) of 1526 went much further in the direction of liturgical innovation. It was above all Luther's twofold stress upon the proclamation of the word of God as central to worship and upon the participation of the worshiping congregation as priests before God that was responsible for the innovation. Theodor Kliefoth and Paul Graff have charted, in meticulous detail, the fate of various liturgical practices in the Reformation itself and then in the centuries that followed, as Orthodoxy, Pietism, and Rationalism, each in its turn, created new liturgical structures and revised or rejected old ones, in accordance with their several definitions of what was Christian and Lutheran in worship.

An epitome both of this inventiveness and of the confusion that it could cause is the usage, in Swedish Lutheranism both in Scandinavia and in America, of the term *High Mass* to designate a service that included preaching but did not include the Eucharist. The Lutheran version of the high-church movement in the nineteenth century—among whose leaders, because of his great influence in America, Wilhelm Loehe deserves specific mention—sought to purge out Pietist and Rationalist elements in worship, and eventually, not without influences from other communions, led to a recovery of various Catholic rites and practices, most significantly to a weekly celebration of the Eucharist, replacing the monthly (or even quarterly) celebration that had become standard in Lutheran churches during the periods of Pietism and Rationalism. All of this, too, was, for the reasons enumerated earlier, of special significance for Lutheranism in America.

In another major area of Lutheran culture, however, Lutheranism in America has been far less productive: theological scholarship. The Lutheran Reformation began in the university; unlike the Methodist Reformation, however, it also remained in the university. Within the structure of the four faculties of the European university—philosophy (what today would be called the arts and sciences), law, medicine, and theology—the theological faculty carried on its activities of teaching and research in a style that was required to be responsible to the standards of the university and that was intended to be (but was not always required to be) responsive to those of the church. The decisive place of the university and of its theological faculty in the life and culture of Continental Lutheranism is symbolized by the city of Lund in Sweden: it was the site of an archiepiscopal see from 1104 to 1536, but from 1668 to the present it has been the site of a university, whose faculty of theology has, especially by its Luther scholarship, made a major contribution to the theology of the twentieth century.

It is a considerable extravagance, but not a total distortion, when Albert Schweitzer, in the opening sentence of his epoch-making book *The Quest of the Historical Jesus,* declares:

> When, at some future day, our period of civilisation shall lie, closed and completed, before the eyes of later generations, German theology will stand out as a great, a unique phenomenon in the mental and spiritual life of our time. For nowhere save in the German temperament can there be found in the same perfection the living complex of conditions and factors—of philosophic thought, critical acumen, historical insight, and religious feeling—without which no deep theology is possible.

That "complex of conditions and factors" in German and Scandinavian Lutheranism helped to produce, in the age of orthodoxy, the massive works of dogmatics, of which the *Loci Theologici* of Johann Gerhard is the outstanding example. In the Enlightenment, the same conditions and factors were responsible, through the researches of scholars like Johann Salomo Semler and Johann Lorenz von Mosheim, for the development and refinement of the critical-historical method of studying the Bible and the tradition of the church and for the fundamental reconsideration of every aspect of the meaning of Christianity in the light of that method. And during the nineteenth and twentieth centuries, books by university scholars coming out of European Lutheranism set much of the agenda for theological and historical debate well beyond its borders. From the embarrassment of scholarly riches, three names in the nineteenth century require mention: Ferdinand Christian Baur, Albrecht Ritschl, and Adolf von Harnack. The prominence of many of these people in the history of theological education and of theological controversy throughout American Protestantism is evidence of their decisive place in the New World as well as the Old. It is likewise an index of the relative unimportance attached to scholarship by much of American Protestantism, including American Lutheranism, whose system of theological education, reacting against the alleged worldliness and rationalism of European theological faculties in the universities, sought to create, through the establishment of seminaries, patterns of ministerial training that were both responsive to the church and responsible only to it.

The distinction between "The Lutheran Heritage" and "Lutheranism" represented by the division of labor between this article and its companion article is certainly justified in the light of the historical complexity and scholarly intricacy of both areas. If the distinction were to be taken as a dichotomy, however, it would result in a grave misunderstanding both of the Continental heritage and of the American experience. Repeatedly it has happened that patterns of church life arose within American Lutheranism and only then found their way into the mother churches of Europe: *stewardship* has now become a German word of sorts. In Europe, moreover, a conservative pattern in the relation between Christianity and culture and between church and state, which created the anomaly of the teaching of Luther's Catechism in state schools and even the teaching of Lutheran theology in the Karl-Marx-Universität of Leipzig, has been accompanied by a far more radical secularization of society than is characteristic of American history, despite the First Amendment to the U.S. Constitution. Therefore there are many ways in which America is the Old World and Europe the New World, rather than the other way around. The interaction between the Lutheran heritage and the American experience is in many ways the key to the understanding of American Lutheranism; but it is not without significance for the understanding of the Lutheran heritage as well.

BIBLIOGRAPHY

Paul Althaus, *The Theology of Martin Luther* (1966); Roland H. Bainton, *Here I Stand: A Life of Martin Luther* (1950); Julius Bodensieck, ed., *Encyclopedia of the Lutheran Church,* 3 vols. (1965); Edgar M. Carlson, *The Reinterpretation of Luther*

(1948); Wilhelm Dilthey, *Weltanschauung und Analyse des Menschen seit Renaissance und Reformation* (1957); Gerhard Ebeling, *Luther: An Introduction to His Thought* (1970); Werner Elert, *Morphologie des Luthertums,* 2 vols. (1931–1932; vol. 1 trans. as *The Structure of Lutheranism,* 1962); Karl Holl, *Luther* (7th ed., 1948); Charles Porterfield Krauth, *The Conservative Reformation and Its Theology* (1871; rev. 1888).

Erwin L. Lueker, *Lutheran Cyclopedia* (1954); Steven E. Ozment, *The Age of Reform, 1250–1550: An Intellectual and Religious History of Late Medieval and Reformation Europe* (1980); Jaroslav Pelikan and Helmut T. Lehmann, eds., *Luther's Works: American Edition* (1955–) and *Reformation of Church and Dogma (1300–1700)* (1984); Regin Prenter, *Spiritus Creator* (1953); Hermann Sasse, *Here We Stand: Nature and Character of the Lutheran Faith* (1946); Edmund Schlink, *Theology of the Lutheran Confessions* (1961); Theodore G. Tappert et al., eds., *The Book of Concord: The Confessions of the Evangelical Lutheran Church* (1959); Ernst Troeltsch, *The Social Teaching of the Christian Churches* (1960).

[*See also* LUTHERANISM.]

LUTHERANISM

Christa R. Klein

LUTHERANISM, wrote the late Sydney Ahlstrom in 1957, cannot be understood "as something indistinguishably blended in with the luxuriant foliage of American denominationalism but as a tradition living in a real but fruitful state of tension with American church life." This tension was most conspicuous during the immigrant era of the late nineteenth century when the full panoply of Lutheran ethnic and theological diversity was on display. Never before on so grand a scale had the descendants of the Continental and the British Reformation been in such close proximity. Lutherans, indeed, stood out from the dominant American evangelicalism because of their foreign-language institutions, exclusiveness, liturgical worship, commitment to the Lutheran confessional writings, especially the principal statement of their identity, the Augsburg Confession of 1530, and doctrinal infighting. At other times differences were more muted, as in the early nineteenth century and after World War II, when Americanized Lutherans themselves contributed to the ethos of the Protestant mainstream. Moreover, at all times Lutherans have behaved wholeheartedly as Americans in their enthusiasm for launching campaigns and founding institutions to advance their convictions.

The tension between Lutheranism and American church life is probably best understood as a strain within Lutheranism itself. For the most part Lutherans have fought out their differences with contemporary European and American currents of thought and practice by seeking, finding, and castigating them in each other. Although the issues debated arose in such transcontinental movements as rationalism, revivalism, and the renascent interest in Protestant beginnings, the resolutions were deeply affected by the American environment. American Lutherans have tended to be more conservative in matters of faith and more pragmatic in matters of practice than their European counterparts. This article traces first the issues that shaped Lutheran denominationalism and then Lutheran patterns of piety and morality and of social and intellectual responsibility.

COLONIAL LUTHERANISM

Colonial Lutherans were as unprepared to provide for the practice of the faith in the New World as were any other Europeans who depended on their state churches to provide them with a learned ministry. In the absence of a well-defined polity Lutherans were probably more bewildered by the task. The few earliest Lutherans from Sweden and the Netherlands left resources for the later influx of Germans. Lutherans, under Dutch rule, although fully part of the commercial venture in New Netherland, did not have the same permission to practice their faith as they had in the Netherlands, where large freestanding, heavily German congregations existed in the major cities. Particularly from the 1640s to 1664, when the English succeeded in establishing control, Lutherans were subjected to the same oppression Catholics faced in their homeland: they were allowed to reside and work but not to exercise their faith publicly. Beginning in 1649, the pleas of the first Lutheran congregation in North America for a pastor to serve their 150 families in New Netherland were denied. In 1657 the Lutheran consistory of Amsterdam, which oversaw matters of Lutheran doctrine and practice in the Netherlands on a Reformed model of polity, sent a pastor who was harassed and finally deported in 1659. Dutch authorities wanted the Reformed faith to take its stand on the Hudson and provide cohesion for the colony.

When the English took over New Netherland in 1664, Lutherans were free to adapt the Amsterdam church order to their congregations. By 1669 they were organized in what became the two oldest Lutheran congregations, one at Albany and the other in Manhattan, both of which survive to the present day. Their church order provided for a church council with lay officers; it was carried from New York to the Swedes on the Delaware River by the next pastor sent from Amsterdam. A century later the order was further refined in the congregational constitution commonly used by the Germans.

The Finns and Swedes who settled along the Delaware in the 1630s were the only Lutherans in the mainland colonies to have their faith established by government edict. The governor of New Sweden was charged by the Swedish crown in 1642 to provide for worship according to the Augsburg Confession (1530), the founding confession of Lutheranism; the Council of Uppsala (1593), which decreed the shape the Reformation would take in Sweden; and the ceremonies of the Swedish church. The first Lutheran pastor of the settlement, John Campanius, also translated Luther's Shorter Catechism into the language of the Delaware Indians for his missionary labors. These links with the Church of Sweden were of necessity not so strong once other powers assumed control of New Sweden. When the Dutch annexed the colony of some four hundred persons in 1655, they were in no position to impose their Calvinism as they had in New Netherland. By the time the British took over in 1664 and offered an explicit policy of toleration, the Swedes—who had relied on the homeland for pastors, religious books and the maintenance of church properties—began to feel neglected. By the 1680s their two aging pastors were too infirm to serve, and their log churches were in decay. The Swedish king responded to the appeal of some one thousand Lutherans in the 1690s by sending two young pastors and designating the congregations as missions of the church, part of the diocese of Skara or (after 1736) the archdiocese of Uppsala. One pastor who was designated "provost," a deputy of the archbishop with local authority, ordained a German, Justus Falckner, for work among the Dutch congregations in New York in 1703.

While Swedish and Dutch Lutheranism remained a reference point, the predominant pattern and ethos came by way of the Germans from the southwestern provinces of the Holy Roman Empire who settled primarily in Pennsylvania and contiguous colonies in the eighteenth century. Gradually they muted the Dutch characteristics of the Lutheran congregations in New York. Nevertheless, their influence was repelled by the Swedes along the Delaware, who, by virtue of their preference for the English language, episcopal polity, and liturgical ceremonial gravitated to the Episcopalians by the close of the century.

The Germans, most often peasants and small landholders from the Palatinate, Alsace, Baden, Württemberg, Nassau, and Hesse, had come to the English colonies for a better life. Along the Rhine, poverty and starvation threatened populations increasing in size and burdened by inheritance laws that permitted the continuous subdivision of land. Even after the close of the calamitous Thirty Years War (1618–1648), the region was periodically plundered and devastated by French kings who found it a convenient battlefield. When the harsh winter of 1708–1709 destroyed the wine and other agricultural industries for the foreseeable future, mass emigration began.

The predominantly Lutheran and Reformed people of these regions, along with the Amish, the Dunkards (Baptists), and other sects, had watched as religious dissenters such as the German and Swiss Mennonites heeded the personal invitation of William Penn and began their pilgrimage down the Rhine toward the religious freedom promised in Pennsylvania. As more Germans settled in the colony, tracts and letters were sent home offering hope that neither economic hardship nor religious oppression need be their lot.

At first the British tried to direct immigration to the Hudson Valley, but they were unable to control its spread. The system of indenturing servants before they left for the colonies added to the numbers. Philadelphia became the favored port of entry, and from 1727 (when records began to be kept) to the Revolution some sixty-five thousand German-speaking men, women, and children arrived. By 1750 one-third to one-half of Pennsylvania's inhabitants spoke German, a proportion that remained constant until the 1830s. Of those, nearly 90 percent were closely divided between the Reformed and Lutheran faiths.

Some Germans settled in the vicinity of Philadelphia but more traveled north and west, sharing the moving frontier with Scotch-Irish newcomers. Many farmed, while others found work in the new villages and towns. They followed the valley of the Susquehanna into Maryland. By the 1770s they had reached the Alleghenies and moved down the Shenandoah into western Maryland, Virginia, and North Carolina. Others had settled in New Jersey and New York. Smaller numbers entered Georgia and South Carolina.

The religious life of these German Lutherans was closely intertwined with the German Reformed. The Lutheran movement had reached their homelands in the 1540s. By the 1560s the German Reformed movement had sprouted from it in the Palatinate, where the Heidelberg Catechism originated in 1563. As rulers chose between traditions and as state churches developed, the other party remained in proximity. Among the results were that Lutherans tended to modify their use of Roman ceremony even further in southwestern German lands than in others and to borrow the lay offices of elder and deacon for church governance from the Reformed. But the variety in Lutheranism warrants few generalizations. One colonial pastor noted some fifty different editions of catechisms and songbooks from these homelands in his Pennsylvania congregations.

Confronted with the welter of German sects in Pennsylvania and a social and political order dominated by English-speaking settlers, the German "church people" tightened their cultural bonds. Reformed and Lutheran regularly intermarried and adapted their faiths to their new setting in similar ways. They shared commitments to the ministry of preaching and the sacraments and would not be deterred by the shortage of educated and regularly ordained clergy in founding congregations. In town and country the teachers they hired for their schools often led services and read from postils, printed collections of homilies on the Gospel or epistle for the day. They also catechized the children and were frequently pressed to seek ordination. In fact, no other religious groups with a tradition of educated clergy had as many "irregular pastors," that is, men who began to preach and administer the sacraments without benefit of license or ordination according to accepted procedures. In addition, fully half of the Lutheran and Reformed congregations founded in the eighteenth century pooled their resources to build "union churches," in which customarily each congregation worshiped according to its own rites every three to four weeks. Nevertheless, lines were drawn: communions were separate and pulpits rarely shared. In mixed households children attended services with the parent of the same gender.

The immigrants moved with deliberation to house their congregations in wooden and then stone churches built on property large enough for a cemetery and a school. They made sacrifices to purchase sacred vessels, record books, and altar linens. Organs and church bells were added as they could afford them. While few members were able at any one time to make the long journey from their isolated farms to attend worship, they were faithful in seeking out the pastor to administer privately the sacrament of baptism to their infants. The service of Holy Communion, although more heavily attended was very infrequent, often occurring only once or twice a year after harvest or spring planting, even after there were more ordained men.

The same lay initiative that figured so strongly in the founding of congregations could not have sustained a coherent Lutheran pattern of teaching and worship. There were too few pastors and lay leaders capable of guiding those confused by the competing messages of such proselytizers as the Moravians and Dunkards. Controversy flared among members who had never before had so much say in the parish. And not a few congregations tried to protect their freedom by keeping their pastors on one-year contracts. From the perspective of Henry Melchior Mühlenberg, who left a pastorate in Saxony for his position in Pennsylvania, "it is easier to be a cowherd or a shepherd in many places in Germany than to be a preacher here, where every peasant wants to act the part of a patron of the parish, for which he has neither the intelligence nor the skill" (*Journals of Henry Melchior Mühlenberg*). When parishes, which frequently were composed of a number of congregations, became vacant, there were no established means of filling them.

Some of the oldest congregations turned to Europe for support of lay initiative with more funding and pastors. In 1734 the United congregations of Philadelphia, New Hanover, and Providence were directed to seek a pastor at Halle, the center of Pietism in Prussia and reputed for its missionary fervor. Pietism, a movement dated to the publication of *Pia Desideria* by Philipp Jacob Spener in 1675, emphasized personal experience of God's saving work; the nurture of Christian faith through a regenerate clergy and through regular Bible study; and the expression of Christian commitment in missionary, educational, and charitable endeavors. August Hermann Francke institutionalized these features in the university town of Halle. For eight years the Halle fathers and the United congregations wrangled over the terms of a pastoral call. Only when the fathers learned that the Moravian leader Nikolaus von Zinzendorf himself had decided to serve the Pennsylvanians did they send thirty-year-old Henry Melchior Mühlenberg. In all, the mission society at Halle sent a dozen pastors between 1742 and 1786. No other center of German Lutheranism was as supportive or supplied as much leadership. The Hallensians maintained contact with each other and Halle as they extended their pastoral efforts to New York, New Jersey, Maryland, and Virginia.

Nevertheless, it would be erroneous to overstate the influence of any Lutheran movement such as Pietism on colonial American Lutheranism. Throughout the era Pietists were far outnumbered by the "irregulars" of uncertain religious identity. During the Great Awakening, when other Protestants delineated their theological differences and founded institutions to further their positions, Lutherans primarily managed to recognize the extent of their religious desolation. Most were too poor and too uneducated to live the life of self-examination and Bible study required of a Pietist. According to his journal, Mühlenberg spent his entire ministry counseling parishioners inexperienced with the idea of their need for repentance and new birth. He also noted that in the 1740s Pietists, who were often the more well-to-do, were most susceptible to the missionary efforts of Moravians who pretended to be Lutherans to gain adherents among the Germans.

Nor was the Orthodoxy of sixteenth- and seventeenth-century Lutheran Scholasticism in the background of many of the immigrants. Mühlenberg found it necessary to teach adults the basics of the faith and often incorporated the catechism in his preaching. Still, there were those able to draw on the religious training of their youth to resist sectarians and to maintain Lutheran doctrine. At least one "irregular," John Casper Stoever, Jr., who did not let his lack of formal theological training in the Palatinate keep him from single-handedly ministering to the scattered Pennsylvania Lutherans in the 1730s, used the Lutheran confessions to define his ministry.

The Hallensians, as a group, succeeded less in impressing a consistent theology or even religious ethos on the immigrants and their children than in shaping the next generation of clergy and establishing the rudiments of an organization to support and extend ministry. The so-called Ministerium established in 1748 was little more than a Hallensian fellowship until the 1760s when, at the instigation of the Swedish provost Carl M. Wrangel, Mühlenberg began to call regular meetings and to establish procedures for incorporating pastors from elsewhere in Europe and the more pliant "irregulars" into the Ministerium. By 1776 three-quarters of the forty-four pastors in the field had joined. Meetings continued to serve primarily as spiritual retreats for pastors.

The Ministerium survived by coopting the latitude in practice and adapting to the need for an indigenous ministry. By 1782 the Ministerium had adopted a liturgy acceptable to southwestern Germans and their offspring. Thoroughly modifying the 1748 liturgy, which Mühlenberg had drawn up from north German sources, the 1782 service eliminated all responses between pastor and people and also made the lectionary and traditional prayers optional. Although communion had originally been proposed three times yearly, in practice the Pennsylvanians celebrated it even less frequently, a significant departure from the four annual receptions of communion Luther judged minimally necessary for a person to be called Christian. (Pennsylvania practice differed radically from that in J. S. Bach's Leipzig, where there were hundreds of communicants every Sunday.) The more scholarly pastors were assigned the task of tutoring ministerial candidates, who then became "catechists," the first gradation on the path to ordination—an American innovation. After the Revolution the Ministerium technically became a synod since laymen were granted voting privileges except on matters pertaining to ordination and clerical discipline. By the time the Pennsylvania

Ministerium joined the ranks of new denominations in the young nation, explicit references to Lutheran doctrine or the confessional writings were rare, and the larger question of accountability to the Lutheran theological heritage was left to another generation. European Lutheranism was similarly adrift.

Lutheran leaders were also ambivalent about voicing their opinions on the matter of the Christian citizen's relation to the state, be it far-off Great Britain, proprietary Pennsylvania, or the new United States. Hesitancy had many roots. Germans enjoyed greater freedom under British rule than they had ever known. Those familiar with Prussian Pietism had witnessed the church as an aggressive advocate of the state. Those schooled in the Württemberg version recalled that Lutherans traditionally did not express their opposition to tyranny through political involvement. In America not only were colonial politics murky but first-generation immigrants also distrusted the deism of the revolutionary leaders—not to mention Benjamin Franklin's xenophobic attitude toward Germans—and thought that God's will for the new nation could not be readily discerned. Moreover, they seemed more open to recognizing the sins of any government—including the failures of the proprietors during the French and Indian War, the oppression of the British, and the antitrinitarianism of American revolutionaries—than they were to advocating an untested political vision.

Neither the Lutheran ministerium nor its Reformed counterpart, the coetus, issued a response to the Revolution. Pastors obediently observed nationally prescribed periods of fasting and thanksgiving and as private citizens seemed relieved and cheered by the outcome of events. They had enjoyed their freedom to develop a German subculture in a new land. Slow to seek naturalization under the British, as American citizens they persisted both in using their own language and in their wariness—even as they increasingly became bilingual.

THE RISE OF "AMERICAN LUTHERANISM"

As citizens of a new republic German Lutherans continued to practice their faith and organize their work along the lines they had chosen during the revolutionary era. Those in predominantly German-speaking areas found their cultural allies among their Reformed kin and neighbors. Those among the English-speaking in the larger towns and cities and along the western frontier discovered some religious compatibility also with English-speaking Protestant evangelicals.

Nevertheless, when one immigrant's son, Samuel Simon Schmucker, thoroughly explored this congruence beginning in the 1820s, institutionalized some of it, and tried to raise it to the status of doctrine in the 1850s, he met with resistance. Schmucker thought German Lutherans ought to assume their rightful place, earned in the sixteenth century, at the core of American evangelicalism—God's new reforming movement to complete the work of the Reformation, to spread the Gospel, and to confound both infidels and Roman Catholics, thereby inviting Christ's return. His platform aroused a theological debate among Lutherans, newly augmented by numbers of immigrants, that kept them preoccupied and out of the American Protestant mainstream until well into the twentieth century.

The number of German Lutheran immigrants increased briefly after the Revolution, but then dwindled while Europe warred for the two decades following the French Revolution. Meanwhile, German-Americans would not stay put. They joined the throngs following the Shenandoah Valley to the Carolinas and crossing the Appalachians to Ohio, Kentucky, Tennessee, and Canada at the expense of the Amerindians. Not a few from the same communities traveled and settled on the frontier together. By the 1790s the Pennsylvania Ministerium could no longer provide for such distant settlements, and new synods with the power to ordain were formed in South Carolina (1787), North Carolina (1791), and New York (1792). Elsewhere, regional "conferences" served as agents of the Pennsylvania Ministerium. The Ohio Synod (1818) marked the beginning of a new generation of synods on the frontier. Polity issues were dealt with at the synodical level with considerable variation.

The halt in immigration led Lutherans to reconsider their place in American society. Language became a matter of debate. Wherever German-speaking Lutherans found themselves in a minority, as in the cities and on the frontier, they became bilingual and their children pressed for English services, religious instruction, literature, and record keeping. Frequently, congregations could not resolve their differences, and the new English-speaking assemblies split off.

In rural isolation, where German remained the primary tongue, language was not a religious issue. Those committed to the mother tongue shared in publishing and educational ventures with the Reformed. Across the Atlantic the union of Lutheran and Reformed churches by the king of Prussia in 1817 heartened them. Some thought it presaged a wider union of all Protestants. Both the more educated Lutheran pastors in the Pietist tradition and their former students on the frontier found that their Americanized tradition flowed easily into the channels of revivalistic American evangelicalism not only to create a distinctive form of Lutheranism but also to contribute to an emergent American ethos.

Whereas Mühlenberg had used both piety and doctrine to help Lutherans define themselves in America, his successors, such as Justus Christian Helmuth, put more stock in subjective experience and moral living, including Sabbath observance, as the antidote to the infidelity of German rationalism, American deism, and the emerging Unitarian movement. They tended to reduce doctrine to the "fundamentals" of biblical revelation without reference to the formal distinctions of Lutheran Orthodoxy. They favored such theologians as Johann Anastasius Freylinghausen of Halle, who sought to express the "elements" or "fundamentals" of the faith directly from the Bible without reference to the confessions, and Johann Albrecht Bengel of Württemberg, who treated the Bible's apocalyptic literature as prophetic of the end times. A millennial view of history took firm hold of this generation. For devotional literature they drew from German Pietism and English Puritanism and Methodism.

Some itinerant missionaries experimented with revival meetings on the frontier. Others, such as Samuel Schmucker's father, John George Schmucker, were early members of the American Tract Society and active in the Sunday school and temperance movements. Not surprisingly, the emergent national denominationalism also affected Lutherans. Those most interested in the Protestant ecumenism of the day desired a more uniform, efficient, and purposive organization than regional synods could provide.

By 1819 the Lutheran synods were entertaining a proposal for a national body, vaguely modeled after the Presbyterian General Assembly, to conduct on a triennial basis its work of regulating worship practices and literature, determining gradations of the ministry, overseeing the formation of new synods, and hearing appeals. But Lutherans were not willing to delegate such powers to a central body and elected instead an advisory body, the General Synod of the Evangelical Lutheran Church, founded in 1820. They also directed the denomination to erect seminary and missionary institutions and to care for infirm pastors and their survivors.

Controversy surrounding the Synod's origins proved to be chronic. Of immediate significance for its future was a debate within the Pennsylvania Ministerium, where rural Lutherans, witnessing an imbroglio within the German Reformed Coetus over a similar proposal, argued that the General Synod threatened local autonomy and lay influence and could prove an obstacle to cooperation with the Reformed. Lutherans in towns and cities who were sympathetic to the General Synod and would participate in its projects anyway agreed to withdraw from the organization rather than split the Ministerium. At the other extreme leaders west of the Susquehanna, at the behest of the young Samuel Schmucker, held an organizational meeting and formed the West Pennsylvania Synod earlier than planned in order to affiliate with the General Synod and prevent its dissolution. Thus the denominational idea embodied in the General Synod survived but was weakened from the outset by the absence of the Pennsylvania Ministerium, which would have been its strongest member in numbers and wealth.

A somewhat less potent, but more prescient voice from North Carolina opposed the entire principle of the General Synod. David Henkel, the son of a frontier missionary, who had immersed himself in the Book of Concord, the 1580 collection of Lutheran confessions, in his preparation for the ministry, determined that the Augsburg Confession was sufficient for Lutheran unity and that the hierarchical General Synod was "papistical." Henkel had embarrassed proponents of the General Synod before with his insistence on the Orthodox view over and against the rising tide of American evangelicalism, which held that regeneration occurred in Baptism and that Christ was truly present in the bread and wine. He helped to found the Tennessee Synod, a confessional movement that cut across several southern states, opposed incorporation, and actively publicized its position. A beacon to the incoming German Lutheran immigrants who had experienced a confessional awakening, the Tennessee Synod also encouraged in newer western synods a fear of domination by easterners.

By his mid-twenties Samuel Schmucker had already shaped the governance of both the General Synod and the Gettysburg Seminary (1826), where he taught for nearly forty years. Few individuals felt more personal responsibility for the course of American Lutheranism in the nineteenth century. By the time he left Princeton Seminary in 1820, he had had more formal schooling than any other native Lutheran ministerial candidate. Steeped in the modified Pietism of his father's generation, he had also come under the influence of two European schools of theology, one Scottish Common-Sense philosophy, the other the German "old" Tübingen school advanced by such individuals as Gottlieb Christian Storr and Carl Christian Flatt. Both schools took seriously the Enlightenment concern for verification and claimed the authority of biblical facts as the middle ground against the extremes of rationalism on the one hand and the confines of Lutheran Orthodoxy on the other. The irenic evangelicalism of Princeton's Archibald Alexander meshed with Schmucker's father's convictions and gave focus to the polemical task of countering Socinians who denied the divinity of Christ, Universalists who claimed that salvation was meant for all and not just the predestined, and other enemies of the "fundamental" doctrines. From Samuel Miller he gained an appreciation for Presbyterian polity and for creeds and confessions as the means to denominational unity.

More conscious of the need for a confessional center than older leaders, Schmucker had vowed as a seminarian to raise Augsburg "out of the dust" and to place Lutheranism at the center of the American evangelical movement. He drew on the Augsburg Confession in a variety of ways.

Because it provided an outline of the "fundamental" doctrines of the Christian faith, he used it to shape his dogmatics, *Elements of Popular Theology* (1834). It also framed the apostolic creed he proposed for Christian unity among the Evangelical Protestants in his *Fraternal Appeal* (1838).

Nevertheless, he made only selective use of the founding confession of Lutheranism. Augsburg was always treated as instrumental to some other agenda and not as normative for Lutheran practice. Schmucker argued that the genius of "American Lutheranism" lay in its capacity for progressive improvements, and he celebrated its tendency "not to bind her ministers to the minutiae of any human creed. The Bible and the belief that the *fundamental doctrines* of the Bible are taught in a manner substantially correct in the Augsburg Confession, is all that is required" (*The American Lutheran Church*).

But what of those who chose to bind themselves in the "minutiae" of the Augsburg Confession and the rest of the Book of Concord? Schmucker had rejoiced in 1824 upon learning of Claus Harms's confessional attack on Rationalism during the German celebration of the three hundredth anniversary of the Reformation. But he was not prepared for, nor was his plan for an "American Lutheranism" adaptable to, the recovery of Lutheran scholasticism and liturgical practice that came with European confessionalism. Nor could he have foreseen the staggering numbers of Germans and Scandinavians who would leave their homelands for America and make of the already assimilated Lutherans a minority.

IMMIGRANT DENOMINATIONALISM

Immigrants arrived by the hundreds of thousands during each decade between 1830 and World War I. By 1880 some three million Germans—about one-third Roman Catholic and two-thirds Lutheran, Reformed, or Evangelical (from the union churches)—and some 250,000 Norwegians, 150,000 Swedes, and 54,000 Danes had arrived. Land reform, overpopulation, and industrialization were altering European economies, raising expectations, and creating greater vulnerability to financial hardship, especially among peasants, small landowners, laborers, and craftsmen. The locus of German emigration now shifted from the southwestern states to the North and later to the Northeast. The threat of the military draft under Chancellor Bismarck was an added incentive. Ease of transportation promoted emigration, especially after 1850 when steamships drastically reduced the time of an Atlantic crossing from months to days. The Midwest, in particular, held an allure. Land and burgeoning towns looked promising to those who wanted to own their farms, practice their crafts, or find factory work. A German triangle of settlement from St. Louis, to Cincinnati, to Milwaukee overlapped with the Scandinavians' more northwesterly pattern. Middle Atlantic cities also attracted many. Immigrants who came before 1880 established the Lutheran denominations that attracted those who come after them.

Many pastors emigrated before 1880 and brought with them the theological commitments of the confessional movements afoot in European Lutheranism since 1817. Not a few had had their careers, and therefore influence, blocked for their stringent criticisms of state churches. Most significant for the future of American Lutheranism was the strength of the "Old Lutherans," who viewed the Lutheran confessions and the writings of Luther and Orthodox theologians as one-time and all-sufficient instruction to the church. Their position was distrustful of all philosophical developments in epistemology and historical methodology since the seventeenth century. Highly critical of state churches and the state-decreed union worship of the Lutheran and Reformed, they advocated separation and free congregations. Because such "Old Lutherans" as the founders of the German Evangelical Lutheran Synod of Missouri, Ohio, and other states (the official name of the Missouri Synod, formed in 1847) left Saxony and Prussia before the mid-1840s when free assembly became legal and had experienced persecution, they were jealous of their opportunities to form doctrinally pure synods in America and could not imagine why the Lutherans already here should have such a cavalier attitude to doctrine and "unionism." These newcomers set a tone and developed an esprit that contributed to their success not only in attracting the more numerous Germans who came later, but also in raising issues that tugged American Lutherans toward more conservative positions.

A second strain, "Neo-Lutheranism," had less of an initial impact on the immigrants, although it offered an attractive option to American Lutherans in the twentieth century. In Germany "Neo-Lutherans" chose to work for renewal within the state churches. They held a more dynamic view of the Lutheran heritage within the history of Christianity. While affirming the rich contribution of their tradition to the whole church on earth, they were willing to consider both the historical context in which it arose and the contemporary one to which it must relate. Wilhelm Loehe, a pastor in the small town of Neuendettelsau, Bavaria, held such views and sent missionaries to America who shared his perspectives and eventually founded the Iowa Synod in 1854. Phillip Schaff and John Nevin at the German Reformed Seminary in Mercersburg, Pennsylvania, provided a parallel impetus among the Reformed.

This immigration initiated a second planting of German Lutheranism in America. Eastern-based Lutherans could not have met the religious needs of so many new immigrants, even if they had tried harder. More pastors and lay leaders accompanied these immigrants than had joined those of the eighteenth century. In addition, the new German missionary institutes were a frequent source of candidates for the ministry. The isolation of the frontier allowed immigrants to shape their own ethnic communities around their churches, homes, and parochial schools. Ethnic neighborhoods in the burgeoning cities of the Midwest and the eastern seaboard afforded similar opportunities. Leaders especially enjoyed the luxury of using doctrine to define the character of their new church bodies and became adept at promoting their positions among immigrants who were seeking religious certainty during the years of resettlement.

After an initial period of sifting, new synods emerged quickly among the Germans. Some of Loehe's missionaries at first affiliated with the older Ohio Synod (later, Joint Synod of Ohio) but suspected doctrinal laxity when they discovered that theological education was conducted primarily in English and that the Synod used the same ambiguous formula, *"Jesus said,* Take, eat, this is my body," for the distribution of communion as did the liturgy of the Prussian Evangelical Church. This reflected the Reformed concern to reenact and memorialize the Lord's Supper.

LUTHERANISM

Lutherans were concerned to affirm the real presence of Christ and used formulas that stated *this is* the true body. In 1847 they met with Saxon pastors from Missouri to found the Missouri Synod.

The Saxons, who had arrived a decade earlier, had experienced their own crisis. Seven hundred followers of Martin Stephan, the charismatic "Old Lutheran" pastor of a Bohemian congregation in Dresden who could no longer conduct his ministry without state interference, had pooled their resources, pledged their fidelity to Stephan as bishop, and come to Missouri to found a colony centered in a "true" church. After Stephan was deposed and exiled across the Mississippi River for his illicit relations with a number of women and his misuse of funds, the immigrants agonized over their misjudgment, fearing that they were guilty of establishing a sect, rather than a "true" church.

A young pastor, C. F. W. Walther, emerged as leader of the colonists when he provided a theological justification, drawn from Luther, for their identity as a true church, both in the sense of their membership in the "invisible church" of all true believers and as members of the Missouri congregations where the Word was preached in its purity and the sacraments administered according to Christ's institution. Distrustful of clerical authority since Stephan had misled even the pastors among them, the colonists also accepted Walther's rationale for congregational polity: since congregations embodied the church, they were the instruments, rather than bishops or consistories, through which God called individuals to the public ministry of the church. This stand placed the synod in conflict with two other new German synods, Buffalo (1845) and Iowa (1854), which held the more traditional view giving the primary authority for the ministry to the ministerium and/or bishops and accused Missouri of bowing to "mob rule." Walther, who had begun editing *Der Lutheraner* (The Lutheran) in 1844 to comment on the Lutheran tradition and the state of the church in Europe and America, quickly became the leading voice in midwestern Lutheranism. The Missouri Synod, with its combination of Orthodoxy and pragmatic organization, became the largest of the immigrant bodies. By 1900 its nearly 360,000 members constituted a quarter of all Lutherans in the United States.

Although the foundations of Scandinavian-American church bodies were laid in the mid-1800s, readjustments occurred with the tide of immigrants arriving in the last third of the century. The two earliest Norwegian bodies represented the poles of Lutheran practice in Norway. Eielsen Synod (1846), named after the Norwegian lay preacher Elling Eielsen, was founded in the tradition of Hans Nielsen Hauge, the lay evangelist who had traveled the isolated farmlands of Norway preaching repentance and regeneration to peasants largely ignored by the upper-class, rationalistic clergy of the state church. Informal worship, lay preaching, and a strict personal ethic characterized the synod. Within thirty years it had become a more centralized denomination with a seminary and was renamed Hauge's Synod. Pastors from the state church of Norway established the Norwegian Evangelical Lutheran Church in America (Norwegian Synod) in 1853. Their tradition emphasized formal liturgy and educated clergy. Under the influence of Gisle Johnson's confessionalism at the University of Oslo, pastors of the Norwegian Synod blended Orthodoxy with a Haugean emphasis on preaching for conversion and pious living. Almost immediately this synod allied itself with the Missouri Synod and sent its ministerial candidates to Missouri's Concordia Seminary in St. Louis. Other Norwegians, who eventually founded synods midway between the poles, first joined with the Swedes, Germans, and German-Americans to form the Northern Illinois Synod (1851), which affiliated with the General Synod. Such cooperative ventures arose from experience and tended to unravel quickly with the arrival of more immigrants. Later, Danes, Finns, Icelanders, and Slovaks tried their hand at such experiments.

In general this ethnic organization of church bodies in America matched the pluralism of European Lutheranism, even to the naming of synods after states. What is more, Lutherans who had never known the freedom in Europe to base church bodies on differences of theological interpretation organized, reorganized, and splintered again in America at a frenetic rate. Between 1840 and 1875 they started some sixty new church bodies, many of them short-lived.

Other American Protestants were also in the throes of regional and theological controversy. Like them Lutherans founded seminaries, colleges, and publications to proclaim and support their positions. Lutheran institutions of higher education, maintained at first for education of the clergy, were often hybrids of continental and American schools. Germans and Norwegians usually structured their liberal arts schools after the German "gymnasium," which centered on the study of Latin and was equivalent to a secondary school and two years of college. In Europe study in the gymnasium preceded theological study at the university; in America studies preceded attendance at seminary. One measure of assimilation was the adoption of the British system of four-year colleges. The Swedes moved quickly on this plan at Augustana College in Rock Island, Illinois. The Missouri Synod's system of Concordias (named after the Book of Concord) maintained the marks of the gymnasium until the mid-twentieth century. The Norwegian Synod's Luther College in Decorah, Iowa, moved into the American pattern more quickly.

The immigrants tended to perceive their seminaries either as lone-standing theological faculties that ought to be in a university setting or as missionary institutes. These latter schools had sprung up in Europe in the nineteenth century to educate men for the mission field who were not prepared for theological studies at the university. Since university standards were difficult to maintain in America at the so-called theoretical seminaries, and as the briefer course of the "practical" seminaries was regularly upgraded, the two forms came increasingly to resemble one another. The dual system of "theoretical" and "practical" seminary proved effective in the Missouri Synod, where most of the synodical leaders came from the former at St. Louis, while the majority of pastors came from the latter at Springfield, Illinois.

NINETEENTH-CENTURY ALIGNMENTS

Conflict within the nation over slavery and states' rights was also reflected among Lutherans. Prior to the anti-slavery movement and the slave rebellions of the 1830s some southern Lutherans had been willing to voice opposition to slavery. More commonly, southern Lutheran members of the General Synod expressed their concern for the religious life of the slaves. Thus, for example, by 1860 about a quarter of the Lutherans in South Carolina were black. In the northern synods of the General Synod positions ranged from the Franckean Synod (1837) in New York, which was formed to advocate an immediate abolitionist stance and viewed slavery as a sin against God, to synods which considered slavery a moral evil. Leaders of the General Synod were foiled in their attempt to avoid rupture once the southern states had seceded. A report to the General Synod convention in 1862 condemned the revolt of the southern states. In 1863 five synods south of the Mason-Dixon line broke with the General Synod to form the Evangelical Lutheran Church in the Confederate States of America (later, the United Synod, South).

Most of the new immigrant synods were northern bodies untried by the historical circumstances of slavery. The Scandinavian and German immigrant press expressed moral outrage at slavery and favored the new Republican party. Immigrant Lutherans shared these convictions. However, leaders of the Missouri Synod, centered in a border state, discussed the issue at length and justified the existence of slavery on the basis of Scripture as a relationship in which masters and slaves had obligations to each, a position not unlike that held by southern Protestants generally. When pastors of the Norwegian Synod tried to teach this position to their members, they were rebuffed, and a resolution was passed in church convention to begin a course of theological education apart from the Missouri Synod, where they had previously turned for help in preparing pastors.

The most telling controversy for the organizational life of Lutherans centered on the issue of confessional subscription. How binding was the Augsburg Confession for faith and practice? Immigrant pastors and people with varying degrees of exposure and commitment to the confessionalism had also found their way into the General Synod and its largest competitors in the East, the Pennsylvania and New York ministeriums. At the same time native-born Lutherans were reading the literature published during the German celebration of the three-hundredth anniversary of the Reformation. One of the most influential writings was Henrick Schmid's *Dogmatik* (*Dogmat-*

ics, 1843), a classification of positions held by sixteenth- and seventeenth-century Lutheran theologians. As many of Schmucker's former students grew restless with the limited commitment "American Lutheranism" made to the Reformation heritage, they also grew critical of the low standards of theological study at the Gettysburg Seminary. The *Evangelical Review* was established in 1849 at Gettysburg College to voice their objection. Members of the more culturally conservative Pennsylvania Ministerium—which had preserved the German language and such traditional Lutheran usages as vestments, communion wafers, and communion separate from the Reformed—found in confessionalism definition for the inchoate Lutheran identity they had preserved.

The Pennsylvania Ministerium rejoined the General Synod in 1853 confident that confessionalism would hold sway since it augmented the clergy roster by one-third and communicants by one-half. To counter increased pressure for unequivocal subscription to the Augsburg Confession, Schmucker proposed—at first anonymously—a codification of "American Lutheranism" to be adopted by member synods and used in the screening of ministerial candidates. The *Definite Synodical Platform* (1855) called for agreement on a recension of the Augsburg Confession and for recognition that the Confession was in "error" on approval of ceremonies of the mass, private confession and absolution, denial of the divine obligation of the Christian Sabbath, baptismal regeneration, and the real presence of the body and blood of Christ in the Eucharist.

Reverberations from Schmucker's proposal immediately passed through the General Synod to the churches outside. Members were badly divided over both the theological substance and the ecclesiological implications since the General Synod had never before stipulated any form of confessional subscription. Discussion was avoided at the next convention, and the board of publication was forbidden to issue any volumes on the subject. Nevertheless, bonds were breaking. A fragile General Synod held together two-thirds of all Lutherans in 1860. By the end of the decade only one-quarter remained.

The emerging configuration of Lutheranism was clarified by Schmucker's proposal. Between 1856 and 1859 individuals from the Missouri, Ohio, New York, Pennsylvania, Pittsburgh, Tennessee, and Norwegian synods met together to discuss the Augsburg Confession article by article. The agreement they discovered set the stage for later efforts toward unity. At the same time controversy between the "Platformists" (advocates of the *Definite Synodical Platform*) and "Symbolists" (confessionalists) in the Northern Illinois Synod ruptured the detente among ethnics, and in 1860 the Scandinavian Augustana (Latin for the Augsburg Confession) Synod split off. Controversy over confessional subscription created theological and educational agendas for the fledgling church bodies. But this was no simple importation of a European theological movement. Positions were forged and institutionalized in America over and against "American Lutheranism" in particular and Protestant evangelicalism in general, which made "Old Lutherans" a far more potent force in the New World than they were in Europe.

By the time the General Synod itself tottered toward schism, it had attracted a national Lutheran audience. The first open break after the circulation of the *Definite Synodical Platform* occurred at Gettysburg Seminary, where the student body had been polarized between two professors: Schmucker and Charles F. Schaeffer, appointed by the Pennsylvania Ministerium to teach the curriculum in German. Although the General Synod elected one of Schmucker's chief critics to succeed him when he retired in 1864, the Ministerium was not satisfied. Shortly after a convention battle in the same year over the admission of the Franckean Synod, which had no mention of the Augsburg Confession in its constitution, the Ministerium founded its own seminary in Philadelphia. Charles Porterfield Krauth, who became its premier theologian and wrote *The Conservative Reformation and Its Theology* (1871), explained the cultural, theological, and liturgical reasons for its founding:

> It is most unnatural and dangerous that in the same communion, and under the same roof one set of students should be taught to regard as Romish abominations and dangerous errors what others are taught to consider as the very truth of God. . . . We need it for the sake of the true co-ordinating and harmonious working of the two languages, English and German. It is

one great want of our church that the two tongues should work in sisterly harmony.

(*The Lutheran and Missionary,* III
[1864], p. 166)

When the final break with the General Synod occurred in 1866 and the Ministerium issued a broad appeal to American Lutherans to consider unity based on the "Unaltered Augsburg Confession in its native, original and only true sense," some thirteen synods convened in Reading, Pennsylvania. Five were former members of the General Synod: Pennsylvania, New York, Pittsburgh, Minnesota, and English Synod of Ohio. Another eight, heavily immigrant and primarily midwestern, joined them: the Joint Synod of Ohio, the English District of Ohio, and the Iowa, Norwegian, Missouri, Wisconsin, Michigan, and Canada synods. (The Scandinavian Augustana responded by letter.) Although the convention unanimously adopted Krauth's "Fundamental Principles of Faith and Church Polity," subscription to the Augsburg Confession was not sufficient to hold this mélange of cultures and theological opinions together.

The next year the General Council of the Evangelical Lutheran Church in North America was founded without the young midwestern German synods. These dissidents held out for unity not only in doctrine but also in practice. Four points in particular troubled these bodies. How would the Council address the issues of communing with non-Lutherans, exchanging pulpits with non-Lutherans, membership in secret societies (fraternal orders, such as the Masons, known to have antitrinitarian rituals and traditionally anticlerical in continental Europe), and chiliasm (the Anglo-Greek word for millennialism). Because the Council would not enforce its opposition to the first three (all commonplace in the General Synod) and because the German synods were themselves divided on chiliasm, most severed their connections with the Council. Only the Augustana Synod remained, while the Iowa Synod maintained informal affiliation.

Even within the General Council opinion remained divided on the implications of confessional subscription for practice, especially on pulpit and altar fellowship with other Christians who did not affirm Augsburg as the confession of biblical truth. "Old Lutherans" among them, who defined the church as a divine institution constituted by its confession of Christ, wrangled for two decades with those who held the older American Lutheran view of the church as a voluntary association of Christian believers. Although the latter were wary of "easy" fellowship, especially with Protestant evangelicals, they thought "discriminate" fellowship could be a matter of pastoral discretion. The "Old Lutherans," on the other hand, who were always looking for the marks of a "true church," favored the policy of "close" communion (admission based on doctrinal agreement, not denominational membership as in "closed" communion) and noninterchange of pulpits.

Although the "Old Lutheran" principle won out, it was the practice of the Council to use education rather than discipline to achieve its ends, and individual synods and pastors continued to have considerable leeway. Neither side wished to call the salvation of other Christians into question, but only to express their concern that church practice reflect and give testimony to the truth claims of Christianity. The Council developed a reputation as "a central debating society."

Meanwhile, the midwestern German synods, along with the Norwegian Synod, were able to achieve sufficient agreement on doctrine and practice based on subscription to the entire Book of Concord to join in the Synodical Conference in 1872. Initially they considered visions of orderly regional synods and a national seminary with a scholarly faculty of the caliber known in German universities. But their principle of unity did not survive a decade before differences of interpretation over the doctrine of predestination emerged. At issue was the relation between the doctrine of God's election of humankind to salvation and the doctrine of individual salvation by grace through faith. C. F. W. Walther of the Missouri Synod, labeled a "Calvinist" by his opponents, was concerned to make clear that God was entirely responsible for election. Friedrich Schmidt and Matthias Loy, of the Norwegian and Ohio synods, decried as "synergists," hoped to clarify the role of faith worked by the Holy Spirit for salvation. The vehemence of the conflict kept the immigrant synods from discussing fellowship until the 1920s, when the dread of Protestant liberalism with its emphasis on religious experience to the degeneration of classic Christian formulations of doctrine and its general humanistic optimism outweighed their doubts about each other. The Missouri and Wisconsin synods emerged from the conflict refusing even to engage in "prayer fellowship" with their theological opponents.

LUTHERANS IN THE TWENTIETH CENTURY

Denominational Mergers. There were impulses to merge elsewhere in Lutheranism. Controversy over predestination had the effect of creating the Anti-Missourian Brotherhood in the Norwegian Synod, which withdrew to work for Lutheran unity among the half-dozen competing Norwegian bodies. Moderates between the Haugean and Missouri poles were the first to merge in 1890 and to work toward a union of the more theologically divergent groups. In 1917 the Norwegian and Haugean synods joined with them to create the Norwegian Evangelical Lutheran Church in America centered in Luther Seminary, St. Paul, Minnesota. Likewise, increasing confessionalism in the General Synod paved the way for the 1918 reunion of Eastern-based Lutherans in the United Lutheran Church in America (ULCA). The General Synod, General Council, and the United Synod, South (made up of the Tennessee and Holston synods, and the General Synod, South) began their journey toward reunion with an effort to formulate a common liturgy in the 1880s based on the most pervasive forms of the sixteenth century.

As American Lutherans explored the meaning of religious freedom for themselves as ethnic bearers of a Reformation tradition in America, they came up with many options. They fought among themselves with passion if they detected tendencies they found dangerous in American Christianity or remembered as corrosive of Lutheranism in Europe. While the frenzy of disagreement bewildered other Protestants, embarrassed the more Americanized among their number, diluted the meager resources they had to support schools and churches, and belied the irenic character of their founding confession, it also contributed to the vitality of American Lutheranism. The range of options within ethnic groups allowed immigrants to choose a religious style appropriate to their convictions and instincts about their place in society. Conflict also

generated support for a host of missionaries, schools, and publications engaged in outreach to immigrants. The deeply divided Norwegians, for instance, were far more successful than the Swedes in attracting church members. Although Swedish immigrants outnumbered Norwegians, members of Norwegian Lutheran congregations outnumbered their Swedish counterparts by two to one.

For the Swedes there were other determining factors. The liberalization of Swedish society and revivals by Methodists and Baptists had already made inroads on Lutheran fidelity before the Swedes emigrated. Even the single rupture in the Augustana Synod in 1885 with the founding of the Swedish Evangelical Mission Covenant in America was rooted in the "Mission friends" movement in the Swedish state church and a controversy over the doctrine of the atonement.

World War I, which interrupted the flow of immigrants to America, also made Lutherans more conscious of their corporate image in America and speeded the process of assimilation and denominational merger. German Lutherans, more than any other German community except the Mennonites, suffered persecution during one of the worst waves of xenophobia in American history because of their highly visible parochial schools and their public use of the German language. Once the U.S. government's policy of neutrality had failed and the nation entered the war, most German Lutherans were eager to demonstrate their loyalty and to defend their religious institutions. They joined the liberty bond drives, and many moved to conducting their worship services and schools in English.

The pace of change quickened among all the immigrant bodies generally as they took responsibilities for Lutheran soldiers at home and abroad and for refugee work. Fund drives, publicity campaigns, and the increase in English-language publications had the effect of enlarging the work, staff, and structures of the Lutheran denominations.

Inter-Lutheran activity prompted by the war led to a new tripartite configuration that with some variation held through the late 1980s. Most of the Lutheran bodies that had banded together in the Commission for Soldiers' and Sailors' Welfare or cooperated with it came to recognize the value of a permanent agency to represent their interests and coordinate their common efforts in relation to the government and the wider American society. Exclusive of the Missouri Synod Germans, the resulting National Lutheran Council (1918) assembled the new ULCA and other midwestern Germans, the Swedes, the Norwegians, and several smaller ethnic bodies for common work. Very soon, however, differences over policy on Lutheran relationships to non-Lutheran churches created fissures.

While the National Lutheran Council continued to coordinate the military chaplaincy and represent American Lutherans abroad in their extensive relief work during World War II, theological differences prompted another alliance for the more sensitive areas of cooperation such as evangelism, parochial and higher education, campus chaplaincies at non-Lutheran schools, the publication of literature, and future negotiations for Lutheran unity. The ULCA had declared that no more doctrinal agreements were necessary to achieve Lutheran unity. The midwestern-based synods held that the practice of the ULCA did not match its doctrinal commitments and gathered in 1930 to form The American Lutheran Conference, which nonetheless failed to enlist the Missouri Synod. In this conference the Iowa Synod and the Joint Synod of Ohio, both of which merged with the Buffalo Synod later the same year to form the American Lutheran Church (ALC), had a working association with the Swedes, a small Danish church, and the two major Norwegian bodies, the Norwegian Lutheran Church and the Lutheran Free Church.

The alliances forged in the post–World War II period resulted in continuous negotiations for merger among all three sectors of Lutheranism, the Missouri Synod, the ULCA, and the American Lutheran Conference. Nevertheless, the best that could be achieved by the 1960s were "marriages of those already betrothed" (Tietjen, *Which Way to Lutheran Unity?*). In 1960 the American Lutheran Church merged all of the bodies that had participated in the American Lutheran Conference—Germans, Norwegians, and Danes of the Pietist tradition—except for the Augustana Swedes, among whom contemporary biblical scholarship and ecumenical interests carried greater weight. Meanwhile the Augustana Synod had moved squarely into the orbit of the ULCA, as did the Suomi (Finnish) Synod and the Danish body shaped by the theological and cultural movement initiated by Nicolai Grundtvig to renew church and society in Denmark. These bodies formed the Lutheran Church in America in 1962 (LCA). The LCA, the only Lutheran body to join the National Council of Churches, quickly gained national recognition for the able leadership of its president and Protestant ecumenical pioneer Franklin Clark Fry. By the late 1960s the ALC and the LCA, along with a more cooperative Missouri Synod, were able to design a new and more inclusive agency for common work, the Lutheran Council in the United States of America. By 1973 the ALC had joined the LCA in the World Council of Churches.

In the early 1960s it appeared that the era of denominational separation of Lutherans was drawing to a close. In the Missouri Synod, for example, numerous leading pastors, church officials, seminary and college professors, and many lay members had developed a strong sense of kinship with other Lutherans. The social and geographic mobility of Lutherans, the excitement in biblical and Luther studies, the liturgical movement, and civil rights efforts all created common experiences that cut across denominational lines. Nevertheless, a movement radically conservative, paralleling and intersecting the growth of Protestant fundamentalism, was simultaneously gaining momentum in the midwestern heartland of the Synod. Suspicion grew that relaxing the guard in relations with other Lutherans and other Christians was leading to Protestant liberalism.

After the election of J. A. O. Preus to the presidency of the Missouri Synod in 1969, new procedures and key appointments within the denomination had the effect of circumscribing and halting the advance of moderating tendencies within the Synod. A showdown at Concordia Seminary in St. Louis led to the exodus of some forty professors in 1974 and the opening of a competing seminary, Christ Seminary–Seminex (Seminary in Exile). The Association of Evangelical Lutheran Churches (AELC) was founded soon afterward but never attracted as many moderates as leaders had hoped. It saw its chief task as the unification of the rest of American Lutheranism.

The ALC and the LCA were themselves ready for such negotiations by the 1980s, and a seventy-member commission made up of delegates from those bodies and the AELC set to work to formulate the procedures, design, and theological affirmations for a new body. Their discussions were marked by the persistent concerns of Lutherans in the twentieth century for organizational stability, efficiency, and democratic representation on the one hand and the preservation and renewal of the Lutheran tradition on the other. Questions about the understanding of biblical authority, the role of Lutheran bishops, the nature of the ministry and theological education, the practice of church fellowship, and the dimensions of social activism loomed large. The significance of the merger, anticipated by 1988, for the vitality of the Lutheran tradition or for ecumenical relations is questionable, since a third of American Lutherans, members of the Missouri Synod, are not a party to the discussion, and the entrance of Lutherans into the Protestant mainstream has had the effect of diluting traditional zeal for unity in doctrine and practice.

According to the statistical records of the Lutheran Council, in 1984 there were 8.5 million baptized Lutherans in the United States and another 305,000 in Canada. More than two-thirds of the Canadians were affiliated with either the LCA or the Lutheran Church–Missouri Synod. The smaller Evangelical Lutheran Church of Canada and the Lutheran Church in America-Canada section merged to form the Evangelical Lutheran Church in Canada with 210,000 baptized members in January of 1986. In the United States, the LCA numbered 2,910,000; the Missouri Synod, 2,638,000; and the ALC, 2,339,000. The AELC counted 112,000, while the Wisconsin Synod was the largest of several bodies unaffiliated with the Lutheran Council and numbered 416,000.

Piety: Evangelical and Catholic. An account of the denominational lineage of American Lutheranism may do justice to the passions of theological conviction and the powers of assimilation, but it cannot characterize the piety and ethos of worshiping communities. The evangelical and catholic strains in Lutheran piety make for a rich blend and manifest themselves in practices that range from the charismatic to the Roman Catholic.

The Lutheran emphasis on preaching, Bible study, and the existential appropriation of the meaning of the Gospel has created an ambiguous alliance with American evangelicalism. Nowhere are the connections more apparent than in the twentieth-century hymnals of all American Lutherans, in which the classics of American and British evangelicals are well represented. Most Lutherans were raised on "Just As I Am Without One Plea" or "There Is a Fountain Filled with Blood," along with "A Mighty Fortress Is Our God" and "Lord Keep Us Steadfast in Your Word." Sunday schools, founded in the General Synod in the 1820s and not widely acceptable in the Missouri Synod until the 1920s, have been the most important bridge to American evangelicalism for the Lutheran laity. There are deeper roots as well.

Confessionalism, after all, had grown out of the neo-Pietist awakening in Europe at the beginning of the nineteenth century. Such an unlikely couple as the Prussian university pastor Friedrich Schleiermacher and the Norwegian lay evangelist Hans Nielson Hauge had discovered a hunger for religious experience that pastors educated in the rationalist tradition had been unable to nourish. Others built more theological substance on to the foundations they had laid. The rediscovery of Luther's vivid personal experience of sin and grace made him a soul mate for the confessionalists. Among "Old" and "New" Lutherans feelings of worthlessness and abandonment, most pronounced in a personal crisis, created the foil for the liberating sense of the "sweetness of God's grace in Christ," in C. F. W. Walther's words (*The Proper Distinction Between Law and Gospel*, 1929). It is little wonder that the seemingly Catholic rite of confession and absolution was prominent among confessionalists.

Walther, who himself had had such times of despondence and release, thought them not the source of salvation but nonetheless essential to Christian living. For Walther, who never wrote a dogmatics, education in Lutheran Orthodoxy was a necessary foundation for preaching and pastoral counseling so that a pastor could clearly distinguish between the "law"—the objective judgment on human sinfulness—and the "gospel"—the promise through Christ of salvation unqualified by any human behavior. Within this ethos the rite of confirmation, which preceded first communion and was an affirmation of baptismal vows by adolescent Lutherans, served as an initiation into the life of self-examination. It was adaptable to the neo-Pietism of midwestern Lutherans or to the programmed revivalism of the General Synod.

The legalism of American evangelicals also

had its immigrant Lutheran counterparts. Religious awakenings in Scandinavia included a strong emphasis on personal morality. In Norway Hauge, for example, had preached the conversion of the will to a life of obedience, while Gisle Johnson incorporated the ethic into a confessional framework. Card playing, theater going, dancing, and drinking all signified the dissolute life of unbelievers.

Methodist revivalism in Sweden had been closely associated with the temperance movement. The distilling of grain and potatoes had become a major farm industry in Sweden and the per capita use of liquor had been increasing at an alarming rate since the eighteenth century. On the other hand, German Lutherans—who came to America with equally strong proscriptions against dancing, cards, and the theater—thought temperance, which by the 1830s meant abstinence from fermented as well as distilled beverages, violated Christian freedom. For them the moderate use of beer and other alcoholic beverages was customary on Sundays no less than other days.

Eastern Lutherans, particularly in the General Synod, where temperance was closely tied to Sabbatarianism, were horrified with the corruption and therefore seeming religious insincerity of the German newcomers and would have felt more kinship with the Augustana Swedes and some of the Norwegian synods. Eastern clergy in particular enthusiastically supported Prohibition and welcomed the Eighteenth Amendment. The Women's Christian Temperance Union attracted members from General Synod congregations. In the same region of central Pennsylvania and Maryland, and solely in that region, total abstinence was applied to sacramental wine. Standard arguments built on an alleged biblical distinction between fermented and "unfermented" wine circulated from the last quarter of the nineteenth century and by the 1930s even rural parishes had switched to grape juice.

The synods most open to temperance were also those least scandalized by the increasing organizational activity of women. Where the church was expected by pastors and people to promote moral reform, the expansion of women's roles in church and society was generally deemed less threatening than in the more culturally conservative and doctrinally strict bodies. While Missouri Synod leaders viewed the prohibitionist movement not only as foolishness but also as a dangerous opportunity for women to pursue improper authority over men, the wives and daughters of leaders in the General Synod in 1879 and the Augustana Synod in 1892 were among the founders of national women's missionary societies. These two bodies were also the first to grant lay voting privileges to women near the turn of the century.

In the General Council the women's missionary society had less freedom to plan and fund its own projects, including the support of single women missionaries, and served more as an auxiliary to the denomination's mission boards. Women did not have a national mission board in the Missouri Synod until 1942, nor did the Synod approve congregational voting privileges for women until the late 1960s. When the movement for women's ordination gained advocates among Lutherans, the Missouri Synod rejected it while the ALC and LCA adopted the practice in 1970.

The catholic strain in American Lutheranism has always been theologically implicit, but historically it has been more controversial than the evangelical facets of piety. Emphasis on the sacraments as means of grace gives a priestly character to the ministry, which has set Lutherans apart from most evangelical Protestants. The liturgical expression of sacramental doctrine has varied across ethnic traditions, as between the colonial Swedes and Germans, and within them, as among the Haugean and state church Norwegians. Nevertheless, there has been a steady increase in the attention given to the sacraments in Lutheran practice since the nineteenth century.

"American Lutherans" in the General Synod had abandoned most of the structure of the Roman Catholic Mass and all vestments before the mid-nineteenth century. They had also incorporated the Reformed practice of using leavened bread, and had issued an open invitation to all baptized Christians to join in their communion services. Confessionalism included a deep interest in sixteenth-century liturgical practice, especially in the General Council, where Beale Schmucker, Samuel's son, gathered a library of sixteenth-century orders of worship, and in the Iowa Synod, which received the benefit of Wilhelm Loehe's research and liturgical agenda. The Swedes and most Norwegians brought with them the ceremonial of their state churches.

In the twentieth century the frequency of

communion increased in all sectors of Lutheranism. Once the liturgical movement became ecumenical in scope after the Second Vatican Council and Lutherans went back beyond the sixteenth century to explore the practices of the early churches, celebration of the Eucharist every Sunday became an expressed ideal, as did recovery of the full range of observances for Holy Week and Easter and the inclusion of baptism in regular congregational worship. Vestments, ceremonial chanting, and liturgical music became once more common, and the piety surrounding communion became less penitential and private and more celebrative and corporate.

The liturgical agenda has been slowed by at least two factors. First, the tradition of anti-Catholicism, so strong among the "American" and "Old" Lutherans, has not been overcome especially among the laity, even though Lutherans have reached considerable theological consensus in their official American dialogue with Roman Catholics. Liturgical ceremony strikes many as "Roman," and therefore anathema. Second, the liturgical movement has been largely clerical. Because the liturgy is a corporate, public event at which an ordained minister presides, lay people have been dependent on the clergy for their exposure to western catholic forms of worship. Pastors and their seminary professors of worship are free to practice as much or as little of the liturgical rite available in the Lutheran books of worship produced in the 1970s. Thus the catholic strain of piety, although officially present in Lutheranism, is only slowly and selectively coming to the laity.

Lutherans in Mission and Dialogue. Lutherans kept their distance from the Social Gospel movement that was significant in the liberal Protestant Community from the 1870s through the 1920s. Advocates of this form of Christian social responsibility focused on the reform of society's structures to eliminate tension between labor and industry, to improve urban life for the poor, and to end war among nations. Although the call went out among the eastern-based Lutherans for greater social awareness and the General Synod joined the Federal Council of Churches in 1908, Lutheran leaders generally did not steer their church bodies in the direction of advocating particular social reforms.

Leery of deflecting the church from its central work of proclaiming the Gospel and critical of those who would equate social progress with God's coming kingdom, American Lutherans were far more influenced by the widespread European Lutheran "inner missions" movement, which—like the writings of Karl Marx and massive emigration—was a response to the social and economic travail induced by industrialization. "Inner mission" in the work of Johann Heinrich Wichern, Wilhelm Loehe, and Theodor Fliedner meant voluntary service to and the revitalization of the faith of rootless Germans who were Lutherans only by baptism. Society, they believed, would improve to the degree that committed Christians provided the leaven. Such a massive task required the enlistment of the laity, and the ancient offices of deacon and deaconess were recovered for labors in hospitals, orphanages, and in slum districts.

In the mid-nineteenth century William A. Passavant of the General Council had advocated "inner missions" among American Lutherans and introduced deaconesses. He drew distinction between home missions, a familiar effort in America to provide pastors and churches where there were none, and inner missions, a call to renewal in all aspects of church life, including relief of the neglected, sick, and poor. Immigrant churches struggling to keep up with the massive influx of newcomers after 1880 were largely dependent on their own resources to provide both forms of service.

The call to mission directed the Synodical Conference, the federation of midwestern strict confessionalist synods dominated by the Missouri Synod, beyond their ethnic parameters to begin work among American blacks in the last quarter of the nineteenth century. Most southern blacks had left Lutheranism in the wake of Emancipation. Missionaries were sent primarily to Alabama, Louisiana, and North Carolina. Parochial schools and inadequately staffed and funded academies and theological schools were begun to prepare black converts for teaching and the ministry. Mission status left black Lutherans in ambiguity. The proposal for a Negro Synod within the Synodical Conference failed to win support among whites.

Beginning in the 1940s, the Missouri Synod and other Lutheran bodies began receiving black congregations into full membership. Separate theological education ended in the early 1960s. By then both black and white Lutherans were facing a dilemma that had become a national one for all Christians. Full integration of black Lutherans into denominational church life embodied the ideal of oneness in Christ, while at the same time it deprived blacks of the independence and self-definition that European-American ethnic groups had enjoyed in their formative years. The caucus, a solution borrowed from contemporary political parties, was adopted by black Lutheran pastors in the 1960s and Native-American, Hispanic, and Asian minorities in the 1970s and 1980s.

Inner missions were only gradually supplemented by another style of social witness among Lutherans. World War I provoked Lutherans to reexamine their relation to society and the state. As they became more self-conscious about their public image and assumed responsibility for ministering to soldiers, refugees, and war-industry communities, they focused on the corporate dimensions of social responsibility. The Swedes and the older eastern bodies were already in the habit of passing resolutions in convention to comment on national and international affairs. Often their commentary echoed the disenchantment of the broad-based post–World War I peace movement, which put little stock in national diplomacy and worked to outlaw war, to disarm, and to build international agencies of peace. In some instances the missionary movement and the Christianization of the world were viewed as the last best hope for peace. Leaders of the midwestern-based churches had begun to comment on foreign affairs and public policy for the first time during the war because of their own divided cultural allegiances and their desire to uphold their freedom to dissent and to conduct their own elementary schools.

Further enticement for Lutherans to formulate their own social ethic came with Hitler's rise to power and the advent of World War II, Protestant Neo-Orthodoxy, the new scholarship in Luther's thought, and the civil rights movement. Lutherans grew sober in their social statements and developed a higher profile in American politics and social activism as they clarified their expectation that the justice which is politically achievable within a society and among nations and for which the state is accountable is an expression of God's rule and therefore the business of Christian citizens.

Such an orientation should not be confused with a consensus on public policy. The more politically conservative remained uncomfortable with their church bodies' taking too active a role in public policy, while the more liberal tended to value their denominations increasingly as political lobbies. Political disagreements among Lutherans in the second half of the twentieth century have exacerbated theological disagreements, as in the debate between conservatives and moderates over the nature of biblical authority in the Missouri Synod and the American Lutheran Church.

During the 1969–1975 maelstrom in the Missouri Synod leading moderates in Concordia Seminary's faculty and student body and throughout the church body were opponents of the United States policy in Vietnam. Their conservative counterparts interpreted the moderates' politics as yet one more indication of the desecration of standards. They tended to emphasize the vulnerability of the social order and the church to chaos when traditional standards were loosened. Moderates, on the other hand, were more likely to express hope for renewal in nation and church through a critical reassessment of tradition.

Although Lutherans were preoccupied with their own concerns throughout the period of heavy immigration preceding World War I, they were not unmindful of the intellectual issues shaking the rest of American Protestantism. Eastern-based Lutherans were more likely than midwestern to recognize that the church would have to engage more seriously in biblical scholarship and scientific thought to respond to the challenge of Darwinism and biblical criticism.

"Inerrancy" did not become a slogan for the more conservative Lutherans until the 1920s, although their understanding of the Bible, drawn from seventeenth-century Orthodoxy, certainly emphasized its verbal inspiration, infallibility (reliability), and errorlessness—attributes deemed necessary for the defense of its authority against the Council of Trent. Under modern American conditions the doctrine surrounding the Bible came to be regarded as more than a defense. American Protestant heresy trials of biblical scholars in the late nineteenth century and the mounting fundamentalist-modernist divide had prompted leaders of the German and

Norwegian bodies in particular to require formulas about verbal inspiration, infallibility, and inerrancy in the doctrinal accords they drew up for interchurch cooperation and merger. These teachings came to be seen by some as foundational and even constitutive of Lutheranism.

In 1920 the ULCA, led by theologians already exploring Higher Criticism, claimed that "in the Holy Scriptures we have a permanent and authoritative record of that apostolic truth which is the ground of Christian faith" (Washington Declaration, in Wolf, *Documents of Lutheran Unity*). This formulation emphasized that the Bible contained the *infallible* Word of God but diverged from the strict interpretation of the Bible as the *inerrant* Word of God. It defined the other pole of an argument that has continued to smoulder. The doctrine of Scripture flared as the chief point of contention in the Missouri Synod in the 1970s and appeared again as the other Lutheran bodies worked toward merger in the 1980s.

The new biblical scholarship, which had been evident in the ULCA's seminaries in the 1920s and in the Augustana seminary in the 1930s, became dominant in the rest of Lutheranism after World War II. While Neo-Orthodoxy had some effect on the more Americanized Lutheran denominations before the war, the German- and Norwegian-American churches were awakened to contemporary theological currents primarily through their contacts with the European Lutheran churches after 1945. Their historically strong presence in foreign missions also induced thought about comparative religions. With the foundation of the Lutheran World Federation in 1947 and the availability of scholarships for study abroad, increasing numbers of American seminary graduates attended European universities. By the 1960s, American Lutherans were actively in dialogue with European theologians for the first time since the heyday of confessionalism in the nineteenth century. Nevertheless, by the late twentieth century, few American Lutherans were professors of theology at schools other than those of their own denominations. Moreover, for the most part American Lutherans were still junior partners in international theological discourse.

Lutherans have been ready participants in ecumenical dialogue with American Protestants and Roman Catholics. By the early 1980s the major groups had entered interim eucharistic fellowship with Episcopalians and were exploring similar arrangements with the Presbyterians and other Reformed denominations. The Lutheran–Roman Catholic dialogue produced the most substantive theological research and consensus but still awaited implementation in 1985.

From the postwar era into the 1970s Lutherans, aligned in three major church bodies, were confident of the contribution they brought to the Protestant mainstream. In 1961 Winthrop Hudson had thought that Lutherans would contribute to its revitalization because of their "confessional tradition, a surviving liturgical structure, and a sense of community" (*American Protestantism*). However, during those years a Lutheranism released from its ethnic moorings proved increasingly adaptable to and in some instances imitative of the main currents of American Protestantism.

By the 1980s, even though the Missouri Synod had backed away from the moderate theological consensus, it shared with the American Lutheran Church and the Lutheran Church in America a tendency to rely on denominational rules voted at conventions, rather than traditional theological norms, to maintain stability and harmony. At the same time earlier Lutheran doctrinal commitment had been losing ground in diversified seminary curricula and in the faculties of Lutheran colleges. Tensions within Lutheranism over these and other developments abounded, and although continuing debate may signify that Lutherans still prefer their own internal conversation, such self-consciousness may well prove instrumental in the continuation of the tradition.

BIBLIOGRAPHY

Sydney Ahlstrom, "The Lutheran Church and American Culture," in *The Lutheran Quarterly* 9 (1957); James W. Albers, "Perspectives on the History of Women in the Lutheran Church—Missouri Synod," in the Lutheran Historical Conference, *Essays and Reports* 9 (1980); Willard D. Allbeck, *A Century of Lutherans in Ohio* (1966); G. Everett Arden, *Augustana Heritage* (1963); "The Augsburg Confession in the United States," in *Currents in Theology and Mission* 7 (1980); Richard C. Dickinson, *Roses and Thorns: The Centennial Edition of Black Lutheran Mission and Ministry in the Lutheran Church—Missouri Synod* (1977); Vergilius Ferm, *The Crisis in American Lutheran Theology* (1927); Mary Fulbrook, *Piety and Politics*

(1983); Charles H. Glatfelter, *Pastors and People: German Lutheran and Reformed Churches in the Pennsylvania Field, 1717–1793*, 2 vols. (1980–1981); Alan Graebner, *Uncertain Saints: The Laity in the Lutheran Church—Missouri Synod, 1900–1970* (1975).

James L. Haney, Jr., "The Religious Heritage and Education of Samuel Simon Schmucker: A Study in the Rise of 'American Lutheranism' " (Ph.D. dis., Yale, 1968); Donald Huber, "The Galesburg Rule," in the Lutheran Historical Conference, *Essays and Reports* 8 (1978); Winthrop S. Hudson, *American Protestantism* (1961); Leigh D. Jordahl, "American Lutheranism: Ethos, Style and Polity," in John E. Groh and Robert H. Smith, eds., *The Lutheran Church in North American Life* (1979); Wolfgang Kollmann and Peter Marschalck, "German Emigration to the United States," in Donald Fleming and Bernard Bailyn, eds., *Perspectives in American History* 7 (1973).

Harold C. Letts, ed., *Christian Social Responsibility*, 3 vols. (1957); Frederick C. Luebke, *Bonds of Loyalty: German-Americans and World War I* (1974); Myron A. Marty, *Lutherans and Roman Catholicism* (1968); Fred W. Meuser, *The Formation of the American Lutheran Church* (1958) and "Pulpit and Altar Fellowship among Lutherans in America," in Vilmos Vajta, ed., *Church in Fellowship* (1963); Carl S. Meyer, ed., *Moving Frontiers: Readings in the History of the Lutheran Church—Missouri Synod* (1964); E. Clifford Nelson and Eugene L. Fevold, *The Lutheran Church Among Norwegian-Americans*, 2 vols. (1960); E. Clifford Nelson, ed., *The Lutherans in North America* (1975) and *The Rise of World Lutheranism* (1982).

Samuel Simon Schmucker, *The American Lutheran Church* (1851); Theodore G. Tappert and John W. Doberstein, eds. and transls., *The Journals of Henry Melchior Mühlenberg*, 3 vols. (1945–1958; repr. 1982); Theodore G. Tappert, ed., *Lutheran Confessional Theology in America: 1840–1880* (1972); Jane Telleen, "Emmy Evald and the Woman's Missionary Society of the Augustana Lutheran Church, 1892–1942," in the *Swedish Pioneer Historical Quarterly* 30 (1979); John H. Tietjen, *Which Way to Lutheran Unity?* (1966); C. F. W. Walther, *The Proper Distinction Between Law and Gospel* (1928); Frederick S. Weiser, *Love's Response: A Story of the Lutheran Deaconesses in America* (1962); Abdel Ross Wentz, *Pioneer in Christian Unity: Samuel Simon Schmucker* (1967); Richard C. Wolf, ed., *Documents of Lutheran Unity in America* (1966).

[*See also* ETHNICITY AND RELIGION *and* LUTHERAN HERITAGE.]

CALVINIST HERITAGE

Baird Tipson

AS the dominant theological tradition in the English-speaking colonies of North America, Calvinism left its imprint on the religious life of the majority of colonists. The eminent historian of American religion Sydney Ahlstrom once estimated that at the outbreak of the American Revolution, as many as 85 percent of American Christians "bore the stamp of Geneva" on their religious life. Furthermore, despite frequent reports of its decline, Calvinism continued to exert a powerful influence on American life and thought through the nineteenth century and into the final quarter of the twentieth. Throughout American history, immigrants from Scotland, France, Germany, England, and the Netherlands were always adding their distinctive Calvinisms to that of the earliest settlers.

This article will begin by describing the origins of the Calvinist tradition in Calvin's own writings and his career in Geneva. It will sketch the extension of Calvinist ideas into Germany, the Netherlands, France, and Scotland and the development of a pan-Calvinistic "Reformed scholasticism." Special attention will be paid to the reception of Calvinism in England, for it was English Calvinism that most directly shaped religious life in early America.

Like the term *Lutheran, Calvinist* began as a term of abuse. But unlike the Lutherans, who learned to accept being identified with their most powerful theological spokesman, members of Calvinist traditions have generally preferred either to call themselves "Reformed" or to identify themselves by their form of church organization, e.g., "Presbyterian" or "Congregationalist." The difference in usage stems in part from the different roles played by Luther and Calvin in the formation of their respective traditions.

Luther's forceful personality and penetrating writings dominated Lutheranism from the beginning, while Calvin was a second-generation reformer whose distinctive theology only gradually won special authority among his fellow Reformed thinkers. The Swiss Reformation broke out more or less spontaneously in a number of places in the sixteenth century. Huldreich Zwingli, preacher at the Great Minster of Zurich, assumed its early leadership, but other leading Swiss cities attracted talented leaders as well. Johann Huszgen (Oecolampadius) in Basel, Bertold Haller in Bern, and Pierre Viret in Lausanne were only the most prominent. At Strasbourg, furthermore, Martin Bucer tried to bridge the gap between the Lutheran and Swiss Reformers and labored with some success to keep them in verbal contact with one another. Bucer's reputation attracted men like Wolfgang Köpfel (Capito) and Calvin himself to Strasbourg, where the latter spent several years.

Such leaders did not carry the Reformation on their shoulders; their success depended in turn on their ability to represent and articulate the sentiments of the large number of citizens who had come to find traditional religious forms oppressive and who looked for relief to a Christianity reformed along strictly biblical lines. These leaders and their followers had already laid a foundation before Calvin began to build.

Jean Cauvin (Calvinus) was born the son of a notary in 1509 in the north of France in Noyon, Picardy. He began preparing for the priesthood at the University of Paris, and in 1528 he received his Master of Arts degree. Shortly thereafter, however, his father quarreled with the bishop of Noyon and ordered the young Calvin to transfer to the University of Orléans to prepare for a career in the law. Calvin obeyed and pursued legal studies first in Orléans and then in

Bourges. Although his father died in May 1531, he nonetheless brought his studies to their appropriate conclusion and received a doctorate of law six months after his father's death.

During his time as a university student, Calvin had come under the influence of French and Italian humanists. No sooner was his legal training complete than he returned to Paris to continue humanistic studies in philosophy and theology. It was during this period that his humanism drove him to identify with a party of open protest against the church; he was among those against whom heresy proceedings were initiated late in 1533. He fled the city, and in May 1534 he surrendered the clerical benefices that had financed his education since the age of twelve. The precise moment of his "conversion" to a scripturally based protest against the established church is still debated, but it must have occurred before this date.

The year 1536 saw two milestones in Calvin's career: he published the first edition of his classic text of Christian instruction, *The Institutes of the Christian Religion,* and he was persuaded to assist Guillaume Farel in reforming the religion of the city of Geneva. Calvin and Farel hoped to achieve a thorough reformation of Genevan doctrine and morals, but their success was limited. By 1538 the political climate of the city had changed, and the two ministers were forced to leave.

Calvin then moved to Strasbourg, where Bucer persuaded him to accept the post of pastor to the French refugee congregation. During the three years he spent in this position, Calvin served as preacher, pastor, and public lecturer. His writings during this period bear eloquent witness to the many responsibilities he assumed for the people of his church, for he published a book of musical settings of psalms and canticles in French translation, a manual of worship, a treatise on the Eucharist, and an important commentary on Paul's Epistle to the Romans.

But the political situation in Geneva had changed once again, and in 1541 Calvin finally accepted the city's call to return. He was to remain there until his death in 1564.

Within six weeks of his arrival, Calvin had submitted new *Ecclesiastical Ordinances* to the city fathers. These *Ordinances* affirmed that Christ had instituted four classes of office bearers in the church: pastors, doctors, elders, and deacons.

Pastors were to preach, instruct, administer the sacraments, and admonish the people. Doctors guarded the purity of doctrine and trained pastors and other ministers. Deacons managed church funds and ministered to the poor and the sick.

Most notable were the elders. As amended by the Geneva magistrates, the *Ordinances* provided for the appointment by the three city councils of twelve elders from among their own number. These lay elders were charged to "oversee the life of everyone, admonish amicably those whom they see to be erring or living a disordered life, and where it is required, enjoin fraternal correction." Primary responsibility for the moral life of the city was thus placed in the hands of laypeople.

With the six pastors, the elders also sat on the Consistory, a judicial body that advised the magistrates on moral and religious issues. This system ensured that the Geneva city councils always maintained a controlling influence on Consistory business; failure to recognize this control has led many scholars to overestimate Calvin's power over the moral and religious life of the city. Until 1555, when Calvin succeeded in gaining for the Consistory the right to excommunicate, its authority was largely advisory; only the lay magistrates could ban Christians from the sacraments.

Even in matters that were clearly ecclesiastical, such as the character of worship in Geneva, the power of the magistrates could frustrate Calvin's intentions. Calvin believed strongly that Christians should have frequent access to Christ's body and blood in the Eucharist, and he repeatedly expressed his desire that the sacrament be celebrated weekly in Geneva's churches. But despite his best arguments, only four Eucharists were celebrated a year. On the other hand, he did succeed in bringing the ministry of the word—which included both the reading and explication of Scripture—to the center of Sunday worship; to supplement such preaching, the congregation sang metric versions of the psalms. Some of these metric psalms can still be heard in Reformed churches today, especially those set to music by Louis Bourgeois.

The historian Steven Ozment has reminded us that while religious and moral discipline was new neither in theory nor in statute in Geneva, it came to be more successfully enforced there than elsewhere largely because of Calvin's devotion to it. He worked tirelessly to shape the city's will to his own, and both admirers and detractors still speak of "Calvin's Geneva." The Scottish refugee John Knox called the city "the most perfect school of Christ that ever was in the earth since the days of the Apostles."

From the beginning, the Swiss reformers had committed themselves to a thoroughgoing principle of *sola scriptura:* "by scripture alone." Luther had often been willing to retain a traditional practice if it did not conflict with biblical teaching; the Swiss used a "negative scripture principle" to eliminate every tradition not specifically sanctioned by the Bible. Adoration and invocation of Mary and the saints, pilgrimages, indulgences, images, instrumental music in worship, and many traditional prayers were stripped away.

One cannot forget, however, that the reformers could never have succeeded in making such radical, visible changes in traditional worship unless large numbers of sixteenth-century Christians, lay and clerical alike, had not become disenchanted with existing religious institutions. *Sola scriptura* offered these people the hope of a biblical Christianity purified of all merely human tradition. If such a biblical Christianity invited laypeople to assume a more central role and appeared to weaken the authority of the priesthood and the hierarchical church, that did nothing to lessen its appeal.

The aspect of this biblical Christianity that most impressed Knox and his fellow refugees at Geneva was its discipline. Following Philipp Melanchthon, Calvin recognized a threefold use of the biblical law. First, the biblical commandments set forth the divine will as a "rule" for all human governments, Christian or pagan, to follow in making and enforcing their laws. The purpose of the first use of the law was to restrain the sinful tendencies of subjects. Second, the biblical law served as a "mirror" in which every person could see himself reflected as a sinner. Against the impossible standard of God's will, all human beings would find themselves wanting and would recognize their need for a redeemer. The second use of the law therefore forced those who were not yet Christians to recognize themselves as sinners; it then drove them to seek the help of Christ.

These two uses, to restrain lawlessness and to impel conversion, were admitted by all Christians except those sectarians who separated from civil society. The third use was to prove more controversial.

The third use of the law was confined to Christians. Though they would no longer be condemned for each infraction of the law, Christians were still obligated to use the law as a "guide" for their behavior. Even as they believed that Christ's atoning death had redeemed them from the guilt and punishment they would otherwise incur by breaking God's commandments, true Christians would still order their lives by the standards the commandments set forth. Not that they could succeed completely; as sinners they would still transgress and need to seek divine forgiveness. But Christians who failed even to try to use the law as a guide gave strong evidence that their faith was hypocritical.

Many Lutherans found that this "legalism" undermined the Christian freedom that lay at the heart of the Gospel. But such an understanding of the Christian's continued obligation to observe the moral portions of the biblical law gave the Geneva elders ample justification to oversee the moral life of the city (the judicial and ceremonial portions were believed to refer exclusively to the situation of the biblical Hebrews and were assumed to be no longer in force).

Furthermore, Calvin stressed another justification for the enforcement of discipline: the need to preserve the purity of the Lord's Supper. The Eucharist had been ordained and instituted "to join together the members of Our Lord Jesus Christ with their Head, and among themselves in one body and one spirit." If this communion were not to be contaminated, unworthy participants had to be excluded.

In these justifications for church discipline, we find two elements united that more often appear in tension in the Calvinist tradition: commitment to the church and its sacraments, and concern for the spiritual status of the individual Christian. At Geneva, Calvin succeeded in holding them together. Because the failure of his followers to duplicate his success had immense consequences for the future of the Calvinist tradition, we must examine the tension further.

Calvin inherited from Augustine, whom he cited with great frequency in the *Institutes,* the distinction between the visible and the invisible churches. Augustine's invisible church consisted of the true Christians of every age; until the end of time its exact membership was known only in the mind of God. God knew the members of the invisible church because he had elected them before the creation of the world; they were predestined to enjoy eternal fellowship with him.

The visible church, on the other hand, was the historical institution known on earth. At any given time this would have contained only a portion of the living members of the invisible church, for some of the elect would not yet have been converted. More important, some of its members would not have been among the elect and would ultimately have turned out to be false Christians. Membership in one church was never identical to membership in the other, and the visible church could be no more than an imperfect image of the invisible.

Augustine believed that God alone knew the identity of those he had elected, and further that God almost invariably called his elect through the ministrations of the visible church. So membership in that church and regular participation in its worship and sacraments still represented the best possible evidence (short of the "special revelation" granted only in exceptional circumstances) that any individual was numbered among those predestined to salvation. Yet the doctrine of divine election always had the potential to undercut any human activity, including participation in worship and sacraments. If people's final destiny were known to God even before their birth, what contribution could their membership in the visible church make?

Calvin's theology maintained this Augustinian tension between the church and sacraments on the one hand and election on the other. Although both his followers and his detractors have sometimes allowed his notorious doctrine of predestination to cast a shadow over the rest of his theology, Calvin himself balanced his discussion of individual election with an insistence that Christians encountered God primarily through the means of grace offered by the church.

In Calvin's view, Jesus founded the church to serve as the agency through which faith would be nurtured and sins forgiven. So long as it preached true doctrine and administered the sacraments according to Christ's institution, it remained true to its founder, and Christians could have no justification for separating from it. Calvin had no sympathy for Christians who chose to cultivate their piety apart from the "communion of saints."

Calvin had equally high regard for the church's ministers. Those responsible for preaching and administering the sacraments, the order of pastors, inherited the function of the Apostles; there was no need for a separate order of bishops to ordain and regulate the pastors. On the other hand, so long as this equality of pastors was respected, Calvin had no fundamental objection to an episcopal polity.

Since in Calvin's teaching God had chosen to gather all Christians into the church and to nurture their faith through preaching and the sacraments, the critical link between the visible and invisible churches had to occur in the way Calvin understood the transmission of grace within the visible church. It is no accident that interpreters have found considerable tension at precisely this point in Calvin's system.

Calvin's position can be simply summarized. During a sermon or the administration of baptism or the Lord's Supper, the Holy Spirit promised and truly offered the benefits of Christ's death—forgiveness of sins and acceptance as a child of God—to the worshipers. But unless an individual worshiper believed the promise, he would have no way of accepting the offer. Divine grace was not tied to the words of the sermon or the elements of the sacrament; without divine activity words were merely words and the material elements merely material. Calvin could therefore subscribe to the revised version of the Lutheran Augsburg Confession—that the body and blood of Christ were "truly held forth" (*vere exhibeantur*) in the bread and wine of the Eucharist—but not to the original version—that the body and blood were "truly present" (*vere adsint*) in the elements. Calvin was convinced that without faith a person could derive no lasting benefit from word or sacrament.

Yet the very faith that was a condition for the efficacious hearing of a sermon or the worthy reception of a sacrament was understood in turn as a free divine gift, given only to the elect. Unless the Holy Spirit chose to anticipate any purely human effort with his supernatural aid, faith in God's promises to forgive and adopt was totally beyond human power. Like Augustine, Calvin considered the human will "free" only in the sense that it would freely sin. Without grace no one would choose to repent and believe, so Christians could take no credit for their faith.

Where then did credit belong? To the divine will alone, expressed in the divine decrees of election and reprobation before the creation of the world. More clearly than had Augustine, Calvin taught that God had consciously determined to leave many of his human creatures without the divine aid necessary for them to profit from Christ's atoning death. Their sins would inevitably remain unforgiven, and they were therefore predestined to eternal damnation. These unfortunate people would freely choose the very sin whose punishment would determine their fate, but their destiny ultimately stemmed from a deliberate divine choice. Augustine had used the term *predestination* almost as a synonym for "election"; it described the singling out of those who would believe. Calvin and his followers spoke of a "double" divine predestination, emphasizing God's active involvement in the decree of reprobation as well as that of election.

Most of the elect would have been children of Christian parents, regularly exposed to the church and its sacraments. A few would have been adult converts. In either case, conscious faith was thought to begin and be nurtured during the preaching of the word; Calvin even suggested that the fact that some hearers responded positively to sermons and others negatively gave empirical support to the doctrine of predestination. If someone could make a confession of faith, was willing to participate in the sacraments, and lived a visibly Christian life, Calvin accepted him into the church.

Yet he recognized that this acceptance into the visible church had to be by the "judgment of charity," for God alone could probe the heart and know whether faith was genuine. The church would inevitably make mistakes and admit as members some who were hypocrites, people who had deceived themselves and the church but who had never actually believed.

What advice could Calvin give to church members who feared that they might not be members of the invisible church because their faith might be hypocritical? He reminded them of their membership in the visible church. Doubters would be told to remember that they had been baptized and would be encouraged to participate fully in the church's preaching and celebration of the Eucharist.

Yet this advice might prove small comfort, for good Calvinists knew that neither baptism nor the Eucharist could be efficacious without faith, and preaching could do no good unless the Spirit chose to create faith through it.

Calvin resolved this problem by turning doubters away from their own fears and back to the all-sufficient grace of Christ. Christians should not dwell on their insufficiencies; they should trust Christ to overcome all their anxieties.

But Calvin did not anticipate the extent to which many of his followers would find their ability to trust undermined by the fear that God had never intended them to believe. He asserted that assurance of salvation was simply a part of faith; if one believed, one could be sure one had been chosen to share eternal life.

This lack of congruence between membership in the visible and the invisible churches created two major problems for the Calvinist tradition. One was the problem of assurance: Christians began paying inordinate attention to the question of their election or reprobation. The other was the problem of infant baptism: Christians began questioning the value of administering a sacrament to those incapable of conscious faith.

The problem of assurance surfaced clearly in the writings of Calvin's immediate successor in Geneva, Theodore Beza. Beza moved the doctrine of predestination to a controlling position in his theological system; he even constructed a chart on which the reader could follow the contrasting fates of the elect and the reprobate from their first existence in the mind of God, before their creation, to their final salvation or damnation. Those reading such a chart could not avoid asking which fate lay in store for them.

But Beza had not created his chart to leave his readers in despair. He had advice for such questioners. Those in doubt over their election could turn to the evidence of their own behavior: 1 John 2:3, for example, stated that Christians knew that they knew Christ "if we keep his commandments." Doubters could examine their own practice to see whether they did in fact make a sincere effort to keep the commandments. In effect, Beza took the third use of the law—as a guide to Christian behavior—and turned it into a test of election. Christians who tried to believe but who doubted their faith could still gain assurance so long as they found themselves loving God and their neighbors.

Sixteenth-century writers knew this technique as the "practical syllogism," so called because the minor premise of the syllogism was the *praxis* (behavior) of the doubting person. It took the following form:

People who love God and their neighbors truly believe; (major premise)

The doubting person actually does love God and his neighbor; (minor premise: the doubting person's *praxis*)

Therefore he truly believes. (conclusion)

By means of such practical syllogisms, doubting Christians could test their faith by the evidence of their behavior and gain some assurance that they were destined for salvation.

Doubts over the validity of infant baptism took longer to surface, but by the early seventeenth century many in the Reformed tradition could see no reason to continue the traditional practice. If infants died, their fate depended not on whether they had been baptized but rather on their status as elect or reprobate in the mind of God. If they grew to adulthood, they would be saved only if God chose to justify them through faith. Faith without baptism would suffice for salvation; baptism without faith could not prevent damnation.

The inevitable result was believer's baptism, the practice of reserving baptism to those old enough to demonstrate a conscious faith. Calvin's Roman Catholic opponents had conceived of baptism as a sacrament in which regenerating grace was promised and actually given. Calvin himself taught that the Holy Spirit would confer such grace only upon believers, yet he retained the practice of infant baptism. If God chose to regenerate infants, he could create the necessary faith within their hearts by his own mysterious processes. But Calvin's Baptist followers found this notion of infant faith unnecessary; they eventually came to understand baptism as no more than an ordinance in which the already regenerate Christian made a public profession of faith.

Before taking leave of Switzerland to examine the spread of Calvinism in other parts of Europe, one needs to recall that Geneva was not the only important Swiss center of Reformed activity. Zwingli's successor in Zurich, Heinrich Bullinger, rivaled Calvin and Beza as the leading spokesperson of Reformed Christianity. Bullinger's *Confessio Helvetica Posterior* (Second Helvetic Confession, final version 1566) gained Calvin's approval and served to unite Reformed Christians for centuries to come. Like Calvin, Bullinger offered his hospitality to Protestant refugees, many of whom continued to look to him for guidance after returning to their home countries.

Bullinger's hospitality assumed particular importance for the transmission of the Reformed tradition to England, for a number of prominent English Protestants came under his influence. Reformed ideas gained currency in England during the final years of the reign of Henry VIII and particularly under the boy-king Edward VI. Both Martin Bucer and the Italian Reformed theologian Peter Martyr Vermigli held Regius Professorships of Divinity, Bucer at Cambridge and Peter Martyr at Oxford.

But the ascendancy of Mary Tudor in 1553 drove many Protestants into exile. They turned for refuge to the major Protestant cities on the Continent; important communities of English refugees arose in Geneva, Frankfurt, and Zurich. The Zurich refugees developed unusually strong ties with their adopted city, and they maintained an extensive correspondence with Bullinger after returning to England when Mary's half-sister, Elizabeth, became queen in 1558. Since several of these "Marian exiles" to Zurich became important bishops in the Elizabethan church, Bullinger's influence there remained strong.

The career of Edmund Grindal is a case in point. Grindal had studied with Bucer at Cambridge, but when Mary returned the Church of England to communion with the pope, he left the country and settled in Zurich. There he came to know Bullinger and his writings. After his return to England, Grindal rose rapidly in the Elizabethan church, serving as bishop of London, archbishop of York, and finally archbishop of Canterbury. Grindal often consulted with Bullinger by letter, and he and his old Zurich colleagues were instrumental in having Bullinger's *Decades*—fifty weighty theological sermons—made required reading at both Oxford and Cambridge. During the first half of Elizabeth's reign, Bullinger's influence with the hierarchy undoubtedly outstripped Calvin's.

Relations between Geneva and Canterbury during this period were hampered because two British members of the Geneva refugee community—John Knox and Christopher Goodman—had published tracts defending the right of subjects to overthrow tyrannical rulers. The publication of Knox's *A First Blast of the Trumpet Against the Monstrous Regiment of Women* had a particularly chilling effect, for although it was directed against Mary Tudor, it appeared just in time to greet Elizabeth's ascent to the throne. Despite protests from both Calvin and Beza that they did not share Knox's opinions, Elizabeth found it hard to look kindly on the Geneva version of Reformed theology.

By the last twenty years of her reign (1583–1603), however, matters had changed considerably. Beza's brand of Geneva Calvinism took firm hold at both Cambridge and Oxford, and the doctrine of the late Elizabethan and Jacobean Church of England leaned heavily on the third- and fourth-generation Reformed theology that has since come to be known as Reformed scholasticism.

To understand how Reformed scholasticism came to dominate the Calvinist tradition in the seventeenth and early eighteenth centuries, one must follow the spread of Calvinism as it developed into an international movement. It will be evident that dogmatic theology became largely the province of university professors, men who wrote for an international audience. The result —a pan-Calvinist "school theology"—drove all opposition before it.

Few parts of Europe escaped the influence of Calvinist ideas, but the most important Calvinist centers arose in Germany, the Netherlands, France, Scotland, and England. A brief sketch of all but the last must suffice here.

Heidelberg led the Reformed movement in the Palatinate. Upon his assumption of the electorship in 1559, Frederick III determined to lead his territory away from a ritualistically oriented Lutheranism toward Reformed theology and practice. He attracted to his new theological school at Heidelberg two promising young scholars: Zacharias Bär (Ursinus, who had studied with Melanchthon in Wittenberg before coming under the influence of Bullinger and Peter Martyr at Zurich), and Caspar von Olewig (Olevianus, who had studied in Geneva and come under the direct influence of Calvin). Working together, Ursinus and Olevianus produced the Heidelberg Catechism (1563), a statement of faith in 129 questions and answers that was rapidly accepted in Reformed churches throughout Europe and continues to be widely used in the twentieth century.

In the words of Thomas Torrance, the Heidelberg Catechism "is mainly concerned with God's work in man. It is much more closely oriented

than the other Reformed Catechisms to the religious needs of man, to the hunger of his soul, and its exposition at important points is given from the perspective of human experience of redemption" (*School of Faith*, p. xlx). The catechism gave clear definition to the Reformed character of Christianity in the Palatinate, and other distinguished scholars, among them the Frenchman François du Jon (Junius), and the Italian Girolamo Zanchi (Zanchius), were attracted to the theology faculty at the University of Heidelberg. Upon Frederick's death in 1576, his successor, Ludwig VI, reestablished confessional Lutheranism in the Palatinate and expelled 600 Reformed professors and pastors. But Ludwig lived only until 1583. His brother, the protector Johann Casimir, once again made Heidelberg a Reformed haven, and it remained so until the outbreak of the Thirty Years War.

The governments of other German-speaking areas also embraced Reformed Christianity. Nassau, Bremen, and Hesse were all centers of Reformed influence, and each produced distinguished thinkers, particularly the Marburg professor Andreas Hyperius and the encyclopedist Johann Heinrich Alsted of Nassau.

In France the fortunes of Reformed Christianity became deeply entangled in national political struggles. Throughout most of the sixteenth century the power of church and state combined to repress the Huguenots, as French Reformed Christians came to be known. Such repression could be savage, as in the numerous public burnings for heresy or the 1572 St. Bartholomew's Day Massacre, in which 70,000 Huguenots were murdered in Paris and other Protestant centers.

But the Huguenot party remained a force to be reckoned with, and in 1594 one of its number was crowned King Henry IV. To function as ruler, Henry had to convert to Catholicism— prompting his famous comment that Paris was worth a Mass. Nevertheless, his 1598 Edict of Nantes guaranteed considerable toleration to Huguenots. The terms of the edict had been seriously eroded by the middle of the next century, and it was revoked by Louis XIV in 1685. Yet during the brief period of relative freedom, Huguenot thinkers commanded respect throughout the Reformed world. The universities of Nîmes, Montpellier, Montauban, Saumur, and Sedan were formed from older Huguenot academies, and the works of Philippe du Plessis-Mornay,

Pierre du Moulin, and Paul Ferry were cited as far away as the New England colonies.

In the Low Countries, Reformed Christianity served as a rallying point for resistance to the rule of Catholic Spain. The brief *Confessio Belgica* (Belgian Confession), written by the Flemish martyr Guy de Brès in 1561 in defiance of Spanish authority, became the doctrinal standard of the Netherlandish movement. But it was the military commanders—first William of Orange, who publicly embraced Reformed religion in 1573, and after William's assassination, his son Maurice—who led the Dutch forces to the victories that made it possible to establish a Dutch republic.

The leading sixteenth-century thinker in the Dutch church was du Jon, who had left Heidelberg to assume a professorship at the University of Leiden. But the liberal Calvinist Jacob Harmensen (Arminius, who succeeded Junius at the university in 1603), was destined to enjoy far greater prominence.

The early years of the Scottish Reformation were dominated by the figure of John Knox, whom we encountered earlier in Geneva. Knox returned to Scotland in 1559 and quickly assumed the leadership of the Reformed movement. A year later, he and five other ministers wrote and gained parliamentary approval for the First Scottish Confession, which reflected the Calvinism Knox had learned in Geneva.

The opening sentence sets the Confession's tone and reveals the strength of its language:

> Long have we thrustede, deir Brethrene, to have notified unto the warld the soume of that Doctryne quhilk we profes and for the quhilk we have susteaned Infamye and dangeare.

In twenty-five articles the authors affirm a doctrine similar to what Knox encountered in Geneva. God "of meare grace electit us in Christ Jesus his Sone." Faith and assurance proceed "nocht frome fleshe and blude" but from the inspiration of the Holy Spirit. The eucharistic bread and wine are not "nakit and bair signes"; rather, "the faithfull, in the rycht use of the Lordis table, do so eat the body and drink the blude of the Lord Jesus, that he remaneth in thaim and thay in him."

In 1564 Knox's *Book of Common Order,* a liturgy based on the Geneva model, became the authorized standard of Scottish worship. After Knox's death in 1572, leadership passed to Andrew Melville, who returned to Scotland from his studies in Geneva in 1574. Unlike Knox, who had followed Calvin in allowing a variety of systems of church polity, including modified episcopacy in certain circumstances, Melville rejected any system that included higher clergy and held out for a "classical" or "presbyterian" system. The *Second Book of Discipline,* adopted by the Scottish General Assembly in 1581, insisted that the term *bishop* be applied to every pastor in the church.

Presbyterian polity provided for the lay and teaching elders (Greek, *presbyteroi*) of each congregation to meet periodically as a "session" or "consistory"; the session would then send its teaching elders and representatives from its lay elders to meet in "classes" or "presbyteries" with elders from other nearby congregations. "Synods," representing much larger territories, drew representatives from the presbyteries. Overseeing the religious life of the entire nation was the General Assembly, made up of representatives from each of the synods.

The monarchy and much of the aristocracy continued to resist presbyterian government, and attempts to reestablish an episcopal system in Scotland—some of which succeeded for a time—occurred periodically until the English civil war. The intensity of the struggle over episcopacy focused attention away from theological developments, but a closer look reveals the ascendancy of a Reformed scholasticism on the Bezan model. Robert Rollock, professor of divinity at the University of Edinburgh, typifies this development; his *Treatise on Effectual Calling* was read widely both in Latin and in English translation.

By the beginning of the seventeenth century, the Reformed movements in Germany, the Netherlands, Scotland, and France had all entered a period of consolidation. For the most part, systematic theology had become the province of learned scholars at universities, men like Zanchius at Heidelberg, Junius at Leiden, du Moulin at Sedan, and Rollock at Edinburgh. Building on the foundation of the Heidelberg Catechism, the Second Helvetic Confession, and the various national confessions like the Scottish and the Belgic, these scholars molded Reformed theology into a framework that dealt with theological questions in a fashion similar to that of the late medieval schools. Traditional theological questions—e.g., the nature of God, the work of Jesus Christ, the character of divine revelation—were handled one by one in a rigorous academic manner governed by Aristotelian or the newer Ramist logic. (Ramist logic divided a subject into two parts, subdivided each of these into two, then again dichotomized each subdivision, and so on. The resulting structure, often arranged in a chart or "table," was thought to correspond both to the subject in its actuality and to the contents of the mind.)

These schoolmen of the seventeenth century reached remarkable consensus on most theological issues, so Reformed scholasticism quickly became a pan-Calvinistic "Reformed orthodoxy" that dominated formal theology in the Reformed tradition well into the eighteenth century. The *Compendium Theologiae Christianae* of Johannes Wollebius, which was used as a textbook at seventeenth-century Harvard, represents a typical example of such orthodoxy. Though modern scholars see crucial differences between works like Wollebius' *Compendium* and Calvin's own writings, it was to this kind of theology that seventeenth-century thinkers referred when they spoke of Calvinism.

Before Reformed scholasticism could carry the day, however, it had to beat back liberal Calvinistic challenges from theologians like Arminius. Arminius had studied in Marburg, Leiden, and in Geneva under Beza, but after his call to minister to an Amsterdam congregation in 1587 and his subsequent ordination in 1588, he found he could no longer defend the orthodox version of the doctrine of predestination set out by Beza and the Englishman William Perkins. Through an extensive correspondence with Junius and by working out his disagreements with Perkins on paper, Arminius developed a version of Calvinism that attempted to allow more freedom to the human will without abandoning divine sovereignty.

Arminius' challenge provoked a heated reaction from Dutch Reformed scholastics, of whom the most vocal was the Leiden professor Francis Gomar (Gomarus). Arminius' supporters became known as Remonstrants from the title of their *Remonstrance*, published in 1610 as a statement of their position. Gomarus' party predicta-

bly published a *Counter-Remonstrance* in the following year and took the title Counter-Remonstrants.

Matters came to a head at the Synod of Dort (1618–1619). A hand-picked group of Counter-Remonstrants, assisted by some sympathetic foreign theologians and backed by the power of the state, condemned Remonstrant views and outlawed the Remonstrants. The *Canons* of Dort reaffirmed a strict Calvinist orthodoxy, popularly summarized in five points whose initial letters form the acronym TULIP:

1. Total Depravity (of persons without saving grace)
2. Unconditional Election (God chooses those whom he will save without regard to any good work or "condition" they might perform during their lifetimes)
3. Limited Atonement (Christ died only for the elect)
4. Irresistible Grace
5. Perseverance of the Saints

To remove any remaining doubts, the Counter-Remonstrants published a fuller statement of their position in the 1625 *Synopsis Purioris Theologiae* (literally, Synopsis of Especially Pure Theology) drawn up by the theologians of Leiden.

A number of lecturers at the English universities were active contributors to this Reformed scholasticism; through them it reached generations of English students. Calvinist scholastics like William Whitaker, Lawrence Chaderton, William Perkins, and John Davenant of Cambridge, and Sebastian Benefield, Robert Abbot, and John Reynolds of Oxford, were the reigning theological lights in late Elizabethan and Jacobean England.

The most prolific and influential of these was Perkins, whose lifetime almost exactly spanned Elizabeth's reign. In English translation, Perkins' works fill three huge folio volumes, but it is misleading to judge this scholar's importance only on the evidence of the English edition of his collected *Works*. Many of his treatises were written in Latin and intended for a learned and international audience; only later did admirers translate them into the vernacular. Others were explicitly pastoral, such as *How to Live and That Well* and *The Government of the Tongue*. Perkins wrote these treatises for lay audiences in a direct, engaging English style. Calvinists from abroad found both types of writing useful and made translations of the learned and the pastoral works into their own languages—Dutch, German, French, Welsh, Flemish, even Hungarian. As a result, Perkins' Calvinism reached large audiences, learned and popular, both in England and on the Continent. Though his writings are unknown today except to scholars, Perkins was undoubtedly the most widely read representative of the Church of England in the late Elizabethan and Jacobean periods.

Perkins urged each of his readers to make the question "How a Man May Know Whether He Be the Child of God or No" the paramount concern of the spiritual life. And like Beza and his fellow Reformed scholastics, Perkins directed doubting Christians to the practical syllogism. True Christians could authenticate their faith by the evidence of their behavior. Did they love Christ and their neighbors; did they strive to keep the commandments? Then they could take comfort from their knowledge that this behavior was probably a fruit of true faith and therefore a sign of divine election. If they could find no evidence in themselves of Christian behavior, they should question the authenticity of their faith.

Yet Perkins recognized that it would rarely be so simple for doubters to draw reliable conclusions about their spiritual state. If hypocrites could persuade both themselves and their neighbors that their behavior qualified them for church membership, how reliable could the evidence of behavior be? Though God would always know the heart, his human creatures could and did draw erroneous conclusions on the basis of the evidence available to them. Only when a person carefully examined his conscience—the way his soul passed judgment on his behavior and the motives behind it—over a long period of time could he gain some confidence in the reliability of his conclusions.

At the same time, Perkins held out the hope that the smallest spark of faith, the most hesitant desire to believe, a mere hungering and thirsting after righteousness from those who recognized their own failures might be the first sign of God's favor. Just as he warned would-be Christians to avoid false security, so he also offered encouragement to the downhearted. Because it would

grow in time to a confident trust in divine mercy, even an embryonic "weak faith" would suffice to fulfill God's conditions for salvation.

Perkins and his followers actually encouraged doubting Christians to imagine the process of salvation as a kind of contract. Expanding on Bullinger's distinction between the old covenant (or testament) and the new, Perkins used contractual language to explain the nexus of obligation between God and human beings. In this "covenant theology," God contracted to grant salvation to everyone who could meet the condition stipulated by his covenant; those who failed to meet the condition would be left in their sin and would earn damnation as a just punishment. Under the old covenant, or "covenant of works," the condition was perfect obedience to the law. Once Adam had fallen, however, no one would have been able to meet this condition, so everyone would inevitably have been condemned.

But to all who stood condemned under the covenant of works, God had mercifully offered a new covenant, the "covenant of grace." Because Jesus Christ's sin-free life had fulfilled the condition of the covenant of works, and because God had accepted Christ's undeserved death as a substitute for the punishment due to all those who had disobeyed his law, God could offer salvation in the covenant of grace upon a different condition: faith. Under the terms of this new covenant, God was understood to have obligated himself to grant salvation to anyone who believed in Christ and the power of his redeeming work. And since even a sincere desire to believe would count as faith in God's eyes, only a lack of good intent could keep a person from accepting God's offer. (Even those who had died before the coming of Christ could be saved if they, like Abraham, had believed God's promises.)

The influential writings of Perry Miller caused many modern scholars to interpret the appearance of covenant theology as a sign that the doctrine of election was being undermined. But Perkins and his followers took pains to show that the freedom of the divine decrees was left intact. Faith, the condition of the covenant of grace, was not finally within human power; only the elect would be able to sustain an initial desire to believe until it became a strong faith. By demanding that would-be Christians search their consciences for signs of this condition, the covenant theology was actually intended to complement the doctrine of election. Those who met the condition of the covenant could be certain that God would never allow their faith to fail; they could therefore be certain of their final salvation.

But the emergence of contractual metaphors did signify an important shift in Calvinism. As they expressed the concepts of traditional theology in the language of the marketplace, English Calvinist ministers were responding to the need to preach intelligibly and persuasively to laypeople. Even more strongly than had Calvin, Perkins and his colleagues emphasized the uselessness of sacraments to the unbeliever. Preaching, the means by which faith was first provoked and then sustained, immediately became the liturgical center of English Calvinism.

But to edify, the sermon had to be intelligible. If the laity were to assume the burden of searching their own consciences for marks of election, then preaching had to meet them at their own level. In the years before the colonization of North America, one finds in English Calvinist preaching and in the theology that informed it a sensitivity not only to the *precedent* of the Calvinist tradition but also to the *pressure* of lay demands. Laypeople came to sermons with practical concerns, especially the concern over their own status before God. If their parish preacher failed to address such concerns, many were willing and able to travel to worship services where more satisfactory sermons could be heard.

The full extent of lay involvement in the English Calvinist movement has become clear to historians only very recently. For a long time, it was assumed that English Calvinism was an ideology of disaffected ministers who were trying to impose an alien system of theology and church order on the indigenous "Anglicanism" of the English church. These ministers, called Puritans by historians because of their efforts to purify the Church of England of all unscriptural elements, were trying to enlist the laity in a revolutionary campaign. Their goal, it was argued, was to overthrow the hierarchy of the established church and to create communities of visible saints led by men like themselves: godly preaching ministers who would be free to criticize the government whenever it threatened their authority to direct their congregations on matters of the spirit.

Such a movement could obviously not have been tolerated by Queen Elizabeth and her bishops, the argument continued, so the Church of England resolutely opposed Puritanism. Although the Puritan ministers succeeded in marshaling considerable lay support, especially in the House of Commons, the monarch and the bishops combined to thwart all attempts to change the "Anglican" character of the Church of England. Only after Charles I's attempt to rule without calling a Parliament had thoroughly alienated the country gentry were the Anglican bishops seriously challenged. By the early 1640s, deprived of the support of a king who was now fighting for his survival, the bishops could no longer resist Parliament's demands for a thorough reformation of the Church of England. They were soon deprived of office, and church power passed to the very Puritans they had despised.

It now seems likely that this picture is misleading in at least three important respects. First, Calvinism was far more pervasive, particularly in the late Elizabethan and Jacobean periods, than historians had suspected until quite recently. Not that the majority of English people were Calvinists, for there were many who regretted the demise of the "old religion," Catholicism, and still more who, then as now, were relatively indifferent to religious matters. But most serious Protestants found the Calvinist position persuasive and were not uncomfortable imagining themselves as part of an international "Reformed" Christianity. A self-conscious non-Calvinist "Anglicanism" was late in developing; it was only in the 1620s that the term *Puritanism* came to be used regularly against those within the Church of England who held a Calvinist theology. Earlier it had been reserved for nonconformists. George Abbot, archbishop of Canterbury for most of King James's reign, was a Calvinist; so were all five of the delegates sent by James to represent England and Scotland at the Synod of Dort.

Second, English Calvinism was seldom perceived by contemporaries as a revolutionary ideology. Though its enemies, like Archbishop Richard Bancroft, stressed its foreign origins, it appealed to the gentry because it promised to reinforce the existing social order. The ideal of the godly preaching minister—exhorting the people to observe a strict code of outward behavior, urging them to examine their consciences for the love of righteousness and hatred of sin that was the mark of election, and exemplifying in his own life the practice that he preached—seemed made to order for a squire eager to keep his clients under control.

It is foolish to pretend that English Calvinism ever entirely abandoned its prophetic side, its ability to call down divine judgment upon an unrighteous people. But there is little reason to doubt that, by the early seventeenth century, most English Calvinists felt at home in the Church of England and were willing to defend its legitimacy against Roman Catholic opponents. Similarly, lay magistrates were far more likely to see the local godly preacher as an ally than as an opponent.

Third, the character of the English Calvinist movement was by no means shaped exclusively by clerics. Not only was Calvinist preaching self-consciously tailored to the capacities of the laity, but the preacher's very ability to function also depended heavily on lay patronage. Nowhere is the critical role of the influential gentleman or court official clearer than in the correspondence of the clergy themselves. A layman might hold the right of presentation to a parish benefice or town lectureship; he might have connections that could assist a minister in securing a desired promotion; he might protect the minister from an unsympathetic bishop or archdeacon. We have seen above how the covenant theology reflected lay pressure as well as Calvinist precedent; many cases of clerical nonconformity probably reveal the presence of an equally significant lay influence. Bitter conflicts between bishops and clergy over issues that appear inconsequential to modern minds often turned on a minister's need to preserve his credibility with his own congregation.

But we must beware of assuming that the bishops were invariably unsympathetic. Many late Elizabethan and Jacobean bishops—one thinks especially of Thomas Morton, Joseph Hall, and Arthur Lake—took it as their major challenge to retain the allegiance of all but the most extreme reformers. To a remarkable degree, they succeeded. These prelates were generally willing to tolerate nonconformity in minor matters if they could assure the continued services of godly preaching ministers. In return, they won the esteem of the godly preachers and their lay supporters. One must remember that Lewis Bayly, whose *The Practice of Pietie* was the most influential manual of devotion in seventeenth-century England *and* New England, was a bishop in the Jacobean church, and that Arthur Lake, bishop of Bath and Wells under James, was involved in the formation of the Massachusetts Bay Company.

What counted as Puritanism at any given time was therefore strongly conditioned by the prevailing attitude of the hierarchy. When Bishop William Laud privately composed a list of influential clergy and marked each name either "Puritan" or "Orthodox," most of his "Puritans" would have taken strong exception to the label. The bishop of Salisbury, John Davenant, certainly did so in a letter to his friend Samuel Ward, the Lady Margaret Professor of Divinity at Cambridge and another whom Laud would have called "Puritan."

If one takes a narrower view, and confines "Puritan" to that group of ministers and laypeople who subscribed to the presbyterian *Book of Discipline* and could see no legitimate place for an episcopal hierarchy in the Church of England, then Puritanism reached the height of its influence in the middle of Elizabeth's reign. Under the leadership of John Field, who secretly directed the movement from his base in London, it hoped to replace episcopal supervision with a network of presbyterian "classes." The complete system, which included a form of worship patterned on the Geneva model, procedures for congregational discipline, provision for ruling and teaching elders, directions for government of the local church, and the "classical" system, was contained in the *Book of Discipline,* which Field persuaded Walter Travers (and probably Thomas Cartwright as well) to write early in 1587. Field's correspondence reveals the existence of a number of clerical associations, some of which may in fact have considered themselves presbyterian. But Elizabeth and her bishops succeeded in isolating the more radical of these "Puritans" from their more moderate sympathizers by requiring of all clergy an oath that the Book of Common Prayer contained nothing contrary to the Bible. By the 1590s the presbyterian threat had been effectively blunted.

At this point, so the traditional argument went, Puritans changed tactics. If they could not overthrow the hierarchy by attacking it from without, they would undermine it from within by placing godly preaching ministers in every parish. These ministers would eventually turn the whole populace into Puritans, and episcopacy would collapse from lack of support.

There can be no doubt that Oxford and Cambridge were in fact sending out a stream of godly preaching ministers to the parishes of England throughout the late Elizabethan and Jacobean periods. These men did preach a Calvinist theology, did devote themselves chiefly to the edification of their parishioners, and did attempt to exemplify godly living in their behavior. But there is no reason to see them as the successors to Field and the presbyterians. Their professors, men like Laurence Humphrey and Henry Robinson at Oxford and Robert Some and William Whitaker at Cambridge, had not been active in the presbyterian movement, though the influential Lawrence Chaderton of Emmanuel College had supported "the discipline" before abandoning it in the 1590s. The presence of large numbers of Calvinist clergy in the late Elizabethan and Jacobean church does not need to be traced to a change of tactics on the part of failed revolutionaries; it was a logical result of the pervasiveness of a moderate Calvinism that had always placed more emphasis on piety than on polity and had always been willing to coexist with the right kind of bishops. Nor, given the degree of lay involvement, need it be seen as an attempt to propagandize an indifferent laity. It was often the laity who sought out a Chaderton or a Samuel Ward for advice on the proper candidate for a vacant position, sure that these tutors would recommend a suitably godly man.

Indeed, local historians have been struck by the extent to which individual communities of English Calvinist laity appear to have needed very little external regulation. Though they relied on the preacher for edification and advice, the men and women in these communities had successfully internalized their code of behavior; their consciences really were their guides.

It is in this context that Max Weber's famous thesis must be evaluated. In *The Protestant Ethic and the Spirit of Capitalism,* Weber argued that "ascetic Protestantism," particularly in its English Calvinist version, produced a type of individual uniquely suited to succeed in an emerging capitalist order. Such individuals arose, in Weber's opinion, because Calvin had conceived of God as radically independent of the natural order. As his creatures, human beings were obligated to obey him, but their obedience would not occur "naturally," simply because they were human. People would need to make a conscious decision to order their lives according to God's will. After the Fall, this kind of voluntary obedience would no longer have been within human power; only in the life and death of Christ could Christians find an example of the type of obedience God still required of all human beings.

Christ's example was carried forward in the church, the continuing presence of Christ's body in history. Composed of those whom God had elected not because of their "natural" abilities but for reasons known only to himself, the church became the community of those who voluntarily organized their lives around God's will. The community of Calvinist saints, governed by divine law, stood self-consciously over against the traditional order of society, governed by custom and self-interest.

Individual Calvinists, argued Weber, had therefore freely rejected the traditional order in favor of a "rational" order where all activities were consciously directed toward God's glory. Their adherence to a rigorous code of conduct that was not shared by the society as a whole demanded a high degree of internal self-discipline; Weber called it "this-worldly asceticism." Weber was particularly impressed by the Calvinist use of the practical syllogism. If individuals were constantly examining their behavior for signs that they were elect, they would be constantly reinforcing their propensity to set their voluntary adherence to God's standards over against the thoughtless adherence to the traditional order that characterized "the world."

Weber believed that the same sort of behavior that was required of Calvinist saints was also required of successful capitalists. The "spirit of capitalism"—rational capitalism as a whole way of life—demanded voluntary, self-initiated activity that contributed to a long-term goal, even though that activity might violate traditional social norms; it rewarded methodical, systematic mastery over one's natural impulses. Both Calvinism and capitalism undercut the traditional social order in the name of a higher, more "legal-rational" order. There was therefore a strong affinity between Calvinist Protestantism and the spirit of rational capitalism. Weber concluded that it was no accident that rational capitalism arose first and most successfully in those areas of Europe where Calvinism had been most pervasive.

In the eighty years since Weber first propounded this thesis, it has never ceased to provoke heated controversy. Some have argued that he misunderstood the conditions for the rise of capitalist economies; others that he misunderstood Calvinism. Here it will have to suffice to point out one undeniable weakness shared by Weber and most of his defenders: Weber assumed that theological statements by clergymen provided an adequate description of the ideals toward which the laity strove. Today it seems clear that the Calvinist laity did not derive its notions of religious behavior entirely from the clergy, and that some English clerical expressions of Calvinism took a distinctive shape because of lay concerns. Though it is premature to suggest that the spirit of rational capitalism may have had as strong an influence on ascetic Protestantism as the other way around, it is plain that the influence was mutual.

Despite all reservations, it is likely that Weber's thesis will continue to provoke fruitful discussion for some years to come. Weber was certainly correct in insisting on the importance of the separation between those who embraced Calvinism and those who clung to more traditional ways of life. Just as English Calvinism formed powerful bonds among its followers in a given community, so it also served in town after town as a divisive force, creating a barrier between those followers and the rest of the townspeople.

English Calvinism never succeeded in becoming a "popular" religion; its appeal was always to a spiritual elite. Calvinists used a specialized religious language to interpret as signs of divine favor the same setbacks and achievements that seemed ordinary enough to others. They approached life seriously as a spiritual warfare against the world, the flesh, and the devil. They were constantly examining their motives and castigating themselves for imperfections that seemed trivial to those outside the group. The same godly preaching that attracted many to the cause drove others away. Opponents often spoke derisively of the Calvinist "faction." When substantial theological opposition did arise, as it did in the 1620s with the rise to power of William Laud, it could attach itself to strong anti-Calvinist sentiment in many parts of England.

Though Arminianism would eventually evolve into a powerful tradition in its own right, the earliest Arminians shared many convictions with their Calvinist contemporaries. Some twentieth-century scholars (most recently R. T. Kendall) find Arminius to have been no less faithful to the theology of the *Institutes* than were those who attacked him in Calvin's name.

But seventeenth-century English Calvinists overlooked the similarities; they were shocked by two central Arminian assertions. First, Arminians insisted that God provided all people with sufficient grace to enable them to believe. Of course even before he had created the world, God already knew that all would not avail themselves of this grace; some would be saved and others damned. But he also knew, through his omniscient foreknowledge, precisely which individuals would believe. Only after he had foreseen their faith did he elect them to eternal fellowship with him. Conversely, he only abandoned the reprobate after he had already foreseen their unbelief.

Such divine election "from foreseen faith" (*ex praevisa fidei*) not only assumed a willingness on God's part to consider people's actions before making a final decision on their fate; it also emphasized their ability to make moral choices. Arminianism humanized the economy of salvation by reserving a real role for the human actors. Arminian writers like Richard Montague and Samuel Hoard portrayed the Calvinist God as a capricious tyrant who saved and damned without any apparent rationale. They hoped to eliminate this harsh image and replace it with that of a scrupulously moral divinity, a God who gave a capacity to believe to all and who damned only those who turned a deaf ear to the biblical promises of salvation. People who attended church regularly and did their best to live by the Ten Commandments had no need to agonize over whether they had been predestined to salvation or eternal punishment.

Second, Arminian writers moved the church and its sacraments back to the center of the salvation process. They emphasized the continuity between the rituals of the Book of Common Prayer and the pre-Reformation church, and they attempted to restore the "beauty of holiness" to worship services that had often been drastically simplified by the godly preachers. In his countless confrontations with embittered Calvinists, Archbishop Laud insisted that the altar, where Christ's body became physically present in the Eucharist, was superior to the pulpit, where only his word was preached. The Calvinist Peter Smart asked the Arminians in Durham:

> Why should you cast out the Lord's Tables, and erect Altars, never so called in our Church-bookes? Why make ye so many crosses, and sett up crucifixes in churches, with other images. . . . Why light ye so many wax candles, to the honour of our Lady, and sett tapers and candlesticks upon your Altar, for a dumb shew . . . ?
> (Cosin, *Correspondence*, vol. 1, p. 162)

To Smart, it seemed obvious that Arminians intended to "bring in Popery againe"; they had even gone so far as to term the English Reformers "ignorant and unlearned Calvinisticall bishops." To Laud, who was no friend to Rome, it was a matter of restoring the sacraments to their rightful place at the heart of Christian worship. Since effective ritual required well-maintained churches, Laud also worked tirelessly throughout his career to force churchwardens to make needed repairs on the physical fabric of their churches, for upkeep on buildings, hangings, and vestments had often been neglected by those who saw external beauty in worship as a distraction from their primary business: the upkeep of souls.

No sooner had Charles I succeeded to the throne in 1625 than he began to show his preference for the Arminians. Laud was named bishop of London in 1628, and upon the death of the Calvinist George Abbot in 1633 he became archbishop of Canterbury. His efforts to enforce a stringent conformity stood in sharp contrast to the laxer policies of his predecessor and convinced many Calvinists that their future in the Church of England was dim. To such people the opportunities for colonization in the New World could seem providential. Ministers like John Cotton and Thomas Hooker claimed that God had given England time enough to repent of her worldly ways; he was now ready to transport his Gospel to the New World and focus his primary attention there.

But Laud's victory proved temporary. By 1640, Charles was so desperate for funds that he convened the Long Parliament, so called because it continued in session despite all Charles's efforts to disband it. During its existence the Parliament abolished episcopacy, executed Laud, and finally saw Charles himself beheaded.

It also summoned the Westminster Assembly composed of Calvinist ministers from all over England and Scotland. After long debates, the assembly published its "standards"—a confession of faith as well as a long and a short catechism—in 1648. The Westminster Confession, with its covenant theology and its stress on predestination and assurance of salvation, long endured as a continuing monument to the state of English Calvinism in the mid-seventeenth century: it was widely used by American churches in the Calvinist tradition—Presbyterian, Baptist, and Congregationalist—up until the middle of the twentieth century.

English Calvinism finally failed in its bid to become the dominant ideology of the Church of England. But disaffected English Calvinists were more successful in New England, where the story logically continues.

BIBLIOGRAPHY

William Ames, *The Marrow of Theology*, John Eusden, ed., (1968); Brian Armstrong, *Calvinism and the Amyraut Heresy: Protestant Scholasticism and Humanism in Seventeenth-Century France* (1969); John Calvin, *Institutes of the Christian Religion*, F. L. Battles, trans., 2 vols. (1960); Patrick Collinson, *The Elizabethan Puritan Movement* (1967), *Archbishop Grindal 1519–1583: The Struggle for a Reformed Church* (1979), and *The Religion of Protestants: The Church in English Society 1559–1625* (1982); John Cosin, *Correspondence*, 2 vols. (1869); Mark Curtis, *Oxford and Cambridge in Transition 1558–1642: An Essay on Changing Relations Between the English Universities and English Society* (1959).

A. G. Dickens, *The English Reformation* (1964); William Haller, *The Rise of Puritanism* (1938); E. Brooks Holifield, *The Covenant Sealed: The Development of Puritan Sacramental Theology in Old and New England, 1570–1720* (1974); Douglas Horton, ed., *William Ames by Matthew Nethenus, Hugo Visscher, and Karl Reuter* (1965); R. T. Kendall, *Calvin and English Calvinism to 1649* (1979); Peter Lake, *Moderate Puritans and the Elizabethan Church* (1982); W. M. Lamont, *Godly Rule: Politics and Religion 1603–60* (1969); David Little, *Religion, Order, and Law: A Study in Pre-Revolutionary England* (1969).

Edmund Morgan, *Visible Saints: The History of a Puritan Idea* (1963); Irvonwy Morgan, *The Godly Preachers of the Elizabethan*

Church (1965); Wilhelm Niesel, ed., *Bekenntnisschriften und Kirchenordnungen der nach Gottes Wort Reformierten Kirche* (1938); Geoffrey Nuttall, *The Holy Spirit in Puritan Faith and Experience* (1947); William Perkins, *The Workes . . .* (1616–1618); Harry Porter, *Reformation and Reaction in Tudor Cambridge* (1958); W. Stanford Reid, ed., *John Calvin: His Influence in the Western World* (1982); Alan Simpson, *Puritanism in Old and New England* (1955); Keith Sprunger, *The Learned Doctor Ames: Dutch Backgrounds of English and American Puritanism* (1972); Margaret Spufford, *Contrasting Communities: English Villagers in the Sixteenth and Seventeenth Centuries* (1974).

Thomas Torrance, ed., *The School of Faith: The Catechisms of the Reformed Church* (1959); N. R. N. Tyacke, "Puritanism, Arminianism and Counter-Revolution," in *The Origins of the English Civil War,* Conrad Russell, ed. (1973); Gordon Wakefield, *Puritan Devotion: Its Place in the Development of Christian Piety* (1957); Michael Walzer, *The Revolution of the Saints: A Study in the Origins of Radical Politics* (1965); Max Weber, *The Protestant Ethic and the Spirit of Capitalism* (1958); Johannes Wollebius, *Compendium Theologiae Christianae,* in *Reformed Dogmatics,* John W. Beardslee, ed. (1965); David Zaret, "Ideology and Organization in Puritanism," in *Archives Européennes de Sociologie,* 21 (1980).

[*See also* CALVINIST THEOLOGICAL TRADITION; CONGREGATIONALISM FROM INDEPENDENCE TO THE PRESENT; NEW ENGLAND PURITANISM; *and* PRESBYTERIANISM.]

NEW ENGLAND PURITANISM

Baird Tipson

THE English emigrants who founded the New England colonies in the first half of the seventeenth century soon established a distinctive combination of religious beliefs and practices that has come to be known as New England Puritanism. This article will describe that Puritanism and follow its fortunes well into the eighteenth century; it will concentrate its attention on the settlements in Massachusetts Bay, Connecticut, and New Haven (which was soon incorporated into Connecticut), emphasizing those elements that all held in common. Because the small separatist colony at Plymouth was quickly overshadowed by the Bay Colony to the north, it will not receive separate attention.

One must not imagine the Puritanism of the first colonists as a fully developed alternative to some established "Anglicanism" they had left behind in England. It is true that most of them were disenchanted with the worship and hierarchical structure of the Church of England and were eager to experiment with new forms. But, with the prominent exception of the settlers at Plymouth, they had virtually all been baptized and nurtured in the established church, and they deliberately chose not to separate from it. Many of them came from parishes where a "godly preaching minister," given considerable leeway by a sympathetic bishop, had been able to devote his efforts to the edification of an elite group of Calvinist saints within the parish. It is not difficult to find close counterparts to New England Puritan beliefs and practices in the English communities that the emigrants had left behind.

Yet a whole is always more than the sum of its parts. Two elements made the "New England Way" distinctive: its particular combination of religious beliefs and practices, and the rationale that served to justify the combination. We label

the whole *Puritanism* in order to underscore its cohesiveness in the minds of its adherents, and the label is apt only so long as we remember that it is no more than a scholarly construct. Careful studies of early New England towns have demonstrated that even those who most fervently embraced Puritanism continued to behave as traditional English people in most aspects of their lives. One must beware of "Puritan agriculture" or "Puritan architecture," and in this article, Puritanism will designate no more than the particular combination of religious beliefs and practices to which the leaders of early New England were officially committed.

The leaders of the New England settlements, both lay and clerical, had come out of the English Calvinist tradition. During the final years of the reign of Elizabeth and throughout the reign of James I, they had reason to hope that the Church of England would continue to be receptive to Calvinist ideas, particularly the importance of evangelistic preaching and strict moral discipline at the parish level. But the ascendancy of Charles I in 1625 frustrated these hopes. The new "Supreme Governor" of the Church of England threw his support behind William Laud and the anti-Calvinist Arminian party. Laud required strict conformity from his clergy, and the situation in the diocese of Chichester, where the outspoken Arminian Richard Montague succeeded the staunch Calvinist George Carleton as bishop in 1628, was repeated in many parts of England. As a result, many English Calvinists lost hope in the established church.

Of those ministers who eventually immigrated to the New World in the early 1630s, some (for example, Thomas Hooker) had already fled to Holland to escape Laud's penalties; others (such as Thomas Shepard) had been deprived by Laud but had managed to find lectureships elsewhere; still others (like John Cotton of old Boston) presided over large and influential parishes but feared that they might be deprived of their positions in the future. Such ministers were eager to serve new churches free from the control of unsympathetic bishops.

Their lay counterparts had no more love for the Laudian bishops, but it is clear that they also anticipated a larger role for themselves in the religious life of the new colonies. The voluntary communities of Calvinist saints that had long existed in most English towns and cities were not creatures of the clergy; the lay leaders of these communities brought with them a tradition of involvement in religious matters.

By 1635, less than five years after these leaders actually arrived in the New World, they had developed their distinctive system of church order. The final touches were put on the system in 1648 by the ministers from Massachusetts Bay, Connecticut, and New Haven assembled in synod at Cambridge. There they approved a "Platform of Church Discipline" that effectively codified their experiences of the past fifteen years. This Cambridge Platform remains the clearest description of early New England church order. Both the individual elements of that order and the rationale that bound them together need to be described in some detail.

As in old England, the village church constituted the basic ecclesiological unit. But whereas in the old country the individual parish represented only a small part of the larger administrative unit—the diocese—which was in turn a part of the Church of England as a whole, in New England each village congregation was a church unto itself. In old England the minister was presented to the parish "living" by whoever held the right of presentation to the income of the parish tithes, usually a prominent gentleman or the bishop himself. In New England he was called by the congregation, ordained only with the permission of its lay elders, dependent on its goodwill in paying ministerial assessments on time (ministers frequently complained of arrears), and always subject to its disapproval.

Such congregational control over ministerial appointments was possible only because the legitimacy of each local church rested finally upon the religious experiences of its members. New England churches came into being when a small group of founding members, after intense conversation with one another, determined that the work of grace upon each of their souls was authentic. Those whose faith was questionable were weeded out. But if as few as seven authentic saints remained, they could serve as "founding stones" (cf. Eph. 2:19–22) for the new church.

The founders then invited representatives from surrounding churches to examine them and to certify once more that they had not deceived themselves about their experiences of the work of grace. Only when they had passed these examinations too were they ready to "covenant" together as a new church. They drew up a written covenant that specified their responsibilities to God and to one another, and each founder publicly assented to it. At this time, or shortly thereafter, they also formally called their minister, often one of the founders himself.

Because the New Englanders placed such emphasis on the Pauline metaphor of the church being built from the living stones of its members, they further required that the founders each make a public "relation" of the experience of grace upon their souls. A similar relation was demanded of every additional prospective member. This requirement of a relation quickly became the most distinctive mark of the New England Way.

A number of relations from the 1630s and 1640s have come down to us. Close examination of them reveals that they were not "testimonies" or accounts of "conversion experiences" in the modern evangelical sense. Their theological rationale came from the writings of William Perkins and his followers, who urged Christians to search their consciences continually for evidence of the smallest spark of faith. Though the prospective church members did sometimes refer to climactic moments when they first sensed divine favor, the relations emphasized states of mind that continued into the present rather than isolated experiences from the past.

The relators all recognized their utter inability to obey God's commandments when left to their own devices, and they all confessed that without God's help they would surely be damned eternally. With very few exceptions, they then went on to cite specific scriptural passages that had spoken particularly to their condition. Because they had come to believe that the Spirit was addressing them directly in such passages, they had been able to accept Christ's promises of salvation. Passages like Matt. 5:6, "Blessed are those who hunger and thirst after righteousness," occurred frequently, which would not surprise anyone familiar with Perkins' insistence that God would accept even a desire for faith as the beginnings of faith itself. The fact that the relators found themselves able to take continued comfort from such passages, rather than their ability to recall an intense moment of conversion, seems to have authenticated their faith in the eyes of their colleagues.

Unless they could present such a relation to their local church, inhabitants of New England towns were barred from full membership, no matter how orthodox their theology or how blameless their practice. They could not participate in the Lord's Supper, and they had no vote in church matters.

But those who were not full members were not excused from church attendance. All inhabitants were expected to attend regular weekly services as well as any special services for humiliation or thanksgiving that might be called on the spur of the moment. And since those who followed the New England Way clung fiercely to infant baptism, a growing proportion of the oldest congregations came to consist of the baptized children of full members who had not themselves made a relation and been admitted into full communion.

It is helpful to conceive of the New England churches as a blend of the comprehensive, established church and the more sectarian "gathered" church made up of saints alone. The gathered element is revealed in the fact that only those whose faith had passed the test of a public relation could become full church members. But the churches were also established in two important ways. First, the local government taxed all the inhabitants of the town to support the church and its ministry. Second, the government required the attendance of all citizens at church services and would not tolerate any other form of organized worship.

Early New Englanders would have understood this blend of gathered and established church as a necessarily imperfect congruence of two covenants. As inhabitants of a town, New Englanders had covenanted (though wives participated only through their husbands) to form a social community bound together by obedience

to God and mutual love and respect. In an ideal world, each inhabitant would also have experienced the work of grace, have made a relation, and have joined the church. Membership in the town and the church covenants would then have been perfectly congruent, and the established character of the church would have followed naturally from its inclusiveness. But in practice the church covenant always included a smaller circle than the town covenant; the church's gathered character reflected its practical exclusiveness.

Would a tension between the two covenants have been readily apparent? Imagine a typical Sunday service. A visitor would have found three groups of people in the congregation of a New England church. There would have been inhabitants of the town who had not joined the church but who were legally required to attend its services, though in practice many evaded the requirement. There would have been baptized persons—English-born immigrants who had been routinely baptized in the mother country as well as the New England–born children of full members—who had not made a public relation and were therefore not in full communion. Finally, there would have been the full members themselves. On those occasions when the Lord's Supper was celebrated, the special status of this last group would have become unmistakable, for only they would have been allowed to remain for the celebration.

Although it is clear that early New Englanders expected the church to be a unifying force in their communities, such distinctions among citizens were always potentially divisive. So long as a large percentage of adults eventually became full church members—as seems to have occurred in most towns in the 1630s and 1640s—the potential remained latent. But if the New England–born children failed to fulfill the promise of their baptism and did not proceed to full church membership, churches could be faced with a situation in which the majority of eligible adults were barred from the Lord's Supper and unable to participate in church business.

The magistrates of the Massachusetts Bay Colony increased the potential for division still further when they chose in 1630 to make full church membership a condition for voting in the political affairs of the colony. The magistrates reasoned that only those who had demonstrated the presence of grace in their hearts were morally competent to participate in the governing of a commonwealth. Most towns were less restrictive, allowing nonmembers to vote for local officers, but the decision to restrict full political participation to church members only served to increase the possibility that those who had not joined the church would resent the control that the church members held over them.

By the time that the New England–born children married and had children of their own, the conflict inherent in an established church with a gathered membership could no longer be ignored. These children, the grandchildren of church members in full communion, were not eligible for baptism.

Their own parents had been baptized on the traditional ground that they were the "seed" of those in the covenant. In the seventeenth chapter of Genesis, Abraham had been instructed to have himself circumcised as a sign that he stood in a covenant relationship with God. Each of his male offspring was also to be circumcised as soon as he was eight days old, for God had covenanted "to be a God unto thee, and to thy seed after thee."

Just as circumcision had been the sign of the old covenant, baptism became the sign of the new; it, too, was extended to the infant children of believers. But if these infant children grew to adulthood without ever showing any evidence of gracious activity in their own hearts, did they remain in the covenant, and could their children in turn be baptized? Or had their indifference to the Gospel deprived them of any role as covenant seed and removed any justification for the baptism of their own children?

The ministers met at a synod in 1662 to consider this issue, and their response became known as the "Halfway Covenant." Baptized children of full members could have their own children baptized only if they were themselves willing to agree publicly to the church's doctrine, to lead a life free from scandal, and to "own" the covenant before the church. "Owning the covenant" meant that the New England–born children would publicly acknowledge the covenant with Christ and the church that had been made for them in infancy by their parents; this was far short of the relation of the personal reception of grace that was required of those admitted to full communion.

The adoption of the Halfway Covenant demonstrates that a majority of the ministers at the 1662 synod wished to preserve the uneasy tension between gathered church and established church that the founders had instituted. The majority chose to continue to limit full membership to authenticated saints, thereby preserving the original purity of the innermost circle of church members. But by bringing those baptized adults who had only gone so far as to own the covenant into "halfway" membership, the Halfway Covenant gave much-needed legitimacy to the church's monopoly on organized worship and to its demand for support from the entire community.

In addition, the supporters of the Halfway Covenant obviously hoped that owning the covenant would be merely an interim step on the way to full church membership; once the young adults had come so far as to take that public step, it would be but a matter of time before they felt capable of making a public relation. In the meantime, their status as covenant seed would have been reaffirmed.

But unfortunately for its supporters, an articulate minority of those present at the 1662 synod would not admit the validity of its decisions. These ministers openly opposed the admission of halfway members. Whether because of their arguments, or (as is equally likely) unwillingness to change the status quo, most churches were slow to implement the synod's decision. Since the New England Way gave each individual congregation the full status of a church, the synod had no effective mechanism for enforcing its decisions, and in some cases ministers who were strong supporters of the Halfway Covenant could not even adopt it in their own churches.

Such reluctance to adopt the compromise solution suggests that many New Englanders were still more committed to the ideal of a pure church than to the comprehensiveness that established Christian churches had traditionally required. It was not until the end of the seventeenth century that "halfway" memberships became generally accepted as part of the New England Way, and even then individual churches did not hesitate to modify the terms of the Halfway Covenant as it suited their own local circumstances.

But by this time many New Englanders had begun to reject the whole notion of limiting church membership to the demonstrably converted, and they were no longer satisfied with halfway membership. A vigorous presbyterian movement, which exalted the power of the minister over lay members and of synods over local congregations, had arisen in the Connecticut colony. Presbyterian clergy and congregations reinstituted the traditional Calvinist tests of assent to orthodox doctrine and a life free from outward scandal—the same tests demanded of halfway members in the New England Way—as the only requirements for full participation in the sacraments. Churches in presbyterian towns thereby became nearly as comprehensive as those in old England.

In Boston the Brattle Street Church, gathered in 1699, adopted similar requirements and had its minister presbyterially ordained in England. The Brattle Street congregation joined that of King's Chapel, a Church of England congregation founded in Boston in 1686 that worshiped according to the Book of Common Prayer, in open dissent against the New England establishment.

The struggles over church order that preoccupied ministers and laity in seventeenth-century New England point to a still more fundamental concern: creating and nurturing the spiritual life of the individuals who composed the church. Devout New Englanders dedicated enormous psychic energy to the cultivation of their interior lives. Fortunately for the historian, many of them left written records of their "inner history" in diaries, autobiographies, letters of spiritual counsel, and the relations of the work of grace the churches required of prospective members. Research into this area, particularly the ground-breaking work of Charles Hambrick-Stowe, has given historians remarkable insight into the standards of piety that devout New Englanders set for themselves.

New Englanders cultivated a wide variety of devotional practices, but the purpose of virtually all of them was to enable the individual to participate in a redemptive cycle of birth, death, and resurrection. In acts of prayer that were a regular part of their daily lives, members of New England churches brought to mind Christ's death and rebirth, and they did so not simply to think about them but also to participate emotionally in their salvific power. These activities deserve careful description.

As one would expect, church members were encouraged to devote part of each day to the reading of Scripture. The ability to read was unusually widespread in New England because private Bible reading was often the necessary precondition for religious discussions and full understanding of sermons.

But New Englanders were expected to read not only for instruction but also for edification. If Bible readers could feel that the words were a message intended particularly for themselves, their hearts could be moved while their intellects were enlightened. In the opinion of most New England ministers, Bible reading could even serve as the occasion for the first work of saving grace upon a person's soul, though that event would more likely occur while he was listening to a sermon.

The good Christian would also take time out to meditate. Bible reading might lead naturally to systematic meditation, but the most natural moment would be at day's end. Before going to bed, Christians were expected to look back over the events of the day and allow their consciences to pass judgment over their experiences. Had their actions been consistent with their Christian profession, or had they been characterized by pride and self-love? If the results were reassuring, such self-examination could provide evidence that would ease nagging doubts about whether one was truly among those whom God had elected.

But meditation also served to edify. As New Englanders recalled their shortcomings, they repented, believed that they had received forgiveness, took comfort from that belief, and gave thanks, just as they had in their initial conversion. Meditation allowed Christians to recapitulate the experience of dying to self and being reborn as a member of Christ's body, to participate daily in Christ's death and resurrection.

Besides incorporating the more structured devotions of Bible reading and meditation into their everyday lives, devout New Englanders were expected to set time aside for prayer. True prayer was believed to come spontaneously from within; the presence of the Holy Spirit caused it to arise from the heart. New England ministers hoped to bring all church members to the point where such an "internal spirit of prayer" would guide their spiritual lives. Though the devotional manuals suggested examples, prayer was intended to be personal and free flowing. But ideally it, too, carried the sinner through the stages of the redemptive process: recognition of sin, repentance, sense of forgiveness, assurance of salvation, thanksgiving.

Two institutions provided the link between these purely private devotions and the corporate piety of the Sabbath worship service: family prayer and meetings at private homes. The ideal New England family met as a "little church" both morning and evening for organized devotions. The father played the minister's role on these occasions, leading the family in psalm singing, Bible reading, and prayer.

After reading Hambrick-Stowe's sensitive accounts, the modern student is struck by the similarity between morning and evening prayer in the New England family and the traditional Catholic daily office, particularly matins and compline. A mood of reflective penitence characterized evening prayer; one confessed the sins of the day and in contrition asked that one might die to sin. One prepared for sleep as a kind of death, meditating on the connection between death and darkness and reminding oneself of the resurrection and judgment to come.

When the family gathered for morning devotion, the mood had changed. Now the prayers portrayed the awakening of the body from sleep as an emblem both of natural birth and of the new birth in Christ. One greeted the day in hope and expectation. Taken together, evening and morning prayer recapitulated the cycle of death and rebirth that lay at the heart of the ideal pattern of devotional life in early New England.

Even the prayers before and after meals contained a small reenactment of the Christian's progress from death to life. Before each meal the family recognized its need for spiritual sustenance, a need equal to the need for the material sustenance it was about to receive. When family members had finished eating, they gave thanks for their sustenance and looked forward to the fulfillment of all their hopes in the eschatological kingdom of God.

Max Weber found in Calvinistic Protestantism, and particularly in its English variety, a this-worldly asceticism that could achieve success in the world without becoming attached to its natural and traditional orders. If one remembers that Christian asceticism has always relied closely on the natural rhythms of the day and the year, it is impossible to ignore the parallels between the structured prayers of the monastic orders and the disciplined devotions of pious New England families and individuals. Both reminded Christians that material needs were always to be subordinated to spiritual obligations.

Just as family prayer bridged the gap between the private exercises of its members and their corporate public worship, so, too, did the meetings at private houses that occurred regularly in New England towns. But these meetings also served another function: as a bridge between the larger society and the church. Continuing a practice that many of them had begun in England, groups of church members would meet weekly or biweekly in different homes for prayer, psalm singing, and discussion of a recent sermon or some other religious subject. Though ministers made occasional guest appearances, lay people ordinarily presided.

The meetings allowed Christians an opportunity to reinforce their common values, to comfort the bereaved, encourage the despondent, and exhort the potential backslider. But they also provided a means whereby the newly joined member could be socialized into the community of full church members. They guaranteed that every member of the church would become familiar with the full range of family and private devotions and would be encouraged to incorporate those devotions into everyday routines.

Now that the distinctive polity of the New England churches has been sketched out and the variety of New England devotional practices examined, the heart of organized worship in New England, the sermon, can be placed in its proper context. Most studies of New England sermons have been inclined to emphasize the process by which ministers tried to lead the members of their congregation to become converted and join the church. Such an emphasis is far too narrow, as anyone familiar with devotional practices would suspect.

New Englanders gathered for public worship on the Sabbath, on "lecture days" during the week—occasions when a minister would expound regularly on a particular part of the Bible —and on special days of fasting or thanksgiving. Though there was a clear structure to the service, set prayers were frowned upon. Long extempore petitions, inspired by the same "internal spirit of prayer" that animated private devotion, were the ideal toward which the minister strove. There would be opportunities to sing psalms and to hear the Bible read. But the dramatic heart of the service was the sermon.

New England ministers preached in a "plain style" that avoided allusions to nonbiblical authors and spoke in clear, direct language to the congregation. The chosen biblical text would be explained, briefly set in context, and then mined for "doctrines": the theological gist of the text. "Reasons" for the truth of each doctrine would usually be attached, and the treatment of the text would conclude with a list of "uses." It was in the uses that the minister would drive home the relevance of the text to the situation of his hearers.

Careful examination of New England sermons reveals that they were rarely designed merely to bring the unconverted to repentance and belief. Though the doctrines may often have described what had to happen to an unconverted person before that person would be capable of faith, the uses spoke more consistently to the situation of those who hoped that they had already experienced the first signs of saving grace.

Ministers like Thomas Hooker of Hartford and his son-in-law Thomas Shepard guided the members of their congregations carefully between two dangerous extremes. Were some hearers doubtful that they had ever experienced saving grace and fearful that God had not chosen them for final salvation? These people were reminded that grace often worked secretly, that not everyone would be overpowered by the first movements of divine activity within the heart. Were other hearers so confident of their elect status that they had ceased to be concerned over the state of their souls? It was the minister's responsibility to knock the props out from under their false security, for their overconfidence might be the first sign that their faith had never been authentic.

True saints never took their condition for granted. Both in public worship and in their private devotions, they were constantly striving to expose and confess the pride and wickedness that kept their faith weak and their hearts turned toward themselves rather than God.

From the evidence of early-seventeenth-century sermons, the New England minister's most insidious enemy was not the unconverted person. It was the hypocrite. In the English Calvinist tradition, spiritual hypocrisy was the state of having deceived not only one's neighbors but also oneself about the state of one's soul. Hypocrites thought that they had genuinely confessed their sins, repented of them, been offered the Gospel promises of forgiveness, and accepted those promises in faith. Hypocrites had convinced themselves that their faith was authentic and that they deserved to be admitted into the church.

More ominously, they had also convinced their neighbors. New England ministers all admitted that even their strict standards of church membership could not guarantee that every hypocrite would be weeded out. In considering prospective church members, ministers reminded themselves and their congregations to make decisions with the "judgment of charity," to give the benefit of the doubt to those whose relations of the work of grace might not be completely convincing. Since everyone knew what the experience of grace was supposed to be like, hypocrites might falsely convince themselves that they had had authentic experiences of grace, just as they had falsely convinced themselves that they truly believed. "The wickedness of mans nature, and the depth of hypocrisie is such," William Perkins had warned, "that a man may and can easily transforme himselfe into the counterfeit and resemblance of any grace of God" (*The Whole Works*, 1616–1618, vol. I, p. 642).

To be sure, it is just as misleading to assume that every member of an early New England church lived in constant anxiety over hypocrisy as it is to assume that New Englanders lost all interest in their spiritual life once they had passed beyond a certain point on a "morphology of conversion." But the diarist wrote far too often of hypocrisy, and the printed sermons devoted far too many paragraphs to distinguishing between true faith and the various kinds of hypocrisy, for concern over it to have been limited to a few overscrupulous consciences. It seems more likely that the primary purpose of most sermons was closely analogous to that of the private devotional practices: to enable those already in the fellowship of the church to renew their conversions, to lead them over and over again through the cycle of contrition, repentance, and faith, through despair to hope, through death to resurrection.

In fact, neither the New England ministers nor their English Calvinist counterparts understood conversion as a once-for-all-time event. They did construct an "order of salvation," a theological construct that explained how people who became Christians would pass through a series of stages: recognition of sin, sorrow for having committed it, admission that they were powerless to help themselves, desire for the help of grace, and belief that Christ had extended that help particularly to them.

But this morphology of conversion was an explanation that worked chiefly in retrospect. William Perkins, the father of this kind of explanation as well as of much else that was central to New England spiritual life, did not make the mistake that has plagued many modern interpreters. Perkins did not intend that descriptions of the stages of conversion be understood as accounts of how people would actually experience the work of grace, for he stated clearly that the final stages would be the first to be felt.

Ministers explained the order of salvation to their congregations not primarily to guide them through it, but rather so they could look back upon their own experiences and evaluate their authenticity. If Christians could recall occasions where they had been truly contrite, truly humbled, truly thankful, they could take some comfort from their recollection. The experiences that they brought to mind need not have occurred before their first conversion; the surviving relations bear eloquent testimony to the fact that churches were more interested in behavior that persisted over time than in once-for-all-time experiences.

Just as devout New Englanders moved cyclically from death to rebirth in their private devotions, so in their reflections about their own conversion they traced their progress from a weak to a strong faith. Following Perkins once more, most New England ministers taught that a weak faith, the mere desire to believe, was a sign of grace already at work in the heart; it would therefore suffice for justification in God's eyes. But such weak faith could easily be confused with the false faith of hypocrites. The only way to know whether an initial "spark" of faith was genuine was to attempt to fan it into flame:

> If a man at the first have but some little feeling of his wants, some weake and faint desire, some small obedience, he must not let this sparke of grace goe out, but these motions of the Spirit

must be increased by the use of the word, Sacraments, and praier; and they must daily be stirred up by meditation, endeavouring, striving, asking, seeking, knocking.
>
> (Perkins, *Works,* I, 642)

Even a mite of faith no larger than a mustard seed was believed to be large enough to stir people into striving to increase it. Significantly, Perkins saw both daily private meditation and corporate public worship as appropriate means to strengthen the "motions of the Spirit."

Those who made every effort to increase their faith might eventually discover that it had become a "strong faith," fully assured of God's favor. If "poor doubting Christians" not only took advantage of the available means but also scrutinized their practice for signs of the presence of grace, the ministers assured them that they could use this sanctified behavior (*praxis*) as a reliable sign that they had been elected.

Even a strong faith was not thought to be immune from all doubting. The staunchest Christians would still find their faith "mingled with contrary unbelief" and "assaulted with temptations." "God will not have men perfect in this life," argued Perkins, "that they may alwaies goe out of themselves, and depend wholly upon the merit of Christ" (*Works,* I, 127).

This theology created a situation in which even the most stalwart church members could fall into dark temptation. The more carefully Christians searched their hearts, the more pride and imperfection they were likely to discover. The same self-examination required to strengthen a weak faith might undercut a strong one.

So unsettling could the self-scrutiny become that some ministers, such as John Cotton of Boston, distrusted it. Cotton was wary of asking his hearers to deduce their spiritual estate from their behavior (the "practical syllogism"); he feared that many Christians would uncover in their own *praxis* such a massive catalog of weaknesses and failures that it would utterly discourage them from hoping for God's favor.

But Cotton was in the minority; most ministers followed Hooker and Shepard in devoting large portions of their sermons to explaining the marks of true grace and helping their congregations take their spiritual temperature. Most sermons were therefore meant to encourage members of the congregation to renew their conversion. The evidence of the diaries, autobiographies, and relations suggests that most Christians were constantly working to nurture a weak faith into a confident assurance of salvation. No less than the acts of private devotion, then, public worship served to assist individuals in their efforts to experience over and over again the central drama of Christian redemption.

The blend of personal piety, corporate worship, and established congregational church order that characterized the New England Way did not go unchallenged in seventeenth-century New England. Part of the challenge stemmed from simple indifference: many colonists did not share the leaders' compelling desire to define their personal and social identity in Christian terms. One result of this lack of interest, the crisis caused by the ever-shrinking percentage of colonists who were full church members, has already been discussed.

But the most dramatic challenges came from men and women who were every bit as zealous as the defenders of the New England Way. These people had their own convictions about how the Christian life should be lived, and they often advanced them with great courage. One of the first such challenges, and one of the most decisive for the future of the New England colonies, was posed by people whom their opponents called Antinomians.

The Antinomian Controversy, which shook the Massachusetts Bay Colony from 1636 to 1638 and eventually involved Connecticut ministers as well, challenged the most basic assumptions of the religious establishment. Mistress Anne Hutchinson and her brother-in-law, John Wheelwright, who spoke for the alleged Antinomians, offered a different model of personal piety, a different kind of corporate worship, and a different pattern of church order. Had their opinions prevailed, the positions held by all but a few of the ministers would have been rendered obsolete.

The ministers recognized the threat early on. After conducting their own investigations, they attributed a series of errors to the Antinomians and brought them to the attention of the civil authorities. At this point two further issues cloud the controversy.

The first, of even more interest today than it was to people in the early seventeenth century, was Anne Hutchinson's gender. The Bay Colony leaders were unwilling to separate the issue of the validity of her ideas from the fact that she, a mere woman, was expressing them. Saint Paul had stated clearly that women were to be subservient to their husbands and to remain silent in church, and the male clerical establishment started with the assumption that her ideas could be no better than their source. A woman might legitimately lead a private meeting, but only if the membership were exclusively female. No sooner had Anne Hutchinson assumed the leadership of a "mixed" meeting than she was accused of "unnatural" behavior. The fact that the meeting was unusually large—sixty to eighty members—only compounded her departure from traditional female roles.

Anne Hutchinson's gender and the clergy's prejudice against it was a central issue in the controversy. But despite what some recent interpreters have suggested, it was not the major issue.

Still closer to the heart of the controversy, and even more difficult to disentangle from the positions of the two parties, were the political interests of the participants. Each party wished to impose its notion of the correct form of a Christian commonwealth upon the other, so the clash of ideas inevitably occurred in the context of a struggle for political power. It is certainly possible that the achievement of personal political power took precedence over the clash of ideas in the minds of some of the participants. But since the ideas advanced by Hutchinson and Wheelwright challenged the very assumptions upon which the Massachusetts Bay Colony had been erected, the notion that political questions could be separated from their religious underpinnings would have occurred to few of those involved on either side.

As is frequently the case in such struggles, the historiography of the Antinomian Controversy was controlled by the winning side. The standard account was compiled by John Winthrop, one of the magistrates and a bitter opponent of the Hutchinson–Wheelwright party; historians have therefore had to view the Antinomians largely through hostile eyes. The only surviving theological statement directly from the pen of an Antinomian writer is John Wheelwright's "Fast-Day Sermon," preached 19 January 1637, in the heat of the controversy. From the evidence of this sermon, Wheelwright's party had launched an all-out assault on the New England Way.

Wheelwright began with an attack on all those who lived "under a covenant of works." In the language of covenant theology, anyone who lived under a covenant of works had not yet been saved by Christ and his new covenant of grace.

But Wheelwright gave the term a different meaning. He claimed that it referred to all those who concluded that they enjoyed God's favor because they could find some work of sanctification in themselves. Lest there be any confusion, he pointed specifically to the very interior motivations, "hungering and thirsting and the like," which ministers like Hooker and Shepard were constantly encouraging their congregations to take as positive evidence of election. Those who relied on practical syllogisms rather than simple faith, argued Wheelwright, had never really been converted. True Christians looked on Christ "with a direct eye of faith" and had no need to rely on mere "fruits and effects" of faith.

In attacking the practice of self-scrutiny for signs of the work of grace, Wheelwright was undermining the basic assumptions about personal and corporate piety upon which the New England Way was built. He knew how far from the mainstream he stood, for he later admitted that he would include every Bay Colony minister but Cotton and himself in the group that lived under a covenant of works.

Theologically speaking, Wheelwright was certainly an Antinomian; he denied that Christian freedom should be restricted by a need to seek evidence of election in obedience to God's law. But he did not argue that Christians had no civil obligation to obey the law, as some interpreters have assumed. His rejection of the practical syllogism was not necessarily a prescription for civil disobedience.

On the other hand, he did attack the notion that ungodly ministers and magistrates could dictate the conditions under which the true saints could operate. By his standards most churches had hypocritical ministers who preached heretical sermons to congregations of hypocrites. The time had come for the small band of true saints to throw off the control of the ungodly.

Such convictions did not breed moderation, and Wheelwright's rhetoric quickly became inflammatory. Wheelwright called upon the saints to participate in an apocalyptic battle. He identified those ministers and magistrates who lived under a covenant of works as part of the army of the Antichrist; they were Pharisees and hypocrites who had usurped God's place in his own temple and who were resisting the second coming of Christ. In rejecting the Gospel to follow Antichrist, they had even sinned against the Holy Spirit, the one sin that could never be forgiven. True Christians had an obligation to confront anti-Christian tyranny. Though their numbers were few, their struggles would hasten the final cosmic confrontation between Christ and his antitype and bring in the kingdom of God.

Underneath Wheelwright's incendiary rhetoric stood a thoroughgoing alternative to the New England Way. Until the apocalyptic confrontation at the end of time, true believers would be few. Even in a so-called Holy Commonwealth, they would have to expect opposition from the established ministers and magistrates, for hypocrisy flourished most where outward holiness was most highly prized. Real saints would have no need for painstaking self-scrutiny to prove their election; they would recognize one another immediately by the quality of their faith and by their opposition to hypocrisy in high places.

Ordinarily such embattled Christians could hope for little more than survival, but Wheelwright was convinced that his were no ordinary times. The *eschaton* was near, the need for earthly kingdoms almost at an end. Saints must band together and confront the creatures of Antichrist, even against impossible odds. Then worldly concerns would vanish in the cosmic conflagration at the end of history.

Wheelwright's rhetoric might have been designed primarily to give identity and purpose to a small party of colonists, but it found more than a little inspiration in the New Testament itself. There, too, small groups of Christians had waited expectantly for the second appearance of Christ, an event that many early Christians also believed would occur during their own lifetimes (e.g., Mark 9:1; I Thess. 4:15–17). There, too, Christians often faced a hostile religious establishment with strong political connections.

Such obvious parallels with New Testament Christianity could not escape the attention of a

Bible-reading society. Both the ministers and their supporters among the magistrates immediately perceived the Antinomians as a serious threat. In their private writings, even such staunch opponents as Winthrop and Shepard reveal that they were attracted to the Antinomian position because it seemed to offer a shortcut around the painstaking self-scrutiny to which they were officially committed.

But against the Antinomian model of Christian behavior, leaders like Winthrop reasserted the assumptions of the New England Way: society ought to be based on Christian values, governed by Christian magistrates, and filled with established, comprehensive churches whose members were both visible saints and solid citizens. These assumptions had governed Christian political thinking since the time of Constantine, and the established orders of Massachusetts Bay and Connecticut were not yet ready to repudiate them. Winthrop was convinced that all of New England was in an implicit covenant with God. New England's fortune as a society would depend upon how faithfully she enforced God's commandments.

In the end the ministers and their allies maintained control of the institutions of government, and the Antinomians were convicted of sedition and disarmed. Those who refused to abandon their position had been banished from the colony by 1638. Their defeat closed the door on any future experimentation in the direction of purer churches; when the Quakers "invaded" Massachusetts a generation later, they found the ranks of the establishment solidly closed against them. Nor were the Baptists any more successful, though the logic of their restriction of baptism to the saints must at least have piqued the curiosity of Christians who used similar logic in restricting access to the Lord's Supper. Henry Dunster, the second head of Harvard College, found it compelling, but once Dunster openly rejected infant baptism in 1654 he was forced to leave the Bay Colony.

The most famous New England Baptist, Roger Williams, had already been banished from the Massachusetts Bay Colony in 1635, before the outbreak of the Antinomian Controversy. Williams' downfall was his refusal to recognize the Church of England as a true church; he did not become a Baptist until after his departure. Along with a few other refugees, he purchased land from the Indians and eventually settled at the head of Narragansett Bay in May 1636, thereby founding the community of Providence.

Williams intended that Providence and the other towns in what soon became the Rhode Island Colony be open to settlers of any religious persuasion. He insisted on complete separation of church and state and full religious toleration. For this reason Rhode Island soon became a haven for religious refugees. Anne Hutchinson settled there briefly in 1638 after her expulsion from the Bay Colony; many of her followers stayed permanently. The Society of Friends used Rhode Island as a base from which to launch courageous missions into hostile territory.

The aftermath of the Antinomian Controversy led to the codification of the New England Way in the Cambridge Platform of 1648 and eventually to the Halfway Covenant of 1662, events that have been described above. After 1662, the defenders of the New England establishment began increasingly to refer to the first twenty years of settlement as a golden age from which they had declined. Now-deceased leaders like Hooker, Shepard, and Winthrop assumed almost mythological stature. The fact that the Antinomian Controversy had almost torn the Massachusetts Bay Colony apart was conveniently forgotten; even John Cotton, whom Hooker and Shepard had never forgiven for his support of Anne Hutchinson, took his place among the revered founders. The New England Way, the result of the efforts of those founders to adapt their English Calvinist heritage to the colonial situation, now took on a status closely akin to that of divine revelation.

Given such an apotheosizing of the first generation, it was inevitable that subsequent generations would suffer by comparison. This was precisely the intent of many ministers in the decades after 1662. They used the romanticized memory of the virtues of the founders to browbeat their congregations. Their sermons lament New England's decline from the high standards of the earliest settlers. An entire genre of such sermons developed, which scholars have come to call "jeremiads" after the Hebrew prophet who so frequently lamented the shortcomings of his contemporaries. Like Jeremiah, the jeremiads also predicted that God would vent his anger on a backsliding people unless that people repented and changed its ways.

The rhetoric of declension found more formal expression in the "Reforming Synod" of 1679. There the gathered clergy proposed a remedy for the sad state of New England morality; each church should publicly renew its allegiance to the covenant that its founders had made when the church was first gathered. The ministers made much of the series of formal covenant renewals that ensued, but the level of religious and moral life did not increase dramatically.

In 1691, following the Glorious Revolution in England, the charter of the Bay Colony was rewritten and toleration formally imposed by the English government. Church membership could no longer serve as a condition for the franchise. Baptists and Quakers could no longer be banished, though they could still be taxed to support the religious establishment. The New England Way could no longer be enforced.

The New England establishment was far from dead at the turn of the eighteenth century, but it had become old-fashioned. The stress on free will and moralism that dominated the Church of England after the Stuart restoration could not be resisted forever, and many of the older churches in cosmopolitan Boston became almost imperceptibly Arminian. Ministers like Ebenezer Gay, Lemuel Briant, and Charles Chauncy preached a liberal Christianity to responsive Boston congregations; their churches and others like them would become Unitarian in the nineteenth century. The efforts of conservatives like Increase and Cotton Mather to halt the movement toward liberalism by bringing churches into closer association with one another were unsuccessful. Increase Mather was forced to resign as president of Harvard College; his replacement was a leading liberal.

Many of the Connecticut clergy were alarmed by the developments in Boston, and their efforts at "consociation" were more successful. The Saybrook Platform of 1708 recognized ministerial associations, though with limited powers, and Yale College, which finally settled in New Haven after some inauspicious wanderings just after its founding in 1701, became a bastion of orthodoxy.

Older controversies were overshadowed by the onslaught of the great religious revivals of the 1740s, an event now known as the Great Awakening. A series of local revivals, in which numbers of people believed they had experienced the converting work of the Holy Spirit and subsequently joined the church, had occurred in Solomon Stoddard's Northampton, Massachusetts, congregation in the early years of the eighteenth century. In 1734 Stoddard's grandson, Jonathan Edwards, presided over more revivals in the same church. He quickly published descriptions of the experiences of the converts, and Christians began taking positions for and against the authenticity of the revivals.

In 1740 the English minister George Whitefield, a friend of John and Charles Wesley but a Calvinist in theology, made his first missionary tour of the American colonies. Though his tour of New England lasted less than two months, the "Grand Itinerant" stirred emotions and provoked conversions wherever he preached. The New Jersey Presbyterian minister Gilbert Tennent quickly followed Whitefield with a tour of his own, and Tennent had similar success. Many shorter tours by local itinerant ministers came in quick succession.

The effects of the revivals stunned many New Englanders. People accustomed to hearing staid sermons by eminently respectable preachers suddenly found themselves overwhelmed by a series of unexpected emotions: fear of the pains of hell, guilt for the heinousness of their sins, despair that no remedy seemed possible, hope that Christ's promises of redemption might apply to them, relief that they could apply those promises particularly to themselves. The doctrine that provoked such emotions was traditional Calvinism, though the rhetoric of the sermons in which that doctrine was contained was often deliberately sensational. But revival fervor swept the majority of the New England churches.

Among the learned ministers, debate raged over the authenticity of sensational conversions. Some attributed them to Satan, others to a special outpouring of the Holy Spirit. But soon a more important question emerged. Given that the revival conversions were authentic, should they be normative? Should Christians who could not point to a decisive "conversion experience," in which they were thrown down to hell before being lifted up to heaven, doubt the validity of their faith?

Such doubting was encouraged by the itinerants themselves, who responded to criticism of their ministries by suggesting that the attacks of their critics showed that the critics had never experienced authentic conversion themselves. How could one who had never experienced the work of the Spirit presume to question God's converting work? Furthermore, how could an unconverted minister possibly be the means of converting his people, and how could he counsel them in the event that they did have an authentic experience of conversion?

All over New England, church members began to debate the normative character of revival conversions. Those who had had such experiences frequently found themselves unable to accept the argument that some conversions might occur gradually and almost imperceptibly, even though the earliest New Englanders had founded their churches on such gradual conversions. Those who had not shared the revival experiences found it hard to understand the intensity of their opponents and felt threatened and defensive. If the revival converts suspected that their own minister was himself unconverted, the tension increased.

As a result of all the turmoil, a party of "New Light" supporters of the revivals lined up against "Old Light" opponents. Many churches split acrimoniously, and new churches sprang up in the aftermath of their struggles. The New England Way was in shambles. One incident encapsulates the aftermath of the Great Awakening: the expulsion of the leading New Light thinker, Jonathan Edwards, from his Northampton pulpit.

After years of preaching conversion sermons and observing their effects on the members of his congregation, Edwards came to the conclusion that the membership requirements of his church were too lenient. Full membership and admission to the Lord's Supper should be restricted to demonstrably converted Christians. His insistence on this point, along with his determination to discipline some of the young people in his congregation for circulating mildly pornographic books, led to his ouster in 1750 from the pulpit he had served for twenty-three years.

At first glance it appears that Edwards was merely requesting a return to the standards of the founders. He was completely convinced that the revival conversions were the work of the Holy Spirit, and he also felt sure that truly con-verted Christians would be able to describe the work of the Spirit upon their hearts. He therefore questioned the value both of the Halfway Covenant and of his grandfather Stoddard's practice of encouraging all members of his congregation to partake of the Lord's Supper in the hope that it might serve as a "converting ordinance."

But in fact Edwards had abandoned the founders' claim to comprehensiveness. The idea of a "Holy Commonwealth," where the government was entrusted to those certified by the church, and the church enjoyed the formal support of the government, formed no part of his argument. The corporate errand of New England was no longer part of God's design; the true church had to be gathered out of the world.

Edwards' cousin and opponent, Solomon Williams, felt he had an equal claim to the tradition of the founders. Though the church no longer required a formal relation from prospective members, did it not apply the "judgment of charity" to the evidence of their behavior and their willingness to make a profession of faith? Short of a special revelation to the church from God himself, was not outward appearance, visible sainthood, the best evidence for inward regeneration?

Williams' claim was obviously flawed, for the requirement of a relation had been from the start a distinctive mark of the New England Way. But the controversy illustrates the impossibility of returning to the piety of the founders. If the establishment, in this case the majority of the Northampton church members, was no longer willing to restrict church membership to those who grounded their Christianity on the experience of the work of the Spirit, then the true saints would have to separate from the world. If the saints could not lead, they would have to withdraw.

After the upheavals of the Great Awakening, New England Puritanism had lost any recognizable form. But the institutions established by the founders survived for many years more. Although both the liberal and revivalistic factions generally supported the revolutionary cause, the established churches showed little enthusiasm for relinquishing government support. Connecticut did not completely disestablish her churches until 1818, when a coalition of Baptists, Methodists, Episcopalians, and political Jeffersonians voted an antiestablishment governor into office. New Hampshire followed a year later. Massachusetts held out another fourteen years, finally following suit in 1833. By then the New England Way was but a memory.

BIBLIOGRAPHY

Emery Battis, *Saints and Sectaries: Anne Hutchinson and the Antinomian Controversy in the Massachusetts Bay Colony* (1962); Sacvan Bercovitch, *The Puritan Origins of the American Self* (1975); Timothy Breen, *Puritans and Adventurers: Change and Persistence in Early America* (1980); Richard Bushman, *From Puritan to Yankee: Character and the Social Order in Connecticut, 1690–1765* (1967); John Demos, *Entertaining Satan: Witchcraft and the Culture of Early New England* (1982); Norman Fiering, *Moral Philosophy at Seventeenth-Century Harvard: A Discipline in Transition* (1981).

David D. Hall, *The Faithful Shepherd: A History of the New England Ministry in the Seventeenth Century* (1972), and, as ed., *The Antinomian Controversy, 1636–1638: A Documentary History* (1968); Charles Hambrick-Stowe, *The Practice of Piety: Puritan Devotional Disciplines in Seventeenth-Century New England* (1982); Alan Heimert, *Religion and the American Mind, from the Great Awakening to the Revolution* (1966); David Leverenz, *The Language of Puritan Feeling: An Exploration in Literature, Psychology, and Social History* (1980); Kenneth Lockridge, "The History of a Puritan Church," in *New England Quarterly*, 40 (1967); Ernest Lowrie, *The Shape of the Puritan Mind: The Thought of Samuel Willard* (1974); Paul Lucas, *Valley of Discord: Church and Society Along the Connecticut River, 1636–1725* (1976).

J. F. Maclear, "New England and the Fifth Monarchy: The Quest for the Millennium in Early American Puritanism," in *William and Mary Quarterly*, 3rd. ser., 32 (1975); Robert Middlekauff, *The Mathers: Three Generations of Puritan Intellectuals, 1596–1728* (1971); Perry Miller, *The New England Mind*, 2 vols. (1939, 1953), and, as ed., with Thomas H. Johnson, *The Puritans: A Sourcebook of Their Writings*, 2 vols. (1963); Edmund Morgan, *The Puritan Dilemma: The Story of John Winthrop* (1958); Robert Pope, *The Half-Way Covenant: Church Membership in Puritan New England* (1969); Darrett Rutman, *Winthrop's Boston: Portrait of a Puritan Town, 1630–1649* (1965) and *American Puritanism: Faith and Practice* (1970).

George Selement and Bruce Wooley, eds., *Thomas Shepard's "Confessions"* (1981); David Stannard, "Death and Dying in Puritan New England," in *American Historical Review*, 78 (1973); William Stoever, *"A Faire and Easie Way to Heaven": Covenant Theology and Antinomianism in Early Massachusetts* (1978); Baird Tipson, "How Can the Religious Experience of the Past Be Recovered? The Examples of Puritanism and Pietism," in *Journal of the American Academy of Religion*, 43 (1975); Williston Walker, *The Creeds and Platforms of Congregationalism* (1893; repr. 1960); John Winthrop, *History of New England*, James Savage, ed. (1853); Larzer Ziff, *The Career of John Cotton: Puritanism and the American Experience* (1962).

[*See also* CALVINIST HERITAGE; CALVINIST THEOLOGICAL TRADITION; *and* IMPACT OF PURITANISM ON AMERICAN CULTURE.]

CONGREGATIONALISM FROM INDEPENDENCE TO THE PRESENT

Mary K. Cayton

SOMETIME during the late eighteenth century the New England churches, which had been founded on the tenets of Calvinism in theology and the principle of localism in church government, began to evolve into what became modern Congregationalism. Until the time of the Great Awakening, Puritanism as embodied in the churches of "the New England way" was virtually without rival for the religious loyalties of most New Englanders. Beginning with the Awakening, however, dissenting religious groups proliferated, especially on the frontier, and they eventually forced the members of the old establishment to redefine themselves in contradistinction to the newer sects.

What had been features of "the church" of New England were refined and transformed in the crucible of religious controversy. In the process New England Puritanism as a recognizable entity died, and the modern denomination of Congregationalism was born. Centered in the Northeast and northern parts of the Midwest, Congregationalism has remained localist in its orientation, but not parochial, adapting both theology and social orientation to the conditions of life in an increasingly urbanized world.

FROM CHURCH TO DENOMINATION: CONGREGATIONALISM IN NEW ENGLAND, 1783–1835

In 1783 the Treaty of Paris ended the American War of Independence. That same year Reverend Ezra Stiles, president of Yale, predicted that America's religious future would lie in the hands of three sects—Congregationalism, Presbyterianism, and Episcopalianism. At that time his observation was eminently reasonable: Congregationalism was the religious persuasion of most of New England, Presbyterianism of the Middle States, and Episcopalianism of the South. What Stiles could not have known in 1783, however, was that the Revolutionary War was only the beginning of a half-century of social revolution in American manners and mores, in which Congregationalism found itself transformed into a national denomination competing with others for influence.

At the end of the war Congregationalism was confined almost exclusively to New England, with its position in Massachusetts, Connecticut, and New Hampshire established by law. Though dissenting sects, most notably Baptists, had been growing in numbers and political leverage since the Great Awakening in the 1730s and 1740s, William Warren Sweet has estimated that only about 16,500 out of a total New England population of 1,090,000 belonged to the dissenting Baptist and Episcopalian churches or Quaker meetings in 1783. Congregational churches outnumbered Baptist, the next most populous group in the region, by more than five to one.

Despite its well-entrenched position, there were also clear signs that New England Congregationalism was in trouble. The social and economic disorganization of the Revolution had resulted in a decline in religious practice and in financial support of religious institutions in settled areas. And while frontier areas such as New Hampshire, Vermont, and the territory that later became Maine saw a rapid growth in the number of Congregational churches, sectarian growth among Free Will Baptists, Universalists, Christians, Shakers, and others was nearly as rapid, and in few cases did Congregational church growth keep pace with frontier population growth.

Another effect of the ideological upheaval of the revolutionary period was the spread of natural theology and rationalist philosophy. Ethan Allen's *Reason, the Only Oracle of Man* (1784) and Thomas Paine's *The Age of Reason* (1794–1796) were more extreme expressions of a secularly oriented tendency to regard traditional theology and religious institutions as at best instruments for the maintenance of social order. To the Congregational clergy, whose portrayal of the new United States as a chosen nation transformed the Revolution into a sacred cause, the situation in postrevolutionary New England seemed grave indeed. The falling away from religion seemed to threaten the very survival of the nation.

The established clergy's perception that the moral foundations of the "city upon the hill" were rotting was exacerbated by a rising chorus of dissenting voices, both religious and political. Following the war Baptists and other dissenting sects stepped up their efforts toward disestablishment in the three states where establishments still remained. Laws permitting Episcopalians, Baptists, Quakers, and Methodists to "sign off" —that is, to designate their taxes for the support of their own denominations—were liberalized; and by the 1790s these newly legitimized religious differences began to take shape as clear political differences as well. Religious dissenters began to affiliate with the Democratic-Republican party, which in New England stood in opposition to the conservative, wealthier—and predominantly Congregational—interests represented by the Federalist party. In a society where pluralism of belief was not accepted as the norm, political dissension was yet another cause for concern over the moral soundness of the state.

By the late 1790s the Congregational clergy, feeling besieged and on the verge of crisis, expressed its anxiety in the form of jeremiadic sermons warning of civil decline and moral disorder. The clergy's discomfort crystallized from 1798 to 1800 in an outcry against the conspiracy of a secret political organization whose members were purported to be rationalist in belief and dedicated to the overthrow of all religion and legitimate social order. The Bavarian Illuminati, as they were called, were opposed chiefly by Jedidiah Morse, a Congregationalist minister from Connecticut then settled in Charlestown, Massachusetts. Morse's campaign to bring to light this "conspiracy" of infidel philosophers coincided with heated political debate between Federalists and Jeffersonians over an alliance with rationalist, revolutionary France. Morse's revelation of the conspiracy in a sermon on Fast Day 1798 seemed to many to explain the rise in democratic sentiment, the subversion of true authority, and the decay of true religion that Federalists believed plagued the early American republic.

Congregationalism's most notable response to the fragmenting tendencies of postrevolutionary society was the Second Great Awakening. It resulted nationwide in far more Baptist and Methodist conversions than Congregational; nevertheless, the movement profoundly affected the organization and theological orientation of Congregationalism. In a narrow sense, the New England version of the Awakening encompassed a series of revivals in the late 1790s and early 1800s. In a larger sense, however, these revivals symbolized a process of religious revitalization and social reorganization that did not play itself out until about 1830.

The Awakening arose largely in response to the lack of clear-cut, authoritative institutional structures and codes of behavior. As the democratic revolution gained momentum and rendered traditional forms of social organization outdated, Calvinist Congregationalism began to create in the name of a revitalized Puritanism new, voluntary organizations for the extension of "true" religion and morality.

The Awakening sprang from two major impulses that colored the entire period of Congregational reorganization (1795–1835): the effort to extend Congregational doctrine and polity to new frontier areas through intensive missionary efforts, and the crusade to revitalize emotionally and theologically the existing core of New England Congregational culture through revivals of religion. Missionary efforts on the frontier began in June 1774, when the Congregational General Association of Connecticut voted to raise funds and send missionaries to wilderness settlements of New York and Vermont. The project foundered during the war, but by the early 1790s interest in missions had revived. In 1792 the General Association established a committee to coordinate the efforts of itinerant evangelists on the frontier; in 1798 it formally organized the Missionary Society of Connecticut. The society's purpose was to care for the spiritual needs of the Connecticut emigrants now pouring northward and westward. Massachusetts followed suit in 1799 with the Massachusetts Missionary Society, and New Hampshire organized its own missionary society in 1801. This new interest in missionary activities was accompanied by a series of scattered and sporadic revivals—in Boston in 1790, in various New England locations after 1792, and in western New York by 1798.

The frontier missionary campaign and the isolated revival impulses that accompanied it came together in the first decade of the new century in a flowering of interrelated organizations to improve morals, revive religious fervor, spread humanitarian benevolence, and extend the Gospel. The diffuse anxiety the clergy expressed in jeremiads translated itself into a plethora of voluntary organizations designed to deal with the rising moral threat to the republic. The decade from 1800 to 1810 saw an incredible flurry of activity among New England Congregationalists with the formation of dozens of missionary, tract, and education societies. These organizations established a strong tie between personal piety as experienced through revivals and the support of denominational expansion into new territories. Moreover, they encouraged the pursuit of voluntarism as the principal means of increasing popular religious involvement and promoting individual virtue. New England Congregationalism, whose hallmark up until this time had been its localism, now began to be characterized by a network of regional organizations designed to promote denominational expansion via personal piety.

The following decade saw these local and state voluntary associations join forces to form organizations that purported to be national in scope, although their energies were mainly confined to areas of Congregational or Presbyterian hegemony. The new benevolent societies were, in many cases, interdenominational. Presbyterians and Congregationalists engaged in a number of cooperative efforts, including the American Education Society (1815), the American Bible Society (1816), the American Colonization Society (1817), and the American Temperance Society (1826). While the influence of these organizations was concentrated in New England, New York, and regions settled by emigrants from those areas, the formation of this "benevolent empire" transformed the Congregational sense of mission permanently from a local to a national one.

Missionary societies such as the American Board of Commissioners for Foreign Missions, founded in 1810 by several students from Andover Theological Seminary, also broadened the denominational sense of mission. The ABCFM was organized as much to evoke religious fervor and unity at home as to evangelize the heathen, and it exemplified the tendency to use voluntarism as a means of promoting ideological and social solidarity in a fragmenting culture. The ABCFM sponsored missions to places as diverse as India, the Sandwich Islands (later Hawaii), and Palestine before 1830, but perhaps its most important function was the involvement of the minds of a large number of Congregationalists in denominational concerns that transcended the local.

Missionary efforts abroad assumed heightened importance at home in direct proportion to the perceived threat from a dissident faction within Congregationalism itself—the liberal wing of the church that in time became known as Unitarianism. Unitarianism emerged gradually in the parishes of eastern Massachusetts in the late eighteenth century, as liberal Congregationalists adapted the natural theology that arose from Enlightenment rationalism to the Puritan tradition, emphasizing ethics and a rational understanding of Scripture. Their principal difference with the more "orthodox" Congregationalists, as the Calvinistic tradition had come to be known, lay in their denial of the divinity of Jesus Christ (hence the name Unitarian, signifying a belief in one person possessing supreme divinity) and their denial of the necessity for conversion. Arminian in their orientation, liberals believed that individuals cooperated in the process of their salvation through the cultivation of moral attitudes and behaviors. Until the beginning of the nineteenth century, no formal distinction existed between this eastern liberal wing of the church and the moderate and conservative wings of western Massachusetts and Connecticut. Moderates were those who had condemned the excesses of the Great Awakening while continuing to preach traditional doctrine and adhere to traditional ideas regarding church polity.

CONGREGATIONALISM

Their allies against religious liberalism were the more conservative followers of Jonathan Edwards' student Samuel Hopkins, whose New Divinity conflated Enlightenment rationalism, revivalistic fervor, and Calvinist doctrine to produce a theology that defined all sin as self-love and conversion as the transformation of the will to a state of disinterested benevolence. With the advent of the Second Great Awakening and the foundation of the benevolent and missionary societies that accompanied it, there arose among both moderate and conservative Congregationalists a movement to distinguish themselves from the liberals.

The key figure in this movement was the same Jedidiah Morse who had launched the crusade against the Bavarian Illuminati. In 1805 he extended his war against the forces of infidelity to the rationalists within his own church by leading the fight against the appointment of a liberal, Reverend Henry Ware of Hingham, Massachusetts, to the Hollis Professorship of Divinity at Harvard College. Morse's *True Reasons on Which the Election of a Hollis Professor of Divinity in Harvard College Was Opposed at the Board of Overseers* (1805) was both a defense of the conservative opposition to the appointment and a warning against the liberal tide within Congregationalism. Not only did the conservatives lose the battle over the professorship, but in 1810 the presidency of Harvard College was lost as well to an avowed liberal, Reverend John Thornton Kirkland.

From this time on the conservatives, led by Morse, began self-consciously to reject affiliation with the liberals. In 1808 a coalition of moderates and of conservative Hopkinsians founded Andover Theological Seminary as an orthodox alternative to liberal-dominated Harvard. Other orthodox colleges in Massachusetts included Williams (1793) and Amherst (1821), founded to provide an appropriately orthodox theological education, especially for indigent young men intent upon entering the ministry. In Boston, the liberal stronghold, a group of Hopkinsians organized Park Street Church (1809) as an alternative to the city's Arminian churches. Hostilities reached their zenith in 1815 with the publication of a tract by Morse entitled *Review of American Unitarianism,* which accused the liberals of infidelity. Exclusion of avowed liberals from orthodox pulpits continued until, by the early 1820s, it had become clear to all that a schism had oc-

curred. In 1825 Unitarian ministers formally recognized the situation, forming the American Unitarian Association.

In the charged, controversial atmosphere that surrounded the transformation of the New England Congregational church into two separate denominations, Congregationalism and Unitarianism, the benevolent societies and missionary organizations played a crucial role. Unitarian reluctance to enter wholeheartedly into the moral reform measures advocated by evangelicals offered apparent confirmation that the group espoused unchristian attitudes. Moreover, Unitarians seemed to orthodox leaders to be unconcerned with the secular and grasping tendencies of the period, a perception reinforced by the fact that Unitarians dominated the positions of wealth and influence in the commonwealth. By not urging personal transformation in a conversion process, Unitarians seemed to be endorsing the decrepit state of public morals and to be undermining the one means available for ensuring national morality.

The career of Lyman Beecher, the most significant Congregational evangelist of the period, illustrates the progress of the Second Great Awakening in Congregationalism from personal revival to organizing impulse to instrument of denominational self-definition. Beecher, the son of a blacksmith, was born in Connecticut in 1775. Converted in one of Timothy Dwight's Yale revivals, he was ordained in 1799. For the next twenty-seven years he served as pastor of Congregational churches in East Hampton, New York, and Litchfield, Connecticut. His theology was of the "new school," emphasizing the sinfulness of humankind, the necessity for conversion, and the evidence of conversion in benevolent activity. A revivalist of great power, Beecher channeled the religious impulses he generated into moral reform societies bent on effecting political change. His fervor resulted in the formation of the Connecticut Society for the Promotion of Good Morals, an instrument for dealing with the growing prevalence of vices such as drinking, dueling, and breaking the Sabbath. Called to the pastorate of Boston's Hanover Street Church in 1826, Beecher used his pulpit to promote benevolent activity, participation in Sunday schools and young men's societies, and theological education for indigent young men as ways of extending the influence of a denomination that increasingly defined itself by opposition to Unitarianism.

At first, ministers like Beecher were greatly discomfited by the rising agitation of dissenters for disestablishment. Identifying the fate of the republic with the fate of its churches, they foresaw only an increase in irreligiosity as the result of the severing of ties between church and state. As voluntarism took root as the principle underlying the new evangelical denominationalism, however, disestablishment suddenly appeared as a way of transforming lukewarm conformity to true religious fervor. By the time Connecticut Baptists, Methodists, and Episcopalians succeeded in including in the new state constitution of 1818 a provision for disestablishment, the Congregational clergy had come to believe that the severing of the church-state bond need not mean the abandonment of the Christian mission of the nation. New Hampshire's Toleration Act, passed the following year, effectively provided for disestablishment there as well.

Massachusetts was the last state to abolish a religious establishment—by means of a constitutional amendment in 1833—but not without complicated legal disputes. As a result of the Congregational-Unitarian controversy, factions —usually orthodox—often seceded from congregations to form churches of their own. In 1820 the Supreme Court of Massachusetts dealt with the question of who owned the parish property of these fractured congregations, the church members who seceded or the society and parish who remained. In the important "Dedham decision," Chief Justice Isaac Parker, a Unitarian, ruled that a church separating from its parish for any reason lost its existence in the eyes of the law, forfeiting not only all church property but its status as an established church. The Congregational churches emerged as losers: eighty-one churches, with 3,900 communicants, were disenfranchised, leaving behind property valued at $600,000. Following the decision, orthodox churches became far less averse to the breakdown of the parish system and to disestablishment in general. By 1833 the Massachusetts establishment was abandoned, with only the Unitarian stronghold of Suffolk County opposing the disestablishment amendment.

With disestablishment and the firm establishment of the principle of voluntarism, the transformation of Congregationalism from official church to denomination was complete. No longer would the church maintain moral order through a position mandated by state law. Rather, in the tumult of the new laissez-faire democratic society that was the legacy of the Revolution, Congregationalism, in cooperation with like-minded denominations, would compete for the souls of individuals and for control of the republic. The New England Congregationalists were certainly not ready in 1835 to recognize the moral legitimacy of pluralism in beliefs and values, but there could be no question that by then they had come to accept denominationalism as a fact of life and had done so with some enthusiasm.

EXTENSION WESTWARD: THE EMERGENCE OF CONGREGATIONALISM AS A NATIONAL FORCE

The impetus to denominational organization came not only from the incipient challenge of pluralism within New England, but also from the challenges of westward expansion. On the frontier the failure to establish any church and the rise to prominence of Methodists and Baptists meant that Congregationalism had to alter some of its traditional assumptions about social organization and church polity if it were to flourish there. In addition, some not-so-intentional innovations in doctrine, partly in response to questions raised by western revivalism, led to a permanent theological reorientation of Congregationalism.

The first missionary efforts of Congregationalism, directed at emigrants from Connecticut and Massachusetts in the 1790s, are best viewed as attempts at extending established forms of doctrine and polity to a population already receptive to them. It rapidly became clear, however, that New England Congregationalism, relying as it did on a homogeneity not common in frontier populations and on the compact organization of the town or village pattern of settlement, did not readily lend itself to large-scale expansion. Moreover, the loose-knit character of Congregational church discipline made coordinated expansion efforts difficult.

Recognizing these problems, New England Congregationalists in 1801 entered into a Plan of

Union with Presbyterians for the evangelization of the West. The two denominations resembled each other doctrinally, both expressing adherence to the Westminster Confession, the doctrinal statement of Reformed British Protestantism, issued by the Westminster Assembly in 1643–1645. Connecticut Congregationalism, whose "consociation" form of church government had relied on ministerial associations to enforce church discipline and regularize church practice, had also long resembled Presbyterianism in its form of polity. As early as 1791, delegates from the Presbyterian General Assembly and the General Association of Connecticut had begun to attend regularly one another's sessions; after 1794 these delegates had full voting power. When Jonathan Edwards the younger, president of Union College in New York and representative of the Presbyterian General Assembly to the General Association of Connecticut, proposed a missionary union of the two groups, his idea was quickly adopted. In an atmosphere of concern over the spread of heretical tendencies, infidelity, and immorality, doctrinal unity enabled the two groups to overcome what differences in traditions and polity divided them.

The Plan of Union forged an alliance between Congregationalists and Presbyterians in which each agreed to promote cooperation and forbearance among the separate polities in the interest of the spread of doctrinal orthodoxy. On the western frontier, where there might not be sufficient numbers of either denomination to form a separate church, the two groups might form a common church. The pastor might be of either denomination, and the church might vote to affiliate with either the local presbytery or the local general association. Church disputes would be referred first to the presbytery or council to which the minister belonged, then, if necessary, to a council composed of equal numbers of Presbyterians and Congregationalists. In mixed churches, standing committees of members of both persuasions administered discipline, with appeal to presbyteries or associations possible in cases of disagreement. Thus the new churches west of the Hudson River became "presbygational" in character.

The plan was designed to advance the cause of Christianity rather than that of any particular denomination, but over time it became apparent that Presbyterianism benefited more from the union than did Congregationalism. Williston Walker, a historian of Congregationalism, has estimated that in the period the plan remained in effect (1801–1852), approximately two thousand churches in western New York, Ohio, Illinois, and Michigan that had been Congregational in origin and usage became Presbyterian. Ironically, the reasons for Presbyterianism's success on the frontier lay in the rationale that had persuaded Congregationalists to adopt the plan in the first place. The presbytery as a form of church government met the needs of the widely scattered western settlements better than the more loosely organized associations did. Moreover, the more firmly established denominational consciousness of Presbyterianism, a product of its more centralized ecclesiastical structure, overpowered the localist, parish orientation of the Congregational tradition. The result was a strong tendency of Presbyterianism rather than Congregationalism to color the usage of frontier churches born of the Plan of Union.

The formal union also bore fruit in the activities of the many interdenominational benevolent societies that flourished in the West. The American Home Missionary Society (1826), for example, was instrumental in the large-scale evangelization of the West. The American Sunday School Union (organized 1824) and the American Bible Society, though Presbyterian in origin, for a period of time also served Congregational interests. The American Education Society, founded by Congregationalists to provide funds for indigent youth to receive training for the ministry, opened its ranks early in its history to Presbyterians. The insistence of both denominations on an educated ministry led to the founding of a number of Plan of Union colleges and seminaries, such as Hamilton in New York (1812), Western Reserve in Ohio (1826), and Illinois (1829) and Knox (1837) colleges in Illinois.

The Plan of Union operated with relative success for thirty-six years, until social and theological differences stemming from the Awakening on the frontier led to its partial dissolution in 1837. The controversy that destroyed it centered on certain "new measures" employed in revivals in western New York and on a new theology that seemed to many conservatives to verge on Arminianism. The results were not only a split between the two cooperating denominations, but also schisms within both. The catalyst for the controversy was a Presbyterian—the prominent frontier revivalist Charles Grandison Finney.

Finney's "new measures" swept upstate New York in the 1820s. Explicitly rejecting the Hopkinsianism at the base of much Congregational theology, Finney preached a doctrine that came to be known as "perfectionism" and that seemed to Hopkinsians to be nothing short of Arminianism. He believed that human beings not only might assist in the process of their own conversions through participation in carefully contrived "measures," but might actually achieve a state of perfection on this earth by the grace of God. Finney's position seemed to more conservative elements within both denominations to encourage hyperemotionalism, especially among the lower orders, who, it was thought, took their conversion as license to revolt against their betters anyhow. Within Presbyterianism, two factions began to develop over the issue of Finneyite "measures." The New School wholeheartedly embraced Finney's position as starting up the flames of vital religion, while the Old School believed that Arminian theology had fueled the fires of revivalism until they burned unchecked. (The latter eventually severed ties with Congregationalism because of the "tainted" new doctrines and practices.)

Within New England Congregationalism, controversy also arose concerning both Finney's technique and his theology. Congregationalists had long advocated a style of revivalism that was marked by strict decorum and that rejected as dangerous the use of the anxious bench, loud prayer meetings, protracted night meetings, and "promiscuous assemblies" (meetings where both men and women were present and to which women spoke). They had also opposed itinerancy, a practice common among Methodists and Baptists and one increasingly employed by the western Presbygationals, who licensed evangelists as home missionaries to areas without churches. By 1826 Finney's opponents in western New York acted to put a stop to the revivalist's "excesses" by appealing to New England leaders, particularly Lyman Beecher and Asahel Nettleton, for help in squelching the "new measures."

In July 1827 a meeting was arranged between Finney and Beecher in New Lebanon, New York. Beecher intended to use the encounter as an oc-

casion to bring Finney back into line with orthodox Congregational practice, but the meeting ended bitterly. Beecher's attempt to tone down Finney was motivated in part by a desire to avoid a schism within the ranks of Congregationalism. The denomination had been driven by revivalism to the edge of explicitly Arminian theology, and the Beecherites feared the potential effects of a connection between that theology and "new measures."

The leader of the new theology (called the New Haven theology, after the place where it had originated) was Nathaniel William Taylor, Dwight Professor of Didactic Theology from 1822 to 1857 at the newly organized Yale Divinity School. Taylor's revisionist views of Edwards' experiential, Calvinist theology asserted that man's utter depravity consisted in his own choice of some chief good other than God. "Certainty with power to the contrary" became the watchword of a viewpoint that Taylor articulated for the clergy in *Concio ad Clerum* (1828): the circumstances of human nature were such that man would sin, but he had the power not to do so. Beecher himself was sympathetic to Taylor's position, but a number of the Congregational clergy grew alarmed at his willingness to redefine the concept of utter depravity almost out of existence, thereby opening the door to unrestrained Arminianism.

The result was schism. Responding to the New Haven theology and *Concio ad Clerum,* the Hopkinsian Congregationalists under the leadership of Bennet Tyler, the former president of Dartmouth College and pastor of the Second Congregational Church of Portland, Maine, formed a pastoral union in 1833. Its purpose was to found a new seminary to block the inroads of the New Haven theology. Hartford Theological Seminary opened in 1834, with Tyler serving as its first president.

Old School, or conservative, Presbyterians, equally disturbed about Finneyite "new measures" and the New Haven theology, accused Yale professors of subverting orthodoxy by their denial of the doctrine of utter depravity. Beginning in 1831 they initiated among those affiliated with presbyteries a series of heresy trials that eventually extended to the arraignment of the president of Lane Seminary, Lyman Beecher, before a presbytery in Cincinnati in 1836. In 1837, when the conservative faction finally gained control over the Presbyterian General Assembly, the Old School took punitive measures against the liberals, severing its relationship with the jointly run American Home Missionary Society and the American Education Society and expelling from the church three synods from New York and Ohio. Finally, fearing the taint of moral infection from the New Haven theology, they dissolved the bond with Congregationalism created in the Plan of Union. This action marked the beginning of the end of Presbyterian-Congregational cooperation in the West, although New School Presbyterians, themselves retroactively expelled from the assembly for their cooperation in the Plan of Union, continued to adhere to it as they reorganized separately from Old School men.

The deathblow to the Plan of Union was finally struck by Congregationalists. In the West, beginning in the 1830s, growing resistance to the Plan of Union form of church government resulted in an increasing number of churches that were, from the very beginning, Congregational in polity. State associations began to rise in Plan of Union territories, beginning with New York in 1834. In areas where denominational competition was particularly fierce, identification with a particular form of polity began to override the cooperation that had resulted from similarities in doctrinal positions.

What accounts for the rebirth of denominationalism among Congregationalists during this period? One explanation might be that the proliferation of doctrinal positions within both Congregationalism and Presbyterianism destroyed the basis for the Plan of Union, leaving polity the only sure mark of denominational identity remaining. Another impetus for the movement toward separation may have been the growing tension of sectional dispute. Presbyterianism, a national denomination, could ill afford to take strong positions on issues such as slavery that might alienate a large portion of its membership. As the Civil War approached, Congregationalism grew more socially reformist, while Presbyterianism became more rigid in its support of the status quo. Individuals within each denomination expressed discomfort with the public positions taken by the other, especially in western border states.

The move back toward denominationalism within Congregationalism reached its high point in 1852 at the Albany Convention. The first council of Congregationalism as a whole since the Cambridge Synod of 1646–1648, it followed an 1846 convention in Michigan City, Indiana. There a few delegates, mostly from the West, had discussed abrogating the Plan of Union, which still served as a bridge between Congregationalism and New School Presbyterianism. The 1852 convention unanimously abandoned the plan, and the following year the American Congregational Union was organized to promote Congregationalism, especially the building of Congregational meeting houses. The Albany Convention also formed a Congregational Library Association to serve as the storehouse of Congregational literature and as keeper of its heritage. Thus Congregationalism firmly established itself in the minds of its adherents as an entirely separate and independent denomination on a national scale.

CONGREGATIONALISM IN THE ANTEBELLUM ERA: THE CLERGY, WOMEN, PUBLIC ISSUES

The increasing privatization of individual and family religious practice after disestablishment meant that Congregationalism lost its role as a public moral force in a society organized around religious concerns. Nevertheless, interdenominational benevolent reform movements—most notably, antislavery—had significant impact on the public sphere and demonstrated just how strong the influence of American Protestantism remained. If Congregationalism no longer had a privileged status in public life, and membership and practice became largely private matters, its private influence came to embody an emphasis on ethics that was translated into an issue-oriented politics—the church's public legacy to this day. The shift in emphasis from public to private religion had important effects on two groups within the denomination—the clergy and women—and altered permanently the form that its involvement in public issues took.

The clergy experienced a decline in status during this period that is best understood in the context not only of the rise of denominationalism, but also of the democratization of manners and modernization of society that took place in the period following the Revolution. In colonial New England the minister was a member of the educated elite of a region, perhaps the only educated member of a town. He had a privileged status among the people, for he served as a conduit of information and an interpreter of learning of all sorts. With the increase in non-ministerial graduates of New England colleges in the late eighteenth century, he now faced the competition of educated non-clerics who could also claim the status learning accorded them. In addition, as newspapers and roads connected isolated New England towns and made information more accessible, the minister might no longer be looked upon as the only cosmopolite of a particular region. Many might claim to know as much, especially about the increasingly fascinating and influential world of politics. Finally, the general decline in deferential behavior during the period left its mark on ministerial stature. The result was a sharp decline in the public power of the clergy in the late eighteenth and early nineteenth centuries.

The rise of denominationalism also contributed to this decline in subtle ways. Itinerants, many without formal education, changed the popular expectation that ministers ought to be learned; more important in the new view was that clergy be of righteous heart as evidenced by religious conversion. Moreover, as the number of denominations in a particular region proliferated, Congregational ministers lost their privileged status as publicly supported "town ministers" and found themselves in competition with others—at first for hearts and souls only, but later for financial support as well. The trend gave rise to a new tendency among towns to hire clergymen who were compelling speakers, capable of holding the attention of people. The pattern first became evident in the poll parishes of Boston, congregations that survived on their ability to recruit new, paying members. Later small-town congregations developed justifications for luring away articulate or popular ministers from even smaller congregations, a heretofore unheard-of practice, as ministers had been expected to settle for life in one parish. Thus by the early nineteenth century, the clergy became increasingly mobile, with ministers often moving up a career ladder from smaller, poorer parishes to larger, wealthier ones. In the process the minister came less to seem the divinely called patriarch of his people than their employee, a hired hand subject to popular approval.

Increasingly the congregation was likely to be composed mainly of women. By 1835 the percentage of women in the population belonging to the Congregational church was double that of men, the Second Great Awakening among New England Congregationalists having been primarily a feminine phenomenon. What this shift in membership may have meant for ministers increasingly subject to congregational influence is an interesting question. Ann Douglas contends that the dominance in churches of individuals consigned primarily to the private sphere meant that the clergy began to appeal to the emotions rather than to the intellect. Theology during the antebellum period took on a sentimental character, culminating in Horace Bushnell's *Christian Nurture* (1847). This work emphasized the potential goodness of the child rather than his innate depravity, and elevated mothers, the purveyors of this Christian nurture, to a position of prominence within Christianity. In their preoccupation with sentimental religion and individual consolation, the concerns of the ministry came to resemble those otherwise reserved for women in antebellum America.

The large influx of women into the Congregational church may also have been a major impetus for its involvement in public issues. Denied a legitimate place in the public sphere by a cultural philosophy that restricted their role to the domestic sphere, women used churches to agitate on public issues of concern to themselves and their children. Ministers found the role of mother—the "minister within the home"—most acceptable for women, and gradually that role came to include an expanded number of religious activities outside the home as well. The sexually segregated prayer meeting fostered community-wide revivals; maternal associations explored the techniques and implications of Christian child rearing; female "mite" societies supported missionary activity through the contribution of women's "mites" and prayer. In urban settings, benevolent women of wealth founded charity schools, provided shelter for the homeless, and disseminated sacred literature. As Dorothy C. Bass has noted, these benevolent activities outside the home were considered only externalizations of women's natural and primary domestic function, but they led directly into associations of women for extrafamilial purposes, such as the female auxiliary of the American Anti-Slavery Society, founded in 1833.

Despite the inclination of some women to evangelize in the public sphere, Congregationalism throughout the period remained committed to the notion that women's proper role lay in the private sphere. Congregationalists such as Catharine Beecher were instrumental in founding the first female seminaries for women, but these schools existed in order to shape the characters of those responsible for Christian nurture, future teachers and mothers. Even Oberlin College, founded in Ohio in 1833 by Congregationalists as the first coeducational college in the United States, committed itself to women's education only as a means of enabling women to educate others in religious perfection through women's traditional callings. In 1853, after several years of lecturing in the abolition and temperance movements, an Oberlin graduate, Antoinette Brown, became the first fully ordained woman in a recognized American denomination. However, both her ordination and her subsequent career met with enough resistance to suggest that Congregationalism was not yet inclined to welcome women into public positions.

Benevolent movements enjoyed interdenominational support of women as well as men and became the predominant form of church participation in public affairs. The American Temperance Society, begun in Boston in 1826, was organized by men active in missionary movements; by 1836 the American Temperance Union had begun to spread its platform of total abstinence across the country, usually in the wake of revivals. The American Peace Society, founded in 1828 and a successor to the Massachusetts Peace Society (1815), by 1838 had evolved into the New England Nonresistance Society, with involvement in antislavery and women's rights.

By far the most influential movement to spring out of the Second Great Awakening and to involve Congregationalists was the antislavery movement. The idea of African colonization had begun in 1776 with Samuel Hopkins, the originator of the Hopkinsian theology, who advocated the return of former slaves to Africa for the purpose of evangelizing that continent. The American Colonization Society was formed in 1817, and in 1825 the ABCFM instructed its prudential committee to train blacks in its Cornwall, Connecticut, school for missionary work in Africa. By the late 1820s and 1830s, many young white missionaries became suspicious of the American Colonization Society's intentions, having learned that it was supported financially by slaveholders. Their misgivings became the basis for "immediatism" (the call for immediate enfranchisement of slaves), most prominently championed by William Lloyd Garrison and the American Anti-Slavery Society. Though the organization as it evolved was far from a Congregational organ, many Congregationalists, especially in western border states, were by the 1840s strongly antislavery.

The antislavery tenor of Congregationalism led most of its clerics to oppose the Mexican War and many to interpret the Civil War in religious terms. Later the Civil War was seen through the eyes of the Congregational clergy as an instrument of God's wrath wielded against the South for its sins and against the North for tolerating them. It was also seen as God's means of molding the factious and erring people of the antebellum era into an organic nation now prepared to advance God's kingdom on earth. Without a single prominent exception, Congregationalists viewed it as a holy cause. By 1865, with the victory of a chastened North, Congregationalists saw themselves, as did other northern religionists, on the verge of the millennium held out to Americans since the end of the Revolution.

DENOMINATIONAL CONSOLIDATION: CONGREGATIONALISM IN THE POST–CIVIL WAR PERIOD

Elwyn Smith identifies three elements of American denominationalism: a purposive system of executive and promotional agencies; the association of this structure with a particular American religious tradition; and a conservative, sometimes legalistic determination to maintain a distinctive identity in the face of change. In light of this definition, the post–Civil War period might be seen as the heyday of the denominational spirit in Congregationalism.

Beginning in 1865 Congregationalism undertook in a series of national councils to define formally its nature, theology, and denominational organization. Nevertheless, these self-consciously denominational agencies also expressed a wish for unity and cooperation with other denominations. This concern with ecumenism and joint social action among Protestants has been a characteristic of Congregationalism since the Civil War.

Continuing the pre–Civil War tendency to meet in national councils, the Pilgrim Memorial convention met in Boston on 14 June 1865. This collection of 502 representatives of local conferences or associations ended their meeting by issuing the Burial Hill Declaration, a summary of the beliefs and practice of Congregational Christianity in the United States. The only formal statement of faith by American Congregationalists since 1648, it held out the example of federal cooperation as a model for ecumenism and condemned "the division of . . . communities into several weak and jealous societies" as "a sin against the unity of the body of Christ, and at once the shame and scandal of Christendom."

Firmly rooted by this time in a denominational consciousness, Congregationalists at the Pilgrim Memorial convention also recommended the establishment of a permanent national conference. It met for the first time in November 1871, at Oberlin, Ohio, where a constitution establishing the National Council of Congregational Churches as the permanent executive body of Congregationalism was adopted. Meeting triennially, the body was to be the primary agent of Congregational extension. Other moves toward denominational consolidation had included the establishment of a national newspaper, the *Congregational Quarterly,* in 1859, and of new, explicitly Congregational seminaries, Chicago Theological Seminary (1855) and Pacific Theological Seminary at Berkeley (1866).

During the late nineteenth century doctrinal statements were, as Williston Walker has commented, "more important for what is left unsaid than for what is distinctly affirmed," as Congregationalism concentrated on establishing a clear denominational structure. The most emphatic statement of the Oberlin Council was a "Declaration for Christian Unity," in which interdenominational cooperation was seen simply as another version of local congregational cooperation writ large. As with the 1801 Plan of Union, this new manifestation of enthusiasm for church unity could emerge only in an atmosphere in which social action and evangelical extension took precedence over theological distinctions. Such was the case in the post–Civil War North, where pronounced theological distinctions were lost in the glow of victory. In addition, the emergence of a "liberal theology" did more to mute doctrinal discussion among Congregationalists than any other factor, in that it shifted the focus of discussion from proper interpretations of Calvinist orthodoxy to experience-based explanations of the implications of Christian theology for evangelical action.

Horace Bushnell's "progressive orthodoxy" paved the way for this major reinterpretation of the Christian belief system. Bushnell maintained that Scripture and creedal statements were only testimonies to that which lay beyond them. The implication was that doctrinal pronouncements as approximations of the unutterable remain open to reinterpretation in the light of experience. Thus religion itself became self-authenticating, intuitive, experiential. Emphasis shifted from discussions of utter depravity and the ability of individuals to contribute to their own salvation to consideration of the social uses to which Christian theology might be put. It is significant that successive councils after the Civil War made evangelical Christianity, not Calvinism, the basis of church unity and that the "Commission" Creed, a statement adopted by the national council in 1883 and designed to be representative of Congregationalism, had no binding force.

The advent of Darwinism in this period provided a challenge to the "new theology" of humanitarianism and divine immanence that Bushnell had begun to articulate, and evolutionism ended up shaping Congregational theology in significant ways. Though Mark Hopkins, the president of Williams College, denounced Darwinism as "essentially atheistic," major theologians of the new movement quickly came to terms with Darwinism's challenge to traditional theology. For Henry Ward Beecher, son of Lyman and pastor of Brooklyn's prominent Plymouth Congregational Church, evolution could be seen simply as "God's way of doing things." Theologians such as Newman Smyth (*Old Faiths in New Light,* 1879), Lyman Abbott (*The Evolution of Christianity,* 1892, and *Theology of an Evolutionist,* 1897), and Theodore Thornton Munger (*Through Science to Faith,* 1902) conflated the progressive tendencies of Darwinism and evangelical Christianity, so that the one became the justification for the social reform efforts of the other. The kingdom of God suddenly seemed immanent in natural and social processes.

The first fruits of the revivified evangelical impulse were major missionary efforts in the half-century that followed the Civil War. At first these efforts were strongly denominational in character. Congregationalism led the way with more contributions in proportion to its congregants than any other Protestant denomination. In 1865 the same Congregational general council that issued the Burial Hill Declaration discussed the responsibilities of the Congregational churches for the home evangelization of the West and South. The general council authorized the raising of a large sum to be used in the West for church building and endorsed the efforts of the interdenominational American Missionary Society among the freed persons in founding and staffing schools for blacks in the South. By 1867 the society had 528 teachers in the field, primarily Congregationalists; by 1876 it had been instrumental in founding eight institutions of higher education for blacks, with five directly under Congregational control: Fisk University (1866), Talladega College (1867), Tougaloo University (1869), Straight University (1869), and Tillotson Collegiate and Normal Institute (1876). (Fisk, Talladega, and Tougaloo still exist, though not under Congregational auspices.)

The post–Civil War years also saw a change in women's roles in missionary activity. Before the war the only missionary roles available to women were as missionary wives. Mission boards had sometimes arranged marriages with male missionaries for women who felt called to missionary work. The 1860s and 1870s witnessed the large-scale entry of single women into missionary fields. The Women's Missionary Society of America for Heathen Lands, a nondenominational agency, was formed in 1861 to send single women to foreign missions. In 1868 forty Congregationalist women formed the Women's Board of Missions, a self-governing auxiliary to the ABCFM, and the Congregational Women's Home Missionary Association was formed in 1880 on the same model. These auxiliaries differed from their antebellum counterparts in that

they actually trained women for missionary work and held conventions and conferences to publicize missionary information rather than assuming an exclusively supportive role. These missionary societies provided women with lay leadership roles within the church and paved the way for fuller participation in denominational affairs.

The denominational impulse to evangelize gave rise, as liberal theology came to gain currency within the church, to an interdenominational movement that has come to be called the Social Gospel, or Social Christianity. This pragmatic and issue-oriented "sociological Christianity" emphasized the saving of society rather than of individuals. The ethical ideas at bottom of this progressive theological position included a belief in the dignity of humankind, the eradication of distinctions between secular and religious, the inseparability of personal and social salvation, and the importance of outside forces in character development. Rising concern over heightened class tensions, violent strikes, increasing economic inequality, and the growth of cities forced many Protestant denominations to reexamine their long-standing support of the status quo.

From the beginning Congregationalists were in the forefront of the Social Gospel movement. Andover Seminary pioneered in the discussion of social issues when its journal, *Biblioteca Sacra*, opened its pages to social commentary in 1866. In 1868 Professor John Bascom of Williams College criticized the conservatism of Protestants in a series of articles entitled "The Natural Theology of Social Science." By the 1880s seminaries began to reform their curricula to include courses in sociology, Higher Criticism of the Bible, and pastoral service. Chicago Seminary, Bangor Theological Seminary, Andover, and Hartford all expanded their curricula during these years to accommodate the new "scientific" interests. A graduate program was added at Andover; at Oberlin, Hartford, Andover, and Union, elective systems were instituted before the turn of the century.

The trend toward liberalism in the seminaries was not without its opponents. Five Andover instructors were tried before the seminary's board of visitors, the charges against them brought by alumni who feared a departure from the old orthodoxy. As a result, Professor E. C. Smyth, president of the faculty, was removed from his chair of instruction. (The visitors' decision was set aside in 1891 on technical grounds.) Nor was the Social Gospel the creed of all Congregationalists. In fact, as with most Protestants during the latter part of the nineteenth century, most Congregationalists probably remained dedicated to conservative values, personal piety, and the upholding of the status quo. Nevertheless, the lack of hierarchical organization and the emphasis on education within Congregationalism meant that the Social Gospel could take root and spread quickly. Congregationalists, as Henry F. May has observed, were second only to Episcopalians in early participation in the movement.

Congregational ministers were among the most prominent individuals in the movement. Washington Gladden, "the father of the Social Gospel," was influential in bringing attention to the problems of capital and labor. Cincinnati minister Josiah Strong, like Gladden an admirer of Horace Bushnell's, wrote a bestseller (*Our Country: Its Possible Future and Its Present Crisis*, 1885) that made him a national figure as an advocate of the Social Gospel (as well as, unfortunately, of Anglo-Saxon racial superiority). As organizer of the interdenominational Evangelical Alliance (1886) and the League for Social Service (1898), his advocacy of social reform in the cities was practical, not theological. Strong's and Gladden's efforts led to the appointment of a committee on capital and labor by the Congregational national council in 1892 to investigate the inequities of the nation's economic system.

Congregationalists participated in the establishment of a variety of denominational and interdenominational organizations to deal with the challenge of social change. The 1865 national council, in recognition of the declining percentage of the national population who saw themselves as active church members, recommended a program of home evangelization designed to overcome the class differences between the affluent native-born and the foreign-born, who tended to remain outside the church. One local response to the increasing involvement of the church in social problems was the establishment of the institutional church. It was defined by Edward Judson in 1908 as "a congeries of institutions, which, by touching people on physical, social, and intellectual sides, will conciliate them and draw them within reach of the gospel." A movement away from individual-oriented

schemes of evangelization, the first institutional church was established by Thomas K. Beecher (son of Lyman, brother of Henry) at the Park Congregational Church in Elmira, New York, in 1872. The institutional church made available a variety of social services that reached out into the community. It was not an exclusively Congregational phenomenon but was most utilized among Congregationalists and Episcopalians. By the turn of the century, institutional Congregational churches were reporting six times as many new members as their noninstitutional counterparts.

In urban areas Congregationalist churches increasingly began to cooperate with each other to form citywide missionary societies. In Chicago, for example, the Chicago City Missionary Society, formed in 1883, emphasized industrial education and church extension. In St. Paul, Minnesota, a Congregational union of ten churches provided money and workers for the parish house of the People's Church in 1885. Agencies such as the American Home Missionary Society and the American Congregational Union (organized in 1853 as part of the Formal Congregational rejection of the Plan of Union) began to direct subsidies to the building of urban churches and support of urban missionary societies rather than to frontier and rural churches, as before. Ministerial education too was revised to provide the necessary background in foreign languages for ministries to immigrants.

THE ECUMENIST IMPULSE: CONGREGATIONALISM IN THE MODERN ERA

The organizational beginnings of ecumenism lay in the various interdenominational societies, councils, and agencies formed to spread the Social Gospel. Josiah Strong's pioneering Evangelical Alliance led the way to the formation of such joint efforts as the American Congress of Churches, the Convention of Christian Workers, the Brotherhood of Christian Unity, and the League of Catholic Unity in the 1880s and 1890s. The aim of these groups was to overcome theological barriers that stood in the way of Protestant Christians seeking to form a united front against the evils of industrial America. These loose federations encouraged participants to think in terms of broader and more far-reaching ecumenical movements. In 1905 the Inter-Church Conference on Federation met in Carnegie Hall, New York City, to draw up plans for the Federal Council of Churches. Instrumental in its foundation was Elias B. Sanford, a New England Congregational minister who in 1894 had directed the interdenominational "Open and Institutional Church League" and founded the National Federation of Churches and Christian Workers. In Philadelphia in 1908, the constitution of the Federal Council of Churches was formally approved by delegates from thirty-three denominations. Though its powers were only advisory, its purpose and orientation were clear from the first. A report on "The Church and Modern Industry" was adopted at the first meeting, and a commission on the church and social service was established.

The years after World War I reinforced the Progressive bias of much of the Social Gospel movement. The national council in 1919 vowed to "work for a social order in which there will be none without opportunity to work and in which it will be impossible for idlers to live in luxury and for workers to live in poverty." The Federal Council of Churches and the national council supported such liberal causes as pacifism, labor organizing, the eight-hour day, the minimum wage, collective bargaining, unemployment insurance, and action against racial discrimination. The national council's "Statement on Social Ideals" (1925), a product of a committee of the commission on social service formed in 1913, attacked the profit motive as the basis for social relationships. It was offered to the Federal Council of Churches' denominations for discussion and was used as a model creed by the Reformed church (1926) and the Methodists (1928).

In the 1920s a primary concern with personal morality colored a majority of Congregationalists' visions, reflecting the national tendency to define religion as an exclusively private phenomenon. Like most Protestant denominations, Congregationalists wholeheartedly supported Prohibition and had done so since 1865, when the national council expressed a belief in the connection between temperance and religion. Temperance reform had been incorporated into the missionary effort as well and grew to be a vital plank of the Social Gospel platform. The denominational journal *Congregationalist* (founded in 1849) devoted much space to discussions of the enforcement of the Volsted Act in the 1920s. For many Congregationalists, preoccupied with religion as private experience, this was the sole extent of their involvement in any kind of "social issue." For a vocal minority within the denomination, however, the transformation of the social order remained crucial to their definition of piety. This faction became highly influential in the affairs of the national council.

With social conditions reaching a crisis state during the Depression, Congregationalists acted to transform their educational agency, the Commission on Social Service (renamed the Commission on Social Relations in 1927), into an independent body capable of sponsoring direct social action. Formed at the national council of 1934, the Council for Social Action not only sought to educate the public on race relations, labor, civil liberties, and economic democracy through its semimonthly journal, *Social Action,* but also attempted to support local church study groups that would form community action committees to deal with slums, labor problems, and industrial relations on the local level. Its purpose was "to work toward the abolition of . . . our present competitive profit-seeking economy." The *Congregationalist* affirmed that the formation of the council was in fact "a testimony that the entire Congregational denomination believed in the social gospel."

Paul A. Carter has observed that the Council for Social Action, under Hubert C. Herring, did much for pastoral morale, in that it reinforced the Social Gospel commitments of the clergy against the bourgeois inclinations of the laity on social issues. The formation of the council also marked a further strengthening of the central organization and denominational identity of Congregationalism. This arm of the national council had the ability to take action independent of the individual constituent churches of the denomination. Nevertheless, the existence of the council also pointed to some tension between the neo-liberal Social Gospel concerns of the clergy and the preoccupations of local congregations, who often tolerated leftist clergy viewpoints rather than wholeheartedly endorsing them. Thirty-three percent of the Congregational clergy polled by *World Tomorrow* in 1934 preferred some system of socialism to capitalism; their congregations tended to be drawn from the upper middle class—individuals who had done well under the capitalist system.

The ecumenical movement that had begun as

a result of social concern increasingly picked up momentum in the twentieth century in consequence of a renewed interest in theology. The Congregational tradition of cooperation with other denominations made that church particularly open to ecumenical overtures. As early as 1871 the national council declared its dedication to Christian unity and opposed the spirit of exclusive sectarianism. Because Congregationalists by and large saw themselves as individuals united for a common purpose rather than for the furtherance of specific creedal positions, they had always sought mergers with other groups whose notion of an independent congregational polity was similar to their own.

Proposals for unions had been advanced since the late nineteenth century. In 1886 in Chicago, the council accepted a report that proposed cooperation and merger with the Free Will Baptist churches, a proposal that never reached fruition because of dissension among the Baptists. The merger of Congregationalists with the Methodist Protestant churches and the United Brethren was discussed in conferences and national councils beginning in 1898. Delegates from the three denominations met in Chicago in 1907 to issue an Act of Union to serve as the basis for a new body, the United Churches. A milestone in the movement toward church unity, the agreement was eventually rejected by the Congregational council on the grounds that the three groups held different interpretations of the role of local church autonomy. A proposal for the resumption of an organic union between Presbyterianism and Congregationalism was advanced to both the general assembly of the Presbyterian Church of the United States and the Congregational national council in 1927. Although the council authorized a commission to work toward fulfillment of the plan, no action was taken.

Despite these unsuccessful gestures toward church unity, discussion did produce three successful mergers in the twentieth century. Though differing theologically, ethnically, and socially from the majority of Congregationalists, the merging denominations shared with them a common belief in the independence of local congregations. In 1925 the Evangelical Protestant church, a small pietistic denomination of German and Swiss origin numbering about six thousand and espousing liberal theology and social activism, sought union with the larger Congregational church in order to overcome some of the disadvantages of smallness and isolation in mass society. Two years later a formal merger took place that left local churches free to work out their own relations with state Congregational associations but gave Evangelical Protestant churches seats on the national council of Congregational churches.

In 1931 negotiations with the Christian churches, which had been undertaken in the 1890s, led to their merger with Congregationalism. The Congregational Christian churches, as they were now called, included the churches formed between 1790 and 1810 by Abner Jones, James O'Kelley, and some of the followers of Barton W. Stone. With membership originally drawn from rural areas and groups of lower socioeconomic status, the Christian churches differed from Congregationalists socially but shared certain fundamental beliefs and practices in common: "Both believed in the principle of the local autonomy of churches; both emphasized the freedom of individuals in matters of belief; both expressed their desire for fellowship through regional and national organizations; and in both denominations there was a strong spirit favoring church union" (Fagley and Atkins, p. 357).

In 1957 the union that resulted in the current denominational identity of Congregationalism took place, as the Evangelical and Reformed church merged with the Congregational Christian churches to form the United Church of Christ. The Evangelical and Reformed church, itself formed of a 1934 merger of the Reformed Church in the United States (or the German Reformed church) and the Evangelical Synod of North America, consisted of a gathering of German Pietists. The general synod of that church voted in favor of union with Congregationalism in 1947 despite doctrinal differences. The plan was submitted to local Congregational churches for an advisory vote, and upon receiving 75 percent approval it was accepted by the general council of the Congregational Christian churches, the national body of that denomination, in 1949.

The merger vote produced the one modern instance of schism among American Congregationalists, an action that delayed the official merger of the two denominations until 1957. A minority, fearing that local churches would lose independence if the union were to take place, fought the merger, taking their case to the New

York courts. In their view the bureaucracy arising from the new denomination threatened a loss of power on the part of local congregations and absorption into a larger organizational structure of dubious theological and ecclesiastical character; therefore, the proposed union sacrificed essential elements of Congregationalism and essential rights of local congregations. A 1950 judgment ruled in favor of the dissenting minority, but the case was appealed and the decision reversed in 1952. The minority opposition, with the meeting of the first general synod of the united body in Cleveland in 1957, formed two separate denominations, the Conservative Congregational Conference and the National Association of Congregational Christian Churches. At first these two represented about a hundred local churches; eventually affiliation grew to about three hundred.

Twentieth-century Congregationalism, in keeping with its emphasis on localism in matters of doctrinal interpretation and church polity, has harbored a broad range of theological orientations. In the early part of the century Congregational thought tended to be characterized by the liberal desire to bring the tenets of the Gospel into harmony with modern life and thought. The Depression and the two world wars shook the faith of many Americans in modernism; such thinkers as Reinhold Niebuhr and H. Richard Niebuhr, theologians of the Evangelical Protestant denomination, which merged with Congregationalism in 1925, translated this malaise into Neo-Orthodoxy, the position that Christians must stand in opposition to an evil social order rather than identify with it.

When the United Church of Christ was formed in 1957, the statement of faith adopted was based on the historic confessions of faith of the component churches but remained intentionally broad and open to interpretations. A testimony of faith rather than a creed, the statement contains only seven sentences. According to Roger Lincoln Shinn and Daniel Day Williams, who participated in the preparation of the statement and were invited by the United Church Board for Homeland Ministries to comment upon it, it "does not intend to state the peculiar faith of the people who came together in the United Church of Christ; it aims to state the Christian faith as this church, in conversation with other groups of Christians, apprehends that faith" (1966, p. 28).

Harold E. Quinley, in a study of Protestant clerical positions in 1974, found that United Church of Christ ministers tended to characterize themselves as theological liberals, religious modernists, and social activists. Only in recent years has the denomination's ministry welcomed women to anything approaching full and equal status in its ranks, although Congregationalism has been in the forefront of American Protestant denominations in admitting women to leadership roles. Nine fully ordained women ministered in various capacities in Congregational churches in 1893, but at that time most Congregational seminaries refused to accept them on equal terms with men. Hartford Seminary, the first to open its doors to women (1889), declared that its intent was not to encourage women to enter the ministry; not until 1920 did it drop the requirement that its women students state that they did not intend to enter the ministry.

In the 1910s and 1920s the opening of positions for paid, specialized church workers other than ministers led to the hiring of women to fill positions such as youth worker or social worker, but the introduction of these separate professional roles was long used to justify the exclusion of women from the ministry. Many women who did acquire pastorates did so upon the death of their minister-husbands. In 1952 the United Church Women of the National Council of Churches urged study of the role of women in the church, and the *Christian Century* urged ordination of women. Though women have been admitted to United Church of Christ seminaries with increasing frequency since the 1950s, they still do not enjoy equal access to positions of leadership. Women ministers face longer periods of unemployment, lower salaries, and less opportunity for full responsibility for parishes.

The United Church of Christ reached a peak in membership in 1960, with over 2.2 million members. Since that time the denomination has shown a decline in members as a result both of the schism and of a general decline in membership among liberal Protestant denominations since the mid-1960s, mainly among youth and young adults. The 1985 United Church of Christ report listed a membership of almost 1.7 million, distributed in 6,408 churches, and a clergy of more than ten thousand. About 83 percent of the members today live in urban areas, with the majority concentrated in cities and towns of the Northeast and upper Midwest. Most live in counties where the proportion of United Church of Christ members in the population as a whole is less than 5 percent. They tend to be well educated and upper middle class.

As recently as December 1985 the church renewed its commitment to the cause of ecumenism, entering into a set of accords with eight other Protestant denominations intended to pave the way for an eventual merger of the churches. Liberal in theology and social stance, the United Church of Christ sustains a tradition of cooperation with like-minded denominations while maintaining a sense of local congregational autonomy.

BIBLIOGRAPHY

Aaron Ignatius Abell, *The Urban Impact on American Protestantism, 1865–1900* (1943); Sydney E. Ahlstrom, *A Religious History of the American People* (1972); John A. Andrews III, *Rebuilding the Christian Commonwealth: New England Congregationalists and Foreign Missions, 1800–1830* (1976); Dorothy C. Bass, "'Their Prodigious Influence': Women, Religion and Reform in Antebellum America," in Rosemary Ruether and Eleanor McLaughlin, eds., *Women of Spirit: Female Leadership in the Jewish and Christian Traditions* (1979); Virginia Lieson Brereton and Christa Ressmeyer Klein, "American Women in Ministry: A History of Protestant Beginning Points," in Ruether and McLaughlin (1979); Jackson W. Carroll, Douglas W. Johnson, and Martin E. Marty, *Religion in America: 1950 to the Present* (1979); Paul A. Carter, *The Decline and Revival of the Social Gospel* (1954); Samuel McCrea Cavert, *Church Cooperation and Unity in America: A Historical Review: 1900–1970* (1970); Charles C. Cole, Jr., *The Social Ideas of the Northern Evangelists, 1826–1860* (1954); Nancy F. Cott, "Young Women in the Second Great Awakening in New England," in *Feminist Studies*, vol. 3 (1975).

Henry Martyn Dexter, *The Congregationalism of the Last Three Hundred Years, as Seen in Its Literature*, 2 vols. (1880; 1970); James Dombrowski, *The Early Days of Christian Socialism in America* (1966); Ann Douglas, *The Feminization of American Culture* (1977); Chester A. Ellsworth, "The American Churches and the Mexican War," in *American Historical Review*, vol. 45 (1940); Frederick L. Fagley and Gaius Glen Atkins, *History of American Congregationalism* (1942); Charles I. Foster, *An Errand of Mercy: The Evangelical United Front, 1790–1837* (1960); Lori D. Ginzberg, "Women in an Evangelical Community: Oberlin 1835–1850," in *Ohio History*, vol. 89 (1980); Colin Brummitt Goodykoontz, *Home Missions on the American Frontier* (1939); M. Louise Greene, *The Development of Religious Liberty in Connecticut* (1905; 1970); Clifford S. Griffin, *Their Brothers' Keepers: Moral Stewardship in the United States, 1800–1865* (1960); Nathan O. Hatch, *The Sacred Cause of Liberty: Republican Thought and the Millennium in Revolutionary New England* (1977); C. Howard Hopkins, *The Rise of the Social Gospel in American Protestantism: 1865–1915* (1940); Edward Judson, "The Church in Its Social Aspect," in *The Annals of the American Academy of Political and Social Science*, vol. 30 (1908).

Charles Roy Keller, *The Second Great Awakening in Connecticut* (1942); Rosemary Skinner Keller, "Lay Women in the Protestant Tradition," in Rosemary Radford Ruether and Rosemary Skinner Keller, eds., *Women and Religion in America*, vol. I (1981); Charles B. Kinney, Jr., *Church and State: The Struggle for Separation in New Hampshire, 1630–1900* (1955); Donald G. Mathews, "The Second Great Awakening as an Organizing Process, 1780–1830: An Hypothesis," in *American Quarterly*, vol. 21 (1969); Henry F. May, *Protestant Churches and Industrial America* (1949); William G. McLoughlin, *Modern Revivalism: Charles Grandison Finney to Billy Graham* (1959); *Revivals, Awakenings, and Reform: An Essay on Religion and Social Change in America, 1607–1977* (1978); Donald B. Meyer, *The Protestant Search for Political Realism, 1919–1941* (1960); Jacob C. Meyer, *Church and State in Massachusetts from 1740 to 1833: A Chapter in the History of the Development of Individual Freedom* (1930); Robert Moats Miller, *American Protestantism and Social Issues, 1919–1939* (1958); James H. Moorhead, *American Apocalypse: Yankee Protestants and the Civil War, 1860–1869* (1978).

Joseph W. Phillips, *Jedidiah Morse and New England Congregationalism* (1983); Harold E. Quinley, *The Prophetic Clergy: Social Activism Among Protestant Ministers* (1974); Mary P. Ryan, *Cradle of the Middle Class: The Family in Oneida County, New York, 1790–1865* (1981); Donald M. Scott, *From Office to Profession: The New England Ministry, 1750–1850* (1978); Richard D. Shields, "The Feminization of American Congregationalism, 1730–1835," in *American Quarterly*, vol. 33 (1981); Roger Lincoln Shinn and Daniel Day Williams, *We Believe: An Interpretation of the United Church Statement of Faith* (1966); Elwyn A. Smith, "The Forming of a Modern American Denomination," in *Church History*, vol. 31 (1962); Vernon Stauffer, *New England and the Bavarian Illuminati* (1918); William Warren Sweet, *Religion on the American Frontier, 1783–1850*, vol. 3: *The Congregationalists* (1939); Williston Walker, *A History of the Congregational Churches in the United States* (1894); Barbara Welter, "She Hath Done What She Could: Protestant Women's Missionary Careers in Nineteenth-Century America," in Janet Wilson James, ed., *Women in American Religion* (1980).

[See also CALVINIST HERITAGE; NEW ENGLAND PURITANISM; NINETEENTH-CENTURY EVANGELICALISM; SOCIAL CHRISTIANITY; and UNITARIANISM AND UNIVERSALISM.]

PRESBYTERIANISM

Louis Weeks

THE distinctiveness of Presbyterianism as a branch of Reformed Christianity lies in its way of balancing lay and clerical power, in its representative form of government, and in its inclusive understanding of the nature of the church. In other respects—its confessionalism, its Calvinism, and its evangelical focus on missions and Christian living—Presbyterianism is not significantly different from other Reformed bodies in America.

During the eighteenth century, Presbyterianism emerged as a potent force in American religious life. Especially in the Middle Colonies, from New York to South Carolina, English Puritans and the Scotch-Irish collaborated to form congregations and church courts that became increasingly influential and popular. By the time of the American Revolution, Presbyterianism had come to be identified with the movement for national independence. Since then Presbyterian bodies and personages have remained important in both the theology and culture of the United States. Today the Presbyterian Church (U.S.A.) has more than 3 million members, with congregations in most cities and towns in every state. Smaller denominations of Presbyterians also represent particular traditions and emphases within this wing of Reformed Christianity.

Though Presbyterians share thoroughly the language of Zion common among Western Protestants, certain terms have characteristic use within the communions. A general assembly, for example, is a national governing body in a particular country. A synod is a regional, middle court. A presbytery usually encompasses a specific portion of a state (or contains Presbyterian churches in a metropolitan community). A session governs a particular congregation. A stated clerk serves a higher governing body, such as a synod or an assembly, as the coordinator of meetings but not as a bishop or superintendent.

Though many early Puritans held a more universal than congregational view of the nature of the church, and though Presbyterian congregations existed during the seventeenth century, it was not until 1706 that an organized presbytery was formed in North America. Since by definition Presbyterians depend for government upon presbyteries—regional gatherings of representative leaders—the real start of connectional Reformed Protestantism can be dated from that point.

"The Presbytery," as it was first called, brought together diverse elements among the colonists—English Puritans who had moved into the Middle Colonies, Scots who adhered to the Church of Scotland, Scots who had sojourned in Northern Ireland and came in America to be called Scotch-Irish, and Welsh Calvinists. Dutch, German, and French Reformed Christians joined Presbyterian churches as they formed, though communions of their particular traditions grew up as well. (Actually, Dutch and Scots churches had already existed for decades, but both strains of Calvinists had hailed from establishment traditions. French Huguenots had also formed congregations in New York during the 1680s.)

Francis Makemie, a merchant who had also received ordination as a minister in the Presbytery of Laggan in Northern Ireland, helped gather "the Presbytery" and served as the convenor of their organizational meeting. Makemie, who had arrived in Maryland in 1683, organized particular churches during that very year. He also persuaded other Presbyterian ministers to come to the New World. After the 1706 gathering of the Presbytery, Makemie journeyed to

New York, where he preached in a home and was arrested for leading worship illegally. His incarceration and exoneration have been hailed as milestones in the process that led to religious freedom in America.

Historians of Presbyterianism, especially Leonard Trinterud, have pointed to the plural origins of that presbytery as indicative of the distinctive nature of the communion in America. That British Puritans, with their emphasis on the authority of the Scriptures and the living of the Christian life, united with Scots and Scotch-Irish, folk wedded to the Westminster Standards and focused on doctrinal orthodoxy, meant American Presbyterians melded confessional, biblical, and ethical norms from the very beginning of communal life.

By 1716, American Presbyterians considered that enough congregations existed to constitute the communion as a synod. A general synod was formed, consisting of three presbyteries—in Maryland, Delaware, and New York and New Jersey. Even in its first years, differences among Presbyterians occupied a large portion of the time and energy of the general synod. In 1729 the Adopting Act proved a compromise position between the party of Scots and Scotch-Irish that sought subscription to the Westminster Standards on the part of all ministers and the party from other ethnic sources that considered matters of life-style and biblical teachings most important. (The Westminster Standards included a Confession of Faith, a written document spelling out a covenantal system of doctrine that they believed to have been taught in Scripture; a larger and a shorter catechism; a Book of Order, rules for church government and discipline; and a Directory of Worship, guidelines for praise and public worship.)

The Adopting Act required ministers to declare their "agreement in and approbation of" the Westminster Confession of Faith and the catechisms. If ministers disagreed with portions of the Standards, it would be a matter for the Presbytery to decide whether that difference was essential or superficial.

Colonial Presbyterians united, however, in their respect for education and in their willingness to engage in and support it. While many Presbyterians had to learn the arts and sciences in informal, family settings, institutions did spring up when ministers and their spouses served as teachers of young people and those preparing for the ministry. One pioneering venture was begun by William Tennent in Neshaminy, Pennsylvania. Followers of this pastor-teacher in 1746 opened the College of New Jersey, which later became Princeton College and then Princeton University. Many ministers studied there, and they opened "log colleges" throughout the Middle Colonies patterned on the first one. A number of American universities started this way.

Like all Calvinists, Presbyterians sought a thorough education for their clergy, especially as an article of faith. In fact, most considered literacy of all people important for human accountability to the demands of the Gospel as set forth in Scripture. The proclamation of the Gospel and its application to contemporary life demanded knowledge of God, knowledge of the languages in which the writers of Scripture had worked, knowledge of church history, and knowledge of the world in all its complexity. The Presbyterian log colleges, moreover, prepared ministers for the American milieu by encouraging them to begin new congregations and to evangelize the unchurched.

The new institutions and their adherents also experienced the Great Awakening in the American colonies. Gilbert Tennent imbibed the teachings of Jacob Frelingheusen, a Dutch Reformed pastor, and communicated them to his father, William, in the log college environment. George Whitefield, the English evangelist who witnessed throughout the colonies, and Jonathan Edwards in New England found common spirits among these New Side Presbyterians. Old Side Presbyterians forbade "intrusions" by these evangelicals into their parishes, and the general synod split in 1741. The synod of New York, or New Side, flourished; and soon the Old Side synod of Pennsylvania compromised to permit a reunion in 1758 with room for pro-revival Presbyterians. Through the remainder of the colonial period the Presbyterians grew in numbers and in self-identity. Active missionary endeavors in Virginia and the Carolinas, led by Samuel Davies and others, helped the Presbyterianism flourish.

Colonial Presbyterians worshiped characteristically amid a "Puritan Sabbath" that forbade other activity. The Lord's Supper, celebrated semiannually or at the most quarterly, consisted of a week-long preparation period of examinations, the preaching of a sermon that focused on the solemnity of the event and the action of the Holy Spirit, a fencing of the table to warn the ill-prepared of the dire consequences of their partaking, and the administration of the sacrament to believers seated at table in as many consecutive seatings as necessary. Family worship with reading of the Bible and prayers took place daily among the pious.

Though they constituted a significant body by the time of the American Revolution, Presbyterians were not an established church in any colony. Instead they learned to fend for themselves in a pluralistic environment—a lesson that prepared them to thrive in the atmosphere of the new nation.

Presbyterians generally supported American separation from Great Britain, and most sided forcefully with the revolutionaries. Many Presbyterians, like Benjamin Rush in Pennsylvania and David Caldwell in North Carolina, were stalwarts in the movement for independence. John Witherspoon, a Scot who arrived at Princeton in 1768 to begin service as the president of the College of New Jersey, quickly moved to political leadership as well and served in the Continental Congress for several terms. He became the only minister to sign the Declaration of Independence. Though some Presbyterians remained loyal to Great Britain, the conflict itself was perceived by King George III as "the Presbyterian War." Of the Presbyterians, the Scotch-Irish especially joined the Continental Army.

In 1788 the Presbyterian general synod moved to constitute itself as a general assembly —with four synods and sixteen presbyteries in the new Presbyterian Church in the U.S.A. (PCUSA). The following year, that general assembly began governing the Presbyterians throughout the land. Certain changes were necessary in the Standards, since initial adoption of the Confession of Faith, the catechisms, the Book of Order, and the Directory for Worship had taken place in a colonial environment. Civil magistrates, for example, were now admonished "to protect the church of our common Lord, without giving preference to any denomination of Christians above the rest." Previously, they had been charged with suppressing heresy and keeping the "unity and peace in the Church." That initial assembly sent a delegation to greet newly elected George Washington, first president of the United States; and Presbyterians pledged fealty to him as citizens of the new nation.

Numbers of Scots and Scotch-Irish took exception to such pledges of loyalty and many did not vote in presidential elections subsequently because the new nation did not explicitly declare itself a Christian nation. These Covenanters and Seceders had not joined the general synod either, for they practiced closed communion. Some Seceders had organized a separate presbytery in 1758. Portions of those in both traditions united in the new nation to form the Associate Reformed Church (ARC) in 1782. That body split in the 1820s, but in 1858 most of the ARC Presbyterians joined with many members of the Associate Presbyterian Church (Seceders) to form the United Presbyterian Church of North America (UPNA). By that time the Scottish traditions had become more acculturated, but the UPNA still was comparatively conservative in its theology. It was centered in western Pennsylvania, with strength particularly in surrounding states. Yet another Scots-derived denomination —the Associate Reformed Presbyterian Church (ARP)—arose, with most of its adherents in the South. Other, tiny Presbyterian bodies have existed as well. Thus while the PCUSA was the major, national denomination, it did not represent the affiliation of all Presbyterians, even at its inception. Soon, however, the PCUSA itself divided, and Presbyterians have only recently reunited—in 1983—to form a communion comparable to it.

In the new nation all Presbyterians continued to practice their "Puritan Sabbath," as many streams of Reformed Christianity had developed it. Emphases on Sabbath observance followed from the authority of Scripture, from respect for sober and lengthy worship, and especially from the confluence of natural and moral law. After all, the creation accounts indicate that God rested on the Sabbath (Gen. 2:3) and the moral law required people to "Remember the Sabbath Day, to keep it holy" (Ex. 2:8). Psalms, prophets, and wisdom writings, such as Proverbs, all confirmed the importance of the Sabbath for God's people. Jesus explicitly advocated observance of the Sabbath (Matt. 5:17) and modeled his respect for all to see (Luke 4:16). According to Reformed theology, in which Christology offered perspective on Old Testament and subsequent church activity, the early Christians began Sabbath observance on the first day of the week. Hence contemporary followers should do likewise, and state laws should conform to the natural and moral law. Therefore Presbyterians throughout the nineteenth and early twentieth century gave great attention to maintaining Sunday (or "blue") laws, and they cooperated with Baptists, Methodists, and especially Congregationalists in this enterprise.

The PCUSA and the Congregational Church, colleagues in Calvinism, joined in a Plan of Union in 1801, an agreement by which particular churches could be joined to both denominations and be served by pastors from either. This agreement permitted Presbyterian dominance on the frontier, that part of the West in which presbyteries had already begun to develop—Kentucky, Ohio, and Tennessee. It also explains why Presbyterians remained scarce in New England, where they felt no need to found churches competing with the Congregationalists already there.

In the West also at the beginning of the nineteenth century the Great Revival took place—a movement initiated by Presbyterians but assisting other Protestant denominations more than their own. In the 1780s emotional awakenings had taken place among Presbyterians in Virginia and North Carolina. In 1799, James McGready, a minister in southern Kentucky, offered several "sacramental occasions," communion celebrations that attracted great crowds and created much religious fervor. From that beginning, the revival movement, also called the Second Great Awakening, spread throughout Kentucky and more broadly back toward the seaboard churches from the frontier. In the summer of 1801, Barton Stone, another Presbyterian pastor, organized and led the mammoth Cane Ridge revival, in which more than a score of ministers and thousands of believers gathered in what became the model for the camp meeting in America. Unbelievers by the hundreds experienced conversions and "religious exercises"—falling, barking, "melting" (crying), and many more.

Frontier Methodists and many Baptists thrived on such expressions, and many Presbyterians considered camp meetings obvious works of the Holy Spirit. These Presbyterians were termed New Lights, and their perspective was criticized by other ministers and leaders who sought to retain dignity and order in all worship. Stone and other pro-revivalists founded a sepa-

rate, Springfield presbytery in 1803; but soon those advocating camp meetings divided again. Stone led many Presbyterians into the "Christian movement" that eventually united with ex-Presbyterian "Campbellites," followers of Alexander Campbell, and with restorationists from among the Baptists and Methodists to form the Christian Church (Disciples of Christ). Others from the New Lights joined the Shakers to form a significant part of that communitarian movement. Still others returned to the PCUSA, repenting of their schism.

Simultaneously, other frontier Presbyterians disagreed in Kentucky on the sequence of training for ministers and on the necessity for maintaining certain of the "hard doctrines" of Calvinism. Ministers and leaders of what became the Cumberland Presbyterian Church (CPC) argued that certain Calvinist emphases led people to misunderstand the central message of the Gospel, a word of God's love and mercy for all who repented and believed. They denied the doctrine of double predestination, the belief that God ordained those rejecting the Gospel to be condemned, as God chose those affirming Jesus Christ to be redeemed. They likewise sought to train ministers in the field, as they worked, rather than demand so much formal education before ordination. A majority of leaders in the synod of Kentucky disagreed with these perspectives and moved to discipline their colleagues. Many Presbyterians in the East confused the "Cumberland men" with the New Light dissidents, and the assembly upheld the synod in its actions. Though Cumberland Presbyterians did seek religious revivals, they did not wish to separate. Nevertheless, they were forced to form a separate denomination in 1810, one that became popular especially in rural America and that by 1850 had about 200,000 members.

Though in most respects it was less dramatic than the revival movement, the movement to address particular religious and social issues by forming single-purpose voluntary societies proved equally important for Presbyterians. Moreover, in antebellum America, the two movements remained deeply related through such revivalist-reformers as Lyman Beecher and Charles G. Finney.

In the early nineteenth century, Presbyterians collaborated with other evangelical Protestant bodies to form the American Bible Society (1816), the American Tract Society (1823), and the American Sunday School Union (1824). The purpose of the American Bible Society was to place Scripture in the hands of all people; the American Tract Society was to provide interpretive and educational materials; and the ASSU was to assist in the formation of Sabbath schools to aid and teach poor children, especially in coming to a profession of Christian faith. The first national voluntary society, the American Board of Commissioners for Foreign Missions (1810), sent its members to work among the Indians and to other lands. A parallel society, the American Home Missionary Society (1826), worked harmoniously at first with the Presbyterian Standing Committee of Missions (later, the Board of Missions).

In addition to these church-oriented societies, American Presbyterians formed societies in behalf of peace, education, prison reform, the abolition of Sunday mail delivery, and many other reform objectives. Especially important were the American Colonization Society (1817) and the subsequent American Anti-Slavery Society (1833). Early denominational pronouncements had called American slavery "utterly inconsistent with the law of God" (1818). The ACS, founded by a Presbyterian minister with the usual collaboration of Congregationalists, Methodists, and others, was roundly supported as well in that statement. The ACS sought to relocate manumitted American blacks in newly established Liberia. The American Anti-Slavery Society sought immediate, uncompensated emancipation of slaves.

Disagreements among Presbyterians concerning slavery, and even on the methods of abolishing the institution among those who opposed it, helped cause the Presbyterian denominational division that occurred in 1836–1838 between the Old School and the New School. Historian George Marsden argues that theological differences and questions of denominational polity actually proved even more important in that split. New Schoolers, pleased with the Plan of Union and the cooperation with Congregationalists, embraced the thought of Samuel Hopkins and Nathaniel Taylor from that tradition. The "softer" Calvinism of these theologians was more compatible with revivalism than was the stricter version derived from the Westminster Standards themselves.

With a majority in the general assembly of 1837, the Old School threw out the Plan of Union, ended cooperation with the Congregationalists, and demanded theological conformity from all to the Standards. About half the Presbyterians failed to recognize these actions and declared themselves the "true" denomination in the United States. Secular courts provided scant resolution of the dilemma, and two major Presbyterian communions continued as Old School and New School denominations.

The Old School Presbyterians, especially with leadership from Princeton Seminary, developed a conservative theology and social program that transcended regionalism in America. Their special strength, according to Lefferts Loetscher, came from their inserting new mission functions into the church courts themselves. Old Schoolers established a number of schools and seminaries as well, and by 1869 the denomination numbered about 250,000. An agreement within the general assembly forbade pronouncements on the matter of slavery, and most pro-slavery Presbyterians belonged to this church.

The New School Presbyterians maintained close ties with other evangelical denominations, continued their affinity for revivals, and supported such reform efforts as prohibition and antislavery. Union Theological Seminary in New York became the theological center for New Schoolers. In 1869 the New School claimed almost 175,000 members.

The New School assembly split in 1856–1857 along regional lines, though the denomination had never been strong in the South. The Old School church did not split until 1861, when Union loyalists in its assembly demanded that southern members join them in praying for and supporting the United States at a time when several states had already seceded. Southern Old School Presbyterians withdrew to form the Presbyterian Church in the Confederate States of America (PCCSA). At the close of the Civil War, the Old and New School denominations in the North united to form one PCUSA. The PCCSA, with the addition of some ex–New School Presbyterian congregations and with considerable support from the border states of Kentucky, Missouri, and Maryland, formed the Presbyterian Church in the United States (PCUS).

The Cumberland Presbyterian Church avoided splitting during the war simply by continuing to meet annually and to treat southerners as though merely absent. After the war, the southerners returned and took their seats. The

CPC divided along racial lines in 1869, and the Second Cumberland Presbyterian Church was formed for blacks. The UPNA had few members with Confederate sympathies even in the border states, for it had taken an antislavery position at its inception; but its conservative stance also precluded deep political involvement in the war effort.

After the Civil War, the reunited PCUSA undertook extensive missionary efforts at home and abroad. New judicatories were organized in the South, especially for blacks, many of whom had previously belonged to the two prewar Presbyterian denominations. A network of schools and colleges arose to educate black people generally and to assist in forming black Presbyterian leaders particularly. In this effort, the UPNA served freed slaves especially in Nashville and in Knoxville, but also in five other southern states besides Tennessee.

All the Presbyterian denominations of the latter half of the nineteenth century engaged extensively in foreign missions. Missionaries had served in other countries since 1812, supported by the PCUSA. But in the 1870s and afterward, missions in China, in various locations in Africa, in Mexico, and elsewhere became significant in the life of the churches. Women's groups supporting missions were the first within American churches to give some autonomy to female believers. The sense of a worldwide church, one Presbyterian doctrine in self-identity, received particular substance as congregations and governing bodies arose in other lands with close ties to American Presbyterians.

What now can be seen as Presbyterian "expansion" took place as a portion of the missionary effort in this era. Sheldon Jackson and many other "home missionaries" developed congregations among believers in the Plains states, in the Far West, and even in Alaska. Meanwhile in Appalachia, in county-seat towns throughout the East, and in the growing cities, Presbyterian "church planting" took place at a rapid rate.

Within all the major denominations, issues involving science and religion strained belief systems in the post–Civil War era. Among southern Presbyterians, the situation of Dr. James Woodrow attracted considerable attention. He taught at Columbia Seminary (originally in Columbia, South Carolina, but now in Decatur, Georgia), and in 1884 stated that the Bible taught nothing

concerning the "method of creation." Thus he held that God could have used evolution as a "method." Uproar and declamation from supporting synods led to a condemnation of his teaching at the 1886 assembly of the PCUS.

The greatest strains, however, came where the most Presbyterians belonged—in the PCUSA. There what had come to be known as the Princeton theology encountered the new scientific insights in several areas. The traditional, biblical doctrines concerning creation and ancient history came under attack in light of Darwinism and paleontology. Mosaic authorship of the Pentateuch and a single author of Isaiah were questioned, as were attendant assumptions about the New Testament, when scholars applied historical-critical methods to the study of the Bible. And advocates of the nascent social sciences were critical of the Calvinist doctrines of human depravity and atonement as fostering immaturity. Many Presbyterians, especially those affiliated with colleges and universities, advocated revision of the confessions to accommodate the new truths and to tell of the love of God for all people. Some even derided those who would not make way for the sciences.

Proponents of the Princeton theology organized and fought against the incursions of the "modernists." Articulated first by Archibald Alexander, then by Charles Hodge, and for a third generation by Archibald Alexander Hodge, B. B. Warfield, and many other Princeton graduates, the theology gathered "evidences" in behalf of a rationally defensible and consistent world view. The Princeton theology alleged objective and assured proof that the Bible was inspired, that the Christological councils and the Westminster Standards accurately represented the Bible's teachings, and that systematic exposition of these teachings would lead reasonable people to make professions of faith (should God grant the Spirit's work among them). The Calvinism of Charles Hodge's *Systematic Theology* (1872–1873) bore a close resemblance to seventeenth-century scholastic Reformed theology, a fact not lost on those who disagreed with him.

Following the Princeton theology, if people could decide some parts of Scripture were inspired while others were in error, what was to keep any authority of Scripture for the church? In the 1870s David Swing of Chicago was tried for heterodoxy; and though exonerated, he left the Presbyterians. More celebrated and definitive trials took place in 1891–1893 of Charles A. Briggs, a professor at Union Seminary in New York, and Henry Preserved Smith of Lane Seminary in Cincinnati, leaders in institutions received from the New School branch of the church at reunion. The convictions of these two, together with other trials, effectively exhibited the power of the Princeton theology and the force of what became the intellectual center of the Fundamentalist movement.

In the Briggs trial, which extended over a three-year period, at least eight charges were brought, including that he denied Mosaic authorship of the Pentateuch, taught that the Book of Isaiah came from various hands, honored reason over Scripture itself, and considered even the original manuscripts of the Bible to contain errors. Smith was accused, and convicted, on narrower terms: he did not believe that a lost autograph manuscript contained an inerrant version of Scripture. In the course of these trials, Princeton theologians argued that there were a few Christian "fundamentals," including inerrant Scriptures. Such fundamentals increasingly occupied the center of attention, as in the trial of Arthur C. McGiffert, which resulted in his withdrawal from the PCUSA without having been convicted. The assembly of 1899 offered four "fundamentals" of Reformed doctrine, and these became standards on which McGiffert would be tried. Again, in 1910, the assembly asserted that there were five Presbyterian fundamentals: inerrant Scripture, the virgin birth of Jesus Christ, a satisfaction theory of the atonement, bodily resurrection, and Christ working miracles.

The turn of the PCUSA toward these more commonly named fundamentals rather than those distinctively associated with the tradition—predestination, for example, or total depravity of humanity—occurred as that denomination invited the Cumberland Presbyterian Church to reunite. Modest revision of the Westminster Confession and catechisms made the PCUSA attractive again for most of the CPC. More than 100,000 Cumberland Presbyterians joined with the PCUSA between 1906 and 1910, while about 75,000 remained in a continuing CPC. That reunion, together with another in 1920 that brought Welsh Calvinistic Methodists into the PCUSA, along with the growth of black judicatories, particularly in the South, made the PCUSA increasingly a national and ethnically pluralistic denomination.

Fundamentalists again sought to rid the denomination of liberal thinkers during the 1920s. This time they were aggravated by Harry Emerson Fosdick, a New York pastor who remained a Baptist while also serving a Presbyterian church. He preached against theological rigidity and the Presbyterian preoccupation with what he termed nonessential doctrines. Fosdick, too, was disciplined by the denomination, but by then the mood of the Presbyterians had changed. Most members did not support attempts by conservatives to rid the Presbyterian mission of so-called liberal thinkers. More than 1,200 ministers signed the "Auburn Affirmation" asking for toleration for Presbyterians with a variety of theological positions. The general assembly of 1927 refused to name any particular doctrines as essential, save those central in the historic creeds of Christianity. In doing so, it took a middle position between the Fundamentalists and the "Auburn ministers." The general assembly of 1929 also wrested denominational control of Princeton Seminary from an extremely conservative faction within the board and faculty.

Presbyterian Fundamentalists and other radical conservatives founded a rival seminary, Westminster in Philadelphia, and an Independent Board of Foreign Missions. When told to desist from their schismatic efforts, these Presbyterians, led by J. Greshem Machen, refused. Machen was disciplined and moved to the lead in founding the Presbyterian Church of America in 1936. That denomination divided almost immediately into the Bible Presbyterian Synod (later, Church) and the Orthodox Presbyterian Church, both of which remain tiny denominations in the 1980s.

The Fundamentalist-modernist feud did not completely die, but did abate in the 1930s as other theological movements affected Presbyterians. The movement called neo-orthodoxy, or crisis theology, was the first and perhaps the most important.

The Swiss theologian Karl Barth, together with the American Reinhold Niebuhr, both Reformed in their Christianity, emphasized human sin and God's transcendence. The neo-orthodoxy of Barth, Niebuhr, and others gave positive expression to the faith of conservative Presbyterians, while it honored, sometimes in radical fashion, the historical-critical methods sought by more liberal Presbyterians. All the Presbyterian seminaries, the Christian Faith and Life curriculum undertaken by the PCUSA in 1948, and the Covenant Life curriculum of the PCUS, CPC, and ARP taught Bible and theology for decades following general insights from neo-orthodoxy. It still retains currency among a number of Presbyterians. Many teachers in Presbyterian seminaries, and therefore many pastors, have also been influenced considerably by the related biblical theology movement, by liberation theology, and by the theology of hope.

Since the Fundamentalist-modernist controversy, no pattern of subsequent Presbyterian-Reformed theology has emerged with any distinctiveness. In the words of Lefferts Loetscher: "Memories and scars of the old fundamentalist-modernist controversy still largely inhibit among Presbyterians the frank and realistic discussion of theological questions . . ." (1954, p. 156).

The main body, the PCUSA, really did change institutionally during the 1920s, in part as a natural consequence of America's pattern of urbanization, increasing technology, and changing mores. In part, the change proved to be the fruit of home missions and evangelism, both of which gathered in the churches new strains of believers less enamored of Scottish confessionalism and the Princeton theology. The PCUSA engaged in new ministries, addressed new issues, and began to lead again in American ecumenism.

The PCUS, especially after the Civil War, focused on Christian otherworldliness, what they called "the spirituality of the church." Previously Presbyterians (like other believers) had sought to determine the roles of communions in America, where government and church remained separate institutions. All major Presbyterian bodies paid attention to the admonition of Jesus to "render unto Caesar . . ." (Luke 20:25). But the PCUSA, perhaps out of its memory of the "lost cause," developed a special affinity for avoiding involvement in any matters of peace or justice in the name of the church's "spirituality." From the 1870s to the 1930s, southern Presbyterians frequently addressed matters concerning Sabbath observance and prohibition. However, they generally did not speak corporately or seek church-wide action in matters related to race, economics, or politics. Even in the subsequent decades,

until the middle 1960s, the PCUS seldom dealt with matters of race, labor, or human rights in any but the most general terms.

Presbyterians in the PCUSA who had spearheaded the Protestant attempts for civil regulation of Sunday, and who had cooperated in the temperance and prohibition movements, began in the twentieth century corporately to work for peace and justice in other areas as well. In 1903 the PCUSA created a Working Men's Department to seek legitimation of the union movement and to force oppressive employers to desist from their actions. In the midst of the patriotic fervor of World War I, the PCUSA cautioned its members and the nation generally to seek justice and peace. The denomination unsuccessfully sought to have the United States join the League of Nations.

In fact, an examination of American Presbyterians at the time of World War I serves to illustrate how complex the attitudes and involvements of the members of the denomination had become by that time. At the beginning of 1917, both President Woodrow Wilson and Secretary of State William Jennings Bryan were deeply committed Presbyterians. Wilson moved to sever diplomatic relationships with Germany, and Bryan resigned in protest. Presbyterian minister and revivalist Billy Sunday stirred anti-German fervor among Americans, while Francis J. Grimke, minister among black Presbyterians in the nation's capital, urged patriots to remain at home and fight American racism. The general assemblies of the PCUSA, the PCUS, and the UPNA expressed support for the military effort, and many of the churches and denominational bodies bought Liberty Bonds to help. But Presbyterian Norman Thomas resigned from his charge to help found the Fellowship of Reconciliation, a new pacifist group. Obviously, Presbyterian stances had become numerous, and Presbyterians have attained even more complexity in the intervening years.

In matters of racism, too, the PCUSA especially has sought to heal the wounds of injustice. At other times, it and the other denominations have acceded to national norms. Both the PCUSA and the PCUS responded to America's era of intense racism (or Jim Crow) by establishing segregated governing bodies rather than, as the CPC had done, setting up a separate black denomination. Though both the PCUS and the

PCUSA ordained black clergy during the nineteenth century, most regular church courts met under segregated conditions until well into the twentieth century.

In the early decades of this century, local Presbyterian churches, like churches of other denominations, frequently grew to become very complex organizations. Congregational singing, which initially had focused on the Psalter, and then had developed into instrument-accompanied rendering of hymns from diverse sources, now was supplemented by "special music," frequently offered by a quartet of major voices (sometimes paid). Only the ARP, and the UPNA to a lesser extent, resisted the changes in music. Pastors hired secretaries, worked in offices, and led annual campaigns to meet organization budgets. Flowers, flags, and other "decorations" began to appear in the sanctuaries of Presbyterian churches, sometimes even in chancels, with various committees responsible for seeing that they did. Sunday schools had become complicated, graded-curriculum affairs by this time. Directors of Christian education began in the 1910s to open a new, quasi-ministerial occupation, sometimes also expanding the role of women in the various churches.

Though women have been a majority in the Presbyterian churches in America from the beginning, not until the latter part of the nineteenth century did they start to speak publicly in congregations and to organize thoroughly in behalf of missions and ministry. Earlier, women had taught in Sabbath schools, and some had gathered friends informally in homes. But the denominations had followed general Christian tradition in interpreting literally and for their own day the admonitions of I Corinthians (14:34) and I Timothy (2:12). Formal actions in the PCUSA and the UPNA in 1874 permitted women to sing psalms, read Scripture, lead prayer, and perform other tasks under certain conditions.

The Cumberland presbytery of Nolin, in western Kentucky, ordained the first Presbyterian woman pastor in 1889. Louisa Woosley served for more than two decades as a minister, though the Cumberland general assembly argued several times over whether her ordination by her presbytery was valid. By 1921 the CPC general assembly voted to remove discriminatory language from its book of discipline. The ordination of women in the larger denominations occurred later, but they began discussions of the possibility in this period.

The UPNA permitted women to become deacons in 1906, and after years of discussion the PCUSA authorized the special office of deaconess for women in 1915. In 1930 the PCUSA amended its constitution to allow women to serve as elected lay leaders, and in 1956 the general assembly ratified the action for women to become pastors. The PCUS in 1963–1964 voted to ordain women to church offices. During the 1970s the United Presbyterian Church in the United States (UPCUSA; formed in 1958 from the PCUSA and the UPNA) and the PCUS moved to ordain significant numbers of women. Lois Stair was elected the first woman presiding officer of the UPCUSA in 1971. Sara B. Moseley served as the first woman to moderate the PCUS in 1978.

By the time of reunion, with some exclusions among ex-PCUS congregations, particular churches were supposed to elect women to the session in numbers representative of the whole church. Presbyteries asked pulpit nominating committees to give serious consideration to calling women to serve as pastors. The matter of ordination of women still produced differences of opinion in 1985, however; and congregations that have tried to leave or have left the denomination have frequently cited that issue as the reason for withdrawal.

As previously indicated, Presbyterians might disagree over many issues, but they have remained remarkably unified in their appreciation for education and their support of it—for ministers in particular and for people in general. They established more than sixty colleges before the Civil War, and Presbyterians have kept on founding institutions of higher education in every decade since, at least until 1960. At present, seventy colleges are related to the Presbyterian Church (U.S.A.), formed in 1983, and more than a dozen are related to other Presbyterian denominations.

The communions founded numerous seminaries, sometimes in competition along denominational lines. In the twentieth century, seminaries have continued to spring up with each split among Presbyterians. At the present time the Presbyterian Church (U.S.A.) has ten theological seminaries: Dubuque Theological Seminary; Louisville Presbyterian Theological Seminary; McCormick Theological Seminary in Chicago; Pittsburgh Theological Seminary; Princeton Theological Seminary; San Francisco Theological Seminary; Johnson C. Smith Theological Seminary in Atlanta; Austin Presbyterian Theological Seminary; Columbia Theological Seminary in Decatur, Alabama; and Union Theological Seminary in Richmond, Virginia. The continuing Cumberland Presbyterian Church has one seminary: Memphis Theological Seminary. The ARP has one: Erskine Theological Seminary in South Carolina; and the Presbyterian Church in America (PCA; formed in 1973) has one accredited seminary, Reformed Theological Seminary in Jackson, Mississippi.

Education doubtless was increasingly related to ecumenism for Presbyterians as they came to depend upon other Christian traditions, upon Judaism, and upon other living religions for mutual education and cooperation. Several of the Reformed denominations collaborated in the comity arrangements in the missionary movement of the nineteenth century. They cooperated well in what came to be the World Alliance of Reformed Churches. The PCUSA especially led in the forming of the Federal, National, and World councils of churches. Among Presbyterian denominations themselves, attempts to become more inclusive have increased in recent decades.

In the 1940s serious attempts to join the PCUSA and the PCUS produced cooperation but not union. In the early 1950s, however, the PCUSA, the PCUS, and the UPNA did develop a plan for union that was presented to all three denominations in 1956. PCUS presbyteries demurred, motivated by fear of northern "liberalism" and also by regional parochialism. The PCUSA and the UPNA did affirm the plan, to become in 1958 the United Presbyterian Church in the United States (UPCUSA). About 250,000 UPNA members joined the 3-million-member PCUSA to make up the new communion, with most corporate offices in New York City and with scores of seminary and educational and service institutions.

When the new UPCUSA met in its general assembly, it voted in 1958 to undertake development of an appropriate statement of belief for the denomination. That statement was finally adopted in 1967, after having been approved by previous assemblies and with the necessary presbyteries concurring. The Confession of 1967 (C-67) uses the theme of reconciliation to affirm belief in God's work and human responsibility for Christians. Though C-67 remains characteristically Christocentric, it emphasizes more than other Reformed confessions ethical implications of the faith for all of life: "social and cultural, economic and political, scientific and technological, individual and corporate." As the UPCUSA adopted the C-67, it also embraced a Book of Confessions as bearing authority for the Church. The book contains the two major creeds from the early church, the Apostles' Creed and the Nicene Creed; three creeds from the sixteenth century—the Scots Confession, the second Helvetic, and the Heidelberg Catechism; the Westminster Confession of Faith and the Shorter Catechism; and the Theological Declaration of Barmen as well as the newest offering, C-67.

In America's civil rights movement, in the ecumenical movement, and elsewhere, the UPCUSA remained a central body. Several leading Presbyterians, including Stated Clerk Eugene Carson Blake, were arrested in demonstrations and sit-ins. Local congregations, many of them integrated, became centers of civil rights activity. Within the denomination itself, racially segregated governing bodies were eliminated, and some black Presbyterians moved into positions of authority and responsibility. The first black moderator of the UPCUSA general assembly, Edler Hawkins, was elected in 1963.

The PCUS in 1965 changed the location for a meeting of its general assembly when a host church chose to remain segregated. Shortly afterward, right-wing congregations began to seek withdrawal from the PCUS and formed a new Presbyterian Church in America (PCA). The PCUS elected Lawrence Bottoms as its first black moderator in 1974. Many of the Presbyterians who left the PCUS—about 75,000 between 1965 and 1980—had also opposed the ordination of women and the reunion of the PCUS with what was now the UPCUSA.

Both the PCUS and the UPCUSA began in the 1960s actively to support a number of social causes in addition to those already mentioned. Minutes of the assemblies of both organizations in 1976, for example, show they addressed political and social matters in similar fashion. The UPCUSA moved further from a sense of overall moral policy, while the PCUS continued to move more tentatively for the most part. However, moral and ethical issues broached included the sovereignty of Panama, America's evenhandedness in dealing with the Middle East, world hunger, abortion, and Indian rights.

As American mobility, urbanization in the Sun Belt, and southern industrialism increased, the two denominations moved toward one another and forgot previous antipathies. Finally, in 1982, general assemblies of both the PCUS and the UPCUSA voted affirmatively on a plan for reunion. Already the denominations shared a Worshipbook and many joint functions. When presbyteries in both communions ratified the merger, the two joined together in a general assembly in Atlanta, Georgia, in June 1983. The Presbyterian Church (U.S.A.) was created. A pastor from Charlotte, North Carolina, J. Randolph Taylor, was elected moderator of the new communion.

The Presbyterian Church (U.S.A.) has 3,057,226 members, 19,439 ministers, and 11,621 particular churches (1985 figures). Congregations exist in all fifty states. Partnership efforts in Christian missions exist with churches in sixty-three different nations. Twenty synods and 195 presbyteries in the new church began the process of negotiating boundaries, a process that continues to this day.

Finances in the merged denomination indicated that members were mostly middle class. Those coming from the UPCUSA had contributed a total of $353 per capita during 1982, while members from the PCUS had given an average of $410 per person. Giving in the new communion has increased substantially in the mid-1980s.

Another reunion is taking place among the CPC and the Second Cumberland Presbyterian Church, which had separated during Reconstruction. By 1990 that combined denomination will once again become a racially pluralistic body.

Contemporary American Presbyterianism is extremely pluralistic in congregational organization, in belief, and in worship. Some small, rural congregations have changed little since the nineteenth century. Other, sophisticated urban congregations may have as many as nine full-time clergy and more than a hundred staff serving thousands of members. Such churches may have day-care, social service, club, and educational programs that help members and others in the community from birth to death. In fact, some now possess mausoleums as well.

Some presbyteries gather elders and ministers from a wide area of farmlands and towns. But most presbyteries center in metropolitan communities, drawing surrounding country churches into their urban spheres. Thus "urban bias" has an effect on the Presbyterians, whose offices for higher church bodies are in large cities.

Most particular churches in the Presbyterian Church (U.S.A.) have a "unicameral" system for governance, in which the session of elders with the minister(s) direct the worship and work of the corporate body. A minority of congregations still retain a board of deacons as a distinct unit separate from the session; the board helps with the stewardship and maintenance functions of the church under direction of the session. In 1985 the denomination had a total of 120,822 elders, of whom 47,476 were women; at the same time it had but 78,963 deacons in all—32,861 men and 46,102 women.

Theological emphases of the Presbyterians remain on the Bible, on the historic confessions adopted by the church, and upon the confluence of faith and life. It is increasingly difficult to point to systematic theology that is specifically Presbyterian in nature. However, much of the work with scholarly study of Scriptures, much American process and liberation theology, and much study of relationships between theology and the arts, sciences, and humanities is being done by those with discernibly Reformed perspectives. The Presbyterian Church (U.S.A.) is currently at work on the formulation of an appropriate theological statement or creed.

Distinctive traditions continue, although the mobility of members and the coming into Presbyterianism of those with other religious backgrounds has greatly diminished the intensity of particular habits and customs. In western Pennsylvania, for example, one can still locate congregations and ministers deeply immersed in rational Calvinism, interested in "proving doctrine," and thoroughly conversant with the historic standards of Westminster. In black Presbyterian congregations, members still sometimes expect to hear intellectually framed sermons that differ from those in neighboring churches. Congregations with special Scottish, Welsh, Hungarian, or German backgrounds may differ in some habits and language. In these instances, and throughout the newer Presbyterian congregations, one can find amazing diversity in theology. Some value glossolalia; others emphasize social service of a particular kind; still others grow now among particular populations, including Korean Americans and Native Americans. Some may have more than one of these characteristics.

Historically, Presbyterians have ranged in practice of worship from the very liturgical to the very informal and free; in ecclesiological terms, from high to low church. This diversity has become even more pronounced and multidimensional in recent decades. Presbyterian directories for worship have for the most part become less restrictive over time.

Baptism, for example, can be celebrated among Presbyterians using modes of immersion, effusion, or sprinkling. At present, many Presbyterians continue to present their infants for baptism. Many others wait until their children make personal professions of faith and receive believer baptism. Again, many Presbyterians sing traditional hymns accompanied by an organ (and less frequently by other musical instruments such as trumpets or guitars). A number of ARP churches still sing psalms with no accompaniment. A great number of congregations employ a piano, from either choice or necessity, and some of those follow other traditions in hymnody—from black gospel music, from Appalachian shape-note music, or from Asian heritages, for instance.

In recent worship, congregations in the Presbyterian Church (U.S.A.) have permitted children of believers to share in the Lord's Supper, or Communion. Though many parents and some sessions maintain traditional practices of denying communion to younger children, this is one example of the continual reinterpretation of Scripture that has characterized Presbyterian life throughout American history.

Sometimes the new emphases embrace historic priorities again. The Presbyterian Church (U.S.A.), for example, recently voted to focus heavily on evangelism. Yet throughout the nineteenth century and during most of the twentieth century, the denominations laid great stress on the presentation of the Gospel to all persons and on assisting people in learning about the Christian faith. Presbyterians, active in all the major revival movements in previous generations, are mixing this emphasis with continued attention to the needs of people throughout the nation and throughout the world.

BIBLIOGRAPHY

Maurice Armstrong et al., eds., *The Presbyterian Enterprise* (1956); Ben M. Barrus et al., *A People Called Cumberland Presbyterians* (1972); Lois Boyd and R. Douglas Brackenridge, *Presbyterian Women in America* (1983); Charles Hodge, *Systematic Theology* (1952); *Journal of Presbyterian History* (1922–); Walter Lingle and John Kuykendall, *Presbyterians: Their History and Beliefs* (1978); Lefferts Loetscher, *The Broadening Church: A Study of Theological Issues in the Presbyterian Church Since 1869* (1954) and *A Brief History of the Presbyterians* (3rd ed., 1978).

George Marsden, *The Evangelical Mind and the New School Presbyterian Experience* (1970); John T. McNeill, *The History and Character of Calvinism* (1954); John Mulder, *Woodrow Wilson: The Years of Preparation* (1978); Andrew Murray, *Presbyterians and the Negro: A History* (1966); Harold Parker, *Studies in Southern Presbyterian History* (1979); Ernest T. Thompson, *Presbyterians in the South*, 3 vols. (1963–1973); Robert E. Thompson, *A History of the Presbyterian Churches in the United States* (1902); Leonard Trinterud, *The Forming of an American Tradition* (1970); Louis Weeks, *Kentucky Presbyterians* (1983) and *To Be a Presbyterian* (1983); *The Worshipbook* (1970).
[See also CALVINIST HERITAGE; CALVINIST THEOLOGICAL TRADITION; FUNDAMENTALISM; LIBERALISM; NEW ENGLAND PURITANISM; *and* RELIGIOUS THOUGHT SINCE WORLD WAR II.]

DUTCH AND GERMAN
REFORMED CHURCHES

Milton J Coalter, Jr., and John M. Mulder

DUTCH and German Reformed churches (along with the Presbyterians and Congregationalists) are part of the larger family of communions that trace their origins to the Swiss Reformation. The reform movement in Switzerland was a sister to that led by Martin Luther in Germany, and it drew its initial genius from two centers, Zurich and Geneva. Ulrich Zwingli and John Calvin, the respective leaders of these urban centers of early Protestantism, initiated during the sixteenth century a brand of thought known as Reformed theology and a form of polity known as presbyterian church government.

The term *Reformed* indicates both a common link with other Protestant groups and a unique theological outlook. Like other Protestant traditions, the Reformed churches perceived themselves as restoring the church to the purity of life-style, worship, and belief found in the New Testament community of Christians. They believed that the Bible provided a blueprint for the church's structure and theology, which the Roman Catholic church had corrupted through the gradual addition of unscriptural dogma, rituals, and offices.

The Reformed tradition emphasized the sovereignty of God and the utility of the Old Testament's ethical injunctions as guides for civil and Christian conduct. Where some Protestant churches, like the Baptist and Methodist communions, have focused on the importance of the individual's free will in salvation, Reformed Christians, in varying degrees, concentrated attention on the Pauline doctrine of God's election of only certain individuals for salvation. Indeed, theologians such as Calvin maintained that this determination of a person's future rewards extended even to "double predestination"—election and damnation.

Similarly, Reformed churches distinguished themselves from other Reformation traditions by assigning a civil purpose to Old Testament moral laws. The Reformed believed with other Protestant groups that the fulfillment of such ethical injunctions as the Decalogue was a sign of the converted sinner's progress toward salvation. But the Reformed also claimed that civil law must be based on Old Testament moral instruction. In contrast to the Lutherans, who perceived the state as a temporary expedient for maintaining order until Christ's second coming, the Reformed regarded the state as an agent for bringing the Kingdom of God on earth by enforcing divine law through its civil code.

By removing all icons and statues from their sanctuaries, whitewashing church frescoes, and reducing ecclesiastical vestments to a minimum, the Reformed churches made the sermon and the Lord's Supper (communion) the focal points of their worship. Of the seven Roman Catholic sacraments, only baptism and the Lord's Supper were accepted as true, and the elements of the supper, bread and wine, were not considered the actual body and blood of Christ in either the Roman Catholic sense of transubstantiation or the Lutheran sense of consubstantiation. (The doctrine of transubstantiation assumed that the bread and wine were transformed into the actual body and blood of Christ after being consecrated by the priest. In contrast, consubstantiation meant that the elements of the supper and the body of Christ coexisted in union with one another after the consecration.)

The Dutch and German Reformed churches' presbyterian church government stands in contrast to both democratic forms of church government, in which each church member is accorded an equal vote, and episcopal polities, in which bishops exercise primary ecclesiastical authority. The term *presbyterian* is taken from the New Testament Greek word *presbuteros,* meaning "elder," and presbyterian polity functions through the authority of elders elected as representatives of the entire church.

The foundation of the presbyterian polity of Reformed churches is the Protestant doctrine of the universal priesthood of all believers. According to this concept, all Christians are priests and, therefore, worthy to share in the leadership of the church. The minister is not a different class or order of Christian. Instead, he or she is simply a member of the church set apart by the congregation for the performance of a particular office. Of the four offices of minister, doctor or teacher, elder, and deacon, the latter two were reserved for the laity. Deacons oversaw the financial operations of the church and alms to the poor and the ill. Elders participated with pastors in the maintenance of discipline and true doctrine and were either appointed by civil authorities (as was the pattern in some areas of Europe) or elected by church members (which was the dominant procedure in America). These elders served in the Reformed churches' presbyterian hierarchy of governing bodies, also called judicatories or courts.

The governing body of a Reformed church congregation was known as a consistory or session. Ministers and representative elders from each congregation formed a regional body known as a classis, or presbytery. Clerical and lay representatives of several classes formed a synod, and several synods might be united in a general synod or general assembly, also composed of representative ministers and elders.

The theology and polity of the Swiss Reformation provided the foundation on which both the German and Dutch Reformed churches built, but the specific circumstances of the two churches' early development in their homelands generated different products of the common Reformed spirit. Nowhere is this more evident than in their polity and confessional stances.

In Germany during the sixteenth and seventeenth centuries the local prince or elector was ultimately responsible for the spiritual and ecclesiastical life of his people, but he allowed a multileveled church structure to advise him. The Reformed Church of Germany maintained four levels of polity. At the base were local church consistories made up of three religious officials and three secular members appointed by the civil leader. Above the consistory were classes or districts, each under the oversight of a superintendent, who also was appointed by the civil authority. Synods, containing all the ordained clergy as well as two lay and two ministerial delegates from the civil leader's church council, or *kirchenrath,* lay above the classes. These synods met annually to review the general activities of the churches. Finally, a general synod composed of all superintendents gathered occasionally at the pleasure of the *kirchenrath* for major church decisions.

The Reformed church in the Netherlands had a slightly different presbyterian structure. The four-court system of church government was maintained. Each congregation had a consistory, composed of equal numbers of elders and deacons, and the pastor presided over the consistory. A classis consisted of the minister and one elder from each consistory in a group of churches. The provincial synods brought together two ministers and two elders from each classis in a province. The national synod, which was the highest court, had two ministers and two elders from each provincial synod. The absence of explicit secular political power in church affairs was a pattern later reproduced in the Dutch Reformed churches in North America.

In North America the German Reformed churches maintained a singular allegiance to the Heidelberg Catechism of 1563 while the Dutch Reformed churches adhered to the canons of the Synod of Dort (1618–1619) as the key interpretive document for all creedal statements. The Heidelberg Catechism was uniquely the product of the German Reformed tradition. Frederick William III, elector of the Palatinate, encouraged the birth of the Reformed church in Germany during the sixteenth century by overseeing the creation of this creed. A moderate Reformation churchman himself, Frederick chose for this task two theologians who had personal experience of and sympathies for the range of positions represented in the Reformed and Lutheran churches of Europe. Zacharius Ursinus and Kasper Olevianus created a catechism whose overall tone was devotional with an emphasis on ethics and a theology more moderate than Calvin's, since it avoided all discussion of predestination. As historian Max Goebel has described its creation, the catechism's irenic spirit represented a harmonious blend of "Lutheran inwardness, Melanchthonian clearness, Zwinglian simplicity, and Calvinistic fire."

Although the Dutch Reformed also accepted the Heidelberg Catechism, their history forced them into a more rigid stance on several points of Calvinist doctrine that were never accepted by the German Reformed communion. The Netherlands' Reformed community contained a significant contingent of Arminians who did not accept predestination as a valid biblical concept. Known as Arminians because they accepted the objections to contemporary Calvinism formulated by the Dutch Reformed theologian Jacobus Arminius, they insisted that all humanity enjoyed free will and the possibility of salvation. At the Synod of Dort this segment of the church was roundly condemned, and certain canons were accepted as the only true doctrine of the church. These five points of Dutch Calvinism have popularly been summarized by the acronym TULIP: total human depravity, unconditional election of those who are saved, limited atonement, irresistible grace, and perseverance of the saints (i.e., once saved the converted could not fall from grace). The polemic circumstances out of which the canons developed produced a much more doctrinaire outlook in the Dutch Reformed communion than was to be found in the German Reformed. Although the historical experiences of the German and Dutch Reformed in America were similar and the two churches cooperated during their early work in the colonies, their differing confessional stances prevented them from uniting into a single communion.

In North America the Dutch and German Reformed churches were part of the larger body of Reformed Protestants. The most numerous of these were the Puritans (later known as Congregationalists), who settled primarily in New England, and the Presbyterians, who immigrated to the Middle Colonies and the South. Other smaller groups of Reformed Protestants came from Switzerland, France, the British Isles, and other areas of Europe during the colonial period. While differing in various ways on theology, worship, and church government, all Reformed Protestants trace a common lineage to the Swiss Reformation and to Calvin and are therefore referred to as Calvinists.

DUTCH REFORMED CHURCHES

The first Dutch Reformed churches were established during the seventeenth century in New York, New Jersey, and Delaware, and they represent some of the earliest congregations of the Reformed tradition on the North American continent. The Dutch West India Company at first did not provide support for any church, but through the initiative of Peter Minuit, director general of New Netherland (today New York), the first pastor, Jonas Michaelius, arrived in the colony in 1628. He established the "church in the fort" (now known as the Collegiate Church), and 1628 marks the birth of the Dutch Reformed church in America.

During the seventeenth century migration from Holland accentuated the need for new churches and more ministers. Dutch Reformed congregations were begun throughout New York and New Jersey. Some attempted to attract the highly diverse population of the area into their communion, but generally these churches were composed of Dutch people, with worship services conducted in Dutch. Control over the Dutch Reformed parishes was exercised by the Classis of Amsterdam, which also governed the German Reformed congregations during the early eighteenth century.

When New Amsterdam was conquered by the English in 1664, the Dutch Reformed congregations lost their privileged status, and they opposed various attempts to establish and strengthen the Church of England in New York. In this they were successful, influencing the passage of legislation tolerating other churches in the colony and earning for themselves legal protection as a recognized church next to the Church of England. In 1700 there were fifty churches in New York, twenty-nine of them Dutch Reformed.

As the economic, political, and religious reasons for emigration from Holland became less compelling, the growth in the colonial Dutch population slowed during the latter part of the seventeenth century, and the churches languished in both numbers and spiritual vitality.

However, in 1720 a young pastor of German origin, Theodore J. Frelinghuysen, arrived in New Jersey. Frelinghuysen's pietistic preaching revived the Dutch laity's concern for personal conversion and the practice of piety just prior to the First Great Awakening of the 1740s.

In 1738 a group of Dutch Reformed pastors petitioned the Classis of Amsterdam for freedom to establish their own classis. At stake was the power to ordain ministers in the colonies and to conduct eccelesiastical business independent of Amsterdam's control. They were opposed mainly by other Dutch Reformed ministers in New York, who preferred an alliance with church authorities in Amsterdam and wanted theological training for Dutch pastors to be carried out at King's College (today Columbia).

In 1747 the Classis of Amsterdam granted the Dutch Reformed colonists permission to establish a coetus, or association of churches without full ecclesiastical authority. The restrictive terms did not give them true independence from Amsterdam, and in 1754 the Coetus party formed its own classis, causing further alienation from their opponents, who were known as the Conferentie. The Coetus party also moved to begin its own educational institution, and in 1766 the group received a charter for Queen's College (now Rutgers) in New Brunswick, New Jersey. In 1771 the Coetus and the Conferentie were reconciled through a plan drafted by the Classis of Amsterdam but shaped by John Henry Livingston, "the father of the Reformed church." Livingston was an American trained in Holland, and through his mediation the breach was healed. The plan gave the colonial church far greater autonomy, signified by the establishment of New Brunswick Theological Seminary in 1784, the oldest Protestant seminary in the United States.

During the American Revolution, the Dutch Reformed churches generally supported the revolutionary cause, partly out of fear of domination by the Church of England. When independence was won on the battlefield, it carried with it freedom from the control exercised by the Classis of Amsterdam. In 1784 a synod and classis were founded, and in 1792 the church was organized as the Reformed Protestant Dutch Church. In 1867 it changed its name to the Reformed Church in America (RCA), the title that it bears to this day.

As the American population grew and moved westward during the early nineteenth century, the Dutch Reformed remained concentrated primarily in their traditional strongholds of New York and New Jersey and restricted by their own ethnicity. They debated the use of the Dutch language in worship services, and although English was used increasingly, the church remained primarily Dutch in both its language and its membership. Various attempts were made to cooperate in mission work with other Reformed churches, especially the German Reformed and the Presbyterians, but these efforts were not met with conspicuous success.

Also inhibiting the vitality of the Dutch Reformed was a theological schism that occurred in 1822. The dissenters, known as the True Dutch Reformed Church, withdrew because of what they perceived to be growing liberalization of rigorous Calvinism of the main church, which had been influenced by the revivalistic and Arminian ethos of the era. These conservatives barely survived as an independent group, but their forces were augmented due to another theological division in the mother church in Holland. In 1834 conservative Calvinists broke away from the state church. They desired a church with a more vital piety, a stricter application of moral laws to guide Christian behavior, and a more rigorous interpretation of Calvinist orthodoxy. Many dissenters migrated to the United States in 1846–1847 in what is described as the second Dutch migration. Religious and political persecution of the dissenters, as well as an agricultural depression during the 1840s, spurred their departure. One contingent, led by Albertus van Raalte, established a settlement in western Michigan, and another, led by Hendrik Scholte, moved to central Iowa. While both of these Dutch Reformed groups attempted to remain independent, only Scholte's was successful; by 1850 van Raalte's group had united with the Reformed church.

In 1857 the Reformed Church in America was split again by a small group of conservative pastors and lay leaders in Michigan who were unhappy with what they perceived to be the lax practices and liberal theological doctrine of the Reformed church. Initially known as the True Holland Reformed Church and later as the Christian Reformed Church, it attracted few supporters until the 1880s, when the RCA was wracked by a dispute over Freemasonry. The church refused to prohibit its members from belonging to secret organizations such as the Masons, and because of its stance several congregations withdrew in 1882. In 1890 the 1822 secessionists joined the 1857 dissenters and established the Christian Reformed Church, which grew steadily during the late nineteenth and early twentieth centuries because of new Dutch immigration.

The Reformed Church in America and the Christian Reformed Church are nearly identical in their geographical distribution, for their strength is concentrated primarily in the East (New York and New Jersey), the Midwest (Michigan, Illinois, Wisconsin, and Iowa), and the West (California). The Christian Reformed Church, however, has a significant number of members in Canada. Both remain heavily dependent on the ethnic Dutch population for their membership, although in the East they are more pluralistic and both denominations are engaged in mission work with other ethnic and racial groups in the American population.

Like other Calvinists, the Dutch Reformed have devoted significant energy and resources to education, witnessed by the early founding of Queen's College (Rutgers), which became the State University of New Jersey in 1945, and New Brunswick Theological Seminary. In 1866 the Reformed Church in America established Hope College in Holland, Michigan, and in 1884 it launched a second seminary, Western, in the same city. The denomination also assumed sponsorship of Central College in Pella, Iowa, in 1916, an institution begun by Baptists in 1853, and in 1882 it founded Northwestern College in Orange City, Iowa.

Similarly, the Christian Reformed Church founded Calvin College and Calvin Theological Seminary in Grand Rapids in 1876, and its members established Dordt College in Sioux Center, Iowa, in 1955, as well as several smaller colleges in the United States and Canada. But the most notable feature of the Christian Reformed Church's activity in education has been its extensive network of primary and secondary Christian schools, which are not sponsored by the church per se but mainly by Christian Reformed parents. It is the largest Protestant private school

system in the United States, and control by parents is a product of the Christian Reformed conviction that education is part of the parental responsibility assumed during a child's baptism.

The Dutch Reformed commitment to education can also be traced through the large numbers of church members who have made important contributions in education, science, medicine, religion, the fine arts, and literature, as well as politics and business. Among the better-known contemporary writers is the comic novelist Peter DeVries, who frequently draws on his Christian Reformed heritage for acerbic and sarcastic treatments of the foibles of modern America.

The Reformed Church in America participated in the international missionary movement of the nineteenth and twentieth centuries far out of proportion to its numerical strength and in sharp contrast to its inability to expand greatly beyond the ethnic base of its own membership in the United States. Its missionaries were pioneers in India, China, Japan, and Saudi Arabia, and mission work continues today in Japan, India, Arabia, Africa, and Mexico. During the twentieth century the denomination has demonstrated its willingness to join forces with other Reformed bodies and other Christian churches.

The ecumenical movement of interdenominational cooperative work was spawned in great measure by the missionary zeal of Protestants during the nineteenth century, and the Reformed Church in America became one of the founding members of the Federal Council of Churches (1908) and the National Council of Churches (1950), as well as being active in the World Council of Churches (1948). Its ecumenism has been limited to cooperation, rather than ecclesiastical merger, for the RCA has resisted formal union with Presbyterians and the German Reformed. While the reasons for its refusal to unite with other churches are complex, the continued force of ethnic loyalty and the fear of losing its identity in a larger, more diverse church have been powerful factors.

The Christian Reformed Church also launched its own missionary program during the twentieth century, and today it is active in work with American Indians and in Japan, South America, Nigeria, Mexico, and Taiwan. After

World War II the denomination benefited from a large Dutch migration to Canada, and these settlers now constitute approximately one-quarter of the church's membership.

The Christian Reformed Church has shown little ecumenical involvement, even with its sister denomination, the Reformed Church in America. Theologically, the church has retained a strong commitment to Dutch Calvinist orthodoxy, and throughout the twentieth century it has been heavily influenced by the theology of Abraham Kuyper and the Calvinist revival in the Netherlands. Kuyper adamantly opposed theological liberalism but at the same time embraced modern culture for its potential to be reshaped by Calvinist institutions, such as Christian labor unions and Christian schools. His legacy, plus the theological tradition represented by the Belgic Confession, the Heidelberg Catechism, and the Canons of Dort, has produced a Christian Reformed theology marked by rigorous rationalism.

By the early twentieth century English had replaced Dutch in the worship services of nearly all congregations in both major branches of the Dutch Reformed church in America. The style of worship can vary from one congregation to another, ranging from the highly liturgical to the starkly simple. However, the Dutch Reformed retain a commitment to worship according to established liturgical forms that are set by the denomination and recommended for congregational use. The Reformed Church in America has been more open to the modern liturgical renewal in American Protestantism, while the Christian Reformed Church has generally retained a more reserved and traditional form of worship. Like other Calvinists, the Dutch Reformed also stress the importance of preaching and the regular celebration of the Lord's Supper. Both churches practice infant and adult baptism, although only the children of church members may be baptized.

The Dutch Reformed church has traditionally been strict in censuring certain "worldly" amusements and behavior, such as card playing, dancing, and movies. In the late twentieth century both denominations have become more lenient in this regard, but the Christian Reformed Church is the more rigorous of the two in its strictures and definition of what it deems Christian behavior. The Christian Reformed has also been more consistent in condemning divorce, except in cases of infidelity.

The history of the Dutch Reformed in America is an instructive case study of the interaction of religious belief, ethnic identity, and American culture. Unlike the German Reformed the Dutch have resisted assimilation and formal union with each other or with churches of a similar theological commitment. They have also encountered difficulty in expanding beyond a narrow ethnic base for their membership as a result. But they have retained both an institutional and theological identity that the German Reformed had largely lost by the late twentieth century.

The ministries of Norman Vincent Peale and Robert H. Schuller in the twentieth century indicate a contrary tendency within segments of the Dutch church. Although both men are ministers of the Reformed Church in America, they are also popular spokesmen for "positive thinking," or "possibility thinking." Both thought forms represent new variations on an older "mind cure" theme found commonly in American religious and cultural history.

In 1983 the Reformed Church in America had approximately 350,000 members, and the Christian Reformed Church approximately 300,000. Other small Dutch Reformed churches in America formed as a result of schisms are the Protestant Reformed Churches of America (1926), the Orthodox Reformed Church (1970), the Free and Old Christian Reformed Church of Canada and America (1961), and Netherlands Reformed Congregations (1907).

GERMAN REFORMED CHURCHES

German immigration to North America began in earnest after the founding of Germantown, Pennsylvania, in 1683. By 1776 more than 225,-000 Germans resided in the thirteen colonies. German Reformed immigration peaked during the mid-eighteenth century, when natives of northern Switzerland and the Palatinate predominated. German Reformed settlers attempted to establish themselves in New York, North Carolina, and Virginia in the early eighteenth century. When these efforts yielded meager results, the majority migrated to the frontiers of William Penn's colony.

The German Reformed community was orphaned at birth. The territories of the Reformed Church of Germany served as Europe's battlefield during the late sixteenth and early seventeenth centuries as Protestant and Catholic fought over issues raised by the Reformation. Consequently, the mother church had few financial resources or personnel to spare for its fledgling offspring in America. The American laity compensated for a crippling shortage of ministers by turning to their lay leaders. Men such as Conrad Templeman and John Philip Boehm were persuaded to assume the role of "reader" of sermons and liturgy during worship and later to conduct the rites of baptism and communion.

Boehm became the principal organizer of German Reformed church groups during the early eighteenth century. In 1728 he requested and received ordination from the Dutch Reformed Classis of Amsterdam. Boehm's ordination in 1729 began a formal association between the Continental Dutch Reformed church and the colonial German Reformed communion that lasted until 1793.

The relationship proved difficult from the first. The great distance between the two ecclesiastical communities and the difference in their native tongues made communication slow and cumbersome. Dutch authorities also refused to relinquish the right of ordination to the colonial church structure. Nevertheless, the German Reformed profited from Amsterdam's patronage in several ways. The Dutch provided financial assistance, albeit limited; they attempted to secure German clergy on the Continent for work in the colonies; and, most important of all, they sent Michael Schlatter in 1746 with sufficient official authorization to organize the colonial German Reformed church above the level of local consistories.

Schlatter organized the first German Reformed coetus, or classis, in America in September 1747. The church had by then organized approximately eighty congregations. Two years later Schlatter effected the adoption of a constitution (the Kirchen-Ordnung of 1748) by the new ecclesiastical body. The coetus remained the highest judicatory of the church until 1793. Its ability to provide ministers never extended much beyond Maryland and Pennsylvania (where half of the German population in America was concentrated), even though it assumed authority for congregations stretching from the upper Hudson River Valley to South Carolina.

The ecumenical enthusiasm of the First Great Awakening tested the German Reformed community's integrity. During the movement's peak in the 1740s, Count Nicholas Ludwig von Zinzendorf visited the Middle Colonies. Zinzendorf's church, the *Unitas Fratrum* (Society of Brethren), or Moravians, promoted a unique brand of German pietism. It advocated a communal life-style, spiritual renewal of the heart over doctrinal conformity, and ecumenical alliances of churches. In the colonies, Zinzendorf hoped to establish a united church of Protestants in which persons of different confessional stances would work and worship together. German religious groups in the region responded favorably to Zinzendorf's call. But closer contact with the Moravians and the issuance of anti-Zinzendorf broadsides by leaders such as Boehm and Samuel Guldin led the majority of the Reformed laity to pull back from the *Unitas Fratrum.*

The outbreak of rebellion against Great Britain presented a different challenge. English colonials questioned their German neighbors' loyalties since so many German church groups held pacifist convictions. The German Reformed did not share such qualms about war, so they were able to prove their allegiance by actively promoting the revolutionary cause from the pulpit as well as in the ranks of the Continental Army. On the whole, the church fared well in the colonial conflict. In fact, its membership around Baltimore, Maryland, experienced a revival of enthusiasm under the leadership of Philip Otterbein during 1776. This later led to the formation of a rival denomination, the United Brethren in Christ, when opposition developed over Otterbein's revivalistic emphases, and Otterbein himself began to associate more frequently with Methodist clergy in the area.

The excitement of civil independence following the Revolution inspired the German Reformed church to declare its separation from the Classis of Amsterdam. In 1791 the coetus unilaterally claimed the right to ordain its own clergy, and two years later Der Synod der Reformierten Hoch Deutschen Kirche in Den Vereinigten Staaten von America (the Synod of the Reformed German Church in the United States of America) met for the first time. The first synod meeting listed twenty-two ministers on its roll. It served

178 congregations stretching from Nova Scotia to North Carolina, with the primary concentration of its 15,000 communicants (full members) and 40,000 adherents (nonmembers who attended regularly) in eastern Pennsylvania.

At the close of the eighteenth century the synod faced three major problems. First, it conducted its worship and church governance in German, while the majority of the population spoke English. Second, many of its members soon joined the burgeoning migration of Americans to the Old Northwest, yet the synod's ability to supply clergy leadership and financial assistance was taxed by its present territories. Finally, over a third of the church's congregations lacked a pastor in 1793.

A significant portion of the church's membership clung to the German language in worship and in church courts in order to retain their ethnic identity. However, a growing number of second- and third-generation German Americans who were also German Reformed wished to attract their English-speaking neighbors. They recognized that English would remain the common language of the nation, and any church that refused to use it would cut itself off from the majority of the unchurched.

Agitation for the introduction of English services centered in urban areas, in Maryland, and west of the Susquehanna River where frequent contact with English-speaking people was unavoidable. Major concentrations in both Philadelphia and Baltimore experienced serious schisms over this issue in 1804 and 1808, respectively. Time proved favorable to the proponents of English, but progress was very slow until the late nineteenth century, when the issue was resolved.

Migration of church members into western Pennsylvania, Ohio, and beyond presented a further threat to German Reformed survival. The synod did not consider establishing mechanisms for evangelizing the unchurched and organizing churches among its scattered members on the frontier until 1812, and seven more years elapsed before it created a home missions committee for this purpose. The synod placed the committee's work under its immediate supervision in 1832 by establishing a Board of Missions. Regional classes preempted the board's power, however, by conducting their own home missions programs.

In 1819 the synod created new classes in the western counties of Pennsylvania and the Ohio territory. The synod withheld from these classes the right to ordain and required that delegates travel once a year to its meetings in the East. These stipulations created difficulties for the Ohio classis similar to those that the colonial church had experienced in its relationship with Amsterdam. Consequently, in 1824 the Ohio classis declared its independence from the synod and assumed the role of a synod in its own right.

This High German Evangelical Reformed Synod of Ohio experienced a rapid growth in new English congregations, and several of its clergy adopted the manipulative revival techniques and perfectionist theology of Charles Grandison Finney's "new measures." Finney believed that any converted Christian could perfectly follow Christ's ethical teachings with sufficient human effort. He also fostered conversions during his revivals by organizing peer pressure and publicly naming individuals in need of spiritual rebirth during his sermons and prayers. The Columbiana classis considered these practices objectionable innovations and in 1846 separated from its parent body to form the German Synod of the High German Reformed Church of Ohio and Adjacent States. Seven years later the Ohio synod healed this division amicably.

Both the Ohio synod and its eastern counterpart suffered from a critical shortage of clergy during the first half of the nineteenth century. The synod in the East moved first to establish a theological school within its jurisdiction. Until the early part of the century, church pastors had privately tutored candidates for the ministry, but the synod ended this system abruptly in 1820 by adopting a plan for a church-sponsored theological school. All clergy were instructed to cease their private instruction. This action precipitated a schism. Lebrecht Frederick Herman, a private educator of new ministers, felt this synod action slighted his prior contribution to theological education, so he organized the Synod of the Free German Reformed Congregations of Pennsylvania. As with many German Reformed schisms, this breach was repaired seventeen years later.

The schism did not affect development of the theological school, but other factors did. Several candidates for professor of theology declined their election by the synod, and the church had difficulty finding a home for the school. Known as the Theological Seminary of the Reformed Church, the school was opened at Carlisle, Pennsylvania, in 1825. It was moved in 1829 to York, Pennsylvania, and again in 1837 to Mercersburg, Pennsylvania. During the early 1840s the synod chose for its fledgling seminary two professors who quickly put Mercersburg on the map of American Christianity.

John Williamson Nevin was a Presbyterian by birth and training, but he swiftly illustrated his compatibility with his new home in the German Reformed church by publishing in 1843 the *Anxious Bench*. The work promoted revivals prompted by the Spirit, but condemned those generated by the New Measures of the Second Great Awakening as superficial manipulation of emotion.

Nevin's study of the early church fathers convinced him that the American Reformed community's emphasis on individual conversion and unchanging dogma, its antipathy to set liturgies, and its indifference to the sacraments grew out of a profound historical illiteracy. Nevin attempted to counteract these ill-informed prejudices by highlighting the church's traditional communal identity, the organic development of its worship and creedal witness, as well as the objective presence of Christ in the sacraments.

In 1843 the eastern synod elected Philip Schaff professor of historical and exegetical theology at Mercersburg. Schaff's inaugural address contradicted the contemporary belief in American Protestant circles that the Reformation was a simple restoration of early Christianity's purity. A disciple of the German view that the church's theology and practice had experienced no radical shifts, Schaff maintained that the Roman Catholic church of the Middle Ages had been the bearer of Christian truth, even though it also introduced serious corruptions into the church's dogma, polity, and liturgy. Reformation Protestantism was for Schaff the heir of the best in Roman Catholicism rather than the righteous usurper of Catholicism's claim to be the church of Jesus Christ.

The Mercersburg movement prefigured the direction American theology would take in the 1880s and 1890s, but the school's leaders faced heresy charges in their own day and the most immediate effect of their theology proved contrary to their intention of fostering catholic unity. Mergers with the Dutch Reformed, Presbyterian, and Lutheran communions had been contemplated since colonial days. The German Reformed thwarted early efforts at union by refusing to adopt any other Reformation creed that lacked their catechism's broad outlook. The Mercersburg theology completely overshadowed this objection in the mid-nineteenth century and, in effect, turned the tables on the German Reformed. The Dutch Reformed and Presbyterian churches now spurned German Reformed overtures of merger because they suspected their German brothers and sisters of trading their Reformed principles for a decidedly Roman Catholic perspective on the sacraments and the clerical office.

The Ohio synod harbored similar doubts. The synod had established Heidelberg College as its theological school at Tiffin, Ohio, in 1850, and several of the seminary's early professors strongly opposed the ideas emanating from Mercersburg. However, the western German Reformed were finding it increasingly difficult in the mid-nineteenth century to command attendance at synod meetings and to maintain loyalty to their church government, as frontier individualism and the experiential emphasis of the Second Great Awakening exacted its toll on communal church life. The awakening refocused attention on the individual's experience of conversion and largely ignored the role of the church's collective life in the promotion of faith development. Therefore, in spite of its misgivings about Mercersburg, the Ohio synod began to find the idea of consolidating German Reformed authority in a single denominational body appealing.

At the suggestion of the Mercersburg classis, the eastern synod proposed a Tercentenary Convention of all German Reformed church people to celebrate the three hundredth anniversary of the Heidelberg Catechism in 1863. The same year in Pittsburgh the synod in the East and the Ohio synod healed their broken fellowship by establishing the first General Synod of the German Reformed Church in the United States. The General Synod included twenty-seven classes within its territories. Five hundred ministers served 1,200 congregations with a baptized membership of over 100,000 and a confirmed membership of approximately 130,000. The churches of its western synod stretched all the way to the Great Plains, but its strength in the

West never approximated what might have been expected from the number of Germans who had settled in the upper Mississippi Valley. Two factors conspired to produce this weakness. First, German Reformed home missions remained under the control of local classes until the late nineteenth century, so the resources of the church were never coordinated in the West. Second, the German immigrants who flooded into the western territories during the antebellum period found the practice and doctrine of local German Reformed classes in conflict with their understanding of religion in general, Christianity, or the Reformed faith.

Between 1830 and 1845 an average of 40,000 new German immigrants entered the territories of the United States annually. Most settled in the upper Mississippi Valley. This immigrant population broke down into three distinct groups, each of which opposed the current German Reformed church on different grounds. Political radicals and rationalists distrusted all religions. Saxon Lutherans emigrated when King Frederick William III forced the union of the Lutheran and Reformed churches in Prussia. They believed that the Church of the Prussian Union was a purely political creature and that all similar ecumenical alliances would be an abomination of the pristine Christian witness that German Lutheranism represented. A final contingent were German Pietists. These individuals regarded their allegiance to Christ as more important than their ecclesiastical affiliation, their practical discipleship as more significant than theological orthodoxy, and interconfessional fellowship as a fundamental principle of the Christian life.

The Pietists formed a Kirchenverein, or church association, that soon became the major western rival of the Ohio synod for the loyalty of Reformed churchgoers. Its constituency found the western German Reformed unreceptive to a Lutheran-Reformed union, an ideal that had been effected in contemporary Prussia and that the Kirchenverein's membership wished to transplant to the New World.

In October 1840 the Kirchenverein organized itself formally as Der Deutsche Evangelische Kirchenverein des Westens (the German Evangelical Church Society of the West). Technically, the church had only six members. The six organizing missionaries were all graduates of Pietist missionary societies in Germany. The most prominent of these, the Evangelical Mission Society of Basel and the Rhine Mission Society of Barmen, intentionally trained a mission force of educated laymen rather than theologians. Consequently, the Kirchenverein's early leadership tended to emphasize practical discipleship over confessional propriety, or, put another way, living the faith over correct doctrine.

At its first formal assembly in 1841, the society demonstrated this bias by declaring the Scriptures its sole and infallible guide of faith and life. Where the major confessional documents of the Lutheran and Reformed churches agreed, they might serve the interpretation of the Bible, but wherever they differed, the Kirchenverein adhered strictly to the passages of Holy Scripture dealing with the subject and availed itself of the liberty of conscience prevailing then in the Evangelical Church. The society also declared that it would not interfere in either the internal or external affairs of local congregations that voluntarily joined the society.

The unusual theological tolerance and ecclesiastical liberty built into the Kirchenverein's system proved to be both its greatest strengths and its greatest weaknesses. On the positive side, these qualities neutralized the criticisms of the Kirchenverein's two chief rivals: conservative Lutherans, who charged it with perpetuating the Prussian Union church by mingling Lutheranism with Reformed theology and practice, and rationalists, who depicted the new church society as a subtle attempt to establish in the New World the same priestly domination that had existed in their homeland. The Kirchenverein paid a price for its permissiveness, however. During the 1840s and 1850s, the society lacked the ecclesiastical structures to force individual congregations to provide adequate financial support to the clergy, and its members continued to harbor an inordinate suspicion of all administrative structures.

In 1872 the Kirchenverein, now called the Evangelical Synod of the West, merged with two kindred regional bodies, the United Evangelical Synod of the Northwest and the Synod of the East. All three churches realized they could extend their mission fields, particularly in the West, far beyond their present capabilities as separate bodies. Their union created a national denomination called the German Evangelical Synod of North America, which contained approximately

280 pastors and 340 congregations. Individual churches existed as far east as New York and New Jersey, as far south as Texas and Louisiana, and as far west as California, but the majority of the denomination's members resided in the Midwest.

The new denomination's strong identification with Germans and its customary use of the German language proved advantageous in the late nineteenth century as a third wave of immigration dwarfed all previous migrations from Germany to the United States. Although the average annual emigration from Germany had reached only 42,000 in the years 1876 to 1880, it surged in the next three years to nearly 200,000 new German immigrants per year.

The denomination made some efforts in the 1890s to offer ministerial and financial assistance to this burgeoning population of potential members. In 1898 the German Evangelical Synod established a board of home missions. A similar board had been created in 1870, but the synod had abolished it after the merger of 1872 and returned the responsibility for home missions to local districts. Initially, the board of 1898 did not receive full support. Its income fell below that given to the districts during the previous three years and so it only partially fulfilled its potential harvest of new numbers.

Denomination officials began to warn their constituency in the last three decades of the nineteenth century that the church must make accommodations to the assimilation of its younger members into American society. The church responded by slowly adopting the English language. Its first English catechism appeared in 1892. By 1898 an English-language hymnal had almost reached completion, and an English counterpart to its major journal, the *Friedensbote,* was created in 1902 with the publication of the *Messenger of Peace.* However, the church did not use English extensively in its minutes until 1925, and it did not drop the word *German* from its name for another two years.

During this same period of adjustment, the Evangelical Synod's Elmhurst College in Elmhurst, Illinois, and its Eden Theological Seminary in St. Louis, Missouri, nurtured the early intellectual development of the two Niebuhr brothers. Reinhold Niebuhr and H. Richard Niebuhr significantly shaped American Christian theology in the mid-twentieth century. Reinhold Niebuhr's "Christian realism" relocated original sin in finite humanity's overweening pride and in the hypocrisy of social classes and national policy. H. Richard Niebuhr awakened the church to the social context out of which its religious beliefs arise and to how modifications in social systems had required and continued to demand that the church reinterpret its doctrine over time.

The Evangelical Synod's final name change in 1927 signaled the culmination of a mental shift within the denomination. Where its German ancestry and language were paramount features of the church's identity prior to 1927, its leadership now acknowledged the need to attract members from the larger English-speaking community. The Reformed Church in the United States had made a similar alteration in its title and thinking by 1869. Perhaps even more important, though, both the Evangelical Synod of North America and the Reformed Church in the United States shared a history of cooperation in foreign missions and ecumenical activities.

As early as 1839 the eastern synod of the German Reformed communion formed a Board of Foreign Missions. The board conducted its work through the American Board of Commissioners for Foreign Missions (ABCFM), a body that coordinated the mission activities of the Dutch Reformed, Presbyterians, and Congregationalists. When the two synods of the German Reformed united in 1864, the new General Synod withdrew from the ABCFM and affiliated with the German Evangelical Mission Society in the United States. The society was also supported by the Evangelical Synod of the West. The latter body had been deeply concerned with foreign missions from its inception, since its charter members were themselves foreign missionaries from Germany. During the 1870s the Evangelical Synod's membership contributed so heavily to the foreign missions effort that their president pleaded for equal support for home seminaries.

In the early twentieth century the Evangelical Synod and the Reformed Church in the United States were drawn together by their common involvement in the development of the Federal Council of Churches and the universal Conference on Life and Work, an interdenominational gathering considering the problems of humanity in an industrialized world. The 1925 Stockholm "Life and Work" meeting prompted Evangelical Synod leaders to create a Commission on Closer

Relations with Other Church Bodies. This group negotiated a plan for union with the Reformed Church and the United Brethren in Christ in 1929. The Brethren dropped out of merger talks within the year, and for a time the Reformed Church pondered an alternative alliance with the United Brethren again but including on this occasion the Presbyterian Church in the United States as well. When these discussions broke down, the Reformed Church agreed to join forces with the Evangelical Synod of North America. At the time of the union in 1934, the latter body contained 250,000 members and the Reformed Church had approximately 350,000 members. Together they held nearly 3,000 churches concentrated in Pennsylvania, the Midwest, and pockets of the Plains states, Oregon, and California.

The twelve articles that defined the Evangelical and Reformed merger are noteworthy for their indifference to the organizational structure and doctrinal stance of the new body. In essence the two participating denominations agreed to postpone the definition of their organization until after the union. This required great courage from both church groups since their current constitutions differed on several significant points. The Reformed Church emphasized the critical importance of the Heidelberg Catechism; the Evangelical Synod emphasized liberty of conscience over all creedal statements. The Reformed Church organized its ecclesiastical life on a presbyterian model; the Evangelical Synod maintained a congregational structure, but its administrative boards were more centralized than those of the Reformed Church.

Despite these differences, the two constituencies completed a constitution in 1938 that involved concessions from both parties. The Reformed conceded to the Evangelicals that the new denomination's doctrinal stance need not be rigidly delineated, and the Evangelical membership agreed to a presbyterian system of church government. Thus, where pastors and individual congregations had played a critical role in the Evangelical Synod's organization, elders and higher judicatories were now more significant.

The Evangelical and Reformed Church developed an extensive national bureaucracy between 1940 and 1957. This attempt to provide more efficient leadership for the denomination, however, never produced its intended results. Although national in scope, the denomination remained local in strength, and its membership did not keep pace with the general population growth. In 1940 the denomination had slightly fewer than 700,000 members. By 1950 that number exceeded the 700,000 mark, and by 1957 it had reached 800,000. The church's total number of congregations, on the other hand, declined to such an extent that in 1959 fewer churches existed than had twenty years previous.

The method of the Evangelical and Reformed merger was hailed by the *Christian Century* as an example to be followed throughout the ecumenical movement. It was not imitated by other denominations, however, because other communions remained unwilling to relinquish elements of their polity or to provide the latitude in doctrine that was required for such an effort. Nevertheless, the ease with which the Evangelical and Reformed union was accomplished encouraged the new church's leadership to pursue a further merger with the General Council of Congregational Christian Churches. Formally organized in 1931, the Congregational Christian Churches was a loosely organized national body of congregations that had assumed the commonplace title *Christian* to make a theological statement against all party distinctions. Its members insisted on the liberty of individual conscience and the union of all Christ's followers in the church.

The Congregational Christian Churches approved a plan of union with the Evangelical and Reformed in 1944. This act partially fulfilled a project formulated in 1918 at the Conference on Organic Union, an interdenominational meeting investigating possibilities for ecumenical mergers. Known as the Philadelphia Plan, it proposed the formation of a United Churches of Christ in America out of eighteen denominations, including the Congregational Christian Churches, the Reformed Church in the United States, and the Evangelical Synod of North America.

The Philadelphia Plan never materialized, and many doubted whether a more limited United Church of Christ composed of the Evangelical and Reformed and the Congregational Christian Churches would ever be realized. Although the two communions approved the idea of merger in 1944, they were not united until 1957. The delay was caused primarily by opposition from a small group within the Congregational Christian Churches. The Evangelical and Reformed eagerly sought a union that paralleled the creation of their denomination; that is, official sanction for the merger would precede concrete negotiations for a new constitution. The views of George W. Richards, a prime mover in both the Evangelical and Reformed union and the merger with the Congregational Christian Churches, best exemplify the rationale behind this program of action. The Mercersburg theology's stress on the church's organic nature led Richards to insist that real unity grew out of the practical experience of a people's common pilgrimage rather than out of legislation prior to their collaboration.

A significant and vocal minority in the Congregational Christian Churches perceived the same process quite differently. For them, union could occur only if one of the participating bodies renounced its former identity since the systems of the two denominations were fundamentally at odds with one another. Theologically, the Congregational Christian Churches presented what Reinhold Niebuhr called "a modern liberalism shading off to Unitarianism," whereas the Evangelical and Reformed perpetuated a tradition of liberal or tolerant evangelicalism. With respect to polity, the Congregational Christian Churches preferred the local independence of a congregationalist structure, while their counterpart in the proposed union maintained a presbyterian organization with a strong national judicatory. The failure of nine different drafts of a basis of union plus numerous court battles between 1949 and 1953 testify to the seriousness of these differences. However, all these obstacles were overcome in 1957, when the new denomination of over 2 million members met officially for the first time as the United Church of Christ in Cleveland, Ohio.

Throughout their histories in the United States, the Dutch and German Reformed churches have provided an ecclesiastical home for the spiritual and ethnic sustenance of two significant segments of the American immigrant population. The paths of these two traditions, however, diverged sharply in the twentieth century. Where the Dutch Reformed have sustained a faithful allegiance to traditional Reformed theology and to the Dutch ethnic, the German Reformed have contributed a singular example of theological and ecclesiastical tolerance and ecumenical cooperation.

BIBLIOGRAPHY

Dutch Reformed

Henry Beets, *The Christian Reformed Church, Its Roots, History, Schools and Mission Work, A.D. 1857 to 1946* (1946); James D. Bratt, *Dutch Calvinism in Modern America: A History of a Conservative Sub-Culture* (1984); Arie R. Brouwer, *Reformed Church Roots* (1977); Willard D. Brown, *A History of the Reformed Church in America* (1928); Charles E. Corwin, *A Manual of the Reformed Church in America* (5th ed., 1922); Edward T. Corwin, "History of the Reformed Church, Dutch," in *American Church History Series*, vol. 8 (1895), and *A Digest of Constitutional and Synodical Legislation of the Reformed Church in America* (1906).

Gerald F. De Jong, *The Dutch Reformed Church in the American Colonies* (1978); Peter De Klerk and Richard R. De Ridder, eds., *Perspectives on the Christian Reformed Church* (1983); Elton M. Eenigenburg, *A Brief History of the Reformed Church in America* (n.d.); D. H. Kromminga, *The Christian Reformed Tradition, from the Reformation Till the Present* (1943); John H. Kromminga, *The Christian Reformed Church: A Study in Orthodoxy* (1949); Peter N. VandenBerge, ed., *Historical Directory of the Reformed Church in America, 1628–1978* (1978); Jacob van Hinte, *Netherlands in America* (1985); Henry Zwaanstra, *Reformed Thought and Experience in a New World: A Study of the Christian Reformed Church and Its American Environment, 1890–1918* (1973).

German Reformed

J. H. Dubbs, "The Reformed Church, German," in *American Church History Series*, vol. 8 (1895); David Dunn, et al., *A History of the Evangelical and Reformed Church* (1961); James I. Good, *History of the German Reformed Church in the United States, 1725–1792* (1899), and, as ed., *History of the Reformed Church of Germany, 1620–1890* (1894) and *History of the Reformed Church in the U.S. in the Nineteenth Century* (1911); Louis H. Gunnemann, *The Shaping of the United Church of Christ: An Essay in the History of American Christianity* (1977).

William J. Hinke, *Ministers of the German Reformed Congregations in Pennsylvania and Other Colonies in the Eighteenth Century* (1951); James Hastings Nichols, ed., *Romanticism in American Theology: Nevin and Schaff at Mercersburg* (1961) and *The Mercersburg Theology* (1966); Carl E. Schneider, *The German Church on the American Frontier* (1939).

[See also CALVINIST HERITAGE and ETHNICITY AND RELIGION.]

WESLEYAN HERITAGE

Charles I. Wallace, Jr.

Often referred to as Methodism, the Wesleyan heritage denotes a popular form of Protestantism centering around the work of the Anglican priest John Wesley in the Evangelical Revival of eighteenth-century England. Originally organized as lay-led societies for the spreading of "scriptural holiness" within the state church, the movement soon developed into a separate denominational tradition, first in the newly established United States and, after the founder's death, in Great Britain. Its subsequent heirs may be found in the nations of the former British Empire and in other countries touched by later Methodist missionary outreach. In addition to its own considerable institutional success (and perhaps because of it), the heritage has influenced other denominations with such innovations as hymn singing, the use of lay preachers, an efficient "connexional" polity, and an emphasis on religious experience and Christian perfection.

This essay will examine the life and work of John Wesley, the social and ecclesiastical context in which the Wesleyan tradition arose, and the Wesleyan ethos and its legacy.

THE LIFE AND WORK OF JOHN WESLEY

John Wesley was born in 1703 in Epworth, Lincolnshire, son of the parish's rector, Samuel Wesley, and his wife, Susanna, the seventh of ten children surviving infancy. The same union also produced in 1707 another remarkable son, Charles, whose influence on the tradition that bears the family name was second only to that of his older brother. Both parents had been raised as Nonconformists (each was the child of a Puritan minister ejected from his parish at the Restoration), but had become Anglicans as adolescents. Samuel Wesley's incumbency at Epworth was not altogether a happy one, his Tory politics and ecclesiastical ambitions militating against good relations with his parishioners. Susanna Wesley, however, made the best of rectory life, raising and educating her children "methodically," with long-reaching implications for young John's later life and work. Two noteworthy childhood incidents were a devastating fire, from which the six-year-old John was miraculously rescued, and his presence several years later at "irregular" prayer services held by Mrs. Wesley in the rectory kitchen against her absent husband's wishes.

In 1714 the boy was sent on scholarship to the Charterhouse School in London. From there in 1720 he went up to Christ Church, Oxford, one of the university's better colleges in a period not noted for academic rigor, and graduated Bachelor of Arts in 1724. With encouragement from his parents he began to prepare for Anglican orders, prerequisite for the scholarly calling he wished to follow. This preparation involved the intentional pursuit of "holy living" enjoined by such Catholic and Anglican devotional authors as Thomas à Kempis, Jeremy Taylor, and William Law and was evidenced by the constant monitoring of his spiritual pulse in a meticulously kept private diary.

Career plans continued apace with his ordination as deacon in 1725, his election as a fellow of Lincoln College in 1726, the taking of his M.A. degree in 1727, and his ordination as a priest in 1728. A brief summer in 1726 and a two-year leave time from 1727 to 1729 found him in Epworth, gaining pastoral experience as curate to his father, who was becoming infirm. Returning to take up his fellowship in the autumn of 1729, he joined his younger brother Charles, by then an undergraduate at Christ Church, who had recently formed a small group of students seeking to deepen their own faith and serve others. These "Methodists," as they were derisively called (other names cast at them were Bible Moths, Sacramentarians, and the Holy Club), soon drafted the older Wesley brother as their leader. For some five years John Wesley met with them, guiding them in their study of Scripture and primitive Christianity in general, in their devotional life, and in various social projects (e.g., jail visitations and attempts at educating poor children and distributing clothes and food to their families). Wesley looked back on this experience as "the first rise of Methodism." From this episode he took not only the name that was to identify his future work, but also an example of disciplined organization that was to be its hallmark.

On the whole Wesley found Oxford a congenial locus for his own spiritual growth and ministry. In fact, when his ailing father suggested that he succeed him as rector of Epworth, the young tutor went to great lengths to justify his decision to stay at the university. Yet less than a year later, in October 1735, his father having died, Wesley set sail with his brother Charles and another member of the Holy Club for the colony of Georgia, where he hoped to minister to the Indians under the auspices of the Society for the Propagation of the Gospel. Georgia presented Wesley with an escape from the various distractions of Oxford society; there would be no opportunity for indulgence in sensual pleasures in the colonial wilds. The setting and the prospect of preaching to the simple natives (unencumbered, he thought, by the corruptions of civilization) would suit his chief motive in going: the hope of saving his own soul.

Any external account of the Georgia episode, from Wesley's embarkation until his return in early 1738, must classify it as a disaster, at least in the short term. Wesley was soon disabused of his image of the Georgia Indians as "noble savages," and, in fact, never had the opportunity to go among them, the trustees of the colony having pressed him into service as a priest among the settlers in Savannah. He soon also found that

Georgia was no escape from amorous temptations, for into his life of disciplined devotion came a young woman, Sophia Hopkey, niece of the colony's chief magistrate. Their bungled relationship, attributable to Wesley's naiveté and ineptness with the opposite sex, led finally to his precipitous withdrawal from Georgia. He at first backed away when the subject of marriage came up and then felt betrayed when she married another. He refused to serve the couple at Holy Communion—for reasons more personal, perhaps, than the canon law he cited.

This final act became the occasion for numerous trumped-up charges against Wesley in civil proceedings. Many parishioners who had been offended by his high-church zeal supported the indictment, as did the aggrieved Sophia's uncle, who was in charge of the grand jury. Wesley began to prepare his case, but ultimately despaired of obtaining justice and of successfully exercising his ministry any further in Georgia. Consequently, one December evening after prayers he slipped away and took ship for England, depressed and discouraged.

Nevertheless, Wesley could look back years later and discern "the second rise of Methodism" in some of his activity with the congregation in Savannah. Here, for instance, he experimented with small societies of parishioners who met for weekly prayer and fellowship; he also employed extempore prayer, outdoor preaching, early-morning weekday services, Love Feasts, and lay assistants. Moreover, it was during the Georgia sojourn that he first tried hymn singing in worship and published the innovative *Collection of Psalms and Hymns,* foreshadowing another distinctive trait of Methodism.

Perhaps the most important feature of Wesley's Georgia experience was his meeting with the Moravians, the German Pietists who profoundly influenced his theological development and provided him with several useful ecclesiastical examples. The first and most provocative encounter was on board ship en route to Georgia when Wesley, fearing for his life during a storm, noticed the calm faith of some two dozen Moravian passengers, women and children included. Upon landing Wesley made the acquaintance of their leader, Augustus Gottlieb Spangenberg, who began sharing Pietist notions of personal conversion and assurance. Continued interest in their life and message led the discouraged Wesley toward other Moravians when he returned to London.

In many ways the missionary and personal failures of Georgia set the stage for the spiritual triumph of Aldersgate Street, the site of Wesley's legendary conversion. He was certainly in a troubled, searching mood when he met the Moravian Peter Boehler in early 1738. Their intense conversations led Wesley to acknowledge the difference between faith as assent (the intellectual sort that he had possessed heretofore) and faith as total reliance upon Christ, a faith that might be received and experienced in a sudden moment of assurance. It was then but a short step to the wholehearted seeking of such faith. Encouraged by his Moravian friends and by his brother Charles's recent dramatic conversion, John Wesley was ripe for an experience of his own. His own account, often exaggerated in Methodist hagiography (to the point of becoming not only the focus of Wesley's biography, but also a virtual paradigm of conversion within the tradition), nevertheless sheds light on a crucial turning point in his life. Looking back, he saw the day's activity (his morning meditation over Scripture, attendance at an afternoon service at St. Paul's Cathedral, going unwillingly in the evening to a society meeting in Aldersgate Street) as leading to a climax, his hearing the reading of Luther's preface to the Epistle to the Romans:

> About a quarter before nine, while he was describing the change which God works in the heart through faith in Christ, I felt my heart strangely warmed. I felt I did trust in Christ, Christ alone for salvation; and an assurance was given me that He had taken away *my* sins, even *mine*, and saved *me* from the law of sin and death.
> (*Journal*, 24 May 1738)

Aldersgate was not Wesley's only important spiritual conversion (scholars correctly point to an "Oxford conversion," Wesley's determination in preparation for ordination to seek God through "holy living"), nor did it totally release him from doubt and despair, as a number of his later journal entries and letters reveal. But it did give him the sense of personal assurance without which his role in the coming revival would have been impossible.

Nevertheless, the direction of his public ministry was not yet clear. He was full of his newly experienced gospel when he preached on "Salvation by Faith" to a congregation at St. Mary's, Oxford. But he still sought external direction from the Moravians, journeying that summer to their headquarters in Germany. There he noted firsthand their attempts at incarnating primitive Christianity: the "choirs" and "bands" into which they divided their membership; the Love Feasts and Watch Night services; and the hymn singing. Here also he experienced his first doubts about Moravian theology. Back in England, other influences presented themselves: Jonathan Edwards' *Faithful Narrative* of the Great Awakening in New England excited him; and he discovered his new view of faith corroborated in, of all places, the homilies of the Church of England. Meanwhile he and his brother began preaching "strong words" in workhouses and prisons, at public executions, in the religious societies of Oxford and London, and (until a developing reputation for enthusiasm or fanaticism caught up with them) in parish churches.

The decisive turn his career then took owes much to his friend George Whitefield, a young priest already making his name as a dramatic preacher to thousands in the fields around Bristol in the west of England. About to return to America on a missionary journey of his own, Whitefield persuaded Wesley to preach in his place. Not without some Anglican misgivings, Wesley agreed. "I submitted to be more vile," he wrote in his journal for 2 April 1739, "and proclaimed the glad tidings of salvation, speaking from a little eminence in a ground adjoining to the city to about three thousand people." The results of such measures, conversions much like his own, if sometimes more spectacular in their bodily expression, confirmed him in this singular departure from Anglican decency and order. If other priests and prelates were scandalized by a man preaching in another's parish, Wesley would maintain that it was not only his canonical right (as a fellow of a college), but his evangelical duty. "I look upon all the world as my parish," he wrote, aptly summing up his position and contributing another phrase that acquired mythic power in the Wesleyan heritage.

Wesley now began his life's work in earnest, preaching and organizing revivals throughout the British Isles. The preaching successes in the fields of Bristol led to the establishment of the

"New Room," a small building that later became Wesley's western headquarters. In London, meanwhile, Wesley grew restive with the Moravian-dominated religious society he had been attending in Fetter Lane. He was particularly disturbed by their emphasis on quietism, a doctrine that forbade any human effort (including using the sacramental "means of grace") in the process of salvation. Wesley, surer now of his own direction, left the Fetter Lane Society to the Moravians in July 1740 and established his own wholly Methodist society in a renovated cannon factory. "The Foundery" became his headquarters in the metropolis, succeeded by the City Road Chapel, constructed nearby in 1778.

Further preaching brought more conversions, but also considerable opposition, some of it violent. The emotional component of the early revival provided an easy target for authorities who deplored fanaticism and suspected papist intrigue or the leveling tendencies associated with religious dissent in the previous century. Riots occasionally broke out, the mob often recruited by disgruntled parish clergy. Wesley and his cohorts for the most part escaped without serious injury, often winning over hostile crowds by facing them with calmness and courage. As in the early church, violent persecution probably did more good than harm to the cause.

Less spectacular opposition in the form of literary attacks also had to be met, whether it was a slanderous dredging up of the Georgia episode or the more high-minded ecclesiastical arguments of scandalized bishops. To set the record straight, Wesley published the first of many extracts of his journal and, when sufficiently provoked, responded in kind with point-by-point rejoinders in pamphlets of his own. Here began a career in editing and publishing that included not only his journal and polemical and apologetical works, but sermons, abridgments of Christian classics (his *Christian Library*), a magazine, grammars, histories, and such oddities as his *Primitive Physick,* a book of home remedies. *The Bicentennial Edition of the Works of John Wesley,* currently in progress, will contain some thirty-four volumes.

The organization and expansion of the revival proceeded under Wesley's careful autocratic direction. His own regular itinerary took him for the most part along the sides of a triangle connecting London, Bristol, and Newcastle-upon-Tyne (his northern headquarters after 1742). He later added Ireland (1747) and Scotland (1751) to his circuit, though without as much success in either realm as in England. Even there the revival fared better in the new industrial towns and among the working classes than among the rich or among rural farmers and laborers. Preaching was a primary preoccupation (Wesley averaged about fifteen sermons a week during his career), but proclamation was balanced by organization. His journeys more and more involved the establishment and regulation of the local societies and the development of lay leadership to assist him in both preaching and organizing the far-flung Methodist "connexion." And his concern for individuals' souls did not blind him to the physical needs of the poor and outcast to whom he ministered. His call to holiness had a definite social dimension, albeit usually expressed more in terms of individual aid than systemic political action. Nevertheless, his support late in life of William Wilberforce's parliamentary campaign against the slave trade is in direct line with the young Oxford don's collections for the poor and imprisoned years before.

As Methodism grew, strains developed between it and Anglicanism. Wesley himself had not intended to form a new denomination and remained, he believed, a loyal priest of the Church of England throughout his life. Even though he conscientiously urged his Methodists to attend Anglican services and warned his preachers against trying to play the role of clergymen, pressures toward separation were building. The issue came to a head in 1784. Wesley, capitulating to expediency (the Treaty of Paris having just been signed in ratification of American independence), but not before rationalizing his behavior as scriptural, "set apart" the Anglican priest Thomas Coke as "superintendent" of Methodism in North America and sent him there to expedite the founding of a new church with doctrine, liturgy, polity, and ordained clergy who would perform in a sacramental as well as a preaching ministry.

This colonial precedent would be imitated in England literally only "over Wesley's dead body," as one scholar has daintily put it. The eventuality was already in Wesley's mind in 1784, as he made provision for the legal transfer of the work after his death. Rather than leave the superintendency of Methodism to an individual (his previous intention), Wesley drafted a "Deed of Declaration" that named one hundred members of the conference (an annual gathering of his itinerant preachers) as heirs of his ecclesiastical power. The movement would have a solid institutional basis after its founder's death, but not one that could avoid the eventual slide into de facto dissent.

Wesley outlived many of his contemporaries, including his brother Charles and his wife, Mary Vazeille (the ill-advised marriage took place in 1751, soon foundering on the rocks of her jealousy and his refusal to accommodate his work to the demands of a relationship). He also lived to see the demise of the harsh opposition that had reared up against him in the revival's early days. With society's gradual acceptance of Methodism, pulpits were once again open to him, and as he traveled around Britain crowds thronged just to catch a glimpse of this latter-day patriarch.

When the years finally did overtake Wesley, he obliged the tradition by dying well. Friends and family gathered around the bed in his house, next to the City Road Chapel, praying, singing hymns, and listening to the last words of their venerable father in God. The simple funeral Wesley had desired was followed by a flow of sermons and other appropriate memorials, and not only from the pens of Methodists. Concluded an obituary in the March 1791 *Gentleman's Magazine,* "His history, if well written, will certainly be important, for in every respect, as the founder of the most numerous sect in the kingdom, as a man, and as a writer, he must be considered as one of the most extraordinary characters this or any age ever produced."

A neutral assessment of this sort is likely to satisfy neither the hagiographers nor the debunkers. Such is not just the price of greatness, but also of a voluminous record that has tempted biographers of all stripes—the Marxist and the psychohistorian as well as the sentimental purveyor of pious legend. Inevitably, no one portrait will be complete or without its bias. It is perhaps enough to recognize in all the particulars a self-conscious man of God whose story continues to nurture (for better and for worse) the tradition that bears his name.

THE SOCIAL AND ECCLESIASTICAL CONTEXT

The Wesleyan heritage, as much as it owes to the exploits of one man, cannot be completely understood without reference to the social, ecclesiastical, and intellectual context of eighteenth-century England.

For social historians John Wesley's England is a notable chapter in the process of modernization. Nascent industrialization, population growth and mobility, evolving political and educational institutions, and new cultural forms all made their appearance during the eighteenth century. Religion, and notably the religious revival that Wesley helped lead, played an important role in this complex mix of historical forces. It may be that the Evangelical Revival (like other religious awakenings and reformations) was a "revitalization movement," a means by which anxious people were "converted" and society itself was transformed to meet new realities while maintaining continuity with a core of cultural values from the past. The reciprocal relationship of Methodism to eighteenth-century English society and culture helps explain the success of Wesleyanism, and, some would add, the success of England as it entered the modern world.

The Toleration Act of 1689 symbolized the growing pluralism of English society, a process that began at the Reformation (if not before) and intensified during the Puritan Revolution of the seventeenth century. Where hereditary power, whether at court or in the manor house, had presided over a static, structured society buttressed at all levels by the prayers of the Anglican church, alternative structures, albeit still closely regulated, began to assert themselves. Even the ensuing series of political pendulum swings (the Restoration of 1660 followed by the Glorious Revolution, the Tory ascendancy under Queen Anne succeeded by the Whig triumph as the Hanoverians came to the throne in 1714) moved the nation in the new direction. Parliamentary supremacy increasingly took the place of royal prerogative; pluralism and voluntarism supplanted uniformity and coercion; and acquired status began to compete with, if not eliminate, ascribed status.

The Hanoverian era, however, was notable for resistance to change, an inertia motivated by a general revulsion against the violent and wrenching events that preceded it. Alexander Pope's poetical announcement "Whatever is, is right" was matched in the sphere of practical politics by the famous dictum of England's first prime minister, Sir Robert Walpole: "Let sleeping dogs lie." Nevertheless, the processes begun earlier would not slumber long, especially when an increasing population began moving about to the din of industrialization.

Under such pressures various institutions began to feel the strain. In some cases, reform and evolutionary development were possible; seen in the long term, Parliament and electoral politics followed this pattern, and indeed England as a whole came into the modern world relatively unscathed, while decisive change occurred in the rest of Europe and the stage was set for democratic pluralism in North America. But there were institutions within the nation that did not immediately respond to new realities. One such was the Church of England.

Precedent already existed for extra-establishment religion. The groups tolerated after 1689 were the Protestant Dissenters, or Nonconformists, who shared, broadly speaking, a reformation theology with the Anglican church, but who dissented from its "unreformed" polity and refused to conform to the liturgy prescribed in the Book of Common Prayer. Insofar as these less vociferous successors of the Puritans would pledge allegiance to the Crown and subscribe loosely to the Thirty-nine Articles of Religion, they might worship unharassed in their duly registered meetinghouses. This tradition, into which both of John Wesley's parents were born, was alive but not very lively at the beginning of the eighteenth century. The tenor of the times led many, including the young Samuel Wesley and the young Susanna Annesley, to conform to the Church of England. Dissent declined, both in zeal and in numbers, finally representing not more than 5 percent of the population.

Alternatives of a sort were available even within the church. Anglicans who wished voluntarily to deepen their own spiritual life or to support a moral or missionary endeavor over and above ordinary church attendance could join a religious society, a small group of communicants who met for prayer, spiritual discourse, and the expression of charitable concerns, under the direction of a clergyman. This scheme, initiated in the late 1670s on the German Pietist model, was supported by such highly placed clergy as Archbishop Thomas Tenison—and such relatively obscure country rectors as Samuel Wesley.

The movement persisted well into the eighteenth century, providing John Wesley with a model for the Holy Club and for his later organizational exploits during the revival. Closely allied were other expressions of Anglican voluntarism: the Societies for the Reformation of Manners (pious Dissenters were even welcomed in this crusade against vice of all sorts), the Society for Promoting Christian Knowledge (1698), and the Society for the Propagation of the Gospel (1701). These all represent attempts to enliven a state church that often seemed unwilling or unable to meet the deeper needs of its members and of the world.

Methodism was thus not without its predecessors, positive models of alternative religion both within and without Anglicanism. However, there were also negative factors at work fighting against these pluralistic tendencies. Anglicanism had organizational problems; it was wedded to politics at all levels (every bishop a government appointee with a seat in the House of Lords, most local clergy under the thumb of the local squire), and yet the church had meager institutional means by which to adjust to the requirements of a new age. The convocations of Canterbury and York, the only instruments of Anglican self-government, were prorogued in 1717 because of ecclesiastical controversies and did not resume their role for well over a century. In the meantime a parish that wished to respond to demographic trends would have to pursue the cumbersome process of getting an act of Parliament to permit the building of an additional church.

The Church of England's sluggish response to change is reflected in its inability to provide effective pastoral care to its growing (and moving) body of potential constituents. The parish system, a relic of the Middle Ages, still reflected the settlement patterns of that era. Some parishes continued to be more amenable to the Anglican church, particularly the smaller agricultural parishes, each of which was presided over by a single squire who maintained his ancestors' monopoly on land and work and who found in the church a convenient instrument of social control. However, larger parishes in wilder terrain more suited for pasturing flocks than for intensive tilling often resisted Anglicanism; settlements were scattered, sometimes quite distant from the parish church, and in place of an all-powerful squire there were dozens of small free-holders and hundreds of others who felt no particular deference toward either gentleman or priest. The same independence from the squire-parson alliance could be found in market towns and the growing manufacturing areas, where nonagricultural occupations began to predominate. The problem for Anglicanism in the last situation was exacerbated by population growth, particularly in those northern and urban areas where the parish system was already under strain.

Then, too, the church could not catch up with those people who were more or less constantly on the move, never settled in any parish: soldiers, sailors, chapmen, apprentices, and the like, young men out of their element and susceptible both to the allure of city vice and to the appeal of evangelical preaching. It was not uncommon for a hapless parish priest to have thousands of souls under his care and a church that could accommodate only two hundred—if they cared to attend.

The hapless priest, indeed, was part of the problem, though this was not necessarily his fault. In more than half the 10,000 "livings," he was likely to be scandalously underpaid. This resulted in the well-known "abuses," condemned in canon law but tolerated throughout the century as the only way some clergy could make ends meet: pluralism (the holding of more than one clerical position simultaneously) and nonresidence (living outside one's "cure" while attending to one's other pursuits). Nearly half the clergy in the diocese of York were nonresidents and/or pluralists in 1743. As conscientious as the clergy might have been (and many were, in village rectories as well as in episcopal palaces), they simply could not maintain a consistent sacramental and preaching ministry, let alone deliver effective pastoral care.

If Methodism developed in response to an ecclesiastical vacuum, it also stepped into a theological breach. The intellectual elite was caught up in an Age of Reason, working out the implications of a well-ordered Newtonian universe and empathizing with John Locke's *The Reasonableness of Christianity* (1695). Progressive thinkers, em-

barrassed by the irrationality associated with traditional religion, spoke of God as an abstract First Cause, denied biblical miracles, and were ready to replace supernatural revelation with reason. If Deism or Unitarianism did not triumph, their close relative latitudinarianism, a genteel disdain for precise dogmatic formulations, did win the day. Some, like Bishop Joseph Butler, defended orthodoxy against the rationalists on their own terms. The more usual response, however, followed the example of Archbishop John Tillotson in preaching an inoffensive, prudential version of Christianity.

While Wesley was not immune to the blandishments of reason (Locke's empiricism provides a useful rationalization of "experience"), Methodism's real advancement was among the lower classes, who were relatively untouched by the intellectual approach. Even among the upper classes rationalism sometimes appeared to be a thin veneer over a persisting supernaturalism. Wesley himself believed in poltergeists and witches, and the London and Lisbon earthquakes at mid-century filled even some nominal rationalists with dread of divine retribution. Recent scholarship on popular religion has uncovered powerful currents of superstition persisting well past the eighteenth century, and often in connection with Methodism. It is quite likely that Wesley's gospel established a point of contact between popular supernaturalism and the abstract orthodoxy, veiled in rationalism, of the state church.

Wesley's theological answer to the intellectual spirit of the age was itself a product of existing theological currents. Heir to a rich legacy, he learned both high Anglicanism and Puritanism at his mother's knee; both were part of his family inheritance. The one grounded him in Anglican orthodoxy and resulted in his Oxford "conversion" to holy living; the other, the tradition of his grandfather Annesley and of Jonathan Edwards, influenced him more and more as he organized the revival and realized the practical lessons it might teach him. Catholicism, both in the form of the church fathers and in continental spirituality, had a lasting effect on him, as is evidenced by their inclusion in his *Christian Library*. The Lutheran tradition, as filtered through Pietism, was indelibly stamped on him through his association with the Moravians, Martin Luther's own words being the immediate occasion of the Aldersgate experience. Add to this mix his claim to be a "man of one book"—the Bible—and his acceptance of Locke's philosophical empiricism (among other current intellectual trends) and one may see the creative possibilities open to a capable and zealous practical theologian.

THE WESLEYAN ETHOS AND ITS LEGACY

Methodism, more obviously than most denominational traditions, was not only a set of beliefs or a particular form of church government; it was also an ethos, a way of life.

Doctrine. Wesley's writings provide proof for those who have accused the tradition of theological indifferentism: "Orthodoxy, or right opinions, is, at best, a slender part of religion, if it can be allowed to be any part at all" (*Works,* 8:249). Yet even in the classic statement of Wesleyan theological ecumenism, the sermon "Catholic Spirit" (*Sermons,* 2:129–146), he guards himself against the charge of an "indifference to all opinions" or "muddy understanding." Nevertheless, the popular image of Wesley as an unthinking revivalist persists—so much so that the rehabilitation of his reputation as a theologian (albeit a "folk theologian"), let alone as the "most important Anglican theologian of the 18th century" (in the words of Albert C. Outler), is still not complete.

At least two factors are at work here. First, Wesley was not a systematic or speculative theologian. His was the theology of an itinerant preacher, written literally on the move, and aimed at people on the move, who were "fleeing the wrath to come" or already on the "way to heaven." Second, as an Anglican priest organizing voluntary societies within the church, Wesley could assume basic Christian orthodoxy. The Anglican Church would (or should) expose its communicants to Scripture, the ancient creeds, the Thirty-nine Articles of Religion, and the Reformation theology that infused the Book of Common Prayer and the Book of Homilies. Much like a founder of a Roman Catholic religious order, Wesley did not need to proclaim a new doctrinal system; he did, however, wish to accent several neglected areas of faith and life. These emphases, he believed, were thoroughly scriptural, consistent with the Christian tradition and reason, and confirmed in experience; they

represent a significant, though not always conspicuous, component in the Wesleyan heritage. Taken together, these emphases express what Gordon Rupp has called Wesley's "pessimism of nature" in conjunction with his "optimism of grace."

The first two doctrines (original sin and justification by faith) are relatively noncontroversial —apart from the times when the latter became an occasion for Wesley's Arminianism to be challenged by the hyper-Calvinism of the day. In fact, original sin for Wesley was close to the Calvinist doctrine of total depravity. Divine intervention is necessary in the process of salvation; but that intervention is already visible in certain alleviations provided humanity after the Fall (the law, natural conscience, reason, and freedom), all instances of God's prevenient grace, grace that "comes before" one's awareness of it.

Grace is also operative in the second Wesleyan emphasis, justification by faith, the applying of the merits of Christ's death in a process that includes baptism, repentance, justification, adoption, regeneration, and the restoration of the divine image. Such a faith is not merely intellectual assent, the "divine conviction of God and the things of God" that Wesley called the "faith of a servant," but the "faith of a son," that is, a "sure trust and confidence that Christ died for my sins, that he loved me and gave himself for me" (*Sermons,* 1:125; *Works,* 7:199).

The doctrine of assurance (or the "witness of the Holy Spirit") introduces the more controversial area of religious experience, calling to mind the emotional manifestations that opened Wesley to the charge of "enthusiasm." His early position, based on his own experience, was that assurance necessarily comes with justification. He later backed down from this insistence, still maintaining that in most cases a believer might expect "an inward impression on the soul, whereby the Spirit of God directly witnesses to my spirit, that I am a child of God" (*Sermons,* 1:208). Far from opening the door to salvation by emotion, Wesley maintained that this experience, if it were genuine, would be confirmed in a changed life. Critics were not particularly convinced that fanaticism did not result from Methodist preoccupation with assurance. Doubtless there were (and are) abuses. But this doctrine gave theological substance to the revival's rediscovery of affective religion.

Finally, and most provocatively, Wesley

preached sanctification, also known as perfect love, Christian perfection, holiness, or the great salvation. Wesley claimed this as the most distinctive Methodist doctrine, though it has been variously distorted, overemphasized, and totally forgotten by his spiritual descendants. Wesley himself saw it as the plain teaching of Scripture, defining it in deceptively simple terms: loving God with all one's heart and one's neighbor as oneself. Nevertheless, the notion that perfection was achievable in this life rankled many, then as now. Against those who saw it as a backdoor version of works righteousness, Wesley replied that sanctification no less than justification was an act of divine grace appropriated by faith. Just as justification is "what God does for us through his Son," so sanctification is "what he works in us by his Holy Spirit" (*Sermons*, 1:119).

Answering those who were offended by the extravagant effusions of some Methodists prematurely claiming "sinless perfection," Wesley admitted that perfection is not freedom from ignorance, error, infirmity, or temptation, or from a subsequent fall back into sin. Wesley is, therefore, speaking of a relative, not an absolute, perfection, a dynamic that includes every believer, no matter how far along in the way of salvation. If there is any perfection in the normally accepted sense of the word, it is a freedom from conscious sin, both the outward act and the inner intention. The process, Wesley taught, was gradual, beginning at the point of justification; but at the end of the process, one ought to look to that moment when sin is eradicated. Some might not be completely aware of the instantaneous change, but when that moment comes, most will experience the same witness and fruit of the Spirit at sanctification as they did when they were justified.

Despite the controversy, Wesley regarded sanctification as the mainspring of the revival. It provided the dynamic that sustained the inner life of his converts and his societies after the individual's conversion crisis was resolved or the initial wave of revival had crested. The Christian life is not over, God's law is not set aside, at justification; one must strive expectantly for perfect love of God and neighbor, one must complete the process of salvation. The doctrine of sanctification, drawing on those sources of the "holy living" tradition that had so influenced Wesley in his pre-Aldersgate days, thus stands in creative tension with the Reformation emphasis on justification. In fact, Wesley's genius as a practical theologian may well be the bringing together of Protestant *sola fide* and Catholic "holy living," of justification and sanctification, of faith and works. Furthermore, Christian perfection—holiness of heart and life—provides the theological undergirding for Wesleyan ethical activism, whether it tends toward individual morality (as it did most usually in the eighteenth century) or toward corporate social action (as it has in some of its more recent incarnations).

Necessarily missing from this brief sketch of Wesleyan theology are discussions of, for example, his clashes with Anglican antagonists, with Calvinist Evangelicals, and with his former friends the Moravians; his interesting approach to Roman Catholicism; and his views on certain other doctrines, to the extent that they can be culled from his voluminous, unsystematic writings. The interested reader should check the bibliography.

Hymns. More important in our pursuit of a Wesleyan ethos, yet still closely connected to doctrinal emphases, is a discussion of Methodist worship. Though one might speak of extempore preaching, of Love Feasts and Watch Night services (adopted from the early Christian *agape* and the vigil as revived by the Moravians), or of the Covenant Service (Wesley's liturgical adaptation of a Puritan idea), one necessarily turns first to the hymns of Charles Wesley. The younger Wesley deserves preeminence in his continuing, direct influence on generations of English-speaking Christians. A small minority (theologians, ministers, students) actually read and ponder the sermons and treatises of John Wesley, but untold thousands of ordinary people sing Charles Wesley's hymns on a given Sunday morning. The Wesleyan doctrinal emphases (as well as virtually all other phases of evangelical life) are more likely to be heard (though not necessarily with understanding) in such hymns as "Jesus, Lover of My Soul," "O, for a Thousand Tongues to Sing," and "Love Divine, All Loves Excelling."

Wider theological ideas are also poetically celebrated—high Anglican ones, at that—in hymns written for various festivals of the liturgical calendar (of which "Christ the Lord Is Risen Today" and "Hark, the Herald Angels Sing" have been the most lastingly popular) and for the Eucharist (for example, "Oh, the Depth of Love Divine" and "Come, Sinners to the Gospel Feast"). The careful student will also learn much about early Methodist life from the hymns composed to complement the society's activities: gathering, praying, celebrating a Love Feast, renewing the covenant, and parting.

John Wesley recommended the often-reprinted 1780 *Hymnbook* as "a little body of experimental and practical divinity" and as a manual of private devotion (*Oxford Works,* 7:1–22, 74). Hymn singing among the "people called Methodists" certainly fulfilled these two functions, reinforcing Wesleyan teaching and inspiring them to deeper piety. Moreover, hymn singing became a popular and distinctive characteristic of Methodist worship. Strictly speaking, Wesley's hymns might be considered the functional equivalent of the psalms chanted in the parish churches, but in practice they bore much more weight. The *Hymnbook* served as a kind of Methodist Book of Common Prayer—not, that is to say, as the liturgy itself, but as the affective, responsive center of the worship experience. Methodism cannot take full credit for the Protestant hymn; Luther, Paul Gerhardt, and Isaac Watts must also be reckoned with. But "Our Hymns," as the early Methodist leaders referred to them, became a distinguishing and enduring feature of the Wesleyan heritage, a focal point of the Methodist subculture, and a gift to the wider church.

Organization. Wesley maintained that Methodism's raison d'être is: "to reform the nation, particularly the Church; and to spread scriptural holiness over the land" (*Works,* 8:299). To do so required an organization and a discipline capable of harnessing all the energy generated by preaching and singing. Here John Wesley excelled. While other revivalists (such as his Calvinist friend George Whitefield) may have been more effective preachers, none could match his ability to provide a social context for the long-term nurture of his converts and for the subsequent multiplication of the evangelical effort. This institutional factor explains not only why organization seems always to loom large in the Methodist family of denominations, but also why we are concerned with tracing the influence of a Wesleyan heritage at all—rather than, say, a "Whitefieldian" one.

Drawing on a variety of sources and often improvising as he went, Wesley developed a tightly articulated "connexion," a strong organization binding every local branch of the movement to-

gether and to Wesley at the center. The system worked well in early industrial England and proved adaptable to the American frontier as well. Several features deserve brief discussions, including the various key units of early Methodism (the society, the class, the circuit, and the conference) and the basic offices or roles to which Methodists could aspire (itinerant preacher, local preacher, class leader, steward, and trustee).

The society, based loosely on the model of the older Anglican religious societies and the Holy Club at Oxford, was the first sociological expression of Methodism and remained its basic local unit. As with most early Methodist nomenclature, the term guarded against the implication that a new dissenting congregation was being set up to rival the parish church. The Methodists met weekly for prayer, singing, exhortation, and mutual care in the society, not for prayer book liturgy, not during church hours, and not necessarily led by a clergyman: the society was not to take the church's place. Accordingly, membership did not depend upon any creedal or ecclesiastical test, but upon a sincere "desire to flee from the wrath to come, to be saved from their sins" (*Works,* 8:270). Entrance into the society was relatively easy; continuance was another matter, since sincerity could be measured against a rather stringent set of rules governing moral conduct and religious duty.

Early on Wesley followed the Moravian practice of forming "bands," small groups of people at a similar stage in their spiritual pilgrimage who met together for mutual spiritual encouragement. A more lasting and important subdivision of the societies, however, was the class, a dozen or so Methodists organized without regard to age, sex, marital status, or spiritual attainment under the leadership of a layperson especially chosen by Wesley. Instituted as a means of collecting a "penny-a-week" from each member of the Bristol society, the class soon took on its more important function as the primary locus of Methodist fellowship and discipline. Class membership became a requirement for every Methodist, and it was in the class meeting that Wesley himself (or one of his "assistants") examined each class member and presented or withheld the quarterly "ticket" necessary for admission to the other society functions.

The circuit and the conference arose as means

to strengthen the work of the local societies and link them in an efficient national movement. The circuit was the regional collection of societies placed under the care of one or more of Wesley's preachers in a regular pattern of itinerancy. This enabled rather far-flung groups of Methodists to receive the attention of specially called and approved persons who superintended local affairs in Wesley's stead. There were seven circuits in England and Wales in 1746 (some of gargantuan proportions, taking a preacher as much as two months to negotiate); by the time of Wesley's death in 1791 they had multiplied to 114 more compact areas throughout the British Isles.

The conference first met in 1744, a small gathering of evangelical clergy and lay preachers invited by Wesley to advise him on matters of doctrine and discipline. It became an annual affair and eventually included all of Wesley's itinerant preachers, though it remained under his firm control. In addition to setting theological and ethical standards, it examined, admitted, and stationed preachers wherever they were needed, oversaw financial matters (for example, a common fund out of which societies in any part of the kingdom could be helped), and collected membership statistics. Only after Wesley's death did his supreme legislative and administrative authority devolve upon the conference. More than any other Wesleyan institution, the conference came to represent the "connexion" with its fusion of Catholic-style centralized authority and evangelical zeal.

Lay Leadership. A signal characteristic of the Methodist ethos is the important part given the laity. At first reluctant to employ unordained people in the preaching of the Gospel, Wesley soon saw the usefulness of such a program and, from 1744 on, the burden of evangelization and discipline fell increasingly on these "helpers" or "assistants." Also known as itinerants or traveling preachers (note again that all designations scrupulously avoid church usage: these were "extraordinary messengers," not clergy), they were to exercise pastoral and administrative oversight in the circuits in Wesley's place. Wesley's famous injunction to them was: "You have nothing to do but to save souls. Therefore spend and be spent in this work" (*Works,* 8:310). Submitting themselves as "sons in the gospel" to Wesley's authority, they became the shock troops of the Evangelical Revival, traveling great distances, spending weeks at a time away from home, and living off the land (or the local Methodists) with scarce if any recompense for themselves or their families. "Local preachers," men who possessed the "grace and gifts," but were constrained, usually by financial necessity, from leaving their trades and entering the full-time itinerancy, did yeoman service whenever the regular preachers were unavailable.

The class leader was, religiously speaking, only a cut below the traveling preacher in the Methodist hierarchy. Wesley sought out men and women of spiritual maturity and appointed them to shepherd the small but important classes. The leader's more "worldly" equivalent was the society steward, chosen to handle financial affairs. These included collecting and spending money, keeping strict accounts, and relieving the poor. As Methodism grew, one of the chief jobs of the stewards was to supervise the building of "preaching houses" (again, a name carefully picked to avoid comparison either with Anglican churches or with Dissenting meeting-houses), some 470 of which had been built by Wesley's death. But a new class of officials, the trustees, soon arose to fulfill this function—with the aid of deeds ensuring that only duly appointed Methodist preachers expounding Wesleyan doctrine could officiate in them.

Over half of the early Methodists were women and, although the "connexion" was run by men, there were considerable leadership opportunities for the women, more than had been available in English Protestantism since the rise of Quakerism in the previous century. They led classes and bands, founded and staffed schools and orphanages, visited the sick and imprisoned, and in certain extraordinary circumstances preached and even "itinerated," though never with the formal appointment of the conference. Wesley preferred that his preachers not marry, but many did, and their wives became adjuncts in ministry both by enduring the inconvenience of biennial moves and a frequently absent husband and by actively involving themselves in local class and society work. Women also figured heavily in the pages of Wesley's *Arminian Magazine,* both in editorial correspondence and as subjects of biographical articles. There is evidence also that active Methodist women formed informal support networks to encourage one another in their various ministries.

Discipline. The spirit of early (and subsequent) Methodism is also caught in the various sets of rules drawn up by Wesley to aid his people in their pursuit of holiness. Note, for instance, the small-group discipline found in the "Rules of the Band-Societies, drawn up December 25, 1738." Potential members were asked, among other things:

> Do you desire to be told of all your faults, and that plain and home? . . . Consider! Do you desire we should tell you whatsoever we think, whatsoever we fear, whatsoever we hear, concerning you? . . . Do you desire that, in doing this, we should come as close as possible, that we should cut to the quick, and search your heart to the bottom?
>
> (*Works*, 8:272–273)

"The General Rules," composed in 1743, is a classic expression of Methodist concern for holy living. A member's "desire to flee from the wrath to come" must be evidenced by fruits, here listed under three headings: doing no harm; doing good; and attending upon all the ordinances of God. In the list of evils to be avoided are sabbath breaking, drunkenness, "the buying or selling uncustomed goods" (Wesley was death on smugglers), participating in inappropriate diversions (those that "cannot be used in the name of the Lord Jesus"), and "needless self-indulgence." Positive standards include visiting people in need and providing them with food and clothing as well as instruction, reproof, and exhortation, "doing good especially to them that are of the household of faith" (in other words, patronizing Methodist businesses), and the taking up of one's cross. In the ecclesiastical realm, Methodists are enjoined to attend public worship, including the Lord's Supper (that is, they should be present at Anglican services as well as at Methodist preaching), and to practice family and private prayer, Scripture reading, fasting, and abstinence (*Works*, 8:270–271). The life Wesley demanded of his followers does indeed resemble that of a "married and secular monasticism" (Davies and Rupp, 1966).

It is not easy to say how successfully discipline was applied. There probably were the legendary reformations of previously notorious sinners, and Wesley was quick to exclude from society membership those who did not match up to his strict expectations. But the morality inculcated here is traditional and conservative, and would not have appeared foreign to a majority of Methodists, especially those brought up in relatively devout, upstanding working-class or lower-middle-class families.

In fact, there is evidence that Wesley had better luck with his moral than with his ecclesiastical rigor. Loving one's neighbor as oneself was in many ways easier to contemplate than rising early for 5 A.M. preaching, attending the sacrament at the parish church, and fasting every Friday. Yet even the ethical imperative could begin to slip, as Wesley foresaw in a burst of Weberian insight in 1786: the holiness he had inculcated would lead to diligence, frugality, and economic improvement, which in turn would lead to worldliness and a consequent loss of zeal and holiness. The form of religion might remain, but the spirit might well vanish (*Works*, 13:227).

Legacy. If the Wesleyan tradition was, indeed, a way of life as well as a system of belief, it is not surprising that its legacy should be played out beyond the preaching house walls. And if it did change individuals (nearly 92,000 ticket-carrying Methodists out of a 5.5 million population in 1801, a decade after Wesley's death), it must have had some bearing on the course of the society in which it grew and flourished.

In fact, Methodism has been scrutinized from Wesley's day to the present, by religious and secular historians alike, to determine the nature of its influence. The issue has been grossly oversimplified in the proposition that Methodism "saved England from a French-style revolution." In this view Wesley assisted the process of social change by bringing members of the nascent working class to literacy, training them for leadership roles (for instance, in the early labor movement), and unconsciously providing them with an ideology that legitimated independence and improvement and included a religious subculture that met the associational and communal needs of people caught between the old order and the new.

On the other side Marxist historians, notably E. P. Thompson, emphasize Wesley's natural conservatism and see Methodism, both in its revivalistic exuberance and in its exact discipline, as a regressive feature of the era, playing into the hands of bourgeois factory owners. Revolutionary ardor was drained in the emotional release of worship, and a sober, tractable work force was on the job ready to be exploited early Monday morning. The debate continues, attesting to the general perception that the Wesleyan heritage was an important factor in the development of modern Britain.

The legacy, of course, was not limited to its social impact—nor to the British Isles. Methodism, as we have seen, incorporated all the rich complexity of human religion (experience, myth, doctrine, worship, morality, community). And while it emerged as a popular and powerful religious alternative in the crucible of eighteenth-century England, the Wesleyan heritage also proved eminently exportable and ready to shape, and be shaped by, the American experience.

BIBLIOGRAPHY

Primary Sources

Stuart Andrews, *Methodism and Society* (1970); Frank Baker et al., eds., *The Oxford Edition of the Works of John Wesley*, 4 vols. (1976–1983), cont. as *The Bicentennial Edition of the Works of John Wesley* (1984–   ); Richard M. Cameron, ed., *The Rise of Methodism: A Source Book* (1954); Nehemiah Curnock, ed., *The Journal of the Rev. John Wesley, A.M.*, 8 vols. (1909–1916); Richard P. Heitzenrater, ed., *The Elusive Mr. Wesley*, 2 vols. (1984).

Thomas Jackson, ed., *The Works of the Rev. John Wesley, M.A.*, 14 vols. (1829–1831; repr. 1978); Albert C. Outler, ed., *John Wesley* (1964); Alan Smith, *The Established Church and Popular Religion, 1750–1850* (1971); Edward H. Sugden, ed., *Wesley's Standard Sermons*, 2 vols. (1921); John Telford, ed., *The Letters of the Rev. John Wesley, A.M.*, 8 vols. (1931); Frank Whaling, ed., *John and Charles Wesley: Selected Prayers, Hymns, Journal Notes, Sermons, Letters and Treatises* (1981).

Critical and Biographical Studies

Anthony Armstrong, *The Church of England, the Methodists and Society, 1700–1850* (1973); Stanley Edward Ayling, *John Wesley* (1979; rev. ed, 1983); Frank Baker, *Charles Wesley as Revealed by His Letters* (1948) and *John Wesley and the Church of England* (1970); Earl Kent Brown, *Women of Mr. Wesley's Methodism* (1983); Horton Davies, *Worship and Theology in England*, vol. 3: *From Watts and Wesley to Maurice, 1690–1850* (1961); Rupert E. Davies, *Methodism* (1963; rev. ed., 1976) and, with E. G. Rupp, eds., *A History of the Methodist Church in Great Britain*, vol. 1 (1966); Frederick Dreyer, "Faith and Experience in the Thought of John Wesley," in *American Historical Review*, 88 (1983).

Alan D. Gilbert, *Religion and Society in Industrial England: Church, Chapel and Social Change, 1740–1914* (1976); V. H. H. Green, *The Young Mr. Wesley* (1961); Elie Halévy, *The Birth of Methodism in England* (1906; ed. and trans. by Bernard Semmel, 1971); Nolan B. Harmon, ed., *Encyclopedia of World Methodism*, 2 vols. (1974); Thomas A. Langford, *Practical Divinity: Theology in the Wesleyan Tradition* (1983); Harald Lindström, *Wesley and Sanctification* (1946; rep. 1984).

M. Douglas Meeks, ed., *The Future of the Methodist Theological Traditions* (1985); Kenneth E. Rowe, ed., *The Place of Wesley in the Christian Tradition* (1976) and *United Methodist Studies: Basic Bibliographies* (1982); Theodore Runyon, ed., *Sanctification and Liberation: Liberation Theologies in Light of the Wesleyan Tradition* (1981); Bernard Semmel, *The Methodist Revolution* (1973); E. P. Thompson, *The Making of the English Working Class* (1963; rev. ed., 1968); John D. Walsh, "Elie Halévy and the Birth of Methodism," in *Transactions of the Royal Historical Society*, 25 (1975); Colin W. Williams, *John Wesley's Theology Today* (1960).

[*See also* UNITED METHODISM.]

UNITED METHODISM

Charles Yrigoyen, Jr.

THE United Methodist Church was created on 23 April 1968 in Dallas, Texas. It was formed by a union of the Methodist Church and the Evangelical United Brethren Church, both of which were the result of earlier unions. The Methodist Church was constituted in 1939 in Kansas City, Missouri, when the Methodist Episcopal Church, the Methodist Episcopal Church, South, and the Methodist Protestant Church were joined. In 1946 in Johnstown, Pennsylvania, the Evangelical United Brethren Church was organized by a merger of the Evangelical Church and the Church of the United Brethren in Christ. The two churches shared similar theological views and organizational structures; they also enjoyed generally congenial relationships long before their union was consummated.

BEGINNINGS

Methodism began in eighteenth-century England under the leadership of John Wesley and his brother Charles. Their father, Samuel, was a priest in the Church of England; their mother, Susanna, who had family roots in the Dissenting tradition, was unusually intelligent and pious. In the Anglican rectory in which they were reared, John and Charles Wesley developed a high respect for scholarship, biblical faith, and the practice of the Christian life. Both attended Oxford University, where they became active in a small group called the Holy Club that met regularly for serious Christian fellowship, prayer, and biblical study. Since they lived by a strict and systematic schedule, this small assembly was derisively named the Methodists by other Oxford students.

After being ordained priests in the Church of England, both John and Charles Wesley volunteered for mission work in America. They arrived in the Georgia colony in February 1736, prepared to minister to the English settlers and hoping to convert the Indians to "true religion." Although the Georgia mission was not successful, the brothers met and were positively influenced by Moravians in connection with it. Charles returned to England later in 1736; John in 1737.

Within a few days of each other, in May 1738, the Wesley brothers experienced a spiritual transformation. John described it as feeling his "heart strangely warmed." From that point forward, their ministries were characterized by lively evangelical preaching and effective organizing. They began to preach wherever a group could be gathered. Churches, homes, fields, markets, and mines were the scenes of their evangelical proclamation, at which many experienced conversion. Charles often wrote hymns to be used in their gatherings.

The Wesleys organized their followers into groups called societies, usually composed of smaller groups known as classes. The societies met for preaching and worship, led either by one of the Wesley brothers or by one of their designated lay preacher assistants. The classes, which served as assemblies for study, prayer, and mutual encouragement, were supervised by lay persons commissioned to be class leaders. In no case, however, was the society or class to pre-empt membership and participation in the local Church of England parish. The Wesleys originally intended Methodism only to be a renewal movement within the established church. At first hundreds, and then thousands, of people in England and Ireland were attracted to Methodism. The Wesleyan revival was under way.

The first persons who were products of the

blooming Methodist movement arrived in America about 1760. By the end of the decade a handful of these lay people had begun preaching and had organized Methodist societies. Among the earliest leaders were Robert Strawbridge, a strong-willed immigrant farmer from County Leitrim, Ireland, who established Methodist work in Maryland about 1760; Barbara Heck and her cousin Philip Embury, also immigrants from Ireland, who started a Methodist society in New York City in 1766; and Thomas Webb, a retired officer in the British army, who was responsible for the founding of Methodist societies in Philadelphia and on Long Island. Captain Webb created an interesting spectacle when he preached in his colorful regimental uniform, sporting a green patch over his right eye, which he had lost in battle in Quebec. These lay persons, without express authorization from the Wesleys, launched Methodism in America.

As Methodism took hold in the New World, John Wesley was notified of its existence there. Thomas Taylor, a Methodist in New York, wrote to Wesley on 11 April 1768 imploring him to send preachers to America. If the money for their passage could not be raised in England, Taylor wrote, "we would sell our coats and shirts and pay it. I most earnestly beg an interest in your prayers, and trust you and many of our brethren will not forget the church in this wilderness" (Norwood, ed., *Sourcebook of American Methodism*, pp. 33–34).

Two of Wesley's preachers, Richard Boardman and Joseph Pilmore, were willing to answer the call to America. Arriving in Philadelphia late in October 1769, they immediately set to work to strengthen the Methodist societies and to start new groups. Following Wesley's intention, Pilmore attempted to show that the Methodist societies were not designed to cause a schism within the Church of England parishes in America. In fact, Pilmore claimed, the Methodist groups were "intended for the benefit of all those of every Denomination who being truely convinced of sin, and the danger they are exposed to, earnestly desire to flee from the wrath to come" (Maser and Maag, eds., *The Journal of Joseph Pilmore*, p. 29).

As Methodist work in America continued to show promise of greater growth, Pilmore wrote to Wesley in 1770 asking for at least two more preachers. Wesley selected Richard Wright and Francis Asbury to labor with Boardman and Pilmore. Wright was not very successful, but Asbury was to become a premier leader of American Methodism.

Asbury was born near Birmingham, England, in 1745. He was converted under the ministry of one of Wesley's itinerant preachers and began to hold public services on his own. By 1769 he was appointed to lead the Methodist work in Northamptonshire. Two years later Asbury arrived in Philadelphia. His journal and letters are an invaluable source of information concerning the development of early American Methodism.

While crossing the ocean, Asbury pondered his mission: "Whither am I going? To the New World. What to do? To gain honour? No, if I know my own heart. To get money? No: I am going to live to God, and to bring others so to do. . . . I feel my spirit bound to the New World, and my heart united to the people, though unknown." Shortly after his arrival in America, he observed, "My brethren seem unwilling to leave the cities, but I think I shall show them the way" (Clark, ed., *Journal and Letters of Francis Asbury*, pp. 4, 10). And show the way he did. Asbury rode approximately 250,000 miles on horseback during the span of his ministry in America as he preached, organized Methodist societies, presided over important meetings, settled quarrels, attempted to prevent schisms, imposed discipline, and finally became a bishop of the Methodist Episcopal Church. No other figure in American Methodism exerted more influence on its life and ministry than Asbury, especially during the early years of its history.

In 1773 John Wesley sent two more preachers to America, Thomas Rankin and George Shadford. One of Rankin's duties was to convene the first conference of American Methodist preachers. Ten of them met in Philadelphia in July 1773 and reported 1,160 members in various Methodist societies in Maryland, New Jersey, Virginia, Pennsylvania, and New York. The conference made several important decisions regarding the organization of Methodism in America. It officially committed itself and its people to the spiritual leadership and authority of John Wesley. The preachers were forbidden to administer the Lord's Supper since they were not ordained. They agreed that none of their number was to reprint any of Wesley's books without his consent and the approval of the other preachers.

Finally, they stipulated that although anyone was invited to the general preaching services, their society meetings and love feasts (special gatherings where Methodists shared bread and water, prayer, hymns, personal testimonies, and an offering for the poor) were usually to be reserved for members of their societies. The preachers also agreed that they would give semiannual reports of their work. This gathering foreshadowed the establishment of the Annual Conference, a basic organizational unit of the church.

John Wesley continued to appoint preachers for America until the eve of the American Revolution, when relations between the colonies and England were becoming acutely strained. The Revolution caused a major crisis for Methodists in America. While Wesley advised his American preachers to remain neutral on the matter, he staunchly opposed independence. In 1775 he published *A Calm Address to Our American Colonies*, in which he defended the right of the king and the Parliament to control the colonists' lives, liberties, and properties.

By their religious identification with Wesley, Methodists in America were assumed to share his Tory politics and disdain for colonial independence. Furthermore, a number of Methodist preachers were criticized because they refused to bear arms in the revolutionary cause. Asbury, for example, who opposed violence, moved to Delaware, where he took refuge in the home of Judge Thomas White. Delaware, unlike other colonies, did not require a promise to bear arms in its oath of allegiance. Nevertheless, many Methodists served in the colonial army and offered their encouragement and assistance to the struggle. By the war's end, the opposition to Methodists as unpatriotic had subsided.

A second crisis during the early years of American Methodism centered on the right of the unordained preachers to administer the sacraments, especially the Lord's Supper. Led by Robert Strawbridge, a small group became persuaded that they were called to baptize and to administer the Lord's Supper as well as to preach. They were especially determined to do this since a number of Anglican clergy had returned to England, leaving many Methodists without access to the sacraments. And the Methodist preachers often did not feel as friendly as they once had toward the Anglican clergy who remained. Wesley, Asbury, and others were adamantly opposed to sacramental administrations by the unordained. Between 1778 and 1780 arguments were offered by each side, and the prospect of schism loomed among American Methodists. Division was averted in 1780, when those advocating the administration of the sacraments agreed to suspend the practice until they received further advice from Wesley.

In the years following the Revolution, Wesley realized that the situation of the Methodists in America was considerably different from that of his followers in England. America had achieved political independence. Many of the Anglican parishes were without clergy, making it difficult for American Methodists to receive the sacraments. While his people in England could be both Anglican and Methodist, it was increasingly difficult for Americans to be both. After much careful thought, Wesley decided on a drastic course. His American preachers would have to be ordained, and the Methodist societies in America would have to be free to organize as a church. However, they were to remain loyal to him and to Methodist theological principles and discipline.

In September 1784 Wesley, with his friends Thomas Coke and James Creighton, both Church of England clergymen, ordained two of Wesley's English lay preachers, Richard Whatcoat and Thomas Vasey. Wesley had become convinced that both bishops and presbyters had the right to ordain. Therefore, he felt at liberty to ordain Whatcoat and Vasey both deacon and elder. He also ordained Thomas Coke as superintendent for the work in America. He then dispatched Coke, Whatcoat, and Vasey to America to assist in the formal organization of American Methodism. They took with them a letter of instruction to the Brethren in America, a prayer book entitled *The Sunday Service of the Methodists in North America*, and twenty-four Articles of Religion, which Wesley had reduced from the Thirty-Nine Articles of Religion of the Church of England. The Americans later added a twenty-fifth article.

Wesley's emissaries landed in New York and traveled south through Philadelphia into Delaware, where they met Francis Asbury at Barratt's Chapel. There they agreed to convene a meeting of all the Methodist preachers in the Lovely Lane meetinghouse in Baltimore in late December 1784. Freeborn Garrettson, one of the lay preachers, was commissioned to notify the others of this meeting. On Christmas Eve 1784, about sixty of the eighty-one preachers assembled in Baltimore and commenced the task of forming the Methodist Episcopal Church in America.

The preachers reaffirmed their allegiance to Wesley, adopted an episcopal form of government, and stated the purpose of the new church: "To reform the continent, and spread scriptural holiness through these lands!" Ordinations of the lay preachers were performed, including the ordination of Asbury. On consecutive days he was ordained deacon, elder, and superintendent. Wesley had directed that Asbury become a superintendent with Coke, but Asbury would not accept the office until elected by the other preachers. This they did unanimously. (Wesley was angry when he learned that a few years later Asbury and Coke accepted a change in title from superintendent to bishop.) Known popularly as the Christmas Conference, the assembly resolved to found an educational institution in Abingdon, Maryland, to be called Cokesbury College in honor of the church's two superintendents. It also promulgated rules forbidding the preachers from using intoxicating liquors and expressed strong opposition to slavery.

As Methodism was securing its foothold in America, the foundations for another church were being laid. Philip William Otterbein, born, educated, and ordained in Germany, migrated to America in 1752. He became pastor of the strong German Reformed congregation in Lancaster, Pennsylvania. While serving there in 1754, Otterbein underwent a profound religious transformation in which he experienced divine forgiveness and power in a way he had not previously known. This resulted in his preaching a more fervent, evangelical message. About 1767 Otterbein met Martin Boehm in a "great" meeting at Isaac Long's barn near Lancaster. Following Boehm's stirring sermon, Otterbein embraced him and exclaimed, "Wir sind Brüder!" (We are brothers!). Boehm, a Mennonite, was later dismissed from his church for evangelical irregularities, but his friendship with Otterbein continued and deepened.

Otterbein and Boehm attracted other preachers and lay people, particularly among the German-speaking, with their evangelical message. Their classes were organized in the Methodist style. The preachers met occasionally for sharing and worship, and their relationships with the Methodists were excellent. Asbury requested the presence and assistance of Otterbein at his ordination in Baltimore. Boehm's wife and children at one time were members of a Methodist class.

On 25 September 1800 a small group of preachers who were followers of Otterbein and Boehm met at the home of Peter Kemp near Frederick, Maryland, and decided to constitute a formal ecclesiastical body. They called it the United Brethren in Christ and named Otterbein and Boehm its superintendents.

Yet another church was in the process of formation as the Methodist Episcopal Church was beginning its work. Its founder was Jacob Albright. Born in 1759 near Pottstown, Pennsylvania, Albright was a farmer and tile maker. After the sudden deaths of some of his children in 1790, he went through a period of deep despair and doubt. An intense religious experience in 1791 changed his life and led to the inauguration of his preaching among his fellow Pennsylvania Germans in 1796. As people were drawn to his sincere and persuasive witness, Albright organized them into societies known at first as "Albright's People."

As its numbers grew and preachers were enlisted, the group was organized into a formal church in 1803, with Albright designated "elder preacher." He was ordained and "given the right to govern all meetings." In 1807 he was declared bishop of the church, which in 1816 adopted the name *Die Evangelische Gemeinschaft* (The Evangelical Association). Bonds between this church and Methodism were evident in an earlier name Albright's followers had chosen, the Newly-Formed Methodist Conference, and in their adaptation of the Methodist Episcopal *Discipline* (which contained its law, doctrine, organizational principles, and administrative procedures) as a guide for their polity.

GROWTH AND DEVELOPMENT

The most important religious development in early-nineteenth-century America was the Second Great Awakening. This movement of religious fervor, which spread across the young nation, had as its major thrust bringing the wayward to salvation. Thousands of people experienced conversion under the preaching and exhortation of its leaders. Methodists, United Brethren, and Evangelicals were comfortable in this religious setting. All of them emphasized the possibility that everyone could experience the assurance of divine forgiveness. Their preachers and lay people encouraged the unconverted to surrender to the claims of God's love. Each of the churches flourished during the Awakening.

In addition to the advantage they obtained from the favorable religious climate of the period, Methodists, United Brethren, and Evangelicals were also aided in their growth by the work of circuit riders, by the use of the camp meeting, and by their connectional structures.

The circuit-riding preacher was able to take the Gospel wherever the people were. He had a designated circuit of preaching places, often the homes of committed people, that he visited as frequently as his circuit schedule allowed. He was underpaid and overworked. It was not unusual for him to sleep outdoors, enduring the elements and risking the dangers of the wilderness. He preached a simple message of rebirth and hope. Sometimes he encountered hostility from those who belonged to other churches, as well as antagonism from unbelievers. Between the circuit preacher's visits, which might be as long as a month or two, a lay person appointed by him would preside over a weekly meeting of the members to lead them in prayer, study, and adherence to the disciplines of the church.

Camp meetings were effectively employed by the churches. Held in the warm-weather months for a week or two, they were located at a spot in the countryside where a large number of people could erect tents, cook food, and care for the horses and cattle they had to bring with them. Usually close to this tent settlement, sometimes at its center, was an open area where rows of rough planks or logs faced a speaker's platform. At various times each day the campers gathered to sing, to pray, and to hear from the platform the exhortations of preachers and lay people. A powerful appeal was made to the emotions, frequently evoking strange and unusual responses. There were often mourning and crying by those lamenting their sins. Many were "slain in the Spirit" and fell on the ground in a trance. Some danced for joy "in the Spirit." Others experienced the "jerks" or rolled on the ground. Despite the emotional excesses, however, the camp meeting was an exceedingly important event for socializing activities and a very productive means of bringing men, women, and young people to Christian commitment. Francis Asbury wrote ecstatically of its spiritual successes: "Campmeetings, campmeetings. Oh Glory, Glory!" (Bucke, ed., *History of American Methodism,* vol. 1, p. 520). The continued existence of camp meetings today, though they are significantly different in most cases from their primitive form, attests to their long-term usefulness in the Wesleyan tradition in America.

The connectional organization of the Methodists, United Brethren, and Evangelicals was also an important factor in their development. As these churches expanded numerically and geographically, it became increasingly difficult for all their preachers to gather in one place annually to conduct the necessary business. Therefore, smaller geographical areas, called Annual Conferences, were instituted so that preachers could meet annually with their brothers in the same region. Bishops presided over the Annual Conferences, which were divided into smaller units called districts, administered by presiding elders, today known as district superintendents. Each district comprised a number of circuits or churches served by preachers appointed by a bishop.

In 1808 the Methodists decided to continue their practice of holding a quadrennial General Conference to set the policies for the whole church. However, instead of all the preachers being eligible to attend this meeting as previously, it was agreed that each Annual Conference should elect delegates to be present. Only the General Conference had the authority to change the church's *Discipline.* The United Brethren and Evangelicals adopted the delegated General Conference system a few years later. This organizational pattern of General Conference, Annual Conference, district, and local church clarified lines of authority and responsibility and made it possible to marshal resources and monitor progress more effectively.

During the early years of the nineteenth century, the three churches were especially interested in education, publication, and missions. Considerable effort was devoted to each of these important activities.

Following the example of their founder, John Wesley, Methodists recognized the importance of developing the mind and set out to establish schools and colleges. Among the earliest were Bethel Academy in Kentucky (1794), Asbury College in Maryland (1816), and Wesleyan University in Connecticut (1831). The United Brethren opened their first college, Otterbein University, in Ohio in 1847. The Evangelical Association started Albright Seminary in Pennsylvania in 1852. While there was ample disagreement in the three churches as to whether their preachers should be educated, particularly in theological seminaries, each of them had authorized a course of study for their ministry before 1850. Furthermore, each of the churches actively promoted the founding of Sunday schools. The Methodist Episcopal General Conference of 1824 ordered its preachers "to encourage the establishment and progress of Sunday schools."

Methodists, United Brethren, and Evangelicals also admitted the necessity of providing their preachers and lay people with appropriate religious literature. The Methodist Book Concern, founded in Philadelphia in 1789, was the first denominational publishing house in America. It not only made available many of the works of John Wesley, but also printed a wide selection of other books, pamphlets, and materials for its people and Sunday schools. In 1826 it began to publish the *Christian Advocate,* a weekly newspaper for the general membership. The Evangelical Association began to publish materials in New Berlin, Pennsylvania, in 1816 on a press owned by John Dreisbach, and the United Brethren authorized a "Printing Establishment" in 1833. Preachers served as book agents, selling the materials produced by the denominational presses. Profits were used for retired and "indigent" preachers and their families.

The churches gave evidence of a desire to reach the unbeliever at home and abroad. They organized missionary societies to raise funds and to develop strategies to bring others into their folds. Although there were earlier unofficial missionary efforts, the Methodist Episcopal Church General Conference of 1820 was the first to authorize a denominational missionary society. Its first mission projects abroad were in Liberia (1833) and South America (1835). The Evangelical Association formed its Missionary Society of the Evangelical Association of North America in 1839, and the United Brethren launched its Parent Missionary Society in 1841.

The rapid growth of the churches in the first quarter of the nineteenth century is evident in their 1825 membership statistics. The Methodist Episcopal Church reported over 341,000 members, an increase of more than 500 percent since 1800. The United Brethren in Christ recorded about 12,000 members, and the Evangelical Association listed approximately 2,000 members.

The antebellum years were not without problems, some of which resulted in divisions within the Methodist family. While some issues were dealt with in ways that avoided schism, such as the sacramental controversy mentioned above, others could not be settled short of dividing the Methodist Episcopal Church.

One of the earliest disputes involved James O'Kelly. Born in Ireland in 1757, O'Kelly migrated to America, became a Methodist preacher, and was one of those ordained elder at the Christmas Conference. O'Kelly and his supporters were increasingly displeased with the growing power of the episcopacy. He believed that every preacher should have the right to appeal his appointment by the bishop if he were dissatisfied with it. At the 1792 General Conference of the Methodist Episcopal Church, he offered the following motion: "After the bishop appoints the preachers at conference to their several circuits, if any one thinks himself injured by the appointment, he shall have liberty to appeal to the conference and state his objections; and if the conference approve his objections, the bishop shall appoint him to another circuit" (Bucke, ed., vol. 1, p. 436). When his motion failed, O'Kelly and his associates withdrew from the church and formed a new body, the Republican Methodist Church. In 1801 its name was changed to the Christian Church. Gradually, this church declined and disappeared.

A more serious division in the Methodist Episcopal Church was precipitated over the matter of race. Blacks had been participants in American Methodism from its beginning. Among its prominent early preachers were two blacks, Harry Hosier and Richard Allen. Both were highly regarded orators, and many believe that both were present at the Christmas Conference. An unfortunate incident at St. George's Methodist Episcopal Church in Philadelphia involving racial discrimination provoked Allen to leave the church he loved. In 1816 he organized the African Methodist Episcopal Church in Philadelphia and became the first bishop of this important body, which remains a significant force in American religious life. About the same time, black Methodists in New York City led by Peter Williams and James Varick formed the African Methodist Episcopal Zion Church. This body also continues to be a notable church in America.

Yet another critical schism occurred in the Methodist Episcopal Church in 1830. It was the consummation of nearly three decades of dispute primarily concerning the power of the episcopacy and the right of lay people to representation in the policy-making and administrative conferences of the church. In the 1820s a "reform party" emerged that advocated at least four principal changes in the church's structure: the elimination of the office of bishop; the election rather than the appointment of presiding elders; equal representation of laity and clergy in the Annual and General Conferences; and full ministerial rights for local preachers (who were appointed to serve churches, but were not recognized as members of an Annual Conference).

The agitation of this reform party resulted in some of its preachers and lay people being expelled in 1827. The reformers argued their case at the 1828 General Conference, but made little progress. As their numbers grew, the leaders decided that separation was their only alternative. In November 1830 in Baltimore, Maryland, the geographical center of their strength, they organized the Methodist Protestant Church, with an initial membership of approximately 5,000. The reforms originally proposed were incorporated into its policy, with the exception of full ministerial rights for local preachers. The Methodist Protestant Church enjoyed nearly a century of vigorous ministry until its union in 1939 into the Methodist Church.

THE SLAVERY CRISIS

John Wesley expressed his abhorrence of slavery on many occasions, most notably in his 1774 tract *Thoughts upon Slavery.* He referred to slavery as "the sum of all villainies." American slavery, he said, was "the vilest under the sun." When American Methodism organized in 1784, therefore, it was not surprising that the church stated its opposition to slavery. The 1785 *Discipline* of the Methodist Episcopal Church said, "We view

it as contrary to the Golden Law of God . . . and the unalienable Rights of Mankind, as well as every Principle of the Revolution, to hold in the deepest debasement . . . so many souls that are all capable of the Image of God." Methodists were given one year to begin the emancipation of any slaves they held. Otherwise, they were free to withdraw from the church or face expulsion. The General Rules of the new church prohibited the members from both holding and trading slaves.

The church began to moderate its views on slavery during the last years of the eighteenth century and the early years of the nineteenth century, despite the vehement protests of a few who wanted to remain faithful to the original antislavery stance. In 1816 the General Conference received a report from one of its committees describing the despair of those who desired to see slavery abolished among the Methodists. The report sadly stated that "the evil appears to be past remedy" (Norwood, p. 187).

As abolitionist strength grew in the nation in the 1830s and 1840s, the church, which had substantial membership in both the North and the South, felt the stress of the slavery question more keenly. The issue was debated at the General Conferences of 1836 and 1840. Many began to fear that the church would be divided over the problem. In 1836 the bishops advised that "the only safe, scriptural and prudent way for us, both as ministers and people to take, is wholly to refrain from the agitating subject" (McEllhenney, ed., *Proclaiming Grace and Freedom,* p. 65).

When the Methodist Episcopal Church refused to adopt a strong antislavery platform, some people withdrew from membership. One was Orange Scott, a prominent preacher in the New England Conference who was devoted to restoring Methodism to its original position against owning and trading slaves. When his efforts failed, Scott and those sympathetic to him organized the Wesleyan Methodist Connection in 1843, with about 15,000 members. Since 1968 this body has been incorporated into the Wesleyan Church.

The United Brethren and the Evangelical Association did not experience the intense pressures of the abolitionist controversy, primarily because they did not have large numbers of members in regions that favored slavery. Both churches maintained strong positions against the practice. In 1821 the United Brethren General

Conference declared that "in no sense of the word shall slavery in whatever form it may exist, be permitted or tolerated in our church . . ." (Behney and Eller, *The History of the Evangelical United Brethren Church,* p. 124).

The full impact of the antislavery dispute in the Methodist Episcopal Church was finally realized at its 1844 General Conference in New York City. Two cases brought the issue into sharper focus and aroused bitter debate. The first involved Francis Harding, a ministerial member of the Baltimore Annual Conference, who had been suspended from his conference membership for refusing to free slaves he had acquired in marriage. He lost his appeal to the General Conference to reverse the suspension. This was obviously a victory for those favoring abolition.

The second case decided by the General Conference was more critical. It concerned James O. Andrew, one of the five bishops of the church. Andrew, a native of Georgia, had also acquired slaves through marriage. When his first wife died, she bequeathed him two slaves. His second wife also owned several slaves, over whom, Andrew asserted, he had no control or ownership. While he correctly claimed that he had neither bought nor sold slaves, the antislavery delegates called for his resignation. Following extensive and turbulent debate, the assembly voted 110 to 68 to request Andrew to suspend the exercise of his episcopal functions as long as the slavery "impediment" existed.

Within a few days of the action against Bishop Andrew, the delegates were presented with a Plan of Separation, which provided that Annual Conferences in the slaveholding states could withdraw from the church in order to form a new ecclesiastical body. Annual Conferences and local churches located in border states could determine by majority vote whether they would remain in the Methodist Episcopal Church or affiliate with the new church. Clergy were offered the choice of which church they preferred, and arrangements were proposed for the distribution of church property.

The implementation of the Plan of Separation resulted in the creation of the Methodist Episcopal Church, South, in 1845, when delegates from Annual Conferences in the slaveholding states met in Louisville, Kentucky. Bishops Andrew and Joshua Soule were accepted as the episcopal leaders of the newly organized church. A *Discipline* and hymnbook were authorized, and it was resolved to maintain educational, mission, and publishing enterprises. The first General Conference of the Methodist Episcopal Church, South, convened on 1 May 1846 in Petersburg, Virginia.

Although the Southern Methodists hoped to maintain fraternal relationships with their brothers and sisters in the North, animosity grew between the two. Many northern Methodists declared the Plan of Separation and the formation of the new church unconstitutional. They attempted to retain all the assets of the publishing house, a share of which the southern church was later awarded by the federal courts. There were arguments in local churches on the border as to whether they were members of northern or southern Methodism. At the same time that sectionalism was dividing the nation, relations between the two churches steadily deteriorated. In 1850 the Methodist Episcopal Church boasted a membership of almost 800,000, while the Methodist Episcopal Church, South, reported more than 600,000 members.

POST–CIVIL WAR CHALLENGES

When the Civil War began on 12 April 1861 with the attack on Fort Sumter, the northern and southern Methodist churches were the largest and wealthiest denominations in their respective areas. It was impossible for them to be disinterested in the conflict. Depending on where they lived, bishops, preachers, lay people, and the religious press supported the Union or the Confederacy. Methodists on both sides of the Mason-Dixon Line were convinced that they were fighting on God's side.

When Abraham Lincoln was assassinated in April 1865, it was Methodist Episcopal Bishop Matthew Simpson who was selected to hold the funeral services at the White House and to deliver the eulogy at the burial in Springfield, Illinois. Simpson praised the martyred president: "Chieftain! Farewell! The nation mourns thee. Mothers shall teach thy name to their lisping children. The youth of our land shall emulate thy virtues. Statesmen shall study thy record and learn lessons of wisdom" (Norwood, pp. 326–327).

The Methodist Episcopal Church, South, was

faced with a number of critical problems when hostilities ended. Many of its church buildings and properties had been destroyed. Its ministerial ranks were depleted. Membership had fallen from 750,000 to less than 500,000. Some southern Methodists were convinced that their church could not be rebuilt. A few even suggested that they reunite with the northern Methodists, but others were not discouraged by the circumstances. In 1865 a Manifesto was drafted in Palmyra, Missouri, that called for the revitalization of the Methodist Episcopal Church, South. Later that year the southern bishops issued a Pastoral Address in which they affirmed loyalty to their church and summoned a General Conference for 1866. It was clear that the church was determined to recover its earlier strength.

In 1870 the General Conference of the Methodist Episcopal Church, South, settled the question of what to do with its black membership, which at the time was declining. It assisted in the formation of a new church in December 1870, called the Colored Methodist Episcopal Church. All of the black members of the Methodist Episcopal Church, South—approximately 60,000 people—were transferred into the new church. William H. Miles and Richard H. Vanderhorst were elected bishops of the Colored Methodist Episcopal Church and were properly consecrated by bishops of the Methodist Episcopal Church, South. Today it is known as the Christian Methodist Episcopal Church.

The decades between the Civil War and 1920 were characterized by substantial growth in the churches that now constitute United Methodism. The Methodist Episcopal Church grew from 1 million to more than 4 million. The Methodist Episcopal Church, South, increased from about 500,000 to more than 2 million. Membership in the United Brethren in Christ rose from 95,000 to 350,000; the Evangelical Association from 40,000 to 160,000; and the Methodist Protestant Church from 60,000 to 185,000. Increases in membership were accompanied by growth in the number of churches and clergy in each denomination.

The churches continued to strengthen and extend educational, publishing, and mission programs in the latter decades of the nineteenth century. They were especially successful in expanding their Sunday schools so that almost every local congregation had one. Lay people occupied leadership and teaching positions in the Sunday schools. A large number of colleges and universities were founded during this period. Particularly notable was the Freedmen's Aid Society of the Methodist Episcopal Church, which was responsible for starting and maintaining educational institutions in the southern states for freed slaves. Shaw University, now Rust College, in Mississippi (1866), Clark College in Georgia (1869), Claflin College in South Carolina (1869), and Meharry Medical College in Tennessee (1876) were among the schools begun by the Freedmen's Aid Society. Furthermore, the churches endeavored to implement higher educational standards for their preachers. Not only were the courses of study improved, but by 1900 each of the churches had also opened at least one theological seminary to train its clergy.

Periodicals, books, pamphlets, and Sunday school literature were published in a steady stream by the denominational presses. Not only did these publications supply the clergy and laity with inspirational and educational reading, but the official magazines and newspapers also nurtured denominational solidarity and loyalty.

Perhaps the outstanding accomplishment of the churches during the decades between the Civil War and World War I was the extension of missionary programs. Both at home and overseas, the churches sought to expand their ministry to the unconverted and unchurched. Their missionary societies, founded earlier in the nineteenth century, began to receive more attention and greater financial support.

At home there was an attempt to reach more people in urban as well as less-populated areas. For example, in its Board of Home Missions and Church Extension, the Methodist Episcopal Church set up separate departments for city and rural work. The churches conducted missions among the American Indians and among such immigrant groups as Hispanics, Scandinavians, Asians, and Germans. Mission work sometimes resulted in those who had affiliated with the church in the United States returning to their native lands to begin Methodist work there. With their German cultural and language origins, the United Brethren in Christ and the Evangelical Association were well suited to attract German immigrants in America.

Both northern and southern Methodists maintained and strengthened missions in China and

India that they had instituted before the Civil War. They also began work in Asia and Africa. The Methodist Protestants carried on effective work in Japan. The United Brethren and the Evangelicals supported missions in Africa, China, Japan, the Philippines, and Germany.

Women were in the forefront of the churches' missionary movement. They organized home and foreign missionary societies and through these organizations raised funds, developed educational programs, and recruited personnel for the mission field. Outstanding leaders such as Isabella Thoburn, Belle Harris Bennett, and Lucy Rider Meyer were among the Methodist women, both North and South, who not only contributed to the advancement of the missionary societies, but were also instrumental in the origins of the Methodist deaconess movement. Deaconesses were women trained and licensed by the church for mission work at home or abroad.

The years before World War I were not free from conflict within the churches. Lay representation, the role of women, and theological and social issues were among the problems they sought to solve.

The struggle to give lay people an official voice in the churches' policy-making bodies could be dated in Methodism to the 1820s. Conflict over the role of the laity had been one factor in the formation of the Methodist Protestant Church in 1830. At that time the new church granted the laity equal representation in its Annual and General Conferences. Although the Methodist Episcopal Church, the Methodist Episcopal Church, South, the United Brethren in Christ, and the Evangelical Association were unwilling to grant lay people official voting representation, after decades of deliberation all four churches finally admitted lay people as delegates to their Annual and General Conferences. Equal representation of the laity with the clergy in the Methodist Episcopal Annual Conferences, however, did not occur until 1932.

The role of women in the churches also stirred considerable disagreement. One of the major questions concerned the eligibility of women to hold office and to serve as delegates to various assemblies. In the Methodist Episcopal Church, this matter came to the fore at the 1888 General Conference. Five women had been properly elected delegates to this meeting by their Annual Conferences. One of the women was the famous temperance leader and reformer Frances E. Willard. Since no woman had previously been seated as an official voting delegate at a General Conference, there was a lengthy discussion as to whether Willard and the others should be granted admission. It was decided that they were not eligible because the constitution of the church specifically stated that only "laymen" could occupy the seats reserved for the laity. Not until 1904 did the Methodist Episcopal Church seat women as delegates at its General Conferences.

The right of women to be licensed and ordained preachers in the churches was another major issue with which the churches dealt. If women could serve the church as Sunday school teachers, missionaries, and deaconesses, some argued, why couldn't they enjoy full ministerial rights? The United Brethren in Christ licensed women as early as 1851 and approved the ordination of women in 1889. The Evangelical Association never ordained women. Anna Howard Shaw received orders in 1880 in the Methodist Protestant Church, but her ordination was a source of dissension in the denomination. The northern and southern Methodist churches did not grant full clergy status to women until well after their 1939 reunion.

There was considerable theological discord in the churches over holiness, sanctification, and Christian perfection. John Wesley had emphasized these as essential to the Christian's life and purpose. Many held that by holiness and Christian perfection Wesley meant the believer's gradual maturing in God's grace. Others interpreted holiness to be an instantaneous divine gift, a "second blessing" that followed one's conversion or "first blessing." The Evangelical Association and the Methodists experienced lively quarreling over this matter. A number of Methodists who favored the instantaneous "second blessing" doctrine were prompted to organize a holiness movement among American Protestants. By the end of the nineteenth century, many of these holiness people decided to withdraw from Methodism and later assisted in the formation of new churches, such as the Church of the Nazarene.

Theological liberalism was another subject that generated disharmony in the churches. Biblical criticism, Darwin's theory of evolution, an emphasis on Jesus' humanity rather than his divinity, and stress on the immanence of God as opposed to God's transcendence produced ample contention among the clergy and in the pages of the denominational periodicals. One specific expression of liberal thought contributed by Methodist theologians was "Boston personalism." Borden Parker Bowne, a Methodist clergyman, philosopher, and professor at Boston University, was its chief architect and proponent. Personalism held that the starting point of Christian theology is the human personality.

The churches responded to some of the most pressing social issues of the late nineteenth and early twentieth centuries. They shared many of the concerns of the Social Gospel movement, including compassion for the manual laborer. The Methodist Episcopal Church drafted a Social Creed in 1908, expressing its conviction that workers were entitled to fair and adequate wages. There was one social issue, however, that drew far more attention and organizational energies than any other: temperance. The Methodists, United Brethren, and Evangelicals were of a common mind that alcoholic beverages were a major cause of individual and social decay. In their periodicals, from their pulpits, and in their communities they worked tirelessly to outlaw the production, sale, and consumption of beverage alcohol. The adoption of grape juice for their communion services was a witness to their dedication to temperance.

During the later years of the nineteenth century, there were attempts to improve relations among the churches and even some efforts to achieve unions. Conversations between the Methodist Episcopal Church and the Methodist Episcopal Church, South, took place in Cape May, New Jersey, in August 1876. Delegates discussed their mutual characteristics and common heritage and agreed that "each of said Churches is a legitimate branch of Episcopal Methodism in the United States, having a common origin in the Methodist Episcopal Church organized in 1784" (Bucke, ed., vol. 2, p. 409). Although many signs of animosity existed between northern and southern Methodists, this conference laid some of the groundwork for their later reunion. Other negotiations, between the Evangelical Association and the Methodist Episcopal Church from 1859 to 1871, and between the United Brethren in Christ and the Methodist Protestant Church after 1900, failed to achieve unions. However, in

each case there was recognition of a shared theological ancestry and of the structural similarities that produced a basis for what is now the United Methodist Church.

Churches of the Methodist family devised a worldwide forum to consider ways in which they could cooperate and improve their moral and evangelical influence. Known initially as Ecumenical Methodist Conferences, these meetings began in 1881 and were held every ten years until World War II. In 1951 the name of the assembly was changed to the World Methodist Council. At that time more than twenty Methodist denominations agreed to establish the council as a permanent administrative body. Since 1951 the World Methodist Council has held World Methodist Conferences every five years. According to its constitution, the organization "does not seek to legislate" for its members "nor to invade their autonomy. Rather it exists to serve them and to give unity to their witness and enterprise" (Harmon, ed., *Encyclopedia of World Methodism*, vol. 2, p. 2602).

The churches that presently make up United Methodism were dedicated to the larger ecumenical movement which began to unfold in the decades prior to World War I. When the Federal Council of Churches was constituted in 1908, each of the five churches became members and provided leadership for the council during the ensuing years. The council's first president was Bishop Eugene R. Hendrix of the Methodist Episcopal Church, South. As the ecumenical movement continued to evolve in the twentieth century, the churches also provided important support for both the National Council of Churches, successor to the Federal Council, and the World Council of Churches. This support has not gone unchallenged in recent times as some members of the United Methodist Church have questioned the mission and strategies of each of these ecumenical councils.

BETWEEN THE WORLD WARS

World War I marked the end of an important era in the churches' history and the beginning of a new one. In the twenty-five years between the start of World War I and World War II, there were several significant changes in church life and structure and two important unions.

UNITED METHODISM

The first union involved the Evangelical Association. In 1891 this church had been divided over the site of its General Conference and other issues, some of which were personality conflicts rather than substantive. There was so much dissension that a minority group separated from the church and in 1894 formally organized the United Evangelical Church. It had 61,000 members and 400 clergy. After nearly three decades of separation, the United Evangelical Church and the old Evangelical Association reunited on 14 October 1922 in Detroit, Michigan. The united body, the Evangelical Church, numbered 260,000 members and 1,850 clergy in its first year.

The second union involved the three Methodist churches—the Methodist Episcopal Church, the Methodist Protestant Church, and the Methodist Episcopal Church, South. At a Uniting Conference from 26 April to 10 May 1939, held in Kansas City, Missouri, the Methodist Church was formed. Preparations for the reunion had been made over several decades. The churches had exchanged fraternal delegates and had adjusted rivalries in various areas, particularly the mission field. The Methodist Episcopal Church and the Methodist Episcopal Church, South, had produced a common hymnal in 1905 and another in 1935, with the cooperation of the Methodist Protestant Church. Furthermore, all three were members of the Federal Council of Churches.

A joint commission devised a plan for union that provided for one General Conference and six jurisdictions, five of which were to be geographical. The other was to accommodate the 300,000 blacks who were members of the Methodist Episcopal Church, mostly placed in segregated Annual Conferences. The office of bishop was retained with no major objection from the Methodist Protestants. The jurisdictions, meeting quadrennially, were given the task of electing the bishops. A Judicial Council was designated to act as the supreme interpreter of the law of the church. Equal representation of laity and clergy was determined for the General and Jurisdictional Conferences, which would meet quadrennially, as well as for the Annual Conferences. The twenty-five Articles of Religion were retained as the doctrinal standards of the church. Despite the vocal protests of some in each of the three churches, particularly blacks who objected to the racism of the plan, the union was completed and the Methodist Church was formally organized with approximately 7,691,000 members.

In the meantime, Evangelicals, United Brethren, and Methodists also found themselves entangled in a theological struggle that affected American Protestantism as a whole. It was the battle between theological liberals and conservatives, often referred to as the Fundamentalist-Modernist controversy. While the liberals viewed themselves as bringing the Christian faith into modern times, the conservatives saw them as undermining the essential doctrines and practices of true Christianity. Liberals tended to be skeptical about sudden conversion, preferring the individual's more gradual introduction to and growth in faith. They were more convinced about the inherent goodness of persons and, therefore, less prone to accept any concept of original sin. The liberals raised questions about the authority of the Bible and such traditional doctrines as the virgin birth and the atonement. The conservatives were horrified by what they considered the liberals' subversion of the truth. Harold Paul Sloan, pastor in the New Jersey Annual Conference of the Methodist Episcopal Church, was a leader in the fight against liberalism in the 1920s and 1930s. In 1922 Sloan published a book about the threat of liberalism called *Historic Christianity and the New Theology* in which he attacked the liberals and listed thirteen books in the church's course of study for ministers that contained false and erroneous ideas. It was difficult for the conservatives to stem the tide, however, as liberals increasingly occupied seminary, episcopal, and administrative offices in the denominations as well as pulpits and Sunday school classes.

Temperance remained a major social concern of the churches. They added their influence to the political pressures that resulted in the passage of the Prohibition (Eighteenth) Amendment to the U.S. Constitution in 1919. Even after Prohibition was repealed in 1933, the churches continued their attack against the production and use of beverage alcohol, although the vigor of their opposition began to decline in the 1960s.

WORLD WAR II AND ITS AFTERMATH

When Pearl Harbor was attacked on 7 December 1941, the churches put aside their hope that the world's problems could be settled peacefully,

550

a desire they had nurtured even prior to World War I. Although many chose pacifism and the right of conscientious objection, the vast majority of church members supported the Allied cause, as they had in World War I. As the war progressed, however, some church leaders began to conceive a new world order in which the violence and destruction evident in their time would be mitigated, if not eliminated forever. Methodist Bishop G. Bromley Oxnam was among the leaders who envisaged a new direction for the governments of the world. The creation of the United Nations in 1945 was a partial realization of their dream, and they supported it enthusiastically.

By the end of World War II, the Evangelical Church and the United Brethren in Christ were prepared to enter into a union that had been discussed seriously for more than two decades. A Plan of Union had been drafted in 1928, but sufficient approval could not be enlisted for its passage. Commissioners from both churches met again in the early 1930s and by 1937 had drawn up a Basis of Union. During the following years, each church carefully considered the proposal that would join them into one. On 16 November 1946, in Johnstown, Pennsylvania, the union finally took place, and the Evangelical United Brethren Church was formally organized, with 705,000 members. The doctrinal views of the new denomination were designated as the Confession of Faith of the United Brethren in Christ and the Articles of Faith of the Evangelical Church. In 1962 these two documents were consolidated into the Confession of Faith of the Evangelical United Brethren Church.

From 1946 to 1968 the Methodist Church and the Evangelical United Brethren Church continued to grow. By 1968 the Methodists claimed approximately 10,289,000 members while the Evangelical United Brethren numbered 775,000. During this period the two denominations made adjustments in their structure, maintained active missionary programs, and actively participated in ecumenical ventures.

Among the Methodists the establishment of the Television, Radio, and Film Commission in 1956 signified the church's determination to make effective use of developments in the communications media. The Methodist Youth Fellowship, successor to the Epworth League, became an important and influential means of organizing the interests and energies of young people. The church also began to pay serious attention to the all-black Central Jurisdiction it had created in 1939. In the 1950s and early 1960s there was growing sentiment to eliminate this representation of structural racism. At the General Conference of 1964 a plan was adopted to abolish the Central Jurisdiction and to transfer its black Annual Conferences into the five regional jurisdictions. Although the Central Jurisdiction ceased operations in 1967, the plan to integrate all the black Annual Conferences was not fully implemented until a few years later. Eventually the black Annual Conferences were abolished and black and white churches became partners in the same Annual Conferences. In 1956 the Methodist Church also approved full clergy rights for women. Its *Discipline* stated: "Women are included in all provisions of the *Discipline* referring to the ministry."

In addition to making some changes in its administrative structure, the Evangelical United Brethren remained strongly committed to missionary work. Its established missions flourished. For example, the work in Sierra Leone was successful to the point that in 1958 it became one of the Annual Conferences of the church. New missions were also instituted, including those to the South Pacific, Ecuador, and Nigeria. The denomination's Division of North American Missions was also active. Its attention was centered on inner-city programs, ministries among ethnic groups, and service to Appalachia. The Methodist Church was also dedicated to the expansion of its mission program in the United States and abroad.

In the 1960s both churches were active in ecumenical ventures. In addition to their participation in the National and World Councils of Churches, they were in conversation with other denominations regarding possible unions. The Evangelical United Brethren held negotiations with the Church of the Brethren, the Church of God in North America, and the United Presbyterian Church. Inconclusive conversations were also held between the Methodists and the Protestant Episcopal Church. In 1960 both the Methodists and the Evangelical United Brethren participated in the Consultation on Church Union, the announced goal of which was to unify ten Protestant denominations into one church that would be "truly catholic, truly evangelical, truly reformed."

Discussions between the Evangelical United

Brethren and the Methodists regarding a possible union began in 1956. By 1966 a blueprint had been developed to unite them. Underlying the prospective union were similarities in polity, common theological lineage, and many points of contact during the course of their histories, some of which have been mentioned above. When the two churches' General Conferences met in Chicago in November 1966, the delegates were presented with a plan for union and, after due consideration, approved it. The Annual Conferences ratified the plan, and on 23 April 1968 the United Methodist Church was formed. At the time of its creation the new church had 11,027,000 members.

SINCE 1968

Within a few years of its inception, United Methodism began to alter its structure to meet the needs of the new church and of the rapidly changing world in which it ministered. Cognizant of the problems of racism and sexism and desiring to be an inclusive church, it established a Commission on Religion and Race at the time of union and granted it permanent status in 1972. Four caucuses were formed by ethnic groups to provide each with a forum to present its views and to lobby for support. Black Methodists for Church Renewal, the National Federation of Asian American United Methodists, the Native American International Caucus, and Methodists Associated Representing the Cause of the Hispanic Americans have been influential in calling attention to the concerns of these groups. Since 1976 these caucuses have been effective in persuading the denomination to develop and maintain its ethnic minority churches as one of its highest priorities.

The place of women in the United Methodist Church has also been a major concern since union occurred. A Commission on the Status and Role of Women was authorized in 1972 to interpret the concerns of women in the church and to ensure their proper inclusion in its programs and leadership. The denomination has welcomed an increasing number of women to the ranks of its clergy. A major event for the church occurred in 1980, when Marjorie S. Matthews became its first female bishop. In 1984 two more women were elected to the episcopal office.

By the time of its Bicentennial General Conference in Baltimore in May 1984, United Methodism could celebrate not only a heritage reaching back to the Wesleys, Otterbein, Boehm, Albright, and Asbury, but also a financial prosperity and institutional vitality that seemed to hold promise for the future. Its destiny was not unclouded, however. Since the union of 1968, the denomination's membership has steadily decreased. By 1984 it had fallen to 9,340,000, a net loss of 1,687,000 since union, moving the church from the largest Protestant denomination in America to the second largest.

Various reasons have been cited for the decline. Many attribute it to a lack of evangelical zeal and an abandonment of the church's earlier commitment to Wesleyan theological principles. Even though United Methodism has paid regular attention to social issues, especially in its *Social Principles* document, some claim that it has become captive to American culture and therefore has lost its prophetic passion. Still others dismiss the decline as a phenomenon experienced by many of the major Protestant bodies in the United States, symptomatic of a population less inclined to join and attend churches.

At the time of the 1984 Bicentennial, the United Methodist Church counted 38,000 churches and 39,000 active clergy. Its General Conference, which meets every four years, remains the official policy-making body of the denomination. The *Book of Discipline* contains its doctrinal standards, descriptions of its administrative structure, and its social principles. Five regional jurisdictions, the Northeastern, North Central, Southeastern, South Central, and Western, also convene quadrennially, primarily to elect bishops. There are seventy-three Annual Conferences in the United States and eight Central Conferences overseas (Africa, West Africa, China, Central and Southern Europe, German Democratic Republic, Federal Republic of Germany and West Berlin, Northern Europe, and the Philippines). Sixty-six active bishops are responsible for administering the Annual and Central Conferences. Thirteen general agencies, established by the General Conference, are authorized to assist the church in developing and implementing its program.

United Methodism began with a handful of men and women in the eighteenth century. It has evolved from a small group of religious societies seeking to renew already existing churches into a fully organized church in its own right. Its rapid growth and geographical spread have made it one of the most respected Christian bodies in the world.

BIBLIOGRAPHY

Frank Baker, *From Wesley to Asbury* (1976); Wade Crawford Barclay and J. Tremayne Copplestone, *History of Methodist Missions,* 4 vols. (1949, 1950, 1957, 1973); J. Bruce Behney and Paul H. Eller, *The History of the Evangelical United Brethren Church* (1979); Emory Stevens Bucke, ed., *The History of American Methodism,* 3 vols. (1964); Richard M. Cameron, *Methodism and Society in Historical Perspective* (1961); Robert E. Chiles, *Theological Transition in American Methodism, 1790–1935* (1965); Elmer T. Clark, ed., *The Journal and Letters of Francis Asbury,* 3 vols. (1958).

Edward J. Drinkhouse, *History of Methodist Reform and the Methodist Protestant Church* (1899); Charles W. Ferguson, *Organizing to Beat the Devil: Methodists and the Making of America* (1971); Carol V. R. George, *Segregated Sabbaths: Richard Allen and the Emergence of Independent Black Churches, 1760–1840* (1973); Nolan B. Harmon, ed., *Encyclopedia of World Methodism,* 2 vols. (1974); John G. McEllhenney, ed., *Proclaiming Grace and Freedom: The Story of United Methodism in America* (1982); John G. McEllhenney and Charles Yrigoyen, Jr., *200 Years of United Methodism: An Illustrated History* (1984); Frederick E. Maser and Howard T. Maag, eds., *The Journal of Joseph Pilmore* (1969); Gerald F. Moede, *The Office of Bishop in Methodism, Its History and Development* (1964); Frederick A. Norwood, *The Story of American Methodism: A History of the United Methodists and Their Relations* (1974) and, as ed., *Sourcebook of American Methodism* (1982).

J. Steven O'Malley, *Pilgrimage of Faith: The Legacy of the Otterbeins* (1973); Harry V. Richardson, *Dark Salvation: The Story of Methodism as It Developed Among Blacks in America* (1976); Kenneth E. Rowe, ed., *United Methodist Studies: Basic Bibliographies* (1982); L. C. Rudolph, *Francis Asbury* (1966); Hilah F. Thomas, Rosemary S. Keller, and Louise L. Queen, *Women in New Worlds: Historical Perspectives on the Wesleyan Tradition,* 2 vols. (1981, 1982); Jack M. Tuell, *The Organization of the United Methodist Church* (1970; rev. 1982).

[*See also* WESLEYAN HERITAGE.]

THE BAPTISTS

Eldon G. Ernst

BAPTISTS represent a multifarious free church tradition of Protestant Christianity that originated in seventeenth-century England. Today, because of migrations and missions, there are Baptists in many nations on all continents. Of the more than 33 million Baptist church members worldwide in the 1980s, about 28 million are Americans. Approximately 90 percent of these, or 25 million people, are members of churches affiliated with four major denominations. The Southern Baptist Convention is by far the largest, with 13,900,000 congregants; the others are the National Baptist Convention of the U.S.A., Inc. (6,500,000); the National Baptist Convention of America (3,500,000); and the American Baptist Churches in the U.S.A. (1,600,000; originally the Northern Baptist Convention, then the American Baptist Convention). The remaining 2½ million or so Baptists are members of churches affiliated with more than thirty smaller denominational bodies and of numerous independent congregations with no affiliation outside of themselves.

Baptists share no authoritative ecclesiastical structure, creed or confession, catechism, or manual of worship. But nearly all Baptists embrace the following: (1) a regenerate church membership expressed in the practice of believers' baptism by immersion; (2) the equality of all Christians, lay and ordained, in the life of the church, with no sacerdotal status of ordained clergy; (3) an ecclesiastical polity in which primary power and authority resides in the local congregation; (4) individual freedom and responsibility in matters of faith and morals; (5) the Scriptures, understood through the guidance of the Holy Spirit, as the authoritative basis of doctrine and practice; and (6) the separation of church and state to protect religious freedom.

Throughout their history the majority of Baptist churches have identified theologically and liturgically to varying degrees with the Reformed-Calvinist Protestant heritage, while finding some indirect "spiritual" affinity with the more radical Anabaptist dissent from civil enforcement of religious uniformity (including infant baptism). The interacting of these two strands of the sixteenth-century Reformation in subsequent Baptist self-consciousness helps account for some of the tensions and diversity in their American history.

The large present-day Baptist denominations, and with few exceptions the smaller bodies also, trace their formal organizational origins to the nineteenth century. They were distinguished primarily according to region (North and South), race (black or white), or ethnic identity (German, Swedish, etc.). They did not emerge directly or exclusively from identifiable groupings of Baptists in colonial America, but rather they inherited the theological and ecclesiastical tendencies that developed among various informal groupings of Baptists of the colonial period.

THE COLONIAL PERIOD

Baptists first appeared in colonial America as part of the "great migration" of nonconformist English Puritans during the reign of King Charles I, from 1625 to 1649. Identifying with Puritan Independency (Congregationalism), Baptists had distinguished themselves by their rejection of infant baptism and insistence upon the baptism of adult believers as the necessary basis of church membership. Like other Congregationalists, Baptists recognized the primacy of the local congregation in matters of faith and practice; this brought them into sharp conflict with the Anglican hierarchy and with state enforcement of the established Church of England. Yet when Baptists arrived in the New England colony of Massachusetts Bay, they found themselves identified and treated as illegal dissenters from the established Congregational churches.

Early New England Baptists thus experienced no more toleration of their religious practice than they had known in the mother country. The Massachusetts authorities strictly forbade Baptist gatherings for worship. When they persisted in so gathering, Baptists (along with Quakers) suffered persecution. This led to two critical events in Baptist history.

During the 1630s the Puritan "seeker" Roger Williams came into conflict with the Massachusetts authorities over a variety of issues, among them insistence on believers' baptism and the freedom of congregations from civil interference. When Williams was banished from Massachusetts in 1635, he moved to the head of Narragansett Bay in Rhode Island, where he organized a colony that he named Providence. There he founded a Baptist church in 1638 or 1639. Meanwhile John Clarke, a Puritan of separatist convictions, arrived in Massachusetts in 1637 or 1638. Conflict with the authorities over religious matters soon followed, and Clarke also moved to Rhode Island, where he helped found a church at Newport in 1639; he served as its minister for nearly forty years. Sometime after 1641 the church declared itself to be Baptist. These two congregations, in Providence and Newport, were the first Baptist churches founded in America. Rhode Island (which received a charter in 1663 largely through Clarke's efforts) became a refuge for Baptist and other Christian dissenters from the Massachusetts and Connecticut Puritan establishments. Baptists who continued to live in the other New England colonies and formed a few small congregations experienced abuse for their nonconformity during the later decades of the seventeenth century.

The earliest distinction among the variety of Baptists in colonial America reflected the controversy within Calvinism over the thought of Dutch Reformed minister and professor Jacobus Arminius. Arminius had opposed the strict Calvinist position on predestination and human freedom. In England General Baptists expressed the "Arminian" belief that Christ's atonement applied to the salvation of all (general atonement) and implied human freedom in the salvation process. Particular Baptists followed the more orthodox Calvinist doctrine of predestination, namely that Christ's atonement applied only to the elect (particular atonement), unqualified by human freedom in the salvation process. "Arminianism" became the common label in seventeenth- and eighteenth-century American as well as English and European theological challenges to Calvinist-Reformed confessional orthodoxy; it thereby helped distinguish among Protestant identities. Arminianism deeply influenced the Church of England, for example, and it penetrated both the Unitarian-Universalist expression of Enlightenment thought and the Methodist expression of the eighteenth-century evangelical awakenings.

Baptists in the colonies interacted with all of these theological movements and encompassed within their membership varieties of theological orientations ranging from professedly Arminian to strict Calvinist. The Arminian-Calvinist tension over the understanding of divine initiative and human responsibility in the salvation process would persist among Baptists throughout the nineteenth century as they became involved in programs of evangelistic missions, social reform, the rise of theological liberalism, and ecumenical relationships.

General Baptists. Within the small, scattered, and often persecuted New England congregations that dissented from the rigidly Calvinist Puritan state church establishments in Massachusetts and Connecticut, many Baptists leaned toward the Arminian emphasis on general atonement, free will, and the possibility of falling from grace. Their position not only distinguished them from the eventually more numerous strict Calvinist Baptists but also increased their sectarian identity vis-à-vis the professed Puritan orthodoxy of the establishment. Some of the earliest Baptists to settle in the southern colonies of Virginia (where they also were harassed by the Anglican establishment) and the Carolinas (where they experienced greater toleration) were of the General persuasion.

Though never a large or widely influential segment of colonial Baptist life and thought, General Baptists nevertheless have survived in several historic denominational bodies to the present day. The tiny General Six-Principle Baptists (with about 160 members) is the oldest General Baptist group in the United States. (They interpret the six principles outlined in Hebrews 6:1–2 to include the rite of confirmation or laying on of hands after baptism for reception of the gifts of the Holy Spirit.) It also is the only surviving group with New England roots (Providence, Rhode Island) and a contemporary northern orientation. All other General Baptist groups are primarily southern-oriented. The only surviving group of colonial origin is the National Association of Free Will Baptists (229,500 members), founded in Virginia in 1714.

Particular-Regular Baptists. In contrast to their coreligionists' experience in most of New England and the South, Baptists enjoyed religious toleration and freedom from church taxation in the middle colonies of New Jersey and Pennsylvania. Consequently their churches achieved enough stability and influence to make these colonies the center of Baptist strength by the eighteenth century. Since Particular Baptists dominated the churches in this region, the Philadelphia Association, founded in 1707, promoted the Calvinist orientation among Baptists throughout the colonies. From this Philadelphia center Particular Baptists in America came to be known as Regular Baptists; the name highlights their identity as the major Baptist tradition and an important denominational expression of the broadly Calvinist-rooted churches that comprised the colonial American Puritan heritage.

The Philadelphia Association had no binding power over individual churches; rather it advised, consulted, and in other ways facilitated the interaction and combined strength of local churches. In so doing, it influenced the course of Baptist life and thought in America, both in theological affirmation and in the pattern of ecclesiastical organization beyond the local church congregation. That pattern had been set in the seventeenth century, when English Baptist churches entered into regional associations for the purpose of mutual edification, fellowship, and the strength of united identity. As expressions of this common identity, which distinguished doctrinal emphases of one or another group of churches, Baptist associations frequently prepared confessional statements—not as a rigid condition of fellowship or a test of orthodoxy so much as an expression of underlying unity. It was this associational-confessional principle that defined the Philadelphia Association at its founding.

The Philadelphia Association adopted a confessional statement that reflected the 1677 English Baptist Assembly, or Second London Confession. That confession was based on the Calvinist-oriented Westminster Confession (1646) and was intended to identify Baptists theologically with other Puritan Nonconformists in England. The Regular Baptists in America found in this 1677 confession an underlying theological unity both among their own churches and with other Puritan church traditions. This theological base tended to ameliorate somewhat the New England and southern colonial sectarian character of Baptist identity. During the eighteenth century this confessional practice became common throughout the colonies among Baptist churches that followed the Philadelphia pattern of entering into regional associations for mutual spiritual benefit, preaching and ministry, and common mission. The Regular Baptists thus spread their theological and ecclesiastical influence widely.

It would be misleading, however, to suggest that even the influential Philadelphia Association either reflected or fostered a prospering Baptist tradition in colonial America during the early decades of the eighteenth century. To the contrary, the association simply provided a new foundation upon which Baptists might begin to build a stable tradition beyond the period of their dissent and persecution. During the first century of their New England existence Baptists had felt compelled to disassociate themselves from the radical sixteenth-century Anabaptists, who were widely judged to be religious heretics and civil anarchists.

This defensive posture of Baptist dissent did not stimulate much increase in the number or size of Baptist churches. The memory of Obadiah Holmes, publicly whipped in seventeenth-century Massachusetts for conducting unauthorized worship in a private home, and other such victims provided inspiration to harassed congregations later in the century; but Baptists did not thrive by virtue of their persecutions. Rhode Island had represented a haven for Baptists, but church growth there was stifled by internal theological strife and regional isolation. Although the Philadelphia Association represented unity and organization in a more tolerant and cosmopolitan atmosphere, new adherents were few, apart from successive family generations within their churches and some new Baptist immigrants. Baptist churches had come to resemble the more numerous and prestigious Congregational and Presbyterian churches surrounding them. Proving to be not much of a threat to the established order after all, Baptists had gained toleration in most areas, though they continued to struggle economically in various locales. They were taxed to support established churches while voluntarily supporting their own congregations. By 1740, after a century of existence in colonial America, Baptists thus remained a small, scattered, weak collection of churches.

Separate Baptists. The religio-social movement of the 1740s and 1750s called the Great Awakening marked a turning point in the colonial Baptist experience. As part of the revival of enthusiastic religion that swept through much of western Europe and England in the form of Pietism, quietism, and evangelicalism, the Great Awakening represented a popular movement that challenged established religious customs, practices, and order. Baptist churches were challenged along with the rest. Some of the older Baptist churches, especially among the Regular Baptists who had brought stability and order to church life, did not identify with the new enthusiasm and innovations. Others found in the popular movement support for their century-old witness to a regenerate "believers" church unhindered by official church or state interference.

The Great Awakening's impact on the New England Baptists came not only from revival conversions of hitherto unchurched persons who joined congregations, but even more from those "Separate" Congregationalists ("new lights embracing the revivals") who left the established order and declared themselves Baptists. The doctrine and practice of believers' baptism, no longer carrying quite the public stigma of heresy and anarchy, became a fitting expression of the Separates' revived commitment to regenerate churches. At least 130 new Baptist churches were formed by the disaffected Congregationalists, which helped transform the Baptists from an obscure sect into a thriving popular religious movement within the public social order.

The Congregationalist-turned-Baptist movement is well-illustrated in the career of Isaac Backus. A New Light Congregational minister in Middleborough, Massachusetts, from 1748 to 1756, Backus was among those harassed by civil authorities for challenging orthodox practices. In 1749 he married Susanna Mason, a Baptist, and was immersed according to Baptist principles. In 1756 he covenanted with a remnant of his congregation to separate and form a new Baptist church. During the remaining years of his life Backus was a leader in Baptist life and thought as a church pastor, writer (of some forty published works), organizer, and evangelist-lobbyist for religious freedom and the separation of church and state.

Separate Baptists thrived throughout much of New England, including among the hitherto largely unchurched and less socioeconomically privileged persons on the backwoods frontier and in the rural villages. During the later eighteenth century the revivalistic Separate Baptist movement flourished most widely in the South, where Regular Baptist churches were almost nonexistent. Much of this new Baptist church life in the South resulted from the itinerant missionary efforts of such New England Separate Congregationalists-turned-Baptists as Shubael Stearns, who went south in 1754 and helped found churches in Virginia and North Carolina that eventually resulted in the Sandy Creek Association. Some of the Great Awakening innovations, such as lay preaching (including women), thrived unhindered by traditional structures in the South except where the Anglican establishment resisted.

However, the Separate Baptist challenge to Regular Baptist traditions was not essentially theological. The scholarship of New England's Great Awakening apologist Jonathan Edwards, plus the wide influence of the intercolonial "grand itinerant" revival preacher George Whitefield, infused a rejuvenated Calvinist theology into the New Light churches. This Calvinist thrust, to be distinguished from the Arminian Methodism of John Wesley, thus helped bridge the gap between Regular and Separate Baptists. Although in tension with the Regular Baptist Philadelphia Association for decades to come, the Separate Baptist churches slowly reconciled their differences with the Philadelphia-centered churches. During the upheavals of the revolutionary period both groups made major contributions to the stability, growth, and unity of Baptist church life. The Regular Baptists contributed organizational and intellectual cohesion, while the Separate Baptists engaged the churches in the social-economic-political dynamics that accompanied the birth of the new nation.

THE REVOLUTIONARY PERIOD

During the late-eighteenth-century growth and expansion of Baptist churches, the Philadelphia Association helped to facilitate the institutional stability and orderly faith and practice of the emerging denomination as a whole. Not only did the association stimulate the formation of other regional associations; it also developed programs and institutions that benefited churches in other regions. For example, in 1764 the association commissioned James Manning to found and become first president of Rhode Island College (later Brown University) in order that Baptists might have a strong program of liberal arts education equivalent to those of Harvard, Yale, College of New Jersey (later Princeton), and William and Mary. The college directly served the churches by recruiting and training ministers. It contributed to the advancement of Baptists into the educated and professional circles of society. Rhode Island College became a center of colonial Baptist interaction with British and European Baptists and with other colonial religious and civic centers of life and thought.

The Philadelphia Association also became a publishing facility for Baptists, providing churches with such materials as a confession of faith, a catechism, and a hymnal; various treatises on discipline, apologetics, and worship; English Baptist writings; and the first two volumes of Morgan Edwards' history of Baptists in the colonies (1770, 1792). Finally, the association became instrumental in the development of organized mission activity: in the founding and assistance of new churches, in benevolent social services, in work among Indian tribes, and eventually in missions overseas.

The Philadelphia Association thus contributed to the organizational and intellectual cohesion of colonial Baptist churches. This Regular thrust, along with the popular increase and spread of Baptist congregations through the Separate movement in the wake of the Great Awakening, formed the basis of a thriving, well-organized denominational tradition and brought Baptists into the mainstream of intercolonial life and American Protestantism during the years of the revolutionary war and the constitutional birth of the new nation.

By the end of the seventeenth century the Regular and Separate Baptists had lost most of their distinguishing characteristics. In 1801 the majority of them in Virginia and Kentucky combined their organization and enthusiasm into a merger that became known as United Baptists. This action symbolized the actual move toward unity among Baptists throughout the nation.

The Separate Baptist churches, however, had made a large impact on colonial Baptist life that also contributed to the Baptists' rise to prominence within the new national ethos. The Separate Baptist emphasis on the possibility of individual inspiration and enlightenment through the Holy Spirit detracted somewhat from the importance of fixed written confessional standards while stressing reliance on the Bible alone as containing the sufficient statement of their belief. More far-reaching, their spiritual independence also made them suspicious of associational authority over local congregations, as well as of the clerical authority within their churches. Overall these emphases contributed religious sanction for individualism in social-political attitudes and concerns, which also helps account for the prominence of such Baptist leaders as Isaac Backus in the struggle for religious and civil liberties during the revolutionary era and the rising popularity of Baptist churches at the close of the eighteenth century.

It is significant that Baptists fused their long struggle for religious toleration in the colonies with the American revolutionary cause. Such an alliance was not automatic in the earlier stages of the American struggle against England. Baptists had continued to experience abuse in some colonies. As they gained in strength, Baptists began to advocate, publicly and aggressively, religious freedom and church-state separation. By mid-century some Massachusetts Baptists even petitioned the king of England for greater religious freedom. Then the Rhode Island Warren Association joined with the Philadelphia Association to send Hezekiah Smith to England to present their grievances. But this only intensified the abusive treatment of Baptists in Massachusetts and Connecticut, which led them to petition the colonial general courts for redress. As the war approached, some Baptists were uncertain whether the British or the Americans would provide a greater measure of religious liberty. It finally became clear to most, however, that religious and civil liberties were intertwined; and Baptists overwhelmingly supported the American cause.

Having struggled for a century and a half for toleration and freedom, Baptists were able to apply some of their religious zeal to the revolutionary effort. Separate Baptist leaders led the way. Hezekiah Smith and John Gano, itinerant evangelists to the South who later became pastors in Massachusetts and New York, respectively, were among those who became revolutionary war chaplains. Baptists' support of the Revolution entailed their strong advocacy of a religious settlement granting religious freedom and church-state separation. John Leland, a Virginia Baptist minister, was instrumental in the passage of Jefferson's Statute for Religious Freedom in the Virginia Assembly in 1785, which led to disestablishment of the Anglican Church in 1786. Isaac Backus, the Massachusetts pastor, was appointed by the Warren Association as agent (evangelist-lobbyist) to promote the cause at the Continental Congress. His tract *Government and Liberty Described and Ecclesiastical Tyranny Exposed* (1778) was widely influential in the debates that culminated in the ratification of the First Amendment to the federal Constitution in 1791.

The Baptists also benefited in the new nation from the nature of their congregational orientation and membership. Their lay-oriented local church polity helped them ride the crest of popular enthusiasm for civil democracy. Because Baptist congregations had been organized among all kinds of people in all regions of the country, including frontier territory, they were not identified primarily with any region or social class. They had become identified as a nationwide people's church. Moreover, their long experience of survival and growth on the basis of voluntary support without civil tax assistance, and their persuasive appeals to religious affections, theological concerns, and personal and social needs, placed them in an ideal position to thrive. Having increased from about 500 churches in 1775 to an estimated 1,150 churches in 1797 (according to Backus) and growing rapidly, Baptists had become the largest religious denomination in the new nation.

THE PRE–CIVIL WAR PERIOD

Baptists moved into the nineteenth century with a widespread but largely informal sense of unity. No centralized denominational structure had been created. Rather, Baptist polity continued to develop along the lines of essentially independent congregations entering into regional associations of churches, on the one hand, and Baptist individuals and groups joining together in societies for particular mission-oriented tasks and goals, on the other hand. This nationwide organizational network may best be described as the Baptists' participation in the emerging evangelical mainstream that vigorously set about to implant Christianity in all aspects of American life as the nation began its westward expansion. Baptists not only formed societies for education, publishing, benevolence, moral reform, and other forms of mission; they also joined with other Protestants in cooperative local, regional, and national societies for similar purposes. The overall thrust of this cooperative Protestant impulse became known as the Second Great Awakening, marked by a new wave of revivalism, institutional formations, and theological productivity.

United Efforts. The phenomenon of revivalism that had contributed much to late-eighteenth-century Baptist growth and expansion became one means by which the major Protestant denominations adapted themselves to the westward expansion during the early nineteenth century. Baptists were among them. Although the more established eastern towns also experienced a resurgence of revivalistic praying, preaching, and singing that became organized into an evangelistic method, on the frontier revivalism inspired excessive emotionalism and physical excitement. Baptists often joined Presbyterians and Methodists in revival "camp meetings," to which hundreds of people came for the inspiration of preaching and fellowship in the open air or under large tents. More common among Baptists, however, were "protracted meetings" in their churches at which revival preaching lasted for several days or even weeks. Although Baptists were not universally supportive of revivals, they did generally utilize them successfully as one means of evangelistic outreach. Eventually they combined the roles of professional traveling evangelists (itinerant ministers), for example, with other forms of mission programs that helped foster a denominational strength and identity.

Institutionally, the majority of Baptist churches expressed their sense of denominational identity through the formation of mission-oriented societies that were independent of regional associations. This departure from associational sponsorship allowed a wide variety of local churches to maintain their essential independence while combining their resources and efforts. Although associations continued to thrive on the local and regional level, frequently lending support to particular societies for mission, denomination-wide societies facilitated singular mission goals. With direct support by individuals, churches, and associations, mission societies were bureaucratic organizations for the practical work of churches—in no sense functioning as churches themselves and not identified as ecclesiastical bodies.

The impetus for organizing the first national Baptist society came from foreign mission activity. In 1795 English Baptists had organized a society to support the mission of William Carey in India; and the American churches, led by those of the Philadelphia Association, were eager to identify with this work and to support it economically. In years following, the foreign mission movement spread among most American Protestant denominations as part of the Second Great Awakening fever.

When Congregationalists Adoniram Judson, Ann Hasseltine Judson, and Luther Rice, sent by the American Board of Commissioners for Foreign Missions (Congregationalist) to India, became convinced of the Baptist view of baptism and resigned from the Congregational Board, Baptists in America felt called to assume support of them. In 1812 the Judsons went to Burma as Baptist missionaries while Rice returned to the United States to promote support of the now Baptist missions in the Far East. The result was the formation in 1814 of the Philadelphia-centered General Missionary Convention of the Baptist Denomination in the United States for Foreign Missions. Soon known as the Triennial Convention (it met every three years), the convention secured the support of nearly all Baptist associations in the country.

The Triennial Convention (later renamed the American Baptist Foreign Mission Society) at first intended to facilitate various kinds of domestic mission activity as well; but church fears of concentrating too much of their total mission outreach in one organization convinced the convention to limit its concerns to foreign mission. Other societies might concentrate on different activities. In 1824, for example, the Baptist General Tract Society (later called the American Baptist Publication Society) was formed, to be followed by other similar societies for particular tasks. With power thus diffused among various unconnected societies, the primary ecclesiastical authority located in local congregations could be maintained.

Meanwhile, as part of the migrations westward, Baptist families were becoming diffused throughout the states and beyond into frontier territory. To help facilitate the establishment of churches and schools among pioneer settlers, to reach unchurched persons, to engage in mission work among Indian tribes, and generally to "promote the preaching of the Gospel in North America," the American Baptist Home Mission Society was organized in 1832 in New York City. Instrumental in achieving this new organization were John Mason Peck, a Baptist frontier missionary in St. Louis, and Jonathan Going, pastor of the First Baptist Church of Worcester, Massachusetts. Immediately a flurry of missionary appointments were made by the society, with concentration around the frontier centers of Cleveland, Detroit, Indianapolis, Louisville, and Chicago.

By mid-century the society was establishing churches and supporting mission activity in the Southwest Territory, the Midwest, the Rocky Mountain region, and the Pacific Coast. In 1845 Hezekiah Johnson and Ezra Fisher traveled seven and a half months across the continent to begin organizing churches in Oregon. Four years later the society sent Osgood Church Wheeler and Elizabeth Hamilton Wheeler, from a New Jersey parish, to establish a mission in San Francisco, where the rush for gold was creating an urban center almost overnight. Within a year the Wheelers had helped organize the San Francisco Baptist Association of three churches and had begun plans to form a school for liberal arts and theological education. Their efforts illustrate the role of the society organizations in the expansion of Baptist life throughout the nation.

There was nothing unusual about the San

Francisco association's early preoccupation with establishing a school. For Baptists, as for other Protestant denominations expanding westward, educational programs and institutions had become a priority. By the early years of the century Baptists had begun to organize Sunday schools for secular and religious education—prior to the emergence of large-scale public education in the United States. Soon schools for exclusively religious instruction were being organized in churches. The popularity of the Sunday school movement among Protestants of various denominations led to the formation of the cooperative American Sunday School Union in 1824. Baptists thrived within the movement, which became a means of evangelism and, especially in the West, a stimulus to the formation and growth of churches. Through their local, regional, and finally national society structure, Baptist Sunday schools and educational literature became a basic ingredient in the development of national church life.

Baptists also combined their resources in all regions to establish specialized academies, liberal arts colleges, and theological schools for ministerial training. The college chartered at Newport, Rhode Island, in 1764 (later moved to Providence and eventually renamed Brown University) contributed to the strength and interaction of Baptist life throughout the colonies on the eve of the Revolution. From then on, Baptists made higher education part of denominational life. The following colleges and universities—all still thriving and all with national stature—are among those that trace their origins wholly or in part (through mergers) to pre–Civil War Baptist foundations: Brown University in Rhode Island; Colby College and Bates College in Maine; Hamilton College in New York; Andover-Newton Theological Seminary in Massachusetts; Furman University in South Carolina; Denison University in Ohio; Mercer University in Georgia; Wake Forest University in North Carolina; Franklin College in Indiana; Baylor University in Texas; Bucknell University in Pennsylvania; Linfield College in Oregon; Kalamazoo College in Michigan; William Jewell College in Missouri; Colgate University, the University of Rochester, and Colgate Rochester Divinity School in Rochester, New York; the University of Chicago and its Divinity School in Illinois; Southern Bap-

tist Theological Seminary in South Carolina (later Kentucky); and Ottawa University in Kansas.

Baptists related to the intellectual world in which they lived through their colleges and seminaries as well as through their churches. Although theological disagreements have divided Baptists since the seventeenth century, in the years after the Civil War theology also provided support to the United Baptist efforts. Most Baptists embraced some modified form of Calvinism—ranging from affinity with the more liberal Yale Congregationalist theologian Nathaniel William Taylor to the more orthodox-minded Princeton Presbyterian theologian Charles Hodge. These theological "schools" found common intellectual support in the natural law and Scottish common-sense philosophy that permeated much of American political, economic, scientific, and religious thought of the day. No better example of this philosophical-theological framework can be found than the writings of Francis Wayland, Baptist president and professor at Brown University and later a minister in Providence. His *The Elements of Moral Science* (1835) and *The Elements of Political Economy* (1837) were widely read for decades by Baptists and other Protestants as almost normative doctrine. The same integration of philosophy and theology informed the teaching and writing of John Leadley Dagg, professor of theology at Mercer University, who published in 1856 a *Manual of Theology* that became a standard text in the Southern Baptist Theological Seminary and a formative book in Baptist churches in the South. Within this rationalist intellectual framework Baptist theologians could, for example, argue their position on baptism on rational grounds to buttress their scriptural interpretation. In so doing a wide variety of Baptists could participate in the larger world of theological discourse with a sense of intellectual support for those affirmations and practices they shared as a distinctive tradition within Protestant Christianity.

A nineteenth-century quest for Baptist unity based on a common affirmation of faith also found confessional and catechetical expression. The New Hampshire Confession of 1833, for example, had become widely disseminated in revised form among a wide variety of Baptist churches by mid-century. Its moderate Calvinistic flavor touched the essential doctrinal nerve of churches rooted in the Regular and Separate strands of the Baptist heritage. As sectional strife leading to the Civil War made a deep impact on Baptist denominational life, the American Baptist Publication Society in 1851 printed *The Baptist Catechism,* a slight revision of the edition published in London in 1794, which was based on the 1677 Confession of Faith set forth by London Baptists and adopted by the Philadelphia Association in 1742. The American Baptist Publication Society intended the catechism to express the historic Baptist tradition common to most northern and southern Baptist churches, thereby to reaffirm an essential theological unity of the regions and solidify Baptist identity within the broader spectrum of denominational Protestantism.

Dissent, Division, Plurality. Unity among Baptists in America, however, was not to be. Deeply embedded in the tradition was a sectarian instinct that challenged Baptists' efforts both toward internal unity and toward cooperation with wider expressions of denominational Christianity. The very search for a distinctive identity, as Baptist churches prospered in concert with other exponents of popular evangelicalism, led full circle to new sectarian Baptist expressions. The plurality that became divisive reflected the political and cultural regionalism of the nation, as well as the new historical consciousness that marked the transition in American thought from the Enlightenment legacy of latitudinarian common-sense reason to the romantic emphasis on the particular, distinctive, and unique in human experience. In this changing intellectual climate, how churches differed from one another became as important as what they had in common. As a result, cooperative organizations fostered dissenting nonconformity in the cause of preserving the distinctive tradition; broad-based evangelical theology became characterized as doctrinal reductionism; and confessional statements excluded more than they included. Baptist plurality finally prevailed at the cost of unity.

Regional feeling and the quest for particular historical identity had found extreme expression by mid-century in the Old Landmarkism movement, which had a deep impact on Baptists in the South. A key fomenter of the movement was James R. Graves, editor of *The Tennessee Baptist* and publisher of such Baptist writings as James M. Pendleton's *An Old Landmark Re-Set* (1854) and G. H. Orchard's *Concise History of Foreign Baptists* (1855).

The Landmarkists sought to locate the distinctive Baptist identity within Christian history on the basis of autonomous local congregations as the only true visible manifestation of the church. These local churches were "marked" by exclusive adherence to adult believers' baptism by immersion and nonrecognition of "alien immersion"; by use of the New Testament as the "only sufficient rule of faith and practice" (as against confessions and catechisms); and by disassociation from all other organizations claiming to be expressions of Christianity (such as mission societies and denominations).

The Landmark movement thus countered Baptist efforts toward unity on the basis of mission societies and confessional affirmations. Crossing the thin line that often separates extreme sectarian from extreme churchly expressions of Christianity, Landmarkism embraced an interpretation of church history in which a succession of true Baptist congregations are located in conflict with established Christendom and traced throughout history from apostolic times. This "high church" view allowed nineteenth-century Baptists to identify with sixteenth-century Anabaptists, for example, as well as persecuted "heretics" of Western Christendom. It also helped define the subsequent Southern Baptist Convention's "churchly" identification with the South as the original and authentic Christian expression that in sectarian fashion made it aloof from institutions of ecumenical Protestantism. Overall, Landmarkism called attention to distinctions among Baptists that had emerged throughout the antebellum years and would proliferate after the Civil War.

The Arminian tendencies that had defined the early colonial General Baptist churches also remained alive not only in the two groups formed in the colonial years (the General Six-Principle Baptists and the National Association of Free Will Baptists), but also in the Free Will Baptists, which arose in New England in 1780. Led by Benjamin Randall, the group continued throughout the nineteenth century. The resurgence of Free Will Baptists exemplified the impact on nineteenth-century American Protestantism of such popular movements as Methodism and the Campbellite "Christians" or Disciples of Christ. Each of these new denominational traditions openly challenged Calvinistic theology at its core by emphasizing free will in the acceptance of saving grace offered by God through Christ to all persons. This popular Arminianism harmonized with revivalistic preaching for mass conversions. Whereas various Free Will Baptist groups found support in the Arminian impulse, they also lost members to the Methodists and Disciples of Christ and thus remained small. Baptists of the Regular-Separate heritage tended to react to resurgent Arminianism by reaffirming their Calvinistic heritage yet modifying it so as to harmonize with revivalistic appeals for conversion and commitment. But modified Calvinism satisfied neither the Arminians nor the orthodox-minded. Meanwhile the Landmarkists' diatribes against the churchly claims of Methodists and Disciples (rather than dealing with the Calvinist-Arminian issue) accentuated both the variety of differences among Baptists and the distinction between Baptists and other evangelical denominations.

At the other extreme, some Baptists distinguished themselves from the Regular-Separate unity by their adherence to an extreme interpretation of the Calvinist doctrine of predestination. Daniel Parker, for example, pushed the extreme in founding (about 1826) the Two-Seed-in-the-Spirit Predestinarian Baptists, meaning that both good and bad seeds are planted and transmitted biologically and (according to divine election) result in either salvation or damnation. Radical Predestinarian Baptists rejected organized mission societies as humanly devised methods to obtain conversions, which they believed to be entirely an act of God.

Theological arguments bolstered the social and economic reasons these Baptists had for opposing mission programs. Especially in the South and West, for example, some Baptists resisted the centralized eastern-based power of mission organizations whose educational and paid lay and ordained leaders might control western church resources for the benefit of northeastern programs. Local church autonomy thus seemed at stake, including economic independence, as well as perceived doctrinal purity.

The radical anti-mission Calvinists became a permanent sectarian Baptist presence, especially in the South, where they distinguished themselves from the increasingly powerful, missionary-oriented Baptist majority. Today they include perhaps 100,000 church members in a dozen or so bodies.

A Regular Baptist body with seventeenth-century roots that remained outside the Regular-Separate unity is the Seventh Day Baptist General Conference. Seventh Day Baptists, who formed their first church in 1671 in Newport, Rhode Island, distinguished themselves from other Regular Baptists by holding to the seventh day as the Sabbath. Their membership, which has remained about the same size for the past century (5,000 members), today is strongest in Rhode Island, New York, New Jersey, West Virginia, Wisconsin, and California.

Black Baptists. By the end of the eighteenth century the influence of Christianity on Afro-American slaves and freedmen began to take institutional form. Plantation slave churches had appeared as early as 1758 in Virginia, and similar churches were organized in other regions of the South. By the end of the century Savannah, Georgia, had become an important center of black Baptist church life. Soon black Baptist churches were organized in Boston (1805), New York (1808), and Philadelphia (1809). Under southern plantation conditions, slaves sometimes openly heard white church preaching, and other times gathered secretly; in the latter cases, African religious expressions mixed with evangelical Christianity. Distinctively black congregations also developed a vigorous life, though in the South they were restricted by white church control. Baptist local congregational polity helped to facilitate the growth of black congregations, where black Christians could maximize the possibilities for corporate self-definition and regulation. The larger black church vision found expression in Lott Cary and Collin Teague, members of the Richmond African Baptist Missionary Society (founded in 1815), who in 1821 became the first American missionaries to Africa. So too, slave rebellions such as that led by black Baptist preacher Nat Turner in Southhampton County, Virginia, in 1831 suggest the degree to which black religion had become integrated into the total slave experience.

Outside southern slave regions, independent black church associations were constituted in Ohio, Illinois, and Indiana during the 1830s and

1840s. In New England and the Middle States the black American Baptist Missionary Convention was formed in 1840; and in the 1850s the Colored Baptist Convention received support in Illinois and Missouri. By that time blacks had joined the rush for gold in California, and permanent black church communities had appeared in the San Francisco area. Finally, following the Emancipation Proclamation abolishing slavery, black Baptists in the South began to organize associations and state conventions, such as the Virginia Baptist State Convention in 1867 and the North Carolina State Convention in 1886.

The 1845 North-South Schism. The movement to abolish slavery contributed greatly to the 1845 institutional division between Baptists of the North and South, thereby rupturing the movement toward national denominational unity that had begun in the early nineteenth century. Prior to 1830 Baptist pronouncements against slavery had come almost equally from churches in the South and in the North. As the abolitionist movement became increasingly widespread and aggressive in the North, however, and as southern defense of the institution of slavery hardened, Baptists became increasingly caught up in the ensuing sectional strife.

Actually, the process of regional differentiation among Baptists had developed long before the 1845 schism. Cultural nuances and regional loyalties exacerbated social differences between the two groups, for example. Baptists in the North had deeper institutional roots, including churches of many generations and a major college. They tended to have a middle-class laity and an educated ministry plus a westward expansion program led by missionaries trained and sent by societies headquartered in northern cities. They represented the Yankee cultural ethos moving westward. Southerners tended to be more recent Baptists representing a lower socioeconomic status, caring less for an educated clergy, and moving westward by means of farmer preachers. Baptists in the South thrived as a popular religious movement deeply assimilated into the prevailing culture. Baptists in the North and in the South, therefore, both manifested their respective regional cultures and differed somewhat in their social backgrounds. But these differences alone do not account for the schism that was to come.

Regional differences became increasingly important as Baptists from the North and the South moved westward. The major societies of the denomination had originated in the North—in Philadelphia, New York, and Boston. Baptist leaders in these centers greatly influenced the policies of the denomination. During the 1830s it became increasingly clear that the General Missionary Convention and the American Baptist Home Missionary Society reflected the organizational preferences and program interests of the northerners at the expense of the southerners. Southern leaders, for example, felt that the Home Mission Society concentrated its work in areas of the West where Baptists from the North were settling. The increasingly acute sectional strife over the issues of western territories being admitted as free or slave states contributed to the eventual rupture of Baptist life into separate northern and southern organizations.

The rupture finally came in 1845. For years the mission societies had tried to maintain unity by declaring neutrality on the issues related to slavery and thereby containing both northern and southern views of their Baptist constituents. Eventually northern abolitionist sympathizers gained the balance of power, however, and through a complex series of resolutions and test cases, the neutrality of the societies was broken. When the societies' leaders attempted to prohibit the appointment of slaveholders as missionaries, and Baptist leaders in the South rejected this action, both sides concluded that it would be expedient if mission work were to be carried on by separate organizations in the North and in the South. In 1845, 328 delegates from the churches of the South met in Augusta, Georgia, to organize the Southern Baptist Convention (SBC). This schism over the issue of slavery thus formalized regional differences that long had been developing within Baptist life.

Schism, however, was not easily accepted. The American Baptist Home Mission Society continued to claim national identity without territorial limitations, and many southern churches maintained contact with the society despite the formation of the Southern Baptist Convention. The convention itself in 1845 insisted that "Northern and Southern Baptists are still brethren. They differ in no article of faith" (1845 *Proceedings*). As war approached, however, sectional differences became exaggerated beyond repair. Churches north and south identified with their respective armies; and some far western congregations split into southern and northern factions.

The wartime experience completed the rupture. The devastation of the South usually did not spare churches. The American Baptist Home Mission Society asked the U.S. War Department for permission to occupy and preserve abandoned churches in Union-occupied territory; but their motives were misunderstood by some when in 1864 the federal government granted the society permission to occupy all churches lacking a pastor loyal to the Union. Few southern churches would have escaped this action had the society decided to follow the government's lead (which, in most cases, it did not). Still, the impression of civil-religious entanglement was oppressive to southern Baptist sensibilities, especially when ministers were arrested and imprisoned for their Confederate loyalty. In 1866 the Southern Baptist Convention reaffirmed the principle of "soul liberty," opposed government intervention in church matters, resolved as churches to remain outside of political affairs, and thus identified with the early Baptist dissenting tradition. With this outlook, the Southern Baptist Convention declared itself a permanent organization in 1868.

THE POST–CIVIL WAR YEARS

After the Civil War, Baptists in the United States were involved in three major regional enterprises. First, they became integral to the reconstruction and development of southern culture. Second, they became increasingly pluralized in cosmopolitan centers and in relationship to the masses of immigrants who poured into northern cities. Third, they helped "develop" the Far West and became part of its cultural ethos and diversity.

Baptists in the South. In post–Civil War America, the Southern Baptist Convention became a major institution facilitating cultural identity and expression. The Baptist local church emphasis gave grass-roots religious identity to southern citizens, while the convention's centralized structure brought local churches into a sense of regional unity. The Southern Baptist Convention became the South's dominant religious force by the late nineteenth century and the largest Protestant denomination in the United States (1,482,274 members in 1900). From a position of dissenting sectarian congregations in colonial Anglican establishments, Baptist themselves had become virtually territorial. As a relatively homogeneous religious tradition, the Southern Baptist Convention emerged from the Reconstruction period prepared to propagate its piety with evangelistic zeal throughout its homeland, across the continent, and into other lands through well-organized mission programs.

The Southern Baptist Convention's dominance was achieved only gradually and with struggle, and with a major limitation. The struggle involved completing the separation of southern churches from the American Baptist Home Mission Society, consolidating the convention's primacy in mission work in the South, and establishing a stable organization out of the socioeconomic ruins of the Civil War. SBC churches had to reconstruct their own unity among themselves, but the urge to reunite with northern Baptists persisted as well. Proclaiming its "North America for Christ" motto, the American Baptist Home Mission Society refused to acknowledge territorial limits. The society gave financial assistance to southern churches and was instrumental in founding schools and ministerial institutes for freedmen.

Southern Baptist Convention leaders recognized this constructive work by northerners, but increasingly they asserted territorial control. In 1882 Isaac T. Tichenor became corresponding secretary of the convention's Home Mission Board. During his tenure, from 1882 to 1899, the convention's overall mission program and local church support gained strength. In addition to the Home Mission Board, the Foreign Mission Board, the Woman's Missionary Union, and the Sunday School Board were formed. By the century's end the Southern Baptist Convention had become a base of world missions and of missions in the American West among migrating settlers, native Indian tribes, and immigrants. With the formation in 1907 of the Northern Baptist Convention (later the American Baptist Convention and then the American Baptist Churches in the U.S.A.), the regional separation of Baptists north and south reached a climax.

The limitation of the Southern Baptist Convention's control of Baptist church life in the South came with the separation of most black

Baptists from white-dominated churches, the increase in independent black Baptist churches and associations, and finally the formation of the National Baptist Convention of America in 1895. (In 1915 a schism resulted in the formation of a second denomination, the National Baptist Convention of the U.S.A., Inc.; and in 1961 a schism from the incorporated body led to the formation of the Progressive National Baptist Convention.) This development of black Baptist denominationalism manifested both the integrity of Afro-American religion rooted in the slavery experience and the fact of racial segregation in the New South following Reconstruction. If black citizens were to experience discrimination and segregation in white-dominated religious and civil institutions, at least they could assume control of their corporate religious life. Baptist congregational polity maximized this black independence, and black churches became community centers wherever they existed. Although many black churches maintained contacts with the Southern Baptist Convention and some related to the churches of the North, most came to identify primarily with the independent black denominations. By the mid-twentieth century these had grown to a combined estimated membership of over 7 million, and they have continued to grow rapidly. By that time, black Baptists, along with other Baptists of southern origins, had long since migrated into northern cities and westward throughout the nation.

Baptists in the North. Baptists in the North survived the Civil War with something of the strength and prestige of victors. Only with reluctance did the northern-based societies relinquish their claims to being the instruments of denominational unity nationwide. During their gradual loss of influence in the South, the northern societies vigorously resumed their overall programs of foreign and domestic missions, expanding into new lands and into new dimensions of social outreach as the urban-industrial revolution transformed the American environment. The most notable new societies were the Women's Baptist Foreign Mission Society (1871), the Women's Baptist Home Mission Society (1877), the American Baptist Education Society (1888), and the Baptist Young People's Union of America (1891).

Identifying with the so-called American Protestant mainstream, Baptists in the North eagerly participated in cooperative ventures with other denominations. Through these developing ecumenical contacts, through cosmopolitan influences in urban centers and within their educational institutions in the Boston, Rochester (New York), Philadelphia, Chicago, and San Francisco areas, northern Baptists participated in the new diversity of theological expression that characterized Protestantism during the late nineteenth and early twentieth centuries. All of this, plus the new immigration of peoples of widely diverse ethnic and national identities, contributed to the transformation of Baptists in the North as a denomination. By 1907, when the various societies joined together into a unified convention structure, the Northern Baptist Convention, they were a broadly pluralistic denomination, with more than one million members.

During the late nineteenth century Baptists in the North thus established themselves as major participants in the intellectual and social forces of American Christianity. In New York City alone such Baptist ministers as Cortland Myers, Cornelius Woelfkin, W. H. P. Faunce, George C. Lorimer, Edward Judson, and William C. Bitting were prominent religious personalities. In other cities, such preachers as George Dana Boardman, Russell H. Conwell, and Clarence Barbour gained national fame. Within the ecumenical ranks of powerful leaders of the women's movement few names loomed larger than Lucy Peabody and Helen Barrett Montgomery, whose denominational thrust reached international dimensions, for example, in the formation of the World-wide Guild of Northern Baptist Young Women. Baptist seminary faculties likewise included some of the premier theologians on the American scene, such as Alvah Hovey, William Newton Clarke, Augustus Hopkins Strong, Henry C. Vedder, and the illustrious scholars gathered by William Rainey Harper for the theological faculty of the University of Chicago—among them Ernest De Witt Burton, Shailer Mathews, Edgar J. Goodspeed, Charles Henderson, Shirley Jackson Case, Gerald Birney Smith, and George Burman Foster. Perhaps of most lasting influence was Walter Rauschenbusch, whose teaching and writing on the Social Gospel brought mission and theology together in ways that challenged Baptists (and others) to meet the twentieth century with creative vision.

Within this context the Northern Baptist Convention formalized a denominational identity that included widely divergent theological orientations—from the most liberal to the most conservatively orthodox—a commitment to social action in mission endeavor, and close cooperation with other denominations. The convention joined the Federal Council of Churches of Christ in America, even as Baptist societies previously had been members of the various interdenominational federations that had come together in 1908 to form the council. Meanwhile the denomination's scope of identity had expanded to the Far West and become increasingly pluralistic along racial and ethnic lines.

Baptists in the West. Baptists, both black and white, continued to move westward during the late nineteenth century as the frontier gave way to new towns and cities. Both the Southern Baptist Home Mission Board and the American Baptist Home Mission Society labored to build churches and schools, to establish ministries in mining and lumber camps, and to work among immigrants and Indian tribes.

Baptist missions to Indian tribes spanned most areas of the West, from the Oklahoma Territory to the Pacific Coast, wherever reservations were located. Like other denominations, Baptists cooperated with the Board of Indian Commissioners during the years of President Grant's Peace Policy, from 1869 to 1897 (the policy lived on after his death). By the end of the century, however, Baptists were among those who favored separation of church missions to Indians from government agencies.

The most constructive results of Baptist contacts with tribal peoples came as indigenous Indian leadership was developed. An important step in this direction came with the founding of the Indian Normal and Theological School (under American Baptist Home Mission Society auspices) at Tahlequah, Oklahoma, where in 1880 Almon C. Bacone (a Native American) became principal. The school was moved to Muskogee in 1885 and renamed Bacone Junior College. During the course of the twentieth century, Indian congregations stabilized in relationship to both the Northern and Southern Baptist Conventions in the West, adding richly to the plurality of Baptist cultural life.

During the late nineteenth and early twentieth centuries, much western Baptist life developed in conjunction with the northern denomination.

The American Baptist Home Mission Society and the American Baptist Publication Society cooperated to support new church building. They also financed railroad chapel cars to carry colporteur missionaries into more remote areas to reach unchurched people. Regional and local associations, mission societies, and conventions became the immediate facilitators of Baptist church growth and development. Permanent Baptist institutions of higher education were founded in strategic locations, such as Linfield College in Oregon, Sioux Falls College in South Dakota, Berkeley Baptist Divinity School across the bay from San Francisco, the University of Redlands in southern California, and Central Baptist Theological Seminary in Kansas.

Baptist life in the Far West assumed a regional flavor. With the denominational bureaucratic structures of both the Northern and Southern Baptist Conventions reflecting eastern cultural orientations and circumstances, far western Baptist churches in many ways lived in relative isolation. Twentieth-century transportation and communication made denominational ties closer, but the sense of independence continued. All kinds of Baptists coexisted in the Far West on fairly equal terms, including Northern and Southern Convention adherents, Landmarkists, strict Calvinists, Arminians, Seventh Day Baptists, and newly formed groups trying to rejuvenate the old Regular Baptist identity. Along with these were black Baptists, Native American Baptists, Hispanic Baptists, Asian Baptists, and Baptists of many European national identities.

Although successive waves of SBC migrants after World War I altered the demography of the Far West—some areas of which are the most secular in the nation—no Baptist group represented a dominant religious force or even a strong mainstream identity. Under these conditions the separatist, even sectarian tendency inherent in Baptist roots easily surfaced. Overall, the Far West included the largest dimensions of plurality that eventually defined the Baptist experience in the nation as a whole.

BAPTISTS AND THE IMMIGRANTS

Baptist life in the United States was dramatically affected by the arrival of peoples from northern European countries during the middle decades of the nineteenth century, followed by the "new immigration" of peoples from eastern and southern Europe during the late nineteenth and early twentieth centuries. The later decades also brought peoples from China, Japan, Mexico, and Latin American nations. Some Baptists were among these immigrants and either related to existing Baptist institutions in the United States or formed their own ethnic churches. Many other immigrants who were either unchurched or identified with other traditions came into contact with and subsequently joined Baptist congregations after their arrival. Much Baptist home mission work became oriented toward these immigrants.

German immigrants settled widely across the nation, with the Midwest becoming home for the majority. German Baptist mission efforts, such as that accomplished by Konrad A. Fleischmann during the 1830s and 1840s, had led to churches being organized in Philadelphia in 1843 and New York in 1851. By 1859, as German people migrated westward, Baptist work among them had grown sufficiently to result in the formation of the General Conference of Baptist Churches in America. Much of its strength in the early years came from German-speaking immigrants from Germany, Switzerland, and eastern Europe (especially German-speaking Russians). Meanwhile the American Baptist Home Mission Society and the Home Mission Board of the Southern Baptist Convention assisted in the formation of German churches in their respective regions.

An especially notable German-American relationship marked the establishment of a German department of the Rochester Theological Seminary in 1858 led by August Rauschenbusch, father of the Social Gospel proponent Walter Rauschenbusch. But distinctively German Baptist life in twentieth-century America flourished primarily within the General Conference, independent of though in cordial relations with the larger Southern and Northern Baptist Convention denominations. Eventually the conference outgrew its largely exclusive German membership and was renamed the North American Baptist Conference (43,000 members in 1982).

Similar developments occurred among Scandinavian Baptists, most notably Norwegian and Swedish immigrants. Having experienced persecution for their illegal dissent from state church practices in their homelands, they welcomed the

freedom of religion in the United States. Norwegian Baptists settling in such states as Illinois, Wisconsin, Minnesota, and North Dakota struggled to survive conflict with the more numerous Lutheran settlers, beginning with the work of Hans Valder in 1837 in Illinois. In Wisconsin, Minnesota, and Illinois, Norwegian and Danish Baptists formed mixed congregations, leading to the formation of the Danish-Norwegian Baptist Conference of the Northwest in 1864.

Meanwhile the Scandinavian groups maintained relations with the American Baptist Home Mission Society, which provided financial aid to new churches and assisted in the training of clergy by encouraging the opening of a Scandinavian department in the Baptist Seminary in Chicago. During the 1880s and 1890s Norwegians settling in large numbers in North Dakota cooperated with both the American Baptist Home Mission Society and Swedish Baptists, all the while experiencing conflict with Lutheran settlers in the region.

Swedish Baptists prospered especially in Minnesota and the surrounding territory, led originally by such immigrant pioneers as Gustaf Palmquist, F. O. Nilsson, and Andreas Wiberg in the 1850s. Migrating Swedish Baptists also organized strong churches in the Pacific Northwest and in central California. In 1879 the Swedish General Conference of America was organized, maintaining cooperation with the Northern Baptist Convention until 1945, when it became wholly separate and began broadening its ethnic identity beyond Scandinavian orientation. Its name was changed to the Baptist General Conference (130,000 members in 1982). Bethel Seminary, founded in Milwaukee (now in St. Paul, Minnesota, as a four-year college), manifests this growing independence of Swedish Baptist church life while enlarging its ethnic identity. At the same time Swedish Baptist identity has remained visible in the Northern Baptist Convention, as illustrated, for example, in the Baptist Scandinavian Seamen's Mission in San Francisco, which has ties to Baptists in both America and Sweden.

Because the new immigrants from southern, central, and eastern Europe, from Asia, and from Mexico settled largely in and around northern cities and in the Far West, they subsequently affected Northern Baptist Convention denominational life more than that of the Southern Baptist Convention. The American Baptist Home Mission Society worked among Italian, Hungarian, Slovak, Polish, Russian, Rumanian, and Czech immigrants—ministering to their needs and helping them form congregations. Although in most cases these churches never became more than a small minority of the largely Roman Catholic population comprising these ethnic communities, they greatly widened the ethnic diversity and cultural orientation of the Northern Baptist Convention.

Illustrative of the ethnic-oriented work was the International Baptist Seminary for non-English-speaking peoples, which operated in East Orange, New Jersey, during the 1920s and 1930s. Since then most of the churches that survived the first- and second-generation assimilation into American society while remaining ethnically oriented (an assimilation greatly assisted by the mission churches themselves) either have become fully integrated into the Northern Baptist Convention or have continued to relate to that denomination as semi-autonomous ethnic church bodies. Examples of the latter are the Czechoslovak Baptist Convention in America, the Hungarian Baptist Union of America, the Association of Evangelicals for Italian Mission, the Union of Latvian Baptists of America, the Portuguese Baptist Convention of New England, the Rumanian Baptist Association of the United States and Canada, the Russian-Ukrainian Evangelical Baptist Union of the U.S.A., and the Polish Baptist Association in the U.S.A. and Canada.

Baptist involvement with Asian immigrants began with a mid-nineteenth-century mission to the San Francisco Chinese. Soon the American Baptist Home Mission Society and the Southern Baptist Convention's Home Mission Board both were in the field. Although the First Chinese Baptist Church was formed in 1880, racial discrimination and unjust immigration laws greatly hindered the growth of Baptist church life among the Chinese. Widespread and often violent discrimination of Chinese immigrants broke out in California during the major economic depression of the late 1870s. The Chinese were a common target of white laborers and the victims of race prejudice.

The federal Chinese Exclusion Law in 1882, plus California legislation limiting the Chinese people's rights to business ownership, housing, and public education, resulted in a declining Chinese population. Baptists were among those who defended the Chinese as well as among those who discriminated against them. Overall, Baptist church involvement with the Chinese people under these conditions suffered for years to come, though it did not end and would take on new life in the twentieth century.

Work began with Japanese people when they began arriving in Pacific Coast ports at the end of the nineteenth century. Slowly, against great social pressures, Asian Baptist churches thrived, though their numbers remained small. Pressures became most extreme during World War II, when Japanese-Americans were placed temporarily in internment camps, a government measure protested by several Baptist denominations but not successfully countered. During the 1960s Asian Baptists expressed a new, aggressive sense of identity by forming a caucus within the American Baptist Convention (formerly the Northern Baptist Convention; the name change occurred in 1950). They have greatly enriched the plurality of Baptist life in America.

Baptists' involvement with Spanish-speaking people in Texas and New Mexico had begun by the mid-nineteenth century, following Mexico's loss of the territory to the United States. The work became more extensive later in the century, especially after 1870 when the American Baptist Home Mission Society began work in Mexico. Following the close of the Spanish-American War in 1898 the society entered Cuba and Puerto Rico; soon after, work began in El Salvador, Nicaragua, Haiti, Jamaica, and Honduras. These Latin American missions helped prepare Baptists in the United States to relate to the increasing numbers of Latin American peoples migrating into the country. After 1910 southern California became a center of Spanish-American Baptist church life. In 1921 the Spanish-American Baptist Seminary was founded in Los Angeles, preparing persons to serve both in Latin America and in California and other states where immigrants settled.

With the enormous increase in migration from Puerto Rico, Cuba, Mexico, and other Latin American countries after World War II, Baptist work has expanded greatly. Eventually Hispanic Baptists formed a distinct tradition, both as independent churches and conventions and as churches related to the Southern and American Baptist Conventions and to other national bodies.

THE BAPTIST DENOMINATIONS IN THE TWENTIETH CENTURY

As the twentieth century progressed, Baptist life and thought in the United States bore the marks of modernity. As the denominations developed along divergent lines of cultural, racial-ethnic, and theological identity, their organizational structures assumed the elements of increasingly complex bureaucracies. With businesslike efficiency, denominational machinery was geared to church mission in modern technocracy. All the while, intellect and piety both reflected and responded to the pragmatic forces of the contemporary world. Despite some points of interaction, Baptists in modern America mostly led separate denominational lives and must be described primarily in their independence and individuality.

No sooner had territorial acknowledgment been made by Baptists north and south at the start of the twentieth century than the two large predominantly white denominations began to expand their visions and activities to national dimensions. Population mobility helped to force the issue. World War I brought massive migrations of black southerners into northern cities seeking employment; and during World War II wartime industries drew many blacks to the Pacific Coast. The two major black Baptist conventions thus also became truly national in their constituencies. As white southerners moved westward in the great dust-bowl migrations of the 1920s and 1930s, the World War II migrations, and the more recent sun-belt migrations, the Southern Baptist Convention became a highly visible presence in regions outside the South. Today SBC churches are among the fastest-growing religious groups in the Far West, including Alaska and Hawaii, and are also growing rapidly in northern cities. The Northern Baptist Convention was also organizing churches in all regions of the nation. By renaming itself the American Baptist Convention in 1950, the denomination identified its national character.

The American Baptist Convention has remained fairly stable in church membership throughout the twentieth century (1,400,000 in 1925 to 1,600,000 in 1980). Its lack of growth resulted from several factors: (1) various European ethnic groups among whom the denomination concentrated much of its mission effort eventually formed independent denominations; (2) it increasingly replaced mass evangelism with programs of Christian nurture and social action, thereby causing some disaffections while not securing large numbers of new converts; (3) it embraced a pluralistic identity theologically and ecumenically, which caused disaffections both through conservative schisms and through loss of members to more singularly liberal-oriented denominations; and (4) it suffered a decline in popular growth along with other major denominations of ecumenical Protestantism, while Fundamentalist-Holiness-Pentecostal and conservative evangelical movements and groups have thrived—including the Southern Baptist Convention.

Major upheavals came to the northern denomination over issues of theology, biblical understanding, mission orientation, and ecumenical relationships during the thirty years following World War I. During the 1920s, a group of Fundamentalists led by J. C. Massee, William B. Riley, I. M. Haldeman, John Roach Straton, T. T. Shields, and Curtis Lee Laws (among others) attempted unsuccessfully to move the denomination into a Fundamentalist identity safeguarded by creedal uniformity. In 1933 fifty congregations withdrew from the convention to form the General Association of Regular Baptists (300,000 members in 1982); and in 1947 more groups withdrew to form the Conservative Baptist Association of America (225,000 estimated members in 1982). Throughout this schismatic period the convention refused to adopt a doctrinal creed, but responded by reaffirming faith in the New Testament as "a trustworthy, authoritative and all-sufficient rule of [their] faith and practice."

Meanwhile in 1925 the Southern Baptist Convention meeting in Memphis, Tennessee, being relatively untouched by theological liberalism, observing the theological disruption of Baptist life in the North, and sensitive to the confusion surrounding the Scopes trial over the teaching of evolution in Tennessee public schools, adopted a confession of faith somewhat akin to the old New Hampshire Confession. Led by internationally known theologian Edgar Young Mullins, who served as a pastor, administered foreign mission work, taught theology, and was president of Southern Baptist Seminary for twenty-nine years, SBC churches maintained an enlightened, conservative, evangelical image that appealed to most Fundamentalists. While the Northern Baptist Convention suffered disaffection, therefore, the Southern Baptist Convention grew by leaps and bounds through evangelistic appeals that offered apparent theological certitude.

If beset by theological upheaval, however, Baptists of the North ploughed undaunted into fields of creative social mission while enriching their ecumenical relationships. Unlike southern Baptists, northern Baptists maintained membership in the Federal Council of Churches and in its successor, the National Council of Churches (organized in 1950), as well as in the World Council of Churches (organized in 1948). During the half-century following World War I, four persons of international renown illustrate the dimensions of Northern (later American) Baptist Convention life.

Helen Barrett Montgomery, a lay church leader, teacher, and preacher from Rochester, New York, a civic leader (known as "Helen of Rochester"), and a public educator, was internationally known in ecumenical circles as a powerful platform speaker. A feminist proponent of women's rights, she was the first woman president of the Northern Baptist Convention (1921–1922), a delegate to the Baptist World Alliance meeting in Stockholm and one of only two women speakers there (1923), and president of the Woman's American Baptist Foreign Mission Society (1914–1924). She also wrote four books and translated the New Testament from the original languages.

Harry Emerson Fosdick was once America's most widely heard liberal Protestant preacher. His famous 1922 sermon "Shall the Fundamentalists Win?" first thrust him into the limelight. As professor of practical theology at Union Theological Seminary in New York (1919–1934), as minister of Park Avenue Baptist Church (renamed Riverside Church) in New York from 1915 to 1946, and as author of a number of widely read books, Fosdick gained international fame. His church became an ecumenical center of social service, and his radio sermons were heard by millions.

Kenneth Scott Latourette, born in Oregon and educated at Linfield College there, was a man of passion for world Christian mission who early in his career acted as traveling secretary of the Student Volunteer Movement for Foreign Missions. Throughout his life he actively participated in numerous international and ecumenical organizations. But he ultimately became known as one of the great historians of modern times. Profoundly Baptist in his identity (he served as president of the American Baptist Convention and was on the American Baptist Foreign Mission Society board for over twenty years), his scholarship covered all Christian traditions throughout their history. While Professor of Missions and Oriental History at Yale (1921–1953), Latourette published his massive seven-volume *The History of the Expansion of Christianity,* one of over one hundred books he wrote.

Martin Luther King, Jr., the Nobel Prize–winning black civil rights leader, an ordained American Baptist Convention minister, represents the distinction in Baptist denominationalism defined according to region and race as well as the crossing of those boundary lines. A native of Atlanta, Georgia, to which he returned in 1959 to become co-pastor of the Ebenezer Baptist Church, King had been educated at Morehouse College, a black school founded under Northern Baptist Convention auspices in SBC territory. He then took his theology degree at Crozer Seminary in Pennsylvania and earned his Ph.D. at Boston University. Most profoundly a black Baptist preacher from the South, King's liberal theological appreciation and social mission orientation (he admired Walter Rauschenbusch) made him a central and controversial figure within the American Baptist Convention. Many criticized him for his leadership in massive non-violent civil disobedience, but other Baptists identified with him. A great preacher-orator, a prophetic social activist, and a widely read author, King thus contributed to the development of American Baptist Convention identity after the mid-twentieth century.

In 1968 the American Baptist Convention formed a Study Commission on Denominational Structure to reexamine and organize their ordered denominational life in keeping with their twentieth-century history. The result was a more churchly sense of denominational association that would reaffirm the essential priority of local congregations whose identity, altogether, seemed to be a rather amorphous plurality. In 1972 the denomination changed its name to American Baptist Churches in the U.S.A.

The Southern Baptist Convention, in contrast, has maintained a consistent course of distinctive identity and growth during the twentieth century. The denomination continues to grow in numbers at a remarkable rate, unlike most other large Protestant denominations. Annual baptisms, Sunday school attendance, mission activity and support, and newly formed churches continue to increase.

By 1984 Southern Baptist Convention church membership approached the 14 million mark. Although the many small congregations contain most of these members, some large urban and suburban institutional churches with enormous budgets also continue to prosper. Such congregations as the Dallas First Baptist Church with 24,000 members, for example, led for four decades by the Reverend W. A. Criswell, with an $8 million annual budget and occupying four blocks of downtown property, wield large influence both within local urban communities and within the convention. Powerful, nearly autonomous churches are balanced within the denomination by the multitude of small churches. Together they influence national and state denominational politics.

There are signs of change that may be bringing the Southern Baptist Convention into greater contact with and similarity to other major Protestant denominations. Its spread throughout the nation, plus the appearance of certain traditional SBC cultural-religious values and style in national political leaders during recent years, have contributed to the breaking-up of the regional identity of the denomination. Yet this spreading-out has also brought challenges to its cultural-religious identity.

Through a self-defined "Bold Mission Thrust," for example, the denomination has concentrated on extending and expanding its organized church life in states throughout the nation with emphasis on reaching people not previously related to the Southern Baptist Convention. This resurgent national orientation has coincided with the increasingly diverse character of SBC life, a phenomenon that has been accompanied by internal denominational tension and conflict. Theology and mission bring focus to the strife. The convention has been experiencing controversy and power struggles over theological liberalism and biblical interpretation (literalism versus Higher Criticism) reminiscent of the modernist-fundamentalist controversy in the Northern Baptist Convention during the 1920s and 1930s. As with other denominations in the past, this theological conservatism has been aligned variously with rejection of liberal-identified social action and reform emphases (i.e., Social Gospel) in church missions, while at the same time identifying with traditional conservative positions on such issues as U.S. military armaments, government social welfare, sexuality issues, and prayers in public schools. The "biblical inerrantists" have brought pressures to bear on Southern Baptist Convention seminaries and denominational power structures to conform to their position. This conservative thrust, moreover, has been buttressed by the national political movement to the right, as reflected in President Richard Nixon's association with Southern Baptist evangelist Billy Graham. Later, in the Reagan presidency, it was linked publicly to the Moral Majority movement led by Lynchburg, Virginia, independent Baptist minister Jerry Falwell.

Significant numbers of Southern Baptists have moved across the traditional boundaries of the denomination's particular brand of theological and social conservatism. Among the reasons: the civil rights movement of the late 1950s and 1960s; the increasing contacts with diverse social and intellectual orientations outside the South (as well as within southern urban centers) during the countercultural and social protest years of the 1960s and 1970s; and the moderately liberal social and religious stance of SBC churchman President Jimmy Carter. These movements and events have made the denomination attractive to a wider variety of new church members. Their local church and state convention structures have allowed dissenting churches to challenge the national denominational positions on critical matters. For example, on such issues as public school prayer, the Equal Rights Amendment, and the nuclear freeze movement, several state conventions have taken stands opposed to the Southern Baptist Convention positions.

Churches and special concern organizations are boldly engaging in controversial social activism. Furthermore, Southern Baptist seminaries and the Home Mission Board have broadened their urban social vision to include concentrated work with racial and ethnic minorities in black, Hispanic, and Asian population centers. This work has stimulated new sensitivity to the experiences of oppression in American society and to the possible role of the churches as social justice advocates and reformers.

Consequently, as the Southern Baptist Convention continues to expand nationwide, its members are becoming an increasingly heterogeneous people intellectually, socially, ethnically, and geographically. They continue to be primarily, even overwhelmingly, a people of the American South who dominate the religious culture there; but increasingly they also are people of the North and Far West who interact with the varieties of religious cultures present in those areas. It remains to be seen how successful the denomination will be in maintaining sufficient common religious identity and organizational cohesion to contain its increasingly pluralistic constituency within a single ecclesiastical body. Historic Baptist convictions, instincts, and precedents may operate to lead some SBC members into separatist and schismatic directions, and others into alignments with different Baptist bodies or even broader Protestant denominational and interdenominational relationships.

Since the mid-twentieth century the directions of Baptist life and thought in the United States have been profoundly influenced by new internal vitality, aggressive social action, and the increased public visibility and influence of the black churches. Several historical forces framed the context of these developments: the civil rights movement of the 1950s and 1960s; the black power movement that emerged during the late 1960s; the widespread resistance to U.S. military involvement in Vietnam that led to a new awareness on the part of many American citizens of their nation's global impact on oppressed Third World peoples during the 1970s; and the 1984 presidential aspirations of the Reverend Jesse Jackson (ordained in the National Baptist Convention, U.S.A., Inc.) after a decade of conservative resurgence in American politics. Black Baptists interacted with these public social forces as individuals, church congregations, church-related organizations, and as denominational conventions.

There has always been a wide variety of social and theological tendencies among the constituents of the black Baptist conventions. The whole spectrum of theological movements and tensions that the predominantly white churches had expressed since the early nineteenth century may be found historically represented among black Baptists as well. Out of their original African cultural-religious roots they had embraced aspects of European-rooted Baptist church thought and practice that met their social and religious needs and inclinations. Because the vast majority of black Baptists lived in the South prior to World War I, they naturally shared some of the experiential piety and Bible-centered conservative theology that characterized much of the Southern Baptist Convention church life and thought. As black people in large numbers migrated to northern cities and to the Far West during the twentieth century, the Baptists among them expressed the increasingly diverse theological modes of their white counterparts in these regions as well. Black and white Baptists thus maintained a measure of theological interaction that allowed them to share a common though diverse tradition. This interaction was enhanced, moreover, by various forms of associations among black and white conventions, especially in educational and mission endeavors.

Black Baptists also developed a tradition distinct from the large, predominantly white churches. They have shared their enforced and oppressive segregated social position with black citizens as a whole, so that in vital ways black Baptists have had more in common with black Methodists and other black religious denominations than they have had with white Baptists. Throughout the nineteenth century black Baptists developed distinctive liturgical forms featuring lively interaction of preacher with congregation and emotionally moving "spiritual" singing. These worship forms expressed their theology of "other-worldly" consolations combined with "this-worldly" hope for social and economic betterment. What especially has distinguished this black Christian tradition is its essentially prophetic social orientation, which has sought to bring relief to black citizens from the omnipresent experience of race prejudice and discrimination. Adjustment to, much less maintenance of, the social status quo could not be a strong religious motivation for most black church members, even though many black churches became socially quiescent in the face of legalized and institutionalized racial discrimination in the white-dominated American civil order of the early twentieth century.

Because black churches have been at the center of black community life generally, they have provided leadership, facilities, and moral and financial support to a wide range of black social advocacy and protest organizations, movements, and leaders. The National Association for the Advancement of Colored People (founded in 1909), the National Urban League (1910), the Congress of Racial Equality (1942), and the Southern Christian Leadership Conference (1957) are significant examples of such organizations that have received widespread black church support. The large black Baptist conventions, distinguished more by nuances of organizational form and leadership style than by basic theological, cultural, or social outlook, have not always been the primary agencies of black church social pronouncement and action. But they have provided a continuous structural network within which black social-religious leaders and organizations could interact and maintain corporate identity and strength. In this manner the conventions have helped facilitate the black churches' advocacy of social reform as a basic element of their mission agenda. The black conventions were reluctant to endorse publicly the more radical ideas and actions of such leaders as black nationalist advocate Marcus Garvey, socialist writer W. E. B. Du Bois, labor leader A. Philip Randolph, and New York congressman Adam Clayton Powell from the 1920s through the 1940s. But these leaders had many followers among the black conventions' constituents.

With the movement for civil rights led by the Reverend Dr. Martin Luther King, Jr., black Baptists along with other black churches brought their tradition of social protest to a new level of massive public expression. Although the National Baptist Convention, U.S.A., Inc., was unable as a body formally to support King and the Southern Christian Leadership Conference, the churches became increasingly caught up in the general thrust of the movement. The formation of the Progressive National Baptist Convention in 1961, a schism over leadership within the National Baptist Convention, U.S.A., Inc., in part also expressed the desire of some church leaders for a more outspoken and progressive black denominational social stance. But despite this schism and the wide variety of positions within the churches on particular matters of theology and social action approaches, black Baptists have maintained widespread unity in their common quest for civil rights. Moreover, through their participation in such new black interdenominational organizations as the National Committee of Black Churchmen, and in their recent attempt with other denominations to form a Congress on Black Churches, black Baptists are maintaining solidarity with the larger black Christian community.

The black churches' involvement in the civil rights movement has enhanced their effectiveness as a social-religious force both within the black communities generally and among the white churches as well. Since his assassination in 1968 while in Memphis, Tennessee, supporting a sanitation workers' strike, King has become widely recognized by Baptists as well as other Americans as a major social-religious leader instrumental in combating racial segregation and civil discrimination against blacks and other minorities. King's bold criticism of America's military involvement in Vietnam brought harsh criticism from black and white religious and secular circles alike; but in the years following his death many of his critics came to recognize the validity of his linking the oppression of black Americans to that of oppressed peoples everywhere in the world. Overall, King helped make black churches more visible and influential in the larger circles of public religious and civil affairs.

Meanwhile the major black Baptist denominations have continued to grow in size, reaching an estimated 11 million members by the mid-1980s. Black theologians have shaped theology out of the American black experience that has had a wide impact throughout the larger Christian world and contributed to theological and social movements of liberation among oppressed peoples in Africa, Central America, and Asia. Black church history, piety and preaching, theology and ethics have altered the curricula of some traditionally white Baptist theological seminaries; and more black aspirants to the ministry have enrolled in these schools than ever before.

However, the black churches recognize that the battle for racial justice still has only begun in the United States. In recent years they have experienced white backlash, civil rights retrenchments, and new economic deprivations as well as apparently permanent steps toward greater opportunity and the respect necessary for full citizenship and human dignity within the civil order. The 1984 campaign of the Reverend Jesse Jackson for the Democratic party's nomination for the U.S. presidency exemplified the new entrée of black citizens into the realm of national political power. That Jackson was a black preacher whose outspoken political agenda emphasized bringing greater justice to oppressed peoples in the nation and the world further expressed the long-standing black church tradition of social reformist mission. That Jackson received most of his support from the black community, including its churches, suggests that many black and white citizens still differ in their sense of social-religious priorities.

If black Baptists must be realistic in assessing the degree of their acceptance as full and equal members of the larger Christian community, they do know that in modern times they have greatly enriched the plurality of publicly expressed Baptist church life in the United States.

Baptist plurality makes generalization about the tradition in contemporary America nearly impossible. Two interdenominational Baptist organizations facilitate some contact among the numerous independent groups, thus fostering a sense of common identity. The Baptist World Alliance, formed in 1905, has engendered a global expression of the tradition. The majority of white and black Baptist conventions in America participate in this fully interracial, international voluntary association that in the mid-1980s includes over 100 Baptist bodies with a combined membership of about 30 million church members in more than 120 countries, including Third World nations. The alliance meets as a congress every few years in different nations, not only to foster international fellowship and conversation among Baptists, but also occasionally to speak publicly on events and issues related to religious freedom and human rights.

The Baptist Joint Committee on Public Affairs, which developed out of concerns about threats to religious liberty and civil rights during the years surrounding World War II, includes the major black and white Baptist denominations plus the Baptist Federation of Canada. Its role has been to engage Baptists in the social and political structures that bear on religious and civil liberty issues. Committee leaders at times have lobbied in Washington, D.C., attempting to influence foreign and domestic policy. They have frequently stated their views to the public media and have researched issues for the benefit of Baptist church leaders. Their power is limited to persuasion. Through both the Baptist Joint Committee on Public Affairs and the Baptist World Alliance, a national and international witness to personal and corporate religious freedom in the civil order links contemporary Baptists to a common 350-year heritage.

A key to Baptist identity, then, is a certain passion for spiritual freedom, not only in faith and order but also in piety and worship. The ideal of a congregation thriving in spiritual fellowship of "newly born" regenerate believers, each one personally experiencing divine grace through Jesus Christ, is a recurring theme in Baptist history. Preaching, praying, and singing freely without uniform directive or constraint, balancing ordered formality with spirit-moved spontaneity, have framed most kinds of Baptist worship. The ordinances (usually not called sacraments) of baptism and the Lord's Supper (or communion) likewise are practiced with a minimum of liturgical formality. At the center of worship is the Bible, which through the guidance of the spirit is expected to provide sufficient resource for understanding and practicing the faith.

Spiritual experience and biblical interpretation together have nourished the Baptist sense of mission to the world. Such famous Baptist personalities as John Bunyan, Roger Williams, William Carey, Adoniram Judson, Walter Rauschenbusch, Billy Graham, and Martin Luther King, Jr., centered their theology and action in the personal religious experiences that they shared within worshiping communities. Indeed most Baptists would look no further for an underlying unity of their otherwise multifarious tradition.

BIBLIOGRAPHY

Robert A. Baker, *The Southern Baptist Convention and Its People, 1607–1972* (1974); Norman A. Baxter, *History of the Free Will Baptists* (1957); William H. Brackney, ed., *Baptist Life and Thought: 1600–1980* (1983); Lawrence B. Davis, *Immigrants, Baptists, and the Protestant Mind in America* (1973); John Lee Eighmy, *Churches in Cultural Captivity* (1972); William R. Estep, *Baptists and Christian Unity* (1966); Leroy Fitts, *A History of Black Baptists* (1985); Sandford Fleming, *American Baptists and Higher Education*, 6 vols. (1965); James L. Garrett, ed., *Baptist Relations with Other Christians* (1974); Clarence C. Goen, *Revivalism and Separatism in New England, 1740–1800* (1962).

Robert T. Handy, "American Baptist Polity: What's Happening and Why," in *Baptist History and Heritage* (14 July 1979); Paul Harrison, *Authority and Power in the Free Church Tradition* (1959); Samuel S. Hill, Jr., and Robert G. Torbet, *Baptists North and South* (1964); Winthrop S. Hudson, *Baptists in Transition* (1979) and, as ed., *Baptist Concepts of the Church* (1959); Eleanor Hull, *Women Who Carried the Good News* (1975); Joseph H. Jackson, *A Story of Christian Activism: The History of the National Baptist Convention, U.S.A., Inc.* (1980); Charles D. Johnson, *Higher Education of Southern Baptists* (1955); William L. Lumpkin, *Baptist Confessions of Faith* (1959) and *Baptist Foundations in the South* (1961); Norman H. Maring and Winthrop S. Hudson, *A Baptist Manual of Polity and Practice* (1963); William G. McLoughlin, *New England Dissent, 1630–1833* (1971); W. Morgan Patterson, *Baptist Successionism* (1969).

Bruce L. Shelley, *A History of Conservative Baptists* (1971); John E. Skoglund, *A Manual of Worship* (1968); Mechal Sobel, *Trabelin' On: The Slave Journey to an Afro-Baptist Faith* (1978); Rufus B. Spain, *At Ease in Zion: A Social History of Southern Baptists, 1865–1900* (1967); Edward C. Starr, *A Baptist Bibliography*, 25 vols. (1947–1976); Robert G. Torbet, *A History of the Baptists* (1950; rev. 1963); James E. Tull, *Shapers of Baptist Thought* (1972); Albert W. Wardin, Jr., *Baptist Atlas* (1980); James M. Washington, *Frustrated Fellowship: The Black Baptist Quest for Social Power* (1986); Charles L. White, *A Century of Faith* (1932); James E. Wood, Jr., *Baptists and the American Experience* (1976); Frank H. Woyke, *Heritage and Ministry of the North American Baptist Conference* (1979).

[*See also* BLACK CHRISTIANITY; CALVINIST HERITAGE; CHURCH AND STATE; NEW ENGLAND PURITANISM; *and* THE SOUTH.]

UNITARIANISM AND UNIVERSALISM

Peter W. Williams

IN May 1961 the American Unitarian Association and the Universalist Church of America brought extended negotiations for a merger of the two groups to a successful consummation, forming the Unitarian-Universalist Association. Thus, two major streams of institutionalized liberal religion in the United States (and Canada) formally converged after over a century and a half of parallel but separate courses, heretofore kept distinct by barriers more sociological than theological. The stories of their emergence, development, periodic decline, and ultimate union illuminate the problems, both past and present, of attempting to institutionalize religious impulses that by their very nature are in tension with structure and definition.

Liberal religion in the American context may be defined as the impulse to reject dogma in favor of free inquiry; to bring to bear the forces of reason in making religious judgments, while not necessarily denying the reality of supernatural forces; to be suspicious of religious authority that conflicts with individual reason; to replace a preoccupation with the metaphysical aspects of theology with an orientation toward living rightly and doing good in this world; and to exhibit an optimistic stance toward the possibilities of transforming the world into a saner and more humane place through the development of human potential by education, self-cultivation, and a beneficent social environment. Although many of these ideas have surfaced in different forms throughout the course of Western history, their fullest flowering was in the eighteenth and nineteenth centuries, when confidence in reason was at its apogee in Europe and the Americas. It was in the context particularly of the influence of Enlightenment ideas on British religious thought in the eighteenth century and their sub-

sequent impact on the American colonies and new nation that an indigenous religious liberalism, both popular and elite, came to take shape on these shores.

Although liberal religion overtly abjures mythology in favor of reason, both Unitarian and Universalist accounts of their history demonstrate the need to create a story that transcends a narrow and prosaically historical interpretation of origins. Such historians as Conrad Wright now generally agree that Unitarianism in its distinctively American form began with opposition to the Great Awakening among those eighteenth-century Massachusetts clergy who were also inclined toward an Arminian interpretation of the relationship between the divine and the human (that is, who affirmed some role for human choice in the process of salvation).

On the other hand, Earl Morse Wilbur devotes nearly three-quarters of his massive two-volume *History of Unitarianism* (1945, 1952) to the careers of such liberal Reformation figures as Serveto (Servetus) and Sozzini (Socinus) and the subsequent development of anti-Trinitarianism and other radical ideas in Poland, Hungary, and Transylvania, before coming to England and ultimately, in the last hundred or so of his eleven hundred pages, to colonial America. Similarly, many Unitarians claim Thomas Jefferson as one of their own, even though he did not actively participate in any institutionalized form of religious life and his specific religious views differed in some important ways from those of his New England liberal counterparts. It is therefore important to distinguish between the *history* of American Unitarianism and the Unitarian *story;* it is a distinction that is not only historiographically significant but also closely related to the ongoing tension in American Unitarian history

579

between the demands of institutionalization and the resistance of the "liberal spirit" to such forces.

The self-interpretation of Universalist history reveals some interesting parallels to that of the Unitarians. For example, Alonso Ames Miner, the president of Universalist-founded Tufts University, traced in a sermon of 1870 the history of Universalism from the early church through the church fathers, Gnostics, Cathars, and Anabaptists to more specific institutional origins in late-eighteenth-century America. Again, the point is important for understanding the character of American liberal movements: their self-conception is based on a sense of mission to spread the message that true religion consists of a pattern of attitudes and actions that may be fostered by specific ideas, movements, and institutions but cannot and should not be confined to them.

Nevertheless, Unitarianism and Universalism in America have taken the form of organized religious institutions with distinctive sets of ideas and programs and equally distinctive clienteles. Although some influence from a British Unitarian movement may have been spread in the colonies and early Republic through such émigrés as Thomas Cooper and Joseph Priestley, the American version of liberal religion that arose primarily in eastern New England never found the philosophical materialism of its transatlantic counterpart particularly congenial.

As Conrad Wright has demonstrated, American Unitarianism had its intellectual and social origins in a small group of Congregationalist clergy in the Boston area who took offense at the "enthusiastic" religion being spread during the 1730s and 1740s by George Whitefield and James Davenport. This small but influential group of "Old Lights" (opponents of the Great Awakening) was not content to defend traditional Puritanism from its "New Light" opponents but instead began to explore theological avenues that were to prove equally subversive of New England Calvinism from another direction. Such men as Charles Chauncy and Jonathan Mayhew of Boston, together with Ebenezer Gay of Hingham, were becoming increasingly uncomfortable with such Calvinistic dogmas as God's predestinating decrees and the universal depravity of humankind. Contemporaries identified their ideas with those of two earlier "heretics": Arius, whose teaching that Jesus Christ was

not a member of the godhead, but a special and subordinate divine emissary to humanity, provoked the convening of the Council of Nicaea in 325; and Jacob Harmensen (Arminius), whose denial of complete human inability to affect the process of salvation brought forth the Calvinistic formulations of the Synod of Dort in 1618.

Although these ideas quickly found favor among many of the Congregationalist churches of eastern Massachusetts, it was an Anglican congregation that was the first in America to formally espouse what became known as a Unitarian position. King's Chapel in Boston (founded by the royal governor in 1688) had for some time been a thorn in the side of orthodox Puritans as a visible sign of the erosion of Calvinist hegemony in that city. Led by their lay reader, James Freeman, the congregation in 1785 amended the Anglican Book of Common Prayer to create a liturgy free from references to the Trinity. When Freeman subsequently (and perhaps not surprisingly) experienced difficulty in obtaining Anglican ordination, his followers took matters into their own hands and imitated their Congregationalist neighbors by performing that ordinance themselves. Unitarianism was thereby launched as a visible presence in American religious life.

Thereafter, the drift toward a liberal position among the churches of Boston rapidly grew into a freshet so that by the time an open rift between liberals and "orthodox" had emerged early in the nineteenth century, some eighty-eight of the hundred oldest Congregationalist churches had allied themselves with the liberal party. The liberals had always been reluctant to declare themselves a separate group, and their desire to work quietly within the tradition of the New England establishment was aided by the decentralized character of their polity.

As the factions began to take firmer shape, however, the issue of the control of the Boston area's preeminent institution of higher learning proved the occasion for the beginnings of open schism and the onset of bitter theological warfare. In 1804 a vacancy in the Hollis Professorship of Divinity at Harvard College attracted candidates of rival views, and the liberals on the governing board prevailed in securing the appointment of Henry Ware, Sr., a known liberal, the following year. From that date, the orthodox regarded Harvard as a lost cause and helped found Andover Seminary in 1808 to preserve the endangered tradition.

The ongoing struggle in which the fall of Harvard to the liberals was the first pitched battle has sometimes been called the "first Unitarian controversy," and the most vocal of the orthodox campaigners was the minister (and geographer) Jedidiah Morse. Morse's relentless pamphlet warfare against the forces of Arianism and Arminianism could scarcely be ignored indefinitely, and the liberals began effectively to give as well as get. Perhaps the most eloquent and telling exposition of the new theology was delivered by William Ellery Channing in his sermon at Baltimore in 1819 at the ordination of Jared Sparks (later to become, among other things, a prominent historian of New England). In this frequently reprinted address, Channing, who would rapidly come to be recognized as the spiritual leader of the movement, articulated the basic tenets of the liberals: rejection of biblical literalism; the value of human reason in interpreting Scripture; the unity of God and the concomitant rejection of the idea of the Trinity; the single human nature of Jesus; a stress on the moral and ethical dimensions of Christianity; the moral nature of God and his parental rather than judgmental character; Jesus' mission to rescue humanity from sin through moral example instead of through a substitutionary atonement; human free will; and the rejection of revivalism and "enthusiastic" religion. Here was an articulate and persuasive platform upon which liberals could unite. Six years later, the American Unitarian Association was founded in Boston to provide a loose institutional structure to give that union more deliberate form.

The milieu in which Unitarianism came so rapidly to flourish was a very distinctive one and gave rise to the observation that Unitarians believed in "the Fatherhood of God, the Brotherhood of Man, and the Neighborhood of Boston." From its beginnings in the parsonages of Boston and the South Shore, the fortunes of Unitarianism were inextricably wrapped up with the culture of prosperity and cultivation emerging among the area's commercial elite and their families. The downplaying of divine mystery and the concomitant stress on human reason and goodness reflected a confident posture toward earthly possibilities, doubtless conditioned by the experience of success and the self-confidence

that success begot. As Harriet Beecher Stowe, daughter of that stalwart foe of Unitarian and Catholic alike, Lyman Beecher, put it in a letter included in her father's autobiography:

> All the literary men of Massachusetts were Unitarian. All the trustees and professors of Harvard College were Unitarian. All the élite of wealth and fashion crowded Unitarian churches. The judges on the bench were Unitarian, giving decisions by which the peculiar features of church organization, so carefully ordained by the Pilgrim fathers, had been nullified.
> (John Harvard Library ed., 1961, vol. 2, p. 82)

Although the Unitarian impulse by no means stayed confined within Suffolk County and environs, it is indisputable that the social, commercial, intellectual, and literary ethos of antebellum Boston—"the flowering of New England"—was inextricably connected with Unitarianism, and even today Boston remains the clearest locus of the Unitarian presence in America. Liberalism also spread along the New England coast, where the cultural influence of Boston had penetrated, but it halted at the margins of the Connecticut valley, where a religious culture better personified in Northampton's Jonathan Edwards and New Haven's Timothy Dwight prevailed. In Connecticut, some of the same impulses that had resulted in the triumph of Unitarianism in Boston emerged in a movement toward Anglicanism heralded by the conversion of several Yale tutors in 1722. To this day, New Haven and its suburbs are dotted with Congregational (now United Church of Christ) and Episcopal churches, but Unitarians remain as scarce as Presbyterians in "the land of steady habits."

Unitarianism was by no means the only institutional form that liberal religion in colonial New England (or elsewhere) assumed. Although such early Unitarian ministers as Joseph Tuckerman distinguished themselves as pioneer workers among the urban poor, their movement never held a great deal of appeal among the less comfortably off, the less sophisticated, and the more rural, and the genteel Unitarian aversion to aggressive evangelism did little to promote their message among such people. However, not all of the less well-to-do classes of rural New England were necessarily content with either orthodoxy or New Light revivalism. As an alternative, enclaves of a more popular liberalism began to emerge along the East Coast during the last decades of the eighteenth century, enclaves that would soon converge to form a movement known as Universalism.

As its name implies, Universalism was distinguished theologically by its optimistic teaching that all of humanity would ultimately be saved, even though early Universalist thought differed on such questions as whether there would be a period of atonement after death for those whose earthly careers had been less than exemplary. Although its optimism about the human condition and the future prospects of humanity were similar in many ways to that of the Unitarians, there is a truth in Thomas Starr King's waggish observation that the distinction between the two lay in the Universalists' belief that God was too good to damn them and the Unitarians' conviction that they were too good to be damned. The central ideas of the unity of the godhead and the certainty of universal salvation neither implied nor excluded one another, but the two movements always tended to converge in their emphasis on a benevolent deity and a confidence in human prospects.

As was the case with nascent Unitarianism, Old World writers and movements helped to mold the early shape of Universalist thought at the time of its origins in revolutionary America. In particular, the ideas concerning salvation of Paul Siegvolck (the pseudonym of George Klein-Nicolai of Friessdorf) and of the Welsh Methodist James Relly began to circulate along the eastern seaboard during the latter half of the century, thus establishing both a German Pietist and British evangelical provenance for the American movement's central idea.

Universalism did not enter the colonies in a religious and cultural vacuum, however. As Stephen A. Marini has demonstrated in his study of the popular sects of New England, a radical evangelical subculture had emerged out of the ambience of the Great Awakening, which rendered many of the more socially marginal inhabitants of the northern colonies susceptible to new religious ideas. New England Universalism sprouted in the same seedbed that nurtured the Shakers and Free Will Baptists, two other "popular" movements that rejected the central tenets of both New and Old Light orthodoxy. It took shape not in the manses of the staid Harvard-

and Yale-trained clergy but rather among the less formally educated, self-appointed prophets of new and sometimes startling versions of the Gospel. Among these prophets were John Murray, an English itinerant preacher and follower of John Relly, and Elhanan Winchester, a Massachusetts-born New Light Congregationalist turned Baptist who was converted to Universalist principles through reading the work of Siegvolck. Murray attracted numerous followers and established one nucleus of the new movement in Gloucester, Massachusetts, where he had settled in 1774 and remained until his move to Boston in 1793. Winchester, though of New England birth, exercised most of his influence in the Philadelphia area, where his Society of Universal Baptists, organized in the 1780s, included the eminent Benjamin Rush. Universalist ideas often combined readily with a general optimism about the millennial prospects of the new nation, and Rush's participation demonstrates that the class lines separating the two forms of institutionalizing liberal religion were not entirely rigid.

Although Universalists, like Unitarians, disliked any rigid ordering of belief or practice, they were nevertheless moved early on—in part out of the necessity of obtaining legal recognition—to draw up loose creedal statements and band together in bodies larger than the local congregations in which the movement subsisted. A 1790 statement by the Philadelphia Convention, which Rush had played a part in drafting, was Christian without being explicitly Trinitarian, and the more widely influential "Winchester Profession" of 1803 (named after a New Hampshire town, not the man) followed similar lines in emphasizing the ultimate restoration through Jesus Christ of all humanity to "holiness and happiness."

Regional organizations began to come into being with the New England Convention of 1785 and the Philadelphia Convention of 1790. The latter group disappeared within a few years, however, and it was the New England organization that was to provide the nucleus of the General Convention of Universalists in the United States, which took formal shape in 1833. Universalism, though still aggressively congregational in polity, had evolved from a group of like-minded but independent, scattered congregations into something resembling a denomination.

Finally, Universalists soon acquired a spokesman who could provide a compelling articulation of the movement's theological principles, a counterpart to the Unitarians' Channing: Hosea Ballou, the New Hampshire–born son of a Baptist farmer-preacher. Ballou had been early exposed to the Universalist message through the preaching of Caleb Rich and other itinerants. Ordained by Elhanan Winchester in 1794, Ballou preached in a variety of New England locales until settling into a long pastorate in Boston in 1817. As preacher, writer, and editor, Ballou firmly allied Universalists with the Unitarian rejection of the Trinity. He also engaged in the temporarily divisive "Restorationist controversy" (not to be confused with the Campbellite movement) by arguing the "ultra-universalist" teaching that no punishment of sin whatever would take place beyond this world. (Adin Ballou, a distant relative and founder of the utopian Hopedale community, participated in a small schism precipitated by this issue.) Ballou's most influential writing was his *Treatise on the Atonement* (1805), in which he argued that a benevolent God had sent Christ to earth not to atone for humanity's sins but to lead them to an ultimately irresistible love, happiness, and salvation—an argument that would later appear in Channing's Baltimore sermon.

Universalism and Unitarianism continued to expand both numerically and geographically as the nineteenth century progressed, but each retained a firm demographic center in the northeastern United States. In 1850, for example, 90 percent of the 246 Unitarian churches of that day were to be found in New England and New York, while 285 of 529 Universalist churches were located in New England. Each denomination established outposts in the South and Midwest—Unitarians in the larger cities, Universalists usually in the smaller towns and rural areas—but neither was ever to attain extraordinary size nor a comprehensively national distribution. (In 1950, 145 of 357 Unitarian churches were in New England, as were 200 of 300 Universalist.) Though representatives of the two (and today, the merged) denominations can now be found in all parts of the country, the character of each has been inextricably tied to its geographical and cultural source.

Unitarianism, in fact, once it had established a clearcut identity as a separate denomination, rapidly displaced its orthodox rival as the dominant church of eastern Massachusetts, and in the process helped to bring about formal disestablishment of religion in the last state to hold out against the trend. In 1820, the Massachusetts Supreme Court held in its "Dedham Decision" that the ultimate control of the individual churches of the state resided not in the "church," the relatively small body of committed full members, but rather in the "parish," or the entire community that a particular church was intended to serve. Although "churches" tended to be more orthodox in their sympathies, the reverse was true of parish membership; consequently, control over ministerial appointments and fabric ownership reverted to the liberals in most of the parishes of the eastern part of the state. Orthodox sympathizers now faced the alarming prospect of being reduced to the status of sectarian dissenters and seeing tax money turned to the support of the upstart liberals, and consequently rallied to bring about final disestablishment of religion and the end of any state support in 1833.

By this time, as Harriet Beecher Stowe's earlier quoted appraisal indicates, Unitarians were firmly in control of the social, political, economic, and cultural ethos of Boston and environs. Harvard College, the "first flower" of the Puritan "wilderness" (in the words of Samuel Gilman, Unitarian minister in Charleston, South Carolina, and author of "Fair Harvard"), had been virtually conceded to Unitarian control by all challengers since 1805, and its newly formed Divinity School set about the task of supplying Boston's churches with well-educated liberal clergy. The clergy, the professoriate, the political leadership, and the worlds of literature and publishing all reflected Unitarian hegemony, and the local intelligentsia freely moved among these several interrelated professional worlds in an era not yet characterized by intense vocational specialization. Since Unitarians were averse to creeds, and since even the Divinity School at Harvard was overtly nondenominational, though de facto Unitarian, it was not always easy to tell the exact character of belief or degree of commitment among this intellectual elite. The calculated blurring of boundaries expressed the Unitarian encouragement of the "free spirit" in the realm of the intellect.

The intellectual core of the Unitarian culture of Boston was fashioned by the work of the Harvard faculty, particularly the moral philosophers of the Divinity School, and reflected in the writings, lectures, and sermons of their students as well. Their basic philosophy has been described by Conrad Wright as a "supernatural rationalism" and by Daniel Walker Howe as a revived form of "Christian humanism."

Antebellum Unitarian thought was a mixture of Protestant moral seriousness and Enlightenment assumptions about human nature and epistemology, particularly as filtered through the Scottish "common-sense" philosophy, which was to prove so influential for nineteenth-century American Protestant thought in general. The operative premise of this moral philosophy was that humanity possesses an innate, God-given moral sense that is ultimately reliable as a guide to action in this world. Metaphysics and speculative theology were thus subordinated to ethics, broadly defined, and the primary imperative for the Christian was action for practical good in this world. This imperative, however, was constricted by a simultaneous commitment to the preservation of the social order, and a concomitant revulsion from programs, such as abolitionism, for radical institutional change. Individual and social perfection was possible through gradual change based on the assumptions of human goodness and the harmony of class interests, and the Harvard faculty and Boston clergy saw themselves as primary agents through which this transformation might take place. Their ultimate vision was of a properly ordered and stable society permeated by a genteel culture shaped by a benevolent elite.

In many ways, the Boston of their day did see the emergence of such a culture of gentility. Most of the beloved "Fireside Poets"—Henry Wadsworth Longfellow, James Russell Lowell, Oliver Wendell Holmes, Sr., William Cullen Bryant—were Unitarian at least by nurture, and Longfellow and Lowell both held the Smith Professorship of Romance Languages at Harvard for a time. Historical writing, often of a high order, abounded during the era, and Francis Parkman, William Hickling Prescott, George Bancroft, George Ticknor, and Jared Sparks all combined a romantic interpretation of the past with the beginnings of an interest in rigorous historiography shaped, again, by the assumptions of the Boston milieu. It was in Parkman that the streak of pessimism began to emerge which

would manifest itself more fully in Charles Eliot Norton and Henry Adams, agnostic Unitarian scions of the postbellum era. Basically, the failure of the ethos to deal, on the one hand, with the drastic implications of human fallenness and, on the other, with the increasing tensions in a rapidly modernizing and sectionalizing American society were flaws that both contemporary critics and subsequent analysts would identify as the sources of the short-lived character of the Boston Unitarian cultural hegemony. These flaws would lead many of the region's intelligentsia of a later epoch either to the Episcopal church or to a suspension of belief entirely.

The first of a series of disharmonies within Boston Unitarianism arose on neither of these grounds explicitly. Almost from the beginning, the confidence in the ability of human reason aided by supernatural revelation to know the truth, and in the ability of the human will instructed by God-given conscience to do the good, did not seem a satisfactory account of human possibilities to a small but highly articulate group of young Unitarian clergy and their lay friends. This group of about three dozen began during the 1830s to meet from time to time at one another's homes to discuss the new ideas that were filtering into Boston, Cambridge, and Concord from Germany—frequently mediated through the British romantic writers Thomas Carlyle and Samuel Taylor Coleridge—as well as the astonishing documents of classical South Asian religion and culture that were beginning to be accessible in modern translations. Those in the group, who almost in spite of themselves began to be known as Transcendentalists after their fascination with German "transcendental" philosophy, were too jealous of their individual independence ever to unite in a formal organization or fashion a common creed, but their rejection of rational and empirical epistemology in favor of an intuitive sense that could put the individual in touch with a realm which transcended the mundane was a keystone in their discontent over what by now had emerged as "classical" Unitarian belief.

The salvo that brought this growing tension into the explosion sometimes called the "Second Unitarian Controversy" was fired by a man who has since, and somewhat ironically, taken a position in the American cultural pantheon together with the "Fireside Poets" as an "inspiring" writer, even though recent scholarship has discovered far deeper dimensions to his thought than that manifested in innumerable rhetorical invocations of "self-reliance." Ralph Waldo Emerson had studied for the Unitarian ministry at Harvard and had been settled as the pastor of Boston's Second Church. In 1832, however, he developed qualms about the appropriateness of his administering the Lord's Supper and withdrew from the ministry, turning his attention to European travel, lecturing, and writing the essays that became a major vehicle for spreading his ideas and gained him a widespread popular following.

In 1838, the senior class of Harvard Divinity School invited Emerson to deliver the commencement address, but their mentors were hardly prepared for the result. In what has come to be known as the "Divinity School Address," he attacked the assumption, which Unitarians shared with their more traditional brethren, that Christianity was ultimately dependent for its validity on the supernatural person and miraculous work of the historical Jesus. Emerson denounced this insistence on the historical grounding and miraculous authentication of religious trust as formalistic, and compared it in its impotence to a preacher whom he had heard whose presence seemed pallid and lifeless in contrast with the snowstorm that raged about the church as he preached. (Appropriately, this unfortunate divine bore the name of Barzillai Frost.) Emerson went on to characterize an insistence on Jesus' wonder working as virtually blasphemous, and declared all life to be a miracle. True religion arose instead from an individual realization of the presence of an immanent spiritual force that existed potentially already within each individual; Jesus had exemplified the realization of this force as fully as ever any human had, but his significance lay not in his miracle working nor his alleged supernatural status but rather in his exemplary spiritual character.

All of this was simply too much for that redoubtable "pope" of Unitarianism, Andrews Norton, the Dexter Professor of Sacred Literature at Harvard. Norton now ironically assumed the role of his old nemesis, Jedidiah Morse, and rose to smite the Emersonian "heresy" in his pamphlet *A Discourse on the Latest Form of Infidelity* (1839). The issue on which Norton and the "more conservative" Unitarians chose to take

their stand was what became known as the "miracles question." They asserted, contrary to Emerson, that the evidence for Jesus' having worked miracles was reliable, and that the miracles were necessary as supernatural legitimations of Jesus' teaching. This position highlighted several characteristics of what had emerged as received Unitarian belief: that Unitarianism was not only theistic but explicitly Christian in its insistence on the unique historical mission of Jesus; that supernatural events of divine causation were a necessary and verifiable course of God's interaction with creation (and not, as Emerson styled them, "monsters"); and that God-given human faculties were capable of accurately receiving and correctly interpreting revelatory events as complementary to the moral truths known through reason and conscience. Although this position stood at a far remove from the transcendent and mysterious God of their Calvinist forebears, it was equally distant from the stress on immanence and intuition that was being developed by their restless contemporaries.

The metaphysics, epistemology, and morals represented in this formulation were based on the assumption that, fundamentally, things are as they ought to be: God has created the world deliberately and rather considerately, and humanity has the ability to respond in such a way as to make it a pleasant and sensible place to inhabit. Another challenge to what by this time had become virtual orthodoxy among more conservative Unitarians was presented by Theodore Parker, the self-educated scholar and minister who in 1841 delivered an ordination sermon entitled "The Transient and Permanent in Christianity." In it, Parker totally dissociated lasting religious truth from any specific historic event or formulation, thereby claiming that the truth of Christianity lay not in its uniqueness and specificity but rather in its sharing in the broader, everlasting truth of "pure religion." To this theological radicalism Parker added a passionate commitment to the emergent cause of abolitionism, and made it clear early on that he was prepared to offer not only comfort but material aid to the cause of the fugitive slaves.

The issue of slavery was one that proved extremely problematic for the Unitarian "establishment." On the one hand, their principal emphasis was on a this-worldly faith that stressed responsible ethical action for the alleviation of human distress. On the other, they feared any extreme disruption of the well-balanced world around them and were buttressed in their caution by the dependence of many of their wealthy parishioners on a thriving mill economy based on slave-grown cotton. Furthermore, the general emphasis within the community of Unitarian thinkers had been on the gradual improvement of society through self-cultivation rather than through collective, and possibly violent, social action. Eventually, a few leaders such as William Ellery Channing (in his brief 1835 book, *Slavery*) took a stand on the issue, but they were largely unsuccessful in commanding the sympathy of their fellows and followers.

There were, to be sure, exceptions to this general policy of intellectual and moral caution. John Gorham Palfrey, to give a strenuous example, was a Boston minister and scholar who briefly served in Congress as a "conscience Whig" opponent of slavery. (Palfrey's career, incidentally, is an excellent example of the multiple roles that Boston Unitarian leaders could play in their society. Palfrey served, at times simultaneously, as editor of the Unitarian journal the *Christian Disciple* and the highly influential *North American Review;* minister of Boston's Brattle Street Church; professor and later dean at the Harvard Divinity School; Massachusetts secretary of state; editor of the Free Soil newspaper the *Commonwealth;* Boston postmaster; and author of the four-volume *History of New England,* 1858–1875.) James Freeman Clarke, another versatile member of the clergy, was active in the antislavery movement as well as intellectually and personally sympathetic with his Transcendentalist brethren and was one of the few clergy of his time to defy the Boston Association of Ministers' "disfellowshipping" of Theodore Parker in 1841 on grounds of heterodoxy. Clarke was also something of a rebel in his leadership of the Church of the Disciples, which he organized in 1841 and which he served as minister until his death in 1888. Along with demanding a more active participation of his congregation in worship, study, and benevolent work than was usual at the time, Clarke abolished the traditional New England practice of renting or selling pews and made his church entirely dependent on voluntary contributions. This daring practice earned him the suspicion of many of his colleagues but was never deemed sufficiently drastic to deserve the ostracism that had been Parker's fate.

After the Civil War had put the question of slavery to rest, Unitarians did not lack either for issues to divide them or for forces seeking to reconcile differences and bring about a spirit of unity and structures to foster it. Two related forces were at work during these years that brought about contention. The first was the emergence of a new group of "radicals" who, following the lead of Parker and others of the Transcendentalists, denied that Unitarianism should consider itself Christian in any sense that implied that Christianity could claim any special or exclusive character as a form of religious truth. These dissidents included Octavius Brooks Frothingham, author of the classic study *Boston Unitarianism* (1890); Samuel Longfellow, the brother of the poet; and William J. Potter, Cyrus Bartol, and Francis Ellingwood Abbot, Unitarian ministers, respectively, of New Bedford, Boston, and Dover (New Hampshire), each of whom entertained serious doubts about the validity of Unitarianism as a form of Christianity. Following their failure in 1866 to persuade the recently founded National Conference of Unitarian Churches, meeting in Syracuse, to eliminate the term "Christian" from its self-definition, this small band withdrew in 1867 to form the Free Religious Association (FRA) with Bartol and then Frothingham as president. The group's purposes were "to promote the interests of pure religion, to encourage the scientific study of theology, and to increase fellowship in the spirit" (Wilbur, vol. 2, p. 474). A new enthusiasm for the "scientific" study of human history and nature as a means of discovering ultimate truth was a moving force for the group, as was their desire—one that had run through American religious liberalism from its earliest origins—to escape from the alleged tyranny of creeds and institutions so that independent individuals could be free to pursue truth wherever it might lead. It is perhaps not surprising to note that such a loosely bound fellowship was not destined to achieve a great deal of success in founding new churches or other activities involving organized, cooperative effort. The FRA enjoyed only a marginal existence until its ultimate dissolution in 1938. It should be noted, however, that Felix Adler, who would later found the Society for Ethical Culture, served as its president from 1879 to 1882.

A similar question of inclusiveness arose in the context of the ongoing westward expansion of the Unitarian movement as the frontier began to approach the Pacific Coast. Unitarianism never possessed a great deal of appeal for rough and ready pioneers, and James Freeman Clarke, who had served a stint as a missionary of liberalism in Louisville during the 1830s, soon came to the conclusion that Boston was more to the taste of a young clergyman with cultural and intellectual aspirations. (Clarke did collaborate on the editorship of the *Western Messenger,* an attempt to spread liberal religious culture through what was then the West, with first Ephraim Peabody and then William Henry Channing, each at the time resident in Cincinnati.)

As liberalism gained a following in these regions increasingly remote from Boston, it sometimes assumed a form that did not sit very well with its adherents on Beacon Hill. A leader arose in the person of Jenkin Lloyd Jones, whose career stretched from service in the Civil War to opposition to World War I. Jones, whose work included the authorship of Sunday school materials, the supervision of Unitarian missionary work on the West Coast, and a major role in the organization of the 1893 World's Parliament of Religions, was one of the leaders of the "Unity Men" (named after the periodical *Unity*) in the West who objected to an overly narrow definition of the movement and the terms for ministerial good standing.

"The Western issue," which pitted Jones and his allies against more conservative "westerners" such as Jabez Sunderland of Ann Arbor, focused on attempts by the Western Unitarian Conference, a regional group of liberals founded in 1852, to draft a statement of belief. At issue particularly, and reminiscent of the controversies that had given rise to the Free Religious Association in the East, was the question of whether non-Christians and even nontheists could be welcomed into the liberal fellowship. By 1894 the issue had resolved itself through compromise, as a new generation became tired of the issues and personalities that had exercised their predecessors. It was to be in the "West," however, that the forces of increasing inclusiveness and the rejection of a specifically Christian or even theistic identity in favor of the designation "humanist" were to exert the strongest force during the twentieth century.

Although such controversies over the question of inclusiveness were to continue for decades more, counterforces toward unity and centralization were also at work within the movement. One sort of drawing together was exemplified in the leadership provided by Thomas Starr King, the son of a New York Universalist minister, who had begun his own ministry in that denomination in Charlestown, Massachusetts, in 1846. King left the Boston area to visit California to recover his health near the time of the outbreak of the Civil War, and stayed both to lead the Unitarian community that had been founded in San Francisco in 1850 and, more important, to rally the opponents of slavery in that area in support of the Union. King died prematurely before the war's end, but his contribution to the life of California was later recognized in his being named one of the state's two representatives in the National Hall of Fame. (Junípero Serra, the Franciscan founder of missions, was the other.)

Another commanding figure of midcentury who exemplified both the rallying of Unitarians to the cause of the Union as well as the consolidation of denominational unity was Henry W. Bellows, minister for decades at New York's All Souls Church. Where King had strongly supported the work of the humanitarian United States Sanitary Commission in California during the war, Bellows was one of its chief organizers and moving spirits, and even found in the war-caused suffering a source of inspiration and invigoration for the American people. Bellows was still more notable for his work in articulating a theological stance and molding a denominational structure that would help to overcome the centrifugal forces that were perennially weakening organized liberalism. In particular, he was instrumental in revitalizing the American Unitarian Association (AUA), which had fallen on bad days since its founding in 1825, as well as helping in 1865 to found the National Conference of Unitarian Churches (NCUC) to aid the AUA in its work. The AUA continued to be composed entirely of individual members, while the NCUC now was to serve as an advisory representative body, with clerical and lay delegates sent by participating churches. Even though the irenic efforts of Bellows (and James Freeman Clarke) were not sufficient to prevent the breaking off of the Free Religious Association radical faction, Unitarian institutional life was substantially strengthened during the ensuing decades by these and innumerable other efforts of the redoubtable New York minister, ecclesiastical politician, European traveler, and bon vivant. Bellows is also remembered for his 1859 address to the Harvard Divinity School entitled "The Suspense of Faith," in which he called for "a new catholic church"—free, needless to say, of papacy and episcopacy—that would draw contemporary secularized society into a more organic and institutionalized expression of religious life and sentiment.

By the late nineteenth century, Unitarianism had become institutionally reinvigorated and geographically national in scope, though its numbers remained relatively small and still concentrated in New England. Its extension from coast to coast—largely following the line of Yankee migration across upstate New York, through the Old Northwest, and into northern California and the Pacific Northwest—was reflected in the modest but significant expansion of its facilities for ministerial preparation. During the earlier decades of the nineteenth century, of course, Harvard College and its newly formed Divinity School provided nearly the totality of the movement's clergy. By the 1840s, the liberal presence west of the Alleghenies had been sufficiently established that Meadville, Pennsylvania, had emerged as a center of Unitarian culture. A theological school was founded there in 1844 through the efforts of Harm Jan Huidekoper, a self-educated Dutchman whose studies had led him to religious liberalism, and George W. Hosmer, a minister of the Christian Connection who had been working with Huidekoper. (Unitarians and members of the Christian Connection, a group with a provenance similar to that of the Disciples of Christ, also collaborated in the founding of Antioch College in Yellow Springs, Ohio, in 1852. Horace Mann, active Unitarian layman and "father" of the American public school system in his role as secretary of the Massachusetts Board of Education, served as its first president.) The Meadville Theological School moved its operation to Chicago in 1926 to allow its students fuller exposure to the conditions of the modern world. In 1912 the Ryder Divinity School, associated with Universalist-founded Lombard College in Galesburg, Illinois, had already moved to Chicago. Ryder and Meadville became affiliated in 1928 and finally entered into a full merger in 1963. In addition to Harvard and Meadville/Lombard, theological education was and still is also provided on the West Coast at the Starr King School for the Ministry in Berkeley, California, founded in 1905 with the historian Earl Morse Wilbur as its first president.

It was partly in these institutions of higher learning and their Universalist counterparts, such as Tufts and St. Lawrence universities, that organized liberalism made contact with the new liberal movement in American Protestantism of which Unitarians and Universalists could claim to be forerunners. Many of the themes that were to have such an impact on the mainstream of American Protestantism—the benevolence of God; the possibilities of humanity; the influence of environment on human character; the role of Jesus as moral teacher and exemplar; the critical interpretation of Scripture on historical principles; and an emphasis on ethics and self-cultivation rather than speculation on the nature of the deity—had been eloquently articulated by Channing and Norton decades before they were appropriated by Phillips Brooks and Harry Emerson Fosdick. By 1880 the Harvard Divinity School, reinvigorated with the support of Charles William Eliot as university president, had become formally a nondenominational institution, and its theologically pluralistic faculty rapidly shaped it into a leading force in promoting a learned and liberal approach to religious scholarship and ministerial training among a broad spectrum of Protestant groups.

Another dimension of Protestant liberalism that Unitarianism had foreshadowed and in which it now actively participated was the Social Gospel. Throughout the nineteenth century, Unitarian clergy and laity alike had been active in the promotion of social reforms. Joseph Tuckerman's "ministry at large" among the poor of Boston; Samuel Gridley Howe's pioneering work in the education of the blind and deaf; and Dorothea Dix's campaigns to improve the treatment of the mentally disturbed were some of the more prominent involvements of Unitarians in humanitarian movements before the era of massive urbanization and immigration. As social Christianity began to achieve articulation and implementation as a distinct movement, the career of Francis Greenwood Peabody emerged as representative of Unitarian sympathies with the effort to apply the teachings of Jesus to the betterment of the social order. Peabody, who served as Plummer Professor of Christian Morals from 1886 to 1913 and for five years as dean of the Harvard Divinity School, was probably the first American academic to introduce a course on Christian social ethics into the university curriculum. Among his many books, *Jesus Christ and the*

Social Question (1900) was the most instrumental in spreading his message of what by later standards would seem a rather cautious and even paternalistic program of social reform on Christian principles.

The Social Gospel was also expounded at Meadville by Nicholas Paine Gilman, the first incumbent of the Caleb Brewster Hockley Professorship of Sociology and Ethics at that institution, as well as by George Beals Fisher, Ryder Professor of Pastoral Theology at Canton Seminary, the theological school of Universalist St. Lawrence University. (Tufts also established a professorship of applied Christianity in 1893.) On a denominational level, the American Unitarian Association in 1908 established the Department of Social and Public Service, which published a lengthy series of bulletins reporting on social problems over the next several years.

By the beginning of the present century, the fortunes and future of organized religious liberalism had begun to appear questionable. As other Christian groups began to adopt theological and social attitudes that had once been advocated almost solely by Unitarians and Universalists, the role of those pioneers seemed less certain. In addition, erosion from within the very matrix of Unitarian culture was increasingly perceptible. Henry Adams, scion of the most venerable and distinguished of all of Boston's Unitarian families, would present a sardonic and at times even savage caricature of his antecedents' religious culture in his autobiographical *Education of Henry Adams* (1907). Boston, he stated, meaning its Unitarian elite, believed that it had "solved the universe," and went about its business oblivious to the new political, social, and intellectual forces that Adams captured in the image of the Dynamo. The Episcopal Church was even luring away many among the Boston elite by the elaborate liturgy of the Church of the Advent and Phillips Brooks's charismatic preaching at nearby Trinity. At the other extreme, the Irish Catholic immigrants who had begun to flood into Boston early in the nineteenth century had wrested political control of the city by the 1880s, and John "Honey Fitz" Fitzgerald would soon seem more representative of the local political culture than Charles Francis Adams.

Despite these reverses, Unitarianism in Boston and elsewhere was hardly moribund. It was during this period of apparent declension that the most talented organizational leader of the movement since Henry Bellows emerged in the person of Samuel Atkins Eliot. Son of Harvard president Charles William Eliot and nephew of Francis Greenwood Peabody, the young Eliot began his ministerial career in the unlikely locale of Denver, Colorado, in 1889. Returning East four years later, Eliot rapidly began to gain influence within the national administrative structure of the denomination. In 1900 he began service as president of the AUA, which would last till his acceptance in 1927 of a call to Boston's Arlington Street Church, the "Cathedral of Unitarianism," where Channing had once presided.

Eliot was an administrative genius, and he regarded the condition of the denomination's organization at the time of his election as sad indeed. He immediately set to work at implementing a whole panoply of changes, including a reform of denominational financial management; the development of a realistic and well-organized strategy of extension and missionary work; establishment of a church building loan fund; refusal to continue financial support of congregations unable to pay their own way; rationalization of the program of publishing, including establishment of a distinctive Unitarian imprint, Beacon Press; revision of the hymnal, which he himself undertook in collaboration with the distinguished scholar Henry Wilder Foote; and, in 1925, the implementation of a set of organizational changes recommended by his committee on polity, which resulted in a merger of the General Conference (the successor of the National Conference of Unitarian Churches) and the AUA.

Although Eliot enjoyed considerable success in his programs for denominational consolidation and revitalization, his was a career hardly lacking in conflict. His businesslike approach to religious affairs did not win him universal admiration, and his seemingly complete lack of sympathy with the efforts of the unfortunate Egbert Ethelred Brown, a Jamaican-born black, to undertake a liberal ministry in Harlem, revealed the impress of State Street attitudes and methods on his rather paternalistic character. Another conflict involving Eliot was the repudiation of the denomination in 1919 by John Haynes Holmes after Eliot and the AUA had taken a firm stance in favor of American involvement in the war. Holmes, the longtime minister of the Church of the Messiah (later the Community Church of New York), was a lifelong advocate of pacifism, even during the strenuous years of World War II, as well as a civil liberties activist. (He was one of the organizers of the American Civil Liberties Union as well as the National Association for the Advancement of Colored People.) Holmes continued for decades in an unfailing advocacy of such causes as minister, author, and editor of *Unity* magazine, and finally restored ties with what had by then become the Unitarian-Universalist Association (UUA) near the end of his life.

Eliot's successor as AUA president, Louis C. Cornish, was a well-meaning but rather ineffectual counterpart of his contemporary Herbert Hoover. With the onset of the Depression the denomination had found itself come again on hard times. The "lyrical theism" that characterized the theology of many of the liberal clergy of the time was challenged on the right by a more tough-minded Neo-Orthodoxy within the Protestant mainstream, and the left flank of liberalism was increasingly attacked by the humanist movement, which would come to gain greater influence within both the Unitarian and Universalist camps as the century progressed. Membership and financial contributions both were hit hard by the events of the 1930s, and in 1934 a Committee of Appraisal chaired by Frederick May Eliot issued its influential report, *Unitarians Face a New Age.* The report, which was adopted virtually in its entirety in 1937, brought about simultaneously an increased centralization of leadership in the presidency and a decentralization through the distribution of administrative functions among regional organizations. The result was an enhancement of grassroots influence in the formulation and implementation of denominational policy and an at least modest revival of liberal fortunes.

Eliot (by now a familiar surname in Unitarian history) rapidly succeeded Cornish as AUA president, and his career was in many ways as productive as that of his kinsman Samuel Atkins Eliot. It was during his administration, which lasted until his death in 1958, that Sophia Lyon Fahs developed her highly successful New Beacon Series in Religious Education. It was also during these years that Beacon Press began to emerge as more than simply a denominational publishing organ and embarked on a program of publication on a wide variety of social and intellectual issues that continues to this day. Most controversial, perhaps, was the appearance in 1949 of Paul Blanshard's *American Freedom and Catholic Power,* in which the author denounced the attempt of the American Catholic hierarchy to exert what seemed to him undue influence on political issues and public morals through its vast wealth and popular following.

Nor was Blanshard's book the only controversial issue among Unitarians of the 1940s and 1950s. As was not unusual among Protestant denominations following World War II (during which the AUA supported its conscientious objectors firmly), charges of Communist infiltration were leveled against Unitarians. The most visible object of suspicion was Stephen Fritchman, who had in 1943 been appointed editor of the official denominational newspaper, the *Christian Register.* Fritchman's editorial sympathies were clearly with the Soviet Union and, after attempts at compromise had failed, he was dismissed from his position in 1947. He soon thereafter received a call from a church in Los Angeles, where he continued his colorful and controversial political advocacy.

Another controversy of the present century that affected Unitarians and Universalists alike was really a continuation of a long-developing issue, namely, whether liberal religion in either of its principal organized forms was necessarily Christian or even theistic. Humanism was the watchword for this "latest form of infidelity," and its principles were asserted most clearly and publicly in the 1933 "Humanist Manifesto." (A newer and even more controversial version was published in 1973.) Signers of the original document included the philosopher John Dewey, one Universalist clergyman, and a considerable number of Unitarian ministers. Another significant publication on the topic was the 1927 collection *Humanist Sermons,* edited by Curtis W. Reese. It included work by such diverse figures as John Haynes Holmes, John H. Dietrich, and Frederick May Eliot himself. As AUA president, Eliot refused to yield to conservative pressures on the issue; his Universalist counterparts Robert Cummins, Brainard F. Gibbons, and Philip R. Giles, who served as general superintendents of that denomination from 1938 until the time of the merger, similarly took stands in favor of philosophical inclusiveness.

A related issue was the relationship of both groups to other, non-Christian world religions. James Freeman Clarke had done pioneering work in the sympathetic exposition of other faiths in his *Ten Great Religions* (1871, 1883), which had grown out of his class lectures at Harvard. Unitarians had also engaged in a rather mild form of missionary activity in India and Japan during the nineteenth century, but were more interested in a general stimulation of interest in liberal principles than in making formal converts. Universalists, whose philosophy was similar, also undertook a mission to Japan in 1890. A specific case that generated controversy in this area was that of Kenneth L. Patton of the Charles Street Meeting House in Boston, an avowed humanist who employed syncretistic elements taken from a variety of religious traditions in his liturgy and in the ornamentation of the building. His admission to Universalist fellowship in 1949 was indicative of the broadening self-understanding of that denomination's inclusiveness.

Another broad movement within the American churches of the twentieth century, which was to have a direct bearing on both Unitarians and Universalists, was ecumenism. A linkage between this and the question of world religions was the enthusiastic participation of both groups in the World's Parliament of Religions of 1893, behind which Jenkin Lloyd Jones had been a moving force. Since both groups regarded their message as inclusive, they had always been at least in theory open to close relationships with other groups, as indicated in earlier Unitarian relations with the Christian Connection in the cases of Meadville and Antioch. In practice, however, differences perhaps mostly of sociology and institutional self-preservation had frustrated earlier attempts on the parts of each to enter into mergers with one another and other denominations, particularly the Congregationalists. Participation in such efforts as the International Association for Liberal Christianity, as well as individual grassroots cooperative efforts, kept relations open until the 1950s, when the obvious duplication of effort in maintaining two separate but virtually identical denominational structures became increasingly and embarrassingly obvious.

Despite some resistance on both sides and, for the first time ever, a contested election for the AUA presidency, in 1958—pro-merger Dana McLean Greeley was victorious—the union of the two groups was accomplished at a joint meeting in Syracuse in 1959, based on a common allegiance, in their statement's rhetoric, to the Judeo-Christian heritage. The merger was made legally binding at the Boston Joint Assembly two years later, and a remarkably small number of individual churches refused to enter the new denomination.

At the time of the formation of the Unitarian-Universalist Association (UUA), a demographic shift in relative strengths over the course of the century was apparent. Greeley estimated that Unitarians outnumbered their counterparts roughly four to one in the late 1950s. (He cited statistics of approximately 120,000 Unitarians and about 30,000 Universalists in his 1971 autobiography.) Although Greeley claims that Universalists were considerably stronger at the turn of the century, it seems safer to follow Edwin Scott Gaustad's estimate in the 1976 edition of his *Historical Atlas of Religion in America*, which gives the Unitarians a slight advantage.

Although neither group enjoyed what one could term a mass following—membership in the merged group has declined in recent years from a peak during the 1960s of around 200,000 —Unitarian fortunes were buoyed beginning in 1948 by an imaginative new approach to recruitment, the Lay Fellowship Plan. Given the small number of liberal sympathizers in many areas, especially outside the larger cities and academic communities that were traditional Unitarian bastions, a new program that invited the formation of a fellowship led by laity and meeting wherever convenient quarters could be found was developed and spread through such unaccustomed devices as newspaper advertisements. The program, moreover, was deliberately conceived not simply as a means to creating nuclei for future churches, but as an end in itself. Although some fellowships did eventually grow sufficiently to apply for church status, a considerable number found that a small, informal group provided a better setting for the sort of community that their members sought. Fellowships, which have generally served parts of the country (especially in the South and West) that had never before enjoyed a widespread Unitarian presence, tend strongly toward the humanistic in philosophy and seldom favor the more formal and basically Congregationalist liturgy practiced in the older churches of the Northeast. Instead, they often incline toward discussions of contemporary issues and ethical concerns, with some recorded classical music providing the "ritual" dimension.

The Unitarian-Universalism that has developed during the quarter-century since the merger resembles in many ways some of the other small liberal denominations of our time, the Episcopalians, the Friends, and especially the United Church of Christ. Each combines a heritage rooted in the American colonial experience, and congregations and families that date back to colonial days, with a geographically more diverse membership of recent converts who may form a large majority in a particular locale and even in the denomination as a whole. (Ninety percent of contemporary "UU's" are not members by birth, compared with a figure of about 80 percent converts for Episcopalians.) Polity, despite the growth over the years of a national administration based at 25 Beacon Street in Boston and a network of twenty-three regional districts dividing up the territory of the United States and Canada, still retains its historic congregational focus. Membership is affluent and extremely well educated, and tends to cluster in either urban areas, academic communities, or "high tech" centers such as Oak Ridge, Tennessee, and Los Alamos, New Mexico. A series of surveys conducted during the 1960s and 1970s indicate that religious education, personal development, and fellowship are the three most important concerns of members.

The distinctive character of contemporary Unitarian-Universalism, however, lies in the realm of social issues and social action, since the political and social attitudes of its followers are overwhelmingly liberal. As Robert B. Tapp, a leading contemporary student of the movement, observed in "The Unitarian Universalist," this concern for issues such as environmentalism and social justice differs from other liberally inclined religious groups not so much in kind but in the degree of consensus and the primacy of this agenda in its self-definition. Since theology and liturgy do not play a central unifying role—UU's continue to resist any consensus on theistic or humanistic orientation—emphasis is rather on a "shared community of values," which involves both questions of personal growth and the achievement of a just and whole society.

The question of racial justice has deep roots in the UU community, as indicated in the earlier discussion of the antislavery question. However, the number of blacks within the UU fold even in the 1980s is very small (less than 1 percent), and in 1983 only about half of the dozen black clergy were serving in parishes. The UU presence during the civil rights movement of the early 1960s was disproportionately high, however, and the murder of James Reeb, assistant minister at All Souls Church in Washington, D.C., in Selma, Alabama, in 1964 provided a witness to the intensity of denominational commitment. The emergence of two groups representing differing degrees of militancy with regard to the question of funds for black "empowerment" gave rise to a long period of conflict over the best means for implementing a generally agreed upon commitment to the promotion of racial justice.

Not surprisingly, perhaps, women have from early on enjoyed a greater acceptance among both Unitarians and Universalists in playing active roles than has been the case in other religious communities. Olympia Brown was ordained by the St. Lawrence Association of Universalists in 1863, and she is generally regarded as the first American woman to receive ordination by denominational action. (Antoinette Brown Blackwell had been ordained by an individual Congregationalist church a decade earlier; she left the ministry after a year and soon became a Unitarian.) In 1871, Celia Burleigh became Unitarianism's first woman minister, in Brooklyn, Connecticut. Nearly two hundred women were ordained by the time of the merger of the two denominations; in 1984, 205 of the UUA's nearly one thousand clergy were female, of whom 90 were settled in parishes. Unitarian women, like their male counterparts, also played a role in leadership of social and reform causes disproportionate to their numbers, and their ranks include Elizabeth Peabody, Margaret Fuller, Elizabeth Cady Stanton, Susan B. Anthony, Lucy Stone, and Julia Ward Howe.

Unitarian-Universalists, then, have been and continue to be a small but influential and committed group, concerned with their own personal development as well as with a host of social issues including, in the 1970s and 1980s, nuclear warfare, American involvement in Southeast Asia and Central America, and gay rights. (UU's have taken an especially positive stance on the latter issue, and do not discriminate against gay clergy.) Their ranks have never been large, and their role in the future appears to be one of a leavening influence in the larger society rather than a broadly popular movement. Perhaps the most remarkable aspect of their history, however, has been their recurrent ability to overcome such potentially radically divisive issues as theistic versus humanistic identity, and to embrace these extremes within one system of tolerant and enduring institutionalized fellowship.

BIBLIOGRAPHY

Sydney E. Ahlstrom and Jonathan S. Carey, eds., *An American Reformation: A Documentary History of Unitarian Christianity* (1985); Charles W. Akers, *Called Unto Liberty: A Life of Jonathan Mayhew, 1720–1766* (1964); Joseph Henry Allen and Richard Eddy, *A History of the Unitarians and the Universalists in the United States* (1894); Laile E. Bartlett, *Bright Galaxy: Ten Years of Unitarian Fellowships* (1960); Arthur S. Bolster, Jr., *James Freeman Clarke* (1954); J. Wade Caruthers, *Octavius Brooks Frothingham, Gentle Radical* (1977); Ernest Cassara, ed., *Universalism in America: A Documentary History* (1971); Arnold Crompton, *Unitarianism on the Pacific Coast* (1957); David P. Edgell, *William Ellery Channing* (1955); Octavius Brooks Frothingham, *Boston Unitarianism, 1820–1850* (1890).

Frank Otto Gatell, *John Gorham Palfrey and the New England Conscience* (1963); Dana McLean Greeley, *25 Beacon Street and Other Recollections* (1971); Catherine F. Hitchings, "Universalist and Unitarian Women Ministers," in *Journal of the Universalist Historical Society* X (1975); John Haynes Holmes, *I Speak for Myself* (1959); Daniel Walker Howe, *The Unitarian Conscience: Harvard Moral Philosophy, 1805–1861* (1970); William R. Hutchison, *The Transcendentalist Ministers* (1959); Walter Donald Kring, *Henry Whitney Bellows* (1979); Charles H. Lippy, *Seasonable Revolutionary: The Mind of Charles Chauncy* (1981); Charles H. Lyttle, *Freedom Moves West: A History of the Western Unitarian Conference* (1952).

Stephen A. Marini, *Radical Sects of Revolutionary New England* (1982); Russell E. Miller, *The Larger Hope: The First Century of the Universalist Church in America, 1770–1870* (1979) and *The Larger Hope: The Second Century of the Universalist Church in America, 1870–1970* (1985); Mark D. Morrison-Reed, *Black Pioneers in a White Denomination* (1984); Eugene B. Navias, *Singing Our History: Tales, Texts and Tunes from Two Centuries of Unitarian and Universalist Hymns* (1975); David B. Parke, "Liberals and Liberalism Since 1900," in *Proceedings of the Unitarian Historical Society* XV, I (1964), 1–21; David Robinson, *The Unitarians and the Universalists* (1985); Douglas C. Stange, *Patterns of Antislavery Among American Unitarians, 1831–1860* (1977); Richard Eddy Sykes, "Massachusetts Unitarianism and Social Change," Ph.D. diss., University of Minnesota (1966).

Robert B. Tapp, *Religion Among the Unitarian Universalists* (1973) and "The Unitarian Universalists: A Church of Converts," in Martin E. Marty, ed., *Where the Spirit Leads* (1980); Earl Morris Wilbur, *History of Unitarianism*, 2 vols. (1945, 1952); George Huntston Williams, *American Universalism* (1976) and, as ed., *The Harvard Divinity School* (1954); Robert J. Wilson, III, *The Benevolent Deity: Ebenezer Gay and the Rise of Rational Religion in New England, 1696–1787* (1984); Conrad Wright, *The Liberal Christians* (1970), *The Beginnings of Unitarianism in America* (1955), and, as ed., *A Stream of Light: A Sesquicentennial History of American Unitarianism* (1975).

[*See also* FREE THOUGHT AND ETHICAL MOVEMENTS; THE GREAT AWAKENING; SOCIAL CHRISTIANITY; THE CALVINIST THEOLOGICAL TRADITION; THE ENLIGHTENMENT; TRANSCENDENTALISM; *and* LIBERALISM.]

THE SOCIETY OF FRIENDS

Melvin B. Endy, Jr.

THE Quaker movement began during the time of political and religious turmoil following the English Civil War (1642–1646). Having defeated King Charles I's military forces and then beheaded him in 1649, the opponents of the king's political and religious tyranny, the Puritans, controlled English political and religious life until the return of the Stuart monarchy and its established Anglicanism in 1660. The Puritans, influenced by the form of Protestantism represented by the French reformer John Calvin, were trying to purify the English church of its "popish" ceremonies, polity, and theology. During their ascendancy the freedom to practice ever more purified versions of the Calvinist faith led to a splintering process. The Puritan movement split into a variety of Presbyterian, Congregationalist, and Baptist groups and then led to the formation of a host of more radical sects that can be labeled "spiritualist" because of their professed reliance on the leadings of the Holy Spirit for their beliefs and actions.

During the 1640s many of those who responded to the purifying impulse spent brief stints in one or more of the Puritan groups and then became more radical, joining religious bodies claiming to rely ever more directly and fully on the guidance of the Holy Spirit. Some finally concluded that none of the myriad sects was God-inspired. They became what were loosely called Seekers, and met together to wait in silence for immediate guidance from the Spirit, which they expected to inaugurate a new and probably final dispensation of Christian world history.

Raised in an Anglican home strongly influenced by Puritanism, George Fox (1624–1691), the founder of Quakerism, began his religious quest in 1643. He met with a variety of spiritualists and Seekers during the next few years and began "declaring Truth," proclaiming "the day of the Lord," and gathering followers in the Midland counties from 1647 to 1650. Imprisoned in 1650–1651 for blasphemy because of his claims of Spirit-possession and his disruption of others' religious services, he started organizing like-minded Christians in the rural northern counties from 1652 to 1654.

Many of those who became associated with Fox in the North as "Friends of Truth" or "Children of Light" had been through a period of seeking similar to his. They believed that all true worship and service to God were the result of the direct leading of the Spirit as spiritualist worshipers sat silent and utterly dependent on the inward or inner light of Christ. They also believed that the light was available to all humanity and had permeated the primitive Christian church, which was their model.

The work in the North was followed by campaigns in London and the southeastern and southwestern counties in 1654–1655. By the end of the interregnum in 1660 the day of the Lord had been proclaimed successfully throughout England and in Wales, Scotland, Ireland, the West Indies, the American colonies, Holland, and Germany. An estimated 30,000 to 40,000 people had become what the world was to call Quakers, because they trembled when under a "leading" of the Spirit.

Those who responded to the message and experienced the indwelling of the Spirit at least fleetingly began to meet with the Friends and to take on their characteristic marks: refusal to doff their hats to superiors; use of plain language, including the pronouns "thee" and "thou" to highborn and lowborn alike; refusal to use "pagan" names for days and months (i.e., Sunday); refusal to take oaths; and simple dress. But unlike most Puritans and spiritualists, they experienced this period as a trial stage of what they called "convincement," which could last for many months or even years and which had its spiritual highs and lows. It was a prelude to true conversion, which was an advanced state of sanctification approaching perfection. The approach to this elevated state might be signaled by a "leading" that produced a first utterance in the pregnant silence of meeting and an overpowering sense of having made the crossing from "the world" to the kingdom of the Spirit.

The Quakers believed that they alone among Christian sects realized that all human thoughts, desires, and activities must be wholly silenced or even extinguished in order for men and women to live in the Spirit. The silence of their meetings for worship reflected this conviction that the quieting of all "fleshly" mental and physical activity was a necessary precondition for the leadings of the Spirit, which in effect infused the human subject with a divine agency.

Despite this emphatic insistence that even the most Calvinist Puritans had failed to plumb the depths of the Quakers' despair over fallen humanity, the second mark of their self-understanding was their belief—shocking to Calvinists, trained to divide the world into the predestined elect and the damned—that all humanity throughout history had experienced at least intermittently the presence of a divine light and life of sufficient power to provide the knowledge and grace necessary for a saving relationship with God. The Friends believed that the revealing and sanctifying Spirit of God known to the world as Jesus Christ had been present to every human heart in the form of what they called the "inward light" or "inward Christ."

Since the Christ they experienced in their own breasts was the same "inward Christ" that had been active in the conversion of sinful humanity throughout history, the Quakers believed that Christ's saving power should not be tied too closely to the physical or "outward" forms that it took, even in Jesus Christ, whose life, death on the cross, and resurrection are the focal point of Christianity. Nor could it be tied, as the vast majority of Christians were wont to do, to such outward forms as the Bible, the theological creeds that "learned" Christians identified with the Word of God, the ordained ministry, or the word and sacrament dispensed in churches.

The Quakers believed that the Christ within was the same as the Savior whose death on a cross atoned for the sins of the world. Although the writer who later became the normative theologian of seventeenth-century Quakerism, Robert Barclay, in *An Apology for True Christian Divinity* (1678), made Christ's historical atonement the cause in some sense of all salvation, the thrust of the new movement was in the direction of contrasting the "visible," "carnal," or "fleshly" knowledge gained through the physical senses with the "inward," "invisible," "spiritual" knowledge made available by the immediate presence of the Spirit. If the Quakers' emphasis on the radical otherness of the Spirit from the humans it possessed amounted to a divine-human dualism, then contrasting of the "outward" and "inward" in religion was based on a spiritual-physical dualism.

Their sense of the imminence of a new age of the Spirit accounts for another characteristic of the earliest Quakers. Just as they combined their Calvinist divine-human dualism with an understanding of the universality of the experience of the Spirit, making a saving relationship with God available at the initiative of every human being, so Quakers linked their spiritualized religion to a belief in religious progress on the plane of history. They believed that the world was at the threshold of the kingdom of God. They were confident that their message would take England by storm and sweep on to the ends of the earth; even the state would be reformed so that social relations would reflect the will of God, the sovereign Lord of history.

It was only after much inner turmoil that the Friends declined to join the Puritan uprisings of 1656 and 1659. Recognizing both their pacifistic opposition to "carnal" ways and their need to dissociate themselves from revolutionaries like the Fifth Monarchists shortly after the Restoration in 1660, they made nonviolence a part of their countercultural witness.

RESTORATION QUAKERISM AND THE NEW WORLD

Although still hoping to turn the world into the kingdom of God and still seeking converts, with the advent of the Restoration the Quaker movement settled down for a strenuous battle against "the world" and took on more of the separatism normally associated with the Religious Society of Friends in the eighteenth and nineteenth centuries. The number of Friends continued to increase but the rate of growth slowed down; there were probably between 40,000 and 60,000 Friends in England by 1690.

Becoming a Quaker during the Restoration required a more clear-eyed commitment than it had in the freer and more intoxicating world of the 1650s. The Conventicle Act of 1664 outlawed on pain of imprisonment or deportation any religious gathering not under the auspices of the reestablished Church of England. Friends were also imprisoned or fined for refusing to take oaths, for appearing to attack political order and authority, and for a variety of additional offenses. Throughout the most repressive years of the Restoration, between 3,000 and 4,000 Friends were in jail simultaneously, and some 500 failed to survive the rigors of confinement.

That the Friends alone, among the myriad religious bodies that grew up during the Interregnum, survived is due primarily to the organizing genius of Fox and the other influential Friends with whom he shared informal authority. In addition to preaching "threshing" meetings for the unconverted and bringing spiritual leadings to local meetings, the traveling Friends helped to sift the local leaders and to appoint as elders those whose activities were in accord with the teachings of Jesus and the messages of the most inspired Quaker leaders. Those who later were called deacons came to the fore in local meetings to organize marriages and burials and to attend to the needs of widows, orphans, and the poor.

In 1668 Fox urged local meetings to take up their social and economic concerns in a monthly "business" meeting, and in the 1670s regional quarterly meetings and a London Yearly Meeting developed with the explicit intent to provide guidance for and even to discipline Friends whose spirituality and way of witnessing or living were discordant with that of the main body. Friends holding to the less structured ways of the first decade, such as John Perrot, John Wilkinson, and John Story, raised a protest that resulted in a schism. In response, preeminent leaders such as Fox, William Penn, and Barclay established convincingly the informal authority of traveling Friends and of the most influential local Quakers.

More than 700 Quakers published over 6,000 religious tracts and broadsides between 1650 and 1700. Writers such as Fox, Edward Burrough, Isaac Penington, and Samuel Fisher were later joined by Barclay, George Keith, Penn, and George Whitehead, who had received enough theological education to make clearer than the earlier writers had the relationship between Quakerism and other Christian religious bodies. In the 1670s the weekly Second-day Morning Meeting of leaders in London took on responsibility for assigning writers to answer anti-Quaker polemics and for expounding "the Truth" and checking on the style and content of Quaker writings. About the same time the London-based Meeting for Sufferings began publishing accounts of Quaker persecution as well as arguing for religious toleration and the establishment of fundamental rights for all Englishmen.

The Quakers' proselytizing urge, and especially their exuberant confidence that they could spread truth to the ends of the earth as a prelude to the coming kingdom, sent them throughout Europe and into the New World as early as 1656. The Puritans of Massachusetts had earlier rid themselves of Roger Williams, who had questioned their use of the coercive authority of the state on behalf of religion, and Anne Hutchinson and her fellow Antinomians, who had claimed a kind of spiritual authority while questioning that of some Puritan ministers. They were in no mood to coddle more dissenters when the Quakers Ann Austin and Mary Fisher arrived from Barbados in July 1656. By October the Puritans had passed a law imposing imprisonment, fines, whipping, and banishment on the "cursed sect of heretics." Undeterred, thirty-three more Quakers arrived between 1656 and 1659, and the laws became more severe until Marmaduke Stephenson and William Robinson were hanged in 1659, followed by Mary Dyer and William Leddra in 1660.

Although a few converts were gathered from among settlers of Massachusetts Bay, Plymouth Colony, Connecticut, and New Haven—all of which passed laws in 1656 and 1657 against the Friends—Quakers became more prominent in the safer outlying areas, such as Cape Cod, Nantucket, Maine, and Rhode Island, to which Massachusetts Bay shipped its unwelcome Friends under the "Cart and Whip" Act of 1661, whereby Charles II forbade capital punishment for the heresy. The first Friends arrived in Rhode Island in 1656, and by 1660 several prominent settlers had joined. Rapid growth around the

Newport-Portsmouth area produced a Quaker majority in the colony by 1670 and Quaker control of the General Assembly, which allowed affirmation instead of oaths and exempted conscientious objectors from military service until the preparations for King Philip's War (1675–1676). The Friends developed regular meetings in Massachusetts Bay and Plymouth Colony in the 1660s. George Fox's visit to New England in 1671 was the occasion of a general meeting for all New England (and Long Island) Friends and led to the institutionalization of the New England Yearly Meeting that year.

Five Friends had arrived in Long Island in 1657. Some of them, along with associates who followed, were fined, jailed, or even banished for proselytizing too actively, especially the women, until the directors of the Dutch West India Company in 1663 restrained Gov. Peter Stuyvesant. With the English takeover of New Netherland in 1664, Quakers, although harassed at times and still controversial, established meetings in Long Island and then spread to what is now northern New Jersey and the mainland of New York and organized a New York Yearly Meeting in 1695.

The Friends took their message to Maryland and Virginia in 1656. Outlawed and harassed, they nonetheless found in both colonies English of Puritan persuasion who were without ministers or services and were ripe for the Quaker message. Local meetings were formed in the 1660s; the West River (later Maryland) Yearly Meeting first met in 1672 and the Virginia Yearly Meeting in 1673. Fox's visit in 1672 aided the growth of the Friends in both colonies. Missionaries to the Carolinas in the 1670s gained converts, and by 1698 a yearly meeting was formed.

The Quakers' success was greatest in areas with no established church and in outlying regions, where they were without many competitors and, despite their unusual ways, provided stability for settlers fearful of the moral decay possible in primitive surroundings. In addition, since the Friends needed no educated or ordained ministry, sanctuary, service books, or sacraments, they could grow as easily on the frontier as in urban areas.

The Quakers John Fenwick and Edward Byllynge, who purchased West Jersey in 1674, were bought out by a group of thirteen proprietors in 1675, all but one of whom were Friends. The Friends became the dominant religious body of West Jersey, and their instrument of government, the Concessions and Agreement of West Jersey, possibly written by Byllynge, reflected what Quakers had previously only called for at the hands of English authorities: trial by jury, freedom of conscience, taxation by consent, and governing authority vested largely in the representative Assembly. A group of proprietors including a majority of Friends also purchased East Jersey, but Quaker settlers were not as prominent as in West Jersey.

William Penn's proprietorship in Pennsylvania provided the Friends the same opportunity to build a religious utopia that Puritans had enjoyed in New England. Having displayed in England more of a reformist ethic than most Friends, Penn turned to the New World when Whig political reforms and his campaign to win toleration for Friends in England faltered. Perhaps hoping to rid England of some of the troublesome Friends in the process of repaying a debt to Penn's father, Charles II in 1681 provided Penn with what became a haven for Quakers. Whatever the king's motives, Penn himself believed—as he wrote at the time—that the colony was founded in order that "an example and standard may be set up to the nations" of an ideal Christian order, demonstrating that a society founded and operated along Quaker lines was the answer to human ills.

Although Pennsylvania's Frame of Government was more conservative than the Jersey Concessions and than some Quakers desired, the Quaker mark on the new colony was seen in the legal provision for marriage without benefit of ordained clergy, the requirement that the common or pagan names for days and months be avoided, the provision for arbitrators or peacemakers to be attached to the courts, the provision for affirmations and attestations in place of oaths, the failure to provide a militia, and the attempt to reach decisions in the Provincial Council and Assembly by general consent.

By the end of 1683 two-thirds of the 4,500 settlers in the Delaware Valley were Quakers. Since Pennsylvania was such a haven for Friends, those who emigrated in the seventeenth century had to convince their meeting in England that they were motivated by desires other than to escape persecution and to gain worldly security. Whether or not Penn agreed with Fox that states needed absolutely no restrictions on religious belief, as a proprietor under the Crown he no doubt felt constrained and restricted religious freedom to believers in God the creator, providential ruler, and author of the moral law that directs the human conscience to live justly and peaceably. To exercise voting rights and serve in government one had to be a Christian. Although Pennsylvania attracted many varieties of Protestant settlers, Quakers predominated until well into the eighteenth century.

A CENTURY OF QUIETISM

The Glorious Revolution of 1688–1689 began a new phase of Quaker history. In England it brought the end of the repressive Clarendon Code, which outlawed dissenters' activities, and the beginnings of toleration for Friends. Promised toleration if they avoided behavior threatening to the authorities, the Friends settled into a respectable sectarian existence and focused on preserving their freedom by emphasizing orthodox beliefs and responsible behavior and on preserving their numbers and vitality by making their speech, dress, and style of living visible marks of their distinctiveness. Their plain living, dependable work habits, and inventiveness enabled many of them to prosper, and they became involved in most areas of English artisan, manufacturing, and commercial activities. What distinguished Friends in their own eyes from other Christians was no longer their position as the vanguard of an eschatological age of the Spirit but their utter "quieting" of human thoughts and activities and their reliance on divine leadings in liturgy and ethics.

The era of the Glorious Revolution placed Friends in Massachusetts, New York, and Maryland under a cloud since the ousted Stuarts had been their protectors and Penn especially was associated with James II. North Carolina in 1691, Maryland from 1692 to 1715, New Jersey in 1702, and South Carolina in 1726 became royal colonies, with Anglican establishments in all but New Jersey. Penn lost his proprietary power in 1692, and when he regained control in 1694 his utopian dreams were largely gone. Anglicans had arrived to question Quaker ascendancy, and their insistence on the illegitimacy of Quaker rule because of heresies on the Trinity, Christ's person and work, and original sin and grace was aided by the Quaker leader George Keith. In the 1690s, after trying to turn the Friends in a more orthodox theological direction, Keith became an Anglican minister and returned from London to Pennsylvania to question both the legitimacy of Quaker power, in light of their heresies, and their right as governmental authority, in light of their pacifistic stance.

Because of the first-generation Quakers' ambivalence about precisely the issues to which Keith was pointing, his protests divided Friends both in the colony and in England. The religious divisions quickly healed when Keith became an Anglican, but they were replaced by a developing social-political split between urban, cultured Friends, represented by James Logan, and the more rural supporters of David Lloyd and his popular party. Moreover, when Penn, who returned briefly to his colony in 1699 for the first time since his visit in the early 1680s, enacted a new Frame of Government, all of the colony's laws had to be reenacted and ratified by the home government. The English government took the opportunity to veto those that represented the Quakers' attempt to improve on English law, such as provisions for affirmations rather than oaths and laws restricting recreation and cursing. With the Crown vetoing the colony's laws and the proprietary and popular parties at a deadlock in a society with a large sectarian majority already ambivalent about worldly authorities, Pennsylvania came closer to riotous anarchy than to the loving consensual society that Penn had envisioned.

By 1725 Pennsylvanians were able to enjoy once again political and social stability along with their continuing economic well-being. Having gradually modified their social egalitarianism and having become accustomed to governing and to accepting the political authority of fellow Quakers, Friends became more cohesive. Penn's "holy experiment" began to shine as the most impressive colonial harbinger of the religious diversity, political freedom, and social mobility that later marked the United States. Although Friends were becoming a smaller percentage of the population, they still made up two-thirds of the Assembly, which often exhibited the consensual behavior of a Quaker meeting.

Statistical estimates are hazardous, but the combination of Quaker immigrants, converts, and offspring may have doubled their size in the half-century from 1700 to 1750, when they numbered around 50,000. After 1760 Philadelphia became the most prominent yearly meeting in the New World, named in 1790 the General Yearly Meeting for Friends of Pennsylvania, East and West Jersey, and of the adjacent Provinces.

In this "classical age" of Quakerism, the Friends became increasingly a sect but retained enough worldly position and hopes of transforming the world to exercise a marked influence on Anglo-American society. Revering their first-generation heroes and martyrs, they developed an intense fellowship, a set of ecclesiastical structures and procedures, and a unified theology and set of ethics. Fox's organizational genius left its imprint on the Friends, and in the eighteenth century they more or less formalized the combination of consensual ways and oligarchical forms he had set up. Local meetings called on their older and more prosperous families for overseers and elders. Overseers regulated the procedures for membership, child rearing, education, marriage, daily living, social witness, and burials, and they served as delegates to quarterly and yearly meetings. They shared their authority with elders, who regulated the ministry by supervising local first-day meeting utterances ("eldering" those who spoke too much or inappropriately) and providing and checking certificates of membership.

For these purposes overseers and elders developed the Books of Discipline. Friends in the Delaware River Valley presented a set of rules "relating to good Order and Discipline" to the Philadelphia Yearly Meeting, which adopted them in 1704, as did New England Quakers in 1708. London codified its rules in 1737. From then on most yearly meetings possessed copies of the Book of Discipline of London and Philadelphia yearly meetings, but the other American yearly meetings also drew up their own books to address peculiar local situations. Books of Discipline included a list of "queries" that Friends were to ask themselves individually and corporately about their spiritual and daily lives. Corporate queries were done quarterly in monthly meetings, and these meetings sent their answers to quarterly and yearly meetings.

The local meeting for worship (first-day meeting) was the heart of Quakerism. Men and women sat separately looking toward the "facing bench" of elders and overseers. Although Quakerism is rightly known for the silence of its meetings, from the beginning of the movement the Friends of Truth had held "threshing" meetings for proselytizing and discussing and had relied especially on traveling Friends to enliven local meetings with utterances of the Spirit, sometimes at great length. In the eighteenth century quietism increasingly tended to exaggerate the insistence on silencing the human and on speaking only when irresistibly moved by the Spirit. As a result, silence came to prevail in some meetings, and the working of the Spirit was attested by the long silence at the beginning and by the ritualistic and unnatural form that speaking took. Speakers chanted or half-sang in a strange cadence ending with an accent that trailed off into a sob. Most speaking was done by "recorded" ministers—including an increasingly large minority of women—who often divided themselves among meetings on a particular first-day. "Sermons" could last a few minutes or more than a half hour. Speakers quoted Scripture freely and often gave an exegesis of a text or spoke directly about death, education, prayer, distinctive Quaker beliefs, spiritual fellowship, and individual testimonies.

Monthly or business meetings were also begun in silence, but their purpose was to deal with practical matters such as marriages and deaths, social witness, and the quality of life in the meeting. Decisions were made according to the united will of the body, with the clerk determining the consensus without votes or majority rule. Discussion continued until the clerk, judging by the content of the most recent utterances, the ensuing silences, and bodily postures and facial expressions, discerned that no active opposition remained.

During the eighteenth century, men and women began to meet for separate monthly meetings. Although the prominence of women in Quaker ministerial roles in this period is striking, it stemmed less from a belief in the equality of men and women than from the Quaker conviction that the Spirit poured forth in its own voice and power completely without the cooperation of its human vessels. For that reason the Spirit might speak by means of the weaker sex if only to make its independence clear. Quakers expected women to follow the biblical injunction to subordinate themselves to men in marriage as in life, and it was only gradually that the egalitarian thrust of the movement made itself felt in gender roles. In the eighteenth century only men's meetings had the power to "disown," or strip a Friend of membership in the meeting.

Quarterly meetings included all of the monthly meetings in a region. They were attended by delegates from monthly meetings and, like the monthly meetings, began in silence and then took up business. Yearly meetings numbered six in the colonies, all formed in the seventeenth century: New England, Baltimore, Virginia, Philadelphia, New York, and North Carolina. There delegates from quarterly meetings met for several days to receive query responses from monthly and quarterly meetings, hear occasional appeals, and arrive by "sense of the meeting" at decisions that were in theory binding on every Quaker meeting and every individual.

The London and Philadelphia yearly meetings —in that order—were the most influential. All American yearly meetings received from and sent correspondence to London but did not always correspond with each other. In America women met separately for yearly meetings through the nineteenth century. Most American yearly meetings also developed a separate annual meeting for ministers and elders to work on publications and general spiritual supervision.

Within this structure what had been intended as guidelines became rules, and this most individualistic body of Christians began to exhibit much uniformity. Although the Friends continued to make converts, especially in the colonies, the long, arduous path from initial "convincement" to full "conversion" became less and less common. Because they did not accept the Christian belief that infants are born bearing the dual burden of impaired faculties of reason and will and actual guilt, Quakers found it easy to regard children as being on a continuum with adults in their spiritual development. Children attended meetings at an early age, received spiritual education and nourishment in the home and at Quaker schools, and were to become "tender" to the leadings of the Spirit. In this setting the idea of birthright membership arose naturally and without discussion by the end of the seventeenth century, although the issue was first confronted explicitly by the London Yearly Meeting in 1737.

Because of their sectarian existence in the eighteenth century and the relative lack of adult converts, Friends were expected to marry within the faith, and, since the family was the locus of piety, wisdom in the choice of partners was of great importance to Quakers. Often those who married outside of the faith could avoid disownment only if they signed a certificate condemning their error and urging their spouse to attend meetings often enough to avoid scandal.

Adult Quakers governed their lives by a strict code laid out in the Book of Discipline. Friends who stepped out of line were discussed at the monthly meeting, which formed a visitation committee of overseers to broach the matter with the offender and get an acknowledgment in writing of his or her intention to reform, if the offense was serious enough. If reform did not follow, the penalty was disownment, a state of spiritual isolation that allowed attendance at first-day meetings but not at monthly meetings and that prevented any other Quaker contact. A disowned Friend could appeal to the quarterly and yearly meeting.

Friends had written many theological tracts in the seventeenth century, and they exhibited some divergence of views despite the editorial work of the morning meeting. Such divergences stemmed from the different levels of education of the writers and the Quakers' lack of clarity about their relationship to traditional Christian theological doctrines such as the Trinity, the person and work of Christ, and sin and grace, especially in relation to the inward light.

Although they were at pains to deny that they were heterodox, early Quakers were influenced by the conviction that spiritual and physical realities are distinct and separate and that the essence of the person is the spiritual part, or what others called the soul. Since Christ was essentially a spiritual reality and almost interchangeable with the Spirit, Quakers had difficulty both differentiating the three persons of the Trinity and regarding Christ's bodily existence as essentially part of his "person" and as essential to anyone's salvation. Thus Christ's death on the cross could not clearly be in any direct sense the cause of human salvation. Moreover, although the Friends believed strongly in human fallenness and in the need for prevenient grace, since they believed that all human beings had a divine light or power enabling them at least at times to respond to God's call, other Christians accused them of weakening the Christian emphasis on sin and grace. In fact, they matched their spiritual-physical dualism with an emphasis on the radical distinction between divine and human reality and therefore regarded the divine Spirit present in all fallen human creatures as clearly distinct from the human mind and body, which were utterly fallen and helpless apart from the presence of the Spirit or inner light. Nevertheless, their belief in the universality of the Spirit to all of humanity both before and after conversion made them suspect to other Christians.

By the eighteenth century Friends only rarely defended their views against detractors, and they increasingly began to see Robert Barclay's *Apology* as an adequate, normative statement of Quaker thought. *An Apology* is by no means devoid of the spiritual-physical dualism that made earlier Quakers uncomfortable with a religion that makes salvation dependent on the atoning actions of the historical Jesus Christ as reported in Scripture. Nevertheless, Barclay attributed all salvation through the inward light to the death and resurrection of Jesus Christ—even the salvation of those who have never heard of Christ—and generally presented accounts of key Christian doctrines that were less offensive to Roman Catholic and Protestant theologians than those of his predecessors. Still, Quakers continued to exhibit differences of perspective among themselves in their theological and ethical self-understanding. The more prosperous urban Friends associated with non-Friends in business and reform efforts, and they tended to downplay distinctive Quaker beliefs and to value the biblical and theological scholarship of evangelical Protestants, such as Congregationalists, Presbyterians, and Methodists. Friends who did not travel in these circles were more likely to see the Spirit and the world in the divine-human and spiritual-physical dualistic terms that had differentiated early Quakers from most other Christians. The differences were minor, however, compared to what they later became.

Although eighteenth-century Quakers in America were in many ways an increasingly sectarian body, the social and political prominence of Friends in some areas, especially in Pennsylvania, served to moderate their prophetic critique of the world. But in the second half of the century a combination of the pressure of events—especially those related to the Revolu-

tion—and a revival of Quaker social witness reminded both Friends and "the world" that spiritual leadings as experienced by Friends obliged them to oppose many forms of injustice rooted ultimately in coercion. One of the most imposing figures in the history of Quakerism, John Woolman (1720–1772), had a major role in this development.

A native of New Jersey, Woolman became influential by traveling widely in the colonies visiting Quaker meetings and by means of his writings and correspondence. Like Fox, Woolman experienced the light as a consuming fire, and his convincement led him to call the light "that which is pure." To him purity meant lack of contamination with any human element, and Woolman was a classic example of eighteenth-century quietism with its divine-human dualism and physical-spiritual dualism and its accompanying lack of resonance to historic Christianity's focus on the life, atoning death, and resurrection of Jesus. Woolman saw a direct causal connection between the human desire for economic security and luxury, on the one hand, and most human oppression and suffering, on the other. He saw slavery and war as attributable largely to the desire for luxury and campaigned to end slaveholding by Friends and to have them rid themselves of the contamination brought by involvement in Pennsylvania politics.

From the beginning of the colony Friends in Pennsylvania's government had simply assumed that, since government was ordained by God, a government that ruled primarily through noncoercive means and eschewed militarism could influence affairs in a righteous direction. With the heating up of the imperial struggle in the New World between England and France after 1690, the Assembly came under pressure to raise a militia and to contribute money for military purposes. Friends in government managed to defeat successive moves to establish a militia from 1690 to 1755 and refused to vote money directly for military purposes. They did, however, vote money "for the king's use" in situations in which they surely realized that they were indirectly assisting a war effort. As the military situation deteriorated in the early 1750s, some Friends began to interpret their pacifism as requiring refusal to pay war taxes. In 1755 twenty-one prominent Friends endorsed such a refusal, thereby placing Friends in the Assembly in the position of potentially punishing fellow Friends and leading to the yearly meeting's request that Friends withdraw from government. Most of them did.

The same reformers who pressured Quakers into withdrawing from government set up committees of visitation to induce Friends to stick more closely to traditional ways of plainness in their economic and social lives. They were especially effective in getting Friends to free their slaves and to oppose slavery. The Quaker-led Pennsylvania Assembly had outlawed the importation of slaves in 1711.

The reformers who wanted Friends to withdraw from all direct participation in government and to maintain distinctive Quaker practices in child rearing, education, speech, and dress began to press for the disownment of offenders. They gained increasing control in the late 1750s and 1760s throughout American Quaker communities. Their argument was given force by the developing political crisis between England and the colonies, and the insurrectionary colonial response to stricter English economic control in the colonies reinforced the Friends' resolve to withdraw from the world.

Despite their increasing desire to dissociate themselves from even indirect participation in the coercive power exercised by governments in enforcing laws, Friends argued that governments were ordained by God to restrain human evil and that spiritual Christians were not to attempt to redress wrongs of even wayward governments. All of the American yearly meetings insisted on neutrality in the political struggle and opposed sedition and rebellion. Friends were neither to vote nor to hold office, and in some colonies Friends were formally advised by their meetings to decline to pay taxes levied to carry on the war, although not on pain of disownment should they decide otherwise.

Friends in all colonies suffered fines and distraints during the Revolution. They experienced the most animosity in Pennsylvania and New Jersey, where they were most prominent and where the largest percentages of male Friends were disowned for war-related offenses. Many such Quakers helped form in 1781 the Society of Free Quakers in support of the war. Drafted Friends were faced with the requirement of hiring a substitute, paying a fee, or being fined. If they remained faithful to the pacifist witness as set forth at the gathering of most yearly meetings in Philadelphia in 1776, they suffered fines or imprisonment.

The Revolution enabled the reformers attempting to raise a wall between Friends and the world to assume control of most meetings. The most visible evidence of their control was the strengthening of the battle against slavery. All of the yearly meetings but Virginia made slave-owning a disownable offense between 1772 and 1780, although Friends were often given a few years to comply, and laws against manumission in North Carolina and Virginia slowed the process. Nevertheless, emancipations seem to have occurred in Virginia after 1782, and in 1808 North Carolina Friends finally gave title to any remaining slaves to the yearly meeting, which let them migrate north, thereby enabling individual slaveowners to manumit them indirectly without bearing individual responsibility for breaking the law.

THE BEGINNINGS OF PLURALISM: THE NINETEENTH CENTURY

The increasing unity of thought and especially of behavior in eighteenth-century Quakerism was made possible by the Friends' steady accretion of the marks of a sect set apart from the larger society. These included a renewed emphasis on peculiarities of speech and dress; social and, to the extent possible, economic separation from non-Quakers; and a critique of many of the norms of the larger society. But Friends of the quietist period did not lose completely the strange Quaker mixture of a sectarian desire for boundaries and purity, on the one hand, and, on the other, a confidence in their ability to serve as a beacon and goad helping to transform the world into the kingdom of God. As the social reform activities that Friends undertook with non-Friends after 1750 indicate, Quakers in America were too prominent socially and economically to avoid involvement in the larger society. Moreover, Friends became increasingly spread out and subject to outside influences as they moved west with the frontier.

By 1800 a developing split in the movement between quietism and evangelicalism became evident. On one side were those most firmly committed to quietism, with its divine-human and physical-spiritual dualisms. Insistent that Quakerism must emphasize its distinctive beliefs and practices—including silent meetings and a devotional life broken only by irresistible urgings of the Spirit, emphasis on the inward light of Christ as the subject of all true religion, and peculiar Quaker dress, speech, and behavior—the quietists saw themselves as distinct from Christians wholly focused on a Trinity of divine persons, the historical atonement of Jesus Christ as the source of all salvation, and the preached Word and physical trappings of revivalism. Moreover, although they distrusted all human faculties, those quietists in contact with the intellectual currents of their era but not trained in theological analysis could see some similarities between their belief in the "inner light" and what some Enlightened thinkers called Reason, especially since Enlightened Christians tended to downplay the same doctrines of Christian orthodoxy as quietists did, including the Trinity, atonement, and original sin.

Although a simple urban-rural analysis of the split does not hold for all Quaker regions, the most prominent evangelicals were urban Friends with leadership positions in the Society and a social and economic prominence that brought them into contact with Protestant evangelicals. Beginning in the early nineteenth century, Friends in both England and America worked in Bible, tract, and reform societies. These groups constituted the main instruments of the interdenominational Protestant effort to Christianize society and, in America, to enable "the first new nation" to realize its potential to lead the world toward the kingdom of God.

Moved by their transformationist ethic to emphasize religious similarities with their partners in Protestant voluntary societies, Friends devoted themselves to religious literature, antislavery activities, poor relief, and prison reform. Friends recognized in evangelicalism early Quakerism's insistence on a conscious, momentous crossing from the world to a "convinced" state, its focus on Jesus Christ, its biblical phraseology and imagery, and its transformationist ethic, and they began to see themselves as part of the evangelical Protestant vanguard. Evangelicalism continued to grow in strength in England until about 1870; in the United States the evangelical pull was even stronger as Quakers moved west away from settled Quaker communities, forming the Ohio Yearly Meeting in 1812 and the Indiana in 1821.

Quaker evangelicalism of the early nineteenth century was most influenced by Dissenter or Anglican low-church piety in England and by the Congregationalist-Presbyterian awakenings in America that were part of the Great Awakening at the turn of the century and the "New Measure" revivals of the 1820s and 1830s initiated by Charles Grandison Finney. In response to the rationalist quietism of, among others, Abraham Shackleton of Ireland and Hannah Barnard of New York, the London Yearly Meeting in 1801 announced that Friends believed in the Trinity, the inerrancy of Scripture, and the importance of doctrinal orthodoxy. The Philadelphia Yearly Meeting followed suit in 1806, declaring it cause for disownment to deny the divinity of Christ, the immediate revelation of the Spirit, or the authenticity of Scripture. Never before had Quaker meetings insisted on predicating membership on subscription to doctrines.

Elias Hicks (1748–1830) of Long Island, one of the most prominent traveling "recorded" ministers in American Quakerism ("recorded" ministers were men and women whose gifts in the spoken ministry were recognized formally by their monthly meeting) was in many ways a striking reminder of George Fox. Largely self-educated and steeped in the Bible, Hicks had theological acumen, great eloquence, a striking appearance, and a forceful personality. A quietist unimpressed by the religious value of formal learning and unmoved by such "outward" forms as the historical Jesus, Scripture, the church, or theological formulas, Hicks emphasized the immediate presence of the divine light as a continuing revelation within all human breasts. Although he had no special interest in denying Christian orthodox beliefs, they were of little concern to him, and he saw insistence on adhering to specific doctrinal formulas as antithetical to traditional Quakerism. From 1819, when he visited Philadelphia and alarmed some weighty Friends, the evangelicals around Philadelphia viewed him as a representative of dangerous tendencies. Division occurred there in 1827, when what became the Orthodox outmaneuvered the Hicksites in a struggle for the clerkship of the yearly meeting. Orthodox and Hicksites began disowning each other in the yearly meetings of Philadelphia, New York, Baltimore, Ohio, and Indiana.

Orthodox Quakers believed themselves to be orthodox Christians of the Protestant evangelical bent and were usually urban dwellers who were associated with evangelicals in reform societies. Hicksites were largely rural Quakers who emphasized the distinctiveness of the Quaker witness and believed that Friends were marked above all by their sense of Spirit-possession and by resisting the notion that theological formulas are the focus of the Bible.

The Hicksites had probably a two or three to one majority in the Philadelphia, New York, and Baltimore yearly meetings and a majority in Ohio, but the Orthodox had the prominent urban Friends, the impetus of a reforming movement linked to the evangelical alliance in America and all of New England, the remains of southern Quakerism, and Indiana. Each side probably numbered between 35,000 and 45,000, but the Orthodox doubled the latter figure by 1900, while the Hicksites, more sectarian and stronger in the old centers of a declining eastern Quakerism, were barely able to hold their own.

Hicks's counterpart as the leading figure among the evangelicals was Joseph Gurney (1788–1847). Educated by private tutors at Oxford, he was a renowned minister and theologian who reintroduced in Quakerism the critical study of the Bible and insisted that the Bible was the final authority in doctrinal matters and that those who disagreed could be disowned. At the same time, Gurney lived and taught a deep Quaker spirituality centered on silent worship, scrupulously Quaker conduct and mannerisms, reliance on spiritual leadings, and energetic reformism. Although he believed that the experience of grace and forgiveness was available even to those who had not heard of Christ, his most striking innovation was his belief that Christians, including Quakers, were justified or reckoned "just" or acceptable to God because of the imputed righteousness of Christ gained in His act of atonement, and that sanctification or personal holiness was logically dependent on justification. This doctrine, with its focus on the atoning deeds of Christ, was stated forcefully in a manner not previously known in Quakerism, which had held that justification was part of the sanctifying repentance brought by the light. Moreover, Gurney explicitly attacked the idea that Quakers were a spiritual vanguard among Christians. He undertook a grand tour as a traveling minister among American Friends from 1837 to 1840, and his thought set the tone for evangelicals for the next forty years. As Quakers followed the westward movement, setting up the Western and Iowa yearly meetings in 1858 and 1863, American evangelicals began to mix Gurneyite views with the revivalism of the followers of Charles Grandison Finney and their distinctive emphasis on sanctification.

The cultured and charismatic Gurney appealed both to eastern cosmopolitans and to frontier Quakers, but his visit also stirred controversy among Friends who had previously identified with the Orthodox. John Wilbur (1774–1856) of the New England Yearly Meeting found Gurney's "creaturely" emphasis on biblical study offensive and held that Gurney's belief in imputed righteousness and his neglect of the inner light were a great danger to Quakerism. When New England tried to rearrange territorial divisions among meetings to reduce Wilbur's influence, he led a schism including 500 of the 6,500 New England Quakers in 1845. Wilburite schisms also occurred in the next several years in Baltimore and New York. A Wilburite Ohio Yearly Meeting was organized in 1854, and Wilburite groups in Iowa coalesced into a yearly meeting in 1877. Separations in Western (1877), Kansas (1879), and Canada (1881) yearly meetings by Wilburite opponents of American developments in the Gurney revivalistic vein fostered the formation of Conservative Friends, the third major body in addition to the Orthodox and Hicksite. Although joined by a small group later in North Carolina, the Conservatives failed to grow and in 1890 numbered just over 4,000, being strongest in eastern Ohio and Iowa. Conservative Quakerism stood somewhere between the mysticism, sectarianism, and increasing rationalism of the Hicksites and the biblicism, creedalism, and evangelical reformism of the Orthodox Friends.

As Quakers moved west, those in Virginia and parts of North Carolina, where Quakerism was not strong, drifted away to Methodism, while Friends became especially numerous in Indiana and Iowa. In the latter areas Gurneyite evangelical Quakerism became increasingly revivalistic, as Gurney's distinction between justification and sanctification pointed to not only a doctrine of imputed righteousness but a separate emphasis on sanctification as a second and possibly more significant stage of spiritual life.

At the Indiana Yearly Meeting in 1860, 1,500 people attended a revival meeting with testimonials and prayer; 120 testified or prayed;

and a hymn was sung for the first time in Quakerism for well over a century. In the next decade significant revivals occurred in Indiana and Iowa; "social-religious" meetings proliferated from Ohio to the west among Friends; and between 1868 and 1870 a number of protracted revival sessions of several days occurred, increasingly using such Finneyite measures as elaborate preparations (including intensive advertising and training in revival techniques), emotional public conversion experiences, and other manifestations of spiritual possession and inducements to rebirth. Indiana appointed a committee in 1867 to hold "General Meetings" to promote and control the revival impulse, and soon most other Gurneyite yearly meetings had a similar committee. "General meetings" were a revival of the "threshing" sessions seventeenth-century Quakers had held for preaching to the unconvinced, doctrinal discussion, and spontaneous testimonies.

It was in the context of these developments that Conservative Friends had felt the need to raise questions and finally to separate. Their concern was that many Friends were going beyond a combination of evangelical and distinctive Quaker themes to a full-fledged Methodist revivalism that dropped the Quaker marks. Long periods of silence gave way to regular preaching; the Books of Discipline replaced the distinctive "plainness" of speech and dress with a call for "simplicity"; the high-pitched chanting of traditional Quaker meeting utterances was frowned upon; and music began to intrude on the silence.

With many new converts and with meetings closer in form to those of evangelical Protestants, Quakers found themselves faced with the task of teaching and training attenders unfamiliar with Quakerism. Moreover, although the midwestern yearly meetings recorded increased numbers of ministers in the 1860s and 1870s, most Friends were spread out over many miles on farms. Local meetings found themselves relying increasingly on one or a few members who, in effect, took on the responsibilities of a pastor. Although still "recorded" rather than ordained they presided over services including hymns, readings from Scripture, and prepared sermons; and they visited and performed other pastoral duties. These arrangements became common in the early 1880s, although most yearly meetings resisted one-person paid pastorates through the

end of the decade. The pastoral system was approved by New York and Iowa in 1886, Kansas in 1889, Ohio in 1890, and Western and Indiana in 1891 (the latter informally).

Quaker pastors tried to minister in ways that developed a sense of pastoral responsibility in others and conceived of their responsibilities in worship as subordinate to their duty to keep the meeting under the immediate guidance of the Spirit. Although worship was planned and programmed, the ideal for the pastor was to sense the direction of the meeting and to adjust accordingly the period of silence and general vocal ministry, music, and even the sermon.

Changes that had even more radical implications for Quakerism than the pastoral system came about between 1870 and 1900 through the influence of birthright Quakers and converts who carried evangelical theological and ecclesiastical themes well beyond Gurney. The most prominent of these was David Updegraff. Updegraff adopted virtually all of the revival practices and tactics of the movements associated with Charles Grandison Finney before the Civil War and Dwight Moody after it. The meetings he ran included Scripture reading, testimonies to rebirth, singing and spiritual "shouting," and long evangelical sermons leading to an altar call, in which those wishing to be saved on the spot were asked to step forward and receive Christ as their Lord and Savior. Throughout Updegraff played the role of the master of spiritual ceremonies, telling the congregation or specific individuals when to rise, kneel, testify, and pray. Even more noteworthy were his theological innovations. Convinced that conversion was necessary for all humanity, Updegraff preached that the inward light was present before conversion only in the form of God's wrath or judgment, thereby denying, in effect, the presence of the inner light as traditionally understood by Quakers.

Updegraff also taught that a second baptism of the Holy Spirit was necessary after the initial conversion if a believer was truly saved and on the necessary path to "entire sanctification." Here Updegraff reflected his reliance on the Holiness movement, with its emphasis on continuing sanctification through spiritual possession and gifts, as he did in his concomitant adherence to the premillennial teaching that Christians were to focus exclusively on saving souls from an increasingly sin-ridden world. (In contrast to the traditional postmillennial Quaker belief that Christ's Second Coming would follow the gradual transformation of history into the kingdom of God, premillennialists believe that sin will increase its power in the world until the sudden return of Christ to set up the millennium after a great battle against the forces of evil.) Updegraff also introduced to Quakerism the ordinance of baptism by immersion.

The implications for Quakerism of this extreme evangelicalism were far-reaching. Despite their divine-human dualism, with its devaluing of human faculties, Quakers had developed in the United States several educational institutions that influenced strongly the development of Quaker leaders and augmented Quaker influence. The Orthodox had founded Haverford (1833), Earlham (1859), Wilmington (1871), William Penn (1873), and Guilford (1888); the Hicksites, Swarthmore (1864). Convinced that modern thought was increasingly under demonic control and that the Bible was the infallible source of all truth, extreme evangelicals founded biblical institutes for "training" in Scripture along fundamentalist lines. The most prominent was the Cleveland (Ohio) Bible Institute, founded in 1892. Others were later started in Westfield, Indiana; Haviland, Kansas; Greenleaf, Idaho; and Los Angeles. Here Quakers learned a Holiness fundamentalist theology and a wariness of the mainstream intellectual developments known as "modernism," including critical biblical study and theology.

Even more significant was the change in the nature of the Quaker social witness. Believing that all humans have within them the divine light in some form and thus that they can understand and respond to truth, Quakers previously had assumed that the non-Christians they encountered, such as Native Americans, possessed spiritual insights and could recognize truth in the Quaker message and way of living. Quakers had at times assumed the superiority of their own form of religious life and hoped that others would join them, but they had recognized the validity of other religious forms and often, as among the Indians in Pennsylvania, had devoted more energy to social reforms than to proselytizing. Quakers of the nineteenth century, including Orthodox, Hicksites, and Wilburites, had continued and even quickened the Quaker social

conscience. They worked to ease the lot of the oppressed, including blacks, Indians, orphans, prostitutes, apprentices, and the poor; they founded ameliorative institutions such as schools, prisons called "penitentiaries" in which character reformation was attempted, asylums, hospitals, and libraries; they spread spiritual light through Bible and tract societies; and they attacked social problems such as war and alcoholism.

Although not radicals who questioned the fundamental institutions of American society—except in their abolitionist and women's rights activity—they viewed the struggle against injustice and suffering and the struggle for the transformation of the world into the heavenly kingdom as central to their witness. Evangelicals who devoted most of their social reform efforts to interdenominational organizations sometimes earned the ire of Friends who feared the pull of this world and wanted a distinctive Quaker witness, but virtually all Quakers before 1875 placed witness against oppression and suffering at least as close to the center of their faith as whatever theological beliefs they possessed. Moreover, whether they had much hope for religious and social progress toward the kingdom in their day or not, they constantly acted as if it was the duty of Christians to judge the world by the standards of the kingdom. Evangelicals like Updegraff, with their premillennialism and their denial that the divine light shines in all breasts, stifled reformist efforts. After 1890 the most extreme evangelical Friends devoted their "spiritual" resources to missionary work and took an increasingly conservative attitude toward political and social issues.

AMERICAN QUAKERISM IN THE TWENTIETH CENTURY

As Quakerism entered the twentieth century it was completing its spread both across the continent and across the American religious and social landscape. The Midwest became more urbanized from 1880 to 1910, and many of the recent converts who had experienced conversion at Quaker meetings drifted into other evangelical denominations when they reached the cities. At the same time, the movement was completing its westward push, and between 1890 and 1910 largely evangelical Quaker local and regional meetings were founded in Texas, Colorado, Nebraska, South Dakota, California, and Oregon, with yearly meetings being organized in Oregon (1893), California (1895), and Nebraska (1900). These meetings were largely of the extreme evangelical or Holiness kind of Quakerism.

Liberal intellectual and religious currents more in accord with Hicksite views were coming to the fore in English Quakerism after 1870 and, as in the case of evangelical views at the beginning of the eighteenth century, were being picked up on the other side of the Atlantic as well. Such currents included a more relativistic view of the religious truths of Christianity, a more critical, historical approach to biblical material, and a reluctance to equate theological formulas and divine truth. English Friends such as John Wilhelm Rowntree, J. Rendel Harris, and Norman Penney hoped to capture the distinctive marks of Quakerism by reexamining its past and using the developments of modern historical scholarship to portray the mystical, rational, and transformationist marks of the movement as well as its evangelical side. They were joined by American Friends from both the Hicksite and Orthodox groups, the most prominent and influential of whom was Rufus Jones (1863–1948), who grew up in an Orthodox meeting but soon outgrew its approach to Quaker self-understanding.

Jones saw Quakerism as having come in on the crest of a revival of mystical religion in the fifteenth and sixteenth centuries and as having turned the movement in the direction of a "positive" or "group" mysticism. Such mysticism combined a reliance on silent waiting for the leading of the Spirit with a conviction that the Spirit would bring to spiritual Christians not only an appreciation for the unifying intellectual and spiritual currents present in all cultures but a powerful thrust in the direction of social reform. Like Penn, Barclay, and Hicks before him, but with more of the optimistic nineteenth-century liberal theological sense of continuity between the human and the divine, Jones stressed the affinities between Quaker thought and witness and the progressive intellectual and social currents of his day.

Despite the effects of these intellectual and theological attitudes on both the far right and far left of the movement in the early twentieth century, Friends had already begun to show signs of a desire for unification. Developments along the evangelical front in the 1870s and 1880s had led not only to the growth of the Conservative schism but also to an attempted meeting of minds among Orthodox Friends. The Indiana Yearly Meeting called all but Hicksite Friends to a meeting in Richmond, Indiana, in 1887 to discuss Quaker thought and practices. Representatives came from all of the American yearly meetings in correspondence with London, although Philadelphia was represented only unofficially. The conference produced a Declaration of Faith that muted the claim of the universality of the divine light, retained reference to the significant Quaker testimonies including that against war, and emphasized evangelical doctrine focusing on the centrality to salvation of the atoning deeds of the divine-human Jesus Christ.

The Richmond Declaration, although not officially responded to by London, Philadelphia, Ohio, or New England, was either adopted or generally approved by most of the yearly meetings and was regarded as the closest that Quakerism had yet come to having a creed. The groups represented at Richmond continued to meet every five years and came to consider the Richmond Declaration and Fox's 1671 Letter to the Governor of Barbadoes (which emphasizes Quaker acceptance of Christian doctrines on the person and atoning work of Christ) as adequately representing Quaker beliefs. In 1902 they formed the Five Years Meeting.

The proposed discipline for the new coordinating body was adopted by New England, New York, Indiana, Kansas, California, Wilmington, Western, Baltimore, Iowa, Oregon, and Canada. The Nebraska Yearly Meeting, set up in 1908, also became a member. Despite the exclusion of Hicksites from the Five Years Meeting, some Orthodox were already renewing contacts with members of their liberal body at summer conferences at Haverford and Earlham, and the openness of the Five Years Meeting was seen in its membership in the Federal Council of Churches of Christ in America beginning in 1908. Meanwhile the Hicksites had shown their own unifying impulse in forming the Friends General Conference in 1900, including the yearly meetings in New York, Philadelphia, Baltimore, Ohio, Indiana, and Genesee, New York (founded in 1834).

Friends from all yearly meetings first began to meet at the Young Friends' Conference at Winona Lake, Indiana, in 1910. By that time London had already sent a letter to Hicksite yearly meetings and from 1921 addressed its general correspondence to "all who bear the name of Friends." Where Orthodox and Hicksites were in close proximity they began to correspond and even to act together. In 1926 the Philadelphia Orthodox Yearly Meeting recognized its Hicksite counterpart, receiving members by certificate and opening its preparatory school, Westtown, to Hicksites. Mutual recognition and cooperation in conferences, joint celebrations, worship, and work in the world were accepted generally by 1940 in New York, Baltimore, and Philadelphia, and full unity came in 1955.

Contacts of an even broader nature involving all Friends continued. English and American Friends participated generally in the Protestant ecumenical movement beginning with the Edinburgh Foreign Mission Conference in 1910. As the movement became better organized and made some progress on a theological formula linking its bodies, Friends retreated to a kind of associate membership and saw the formulas as affirmations of theological tendencies rather than creeds in the strict sense requiring subscription as a prerequisite for membership. Quakers were represented at the Second Vatican Council (1962–1965) and continue to be active in the World Council of Churches in various capacities.

Among themselves Friends convened a conference of all Friends in London in 1920 and in Philadelphia in 1937, when they formed the Friends World Committee for Consultation. Gatherings of all Friends in Oxford (1953), Guilford (1967), St. Louis (1970), and Wichita (1977) and the activities of the World Committee on Consultation highlighted the religious dialogue among Friends of different branches. A continuing organ for theological discussion among Friends of all persuasions has been the Quaker Theological Discussion Group, which began meeting in 1957 and publishes *Quaker Religious Thought*.

Another source of unity has been the American Friends Service Committee (AFSC). Started in 1917 by the Philadelphia Orthodox and Hicksite Quakers and members of Five Years Meetings, it came to include all American yearly meetings. Although its form of witness is more socially oriented than premillennialist Friends would like, its focus on relief work and on alleviating suffering and oppression has allowed Friends of all varieties to join against a common enemy. During and after World War I it provided rebuilding, medical, agricultural, and relief assistance, in conjunction with the English Friends War Victims Relief Committee, in France, Vienna, Serbia, Poland, Russia, Turkey, and Greece. In 1925 separate sections were set up to deal with relief and rehabilitation in Europe and the United States and with peace and interracial concerns.

In the 1930s and 1940s the AFSC provided massive assistance to refugees from Spain, Germany, Poland, Holland, Belgium, and parts of Asia. As a result of its work new meetings began in many countries of Europe and joined the newer Friends meetings stemming from nineteenth- and twentieth-century missionary work in Africa, Central and South America, and Asia. In 1935 the AFSC Friends Fellowship Council was organized to care for local meetings that could not easily establish relationships with an existing yearly meeting, thereby continuing the AFSC's unifying work. In 1947 the AFSC was awarded, with the Friends Service Council of London, the Nobel Peace Prize for its relief work in the late 1930s and 1940s.

In the period of disillusionment on the part of pacifists and optimistic liberals between the two world wars, the AFSC helped turn Quakerism back toward the prophetic and transforming focus on struggle against the world's evils that had marked the early Quaker movement but that had been muted first by quietism and later by the most evangelical of nineteenth- and early-twentieth-century Quakers. With its prominence throughout the world since 1950 in relief work, and as a supplier of humanitarian services to both the North and South Vietnamese during the Vietnam War, the Service Committee has changed the image of Quakerism from that of a sect with a conscience to that of a body of spiritual pacifists who manifest in deed as well as in word their insistence that the world be judged by, and move toward, the kingdom of righteousness and love.

Although Friends have been in dialogue with one another increasingly in the twentieth century, this dialogue has only clarified—and not resolved—the differences between the ends of the spectrum. The unity among Gurneyite Friends represented by the Five Years Meeting was breached by Friends who found the majority of the Five Years Meeting too willing to compromise with theological liberalism. In 1912 the Kansas, Western, and California Yearly Meetings asked that the Richmond Declaration and the Letter of George Fox to the Governor of Barbadoes be made corporate parts of the Uniform Discipline, thereby making them creeds and requiring their acceptance. The Five Years Meeting was willing to label them "historic statements of belief" but said they were "not to be regarded as constituting a creed." Under pressure from western evangelicals, the meeting dropped the latter phrase in 1922, but nevertheless Oregon withdrew from the meeting in 1926 and Kansas in 1937; Western saw a secession in 1926 to form Central Yearly Meeting as an independent; and Nebraska left the Five Years Meeting in 1957.

Representatives of what became the independent yearly meetings, along with the more fundamentalist evangelicals in yearly meetings that were part of the Five Years Meeting, first met in 1927 at Cheyenne, Wyoming, to form what became the Association of Evangelical Friends. Meeting again in Colorado Springs in 1947, representatives of California, Central, Indiana, Iowa, Kansas, Nebraska, Ohio, Oregon, and Western declared the Richmond Declaration and the Barbadoes letter their creed. After meeting again in Wichita, Kansas, in 1950 and Oskaloosah, Iowa, in 1953, they formally organized as the Association of Evangelical Friends in 1956 at Denver to promote the fellowship of the Gospel by making articulate the voice of evangelical Friends, providing them with a means of associating in common endeavors, and working for the speedy evangelization of the world and the revival of Quakerism.

These evangelicals were united in holding to the theology of the Bible school movement under the influence of the National Holiness Association, including the Pilgrim Holiness Church, Church of the Nazarene, and Wesleyan Methodist Church. The association's marks were, first, belief in "entire" or "instant" sanctification by the Holy Spirit after conversion as formulated by the Keswickian Holiness movement; second, belief in the Bible as the divinely inspired, infallible, and sufficient word of God;

third, an apocalyptic emphasis on the Second Coming of Christ, after warning by evident signs fulfilling biblical prophecy, to rescue the world from the grip of sin; and fourth, the identification of modernism, including biblical criticism and theological naturalism, as the main agent of the reign of sin.

From its beginning the Association of Evangelical Friends included both Friends desiring that it serve as a catalytic agent within the existent yearly meetings and Friends who wanted it to bring about the formation of a new counterpart to the Five Years Meeting and the Friends General Conference. The latter group won in 1965 with the formation of the Evangelical Friends Alliance (EFA). It included at first the Rocky Mountain Yearly Meeting (formerly Nebraska), Northwest Yearly Meeting (formerly Oregon), Mid-American (formerly Kansas), and the Eastern Region of Friends' Church (formerly Ohio), but since 1973 monthly meetings that wish to join may do so despite retaining affiliation with another association of yearly meetings.

Although there is some evidence that the Evangelical Friends Alliance is not wholly dominated by the opposition to modernism and peculiar beliefs of the Keswickian Holiness movement, having become somewhat less defensive in the 1960s and 1970s, it is still part of the Fundamentalist movement. For members of the Alliance, the Bible is the infallible and sufficient Word of God; true Christians are those who have experienced conscious rebirth; and the sole focus of faith is the redemptive atonement of Jesus Christ on the cross. Even in its initial silent period, the typical EFA meeting for worship directs the worshiper to meditate on the fully divine and human Christ and on his death and resurrection for sin and rebirth. Quakerism is still seen as a movement of spiritual religion with significant reliance on silence, pacifism, and social concern, but its links are primarily with the wider Evangelical or Fundamentalist alliance, not with more moderate or liberal Friends.

American Quakerism today includes three major groupings of yearly meetings. The largest is the Friends United Meeting (FUM), known as the Five Years Meeting until 1960, with roughly 60,000 members and well more than 500 local meetings. About half of its meetings are pastoral, and, although its membership ranges from lib-

eral to ultra-conservative, its religious and theological center—represented by the theologies
present at the Earlham School of Religion
(founded in 1960)—is moderately evangelical
with a strong emphasis on the distinctive Quaker
theological and social witness. In full communion with the FUM is the Friends General Conference (1900), with 350 meetings and around
33,000 members. It includes most of the descendants of the Hicksites and many attenders
and members who have become allied with
Friends through involvement in pacifism, war
protests, and social concerns or have found it a
congenially liberal and even religiously relativistic spiritual home. The Evangelical Friends Alliance has about 250 meetings and 27,000 members. Although allied with the more conservative
wing of the FUM, it minimizes its Quaker distinctiveness. In addition, the Religious Society of
Friends (descendants of the Conservatives or
Wilburites) number 2,000, and members in various unaffiliated yearly meetings number more
than 6,000.

QUAKERS IN THE CONTEXT OF AMERICAN CULTURE

Quakerism's significance to American culture
and religion is twofold, with one set of influences
relating primarily to the past and the other to the
present. First, it has served as both a model and
a goad for other religious bodies and for American national self-understanding. Thinking that
they could not reform or remake England in
their image, many of the Puritans who came to
the New World, and especially the non-separat-
ing congregationalists of Massachusetts Bay,
hoped to set up a new order based on proper
religious understanding and to approximate as
closely as possible on earth the kingdom of God,
thereby pleasing God and serving as a model for
European nations. William Penn, too, wanted to
set up an example for the nations, or a "holy
experiment," and his relatively noncoercive social order, with few government agents to enforce its laws, was even more utopian than that
of the Puritans and therefore more significant, in
his view, should it work. In many respects Pennsylvania was not a success in Penn's eyes because
of the colonists' fractiousness, but from a later

vantage point it seems to have served as a precursor of sorts for the "first new nation."

Pennsylvania in the eighteenth century was a
pluralistic society run by Quakers with as many
Quaker consensual governmental methods as
pluralism would allow. Its relatively egalitarian
social order, generous observance of fundamental human rights, minimal government, and
prosperous economy pointed toward the American national experiment of the early nineteenth
century. Pennsylvania served as a paradigm for
American religious nationalism in part because it
was a successful religious experiment, but also
because Quakerism's assumptions about human
rights, the "light" available to all of humanity,
and the possibilities of history's movement toward the kingdom of God were even more in
accord than Puritanism with the beliefs of Americans in the Revolutionary era and thereafter.

By the time of the Revolution, Pennsylvania
was no longer strictly a Quaker experiment,
since Quakers were a minority and they had withdrawn from involvement in government. But
Friends were still trying to reform the structures
of history in the direction of a just, egalitarian,
and loving social order, and they did so on the
assumption that all human beings, be they Native
Americans, slaves, criminals, the insane, or even
national enemies, had within them the inner light
of divine truth that would enable them to recognize and to respond to acts of justice and love.
No longer a controlling body in a social order,
the Friends dared other Christian groups and all
Americans to believe that criminals could profit
from penitentiaries, that Indians could become
useful citizens without benefit of Christianity,
and that poor relief, education, and hospitals
would not spoil the poor but instead release the
cramped divine powers within them.

Working increasingly with other Protestant
evangelical bodies, the Friends played an essential role in the common Christian reforming activities and expressed greater confidence than
most Christians in the potential of both the individuals who benefited from their crusades and
the social order. Moreover, with their largely
noncoercive government in Pennsylvania and especially their pacifist witness during the many
wars in American history, they reminded their
fellow citizens that the American model social
order was still far from the kingdom, that their

faith in God was still far too small, and that their identification of themselves as God's latter-day "chosen people" and of their enemies as demonic powers was simplistic and dangerous for fallen humanity.

It was largely the social and political prominence of the Quakers in many colonies that induced several colonies and then the nation to grant pacifists the right to follow a higher law even when the existence of America was at stake. Although in the nineteenth and early twentieth centuries the Friends' witness to pacifism was far from uniform, the congruence between their message and practice and that of the early church described in the Bible increasingly left its mark on Protestant and Roman Catholic Christians. The Quakers' prominent witness against war was influential in giving rise to the non-Quaker peace movement in the nineteenth and early twentieth centuries. Quaker relief efforts on behalf of American enemies, especially the work of the American Friends Service Committee, have helped to reconcile former enemies and have reminded American Christians that they must love even their enemies. As the era of nuclear warfare began, the peculiar form of Quaker pacifism, pointing as it does both to the New Testament ideal and to the practical futility of war, helped convince many Roman Catholics and Protestants that there must and can be a better way to resolve international disputes if the world is to survive the arrival of doomsday weapons.

There can be no doubt that American Friends have been admired for their witness and their social and political goals more than for their theology or world view. But in fact the early Quakers constituted a unique brand of Christianity that combined an adherence to the Christian message of radical fallenness and reliance on divine grace with a belief that the divine light of truth and power was available to all humanity of whatever religion or world view. Unlike most critics of Christian exclusivism, with the possible exception of some late-nineteenth-century idealists, Quakers did not water down Christianity to a few simple rational truths. Rather, Quaker theologians such as William Penn, Elias Hicks, and, for the most part, Rufus Jones have believed that the Christ who is "the same yesterday, today, and forever" comes to all humanity as an agent of

divine knowledge and gracious power enabling us to accept the divine call in whatever cultural and religious forms it is symbolized.

Some Quaker thinkers, struggling with the problem of how to square traditional claims about the cosmic significance of Christ's historical redemption with universal knowledge of God, make Jesus Christ the causal agent of salvation available throughout human religious cultures on non-Christian terms. Others see the Christ-event as a paradigm of the divine-human relationship or simply as the source of the deepest Western insight into the divine nature and the human goal. Although Quakerism has not been widely seen as having much to offer Christian thinkers in an age when the major religions of the world regularly interact, the thought of such theologians as the Roman Catholic Karl Rahner and Protestants Schubert Ogden and John Cobb, Jr., is coming increasingly to resemble the message that the more liberal strands of Quakerism have developed. As Christian theologians attempt to understand other religious faiths as special interpretations of truth with their own dynamics, they may find guidance in the Friends' thought about the inward light of Christ, their practice of silence in the presence of the One, and their identification of Christian witness with acts of justice and love even for enemies.

BIBLIOGRAPHY

Margaret H. Bacon, *The Quiet Rebels: The Story of the Quakers in America* (1969); Hugh Barbour, *The Quakers in Puritan England* (1964) and, with Arthur O. Roberts, as eds., *Early Quaker Writings: 1650–1700* (1973); Robert Barclay, *An Apology for the True Christian Divinity* (1678); Richard Bauman, *For the Reputation of Truth* (1971) and *Let Your Words Be Few* (1984); William C. Braithwaite, *The Beginnings of Quakerism,* 2nd ed., rev. by Henry J. Cadbury (1955), and *The Second Period of Quakerism,* 2nd ed., rev. by Henry J. Cadbury (1961); Howard H. Brinton, *Friends for 300 Years* (1952); Peter Brock, *Pacifism in the United States, from the Colonial Era to the First World War* (1968) and *Twentieth-Century Pacifism* (1970); Edwin B. Bronner, *William Penn's Holy Experiment* (1962); Thomas E. Drake, *Quakers and Slavery in America* (1950).

Errol T. Elliot, *Quakers on the American Frontier* (1969); Melvin B. Endy, Jr., *William Penn and Early Quakerism* (1973); George Fox, *Works,* vols. 3–8 (1831), and *Journal,* ed. by John L. Nickalls (1952); Jerry William Frost, *The Quaker Family in Colonial America* (1973); Joseph John Gurney, *Essays on the*

Evidences, Doctrines, and Practical Operation of Christianity (1825); Francis B. Hall, ed., *Quaker Worship in North America* (1979); Elias Hicks, *Journal of the Life and Religious Labors of Elias Hicks* (1832); James H. Hutson, *Pennsylvania Politics, 1746–1770* (1972); Sydney V. James, *A People Among Peoples: Quaker Benevolence in Eighteenth-Century America* (1963); Rufus M. Jones et al., *The Quakers in the American Colonies* (1911) and *The Later Periods of Quakerism* (1921); David C. LeShana, *Quakers in California: The Effects of Nineteenth-Century Revivalism on Western Quakerism* (1969).

Jack D. Marietta, *The Reformation of American Quakerism, 1748–1783* (1984); Arthur J. Mekeel, *The Relation of the Quakers to the American Revolution* (1979); Phillips P. Moulton, ed., *The Journal and Major Essays of John Woolman* (1971); Geoffrey F. Nuttall, *The Holy Spirit in Puritan Faith and Experience* (1946); William Penn, *A Collection of the Works of William Penn,* 2 vols. (1726); John Punshon, *Portrait in Grey* (1984); Arthur O. Roberts, *The Association of Evangelical Friends* (1975); Elbert Russell, *The History of Quakerism* (1943); Joseph Smith, *A Descriptive Catalogue of Friends' Books,* 2 vols. (1867) and *Supplement* (1893); Allen C. Thomas, *A History of the Friends in America* (1894; 6th ed., 1930); Frederick B. Tolles, *Meeting House and Counting House: The Quaker Merchants of Colonial Philadelphia, 1682–1763* (1948); D. Elton Trueblood, *The People Called Quakers* (1966; 2nd ed., 1971); Richard T. Vann, *The Social Development of English Quakerism, 1655–1755* (1969); Arthur J. Worrall, *Quakers in the Colonial Northeast* (1980).

[*See also* WAR AND PEACE.]

SECTS AND RELIGIOUS MOVEMENTS OF GERMAN ORIGIN

Don Yoder

THE importance of German-language religious groups in the United States can be gauged by the extent of German immigration over the past three centuries. Since the founding of Germantown, Pennsylvania, in 1683—the first German settlement in America—over 7 million German-speaking immigrants have arrived at American ports, making up the largest single European ethnic group in American society apart from the British Isles contingent. Furthermore, German immigrants settled in every corner of the country, in cities as well as rural areas. Many cities, towns, and communitarian colonies were in fact founded by German immigrants.

Because of William Penn and his Quaker colonization projects, Pennsylvania became the focus of the major German immigration before 1800, although other colonies received settlers in lesser numbers via the ports of Boston, New York, Annapolis, Baltimore, Charleston, Savannah, and New Orleans. In 1677 Penn made a missionary tour up the Rhine to the Palatinate and adjoining areas, visiting Pietist and Mennonite centers. His invitation to the persecuted groups of Europe to settle in his colony was taken up by a variety of radical Pietists, mystics, and separatists, including Mennonites, Amish, Brethren, Moravians, and Schwenkfelders. This movement of religious groups across the Atlantic greatly enriched the culture of colonial Pennsylvania and added significant European elements to the religious map of the colonies.

Apart from the earliest waves of immigrants, the majority of the German settlers who came to Pennsylvania and other colonies in the colonial era represented the churchly traditions, the Lutherans and Reformed of Germany and Switzerland. In the Pennsylvania German culture these made up the majority, with the sectarians providing the minority component. Probably no more than 25 percent of the Pennsylvania German population was at any time made up of the sectarian elements.

Emigration from the German-speaking areas of Central Europe continued in the nineteenth century, with large waves after the Napoleonic wars and the revolutions of 1830 and 1848. The majority of emigrants in this period were from the Lutheran, Reformed, and Catholic churches, although a continuing minority of sectarians and communitarians emigrated also. Among these were the Harmonites, the Amana, Zoar, Bethel, and Aurora communities, as well as the Hutterites and other Mennonite groups from Russia.

Since the American-German church groups are considered elsewhere in this work, we shall concentrate on four smaller movements usually referred to as sectarian—continental sectarians of the Reformation and Pietist eras: Mennonites, Amish, Brethren, Schwenkfelders; communitarian sects of European origin: Moravians, the Ephrata Community, Harmonites, Hutterites, the Amana Community; hybrid American-German groups uniting Pietism and Anglo-American revivalism: United Brethren in Christ, Evangelical Association, Church of God; and German-language wings of Anglo-American churches: German Methodists, German Universalists, German Jehovah's Witnesses.

CONTINENTAL SECTARIANS OF THE REFORMATION AND PIETIST ERAS

The Anabaptist movement of the sixteenth century, with roots in Switzerland, Germany, and Holland, produced America's largest German sectarian family of denominations, a grouping of related "peace churches" including the Mennonites and their ultraconservative offspring the Amish. The basing of Anabaptist theology and practice on a literal approach to the Bible, especially on the direct commands of Jesus, created for Protestantism its first authentic sect in the sociological sense. Sects are essentially protest groups of strict constructionists who withdraw from the established churches and reject the common culture of their age, which they refer to as the "world." Because "worldly" fashions, customs, and values are viewed as dangerous, even sinful, sectarians delimit their contacts with the world as much as possible, setting up boundaries, such as plain costume, that serve to differentiate them from worldly church people.

Because of their obedience to what they considered the strict commands of the New Testament church, Anabaptists opposed war, military service, the swearing of oaths, and participation in government. In places like Switzerland, this rejection of the community values made them unwelcome, since the fabric of society was based on these values. Persecution drove them to more hospitable states, for instance the Palatinate of the Rhine. Palatine toleration was, however, not complete, for although Anabaptists were permitted to worship freely, they were not allowed until the nineteenth century to erect meetinghouses. They were in fact second-class citizens, and the government put a *numerus clausus* on them, which limited their expansion in Germany. Hence the migration to North America.

The Mennonites. The Mennonites, as the main or evangelical branch of the Anabaptist movement came to be called, have their oldest roots in Switzerland, where they arose as dissenters from the Zwinglian state-church reformation (after the Swiss religious reformer Huldrych Zwingli) in Zurich. The second source is Holland, where Menno Simons renounced Catholicism in 1536 and began his restorationist church based on the New Testament. Independent Anabaptist leaders of various theological mixes arose also in Germany and Austria. The mainstream of the movement gradually took the name Mennonites, although the original name in Holland was *Doopsgezinde* (Baptists) and in Switzerland and Germany *Wiedertäufer* (Anabaptists) or simply *Täufer* (Baptists). However, the group favored the name Brethren, as in Swiss Brethren, Hutterian Brethren, and other similar names.

As with Puritanism, the Anabaptist movement produced a spectrum of variants. These included spiritual Anabaptists such as Hans Denck, Communitarian Anabaptists (Hutterites) who held everything in common on the model of the primitive church in Acts 4:32, the militant millenarian Anabaptists of Münster, and other positions. The main trunk of the movement was pacifist rather than militant, evangelical, and rooted in a literal understanding of the Gospels and the ethical commands of the New Testament. It was also noncommunitarian, accepting private property but linking participant families in a disciplined community that exercised rigid control over both manners and morals.

The Anabaptist map of Europe was enlarged through the migration of the Swiss Brethren into Germany, France, and Holland; of the Hutterites from Czechoslovakia to Russia and elsewhere; of the Dutch Mennonites to North Germany, Denmark, and Russia; and of additional Mennonite groups to ethnic German enclaves in Poland, Russia, and the Balkans. All of these diverse settlements eventually sent immigrants to North America, making American Mennonite history a complex affair.

The first Mennonites to make permanent settlement in the New World were among those who arrived in Germantown (now part of Philadelphia) from Krefeld on the Lower Rhine in 1683. The majority of the original thirteen families were Quakers, some of them converts from Mennonitism. There were, however, a few Mennonites as such in the first group, and many who came over later. Germantown thus eventually developed a Mennonite congregation, the first permanent one in North America.

North American Mennonite groups stem for the most part from three separate migrations: the colonial Mennonite migration that produced the Pennsylvania German Mennonite and Amish groups; after the Napoleonic Wars, the Amish Mennonites from Alsace, Hessia, and Bavaria, who settled for the most part in the Midwest and Canada; and the Russian-German Mennonites who emigrated in the years 1874 to 1880.

Of the nineteenth-century Amish emigrants from Europe, no more than 20 percent remained Old Order, among them the Ontario Amish and the Swiss Amish of Indiana. The majority of the emigrants, already acculturated in part to Mennonite patterns in Europe, identified with the Mennonites here.

The largest Mennonite body in the United

States today is the Mennonite Church (90,000 members in 1986), formerly called the Old Mennonites. From this main trunk, made up of colonial emigrant stock, various schismatic groups arose. These include, among others, the conservative New or Reformed Mennonites, also known as Herrites, founded in Lancaster County, Pennsylvania, in 1812; the River Brethren or Brethren in Christ, who split in Lancaster County in the eighteenth century; the Funkites, a temporary schism in eastern Pennsylvania during and after the Revolution, who split over the question of paying war taxes; the Eastern District of the General Conference Mennonites, founded in 1847 by John H. Oberholtzer in eastern Pennsylvania; the Evangelical Mennonites, later called Mennonite Brethren in Christ and still later the United Missionary Church, founded in eastern Pennsylvania, Indiana, and elsewhere in the 1850s; and the Old Order Mennonites, who split off at various times from the 1870s to the 1930s.

The Old Order Mennonites are divided into the Wislerites, a schism of 1872 in Indiana opposing the innovations that were entering church work at the time (Sunday schools, protracted meetings, four-part singing, and English preaching). A similar schism arose among the Old Order in southeastern Pennsylvania in the 1930s over the question of the use of automobiles. Bishop Joseph Wenger opposed the auto, and his Wengerites still travel about like the Amish, by horse-drawn transportation. Bishop Moses Horning allowed the use of automobiles, if they were black and without "frivolous" trim. This group is called today either the Horning Mennonites or the "Black Bumper" Mennonites.

The Russian Mennonite migration of 1874 to 1880 brought new German-language religious groups to the United States and Canada. The migration was prompted by the new laws revoking the exemption from military service and other privileges extended to the first settlers by Catherine the Great and by the stepping up of the Russification process through schools and other means. Russian Mennonites, who represented both the Dutch–North German and the Swiss–South German varieties of Anabaptism, had while in Russia split into several subgroups, all of which were transplanted to North America. The largest group in Russia, the "Church Mennonites," affiliated here with the General Conference Mennonite Church of North America. Other groups included the Mennonite Brethren Church (1860), influenced by Moravianism and Lutheran Pietism; the Kleine Gemeinde (1814), an austere group that frowned on cardplaying, smoking, drinking, higher education, musical instruments, mission work, even laughter and joking by children; and the Krimmer Mennonite Brethren (1869) from the Crimea.

The most conservative element among the Russian Mennonites founded the Old Colony Mennonites. They are ultraconservative, even more conservative in a sense than the Old Order Amish. Among their main goals is the point-by-point preservation of their way of life, including village structure, language, clothing, material culture, and customs, all of which are given religious sanction. When threatened in Canada by the government's compulsory education program, they migrated to Mexico from 1922 to 1926, purchasing over 250,000 acres in the provinces of Chihuahua and Durango. Some of the Kleine Gemeinde also settled in Mexico at the same time, and others of the Old Colony went on to Paraguay in 1948. Since then some Old Colony groups have returned to Canada.

The Mennonite Church has spread into many areas of the United States and several provinces of Canada. Although in some areas, such as southeastern Pennsylvania, it has preserved in varying degrees sectarian elements like plain costume, it provides a classic example of the transition from the sect type of Protestantism to the church type, moving through what J. Milton Yinger and other sociologists call the "sect cycle." Hence, it has moved from the German language to the English language of the surrounding American culture; from a lay ministry chosen by lot to a salaried, seminary-educated ministry; from plain meetinghouses to church-like structures decorated with crosses and towers; and from a simple unitary congregational division into men's and women's sides to a relatively complete duplication of the organizational spectrum of the average American Protestant congregation, with Sunday schools, youth groups, women's groups, and other classifications. When the main body modernized or acculturated in these ways, the Old Order groups retained the older ways.

Like the earlier Anabaptist theology, the theology of the Mennonite Church is Bible-oriented and Christ-centered. Anabaptist concepts of peacemaking, peaceful living, charity to one's neighbors, and a strong sense of *Gemeinschaft,* or community, mark the contemporary church programs. The strong current of revivalism and missionary zeal from the Anglo-American church world has redirected the community goals of American Mennonites, sending their young people into many corners of the world as missionaries, teachers, and agricultural, technical, and medical consultants. The Mennonite Central Committee, founded in 1920 and modeled in part on the American Friends Service Committee of 1917, supervises this practical mission in over forty-five countries. A strong foreign mission program as well as home missions among university students, Hispanics, blacks, and other American minorities is creating a new pluralistic image for the church, in part replacing its longtime limitation of ethnic identity to German, Swiss, and Holland Dutch roots.

The twentieth century has produced a strong sense of denominational loyalty and new waves of Mennonite historiography. Historical centers and archives have been organized at Mennonite colleges over the nation, beginning with Goshen College in Indiana, whose collections on Anabaptist-Mennonite history are the most extensive in the world. The influence of such leaders as Harold S. Bender in analyzing what was unique about the Anabaptist message gave direction to whole generations of younger scholars. Two model contributions that are outgrowths of his historical vision are the *Mennonite Quarterly Review,* founded in 1927, and the four-volume *Mennonite Encyclopedia* (1955–1959), now being augmented by a fifth volume. This historical awareness, combined with the new Mennonite evangelism and practical aid to the Third World, has put the Mennonites into a strong position of advancement in the United States and Canada.

The Amish. Those Anabaptists who followed Jacob Ammann, a preacher from Canton Bern, Switzerland, in his differences with the main body of the Swiss, Alsatian, and Palatine Anabaptists are known as the Amish. The division took place in Europe from 1693 on, and Amish families began emigrating to America in the 1730s. They settled first in Bern Township (in what is now Berks County), whence they spread to other Pennsylvania counties and eventually into many states. In most cases their settlements were among or contiguous to those of the Mennonites and other plain sectarians, making up a kind of larger plain community. In Lancaster County, Pennsylvania, there are today at least a dozen plain sects settled together, all with distinct plain costumes. This is one reason why Lancaster County has become a major tourist attraction in the East, with more living folk costumes than any single area of Europe. Furthermore, these costumes are worn every day, not just for holidays, as is sometimes the case in European costume areas.

The Amish are divided principally into ultraconservative and moderate groups. The ultraconservatives are called Old Order Amish, since they hold on to the older ways of practicing their religion that were given up by the progressives. Hence the Old Order retains horse-drawn transportation and farm implements, except in some districts where the bishops have decided in favor of the use of tractors in the field. They have retained an extremely plain costume that differentiates them not only from worldly people but also from other plainly dressed sectarians. They also retain the old European Anabaptist congregational organization. There are no meetinghouses, Sunday schools, or missionary organizations—in fact, no mission to the outside world at all. Their lengthy worship services are for the community alone, which is God's holy church. The preaching and singing are in German. The services are held every two weeks, in a different farmhouse of the district, in rotation. There were some 34,000 members in 1986.

Like the Old Order Mennonites, the Amish retain a prerevivalist morality, which permits the use of tobacco, a traditional moderate use of liquor, and dancing on the part of the young people. Amish dances are barn dances similar to the "play parties" of nineteenth-century evangelical Americans. The "order" (*Ordnung*) is what the Amishman follows in the arrangement of his life and life-style. If he transgresses, he goes under ecclesiastical ban, called the *Meidung,* or shunning, until through penitence he returns to the fold. So strict is the process that a dissident Amishman has to be shunned not only by church and business associates but also by his wife and family (he cannot even eat at the same table with them). Shunning was the principal point of contention between the Amish party and the other Anabaptists at the time of their origin and is still placed in full operation when required. Being on the receiving end of such a religious boycott can be, to say the least, extremely trying. Hence, beginning with the 1860s, there have been legal cases in which the person shunned has sued the church in the state courts, and in some cases won his point.

In the twentieth century some of the Amish wished to modernize their life-style more thoroughly than most bishops were willing to permit. A new type of Amish, called Church Amish from the fact that they build meetinghouses rather than worshiping in homes, or Beachy Amish from their principal founder, Moses Beachy, now exists side by side with the Old Order. They wear trimmed beards and a modified plain costume, and are permitted to drive automobiles and tractors, and use electricity.

For purposes of worship and discipline the Amish population is divided into congregations called "church districts." These contain twenty-five to thirty-five families and three or four leaders chosen by lot and set apart for ministry of various sorts. These are true lay preachers who support themselves. The types of ministry are three: bishops (*völlige Diener;* literally, servants with full power), preachers (*Diener zum Buch;* literally, servants of the book), and deacons (*Armen-Diener,* literally, servants of the poor). When problems over innovations present themselves in the community, the bishop must decide which way the church must go. Where there is disagreement, schism and separate organizations result, as has frequently happened in Amish history.

Among the principal Amish settlements in the United States are Lancaster, Chester, Mifflin, and Somerset counties in Pennsylvania; Holmes County, Ohio; Elkhart and Lagrange counties, Indiana; and Johnson County, Iowa. Approximately 75 percent of the Amish in fact live in three states: Pennsylvania, Ohio, and Indiana. There are also Amish settlements in Ontario. Most of these were formed by migration not from Pennsylvania, as in the case of the Ontario Mennonites, but rather by direct emigration from Germany in 1824 and later.

The most conservative of all Old Order Amish groups is the so-called Nebraska Amish sect in Mifflin County, Pennsylvania. Their dress is the oldest Amish costume still worn in America. For example, the Nebraska women never adopted the plain bonnet when it entered the sectarian world in the early 1800s. Instead they still wear the earlier "flat hat" of the mid-eighteenth century. Also, they refuse to paint their houses and

barns, which makes them an exception to the rest of the Amish world, where neatly painted farm buildings are the rule. The reasons for this appear to be cultural rather than economic, and may indeed reflect the fact that in Canton Bern, Switzerland, where most of the Amish families originated, farm buildings are generally unpainted.

Another Bernese custom still practiced by the Old Order Amish in America is the erection of two houses on the same farm, one of them called in Pennsylvania German the *Grossdaadihaus,* or Grandfather House. (The Swiss word is *Stöckli.*) The Amish have large families and it is customary for fathers to provide farms for their sons when they marry. The daughters are provided for by their husband's families. When the youngest son marries, the parents turn over the farm to him and move into the Grandfather House. This "retirement" (in name only) keeps the aging parents near their children and grandchildren, but in an independent position. For this and other reasons the Amish do not participate in the Social Security system, since they take care of their own families.

The Amish community is the ultimate resource when an individual or family is in need of help. The system of mutual aid grows out of the Anabaptist concept of community as an extended spiritual family where all are brothers and sisters. The most spectacular illustration of Amish mutual aid is what happens when an Amishman's barn burns. The entire community gathers, the men to erect a new barn—in some cases in a single day—while the women prepare and serve copious farm meals. The Amish reject financial insurance schemes as worldly, but continue to practice their own type of community-based insurance.

The conservative, almost archaic culture of the Old Order Amish, and their closed character as an endogamous group, has made them favorite subjects for research by sociologists, anthropologists, and medical historians. The latter, centered at the Johns Hopkins Medical School, have been able to trace genetic disease patterns through Amish genealogy. Among the recessive genetic ailments identified in Amish families are hemophilia, six-fingered dwarfism, and phenylketonuria, a rare type of anemia.

But Amish culture is not static. Although some Americans view them as "contemporary ancestors,'' preserving as they do so much of our earlier rural culture, the Amish have subtly changed through the generations. While many examples of cultural lag can be demonstrated in Amish culture, in some ways they are as modern as their neighbors. For example, while the Amish forbid the use of electricity, their farmhouse kitchens can be as modern as any electric kitchen through the permitted use of bottled gas. There is obviously an Amish resilience in dealing with what seems to the outsider an unyielding body of custom, which finds practical and permitted solutions. Nor does the conservative nature of Amish society make Amish culture derivative to the total exclusion of creativity. In recent decades the museum world's focus on Amish quilts has resulted in a new healthy respect for the Amish aesthetic.

Like other Puritan and plain groups the Amish forbid art for art's sake—that is, public art or art for display—but accept certain permitted forms of artistic expression. Such permitted forms include fraktur Bible records and quilts, both of which are obviously functional. Amish quilts, however, often use large blocks of dissonant colors (greens and purples, for example), forming an innovation in the world of American quilting that has been likened to the more abstract forms in the contemporary art world. This sensational Amish venture into the world of art was of course unintentional. Had Amish women planned anything of the kind, quilting itself would undoubtedly have been forbidden by the bishops, as catering to pride, worldliness, and frivolity.

Most important of all, perhaps, the Amish are now increasingly seen as representatives of a long tradition of respect for agriculture and the natural environment, with something to teach their contemporaries. And as nonviolent rebels against some of the standards of American society, they have proved their point in the Supreme Court on the questions of Amish schools and nonparticipation in Social Security. Like other sectarians at their best in Western civilization, they continue to believe in and insist on the right to be different.

The Church of the Brethren. The third in the triumvirate of the American-German "peace churches" was founded in 1708 in Wittgenstein, Germany, by a Reformed Pietist named Alexander Mack, Sr. The principality of Wittgenstein in Westphalia was in the eighteenth century a major refuge center for all sorts of Pietists and mystics. It became, for example, the continental center for the Philadelphian Society, founded by the English mystic Jane Leade. The Philadelphians, who drew their name from the model church at Philadelphia in Revelation (3:7–13), were mystics, millennialists, and ecumenists. Their principal legacy was the Berleburg Bible, which appeared in eight folio volumes, 1728–1742. This was a fresh new literal translation of the Scriptures, edited by Johann Heinrich Haug, with numerous prefaces and copious annotations to show the mystical and spiritual sense of the text. It was directed to all Christian "parties" looking to the appearance of the "one holy and universal Christian Church, in which no divisions and religious controversies will ever be found again." The Berleburg Bible was a favorite among the Brethren, Mennonites, and communitarian groups of colonial America.

In 1708 Mack and his radical Pietist followers separated from the established churches, rebaptizing each other as adults, much as the first Anabaptist had done two centuries earlier. Migrating to Pennsylvania in 1719 and 1729, they settled in Germantown, where, like the Mennonites, they organized their first American congregation. They then spread to rural areas, settling alongside the Mennonites and Amish. Since as Pietists the Brethren were more evangelistic, they picked up from these many of their American members.

Like the Anabaptists, the Brethren believed that they were reestablishing the primitive church. Their theological world was shaped by the works of the radical Pietist Hochmann von Hochenau, the irenic church historian Gottfried Arnold, and the annotations on biblical theology as published in the Berleburg Bible. The congregational customs of the early Brethren reflected their understanding of the practice of the apostolic church. Hence foot-washing was a religious rite based on Christ's washing of the disciples' feet, the holy kiss was passed from brother to brother and from sister to sister, and the communion service was preceded by a congregational "love feast" based on the early Christian agape. Most radical was their practice of adult baptism. Based on Arnold's description of primitive baptizings, the Brethren practiced what they called "trine immersion," dipping the candidate three times face forward into a running stream of water. Because of their emphasis upon baptism, they were often called in Pennsylvania and elsewhere Tunkers, Dunkers, or Dunkards, from the German word *tunken,* "to dip."

The best-known Dunker in colonial America was Christopher Sauer, Sr., an emigrant from Wittgenstein. Settling in Germantown, he established a press in 1731 whose cultural and political influence on the colonial Germans was immense. He became in a sense the spokesman for the German sectarians in their quest for political relevance. In 1743 he published the first European-language edition of the Bible in America, with a second edition in 1763 and a third in 1776. (The reason why no English edition of the Bible was printed in America until 1782 was that the English universities had a monopoly on the printing of the English Bible in the colonies.)

The Brethren world passed through the same conservative-progressive splits that affected Mennonites and Amish. In the Brethren case it was a three-way affair. The progressives founded the Brethren Church; the ultraconservatives withdrew to form the German Baptist Brethren, the Dunkard Brethren, and other plain groups; and the central body continued as the Church of the Brethren. Both the progressives and the moderates adopted seminaries, colleges, church journalism, the missionary movement, and other accoutrements of Anglo-American revivalism, but kept the pacifism and Bible-centered theology of the earlier generations. In some of the rural congregations a token plain dress has been retained, although today most Brethren, like most Mennonites of the larger bodies, dress like other Americans of their region and class.

Like the Mennonite Church and other branches of the Mennonite tradition in North America, the Church of the Brethren gradually accepted the need for educating its youth and its ministry. There are today six colleges operated by the Brethren: Juniata and Elizabethtown in Pennsylvania, Bridgewater in Virginia, Manchester in Indiana, McPherson in Kansas, and LaVerne in California. The seminary of the denomination is Bethany Biblical Seminary at Oak Brook, Illinois, in the metropolitan Chicago area.

As one of the "peace churches," the Church of the Brethren is officially opposed to military service, although it allows individual members to take up noncombatant and even full military service. The passage of the Selective Training and Service Act of 1940, allowing for conscientious objection to military service for the first time on a national basis in American history, led to the formation of the Brethren Service Committee, later the Brethren Service Commission, established in 1940 to support the denomination's C.O.'s, of which it furnished over 1,000 to Civilian Public Service. After the war the committee devoted its attention to relieving suffering in the world. The development here is similar to that of the American Friends Service Committee and the Mennonite Central Committee.

After World War II the Church of the Brethren reorganized its denominational structure. The congregation presided over by an "elder" remains the basic organizational unit. Congregations are grouped into districts, of which there are forty-nine in the United States and Canada. The national body is still the Annual Conference, first assembled as the Annual Meeting in 1742 (in reaction to Zinzendorf's attempt to Moravianize the colonial German denominations). This body is made up of delegates (elders) from each district and elected representatives from each congregation. The committees and boards, which had mediated the church's work on various fronts since the late nineteenth century, were replaced in 1947 by a General Brotherhood Board of twenty-five members, chosen by the Annual Conference, that can act as a unit but also divides itself into functional commissions. The publishing house of the denomination is located at Elgin, Illinois, and the official periodical is *The Gospel Messenger.* There were some 162,000 members in 1986.

In the twentieth century the Church of the Brethren has participated in the larger currents of American Protestantism, including the National Council of Churches, and has contributed leadership to various religious concerns. An example of such leadership is the University of Chicago professor and labor leader Kermit Eby, whose autobiography, *The God in You* (1954), is a personal commentary on the growth of his church from rural and conservative contexts to national significance.

The Schwenkfelders. A group found today only in Pennsylvania, the Schwenkfelders are the spiritual descendants of a sixteenth-century Protestant reformer named Kaspar Schwenkfeld von Ossig. A Silesian theologian of noble birth and aristocratic education, he developed, without organizing a separate sect, a free mystical Protestant system that dispensed with sacraments and other outward forms. Schwenkfeld's followers gradually organized an informal fellowship and preserved his writings in their communities. As a result of the stepped-up Counter-Reformation in the Austrian Empire, the Jesuits were sent into Silesia in 1726 to reconvert the Schwenkfelders, first by suasion and then by force. After an unsuccessful appeal to the emperor in Vienna, the Schwenkfelder families migrated to the estates of Nikolaus Ludwig, Count von Zinzendorf, in Saxony. From 1734 to 1737 they came to Pennsylvania, settling in parts of a four-county area north of Philadelphia.

Because of their experiential, nonsacramental view of religion, as well as their pacifism, they maintained a close relationship to the Quakers. When they began building meetinghouses, they adopted, as the Mennonites also did, the Quaker meetinghouse format; they also used the Quaker plain language when speaking English. In 1782, when they organized as a religious body, they took the name Society of Schwenkfelders.

During the nineteenth century they drew nearer to their Pennsylvania German neighbors of the church variety, particularly the Reformed. In 1878 they resumed the public administration of the sacraments on which Schwenkfeld had put a moratorium. They adopted a seminary-trained ministry, using the Hartford Theological Seminary in Connecticut, to which they contributed professors and administrators. In 1908 they took the official title Schwenkfelder Church.

Despite their small size (some 3,000 members in 1986), the Schwenkfelders have preserved a strong denominational identity. It was American Schwenkfelder scholars, notably Dr. Chester David Hartranft and Dr. Elmer E. S. Johnson, who initiated and carried through the *Corpus Schwenkfeldianorum* project to edit and publish Schwenkfeld's major writings. The work was done at Wolfenbüttel in Germany, and the nineteen volumes (published 1907–1961) offer a major contribution to Reformation history and theology. The Schwenkfelder Library at Pennsburg, Pennsylvania, contains unrivaled collections on denominational history, including much of the original correspondence that passed back and forth between Pennsylvania and Europe throughout the eighteenth century.

COMMUNITARIAN SECTS OF EUROPEAN ORIGIN

The appeal of communitarianism lies in its provision of an alternative family structure for those who wish to reject the nuclear family. This makes it in a sense a Protestant substitute for monasticism. The American communitarian organizations also provided equality of men and women, offering women an alternative to secular life and work. Not all of them rejected marriage. Some communities combined celibate brethren and sisters with groups of married couples with families. Others, like the Hutterites, were made up of only married couples who had adjusted to communal living patterns.

These sociological appeals were reinforced by elaborate theological systems based on mysticism, millennialism, and ethical reform. Leadership usually combined charisma, practicality, and innovative theology. In his classic book *The Communistic Societies of the United States* (1875), Charles Nordhoff came to the conclusion that of all American communities of this sort, the most successful in their operation were those of German origin. For most of these, Pennsylvania was the original center, from which they spread into other states.

The Moravian Brethren. Having arrived in America in the 1730s and 1740s, the Moravians settled first in Georgia and then in Pennsylvania. They were the spiritual offshoot of the pre-Reformation church of the Unitas Fratrum, founded in what is now Czechoslovakia in 1457. In their present form they were reorganized, or "renewed," by Count von Zinzendorf, one of Protestantism's key leaders in both Europe and America in the eighteenth century. A Lutheran who invited the Moravian exiles to his estates in Saxony, he founded Herrnhut in 1722, which became the world center of an expanding missionary church.

Zinzendorf's university education and his network of contacts on the highest levels of church and state in Europe, including Catholic, Pietist, and other church leaders, gave him the widest possible preparation for leadership. He advanced Protestantism through his ecumenical theology, which made him a pioneer in the ecumenical movement. His concern with Christian missions set him in the forefront of the Protestant missionary advance that began only in the eighteenth century. A third contribution of Zinzendorf and the Moravians is their influence on the conversion of John Wesley and through him on the Methodist organization.

The two centers of American Moravians are Bethlehem, Pennsylvania, founded by Zinzendorf himself in 1741, and Salem (now Winston-Salem), North Carolina, founded by Pennsylvania Moravians in 1753. The Moravians differed from the other Pennsylvania German groups in their insistence on planned towns centering around *Gemeinhaus* and school rather than dispersed farm settlements. (A *Gemeinhaus* was the congregational center, a large multipurpose building designed to house worship services and ministerial living quarters in the days before separate Moravian church buildings were erected.) Among the urban centers they founded were Nazareth, Emmaus, Lebanon, Lititz, Friedenshütten, and Gnadenhütten in Pennsylvania; Hope in New Jersey; Graceham in Maryland; Friedberg, Wachovia, and Salem in North Carolina; and Schönbrunn in Ohio.

These centers were founded as communitarian settlements, made up of married couples and families plus single brethren and sisters. As in all the early German churches and sects, there was a rigid division of the sexes in worship. Moravians carried this even further than the other groups. Their congregations were divided into "choirs," groups arranged according to age and sex. A religious or plain garb was worn as a badge of identity. Moravian women dressed exactly alike except for the color of their cap strings, which indicated the choir of which they were members. Thus the young girls wore red cap strings, the unmarried teenage girls pink, the married matrons blue, and the widows white.

In the Moravian towns in their early stages land ownership and economy were communal; in fact, the organization of Bethlehem into factories and farms and assigned labor was first called the Economy. Later the communal economy was relaxed, with private ownership replacing it. But for many generations the Moravian towns continued under a charter of ecclesiastical domination, which made it difficult for non-Moravians to participate.

The Moravians were radical Pietists, with strong emphasis upon the life and passion of Christ the Savior. In no Protestant group did such extreme devotion to the body of Christ develop as in the Moravian world. Three foci of their Christ cult appeared in the eighteenth century: the cult of the *Jesulein*, or Baby Jesus (an emphasis that made the celebration of Christmas a beloved festival); the cult of the "Blessed *Lämmlein*" or sacrificial Lamb; and the cult of the wounds of Christ. In a very real sense these outward expressions of Moravian piety were adaptations of Catholic popular spirituality into the Protestant world. In the 1750s these tendencies reached the saturation point in sentimental expression. John Wesley, whose debt to Moravianism he himself acknowledged, criticized their spirituality as "namby-pambical," with its affectionate diminutives such as "Lambkin" (*Lämmlein*), cautioning his Methodists to avoid the use of "fondling expressions" in connection with the Deity. By 1760 Zinzendorf's successor, Bishop August Spangenberg, had called the church to a less bizarre spirituality. Jacob John Sessler's *Communal Pietism Among Early American Moravians* (1933) is the most thorough introduction in English to these radical Pietist theological aberrations. But the Conquering Lamb bearing the Cross and Banner is today, as earlier, the symbol of the Moravian Church.

The Moravians were diligent record keepers, which makes them favorites of historians. Each Moravian community kept a *Gemeinde-Diarium*, or community journal, copies of which were forwarded to Bethlehem and eventually to Herrnhut. With their emphasis on conversion and the Protestant need for "saints" as role models, individuals were encouraged to write out their own *Lebensläufe*, or autobiographies, centering on their religious experience, which could be read with profit by others aspiring to holiness. These autobiographies exist by the thousands in all the American Moravian archives and have only now begun to be analyzed.

Zinzendorf's interest in Christian unity created in America in the 1740s a movement called the Congregation of God in the Spirit. Yearly gatherings were held in Pennsylvania to which came representatives from many of the German and some of the English groups. Zinzendorf believed in an overarching spiritual unity, which led him to send missionaries to "awaken" the "sleeping" Christians in other denominations, preaching the Moravian gospel of the *Lämmlein* and the *Jesulein*. This spiritual campaign was misunderstood, and an anti-Moravian reaction set in that led both to the demise of the ecumenical synods and to the stricter organization of the surrounding denominations. Zinzendorf's ecumenism has been more deeply appreciated in the twentieth century than in his own time.

When the Moravians' evangelism among sister denominations was rejected, they redirected their mission, focusing it thenceforth on the Native Americans. This Moravian mission resulted in the first widespread American Protestant interest in the Indian and his soul. The missionaries were also in a sense primitive ethnographers in recording details of Indian life and language. The Moravians even followed some of the Indians from the middle colonies to Canada, and as such formed the vanguard of the Pennsylvania German migration to Ontario after the Revolution.

The Moravian contribution to early American culture was distinctive. In education they are credited with founding the earliest interracial school in the colonies as well as the first higher school for girls. The products of their mills and factories and potteries achieved wide recognition. Their town architecture was massive and professionally designed by Moravian architects, of whom the best known was Benjamin Henry Latrobe. The Moravian portraiture by Valentin Haidt and others provides a unique record of members as well as clergy of a colonial group. Portraiture was encouraged for the same reason as autobiography. Finally, they excelled in music —secular as well as sacred, instrumental as well as choral. This made Bethlehem and other Moravian centers in a sense musical capitals of the American colonies. The Early American Moravian Music Foundation at Winston-Salem is devoted to the study of Moravian music, much of which was composed in America.

American Moravians kept their ties with the German mother organization at Herrnhut even after the Revolution prompted many denominations to sever relations with Europe. In the nineteenth century Moravian settlements were established in Wisconsin and elsewhere in the Midwest, and Moravian missionary work was continued in various new places, including Alaska, although the church has never since the eighteenth century shown the growth it enjoyed in the time of Zinzendorf.

The Ephrata Community. A radical Pietist emigrant named Johann Conrad Beissel, from the

Neckar Valley near Heidelberg, was the founder of this community. Emigrating in 1720 to Pennsylvania, he lived for a time as a hermit and then founded, at Ephrata in Lancaster County, a double cloister, with both monks and nuns under his priorship. This system was similar to the later Shaker communities and, indeed, similar to the double monasteries of the Middle Ages, like those founded in England by Saint Gilbert of Sempringham and the Brigittines. Beissel's followers, who rejected the first-day sabbath and worshiped on the seventh day, were known as Seventh-Day Baptists. Their habit was white and modeled on that of the Capuchins.

Beissel's mystical Pietism and undoubted charisma attracted numerous converts, some of them highly educated and talented, who made the community a beehive of spirituality as well as practical concerns. For example, the cloister operated one of the most productive presses in the colonies, and manufactured its own paper for it.

One of the distinguished converts to Ephrata was Johann Peter Miller, a Reformed pastor and graduate of the University of Heidelberg, who as Bruder Jabez became Beissel's successor in 1768. He maintained correspondence with leading Americans and Europeans, participated in scientific interests, and supervised the compilation of the *Chronicon Ephratense* (1786), a record of Beissel's career and the early development of the cloister.

Ephrata had branches in Virginia and at several places in Pennsylvania, notably Snow Hill in Franklin County. Beissel sent out evangelists to New Jersey, New York, and New England. There are many contemporary descriptions of the cloister and its activities, since in the colonial period Ephrata, like Bethlehem, was on the tourist circuit for all the European and American travelers who based their itineraries in Philadelphia.

After 1800 the membership declined. Descendants of the married "householders" maintained the congregation for about a century under the name German Seventh-Day Baptist Church. The cloister buildings at Ephrata are now preserved as an open-air museum by the Commonwealth of Pennsylvania.

The Harmonites. The Harmonites were disciples of a Swabian charismatic leader of peasant background, George Rapp, from a village in Württemberg not far from Stuttgart. A Lutheran, he became convinced that the state church of

Württemberg was in apostasy and he organized a group of villagers in his area in the 1780s who were arrested as separatists from the established church. Rapp finally solved the problem by emigration to the United States from 1803 to 1805, establishing the communitarian settlement of Harmony, not far from Pittsburgh. When Harmony had become successful from its farm produce and manufactures, he sold it and moved west to New Harmony, along the Wabash River on the border of Illinois and Indiana. There his hardworking German emigrants again created an economic success. In 1825 he sold that town and its lands to Robert Owen, the socialist reformer, and moved back to Pennsylvania to found his permanent settlement, Economy, on the Ohio River north of Pittsburgh.

Each of these moves was justified by elaborate theological reasoning based on mystical interpretations of the Book of Revelation. The Harmonites were millennialists, with a view of the future that derived from the teachings of Jacob Boehme in the seventeenth century and the "Philadelphian" views of the Berleburg Bible in the eighteenth century. Both the Church at Philadelphia (Revelation 3) and the Woman in the Wilderness (Revelation 3) were symbols of the purified Protestantism represented in George Rapp's Harmony Society. To Rapp, as to many other visionaries of the time, the Napoleonic Wars meant that the end was near. The superfluous and useless elements in the old church would be destroyed, but the inner calm of Rapp's "spiritual virgins" would enable his new church to weather the storms. "Harmony," the spiritual church of the elect, called from the four corners of the earth, would triumph over "Babylon," the world, which is disharmony. And of course Pennsylvania's earthly "Economy" was seen as the terrestrial counterpart of the divine and celestial "Oekonomie," the spiritual housekeeping of the universe. The intense longing of the Harmonites for the coming of the Divine Bridegroom is expressed by their prophet, who in a sermon in 1838 called out, "Come! Behold, Thy children are ready, the lamps are prepared."

Like most such movements, the Harmonites believed that they were restoring the true, apostolic church. Unlike some of the Anabaptist groups, they felt that government was necessary and even good, although they refused to take oaths, send their children to state schools, or to serve in military forces.

Several offshoots arose out of Harmonite inspiration. Among these were Dr. P. F. C. Haller's Blooming Grove Community in central Pennsylvania and the Bethel Community in Missouri, later to become the Aurora Community in Oregon. The founder of both Bethel and Aurora was Wilhelm Keil, a Prussian emigrant who had for a time been a German Methodist and later came under Harmonite influence.

In the 1830s the Harmonites were divided and deeply disturbed by a European impostor who called himself the Count de Leon. He used the religious title Lion of Judah, "the anointed of God of the stem of Judah of the root of David." He appeared among them as an emissary announcing the imminent return of Christ and the establishment of the Kingdom. His message appealed to the dissenting elements at Economy, who with their new prophet founded the New Philadelphia Congregation at Philippsburg, later renamed Löwenburg for the Lion of Judah.

Dr. Karl J. R. Arndt's series of documentary volumes on Harmonite history, providing translations of hundreds of key German documents, is the best introduction to the movement and can serve as a model for the study of similar groups. The Harmonite Archive has recently been moved from Economy to the Pennsylvania State Archives at Harrisburg. The town of Old Economy, with its South German architecture and atmosphere, is preserved as a museum by the Pennsylvania Historical and Museum Commission.

The Hutterites. Viewed by some historians as the most successful Christian communal group in the United States, the Hutterites are found in the plains states and western Canada, where they own large tracts of land and European-style villages in common. They are disciples of Jacob Hutter, a sixteenth-century Tyrolese Anabaptist who attracted followers from Austria, Germany, and Switzerland. Organized in Moravia in 1528, they were driven out at the time of the Counter-Reformation and fled to Slovakia, Hungary, Romania, and, in 1770, to the Ukraine. Following the revocation of their exemption from Russian military service, they made a final migration in the 1870s to North America. The largest Christian communal group in the nation (some 4,000 members in 1986), they live today in North and South Dakota, Montana, Manitoba, Saskatchewan, and Alberta.

Hutterite communities or "colonies," as they

are called, are organized as groups of nuclear families who own and till land in common. They eat together and work together, but have private living quarters. As with the Amish, the community is sacred and the individual surrenders his will to its direction. The German language is the official and liturgical language of the group. The members wear a plain costume, but a certain amount of modernization has entered their lives. Their agriculture, for example, is mechanized to a higher degree than is that of the Amish.

Like other communitarians, Hutterites not only engaged in farming but excelled in certain crafts. In Czechoslovakia, for example, they developed majolica pottery manufacture. Even the descendants of the Czechoslovakian Hutterites who were reconverted to Catholicism in the Counter-Reformation, the so-called Habaner, continued the production of majolica.

Living apart from official society as they did, cut off in Europe by censorship from the media of print, the Hutterites preserved manuscript hymnals, chronicles, and other historical works. Many of the latter have been published for the first time in this century and have proved of immense use to historians and sociologists of religion.

A modern movement related to and for a time an affiliate of the Hutterites is the Society of Brothers, founded in 1922 by Eberhard Arnold in Germany. Also known as the Bruderhof movement and the Hutterian Society of Brothers, it is devoted to brotherhood and communal living. Communities exist in Connecticut, Pennsylvania, and New York, as well as in England. Headquarters are in Rifton, New York, where they operate the Plough Publishing House.

The Amana Community. The Amana Community in Iowa had its roots in the Inspirationist movement in Europe, which arose in the Huguenot tradition in the aftermath of the revocation of the Edict of Nantes in 1685. Cut off from their sanctuaries and exiled from their homeland, some elements among the Huguenot population shifted their spiritual focus to trances, trance preaching, prophecy, and similar phenomena. They migrated to Germany and Switzerland, attracting many converts and influencing, among others, Conrad Beissel, founder of the Ephrata Community. Their missionary program in England, initiated in 1706 by the so-called French Prophets, a group of charismatic evangelists, left

its mark on English sectarianism and helped to produce the Shaker movement. Similar evangelists missionized in the Rhineland and Switzerland at the same time, producing the Inspirationists. The founders of the Amana group were Inspirationists in the Rhineland, already seen as a fertile seedbed of Pietistic separation from the Reformation churches.

Persecuted as separatists in Germany, the group emigrated in 1842 to near Buffalo, New York, where they organized the Ebenezer Society. Moving to Iowa from 1855 to 1859, they incorporated there under the name Amana Society. The name Amana derives from the Song of Solomon 4:8.

Amana's founders and their successors were known as "instruments" of God's will, whose preaching formed a continuing revelation. Their technique of trance preaching is a phenomenon found for various reasons in many religious groups in Europe and America. From Amana the practice of preaching while in a trance state spread to the nearby Amish settlements in Johnson County, Iowa, resulting in a schismatic Amish group that for a time operated in Iowa, Illinois, Pennsylvania, and elsewhere.

Like other similar groups, Amana morality was strict, with enforced plainness in dress, limitations on amusements, and a ban on pictures and photographs. The organization of the villages was democratic, with thirteen elected trustees, who in turn elected a president. The elders met in each village to discuss the work schedule. Organized in several villages, each with its own schoolhouse, the Amana Society developed community industries, as did similar groups, to supply its own needs and to support itself. Among these were woolen mills, gristmills, sawmills, printing shops, and knitting mills. Products of the cloth mills, such as gloves and stockings, were exported to the "world."

In 1932 the community voted to convert its economic operations into a joint-stock corporation, in which all members became stockholders. This cooperative has the legal title Amana Society, which holds all real property. Church matters are managed by the Amana Church Society, governed by elders elected by the community. Agriculture (food production and the woolen industry) continued as the major occupation of the residents of the seven Amana villages, although the society is today known best as the producer of the Amana freezers and other home appliances.

HYBRID AMERICAN-GERMAN GROUPS UNITING PIETISM AND ANGLO-AMERICAN REVIVALISM

Most German religious groups in colonial America had brought with them some form of Pietism. Pietism is a product of the seventeenth century, growing out of both the Lutheran and Reformed traditions, linking with Puritanism in England, and eventually producing a spectrum of movements from those within the churches to radical Pietists who separated from them. The main focus of Pietist theology was on Christ the Savior, with conversion and holy living the goal for the individual. This emphasis on conversion —required even for the ministry—broke up the earlier Protestant communities by the formation within the churches of sectlike conventicles for Bible study and prayer, or by the setting up of separatist sects. These withdrew completely from the churches to form spiritual microcosms, countercultures in fact, to oppose both the "dead" churches and the "sinful" world in which they operated. The activistic dynamism of Halle (the center of Lutheran pietism) and Herrnhut (the Moravian center) led to reforms in society based on the founding of hospitals, orphanages, and schools. It led also, through its goal of converting every soul in the world to Christ, to the great Protestant missionary awakening of the eighteenth century and helped to produce both Evangelicalism and Methodism in the British Isles. Certainly Pietism was one of the most pervasive European influences upon American religion throughout the eighteenth and nineteenth centuries, and judging from the recent "born again" movement its influence is still in operation here.

Revivalism, a sharpened form of Pietism, was one of the major systems of organizing Protestant evangelism in the world of Anglo-American religion. It systematized the conversion process and brought it to the masses through revival meetings, protracted meetings, rural camp meetings, urban tent meetings, and other forms of mass evangelism. The movement bears the marks of both Pietism and Evangelicalism in Europe but developed fully on this side of the Atlantic. Beginning in the eighteenth century it invaded most American denominations, capturing some completely—Methodism for example —and dividing others into pro- and antirevivalist parties, some of which split off into separate denominations.

When revivalism invaded the Pennsylvania German region and other American-German settlements, new American forms of religion came into being. What resulted was a union of residual Pietist elements in the German churches and sects with the revivalist system. This merging of traditions was to affect most of the American-German groups in the eighteenth and nineteenth centuries, and the effects are still with us today. Even the Lutherans and Reformed, the major German Protestant traditions in the country, were sharply divided over adherence to the "new" revival system of entering the church via conversion versus the "old" catechetical system of growing up within the church and entering it through confirmation. With the revival system, once it was accepted, came also what can be called the revivalist "package deal" of new church methods. These included Sunday schools; missionary societies; men's, women's, and children's organizations; church journalism; colleges and seminaries; and—difficult sometimes for Germans as well as Anglo-Americans— the temperance movement.

Some American church historians, such as William Warren Sweet and William G. McLoughlin, Jr., have divided the history of revivalism into four major revival periods, of which the first two, the Colonial or First Great Awakening (ca. 1725–1750) and the Second Great Awakening (ca. 1795–1830), are most relevant here. The First Great Awakening, in which the Moravians participated, began to stir up the German population of Pennsylvania and elsewhere. Continuing through the Second Great Awakening, groups were organized here and there, combining Pietist and revivalist elements, that finally developed into separate denominations. Let us look at these in the order of their appearance.

The Church of the United Brethren in Christ. The roots of this church can be traced back to 1767, to the uniting of forces on the part of two evangelists who recognized each other as "brethren." These were the Mennonite preacher Martin Boehm, who had been awakened in 1761 by the "New Lights" in Virginia, and Philip William Otterbein, a Reformed minister who had emigrated in 1752 and represented German churchly Pietism of the Reformed variety. The work of these two leaders led to the establishment of German congregations over a wide area of Pennsylvania and Maryland.

By the time the United Brethren came to be fully organized, in 1789, another tributary stream had influenced them, Anglo-American Methodism. The United Brethren theology combined the Pietist and Methodist doctrines of conversion and free grace. The new group was Arminian and aggressively evangelistic, low church liturgically, and, like Methodism, a religion of joyous song celebrating the conversion experience. The United Brethren system was, like Methodism, connectional, with bishops, circuits, conferences, and camp meetings. The language in the early stages was German, and German evangelism spread the church to Ohio and other states in the Midwest.

The United Brethren suffered the same conservative-progressive divisions that have been noted in connection with the Mennonites. In the Civil War period a small schism arose in southeastern Pennsylvania that produced the United Christian Church. This group, also known as Hoffmanites from their founder, George W. Hoffman, was plain in dress, pacifist, and opposed to higher education. A larger split in 1889 resulted in the continuation of the main body (Church of the United Brethren in Christ) and the establishment of a rival smaller group called the United Brethren in Christ (Old Constitution). The major point at issue was membership in secret societies, including Freemasonry, a subject that other denominations also were debating at the time. In this case the Old Constitution group opposed while the larger body permitted such membership.

The ecumenical movement has led the United Brethren into mergers with similar groups in this century. In 1946, recognizing the common origins they shared with the Evangelical Church (see below), the United Brethren entered into organic union with them as the Evangelical United Brethren Church. In 1968 this union denomination joined with the Methodist church to form what is today the United Methodist Church.

Evangelical Association. A similar group that grew from the same roots as the United Brethren was the Evangelical Association, founded in Pennsylvania in 1800. The product of the conversion of a Pennsylvania German named Jacob Albright, the association likewise combined Pietism with the Methodist system, all in a German-language framework. Even closer to Methodism than the United Brethren, the Evangelicals were often called German Methodists in Pennsylvania. Spreading by revivals and camp meetings into many states, they evangelized the Pennsylvania German communities in both Pennsylvania and the Midwest and also converted newly arrived German emigrants everywhere.

Like Methodists, the Evangelicals passed through the sect cycle to denominational status, with seminary education for the ministry and colleges—like Albright College, for example—for the laity. An almost complete transfer to the English language was made in the twentieth century, although there are still congregations where the old camp meeting spirituals or "choruses" are on occasion sung in German, Pennsylvania German, or a mixture of the two.

Before the Civil War the American Evangelicals had sent missionaries to Germany. There, like both the British and American Methodists, they set up conferences, publishing houses, hospitals, homes, and other institutions. In 1863 they founded a Sunday school in Stuttgart on the American plan, which was widely copied by the state churches. The Evangelical Seminary at Reutlingen near Stuttgart is still flourishing.

In the 1890s a bitter civil war within the Evangelical Association led to a disastrous split. This was the result of a power struggle between rival bishops and of tension between the Pennsylvania German and the European German elements in the church. In 1894 the larger body continued as the Evangelical Association, while the smaller body became the United Evangelical Church. In 1922, when the two agreed to reunite into the Evangelical Church, a small but significant body of clergy and congregations preferred to remain independent, like the "Wee Frees" in Scotland (who remained out of the reunion of the Free Churches of Scotland in 1900). They are still operating as the Evangelical Congregational Church, with some 34,000 members as of 1986. The headquarters is at their seminary in Myerstown, Pennsylvania. And as stated above, the Evangelical Church became part of the Evangelical United Brethren Church in 1946 and since

1968 has been included within the United Methodist Church.

The Church of God. A third product of the union of Pennsylvania German Pietism with Anglo-American revivalism is the Church of God, organized in 1830. The founder was John Winebrenner, Reformed pastor at Harrisburg, Pennsylvania, whose revivalist tendencies led to his expulsion from the German Reformed Church in 1825. While his revival and camp meeting methods show congruence with those of the Methodist circuit riders, he also seems to have absorbed the tendencies of the Church of Christ and the Disciples of Christ. Like the Disciples of Christ and Church of Christ of the South and Midwest, he opposed nonbiblical titles and customs. Hence he called his denomination the Church (or Churches) of God; conferences he renamed "elderships"; and individual church buildings he insisted on calling "bethels." He also popularized the rite of foot-washing, probably borrowed from the Brethren, and wrote hymns in its defense.

This group, often called Winebrennerians, from its founder, also spread to the Midwest and other areas of the United States. For a time it operated a "German eldership" for the Pennsylvania German membership. Now called the Churches of God, General Conferences, it had approximately 35,000 members in 1986. Its national center and archives are at Findlay College and Winebrenner Theological Seminary at Findlay, Ohio.

The Church of God (Anderson, Indiana), a Holiness offshoot of Winebrenner's Church of God, is now much larger than the parent body (185,000 members in 1986). It was founded in 1880 by a Pennsylvania German Winebrennerian named Daniel Sidney Warner. Its headquarters is at Anderson College and School of Theology.

GERMAN-LANGUAGE WINGS OF ANGLO-AMERICAN CHURCHES

In addition to the independent German-language denominations that arose in the middle states as a result of the national awakenings, several of the larger Anglo-American denominations and some smaller movements conducted German-language evangelism during the nineteenth and twentieth centuries.

This movement was rooted in part in Anglo-American concern over the rising tide of emigration from Germany after the revolutions of 1830 and 1848. Not only were there increasing numbers of German Roman Catholics, which sparked the nativist fear of a Catholic "takeover" in the Midwest and an erosion of democratic society, but almost equally feared were the hundreds of thousands of German Protestant emigrants. These brought with them a "new" Continental morality that conflicted directly with the "old" Puritan mores of the Anglo-American churches and the puritanized American-German denominations of the colonial immigration. Two examples of conflicts are the tensions over the "continental Sunday" vs. the "Puritan sabbath" and the immigrant drinking patterns vs. the American temperance movement.

The answer of the American Protestant churches already on the scene seemed to be clear—convert the immigrant, whether Catholic or Protestant—to an American form of Protestantism; that is, transform him into an American Protestant. The home mission program of the "Evangelical Empire"—for example, such organizations as the American Sunday School Union (1824), the American Tract Society (1825), and the American Home Missionary Society (1826)—all developed interest in German evangelism, published German tracts for the immigrants, and sent evangelists and colporteurs to convert the immigrants. The leading denominations of the Northeast and middle states, the Congregationalists and Presbyterians, whose cooperation largely led to this nationwide evangelistic thrust, themselves later developed German-language programs in the eastern cities, the Midwest, and the plains states.

The Northern Baptist denomination also operated a German home missionary movement, the most important product of which for American church history was Walter Rauschenbusch, one of the initiators and shapers of Social Gospel theology.

German Methodists. The most significant of all the German-language missions was that initiated by the Methodist Episcopal Church. This was the result of the conversion to Methodism, at a Pennsylvania camp meeting, of Wilhelm Nast. Nast, scion of a Stuttgart family of Lutheran ministers, was himself destined for the ministry. At the University of Tübingen, where he roomed with David Friedrich Strauss, author of a rationalistic life of Jesus, he discovered biblical criticism and gave up his plans for the ministry. He immigrated to the United States in 1828, taught for a while at West Point, flirted with Universalism, and finally in the early 1830s was converted to Methodism and called to preach.

With Cincinnati as his base, Nast began his mission among the German immigrants. He was joined in this work by another convert, Adam Miller, an ex-Amishman of Pennsylvania German extraction. They converted others who began to preach. Nast was able in 1844 to organize the German missions into German districts under presiding elders. After the Civil War several German conferences were organized, beginning with the Central Conference. This was all an integral part of the Methodist Episcopal Church, which operated missions and congregations across the nation, all in the German language. For a time the German Methodists had their own schools and colleges. But as German Methodists were increasingly acculturated to English, the German conferences were phased out in the twentieth century.

This American-German variety of Methodism was also exported to Europe. In 1849 one of Nast's converts, Ludwig S. Jacoby, a Lutheran immigrant of Jewish birth, returned to Germany and helped organize congregations, conferences, and other institutions, with separate conferences for Switzerland and other lands. In the nineteenth and twentieth centuries German Methodism, with its seminary in Frankfurt, took an honored place among the so-called free—that is, non-state—churches of Germany. One reverse influence that entered American Methodism from this European mission was the deaconess calling as a full-time career for unmarried Methodist women.

German Universalists. One of the smaller groups in American Protestantism, the Universalists soon discovered that they could make converts among those Pennsylvania Germans who were looking for a liberal theology. While Universalism in its organized form was imported from England in the 1770s by John Murray, Pennsylvania Germans such as Dr. George DeBenneville had contributed to its spread before the Revolution.

In the 1820s and 1830s Universalist ministers from New England preached their gospel of universal salvation in southeastern Pennsylvania, making converts like Aaron B. Grosh from the Moravians, Abel C. Thomas among the Quakers, and Jacob Myers among the Dunkers. Jacob Myers published a German Universalist periodical, *Der Fröhliche Botschafter* (The Bearer of Joyful Tidings; 1828–1832), that chronicled the advance of Universalism among Pennsylvania's German-speaking population. Congregations were organized at the time that still exist, although all the work is now in the English language.

German Jehovah's Witnesses. Later in the nineteenth century there was also a German-language program under the auspices of the Jehovah's Witnesses. This was largely the work of the Rev. Otto Ulrich Karl von Zech, a member of a landed family from Thuringia who immigrated to the United States to escape military service in 1865. As a Lutheran minister he settled at Allegheny, Pennsylvania, in 1882, where he met Charles Taze Russell, founder of the Zion's Watch Tower Society, now the Jehovah's Witnesses.

Joining the movement in 1885, Von Zech became editor of *Zion's Wach Thurm,* the German version of *Zion's Watch Tower.* This he replaced with *Die Ernte-Sichel* (The Harvest Sickle) in 1891, which he edited for two decades, even setting its type. He also translated Russell's major tracts into German. Later breaking with Russell, he took his press and founded in 1900 a communitarian settlement in Virginia called Friedheim. Later he moved to Philadelphia, where he continued *Die Ernte-Sichel* until his death in 1906.

CONCLUSION

The German sectarian groups of the United States can provide instructive materials for a variety of scholars in solving four separate but related questions: How are these sectarian groups related as to European theological lineage? How is the religion of immigrants transformed in the new context? How are language and ethnicity related in these groups? How have these immigrant patterns of religion contributed to the Anglo-American and other churches of America?

In answer to the first question, the deeper study of the European roots of the radical Pietist communities (Ephrata, Harmony, and Amana, for example) reveals common influences that also operated on British Isles radicals such as Seekers, Quakers, and Shakers. Among these roots were the theological systems of such Protestant mystics as Boehme, Weigel, and Schwenkfeld, plus the eighteenth-century Inspirationist movement, all of which influenced Ephrata and Amana in particular. Above all it was continental Pietism in its range of forms that provided the unifying thread in much of American-German religion. Rufus M. Jones in his histories of mysticism, particularly *Spiritual Reformers in the Sixteenth and Seventeenth Centuries* (1914), points to many of these common roots.

With respect to the second question, as we have seen from numerous examples, the process of transplantation of religious patterns through migration leads to the gradual transformation of those forms through acculturation with the new environment. The movement of groups like the Mennonites through the so-called sect cycle, with resulting conservative-progressive schisms, and the persistent influence upon them of Anglo-American patterns of organization and thought can be paralleled in many of the larger American groups that started out as sects and ended as denominations, Methodism being a notable example. In the process of acculturation the older European ways of organizing Protestant life and thought were, according to different points of view, eroded, Americanized, or secularized. The least eroded of the Mennonite patterns, the Old Order, Old School, and Old Colony groups, in their tenacious adherence to older life-styles, have proved useful for scientific study by a variety of disciplines.

As for the third question, sectarian religious movements of German origin often used the German language to mark off the boundaries of their sectarian culture against the surrounding English "world." Language thus is viewed as an integral part of their spiritual as well as their ethnic identity. Language loyalty in American ethnic groups has often been consciously stimulated by the church. This has been particularly true of the Pennsylvania German churches and sects. Among them the church was the last institution to press for retention of High German. The Pennsylvania German "old order" groups (Amish, Mennonites, Brethren), whether found in Pennsylvania or Iowa or Ontario, are actually the last holdouts for German in the three-century struggle within the Pennsylvania German culture between the English and German languages. While all these groups can use English where necessary today, they preserve High German or Pennsylvania High German for worship and official communication, and Pennsylvania German dialect for everyday communication.

The sermons of these groups are chanted in High German or, better, Pennsylvania High German. The archaic German hymnody has been studied carefully by folklorists and ethnomusicologists. For example, the Old Order Amish use a German hymnal called the *Ausbund*. Its first-known edition appeared in 1560, making it the oldest Protestant hymnal still in use anywhere in the world. The *Ausbund* hymns, many of which recite the martyrdoms of early Anabaptists, are sung in the biweekly Amish Sunday services to "slow tunes" (*langsame Weisen*). These are related to both folksong and Gregorian chant. But at their "singings," Amish youth sing "fast tunes" (*starke Weisen*), which are mostly Anglo-American gospel song tunes to which favorite German hymn texts have been fitted. Thus the German Pietist hymn "Wo ist Jesus mein Verlangen?" is sung to the tune "What a Friend We Have in Jesus."

The Mennonites and related groups of the midwestern and plains states have likewise used German dialects to the present day. These include Low German, Swiss German, and Hutterite German. Preserving such dialects has helped these groups to define their sense of ethnic identity. To promote ethnic loyalties they have recently begun to sponsor folk festivals and found cultural heritage museums.

Finally, on the broad canvas of American religious history the German sectarian groups can be seen as contributing ideas and directions that though once rejected are now more generally accepted by the majority groups. Certainly the "peace churches" of the American-German world have influenced American ideas of charity and community, peace and pacifist movements, and respect for the natural environment.

The original community concept of both the "peace churches" and the communitarian societies represented an earlier, pre-Pietist model of community shared by all the European Protestant denominations in colonial and early-nineteenth-century America. What it did was subsume both individuals and nuclear families under an overarching holy community. Most of these groups put a high value on marriage and family life, but on the higher levels of community individuals were seen as part of God's family, in which all in the community were brothers and sisters. This is why originally there was a men's side and a women's side in Lutheran and Reformed churches as well as in the meetinghouses of the plain sects. Men and women entered the place of worship by separate doors and were seated separately, divided into age groupings. Thus on the women's side unmarried girls, married women, and widows all sat in separate sections, with similar divisions on the men's side. This separation mirrored the structure of the folk community. While the churches, largely as the result of the individualizing effect of revivalism, eventually gave this system up and seated families together, the system is still illustrated by America's "old order" groups. These also continue to de-individualize the individual by wearing plain costume, which provides a badge of identity both to the wearer and the outside world.

Related to this point is the sectarian concept of charity, directed originally to group needs, but often given to needy individuals from the "world" as well. The relation of hardworking Mennonites to the homeless tramps who circulated through the Pennsylvania countryside provides a pointed example of sectarian charity. The tramps, who rejected family, the economic system, and labor, were treated as equals by the Mennonite farmers, who gave them food, clothing, and a place to stay overnight. Even today, in Lancaster County, the carriage sheds surrounding the plain meetinghouses are still a permitted locale for tramps seeking shelter. In the larger world, sectarian charity provided food and other aid to the European populations in the dark days following the two world wars. A particular Mennonite innovation in this program of feeding the starving populations of Europe was the heifer project after World War II. Developed by Mennonite and other farming sects, it shipped milk cows to Europe to replenish the depleted herds in several countries.

Farmers are not necessarily automatic respecters of the natural environment, but in the case of the Mennonites and other related groups the combination of the emphasis on God's crea-

tion and a genuine love for rural life has often led to such a healthy respect. Farmers in these groups have been pioneers both in the rejection of chemical fertilizers and in the employment of natural means of energy production through windmills and waterwheels. Groups such as the Amish express the belief that God intended them to be farmers, and for those among them who are not farmers only a limited range of alternate occupations is permitted.

The "peace churches" of the American-German world can be seen as influencing general American peace and pacifist movements. Their defense, along with that of the Quakers, of the pacifist position in all of America's war periods finally led in 1940 to the establishment of alternative service programs in war time for conscientious objectors. Because of the tenacity with which these sectarians defended their pacifist position, it is easier today for individuals in the Catholic and Lutheran churches, which have usually defended the "just war" position, to register for alternative service as conscientious objectors.

Perhaps the statement of Benjamin Rush in 1789 on German contributions to the peaceful solution of problems is still relevant today. In *An Account of the Manners of the German Inhabitants of Pennsylvania,* he commented on the place of sectarianism in American society: "Perhaps those German Sects of Christians who refuse to bear arms for the shedding of human blood may be preserved by Divine Providence as the center of a circle which shall gradually embrace all nations of the Earth in a perpetual treaty of friendship and peace."

BIBLIOGRAPHY

General Readings

Joshua A. Fishman, *Language Loyalty in the United States* (1966); Milton M. Gordon, *Assimilation in American Life* (1964); Fredric Klees, *The Pennsylvania Dutch* (1950); J. Gordon Melton, ed., *The Encyclopedia of American Religions,* 2 vols. (1978); Benjamin Rush, *An Account of the Manners of the German Inhabitants of Pennsylvania* (1789; repr. 1875, 1910).

Julius F. Sachse, *The German Sectarians of Pennsylvania, 1708–1800,* 2 vols. (1899–1900); F. Ernest Stoeffler, *The Rise of Evangelical Pietism* (1965), *German Pietism During the Eighteenth Century* (1973), and *Continental Pietism and Early American Christianity* (1976); Steven Thernstrom, ed., *Harvard Encyclopedia of American Ethnic Groups* (1980); George H. Williams,

The Radical Reformation (1962); Ralph Wood, ed., *The Pennsylvania Germans* (1942); J. Milton Yinger, *Religion, Society, and the Individual* (1957).

Peace Churches

Roland H. Bainton, *Christian Attitudes Toward War and Peace* (1960); Harold S. Bender and Henry C. Smith, eds., *The Mennonite Encyclopedia*, 4 vols. (1955–1959); Peter Brock, *Pacifism in the United States, from the Colonial Era to the First World War* (1968) and *Pacifism in Europe to 1914* (1972); Donald F. Durnbaugh, ed. and tr., *European Origins of the Brethren* (1958), and, as ed., *The Brethren in Colonial America* (1967) and *The Church of the Brethren* (1971); Robert Friedmann, *Mennonite Piety Through the Centuries* (1949); Melvin Gingerich, *Service for Peace* (1949).

Guy F. Hershberger, ed., *The Recovery of the Anabaptist Vision* (1957); John A. Hostetler, *Amish Society* (1968; 3rd ed., 1980); Howard W. Kriebel, *The Schwenkfelders in Pennsylvania* (1904); Cornelius Krahn, *Dutch Anabaptism* (1968); W. Kyrel Meschter, *Twentieth-Century Schwenkfelders* (1984); Calvin W. Redekop, *The Old Colony Mennonites* (1969); C. Henry Smith, *The Story of the Mennonites* (1941; rev. 1981); Carlton O. Wittlinger, *Quest for Piety and Obedience: The Story of the Brethren in Christ* (1978).

Communitarian Groups

Karl J. R. Arndt, *George Rapp's Harmony Society: 1785–1847* (1965; rev. 1972) and, as ed., *George Rapp's Separatists: 1700–1803* (1980); Arthur E. Bestor, *Backwoods Utopias* (1950; 2nd ed., 1970); James E. Ernst, *Ephrata: A History* (1963); Gillian L. Gollin, *Moravians in Two Worlds* (1967); J. Taylor Hamilton and Kenneth G. Hamilton, *History of the Moravian Church* (1967); John A. Hostetler, *Hutterite Society* (1974); Walter C. Klein, *Johann Conrad Beissel* (1942); Charles Nordhoff, *The Communistic Societies of the United States* (1875; repr. 1965).

Victor Peters, *All Things Common: The Hutterian Way of Life* (1965); Felix Reichmann and Eugene E. Doll, *Ephrata as Seen by Contemporaries* (1953); Hillel Schwartz, *The French Prophets: The History of a Millenarian Group in Eighteenth-Century England* (1980); Jacob J. Sessler, *Communal Pietism Among Early American Moravians* (1933); Bertha M. H. Shambaugh, *Amana That Was and Amana That Is* (1932); Clifford W. Towlson, *Moravian and Methodist* (1957); Aarni Voipio, *Sleeping Preachers: A Study in Ecstatic Religiosity* (1951); John R. Weinlick, *Count Zinzendorf* (1956).

Revivalist and Other Movements

Raymond W. Albright, *A History of the Evangelical Church* (1942); J. Bruce Behney and Paul H. Eller, *The History of the Evangelical United Brethren Church* (1979); Paul F. Douglass, *The Story of German Methodism* (1939); A. W. Drury, *History of the Church of the United Brethren in Christ* (1924; rev. 1931).

C. H. Forney, *History of the Churches of God in the United States of North America* (1914); William G. McLoughlin, Jr., *Modern Revivalism* (1959); Adam Miller, *Origin and Progress of the German Missions in the Methodist Episcopal Church* (1843); William W. Sweet, *Revivalism in America* (1944); Carl Wittke, *William Nast* (1959); Don Yoder, *Pennsylvania Spirituals* (1961).

[*See also* ETHNICITY AND RELIGION *and* WAR AND PEACE.]

BLACK CHRISTIANITY

IN NORTH AMERICA

Albert J. Raboteau

FROM the beginning of the Atlantic slave trade, Europeans claimed that the conversion of slaves to Christianity justified the enslavement of Africans in the Americas. Despite this rationalization for slavery, the British colonists in North America proved indifferent, if not hostile, to the conversion of slaves. At first, opposition was based on the suspicion that English law forbade the enslavement of Christians and, thus, required slaveholders to emancipate any slave who received baptism. Colonists feared that slaves would seek to be baptized in order to gain freedom.

By the early 1770s, colonial legislators had assuaged these fears by declaring that baptism had no effect upon the status of the baptized with regard to freedom or slavery. Legal obstacles aside, slaveowners, for the most part, still demonstrated scant interest in converting their slaves. Christianity, according to common wisdom, spoiled slaves. Christian slaves thought too highly of themselves, became impudent, and even turned rebellious. Moreover, Anglo-Americans were troubled by a feeling that it was wrong to make a slave Christian. Africans were foreign. To convert them was to make them more like the English and therefore deserving of better treatment. Christianity, like white skin and the rights of Englishmen, constituted the colonists' identity. To mix Christianity, therefore, with black-skinned African slaves confused the distinctiveness of the races and threatened the social order based upon that distinctiveness. Finally, it was the labor, not the souls, of the slaves that concerned most slaveholders.

A concerted attack on these obstacles to slave conversion was mounted by the Church of England in 1701, when it founded the Society for the Propagation of the Gospel in Foreign Parts

to support missionaries in the colonies. The first task was to convince masters that it was their duty to instruct their slaves. In tract after tract, widely distributed in the colonies, officials of the society stressed the compatibility of Christianity and slavery. Masters need not worry that religion would ruin their slaves. On the contrary, it would make them better slaves by convincing them to obey out of a sense of moral duty instead of fear. After all, society pamphlets explained, Christianity does not upset the social order, but supports it by teaching people to remain content in the station that God has given them. Quoting Scripture to prove the point, society preachers dwelled at length on Ephesians 6:5, "Servants, be obedient to them that are *your* masters."

In addition to opposition from the slaveholders, the mission to the slaves faced other obstacles. The linguistic and cultural differences between Africans and the English discouraged missionaries from attempting to convert adult Africans. Instead, they concentrated on children and on slaves born in America. Conversion was also hampered by the way in which the Anglicans conceived of the process—as a lengthy course of instruction, requiring slaves to learn to read and to recite creeds, catechisms, and prayers from memory. The most serious drawback to the whole enterprise was the small number of missionaries and the huge scope of the task. In the southern colonies, where the bulk of the slaves lived, religious conditions were unsettled and regular pastoral care for most whites, let alone blacks, was scarce or nonexistent. In the North, churches were numerous and religious services readily available, but the number of blacks was relatively small.

The success of missions to the slaves was largely dependent upon factors beyond the missionaries' control: the proportion of African-born to native-born slaves, the geographic location and work patterns of the slaves, and the ratio of blacks to whites in a given locale. Blacks in the North and in the Chesapeake region of Maryland and Virginia, for example, experienced much more frequent and intense contact with whites than did those of the lowland coasts of South Carolina and Georgia, where large gangs of African-born slaves toiled on isolated rice plantations with only limited and infrequent exposure to whites or their religion.

Even if a missionary gained regular access to slaves, it didn't follow that the slaves invariably accepted the Christian Gospel. Some rejected it and, according to missionary accounts, laughed at those who accepted the religion of their owners. Others accepted Christianity because they hoped, colonial legislation and missionary pronouncements notwithstanding, that baptism would raise their status and ensure eventual freedom for their children, if not themselves. Still others mixed Christian beliefs with the traditional religions of their African homelands, much to the dismay of the clergy.

Discouraging though the prospects were, colonial clergymen had established a few successful missions among the slaves by the early eighteenth century. When the bishop of London distributed a questionnaire in 1724 requiring ministers to describe their work among the slaves, a few respondents reported impressive numbers of baptisms; the great majority, however, referred to vague intentions instead of concrete achievements. During the first 120 years of black slavery in British North America, Christianity made little headway in the slave population.

Slaves first came to conversion in large numbers in the wake of the periodic religious revivals that swept parts of the colonies beginning in the 1740s. Evangelical revivalists succeeded where Anglican pastors had failed for a variety of reasons. Whereas the Anglicans had depended upon a slow process of indoctrination, the evangelicals made Christianity more accessible by preaching the immediate experience of conversion as the primary requirement for baptism. Due to their emphasis on conversion, Evangelicals tended to deemphasize instruction and to downplay the importance of learning for the Christian life. As a result, all classes were welcome to actively participate in their prayer meetings and revival services, in which the poor, the illiterate, and the enslaved prayed, exhorted, and preached.

As revival fervor continued to flare up sporadically in the South after the Revolution, more and more slaves converted to Christianity under the dramatic preaching of Presbyterian, Methodist, and Baptist revivalists. The emotionalism of the revivals encouraged the outward expression of religious feeling, and the sight of black and white converts weeping, shouting, fainting, and moving in ecstatic trance became a familiar, if sensational, feature of the sacramental and camp meetings.

The religious ecstasy of the revivals was not unlike the behavior characteristic of spirit possession in the festivals honoring the gods of Africa. In both cases, participants manifested bodily the presence and the power of the divine. Moved to ecstatic trance by drumming, singing, and dancing, African mediums spoke and acted in the person of one of their gods. Similarly, Afro-American evangelicals were seized by the Spirit and driven to act, speak, and move under its power. To be sure, there were differences. The slaves believed that they were filled by the Spirit of the Christian God, not possessed by an African spirit. But the rhythmic drumming, repetitive singing, and continuous dancing, characteristic of possession ceremonies in Africa, were replicated in the American South. Slaves used hands and feet to approximate the rhythms of the drum, substituted spirituals for hymns to the gods, and danced in a counterclockwise, circular ring called the shout, the steps of which bore a striking resemblance to those of possession dances in Africa and the Caribbean. The analogy between African styles of worship and the evangelical revivals enabled the slaves to reinterpret the new religion by reference to the old, thus making Christianity seem more familiar.

The rise of the evangelical denominations, particularly the Methodists and the Baptists, threatened the established Anglican Church in the South. The evangelicals, who appealed to the "lower sort," suffered persecution at the hands of the Anglican authorities. Their preachers were jailed, and their services disrupted. Their challenge to the social order seemed all the more radical when the general conference of the Methodists in 1784 and some individual Baptists by the 1790s took a stand against slavery on religious grounds. Though both Methodists and Baptists rapidly retreated from their antislavery stand, their struggle with the established order and their uneasiness about slavery gave slaves, initially at least, the impression that they were "friendly toward freedom."

The egalitarian impulse within evangelicalism prompted the Methodists and the Baptists to license black men to exhort and to preach, the most significant single step in the conversion of the slaves. By the 1770s pioneer black preachers had begun to convert and to pastor their own people, without the involvement of whites. From that time on, blacks had the opportunity to receive the Christian Gospel not only from whites but from their fellow blacks.

The spread of evangelical revivalism between 1770 and 1820 changed the religious complexion of the South by bringing unprecedented numbers of slaves into membership in the church and by introducing even larger numbers to at least the rudiments of Christianity. During the decades before the Civil War, Christianity gradually filtered into the slave quarters, though the great majority of slaves were not church members at the time of emancipation. The slaves most likely to gain access to institutional church care were house servants and those living in proximity to towns.

Concern over the lack of regular church care among the masses of plantation slaves led some antebellum clergymen, like the Presbyterian Charles Colcock Jones and the Methodist William Capers, to propose an extensive system of plantation missions designed to reach even the most isolated slaves. While the plantation mission did raise the consciousness of some southerners about the religious state of their slaves, its more significant influence was upon the creation of a slaveholding ethic based on the idea that masters owed duties to slaves and that slaves owed duties to masters. This reciprocal relationship created the possibility, according to Jones and Capers, for Christianizing the institution of slavery. As both men were well aware, the harsh realities of slavery constantly corroded this ideal. And yet, to abandon the attempt to bring slavery "under the rule of gospel order" was tantamount to agreeing with the abolitionists that slavery was fundamentally wrong. And so they labored on.

By 1850 the majority of slaves attending church did so with whites. But as early as the 1760s, separate black churches began to emerge. Mainly Baptist, due to that denomination's policy of congregational autonomy, black churches grew in size and number during the nineteenth century, even in the slave South. The First African Baptist Church of Savannah, Georgia, for example, was organized in 1788 by Andrew Bryan, a former slave, despite severe persecution by white opponents of the church. In 1830, First African boasted a congregation of 2,417 slaves and free blacks pastored by Bryan's nephew, Andrew Marshall. Though nominally supervised by whites, these separate congregations were frequently pastored in fact by black ministers, some free, some slave. Often they outnumbered the largest white churches in the local Baptist associations. Never numerous, the separate black churches were extremely important as the only institutions over which blacks exercised control. They served as the major source of black leadership during slavery and long after.

Slave codes—forbidding literacy, prohibiting night meetings, and restricting mobility off the plantation—severely limited the independence of black churches and black ministers in the South. But in the North the abolition of slavery after the Revolution gave black congregations and clergy much more leeway to assert control over their religious lives. Between 1790 and 1820, black Episcopalians, Methodists, Baptists, and Presbyterians struggled with white church authorities to gain religious autonomy. Among the first to do so was Bethel Church in Philadelphia. Founded in 1794 by Richard Allen, a former slave who had become a licensed Methodist preacher, Bethel had been organized after discriminatory treatment had forced black Methodists to abandon St. George's, the white church they had attended for years. When the white elders of St. George's tried to take control of the Bethel Church property, the black congregation went to court to retain their rights to the church they had built themselves. In 1816 the Pennsylvania Supreme Court declared in their favor.

Similar conflicts between black Methodists and white elders elsewhere prompted Allen to call for a convention of African Methodists to meet in Philadelphia in 1816. Delegates organized an independent black denomination, the African Methodist Episcopal Church, and elected Richard Allen as its first bishop. Two other denominations of black Methodists were formed around the same time: the Union Church of Africans led by Peter Spencer in Wilmington, Delaware, in 1815, and the African Methodist Episcopal Zion Church (called "Zion" to distinguish it from Allen's group), established in New York City in 1821.

The African Methodists were the first to take independent control of their church property, finances, and governance on the denominational level, but northern black Christians in other churches demonstrated their spirit of independence as well. The first black Episcopal church, St. Thomas, was built in Philadelphia in 1794, with Absalom Jones, a former Methodist and close associate of Allen, serving as pastor. John Gloucester, a freed slave, gathered the First African Presbyterian Church in 1807, also in Philadelphia. And African Baptist churches were organized in Boston, New York, and Philadelphia between 1804 and 1809. As centers of social, economic, educational, and political life, these churches formed the institutional core for the development of free black communities in the North. They also formed a platform from which black leaders, frequently the ministers themselves, addressed the issues confronting their people.

Northern black clergy spoke out against slavery from pulpit, platform, and press, condemning it as antithetical to the ideals professed by a Christian and democratic people. When the American Colonization Society was formed in 1816 to solve the problem of slavery by fostering the repatriation of free blacks in Africa, they actively opposed it. At the same time, black clergy like Allen and the Baptist elder Jeremiah Asher supported the notion of voluntary emigration and encouraged Afro-American missions to Africa and Haiti. In 1821, Lott Carey, a black Baptist preacher from Richmond, Virginia, sailed to Liberia, preceded by Daniel Coker, a leader in the founding of the African Methodist Episcopal Church, who emigrated in 1820 and settled in Sierra Leone. Black ministers and congregations helped to organize and support local antislavery societies and actively participated in the growing antislavery campaign. Eight of the black founders of the American and Foreign Anti-Slavery Society, which split from the American Anti-Slavery Society in 1840, were clergymen: Jehiel Beman, Amos Gerry Beman, Christopher Rush, Samuel Cornish, Theodore Wright, Andrew Harris, Stephen Gloucester, and Henry Highland Garnet.

With the notable exception of Frederick Douglass, the most outspoken and prominent black abolitionists were ministers. Nor did they confine their antislavery deeds to the platform and the pulpit. Rush, Garnet, and Wright—the first an African Methodist Episcopal Zion leader, the other two, Presbyterian clergymen—formed a committee of vigilance to give aid and sanctuary to fugitive slaves. Richard Allen and his wife, Sarah, sheltered fugitives in their Philadelphia home, and the basement of Bethel Church also furnished a safe stop for travelers on the Underground Railroad. Leonard Grimes, a black minister in Boston, served a jail term for assisting escaping slaves.

Black clergymen also spoke out in favor of temperance and other moral reforms of the day. They were not willing to ordain women, however, and a talented preacher such as the African Methodist laywoman Jarena Lee faced opposition from an all-male clergy when she began to exercise her gift.

The centrality of the church in the lives of free blacks in the North was symbolized by the fact that the first national black political organization met in 1830 at Bethel Church in Philadelphia. The forty delegates to this First National Negro Convention elected Allen as president and proceeded to discuss the discrimination and poverty that confronted black Americans at every turn.

In sermons, pamphlets, and tracts, black ministers wrestled with the agonizing problem of black suffering: Why did God permit slavery? Trying to discern what meaning the history of their people had in the providence of God, black preachers affirmed that God would turn evil into good, and in His own time would free black Americans from slavery, as He had the Israelites of old. One of the most trenchant theological reflections upon suffering and the meaning of Afro-American history was written not by a cleric but by a Boston clothing merchant named David Walker, whose *Appeal to the Coloured Citizens of the World* (1829) has been aptly called a black jeremiad (a warning to the nation to repent the evil of slavery and race prejudice before it was too late). The American nation, Walker warned, was doomed to fall under the wrath of God, unless she rapidly repented the sin of slavery. Recounting the history of European wars and bloodshed, he concluded that if ever the world were to become Christian, it would have to be through the ministry of blacks.

Slaves, no less than free blacks, condemned the hypocrisy of slaveholding Christians, but they had to do so in secret. Outside the formal structures of the institutional church, slaves constructed their own "invisible institution" of prayer meetings and worship services in which they made Christianity truly their own. Much of the religious life of the slaves was invisible to the extent that it was hidden from the masters. Since slaves were illiterate, until recently historians assumed that their religion remained invisible to history as well. However, in the last decade or so, historians using slave narratives, black autobiographies, and folklore have been able to sketch a picture of slave religious life.

From the testimony of fugitive and former slaves, it is apparent that slaves were motivated to hold their own religious meetings out of dissatisfaction with the version of the Gospel preached by whites, a Gospel that justified slavery and incessantly instructed them to obey their masters. They risked punishment to attend illicit services, gathered in woods, cabins, and brush arbors (aptly named "hush harbors") where they might pray, preach, and sing "out from under the eye of the master." In these private spaces they prayed and preached about deliverance in this world, not just in the next. Though some slaveholders permitted their slaves to hold prayer meetings and even enjoyed listening to the slaves' singing and preaching, a fundamental contradiction remained between the masters' religion and that of the slaves. For slaves refused to believe, as masters did, that the Gospel of Jesus was compatible with slavery.

Slave preachers presided over the "invisible institution" and enjoyed a good deal of influence among slaves generally. Despite illiteracy, the eloquence of some slave preachers earned them the respect of blacks and sometimes of whites. The slave preacher had to take care that his sermons not explicitly endorse freedom or equality for blacks, except in heaven. Slaves understood his situation and became attuned to veiled and indirect references designed to sound innocuous to whites; for example, references to the impartiality and justice of God to all, rich and poor, black and white. Slaves preferred their own

preachers, with whom they readily identified, and they took pride in the verbal skill of slave preachers as evidence of black intelligence, which slavery attempted to deny.

Prohibited from literacy by law or custom, slaves learned the Bible by hearing it preached. Biblical stories, images, and passages were committed to memory and became part of the slaves' oral culture. The Bible itself became an object of veneration for slaves. After emancipation, teachers were amazed at the freedmen's desire to learn to read so that they could study the good book for themselves. Most of all, it was in their songs that the slaves brought the biblical stories to life.

Spirituals, based upon the Bible, Protestant hymns, and African styles of music, were sung in the fields and the big-house kitchens, at work and at prayer, in groups and alone. They were not only sung, they were performed—with hand-clapping, foot-stamping excitement. And they were danced in the counterclockwise, circular shuffle known as the shout. The shout dramatized the biblical scenes depicted in the words of the spirituals. As the dancers circled around in the ring, time and distance disappeared in the ecstasy of the moment, and the slaves became the children of Israel crossing the Red Sea or marching to the battle of Jericho. Like all good poetry, the words of the spirituals were frequently ambiguous. They spoke of freedom from slavery to sin, but referred as well to freedom from slavery to whites. They were used as signals to warn when an overseer approached or to announce that a prayer meeting was planned.

Slaves created the spirituals by a process of communal composition in which one singer extemporized the verses as the group joined in with a chorus familiar to all. This open and spontaneous structure allowed the singers to refer to daily events and to incorporate them in the song. In this way, the sorrows and joys of individual slaves were shared by the community. The spirituals dealt also with the events of the Christian life, beginning with conversion "down in some lonesome valley" and ending across the "last river" of death in the promised land of rest and peace.

The wisdom and poignancy of these songs have touched people around the world. As W. E. B. Du Bois remarked in *The Souls of Black Folk* (1903), the slave spirituals represent one of America's major contributions to world culture.

In songs of simple eloquence, anonymous slave communities articulated the ability of the human spirit to transcend suffering:

> I know moon-rise, I know star-rise
> Lay dis body down.
> I walk in de moonlight,
> I walk in de starlight,
> To lay dis body down.
> I'll walk in de graveyard,
> I'll walk through de graveyard,
> To lay dis body down.
> I'll lie in de grave and stretch out my arms;
> Lay dis body down.
> I go to de judgement in de evenin' of de day,
> When I lay dis body down;
> And my soul and your soul will meet in de day
> When I lay dis body down.
>
> (Allen, 1951)

An essential feature of the Christian life, according to the evangelical piety that the slaves increasingly made their own, was the experience of conversion. Testimony of conversion before the assembled Christian community was required for baptism. Slaves, ignorant of the date of their actual birth, recalled, long after the fact, the day and the hour of their "rebirth." As recounted by former slaves, their conversion experiences conformed to the classic tripartite division of awakening, conviction, and pardon, frequently visualized in imagery drawn from the Bible, sermons, spirituals, and the testimonies of other converts recited at recurring "experience meetings." "God struck me dead" was the vivid expression used by former slaves to describe the onset of conversion, an experience of personal transformation in which individuals felt sadness, fear, and rejection change to joy, confidence, and acceptance. Believing that God had chosen them to be saved, they felt totally renewed. "I looked at my hands and they looked new; I looked at my feet and they were new; and I just loved everything and everybody" (Johnson, 1969).

From colonial slaveholders to modern historians, one question has troubled every observer of slavery: Did Christianity make slaves accept their enslavement, or did it make them resist slavery? Slave testimony indicates that it did both. On the one hand, Christianity consoled slaves for suffering injustice in this life by promising them redress in the next. Moreover, Christians were taught to love their enemies and to do good to those who injured them. Some slaves internalized these doctrines and accepted their situation. In effect, the compensatory and otherworldly tendency of Christianity distracted slaves from rebelling against the system that oppressed them. On the other hand, the three major slave revolts in the United States depended upon Christianity as a justification.

In 1800, Gabriel Prosser recruited slaves for his plot to rise against Richmond, Virginia, by quoting Scripture to prove that God had assured their success. The leaders of the Denmark Vesey conspiracy in Charleston, South Carolina, in 1822 were active members of that city's African Methodist Church, and Vesey reportedly appealed to the Bible to convince blacks to join his cause. Nat Turner, the leader of the bloodiest slave revolt (1831) in United States history, was a preacher, healer, and seer who claimed that God had instructed him by signs to strike against the whites.

Christianity, then, as slaveholders had all along suspected, was a two-edged sword. Even though the Bible did not condemn slavery explicitly, Exodus and the apocalyptic and prophetic books contained enough passages that posed a threat to slave control. In the contest of wills between slaves and masters, Christianity helped the slaves to resist. When, for example, slaves attended prayer meetings against the master's command, they chose to obey their consciences and demonstrated that there were limits to any human's authority over another.

Beyond the issue of docility and rebellion, Christianity affected the slaves' sense of identity and self-worth as individuals and as a people. The conversion experience convinced the individual of his or her ultimate value in the eyes of God. In the midst of the degradation of slavery, the slave converts gained a system of values, a core of meaning, and a sense of purpose that transcended the status of slaves. Taking the story of Exodus as a symbol of their experience, they believed that they were a chosen people, with a special destiny of their own. These individual and communal identities were reaffirmed in emotion-filled prayer meetings in which singing, shouting, and preaching helped them to transcend and transform, if only for a while, the hopelessness and suffering of slavery. After slavery ended, freedmen continued to worship as they or their parents had during slavery, their religion a source of stability in the chaos and failure of Reconstruction.

Following the advance of the Union armies, northern missionaries traveled south to offer material aid, education, and church membership to the freedmen. Northern white churches, including Congregationalist, Baptist, Methodist, and Presbyterian, established freedmen's aid societies to support missions and schools. Former slaves enthusiastically welcomed schooling as tangible proof that freedom had really arrived. The intense desire for education led freedmen to contribute whatever they could despite their desperate poverty. Morehouse College in Atlanta, Fisk University in Nashville, Hampton Institute in Hampton, Virginia, Talladega College in Talladega, Alabama, and several other contemporary black colleges and universities trace their origins to freedmen's schools founded under church auspices in the 1860s and 1870s.

After emancipation, black Christians swarmed out of white-run churches in order to form their own. In rapid succession, the Colored Primitive Baptists, the Colored Cumberland Presbyterian Church, and the Colored Methodist Episcopal Church were established between 1865 and 1870 as blacks seceded from white parent denominations. Numerous black Baptist churches united in separate black state conventions throughout the South, leading eventually to the organization of the National Baptist Convention in 1895. (In 1907 the denomination would split into two. The larger faction took the name National Baptist Convention of the U.S.A., Inc., in 1915; the smaller body kept the old name, National Baptist Convention.)

At the same time, missionaries from the northern black denominations actively recruited former slaves for their church rolls. African Methodist Episcopal missionaries arrived in the field first; James Lynch from Baltimore and James D. Hall from New York opened missions in the Sea Islands as early as 1863. Two years later, Bishop Daniel Alexander Payne returned to his native Charleston in order to organize the South Carolina Conference of the African Methodist Church. Payne's return was triumphant since he had been forced to leave thirty years earlier when his school for free black children was declared illegal by the South Carolina legislature. As a result of their missions, northern

black denominations grew to unprecedented size and geographical extent. The increase in southern members meant that the northern-based leadership and character of the black church had to change if the new constituency were to be fairly represented.

Though some of the black missionaries, like Payne, were native southerners returning home, tension marred their relationship with less-educated indigenous preachers, who viewed the northerners as outsiders. Personal conflicts reflected larger cultural dissonance between the more sedate piety of the educated clergy and the emotionally expressive worship of the illiterate folk. Payne himself underscored the difference when he attempted to stamp out the shout as a "heathenish" custom that disgraced blacks. Payne represented the intelligentsia, who identified religion with moral and educational uplift of the race; the shouters stood for the old-time religion in which learning and morality were not nearly so important as experiencing the power of God.

So-called radical Reconstruction of the former Confederate state governments gave blacks, for a while at least, the opportunity to exercise political rights. As prominent leaders, black ministers took an active role in Reconstruction politics. Richard H. Cain, for example, an African Methodist missionary assigned to Charleston, gathered a congregation of several thousand, started a newspaper, worked for the Republican party, and represented South Carolina in the U.S. Congress.

Historians have described the growth of the black church after emancipation as a merger between the invisible institution of the slave South and the independent churches of the North. While no doubt true, a more significant event was the emergence of indigenous black preachers who had been pastoring their people for years under the restrictive conditions of slavery. Freed of white supervision, these men rapidly formed numerous black churches, scattered across the landscape of the South. Mainly Baptist, these congregations were, by and large, small, poor, and rural. Physically unimpressive, the churches that emerged after emancipation served as the nucleus for the former slaves' social, economic, educational, and political life. As the distance from slavery widened, the church remained a profoundly conservative force as well as a source of adaptation to new and different circumstances.

The period between the end of Reconstruction in 1877 and the entrance of America into World War I in 1917 has been labeled the nadir by historian Rayford Logan, because conditions for blacks steadily worsened as freedom proved incomplete. During those years, blacks were disfranchised, white supremacists returned to power in the southern states, lynching increased, black sharecroppers and tenant farmers lived under a system of peonage, in *Plessy* v. *Ferguson* (1896) the Supreme Court accepted segregation, and pseudoscientific racism propagated the myth of black inferiority. Black response to virulent racism was still largely formulated through the church, but increasingly the voices of secular leaders, not just those of the clergy, began to be heard and heeded.

Two nonclerical figures, Booker T. Washington and W. E. B. Du Bois, have dominated discussion of the period. Their diametrically opposed positions on issues of education and race relations have come to symbolize black response to the nadir. While Washington, the founder and principal of Tuskegee Institute in Alabama, advocated industrial education as the most realistic path of progress for a largely peasant people, Du Bois, the scholar and activist, stressed the need for liberal education to train an intellectual elite to lead an uneducated race. Washington emphasized black economic development, and counseled patience concerning social equality between the races. Du Bois encouraged protest for black civil rights and argued that without political participation economic advance would prove impossible for blacks in a racist society. Washington's Tuskegee machine and Du Bois's National Association for the Advancement of Colored People (NAACP) both had their clerical supporters, though it would be simplistic to divide them into accommodationist and protestor camps. Black churchmen might support compromise or radical protest, depending on the issues and circumstances involved.

The experience of the nadir drove the clergy to sustained theological reflection on the meaning of Afro-American history, as they sought to make sense of slavery, freedom, and oppression to themselves and their congregations. According to some, black Americans were "suffering servants" destined to save Christianity in America from racism, militarism, and materialism. God permitted—but did not will—the enslavement of Africans, so that Afro-Americans, not Europeans or Anglo-Americans, would bring the true Gospel of Jesus to Africa uncorrupted by the racism of whites. A few black theologians, like Theophilus G. Steward and James Theodore Holly, predicted that the age of European Christianity was nearing its end and was about to be succeeded by a new age in which the darker races of the world would finally put Christianity into practice.

In the late nineteenth century some Afro-Americans turned to emigration as the only solution to the racism that surrounded them in America. According to Henry McNeal Turner, a bishop of the African Methodist Episcopal Church, Africa offered Afro-Americans the opportunity to assert their rights without the debilitating limits of racism. Moreover, it was the mission of black Americans, according to the black Episcopalian Alexander Crummell, to Christianize and civilize pagan Africa. Crummell, a missionary to Sierra Leone, declared that slavery, for all its evils, had been a school in which Africans had been educated by a technologically advanced society. Now it was the descendants' duty to share their education with the homeland.

The idea of settling and spreading Christian civilization in Africa stood as a challenge to racial pride. Nowhere was this challenge more clearly stated than in the words of Turner, who urged blacks to respect blacks and argued that they, just as much as whites, ought to imagine and depict God in their own image, a black God for black people. Interest in emigration was also stirred by Edward Wilmot Blyden, a Presbyterian minister from the West Indies, who served as a minister in the government of Liberia. Blyden lectured widely on Africa throughout the United States and urged Afro-Americans to fulfill their duty toward her.

The redemption of Africa was far more powerful as an ideal than as a practical project for black churches lacking the money for large-scale foreign missions. Nevertheless, Afro-American missionaries did labor in Africa, some under the auspices of black churches, others with support from whites.

Bleak as the racial situation was, few black Americans immigrated to Africa. They did move, however, and on a large scale, but they went west, north, and especially from country to city. After the turn of the century, the great migration began. In the 1890s agricultural depression and a series of crop failures combined to push impoverished rural blacks off the land into the cities of the South, West, and North, in search of work. As World War I curtailed the supply of immigrant workers and increased demand for cheap labor to handle greater industrial production, the tide of black migration gathered momentum. Crowded into ghettos in the unfamiliar urban environment, black migrants sought security in the church.

Some of the large city churches, such as Olivet Baptist in Chicago, developed social programs to assist the migrants in finding jobs, housing, and basic education. Olivet, under pastor L. K. Williams, staffed a day nursery, gym, kindergarten, music school, employment bureau, and Bible school. Socially conscious ministers, such as Reverdy C. Ransom of the Institutional Church and Settlement in Chicago, Baptist pastor J. Milton Waldron in Jacksonville, Florida, Congregationalist H. H. Proctor in Atlanta, and Episcopalian Hutchens C. Bishop in New York City, encouraged their congregations to take seriously the social implications of Christianity. The migrants, however, found it difficult to feel comfortable in the large urban churches, so different from the small rural chapels back home. It was not possible to re-create the familiarity and intimacy of the old congregations in a new institution where they were unknown and perhaps unappreciated. As a result, they formed new churches, usually located in homes or rented storefronts that became familiar features of the black urban landscape.

Between 1890 and 1930 the number of black churches and small denominations increased rapidly, prompting some sociologists to decry black communities for being overchurched. Meager resources spread too thin among competing religious bodies, they argued, might have advanced the cause of black progress more effectively had they been invested in fewer, more centralized institutions of social reform. However this may be, much of the growth in religious organization was due to the efforts of black migrants to reorder lives and communities disrupted by the experience of migration.

One of the most significant of the new religious movements to attract blacks during this period of migration and ecclesiastical ferment was in many ways a return to the ecstatic worship of the old-time religion from which Baptists and Methodists had reputedly strayed. The late-nineteenth-century Holiness movement, and the Pentecostalism that developed from it, reemphasized the experiential dimension of Christian life to a greater degree than most Methodists or Baptists were willing to accept. When C. H. Mason and C. P. Jones began to preach the Holiness doctrine of entire sanctification (a second experience of grace after conversion that made the Christian holy) to black Baptists in Mississippi, they were expelled by the local association. Undaunted by this rebuke, Jones and Mason organized in 1897 in Memphis, Tennessee, the Church of God in Christ.

About the same time, some advocates of Holiness began to speak of another experience beyond sanctification: the experience of baptism with the Spirit. Endowed with the Spirit's power, modern-day Christians expected to speak in unknown tongues just as the disciples did on Pentecost. In 1906, William J. Seymour, a black Holiness preacher, dismissed from his congregation in Los Angeles for teaching about speaking in tongues, started a prayer meeting in a private home. As people began speaking in tongues and the crowds increased, Seymour moved the budding revival to an old building on Azusa Street. For three years the Azusa Street Revival attracted white and black Christians from all over the nation, indeed from around the world, eager to receive baptism with the Spirit and the accompanying gift of tongues.

Among the thousands who flocked to Los Angeles was C. H. Mason. Receiving the gift of Spirit baptism, Mason returned to Memphis in 1907 to preach the doctrine of speaking in tongues. When Jones rejected this message, a schism emerged. Mason and his followers kept the name Church of God in Christ, while Jones and his group took the name Church of Christ (Holiness) U.S.A. The Church of God in Christ, under the leadership of Mason, became the largest black Pentecostal denomination.

The "sanctified" churches, as the Holiness and Pentecostal congregations were called, renewed the ecstatic emphasis in black liturgical life by encouraging prophecy, healing, and speaking in tongues as the "normal" characteristics of the Christian church. Ridiculed as "holy rollers," due to the emotionalism of their services, they incorporated the use of "secular" instruments, such as guitars, pianos, and drums, into worship, and in the process made a major contribution to the development of black religious music. Prohibiting the use of alcohol, drugs, cosmetics, and secular entertainment, the "saints" created little societies within the larger, often hostile, white society. Here members were encouraged to develop habits of industry, honesty, and thrift, which eventually lead to upward mobility, within the limits set by segregation. Interestingly, the Holiness-Pentecostal movement had initially inspired extensive interracial cooperation, but by the 1920s sanctified churches had separated along racial lines. A century after the Baptists and Methodists had tried and failed, Holiness and Pentecostal churches discovered that Americans could not yet sustain biracial Christian community.

A wide range of new religious options confronted Afro-Americans in the pluralistic context of twentieth-century America. Various groups of black Jews and Black Muslims rejected Christianity outright as a religion for whites and offered Afro-Americans new religious and racial identities that contradicted the myth of black inferiority. They claimed that the so-called Negroes were in reality the descendants of Moors or Jews of the ten lost tribes of Israel. Viewed as prophets of God by their followers, men like the Noble Drew Ali, founder of the Moorish Science Temple (around 1913), offered to restore the true identity of black people robbed from them by Christian slaveholders. These heterodox versions of Islam and Judaism buttressed the new identities of their members with strict codes of dress, diet, and morality. Most forbade eating pork, dancing, emotional worship, and other stereotypical features of Afro-American popular culture. The most formidable of the new religious opponents of black Christianity, the Nation of Islam, developed from the teaching of Wallace D. Fard in Detroit in 1930 and expanded under the leadership of Elijah Muhammad over the next forty years.

During the 1920s and 1930s new messiahs, such as Father Divine and Daddy Grace, appeared and attracted sizable followings. Tired of deferring happiness to a future heaven, the disciples of these "black gods" sought tangible and immediate salvation in this world from the evils of sickness, poverty, and hunger. According to many of his converts, Father Divine had cured their illnesses, physical as well as moral, even at a distance. Proposing a system of economic and political justice, Father Divine abolished all references to race and forbade sexual intercourse among his followers, who lived in communities called "heavens." Illness and unhappiness were due to sin and lack of belief in "Father."

The largest of the new movements, and the biggest mass movement ever among Afro-Americans, was the Universal Negro Improvement Association (UNIA), founded in 1914 by Marcus Garvey, a Jamaican who settled in the United States in 1916. Garvey appealed to the racial pride of Afro-Americans and directed their hopes toward the creation of an African republic that would serve as a black Zion destined to unite the peoples of Africa scattered around the world. Through his journal, the *Negro World,* and numerous local branches of the UNIA throughout the nation, Garvey influenced the black masses like no other leader before or since.

The UNIA has appropriately been described as a black civil religion. While Garvey carefully endorsed no particular denomination, he did adopt religious symbols and rituals to convey the serious purpose and moral commitment of the movement he led. UNIA meetings began with the organization's hymn. Sunday morning services, afternoon Sunday schools, a UNIA catechism, creed, and baptismal ceremony all encouraged Garvey's disciples to dedicate themselves to a transcendent cause. Garvey's refusal to ally the UNIA with a particular religion reflected the quasi-religious ethos that he identified with racial unity. He also kept from alienating the most powerful black community leaders, the ministers. As a result, it was not unusual for prominent clergy to deliver the principal address at Sunday evening meetings of the UNIA.

Though he did not stint in criticizing the racial attitudes and behavior of white Americans and Europeans, Garvey denied that he was racist and affirmed his belief in the "Fatherhood of God and the brotherhood of man." Branded as a subversive by U.S. intelligence agents, he was deported in 1927, after serving two years in prison on a conviction for mail fraud. Without his personal involvement, Garvey's movement languished. Despite his apparent defeat, Garvey's doctrines of racial unity and pan-African liberation had a profound impact upon black Americans, influenced the native church movements in Africa and the West Indies, and led nationalist groups as diverse as the Rastafarians and the Black Muslims to regard him as a forerunner.

Urbanization introduced significant numbers of Afro-Americans to Roman Catholicism for the first time. Black Catholics had been present in colonial Maryland and Louisiana. As John Carroll, the first American bishop, reported in 1785, about 3,000 of the 15,800 Catholics in Maryland were black slaves. Unless they were owned by a religious order, they and their fellow black Catholics in Louisiana rarely received instruction or regular pastoral care in a widely scattered and undermanned mission church. There were also small pockets of black Catholics by the early nineteenth century in areas of Kentucky settled by Catholic Marylanders, who were accompanied by their slaves.

In New Orleans and Baltimore, French-speaking "free people of color" constituted sizable communities of black Catholics, augmented after 1792 by refugees from the Haitian revolution. In these cities, two congregations of black nuns arose, the Oblate Sisters of Providence in 1829 in Baltimore and the Sisters of the Holy Family in 1842 in New Orleans. Besides educating black children and caring for the aged and infirm, these black sisters were crucial symbols of the black presence in the church, all the more so since there were only a handful of black priests until the mid-twentieth century.

The first black Americans ordained to the priesthood were James Augustine, Patrick, and Alexander Sherwood Healy, the sons of a slave mother and an Irish immigrant father. Educated for the priesthood abroad and ordained in Europe, James (ordained 1854) became chancellor of the diocese of Boston and bishop of Portland, Maine; Patrick (ord. 1864), a Jesuit, served as president of Georgetown University; Alexander Sherwood (ord. 1858) died young in 1875. The race of the light-skinned Healys was generally known, but they were not identified as black priests, nor did they work among black Catholics, as did Augustus Tolton, ordained in Rome in 1886. Upon his return to the United States Tolton was acclaimed by black Protestants, as well as Catholics, as "our Colored priest." The first black priest ordained in this country was Charles Randolph Uncles in 1891, more than a

century after the first black Baptist and Methodist clergy had emerged to pastor their people.

In the absence of black priests, black laity took up the task of defining the meaning of Roman Catholicism for Afro-Americans. From 1889 to 1894, five congresses of black Catholics met to discuss common issues. They protested racial discrimination in the church, particularly the refusal of Catholic schools to accept black youths past the age of twelve. The leader of these congresses, black layman Daniel A. Rudd, edited a black Catholic newspaper, the *American Catholic Tribune* (1887–1895). In the pages of the *Tribune*, Rudd argued that salvation for Afro-Americans lay not in Protestantism, with its separate "race" churches, but in the universalism of the Roman Catholic church, with its age-old liturgy and its history of accepting all races into the calendar of saints. While extolling Catholic universalism, Rudd and his colleagues recorded instances of discrimination and condemned them as unworthy of the church. In the twentieth century the lay activism of Rudd and the black Catholic congresses was carried on by the Federated Colored Catholics, founded in 1917 by a biology professor from Howard University, Thomas Wyatt Turner. Until its demise in the 1950s, this organization encouraged black lay leadership and condemned racism within and outside the church.

As rural southern blacks migrated to northern cities, they encountered black Catholics who had migrated from Louisiana or Maryland and white Catholics of European immigrant background. Catholic parochial schools, as time went on, offered urban blacks an appealing alternative to public education and became an important source of black converts. By midcentury the number of Afro-American Catholics had increased dramatically due to conversion. The number of black priests grew slowly and in the 1980s most black Catholics were still pastored by white priests. Today there are about 1 million black Catholics out of 50 million Catholics in the United States. They constitute a minority in population of roughly 28 million Afro-Americans of whom perhaps 18 million are Protestant.

The black Catholic population was also augmented by mid-twentieth-century immigration from Haiti, Cuba, the Dominican Republic, and Puerto Rico. These West Indian immigrants, many of African descent, also introduced the religions of voodoo and Santería in which the gods of Nigeria and Dahomey blend with Catholic saints. In the black and Hispanic sections of many American cities, *botánicas* (religious goods stores) present crowded shelves of herbal medicines, blessed candles, holy oils, statues of saints, and emblems for African gods to a large and regular clientele.

By the mid-twentieth century, the black Protestant churches faced increasing criticism from black intellectuals for alleged otherworldliness and apolitical conservatism. Leadership no longer fell exclusively to the ministers now that the number of other professionals—teachers, lawyers, doctors—was increasing in the black community. Ministers found themselves grappling not only with the old problems of poverty and segregation, but also with new threats to the traditional faith—evolution, biblical criticism, and secularism. Despite these new pressures, the black church remained the central institution for black social and political life. Though many churches were small and poor, some, such as Olivet Baptist in Chicago or Abyssinian Baptist in New York, to name only two, counted their membership in the thousands and served as important power bases for political activism on the local and even national level.

While some black intellectuals questioned the relevance of religion for the advancement of the race, others celebrated its contribution to the development of Afro-American culture. As noted above, the spirituals inspired W. E. B. Du Bois's evocative essay "Of the Sorrow Songs," in *The Souls of Black Folk*. Concertized versions of the spirituals were spread around the world, first by the Fisk Jubilee Singers (of Fisk University) in the late nineteenth century, and then by a succession of talented black virtuosos, including Roland Hayes, Paul Robeson, Marian Anderson, and William Warfield. Reflecting on the poetry and the theology of the spirituals, the black mystic, theologian, and ecumenist Howard Thurman wrote two eloquent and insightful commentaries, *Deep River* (1945) and *The Negro Spiritual Speaks of Life and Death* (1947). James Weldon Johnson arranged two volumes of spirituals and also attempted to convey the dynamic rhythms of the black chanted sermon in a volume of poetry called *God's Trombones* (1927).

Even more pervasive has been the influence of the black religious music called Gospel, which has had a symbiotic relation with secular music down to the present day. Many black musicians and singers readily acknowledged black church music as the origin of their art. A veritable collage of spirituals, Gospel, the sermon, and black religious culture was skillfully crafted by James Baldwin in his novel *Go Tell It on the Mountain* (1952), the story of one sanctified family whose life reflects the history of black Americans.

Granting the centrality of Christianity to black culture, what about the critique of the black church as politically conservative? Much of the legal struggle for civil rights as well as protest activities against segregation was led by the NAACP, a "secular" organization. But the NAACP depended heavily, particularly in the South, upon the support of local black churches and black clergy. The support of the clergy was critical. Since the minister depended upon his congregation and not upon white employers for financial support, he was less vulnerable than most southern blacks to immediate economic reprisals by whites. Moreover, during the civil rights movement of the 1950s and the 1960s the clergy lent moral support as well as considerable organizational skill to the NAACP cause on the local level. This is not to say that all black ministers supported the NAACP or protest as the best means of achieving racial justice. Some stressed black economic advance and viewed the church as a spiritual and ethical community, not a political organization. Conversely, the activism of particular congregations or individual ministers did not constitute the sole significance of religion for the civil rights movement. For many black people (and whites as well), the civil rights struggle was itself a religious crusade meant to convert the nation to the justice of this cause.

Nowhere was the connection between social activism and Christian ethics more clearly articulated than in the career of Martin Luther King, Jr. Born in 1929 in Atlanta, the son and grandson of prominent Baptist preachers, King was shaped from childhood by the black church. His style of oratory, the very cadence of his voice, was deeply rooted in the tradition of black Christianity, as were the biblical images and the historical echoes that suffused his speeches. For King and his followers the civil rights movement had as its goal the salvation of the soul of the nation. After seminary and graduate education in the North, where Walter Rauschenbusch's writings on the Social Gospel, Gandhi's theories of nonviolent resistance, and the ideas of personalist philosophy deeply influenced his thought, King returned to the South in 1954 to pastor the Dexter Avenue Baptist Church of Montgomery, Alabama. Shortly after his arrival, the Montgomery bus boycott (1955–1956) began and King was asked to act as spokesman. In this role, he articulated a philosophy of nonviolent resistance that supported protest not only in Montgomery, but in city after city in the 1960s.

Nonviolence, according to King, involved active resistance rather than aquiescence to evil. The purpose was to convert, not defeat, the opponent. Internal as well as external violence must be rooted out, since hatred and bitterness, as much as fighting, depersonalized the individual. Fundamentally, nonviolence, King claimed, was based on the belief that suffering is redemptive: by accepting the violence of the oppressor, without retaliation, the demonstrators would transform the oppressor's heart.

Vaulted to national attention by the Montgomery bus boycott, King helped organize the Southern Christian Leadership Conference (SCLC) in 1957, a church-based organization designed to coordinate protest efforts throughout the South. In demonstration after demonstration, nonviolent blacks provoked the hatred and violence of white crowds and police, revealing to the nation and the world the extent of racial injustice. Demonstrations invariably began with rallies in the black churches, including songs, prayers, Scripture readings, discussions of tactics, and an exhortation to action that sounded like a sermon. From the churches, the demonstrators moved out into the public arena to face the beatings and jailings with which white authorities greeted their demands for justice.

Though King attracted widespread support from the local black churches, it was never unanimous. Some clergymen disagreed with his philosophy of social activism because they believed that Christian ethics was a matter of personal morality and salvation. Society would be changed by obedience to God, not by political agitation. Others thought that King's appeal to obedience to a "higher law" as justification for breaking an unjust law would lead to anarchy, with each person deciding whether a law was just or not.

The most cogent critic of King's theory of nonviolent resistance came from outside the Christian churches. Malcolm X rejected King's tactics and insisted that blacks use any means necessary to achieve freedom, including violence. Malcolm, and the Nation of Islam, for which he spoke, scorned Christianity as the religion of the oppressor. Integration, they claimed, was a misguided fantasy and nonviolence only exacerbated the self-hatred that blacks already suffered. Malcolm's critique was all the more powerful because of his eloquence and integrity.

Confident optimism about the efficacy of King's nonviolent approach to civil rights peaked in 1963–1965, the years of the march on Washington, Selma, and the passage of important civil rights legislation by Congress. At that time King's dream was still "deeply rooted in the American dream." But rioting in black ghettos around the nation, the escalation of the Vietnam War, the subtlety and intransigence of racism in the North, where King's campaigns seemed to falter, all tended to threaten the dream that had seemed so hopeful in 1963. Despite opposition from many of his advisers, King spoke out against the Vietnam War, which he saw as morally evil and as a distraction from the war on poverty and racism at home. Increasingly concerned about the relationship between racism and economic injustice, King was planning to mount a "Poor People's Campaign" when he was assassinated in Memphis in April 1968.

During the last years of King's life, disappointment over the slow pace of change and disillusionment with the tactics of nonviolence had led some black activists to adopt a more militant stance and to join in the demand for "black power." For them, King's assassination sealed the demise of nonviolent resistance as a viable means of achieving equality for blacks in America. In some quarters, the rejection of nonviolence was coupled with strong criticism of the black church as a detriment to black liberation. Integration as the goal of the struggle was replaced by calls for liberation, self-determination, and community control. Black pride and the recovery of black cultural identity represented a new mood of independence—some called it separatism—among Afro-Americans.

Black clergy in white churches founded separate black caucuses to deal with questions of black identity and power within white-controlled denominational structures. Responding in part to the militant criticism of the church and in part to their own agenda, the National Conference of Black Churchmen, began in the late 1960s and early 1970s to develop a black theology in opposition to the neglect of issues of justice in white theology, as they viewed it. God, according to black theologians like Gayraud Wilmore and James Cone, is on the side of the oppressed and His presence is to be found primarily among the poor and the outcast. Jesus, they proclaimed, is the liberator of black people. Entering into dialogue with feminist and Third World theologians, black theologians such as Cone, Wilmore, and Cornel West have asserted that poverty, injustice, sexism, and racism must be taken seriously for theological reflection to be adequate.

Despite pluralism, secularization, and criticism, black Christianity remains a vital force in Afro-American life and culture in the late twentieth century. Though church statistics are notoriously inexact, some idea of the strength of the traditional black churches can be gained from a quick survey of their numbers. According to the 1984 edition of the *Yearbook of American and Canadian Churches,* the three major black Baptist denominations—the National Baptist Convention of America, the National Baptist Convention, U.S.A., Inc., and the Progressive National Baptist Convention, Inc.—claimed a combined membership of over 8.5 million. Black Methodists, including African Methodist Episcopal, African Methodist Episcopal Zion, and Christian (changed from Colored) Methodist Episcopal churches, accounted for more than 4 million members. The family of black Holiness and Pentecostal churches, with the Church of God in Christ alone claiming over 3 million members, probably numbers in excess of 4.5 million. These figures take no account of the numerous smaller religious bodies or of the significant number of black members of predominantly white churches. In a total population of approximately 28 million, the number of black church members remains high. Statistics of church membership aside, the black church remains very much at the center of black community life throughout the country.

BIBLIOGRAPHY

William Francis Allen et al., eds., *Slave Songs of the United States* (1951; orig. pub. 1867); Randall K. Burkett, *Garveyism as a Religious Movement* (1978) and with Richard Newman, as eds., *Black Apostles: Afro-American Clergy Confront the Twentieth Century* (1978); W. E. B. Du Bois, *The Souls of Black Folk* (1903); Arthur H. Fauset, *Black Gods of the Metropolis* (1944; repr. 1971); Carol V. R. George, *Segregated Sabbaths: Richard Allen and the Emergence of Independent Black Churches* (1973); Clifton H. Johnson, ed., *God Struck Me Dead: Religious Conversion Experiences and Autobiographies of Ex-Slaves* (1969); Martin Luther King, Jr., *Stride Toward Freedom: The Montgomery Story* (1958); Donald G. Mathews, *Religion in the Old South* (1977).

Albert J. Raboteau, *Slave Religion: The "Invisible Institution" in the Antebellum South* (1978); Milton C. Sernett, ed., *Afro-American Religious History: A Documentary Witness* (1985); Mechal Sobel, *Trabelin' On: The Slave Journey to an Afro-Baptist Faith* (1979); Vinson Synan, *The Holiness-Pentecostal Movement in the United States* (1971); Ethel L. Williams and Clifton F. Brown, comp., *The Howard University Bibliography of African and Afro-American Religious Studies with Locations in American Libraries* (1977); Walter L. Williams, *Black Americans and the Evangelization of Africa, 1877–1900* (1982); David W. Wills and Richard Newman, eds., *Black Apostles at Home and Abroad: Afro-Americans and the Christian Mission from the Revolution to Reconstruction* (1982); Gayraud S. Wilmore, *Black Religion and Black Radicalism* (1972; rev. ed., 1983) and with James H. Cone, as eds., *Black Theology: A Documentary History, 1966–1979* (1979); Carter G. Woodson, *The History of the Negro Church* (1921; 2nd ed., 1945).

[*See also* AFRICAN HERITAGE IN CARIBBEAN AND NORTH AMERICAN RELIGIONS; BLACK MILITANT AND SEPARATIST MOVEMENTS; BLACK RELIGIOUS THOUGHT; *and* MILLENNIALISM AND ADVENTISM.]

THE LATTER-DAY SAINTS

Jan Shipps

MORMONISM was introduced to the world early in 1830, first with the publication of the Book of Mormon and, shortly afterward, with the organization of what its members maintained was "the only true and living church upon the face of the whole earth." They believed this institution had been miraculously restored after a "Great Apostasy" that had led to the loss of the true Church of Jesus Christ and of the ancient priesthoods at the end of Christianity's apostolic age. Because Christ's followers in that earlier era had been known as "saints," those associated with this new Church of Jesus Christ understood themselves to be saints of the "latter days." This led to the official name later adopted by the organization, the Church of Jesus Christ of Latter-day Saints.

The "first elder" of the new church and the leader of the group was Joseph Smith, Jr., a young farmer who had become the Mormon prophet. Even though he was only in his early twenties, Smith had a regional reputation as a scryer, a crystal-gazer who with the help of a "peepstone" could tell people where to dig to find buried treasure. He was also known as a "diviner" who had been visited periodically by an angel named Moroni. He described this supernatural being as one who visited him three different times on the evening of the fall solstice in 1823, telling him each time of a book written upon gold plates buried in the Hill Cumorah in Manchester, New York, not far from the Smith home. When young Joseph went the next day to the exact spot he had seen in a vision the night before, he said Moroni was also there. Smith reported not having been allowed to take the gold plates then, nor for three years thereafter, even though he said he had gone to meet the angel at the appointed place on the night of the fall sol-

stice each year. He reported having obtained the plates on the night of September 22/23, 1827.

The earliest Mormon circle included most of the members of Smith's immediate family, plus a few of his more distant kinfolk and a small number of close associates. This small band was held together by a shared belief that Smith had used "ancient seers," stones known as the "Urim and Thummim," to decipher "reformed Egyptian" hieroglyphics that were engraved on the golden plates. Smith described the deciphering process as "translating."

Smith published the ancient record as the Book of Mormon. This work recounted a history of various Hebraic-American peoples, some of whom had come to the Western hemisphere at the time of the building of the Tower of Babel; others came shortly before the Babylonian captivity. The Book of Mormon identified one of these Hebraic-American peoples, the "Lamanites," as the progenitors of Native Americans. According to the text translated from the engravings on the gold plates, the ancient record also told of a visit the resurrected Jesus had made to the New World. It further said that the bringing forth of this record "out of the ground to speak to the children of men" would inaugurate the final dispensation of the "fulness of times," an era that would be marked by the reorganization of the true Christian church and later by the Second Coming of Christ.

In addition, the text indicated that in the day when it "spoke out of the ground" a prophet would come forth. Since the Book of Mormon explained that this prophet's name, like that of his father, would be Joseph, his adherents naturally concluded that Joseph Smith, Jr., was the prophet whose coming forth the ancient text foretold. Opponents made the connection, too,

649

and derisively referred to Smith's followers as "Mormonites." The Saints shortened this to "Mormon," however, and wore it as a badge of honor, making the terms *Mormons* and *Saints* (or Latter-day Saints) more or less interchangeable.

That Mormonism initially appeared in western New York State might have been expected, for this was an area where religious enthusiasm so often set the region aflame and so many extraordinary sects and strange cults flourished that it was known as the "burned-over district." This district extended along both sides of the Erie Canal west of the Catskills and Appalachians all the way to Rochester, an industrial town that became one of the great centers of the ministry of evangelist Charles Grandison Finney. In addition to the many Protestant denominations adopting "New Light" measures, many schismatic groups (sects) were organized because their members differed with the existing denominations over ritual, doctrine, or church organization. Other groups (cults) coalesced around leaders who espoused religious doctrines that departed significantly from what could be described as Protestant "orthodoxy." Among these in this region were several communities of Shakers, the followers of Jemima Wilkinson, "the Public Universal Friend," as well as followers of a variety of other lesser-known, but no more orthodox, religious leaders.

At first, the movement that Smith's small group had started seemed to be merely one more unusual cult that would fire the imaginations of people for a while and then quickly subside. But Mormonism has endured and prospered for more than a century and a half. During this time the church that was organized in 1830 with six elders and about fifty members has changed so dramatically that what began as a form of "primitive" Christianity has become a full-scale religious tradition.

In the earliest days of Mormonism, the claim that Joseph Smith was a prophet was probably less important to potential converts than the claim that this young farmer had somehow gained possession of the formula for restoring the only true Christian church. Insofar as this was the case, Mormonism had much in common with the primitive Baptists, the Campbellites, and many other contemporary Christian movements whose goal was the restoration of the so-called "primitive" or apostolic church.

But even as they accepted the New Testament as Scripture, early Latter-day Saint (LDS) converts soon discovered that the presence of a prophet in their midst made theirs a primitivism of a very different sort. For example, by the early to mid-1830s the followers of the Mormon prophet had become convinced that the ancient Aaronic priesthood (lesser priesthood) had been conferred on the Saints through an epiphany in which John the Baptist appeared to Joseph Smith and his scribe, Oliver Cowdery, prior to the formal organization of their church. The Saints came to believe that through Peter, James, and John, the priesthood of Melchizedek (higher priesthood) was restored to them as well, although the precise place and time in which this occurred is a matter that Mormons still debate. Within Mormonism's organizational and doctrinal structure, males elevated to the Aaronic priesthood may administer "outward ordinances" such as baptism, but spiritual blessings may only be conferred by persons who hold the Melchizedek priesthood.

Among a host of other revelations given through Joseph Smith, one in 1830 called for the "gathering of the Saints," which would bring the prophet's followers together in one place "to prepare their hearts and be prepared in all things against the day when tribulation and desolation are sent forth upon the wicked." Another prescribed the ordaining of the prophet's father, Joseph Smith, Sr., as patriarch. The Saints were also instructed to build a temple where the ancient ordinances could be performed.

The Saints' compliance with these revelations attenuated Mormonism's Christian connection, at least as Christianity existed in the nineteenth century, and additional changes that were made during Mormonism's first half-century revealed that it would have as much in common with ancient Israel as with the Christianity of the apostolic age. Consequently, despite the LDS perception that the Saints alone are truly Christian, Mormonism's relationship to Christianity has never been clear and simple for anyone other than the Saints themselves.

Nevertheless, Mormonism was and is related to the Christianity that existed before 1830 in much the same manner that Christianity itself was and is related to the Judaism that existed at the time of the birth of Jesus. Indeed, Mormonism was transformed from cult to religious tradition in much the same way that Christianity developed from a cultic form of Judaism into a separate and distinct religious tradition.

Just as Christianity built on a foundation supplied by the Hebraic Scriptures, Mormonism contributed new elements to the foundation provided by the Judeo-Christian Scriptures. In each case three elements were added, all of which have become fundamentals of the new traditions. Christianity added the life and ministry of Jesus; the Crucifixion and the miracle of the Resurrection; and the experiences of those who first believed, especially in the years immediately after the death of Jesus. The Saints accepted these as basic elements of Christianity, but added the miracle of the Book of Mormon; the prophetic leadership of Joseph Smith; and the experiences of those who first believed, especially in the years immediately after Smith's death.

A canon of Scripture that had appeared to be closed was reopened in both traditions. The early Christians did not reject the Hebrew canon as it then existed, but they added to the *Old* Testament, eventually canonizing a *New* Testament before sealing the canon once again. Similarly, the early Mormons did not reject the prevailing Jewish and Christian canons. As far as these works "are correctly translated," the Saints accept both the Old and New Testaments as Scripture, but in reopening the canon, Mormonism added three new volumes of Scripture. Besides the Book of Mormon, these are the Doctrine and Covenants, a book containing "the Revelations given to Joseph Smith" plus a small number of revelations that came to later LDS prophets, and the Pearl of Great Price, a slender volume that includes selections from the writings of ancient prophets such as Abraham and Moses that were either translated by or revealed to Joseph Smith, as well as an autobiographical account of the prophet's early years. Unlike Christianity, however, Mormonism did not seal its canon when the movement became fully institutionalized. Because current presidents of LDS churches are also prophets who continue to speak for God, announcing revelations that the faithful accept as divine writ, Mormonism still has an open canon.

The form and content of the new Mormon Scriptures differ considerably from the Gospels, letters, and concluding Book of the Apocalypse that Christianity added to its canon. While the New Testament supplies the Christian tradition with descriptive narratives of all three of its added fundamentals, works formally canonized by the LDS Church include narrative accounts of only two of the fundamentals that separate Mormonism from the rest of the Judeo-Christian tradition. The miracle of the Book of Mormon is explained by the existence of the book itself, and Joseph Smith's prophetic leadership is made manifest through the translations, revelations, and narrations found in the Doctrine and Covenants and the Pearl of Great Price. But in contrast to Christianity's accounts of the movement after the death of Jesus, which are contained in the Book of Acts and the letters of Paul and others, Mormonism has no scriptural narrative detailing the experiences of the Saints in the years after the death of their first prophet.

Whereas the Christian canon includes only sketchy information about the early life of Jesus, however, a short section in the Pearl of Great Price provides the Saints with their founder's own retrospective description of his early life. Written in 1838, but describing events that occurred many years earlier, Smith's autobiographical narrative (formally canonized in 1880) is especially significant in modern Mormon understandings of the Mormon story. Of particular importance is the modern Saints' emphasis on Smith's description of his visionary experience in the spring of 1820, an experience Mormons describe as the First Vision.

The prophet had written about this experience in his diary in 1832, describing it in a manner not unlike contemporary evangelical accounts of conversion experiences. But in the 1838 version, he described the experience as a vision in which he perceived "the Father and the Son" as personages as distinct from each other as ordinary mortals with "bodies and parts." Smith said he also learned during this vision that existing churches were all false and that, as the one to whom this vision was manifested, he would play a prominent part in the forthcoming restoration of the true church.

This account of the prophet's vision nicely illustrates the Mormon rejection of the Trinity and of descriptions of God as an incorporeal being. It explains why the Saints believe that the only true church is the one founded by the Mormon prophet, and it dramatizes Smith's divine calling. Perhaps because it makes these important theological points with such economy,

Smith's 1838 account of his First Vision is often identified by modern Latter-day Saints as the event that opened the "new dispensation of the fulness of times."

The decision to canonize "Joseph Smith's History," with its emphasis on his early spiritual experience, has given the prophet's First Vision an aura of authenticity as the beginning of the movement. But the members of Smith's family and his early followers apparently had no knowledge of the divine manifestation that came to the prophet in 1820. This does not indicate that the vision never happened, as some of Mormonism's evangelical Protestant opponents have charged. But it is a reminder that in the beginning Smith placed much greater stress on the thrice-repeated vision he had in 1823 in which he beheld the heavenly being who directed him to the golden plates buried in a hill near his home.

As indicated, accounts of the experiences of the Saints after Smith's death, while vitally important, are not canonized. Instead, these reports are located in a multitude of diaries, letters, and various documentary records. An immense number of historical works have drawn upon such sources to form narrative accounts of the experiences of the Mormon pioneers, and some of the ones written by official LDS Church historians have taken on quasi-canonical status. Still, the lack of a scriptural narrative imposing a modicum of order on conflicting historical accounts—as order is imposed on the history of the Hebrews in the historical books of the Old Testament and on stories of the life of Jesus and the history of his early followers in the New Testament—has meant that, in Mormonism, history has always been at one and the same time unusually significant and very problematic.

MORMON DIVERSITY

A canonized history of the inaugural era of a religion signals a high level of agreement in perceptions of what happened "in the beginning." By the same token, the absence of fixed understandings of the generative period of Mormonism signals, if not a total lack of agreement among the Saints, at least the presence of alternative understandings of the events of those years. During the lifetime of Joseph Smith, the Saints' varying perceptions of Mormonism's

genesis were never sharp enough to cause full-scale schism within the church. But after the prophet's murder in 1844, subdivisions developed that reflected an increasing lack of agreement about whether Mormonism was primarily a restoration of apostolic Christianity or a restoration of both the New Testament church and the kingdom of God established according to a pattern drawn from ancient Israel. This dissension within the larger body led inexorably to the creation of distinct LDS organizations in the second half of the nineteenth century.

Bound together mainly by a belief that the Book of Mormon is Scripture and that Joseph Smith was a prophet, the principal ecclesiastical units in the Mormon tradition are now the Church of Jesus Christ of Latter-day Saints (the LDS Church), whose headquarters is in Salt Lake City, Utah, and the Reorganized Church of Jesus Christ of Latter Day Saints (the RLDS Church), based in Independence, Missouri. The initial disagreement that separated these two Mormon groups was the matter of prophetic succession. Those who believed that Smith's successor should be a sitting member of the Council of Twelve Apostles, the church's governing body, followed Brigham Young, who led the LDS branch of the movement; those who believed that the prophetic line would be perpetuated only if one of Joseph Smith's lineal descendants was selected followed the Mormon leader's eldest son, Joseph Smith, III, who led the Reorganization. Because the break between them was precipitated by Smith's death, these two organizations are considered divisions of Mormonism, not schismatic movements.

As will be shown, a much deeper issue underlay this rending of the Mormon fabric. In spite of the fact that Smith's revelations mandating the ordaining of a patriarch, inaugurating plural marriage, building temples, and establishing a theocratic kingdom started to give Mormonism an Old Testament as well as a New Testament character during his lifetime, the RLDS Church adopted the position that, while Mormonism has a prophet at its head, it originally was and continues to be primarily a restoration of the Church of Jesus Christ. Saints associated with Brigham Young did not disagree about Mormonism's status as a movement of Christian restoration. But until the end of the nineteenth century, when, under extreme pressure from the U.S. government and the nation's evangelical Protestant community, the Saints agreed to discontinue the practice of plural marriage and to dissolve the temporal kingdom (in which church authorities had directed social, political, and economic as well as ecclesiastical affairs), the LDS Church fashioned a very different form of Mormonism. It was a form that so nearly included "the restoration of all things" that the LDS movement appeared to be as Hebraic, according to a literal reading of the Old Testament, as it was Christian.

As a reaction against existing Catholic and Protestant forms of Christianity, Mormonism developed a pattern of leadership different from that in other religious organizations. Instead of a system of local congregations led by what many early LDS preachers called "hireling clergy," the Mormons established settlements, lived in close proximity, and worshiped together. Although the goal set by the revelation calling for the gathering was the creation of a single community in which all the Saints would reside, centers of Mormonism existed in both Ohio and Missouri in the first half of the 1830s. Described by Joseph Smith as "stakes in the tent of Zion," these settlements provided the pattern for organizing the church into stakes (dioceses) and wards (parishes).

Since virtually all Mormon males are elevated to the priesthood at the age of twelve, the LDS population is not divided vertically into a two-tiered, clergy-laity structure, with clerics serving as preacher-pastors. The male population of Mormonism is separated instead into priesthood quorums that rank from lowest, the deacons' quorum in the Aaronic order, through quorums of teachers and priests that are also in the Aaronic order, to the higher quorums of elders, seventies, and high priests in the priesthood order of Melchizedek. While these various quorums have particular responsibilities assigned to them, the leadership cadre in the church is made up of members of the priesthood and Mormon women who are fulfilling "callings." All the areas in the world where the church is organized are divided into stakes and a presidency; an executive (president) and two counselors are called to preside over each one. Stakes are divided into wards and a bishopric; a pastor (bishop) and two counselors are called to preside over each one.

The central administration of the church is carried out by the First Presidency, composed of a president, who by virtue of his office is also "prophet, seer, and revelator," and two counselors, and by a Council of Twelve Apostles, a Quorum of Seventy, and a Presiding Bishopric. The Saints who fulfill these callings are known corporately as General Authorities.

Stake presidents and their counselors, bishops and their counselors, mission presidents, and other middle- and lower-echelon ecclesiastical administrators in the LDS Church all serve without financial compensation. In the RLDS Church, however, while there are some local leaders who serve without pay, a corps of paid ministers slowly came into being. From the mid-twentieth century forward, however, members of the central administration of both churches have been given living allowances that take the place of salaries earned from lay activities. In addition, the RLDS and LDS ecclesiastical structures differ in two other important areas. RLDS women may be ordained to the priesthood, but LDS women may not. In the LDS Church custom dictates that, upon the death of a church president, the new president will be the apostle who has the longest tenure in the Council of the Twelve and he will be president as long as he lives. This system almost guarantees that all LDS church presidents will be aged men. In the RLDS Church, church presidents, who must be direct descendants of Joseph Smith, usually assume the office in middle age and generally retire before they reach the age of seventy.

By the mid-1980s the LDS and RLDS churches in the United States had well over 6 million members in a ratio of about 20 LDS to 1 RLDS. Yet this total does not begin to encompass all those who fit in one way or another into the Mormon category. An almost bewildering variety of other organizations, none of them connected to the LDS Church (which is often referred to as Utah Mormonism) or the RLDS Church (which is officially known as the Reorganization), are also included within the Mormon tradition. Many—but by no means all—of these Mormon organizations are underground groups composed of people who believe that Mormonism so accommodated itself to "the world" when the practice of plural marriage was officially discontinued that the LDS Church is no longer truly the Church of Jesus Christ. There are also a number, perhaps 25,000, of so-called "cultural" Mormons, i.e., individuals who are

Latter-day Saints solely from the standpoint of family heritage, not from active membership in any LDS ecclesiastical unit.

In other words, Saints come in many varieties. Some Saints take LDS theological claims very seriously and some Saints reject these claims out of hand. And there are Saints on every point along a spectrum in between. Some LDS life patterns are determined by Mormon behavioral standards, which include total abstinence from alcohol, tobacco, coffee, and tea; some LDS life patterns are practically unaffected by Mormon affiliation. And, again, there are LDS life patterns located at every point along a spectrum in between. Such diversity makes it clear that Mormonism is not just a belief system. The Mormons are as much an ethnic group as are Irish Catholics or Eastern European Jews.

CULTURAL BACKGROUND AND MORMON BEGINNINGS

Economic opportunity in the area along the Erie Canal had drawn Joseph Smith, Sr., and his family to the region around Palmyra, New York, a village about twenty miles east of Rochester. Along with thousands of other families whose members came from venerable New England stock, the future prophet's father and his mother, Lucy Mack Smith, had abandoned their struggle to gain a living along the Vermont–New Hampshire border and crossed the Adirondacks seeking a better life for themselves and their eight children. When they arrived in 1816 they found, however, that day-to-day existence was difficult in western New York as well. In addition to working land for themselves, the elder Joseph Smith and his sons often worked for wages on neighboring farms while his wife and daughters sold handmade items and foodstuffs at local markets and fairs. Yet, as in New Hampshire and Vermont, the Smith family was so plagued with hard luck that they were never able to become the sort of independent landowners that their paternal and maternal ancestors in New England had been. So it was that the Mormon prophet grew to manhood in a family located on the economic fringes of society.

Yet from the standpoint of their sociocultural situation, the Smith family did not occupy a marginal position. Its members were, rather, reasonably central figures in a substantial subculture mostly made up of rural farming people, some of whom were quite successful, but most of whom were of the middling and poorer sorts. Populated by persons in the rural areas in other parts of the nation, as well as in western New York, this subculture subscribed to the great republican synthesis that held together the nation's various sections and heterogeneous groups of people in the first half of the nineteenth century. But people in this rural subculture also held on to an older folk-culture outlook characterized by a concern for families as corporate units and an inordinate fear of societal disorder.

Essentially premodern in worldview, this subculture was set apart from the rest of the nation by its attitudes toward religion and its perspectives on magic, alchemy, and other forms of the occult. While many found religious assurance through participation in "New Light" evangelical denominations, many others became "seekers," trying out several evangelical denominations before becoming so confused by the ever-present competing religious claims that they came to doubt whether ecstatic spiritual experiences constituted absolute evidence of religious authority. Repudiating the legitimacy of existing churches, they sought what they believed to be the unambiguous truth inherent in "primitive" Christianity and the unconditional authority inherent in the "correct" organizational form of the apostolic church. Depending on the Bible for definitive answers to their religious questions, the persons who made up this subculture usually read that ancient text with a literal cast of mind and presentist perspective.

Yet, even as they firmly and surely regarded the Bible as the source of truth, their folk religion allowed them to embrace the occult as well, although neither in a mystical sense nor in a superstitious frame. Like most Americans of the time, they were essentially empiricists. On the basis of the testimony of trusted persons who reported first-hand observations of competent diviners (who could use rods or seer stones to find buried treasure) and expert adepts (who were skilled in performing magic rituals that produced desirable results) they accepted the efficacy of the formulas treasured by diviners and adepts in much the same way that people in the larger culture were coming to accept the effectiveness and reliability of scientific formulas.

These people cultivated their religious attitudes and their beliefs about clairvoyant gifts, enchanted treasure, talismans that protected wearers from evil, and the possibility of turning base metal into gold in the heady atmosphere of religious ferment and intellectual freedom emanating from the absence of ecclesiastical order and standards of orthodox belief that prevailed in the wake of the young nation's separation of church and state. Further, the romantic ambience of the early nineteenth century encouraged speculation about such diverse matters as Egyptian hieroglyphics, a plurality of worlds, and the racial origins of Native Americans.

Thus, instead of seeming peculiar or fantastic, the coming forth of the Book of Mormon, Joseph Smith, Jr.'s taking up of the prophet's mantle, and the restoration of the apostolic church appeared almost as natural events, not unexpected in the subculture of which the Smiths were a part. It is likely that the treasure-seeking activities of the family, their acceptance of occult teachings, their connection with folk magic, and young Joseph's reputation as an adept were not detrimental to early Mormonism. Indeed, the intimate connection between magic and religion at Mormonism's beginning probably accounted for some of the movement's early appeal. Moreover, the rapid growth of Mormonism could have partially been the result of the unusual appeal that Joseph Smith's story had for persons who were a part of the subculture from which the Mormon prophet came.

Whatever the role of magic and the occult, the historical record reveals that the persuasiveness of the LDS religious claims and the millennialist character of the movement were elements of far greater importance in Mormonism's success in attracting adherents. Because early Mormon theological propositions rested heavily on prophetic and apocalyptic biblical passages describing preludes to a new age, these two elements were interrelated. The Saints established a direct connection between the record Smith translated from metal plates and the promises set forth in the Old and New Testaments by identifying the Book of Mormon as the "book that is sealed" described in Isaiah 29:11, for example. This not only legitimated the new Mormon Scripture, but since the rest of Isaiah 29 could be read as a prediction that the appearance of the sealed book would initiate "a marvelous work and a

wonder," this text was also used to support the assertion that Smith's discovering and translating the plates opened a new dispensation that would be the occasion for the "turning of things upside down." How comforting to the new Saints to read that on that day the deaf would hear, the blind would see, the meek would increase their joy, and Israel's house would be redeemed.

Two passages in Smith's "gold bible," as skeptical contemporaries called it, referred to the prophecy concerning the "sticks" (writings or histories) of Ephraim and Judah in Ezekiel 37. When the two "sticks" became one in the Lord's hand, according to the prophecy, the children of Israel would be gathered from "among the heathen" and the divided kingdom would be no more. Since Mormon converts understood themselves to be children of Israel gathered from among the heathen, this passage was likewise reassuring.

Perhaps of greater theological import was the Mormon identification of Moroni, the being who revealed the location of the plates to Joseph Smith, as the angel who flew "in the midst of heaven having the everlasting gospel to preach unto them that dwell on the earth" (Rev. 14:6). In tying their story to the Apocalypse of Saint John in this way, the Saints placed themselves in "the winding-up scene," awaiting only the final curtain before Christ's Second Coming. Standing at the edge of history, the Mormon prophet and his followers embarked together on an extraordinary set of experiences in a time they described as a new dispensation.

EARLY HISTORY

During the LDS movement's first two decades, the Mormons made what were intended as permanent settlements in four different places: Kirtland, Ohio; Independence, Missouri; Caldwell County, Missouri; and Nauvoo, Illinois. Unfortunately, the non-Mormon inhabitants in each of these places—the Saints called them Gentiles—soon became alarmed by the large numbers of Mormons gathering in their areas. Seeing the Saints' sheer numbers and their abundant energy in establishing strong, cohesive, self-sufficient communities, the Gentiles started to fear that they would be economically overwhelmed and that their political power would be diluted. In addition, most non-Mormons regarded Mormonism as a heretical movement that endangered American religion. In Kirtland, western Missouri, and Nauvoo, the resulting Mormon-Gentile tensions were exacerbated by internal dissension that developed within the LDS circle as Mormonism struggled through the exciting but sometimes disconcerting process of shaping itself into a unique theological and cultural entity.

One byproduct of this early period was a large body of polemical literature that called into question the very foundations of Mormonism. Written by Mormon apostates—persons who, after having joined the LDS movement, either were "cut off" (excommunicated) or left of their own accord—Gentile journalists, foreign observers, Protestant ministers, Roman Catholic priests, and non-Mormon politicians, this literature drew heavily on the interviews with persons who had known the prophet and his family before 1830 first published in *Mormonism Unvailed* (*sic*), a scurrilous work put together by Philastrus Hurlbut and Eber D. Howe. This literature portrayed the Smith family as ignorant and superstitious and pictured Joseph Smith as an itinerant scryer turned religious fraud. Many of these works also charged that the Book of Mormon was produced by someone other than Smith. Perhaps because Mormonism prospered so quickly, this literature took on a life of its own, regularly appearing throughout the nineteenth and twentieth centuries in exposé literature, as well as in the eleventh edition of the *Encyclopaedia Britannica,* William Alexander Linn's much-used history of Mormonism, Alice Felt Tyler's *Freedom's Ferment,* and many other works purporting to be carefully researched history.

A more dramatic result of the events and tensions in this early period was the armed conflict that drove the Saints from Kirtland (January 1838) and Independence (November 1833) to western Missouri and then to an area along the eastern bank of the Mississippi River above Quincy, Illinois (spring 1839). The 12,000 to 15,000 Saints who streamed back across the river were initially welcomed by the residents of Illinois, a state in desperate financial straits and much in need of new citizens who would enlarge the tax base. Purchasing Commerce, a

hamlet, the Saints established a thriving settlement there in less than a year. Explaining that it was a word of Hebrew derivation meaning "beautiful place," the prophet named the town Nauvoo. Amicable Mormon-Gentile relations in Illinois in 1839 and 1840 created an atmosphere that allowed the state legislature to approve a charter for the city liberal enough to permit the Saints to operate Nauvoo almost as an independent municipality. Protected by its own court system and militia (the Nauvoo Legion), Nauvoo flourished; by 1844 it was the largest city in Illinois.

Mormon bloc voting directed by revelation announced from the pulpit aroused fear in the Illinois non-Mormon population, which had already grown anxious about the burgeoning economic power of the state's new citizens. Gentile fear soon turned to outright hostility that was not allayed when the Mormon prophet announced his candidacy for president of the United States in January 1844. Pressure exerted on the Saints by belligerent non-Mormons was exacerbated by developing dissension within the Mormon community generated by the introduction of the practice of plural marriage and the organization of the political Kingdom of God. In addition to the regular city government, in which he served as mayor, Smith was crowned king and a committee known as the Council of Fifty was called to serve, in the words of Joseph Smith, as the "municipal department of the kingdom [of God]."

The combination of internal tension and external animosity created a threatening situation that placed the Mormons and their leaders in jeopardy. In June 1844 Joseph Smith and his brother Hyrum were arrested and, while incarcerated in the jail in Carthage, Illinois, were murdered by members of a militia group that had been called out to protect the state in the event of a Mormon uprising. This led to a subsequent splintering of the LDS movement and the flight of the largest body of Latter-day Saints to the then unsettled basin of the Great Salt Lake.

The years when Smith led the Saints comprise Mormonism's generative period. As he communed daily with his followers, worked, studied the Scriptures, prayed, preached, suffered persecution and imprisonment, Smith announced a steady stream of revelations that carried the Saints ever further from the Trinitarian theology of the Book of Mormon and the Christian primitivism that had been central to the movement at its beginning.

But the first moves Smith made were more geographical than theological. For reasons that may have been connected to Smith's former activities as a diviner who had pledged to share the benefits of all of his discoveries of treasure with the other members of a treasure-seeking band, the prophet, his family, and his associates experienced harassment and ridicule both before and after the publication of the Book of Mormon. They interpreted this unfriendly and often malicious activity as religious persecution. Concluding that under the circumstances it would be best to remove himself and his followers from New York State, Smith led his growing flock westward in 1831.

For the next seven years there would be two major Mormon settlements, one in Kirtland, Ohio, where Campbellite minister Sidney Rigdon and his whole congregation had converted to Mormonism, and the other in western Missouri. Although an early revelation identified Missouri's Jackson County as the "center place for the city of Zion," the majority of the LDS converts settled near the prophet and his family in Ohio. But after land west of Independence was consecrated as the gathering place for the Saints, more than 1,200 Saints settled in the area.

In both Ohio and Missouri, Mormons set themselves apart from non-Mormon residents socially, psychologically, and eventually politically. The straitened circumstances of many of the LDS converts who gathered to these communities were such that, even before revelation required Saints to share their worldly goods with other members of the group, a form of economic communitarianism became a necessity. The law of consecration and stewardship was revealed 9 February 1831. It established an Order of Enoch and called for Saints to enter the order by consecrating all their property and personal possessions to the church. In return they were to be given an "inheritance" or stewardship sufficient for themselves and their families, with the remainder being used for the poor and for general improvements. This allowed the Saints control over whatever possessions they needed to make their livings, while creating a common store

from the surplus. The unsettled situation of the Saints and difficulties encountered in putting this system into practice led to its suspension. In the summer of 1838 a new law was revealed establishing a tithing system as the rule of the church. Nevertheless Mormon communities in the early years functioned as corporate units economically.

Independence was still a frontier outpost in 1831, but a substantial group of early settlers had such a proprietary interest in the region that the security of the Saints was threatened almost from the time they reached the area. While they managed to organize themselves into a "stake in the tent of Zion" and to bring in a press to use in printing tracts, doctrinal works, and an LDS newspaper, the tense situation erupted in violence when an editorial published in the *Evening and Morning Star,* the first Mormon periodical, welcomed free blacks to join the Saints in Missouri, a slave state. In July 1833 the office of the *Morning and Evening Star* was destroyed, and the Missourians mounted a campaign to drive the Saints away.

As soon as news of his followers' fate reached the prophet in Kirtland, he organized a military force called Zion's Camp and set off in May 1834 to help the Missouri Saints regain their Independence land and property. In retrospect this episode in LDS history resembles nothing so much as Joshua setting out with his small band of followers to subdue Jericho. Unlike that famous biblical campaign, however, Zion's Camp was a dismal military failure. Although the operation failed, the Zion's Camp experience was nevertheless extremely significant. It winnowed the weak in faith from the LDS leadership cadre, while those who had proved their loyalty to their Mormon brethren afterward formed the prophet's inner circle.

A familial relationship was engendered in the LDS communities by the forms of address that were universally used. Women joining the Saints became "sisters"; men became "brothers." In addition, persons who joined were not only baptized into the church; they also received patriarchal blessings from "Father Smith" or some other person who had been ordained as a patriarch in which, along with prophecies of their future lives as Saints, they were informed of their Hebraic tribal identity.

The Mormons in and around Kirtland were also united by their common effort to construct the unusual meetinghouse that was dedicated in 1836 as the Kirtland Temple. From the exterior this building resembled a New England meetinghouse, but the interior was divided into upper and lower floors, each of which had, instead of pulpits, "stands" for various priesthood quorums. While high ceilings and tall windows made the meeting area appear spacious when the stands were left open, an elaborate system of curtains (sometimes called veils) and pulleys made it possible for the quorums to meet in private. Considering the financial difficulties and the precarious situation of the Saints, this was a magnificent structure, and the week-long ceremony in which it was dedicated proved to be such a religious high point that it fused the Saints into a spiritual body, much as the tongues of fire that fell on the apostles fused the Christians into one body on the day of Pentecost. Afterward there would be dissensions and divisions, but the covenant was sealed in the hearts and minds of the Saints; the kingdom was organized and would, in the words of the prophet, from thence roll forth.

The open dissension that erupted within the LDS community in Kirtland in 1837 was apparently rooted in the financial machinations of Smith and other leading Mormons, whose bank —organized in spite of their inability to obtain a state charter—failed, causing a virtual collapse of the Kirtland economy. The surviving evidence suggests, however, that the dissension also reflected disagreement about theology and religious practice. The Christian primitivism that had first attracted Saints to the movement had been much less structured and less doctrinaire than the new Mormonism, which featured a systematized doctrine and an increasingly elaborate church organization. By the late 1830s the church not only had deacons, elders, priests, bishops, and apostles whose roles were outlined in the biblical Book of Acts, but it had a First Presidency (made up of a president and two counselors), a high council, a patriarch, a Quorum of Seventy, and a Council of Twelve Apostles. Additionally, revelation had given the prophet ultimate authority by making it clear that "no one shall be appointed to receive commandments and revelations in this church ex-

cepting [the Lord's] servant Joseph Smith, Jun." And while the revelation permitting plural marriage (polygamy) was not disclosed—even to selected Saints—until 1843 and was not made public until 1852, much evidence suggests that a precursor or variant of it was introduced while the Saints were in Kirtland, thus transforming Mormonism ever more dramatically from what it had been only five or six years before.

Although some Saints—likely those who were nostalgic for early Mormonism—remained in Ohio, the prophet and most other LDS leaders were forced to flee in late 1837 and early 1838. They went to join the Saints in Missouri, who by this time were settled in a "Mormon" county that the state legislature had set aside especially for them. This, however, proved to be a temporary way station since tension expressed in the violent clashes of non-Mormons and the Danite Band, an unofficial LDS militia, turned into the so-called Mormon war in September 1838. Heavily outnumbered, the Mormons surrendered on October 31 and Joseph Smith and other LDS leaders were arrested. Their stock slaughtered and their crops destroyed, the Saints had no choice other than flight. Early in 1839 Brigham Young and the Council of Twelve Apostles organized the removal of the Mormon community from Missouri. As discussed earlier, some 12,000 to 15,000 Mormons went back across the Mississippi to Illinois, and when the prophet was permitted to escape, he joined them there.

By the time the Saints reached Nauvoo, the basic belief system was in place, separating the Saints from Roman Catholics and Protestants while keeping them in the Christian fold. The Book of Mormon is affirmed as a "second witness" of Jesus Christ. The Saints maintain, moreover, that the coming forth of this sacred record opened a new dispensation, which is to be the final dispensation before the Second Coming of the Savior. Since they recognize the text of the book as the "everlasting gospel" that the angel flying "in the midst of heaven" had to "preach unto them that dwell on the earth" to which Revelation 14:6 refers, its being published to the world is also understood as a sign that the Second Coming is near.

LDS theological tenets drawn from the Book of Mormon include a rejection of the doctrine of original sin and assurance that "through the

Atonement of Christ," salvation is available to all who have "faith in the Lord Jesus Christ," are willing to repent, and give "obedience to the laws and ordinances of the Gospel." Equally important, the Book of Mormon identified Joseph Smith, Jr., as the prophet whose coming forth would coincide with the coming forth of the book itself. Through him and his successors occupying the prophetic office the Mormons have access to continuing revelation. Mormons further affirm that the presence of a prophet in the position of church president is crucial to the claim that theirs is the only legitimate Church of Jesus Christ. They are also certain that they have the restored priesthoods of Aaron and Melchizedek as well as the restored church.

The framework of the central church organization was likewise fixed before the Mormons were driven from Missouri. Although the disruptions in Kirtland and Missouri had kept the tithing system from operating smoothly, the principle of tithing had been established. And missionaries traveling in England and throughout the eastern and southern United States and eastern Canada were laying the groundwork for the system of missions that would afterward bring a steady stream of converts into the movement.

The shift in emphasis that turned as much of the prophet's attention to the ancient Hebraic order of things as to the apostolic era started to take place in Kirtland, as was indicated by the interior plan of the temple and the ordaining of Smith's father to the office of patriarch. Although it was not written down until 1843 and not announced publicly until 1852, some scholars, including Lawrence Foster and Jan Shipps, are convinced that the prophet also received the revelation dealing with celestial marriage in Kirtland. This important revelation, now Section 132 in the Doctrine and Covenants, is the basis of LDS doctrine concerning marriage for time and all eternity, as well as the basis for a belief in "three degrees of glory," terrestrial, telestial, and celestial. In Nauvoo this revelation also became the basis for the introduction of the practice of plural marriage, a system that allowed "worthy" LDS men to take more than one wife.

Other temple ordinances were introduced in Nauvoo besides celestial marriage, ordinances believed to have been withheld from the world awaiting the construction of a temple that would serve the Saints in the same way that Solomon's temple served the chosen people in the days of the ancient Hebrews. Called *endowments,* these include vicarious ordinances, such as baptism for the dead, in which living Mormons perform ordinances for and in behalf of the dead who had no opportunity to perform the ordinances themselves. The theological import of the introduction of temple ordinances was the introduction of the concept of eternal progression toward Godhood, a concept expressed by Lorenzo Snow, LDS church president from 1898 to 1901: "As man is, God once was; as God is, man may become."

Innovations in theology and liturgy were not the only additions to Mormonism that came in Nauvoo. There on the banks of the Mississippi River a temporal kingdom with a theocratic government came into being. And as the years passed, its leaders were the Latter-day Saints who were willing to follow Joseph Smith into the practice of plural marriage (polygamy). While the full extent of these unusual developments was obscured by the atmosphere of secrecy in which they occurred, the perception that something highly unusual, if not dangerous, was going on stirred enough opposition to provoke both the prophet's death and the Saints' being driven from the state.

DEVELOPMENT OF THE TRADITION

With Joseph Smith's death, Mormonism moved into a second phase. While the canon remained open, the basic pattern for the tradition had been set. Since that time, revelation has sometimes altered doctrine to deal with existing issues, but it has never introduced new doctrine in the manner that new doctrine was introduced in Nauvoo. From 1844 onward, Mormons have dealt with most issues and handled most problems using the same strategies that other religious traditions use: reinterpretation of existing Scripture and reflection on historical precedent.

But Smith's untimely death created a critical problem for which the Mormons had no immediate solution: identifying a new leader. The prophet had not occupied an existing office and he had not been a scion to tradition; he was, in

Weberian terms, a classic charismatic leader. His right to head the church and direct the destiny of the Saints had been rooted in his followers' certainty that he had been called by and that he spoke for God. He had been so successful that it would have been possible for him to designate his successor, or at least to specify how his successor should be chosen, but he did not do that. Instead he left such mixed messages about who his successor should be that a protracted struggle ensued.

Because history has a way of validating winners and making contested outcomes appear inevitable, it is easy to get the wrong impression about the emergence of a new Mormon leader. Despite an oft-repeated reconstruction of events that pictures the contest as having been settled when Brigham Young appeared before the Saints speaking with the voice and having the physical characteristics of the slain prophet, and despite the size and visibility of the "Great Basin Kingdom" built by Young and his adherents, the succession struggle was not definitively settled before the Saints were driven from Illinois.

Rather than a contest between individuals, such as Brigham Young, the president of the Council of Twelve Apostles, Sidney Rigdon, a member of the First Presidency, William Smith, brother of the slain prophet, the LDS leadership struggle was actually a contest between competing ideas about what Mormonism ought to be. In view of the persecution and violence with which they had been forced to contend in Ohio and Missouri, and which threatened them in Illinois, some of the Saints had grown disenchanted with the gathering. They did not deny Mormonism, but they wondered whether an LDS diaspora might not be better than continuing to maintain high boundaries separating the LDS and non-Mormon communities. Others were disturbed by the new theology and practical innovations (theocracy, polygamy) that had been introduced in the last months of Smith's life. They did not deny Mormonism, but wanted to turn back to the days when the restored apostolic church had been at the heart of the movement. But such sentiments were anathema to Brigham Young, who became the champion of those who wished to preserve the movement as it had existed at the time of the prophet's death. And since he was the most powerful member of the group that led the LDS community in the interim between the martyrdom, as

the Saints describe it, and the Mormon flight from Illinois across Iowa to Council Bluffs in 1846, Young has been pictured as Smith's successor.

While there can be no question about Young's importance, understanding Mormonism as a religious tradition requires recognition that a significant proportion of the LDS population—one historian estimates that it might have been more than 25 percent—did not follow "the Lion of the Lord" when in 1847 he led the Saints across the Rocky Mountains to the Great Salt Lake Valley. Some of those who rejected Young's leadership followed James J. Strang to northern Michigan, others went with Lyman Wight to Texas, or with Sam Brannan to California, or back east to join Sidney Rigdon in Pennsylvania. The largest number of Mormons in the group that did not follow Young settled throughout the Midwest, where they organized independent Mormon congregations and continued to regard themselves as Latter-day Saints. In 1860, when the prophet's son, Joseph Smith III, was mature enough to assume a leadership role, many of these independent congregations came together and formed the Reorganized Church.

As significant as these various other groups are, the followers of Brigham Young became the most important Mormon group to survive the death of the tradition's founder. Partly because of sheer numbers (the number of Joseph Smith's followers in 1840 had been 30,000; by 1850, even with the splintering of the movement, Young's followers numbered 60,000; a decade later there were 80,000 and by 1870 the total was 110,000) and partly because they have retained their separate identity, their story has become the Mormon story—appropriately so, because in the Salt Lake Valley these people actually brought the kingdom Smith had envisioned into reality.

Brigham Young had learned about Mormonism almost as soon as the Book of Mormon was published. But this carpenter, cabinetmaker, and glazier from Mendon, New York, the son of pious Methodist parents, did not rush into the movement. In 1832, however, after studying the new Scripture carefully, he was baptized and moved to Kirtland. By the time Young was received into the church, many of Smith's revelations were moving Mormonism away from the strict Christian primitivist camp and toward the "restoration of all things." Although a number of Smith's earliest followers were concerned about this perceived change in the movement's direction, Young never was. He embraced the gathering, the ordination of a patriarch, the growing organizational complexity, and all the other measures that were instituted by revelation, believing that as prophet, seer, revelator, and high priest, as well as church president, Joseph Smith held the keys to salvation. His support of the prophet in the face of internal dissent in the LDS community brought "Brother Brigham" into the prophet's inner circle.

Called to the Council of Twelve Apostles, Young took effective charge of the flight of the Missouri refugees, leading them back across the Mississippi to Illinois, and while he was dismayed by the necessity of doing so, he followed Smith and other leaders who were close to the prophet into plural marriage. In 1839 Young went to England, where he spent two years as a missionary. Although Joseph Smith's murder caused him untold anguish, Young was so totally committed to Mormonism that he was ready to assume the prophet's mantle. If the entire Mormon population failed to follow him, there were so many who did—and in subsequent years, many LDS converts from England, Scandinavia, and elsewhere also joined him—that before his death in 1877 Young's flock numbered nearly 150,000.

The Mormon trek to the Salt Lake Valley is sometimes compared to the movement along the Oregon Trail that took place at about the same time. From the immigrants' standpoint, it is not an appropriate comparison. The Mormons were leaving the modernity of nineteenth-century America, moving at one and the same time backward into antiquity and forward to the promised land. Carrying with them not only the "plat of the City of Zion" but the theology and theocracy of the "kingdom on the Mississippi" as well, these Saints built up Zion in the heart of the American West.

Under the guidance of Young, who had been named president of the church in December 1847, the Saints re-created an ancient order, building temples, practicing plural marriage, and organizing a "theo-democracy" to govern a realm patterned as much on the kingdom over which David and Solomon reigned as on the Constitution of the United States. Set apart from the rest of the nation by a peculiar manner of conducting public affairs—the Mormons had their own political party and voted as a bloc in accordance with directions delivered from the pulpit during Sunday sermons—and by their practice of plural marriage, this kingdom attempted to maintain economic self-sufficiency. Within a decade Mormonism had spread along the Wasatch front, throughout the intermountain region, and southwest all the way to the Pacific.

That the Mormon domain came to be viewed as an alien land is not surprising. The principal town in the enclave the Mormons called the State of Deseret was located on one of the main routes to the California gold fields. This attracted many non-Mormons to the region. In addition to those who were just traveling through, government officials and other non-Mormons came to what was then called Great Salt Lake City intending to stay after the area was organized as a U.S. territory in 1850.

While the LDS kingdom lasted for over forty years, Mormon marriage patterns were too abhorrent and LDS political practices too foreign for most non-Mormons to tolerate. Interpreting Mormonism as a dangerous heresy as well as a threat to the American home and family, the nation's evangelical Protestant majority pressured the federal government to act. The U.S. Congress responded in 1862 by passing a law making plural marriage illegal. After the Civil War the pressure to end polygamy was intensified and force was used in an effort to bring the politics of Utah Territory in line with that of the rest of the nation.

The Edmunds Act, a stringent antipolygamy measure passed in 1882, led to the arrest of dozens of Mormon men. By 1890 it was obvious that the kingdom could not hold out against the pressure. Aware that further attempts to maintain the practice of plural marriage could destroy the church as well as the kingdom, LDS church president Wilford Woodruff struck a political bargain, agreeing that in return for statehood for Utah, plural marriage would be stopped and the Mormon political party disbanded. Accordingly, in September of that year, he issued a Manifesto announcing that the practice of plural marriage had been discontinued by the members of the LDS Church. When Woodruff's statement was formally accepted by the Saints assembled in conference, it took on the force of revelation.

Even though recent research reveals that some Mormons ignored Woodruff's edict, the president's action nevertheless signaled the demise of the kingdom. Henceforth the Saints, who had been set apart from the world by unorthodox marriage practices, would have to find new marks of identity, and Mormonism itself would need to undergo a reorientation. Concentrating its greatest energies on protecting a literal kingdom of God would no longer be necessary.

MODERN MORMONISM

The story of the Latter-day Saints since 1890 can be divided roughly into three chronological periods. The first, which extended from the issuing of the Manifesto into the mid-1930s, was a time of transition. Despite the Gentile presence among them, Saints in the pioneer era had remained physically separated from the rest of the nation by distance and by eastern and western mountain ranges. Socially, they were isolated because of their unusual marriage system. As a result, the Saints' knowledge of themselves as chosen people was corporate. But in the years after 1890 Mormonism changed dramatically, and as it did so new marks of Mormon identity had to be forged. The Word of Wisdom (a directive forbidding the consumption of alcoholic beverages, coffee, tea, and tobacco that Joseph Smith had given the Saints in 1833) was elevated to the status of revelation and adherence to it became the most visible means of differentiating Mormons and Gentiles. But as the decades passed, other peculiarly Mormon practices have served to set the Saints apart. Among these are the effort made by many Saints to pay full tithes and a remarkable increase in ritual "temple work," in which living Saints undergo baptisms and ordinances for the dead, contributing to the salvation of those who had been left out of the fold. As an accompaniment to ceremonial work for the dead, the Saints have become diligent genealogists. Through this activity they have discovered the names of many of their ancestors who lived between the "Great Apostasy" and 1830 and, therefore, had not been baptized as Latter-day Saints.

In the early years of the twentieth century Utah Mormonism systematized its doctrine, especially through lessons prepared for the priesthood organizations and through the publication of James E. Talmage's officially sanctioned *The Articles of Faith* (1899), a book that is considered an authoritative presentation of Mormon canon. The church also sponsored official compilations of its early years, published as the *History of the Church, Period I,* edited by B. H. Roberts, and *Essentials in Church History* (1922), written by Joseph Fielding Smith.

Semiannual conferences of the entire church were established; they continue to be held every year in April and October; Mormon leaders from all over the world attend. Each stake had extended quarterly conferences as well (stake conferences are now held every winter and summer). Sunday school and sacrament meetings were held every Sunday. Priesthood organizations and the Women's Relief Society, the church's women's auxiliary that was founded in 1843, also met once a week, and through these groups systems of home teaching, block teaching, and ward teaching were activated. Other auxiliary programs took on more importance and met on a weekly basis. These included the Primary Association, which offered religious instruction to Mormons ages four to twelve, and the Young Men's and Young Women's Mutual Improvement Associations, which sponsored religious and recreational activity for teenagers. As opposed to the Kingdom-building period, church activity pervaded most Mormon lives in this new era.

The Saints' relationship with the non-Mormon world remained problematical. In what might be described as the secular arena, Mormons and non-Mormons joined forces in a number of political and economic ventures, establishing a *modus operandi* that the two groups would continue to use in working together, not only in Utah but throughout the nation.

Nevertheless an adversarial relationship continued between Mormons and the members of many Christian denominations. Baptist, Methodist, and Presbyterian missionaries, portraying Mormonism as a dangerous heresy, intensified their efforts to convert Saints. The polygamy issue also refused to die, with Evangelicals insisting that plural marriage remained a common Mormon practice. Joseph Smith III, whose followers in the RLDS Church believed that Brigham Young had introduced plural marriage into Mormonism, mounted a public attack on the LDS Church that called into question the accuracy of LDS historical accounts about the Nauvoo years. Protestant organizations and the

RLDS Church also published books and articles that accused the Mormon hierarchy of continuing their "lascivious conduct" in new polygamous liaisons and, more significantly, of extending through devious means their control over the lives of all persons in the intermountain area and in much of the American West.

In order to counter this hostile press, the LDS Church moved into the emerging field of public relations and tried to place articles favorable to the Saints in national and regional publications. Concurrently, the Saints started to introduce Mormonism to the world, establishing in Salt Lake City a Bureau of Information and Church Literature in 1902 and stationing representatives of the church at various Mormon historic sites, many of which were undergoing restoration.

Another development of enormous significance that took place during the transition period was what Douglas Alder has called "the scattering of the gathering." To some extent, this was a movement in which Saints left Utah to search out economic opportunities in other areas of the nation. But more important, a change in church policy and Mormon theology called for persons who converted to the faith to remain in their home areas. In early Mormon thought, Zion had been a particular place; it would henceforth be located "where the people of God are."

Consolidation, more than anything else, characterized Mormonism in the middle years of the twentieth century. LDS church authorities, led by President Heber J. Grant, continued to "preach the Word of Wisdom" and to emphasize tithing and the performance of temple work. Equally important, however, was the inauguration of a Church Welfare Plan, originally intended as a means of dealing with the economic crisis of the 1930s. Sometimes seen merely as an effort to remove the Saints from the public welfare rolls, the welfare plan represents something much more fundamental and much more in keeping with the Mormon tradition. It became a means of rebuilding a Mormon corporate sense, of forging a boundary within which the community of Saints could care for themselves and for each other.

Because the gathering concept was played down, these middle years saw the administrative extension of the church far beyond the intermountain West, with new stakes being organized in California and in metropolitan areas such as New York and Washington, D.C. Until the mid-

1950s, however, most of the administrative divisions of the LDS Church outside what sociologists and anthropologists were beginning to call the Mormon culture region were missionary districts headed by persons dispatched from Utah. The number of Mormons was still small enough for the church to be administered from its handsome but—from the standpoint of size—modest Salt Lake City headquarters. The various auxiliaries nearly all had strong leadership units and there was a high level of cooperation among them. But while they all reported to the First Presidency and the Council of Twelve Apostles, the elaborate LDS bureaucracy that would come into being in the 1970s simply did not exist in these middle years.

Some Mormon intellectuals nostalgically view the mid-twentieth century as a time when Mormonism was still fairly homogeneous culturally, and individual Latter-day Saints were linked with such strong experiential bonds that considerable heterodoxy was tolerable. At the same time, the post-Manifesto Mormon way of life had become so acceptable to American culture that instead of being attacked as foreign and un-American, the Saints were almost idealized. If the Church Welfare Plan did not operate as successfully as planned, the Saints were trying to help their more unfortunate sisters and brothers. And if most Americans were unwilling to forgo tobacco and alcohol and live model family lives, they nevertheless expressed much admiration for the Saints who did. In addition, these middle years witnessed such impressive Mormon-Gentile cooperation and general good feeling that the fundamental differences in the religious claims of Mormonism and traditional Christianity seemed to recede into the background.

In the 1960s the LDS Church turned its attention to bolstering the Mormon missionary movement. Resulting conversions, plus an astonishing natural increase that resulted from an elevated birthrate among the Saints, produced a rate of church growth unknown since the early years of Mormonism. As the movement spread throughout the United States and into many countries around the world, the idyllic interlude of the middle years of the twentieth century came to an abrupt end. In an amazingly short period, new stakes and wards were organized in practically every area on the globe. As Mormon chapels started appearing in cities and small towns all across America and Mormon temples were constructed in major population centers, Gentile worry resurfaced and renewed charges of heresy were raised in Evangelical and Fundamentalist Protestant congregations.

As the Utah Mormons struggled to deal with the church's phenomenal growth, a modern church bureaucracy became a necessity. In little more than a decade, proliferation of administrative units and intervening administrative levels made for an ecclesiastical structure that distanced local Saints from their prophet/president. While Mormonism had always operated from the top down, the authoritarian character of the church had been mitigated by the personal consideration Saints received from the center, Salt Lake City. Now the size of the church made it difficult for the LDS General Authorities to devote close attention to local matters and individual concerns. Meanwhile, the growing cultural diversity in the church and its large proportion of convert members made it necessary to clarify and systematize the church's organizational pattern and its basic teachings about history, doctrine, and church structure. As far back as 1932, correlation of programs had been undertaken to "account for everyone," as the announcement in the official *Church News* put it; in the 1960s this activity was formalized with the organization of a Correlation Department, which is responsible for reviewing all existing and proposed activities and programs, and all practices, policies, and procedures, as well as monitoring the content of and terminology used in handbooks, curriculum materials (at every level), and official church magazines. As a consequence of the mandatory correlation of practically everything Mormon that has been accelerating since 1960, the tolerable heterodoxy of the 1950s and 1960s became intolerable in the 1970s and 1980s.

It is important to keep in mind, however, that the LDS Church did not move outside its own traditions when it streamlined its authority structure at the local level by bringing under the authority of the priesthood—personified by bishops and stake presidents—such auxiliaries as the Relief Society and the youth programs, which had been functioning more or less autonomously, and by arranging the church's central administration so that a line of authority extended from top to bottom. While increased efficiency was the desired impact of this strengthening of priesthood organizations at the expense of the auxiliary programs, LDS leaders saw this as fulfillment of Joseph Smith's early prophecy that, at some unspecified time in the future, the priesthood would be properly organized to allow the gospel to be carried to all the world.

As Saints contemplated this exciting prospect, Mormonism started preparing itself by simplifying its goals. Modern Mormon leaders articulate the responsibilities of the LDS priesthood in perfect harmony with patterns that were set by Joseph Smith and Brigham Young: besides carrying the gospel to the nations, the purpose of the restoration is to perfect the Saints and to redeem the dead. Toward this end, Mormons believe, the Church of Jesus Christ that was founded in 1830 in western New York is absolutely necessary, and it can best serve if it is an efficient organization.

The sesquicentennial of Mormonism in 1980 was a high point for both of the main branches of the LDS movement. As the decade passed, however, modernity created challenges. Historians studying the beginnings of Mormonism found undeniable evidence that Joseph Smith and his father were experienced folk magic practitioners. By linking Mormon beginnings to magic and the occult, their work raised troubling questions about the Saints' early history. For the majority of Mormons, however, questions about the Mormon past seem less important than the strain of living in the midst of cultural change that is altering the family structure on which Mormonism was built and on which the theology of Utah Mormonism rests. While a revelation to President Wallace Smith of the RLDS Church opened the priesthood to women in the Reorganization, the LDS Church appears to be trying to maintain the status quo by articulating a doctrinal position which asserts that women "share" the priesthood that is held by their husbands. The status of women in the church organization remains a thorny and as yet unresolved problem. The reordering of the church structure that brought the auxiliaries under the control of the bishops and stake presidents stripped away from LDS women the autonomy and authority they had exercised since the days of Brigham Young. Moreover, in an effort to protect the family, the LDS Church announced its firm opposition to the Equal Rights Amendment and encouraged its members to work against its passage. It is difficult to measure the impact of Mormon opposition, but many feminists believe that the LDS

Church kept the amendment from being added to the U.S. Constitution.

Of more consequence to the Saints is what may be the greatest challenge of all: the necessity of integrating persons from all races and cultures into Mormonism. Although the RLDS Church had always welcomed persons of all races into the church, the LDS Church had adopted a position—whether it was simply a practice or whether it was church doctrine is a matter of argument—that blacks could become members of the church, but that black males could not hold the priesthood. Because males in the LDS Church are ordinarily ordained to the Aaronic priesthood at age twelve, this position kept most, but not all, blacks from membership in the church. A 1978 revelation to President Spencer W. Kimball extended the priesthood to "all worthy black male members of the Church . . . without regard for race or color," paving the way for Mormonism to become a universal movement. But this is only the first step in overcoming problems that racial and cultural diversity poses to a religious movement whose roots are so firmly set in American soil.

Predicting the future is always risky, but past Mormon experience has usually led to "the making of Saints." Although the situation is now very different—the Mormon diaspora is a reality—Saints have managed over and over again to turn diversity into unity. They have met the challenge of altered situations repeatedly, and if the past is used as the basis for prognostication, if not prophecy, it is likely that today's Saints will also meet the challenges that modern conditions pose. History suggests, then, that it is more than probable that the Saints will once again find ways to build up their kingdom and create LDS community in the process.

BIBLIOGRAPHY

General Works

James B. Allen and Glen M. Leonard, *The Story of the Latter-day Saints* (1976); Leonard J. Arrington and Davis Bitton, *The Mormon Experience: A History of the Latter-day Saints* (1979); Klaus J. Hansen, *Mormonism and the American Experience* (1981); F. Mark McKiernan, Alma R. Blair, and Paul M. Edwards, eds., *The Restoration Movement: Essays in Mormon History* (1972); Thomas F. O'Dea, *The Mormons* (1957); Jan Shipps, *Mormonism: The Story of a New Religious Tradition* (1985).

Studies of Chronological Periods

Thomas G. Alexander, *Mormonism in Transition: A History of the Latter-day Saints, 1890–1930* (1986); Richard L. Bushman, *Joseph Smith and the Beginnings of Mormonism* (1984); Robert B. Flanders, *Nauvoo, Kingdom on the Mississippi* (1965); E. Leo Lyman, *Political Deliverance: The Mormon Quest for Utah Statehood* (1986).

Collections of Documents

James R. Clark, ed., *Messages of the First Presidency of the Church of Jesus Christ of Latter-day Saints,* 6 vols. (1965–1975); Kenneth W. Godfrey, Audrey M. Godfrey, and Jill Mulvay Derr, eds., *Women's Voices: An Untold History of the Latter-day Saints, 1830–1900* (1982); Dean C. Jessee, ed., *The Personal Writings of Joseph Smith* (1984) and *Journal of Discourses,* 26 vols. (1854–1886).

Russell Mortensen and William Mulder, eds. *Among the Mormons* (1958); B. H. Roberts, ed., *History of the Church of Jesus Christ of Latter-day Saints: Period I, History of Joseph Smith, the Prophet,* 6 vols. (1902–1930; 2nd rev. ed., 1955) and *Period II, from the Manuscript History of Brigham Young and Other Original Documents* (1932); Joseph Smith III, Heman C. Smith, and F. Henry Edwards, eds. and comps., *The History of the Reorganized Church of Jesus Christ of Latter Day Saints,* 6 vols. (1965–1985).

Biographies

Leonard J. Arrington, *Brigham Young: American Moses* (1985); Fawn M. Brodie, *No Man Knows My History: The Life of Joseph Smith, the Mormon Prophet* (1948; 2nd rev. ed., 1971); Donna Hill, *Joseph Smith, The First Mormon* (1979); Linda K. Newell and Valeen T. Avery, *Mormon Enigma: Emma Hale Smith, Prophet's Wife, "Elect Lady," Polygamy's Foe* (1984); Lucy Mack Smith, *Biographical Sketches of Joseph Smith, the Prophet, and His Progenitors for Many Generations* (1853; repr., 1969).

Specialized Studies

Leonard J. Arrington, *Great Basin Kingdom: An Economic History of the Latter-day Saints, 1830–1900* (1958), and with Feramorz Y. Fox and Dean L. May, *Building the City of God: Community and Cooperation Among the Mormons* (1976); Paul M. Edwards, *Preface to Faith: A Philosophical Inquiry into RLDS Beliefs* (1984); Lawrence Foster, *Religion and Sexuality: Three American Communal Experiments of the Nineteenth Century* (1981); Sterling M. McMurrin, *The Theological Foundations of the Mormon Religion* (1965); D. Michael Quinn, "The Mormon Hierarchy, 1832–1932, An American Elite," Ph.D. diss., Yale (1976), and *Early Mormonism and the Magic World View* (1986).

Bibliographies

Davis Bitton, ed., *Guide to Mormon Diaries and Autobiographies* (1977); Chad J. Flake, ed., *A Mormon Bibliography, 1830–1930* (1978). See also numerous bibliographical listings and surveys in *Dialogue: A Journal of Mormon Thought, Brigham Young University Studies, Journal of Mormon History,* and *Mormon History Association Newsletter.*
[See also RELIGIOUS ARCHITECTURE AND LANDSCAPE; RESTORATIONISM AND THE STONE-CAMPBELL TRADITION; and REVIVALISM.]